ST/ESA/STAT/SER.S/39

**Department of Economic
and Social Affairs**
Statistics Division

**Département des affaires
économiques et sociales**
Division de statistique

Statistical Yearbook
2020 edition
Sixty-third issue

Annuaire statistique
2020 édition
Soixante-troisième édition

United Nations | Nations Unies
New York, 2020

Department of Economic and Social Affairs

The Department of Economic and Social Affairs of the United Nations Secretariat is a vital interface between global policies in the economic, social and environmental spheres and national action. The Department works in three main interlinked areas: (i) it compiles, generates and analyses a wide range of economic, social and environmental data and information on which Member States of the United Nations draw to review common problems and to take stock of policy options; (ii) it facilitates the negotiations of Member States in many intergovernmental bodies on joint courses of action to address ongoing or emerging global challenges; and (iii) it advises interested Governments on the ways and means of translating policy frameworks developed in United Nations conferences and summits into programmes at the country level and, through technical assistance, helps build national capacities.

Note

ST/ESA/STAT/SER.S/39

UNITED NATIONS PUBLICATION
Sales No. B.20.XVII.12.H

ISBN 978-92-1-259150-6
e-ISBN 978-92-1-005078-4
ISSN 0082-8459

Département des affaires économiques et sociales

Le Département des affaires économiques et sociales du Secrétariat de l'Organisation des Nations Unies assure le lien essentiel entre les politiques adoptées au plan international dans les domaines économique, social et écologique et les mesures prises au plan national. Il mène ses activités dans trois grands domaines interdépendants : i) il compile, produit et analyse une grand variété de données et d'informations économiques, sociales et écologiques dont les États Membres de l'ONU tirent parti pour examiner les problèmes communs et faire le point sur les possibilités d'action; (ii) il facilite les négociations que les États Membres mènent dans un grand nombre d'organes intergouvernementaux sur les moyens d'action à employer conjointement pour faire face aux problèmes mondiaux existants ou naissants; et (iii) il aide les gouvernements intéressés à traduire les orientations politiques établies lors des conférences et sommets de l'ONU en programmes nationaux et contribue à renforcer les capacités des pays en leur apportant une assistance technique.

Note

ST/ESA/STAT/SER.S/39

PUBLICATION DES NATIONS UNIES
Numéro de vente: B.20.XVII.12.H

ISBN 978-92-1-259150-6
e-ISBN 978-92-1-005078-4
ISSN 0082-8459

Preface

The 2020 edition of the United Nations *Statistical Yearbook* is the sixty-third issue of the publication, prepared by the Statistics Division of the Department of Economic and Social Affairs. Ever since the compilation of data for the *Statistical Yearbook* series was initiated in 1948, it has consistently provided a wide range of internationally available statistics on social, economic and environmental conditions and activities at the national, regional and world levels.

The contents of the *Yearbook* continue to be under review. Please send any comments or views to our email address, statistics@un.org. The tables include series covering an appropriate historical period, depending upon data availability and space constraints, for as many countries, territories and statistical areas of the world as available. The tables cover a period up to 2020, with some of the data being estimated.

The *Yearbook* tables are based on data which have been compiled by the Statistics Division mainly from official national and international sources as these are more authoritative and comprehensive, more generally available as time series and more comparable among countries than other sources. These sources include the United Nations Statistics Division in the fields of national accounts, industry, energy and international trade, the United Nations Statistics Division and the Population Division in the field of demographic statistics, and over 20 offices of the United Nations system and international organizations in other specialized fields. In some cases, official sources have been supplemented by other sources and estimates, where these have been subjected to professional scrutiny and debate and are consistent with other independent sources.

The United Nations agencies and other international, national and specialized organizations which furnished data are listed under "Source" at the end of each table. Acknowledgement is gratefully made for their generous and valuable cooperation in continually providing data.

After the first table, which presents key world aggregates and totals, the *Yearbook* is organized in three parts as follows; part one, relating to population and social topics; part two, relating to economic activity; and part three relating to energy, environment and infrastructure. The tables in the three parts are presented mainly by countries or areas, and world and regional aggregates are shown where available.

The four annexes contain information on country and area nomenclature (annex I), summary technical notes on statistical definitions, methods and sources for all tables of the *Yearbook* (annex II), the conversion coefficients and factors used in certain tables (annex III), and a list of those tables which were added, omitted or discontinued since the last issue of the *Yearbook* (annex IV).

The *Statistical Yearbook* is prepared by the Development Data Section, Development Data and Outreach Branch of the Statistics Division, Department of Economic and Social Affairs of the United Nations Secretariat. The programme manager is Matthias Reister, the chief editor is Anuradha Chimata and David Carter, Mohamed Nabassoua, and Zin Lin provide production assistance. Bogdan Dragovic provided IT support.

Comments on the present *Yearbook* and its future evolution are welcome. They may be sent via e-mail to statistics@un.org or to the United Nations Statistics Division, Development Data Section, New York, NY 10017, USA.

Préface

*L'*édition *2020 de l'Annuaire statistique* des Nations Unies est la soixante-troisième édition de cette publication, préparée par la Division de statistique du Département des affaires économiques et sociales. Depuis son instauration en 1948 comme outil de compilation des données statistiques internationales, l'*Annuaire statistique* s'efforce de constamment diffuser un large éventail de statistiques disponibles sur les activités et conditions économiques et sociales, aux niveaux nationaux, régional et mondial.

Le contenu de l'Annuaire est actuellement en cours de révision. Pour tout commentaire, veuillez envoyer un courriel à notre adresse électronique : statistics@un.org. Les tableaux présentent des séries qui couvrent une période historique appropriée, en fonction de la disponibilité des données et des contraintes d'espace, pour autant de pays, territoires et zones statistiques du monde comme disponibles. Les tableaux couvrent généralement la période allant jusqu'en 2019.

Les tableaux de l'*Annuaire* sont construits essentiellement à partir des données compilées par la Division de statistique et provenant de sources officielles, nationales et internationales ; c'est en effet la meilleure source si l'on veut des données fiables, complètes et comparables, et si l'on a besoin de séries chronologiques. Ces sources sont: la Division de statistique du Secrétariat de l'Organisation des Nations Unies pour ce qui concerne la comptabilité nationale, l'industrie, l'énergie et le commerce extérieur, la Division de statistique et la Division de la population du Secrétariat de l'Organisation des Nations Unies pour les statistiques démographiques; et plus de 20 bureaux du système des Nations Unies et d'organisations internationales pour les autres domaines spécialisés. Dans quelques cas, les données officielles sont complétées par des informations et des estimations provenant d'autres sources qui ont été examinées par des spécialistes et confirmées par des sources indépendantes.

Les institutions spécialisées des Nations Unies et les autres organisations internationales, nationales et spécialisées qui ont fourni des données sont énumérées dans la "Source" sur chaque tableau. Les auteurs de l'*Annuaire statistique* les remercient de leur précieuse et généreuse collaboration.

Après le premier tableau qui fournit les principaux agrégats et totaux au niveau mondial, l'*Annuaire* est groupé en trois parties. La première partie est consacrée à la population et aux questions sociales, la deuxième est consacrée à l'activité économique, et la dernière est consacrée à l'énergie, environnement et infrastructures. Dans ces trois parties, les tableaux sont généralement présentés par pays ou régions, mais les agrégats mondiaux ou régionaux sont indiqués si disponibles.

Les quatre annexes donnent des renseignements sur la nomenclature des pays et des zones (annexe I), des notes récapitulatives sur les définitions, méthodes statistiques et techniques utilisées dans les sources de chaque tableau de l'*Annuaire* (annexe II), ainsi que sur les coefficients et facteurs de conversion employés dans les différents tableaux (annexe III), enfin une liste de nouveaux tableaux, de tableaux omis ou supprimés depuis la dernière édition est disponible (annexe IV).

L'Annuaire statistique est préparé par la Section des données de développement, Direction des données de développement et de liaison de la Division de statistique, Département des affaires économiques et sociales du Secrétariat de l'Organisation des Nations Unies. Le responsable du programme est Matthias Reister, le rédacteur en chef est Anuradha Chimata et David Carter, Mohamed Nabassoua, et Zin Lin fournissent une assistance à la production. Bogdan Dragovic est responsable du support en informatique.

Les observations sur la présente édition de l'*Annuaire* et les suggestions de modification pour l'avenir seront reçues avec intérêt. Elles peuvent être envoyées par message électronique à statistics@un.org, ou adressées à la Division de statistique des Nations Unies, Section des données de développement, New York, NY 10017 (États-Unis d'Amérique).

Explanatory notes

Symbols and conventions used in the tables

.   A point is used to indicate decimals.

-      A hyphen between years, for example, 2010-2015, indicates the full period involved, including the beginning and end

/   A slash indicates a financial year, school year or crop year, for example 2014/15.

...   Data are not available or not applicable.

*   Data are provisional, estimated or include a major revision.

\#   Marked break in the time series.

~0   Not zero, but less than half of the unit employed.

—~0   Not zero, but negative and less than half of the unit employed.

A space is used as a thousands separator, for example 1 000 is one thousand. Subtotals and percentages in the tables do not necessarily add to totals because of rounding.

Country notes and nomenclature

As a general rule, the data presented in the *Yearbook* relate to a given country or area as described in the complete list of countries and territories, see annex I.

References to statistical sources and methods in tables

For brevity the *Yearbook* omits specific information on the source or methodology for individual data points, and when a data point is estimated no distinction is made between whether the estimation was done by the international or national organization. See the technical notes to the tables in annex II for the primary source which may provide this information.

Units of measurement

The metric system of weights and measures has been employed throughout the *Yearbook*. For conversion coefficients and factors, see annex III.

Notes explicatives

Signes et conventions employés dans les tableaux

.   Les décimales sont précédées d'un point.

-   Un tiret entre des années, par exemple "2013-2014", indique que la période est embrassée dans sa totalité, y compris la première et la dernière année.

/   Une barre oblique renvoie à un exercice financier, à une année scolaire ou à une campagne agricole, par exemple

... Données non disponibles ou non applicables.

*   Données provisoire, estimatif ou avec une révision majeure.

\#   Discontinuité notable dans la série chronologique.

~0   Non nul mais inférieur à la moitié de l'unité employée

—~0   Non nul mais négatif et inférieur à la moitié de l'unité employée

Le séparateur utilisé pour les milliers est l'espace : par exemple, 1 000 correspond à un millier. Les chiffres étant arrondis, les sous-totaux ou pourcentages ne correspondent pas toujours à la somme exacte des éléments figurant dans les tableaux.

Notes sur les pays et nomenclature

En règle générale, les données renvoient au pays ou zone en question que décrite dans la liste complète des pays et territoires figure à l'annexe I.

Références à des sources et des méthodes statistiques dans les tableaux

Par souci de brièveté, l'*Annuaire* omet les informations relatives aux sources et méthodologies employées pour les points de données individuels. De plus, quand un point de données est estimé aucune distinction n'est faite entre une estimation provenant d'une organisation internationale ou d'une organisation nationale. Voir les notes techniques relatives aux tableaux dans l'annexe II ou se trouvent les références aux différentes sources contentant ces informations.

Unités de mesure

Le système métrique de poids et mesures a été utilisé dans tout l'*Annuaire*. On trouvera à l'annexe III les coefficients et facteurs de conversion.

Contents

Note: See **Annex IV** for table names presented in previous issues of the *Statistical Yearbook* which are not contained in the present issue.

Table des matières

Voir Annexe IV pour les tableaux publiés dans les éditions précédentes de l'Annuaire statistique mais qui n'ont pas été repris dans la présente edition.

Introduction

The 2020 edition of the United Nations *Statistical Yearbook* is the sixty-third issue of this publication, prepared by the Statistics Division, Department of Economic and Social Affairs, of the United Nations Secretariat. The contents of the *Yearbook* continue to be under review and the number of tables has been reduced as a result. Additional tables are expected to be introduced in future editions. Please send any comments or views to our email address, statistics@un.org. The tables include series covering an appropriate historical period, depending upon data availability (as of 31 July 2020) and space constraints, for as many countries, territories and statistical areas of the world as available. The tables cover a period up to 2020, with some of the data being estimated.

Objective and content of the Statistical Yearbook

The main purpose of the *Statistical Yearbook* is to provide in a single volume a comprehensive compilation of internationally available statistics on social, economic and environmental conditions and activities, at world, regional and national levels, for an appropriate historical period.

Most of the statistics presented in the *Yearbook* are extracted from more detailed, specialized databases prepared by the Statistics Division and by many other international statistical services. Thus, while the specialized databases concentrate on monitoring topics and trends in particular social, economic and environmental fields, the *Statistical Yearbook* tables aim to provide data for a comprehensive, overall description of social, economic and environmental structures, conditions, changes and activities. The objective has been to collect, systematize, coordinate and present in a consistent way the most essential components of comparable statistical information which can give a broad picture of social, economic and environmental processes.

The content of the *Statistical Yearbook* is planned to serve a general readership. The *Yearbook* endeavors to provide information for various bodies of the United Nations system as well as for other international organizations, governments and non-governmental organizations, national statistical, economic and social policy bodies, scientific and educational institutions, libraries and the public. Data published in the *Statistical Yearbook* may also be of interest to companies and enterprises and to agencies engaged in market research. The *Statistical Yearbook* thus provides information on a wide range of social, economic and environmental issues which are of concern in the United Nations system and among the governments and peoples of the world. A particular value of the *Yearbook* is that it facilitates meaningful analysis of issues by systematizing and coordinating the data across many fields and shedding light on such interrelated issues as:

- General economic growth and related economic conditions;
- Gender equality;
- Population by sex and rate of increase, surface area and density;
- Unemployment, inflation and prices;
- Energy production and consumption;
- Expansion of trade;
- The financial situation of countries;
- Education;
- Improvement in general living conditions;
- Pollution and protection of the environment;
- Assistance provided to developing countries for social, economic and environmental development purposes.

Organization of the Yearbook

After the first table which presents key world aggregates and totals, the tables of the *Yearbook* are grouped into three parts as follows:

- Part One: Population and Social Statistics (chapters II-VI: tables 2-11);
- Part Two: Economic Activity (chapters VII-XI: tables 12-20);
- Part Three: Energy, environment and infrastructure (chapters XII-XVII: tables 21-32).

The first table provides a summary picture of development at the global level. More specific and detailed information for analysis concerning regions, individual countries or areas are presented in the three thematic parts.

Part One, Population and Social Statistics, comprises 10 tables which contain more detailed statistical series on population and migration, gender, education, health and crime.

Part Two, Economic Activity, comprises 9 tables on national accounts, finance, labour market, price and production indices and international merchandise trade.

Part Three, Energy, environment and infrastructure, comprises 12 tables on energy, environment, science and technology, international tourism and transport, communication and development assistance.

Annexes and regional groupings of countries or areas

The annexes to the *Statistical Yearbook*, and the section "Explanatory notes" preceding the Introduction, provide additional essential information on the *Yearbook*'s contents and presentation of data.

Annex I provides information on countries or areas covered in the *Yearbook* tables and on their arrangement in geographical regions and economic or other groupings. The geographical groupings shown in the *Yearbook* are generally based on continental regions unless otherwise indicated. However, strict consistency in this regard is impossible. A wide range of classifications is used for different purposes in the various international agencies and other sources of statistics for the *Yearbook*. These classifications vary in response to administrative and analytical requirements.

Annex II provide brief descriptions of major statistical concepts, definitions and classifications required for interpretation and analysis of the data.

Annex III provides detailed information on conversion coefficients and factors used in various tables, and Annex IV provides a list of tables added, omitted and discontinued in the present edition of the *Yearbook*. Some Tables do not feature in this edition of the *Yearbook* due to space limitations or an insufficient amount of new data being available. Their titles nevertheless are still listed in this Annex since it is planned that they will be published in a later issue as new data are compiled by the collecting agency and where space permits.

Data comparability, quality and relevance

The major challenge continuously facing the *Statistical Yearbook* is to present series which are as comparable across countries as the available statistics permit. Considerable efforts have already been made among the international suppliers of data and by the staff of the *Statistical Yearbook* to ensure the compatibility of various series by aligning time periods, base years, prices chosen for valuation, and so on. This is indispensable in relating various bodies of data to each other and in facilitating analysis across different sectors. In general, the data presented reflect the methodological recommendations of the United Nations Statistical Commission issued in various United Nations publications, and of other international bodies concerned with statistics. The use of international recommendations promotes international comparability of the data and ensures a degree of compatibility regarding the underlying concepts, definitions and classifications relating to different series. However, much work remains to be done in this area and, for this reason, some tables serve only as a first source of data and require further adjustment before being used for more in-depth analytical studies. While on the whole, a significant degree of comparability has been achieved in international statistics, there will remain some limitations, for a variety of reasons.

One common cause of non-comparability of economic data is different valuations of statistical aggregates such as national income, wages and salaries, output of industries and so forth. Conversion of these and similar series originally expressed in national prices into a common currency, for example into United States dollars, through the use of exchange rates, is not always satisfactory owing to frequent wide fluctuations in market rates and differences between official rates and rates which would be indicated by unofficial markets or purchasing power parities. The use of different kinds of sources for obtaining data is another cause of incomparability. This is true, for example, in the case of employment and unemployment, where data are obtained from different sources, namely household and labour force sample surveys, establishment censuses or surveys, official estimates, social insurance statistics and employment office statistics, which are not fully comparable in many cases. Non-comparability of data may also result from differences in the institutional patterns of countries. Certain variations in social, economic and environmental organization and institutions may have an impact on the comparability of the data even if the underlying concepts and definitions are identical. These and other causes of non-comparability of the data are briefly explained in the technical note associated with each table (see Annex II).

A further set of challenges relate to timeliness, quality and relevance of the data contained in the *Yearbook*. Users generally demand the most up-to-date statistics. However, due to the different development stages of statistical capacity in different countries, data for the most recent years may only be available for a small number of countries. For a global print publication, therefore, a balance has to be struck between presenting the most updated information and satisfactory country coverage. Of course the United Nations Statistics Division's website offers greater flexibility in presenting continuously updated information and is therefore a useful complement to the annual print publication. Furthermore, as most of the information presented in this *Yearbook* is collected through specialized United Nations agencies and partners, the timeliness is continuously enhanced by improving the communication and data flow between countries and the specialized agencies on the one hand, and between the United Nations Statistics Division and the specialized agencies on the other. The development of new XML-based data transfer protocols will address this issue and is expected to make international data flows more efficient in the future.

Data quality at the international level is a function of the data quality at the national level. The United Nations Statistics Division in close cooperation with its partners among the UN agencies and the international statistical system continues to support countries' efforts to improve both the coverage and the quality of their data. Metadata, as for example reflected in the footnotes and technical notes of this publication, are an important service to the user to allow an informed assessment of the quality of the data. Given the wide variety of sources for the *Yearbook*, there is of course an equally wide variety of data formats and accompanying metadata. An important challenge for the United Nations Statistics Division and its partners for the future is to work further towards the standardization, or at least harmonization, of metadata.

A crucial challenge is to maintain the relevance of the series included in the *Yearbook*. As new policy concerns enter the developmental debate, the United Nations Statistics Division will need to introduce new series that describe concerns that have gained prominence as well as to prune data as they become outdated and continue to update the recurrent *Yearbook* series that still address those issues which are most pertinent. Often choosing the appropriate moment when the statistical information on new topics has matured sufficiently so as to be able to disseminate meaningful global data can be challenging. Furthermore, a balance has to continuously be found between the ever-increasing amount of information available for dissemination and the space limitations of the print version of the *Statistical Yearbook*. International comparability, data availability, data quality and relevance will remain the key criteria to guide the United Nations Statistics Division in its selection.

Needless to say, more can always be done to improve the *Statistical Yearbook*'s scope, coverage, design, metadata and timeliness. The *Yearbook* team continually strives to improve upon each of these aspects and to make its publication as responsive as possible to its users' needs and expectations, while at the same time focusing on a manageable body of data and metadata. Since data disseminated in digital form have clear advantages over those in print, as much of the *Yearbook* information as possible will continue to be included in the Statistics Division's online databases. Please feel welcome to provide feedback and suggestions to statistics@un.org.

Introduction

L'édition 2020 de l'*Annuaire statistique* des Nations Unies est la soixante-troisième édition de cette publication, établi par la Division de statistique du Département des affaires économiques et sociales du Secrétariat de l'Organisation des Nations Unies. Le contenu de l'*Annuaire* est actuellement en cours de révision, de ce fait le nombre de tableaux a été réduit. Des tableaux seront inclus dans les prochaines éditions. Pour tout commentaire, veuillez envoyer un courriel à notre adresse électronique : statistics@un.org. Les tableaux présentent des séries qui couvrent une période historique appropriée, en fonction de la disponibilité des données (à la date du 31 juillet 2020) et des contraintes d'espace, pour autant de pays, territoires et zones statistiques du monde comme disponibles. Les tableaux couvrent généralement pour la période jusqu'à 2020, avec certaines des données étant estimées.

Objectif et contenu de l'Annuaire statistique

Le principal objectif de *l'Annuaire statistique* est de fournir en un seul volume un inventaire complet de statistiques internationales concernant la situation et les activités sociales, économiques et environnementales aux niveaux mondial, régional et national, sur une période adéquate.

La plupart des données qui figurent dans l'*Annuaire statistique* proviennent de bases de données spécialisées davantage détaillées, préparées par la Division de statistique et par bien d'autres services statistiques internationaux. Tandis que les bases de données spécialisées se concentrent sur le suivi de domaines socioéconomiques et environnementaux particuliers, les données de l'*Annuaire* sont présentées de telle sorte qu'elles fournissent une description globale et exhaustive des structures, conditions, transformations et activités socioéconomiques et environnementaux. On a cherché à recueillir, systématiser, coordonner et présenter de manière cohérente les principales informations statistiques comparables, de manière à dresser un tableau général des processus socioéconomiques et environnementaux.

Le contenu de l'*Annuaire statistique* a été élaboré en vue d'un lectorat large. Les renseignements fournis devraient ainsi pouvoir être utilisés par les divers organismes du système des Nations Unies, mais aussi par d'autres organisations internationales, les gouvernements et les organisations non gouvernementales, les organismes nationaux de statistique et de politique économique et sociale, les institutions scientifiques et les établissements d'enseignement, les bibliothèques et les particuliers. Les données publiées dans l'*Annuaire* peuvent également intéresser les sociétés et entreprises, et les organismes spécialisés dans les études de marché. L'*Annuaire* présente des informations sur un large éventail de questions socioéconomiques et environnementales liées aux préoccupations actuelles du système des Nations Unies, des gouvernements et des peuples du monde entier. Une qualité particulière de l'*Annuaire* est de faciliter une analyse approfondie de ces questions en systématisant et en articulant les données d'un domaine/secteur à l'autre, et en apportant un éclairage sur des sujets interdépendants, tels que :

- La croissance économique générale, et les conditions économiques qui leurs sont liées ;
- La situation de femmes ;
- La population par sexe et taux de croissance, taux d'accroissement, superficie et densité ;
- Le chômage, l'inflation et les prix ;
- La production et la consommation d'énergie ;
- L'expansion des échanges ;
- La situation financière des pays ;
- L'éducation ;
- L'amélioration des conditions de vie ;
- La pollution et la protection de l'environnement ;
- L'assistance aux pays en développement à des fins socioéconomiques et environnementaux.

Présentation de l'Annuaire

Après le premier tableau qui fournit les principaux agrégats et totaux au niveau mondial, l'Annuaire est groupé en trois parties comme suit :

- Première partie : Statistiques démographiques et sociales (chapitres II à VI, tableaux 2 à 11)
- Deuxième partie : Activité économique (chapitres VII à XI, tableaux 12 à 20)
- Troisième partie : Énergie, environnement et infrastructures (chapitres XII à XVII, tableaux 21 à 32)

Le premier tableau donne un aperçu du développement à l'échelon mondial, tandis que les trois autres parties contiennent des renseignements plus précis et détaillés qui se prêtent mieux à une analyse par régions, pays ou par zones. Chacune de ces trois parties est subdivisée en unités thématiques.

La première partie, intitulée "Population et statistiques sociales", comporte 10 tableaux où figurent des séries plus détaillées concernant la population et la migration, la situation des femmes, l'éducation, la santé et la criminalité.

La deuxième partie, intitulée "Activité économique", comporte 9 tableaux sur les comptes nationaux, les finances, le marché du travail, les indices des prix et de la production, et le commence international des marchandises.

La troisième partie, intitulée "Energie, environnement et infrastructures", comprend 12 tableaux sur l'énergie, l'environnement, la science et technologie, le tourisme international et le transport, la communication et à l'aide au développement.

Annexes et groupements régionaux des pays et zones

Les annexes à l'*Annuaire statistique*, et la section intitulée "Notes explicatives" qui précède l'introduction, offrent d'importantes informations complémentaires quant à la teneur et à la présentation des données figurant dans le présent ouvrage.

L'annexe I donne des renseignements sur les pays ou zones couverts par les tableaux de l'*Annuaire* et sur leur regroupement en régions géographiques et groupements économiques ou autres. Sauf indication contraire, les groupements géographiques figurant dans l'*Annuaire* sont généralement fondés sur les régions continentales, mais une présentation absolument systématique est impossible à cet égard car les diverses institutions internationales et autres sources de statistiques employées pour la confection de l'*Annuaire* emploient, selon l'objet de l'exercice, des classifications fort différentes en réponse à diverses exigences d'ordre administratif ou analytique.

L'annexe II contient les notes techniques de chaque chapitre apportent une brève description des principales notions, définitions et classifications statistiques nécessaires pour interpréter et analyser les données.

L'annexe III fournit des renseignements sur les coefficients et facteurs de conversion employés dans les différents tableaux, et l'annexe IV contient la liste de tableaux qui ont été ajoutés omis ou supprimés dans la présente édition de l'*Annuaire*. Certains tableaux ne figurent pas dans cet *Annuaire* en raison du manque d'espace ou de données nouvelles. Comme ils seront repris dans une prochaine édition à mesure que des données nouvelles seront dépouillées par l'office statistique d'origine, ses titres figurent toujours dans la table des matières.

Comparabilité, qualité et pertinence des statistiques

Le défi majeur auquel l'*Annuaire Statistique* fait continuellement face est de présenter des séries aussi comparables d'un pays à l'autre que le permettent les statistiques disponibles. Les sources internationales de données et les auteurs de l'*Annuaire* ont réalisé des efforts considérables pour faire en sorte que diverses séries soient compatibles, en harmonisant les périodes de référence, les années de base, les prix utilisés pour les évaluations, etc. Cette démarche est indispensable si l'on veut rapprocher divers ensembles de données, et faciliter l'analyse intersectorielle de l'économie. De façon générale, les données sont présentées selon les recommandations méthodologiques formulées par la Commission de statistique des Nations Unies, et par les autres entités internationales impliquées dans les statistiques. Le respect des recommandations internationales tend non seulement à promouvoir la comparabilité internationale des données, mais elle assure également une certaine comparabilité entre les concepts, les définitions et classifications utilisés. Mais comme il reste encore beaucoup à faire dans ce domaine, les données présentées dans certains tableaux n'ont qu'une valeur indicative, et nécessiteront des ajustements plus poussés avant de pouvoir servir à des analyses approfondies. Bien que l'on soit parvenu, dans l'ensemble, à un degré de comparabilité appréciable en matière de statistiques internationales, diverses raisons expliquent que subsistent encore de nombreuses limitations.

Une cause commune de non-comparabilité des données économiques réside dans la diversité des méthodes d'évaluation employées pour comptabiliser des agrégats tels que le revenu national, les salaires et traitements, la production des différentes branches d'activité industrielle, etc. Il n'est pas toujours satisfaisant de ramener la valeur des séries de ce type—exprimée à l'origine en prix nationaux—à une monnaie commune (par exemple le dollar des États-Unis) car les taux de change du marché connaissent fréquemment de fortes fluctuations, et parce que les taux officiels ne coïncident pas avec ceux des marchés officieux ni avec les parités réelles de pouvoir d'achat. Le recours à des sources diverses pour la collecte des données est un autre facteur qui limite la comparabilité. C'est le cas, par exemple, des données d'emploi et de chômage, obtenues par des moyens aussi peu comparables que les sondages, le dépouillement des registres d'assurances sociales et les enquêtes auprès des entreprises. Dans certains cas, les données ne sont pas comparables en raison de différences entre les structures institutionnelles des pays. Des changements dans l'organisation et les institutions sociales, économiques et environnementales peuvent affecter la comparabilité des données, même si les concepts et définitions sont fondamentalement identiques. Ces causes, et d'autres, de non comparabilité des données sont brièvement expliquées dans les notes techniques associée à chaque tableau (voir annexe II).

Un autre ensemble de défis à relever concerne la fraîcheur, la qualité et la pertinence des données présentées dans l'*Annuaire*. Les utilisateurs exigent généralement des données les plus récentes possibles. Toutefois, selon le niveau de développement de la capacité statistique des pays, les données pour les dernières années peuvent n'être disponibles que pour un nombre limité de pays. Dans le cadre d'une publication mondiale, un équilibre doit être trouvé entre la présentation de l'information la plus récente et une couverture géographique satisfaisante. Bien entendu, le site Internet de la Division de statistique des Nations Unies offre une plus grande flexibilité, puisqu'il propose une information actualisée au fil de l'eau, et constitue ainsi un complément utile à la publication papier annuelle. Par ailleurs, étant donné que la plupart des informations présentées dans cet *Annuaire* sont collectées parmi les agences spécialisées des Nations Unies et autres partenaires, la fraîcheur des données est continuellement améliorée, grâce à une meilleure communication et un meilleur échange de données entre les pays et les agences spécialisées d'une part, et entre la Division de statistique des Nations Unies et les agences spécialisées d'autre part. Le développement de nouveaux protocoles de transfert de données basés sur le langage XML devrait contribuer à rendre, à l'avenir, les échanges de données internationales encore plus efficaces.

La qualité des données au niveau international est fonction de la qualité des données au niveau national. La Division de statistique des Nations Unies, en étroite collaboration avec ses partenaires dans les agences de l'ONU et dans le système statistique international, continue de soutenir les efforts des pays pour améliorer à la fois la couverture et la qualité de leurs données. Des métadonnées, comme l'illustrent les notes de bas de page et les notes techniques de cette publication, constituent un important service fourni à l'utilisateur pour lui permettre d'évaluer de manière avisée la qualité des données. Etant donné la grande variété des sources de l'*Annuaire*, il y a bien entendu une non moins grande variété de formats de données et de métadonnées associées. Un important défi que la Division de statistique des Nations Unies et ses partenaires doivent relever dans le futur est d'aboutir à la standardisation, ou au moins l'harmonisation, des métadonnées.

Le défi majeur reste la constance de la pertinence des séries présentées dans l'*Annuaire*. Au fur et à mesure que de nouvelles préoccupations politiques pénètrent le débat lié au développement, la Division de statistique des Nations Unies doit introduire dans l'*Annuaire* de nouvelles séries qui leur sont liées, et, ce faisant, effectuer une coupe sombre parmi les données qui lui semblent dépassées, tout en s'assurant de continuer à actualiser les séries récurrentes de qui paraissent encore pertinentes. Souvent, choisir le moment idoine auquel les données statistiques sur de nouveaux thèmes sont suffisamment matures pour qu'elles puissent, au niveau mondial, être diffusées sans hésitation, est un défi en soi. Par ailleurs, un équilibre doit continuellement être trouvé entre le volume toujours croissant d'informations disponibles à la diffusion, et les contraintes d'espace de la version papier de l'*Annuaire* statistique. La comparabilité internationale, la disponibilité, la qualité et la pertinence des données devront rester les principaux critères à considérer par la Division de statistique des Nations Unies dans sa sélection.

Inutile de dire qu'il est toujours possible d'améliorer l'*Annuaire* statistique en ce qui concerne son champ, sa couverture, sa conception générale, ses métadonnées et sa mise à jour. L'équipe en charge de l'*Annuaire* s'évertue en permanence à améliorer chacun de ces aspects, et de faire en sorte que cette publication réponde au plus près aux besoins et aux attentes de ses utilisateurs, sans toutefois oublier de mettre l'accent sur un corpus gérable de données et de métadonnées. Puisqu'il est avéré que les données diffusées de manière digitale ont des avantages comparés à celles diffusées sur papier, autant d'informations de l'*Annuaire* que possible continueront d'être inclues dans les bases de données électroniques de la Division de statistique. L'*Annuaire* statistique garde toujours une place de choix parmi les produits de la Division de statistique comme une ressource utile pour une compréhension général de la situation sociale, économique et environnementale globale. N'hésitez pas à nous faire part de vos commentaires et suggestions à statistics@un.org

1

World statistics: selected series
Population and social statistics, economic activity and energy, environment and infrastructure

Statistiques mondiales : séries principales
Population et statistiques sociales, activité économique et énergie, environnement et infrastructures

Series Séries	Unit or base Unité ou base	2005	2010	2015	2017	2018	2019	2020
Population and Migration • **Population et migration**								
Population [1]	million	6 541.9	6 956.8	7 379.8	7 547.9	7 631.1	7 713.5	7 794.8
Population density [1] Densité de population [1]	per km² pour km²	50.3	53.5	56.7	58.0	58.7	59.3	59.9
Population, male [1] Population, hommes [1]	million	3 296.5	3 507.7	3 720.7	3 805.5	3 847.5	3 889.0	3 930.0
Population, female [1] Population, femmes [1]	million	3 245.4	3 449.1	3 659.1	3 742.4	3 783.6	3 824.4	3 864.8
Sex ratio [1] Rapport des sexes [1]	males per 100 females hom. p. 100 fem.	101.6	101.7	101.7	101.7	101.7	101.7	101.7
Population age distribution, 0-14 [1] Répartition par âge de la population, 0-14 [1]	percentage of pop. pourcentage de la pop.	28.1	27.0s	26.2	25.9	25.8	25.6	25.4
Population age distribution, 60+ [1] Répartition par âge de la population, 60+ [1]	percentage of pop. Pourcentage de la pop.	10.3	11.0	12.2	12.7	13.0	13.2	13.5

Series Séries	Unit or base Unité ou base	2005	2010	2015	2017	2018	2019	2020
Urban population Population urbaine	percentage of pop. pourcentage de la pop.	49.2	51.7	53.9	...	55.3	...	...
Total annual urban growth rate [2] Taux d'accroissement urbaine annuel [2]	percentage of pop. pourcentage de la pop.	2.3	2.2	2.0	...	...	...	...
Total annual rural growth rate [2] Taux d'accroissement rurale annuel [2]	percentage of pop. pourcentage de la pop.	0.3	0.2	0.2	...	...	...	...

Series Séries	Unit or base Unité ou base	2005	2010	2015	2017	2018	2019	2020
International migrant stock: total Stock de migrants internationaux : total	thousand millier	191 616	220 782	248 861	257 715	...	271 642	...
International migrant stock: total Stock de migrants internationaux : total	percentage of pop. pourcentage de la pop.	2.9	3.2	3.4	3.4	...	3.5	...
International migrant stock: male Stock de migrants internationaux : hommes	percentage of pop. pourcentage de la pop.	3.0	3.3	3.5	3.5	...	3.6	...
International migrant stock : female Stock de migrants internationaux : fémmes	percentage of pop. pourcentage de la pop.	2.9	3.1	3.3	3.3	...	3.4	...
Refugees Réfugiés	thousand millier	...	...	15 098	18 474	20 203	20 232	...
Asylum seekers Demandeurs d'asile	thousand millier	...	...	2 344	2 957	3 174	3 727	...
Other of concern to UNHCR Autres personnes relevant de la comp. du HCR	thousand millier	...	...	40 518	45 980	46 974	55 432	...
Total population of concern to UNHCR Population totale de préoccupation pour le HCR	thousand millier	...	...	57 960	67 408	70 351	79 391	...

Gender • Le genre

Series Séries	Unit or base Unité ou base	2005	2010	2015	2017	2018	2019	2020
Seats held by women in national parliament Pro. de sièges occupés par les fem. au par. nat.	percentage of seats pourcentage du sièges	15.9	19.0	22.3	23.4	23.4	24.3	24.9
Girls to boys in primary education Filles/garçons dans l'enseigne. primaire	ratio rapport	0.95	0.97	1.00	1.01	*1.00	...	...
Girls to boys in secondary education Filles/garçons dans l'enseigne. secondaire	ratio rapport	0.94	0.97	0.99	0.99	*0.99	...	...
Girls to boys in tertiary education Filles/garçons dans l'enseigne. supérieur	ratio rapport	1.05	1.08	1.12	1.13	*1.14	...	...

1

World statistics: selected series *(continued)*
Population and social statistics, economic activity and energy, environment and infrastructure
Statistiques mondiales : séries principales *(suite)*
Population et statistiques sociales, activité économique et énergie, environnement et infrastructures

Education • Enseignement

Series Séries	Unit or base Unité ou base	2005	2010	2015	2016	2017	2018	2019
Students enrolled in primary education Les étudiants inscrits dans l'enseignement primaire	thousand millier	678 920	697 001	720 012	736 227	740 868	750 739	...
Gross enrollment ratio - primary, male Taux brut de scolarisation - primaire, hommes	percentage pourcentage	104.5	104.4	102.5	103.5	103.4	103.8	...
Gross enrollment ratio - primary, female Taux brut de scolarisation - primaire, fémmes	percentage pourcentage	99.7	101.8	102.5	104.4	104.0	*104.1	...
Students enrolled in secondary education Les étudiants inscrits dans l'enseignement second.	thousand millier	509 254	546 192	582 977	586 557	588 390	594 663	...
Gross enrollment ratio - secondary, male Taux brut de scolarisation - secondaire, hommes	percentage pourcentage	65.7	72.2	76.9	76.0	75.8	76.0	...
Gross enrollment ratio - secondary, female Taux brut de scolarisation – secondaire, fémmes	percentage pourcentage	62.3	69.8	74.9	75.2	74.9	*75.1	...
Students enrolled in tertiary education Les étudiants inscrits dans l'enseigne. supérieur	thousand millier	139 578	182 258	217 627	220 187	222 657	223 672	...
Gross enrollment ratio - tertiary, male Taux brut de scolarisation - tertiaire, hommes	percentage pourcentage	23.8	28.5	34.8	35.3	35.6	35.6	...
Gross enrollment ratio – tertiary, female Taux brut de scolarisation – tertiaire, féminin	percentage pourcentage	24.9	30.7	38.9	39.7	40.3	40.6	...
Teaching staff at the primary level Personnel enseignant au niveau primaire	thousand millier	26 890	28 671	31 185	31 161	31 676	32 020	...
Teaching staff at the secondary level Personnel enseignant au niveau secondaire	thousand millier	28 494	32 336	33 479	34 321	34 728	34 984	...
Teaching staff at the tertiary level Personnel enseignant au niveau supérieur	thousand millier	9 229	11 151	12 918	13 066	13 166	13 063	...
Pupils to teachers in the primary level Élèves/enseignant dans l'enseigne. primaire	ratio rapport	*25.3	24.3	23.1	23.4	23.4	23.4	...
Pupils to teachers ratio in the secondary level Élèves/enseignant dans l'enseigne. secondaire	ratio rapport	*17.9	16.9	17.4	17.1	17.0	17.0	...

Crime • La criminalité

Series Séries	Unit or base Unité ou base	2005	2010	2015	2016	2017	2018	2019
Intentional homicide rate [3] Homicides volontaires [3]	per 100,000 population pour 100,000 pop.	6.3	6.0	5.9	6.0	6.0	6.0	...

National Accounts • Comptes nationaux

Series Séries	Unit or base Unité ou base	2005	2010	2015	2016	2017	2018	2019
GDP in current prices PIB aux prix courants	billion US $ milliard $ E.-U.	47 605	66 232	74 883	76 019	80 789	85 693	...
GDP per capita PIB par habitant	US $ $ E.-U.	7 279	9 523	10 149	10 187	10 706	11 232	...
GDP in constant 2005 prices PIB aux prix constants	billion US $ milliard $ E.-U.	56 370	64 700	74 883	76 885	79 429	81 894	...
GDP real rates of growth Taux de croissance	percentage pourcentage	4.1	4.4	3.0	2.7	3.3	3.1	...

Labour market • Marché du travail

Series Séries	Unit or base Unité ou base	2005	2010	2015	2017	2018	2019	2020
Labour force - total Force de travail - total	percentage of pop. pourcentage de la pop.	63.8	62.5	61.4	61.0	60.9	60.7	60.5
Labour force - male Force de travail - hommes	percentage of pop. pourcentage de la pop.	77.3	76.1	75.0	74.6	74.4	74.2	74.0
Labour force - female Force de travail - femmes	percentage of pop. pourcentage de la pop.	50.3	48.8	47.7	47.5	47.4	47.2	47.0
Unemployment rate - total Chômage - total	percent. of active pop. pour. de la pop. active	5.9	5.9	5.6	5.6	5.4	5.4	5.4
Unemployment rate - male Chômage - mâle	percent. of active pop. pour. de la pop. active	5.7	5.8	5.5	5.4	5.3	5.3	5.3
Unemployment rate - female Chômage - femmes	percent. of active pop. pour. de la pop. active	6.2	6.1	5.8	5.8	5.6	5.6	5.6

1

World statistics: selected series *(continued)*
Population and social statistics, economic activity and energy, environment and infrastructure
Statistiques mondiales : séries principales *(suite)*
Population et statistiques sociales, activité économique et énergie, environnement et infrastructures

Series / Séries	Unit or base / Unité ou base	2005	2010	2015	2017	2018	2019	2020
Employment in agriculture - total / L'emploi dans agriculture - total	percent. of employees pourcent. des employ.	37.0	33.0	28.9	27.8	27.3	26.8	26.5
Employment in agriculture - male / L'emploi dans agriculture - hommes	percent. of employees pourcent. des employ.	37.3	33.5	29.6	28.6	28.0	27.6	27.2
Employment in agriculture - female / L'emploi dans agriculture - femmes	percent. of employees pourcent. des employ.	36.5	32.3	27.7	26.5	26.0	25.7	25.4
Employment in industry - total / L'emploi dans industrie - total	percent. of employees pourcent. des employ.	21.2	22.6	23.2	22.9	23.0	23.0	23.1
Employment in industry - male / L'emploi dans industrie - hommes	percent. of employees pourcent. des employ.	24.2	26.2	27.3	27.2	27.3	27.5	27.6
Employment in industry - female / L'emploi in industrie - femmes	percent. of employees pourcent. des employ.	16.7	16.9	16.7	16.3	16.3	16.1	16.0
Employment in services - total / L'emploi dans services - total	percent. of employees pourcent. des employ.	41.8	44.4	48.0	49.3	50.0	50.1	50.4
Employment in services - male / L'emploi dans services - hommes	percent. of employees pourcent. des employ.	38.6	40.3	43.1	44.2	44.6	45.0	45.2
Employment in services - female / L'emploi dans services - femmes	percent. of employees pourcent. des employ.	46.8	50.8	55.6	57.2	57.8	58.2	58.6

Price and production indices • Indices de la production

Series / Séries	Unit or base / Unité ou base	2005	2010	2015	2016	2017	2018	2019
Agriculture (gross) / Agriculture (brut)	2004-2006 = 100	99.9	112.9	125.9	127.3	...	...	...
Food (gross) / Ailmentaires (brut)	2004-2006 = 100	99.9	113.4	126.4	127.8	...	...	...

International merchandise trade • Commerce international des marchandises

Series / Séries	Unit or base / Unité ou base	2005	2010	2015	2016	2017	2018	2019
Exports FOB / Exportations FOB	billion US $ milliard $ E.-U.	10 373	15 102	16 362	15 890	17 482	19 132	18 723
Imports CIF / Importations CIF	billion US $ milliard $ E.-U.	10 577	15 275	16 465	16 054	17 773	19 498	18 964
Balance / Balance	billion US $ milliard $ E.-U.	-204	-173	-104	-164	-250	-365	-241

Energy • Ènergie

Series / Séries	Unit or base / Unité ou base	2005	2010	2014	2015	2016	2017	2018
Primary energy production / Production d'énergie primaire	petajoules pétajoules	477 404	530 934	567 115	570 508	570 167	581 665	...
Net imports / Importations nettes	petajoules pétajoules	-13 321	-12 898	-16 226	-17 407	-21 798	-20 029	...
Changes in stocks / Variations des stocks	petajoules pétajoules	-305	73	2 745	2 553	-4 567	-1 762	...
Total supply / Approvisionnement total	petajoules pétajoules	464 387	517 963	548 145	550 548	552 936	563 396	...
Supply per capita / Approvisionnement par habitant	gigajoules gigajoules	71	74	75	75	74	75	...

Environment • Environnement

Series / Séries	Unit or base / Unité ou base	2005	2010	2014	2015	2016	2017	2018
Land area / Terres superficie	1,000 hectares	12 997 688	12 995 550	12 994 955	12 994 900	13 002 515	13 002 855	...
Arable land / Terres arables	000 hectares	1 356 869	1 347 680	1 367 227	1 382 469	1 386 327	1 390 699	...
Arable land / Terres arables	percentage of land pourcent. de la superf.	10.4	10.4	10.5	10.6	10.7	10.7	...
Forest cover / Superficie forestière	1,000 hectares	4 032 743	4 015 673	4 002 441	3 999 133	3 999 133	3 999 133	...
Forest cover / Superficie forestière	percentage of land pourcent. de la superf.	31.0	30.9	30.8	30.8	30.8	30.8	...

1

World statistics: selected series *(continued)*
Population and social statistics, economic activity and energy, environment and infrastructure

Statistiques mondiales : séries principales *(suite)*
Population et statistiques sociales, activité économique et énergie, environnement et infrastructures

Series Séries	Unit or base Unité ou base	2005	2010	2014	2015	2016	2017	2018
Permanent crops Cultures permanentes	1,000 hectares	145 681	158 259	163 875	165 298	166 639	167 877	
Permanent crops Cultures permanentes	percentage of land pourcent. de la superf.	1.1	1.2	1.3	1.3	1.3	1.3	
Sites protected for terrestrial biodiversity Sites pour la bio. terre. dans aires protég	percentage of sites pourcentage du sites	36.2	40.9	42.9	43.1	43.3	43.5	43.7

Science and technology • Science et technologie

Series Séries	Unit or base Unité ou base	2005	2010	2014	2015	2016	2017	2018
Grant of patents Brevets délivrés	per million population par million d'habitants	633 100	914 800	...	1 233 700	1 345 800	1 397 900	1 422 800
Gross domestic expenditure on R & D Dépenses intérieures brutes de R-D	percentage of GDP pourcentage du PIB	1.5	1.6	1.7	1.7	1.7	1.7	...

Communication • Internet users

Series Séries	Unit or base Unité ou base	2005	2010	2014	2015	2016	2017	2018
Internet usage Utilisation d'internet	% of individuals % de personnes	15.7	28.7	39.7	41.5	44.6	49.7	51.4

Development assistance • Aide au developpement

Series Séries	Unit or base Unité ou base	2005	2010	2014	2015	2016	2017	2018
Net ODA received: bilateral APD nette reçue : bilatérale	million US $ million $ E.-U.	81 833	92 131	119 778	111 374	118 315	123 597	121 932
Net ODA received: multilateral APD nette reçue : multilatérale	million US $ million $ E.-U.	25 620	37 133	41 952	35 368	40 493	41 429	44 346
Net ODA received: total APD nette reçue : total	million US $ million $ E.-U.	108 542	131 574	161 730	152 740	157 011	165 026	166 278
Net ODA received: total APD nette reçue : total	% of recipients' GNI % du RNB des bénéfic.	1.2	0.7	0.6	0.6	0.6	0.6	0.6

Source:
These data are presented in other tables of this Yearbook; please refer to the relevant table for source notes and last access data.

Source:
Ces données sont présentées dans d'autres tableaux du présent Annuaire, veuillez donc vous reporter au tableau correspondant pour les notes de source et la date du dernier accès.

1   Mid-year estimates and projections (medium fertility variant).

2   Data refers to a 5-year period preceding the reference year.

3   Data is for 2020, or latest available data from 2005 onwards.

1   Les estimations et projections approximative (variante moyenne fécondité) au milieu de l'année.

2   Les données se réfèrent a période de 5 ans précédant l'année de référence.

3   Données pour 2020, ou dernières données disponibles à partir de 2005.

Part One

Population and social statistics

Première partie

Population et statistiques sociales

2

Population, surface area and density

Population, superficie et densité

Country or area Pays ou zone	Year Année	Mid-year population estimates and projections (millions) Estimations et projections de population au milieu de l'année (millions)			Sex Ratio (males per 100 females) Rapport des sexes (hommes pour 100 femmes)	Population age distribution (percentage) Répartition par âge de la population (pourcentage)		Population density (per km²) Densité de population (pour km²)	Surface area Superficie (000 km²)
		Total	Male Hommes	Females Femmes		Aged 0 to 14 years old âgée de 0 à 14 ans	Aged 60+ years old âgée de 60 ans ou plus		
Total, all countries or areas	2005	6 541.91	3 296.49	3 245.42	101.6	28.1	10.3	50.3	...
	2010	6 956.82	3 507.70	3 449.12	101.7	27.0	11.0	53.5	...
Total, tous pays ou	2017	7 547.86	3 805.47	3 742.39	101.7	25.9	12.7	58.0	136 162
zones	2020	7 794.80	3 929.97	3 864.82	101.7	25.4	13.5	59.9	...
Africa	2005	916.15	456.65	459.51	99.4	41.9	5.1	30.9	...
Afrique	2010	1 039.30	518.25	521.05	99.5	41.5	5.1	35.1	...
	2017	1 244.22	621.39	622.84	99.8	40.9	5.4	42.0	30 311
	2020	1 340.60	669.88	670.72	99.9	40.3	5.5	45.2	...
Northern Africa	2005	186.42	93.70	92.72	101.1	33.5	7.0	24.0	...
Afrique septentrionale	2010	202.94	101.87	101.07	100.8	32.1	7.4	26.1	...
	2017	232.79	116.95	115.84	101.0	32.7	8.3	30.0	7 880
	2020	246.23	123.72	122.51	101.0	32.7	8.8	31.7	...
Sub-Saharan Africa	2005	729.73	362.95	366.79	99.0	44.0	4.6	33.4	...
Afrique subsaharienne	2010	836.36	416.39	419.98	99.1	43.8	4.6	38.2	...
	2017	1 011.43	504.44	506.99	99.5	42.8[1]	4.7	46.2	22 431[2]
	2020	1 094.37	546.16	548.21	99.6	42.1	4.8	50.0	...
Eastern Africa	2005	295.19	146.04	149.15	97.9	45.5	4.3	44.3	...
Afrique orientale	2010	339.32	167.97	171.35	98.0	44.9	4.3	50.9	...
	2017	411.40	204.01	207.39	98.4	42.9	4.5	61.7	7 005
	2020	445.41	221.04	224.37	98.5	41.8	4.6	66.8	...
Middle Africa	2005	112.01	55.69	56.32	98.9	45.7	4.6	17.2	...
Afrique centrale	2010	131.62	65.53	66.09	99.1	45.8	4.4	20.3	...
	2017	164.04	81.82	82.22	99.5	45.6	4.3	25.2	6 613
	2020	179.60	89.62	89.97	99.6	45.0	4.4	27.6	...
Southern Africa	2005	54.64	26.87	27.77	96.7	31.8	6.9	20.6	...
Afrique australe	2010	58.38	28.74	29.65	96.9	30.5	7.0	22.0	...
	2017	64.83	31.93	32.91	97.0	29.9	7.9	24.5	2 675
	2020	67.50	33.21	34.29	96.9	29.5	8.3	25.5	...
Western Africa	2005	267.89[3]	134.34[3]	133.55[3]	100.6[3]	44.1[3]	4.6[3]	44.2	...
Afrique occidentale	2010	307.04[3]	154.15[3]	152.89[3]	100.8[3]	44.2[3]	4.5[3]	50.6	...
	2017	371.16[3]	186.68[3]	184.48[3]	101.2[3]	43.7	4.5[3]	61.2[3]	6 138
	2020	401.86[3]	202.28[3]	199.58[3]	101.4[3]	43.1[3]	4.6[3]	66.3	...
Americas [2]	2005	884.79	436.52	448.26	97.4	26.5	11.9	20.9	...
Amériques [2]	2010	934.64	461.03	473.61	97.3	24.8	13.1	22.1	...
	2017	998.18	492.19	505.99	97.3	22.6	15.5	23.6	42 322
	2020	1 022.83	504.21	518.62	97.2	21.8	16.6	24.2	...
Northern America	2005	327.29	161.58[4]	165.71[4]	97.5[4]	20.6[4]	16.8[4]	17.5	...
Amérique septentrionale	2010	343.29	169.62[4]	173.67[4]	97.7[4]	19.8[4]	18.5[4]	18.4	...
	2017	361.94[4]	179.12[4]	182.82[4]	98.0[4]	18.6	21.7[4]	19.4[4]	21 776
	2020	368.87[4]	182.58[4]	186.29[4]	98.0[4]	18.1[4]	23.1[4]	19.8	...
Latin America & the Caribbean	2005	557.50	274.95	282.56	97.3	29.9	9.0	27.7	...
	2010	591.35	291.42	299.94	97.2	27.7	10.0	29.4	...
Amérique latine et	2017	636.23	313.07	323.17	96.9	24.9	12.0	31.6	20 546
Caraïbes	2020	653.96	321.63	332.33	96.8	23.9	13.0	32.5	...
Caribbean	2005	39.75	19.68[5]	20.07[5]	98.0[5]	28.2[5]	11.1[5]	175.9	...
Caraïbes	2010	41.22	20.39[5]	20.83[5]	97.9[5]	26.5[5]	12.0[5]	182.4	...
	2017	43.00[5]	21.25[5]	21.75[5]	97.7[5]	24.6	13.9[5]	190.3	234
	2020	43.53	21.49[5]	22.04[5]	97.5[5]	23.9[5]	14.9[5]	192.6	...
Central America	2005	145.95	71.51	74.44	96.1	33.4	7.8	59.5	...
Amérique centrale	2010	157.59	77.24	80.35	96.1	30.9	8.4	64.3	...
	2017	173.33	84.93	88.40	96.1	28.0	9.9	70.7	2 480
	2020	179.67	88.05	91.62	96.1	26.9	10.7	73.3	...
South America	2005	371.80	183.76[6]	188.05[6]	97.7[6]	28.8[6]	9.2[6]	21.3	...
Amérique du Sud	2010	392.54	193.79[6]	198.76[6]	97.5[6]	26.5[6]	10.4[6]	22.5	...
	2017	419.90[6]	206.89[6]	213.01[6]	97.1[6]	23.6	12.6[6]	24.0	17 832
	2020	430.76	212.08[6]	218.68[6]	97.0[6]	22.6[6]	13.7[6]	24.7	...

| Country or area
Pays ou zone | Year
Année | Mid-year population estimates and projections (millions)
Estimations et projections de population au milieu de l'année (millions) | | | Sex Ratio
(males per 100 females)
Rapport des sexes (hommes pour 100 femmes) | Population age distribution (percentage)
Répartition par âge de la population (pourcentage) | | Population density
(per km²)
Densité de population (pour km²) | Surface area
Superficie
(000 km²) |
		Total	Male Hommes	Females Femmes		Aged 0 to 14 years old âgée de 0 à 14 ans	Aged 60+ years old âgée de 60 ans ou plus		
Asia Asie	2005	3 977.99	2 035.22	1 942.76	104.8	27.6	9.1	128.2	...
	2010	4 209.59	2 155.31	2 054.28	104.9	25.9	10.0	135.6	...
	2017	4 519.04	2 311.79	2 207.25	104.7	24.1	12.1	145.6	31 915
	2020	4 641.05	2 373.46	2 267.59	104.7	23.5	13.1	149.6	...
Central Asia Asie centrale	2005	58.45	28.82	29.63	97.2	30.9	7.3	14.9	...
	2010	62.81	31.02	31.79	97.6	28.7	7.0	16.0	...
	2017	70.87	35.07	35.80	98.0	29.9	8.1	18.0	4 103[2]
	2020	74.34	36.81	37.53	98.1	30.5	8.9	18.9	...
Eastern Asia Asie orientale	2005	1 564.19	798.71	765.49	104.3	19.8	12.2	135.3	...
	2010	1 604.86	819.65	785.21	104.4	18.2	13.8	138.8	...
	2017	1 659.77	846.78	812.98	104.2	17.4	17.5	143.6	11 799
	2020	1 678.09	855.48	822.61	104.0	17.1	18.9	145.2	...
South-central Asia Asie centrale et du Sud	2005	1 647.07	851.43	795.64	107.0	33.5	7.0	159.5	...
	2010	1 775.36	916.46	858.90	106.7	31.6	7.5	171.9	...
	2017	1 944.11	1 001.70	942.41	106.3	28.7	8.8	188.3	10 791
	2020	2 014.71	1 037.60	977.11	106.2	27.6	9.5	195.1	...
South-eastern Asia Asie du Sud-Est	2005	561.16	279.66	281.50	99.3	29.9	7.6	129.3	...
	2010	596.95	298.34	298.60	99.9	27.9	8.1	137.5	...
	2017	648.46	323.96	324.50	99.8	26.0	10.0	149.4	4 495
	2020	668.62	333.93	334.69	99.8	25.2	11.1	154.0	...
Southern Asia Asie méridionale	2005	1 588.62	822.61	766.01	107.4	33.6	7.0	248.2	...
	2010	1 712.56	885.44	827.11	107.1	31.7	7.5	267.6	...
	2017	1 873.24	966.63	906.61	106.6	28.6	8.8	292.7	6 688[2]
	2020	1 940.37	1 000.79	939.58	106.5	27.5	9.5	303.2	...
Western Asia Asie occidentale	2005	205.56	105.43	100.13	105.3	33.5	7.2	42.8	...
	2010	232.43	120.86	111.57	108.3	31.1	7.3	48.4	...
	2017	266.70	139.35	127.36	109.4	28.9	8.2	55.5	4 831
	2020	279.64	146.46	133.18	110.0	28.1	8.8	58.2	...
Europe Europe	2005	729.29	351.22	378.06	92.9	15.9	20.6	32.9	...
	2010	736.41	354.62	381.80	92.9	15.5	22.0	33.3	...
	2017	745.41	359.58	385.84	93.2	15.9	24.5	33.7	23 049
	2020	747.64	361.06	386.58	93.4	16.1	25.7	33.8	...
Eastern Europe Europe orientale	2005	297.50	140.21	157.29	89.1	15.4	18.2	16.5	...
	2010	294.87	138.61	156.26	88.7	14.9	19.3	16.3	...
	2017	294.06	138.30	155.76	88.8	16.5	22.4	16.3	18 814
	2020	293.01	137.83	155.18	88.8	17.0	23.7	16.2	...
Northern Europe Europe septentrionale	2005	96.31	47.13[7]	49.18[7]	95.8[7]	18.0[7]	21.1[7]	56.6	...
	2010	100.40	49.28[7]	51.12[7]	96.4[7]	17.4[7]	22.6[7]	59.0	...
	2017	104.68[7]	51.62[7]	53.06[7]	97.3[7]	17.5	24.0[7]	61.5	1 810
	2020	106.26	52.49[7]	53.77[7]	97.6[7]	17.5[7]	24.8[7]	62.4	...
Southern Europe Europe méridionale	2005	149.68	73.24[8]	76.44[8]	95.8[8]	15.1[8]	22.5[8]	115.6	...
	2010	153.02	74.75[8]	78.26[8]	95.5[8]	14.9[8]	24.0[8]	118.2	...
	2017	152.80[8]	74.56[8]	78.24[8]	95.3[8]	14.3	26.6[8]	118.0	1 317
	2020	152.22	74.37[8]	77.85[8]	95.5[8]	13.9[8]	27.9[8]	117.5	...
Western Europe Europe occidentale	2005	185.80	90.64[9]	95.16[9]	95.2[9]	16.4[9]	22.6[9]	171.3	...
	2010	188.13	91.96[9]	96.16[9]	95.6[9]	15.9[9]	24.3[9]	173.4	...
	2017	193.89[9]	95.10[9]	98.79[9]	96.3[9]	15.6	26.4[9]	178.7	1 108
	2020	196.15	96.37[9]	99.77[9]	96.6[9]	15.6[9]	27.4[9]	180.8	...
Oceania Océanie	2005	33.69	16.87	16.82	100.2	25.0	14.0	4.0	...
	2010	36.87	18.49	18.38	100.6	24.1	15.2	4.3	...
	2017	41.01	20.52	20.48	100.2	23.7[10]	16.7	4.8	8 564
	2020	42.68	21.36	21.31	100.2	23.6	17.5	5.0	...
Australia and New Zealand Australie et Nouvelle-Zélande	2005	24.31	12.10	12.22	99.0	20.1	17.3	3.1	...
	2010	26.52	13.23	13.30	99.4	19.3	18.8	3.3	...
	2017	29.29	14.56	14.73	98.8	19.2[11]	20.8	3.7	8 012
	2020	30.32	15.07	15.25	98.8	19.3	21.8	3.8	...

Country or area Pays ou zone	Year Année	Mid-year population estimates and projections (millions) Estimations et projections de population au milieu de l'année (millions)			Sex Ratio (males per 100 females) Rapport des sexes (hommes pour 100 femmes)	Population age distribution (percentage) Répartition par âge de la population (pourcentage)		Population density (per km²) Densité de population (pour km²)	Surface area Superficie (000 km²)
		Total	Male Hommes	Females Femmes		Aged 0 to 14 years old âgée de 0 à 14 ans	Aged 60+ years old âgée de 60 ans ou plus		
Melanesia Mélanésie	2005	8.23	4.19	4.04	103.6	38.1	5.3	15.5	...
	2010	9.19	4.67	4.51	103.6	37.2	5.7	17.3	...
	2017	10.51	5.36	5.16	103.9	35.6	6.1	19.9	541
	2020	11.12	5.67	5.45	104.0	34.7	6.5	21.0	...
Micronesia Micronésie	2005	0.50	0.25[12]	0.25[12]	102.0[12]	33.4[12]	6.4[12]	157.2	...
	2010	0.50	0.26[12]	0.25[12]	102.6[12]	32.1[12]	7.4[12]	158.9	...
	2017	0.53[12]	0.27[12]	0.26[12]	102.3[12]	30.0	9.7[12]	168.1	3
	2020	0.55	0.28[12]	0.27[12]	102.1[12]	29.3[12]	10.9[12]	173.2	...
Polynesia Polynésie	2005	0.65[13]	0.33[14]	0.32[14]	104.6[14]	34.1[14]	7.6[14]	79.8[13]	...
	2010	0.66[13]	0.33[14]	0.32[14]	104.0[14]	32.0[14]	8.4[14]	81.2[13]	...
	2017	0.67[14]	0.34[14]	0.33[14]	103.0[14]	30.2	10.2[14]	83.2[13]	8
	2020	0.68[13]	0.35[14]	0.34[14]	102.9[14]	29.2[14]	11.2[14]	84.5[13]	...
Afghanistan Afghanistan	2005	25.65	13.24	12.41	106.6	47.9	3.7	39.3	...
	2010	29.19	14.94	14.25	104.8	48.2	3.9	44.7	...
	2017	36.30	18.65	17.64	105.7	43.7	4.1	55.6	653
	2020	38.93	19.98	18.95	105.4	41.8	4.2	59.6	...
Albania Albanie	2005	3.09	1.55	1.53	101.1	26.5	12.3	112.7	...
	2010	2.95	1.49	1.46	101.5	22.5	15.0	107.6	...
	2017	2.88	1.47	1.41	103.9	18.0	19.1	105.3	29
	2020	2.88	1.46	1.41	103.7	17.2	21.2	105.0	...
Algeria Algérie	2005	33.15	16.77	16.38	102.3	29.2	7.0	13.9	...
	2010	35.98	18.16	17.82	101.9	27.3	7.8	15.1	...
	2017	41.39	20.91	20.48	102.1	29.6	9.3	17.4	2 382
	2020	43.85	22.15	21.70	102.1	30.8	9.9	18.4	...
American Samoa Samoa américaines	2000	0.06	...	...	104.4[15,16]	38.8[15,16]	5.4[15,16]	287.6	...
	2005	0.06	...	...	...	...	...	295.6	...
	2010	0.06	...	...	103.0[15,16]	35.0[15,16]	6.7[15,16]	278.2	...
	2016	0.06[17]	...	...	# 103.6	# 33.3	# 9.0	278.0[17]	~0
	2017	0.06[17]	...	...	...	...	...	278.2[17]	...
	2020	0.06	...	...	...	...	...	279.0	...
Andorra Andorre	2005	0.08	...	...	109.0[15,18]	15.1[15,18]	16.1[15,18]	167.8	...
	2010	0.08	...	...	108.5[15,18]	14.0[15,18]	18.6[15,18]	179.7	...
	2016	0.08[17]	...	...	102.3[15,18]	14.4[15,18]	19.0[15,18]	164.4[17]	~0
	2017	0.08[17]	...	...	...	...	...	163.8[17]	...
	2020	0.08	...	...	...	...	...	164.2	...
Angola Angola	2005	19.43	9.64	9.79	98.4	46.9	4.0	15.6	...
	2010	23.36	11.55	11.81	97.8	47.0	3.8	18.7	...
	2017	29.82	14.75	15.07	97.9	47.0	3.6	23.9	1 247
	2020	32.87	16.26	16.61	97.9	46.4	3.7	26.4	...
Anguilla Anguilla	2001	0.01	...	...	97.3	27.7	10.2	126.4	...
	2005	0.01	...	...	...	...	...	140.4	...
	2010	0.01	...	...	...	...	...	153.0	...
	2011	0.01	...	...	* 97.6	* 23.3	* 7.6[19]	155.0	...
	2017	0.01[17]	...	...	...	...	...	165.7[17]	~0
	2020	0.02	...	...	...	...	...	169.8	...
Antigua and Barbuda Antigua-et-Barbuda	2005	0.08	0.04	0.04	90.2	26.5	9.8	185.1	...
	2010	0.09	0.04	0.05	91.7	24.3	10.7	200.1	...
	2017	0.10	0.05	0.05	93.0	22.2	12.8	216.9	~0
	2020	0.10	0.05	0.05	93.3	21.9	14.1	222.6	...
Argentina Argentine	2005	38.89	18.90	20.00	94.5	27.3	13.6	14.2	...
	2010	40.90	19.90	21.00	94.8	26.0	14.2	14.9	...
	2017	43.94	21.42	22.52	95.1	24.9	15.1	16.1	2 780
	2020	45.20	22.05	23.15	95.3	24.4	15.5	16.5	...
Armenia Arménie	2005	2.98	1.40	1.58	88.8	21.5	14.4	104.7	...
	2010	2.88	1.35	1.53	87.9	19.5	14.8	101.1	...
	2017	2.94	1.39	1.56	88.8	20.5	16.8	103.4	30
	2020	2.96	1.39	1.57	88.8	20.8	18.5	104.1	...

| Country or area
Pays ou zone | Year
Année | Mid-year population estimates and projections (millions)
Estimations et projections de population au milieu de l'année (millions) | | | Sex Ratio
(males per 100 females)
Rapport des sexes (hommes pour 100 femmes) | Population age distribution (percentage)
Répartition par âge de la population (pourcentage) | | Population density
(per km²)
Densité de population (pour km²) | Surface area
Superficie
(000 km²) |
		Total	Male Hommes	Females Femmes		Aged 0 to 14 years old âgée de 0 à 14 ans	Aged 60+ years old âgée de 60 ans ou plus		
Aruba Aruba	2005	0.10	0.05	0.05	90.7	21.5	12.6	555.7	...
	2010	0.10	0.05	0.05	91.1	20.9	15.5	564.8	...
	2017	0.11	0.05	0.06	90.4	18.0	19.7	585.4	~0
	2020	0.11	0.05	0.06	90.2	17.4	21.8	593.1	...
Australia Australie	2005[11]	20.18	10.07	10.11	99.6	19.8	17.4	2.6	...
	2010[11]	22.15	11.08	11.08	100.0	19.0	18.8	2.9	...
	2017	24.58[11]	12.24[11]	12.34[11]	99.2[11]	19.1	20.8[11]	3.2[11]	7 692[20]
	2020[11]	25.50	12.70	12.80	99.2	19.3	21.8	3.3	...
Austria Autriche	2005	8.25	4.01	4.24	94.6	16.0	22.1	100.2	...
	2010	8.41	4.10	4.31	95.1	14.7	23.3	102.1	...
	2017	8.82	4.33	4.49	96.4	14.2	24.7	107.0	84
	2020	9.01	4.44	4.57	97.2	14.4	25.7	109.3	...
Azerbaijan Azerbaïdjan	2005[21]	8.54	4.21	4.33	97.1	26.2	8.5	103.3	...
	2010[21]	9.03	4.48	4.56	98.2	22.8	8.1	109.3	...
	2017	9.85[21]	4.91[21]	4.94[21]	99.4[21]	23.3	10.1[21]	119.1[21]	87
	2020[21]	10.14	5.06	5.07	99.8	23.5	11.6	122.7	...
Bahamas Bahamas	2005	0.32	0.16	0.17	94.4	28.1	8.6	32.5	...
	2010	0.35	0.17	0.18	94.0	26.9	9.0	35.5	...
	2017	0.38	0.19	0.20	94.4	22.9[21]	10.9	38.1	14
	2020	0.39	0.19	0.20	94.5	21.6	12.2	39.3	...
Bahrain Bahreïn	2005	0.89	0.53	0.36	150.5	25.7	3.4	1 170.0	...
	2010	1.24	0.77	0.47	165.8	20.3	3.5	1 632.7	...
	2017	1.49	0.94	0.55	169.6	19.8	4.6	1 965.9	1
	2020	1.70	1.10	0.60	183.1	18.3	5.3	2 238.9	...
Bangladesh Bangladesh	2005	139.04	71.22	67.81	105.0	34.4	6.7	1 068.1	...
	2010	147.58	75.02	72.56	103.4	32.0	7.0	1 133.7	...
	2017	159.69	80.87	78.82	102.6	28.2	7.4	1 226.7	148
	2020	164.69	83.26	81.43	102.2	26.8	8.0	1 265.2	...
Barbados Barbade	2005	0.28	0.13	0.14	92.3	20.6	16.1	642.6	...
	2010	0.28	0.14	0.15	92.3	19.7	18.1	656.1	...
	2017	0.29	0.14	0.15	93.4	17.6	21.4	665.7	~0
	2020	0.29	0.14	0.15	93.8	16.8	23.2	668.3	...
Belarus Bélarus	2005	9.56	4.46	5.10	87.6	15.6	18.5	47.1	...
	2010	9.42	4.38	5.04	86.9	14.9	19.1	46.4	...
	2017	9.45	4.40	5.05	87.1	16.7	21.3	46.6	208
	2020	9.45	4.40	5.05	87.1	17.2	22.6	46.6	...
Belgium Belgique	2005	10.55	5.17	5.37	96.3	17.2	22.1	348.3	...
	2010	10.94	5.37	5.57	96.5	16.9	23.2	361.3	...
	2017	11.42	5.63	5.79	97.3	17.0	24.6	377.1	31
	2020	11.59	5.74	5.85	98.3	17.0	25.6	382.7	...
Belize Belize	2005	0.28	0.14	0.14	101.1	38.9	4.8	12.4	...
	2010	0.32	0.16	0.16	100.1	35.6	6.0	14.1	...
	2017	0.38	0.19	0.19	99.4	30.9	7.0	16.5	23
	2020	0.40	0.20	0.20	98.9	29.2	7.6	17.4	...
Benin Bénin	2005	7.98	3.96	4.03	98.2	44.4	5.0	70.8	...
	2010	9.20	4.57	4.63	98.7	43.8	4.9	81.6	...
	2017	11.18	5.57	5.60	99.5	42.7	5.0	99.1	115
	2020	12.12	6.05	6.07	99.8	41.9	5.1	107.5	...
Bermuda Bermudes	2005	0.07	...	...	91.8[15,22]	18.4[15]	16.4[15]	1 302.6	...
	2010	0.06	...	...	92.4[15,23]	17.4[15]	18.7[15]	1 279.1	...
	2017	0.06[17]	...	...	91.4[15,23]	14.8[15,23]	24.9[15,23]	1 227.0[17]	~0
	2020	0.06	...	...	...	...	...	1 212.8	...
Bhutan Bhoutan	2005	0.65	0.34	0.31	110.2	35.1	6.8	17.0	...
	2010	0.69	0.36	0.33	110.7	31.2	7.5	18.0	...
	2017	0.75	0.39	0.35	112.4	26.2	8.4	19.6[4][15,2]	38
	2020	0.77	0.41	0.36	113.4	24.9	9.0	20.2	...

Country or area Pays ou zone	Year Année	Mid-year population estimates and projections (millions) Estimations et projections de population au milieu de l'année (millions)			Sex Ratio (males per 100 females) Rapport des sexes (hommes pour 100 femmes)	Population age distribution (percentage) Répartition par âge de la population (pourcentage)		Population density (per km²) Densité de population (pour km²)	Surface area Superficie (000 km²)
		Total	Male Hommes	Females Femmes		Aged 0 to 14 years old âgée de 0 à 14 ans	Aged 60+ years old âgée de 60 ans ou plus		
Bolivia (Plurin. State of) Bolivie (État plurin. de)	2005	9.23	4.65	4.58	101.4	36.3	8.1	8.5	...
	2010	10.05	5.06	4.99	101.3	34.5	8.8	9.3	...
	2017	11.19	5.62	5.57	100.9	31.5[15,24]	9.8[15,24]	10.3	1 099[25]
	2020	11.67	5.86	5.82	100.7	30.2	10.4	10.8	...
Bonaire, St. Eustatius & Saba Bonaire, St-Eustache et Saba	2005	0.01	...	...	...	...	...	43.9	...
	2010	0.02	...	...	...	...	...	63.8	...
	2020	0.03	...	...	...	...	...	79.9	...
Bosnia and Herzegovina Bosnie-Herzégovine	2005	3.77	1.85	1.92	96.5	17.7	17.4	73.8	...
	2010	3.71	1.82	1.89	96.5	15.7	19.3	72.7	...
	2017	3.35	1.64	1.71	96.1	14.8	23.0	65.7	51
	2020	3.28	1.61	1.67	96.0	14.5	25.3	64.3	...
Botswana Botswana	2005	1.80	0.87	0.92	94.7	36.5	5.1	3.2	...
	2010	1.99	0.97	1.02	95.7	35.0	5.3	3.5	...
	2017	2.21	1.06	1.14	93.0	34.4	6.5	3.9	582
	2020	2.35	1.14	1.21	93.9	33.4	7.0	4.1	...
Brazil Brésil	2005	186.13	92.00	94.13	97.7	27.4	8.8	22.3	...
	2010	195.71	96.54	99.18	97.3	24.8	10.2	23.4	...
	2017	207.83	102.23	105.60	96.8	21.7	12.7	24.9	8 516
	2020	212.56	104.44	108.12	96.6	20.7	14.0	25.4	...
British Virgin Islands Îles Vierges britanniques	2001	0.02	...	...	106.1	26.3	7.4	140.6	...
	2005	0.02	...	...	...	...	...	154.5	...
	2010	0.03	...	...	97.1	22.3	9.7	181.5	...
	2017	0.03[17]	...	...	...	...	...	208.0[17]	~0
	2020	0.03	...	...	...	...	...	217.6	...
Brunei Darussalam Brunéi Darussalam	2005	0.37	0.19	0.18	104.3	27.8	4.8	69.3	...
	2010	0.39	0.20	0.19	106.8	26.0	5.4	73.7	...
	2017	0.42	0.22	0.20	108.3	23.5	7.9	80.5	6
	2020	0.44	0.23	0.21	107.8	22.3	9.5	83.0	...
Bulgaria Bulgarie	2005	7.69	3.74	3.95	94.8	13.6	23.1	70.8	...
	2010	7.43	3.62	3.81	94.9	13.5	25.3	68.4	...
	2017	7.10	3.45	3.65	94.6	14.4	27.6	65.4	111
	2020	6.95	3.37	3.57	94.4	14.7	28.2	64.0	...
Burkina Faso Burkina Faso	2005	13.42	6.62	6.80	97.4	46.5	4.1	49.1	...
	2010	15.61	7.74	7.87	98.3	46.2	3.9	57.0	...
	2017	19.19	9.57	9.62	99.5	45.2	3.9	70.2	273
	2020	20.90	10.44	10.46	99.9	44.4	3.9	76.4	...
Burundi Burundi	2005	7.36	3.63	3.74	97.2	47.0	3.4	286.8	...
	2010	8.68	4.29	4.39	97.7	45.1	3.3	337.8	...
	2017	10.83	5.37	5.46	98.2	45.6	3.8	421.6	28
	2020	11.89	5.90	5.99	98.5	45.3	4.1	463.0	...
Cabo Verde Cabo Verde	2005	0.46	0.23	0.24	94.8	37.6	7.2	114.9	...
	2010	0.49	0.25	0.25	99.8	32.3	6.5	122.2	...
	2017	0.54	0.27	0.27	100.7	29.2	7.0	133.4	4
	2020	0.56	0.28	0.28	100.8	28.1	7.6	138.0	...
Cambodia Cambodge	2005	13.27	6.44	6.83	94.3	37.1	5.3	75.2	...
	2010	14.31	6.97	7.34	95.0	33.3	5.9	81.1	...
	2017	16.01	7.81	8.20	95.3	31.3	7.1	90.7	181
	2020	16.72	8.16	8.56	95.4	30.9	7.6	94.7	...
Cameroon Cameroun	2005	17.73	8.84	8.90	99.3	44.2	4.7	37.5	...
	2010	20.34	10.15	10.19	99.7	43.7	4.4	43.0	...
	2017	24.57	12.28	12.29	99.9	42.9	4.3	52.0	476
	2020	26.55	13.28	13.27	100.1	42.1	4.3	56.2	...
Canada Canada	2005	32.16	15.95	16.22	98.3	17.7	17.9	3.5	...
	2010	34.15	16.94	17.21	98.5	16.5	19.9	3.8	...
	2017	36.73	18.22	18.51	98.4	15.9	23.3	4.0	9 985
	2020	37.74	18.73	19.01	98.5	15.8	24.9	4.2	...

Country or area Pays ou zone	Year Année	Mid-year population estimates and projections (millions) Estimations et projections de population au milieu de l'année (millions) Total		Male Hommes	Females Femmes	Sex Ratio (males per 100 females) Rapport des sexes (hommes pour 100 femmes)	Population age distribution (percentage) Répartition par âge de la population (pourcentage) Aged 0 to 14 years old âgée de 0 à 14 ans	Aged 60+ years old âgée de 60 ans ou plus	Population density (per km²) Densité de population (pour km²)	Surface area Superficie (000 km²)
Cayman Islands	2005	0.05		...	...	101.0[15]	...	...	202.6	...
Îles Caïmanes	2010	0.06		...	...	97.8[15,26]	18.1[15,26]	8.6[15,26]	231.3	
	2015	0.06		...	...	100.4[15]	18.3[15]	6.7[15,19]	249.8	~0
	2017	0.06[17]		...	...	...	...	...	256.5[17]	~0
	2020	0.06		...	...	...	...	...	266.2	...
Central African Republic	2005	4.04		2.00	2.04	97.7	43.5	5.0	6.5	...
République	2010	4.39		2.17	2.22	98.0	44.1	4.6	7.0	
centrafricaine	2017	4.60		2.28	2.32	98.3	44.6	4.5	7.4	623
	2020	4.83		2.39	2.44	98.3	43.5	4.5	7.8	...
Chad	2005	10.10		5.03	5.07	99.3	49.1	4.2	8.0	...
Tchad	2010	11.95		5.96	5.99	99.5	48.8	3.9	9.5	
	2017	15.02		7.50	7.52	99.6	47.4	3.9	11.9	1 284
	2020	16.43		8.20	8.23	99.7	46.5	3.9	13.0	...
Channel Islands	2005[27]	0.15		0.07	0.08	96.1	16.3	20.6	798.3	...
Îles Anglo-Normandes	2010[27]	0.16		0.08	0.08	97.1	15.5	21.5	840.7	
	2017	0.17[27]		0.08[27]	0.09[27]	97.8[27]	15.3	22.9[27]	887.7[27]	~0[27]
	2020[27]	0.17		0.09	0.09	98.0	15.0	24.0	915.1	...
Chile	2005	16.18		7.96	8.22	96.9	24.7	11.9	21.8	...
Chili	2010	17.06		8.40	8.67	96.9	22.1	13.3	22.9	
	2017	18.47		9.10	9.37	97.1	20.0[27]	16.1	24.8	756
	2020	19.12		9.43	9.69	97.3	19.2	17.4	25.7	...
China	2005[28]	1 330.78		683.49	647.29	105.6	20.4	10.8	141.7	...
Chine	2010[28]	1 368.81		703.41	665.40	105.7	18.7	12.2	145.8	
	2017	1 421.02[28]		729.46[28]	691.56[28]	105.5[28]	17.9	16.0[28]	151.4[28]	9 600
	2020[28]	1 439.32		738.25	701.08	105.3	17.7	17.4	153.3	...
China, Hong Kong SAR	2005	6.77		3.25	3.52	92.5	14.3	15.6	6 447.2	...
Chine, RAS de Hong	2010	6.97		3.28	3.69	88.8	11.9	18.4	6 634.6	
Kong	2017	7.31		3.37	3.93	85.8	11.5[28]	23.5	6 958.4	1
	2020	7.50		3.44	4.06	84.8	12.7	26.1	7 140.0	...
China, Macao SAR	2005	0.48		0.23	0.25	90.5	17.0	9.6	16 149.1	...
Chine, RAS de Macao	2010	0.54		0.26	0.28	92.3	13.0	10.9	18 000.6	
	2017	0.62		0.30	0.32	92.3	13.3	16.1	20 822.2	~0[29]
	2020	0.65		0.31	0.34	92.5	14.4	18.9	21 716.9	...
Colombia	2005	42.65		20.90	21.75	96.1	30.3	8.4	38.4	...
Colombie	2010	45.22		22.16	23.06	96.1	27.3	9.7	40.8	
	2017	48.91		23.99	24.92	96.3	23.6	12.1	44.1	1 142
	2020	50.88		24.98	25.90	96.5	22.2	13.2	45.9	...
Comoros	2005	0.61		0.31	0.30	101.4	42.3	4.6	328.7	...
Comores	2010	0.69		0.35	0.34	101.6	41.0	4.5	370.6	
	2017	0.81		0.41	0.40	101.8	39.8	4.9	437.3	2
	2020	0.87		0.44	0.43	101.8	39.0	5.1	467.3	...
Congo	2005	3.62		1.80	1.83	98.3	41.8	4.1	10.6	...
Congo	2010	4.27		2.13	2.15	99.0	41.6	4.0	12.5	
	2017	5.11		2.55	2.56	99.7	41.9	4.3	15.0	342
	2020	5.52		2.76	2.76	99.8	41.3	4.5	16.2	...
Cook Islands	2001	0.02		...	...	106.6	30.0	10.6	76.3	...
Îles Cook	2005	0.02		...	...	...	...	...	82.1	...
	2006	0.02		...	...	* 103.1	* 26.1	* 11.9	82.1	...
	2010	0.02		...	...	...	...	...	77.3	...
	2016	0.02[17]		...	...	# 97.4	# 26.9	# 14.2	72.4[17]	...
	2017	0.02[17]		...	...	...	...	...	72.4[17]	~0
	2020	0.02		...	...	...	...	...	73.0	...
Costa Rica	2005	4.29		2.15	2.14	100.5	27.4	9.2	83.9	...
Costa Rica	2010	4.58		2.29	2.28	100.4	24.3	10.8	89.6	
	2017	4.95		2.48	2.47	100.0	21.6	13.5	96.9	51
	2020	5.09		2.55	2.55	99.8	20.8	15.0	99.8	...

Country or area Pays ou zone	Year Année	Mid-year population estimates and projections (millions) Estimations et projections de population au milieu de l'année (millions)			Sex Ratio (males per 100 females) Rapport des sexes (hommes pour 100 femmes)	Population age distribution (percentage) Répartition par âge de la population (pourcentage)		Population density (per km²) Densité de population (pour km²)	Surface area Superficie (000 km²)
		Total	Male Hommes	Females Femmes		Aged 0 to 14 years old âgée de 0 à 14 ans	Aged 60+ years old âgée de 60 ans ou plus		
Côte d'Ivoire Côte d'Ivoire	2005	18.35	9.38	8.98	104.5	44.1	4.7	57.7	...
	2010	20.53	10.43	10.11	103.2	43.6	4.5	64.6	...
	2017	24.44	12.34	12.09	102.1	42.2	4.6	76.8	322
	2020	26.38	13.30	13.08	101.7	41.5	4.7	83.0	...
Croatia Croatie	2005	4.38	2.11	2.27	92.9	15.7	21.9	78.2	...
	2010	4.33	2.08	2.24	92.9	15.4	23.8	77.3	...
	2017	4.18	2.01	2.17	92.7	14.4	27.1	74.7	57
	2020	4.11	1.98	2.13	93.1	14.5	28.3	73.4	...
Cuba Cuba	2005	11.26	5.61	5.65	99.4	19.2	15.4	105.8	...
	2010	11.23	5.58	5.64	99.0	17.7	17.3	105.5	...
	2017	11.34	5.63	5.71	98.7	16.4	20.0	106.5	110
	2020	11.33	5.62	5.70	98.6	15.9	21.3	106.4	...
Curaçao Curaçao	2005	0.13	0.06	0.07	88.2	21.6	17.1	293.1	...
	2010	0.15	0.07	0.08	85.0	20.7	18.6	336.0	...
	2017	0.16	0.07	0.09	84.7	19.3	22.7	364.9	~0
	2020	0.16	0.08	0.09	85.1	18.2	24.5	369.6	...
Cyprus Chypre	2005[30]	1.03	0.52	0.51	102.6	20.0	14.9	111.2	...
	2010[30]	1.11	0.56	0.56	99.7	17.8	16.1	120.4	...
	2017	1.18[30]	0.59[30]	0.59[30]	100.2[30]	16.8	18.5[30]	127.7[30]	9
	2020[30]	1.21	0.60	0.60	99.9	16.6	19.8	130.7	...
Czechia Tchéquie	2005	10.26	5.00	5.26	95.0	14.7	19.8	132.8	...
	2010	10.54	5.17	5.37	96.4	14.2	22.4	136.4	...
	2017	10.64	5.23	5.41	96.7	15.4[30]	25.5	137.8	79
	2020	10.71	5.27	5.44	97.0	15.8	26.2	138.6	...
Dem. People's Rep. Korea Rép. pop. dém. de Corée	2005	23.90	11.67	12.23	95.4	24.7	11.9	198.5	...
	2010	24.55	11.99	12.55	95.5	22.6	12.9	203.9	...
	2017	25.43	12.44	12.99	95.7	20.5	13.5	211.2	121
	2020	25.78	12.61	13.17	95.7	19.8	15.1	214.1	...
Dem. Rep. of the Congo Rép. dém. du Congo	2005	54.79	27.22	27.56	98.8	45.8	4.7	24.2	...
	2010	64.56	32.14	32.42	99.1	46.1	4.7	28.5	...
	2017	81.40	40.61	40.79	99.6	46.3	4.7	35.9	2 345
	2020	89.56	44.71	44.85	99.7	45.8	4.7	39.5	...
Denmark Danemark	2005	5.42	2.69	2.74	98.1	18.7	21.2	127.8	...
	2010	5.55	2.76	2.80	98.5	17.9	23.3	130.9	...
	2017	5.73	2.85	2.88	98.9	16.5	25.3	135.1	43
	2020	5.79	2.88	2.91	98.9	16.3	26.1	136.5	...
Djibouti Djibouti	2005	0.78	0.39	0.39	101.0	37.9	5.2	33.8	...
	2010	0.84	0.45	0.39	113.7	32.6	6.1	36.2	...
	2017	0.94	0.50	0.45	111.3	30.0	6.8	40.7	23
	2020	0.99	0.52	0.47	110.7	28.9	7.4	42.6	...
Dominica Dominique	2001	0.07	...	...	101.5[31]	29.0[32]	13.2[32]	92.9	...
	2005	0.07	...	...	101.4	...	...	94.2	...
	2006	0.07	...	...	103.7	29.5	13.3	94.4	...
	2010	0.07	...	...	101.4	...	...	95.3	...
	2014	0.07	...	...	103.0	...	...	97.0	1
	2017	0.07[17]	...	...	...	...	...	98.6[17]	1
	2020	0.08	...	...	...	...	...	100.1	...
Dominican Republic République dominicaine	2005	9.10	4.58	4.52	101.2	33.0	7.7	188.3	...
	2010	9.70	4.87	4.83	100.8	30.6	8.5	200.6	...
	2017	10.51	5.26	5.25	100.1	28.3	10.2	217.6	49
	2020	10.85	5.42	5.43	99.8	27.4	11.1	224.5	...
Ecuador Équateur	2005	13.83	6.93	6.89	100.6	33.1	7.8	55.7	...
	2010	15.01	7.52	7.49	100.4	31.0	8.6	60.4	...
	2017	16.79	8.40	8.39	100.2	28.4	10.2	67.6	257
	2020	17.64	8.82	8.82	100.1	27.4	11.0	71.0	...

Country or area Pays ou zone	Year Année	Total	Male Hommes	Females Femmes	Sex Ratio (males per 100 females) Rapport des sexes (hommes pour 100 femmes)	Aged 0 to 14 years old âgée de 0 à 14 ans	Aged 60+ years old âgée de 60 ans ou plus	Population density (per km²) Densité de population (pour km²)	Surface area Superficie (000 km²)
Egypt	2005	75.52	38.10	37.43	101.8	33.8	7.1	75.9	...
Égypte	2010	82.76	41.81	40.96	102.1	32.6	7.6	83.1	...
	2017	96.44	48.74	47.71	102.2	33.8	7.9	96.9	1 002
	2020	102.33	51.70	50.63	102.1	33.9	8.2	102.8	...
El Salvador	2005	6.05	2.89	3.16	91.3	34.8	9.1	292.1	...
El Salvador	2010	6.18	2.93	3.26	89.8	31.6	9.9	298.4	...
	2017	6.39	3.00	3.39	88.4	27.4	11.4	308.3	21[33]
	2020	6.49	3.04	3.45	88.0	26.6	12.1	313.0	...
Equatorial Guinea	2005	0.75	0.40	0.35	113.1	39.6	5.0	26.7	...
Guinée équatoriale	2010	0.94	0.51	0.43	119.3	38.5	4.4	33.6	...
	2017	1.26	0.70	0.56	124.6	37.3	4.0	45.0	28
	2020	1.40	0.78	0.62	125.3	36.8	3.8	50.0	...
Eritrea	2005	2.83	1.41	1.42	99.6	38.6	6.1	28.0	...
Érythrée	2010	3.17	1.58	1.59	99.9	39.5	6.2	31.4	...
	2017	3.41	1.71	1.70	100.4	42.0	6.5	33.8	118
	2020	3.55	1.78	1.77	100.5	41.1	6.4	35.1	...
Estonia	2005	1.36	0.63	0.73	86.8	15.2	21.9	32.0	...
Estonie	2010	1.33	0.62	0.71	87.2	15.1	23.2	31.4	...
	2017	1.32	0.62	0.70	88.7	16.2	25.9	31.1	45
	2020	1.33	0.63	0.70	90.0	16.5	26.8	31.3	...
Eswatini	2005	1.03	0.49	0.54	90.4	41.3	5.1	59.9	...
Eswatini	2010	1.06	0.50	0.56	89.3	40.2	5.6	61.9	...
	2017	1.12	0.55	0.58	94.8	38.3	5.7	65.4	17
	2020	1.16	0.57	0.59	96.7	37.4	5.7	67.5	...
Ethiopia	2005	76.35	38.07	38.27	99.5	46.5	4.9	76.3	...
Éthiopie	2010	87.64	43.73	43.91	99.6	44.9	5.1	87.6	...
	2017	106.40	53.21	53.19	100.1	41.3	5.2	106.4	1 104
	2020	114.96	57.52	57.45	100.1	39.9	5.3	115.0	...
Falkland Islands (Malvinas) [34]	2001	~0.00	...	...	121.5	15.0	12.0	0.2	...
	2005	~0.00	...	...	...	...	...	0.2	...
Îles Falkland (Malvinas) [34]	2006	~0.00	...	...	113.2	15.9	14.0	0.2	...
	2010	~0.00	...	...	...	...	...	0.2	...
	2012	~0.00	...	...	110.5[35]	16.4[35]	15.7[35]	0.2	...
	2017	~0.00[17]	...	...	...	...	...	0.2[17]	12
	2020	~0.00	...	...	...	...	...	0.2	...
Faroe Islands	2005	0.05	...	...	108.0[15]	...	...	34.6	...
Îles Féroé	2008	0.05	...	...	108.1[15]	22.0[15]	19.3[15]	34.7	...
	2010	0.05	...	...	108.0[15]	...	...	34.8	...
	2015	0.05	...	...	107.2[15]	21.0[15]	22.5[15]	35.1	1
	2017	0.05[17]	...	...	...	...	...	35.3[17]	1
	2020	0.05	...	...	...	...	...	35.7	...
Fiji	2005	0.82	0.42	0.40	104.1	30.5	6.9	45.0	...
Fidji	2010	0.86	0.44	0.42	104.3	29.0	7.9	47.1	...
	2017	0.88	0.45	0.43	103.0	29.7	8.7	48.0	18
	2020	0.90	0.45	0.44	102.6	29.0	9.6	49.1	...
Finland	2005[36]	5.26	2.57	2.68	95.9	17.3	21.5	17.3	...
Finlande	2010[36]	5.37	2.63	2.73	96.4	16.5	24.8	17.7	...
	2017	5.51[36]	2.71[36]	2.80[36]	97.1[36]	16.3	27.8[36]	18.1[36]	338[36]
	2020[36]	5.54	2.73	2.81	97.3	15.9	29.0	18.2	...
France	2005	61.12	29.59	31.53	93.8	18.5	20.9	111.6	...
France	2010	62.88	30.46	32.42	93.9	18.5	23.1	114.8	...
	2017	64.84	31.40	33.44	93.9	18.1[36]	25.7	118.4	552
	2020	65.27	31.59	33.68	93.8	17.7	26.8	119.2	...
French Guiana	2005	0.20	0.10	0.10	98.2	35.8	5.8	2.5	...
Guyane française	2010	0.23	0.12	0.12	99.9	34.9	6.6	2.8	...
	2017	0.28	0.14	0.14	97.4	32.7	7.9	3.3	84
	2020	0.30	0.15	0.15	97.9	31.8	8.9	3.6	...

Country or area Pays ou zone	Year Année	Mid-year population estimates and projections (millions) Estimations et projections de population au milieu de l'année (millions)			Sex Ratio (males per 100 females) Rapport des sexes (hommes pour 100 femmes)	Population age distribution (percentage) Répartition par âge de la population (pourcentage)		Population density (per km²) Densité de population (pour km²)	Surface area Superficie (000 km²)
		Total	Male Hommes	Females Femmes		Aged 0 to 14 years old âgée de 0 à 14 ans	Aged 60+ years old âgée de 60 ans ou plus		
French Polynesia Polynésie française	2005	0.26	0.13	0.13	105.1	28.2	8.0	70.7	...
	2010	0.27	0.14	0.13	104.9	25.5	9.3	72.8	...
	2017	0.28	0.14	0.14	102.8	22.9	12.2	75.4	4
	2020	0.28	0.14	0.14	102.6	22.2	13.6	76.8	...
Gabon Gabon	2005	1.39	0.70	0.70	100.0	39.3	6.8	5.4	...
	2010	1.62	0.82	0.80	102.4	37.4	6.0	6.3	...
	2017	2.06	1.05	1.01	103.8	36.8	5.4	8.0	268
	2020	2.23	1.13	1.09	103.7	37.3	5.4	8.6	...
Gambia Gambie	2005	1.54	0.77	0.78	98.7	46.3	4.3	152.5	...
	2010	1.79	0.89	0.90	98.5	45.1	4.3	177.2	...
	2017	2.21	1.10	1.12	98.4	44.4	4.0	218.8	11
	2020	2.42	1.20	1.22	98.4	44.0	3.9	238.8	...
Georgia Géorgie	2005[37]	4.21	2.01	2.20	91.1	19.0	18.4	60.6	...
	2010[37]	4.10	1.95	2.15	91.0	18.0	18.9	59.0	...
	2017	4.01[37]	1.91[37]	2.10[37]	91.3[37]	19.5	20.7[37]	57.7[37]	70
	2020[37]	3.99	1.90	2.09	91.1	20.2	21.5	57.4	...
Germany Allemagne	2005	81.60	39.87	41.73	95.6	14.4	24.9	234.1	...
	2010	80.83	39.62	41.21	96.1	13.6	26.1	231.9	...
	2017	82.66	40.74	41.92	97.2	13.5[37]	27.9	237.1	357
	2020	83.78	41.42	42.37	97.8	14.0	28.6	240.4	...
Ghana Ghana	2005	21.81	11.02	10.80	102.1	40.9	4.4	95.9	...
	2010	24.78	12.53	12.25	102.3	39.3	4.6	108.9	...
	2017	29.12	14.75	14.37	102.7	37.8	4.9	128.0	239
	2020	31.07	15.75	15.32	102.8	37.1	5.3	136.6	...
Gibraltar Gibraltar	2001	0.03	...	...	98.5[38]	18.4[38]	20.5[38]	3 137.4	...
	2005	0.03	...	...	97.3[39]	...	...	3 208.5	...
	2010	0.03	...	...	99.2[39]	...	...	3 318.9	...
	2012	0.03	...	...	99.6[15,39]	18.1[15,39]	22.4[15,39]	3 362.3	...
	2015	0.03	...	...	101.8[39]	...	...	3 422.8	~0
	2017	0.03[17]	...	...	...	...	...	3 457.1[17]	~0
	2020	0.04	...	...	...	...	...	3 500.0	...
Greece Grèce	2005	11.22	5.56	5.67	98.0	14.7	22.6	87.1	...
	2010	10.89	5.35	5.54	96.6	15.1	24.8	84.5	...
	2017	10.57	5.19	5.38	96.4	14.2	27.4	82.0	132
	2020	10.42	5.12	5.31	96.4	13.7	28.8	80.9	...
Greenland Groenland	2005	0.06	...	...	113.4[15,18]	25.0[15,18]	9.6[15,18]	0.1	...
	2010	0.06	...	...	112.6[15,18]	22.6[15,18]	10.9[15,18]	0.1	...
	2016	0.06[17]	...	...	112.1[15,18]	21.0[15,18]	13.2[15,18]	0.1[17]	...
	2017	0.06[17]	...	...	...	...	...	0.1[17]	2 166
	2020	0.06	...	...	...	...	...	0.1	...
Grenada Grenade	2005	0.10	0.05	0.05	100.6	28.1	11.5	307.8	...
	2010	0.11	0.05	0.05	102.1	24.0	13.3	312.5	...
	2017	0.11	0.06	0.06	101.7	23.4	14.0	326.1	~0
	2020	0.11	0.06	0.06	101.5	23.8	14.9	331.0	...
Guadeloupe Guadeloupe	2005	0.40	0.19	0.21	89.3	23.4	16.2	247.5	...
	2010	0.41	0.19	0.22	86.7	22.5	19.1	249.4	...
	2017	0.40	0.18	0.21	86.1	19.4	24.1	245.5	2
	2020	0.40	0.18	0.22	85.6	18.4	26.1	245.8	...
Guam Guam	2005	0.16	0.08	0.08	104.0	29.5	9.2	293.3	...
	2010	0.16	0.08	0.08	103.3	27.5	11.1	295.3	...
	2017	0.16	0.08	0.08	102.2	24.8	13.9	304.2	1
	2020	0.17	0.09	0.08	101.8	23.9	15.2	312.5	...
Guatemala Guatemala	2005	13.10	6.42	6.67	96.2	42.3	5.9	122.2	...
	2010	14.63	7.19	7.44	96.5	39.4	6.1	136.5	...
	2017	16.92	8.33	8.59	96.9	35.1	6.9	157.8	109
	2020	17.92	8.83	9.09	97.1	33.3	7.2	167.2	...

Country or area Pays ou zone	Year Année	Mid-year population estimates and projections (millions) Estimations et projections de population au milieu de l'année (millions)			Sex Ratio (males per 100 females) Rapport des sexes (hommes pour 100 femmes)	Population age distribution (percentage) Répartition par âge de la population (pourcentage)		Population density (per km²) Densité de population (pour km²)	Surface area Superficie (000 km²)
		Total	Male Hommes	Females Femmes		Aged 0 to 14 years old âgée de 0 à 14 ans	Aged 60+ years old âgée de 60 ans ou plus		
Guinea	2005	9.11	4.34	4.77	91.1	46.8	4.9	37.1	...
Guinée	2010	10.19	4.86	5.33	91.1	46.2	4.6	41.5	...
	2017	12.07	5.80	6.27	92.6	44.2	4.7	49.1	246
	2020	13.13	6.35	6.78	93.7	43.0	4.7	53.4	...
Guinea-Bissau	2005	1.34	0.65	0.70	93.2	44.1	4.4	47.8	...
Guinée-Bissau	2010	1.52	0.74	0.78	94.1	43.1	4.3	54.1	...
	2017	1.83	0.89	0.94	95.3	42.5	4.6	65.0	36
	2020	1.97	0.96	1.01	95.8	41.9	4.6	70.0	...
Guyana	2005	0.75	0.37	0.37	100.4	36.3	6.4	3.8	...
Guyana	2010	0.75	0.37	0.38	98.5	32.2	7.3	3.8	...
	2017	0.78	0.39	0.39	100.6	28.6	9.6	3.9	215
	2020	0.79	0.40	0.39	101.2	27.7	10.8	4.0	...
Haiti	2005	9.20	4.53	4.66	97.1	38.2	6.5	333.6	...
Haïti	2010	9.95	4.91	5.04	97.3	36.3	6.5	361.0	...
	2017	10.98	5.42	5.56	97.5	33.6	7.3	398.5	28
	2020	11.40	5.63	5.78	97.4	32.5	7.7	413.7	...
Holy See	2000	~0.00	...	...	196.7[18,40]	...	...	1 784.1	...
Saint-Siège	2005	~0.00	...	...	...	...	...	1 813.6	...
	2009	~0.00	...	...	219.2	...	...	1 806.8	...
	2010	~0.00	...	...	...	...	...	1 804.5	...
	2017	~0.00[17]	...	...	...	...	...	1 800.0[17]	~0[41]
	2020	~0.00	...	...	...	...	...	1 820.5	...
Honduras	2005	7.46	3.71	3.74	99.2	40.6	5.4	66.7	...
Honduras	2010	8.32	4.15	4.17	99.5	37.6	5.8	74.3	...
	2017	9.43	4.71	4.72	99.8	32.3	6.8	84.3	112
	2020	9.90	4.95	4.96	99.9	30.6	7.4	88.5	...
Hungary	2005	10.09	4.79	5.30	90.3	15.5	21.4	111.4	...
Hongrie	2010	9.93	4.71	5.22	90.3	14.9	22.1	109.7	...
	2017	9.73	4.63	5.10	90.7	14.4	26.0	107.5	93
	2020	9.66	4.60	5.06	90.8	14.4	26.8	106.7	...
Iceland	2005	0.30	0.15	0.15	100.6	22.2	15.8	2.9	...
Islande	2010	0.32	0.16	0.16	101.5	20.8	16.9	3.2	...
	2017	0.33	0.17	0.17	100.7	20.0	20.1	3.3	103
	2020	0.34	0.17	0.17	100.9	19.4	21.6	3.4	...
India	2005	1 147.61	597.05	550.56	108.4	32.7	7.2	386.0	...
Inde	2010	1 234.28	642.16	592.12	108.5	30.8	7.8	415.1	...
	2017	1 338.68	695.88	642.80	108.3	27.5	9.4	450.2	3 287
	2020	1 380.00	717.10	662.90	108.2	26.2	10.1	464.1	...
Indonesia	2005	226.29	113.59	112.70	100.8	29.9	7.4	124.9	...
Indonésie	2010	241.83	121.82	120.01	101.5	28.8	7.5	133.5	...
	2017	264.65	133.27	131.38	101.4	26.9	9.0	146.1	1 911
	2020	273.52	137.72	135.81	101.4	25.9	10.1	151.0	...
Iran (Islamic Republic of)	2005	69.76	35.49	34.27	103.6	26.9	6.7	42.8	...
Iran (Rép. islamique d')	2010	73.76	37.18	36.58	101.6	24.0	7.5	45.3	...
	2017	80.67	40.82	39.85	102.4	24.2	9.4	49.5	1 629[42]
	2020	83.99	42.41	41.58	102.0	24.7	10.3	51.6	...
Iraq	2005	26.92	13.60	13.32	102.1	42.0	5.1	62.0	...
Iraq	2010	29.74	15.02	14.72	102.1	41.8	4.8	68.5	...
	2017	37.55	18.99	18.56	102.3	38.8	5.1	86.5	435
	2020	40.22	20.36	19.86	102.5	37.7	5.1	92.6	...
Ireland	2005	4.14	2.07	2.07	99.7	20.2	14.7	60.1	...
Irlande	2010	4.55	2.26	2.29	98.8	20.8	15.9	66.1	...
	2017	4.75	2.35	2.40	98.1	21.6	18.6	69.0	70
	2020	4.94	2.45	2.49	98.6	20.8	19.6	71.7	...

Population, surface area and density *(continued)*

Population, superficie et densité *(suite)*

Country or area Pays ou zone	Year Année	Mid-year population estimates and projections (millions) Estimations et projections de population au milieu de l'année (millions)			Sex Ratio (males per 100 females) Rapport des sexes (hommes pour 100 femmes)	Population age distribution (percentage) Répartition par âge de la population (pourcentage)		Population density (per km²) Densité de population (pour km²)	Surface area Superficie (000 km²)
		Total	Male Hommes	Females Femmes		Aged 0 to 14 years old âgée de 0 à 14 ans	Aged 60+ years old âgée de 60 ans ou plus		
Isle of Man	2005	0.08	...	...	96.9[15]	17.3[15]	22.1[15]	133.5	...
Île de Man	2009	0.08	...	...	98.4[15]	16.4[15]	24.1[15]	139.2	...
	2010	0.08	...	...	98.6[15]	...	...	140.5	...
	2016	0.08[17]	...	...	98.2[15]	16.0[15]	26.9[15]	146.9[17]	...
	2017	0.08[17]	...	...	...	...	...	147.9[17]	1
	2020	0.09	...	...	...	...	...	150.7	...
Israel	2005	6.53	3.22	3.31	97.3	27.9	13.2	301.7	...
Israël	2010	7.35	3.63	3.72	97.6	27.3	14.9	339.5	...
	2017	8.24	4.09	4.15	98.7	27.9	16.1	381.0	22
	2020	8.66	4.31	4.35	99.1	27.8	16.5	400.0	...
Italy	2005	58.28	28.30	29.99	94.4	14.2	25.1	198.1	...
Italie	2010	59.33	28.70	30.62	93.7	14.1	26.7	201.7	...
	2017	60.67	29.48	31.19	94.5	13.5	28.6	206.3	302
	2020	60.46	29.44	31.02	94.9	13.0	29.8	205.6	...
Jamaica	2005	2.74	1.36	1.38	98.2	30.1	10.7	253.0	...
Jamaïque	2010	2.81	1.40	1.41	98.9	27.0	11.4	259.5	...
	2017	2.92	1.45	1.47	98.7	24.0	12.4	269.7	11
	2020	2.96	1.47	1.49	98.5	23.4	13.3	273.4	...
Japan	2005	128.33	62.89	65.44	96.1	13.8	26.3	352.0	...
Japon	2007	128.49	62.92	65.58	95.9	13.6	27.9	352.5	378[43]
	2010	128.54	62.87	65.67	95.7	13.4	30.3	352.6	...
	2020	126.48	61.75	64.72	95.4	12.4	34.3	346.9	...
Jordan	2005	5.77	2.97	2.79	106.6	38.2	5.2	64.9	...
Jordanie	2010	7.26	3.70	3.56	104.1	37.5	5.4	81.8	...
	2017	9.79	4.95	4.83	102.5	34.9	5.7	110.2	89
	2020	10.20	5.17	5.04	102.6	32.9	6.1	114.9	...
Kazakhstan	2005	15.40	7.42	7.98	92.9	24.5	10.1	5.7	...
Kazakhstan	2010	16.25	7.86	8.40	93.6	24.1	9.9	6.0	...
	2017	18.08	8.76	9.32	94.0	27.9	11.3	6.7	2 725
	2020	18.78	9.11	9.66	94.3	29.1	12.2	7.0	...
Kenya	2005	36.62	18.17	18.45	98.5	44.0	3.2	64.4	...
Kenya	2010	42.03	20.87	21.16	98.6	43.4	3.2	73.8	...
	2017	50.22	24.95	25.27	98.7	40.4	3.8	88.2	592
	2020	53.77	26.72	27.05	98.8	38.6	4.2	94.5	...
Kiribati	2005	0.09	0.05	0.05	97.1	36.9	5.4	114.0	...
Kiribati	2010	0.10	0.05	0.05	96.9	36.1	5.5	127.1	...
	2017	0.11	0.06	0.06	96.6	35.1	6.1	140.9	1[44]
	2020	0.12	0.06	0.06	96.8	35.9	6.8	147.5	...
Kuwait	2005	2.27	1.34	0.93	144.2	26.0	3.6	127.4	...
Koweït	2010	2.99	1.73	1.26	137.1	23.2	3.4	167.9	...
	2017	4.06	2.43	1.63	149.2	21.4	5.0	227.6	18
	2020	4.27	2.61	1.66	157.9	21.5	6.5	239.7	...
Kyrgyzstan	2005	5.08	2.52	2.56	98.3	31.0	7.1	26.5	...
Kirghizistan	2010	5.42	2.68	2.74	97.7	29.9	6.4	28.3	...
	2017	6.19	3.06	3.13	97.9	32.2	7.4	32.3	200
	2020	6.52	3.23	3.30	97.9	32.6	8.1	34.0	...
Lao People's Dem. Rep.	2005	5.75	2.85	2.91	97.9	40.3	5.5	24.9	...
Rép. dém. populaire lao	2010	6.25	3.10	3.15	98.4	36.4	5.6	27.1	...
	2017	6.95	3.49	3.46	100.9	32.9	6.4	30.1	237
	2020	7.28	3.65	3.62	100.8	31.9	6.8	31.5	...
Latvia	2005	2.25	1.03	1.22	84.7	14.7	22.5	36.2	...
Lettonie	2010	2.12	0.97	1.15	84.5	14.1	23.6	34.1	...
	2017	1.95	0.90	1.05	85.0	15.6	26.5	31.4	65
	2020	1.89	0.87	1.02	85.5	16.4	27.6	30.3	...
Lebanon	2005	4.70	2.39	2.31	103.6	30.3	8.1	459.3	...
Liban	2010	4.95	2.52	2.44	103.2	25.8	9.2	484.2	...
	2017	6.82	3.43	3.39	101.2	26.6	10.1	666.6	10
	2020	6.83	3.44	3.39	101.4	25.1	11.2	667.2	...

Country or area Pays ou zone	Year Année	Mid-year population estimates and projections (millions) Estimations et projections de population au milieu de l'année (millions)			Sex Ratio (males per 100 females) Rapport des sexes (hommes pour 100 femmes)	Population age distribution (percentage) Répartition par âge de la population (pourcentage)		Population density (per km²) Densité de population (pour km²)	Surface area Superficie (000 km²)
		Total	Male Hommes	Females Femmes		Aged 0 to 14 years old âgée de 0 à 14 ans	Aged 60+ years old âgée de 60 ans ou plus		
Lesotho Lesotho	2005	2.00	0.96	1.03	93.4	37.2	6.5	65.7	...
	2010	2.00	0.97	1.03	94.6	34.9	7.0	65.7	...
	2017	2.09	1.03	1.06	97.1	33.0	7.4	68.9	30
	2020	2.14	1.06	1.09	97.4	32.2	7.5	70.6	...
Liberia Libéria	2005	3.22	1.61	1.61	100.0	42.9	5.3	33.4	...
	2010	3.89	1.95	1.94	100.3	43.0	5.0	40.4	...
	2017	4.70	2.36	2.34	100.8	41.5	5.1	48.8	111
	2020	5.06	2.54	2.52	101.1	40.4	5.2	52.5	...
Libya Libye	2005	5.80	2.99	2.81	106.4	30.2	5.9	3.3	...
	2010	6.20	3.16	3.03	104.3	28.8	5.9	3.5	...
	2017	6.58	3.33	3.26	102.2	28.5	6.5	3.7	1 676
	2020	6.87	3.47	3.40	101.9	27.8	6.9	3.9	...
Liechtenstein Liechtenstein	2005	0.03	...	...	97.0[15]	17.5[15]	16.8[15]	217.8	...
	2010	0.04	...	...	97.9	16.0	20.1	225.0	...
	2016	0.04[17]	...	...	98.4[15]	14.9[15]	22.7[15]	235.4[17]	...
	2017	0.04[17]	...	...	...	...	...	237.0[17]	~0
	2020	0.04	...	...	...	...	...	241.5	...
Lithuania Lituanie	2005	3.34	1.55	1.79	86.8	16.8	21.1	53.4	...
	2010	3.12	1.44	1.69	85.3	14.8	22.4	49.8	...
	2017	2.85	1.31	1.53	85.7	14.7	25.7	45.4	65
	2020	2.72	1.26	1.46	86.2	15.5	27.5	43.4	...
Luxembourg Luxembourg	2005	0.46	0.23	0.23	97.4	18.6	19.0	176.8	...
	2010	0.51	0.25	0.26	98.7	17.6	19.0	196.1	...
	2017	0.59	0.30	0.29	101.5	16.1	19.4	228.5	3
	2020	0.63	0.32	0.31	102.3	15.6	19.9	241.7	...
Madagascar Madagascar	2005	18.34	9.13	9.21	99.2	44.7	4.4	31.5	...
	2010	21.15	10.54	10.62	99.3	43.5	4.3	36.4	...
	2017	25.57	12.75	12.82	99.5	41.0	4.8	44.0	587
	2020	27.69	13.81	13.88	99.6	40.1	5.0	47.6	...
Malawi Malawi	2005	12.63	6.21	6.41	96.9	46.4	4.5	133.9	...
	2010	14.54	7.15	7.39	96.9	46.4	4.2	154.2	...
	2017	17.67	8.71	8.96	97.2	44.3	4.1	187.4	118
	2020	19.13	9.43	9.70	97.3	43.0	4.1	202.9	...
Malaysia Malaisie	2005[45]	25.69	13.17	12.52	105.2	30.5	7.1	78.2	...
	2010[45]	28.21	14.55	13.66	106.5	28.0	7.9	85.9	...
	2017	31.10[45]	16.00[45]	15.10[45]	105.9[45]	24.3	9.9[45]	94.7[45]	330
	2020[45]	32.37	16.63	15.74	105.7	23.4	11.0	98.5	...
Maldives Maldives	2005	0.32	0.17	0.15	109.4	31.5	6.5	1 065.4	...
	2010	0.37	0.20	0.17	119.0	25.3	6.2	1 219.1	...
	2017	0.50	0.31	0.19	162.1	20.4[45]	5.8	1 654.7	~0
	2020	0.54	0.34	0.20	173.5	19.6	5.7	1 801.8	...
Mali Mali	2005	12.78	6.36	6.42	99.1	46.9	4.6	10.5	...
	2010	15.05	7.52	7.53	99.8	47.5	4.2	12.3	...
	2017	18.51	9.26	9.25	100.2	47.7	4.0	15.2	1 240
	2020	20.25	10.15	10.11	100.4	47.0	3.9	16.6	...
Malta Malte	2005	0.40	0.20	0.20	98.4	17.4	18.9	1 264.5	...
	2010	0.41	0.21	0.21	98.5	15.0	23.0	1 294.5	...
	2017	0.44	0.22	0.22	100.5	14.2	26.5	1 368.5	~0
	2020	0.44	0.22	0.22	100.6	14.4	28.1	1 379.8	...
Marshall Islands Îles Marshall	2004	0.05	...	...	104.0[24,46]	40.6[24,46]	3.6[24,46]	289.3	...
	2005	0.05	...	...	...	...	...	289.2	...
	2010	0.05	...	...	105.2[24,46]	40.9[24,46]	4.5[24,46]	291.3	...
	2016	0.05[17]	...	...	# 104.5	# 39.0	# 5.5	294.8[17]	...
	2017	0.05[17]	...	...	...	...	...	295.2[17]	~0
	2020	0.05	...	...	...	...	...	295.8	...

Country or area Pays ou zone	Year Année	Mid-year population estimates and projections (millions) Estimations et projections de population au milieu de l'année (millions)			Sex Ratio (males per 100 females) Rapport des sexes (hommes pour 100 femmes)	Population age distribution (percentage) Répartition par âge de la population (pourcentage)		Population density (per km²) Densité de population (pour km²)	Surface area Superficie (000 km²)
		Total	Male Hommes	Females Femmes		Aged 0 to 14 years old âgée de 0 à 14 ans	Aged 60+ years old âgée de 60 ans ou plus		
Martinique Martinique	2005	0.40	0.19	0.21	87.3	21.1	18.0	374.7	...
	2010	0.39	0.18	0.21	85.8	19.5	20.6	372.3	
	2017	0.38	0.17	0.20	85.9	16.5	26.9	354.7	1
	2020	0.38	0.17	0.20	85.2	15.7	29.2	354.0	...
Mauritania Mauritanie	2005	3.02	1.51	1.52	99.5	42.2	4.9	2.9	...
	2010	3.49	1.75	1.75	100.0	41.2	4.8	3.4	...
	2017	4.28	2.15	2.13	100.6	40.3	4.9	4.2	1 031
	2020	4.65	2.34	2.31	100.9	39.7	5.1	4.5	...
Mauritius Maurice	2005[47]	1.22	0.61	0.62	98.3	24.7	9.6	602.0	...
	2010[47]	1.25	0.62	0.63	98.3	21.9	12.1	614.8	...
	2017	1.26[47]	0.63[47]	0.64[47]	97.9[47]	18.4	16.6[47]	622.9[47]	2[48]
	2020[47]	1.27	0.63	0.64	97.4	16.8	18.4	626.5	...
Mayotte Mayotte	2005	0.18	0.09	0.09	97.2	42.4	4.8	474.9	...
	2010	0.21	0.10	0.11	95.6	42.9	5.1	556.6	...
	2020	0.27	0.13	0.14	96.8	39.0	6.1	727.5	...
Mexico Mexique	2005	106.01	51.84	54.17	95.7	31.8	8.1	54.5	...
	2010	114.09	55.83	58.27	95.8	29.5	8.8	58.7	...
	2017	124.78	61.02	63.75	95.7	26.9	10.4	64.2	1 964
	2020	128.93	63.07	65.86	95.8	25.8	11.2	66.3	...
Micronesia (Fed. States of) Micronésie (États féd. de)	2005	0.11	0.05	0.05	103.3	38.9	5.4	151.6	...
	2010	0.10	0.05	0.05	103.1	35.7	5.4	147.0	...
	2017	0.11	0.06	0.05	103.4	32.0	7.0	159.2	1
	2020	0.12	0.06	0.06	103.4	31.2	7.8	164.3	...
Monaco Monaco	2000	0.03	...	...	94.3[15]	13.2[15]	28.9[15]	21 531.5	...
	2005	0.03	...	...	...	...	...	22 679.9	...
	2008	0.04	...	...	94.7[15]	12.7[15]	31.2[15]	24 062.4	...
	2010	0.04	...	...	...	...	...	24 895.3	...
	2017	0.04[17]	...	...	...	...	...	25 969.8[17]	~0
	2020	0.04	...	...	...	...	...	26 373.8	...
Mongolia Mongolie	2005	2.53	1.26	1.27	99.0	28.9	5.6	1.6	...
	2010	2.72	1.35	1.37	98.4	27.0	5.6	1.8	...
	2017	3.11	1.54	1.58	97.5	29.9	6.5	2.0	1 564
	2020	3.28	1.62	1.66	97.1	31.1	7.3	2.1	...
Montenegro Monténégro	2005	0.62	0.30	0.31	96.9	20.2	17.0	45.8	...
	2010	0.62	0.31	0.32	97.6	19.2	17.9	46.4	...
	2017	0.63	0.31	0.32	97.8	18.3	21.1	46.7	14
	2020	0.63	0.31	0.32	97.8	18.0	22.1	46.7	...
Montserrat Montserrat	2001	~0.00	...	...	116.6	19.3	19.9	45.1	...
	2004	~0.00	...	...	112.7	...	...	46.4	...
	2005	~0.00	...	...	...	...	...	47.8	...
	2006	~0.00	...	...	108.7[49]	19.6[49]	19.0[49]	48.5	...
	2010	~0.00	...	...	...	...	...	49.4	...
	2011	0.01	...	...	107.2[15]	19.7[15]	19.6[15]	49.9	...
	2016	0.01[17]	...	...	106.0	...	...	51.5[17]	...
	2017	0.01[17]	...	...	...	...	...	51.8[17]	~0
	2020	0.01	...	...	...	...	...	52.4	...
Morocco Maroc	2005	30.46	15.05	15.41	97.6	30.8	8.2	68.2	...
	2010	32.34	15.95	16.40	97.3	28.5	8.6	72.5	...
	2017	35.58	17.64	17.94	98.3	27.5	10.6	79.7	447
	2020	36.91	18.32	18.59	98.5	26.8	11.9	82.7	...
Mozambique Mozambique	2005	20.49	9.85	10.65	92.5	45.2	4.9	26.1	...
	2010	23.53	11.35	12.18	93.2	45.7	4.7	29.9	...
	2017	28.65	13.89	14.76	94.1	45.0	4.4	36.4	799
	2020	31.26	15.19	16.07	94.5	44.1	4.4	39.7	...
Myanmar Myanmar	2005	48.95	23.67	25.28	93.6	31.2	6.9	74.9	...
	2010	50.60	24.40	26.20	93.1	30.0	7.3	77.5	...
	2017	53.38	25.73	27.65	93.0	26.8	9.1	81.7	677
	2020	54.41	26.22	28.19	93.0	25.5	10.0	83.3	...

Country or area Pays ou zone	Year Année	Mid-year population estimates and projections (millions) Estimations et projections de population au milieu de l'année (millions)			Sex Ratio (males per 100 females) Rapport des sexes (hommes pour 100 femmes)	Population age distribution (percentage) Répartition par âge de la population (pourcentage)		Population density (per km²) Densité de population (pour km²)	Surface area Superficie (000 km²)
		Total	Male Hommes	Females Femmes		Aged 0 to 14 years old âgée de 0 à 14 ans	Aged 60+ years old âgée de 60 ans ou plus		
Namibia	2005	1.94	0.94	1.00	93.2	39.4	5.5	2.4	...
Namibie	2010	2.12	1.02	1.09	93.5	37.4	5.8	2.6	...
	2017	2.40	1.16	1.24	93.9	36.9	5.6	2.9	824
	2020	2.54	1.23	1.31	94.1	36.8	5.6	3.1	...
Nauru	2002	0.01	...	...	104.2	38.1	2.5	504.0	...
Nauru	2005	0.01	...	...	...	...	...	505.7	...
	2010	0.01	...	...	...	...	...	501.3	...
	2016	0.01[17]	...	...	# 101.9	# 39.5	# 4.0	567.4[17]	...
	2017	0.01[17]	...	...	...	...	...	568.0[17]	~0
	2020	0.01	...	...	...	...	...	561.4	...
Nepal	2005	25.74	12.79	12.96	98.7	39.3	6.7	179.6	...
Népal	2010	27.01	13.30	13.72	96.9	36.3	7.5	188.4	...
	2017	27.63	12.56	15.08	83.3	31.3	8.5	192.8	147
	2020	29.14	13.35	15.79	84.5	28.8	8.7	203.3	...
Netherlands	2005	16.37	8.12	8.25	98.4	18.3	19.3	485.4	...
Pays-Bas	2010	16.68	8.28	8.40	98.6	17.5	22.0	494.7	...
	2017	17.02	8.47	8.55	99.0	16.4	25.0	504.8	42
	2020	17.13	8.54	8.60	99.3	15.7	26.6	508.2	...
New Caledonia	2005	0.24	0.12	0.12	101.7	27.9	9.5	12.9	...
Nouvelle-Calédonie	2010	0.25	0.13	0.13	101.5	25.8	11.0	13.9	...
	2017	0.28	0.14	0.14	101.5	23.0	13.0	15.2	19
	2020	0.29	0.14	0.14	101.1	22.1	14.2	15.6	...
New Zealand	2005	4.14	2.03	2.11	96.0	21.5	16.4	15.7	...
Nouvelle-Zélande	2010	4.37	2.15	2.22	96.5	20.5	18.4	16.6	...
	2017	4.70	2.31	2.39	96.7	19.7	20.9	17.9	268
	2020	4.82	2.37	2.45	96.7	19.4	22.2	18.3	...
Nicaragua	2005	5.44	2.68	2.75	97.4	36.2	6.0	45.2	...
Nicaragua	2010	5.82	2.87	2.96	97.1	33.3	6.3	48.4	...
	2017	6.38	3.15	3.24	97.2	30.5	7.9	53.1	130
	2020	6.62	3.26	3.36	97.2	29.5	8.7	55.0	...
Niger	2005	13.62	6.78	6.84	99.2	49.2	4.1	10.8	...
Niger	2010	16.46	8.23	8.24	99.9	50.0	4.2	13.0	...
	2017	21.60	10.84	10.76	100.8	50.1	4.1	17.1	1 267
	2020	24.21	12.17	12.04	101.1	49.7	4.1	19.1	...
Nigeria	2005	138.87	70.12	68.74	102.0	43.7	4.6	152.5	...
Nigéria	2010	158.50	80.16	78.34	102.3	44.0	4.5	174.0	...
	2017	190.87	96.69	94.19	102.7	44.0	4.5	209.6	924
	2020	206.14	104.47	101.67	102.8	43.5	4.5	226.3	...
Niue	2005	~0.00	...	...	94.8[15]	26.1[15]	15.1[15]	6.5	...
Nioué	2010	~0.00	...	...	101.9[15]	25.7[15]	16.8[15]	6.3	...
	2016	~0.00[17]	...	...	# 100.0	# 22.8	# 20.1	6.2[17]	...
	2017	~0.00[17]	...	...	...	...	...	6.2[17]	~0
	2020	~0.00	...	...	...	...	...	6.3	...
North Macedonia	2005	2.06	1.03	1.03	99.9	20.2	15.3	81.7	...
Macédoine du Nord	2010	2.07	1.03	1.04	99.9	17.9	16.4	82.1	...
	2017	2.08	1.04	1.04	100.2	16.7	19.4	82.6	26
	2020	2.08	1.04	1.04	100.1	16.3	20.7	82.6	...
Northern Mariana Islands	2005	0.06	...	...	83.3[24]	22.9[24,50]	3.7[24,50]	138.6	...
Îles Mariannes du Nord	2010	0.05	...	...	106.2	26.7	5.8	118.3	...
	2016	0.06[17]	...	...	# 107.1	# 23.5	# 10.0	119.6[17]	...
	2017	0.06[17]	...	...	...	...	...	119.9[17]	~0
	2020	0.06	...	...	...	...	...	120.3	...
Norway	2005[10]	4.63	2.30	2.33	98.5	19.6	19.8	12.7	...
Norvège	2010[10]	4.89	2.44	2.44	100.0	18.8	21.0	13.4	...
	2017	5.30[10]	2.67[10]	2.62[10]	101.8[10]	17.7	22.4[10]	14.5[10]	386[10]
	2020[10]	5.42	2.74	2.68	102.2	17.3	23.3	14.8	...

Country or area Pays ou zone	Year Année	Mid-year population estimates and projections (millions) Estimations et projections de population au milieu de l'année (millions)			Sex Ratio (males per 100 females) Rapport des sexes (hommes pour 100 femmes)	Population age distribution (percentage) Répartition par âge de la population (pourcentage)		Population density (per km²) Densité de population (pour km²)	Surface area Superficie (000 km²)
		Total	Male Hommes	Females Femmes		Aged 0 to 14 years old âgée de 0 à 14 ans	Aged 60+ years old âgée de 60 ans ou plus		
Oman Oman	2005	2.51	1.42	1.09	130.2	32.5	4.1	8.1	...
	2010	3.04	1.83	1.21	152.0	25.7	3.9	9.8	...
	2017	4.67	3.07	1.59	193.0	22.0	4.0	15.1	310
	2020	5.11	3.37	1.74	194.1	22.5	4.3	16.5	...
Other non-specified areas Autres zones non-spécifiées	2005	22.71	11.49	11.21	102.5	19.0	13.1	641.2	...
	2010	23.19	11.65	11.53	101.0	15.9	15.2	654.8	...
	2020	23.82	11.83	11.98	98.8	12.7	22.9	672.6	...
Pakistan Pakistan	2005	160.30	82.68	77.63	106.5	40.0	6.3	207.9	...
	2010	179.42	92.43	87.00	106.2	37.7	6.3	232.8	...
	2017	207.91	106.99	100.91	106.0	35.5	6.5	269.7	796
	2020	220.89	113.67	107.22	106.0	34.8	6.7	286.5	...
Palau Palaos	2005	0.02	...	...	116.2[15]	24.1[15]	8.2[15]	43.3	...
	2010	0.02	...	...	...	...	...	44.5	...
	2016	0.02[17]	...	...	# 113.3	# 20.3	# 13.1	46.7[17]	...
	2017	0.02[17]	...	...	...	...	...	47.2[17]	~0
	2020	0.02	...	...	...	...	...	48.8	...
Panama Panama	2005	3.33	1.68	1.65	101.3	30.4	8.8	44.8	...
	2010	3.64	1.83	1.81	101.0	29.1	9.7	49.0	...
	2017	4.11	2.06	2.05	100.5	27.3	11.4	55.2	75
	2020	4.31	2.16	2.15	100.2	26.5	12.2	58.0	...
Papua New Guinea Papouasie-Nvl-Guinée	2005	6.49	3.30	3.19	103.5	39.2	5.0	14.3	...
	2010	7.31	3.72	3.59	103.6	38.3	5.3	16.1	...
	2017	8.44	4.31	4.13	104.2	36.1	5.7	18.6	463
	2020	8.95	4.57	4.38	104.3	35.1	6.0	19.8	...
Paraguay Paraguay	2005	5.82	2.96	2.87	103.1	35.5	7.0	14.7	...
	2010	6.25	3.18	3.07	103.5	32.9	7.8	15.7	...
	2017	6.87	3.49	3.37	103.5	29.7	9.3	17.3	407
	2020	7.13	3.62	3.51	103.3	28.9	9.9	18.0	...
Peru Pérou	2005	27.87	13.89	13.97	99.4	32.0	7.9	21.8	...
	2010	29.03	14.47	14.55	99.5	30.1	8.9	22.7	...
	2017	31.44	15.61	15.83	98.6	26.4	11.3	24.6	1 285
	2020	32.97	16.38	16.59	98.7	24.7	12.5	25.8	...
Philippines Philippines	2005	86.33	43.39	42.94	101.0	37.1	5.5	289.5	...
	2010	93.97	47.40	46.57	101.8	34.0	6.5	315.1	...
	2017	105.17	52.88	52.29	101.1	31.5	7.8	352.7	300
	2020	109.58	55.03	54.55	100.9	30.0	8.6	367.5	...
Poland Pologne	2005	38.37	18.58	19.79	93.9	16.6	17.0	125.3	...
	2010	38.33	18.53	19.80	93.6	15.2	19.4	125.2	...
	2017	37.95	18.40	19.55	94.1	14.9	24.2	123.9	313
	2020	37.85	18.34	19.51	94.0	15.2	25.9	123.6	...
Portugal Portugal	2005	10.51	5.08	5.43	93.6	15.4	22.4	114.7	...
	2010	10.60	5.07	5.53	91.8	15.0	24.7	115.7	...
	2017	10.29	4.87	5.42	89.7	13.7[13]	27.9	112.3	92
	2020	10.20	4.82	5.37	89.8	13.1	29.4	111.3	...
Puerto Rico Porto Rico	2005	3.63	1.74	1.89	92.1	22.3	16.9	409.5	...
	2010	3.58	1.72	1.86	92.4	20.6	18.3	403.6	...
	2017	3.16	1.51	1.66	91.0	17.4	23.5	356.7	9
	2020	2.86	1.36	1.51	90.0	15.8	27.7	322.5	...
Qatar Qatar	2005	0.87	0.58	0.28	208.2	21.7	2.5	74.5	...
	2010	1.86	1.42	0.44	324.8	12.9	1.6	159.9	...
	2017	2.72	2.06	0.66	311.0	13.5	2.7	234.7	12
	2020	2.88	2.17	0.72	302.4	13.6	3.6	248.2	...
Republic of Korea République de Corée	2005	48.70	24.43	24.27	100.7	18.8	12.8	500.9	...
	2010	49.55	24.82	24.72	100.4	16.1	15.3	509.6	...
	2017	51.10	25.60	25.50	100.4	13.2	20.1	525.5	100
	2020	51.27	25.67	25.60	100.2	12.5	23.2	527.3	...

Country or area Pays ou zone	Year Année	Mid-year population estimates and projections (millions) Estimations et projections de population au milieu de l'année (millions)			Sex Ratio (males per 100 females) Rapport des sexes (hommes pour 100 femmes)	Population age distribution (percentage) Répartition par âge de la population (pourcentage)		Population density (per km²) Densité de population (pour km²)	Surface area Superficie (000 km²)
		Total	Male Hommes	Females Femmes		Aged 0 to 14 years old âgée de 0 à 14 ans	Aged 60+ years old âgée de 60 ans ou plus		
Republic of Moldova	2005[51]	4.16	1.99	2.17	91.9	18.5	13.6	126.6	...
République de Moldova	2010[51]	4.09	1.96	2.12	92.6	16.5	14.1	124.4	...
	2017	4.06[51]	1.95[51]	2.11[51]	92.3[51]	15.8	17.5[51]	123.6[51]	34
	2020[51]	4.03	1.93	2.10	91.9	15.9	18.9	122.8	...
Réunion	2005	0.79	0.39	0.40	96.4	26.9	10.3	316.6	...
Réunion	2010	0.83	0.40	0.43	93.9	25.4	12.2	332.2	...
	2017	0.88	0.42	0.45	93.9	23.6[51]	16.4	350.5	3
	2020	0.90	0.43	0.46	93.8	22.4	18.3	358.1	...
Romania	2005	21.42	10.44	10.98	95.1	15.7	19.7	93.0	...
Roumanie	2010	20.47	9.94	10.53	94.4	15.8	21.3	88.9	...
	2017	19.65	9.57	10.09	94.8	15.4	24.9	85.4	238
	2020	19.24	9.35	9.88	94.6	15.5	25.9	83.6	...
Russian Federation	2005	143.67	66.85	76.82	87.0	15.2	17.2	8.8	...
Fédération de Russie	2010	143.48	66.54	76.94	86.5	14.9	18.0	8.8	...
	2017	145.53	67.43	78.10	86.3	17.6	21.0	8.9	17 098
	2020	145.93	67.64	78.29	86.4	18.4	22.4	8.9	...
Rwanda	2005	8.84	4.33	4.51	95.8	42.4	4.2	358.3	...
Rwanda	2010	10.04	4.92	5.12	96.1	41.5	4.1	406.9	...
	2017	11.98	5.89	6.09	96.6	40.1	4.7	485.6	26
	2020	12.95	6.37	6.58	96.7	39.5	5.1	525.0	...
Saint Barthélemy	2005	0.01	...	...	...	...	...	388.8	...
Saint-Barthélemy	2010	0.01	...	...	...	...	...	419.7	...
	2020	0.01	...	...	...	...	...	449.0	...
Saint Helena [52]	2005	~0.00	...	...	...	...	...	11.0	...
Sainte-Hélène [52]	2010	~0.00	...	...	...	...	...	10.7	...
	2017	~0.00[17]	...	...	...	...	...	10.4[17]	~0
	2020	~0.00	...	...	...	...	...	10.6	...
Saint Kitts and Nevis	2000	0.05	...	...	101.9	28.0	9.9	174.5	...
Saint-Kitts-et-Nevis	2005	0.05	...	...	* 95.7	...	...	187.0	...
	2010	0.05	...	...	* 95.7	...	...	197.9	...
	2011	0.05	...	...	* 97.0	...	...	200.0	...
	2017	0.06[17]	...	...	...	...	...	212.9[17]	~0
	2020	0.06	...	...	...	...	...	218.5	...
Saint Lucia	2005	0.16	0.08	0.08	96.2	27.8	9.6	267.9	...
Sainte-Lucie	2010	0.17	0.09	0.09	96.9	23.2	11.9	285.4	...
	2017	0.18	0.09	0.09	97.0	18.9	13.6	296.6	1[53]
	2020	0.18	0.09	0.09	97.0	18.0	14.9	301.0	...
Saint Martin (French part)	2005	0.03	...	...	...	...	...	646.2	...
St-Martin (partie française)	2010	0.04	...	...	...	...	...	709.1	...
	2020	0.04	...	...	...	...	...	729.5	...
Saint Pierre and Miquelon	2005	0.01	...	...	...	...	...	27.2	...
Saint-Pierre-et-Miquelon	2006	0.01	...	...	98.2	19.1	17.8	27.2	...
	2010	0.01	...	...	...	...	...	27.3	...
	2017	0.01[17]	...	...	...	...	...	27.5[17]	~0
	2020	0.01	...	...	...	...	...	27.9	...
Saint Vincent & Grenadines	2005	0.11	0.05	0.05	102.1	28.6	9.3	278.5	...
Saint-Vincent-Grenadines	2010	0.11	0.06	0.05	103.7	25.8	11.3	277.6	...
	2017	0.11	0.06	0.05	103.4	22.9	13.7	281.6	~0
	2020	0.11	0.06	0.05	102.7	21.9	14.7	284.5	...
Samoa	2005	0.18	0.09	0.09	107.5	39.6	6.8	63.5	...
Samoa	2010	0.19	0.10	0.09	106.7	38.3	7.1	65.7	...
	2017	0.20	0.10	0.09	107.2	38.5	7.4	69.0	3
	2020	0.20	0.10	0.10	107.3	37.2	8.0	70.1	...

Country or area Pays ou zone	Year Année	Mid-year population estimates and projections (millions) Estimations et projections de population au milieu de l'année (millions)			Sex Ratio (males per 100 females) Rapport des sexes (hommes pour 100 femmes)	Population age distribution (percentage) Répartition par âge de la population (pourcentage)		Population density (per km²) Densité de population (pour km²)	Surface area Superficie (000 km²)
		Total	Male Hommes	Females Femmes		Aged 0 to 14 years old âgée de 0 à 14 ans	Aged 60+ years old âgée de 60 ans ou plus		
San Marino	2004	0.03	...	...	96.2[18]	15.2[18]	21.5[18]	481.1	...
Saint-Marin	2005	0.03	...	...	96.1[18]	...	...	487.3	...
	2010	0.03	...	...	* 93.5	* 20.9[54]	* 21.6[55]	518.5	...
	2015	0.03	...	...	94.9[18]	15.0[18]	24.1[18]	549.3	~0
	2017	0.03[17]	...	...	...	...	...	556.7[17]	~0
	2020	0.03	...	...	...	...	...	563.5	...
Sao Tome and Principe	2005	0.16	0.08	0.08	98.0	44.0	4.7	164.0	...
Sao Tomé-et-Principe	2010	0.18	0.09	0.09	99.9	43.4	4.4	187.9	...
	2017	0.21	0.10	0.10	100.1	42.9	4.7	215.7	1
	2020	0.22	0.11	0.11	100.2	41.8	5.0	228.3	...
Saudi Arabia	2005	23.82	13.26	10.56	125.6	33.9	4.4	11.1	...
Arabie saoudite	2010	27.42	15.43	11.99	128.6	29.7	4.5	12.8	...
	2017	33.10	18.98	14.13	134.3	25.3	5.4	15.4	2 207
	2020	34.81	20.13	14.68	137.1	24.7	5.9	16.2	...
Senegal	2005	11.09	5.42	5.67	95.5	43.7	4.9	57.6	...
Sénégal	2010	12.68	6.17	6.51	94.9	43.5	4.8	65.9	...
	2017	15.42	7.51	7.91	94.9	43.2	4.8	80.1	197[56]
	2020	16.74	8.17	8.57	95.3	42.6	4.8	87.0	...
Serbia	2005[57]	9.19	4.50	4.69	95.9	18.7	18.8	105.1	...
Serbie	2010[57]	8.99	4.41	4.58	96.1	17.3	21.1	102.8	...
	2017	8.83[57]	4.33[57]	4.50[57]	96.1[57]	15.8	24.9[57]	101.0[57]	88[58]
	2020[57]	8.74	4.28	4.46	96.0	15.4	25.3	99.9	...
Seychelles	2005	0.09	0.04	0.04	99.9	25.0	9.1	192.7	...
Seychelles	2010	0.09	0.05	0.04	106.6	22.8	9.9	198.4	...
	2017	0.10	0.05	0.05	105.7	23.5[57]	11.6	209.6	~0
	2020	0.10	0.05	0.05	105.3	23.8	13.0	213.8	...
Sierra Leone	2005	5.65	2.81	2.84	98.7	43.7	5.0	78.2	...
Sierra Leone	2010	6.42	3.19	3.22	99.1	43.0	4.8	88.9	...
	2017	7.49	3.73	3.75	99.5	41.4	4.6	103.7	72
	2020	7.98	3.98	4.00	99.6	40.3	4.6	110.5	...
Singapore	2005	4.27	2.16	2.11	102.2	17.2	10.7	6 093.8	...
Singapour	2010	5.13	2.68	2.46	108.9	14.0	12.7	7 330.2	...
	2017	5.71	2.99	2.72	109.8	12.2	17.8	8 154.3	1[59]
	2020	5.85	3.06	2.79	109.8	12.3	20.9	8 357.6	...
Sint Maarten (Dutch part)	2005	0.03	...	...	93.9[15]	...	...	956.1	...
St-Martin (partie néerland.)	2010	0.03	...	...	91.0[15]	...	...	974.2	...
	2013	0.04	...	...	95.8[15]	21.0[15]	10.4[15]	1 071.7	~0
	2014	0.04	...	...	95.7[15]	...	...	1 108.7	~0
	2017	0.04[17]	...	...	...	...	...	1 180.0[17]	~0
	2020	0.04	...	...	...	...	...	1 216.6	...
Slovakia	2005	5.40	2.62	2.78	94.1	16.8	16.1	112.3	...
Slovaquie	2010	5.40	2.62	2.78	94.2	15.3	17.8	112.4	...
	2017	5.45	2.65	2.80	94.7	15.3	21.8	113.3	49[60]
	2020	5.46	2.66	2.80	94.9	15.6	23.3	113.5	...
Slovenia	2005	2.00	0.98	1.02	95.7	14.0	20.8	99.1	...
Slovénie	2010	2.04	1.01	1.03	98.2	14.0	22.2	101.5	...
	2017	2.08	1.03	1.04	98.9	14.9	26.2	103.1	20
	2020	2.08	1.04	1.04	99.2	15.1	27.7	103.2	...
Solomon Islands	2005	0.47	0.24	0.23	104.4	41.3	4.9	16.8	...
Îles Salomon	2010	0.53	0.27	0.26	103.3	40.8	5.1	18.9	...
	2017	0.64	0.32	0.31	103.4	40.4	5.4	22.7	29
	2020	0.69	0.35	0.34	103.4	40.0	5.6	24.5	...
Somalia	2005	10.45	5.23	5.22	100.1	47.9	4.3	16.7	...
Somalie	2010	12.04	6.02	6.03	99.8	48.2	4.4	19.2	...
	2017	14.59	7.28	7.31	99.5	46.8	4.5	23.3	638
	2020	15.89	7.92	7.97	99.4	46.1	4.6	25.3	...

Country or area Pays ou zone	Year Année	Mid-year population estimates and projections (millions) Estimations et projections de population au milieu de l'année (millions)			Sex Ratio (males per 100 females) Rapport des sexes (hommes pour 100 femmes)	Population age distribution (percentage) Répartition par âge de la population (pourcentage)		Population density (per km²) Densité de population (pour km²)	Surface area Superficie (000 km²)
		Total	Male Hommes	Females Femmes		Aged 0 to 14 years old âgée de 0 à 14 ans	Aged 60+ years old âgée de 60 ans ou plus		
South Africa	2005	47.88	23.61	24.27	97.3	30.9	7.0	39.5	...
Afrique du Sud	2010	51.22	25.27	25.95	97.4	29.7	7.2	42.2	...
	2017	57.01	28.12	28.89	97.3	29.2	8.1	47.0	1 221
	2020	59.31	29.22	30.09	97.1	28.8	8.5	48.9	...
South Sudan	2005	7.54	3.76	3.78	99.6	44.3	5.1	12.3	...
Soudan du sud	2010	9.51	4.75	4.76	99.9	43.5	5.2	15.6	...
	2017	10.91	5.46	5.45	100.2	42.1	5.1	17.9	659
	2020	11.19	5.60	5.59	100.2	41.3	5.2	18.3	...
Spain	2005[61]	44.02	21.72	22.30	97.4	14.2	21.6	88.3	...
Espagne	2010[61]	46.93	23.20	23.73	97.7	14.8	22.2	94.1	...
	2017	46.65[61]	22.90[61]	23.75[61]	96.4[61]	14.7	24.8[61]	93.5[61]	506
	2020[61]	46.75	22.98	23.78	96.6	14.4	26.3	93.7	...
Sri Lanka	2005	19.55	9.64	9.91	97.3	25.6	10.4	311.7	...
Sri Lanka	2010	20.26	9.87	10.40	94.9	25.4	11.9	323.1	...
	2017	21.13	10.16	10.97	92.6	24.4[61]	15.0	336.9	66
	2020	21.41	10.27	11.15	92.1	23.7	16.4	341.5	...
State of Palestine	2005[1]	3.58	1.82	1.76	103.2	45.5	4.0	594.3	...
État de Palestine	2010[1]	4.06	2.06	2.00	103.0	42.3	4.4	673.7	...
	2017	4.75[1]	2.41[1]	2.34[1]	103.0[1]	39.3	4.7[1]	788.6[1]	6
	2020[1]	5.10	2.59	2.51	102.9	38.4	4.9	847.4	...
Sudan	2005	30.95	15.52	15.43	100.5	43.5	4.8	17.5	...
Soudan	2010	34.55	17.23	17.31	99.5	43.0	5.1	19.6	...
	2020	43.85	21.91	21.94	99.8	39.8	5.7	24.8	...
Suriname	2005	0.50	0.25	0.25	101.8	31.3	8.5	3.2	...
Suriname	2010	0.53	0.27	0.26	101.5	29.4	9.1	3.4	...
	2017	0.57	0.29	0.28	101.2	27.4	10.0	3.7	164
	2020	0.59	0.29	0.29	101.0	26.7	10.8	3.8	...
Sweden	2005	9.04	4.48	4.56	98.4	17.4	23.5	22.0	...
Suède	2010	9.39	4.68	4.71	99.2	16.5	24.9	22.9	...
	2017	9.90	4.96	4.95	100.1	17.5	25.5	24.1	439
	2020	10.10	5.06	5.04	100.4	17.6	25.9	24.6	...
Switzerland	2005	7.39	3.62	3.77	95.9	16.3	21.3	186.9	...
Suisse	2010	7.81	3.85	3.96	97.0	15.1	22.8	197.6	...
	2017	8.46	4.19	4.27	98.2	14.9	24.1	214.0	41
	2020	8.65	4.29	4.36	98.5	15.0	25.3	219.0	...
Syrian Arab Republic	2005	18.36	9.37	8.99	104.2	39.3	4.9	100.0	...
République arabe	2010	21.36	10.79	10.58	102.0	37.4	5.0	116.3	...
syrienne	2017	17.10	8.59	8.50	101.0	31.8	6.8	93.1	185
	2020	17.50	8.76	8.74	100.2	30.8	7.5	95.3	...
Tajikistan	2005	6.79	3.41	3.38	101.1	38.0	5.1	48.5	...
Tadjikistan	2010	7.53	3.80	3.73	101.8	35.7	4.8	53.8	...
	2017	8.88	4.48	4.40	101.7	36.5	5.2	63.4	143
	2020	9.54	4.81	4.73	101.6	37.3	5.8	68.1	...
Thailand	2005	65.42	32.17	33.24	96.8	21.3	11.1	128.0	...
Thaïlande	2010	67.20	32.93	34.26	96.1	19.2	12.9	131.5	...
	2017	69.21	33.75	35.46	95.2	17.4	17.0	135.5	513
	2020	69.80	33.97	35.83	94.8	16.6	19.2	136.6	...
Timor-Leste	2005	1.00	0.50	0.49	102.0	44.7	5.9	66.9	...
Timor-Leste	2010	1.09	0.55	0.54	102.2	42.5	6.3	73.5	...
	2017	1.24	0.63	0.61	102.2	38.3	6.4	83.6	15
	2020	1.32	0.67	0.65	102.2	36.8	6.6	88.7	...
Togo	2005	5.61	2.78	2.83	97.9	42.8	4.5	103.2	...
Togo	2010	6.42	3.19	3.24	98.4	42.8	4.4	118.1	...
	2017	7.70	3.83	3.87	98.9	41.6	4.6	141.5	57
	2020	8.28	4.12	4.16	99.0	40.6	4.7	152.2	...

Country or area Pays ou zone	Year Année	Mid-year population estimates and projections (millions) Estimations et projections de population au milieu de l'année (millions)			Sex Ratio (males per 100 females) Rapport des sexes (hommes pour 100 femmes)	Population age distribution (percentage) Répartition par âge de la population (pourcentage)		Population density (per km²) Densité de population (pour km²)	Surface area Superficie (000 km²)
		Total	Male Hommes	Females Femmes		Aged 0 to 14 years old âgée de 0 à 14 ans	Aged 60+ years old âgée de 60 ans ou plus		
Tokelau	2001	~0.00	...	...	98.1	40.7	9.5	150.3	...
Tokélaou	2005	~0.00	...	...		...	...	120.8	...
	2006	~0.00	...	...	102.6	36.6	11.3	116.7	...
	2010	~0.00	...	...	...	...	...	114.0	...
	2016	~0.00[17]	...	...	# 100.0	# 28.3	# 12.2	128.2[17]	...
	2017	~0.00[17]	...	...	...	...	...	130.0[17]	~0
	2020	~0.00	...	...	...	...	...	135.7	
Tonga	2005	0.10	0.05	0.05	100.8	38.2	8.2	140.1	...
Tonga	2010	0.10	0.05	0.05	100.5	37.4	7.9	144.4	...
	2017	0.10	0.05	0.05	100.0	35.8	8.7	141.7	1
	2020	0.11	0.05	0.05	100.2	34.8	8.7	146.8	...
Trinidad and Tobago	2005	1.30	0.64	0.65	98.5	21.9	10.8	252.7	...
Trinité-et-Tobago	2010	1.33	0.66	0.67	98.1	20.7	12.4	258.9	...
	2017	1.38	0.68	0.70	97.7	20.5	15.4	269.8	5
	2020	1.40	0.69	0.71	97.5	20.1	16.9	272.8	...
Tunisia	2005	10.11	5.06	5.05	100.2	25.5	10.1	65.1	...
Tunisie	2010	10.64	5.30	5.33	99.5	23.3	10.4	68.5	...
	2017	11.43	5.67	5.77	98.2	24.1	12.4	73.6	164
	2020	11.82	5.86	5.96	98.4	24.3	13.4	76.1	...
Turkey	2005	67.90	33.42	34.48	96.9	28.6	9.6	88.2	...
Turquie	2010	72.33	35.56	36.76	96.7	26.9	10.4	94.0	...
	2017	81.12	39.98	41.14	97.2	25.0	12.1	105.4	784
	2020	84.34	41.64	42.70	97.5	23.9	13.1	109.6	...
Turkmenistan	2005	4.75	2.34	2.42	96.8	32.6	6.1	10.1	...
Turkménistan	2010	5.09	2.50	2.58	96.8	29.5	6.1	10.8	...
	2017	5.76	2.84	2.92	97.0	30.9	7.3	12.3	488
	2020	6.03	2.97	3.06	97.0	30.8	8.1	12.8	...
Turks and Caicos Islands	2001	0.02	...	...	99.1	28.6	5.2	21.2	...
Îles Turques-et-Caïques	2005	0.03	...	...	99.1[15,24]	...	...	27.8	...
	2010	0.03	...	...	106.7[15,24]	...	...	32.6	...
	2017	0.04[17]	...	...	104.1[15,24]	19.2[15,24]	7.6[15,24]	37.3[17]	1[62]
	2020	0.04	...	...	...	...	...	38.9	...
Tuvalu	2002	0.01	...	...	97.9	36.2	8.6	321.2	...
Tuvalu	2005	0.01	...	...	...	...	...	334.2	...
	2010	0.01	...	...	...	...	...	351.0	...
	2016	0.01[17]	...	...	102.0	31.1	9.9	369.9[17]	...
	2017	0.01[17]	...	...	...	...	...	373.1[17]	~0
	2020	0.01	...	...	...	...	...	383.3	...
Uganda	2005	27.68	13.64	14.05	97.1	49.7	3.2	138.6	...
Ouganda	2010	32.43	15.91	16.51	96.4	49.1	3.0	162.3	...
	2017	41.17	20.25	20.92	96.8	47.3	3.1	206.0	242
	2020	45.74	22.55	23.19	97.2	46.0	3.2	228.9	...
Ukraine	2005[63]	46.89	21.75	25.14	86.5	14.6	20.4	80.9	...
Ukraine	2010[63]	45.79	21.14	24.66	85.7	14.1	21.0	79.0	...
	2017	44.49[63]	20.60[63]	23.89[63]	86.2[63]	15.6	22.8[63]	76.8[63]	604
	2020[63]	43.73	20.26	23.47	86.3	16.0	23.6	75.5	...
United Arab Emirates	2005	4.59	3.23	1.36	237.7	18.3	1.6	54.9	...
Émirats arabes unis	2010	8.55	6.40	2.15	296.9	13.2	1.4	102.3	...
	2017	9.49	6.60	2.89	228.1	14.5[63]	2.2	113.5	84
	2020	9.89	6.84	3.05	223.8	14.8	3.1	118.3	...
United Kingdom	2005	60.29	29.52	30.77	95.9	18.0	21.2	249.2	...
Royaume-Uni	2010	63.46	31.18	32.28	96.6	17.5	22.6	262.3	...
	2017	66.73	32.92	33.80	97.4	17.6	23.7	275.8	242
	2020	67.89	33.54	34.34	97.7	17.7	24.4	280.6	...
United Rep. of Tanzania	2005[64]	38.45	19.14	19.31	99.1	44.8	4.1	43.4	...
Rép.-Unie de Tanzanie	2010[64]	44.35	22.12	22.23	99.5	44.9	4.0	50.1	...
	2017	54.66[64]	27.29[64]	27.37[64]	99.7[64]	44.3	4.1[64]	61.7[64]	947
	2020[64]	59.73	29.85	29.88	99.9	43.6	4.2	67.4	...

Country or area Pays ou zone	Year Année	Mid-year population estimates and projections (millions) Estimations et projections de population au milieu de l'année (millions)			Sex Ratio (males per 100 females) Rapport des sexes (hommes pour 100 femmes)	Population age distribution (percentage) Répartition par âge de la population (pourcentage)		Population density (per km²) Densité de population (pour km²)	Surface area Superficie (000 km²)
		Total	Male Hommes	Females Femmes		Aged 0 to 14 years old âgée de 0 à 14 ans	Aged 60+ years old âgée de 60 ans ou plus		
United States of America États-Unis d'Amérique	2005	294.99	145.57	149.43	97.4	20.9	16.7	32.2	...
	2010	309.01	152.61	156.40	97.6	20.2	18.4	33.8	...
	2017	325.08	160.84	164.24	97.9	18.9[64]	21.5	35.5	9 834
	2020	331.00	163.79	167.22	97.9	18.4	22.9	36.2	...
United States Virgin Islands Îles Vierges américaines	2005	0.11	0.05	0.06	93.5	22.4	16.6	308.0	...
	2010	0.11	0.05	0.06	91.8	20.7	20.4	303.1	...
	2017	0.10	0.05	0.05	90.8	19.9	25.5	299.3	~0
	2020	0.10	0.05	0.05	90.5	19.3	27.6	298.4	...
Uruguay Uruguay	2005	3.32	1.60	1.72	93.2	23.7	17.9	19.0	...
	2010	3.36	1.62	1.74	93.0	22.2	18.5	19.2	...
	2017	3.44	1.66	1.78	93.3	20.8	19.6	19.6	174
	2020	3.47	1.68	1.80	93.5	20.3	20.2	19.8	...
Uzbekistan Ouzbékistan	2005	26.43	13.13	13.30	98.7	32.6	6.5	62.1	...
	2010	28.52	14.18	14.33	98.9	29.1	6.2	67.0	...
	2017	31.96	15.93	16.03	99.4	28.5	7.4	75.1	449
	2020	33.47	16.70	16.77	99.6	28.8	8.3	78.7	...
Vanuatu Vanuatu	2005	0.21	0.11	0.10	104.1	39.7	5.1	17.2	...
	2010	0.24	0.12	0.12	103.1	38.2	5.7	19.4	...
	2017	0.29	0.14	0.14	102.9	38.9	5.7	23.4	12
	2020	0.31	0.16	0.15	102.8	38.4	5.8	25.2	...
Venezuela (Boliv. Rep. of) Venezuela (Rép. boliv. du)	2005	26.43	13.23	13.20	100.2	31.7	7.5	30.0	...
	2010	28.44	14.19	14.25	99.6	29.9	8.4	32.2	...
	2017	29.40	14.55	14.85	98.0	28.0	10.5	33.3	912
	2020	28.44	13.98	14.45	96.8	27.3	12.1	32.2	...
Viet Nam Viet Nam	2005	83.83	41.53	42.30	98.2	27.1	8.6	270.4	...
	2010	87.97	43.75	44.22	98.9	23.6	8.8	283.7	...
	2017	94.60	47.19	47.41	99.5	23.1	11.0	305.1	331
	2020	97.34	48.60	48.74	99.7	23.2	12.3	313.9	...
Wallis and Futuna Islands Îles Wallis-et-Futuna	2003	0.01	...	...	100.6	...	...	104.7	...
	2005	0.01	...	...	...	...	...	104.1	...
	2008	0.01	...	...	98.4	...	...	99.9	...
	2010	0.01	...	...	...	...	...	95.9	...
	2016	0.01[17]	...	...	# 93.4	25.5	15.4	85.0[17]	...
	2017	0.01[17]	...	...	...	...	...	84.1[17]	~0
	2020	0.01	...	...	...	...	...	82.5	...
Western Sahara Sahara occidental	2005	0.44	0.23	0.21	111.5	31.5	3.6	1.6	...
	2010	0.48	0.25	0.23	111.2	29.4	3.8	1.8	...
	2017	0.55	0.29	0.26	110.1	28.1	5.4	2.1	266[65]
	2020	0.60	0.31	0.29	109.5	27.2	6.3	2.2	...
Yemen Yémen	2005	20.11	10.13	9.97	101.6	46.1	4.2	38.1	...
	2010	23.15	11.67	11.48	101.6	42.7	4.3	43.9	...
	2017	27.83	14.03	13.81	101.6	40.0	4.5	52.7	528
	2020	29.83	15.03	14.80	101.5	38.8	4.6	56.5	...
Zambia Zambie	2005	11.86	5.86	6.00	97.8	47.0	3.5	15.9	...
	2010	13.61	6.72	6.89	97.5	47.3	3.3	18.3	...
	2017	16.85	8.34	8.51	98.0	45.4	3.3	22.7	753
	2020	18.38	9.10	9.28	98.1	44.0	3.4	24.7	...
Zimbabwe Zimbabwe	2005	12.08	5.78	6.29	91.9	41.3	4.7	31.2	...
	2010	12.70	6.05	6.65	91.0	41.6	4.4	32.8	...
	2017	14.24	6.78	7.46	90.9	42.6	4.5	36.8	391
	2020	14.86	7.09	7.77	91.3	41.9	4.6	38.4	...

Source:

United Nations Population Division, New York, World Population Prospects: The 2019 Revision, last accessed June 2019.

Source:

Organisation des Nations Unies, Division de la population, New York, « World Population Prospects: The 2019 Revision », denier accès juin 2019.

United Nations Population Division, New York, World Population Prospects: The 2019 Revision; supplemented by data from the United Nations Statistics Division, New York, Demographic Yearbook 2015 and Secretariat for the Pacific Community (SPC) for small countries or areas, last accessed June 2019.

United Nations Statistics Division, New York, "Demographic Yearbook 2015" and the demographic statistics database, last accessed June 2017.

Organisation des Nations Unies, Division de la population, New York, « World Population Prospects: The 2019 Revision »; complétées par des données de l'Organisation des Nations Unies, Division de statistique, New York, Annuaire démographique 2015 et Secrétariat de la Communauté du Pacifique (SCP) pour petits pays ou zones, denier accès juin 2019.

Organisation des Nations Unies, Division de statistique, New York, Annuaire démographique 2015 et recueil de statistiques démographiques, denier accès juin 2017.

1	Including East Jerusalem.	1	Y compris Jérusalem-Est.
2	Calculated by the UN Statistics Division.	2	Calculés par la Division de statistique des Nations Unies.
3	Including Saint Helena.	3	Y compris Sainte-Hélène.
4	Including Bermuda, Greenland, and Saint Pierre and Miquelon.	4	Y compris les Bermudes, le Groenland et Saint-Pierre-et-Miquelon.
5	Including Anguilla, Bonaire, Sint Eustatius and Saba, British Virgin Islands, Cayman Islands, Dominica, Montserrat, Saint Kitts and Nevis, Sint Maarten (Dutch part) and Turks and Caicos Islands.	5	Y compris Anguilla, les îles Bonaire, Saint-Eustache et Saba, les îles Caïmans, la Dominique, Montserrat, Saint-Kitts-et-Nevis, Saint-Martin (partie néerlandaise), les îles Turques-et-Caïques et les îles Vierges britanniques.
6	Including Falkland Islands (Malvinas).	6	Y compris les îles Falkland (Malvinas)
7	Including the Faroe Islands and the Isle of Man.	7	Y compris les îles Féroé et l'île de Man.
8	Including Andorra, Gibraltar, Holy See, and San Marino.	8	Y compris Andorre, Gibraltar, Saint-Siège, et Saint-Marin.
9	Including Liechtenstein and Monaco.	9	Y compris le Liechtenstein et Monaco.
10	Including Svalbard and Jan Mayen Islands.	10	Y compris les îles Svalbard-et-Jan Mayen.
11	Including Christmas Island, Cocos (Keeling) Islands and Norfolk Island.	11	Y compris l'île Christmas, les îles des Cocos (Keeling) et l'île Norfolk.
12	Including Marshall Islands, Nauru, Northern Mariana Islands and Palau.	12	Y compris les îles Mariannes du Nord, les îles Marshall, Nauru et Palaos.
13	Including Pitcairn.	13	Y compris Pitcairn.
14	Including American Samoa, Cook Islands, Niue, Pitcairn, Tokelau, Tuvalu, and Wallis and Futuna Islands.	14	Y compris les îles Cook, Nioué, Pitcairn, Samoa américaines, Tokélaou, Tuvalu, et les îles Wallis-et-Futuna.
15	De jure population.	15	Population de droit.
16	Including armed forces stationed in the area.	16	Y compris les militaires en garnison sur le territoire.
17	Projected estimate (medium fertility variant).	17	Projection approximative (variante moyenne fécondité).
18	Population statistics are compiled from registers.	18	Les statistiques de la population sont compilées à partir des registres.
19	Population aged 65 years and over.	19	Population âgée de 65 ans ou plus.
20	Including Norfolk Island.	20	Y compris l'île Norfolk.
21	Including Nagorno-Karabakh.	21	Y compris le Haut-Karabakh.
22	Data refer to projections based on the 2000 population census.	22	Les données se réfèrent aux projections basées sur le recensement de la population 2000.
23	Data refer to projections based on the 2010 Population Census.	23	Les données se réfèrent aux projections basées sur le recensement de la population de 2010.
24	Estimates should be viewed with caution as these are derived from scarce data.	24	Les montants estimatifs sont à prendre avec prudence, car calculés à partir de données peu nombreuses.
25	Data updated according to "Superintendencia Agraria". Interior waters correspond to natural or artificial bodies of water or snow.	25	Données actualisées d'après la « Superintendencia Agraria ». Les eaux intérieures correspondent aux étendues d'eau naturelles ou artificielles et aux étendues neigeuses.
26	Excluding the institutional population.	26	Non compris la population dans les institutions.
27	Refers to Guernsey and Jersey.	27	Se rapporte à Guernesey et Jersey.
28	For statistical purposes, the data for China do not include those for the Hong Kong Special Administrative Region (Hong Kong SAR), Macao Special Administrative Region (Macao SAR) and Taiwan Province of China.	28	Pour la présentation des statistiques, les données pour la Chine ne comprennent pas la région administrative spéciale de Hong Kong (RAS de Hong Kong), la région administrative spéciale de Macao (RAS de Macao) et la province chinoise de Taïwan.
29	Inland waters include the reservoirs.	29	Les eaux intérieures comprennent les réservoirs.
30	Refers to the whole country.	30	Ensemble du pays.
31	Excluding residents of institutions.	31	À l'exclusion de personnes en établissements de soins.
32	Data have not been adjusted for underenumeration, estimated at 1.4 per cent.	32	Les données n'ont pas été ajustées pour le sous-dénombrement, estimé à 1,4 pour cent.
33	The total surface is 21 040.79 square kilometres, without taking into account the last ruling of The Hague.	33	La superficie totale est égale à 21 040.79 km2, excluant la dernière décision de la Haye.
34	A dispute exists between the Governments of Argentina and the United Kingdom of Great Britain and Northern Ireland concerning sovereignty over the Falkland Islands (Malvinas).	34	La souveraineté sur les îles Falkland (Malvinas) fait l'objet d'un différend entre le Gouvernement argentin et le Gouvernement du Royaume-Uni de Grande-Bretagne et d'Irlande du Nord.
35	Excluding military personnel and their families, visitors and transients.	35	À l'exclusion des personnels militaires et leurs familles, les personnes de passage et les visiteurs.
36	Including Åland Islands.	36	Y compris les Îles d'Åland.
37	Including Abkhazia and South Ossetia.	37	Y compris l'Abkhazie et l'Ossétie du Sud.
38	Excluding families of military personnel, visitors and transients.	38	Non compris les familles des militaires, ni les visiteurs et voyageurs en transit.
39	Excluding military personnel, visitors and transients.	39	À l'exclusion des personnels militaires, les personnes de passage et les visiteurs.

40	Including nationals outside the country.	40	Y compris les ressortissants étrangers.
41	Surface area is 0.44 Km2.	41	Superficie: 0,44 Km2.
42	Land area only.	42	La superficie des terres seulement.
43	Data refer to 1 October.	43	Les données se réfèrent au 1er octobre.
44	Land area only. Excluding 84 square km of uninhabited islands.	44	La superficie des terres seulement. Exclut des îles inhabitées d'une superficie de 84 kilomètres carrés.
45	Including Sabah and Sarawak.	45	Y compris Sabah et Sarawak.
46	Projections are prepared by the Secretariat of the Pacific Community based on 1999 census of population and housing.	46	Les projections sont préparées par le Secrétariat de la Communauté du Pacifique en fonction du recensement de la population et du logement de 1999.
47	Including Agalega, Rodrigues and Saint Brandon.	47	Y compris Agalega, Rodrigues et Saint-Brandon.
48	Excluding the islands of Saint Brandon and Agalega.	48	Non compris les îles Saint-Brandon et Agalega.
49	Intercensus data.	49	Données intercensitaires.
50	Refers to the island of Saipan.	50	Fait référence seulement à l'île de Saipan.
51	Including the Transnistria region.	51	Y compris la région de Transnistrie.
52	Including Ascension and Tristan da Cunha.	52	Y compris Ascension et Tristan da Cunha.
53	Refers to habitable area. Excludes Saint Lucia's Forest Reserve.	53	S'applique à la zone habitable. Exclut la réserve forestière de Sainte-Lucie.
54	Population aged 0 to 20 years.	54	Population âgée de 0 à 20 ans.
55	Population aged 61 years and over.	55	Population âgée de 61 ans ou plus.
56	Surface area is based on the 2002 population and housing census.	56	La superficie est fondée sur les données provenant du recensement de la population et du logement de 2002.
57	Including Kosovo.	57	Y compris Kosovo.
58	Changes in total area per year are the result of new measuring and correcting of the administrative borders between former Yugoslavian countries.	58	Les changements des totaux par année résultent de nouvelles mesures et de corrections des frontières administratives entre pays ex-yougoslaves.
59	The land area of Singapore comprises the mainland and other islands.	59	La superficie terrestre de Singapour comprend l'île principale et les autres îles.
60	Excluding inland water.	60	Exception faite des eaux intérieures.
61	Including Canary Islands, Ceuta and Melilla.	61	Y compris les îles Canaries, Ceuta et Melilla.
62	Including low water level for all islands (area to shoreline).	62	Y compris le niveau de basses eaux pour toutes les îles.
63	Including Crimea.	63	Y compris Crimea.
64	Including Zanzibar.	64	Y compris Zanzibar.
65	Comprising the Northern Region (former Saguia el Hamra) and Southern Region (former Rio de Oro).	65	Comprend la région septentrionale (ancien Saguia el Hamra) et la région méridionale (ancien Rio de Oro).

3

International migrants and refugees
International migrant stock (number and percentage) and refugees and others of concern to UNHCR

Migrants internationaux et réfugiés
Stock de migrants internationaux (nombre et pourcentage) et réfugiés et autres personnes relevant de la compétence du HCR

Region, country or area Région, pays ou zone	Year Année	International Migrant Stock (mid-year) Stock de migrants internationaux (milieu de l'année) Total Total	% of total pop. % de la pop. totale MF HF	M H	F	Refugees and others of concern to UNHCR (mid-year) Réfugiés et autres personnes relevant de la compétence du HCR (milieu de l'année) Refugees& Réfugiés&	Asylum seekers Demandeurs d'asile	Other&& Autres&&	Total pop. Pop. totale
Total, all countries or areas	2005	191 615 574	2.9	3.0	2.9	...	...	...	...
Total, tous pays ou zones	2010	220 781 909	3.2	3.3	3.1	...	...	...	...
	2015	248 861 296	3.4	3.5	3.3	15 097 633	2 343 919	40 518 150	57 959 702
	2019	271 642 105	3.5	3.6	3.4	20 231 932	3 727 291	55 432 149	79 391 372
Africa	2005	15 969 835	1.7	1.9	1.6	...	...	...	...
Afrique	2010	17 804 198	1.7	1.8	1.6	...	...	...	...
	2015	23 476 251	2.0	2.1	1.9	4 493 139	1 044 031	11 530 138	17 067 308
	2019	26 529 334	2.0	2.2	1.9	6 662 807	603 498	22 807 473	30 073 778
Northern Africa [1]	2005	1 747 369	0.9	1.1	0.8	...	...	...	...
Afrique septentrionale [1]	2010	1 948 262	1.0	1.1	0.8	...	...	...	...
	2015	2 138 918	1.0	1.1	0.8	...	...	...	...
	2019	2 955 849	1.2	1.4	1.1	...	...	...	...
Sub-Saharan Africa	2005	14 222 466	1.9	2.1	1.8	...	...	...	...
Afrique subsaharienne	2010	15 855 936	1.9	2.0	1.8	...	...	...	...
	2015	21 337 333	2.2	2.4	2.1	...	...	...	...
	2019	23 573 485	2.2	2.3	2.1	...	...	...	...
Eastern Africa	2005	4 762 817	1.6	1.7	1.5	...	...	...	...
Afrique orientale	2010	4 757 899	1.4	1.4	1.4	...	...	...	...
	2015	6 716 524	1.7	1.8	1.7	...	...	...	...
	2019	7 908 176	1.8	1.8	1.8	...	...	...	...
Middle Africa	2005	1 958 781	1.7	1.8	1.7	...	...	...	...
Afrique centrale	2010	2 430 300	1.8	1.9	1.8	...	...	...	...
	2015	3 494 415	2.3	2.4	2.1	...	...	...	...
	2019	3 785 279	2.2	2.3	2.0	...	...	...	...
Southern Africa	2005	1 582 674	2.9	3.4	2.4	...	...	...	...
Afrique australe	2010	2 352 292	4.0	4.7	3.4	...	...	...	...
	2015	4 060 505	6.4	7.3	5.6	...	...	...	...
	2019	4 481 651	6.7	7.6	5.9	...	...	...	...
Western Africa	2005	5 918 194	2.2	2.4	2.1	...	...	...	...
Afrique occidentale	2010	6 315 445	2.1	2.2	1.9	...	...	...	...
	2015	7 065 889	2.0	2.1	1.9	...	...	...	...
	2019	7 398 379	1.9	2.0	1.8	...	...	...	...
Northern America	2005	45 363 257	13.9	14.0	13.8	...	...	...	...
Amérique septentrionale	2010	50 970 861	14.8	14.7	15.0	...	...	...	...
	2015	55 633 443	15.6	15.3	15.9	416 385	238 989	...	655 374
	2019	58 647 822	16.0	15.6	16.4	420 131	809 134	3 790	1 233 055
Latin America & the Caribbean	2005	7 224 942	1.3	1.3	1.3	...	...	...	...
Amérique latine et Caraïbes	2010	8 262 433	1.4	1.4	1.4	...	...	...	...
	2015	9 441 679	1.5	1.5	1.5	336 552	37 378	6 697 290	7 071 220
	2019	11 673 288	1.8	1.8	1.8	220 962	759 306	12 450 136[2]	13 430 404
Caribbean	2005	1 311 361	3.3	3.4	3.2	...	...	...	...
Caraïbes	2010	1 326 879	3.2	3.3	3.1	...	...	...	...
	2015	1 489 916	3.5	3.8	3.2	...	...	...	...
	2019	1 524 793	3.5	3.8	3.2	...	...	...	...
Central America	2005	1 385 713	0.9	1.0	0.9	...	...	...	...
Amérique centrale	2010	1 749 940	1.1	1.1	1.1	...	...	...	...
	2015	1 878 860	1.1	1.1	1.1	...	...	...	...
	2019	1 927 688	1.1	1.1	1.1	...	...	...	...
South America	2005	4 527 868	1.2	1.2	1.2	...	...	...	...
Amérique du Sud	2010	5 185 614	1.3	1.3	1.3	...	...	...	...
	2015	6 072 903	1.5	1.5	1.5	...	...	...	...
	2019	8 220 807	1.9	1.9	1.9	...	...	...	...
Asia	2005	53 439 306	1.3	1.4	1.2	...	...	...	...
Asie	2010	65 938 712	1.6	1.8	1.4	...	...	...	...
	2015	77 231 760	1.7	2.0	1.5	8 178 380	320 437	19 921 907	28 420 724
	2019	83 559 197	1.8	2.1	1.5	10 005 966	619 941	17 743 970[3]	28 369 877

3

International migrants and refugees *(continued)*
International migrant stock (number and percentage) and refugees and others of concern to UNHCR

Migrants internationaux et réfugiés *(suite)*
Stock de migrants internationaux (nombre et pourcentage) et réfugiés et autres personnes relevant de la compétence du HCR

Region, country or area Région, pays ou zone	Year Année	International Migrant Stock (mid-year) Stock de migrants internationaux (milieu de l'année) Total Total	% of total pop. % de la pop. totale MF HF	M H	F	Refugees and others of concern to UNHCR (mid-year) Réfugiés et autres personnes relevant de la compétence du HCR (milieu de l'année) Refugees& Réfugiés&	Asylum seekers Demandeurs d'asile	Other&& Autres&&	Total pop. Pop. totale
Central Asia	2005	5 235 877	9.0	8.4	9.5	...	...	...	...
Asie centrale	2010	5 264 938	8.4	8.0	8.7	...	...	...	...
	2015	5 392 792	7.9	7.7	8.1	...	...	...	...
	2019	5 543 398	7.6	7.4	7.8	...	...	...	...
Eastern Asia	2005	6 228 684	0.4	0.4	0.4	...	...	...	...
Asie orientale	2010	7 062 527	0.4	0.4	0.5	...	...	...	...
	2015	7 636 397	0.5	0.4	0.5	...	...	...	...
	2019	8 105 764	0.5	0.5	0.5	...	...	...	...
South-eastern Asia	2005	6 718 503	1.2	1.2	1.1	...	...	...	...
Asie du Sud-Est	2010	8 685 564	1.5	1.5	1.4	...	...	...	...
	2015	10 237 687	1.6	1.7	1.5	...	...	...	...
	2019	10 190 867	1.5	1.6	1.4	...	...	...	...
Southern Asia	2005	13 722 314	0.9	0.9	0.9	...	...	...	...
Asie méridionale	2010	14 311 392	0.8	0.8	0.8	...	...	...	...
	2015	14 051 010	0.8	0.8	0.8	...	...	...	...
	2019	14 083 627	0.7	0.7	0.7	...	...	...	...
Western Asia	2005	21 533 928	10.5	12.6	8.2	...	...	...	...
Asie occidentale	2010	30 614 291	13.2	16.5	9.5	...	...	...	...
	2015	39 913 874	15.5	19.2	11.4	...	...	...	...
	2019	45 635 541	16.6	20.6	12.2	...	...	...	...
Europe	2005	63 594 822	8.7	8.8	8.7	...	...	...	...
Europe	2010	70 678 025	9.6	9.6	9.6	...	...	...	...
	2015	75 008 219	10.1	10.0	10.2	1 626 214	678 737	2 368 815	4 673 766
	2019	82 304 539	11.0	11.1	10.9	2 842 904	871 730	2 426 636	6 141 270
Eastern Europe	2005	19 744 557	6.6	6.7	6.6	...	...	...	...
Europe orientale	2010	19 110 686	6.5	6.5	6.4	...	...	...	...
	2015	19 841 537	6.7	6.8	6.7	...	...	...	...
	2019	20 278 745	6.9	7.0	6.8	...	...	...	...
Northern Europe	2005	9 588 814	10.0	9.7	10.2	...	...	...	...
Europe septentrionale	2010	11 344 850	11.3	11.1	11.5	...	...	...	...
	2015	13 269 401	12.8	12.5	13.1	...	...	...	...
	2019	15 094 924	14.3	14.0	14.5	...	...	...	...
Southern Europe	2005	12 004 009	8.0	8.0	8.0	...	...	...	...
Europe méridionale	2010	16 206 134	10.6	10.5	10.6	...	...	...	...
	2015	15 815 447	10.3	9.9	10.7	...	...	...	...
	2019	16 503 552	10.8	10.4	11.2	...	...	...	...
Western Europe	2005	22 257 442	12.0	12.1	11.8	...	...	...	...
Europe occidentale	2010	24 016 355	12.8	12.8	12.8	...	...	...	...
	2015	26 081 834	13.6	13.5	13.6	...	...	...	...
	2019	30 427 318	15.6	15.9	15.2	...	...	...	...
Oceania	2005	6 023 412	17.9	17.7	18.0	...	...	...	...
Océanie	2010	7 127 680	19.3	19.1	19.5	...	...	...	...
	2015	8 069 944	20.2	20.1	20.4	46 963	24 347	...	71 310
	2019	8 927 925	21.2	21.0	21.4	79 162	63 682	144	142 988
Australia and New Zealand	2005	5 717 982	23.5	23.4	23.7	...	...	...	...
Australie et Nouvelle-Zélande	2010	6 830 423	25.8	25.6	25.9	...	...	...	...
	2015	7 769 466	27.2	27.1	27.3	...	...	...	...
	2019	8 618 009	28.7	28.6	28.9	...	...	...	...
Melanesia	2005	104 017	1.3	1.4	1.1	...	...	...	...
Mélanésie	2010	110 685	1.2	1.3	1.1	...	...	...	...
	2015	119 344	1.2	1.3	1.1	...	...	...	...
	2019	123 564	1.1	1.2	1.0	...	...	...	...
Micronesia	2005	128 390	25.8	25.3	26.2	...	...	...	...
Micronésie	2010	115 020	22.8	22.7	23.0	...	...	...	...
	2015	113 523	21.7	21.7	21.7	...	...	...	...
	2019	117 978	21.7	21.7	21.7	...	...	...	...

International migrants and refugees *(continued)*
International migrant stock (number and percentage) and refugees and others of concern to UNHCR

Migrants internationaux et réfugiés *(suite)*
Stock de migrants internationaux (nombre et pourcentage) et réfugiés et autres personnes relevant de la compétence du HCR

Region, country or area Région, pays ou zone	Year Année	International Migrant Stock (mid-year) Stock de migrants internationaux (milieu de l'année) Total Total	% of total pop. % de la pop. totale MF HF	M H	F	Refugees and others of concern to UNHCR (mid-year) Réfugiés et autres personnes relevant de la compétence du HCR (milieu de l'année) Refugees& Réfugiés&	Asylum seekers Demandeurs d'asile	Other&& Autres&&	Total pop. Pop. totale
Polynesia [4] Polynésie [4]	2005	73 023	11.3	12.0	10.6	...	...	...	...
	2010	71 552	10.9	11.5	10.2	...	...	...	...
	2015	67 611	10.1	10.7	9.5	...	...	...	...
	2019	68 374	10.1	10.7	9.4	...	...	...	...
Afghanistan Afghanistan	2005	87 300	0.3	0.4	0.3	32[5]	14[5]	159 551[5]	159 597[5]
	2010	102 246	0.4	0.4	0.3	6 434[5]	30[5]	1 193 523[5]	1 199 987[5]
	2015	489 749	1.4	1.4	1.4	225 714	101	1 195 604	1 421 419
	2019	149 762	0.4	0.4	0.4	72 231	264	2 753 903	2 826 398
Albania Albanie	2005	64 739	2.1	2.1	2.1	56[5]	35[5]	1[5]	92[5]
	2010	52 784	1.8	1.8	1.8	76[5]	23[5]	...	99[5]
	2015	52 031	1.8	1.8	1.8	154	501	7 443	8 098
	2019	49 160	1.7	1.7	1.7	145[6]	233[6]	3 896[6]	4 274[6]
Algeria Algérie	2005	197 422[7]	0.6[7]	0.6[7]	0.5[7]	94 101[5]	306[5]	...	94 407[5]
	2010	216 964[7]	0.6[7]	0.6[7]	0.6[7]	94 144[5]	304[5]	...	94 448[5]
	2015	239 473[7]	0.6[7]	0.6[7]	0.6[7]	94 144[8]	5 892	...	100 036
	2019	249 075[7]	0.6[7]	0.6[7]	0.6[7]	98 282	1 230	...	99 512
American Samoa Samoa américaines	2005	24 233	40.7	...	...	...	...	...	...
	2010	23 555	42.0	...	...	...	...	...	...
	2015	23 513	42.1	...	...	...	...	...	...
	2019	23 539	42.6	...	...	...	...	...	...
Andorra [9] Andorre [9]	2005	50 298	63.8	...	...	...	...	...	...
	2010	52 053	61.6	...	...	...	...	...	...
	2015	42 264	54.2	...	...	...	...	...	...
	2019	45 102	58.5	...	...	...	...	...	...
Angola Angola	2005	61 329[7]	0.3[7]	0.3[7]	0.3[7]	13 984[5]	885[5]	45[5]	14 914[5]
	2010	332 126[7]	1.4[7]	1.4[7]	1.5[7]	15 155[5]	4 241[5]	...	19 396[5]
	2015	632 178[7]	2.3[7]	2.2[7]	2.3[7]	15 555[5]	30 143[5]	2 887	45 698[5]
	2019	669 479[7]	2.1[7]	2.2[7]	2.0[7]	39 900	30 180	...	70 080
Anguilla Anguilla	2005	4 684	37.6	...	...	...	...	...	...
	2010	5 103	38.0	...	...	...	...	...	...
	2015	5 470	38.3	...	...	...	...	...	...
	2018	...	...	...	...	1	...	...	1
	2019	5 679	38.2	...	...	...	...	...	...
Antigua and Barbuda Antigua-et-Barbuda	2005	24 741	30.4	28.6	32.0	...	...	...	...
	2010	26 412	30.0	28.0	31.9	...	...	...	...
	2015	28 083	30.0	27.8	32.1	...	10	...	10
	2019	29 207	30.1	27.8	32.2	2	1	208[2]	211
Argentina Argentine	2005	1 673 088	4.3	4.1	4.5	3 074[5]	825[5]	2[5]	3 901[5]
	2010	1 805 957	4.4	4.2	4.6	3 276[5]	947[5]	...	4 223[5]
	2015	2 086 302	4.8	4.6	5.1	3 523	897	...	4 420
	2019	2 212 879	4.9	4.7	5.2	3 584	7 075	154 933[2]	165 592
Armenia Arménie	2005	469 119[7]	15.7[7]	13.7[7]	17.6[7]	219 550[5]	70[5]	...	219 620[5]
	2010	211 147[7]	7.3[7]	6.4[7]	8.2[7]	3 296[5]	23[5]	82 525[5]	85 844[5]
	2015	191 199[7]	6.5[7]	5.6[7]	7.3[7]	15 690	114	238	16 042
	2019	190 159[7]	6.4[7]	5.6[7]	7.2[7]	17 970	130	913	19 013
Aruba Aruba	2005	32 540	32.5	30.6	34.3	...	...	...	...
	2010	34 327	33.8	31.6	35.7	...	1[5]	...	1[5]
	2015	36 114	34.6	32.5	36.5	...	2	...	2
	2018	...	...	...	...	1	292	...	293
	2019	36 532	34.4	32.3	36.2	...	411	15 598[2]	16 009
Australia Australie	2005	4 878 030[10]	24.2[10]	24.0[10]	24.3[10]	64 964[5]	1 822[5]	8[5]	66 794[5]
	2010	5 882 980[10]	26.6[10]	26.4[10]	26.7[10]	21 805[5]	3 760[5]	15[5]	25 580[5]
	2015	6 729 730[10]	28.1[10]	28.0[10]	28.2[10]	35 582	22 837[11,12]	...	58 419
	2019	7 549 270[10]	30.0[10]	29.8[10]	30.1[10]	66 424[11]	62 680[11]	144[11]	129 248[11]
Austria Autriche	2005	1 136 270	13.8	13.5	14.0	21 230[5]	40 710[5]	830[5]	62 770[5]
	2010	1 275 992	15.2	14.9	15.5	42 630[5]	25 625[5]	470[5]	68 725[5]
	2015	1 492 374	17.2	16.9	17.5	60 747[12]	30 900[12]	570[12]	92 217[12]
	2019	1 779 857	19.9	19.8	19.9	131 366	31 204	1 095	163 665

3

International migrants and refugees *(continued)*
International migrant stock (number and percentage) and refugees and others of concern to UNHCR

Migrants internationaux et réfugiés *(suite)*
Stock de migrants internationaux (nombre et pourcentage) et réfugiés et autres personnes relevant de la compétence du HCR

Region, country or area Région, pays ou zone	Year Année	International Migrant Stock (mid-year) Stock de migrants internationaux (milieu de l'année)				Refugees and others of concern to UNHCR (mid-year) Réfugiés et autres personnes relevant de la compétence du HCR (milieu de l'année)			
		Total Total	MF HF	M H	F	Refugees& Réfugiés&	Asylum seekers Demandeurs d'asile	Other&& Autres&&	Total pop. Pop. totale
Azerbaijan	2005	302 220[7,13]	3.5[7,13]	3.2[7,13]	3.9[7,13]	3 004[5]	115[5]	581 194[5]	584 313[5]
Azerbaïdjan	2010	276 901[7,13]	3.1[7,13]	2.9[7,13]	3.2[7,13]	1 891[5]	17[5]	594 969[5]	596 877[5]
	2015	264 241[7,13]	2.7[7,13]	2.6[7,13]	2.8[7,13]	1 357	262	626 477	628 096
	2019	253 887[7,13]	2.5[7,13]	2.4[7,13]	2.6[7,13]	1 097	132	624 007	625 236
Bahamas	2005	45 595	14.0	15.0	13.1	...	...	...	...
Bahamas	2010	54 736	15.4	16.2	14.7	28[5]	9[5]	...	37[5]
	2015	59 306	15.8	16.5	15.2	7	19	30	56
	2016	...	...	...	...	11	17	97	125
	2019	62 962	16.2	16.8	15.5	17	18	...	35
Bahrain	2005	404 018[9]	45.4[9]	54.0[9]	32.5[9]	...	15[5]	...	15[5]
Bahreïn	2010	657 856[9]	53.0[9]	61.5[9]	39.0[9]	165[5]	69[5]	...	234[5]
	2015	704 137[9]	51.3[9]	60.1[9]	37.2[9]	277	78	...	355
	2019	741 161[9]	45.2[9]	50.8[9]	35.0[9]	260	56	...	316
Bangladesh	2005	1 166 700[7]	0.8[7]	0.9[7]	0.8[7]	21 098[5]	58[5]	250 094[5]	271 250[5]
Bangladesh	2010	1 345 546[7]	0.9[7]	0.9[7]	0.9[7]	229 253[5]	...	...	229 253[5]
	2015	1 422 805[7]	0.9[7]	0.9[7]	0.9[7]	232 975[14]	11	...	232 986
	2017	...	...	...	...	307 424[15]	104	2	307 530
	2019	2 185 613[7]	1.3[7]	1.4[7]	1.3[7]	911 736[16]	44[16]	...	911 780[16]
Barbados	2005	30 624	11.1	10.2	11.9	...	...	...	...
Barbade	2010	32 825	11.6	10.9	12.3	...	...	...	...
	2015	34 475	12.1	11.3	12.8	1	...	...	1
	2019	34 807	12.1	11.3	12.9	1	8	...	9
Belarus	2005	1 106 982	11.6	11.4	11.8	725[5]	56[5]	12 421[5]	13 202[5]
Bélarus	2010	1 090 378	11.6	11.4	11.7	589[5]	66[5]	7 734[5]	8 389[5]
	2015	1 082 905	11.5	11.3	11.6	1 369	257	6 302	7 928
	2019	1 069 395	11.3	11.1	11.5	2 573	151	5 909	8 633
Belgium	2005	1 248 733	11.8	12.0	11.7	15 282[5]	18 913[5]	398[5]	34 593[5]
Belgique	2010	1 503 806	13.7	13.5	14.0	17 892[5]	18 288[5]	696[5]	36 876[5]
	2015	1 783 488	15.8	15.7	15.9	31 115	9 396	5 267	45 778
	2019	1 981 919	17.2	17.1	17.2	61 677	10 893	10 933	83 503
Belize	2005	41 424[7]	14.6[7]	14.8[7]	14.4[7]	624[5]	14[5]	...	638[5]
Belize	2010	46 360[7]	14.4[7]	14.5[7]	14.2[7]	134[5]	30[5]	2[5]	166[5]
	2015	54 674[7]	15.1[7]	15.3[7]	15.0[7]	...	146	...	146
	2019	59 998[7]	15.4[7]	15.5[7]	15.2[7]	28	3 614	2 858	6 500
Benin	2005	221 889[7,9]	2.8[7,9]	2.7[7,9]	2.8[7,9]	30 294[5]	1 695[5]	77[5]	32 066[5]
Bénin	2010	309 124[7,9]	3.4[7,9]	3.1[7,9]	3.6[7,9]	7 139[5]	101[5]	47[5]	7 287[5]
	2015	366 284[7,9]	3.5[7,9]	3.3[7,9]	3.7[7,9]	488	84	...	572
	2019	390 112[7,9]	3.3[7,9]	3.1[7,9]	3.5[7,9]	1 223	351	...	1 574
Bermuda	2005	18 276	27.6	...	...	...	...	...	...
Bermudes	2010	18 884	28.9	...	...	...	...	...	...
	2015	19 126	30.0	...	...	...	...	...	...
	2019	19 336	30.9	...	...	...	...	...	...
Bhutan	2005	40 279	6.2	9.6	2.4	...	...	...	...
Bhoutan	2010	48 420	7.1	10.9	2.8	...	...	...	...
	2015	51 106	7.0	11.3	2.2	...	...	...	...
	2019	53 254	7.0	11.2	2.2	...	...	...	...
Bolivia (Plurin. State of)	2005	107 745	1.2	1.2	1.1	535[5]	3[5]	2[5]	540[5]
Bolivie (État plurin. de)	2010	122 846	1.2	1.3	1.2	695[5]	41[5]	3[5]	739[5]
	2015	142 989	1.3	1.4	1.3	767	8	...	775
	2019	156 114	1.4	1.4	1.3	810[17]	46[17]	...	856[17]
Bonaire, St. Eustatius & Saba	2005[18]	62 205	35.0	...	...	...	...	...	...
Bonaire, St-Eustache et Saba	2010	11 445	54.7	...	...	...	1[5,19]	...	1[5,19]
	2015	13 002	52.9	...	...	...	...	...	...
	2019	15 484	59.6	...	...	...	...	...	...
Bosnia and Herzegovina	2005	* 47 272[7]	* 1.3[7]	* 1.2[7]	* 1.3[7]	10 568[5]	215[5]	188 735[5]	199 518[5]
Bosnie-Herzégovine	2010	* 38 792[7]	* 1.0[7]	* 1.0[7]	* 1.1[7]	7 016[5]	153[5]	171 790[5]	178 959[5]
	2015	* 38 574[7]	* 1.1[7]	* 1.1[7]	* 1.2[7]	6 805	11	137 035	143 851
	2019	* 35 735[7]	* 1.1[7]	* 1.1[7]	* 1.1[7]	5 234	601	145 817	151 652

3

International migrants and refugees *(continued)*
International migrant stock (number and percentage) and refugees and others of concern to UNHCR

Migrants internationaux et réfugiés *(suite)*
Stock de migrants internationaux (nombre et pourcentage) et réfugiés et autres personnes relevant de la compétence du HCR

Region, country or area / Région, pays ou zone	Year / Année	International Migrant Stock (mid-year) / Stock de migrants internationaux (milieu de l'année)				Refugees and others of concern to UNHCR (mid-year) / Réfugiés et autres personnes relevant de la compétence du HCR (milieu de l'année)			
		Total / Total	MF / HF	M / H	F	Refugees& / Réfugiés&	Asylum seekers / Demandeurs d'asile	Other&& / Autres&&	Total pop. / Pop. totale
			% of total pop. / % de la pop. totale						
Botswana	2005	84 614	4.7	5.6	3.8	3 109[5]	47[5]	592[5]	3 748[5]
Botswana	2010	94 614	4.8	5.5	4.0	2 986[5]	249[5]	111[5]	3 346[5]
	2015	103 268	4.9	5.8	4.0	2 164	248	...	2 412
	2019	110 596	4.8	5.6	4.0	2 078	204	7	2 289
Brazil	2005	638 582	0.3	0.4	0.3	3 458[5]	195[5]	4 093[5]	7 746[5]
Brésil	2010	592 568	0.3	0.3	0.3	4 357[5]	872[5]	8[5]	5 237[5]
	2015	716 568	0.4	0.4	0.3	7 762	17 902	40 338	66 002
	2019	807 006	0.4	0.4	0.3	11 629	191 452	68 499[2]	271 580
British Virgin Islands	2005	15 016	65.0	...	...	...	...	...	...
Îles Vierges britanniques	2010	17 074	61.4	...	...	2[5]	...	...	2[5]
	2015	19 132	65.6	...	...	...	...	...	...
	2017	...	...	...	...	...	1	...	1
	2019	20 778	69.2	...	...	1	...	...	1
Brunei Darussalam	2005	98 441	27.0	29.6	24.2	...	...	...	...
Brunéi Darussalam	2010	100 587	25.9	28.3	23.3	...	...	20 992[5]	20 992[5]
	2015	102 733	24.8	27.0	22.4	...	...	20 524	20 524
	2019	110 641	25.5	27.9	23.0	...	...	20 863	20 863
Bulgaria	2005	61 074	0.8	0.7	0.9	4 413[5]	805[5]	...	5 218[5]
Bulgarie	2010	76 287	1.0	0.9	1.1	5 530[5]	1 412[5]	...	6 942[5]
	2015	123 803	1.7	1.7	1.7	11 046[12]	7 840	67	18 953
	2019	168 516	2.4	2.4	2.4	20 015	1 093	102	21 210
Burkina Faso	2005	597 658[7]	4.5[7]	4.3[7]	4.6[7]	511[5]	784[5]	7[5]	1 302[5]
Burkina Faso	2010	674 438[7]	4.3[7]	4.1[7]	4.5[7]	531[5]	534[5]	9[5]	1 074[5]
	2015	704 676[7]	3.9[7]	3.7[7]	4.1[7]	34 027	180	...	34 207
	2019	718 338[7]	3.5[7]	3.4[7]	3.7[7]	25 761	47	170 447	196 255
Burundi	2005	172 874[7]	2.3[7]	2.3[7]	2.4[7]	20 681[5]	19 900[5]	12 988[5]	53 569[5]
Burundi	2010	235 259[7]	2.7[7]	2.7[7]	2.7[7]	29 365[5]	12 062[5]	159 338[5]	200 765[5]
	2015	289 810[7]	2.9[7]	2.8[7]	2.9[7]	54 126	2 733	80 851	137 710
	2019	321 018[7]	2.8[7]	2.8[7]	2.8[7]	72 216	6 986	41 992	121 194
Cabo Verde	2005	12 700	2.7	2.9	2.6	...	...	1[5]	1[5]
Cabo Verde	2010	14 373	2.9	3.0	2.9	...	...	...	...
	2015	14 924	2.8	2.9	2.8	...	...	115	115
	2019	15 664	2.8	2.9	2.8	...	...	115	115
Cambodia	2005	114 031	0.9	0.9	0.8	127[5]	68[5]	207[5]	402[5]
Cambodge	2010	81 977	0.6	0.6	0.5	129[5]	51[5]	...	180[5]
	2015	73 963	0.5	0.5	0.4	80	33	131	244
	2018	...	...	...	...	67	47	...	114
	2019	78 649	0.5	0.5	0.4	...	...	57 444	57 444
Cameroon	2005	265 503	1.5	1.7	1.3	52 042[5]	6 766[5]	7 444[5]	66 252[5]
Cameroun	2010	291 474	1.4	1.6	1.3	104 275[5]	2 383[5]	66[5]	106 724[5]
	2015	508 346	2.2	2.2	2.2	302 293	7 835	81 693	391 821
	2019	505 692	2.0	1.9	2.0	396 698	8 920	1 057 613	1 463 231
Canada	2005	6 078 985	18.9	18.3	19.5	147 171[5]	20 552[5]	12[5]	167 735[5]
Canada	2010	6 761 226	19.8	19.1	20.5	165 549[5]	51 025[5]	7[5]	216 581[5]
	2015	7 428 657	20.6	19.8	21.4	135 888[5]	19 951[5]	...	155 839[5]
	2019	7 960 657	21.3	20.4	22.1	101 279	84 747	3 790	189 816
Cayman Islands	2005[9]	20 679	42.0	...	...	...	...	...	...
Îles Caïmanes	2010	24 057[9]	42.4[9]	...	...	1[5]	4[5]	...	5[5]
	2015	26 177[9]	42.4[9]	...	...	6	1	100	107
	2019	28 985[9]	44.6[9]	...	...	31	6	50[2]	87
Central African Republic	2005	94 449[9]	2.3[9]	2.5[9]	2.2[9]	24 569[5]	1 960[5]	2 167[5]	28 696[5]
République centrafricaine	2010	93 466[9]	2.1[9]	2.3[9]	2.0[9]	21 574[5]	1 219[5]	192 531[5]	215 324[5]
	2015	81 598[9]	1.8[9]	1.9[9]	1.7[9]	7 906	394	508 904	517 204
	2019	90 649[9]	1.9[9]	2.0[9]	1.8[9]	7 265	394	704 990	712 649
Chad	2005	352 062[7]	3.5[7]	3.2[7]	3.8[7]	275 412[5]	68[5]	...	275 480[5]
Tchad	2010	416 924[7]	3.5[7]	3.1[7]	3.8[7]	347 939[5]	110[5]	185 000[5]	533 049[5]
	2015	466 968[7]	3.3[7]	3.1[7]	3.6[7]	420 774	2 749	50 000	473 523
	2019	512 230[7]	3.2[7]	3.0[7]	3.5[7]	464 340	3 707	199 339	667 386

International migrants and refugees *(continued)*
International migrant stock (number and percentage) and refugees and others of concern to UNHCR

Migrants internationaux et réfugiés *(suite)*
Stock de migrants internationaux (nombre et pourcentage) et réfugiés et autres personnes relevant de la compétence du HCR

Region, country or area / Région, pays ou zone	Year / Année	International Migrant Stock (mid-year) Stock de migrants internationaux (milieu de l'année)				Refugees and others of concern to UNHCR (mid-year) Réfugiés et autres personnes relevant de la compétence du HCR (milieu de l'année)			
		Total / Total	% of total pop. / % de la pop. totale			Refugees[&] / Réfugiés[&]	Asylum seekers Demandeurs d'asile	Other[&&] Autres[&&]	Total pop. Pop. totale
			MF HF	M H	F				
Channel Islands [20] Îles Anglo-Normandes [20]	2005	70 941	46.8	45.2	48.3	...	...	...	...
	2010	77 581	48.6	47.0	50.1	...	...	...	...
	2015	82 307	49.8	48.1	51.4	...	...	...	...
	2019	83 833	48.7	47.0	50.3	...	...	...	...
Chile Chili	2005	276 360	1.7	1.7	1.8	806[5]	107[5]	...	913[5]
	2010	375 388	2.2	2.1	2.3	1 621[5]	274[5]	...	1 895[5]
	2015	639 724	3.6	3.4	3.7	1 798	719	...	2 517
	2019	939 992	5.0	4.7	5.2	2 039	10 310	373 186[2]	385 535
China [21] Chine [21]	2005	678 947[9]	0.1[9]	0.1[9]	~0.0[9]	301 041[5]	84[5]	1[5]	301 126[5]
	2010	849 861[9]	0.1[9]	0.1[9]	0.1[9]	300 986[5]	122[5]	...	301 108[5]
	2015	978 046[9]	0.1[9]	0.1[9]	0.1[9]	301 057[22]	564	...	301 621
	2019	1 030 871[9]	0.1[9]	0.1[9]	0.1[9]	321 784[23]	588[23]	...	322 372[23]
China, Hong Kong SAR Chine, RAS de Hong Kong	2005	2 721 235	40.2	36.4	43.7	1 934[5]	1 097[5]	...	3 031[5]
	2010	2 779 950	39.9	35.0	44.2	154[5]	486[5]	3[5]	643[5]
	2015	2 838 665	39.5	33.6	44.6	151	9 940	1	10 092
	2016	...	...	...	...	140	2 315	1	2 456
	2017	...	...	...	...	93	...	1	94
	2019	2 942 254	39.6	33.4	44.8	147	...	...	147
China, Macao SAR Chine, RAS de Macao	2005	279 308	57.8	56.8	58.8	...	...	...	...
	2010	318 506	59.2	56.7	61.5	...	9[5]	1[5]	10[5]
	2015	376 066	62.5	60.4	64.3	...	6	...	6
	2019	399 572	62.4	60.3	64.3	...	2	...	2
Colombia Colombie	2005	107 612	0.3	0.3	0.2	155[5]	41[5]	2 000 009[5]	2 000 205[5]
	2010	124 271	0.3	0.3	0.3	212[5]	167[5]	3 672 065[5]	3 672 444[5]
	2015	139 134	0.3	0.3	0.3	219	56	6 520 304	6 520 579
	2019	1 142 319	2.3	2.3	2.2	328[24]	5 028[24]	9 711 837[2,24]	9 717 193[24]
Comoros Comores	2005	13 209	2.2	2.0	2.3	1[5]	...	...	1[5]
	2010	12 618	1.8	1.7	1.9	...	...	...	...
	2015	12 555	1.6	1.5	1.7	...	...	...	...
	2019	12 504	1.5	1.4	1.5	...	...	...	...
Congo Congo	2005	318 724	8.8	9.6	8.0	66 075[5]	3 486[5]	8 079[5]	77 640[5]
	2010	425 173	9.9	10.9	9.0	133 112[5]	5 524[5]	59[5]	138 695[5]
	2015	390 142	8.0	8.8	7.2	61 492	3 248	1 070	65 810
	2019	402 142	7.5	8.2	6.8	29 777	13 801	146 192	189 770
Cook Islands Îles Cook	2005	3 277	17.2	...	...	...	...	...	...
	2010	3 769	20.5	...	...	...	...	...	...
	2015	3 477	19.8	...	...	...	...	...	...
	2019	3 491	19.9	...	...	...	...	...	...
Costa Rica Costa Rica	2005	358 175[7]	8.4[7]	8.2[7]	8.5[7]	11 253[5]	223[5]	...	11 476[5]
	2010	405 404[7]	8.9[7]	8.5[7]	9.2[7]	19 505[5]	375[5]	40[5]	19 920[5]
	2015	411 697[7]	8.5[7]	8.1[7]	8.8[7]	3 475	1 819	2 613	7 907
	2019	417 768[7]	8.3[7]	8.0[7]	8.5[7]	4 566	44 308	30 287	79 161
Côte d'Ivoire Côte d'Ivoire	2005	2 265 090[9]	12.3[9]	13.4[9]	11.3[9]	41 627[5]	2 443[5]	71 050[5]	115 120[5]
	2010	2 366 537[9]	11.5[9]	12.6[9]	10.4[9]	26 218[5]	256[5]	538 068[5]	564 542[5]
	2015	2 467 984[9]	10.6[9]	11.6[9]	9.6[9]	1 972	667	724 131	726 770
	2019	2 549 141[9]	9.9[9]	10.9[9]	8.9[9]	1 950[25]	237[25]	690 612[25]	692 799[25]
Croatia Croatie	2005	579 273[7]	13.2[7]	12.9[7]	13.6[7]	2 927[5]	8[5]	7 932[5]	10 867[5]
	2010	573 248[7]	13.2[7]	12.9[7]	13.6[7]	936[5]	81[5]	24 463[5]	25 480[5]
	2015	561 093[7]	13.3[7]	12.8[7]	13.7[7]	710	90	16 684	17 484
	2019	518 083[7]	12.5[7]	12.0[7]	13.0[7]	853	231	7 177	8 261
Cuba Cuba	2005	11 935	0.1	0.1	0.1	706[5]	32[5]	...	738[5]
	2010	6 640	0.1	0.1	0.1	411[5]	11[5]	1[5]	423[5]
	2015	5 312	~0.0	~0.0	0.1	313	12	...	325
	2019	4 886	~0.0	~0.0	~0.0	230	44	1	275
Curaçao Curaçao	2010	34 627	23.2	20.7	25.3	7[5]	2[5]	...	9[5]
	2015	37 611	23.5	21.1	25.6	44	41	...	85
	2019	40 883	25.0	22.4	27.2	101	358	25 687[2]	26 146

3

International migrants and refugees *(continued)*
International migrant stock (number and percentage) and refugees and others of concern to UNHCR

Migrants internationaux et réfugiés *(suite)*
Stock de migrants internationaux (nombre et pourcentage) et réfugiés et autres personnes relevant de la compétence du HCR

Region, country or area / Région, pays ou zone	Year / Année	International Migrant Stock (mid-year) / Stock de migrants internationaux (milieu de l'année)				Refugees and others of concern to UNHCR (mid-year) / Réfugiés et autres personnes relevant de la compétence du HCR (milieu de l'année)			
		Total / Total	MF HF	M H	F	Refugees& / Réfugiés&	Asylum seekers Demandeurs d'asile	Other&& / Autres&&	Total pop. Pop. totale
Cyprus / Chypre	2005	117 165[26]	11.4[26]	9.7[26]	13.2[26]	701[5]	13 067[5]	1[5]	13 769[5]
	2010	191 866[26]	17.2[26]	15.1[26]	19.4[26]	3 394[5]	5 396[5]	...	8 790[5]
	2015	192 020[26]	16.5[26]	14.5[26]	18.6[26]	5 763	2 339	6 000	14 102
	2019	191 922[26]	16.0[26]	14.2[26]	17.8[26]	11 508[27]	15 759[27]	6 000[27]	33 267[27]
Czechia / Tchéquie	2005	322 540[9]	3.1[9]	3.6[9]	2.7[9]	1 802[5]	924[5]	...	2 726[5]
	2010	398 493[9]	3.8[9]	4.6[9]	3.0[9]	2 449[5]	1 065[5]	1[5]	3 515[5]
	2015	416 454[9]	3.9[9]	4.6[9]	3.3[9]	3 137[12]	409	1 502	5 048
	2019	512 705[9]	4.8[9]	5.6[9]	4.0[9]	2 267	1 887	1 502	5 656
Dem. People's Rep. Korea / Rép. pop. dém. de Corée	*2005	40 097	0.2	0.2	0.2	...	...	...	...
	*2010	44 010	0.2	0.2	0.2	...	...	...	...
	*2015	48 458	0.2	0.2	0.2	...	...	...	...
	*2019	49 393	0.2	0.2	0.2	...	...	...	...
Dem. Rep. of the Congo / Rép. dém. du Congo	2005	622 869[7]	1.1[7]	1.1[7]	1.2[7]	204 341[5]	140[5]	47 435[5]	251 916[5]
	2010	588 950[7]	0.9[7]	0.9[7]	0.9[7]	166 336[5]	932[5]	2 196 591[5]	2 363 859[5]
	2015	824 492[7]	1.1[7]	1.1[7]	1.1[7]	* 160 271	1 124	1 839 611	2 001 006
	2019	963 833[7]	1.1[7]	1.1[7]	1.1[7]	538 009	1 272	4 518 487	5 057 768
Denmark / Danemark	2005	440 383	8.1	7.9	8.3	44 374[5]	510[5]	573[5]	45 457[5]
	2010	500 772	9.0	8.8	9.2	17 922[5]	3 363[5]	3 238[5]	24 523[5]
	2015	595 876	10.5	10.3	10.6	17 785[12]	4 566	4 984	27 335
	2019	722 878	12.5	12.5	12.6	36 971	1 956	8 507	47 434
Djibouti	2005	92 091[7]	11.8[7]	13.0[7]	10.5[7]	10 456[5]	19[5]	7 668[5]	18 143[5]
	2010	101 575[7]	12.1[7]	11.9[7]	12.3[7]	15 104[5]	732[5]	7[5]	15 843[5]
	2015	112 351[7]	12.3[7]	12.2[7]	12.4[7]	14 787	2 586	...	17 373
	2018	...	...	...	...	17 302	10 129	50	27 481
	2019	115 341[7]	11.8[7]	11.8[7]	11.8[7]	19 158	10 900	...	30 058
Dominica / Dominique	2005	4 744	6.7	...	...	...	...	...	...
	2010	8 110	11.4	...	...	...	...	...	...
	2015	8 093	11.4	...	...	...	...	...	...
	2019	8 264	11.5	...	...	...	...	...	...
Dominican Republic / République dominicaine	2005	376 001	4.1	5.0	3.3	...	...	...	...
	2010	393 720	4.1	4.9	3.2	599[5]	1 759[5]	...	2 358[5]
	2015	549 289	5.3	6.9	3.8	609[28]	752[28]	133 770[28]	135 131[28]
	2019	567 648	5.3	6.8	3.8	170[29]	376[29]	28 392[2,29]	28 938[29]
Ecuador / Équateur	2005	187 404[7]	1.4[7]	1.4[7]	1.3[7]	10 063[5]	2 489[5]	250 001[5]	262 553[5]
	2010	325 366[7]	2.2[7]	2.2[7]	2.1[7]	121 249[5]	49 887[5]	...	171 136[5]
	2015	387 513[7]	2.4[7]	2.5[7]	2.3[7]	121 535[5]	11 583[5]	...	133 118[5]
	2019	381 507[7]	2.2[7]	2.3[7]	2.1[7]	103 101	22 512	294 919[2]	420 532
Egypt / Égypte	2005	285 006[7]	0.4[7]	0.4[7]	0.3[7]	88 946[5]	11 005[5]	203[5]	100 154[5]
	2010	310 017[7]	0.4[7]	0.4[7]	0.3[7]	95 056[5]	14 303[5]	570[5]	109 929[5]
	2015	353 641[7]	0.4[7]	0.4[7]	0.3[7]	226 344	30 019	21	256 384
	2019	504 053[7]	0.5[7]	0.5[7]	0.5[7]	256 020	63 448	4	319 472
El Salvador	2005	36 019[7]	0.6[7]	0.6[7]	0.6[7]	49[5]	1[5]	44[5]	94[5]
	2010	40 324[7]	0.7[7]	0.7[7]	0.7[7]	38[5]	18[5]	...	56[5]
	2015	42 045[7]	0.7[7]	0.7[7]	0.7[7]	48	...	...	48
	2019	42 617[7]	0.7[7]	0.7[7]	0.7[7]	52	17	75 200	75 269
Equatorial Guinea [9] / Guinée équatoriale [9]	2005	6 588	0.9	0.9	0.9	...	...	...	...
	2010	8 658	0.9	0.9	0.9	...	...	...	...
	2015	209 611	17.9	25.0	9.2	...	...	...	...
	2019	227 617	16.8	23.3	8.7	...	...	...	...
Eritrea / Érythrée	2005	* 14 314	* 0.5	* 0.5	* 0.5	4 418[5]	1 591[5]	31[5]	6 040[5]
	2010	* 15 676	* 0.5	* 0.5	* 0.4	4 809[5]	137[5]	13[5]	4 959[5]
	2015	* 15 941	* 0.5	* 0.5	* 0.4	2 944	1	22	2 967
	2016	...	...	...	...	2 293	5	6	2 304
	2019	* 16 101	* 0.5	* 0.5	* 0.4	703	...	223	926
Estonia / Estonie	2005	233 701	17.2	15.0	19.2	7[5]	8[5]	136 000[5]	136 015[5]
	2010	217 890	16.4	14.1	18.3	39[5]	10[5]	100 983[5]	101 032[5]
	2015	194 664	14.8	13.0	16.4	117	117	86 522[30]	86 756
	2019	190 242	14.4	12.9	15.7	324[30]	35[30]	76 639[30]	76 998[30]

International migrants and refugees *(continued)*
International migrant stock (number and percentage) and refugees and others of concern to UNHCR

Migrants internationaux et réfugiés *(suite)*
Stock de migrants internationaux (nombre et pourcentage) et réfugiés et autres personnes relevant de la compétence du HCR

Region, country or area Région, pays ou zone	Year Année	International Migrant Stock (mid-year) Stock de migrants internationaux (milieu de l'année) Total Total	% of total pop. % de la pop. totale MF HF	M H	F	Refugees and others of concern to UNHCR (mid-year) Réfugiés et autres personnes relevant de la compétence du HCR (milieu de l'année) Refugees& Réfugiés&	Asylum seekers Demandeurs d'asile	Other&& Autres&&	Total pop. Pop. totale
Eswatini	2005	33 392[7]	3.2[7]	3.6[7]	3.0[7]	760[5]	256[5]	...	1 016[5]
Eswatini	2010	32 637[7]	3.1[7]	3.3[7]	2.8[7]	759[5]	...	...	759[5]
	2015	32 352[7]	2.9[7]	3.1[7]	2.8[7]	539	321	4	864
	2017	...	...	...	...	770	462	10	1 242
	2019	32 310[7]	2.8[7]	2.9[7]	2.7[7]	923	836	...	1 759
Ethiopia	2005	514 242[7]	0.7[7]	0.7[7]	0.6[7]	100 817[5]	209[5]	4 110[5]	105 136[5]
Éthiopie	2010	568 748[7]	0.6[7]	0.7[7]	0.6[7]	154 295[5]	1 028[5]	47[5]	155 370[5]
	2015	1 161 642[7]	1.2[7]	1.2[7]	1.1[7]	702 467	2 871	348	705 686
	2019	1 253 083[7]	1.1[7]	1.1[7]	1.1[7]	626 957	1 284	4 816 254	5 444 495
Falkland Islands (Malvinas) [31]	2005	1 166	39.7	...	...	...	...	...	...
Îles Falkland (Malvinas) [31]	2010	1 436	49.5	...	...	...	...	...	...
	2015	1 571	55.4	...	...	...	...	...	...
	2019	1 902	56.3	...	...	...	...	...	...
Faroe Islands	2005	4 583	9.6	...	...	...	...	...	...
Îles Féroé	2010	5 096	10.7	...	...	...	...	...	...
	2015	5 485	11.4	...	...	...	...	...	...
	2019	6 454	13.3	...	...	...	...	...	...
Fiji	2005	12 435	1.5	1.6	1.5	...	...	...	...
Fidji	2010	13 351	1.6	1.6	1.5	1[5]	6[5]	...	7[5]
	2015	13 751	1.6	1.7	1.5	12	8	...	20
	2019	14 038	1.6	1.7	1.5	6	14	...	20
Finland	2005	192 169[32]	3.7[32]	3.7[32]	3.6[32]	11 809[5]	...	849[5]	12 658[5]
Finlande	2010	228 481[32]	4.3[32]	4.4[32]	4.1[32]	8 724[5]	2 097[5]	3 133[5]	13 954[5]
	2015	314 856[32]	5.7[32]	5.9[32]	5.6[32]	11 798[12]	2 622	1 928	16 348
	2019	383 116[32]	6.9[32]	7.2[32]	6.7[32]	22 903	9 310	2 759	34 972
France	2005	6 737 600	11.0	11.2	10.9	137 316[5]	41 279[5]	946[5]	179 541[5]
France	2010	7 309 986	11.6	11.7	11.6	200 687[5]	48 576[5]	1 171[5]	250 434[5]
	2015	7 874 172	12.2	12.2	12.2	264 972	53 827	1 290	320 089
	2019	8 334 875	12.8	12.7	12.8	389 680	82 220	1 514	473 414
French Guiana	2005	86 468	42.6	42.5	42.7	...	...	...	...
Guyane française	2010	96 288	41.3	40.0	42.7	...	...	...	...
	2015	106 108	40.7	39.1	42.2	...	...	...	...
	2019	117 372	40.4	38.8	41.9	...	...	...	...
French Polynesia	2005	32 286	12.5	13.9	11.0	...	...	...	...
Polynésie française	2010	31 640	11.9	13.2	10.5	...	...	...	...
	2015	30 058	11.0	12.4	9.6	...	...	...	...
	2019	31 205	11.2	12.6	9.7	...	...	...	...
Gabon	2005	233 824[9]	16.8[9]	19.4[9]	14.2[9]	8 545[5]	4 843[5]	291[5]	13 679[5]
Gabon	2010	270 829[9]	16.7[9]	19.3[9]	14.0[9]	9 015[5]	4 132[5]	84[5]	13 231[5]
	2015	378 686[9]	19.4[9]	24.6[9]	14.1[9]	1 008	1 886	...	2 894
	2017	...	...	...	...	957	105	3	1 065
	2019	411 463[9]	18.9[9]	23.9[9]	13.8[9]	588	94	...	682
Gambia	2005	181 905	11.8	12.5	11.0	7 330[5]	602[5]	42[5]	7 974[5]
Gambie	2010	185 763	10.4	11.0	9.7	8 378[5]	74[5]	31[5]	8 483[5]
	2015	192 540	9.2	9.8	8.7	11 773	2	...	11 775
	2018	...	...	...	...	8 487	301	38	8 826
	2019	215 406	9.2	9.8	8.6	4 030	358	...	4 388
Georgia	2005	72 311[33]	1.7[33]	1.6[33]	1.8[33]	2 497[5]	8[5]	236 097[5]	238 602[5]
Géorgie	2010	73 034[33]	1.8[33]	1.6[33]	1.9[33]	639[5]	44[5]	361 547[5]	362 230[5]
	2015	76 685[33]	1.9[33]	1.7[33]	2.1[33]	1 659	587	266 060	268 306
	2019	79 035[33]	2.0[33]	1.8[33]	2.1[33]	1 998	892	284 534	287 424
Germany	2005	9 402 447	11.5	11.7	11.3	700 016[5]	71 624[5]	12 340[5]	783 980[5]
Allemagne	2010	9 812 263	12.1	12.2	12.0	594 269[5]	51 991[5]	24 378[5]	670 638[5]
	2015	10 220 418	12.5	12.5	12.5	250 299	311 551	11 978	573 828
	2019	13 132 146	15.7	16.7	14.8	1 106 198	339 872	14 932	1 461 002

3

International migrants and refugees *(continued)*
International migrant stock (number and percentage) and refugees and others of concern to UNHCR

Migrants internationaux et réfugiés *(suite)*
Stock de migrants internationaux (nombre et pourcentage) et réfugiés et autres personnes relevant de la compétence du HCR

Region, country or area Région, pays ou zone	Year Année	International Migrant Stock (mid-year) Stock de migrants internationaux (milieu de l'année)				Refugees and others of concern to UNHCR (mid-year) Réfugiés et autres personnes relevant de la compétence du HCR (milieu de l'année)			
		Total Total	MF HF	M H	F	Refugees& Réfugiés&	Asylum seekers Demandeurs d'asile	Other&& Autres&&	Total pop. Pop. totale
Ghana	2005	304 436	1.4	1.4	1.4	53 537[5]	5 496[5]	1 212[5]	60 245[5]
Ghana	2010	337 017	1.4	1.4	1.3	13 828[5]	749[5]	184[5]	14 761[5]
	2015	414 744	1.5	1.6	1.4	18 476	2 855	...	21 331
	2016	...	...	...	...	16 409	2 048	8 871	27 328
	2019	466 780	1.5	1.6	1.5	12 004	1 355	...	13 359
Gibraltar	2005	9 211	27.7	...	...	...	...	...	...
Gibraltar	2010	10 369	30.9	...	...	...	...	...	...
	2015	11 065	32.8	...	...	...	...	...	...
	2019	11 172	33.2	...	...	...	...	...	...
Greece	2005	1 190 707	10.6	10.6	10.6	2 390[5]	8 867[5]	3 000[5]	14 257[5]
Grèce	2010	1 321 149	12.1	12.0	12.3	1 444[5]	55 724[5]	260[5]	57 428[5]
	2015	1 242 924	11.7	10.9	12.4	8 231	29 157	214	37 602
	2019	1 211 382	11.6	10.9	12.2	62 922	79 237	4 892	147 051
Greenland	2005	6 556	11.5	...	...	...	...	...	...
Groenland	2010	6 091	10.8	...	...	...	...	...	...
	2015	5 797	10.3	...	...	...	...	...	...
	2019	5 690	10.0	...	...	...	...	...	...
Grenada	2005	6 902	6.6	6.5	6.7	...	...	...	...
Grenade	2010	6 980	6.6	6.5	6.7	...	3[5]	...	3[5]
	2015	7 057	6.4	6.3	6.5	...	...	...	...
	2018	...	...	...	...	2	3	...	5
	2019	7 124	6.4	6.3	6.5	4	...	3[2]	7
Guadeloupe [34]	2005	89 065	20.0	19.6	20.4	...	...	...	...
Guadeloupe [34]	2010	94 942	21.0	20.3	21.6	...	...	...	...
	2015	98 507	22.1	21.2	22.9	...	...	...	...
	2019	100 030	22.3	21.5	23.1	...	...	...	...
Guam	2005	74 743	47.2	47.8	46.5	...	...	...	...
Guam	2010	75 416	47.3	48.0	46.5	...	...	...	...
	2015	76 089	47.0	47.9	46.1	...	...	...	...
	2019	79 846	47.7	48.8	46.7	...	...	...	...
Guatemala	2005	57 252[7]	0.4[7]	0.4[7]	0.5[7]	391[5]	3[5]	...	394[5]
Guatemala	2010	66 384[7]	0.5[7]	0.4[7]	0.5[7]	138[5]	2[5]	...	140[5]
	2015	78 352[7]	0.5[7]	0.5[7]	0.5[7]	202	73	...	275
	2019	80 421[7]	0.5[7]	0.4[7]	0.5[7]	390	423	146 000	146 813
Guinea	2005	229 611[7,9]	2.5[7,9]	2.6[7,9]	2.5[7,9]	63 525[5]	3 808[5]	29 645[5]	96 978[5]
Guinée	2010	177 998[7,9]	1.7[7,9]	1.9[7,9]	1.6[7,9]	14 113[5]	764[5]	117[5]	14 994[5]
	2015	126 386[7,9]	1.1[7,9]	1.4[7,9]	0.9[7,9]	8 704	293	...	8 997
	2017	...	...	...	...	5 105	105	1	5 211
	2019	120 642[7,9]	0.9[7,9]	1.1[7,9]	0.8[7,9]	4 433	1 980	...	6 413
Guinea-Bissau	2005	20 736[7]	1.5[7]	1.6[7]	1.5[7]	7 616[5]	166[5]	...	7 782[5]
Guinée-Bissau	2010	21 061[7]	1.4[7]	1.4[7]	1.4[7]	7 679[5]	330[5]	5[5]	8 014[5]
	2015	22 333[7]	1.3[7]	1.3[7]	1.3[7]	8 684	123	...	8 807
	2019	26 916[7]	1.4[7]	1.4[7]	1.4[7]	1 852	34	...	1 886
Guyana	2005	10 868	1.5	1.6	1.4	...	...	...	...
Guyana	2010	13 126	1.8	1.9	1.6	7[5]	...	...	7[5]
	2015	15 384	2.0	2.1	1.9	11	1	...	12
	2019	15 699	2.0	2.1	1.9	28	34	36 401[2]	36 463
Haiti	2005	16 360	0.2	0.2	0.2	...	...	...	...
Haïti	2010	17 178	0.2	0.2	0.2	...	4[5]	...	4[5]
	2015	18 036	0.2	0.2	0.1	5	5	...	10
	2019	18 756	0.2	0.2	0.1	4[35]	9[35]	2 992[35]	3 005[35]
Holy See [36]	*2005	798	100.0	...	...	...	...	...	...
Saint-Siège [36]	*2010	794	100.0	...	...	...	...	...	...
	*2015	803	100.0	...	...	...	...	...	...
	*2019	799	100.0	...	...	...	...	...	...
Honduras	2005	27 875[7]	0.4[7]	0.4[7]	0.4[7]	22[5]	50[5]	...	72[5]
Honduras	2010	27 288[7]	0.3[7]	0.3[7]	0.3[7]	14[5]	...	1[5]	15[5]
	2015	38 317[7]	0.4[7]	0.4[7]	0.4[7]	23	19	...	42
	2019	38 933[7]	0.4[7]	0.4[7]	0.4[7]	51	77	251 490	251 618

3

International migrants and refugees *(continued)*
International migrant stock (number and percentage) and refugees and others of concern to UNHCR

Migrants internationaux et réfugiés *(suite)*
Stock de migrants internationaux (nombre et pourcentage) et réfugiés et autres personnes relevant de la compétence du HCR

Region, country or area / Région, pays ou zone	Year / Année	International Migrant Stock (mid-year) / Stock de migrants internationaux (milieu de l'année) Total / Total	% of total pop. / % de la pop. totale MF / HF	M / H	F	Refugees and others of concern to UNHCR (mid-year) / Réfugiés et autres personnes relevant de la compétence du HCR (milieu de l'année) Refugees& / Réfugiés&	Asylum seekers / Demandeurs d'asile	Other&& / Autres&&	Total pop. / Pop. totale
Hungary	2005	366 787[7]	3.6[7]	3.6[7]	3.6[7]	8 046[5]	684[5]	192[5]	8 922[5]
Hongrie	2010	436 616[7]	4.4[7]	4.5[7]	4.3[7]	5 414[5]	367[5]	62[5]	5 843[5]
	2015	475 508[7]	4.9[7]	5.1[7]	4.7[7]	4 192	24 431	128	28 751
	2019	512 043[7]	5.3[7]	5.5[7]	5.1[7]	6 064	196	145	6 405
Iceland	2005	25 492	8.6	8.4	8.9	293[5]	29[5]	53[5]	375[5]
Islande	2010	35 091	11.0	10.9	11.0	83[5]	39[5]	113[5]	235[5]
	2015	39 072	11.8	11.5	12.2	104	225	119	448
	2019	52 404	15.5	16.2	14.7	665	420	69	1 154
India	2005	5 923 945[7]	0.5[7]	0.5[7]	0.5[7]	139 283[5]	303[5]	2 792[5]	142 378[5]
Inde	2010	5 439 758[7]	0.4[7]	0.4[7]	0.4[7]	184 821[5]	3 746[5]	5 109[5]	193 676[5]
	2015	5 240 960[7]	0.4[7]	0.4[7]	0.4[7]	200 383	5 381	...	205 764
	2019	5 154 737[7]	0.4[7]	0.4[7]	0.4[7]	194 873	11 728	...	206 601
Indonesia	2005	289 568[7]	0.1[7]	0.1[7]	0.1[7]	89[5]	58[5]	263[5]	410[5]
Indonésie	2010	305 416[7]	0.1[7]	0.1[7]	0.1[7]	811[5]	2 071[5]	12[5]	2 894[5]
	2015	338 124[7]	0.1[7]	0.2[7]	0.1[7]	5 277	7 911	...	13 188
	2019	353 135[7]	0.1[7]	0.2[7]	0.1[7]	10 658	3 325	...	13 983
Iran (Islamic Republic of)	2005	2 568 930[7]	3.7[7]	4.0[7]	3.4[7]	974 302[5]	140[5]	344 914[5]	1 319 356[5]
Iran (Rép. islamique d')	2010	2 761 561[7]	3.7[7]	4.2[7]	3.3[7]	1 073 366[5]	1 775[5]	10 168[5]	1 085 309[5]
	2015	2 726 420[7]	3.5[7]	3.6[7]	3.3[7]	979 441	42	8	979 491
	2018	...	...	...	...	979 435	82	4	979 521
	2019	2 682 214[7]	3.2[7]	3.4[7]	3.1[7]	979 435	33	...	979 468
Iraq	2005	132 915[7,9]	0.5[7,9]	0.6[7,9]	0.4[7,9]	50 177[5]	1 948[5]	1 526 104[5]	1 578 229[5]
Iraq	2010	117 389[7,9]	0.4[7,9]	0.5[7,9]	0.3[7,9]	34 655[5]	3 073[5]	1 758 603[5]	1 796 331[5]
	2015	359 381[7,9]	1.0[7,9]	1.2[7,9]	0.9[7,9]	288 035	7 420	4 016 205[37]	4 311 660
	2019	368 062[7,9]	0.9[7,9]	1.1[7,9]	0.8[7,9]	257 796[38]	12 935[38]	1 861 682[38]	2 132 413[38]
Ireland	2005	589 046	14.2	15.0	13.5	7 113[5]	2 414[5]	4[5]	9 531[5]
Irlande	2010	730 542	16.0	15.9	16.2	9 107[5]	5 129[5]	1[5]	14 237[5]
	2015	759 256	16.3	16.3	16.3	6 125[5]	4 267[5]	100[5]	10 492[5]
	2019	833 564	17.1	17.1	17.0	6 850	7 412	99	14 361
Isle of Man	2005	41 475	51.6	...	...	...	...	...	...
Île de Man	2010	43 447	51.2	...	...	...	...	...	...
	2015	42 238	50.7	...	...	...	...	...	...
	2019	42 864	50.7	...	...	...	...	...	...
Israel	2005	1 889 503[7]	28.9[7]	26.9[7]	30.9[7]	609[5]	939[5]	...	1 548[5]
Israël	2010	1 950 615[7]	26.6[7]	24.5[7]	28.5[7]	25 471[5]	5 575[5]	9[5]	31 055[5]
	2015	2 011 727[7]	25.2[7]	23.1[7]	27.3[7]	38 500	6 591	88	45 179
	2019	1 956 346[7]	23.0[7]	21.0[7]	25.0[7]	17 951	37 085	42	55 078
Italy	2005	3 954 790	6.8	6.4	7.1	20 675[5]		940[5]	21 615[5]
Italie	2010	5 787 893	9.8	9.3	10.2	56 397[5]	4 076[5]	858[5]	61 331[5]
	2015	5 805 328	9.6	9.0	10.2	93 715[12]	48 307	606	142 628
	2019	6 273 722	10.4	9.9	10.8	193 336	67 207	822	261 365
Jamaica	2005	24 314	0.9	0.9	0.9	...	...	...	...
Jamaïque	2010	23 677	0.8	0.9	0.8	21[5]	...	...	21[5]
	2015	23 167	0.8	0.8	0.8	15	3	...	18
	2019	23 468	0.8	0.8	0.8	15	13	...	28
Japan	2005	2 011 555[9]	1.6[9]	1.5[9]	1.7[9]	1 941[5]	533[5]	1 770[5]	4 244[5]
Japon	2010	2 134 151[9]	1.7[9]	1.5[9]	1.8[9]	2 586[5]	3 047[5]	1 397[5]	7 030[5]
	2015	2 232 189[9]	1.7[9]	1.7[9]	1.8[9]	* 2 419	* 10 705	* 631	* 13 755
	2019	2 498 891[9]	2.0[9]	2.0[9]	2.0[9]	* 1 650	* 29 162	* 710	* 31 522
Jordan	2005	2 325 414[7,9]	40.3[7,9]	39.8[7,9]	40.9[7,9]	965[5]	16 570[5]	329[5]	17 864[5]
Jordanie	2010	2 722 983[7,9]	37.5[7,9]	37.4[7,9]	37.6[7,9]	450 915[5]	2 159[5]	107[5]	453 181[5]
	2015	3 112 026[7,9]	33.6[7,9]	33.4[7,9]	33.8[7,9]	664 102[39]	20 693	...	684 795
	2019	3 346 703[7,9]	33.1[7,9]	33.0[7,9]	33.3[7,9]	700 806[40]	54 449[40]	855[40]	756 110[40]
Kazakhstan	2005	3 103 027	20.1	19.9	20.4	7 265[5]	65[5]	50 598[5]	57 928[5]
Kazakhstan	2010	3 334 937	20.5	20.7	20.4	4 406[5]	314[5]	7 969[5]	12 689[5]
	2015	3 546 060	20.2	20.7	19.7	662	149	7 038	7 849
	2019	3 705 556	20.0	20.4	19.6	561	175	8 204	8 940

3

International migrants and refugees *(continued)*
International migrant stock (number and percentage) and refugees and others of concern to UNHCR

Migrants internationaux et réfugiés *(suite)*
Stock de migrants internationaux (nombre et pourcentage) et réfugiés et autres personnes relevant de la compétence du HCR

Region, country or area / Région, pays ou zone	Year / Année	International Migrant Stock (mid-year) / Stock de migrants internationaux (milieu de l'année)				Refugees and others of concern to UNHCR (mid-year) / Réfugiés et autres personnes relevant de la compétence du HCR (milieu de l'année)			
		Total / Total	% de la pop. totale			Refugees& / Réfugiés&	Asylum seekers / Demandeurs d'asile	Other&& / Autres&&	Total pop. / Pop. totale
			MF / HF	M / H	F				
Kenya	2005	773 354[7]	2.1[7]	2.2[7]	2.0[7]	251 271[5]	16 460[5]	481[5]	268 212[5]
Kenya	2010	954 925[7]	2.3[7]	2.3[7]	2.3[7]	402 905[5]	27 966[5]	320 083[5]	750 954[5]
	2015	1 126 886[7]	2.4[7]	2.4[7]	2.3[7]	552 272	40 341	21 231	613 844
	2019	1 044 854[7]	2.0[7]	2.0[7]	2.0[7]	424 655	49 389	18 500	492 544
Kiribati	2005	2 487	2.7	2.9	2.5	...	...	...	...
Kiribati	2010	2 868	2.8	3.0	2.6	...	...	...	...
	2015	2 919	2.6	2.8	2.4	...	...	...	...
	2019	3 022	2.6	2.8	2.4	...	...	...	...
Kuwait	2005	1 333 327[7,9]	58.7[7,9]	68.5[7,9]	44.6[7,9]	1 523[5]	203[5]	101 000[5]	102 726[5]
Koweït	2010	1 871 537[7,9]	62.6[7,9]	75.7[7,9]	44.5[7,9]	184[5]	3 275[5]	93 000[5]	96 459[5]
	2015	2 866 136[7,9]	74.7[7,9]	84.3[7,9]	61.0[7,9]	593	1 040	93 000	94 633
	2019	3 034 845[7,9]	72.1[7,9]	78.6[7,9]	62.1[7,9]	715	1 005	92 016	93 736
Kyrgyzstan	2005	309 399	6.1	5.1	7.1	2 598[5]	498[5]	100 004[5]	103 100[5]
Kirghizistan	2010	232 065	4.3	3.5	5.0	2 458[5]	554[5]	301 164[5]	304 176[5]
	2015	204 382	3.4	2.8	4.0	433	168	13 678	14 279
	2019	200 260	3.1	2.6	3.7	350	138	108	596
Lao People's Dem. Rep.	2005[7,9]	20 371	0.4	0.4	0.3	...	...	...	...
Rép. dém. populaire lao	2010[7,9]	32 955	0.5	0.6	0.4	...	...	...	...
	2015[7,9]	45 538	0.7	0.9	0.5	...	...	...	...
	2019	48 275[7,9]	0.7[7,9]	0.9[7,9]	0.5[7,9]	5	...	...	5
Latvia	2005	376 725	16.7	15.0	18.2	11[5]	9[5]	418 638[5]	418 658[5]
Lettonie	2010	313 786	14.8	12.8	16.5	68[5]	53[5]	326 906[5]	327 027[5]
	2015	265 418	13.3	11.4	14.9	195	171	262 802[41]	263 168
	2019	237 266	12.4	10.6	14.0	659[42]	38[42]	224 844[42]	225 541[42]
Lebanon	2005	756 784[7]	16.1[7]	16.3[7]	15.9[7]	1 078[5]	1 450[5]	451[5]	2 979[5]
Liban	2010	820 655[7]	16.6[7]	17.0[7]	16.1[7]	8 063[5]	1 417[5]	40[5]	9 520[5]
	2015	1 973 204[7]	30.2[7]	28.8[7]	31.6[7]	1 172 388	10 851	5 813	1 189 052
	2019	1 863 873[7]	27.2[7]	26.0[7]	28.4[7]	930 209	16 258	3 156	949 623
Lesotho	2005[7,9]	6 290	0.3	0.4	0.3	...	...	...	...
Lesotho	2010[7,9]	6 414	0.3	0.4	0.3	...	...	...	...
	2015	6 572[7,9]	0.3[7,9]	0.4[7,9]	0.3[7,9]	44	1	...	45
	2019	6 928[7,9]	0.3[7,9]	0.4[7,9]	0.3[7,9]	116	33	...	149
Liberia	2005	87 188	2.7	3.2	2.2	10 168[5]	29[5]	498 604[5]	508 801[5]
Libéria	2010	99 129	2.5	2.9	2.2	24 743[5]	28[5]	1 855[5]	26 626[5]
	2015	113 779	2.5	2.9	2.2	38 904	18	1 486	40 408
	2019	94 448	1.9	2.2	1.7	8 700	46	6	8 752
Libya	2005	625 212[9]	10.8[9]	14.9[9]	6.4[9]	12 166[5]	200[5]	35[5]	12 401[5]
Libye	2010	683 998[9]	11.0[9]	15.5[9]	6.4[9]	7 923[5]	3 194[5]	37[5]	11 154[5]
	2015	771 146[9]	12.0[9]	16.9[9]	7.0[9]	27 948	8 904	434 869	471 721
	2019	818 216[9]	12.1[9]	17.0[9]	7.0[9]	6 503	46 277	268 629	321 409
Liechtenstein	2005	18 898	54.4	...	...	150[5]	60[5]	...	210[5]
Liechtenstein	2010	22 342	62.1	...	...	92[5]	44[5]	6[5]	142[5]
	2015	23 799	63.5	...	...	107	75	2	184
	2019	25 467	67.0	...	...	170	39	...	209
Lithuania	2005	201 209	6.0	6.1	6.0	531[5]	55[5]	8 709[5]	9 295[5]
Lituanie	2010	160 772	5.1	4.8	5.4	803[5]	71[5]	3 679[5]	4 553[5]
	2015	136 021	4.6	4.3	5.0	1 055	54	3 583	4 692
	2019	117 218	4.2	3.9	4.6	1 790	287	3 039	5 116
Luxembourg	2005	150 618	32.9	33.2	32.6	1 822[5]	...	74[5]	1 896[5]
Luxembourg	2010	163 142	32.1	32.3	32.0	3 254[5]	697[5]	173[5]	4 124[5]
	2015	248 888	43.9	44.3	43.5	1 192	831	81	2 104
	2018	...	...	...	...	2 046[43]	1 015	83	3 144
	2019	291 723	47.4	47.8	47.0	4 571	1 171	...	5 742
Madagascar	2005[9]	26 058	0.1	0.2	0.1	...	...	...	...
Madagascar	2010	28 905[9]	0.1[9]	0.2[9]	0.1[9]	...	...	1[5]	1[5]
	2015	32 075[9]	0.1[9]	0.2[9]	0.1[9]	10	9	...	19
	2019	34 934[9]	0.1[9]	0.1[9]	0.1[9]	111	80	...	191

3

International migrants and refugees *(continued)*
International migrant stock (number and percentage) and refugees and others of concern to UNHCR

Migrants internationaux et réfugiés *(suite)*
Stock de migrants internationaux (nombre et pourcentage) et réfugiés et autres personnes relevant de la compétence du HCR

Region, country or area / Région, pays ou zone	Year / Année	International Migrant Stock (mid-year) Stock de migrants internationaux (milieu de l'année) Total	% of total pop. % de la pop. totale MF / HF	M / H	F	Refugees and others of concern to UNHCR (mid-year) Réfugiés et autres personnes relevant de la compétence du HCR (milieu de l'année) Refugees& / Réfugiés&	Asylum seekers Demandeurs d'asile	Other&& Autres&&	Total pop. Pop. totale
Malawi	2005	221 661[7]	1.8[7]	1.7[7]	1.8[7]	4 240[5]	5 331[5]	49[5]	9 620[5]
Malawi	2010	217 722[7]	1.5[7]	1.5[7]	1.5[7]	5 740[5]	9 362[5]	131[5]	15 233[5]
	2015	232 803[7]	1.4[7]	1.3[7]	1.4[7]	8 963	13 669	...	22 632
	2019	247 652[7]	1.3[7]	1.3[7]	1.4[7]	13 732	25 299	250	39 281
Malaysia	2005	1 918 504[7,9,44]	7.5[7,9,44]	8.6[7,9,44]	6.3[7,9,44]	33 693[5]	10 838[5]	61 555[5]	106 086[5]
Malaisie	2010	2 417 395[7,9,44]	8.6[7,9,44]	10.1[7,9,44]	6.9[7,9,44]	81 516[5]	11 339[5]	120 015[5]	212 870[5]
	2015	3 280 681[7,9,44]	10.8[7,9,44]	12.8[7,9,44]	8.7[7,9,44]	97 573	54 400	120 000	271 973
	2019	3 430 380[7,9,44]	10.7[7,9,44]	12.8[7,9,44]	8.6[7,9,44]	126 603[45]	50 285[45]	89 631[45]	266 519[45]
Maldives [9]	2005	45 045	14.1	16.2	11.8	...	...	...	...
Maldives [9]	2010	54 659	14.9	21.0	7.8	...	...	...	...
	2015	64 273	14.1	20.8	4.3	...	...	...	...
	2019	69 249	13.0	18.1	4.4	...	...	...	...
Mali	2005	256 797[7]	2.0[7]	2.1[7]	1.9[7]	11 233[5]	1 833[5]	...	13 066[5]
Mali	2010	339 375[7]	2.3[7]	2.3[7]	2.2[7]	13 558[5]	1 703[5]	...	15 261[5]
	2015	420 504[7]	2.4[7]	2.4[7]	2.4[7]	14 970	386	132 953	148 309
	2019	468 230[7]	2.4[7]	2.4[7]	2.4[7]	26 820	948	155 160	182 928
Malta	2005	24 560	6.1	5.9	6.2	1 939[5]	149[5]	...	2 088[5]
Malte	2010	33 008	8.0	8.3	7.6	6 136[5]	1 295[5]	...	7 431[5]
	2015	52 642	12.1	13.1	11.2	6 095	425	...	6 520
	2019	84 949	19.3	20.8	17.7	8 726	1 951	11	10 688
Marshall Islands	2005	2 417	4.4	...	...	...	...	...	...
Îles Marshall	2010	3 089	5.5	...	...	...	...	...	...
	2015	3 284	5.7	...	...	...	...	...	...
	2019	3 296	5.6	...	...	...	...	...	...
Martinique	2005	57 034	14.4	14.0	14.7	...	...	...	...
Martinique	2010	59 575	15.1	14.4	15.6	...	...	...	...
	2015	61 731	16.3	15.4	17.1	...	...	...	...
	2019	61 647	16.4	15.6	17.1	...	...	...	...
Mauritania	2005	58 199[7,9]	1.9[7,9]	2.2[7,9]	1.7[7,9]	632[5]	92[5]	29 500[5]	30 224[5]
Mauritanie	2010	84 679[7,9]	2.4[7,9]	2.8[7,9]	2.1[7,9]	26 717[5]	241[5]	9[5]	26 967[5]
	2015	166 552[7,9]	4.1[7,9]	4.6[7,9]	3.6[7,9]	76 851	407	...	77 258
	2019	172 987[7,9]	3.8[7,9]	4.3[7,9]	3.3[7,9]	86 165	1 177	...	87 342
Mauritius	2005[9,46]	19 647	1.6	1.5	1.7	...	...	...	...
Maurice	2010[9,46]	24 836	2.0	2.1	1.9	...	...	...	...
	2015[9,46]	28 585	2.3	2.5	2.0	...	...	...	...
	2019	28 849[9,46]	2.3[9,46]	2.5[9,46]	2.0[9,46]	21	5	...	26
Mayotte	2005	63 176	35.5	35.7	35.2	...	...	...	...
Mayotte	2010	72 757	34.9	33.8	35.9	...	...	...	...
	2015	73 992	30.8	29.0	32.6	...	...	...	...
	2019	74 643	28.0	26.4	29.6	...	...	...	...
Mexico	2005	712 487[7]	0.7[7]	0.7[7]	0.7[7]	3 229[5]	161[5]	...	3 390[5]
Mexique	2010	969 538[7]	0.8[7]	0.9[7]	0.8[7]	1 395[5]	172[5]	6[5]	1 573[5]
	2015	1 028 803[7]	0.8[7]	0.9[7]	0.8[7]	2 158	...	68	2 226
	2019	1 060 707[7]	0.8[7]	0.9[7]	0.8[7]	18 674	50 499	232 916[2]	302 089
Micronesia (Fed. States of)	2005	2 905	2.7	2.9	2.6	...	...	...	...
Micronésie (États féd. de)	2010	2 806	2.7	2.9	2.6	...	...	...	...
	2015	2 756	2.5	2.7	2.4	...	34	...	34
	2016	...	...	...	...	3	1	...	4
	2017	...	...	...	...	4	...	...	4
	2019	2 819	2.5	2.6	2.3	...	...	...	...
Monaco	2005	21 312	63.0	...	...	...	...	...	...
Monaco	2010	21 132	59.3	...	...	...	1[5]	...	1[5]
	2015	25 983	68.9	...	...	33	...	...	33
	2019	26 511	68.0	...	...	25	...	...	25
Mongolia	2005	11 477[9]	0.5[9]	0.6[9]	0.3[9]	...	2[5]	581[5]	583[5]
Mongolie	2010	16 062[9]	0.6[9]	0.9[9]	0.3[9]	12[5]	1[5]	260[5]	273[5]
	2015	19 886[9]	0.7[9]	0.9[9]	0.4[9]	11	5	16	32
	2019	21 128[9]	0.7[9]	0.9[9]	0.4[9]	26	3	27	56

3

International migrants and refugees *(continued)*
International migrant stock (number and percentage) and refugees and others of concern to UNHCR

Migrants internationaux et réfugiés *(suite)*
Stock de migrants internationaux (nombre et pourcentage) et réfugiés et autres personnes relevant de la compétence du HCR

Region, country or area Région, pays ou zone	Year Année	International Migrant Stock (mid-year) Stock de migrants internationaux (milieu de l'année)				Refugees and others of concern to UNHCR (mid-year) Réfugiés et autres personnes relevant de la compétence du HCR (milieu de l'année)			
		Total Total	MF HF	% of total pop. % de la pop. totale M H	F	Refugees[&] Réfugiés[&]	Asylum seekers Demandeurs d'asile	Other[&&] Autres[&&]	Total pop. Pop. totale
Montenegro	2010	78 512	12.6	10.3	14.8	16 364[5]	5[5]	1 886[5]	18 255[5]
Monténégro	2015	71 719	11.4	9.1	13.7	6 203	7	13 602	19 812
	2019	70 967	11.3	9.0	13.5	701	440	12 442	13 583
Montserrat	2005	1 244	25.7	...	...	...	...	...	...
Montserrat	2010	1 291	26.4	...	...	...	14[5]	...	14[5]
	2015	1 351	27.2	...	...	...	...	...	...
	2019	1 375	27.6	...	...	...	...	...	...
Morocco	2005	54 379[9]	0.2[9]	0.2[9]	0.2[9]	219[5]	1 843[5]	4[5]	2 066[5]
Maroc	2010	70 909[9]	0.2[9]	0.2[9]	0.2[9]	792[5]	280[5]	...	1 072[5]
	2015	92 424[9]	0.3[9]	0.3[9]	0.3[9]	2 144	2 216	...	4 360
	2019	98 574[9]	0.3[9]	0.3[9]	0.3[9]	6 388	2 671	...	9 059
Mozambique	2005	264 679[7]	1.3[7]	1.3[7]	1.3[7]	1 954[5]	4 015[5]	40[5]	6 009[5]
Mozambique	2010	306 471[7]	1.3[7]	1.3[7]	1.3[7]	4 077[5]	5 914[5]	1[5]	9 992[5]
	2015	321 794[7]	1.2[7]	1.2[7]	1.2[7]	4 552	14 257	7	18 816
	2018	...	...	...	...	4 993	21 072	21 359	47 424
	2019	334 665[7]	1.1[7]	1.1[7]	1.1[7]	4 666	20 452	...	25 118
Myanmar	2005	83 025[9]	0.2[9]	0.2[9]	0.2[9]	...	...	236 495[5]	236 495[5]
Myanmar	2010	76 414[9]	0.2[9]	0.2[9]	0.1[9]	...	...	859 403[5]	859 403[5]
	2015	73 309[9]	0.1[9]	0.2[9]	0.1[9]	...	...	1 466 501[47]	1 466 501
	2016	...	...	...	...	...	1	1 392 096[47]	1 392 097
	2019	75 998[9]	0.1[9]	0.2[9]	0.1[9]	...	...	883 466[48,49]	883 466[48]
Namibia	2005	107 347	5.5	6.2	5.0	5 307[5]	1 073[5]	2 752[5]	9 132[5]
Namibie	2010	103 826	4.9	5.4	4.4	7 254[5]	1 421[5]	93[5]	8 768[5]
	2015	101 618	4.4	4.9	3.9	1 659	1 100	1 684	4 443
	2019	107 561	4.3	4.8	3.9	2 749	1 519	19	4 287
Nauru	2005[9]	2 253	22.9	...	...	...	...	...	...
Nauru	2010[9]	1 183	11.8	...	...	...	...	...	...
	2015	1 890[9]	18.2[9]	...	...	506[5]	290	...	796
	2019	2 114[9]	19.7[9]	...	...	788	407	...	1 195
Nepal	2005	679 457[7]	2.6[7]	1.8[7]	3.4[7]	126 436[5]	1 272[5]	410 929[5]	538 637[5]
Népal	2010	578 657[7]	2.1[7]	1.4[7]	2.8[7]	89 808[5]	938[5]	800 571[5]	891 317[5]
	2015	509 471[7]	1.9[7]	1.3[7]	2.4[7]	36 287	57	409[50]	36 753
	2019	490 802[7]	1.7[7]	1.1[7]	2.2[7]	18 704[50]	45[50]	549[50]	19 298[50]
Netherlands	2005	1 736 127	10.6	10.4	10.8	118 189[5]	14 664[5]	6 872[5]	139 725[5]
Pays-Bas	2010	1 832 510	11.0	10.6	11.3	74 961[5]	13 053[5]	2 095[5]	90 109[5]
	2015	1 996 318	11.8	11.3	12.3	82 494[12]	8 097	1 951	92 542
	2019	2 282 791	13.4	13.0	13.7	93 378	13 728	1 951	109 057
New Caledonia	2005	55 405	23.4	25.1	21.8	...	...	...	...
Nouvelle-Calédonie	2010	61 158	24.1	25.7	22.5	...	...	...	...
	2015	68 881	25.4	26.5	24.3	...	...	...	...
	2019	72 537	25.7	26.7	24.6	...	...	...	...
New Zealand	2005	839 952	20.3	20.1	20.5	5 307[5]	396[5]	6[5]	5 709[5]
Nouvelle-Zélande	2010	947 443	21.7	21.4	22.0	2 307[5]	216[5]	1[5]	2 524[5]
	2015	1 039 736	22.5	22.2	22.9	1 349[12]	251	...	1 600
	2019	1 068 739	22.3	22.0	22.7	2 182	436	...	2 618
Nicaragua	2005	34 918[7]	0.6[7]	0.7[7]	0.6[7]	227[5]	1[5]	...	228[5]
Nicaragua	2010	37 333[7]	0.6[7]	0.7[7]	0.6[7]	64[5]	12[5]	...	76[5]
	2015	40 262[7]	0.6[7]	0.7[7]	0.6[7]	361	25	5	391
	2019	42 172[7]	0.6[7]	0.7[7]	0.6[7]	326	131	368	825
Niger	2005	124 461[7]	0.9[7]	0.9[7]	1.0[7]	301[5]	48[5]	37[5]	386[5]
Niger	2010	126 464[7]	0.8[7]	0.7[7]	0.8[7]	314[5]	18[5]	5[5]	337[5]
	2015	252 998[7]	1.3[7]	1.2[7]	1.3[7]	82 064	122	120 000	202 186
	2019	294 161[7]	1.3[7]	1.2[7]	1.3[7]	177 583	4 109	229 539	411 231
Nigeria	2005	969 294[7,9]	0.7[7,9]	0.8[7,9]	0.6[7,9]	9 019[5]	420[5]	3 290[5]	12 729[5]
Nigéria	2010	988 679[7,9]	0.6[7,9]	0.7[7,9]	0.5[7,9]	8 747[5]	1 815[5]	34[5]	10 596[5]
	2015	1 199 115[7,9]	0.7[7,9]	0.7[7,9]	0.6[7,9]	1 279	909	1 508 017	1 510 205
	2019	1 256 408[7,9]	0.6[7,9]	0.7[7,9]	0.6[7,9]	42 159	1 009	2 167 924	2 211 092

3

International migrants and refugees *(continued)*
International migrant stock (number and percentage) and refugees and others of concern to UNHCR

Migrants internationaux et réfugiés *(suite)*
Stock de migrants internationaux (nombre et pourcentage) et réfugiés et autres personnes relevant de la compétence du HCR

Region, country or area / Région, pays ou zone	Year / Année	International Migrant Stock (mid-year) Stock de migrants internationaux (milieu de l'année) Total / Total	% of total pop. % de la pop. totale MF / HF	M / H	F	Refugees and others of concern to UNHCR (mid-year) Réfugiés et autres personnes relevant de la compétence du HCR (milieu de l'année) Refugees& / Réfugiés&	Asylum seekers Demandeurs d'asile	Other&& / Autres&&	Total pop. Pop. totale
Niue	2005	522	31.0	...	...	...	...	...	...
Nioué	2010	589	36.4	...	...	...	...	...	...
	2015	588	36.3	...	...	...	...	...	...
	2019	588	36.4	...	...	...	...	...	...
North Macedonia	2005	127 667	6.2	5.2	7.2	1 274[5]	723[5]	2 451[5]	4 448[5]
Macédoine du Nord	2010	129 701	6.3	5.2	7.3	1 398[5]	161[5]	1 731[5]	3 290[5]
	2015	130 730	6.3	5.2	7.3	828	43	717	1 588
	2019	131 175	6.3	5.2	7.3	398	57	17 103	17 558
Northern Mariana Islands	2005	37 542	66.4	...	...	...	...	...	...
Îles Mariannes du Nord	2010	24 168	44.8	...	...	...	...	...	...
	2015	21 648	38.8	...	...	...	...	...	...
	2019	21 815	38.1	...	...	...	...	...	...
Norway	2005	361 144[51]	7.8[51]	7.7[51]	7.9[51]	43 034[5]	...	1 143[5]	44 177[5]
Norvège	2010	526 799[51]	10.8[51]	11.0[51]	10.6[51]	40 260[5]	12 473[5]	3 150[5]	55 883[5]
	2015	746 375[51]	14.4[51]	14.9[51]	13.8[51]	47 043[12]	5 885	1 997	54 925
	2019	867 765[51]	16.1[51]	16.6[51]	15.6[51]	55 336	1 719	2 809	59 864
Oman	2005	666 160[9]	26.5[9]	37.2[9]	12.7[9]	7[5]	4[5]	...	11[5]
Oman	2010	816 221[9]	26.8[9]	35.9[9]	13.0[9]	78[5]	13[5]	...	91[5]
	2015	1 856 226[9]	43.5[9]	55.8[9]	20.5[9]	122	268	...	390
	2019	2 286 226[9]	46.0[9]	58.2[9]	22.2[9]	308	256	...	564
Pakistan	2005	3 171 132[7]	2.0[7]	2.1[7]	1.9[7]	1 084 694[5]	3 426[5]	461 123[5]	1 549 243[5]
Pakistan	2010	3 941 586[7]	2.2[7]	2.2[7]	2.1[7]	1 900 621[5]	2 095[5]	2 248 308[5]	4 151 024[5]
	2015	3 506 520[7]	1.8[7]	1.8[7]	1.7[7]	1 540 854	6 103	1 893 008	3 439 965
	2019	3 257 978[7]	1.5[7]	1.5[7]	1.5[7]	1 410 684	6 978	100 700	1 518 362
Palau	2005	6 043	30.5	...	...	...	...	...	...
Palaos	2010	5 490	30.6	...	...	...	...	...	...
	2015	4 937	27.9	...	...	1	...	...	1
	2016	...	...	...	...	...	1	...	1
	2017	...	...	...	...	5	...	...	5
	2019	5 066	28.1	...	...	...	...	...	...
Panama	2005	117 563	3.5	3.6	3.5	1 730[5]	433[5]	10 273[5]	12 436[5]
Panama	2010	157 309	4.3	4.4	4.2	17 073[5]	479[5]	6[5]	17 558[5]
	2015	184 710	4.7	4.8	4.5	17 303	2 038	2	19 343
	2019	185 072	4.4	4.4	4.3	2 539	16 389	94 598[2]	113 526
Papua New Guinea	2005	30 106[7,9]	0.5[7,9]	0.5[7,9]	0.4[7,9]	9 999[5]	4[5]	135[5]	10 138[5]
Papouasie-Nvl-Guinée	2010	30 425[7,9]	0.4[7,9]	0.5[7,9]	0.3[7,9]	9 698[5]	1[5]	...	9 699[5]
	2015	30 940[7,9]	0.4[7,9]	0.5[7,9]	0.3[7,9]	9 510	400	...	9 910
	2019	31 212[7,9]	0.4[7,9]	0.4[7,9]	0.3[7,9]	9 762	138	...	9 900
Paraguay	2005	168 243	2.9	3.0	2.8	50[5]	8[5]	...	58[5]
Paraguay	2010	160 299	2.6	2.6	2.5	107[5]	8[5]	...	115[5]
	2015	156 462	2.3	2.4	2.3	161	39	...	200
	2019	160 519	2.3	2.3	2.2	284	659	3 350[2]	4 293
Peru	2005	77 877	0.3	0.3	0.3	848[5]	336[5]	1[5]	1 185[5]
Pérou	2010	104 706	0.4	0.4	0.3	1 146[5]	264[5]	1[5]	1 411[5]
	2015	154 774	0.5	0.6	0.4	1 407	366	...	1 773
	2019	782 169	2.4	2.6	2.2	2 636	382 152	475 357[2]	860 145
Philippines	2005	257 468[7,9]	0.3[7,9]	0.3[7,9]	0.3[7,9]	96[5]	42[5]	775[5]	913[5]
Philippines	2010	208 599[7,9]	0.2[7,9]	0.2[7,9]	0.2[7,9]	243[5]	73[5]	139 577[5]	139 893[5]
	2015	211 862[7,9]	0.2[7,9]	0.2[7,9]	0.2[7,9]	254	163	385 746	386 163
	2019	218 530[7,9]	0.2[7,9]	0.2[7,9]	0.2[7,9]	649	297	225 829	226 775
Poland	2005	722 509	1.9	1.6	2.1	4 604[5]	1 627[5]	75[5]	6 306[5]
Pologne	2010	642 417	1.7	1.4	1.9	15 555[5]	2 126[5]	763[5]	18 444[5]
	2015	619 403	1.6	1.4	1.8	15 741[12]	2 470	10 825	29 036
	2019	655 985	1.7	1.6	1.9	12 549	3 108	10 825	26 482
Portugal	2005	771 184	7.3	7.4	7.3	363[5]	...	...	363[5]
Portugal	2010	762 825	7.2	7.3	7.1	384[5]	72[5]	31[5]	487[5]
	2015	864 814	8.3	8.1	8.5	699[12]	641	14	1 354
	2019	888 162	8.7	8.5	8.8	2 228	802	14	3 044

International migrants and refugees *(continued)*
International migrant stock (number and percentage) and refugees and others of concern to UNHCR

Migrants internationaux et réfugiés *(suite)*
Stock de migrants internationaux (nombre et pourcentage) et réfugiés et autres personnes relevant de la compétence du HCR

Region, country or area Région, pays ou zone	Year Année	International Migrant Stock (mid-year) Stock de migrants internationaux (milieu de l'année) Total Total	MF HF	M H	F	Refugees and others of concern to UNHCR (mid-year) Réfugiés et autres personnes relevant de la compétence du HCR (milieu de l'année) Refugees& Réfugiés&	Asylum seekers Demandeurs d'asile	Other&& Autres&&	Total pop. Pop. totale
			% of total pop. % de la pop. totale						
Puerto Rico	2005	352 144	9.7	9.6	9.8	...	...	...	...
Porto Rico	2010	304 969	8.5	8.3	8.7	...	...	...	...
	2015	280 494	8.3	8.1	8.5	...	...	...	...
	2019	266 828	9.1	8.9	9.3	...	...	...	...
Qatar	2005	646 026[9]	74.6[9]	85.3[9]	52.6[9]	46[5]	28[5]	...	74[5]
Qatar	2010	1 456 413[9]	78.5[9]	85.0[9]	57.2[9]	51[5]	16[5]	1 200[5]	1 267[5]
	2015	1 687 640[9]	65.8[9]	72.6[9]	44.1[9]	133	100	1 200	1 433
	2019	2 229 688[9]	78.7[9]	86.5[9]	55.0[9]	199	100	1 200	1 499
Republic of Korea	2005	486 065[9]	1.0[9]	1.2[9]	0.8[9]	69[5]	519[5]	...	588[5]
République de Corée	2010	919 987[9]	1.9[9]	2.1[9]	1.6[9]	358[5]	712[5]	179[5]	1 249[5]
	2015	1 143 087[9]	2.2[9]	2.5[9]	2.0[9]	1 313	5 102	200	6 615
	2019	1 163 655[9]	2.3[9]	2.5[9]	2.0[9]	5 458	22 070	197	27 725
Republic of Moldova	2005	171 122[52]	4.1[52]	3.4[52]	4.8[52]	84[5]	148[5]	1 543[5]	1 775[5]
République de Moldova	2010	129 488[52]	3.2[52]	2.7[52]	3.6[52]	148[5]	81[5]	2 032[5]	2 261[5]
	2015	106 374[52]	2.6[52]	2.2[52]	3.0[52]	389	164	6 233	6 786
	2019	104 713[52]	2.6[52]	2.2[52]	2.9[52]	417	110	3 632	4 159
Réunion	2005	115 076	14.5	15.2	13.9	...	...	...	...
Réunion	2010	123 029	14.8	15.6	14.1	...	...	...	...
	2015	127 209	14.7	15.4	14.1	...	...	...	...
	2019	129 153	14.5	15.2	13.9	...	...	...	...
Romania	2005	145 162	0.7	0.7	0.7	2 056[5]	264[5]	400[5]	2 720[5]
Roumanie	2010	177 211	0.9	0.9	0.9	1 021[5]	388[5]	321[5]	1 730[5]
	2015	281 048	1.4	1.5	1.3	2 426	138	294	2 858
	2019	462 552	2.4	2.6	2.1	4 165	376	225	4 766
Russian Federation	2005	11 667 588	8.1	8.7	7.6	1 523[5]	292[5]	481 282[5]	483 097[5]
Fédération de Russie	2010	11 194 710	7.8	8.3	7.4	4 922[5]	1 463[5]	126 170[5]	132 555[5]
	2015	11 643 276	8.0	8.5	7.6	315 313	2 423	113 474[53]	431 210
	2019	11 640 559	8.0	8.5	7.6	62 470[54]	672[54]	72 323[54]	135 465[54]
Rwanda	2005	423 187[7]	4.8[7]	4.9[7]	4.6[7]	45 206[5]	4 301[5]	14 849[5]	64 356[5]
Rwanda	2010	426 901[7]	4.3[7]	4.3[7]	4.2[7]	55 398[5]	290[5]	2[5]	55 690[5]
	2015	514 647[7]	4.5[7]	4.6[7]	4.5[7]	132 743	253	2 557	135 553
	2019	539 932[7]	4.3[7]	4.3[7]	4.2[7]	144 835	299	4 990	150 124
Saint Helena [9,55]	2005	163	3.0	...	...	...	...	...	...
Sainte-Hélène [9,55]	2010	248	4.8	...	...	...	...	...	...
	2015	377	6.4	...	...	...	...	...	...
	2019	433	7.1	...	...	...	...	...	...
Saint Kitts and Nevis	2005	6 682	14.3	...	...	...	...	...	...
Saint-Kitts-et-Nevis	2010	7 245	14.8	...	...	...	...	...	...
	2015	7 443	14.5	...	...	1	...	...	1
	2019	7 587	14.4	...	...	4	...	...	4
Saint Lucia	2005	9 842	6.0	6.0	6.0	...	...	...	...
Sainte-Lucie	2010	9 051	5.2	5.1	5.3	...	6[5]	1[5]	7[5]
	2015	8 673	4.8	4.7	4.9	2	2	60	64
	2018	...	...	...	...	2	3	...	5
	2019	8 383	4.6	4.5	4.7	2	...	...	2
Saint Pierre and Miquelon	2005	1 147	18.7	...	...	...	...	...	...
Saint-Pierre-et-Miquelon	2010	1 017	16.0	...	...	...	...	...	...
	2015	986	16.5	...	...	...	...	...	...
	2019	990	17.0	...	...	...	...	...	...
Saint Vincent & Grenadines	2005	4 436	4.1	4.0	4.2	...	...	...	...
Saint-Vincent-Grenadines	2010	4 569	4.2	4.2	4.3	...	...	...	...
	2015	4 637	4.2	4.2	4.3	...	...	...	...
	2019	4 692	4.2	4.3	4.2	...	...	...	...
Samoa	2005	5 746	3.2	3.2	3.2	...	...	...	...
Samoa	2010	5 122	2.8	2.7	2.8	...	...	...	...
	2015	4 252	2.2	2.1	2.3	...	...	...	...
	2018	...	...	...	...	3	...	...	3
	2019	4 035	2.0	2.0	2.1	...	1	...	1

3

International migrants and refugees *(continued)*
International migrant stock (number and percentage) and refugees and others of concern to UNHCR

Migrants internationaux et réfugiés *(suite)*
Stock de migrants internationaux (nombre et pourcentage) et réfugiés et autres personnes relevant de la compétence du HCR

Region, country or area / Région, pays ou zone	Year / Année	International Migrant Stock (mid-year) Stock de migrants internationaux (milieu de l'année) Total / Total	% of total pop. % de la pop. totale MF / HF	M / H	F	Refugees and others of concern to UNHCR (mid-year) Réfugiés et autres personnes relevant de la compétence du HCR (milieu de l'année) Refugees& / Réfugiés&	Asylum seekers Demandeurs d'asile	Other&& / Autres&&	Total pop. Pop. totale
San Marino [9] Saint-Marin [9]	2005	4 218	14.4	...	...	...	...	...	...
	2010	4 880	15.6	...	...	...	...	...	...
	2015	5 195	15.6	...	...	...	...	...	...
	2019	5 507	16.3	...	...	...	...	...	...
Sao Tome and Principe [9] Sao Tomé-et-Principe [9]	2005	3 433	2.2	2.2	2.1	...	...	...	...
	2010	2 700	1.5	1.5	1.5	...	...	...	...
	2015	2 394	1.2	1.2	1.2	...	...	...	...
	2019	2 174	1.0	1.0	1.0	...	...	...	...
Saudi Arabia Arabie saoudite	2005	6 501 819[7,9]	27.3[7,9]	33.7[7,9]	19.3[7,9]	240 701[5]	212[5]	70 084[5]	310 997[5]
	2010	8 429 956[7,9]	30.7[7,9]	38.5[7,9]	20.8[7,9]	582[5]	87[5]	70 000[5]	70 669[5]
	2015	10 771 366[7,9]	34.0[7,9]	41.4[7,9]	24.2[7,9]	211	93	70 000	70 304
	2019	13 122 338[7,9]	38.3[7,9]	45.5[7,9]	28.5[7,9]	301	2 209	70 000	72 510
Senegal Sénégal	2005	238 298[7]	2.1[7]	2.3[7]	2.0[7]	20 712[5]	2 629[5]	12[5]	23 353[5]
	2010	256 092[7]	2.0[7]	2.2[7]	1.8[7]	20 672[5]	2 177[5]	1 401[5]	24 250[5]
	2015	266 496[7]	1.8[7]	2.0[7]	1.7[7]	14 304	2 956	...	17 260
	2019	275 239[7]	1.7[7]	1.8[7]	1.5[7]	14 417	1 758	...	16 175
Serbia [56] Serbie [56]	2005	854 848	8.7	8.0	9.4	148 264[5]	33[5]	338 641[5]	486 938[5]
	2010	826 275	9.2	8.3	10.1	73 608[5]	209[5]	238 810[5]	312 627[5]
	2015	807 441	9.1	8.2	10.0	35 309	464	223 949	259 722
	2018	...	...	...	...	30 935	140	219 601	250 676
	2019	820 312	9.4	8.4	10.3	...	...	...	...
Seychelles Seychelles	2005	8 997	10.1	13.1	7.2	...	...	...	...
	2010	11 420	12.5	16.6	8.2	...	...	...	...
	2015	12 791	13.5	18.3	8.3	...	...	...	...
	2018	...	...	...	...	...	1	...	1
	2019	12 926	13.2	18.0	8.1	...	...	...	...
Sierra Leone Sierra Leone	2005	146 050[7]	2.6[7]	2.7[7]	2.4[7]	59 965[5]	177[5]	6 202[5]	66 344[5]
	2010	79 055[7]	1.2[7]	1.4[7]	1.1[7]	8 363[5]	210[5]	38[5]	8 611[5]
	2015	58 813[7]	0.8[7]	0.9[7]	0.7[7]	1 371	16	...	1 387
	2017	...	...	...	...	693	1	...	694
	2019	54 332[7]	0.7[7]	0.8[7]	0.6[7]	370	...	...	370
Singapore Singapour	2005	1 710 594	40.1	35.2	45.1	3[5]	1[5]	...	4[5]
	2010	2 164 794	42.2	35.8	49.2	7[5]	...	...	7[5]
	2015	2 543 638	45.5	38.4	53.3	...	...	1	1
	2019	2 155 653	37.1	31.3	43.6	...	...	1 304	1 304
Sint Maarten (Dutch part) St-Martin (partie néerland.)	2010	26 200	76.7	...	...	1[5]	3[5]	...	4[5]
	2015	27 295	68.3	...	...	3	5	...	8
	2019	28 260	66.7	...	...	6	3	93[2]	102
Slovakia Slovaquie	2005	130 491	2.4	2.2	2.6	368[5]	2 707[5]	...	3 075[5]
	2010	146 319	2.7	2.6	2.9	461[5]	267[5]	911[5]	1 639[5]
	2015	177 624	3.3	3.4	3.2	799[12]	61	1 671	2 531
	2019	187 984	3.4	3.6	3.3	963	7	1 523	2 493
Slovenia Slovénie	2005	217 218	10.9	12.0	9.9	251[5]	185[5]	715[5]	1 151[5]
	2010	253 786	12.4	14.0	10.9	314[5]	121[5]	4 119[5]	4 554[5]
	2015	237 616	11.5	13.1	9.9	283	43	4	330
	2019	253 122	12.2	13.8	10.6	789	360	4	1 153
Solomon Islands Îles Salomon	2005	3 271	0.7	0.8	0.6	...	...	...	...
	2010	2 760	0.5	0.6	0.5	...	...	...	...
	2015	2 585	0.4	0.5	0.4	3	...	...	3
	2016	...	...	...	...	3	...	...	3
	2019	2 532	0.4	0.4	0.3	...	4	...	4
Somalia Somalie	2005	* 20 670[7]	* 0.2[7]	* 0.2[7]	* 0.2[7]	493[5]	98[5]	400 000[5]	400 591[5]
	2010	* 48 106[7]	* 0.4[7]	* 0.4[7]	* 0.4[7]	1 937[5]	24 111[5]	1 463 780[5]	1 489 828[5]
	2015	* 40 990[7]	* 0.3[7]	* 0.3[7]	* 0.3[7]	3 582	9 320	1 152 073	1 164 975
	2019	* 52 131[7]	* 0.3[7]	* 0.4[7]	* 0.3[7]	17 369	17 189	2 660 103	2 694 661
South Africa Afrique du Sud	2005	1 351 031[7]	2.8[7]	3.3[7]	2.3[7]	29 714[5]	140 095[5]	100[5]	169 909[5]
	2010	2 114 801[7]	4.1[7]	4.8[7]	3.4[7]	57 899[5]	171 702[5]	134[5]	229 735[5]
	2015	3 816 695[7]	6.9[7]	7.8[7]	6.0[7]	114 512	798 080	...	912 592
	2019	4 224 256[7]	7.2[7]	8.1[7]	6.3[7]	89 285[17]	184 203[17]	...	273 488[17]

International migrants and refugees *(continued)*
International migrant stock (number and percentage) and refugees and others of concern to UNHCR

Migrants internationaux et réfugiés *(suite)*
Stock de migrants internationaux (nombre et pourcentage) et réfugiés et autres personnes relevant de la compétence du HCR

Region, country or area / Région, pays ou zone	Year / Année	International Migrant Stock (mid-year) / Stock de migrants internationaux (milieu de l'année) Total / Total	% of total pop. / % de la pop. totale MF / HF	M / H	F	Refugees and others of concern to UNHCR (mid-year) / Réfugiés et autres personnes relevant de la compétence du HCR (milieu de l'année) Refugees& / Réfugiés&	Asylum seekers / Demandeurs d'asile	Other&& / Autres&&	Total pop. / Pop. totale
South Sudan / Soudan du sud	2010[7]	257 905	2.7	2.8	2.6	...	...	...	...
	2015	844 122[7]	7.9[7]	8.0[7]	7.7[7]	265 887	632	1 792 014[57]	2 058 533
	2019	865 552[7]	7.8[7]	8.0[7]	7.7[7]	295 986	2 977	1 890 670	2 189 633
Spain / Espagne	2005	4 107 226[58]	9.3[58]	9.9[58]	8.8[58]	5 374[5]	...	27[5]	5 401[5]
	2010	6 280 065[58]	13.4[58]	14.0[58]	12.8[58]	3 820[5]	2 712[5]	31[5]	6 563[5]
	2015	5 891 208[58]	12.6[58]	12.6[58]	12.7[58]	5 798[12]	11 020	440	17 258
	2019	6 104 203[58]	13.1[58]	12.7[58]	13.4[58]	23 462	122 101	3 567	149 130
Sri Lanka / Sri Lanka	2005	39 526[7]	0.2[7]	0.2[7]	0.2[7]	106[5]	121[5]	351 884[5]	352 111[5]
	2010	38 959[7]	0.2[7]	0.2[7]	0.2[7]	223[5]	138[5]	434 903[5]	435 264[5]
	2015	39 706[7]	0.2[7]	0.2[7]	0.2[7]	848	461	50 499[59]	51 808
	2019	40 018[7]	0.2[7]	0.2[7]	0.2[7]	790	798	36 018	37 606
State of Palestine / État de Palestine	2005[60]	266 617	7.5	6.6	8.3	...	...	...	...
	2010[60]	258 032	6.4	5.6	7.2	...	...	...	...
	2015	255 507[60]	5.6[60]	4.9[60]	6.4[60]	...	...	3	3
	2019[60]	253 735	5.1	4.5	5.8	...	...	...	...
Sudan / Soudan	2005	546 419[7,61]	1.4[7,61]	1.4[7,61]	1.4[7,61]	147 256[5]	4 425[5]	878 067[5]	1 029 748[5]
	2010	618 709[7,61]	1.8[7,61]	1.8[7,61]	1.8[7,61]	178 308[5]	6 046[5]	1 767 167[5]	1 951 521[5]
	2015	620 523[7,61]	1.6[7,61]	1.6[7,61]	1.6[7,61]	356 191	11 448	2 400 270[62]	2 767 909
	2019	1 223 092[7,61]	2.9[7,61]	2.8[7,61]	2.9[7,61]	1 087 060	16 979	1 870 023	2 974 062
Suriname / Suriname	2005[9]	33 664	6.7	7.3	6.2	...	...	...	...
	2010	39 713[9]	7.5[9]	8.1[9]	6.9[9]	1[5]	7[5]	...	8[5]
	2015	43 127[9]	7.7[9]	8.4[9]	7.0[9]	1	...	...	1
	2018	...	...	...	...	47	70	2	119
	2019	46 157[9]	7.9[9]	8.6[9]	7.2[9]	48	385	...	433
Sweden / Suède	2005	1 125 790	12.5	12.0	12.9	74 915[5]	15 702[5]	5 785[5]	96 402[5]
	2010	1 384 929	14.7	14.4	15.1	82 629[5]	18 635[5]	9 545[5]	110 809[5]
	2015	1 676 264	17.2	17.0	17.4	142 207[12]	56 135	27 167	225 509
	2019	2 005 210	20.0	20.1	19.9	247 289	31 255	31 819	310 363
Switzerland / Suisse	2005	1 805 437	24.4	25.5	23.4	48 030[5]	14 428[5]	990[5]	63 448[5]
	2010	2 075 182	26.6	26.1	27.0	48 813[5]	12 916[5]	127[5]	61 856[5]
	2015	2 416 394	29.1	28.8	29.4	69 390	17 085	76	86 551
	2019	2 572 029	29.9	29.7	30.2	106 900	13 173	44	120 117
Syrian Arab Republic / République arabe syrienne	2005	878 308[7,9]	4.8[7,9]	4.8[7,9]	4.8[7,9]	26 089[5]	1 898[5]	300 001[5]	327 988[5]
	2010	1 787 561[7,9]	8.4[7,9]	8.5[7,9]	8.3[7,9]	1 005 472[5]	2 446[5]	300 194[5]	1 308 112[5]
	2015	871 174[7,9]	4.8[7,9]	4.9[7,9]	4.8[7,9]	149 200[63]	4 839	7 792 500	7 946 539
	2019	867 848[7,9]	5.1[7,9]	5.2[7,9]	5.0[7,9]	16 797[64]	14 699[64]	6 355 253[64]	6 386 749[64]
Tajikistan / Tadjikistan	2005	280 466	4.1	3.6	4.7	1 018[5]	22[5]	25[5]	1 065[5]
	2010	279 808	3.7	3.2	4.2	3 131[5]	1 656[5]	2 338[5]	7 125[5]
	2015	275 101	3.3	2.8	3.7	1 782	79	10 082[65]	11 943
	2019	274 071	2.9	2.5	3.4	2 287	2 170	6 842	11 299
Thailand / Thaïlande	2005	2 163 447[7]	3.3[7]	3.4[7]	3.2[7]	117 053[5]	32 163[5]	136[5]	149 352[5]
	2010	3 224 131[7]	4.8[7]	4.9[7]	4.7[7]	96 675[5]	10 250[5]	542 505[5]	649 430[5]
	2015	3 486 526[7]	5.1[7]	5.2[7]	4.9[7]	110 372	8 166	506 718[66]	625 256
	2019	3 635 085[7]	5.2[7]	5.4[7]	5.1[7]	100 090	878	475 930	576 898
Timor-Leste / Timor-Leste	2005	11 286	1.1	1.1	1.2	3[5]	10[5]	...	13[5]
	2010	11 540	1.1	1.1	1.1	1[5]	4[5]	...	5[5]
	2015	8 520	0.7	0.9	0.6	...	...	5	5
	2019	8 417	0.7	0.8	0.5	...	...	2	2
Togo / Togo	2005	203 799[7,9]	3.6[7,9]	3.7[7,9]	3.6[7,9]	9 287[5]	420[5]	9 012[5]	18 719[5]
	2010	255 413[7,9]	4.0[7,9]	4.1[7,9]	3.9[7,9]	14 051[5]	151[5]	5[5]	14 207[5]
	2015	277 384[7,9]	3.8[7,9]	3.8[7,9]	3.7[7,9]	21 877	687	...	22 564
	2019	279 142[7,9]	3.5[7,9]	3.5[7,9]	3.4[7,9]	12 333	677	15	13 025
Tokelau / Tokélaou	2005	258	21.4	...	...	...	...	...	...
	2010	429	37.6	...	...	...	...	...	...
	2015	487	38.9	...	...	...	...	...	...
	2019	504	37.6	...	...	...	...	...	...

International migrants and refugees *(continued)*
International migrant stock (number and percentage) and refugees and others of concern to UNHCR

Migrants internationaux et réfugiés *(suite)*
Stock de migrants internationaux (nombre et pourcentage) et réfugiés et autres personnes relevant de la compétence du HCR

Region, country or area Région, pays ou zone	Year Année	International Migrant Stock (mid-year) Stock de migrants internationaux (milieu de l'année)				Refugees and others of concern to UNHCR (mid-year) Réfugiés et autres personnes relevant de la compétence du HCR (milieu de l'année)			
		Total Total	MF HF	M H	% of total pop. % de la pop. totale F	Refugees& Réfugiés&	Asylum seekers Demandeurs d'asile	Other&& Autres&&	Total pop. Pop. totale
Tonga Tonga	2005	4 301	4.3	4.6	3.9	...	...	...	...
	2010	4 604	4.4	4.8	4.1	...	3[5]	...	3[5]
	2015	3 954	3.9	4.3	3.6	...	...	...	...
	2019	3 752	3.6	3.9	3.3	...	1	...	1
Trinidad and Tobago Trinité-et-Tobago	2005	44 812	3.5	3.2	3.7	...	...	...	...
	2010	48 226	3.6	3.5	3.7	29[5]	102[5]	...	131[5]
	2015	50 021	3.7	3.6	3.7	121	59	...	180
	2019	59 249	4.2	4.2	4.3	1 244	14 468	27 306[2]	43 018
Tunisia Tunisie	2005	35 040[9]	0.3[9]	0.4[9]	0.3[9]	87[5]	26[5]	...	113[5]
	2010	43 172[9]	0.4[9]	0.4[9]	0.4[9]	89[5]	23[5]	3[5]	115[5]
	2015	56 532[9]	0.5[9]	0.5[9]	0.5[9]	824	156	3	983
	2019	57 455[9]	0.5[9]	0.5[9]	0.5[9]	1 341	697	9	2 047
Turkey Turquie	2005	1 319 236[7]	1.9[7]	1.9[7]	2.0[7]	2 399[5]	4 872[5]	1 434[5]	8 705[5]
	2010	1 367 034[7]	1.9[7]	1.8[7]	2.0[7]	10 032[5]	6 715[5]	1 086[5]	17 833[5]
	2015	4 346 197[7]	5.5[7]	6.2[7]	4.9[7]	1 838 848[67]	145 335	1 086	1 985 269
	2019	5 876 829[7]	7.0[7]	7.9[7]	6.2[7]	3 622 284[68]	317 820[68]	1[68]	3 940 105[68]
Turkmenistan Turkménistan	2005	213 053	4.5	4.3	4.6	11 963[5]	2[5]	45[5]	12 010[5]
	2010	197 979	3.9	3.6	4.2	62[5]	...	20 000[5]	20 062[5]
	2015	196 376	3.5	3.3	3.7	27	...	7 144	7 171
	2019	195 127	3.3	3.2	3.4	22	...	5 215	5 237
Turks and Caicos Islands Îles Turques-et-Caïques	2005	13 115	46.5	...	...	...	...	...	...
	2010	17 216	52.7	...	...	...	...	...	...
	2015	22 719	63.1	...	...	4	4	...	8
	2019	24 534	64.2	...	...	4	...	...	4
Tuvalu [9] Tuvalu [9]	2005	209	2.1	...	...	...	...	...	...
	2010	220	2.1	...	...	...	...	...	...
	2015	230	2.1	...	...	...	...	...	...
	2019	238	2.0	...	...	...	...	...	...
Uganda Ouganda	2005	593 308[7]	2.1[7]	2.1[7]	2.1[7]	257 256[5]	1 809[5]	1 636[5]	260 701[5]
	2010	492 930[7]	1.5[7]	1.5[7]	1.5[7]	135 801[5]	20 804[5]	437 775[5]	594 380[5]
	2015	851 175[7]	2.2[7]	2.2[7]	2.2[7]	428 397	38 068	180 000	646 465
	2019	1 734 166[7]	3.9[7]	3.8[7]	4.0[7]	1 267 043	26 539	1 152 255	2 445 837
Ukraine Ukraine	2005	5 050 302[69]	10.8[69]	10.0[69]	11.5[69]	2 346[5]	1 618[5]	72 896[5]	76 860[5]
	2010	4 818 767[69]	10.5[69]	9.8[69]	11.1[69]	3 022[5]	2 981[5]	40 357[5]	46 360[5]
	2015	4 915 142[69]	10.9[69]	10.2[69]	11.6[69]	3 232	6 169	1 417 179	1 426 580
	2019	4 964 293[69]	11.3[69]	10.5[69]	12.0[69]	2 627[70]	2 103[70]	1 535 650[70]	1 540 380[70]
United Arab Emirates Émirats arabes unis	2005	3 281 115[7,9]	71.5[7,9]	74.0[7,9]	65.7[7,9]	104[5]	79[5]	...	183[5]
	2010	7 316 697[7,9]	85.6[7,9]	85.4[7,9]	86.0[7,9]	538[5]	86[5]	...	624[5]
	2015	7 995 126[7,9]	86.3[7,9]	90.3[7,9]	76.8[7,9]	424	378	...	802
	2019	8 587 256[7,9]	87.9[7,9]	93.5[7,9]	75.3[7,9]	1 227	7 320	137	8 684
United Kingdom Royaume-Uni	2005	5 926 156	9.8	9.5	10.1	303 181[5]	12 500[5]	909[5]	316 590[5]
	2010	7 119 664	11.2	11.1	11.4	238 150[5]	14 880[5]	229[5]	253 259[5]
	2015	8 411 569	12.8	12.4	13.1	117 234[12]	37 829	16	155 079
	2019	9 552 110	14.1	13.7	14.5	132 700	43 833	176	176 709
United Rep. of Tanzania Rép.-Unie de Tanzanie	2005	771 153[7,71]	2.0[7,71]	2.5[7,71]	1.5[7,71]	548 824[5]	307[5]	81 519[5]	630 650[5]
	2010	309 847[7,71]	0.7[7,71]	0.7[7,71]	0.7[7,71]	109 286[5]	1 247[5]	163 269[5]	273 802[5]
	2015	384 567[7,71]	0.7[7,71]	0.7[7,71]	0.8[7,71]	159 014	1 150	168 019	328 183
	2019	509 166[7,71]	0.9[7,71]	0.9[7,71]	0.9[7,71]	264 601	36 656	19 024	320 281
United States of America États-Unis d'Amérique	2005	39 258 293	13.3	13.5	13.1	379 340[5]	169 743[5]	76[5]	549 159[5]
	2010	44 183 643	14.3	14.2	14.4	264 569[5]	6 285[5]	89[5]	270 943[5]
	2015	48 178 877	15.0	14.8	15.3	* 267 222[12]	224 508	...	491 730
	2019	50 661 149	15.4	15.0	15.7	318 852[72]	724 387[72]	...	1 043 239[72]
United States Virgin Islands Îles Vierges américaines	2005	56 647	52.6	51.3	53.7	...	...	...	...
	2010	56 684	53.4	52.6	54.2	...	...	...	...
	2015	56 721	54.0	53.4	54.6	...	...	...	...
	2019	56 745	54.3	53.8	54.7	...	...	...	...

3 International migrants and refugees *(continued)*
International migrant stock (number and percentage) and refugees and others of concern to UNHCR

Migrants internationaux et réfugiés *(suite)*
Stock de migrants internationaux (nombre et pourcentage) et réfugiés et autres personnes relevant de la compétence du HCR

Region, country or area / Région, pays ou zone	Year / Année	International Migrant Stock (mid-year) Stock de migrants internationaux (milieu de l'année)				Refugees and others of concern to UNHCR (mid-year) Réfugiés et autres personnes relevant de la compétence du HCR (milieu de l'année)			
		Total	MF HF	M H	F	Refugees[&] Réfugiés[&]	Asylum seekers Demandeurs d'asile	Other[&&] Autres[&&]	Total pop. Pop. totale
Uruguay	2005	82 317	2.5	2.4	2.6	121[5]	9[5]	...	130[5]
Uruguay	2010	76 303	2.3	2.1	2.4	189[5]	40[5]	...	229[5]
	2015	78 799	2.3	2.2	2.4	289	68	...	357
	2019	81 482	2.4	2.2	2.5	425	8 428	12 607[2]	21 460
Uzbekistan	2005	1 329 932	5.0	4.5	5.6	43 950[5]	587[5]	5[5]	44 542[5]
Ouzbékistan	2010	1 220 149	4.3	3.9	4.6	311[5]	...	2[5]	313[5]
	2015	1 170 873	3.8	3.5	4.0	118	...	86 703[73]	86 821
	2019	1 168 384	3.5	3.3	3.8	14	...	95 858	95 872
Vanuatu	2005	2 800	1.3	1.3	1.4	...	...	...	...
Vanuatu	2010	2 991	1.3	1.2	1.3	4[5]	...	...	4[5]
	2015	3 187	1.2	1.2	1.2	...	1	...	1
	2019	3 245	1.1	1.1	1.1	...	1	...	1
Venezuela (Boliv. Rep. of)	2005	1 076 474	4.1	4.1	4.1	408[5]	5 912[5]	200 001[5]	206 321[5]
Venezuela (Rép. boliv. du)	2010	1 347 347	4.7	4.8	4.7	201 547[5]	15 859[5]	...	217 406[5]
	2015	1 404 448	4.7	4.7	4.6	174 191	704	...	174 895
	2019	1 375 690	4.8	4.9	4.8	67 588	52	385 000	452 640
Viet Nam	2005	51 768[7,9]	0.1[7,9]	0.1[7,9]	~0.0[7,9]	2 357[5]	...	15 000[5]	17 357[5]
Viet Nam	2010	61 756[7,9]	0.1[7,9]	0.1[7,9]	0.1[7,9]	1 928[5]	...	10 200[5]	12 128[5]
	2015	72 793[7,9]	0.1[7,9]	0.1[7,9]	0.1[7,9]	...	...	11 000	11 000
	2019	76 104[7,9]	0.1[7,9]	0.1[7,9]	0.1[7,9]	...	...	34 110	34 110
Wallis and Futuna Islands	2005	2 191	14.7	...	...	...	...	...	...
Îles Wallis-et-Futuna	2010	1 624	12.8	...	...	...	...	...	...
	2015	1 052	8.6	...	...	...	...	...	...
	2019	1 022	8.9	...	...	...	...	...	...
Western Sahara	*2005	3 891	0.9	1.0	0.8	...	...	...	...
Sahara occidental	*2010	4 493	0.9	1.0	0.8	...	...	...	...
	*2015	5 179	1.0	1.1	0.8	...	...	...	...
	*2019	5 384	0.9	1.0	0.8	...	...	...	...
Yemen	2005	171 871[7,9]	0.9[7,9]	1.0[7,9]	0.7[7,9]	81 937[5]	798[5]	48[5]	82 783[5]
Yémen	2010	288 394[7,9]	1.2[7,9]	1.3[7,9]	1.2[7,9]	190 092[5]	2 557[5]	315 929[5]	508 578[5]
	2015	379 882[7,9]	1.4[7,9]	1.5[7,9]	1.4[7,9]	263 047	9 902	1 267 590	1 540 539
	2019	385 628[7,9]	1.3[7,9]	1.4[7,9]	1.3[7,9]	265 783	9 853	3 647 264	3 922 900
Zambia	2005	252 895[7]	2.1[7]	2.2[7]	2.1[7]	155 718[5]	146[5]	29 833[5]	185 697[5]
Zambie	2010	149 962[7]	1.1[7]	1.1[7]	1.1[7]	47 857[5]	325[5]	9 687[5]	57 869[5]
	2015	132 107[7]	0.8[7]	0.8[7]	0.8[7]	25 737	2 606	23 415	51 758
	2019	170 249[7]	1.0[7]	1.0[7]	0.9[7]	54 926	3 737	23 113	81 776
Zimbabwe	2005	402 226[7]	3.3[7]	4.0[7]	2.7[7]	13 850[5]	118[5]	7[5]	13 975[5]
Zimbabwe	2010	398 307[7]	3.1[7]	3.8[7]	2.6[7]	4 435[5]	416[5]	...	4 851[5]
	2015	400 482[7]	2.9[7]	3.4[7]	2.4[7]	6 085	123	* 301 883	308 091
	2019	411 257[7]	2.8[7]	3.3[7]	2.3[7]	8 706[74]	11 155[74]	969[74]	20 830[74]

Source:

United Nations Population Division, New York, International migrant stock: The 2019 Revision, last accessed January 2020.

United Nations High Commissioner for Refugees (UNHCR), Geneva, UNHCR Population Statistics Database, last accessed March 2020.

Source:

Organisation des Nations Unies, Division de la population, New York, « International migrant stock: The 2019 Revision », derniér accéss janvier 2020.
Haut-Commissariat des Nations Unies pour les réfugiés (HCR), Genève, base de données statistique du HCR, dernier accès mars 2020.

& Number of refugees or persons in refugee-like situations as reported by the Office of the United Nations High Commissioner for Refugees (UNHCR). && Figure includes sum of returned refugees, internally displaced persons (IDPs) protected/assisted by UNHCR, including people in IDP like situations, returned IDPs, Persons under UNHCR's stateless mandate, and others of concern to UNHCR categories.

&Nombre de réfugiés ou de personnes en situation analogue à celle de réfugiés, tel que donné par le Bureau des Nations Unies. && Les chiffres correspondent au total des réfugiés rapatriés, des personnes déplacées protégées ou assistées par le HCR, notamment celles se trouvant dans une situation analogue à celle des personnes déplacées, des personnes déplacées de retour, des apatrides relevant du mandat du HCR et d'autres catégories de personnes relevant de la compétence du HCR.

3 International migrants and refugees *(continued)*
International migrant stock (number and percentage) and refugees and others of concern to UNHCR

Migrants internationaux et réfugiés *(suite)*
Stock de migrants internationaux (nombre et pourcentage) et réfugiés et autres personnes relevant de la compétence du HCR

1	Excluding Sudan.	1	Exclut le Soudan.
2	Including Venezuelans displaced abroad.	2	Y compris les Vénézuéliens déplacés à l'étranger.
3	Excluding Persons under UNHCR's statelessness mandate in Bangladesh and excluding 133000 stateless IDPs in Myanmar.	3	Excluant les personnes relevant du mandat du HCR sur les apatrides au Bangladesh et excluant 133000 personnes déplacées apatrides au Myanmar.
4	Including American Samoa, Cook Islands, Niue, Pitcairn, Tokelau, Tuvalu, and Wallis and Futuna Islands.	4	Y compris les îles Cook, Nioué, Pitcairn, Samoa américaines, Tokélaou, Tuvalu, et les îles Wallis-et-Futuna.
5	Data as at the end of December.	5	Données à la fin de décembre.
6	The statelessness figure refers to a survey conducted in late 2017.	6	Le chiffre de l'apatridie fait référence à une enquête menée fin 2017.
7	Including refugees.	7	Y compris les réfugiés.
8	According to the Government of Algeria, there are an estimated 165,000 Sahrawi refugees in the Tindouf camps.	8	Selon le Gouvernement algérien, les camps de Tindouf accueillent environ 165 000 réfugiés sahraouis.
9	Refers to foreign citizens.	9	Se rapportent aux citoyens étrangers.
10	Including Christmas Island, Cocos (Keeling) Islands and Norfolk Island.	10	Y compris l'île Christmas, les îles des Cocos (Keeling) et l'île Norfolk.
11	Asylum-seekers are based on the number of applications lodged for protection visas.	11	Les chiffres de l'Australie concernant les demandeurs d'asile sont établis sur la base du nombre de demandes de visa de protection présentées.
12	Data relates to the end of 2014.	12	Le nombre se rapporte à fin 2014.
13	Including Nagorno-Karabakh.	13	Y compris le Haut-Karabakh.
14	The refugee population includes 200,000 persons originating from Myanmar in a refugee-like situation. The Government of Bangladesh estimates the population to be between 300,000 and 500,000.	14	Au nombre des réfugiés figurent 200 000 personnes originaires du Myanmar se trouvant dans une situation analogue à celle des réfugiés. Le Gouvernement bangladais estime que le nombre de réfugiés se situe entre 300 000 et 500 000.
15	The refugee population includes 274,000 persons originating from Myanmar in a refugee-like situation. The Government of Bangladesh estimates the population to be between 300,000 and 500,000.	15	Au nombre des réfugiés figurent 274,000 personnes originaires du Myanmar se trouvant dans une situation analogue à celle des réfugiés. Le Gouvernement bangladais estime que le nombre de réfugiés se situe entre 300 000 et 500 000.
16	The figure reported relates to stateless persons who are also refugees from Myanmar, mainly from Rakhine State. This figure exceptionally includes 911,660 stateless refugees who are also counted in the column under "Refugees." UNHCR's statistical reporting currently follows a methodology that reports on one legal status as a person of concern only. However, due to the extraordinary size of the displaced stateless population in Bangladesh, UNHCR considered it important to reflect, on an exceptional basis, the dual status that this population group possesses as both refugees and stateless persons as to do otherwise might convey the mistaken impression that the overall number of stateless persons has declined significantly. This approach will not be replicated in the database and in the Excel version of this table and, therefore, figures may differ.	16	Le chiffre indiqué concerne les apatrides qui sont également des réfugiés du Myanmar, principalement de l'État de Rakhine. Ce chiffre comprend exceptionnellement 911 660 réfugiés apatrides qui sont également comptés dans la colonne «Réfugiés». Les rapports statistiques du HCR suivent actuellement une méthodologie qui rend compte d'un seul statut juridique en tant que personne relevant de sa compétence. Cependant, en raison de la taille extraordinaire de la population apatride déplacée au Bangladesh, le HCR a estimé qu'il était important de refléter, à titre exceptionnel, le double statut que ce groupe de population possède en tant que réfugié et apatride, ce qui autrement pourrait donner l'impression erronée que le nombre total d'apatrides a considérablement diminué. Cette approche ne sera pas reproduite dans la base de données et dans la version Excel de ce tableau et, par conséquent, les chiffres peuvent différer.
17	All data relate to end of 2018.	17	Toutes les données se rapportent à fin 2018.
18	The estimates refer to the former Netherlands Antilles.	18	Les estimations se réfèrent aux anciennes Antilles néerlandaises.
19	Bonaire only.	19	Bonaire seulement.
20	Refers to Guernsey and Jersey.	20	Se rapporte à Guernesey et Jersey.
21	For statistical purposes, the data for China do not include those for the Hong Kong Special Administrative Region (Hong Kong SAR), Macao Special Administrative Region (Macao SAR) and Taiwan Province of China.	21	Pour la présentation des statistiques, les données pour la Chine ne comprennent pas la région administrative spéciale de Hong Kong (RAS de Hong Kong), la région administrative spéciale de Macao (RAS de Macao) et la province chinoise de Taïwan.
22	The 300,000 Vietnamese refugees are well integrated and in practice receive protection from the Government of China.	22	Les 300 000 réfugiés vietnamiens sont bien intégrés et, dans la pratique, reçoivent la protection du Gouvernement chinois.
23	The 321,500 Vietnamese refugees are well integrated and in practice receive protection from the Government of China.	23	Les 321,500 réfugiés vietnamiens sont bien intégrés et, dans la pratique, reçoivent la protection du Gouvernement chinois.
24	Figure of others of concern is provided by the Government of Colombia.	24	Le gouvernement de la Colombie fournit les chiffres sur «autres personnes préoccupantes».

3 International migrants and refugees *(continued)*
International migrant stock (number and percentage) and refugees and others of concern to UNHCR

Migrants internationaux et réfugiés *(suite)*
Stock de migrants internationaux (nombre et pourcentage) et réfugiés et autres personnes relevant de la compétence du HCR

25	The statelessness figure is based on a Government estimate of individuals who themselves or whose parents or grandparents migrated to Côte d'Ivoire before or just after independence and who did not establish their nationality at independence or before the nationality law changed in 1972. The estimate is derived in part from cases denied voter registration in 2010 because electoral authorities could not determine their nationality at the time. The estimation is adjusted to reflect the number of persons who acquired nationality through the special 'acquisition of nationality by declaration' procedure until mid of 2019. The estimate does not include individuals of unknown parentage who were abandoned as children and who are not considered as nationals under Ivorian law.
26	Including northern Cyprus.
27	UNHCR's assistance activities for IDPs in Cyprus ended in 1999. Visit the website of the Internal Displacement Monitoring Centre (IDMC) for further information.
28	Revised estimate includes only individuals born in the country where both parents were born abroad. This estimate does not include subsequent generations of individuals of foreign descent as such it does not include all persons without nationality.
29	UNHCR is currently working with the authorities and other actors to determine the size of the population that found an effective nationality solution under Law 169-14. Since the adoption of Law 169-14 in May 2014, important steps have been taken by the Dominican Republic to confirm Dominican nationality through the validation of birth certificates of individuals born in the country to two migrant parents. Thousands of individuals also are believed to have been issued their Dominican civil documents in 2017, 2018 and first half of 2019, although an official figure was not available for this report.
30	Almost all people recorded as being stateless have permanent residence and enjoy more rights than foreseen in the 1954 Convention relating to the Status of Stateless Persons.
31	A dispute exists between the Governments of Argentina and the United Kingdom of Great Britain and Northern Ireland concerning sovereignty over the Falkland Islands (Malvinas).
32	Including Åland Islands.
33	Including Abkhazia and South Ossetia.
34	Including Saint Barthélemy and Saint Martin (French part).
35	Figure refers to individuals without a nationality who were born in the Dominican Republic prior to January 2010 and who were identified by UNHCR in Haiti since June 2015.
36	Data refer to the Vatican City State.
37	Including an estimate for stateless persons populations in line with Law 26 of 2006, which allows stateless persons to apply for nationality in certain circumstances.
38	Pending a more accurate study into stateless in Iraq, the estimate of stateless persons in Iraq has been adjusted to reflect the reduction of statelessness in line with Law 26 of 2006, which allows stateless persons to apply for nationality in certain circumstances.
39	Includes Iraqi refugees registered with UNHCR.
40	Includes 34,500 Iraqi refugees registered with UNHCR in Jordan. The Government estimated the number of Iraqis at 400,000 individuals at the end of March 2015. This includes refugees and other categories of Iraqis.
41	The figure of stateless persons includes persons covered by two separate Laws; Law on Stateless Persons dated 17 February 2004 and the Law on the Status of Those Former USSR Citizens who are not Citizens of Latvia or of Any Other State.
42	Figure includes persons under UNHCR's statelessness mandate and covered by two separate Latvian laws.
43	Refugee figure related to the end of 2016.
44	Including Sabah and Sarawak.

25	Le chiffre d'apatridie est basé sur une estimation du gouvernement d'individus qui eux-mêmes ou dont les parents ou grands-parents ont émigré en Côte d'Ivoire avant ou juste après l'indépendance et qui n'ont pas établi leur nationalité à l'indépendance ou avant que la loi sur la nationalité ne soit modifiée en 1972. L'estimation est découlait en partie de cas de refus d'inscription des électeurs en 2010 parce que les autorités électorales ne pouvaient pas déterminer leur nationalité à l'époque. L'estimation est ajustée pour refléter le nombre de personnes qui ont acquis la nationalité par le biais de la procédure spéciale «acquisition de la nationalité par déclaration» jusqu'à la mi-2019. L'estimation ne comprend pas les personnes de filiation inconnue qui ont été abandonnées comme enfants et qui ne sont pas considérées comme des nationaux en vertu de la loi ivoirienne.
26	Y compris la partie nord de Chypre.
27	Les activités d'assistance du HCR aux déplacés internes à Chypre ont pris fin en 1999. Pour plus d'informations, visitez le site Web du Centre de surveillance des déplacements internes (IDMC).
28	Cette réestimation concerne uniquement les personnes nées dans le pays dont les deux parents sont nés à l'étranger. Cette estimation ne comprend pas les générations futures de personnes d'origine étrangère tels que les apatrides.
29	Le HCR travaille actuellement avec les autorités et d'autres acteurs pour déterminer la taille de la population qui a trouvé une solution de nationalité efficace en vertu de la loi 169-14. Depuis l'adoption de la loi 169-14 en mai 2014, d'importantes mesures ont été prises par la République dominicaine pour confirmer la nationalité dominicaine à travers la validation des certificats de naissance des personnes nées dans le pays de deux parents migrants. Des milliers de personnes auraient également reçu leurs documents civils dominicains en 2017, 2018 et au premier semestre de 2019, bien qu'aucun chiffre officiel ne soit disponible pour ce rapport.
30	La quasi totalité des personnes enregistrées comme apatrides ont une résidence permanente et jouissent de davantage de droits que ceux prévus par la Convention de 1954 relative au statut des apatrides.
31	La souveraineté sur les îles Falkland (Malvinas) fait l'objet d'un différend entre le Gouvernement argentin et le Gouvernement du Royaume-Uni de Grande-Bretagne et d'Irlande du Nord.
32	Y compris les Îles d'Åland.
33	Y compris l'Abkhazie et l'Ossétie du Sud.
34	Y compris Saint-Barthélemy et Saint-Martin (partie française).
35	Chiffre correspond aux individus sans nationalité qui sont nés en République Dominicaine avant Janvier 2010 et qui ont été identifiés par le HCR en Haïti depuis Juin 2015.
36	Les données se réfèrent à la cité du Vatican.
37	Y compris une estimation des populations apatrides conforme à la loi 26 de 2006,qui permet aux apatrides de demander la nationalité dans certaines circonstances.
38	En attendant une étude plus précise sur les apatrides en Irak, l'estimation des apatrides en Irak a été ajustée pour refléter la réduction de l'apatridie conformément à la loi 26 de 2006, qui permet aux apatrides de demander la nationalité dans certaines circonstances.
39	Y compris réfugiés iraquiens enregistrés par le HCR.
40	Comprend 34 500 réfugiés iraquiens enregistrés auprès du HCR en Jordanie. Le gouvernement estimait le nombre d'Irakiens à 400 000 à la fin de mars 2015. Cela comprend les réfugiés et d'autres catégories d'Iraquiens.
41	Le nombres d'apatrides comprend les personnes couvertes par deux lois distinctes: La loi sur les apatrides du 17 février 2004 et la loi relative au Statut des citoyens de l'ex-URSS qui ne sont pas citoyens de la Lettonie ou d'un autre État.
42	Le chiffre inclut les personnes relevant du mandat du HCR en matière d'apatridie et régies par deux lois lettones distinctes.
43	Chiffre de réfugié lié à la fin de 2016.
44	Y compris Sabah et Sarawak.

3 International migrants and refugees *(continued)*
International migrant stock (number and percentage) and refugees and others of concern to UNHCR

Migrants internationaux et réfugiés *(suite)*
Stock de migrants internationaux (nombre et pourcentage) et réfugiés et autres personnes relevant de la compétence du HCR

45	Updated figure is based on a registration and community legal assistance programme undertaken in West Malaysia by a local NGO with technical support from UNHCR, which began in 2014. During 2017, 906 persons of those registered acquired Malaysian nationality.		45	Le chiffre actualisé est basé sur un programme d'enregistrement et d'assistance juridique communautaire mis en place en Malaisie occidentale par une ONG locale avec l'assistance technique du HCR, qui a débuté en 2014. En 2017, 906 personnes enregistrées ont acquis la nationalité malaise.
46	Including Agalega, Rodrigues and Saint Brandon.		46	Y compris Agalega, Rodrigues et Saint-Brandon.
47	Stateless persons population refers to persons without citizenship in Rakhine State only.		47	Les apatrides s'entendent des personnes dépourvues de nationalité, dans l'État de Rakhine uniquement.
48	The figure of persons of concern under the statelessness mandate relates to stateless persons in Rakhine state and persons of undetermined nationality residing in other states in Myanmar. The figure of stateless persons in Rakhine state has been estimated on the basis of the 2014 census report and 2017 General Administration Department (GAD) of Ministry of Home Affairs (MoHA) data.		48	Le nombre de personnes relevant de la compétence du mandat des apatrides concerne les apatrides de l'État de Rakhine et les personnes de nationalité indéterminée résidant dans d'autres États du Myanmar. Le nombre d'apatrides dans l'État de Rakhine a été estimé sur la base du rapport du recensement de 2014 et des données du Département de l'administration générale (GAD) du ministère de l'Intérieur (MoHA) de 2017.
49	Excluding Persons under UNHCR's statelessness mandate and including 495939 non-displaced stateless.		49	Excluant les personnes relevant du mandat du HCR sur les apatrides et comprend 495939 apatrides non déplacés.
50	Various studies estimate that a large number of individuals lack citizenship certificates in Nepal. While these individuals are not all necessarily stateless, UNHCR has been working closely with the Government of Nepal and partners to address this situation.		50	Selon différentes études, un grand nombre de personnes ne disposeraient pas de certificat de nationalité au Népal. Elles ne sont pas nécessairement toutes apatrides, mais le HCR travaille en coopération étroite avec les autorités népalaises et des partenaires pour régler la situation.
51	Including Svalbard and Jan Mayen Islands.		51	Y compris les îles Svalbard-et-Jan Mayen.
52	Including the Transnistria region.		52	Y compris la région de Transnistrie.
53	Stateless persons refers to census figure from 2010 adjusted to reflect the number of people who acquired nationality since 2011.		53	Le nombre d'apatrides se rapporte aux données du recensement effectué en 2010, ajustées pour tenir compte du nombre de personnes ayant acquis la nationalité depuis 2011.
54	The statelessness figure refers to the census figure from 2010 adjusted to reflect the number of stateless persons who acquired nationality from 2011 to mid-2019.		54	Le chiffre d'apatridie se réfère au chiffre du recensement de 2010 ajusté pour refléter le nombre d'apatrides ayant acquis la nationalité de 2011 à la mi-2019.
55	Including Ascension and Tristan da Cunha.		55	Y compris Ascension et Tristan da Cunha.
56	Including Kosovo.		56	Y compris Kosovo.
57	Internally displaced persons (IDP) figure in South Sudan includes 105,000 people who are in an IDP-like situation.		57	Au nombre des déplacés au Soudan du Sud figurent 105 000 personnes dans une situation analogue à celle des déplacés.
58	Including Canary Islands, Ceuta and Melilla.		58	Y compris les îles Canaries, Ceuta et Melilla.
59	The statistics of the remaining IDPs, while provided by the Government authorities at the district level, are being reviewed by the central authorities. Once this review has been concluded, the statistics will be changed accordingly.		59	Les statistiques relatives au reste des déplacés ont été fournies par les autorités locales au niveau des districts, mais examinées par les autorités centrales, et seront ajustées en fonction des résultats de l'examen.
60	Including East Jerusalem.		60	Y compris Jérusalem-Est.
61	Including South Sudan.		61	Y compris le Sud Soudan.
62	Internally displaced persons (IDP) figure in Sudan includes 77,300 people who are in an IDP-like situation.		62	Au nombre des déplacés au Soudan figurent 77 300 personnes dans une situation analogue à celles des déplacés.
63	The figure for Iraqi refugees is a Government estimate.		63	Le nombre de réfugiés iraquiens est une estimation du Gouvernement.
64	Refugee figure for Iraqis was a government estimate and UNHCR has registered and was assisting 13,800 Iraqis at mid-2019. Figure for stateless persons was an estimate.		64	Le nombre de réfugiés irakiens était une estimation du gouvernement et le HCR s'est enregistré et aidait 13800 Iraquiens à la mi-2019. Le chiffre pour les apatrides était une estimation.
65	Figure refers to a registration exercise in three regions and 637 persons registered as stateless by the Ministry of Internal Affairs of Tajikistan.		65	Les chiffres se rapportent aux enregistrements effectués dans trois régions; 637 personnes ont été enregistrées comme apatrides par le Ministère de l'intérieur tadjik.
66	Figure of stateless persons in Thailand refers to 2011.		66	Les chiffres relatifs au nombre d'apatrides en Thaïlande remontent à 2011.
67	Refugee figure for Syrians in Turkey is a Government estimate.		67	Le nombre de réfugiés syriens en Turquie est une estimation du Gouvernement.
68	Refugee figure is a Government estimate and pertains only to Syrian refugees.		68	Le chiffre des réfugiés est une estimation du gouvernement et ne concerne que les réfugiés syriens.
69	Including Crimea.		69	Y compris Crimea.
70	IDP figure in Ukraine includes 700,000 conflict-affected persons.		70	Le nombre de personnes déplacées à l'intérieur de leur propre pays (PDI) en Ukraine comprend 700 000 personnes touchées par le conflit.
71	Including Zanzibar.		71	Y compris Zanzibar.
72	Figures for asylum-seekers in the United States of America pertain to mid-2019 for claims reported by the Department of Homeland Security and end-2018 for claims reported by the Executive Office for Immigration Review.		72	Les chiffres concernant les demandeurs d'asile aux États-Unis d'Amérique se rapportent à la mi-2019 pour les demandes signalées par le Département de la sécurité intérieure et à la fin de 2018 pour les demandes signalées par le Bureau exécutif pour l'examen de l'immigration.

3

International migrants and refugees *(continued)*
International migrant stock (number and percentage) and refugees and others of concern to UNHCR

Migrants internationaux et réfugiés *(suite)*
Stock de migrants internationaux (nombre et pourcentage) et réfugiés et autres personnes relevant de la compétence du HCR

73 Figure of stateless persons refers to those with permanent residence reported in 2010 by the Government. Information on other categories of stateless persons is not available.

74 A study is being pursued to provide a revised estimate of statelessness figure.

73 Le nombre d'apatrides renvoit au nombre de résidents permanents recensés en 2010 par le Gouvernement. On ne dispose d'aucune information sur d'autres catégories d'apatrides.

74 Une étude est en cours pour fournir une estimation révisée du chiffre d'apatridie.

Proportion of seats held by women in national parliament
Percentage, as of January each year

Proportion de sièges occupés par les femmes au parlement national
Pourcentage, données disponibles en janvier de chaque année

Region, country or area&	Last Election date Dernière date de l'élection	2000	2005	2010	2015	2016	2017	2018	2019	2020	Région, pays ou zone&
Total, all countries or areas		**13.3**	**15.9**	**19.0**	**22.3**	**22.7**	**23.4**	**23.4**	**24.3**	**24.9[1]**	**Total, tous pays ou zones**
Northern Africa		5.4	10.8	13.2	24.6	23.2	23.8	22.6	22.7	20.1[1]	Afrique septentrionale
Sub-Saharan Africa		11.5	14.4	18.4	22.6	23.3	23.7	23.6	23.9	24.3[1]	Afrique subsaharienne
Eastern Africa		11.9	16.6	21.6	27.2	28.9	29.7	30.0	30.2	30.9[1]	Afrique orientale
Middle Africa		8.6	11.2	13.5	18.1	18.1	17.4	16.4	17.0	17.6[1]	Afrique centrale
Southern Africa		22.5	24.6	33.4	33.4	33.4	33.4	33.7	34.0	35.6[1]	Afrique australe
Western Africa		8.2	10.2	11.6	14.5	14.0	14.9	14.8	14.8	14.8[1]	Afrique occidentale
Northern America		16.3	17.5	19.0	21.8	22.3	22.2	22.8	25.0	25.9[1]	Amérique septentrionale
Latin America & the Caribbean		15.2	19.0	22.7	27.4	28.2	29.4	29.5	31.6	32.1[1]	Amérique latine et Caraïbes
Caribbean		20.6	26.0	29.4	33.1	33.0	33.8	33.7	36.1	36.7[1]	Caraïbes
Central America		14.3	17.4	21.6	30.1	32.5	33.1	32.5	36.3	36.9[1]	Amérique centrale
South America		12.5	15.8	19.2	22.2	22.7	24.5	24.8	26.1	26.5[1]	Amérique du Sud
Asia		12.1	13.3	16.8	17.8	17.9	18.4	17.9	18.8	19.5[1]	Asie
Central Asia		7.0	11.6	20.0	21.8	21.1	21.3	21.3	21.1	25.4[1]	Asie centrale
Eastern Asia		18.2	18.1	18.7	20.4	20.4	20.5	20.9	21.4	21.6[1]	Asie orientale
South-eastern Asia		12.3	15.5	19.3	17.8	18.3	19.3	19.1	19.6	20.4[1]	Asie du Sud-Est
Southern Asia		6.8	8.8	18.2	17.6	17.7	18.0	13.9	15.8	17.3[1]	Asie méridionale
Western Asia		5.2	5.7	9.3	12.8	13.2	13.8	14.3	15.3	15.6[1]	Asie occidentale
Caucasus and Central Asia		7.0	9.9	15.1	17.9	17.6	18.4	19.5	20.0	...	Caucase et Asie centrale
Europe		16.8	20.5	23.2	26.7	27.2	28.0	28.9	29.8	31.4[1]	Europe
Eastern Europe		9.7	14.1	15.2	16.9	17.6	19.4	20.0	20.5	22.4[1]	Europe orientale
Northern Europe		27.0	28.0	29.6	30.4	32.5	33.3	33.8	35.1	36.4[1]	Europe septentrionale
Southern Europe		11.0	17.1	23.0	30.0	29.0	29.4	29.9	31.5	33.3[1]	Europe méridionale
Western Europe		23.0	25.8	28.4	32.0	32.2	32.1	34.0	34.2	35.8[1]	Europe occidentale
Oceania		11.3	11.2	13.2	13.2	13.4	15.0	15.5	16.3	16.6[1]	Océanie
Australia and New Zealand		25.5	26.3	30.1	28.8	28.8	31.1	33.0	34.4	35.1[1]	Australie et Nouvelle-Zélande
Melanesia		3.9	3.2	1.4	4.2	4.6	4.6	3.5	4.3	4.9[1]	Mélanésie
Micronesia		2.5	2.4	2.4	4.7	5.5	7.8	7.8	7.8	7.0[1]	Micronésie
Polynesia		4.4	3.2	5.2	4.4	4.4	7.7	8.7	8.7	8.6[1]	Polynésie
Afghanistan	2018-10	...	...	27.3	27.7	27.7	27.7	27.7	...	27.0[1]	Afghanistan
Albania	2017-06	5.2	6.4	16.4	20.7	20.7	22.9	27.9	29.3	29.5[1]	Albanie
Algeria	2017-05	3.2	6.2	7.7	31.6	31.6	31.6	25.8	25.8	25.8[1]	Algérie
Andorra	2019-04	7.1	14.3	35.7	50.0	39.3	32.1	32.1	32.1	46.4[1]	Andorre
Angola	2017-08	15.5	15.0	38.6	36.8	36.8	38.2	30.5	30.0	30.0[1]	Angola
Antigua and Barbuda	2018-03	5.3	10.5	10.5	11.1	11.1	11.1	11.1	11.1	11.1[1]	Antigua-et-Barbuda
Argentina	2019-10	28.0	33.7	38.5	36.2	35.8	38.9	38.9	38.8	40.9[1]	Argentine
Armenia	2018-12	3.1	5.3	9.2	10.7	10.7	9.9	18.1	24.2	23.5[1]	Arménie
Australia	2019-05	22.4	24.7	27.3	26.7	26.7	28.7	28.7	30.0	30.5[1]	Australie
Austria	2019-09	26.8	33.9	27.9	30.6	30.6	30.6	34.4	37.2	39.3[1]	Autriche
Azerbaijan	2015-11	10.4	10.5	11.4	15.6	16.9	16.8	16.8	16.8	16.8[1]	Azerbaïdjan
Bahamas	2017-05	15.0	20.0	12.2	13.2	13.2	13.2	12.8	12.8	12.8[1]	Bahamas
Bahrain	2018-12	...	0.0	2.5	7.5	7.5	7.5	7.5	15.0	15.0[1]	Bahreïn
Bangladesh	2018-12	9.1	2.0	18.6	20.0	20.0	20.3	20.3	20.7	20.9[1]	Bangladesh
Barbados	2018-05	10.7	13.3	10.0	16.7	16.7	16.7	16.7	20.0	20.0[1]	Barbade
Belarus	2019-11	9.1	29.4	31.8	27.3	27.3	34.5	34.5	34.5	40.0[1]	Bélarus
Belgium	2019-05	23.3	34.7	38.0	39.3	39.3	38.0	38.0	38.0	40.7[1]	Belgique
Belize	2015-11	6.9	6.7	0.0	3.1	3.1	9.4	9.4	9.4	9.4[1]	Belize
Benin	2019-04	6.0	7.2	10.8	8.4	7.2	7.2	7.2	7.2	7.2[1]	Bénin
Bhutan	2018-10	2.0	9.3	8.5	8.5	8.5	8.5	8.5	14.9	14.9[1]	Bhoutan
Bolivia (Plurin. State of)	2019-10	11.5	19.2	22.3	53.1	53.1	53.1	53.1	53.1	53.1[1,2]	Bolivie (État plurin. de)
Bosnia and Herzegovina	2018-10	7.1	16.7	19.0	21.4	21.4	21.4	21.4	21.4	21.4[1]	Bosnie-Herzégovine
Botswana	2019-10	17.0	11.1	7.9	9.5	9.5	9.5	9.5	9.5	10.8[1]	Botswana
Brazil	2018-10	5.7	8.6	8.8	9.0	9.9	10.7	10.7	15.0	14.6[1]	Brésil
Brunei Darussalam	2017-01	...	...	...	...	...	9.1	9.1	9.1	9.1[1]	Brunéi Darussalam
Bulgaria	2017-03	10.8	26.3	20.8	20.4	20.4	19.2	23.8	25.8	26.7[1]	Bulgarie

4 Proportion of seats held by women in national parliament *(continued)*
Percentage, as of January each year

Proportion de sièges occupés par les femmes au parlement national *(suite)*
Pourcentage, données disponibles en janvier de chaque année

Region, country or area&	Last Election date Dernière date de l'élection	2000	2005	2010	2015	2016	2017	2018	2019	2020	Région, pays ou zone&
Burkina Faso	2015-11	8.1	11.7	15.3	13.3	9.4	11.0	11.0	13.4	13.4[1]	Burkina Faso
Burundi	2015-06	6.0	18.4	31.4	30.5	36.4	36.4	36.4	36.4	36.4[1]	Burundi
Cabo Verde	2016-03	11.1	11.1	18.1	20.8	20.8	23.6	23.6	23.6	25.0[1]	Cabo Verde
Cambodia	2018-07	8.2	9.8	21.1	20.3	20.3	20.3	20.3	20.0	20.0[1]	Cambodge
Cameroon	2013-09	5.6	8.9	13.9	31.1	31.1	31.1	31.1	31.1	31.1[1]	Cameroun
Canada	2019-10	20.6	21.1	22.1	25.2	26.0	26.3	27.0	26.9	29.0[1]	Canada
Central African Republic	2016-03	7.3	...	9.6	...	...	8.6	8.6	8.6	8.6[1]	République centrafricaine
Chad	2011-05	2.4	6.5	5.2	14.9	14.9	12.8	12.8	14.9	15.4[1]	Tchad
Chile	2017-11	10.8	12.5	14.2	15.8	15.8	15.8	...	22.6	22.6[1]	Chili
China	2018-03	21.8	20.2	21.3	23.6	23.6	23.7	24.2	24.9	24.9[1]	Chine
Colombia	2018-03	11.8	12.0	8.4	19.9	19.9	18.7	18.7	18.7	18.3[1]	Colombie
Comoros	2015-02	...	3.0	3.0	...	3.0	6.1	6.1	6.1	6.1[1]	Comores
Congo	2017-07	12.0	8.5	7.3	7.4	7.4	7.4	11.3	11.3	11.3[1]	Congo
Costa Rica	2018-02	19.3	35.1	36.8	33.3	33.3	35.1	35.1	45.6	45.6[1]	Costa Rica
Côte d'Ivoire	2016-12	8.5	8.5	8.9	9.2	9.2	11.5	10.6	11.0	12.0[1]	Côte d'Ivoire
Croatia	2016-09	0.0	21.7	23.5	25.8	15.2	19.9	18.5	20.5	19.2[1]	Croatie
Cuba	2018-03	27.6	36.0	43.2	48.9	48.9	48.9	48.9	53.2	53.2[1]	Cuba
Cyprus	2016-05	5.4	16.1	12.5	12.5	12.5	17.9	17.9	17.9	19.6[1]	Chypre
Czechia	2017-10	15.0	17.0	15.5	19.0	20.0	20.0	22.0	22.5	22.5[1]	Tchéquie
Dem. People's Rep. Korea	2019-03	20.1	20.1	15.6	16.3	16.3	16.3	16.3	16.3	17.6[1]	Rép. pop. dém. de Corée
Dem. Rep. of the Congo	2019-03	...	12.0	8.4	8.9	8.9	8.9	8.9	10.3	12.8[1]	Rép. dém. du Congo
Denmark	2019-06	37.4	38.0	38.0	38.0	37.4	37.4	37.4	37.4	39.7[1]	Danemark
Djibouti	2018-02	0.0	10.8	13.8	12.7	12.7	10.8	10.8	26.2	26.2[1]	Djibouti
Dominica	2019-12	18.8	19.4	14.3	21.9	21.9	25.0	25.0	25.0	38.1[1,3]	Dominique
Dominican Republic	2016-05	16.1	17.3	19.7	20.8	20.8	26.8	26.8	26.8	27.9[1]	République dominicaine
Ecuador	2017-02	17.4	16.0	32.3	41.6	41.6	41.6	38.0	38.0	39.4[1]	Équateur
Egypt	2015-12	...	...	...	...	14.9	14.9	14.9	14.9	15.1[1]	Égypte
El Salvador	2018-03	16.7	10.7	19.0	27.4	32.1	32.1	32.1	31.0	33.3[1]	El Salvador
Equatorial Guinea	2017-11	5.0	18.0	10.0	24.0	24.0	24.0	20.0	20.0	21.0[1]	Guinée équatoriale
Eritrea	1994-02	14.7	22.0	22.0	22.0	22.0	22.0	22.0	22.0	...	Érythrée
Estonia	2019-03	17.8	18.8	22.8	19.8	23.8	26.7	26.7	28.7	28.7[1]	Estonie
Eswatini	2018-09	3.1	10.8	13.6	6.2	6.2	6.2	6.2	7.2	9.6[1]	Eswatini
Ethiopia	2015-05	2.0	7.7	21.9	27.8	38.8	38.8	38.8	38.8	38.8[1]	Éthiopie
Fiji	2018-11	11.3	8.5	...	14.0	16.0	16.0	16.0	19.6	19.6[1]	Fidji
Finland	2019-04	37.0	37.5	40.0	42.5	41.5	42.0	42.0	41.5	46.0[1]	Finlande
France	2017-06	10.9	12.2	18.9	26.2	26.2	25.8	39.0	39.7	39.5[1]	France
Gabon	2018-10	8.3	9.2	14.7	14.2	14.2	17.1	17.1	17.9	14.8[1]	Gabon
Gambia	2017-04	2.0	13.2	7.5	9.4	9.4	9.4	10.3	10.3	8.6[1]	Gambie
Georgia	2016-10	7.2	9.4	5.1	11.3	11.3	16.0	16.0	14.8	14.1[1]	Géorgie
Germany	2017-09	30.9	32.8	32.8	36.5	36.5	37.0	30.7	30.9	31.2[1]	Allemagne
Ghana	2016-12	9.0	10.9	8.3	10.9	10.9	12.7	12.7	13.1	13.1[1]	Ghana
Greece	2019-07	6.3	14.0	17.3	23.0	19.7	18.3	18.3	18.7	20.7[1]	Grèce
Grenada	2018-03	26.7	26.7	13.3	33.3	33.3	33.3	33.3	46.7	46.7[1]	Grenade
Guatemala	2019-06	7.1	8.2	12.0	13.3	13.9	12.7	12.7	19.0	19.0[1]	Guatemala
Guinea	2013-09	8.8	19.3	...	21.9	21.9	21.9	21.9	22.8	22.8[1]	Guinée
Guinea-Bissau	2019-03	7.8	14.0	10.0	13.7	13.7	13.7	13.7	13.7	13.7[1]	Guinée-Bissau
Guyana	2015-05	18.5	30.8	30.0	31.3	30.4	31.9	31.9	31.9	34.8[1]	Guyana
Haiti	2015-10	3.6	3.6	4.1	4.2	0.0	2.6	2.5	2.5	2.5[1,4]	Haïti
Honduras	2017-11	9.4	5.5	18.0	25.8	25.8	25.8	21.1	21.1	21.1[1]	Honduras
Hungary	2018-04	8.3	9.1	11.1	10.1	10.1	10.1	10.1	12.6	12.1[1]	Hongrie
Iceland	2017-10	34.9	30.2	42.9	41.3	41.3	47.6	38.1	38.1	38.1[1]	Islande
India	2019-05	9.0	8.3	10.8	12.0	12.0	11.8	11.8	12.6	14.4[1]	Inde
Indonesia	2019-04	8.0	11.3	18.0	17.1	17.1	19.8	19.8	18.2	20.4[1]	Indonésie
Iran (Islamic Republic of)	2016-04	4.9	4.1	2.8	3.1	3.1	5.9	5.9	5.9	5.9[1]	Iran (Rép. islamique d')
Iraq	2018-05	6.4	...	25.5	26.5	26.5	25.3	25.3	25.2	26.4[1]	Iraq
Ireland	2016-02	12.0	13.3	13.9	16.3	16.3	22.2	22.2	22.2	20.9[1]	Irlande
Israel	2019-09	11.7	15.0	19.2	22.5	26.7	27.5	27.5	29.2	23.3[1]	Israël
Italy	2018-03	11.1	11.5	21.3	31.0	31.0	31.0	31.0	35.7	35.7[1]	Italie
Jamaica	2016-02	13.3	11.7	13.3	12.7	12.7	17.5	17.5	17.5	17.5[1]	Jamaïque

Proportion of seats held by women in national parliament *(continued)*
Percentage, as of January each year

Proportion de sièges occupés par les femmes au parlement national *(suite)*
Pourcentage, données disponibles en janvier de chaque année

Region, country or area[&]	Last Election date Dernière date de l'élection	2000	2005	2010	2015	2016	2017	2018	2019	2020	Région, pays ou zone[&]
Japan	2017-10	4.6	7.1	11.3	9.5	9.5	9.3	10.1	10.2	9.9[1]	Japon
Jordan	2016-09	0.0	5.5	6.4	12.0	12.0	15.4	15.4	15.4	15.4[1]	Jordanie
Kazakhstan	2016-03	10.4	10.4	17.8	26.2	26.2	27.1	27.1	27.1	27.1[1]	Kazakhstan
Kenya	2017-08	3.6	7.1	9.8	19.7	19.7	19.4	21.8	21.8	21.8[1]	Kenya
Kiribati	2016-01	4.9	4.8	4.3	8.7	6.5	6.5	6.5	6.5	6.5[1]	Kiribati
Kuwait	2016-11	0.0	0.0	7.7	1.5	1.5	3.1	3.1	4.6	6.4[1]	Koweït
Kyrgyzstan	2015-10	1.4	10.0	25.6	23.3	19.2	19.2	19.2	19.2	19.2[1]	Kirghizistan
Lao People's Dem. Rep.	2016-03	21.2	22.9	25.2	25.0	25.0	27.5	27.5	27.5	27.5[1]	Rép. dém. populaire lao
Latvia	2018-10	17.0	21.0	22.0	18.0	18.0	16.0	16.0	31.0	30.0[1]	Lettonie
Lebanon	2018-05	2.3	2.3	3.1	3.1	3.1	3.1	3.1	4.7	4.7[1]	Liban
Lesotho	2017-06	3.8	11.7	24.2	26.7	25.0	25.0	22.1	23.3	23.3[1]	Lesotho
Liberia	2017-10	7.8	5.3	12.5	11.0	11.0	12.3	9.9	12.3	12.3[1]	Libéria
Libya	2014-06	...	...	7.7	16.0	16.0	16.0	16.0	16.0	16.0[1]	Libye
Liechtenstein	2017-02	4.0	12.0	24.0	20.0	20.0	12.0	12.0	12.0	12.0[1]	Liechtenstein
Lithuania	2016-10	17.5	22.0	19.1	23.4	23.4	21.3	21.3	21.3	24.1[1]	Lituanie
Luxembourg	2018-10	16.7	23.3	20.0	28.3	28.3	28.3	28.3	25.0	30.0[1]	Luxembourg
Madagascar	2019-05	8.0	6.9	...	20.5	20.5	19.2	19.2	19.2	15.9[1]	Madagascar
Malawi	2019-05	8.3	14.0	20.8	16.7	16.7	16.7	16.7	16.7	22.9[1]	Malawi
Malaysia	2018-05	7.3	9.1	9.9	10.4	10.4	10.4	10.4	14.4	14.4[1]	Malaisie
Maldives	2019-04	6.0	12.0	6.5	5.9	5.9	5.9	5.9	4.7	4.6[1]	Maldives
Mali	2013-12	12.2	10.2	10.2	9.5	8.8	8.8	8.8	8.8	9.5[1]	Mali
Malta	2017-06	9.2	9.2	8.7	12.9	12.9	12.5	11.9	11.9	13.4[1]	Malte
Marshall Islands	2019-11	3.0	3.0	3.0	3.0	9.1	9.1	9.1	9.1	6.1[1]	Îles Marshall
Mauritania	2018-09	3.8	3.7	22.1	25.2	25.2	25.2	25.2	20.3	20.3[1]	Mauritanie
Mauritius	2019-11	7.6	5.7	17.1	11.6	11.6	11.6	11.6	11.6	20.0[1]	Maurice
Mexico	2018-07	18.2	22.6	27.6	38.0	42.4	42.6	42.6	48.2	48.2[1]	Mexique
Micronesia (Fed. States of)	2019-03	0.0	0.0	0.0	0.0	0.0	0.0	0.0	0.0	0.0[1]	Micronésie (États féd. de)
Monaco	2018-02	22.2	20.8	26.1	20.8	20.8	20.8	20.8	33.3	33.3[1]	Monaco
Mongolia	2016-06	7.9	6.8	3.9	14.9	14.5	17.1	17.1	17.1	17.3[1]	Mongolie
Montenegro	2016-10	...	...	11.1	17.3	17.3	23.5	23.5	23.5	29.6[1]	Monténégro
Morocco	2016-10	0.6	10.8	10.5	17.0	17.0	20.5	20.5	20.5	20.5[1]	Maroc
Mozambique	2019-10	30.0	34.8	39.2	39.6	39.6	39.6	39.6	39.6	41.2[1]	Mozambique
Myanmar	2015-11	...	...	...	6.2	9.9	10.2	10.2	11.3	11.1[1]	Myanmar
Namibia	2019-11	22.2	25.0	26.9	41.3	41.3	41.3	46.2	46.2	42.7[1,5]	Namibie
Nauru	2019-08	0.0	0.0	0.0	5.3	5.3	10.5	10.5	10.5	10.5[1]	Nauru
Nepal	2017-12	5.9	...	33.2	29.5	29.5	29.6	32.7[6]	32.7	32.7[1]	Népal
Netherlands	2017-03	36.0	36.7	42.0	37.3	37.3	38.0	36.0	31.3	33.3[1]	Pays-Bas
New Zealand	2017-09	29.2	28.3	33.6	31.4	31.4	34.2	38.3	40.0	40.8[1]	Nouvelle-Zélande
Nicaragua	2016-11	9.7	20.7	20.7	39.1	41.3	45.7	45.7	44.6	47.3[1]	Nicaragua
Niger	2016-02	1.2	12.4	9.7	13.3	13.3	17.0	17.0	17.0	17.0[1]	Niger
Nigeria	2019-02	...	4.7	7.0	6.7	5.6	5.6	5.6	5.6	3.4[1]	Nigéria
North Macedonia	2016-12	7.5	19.2	32.5	33.3	33.3	31.7	37.5	38.3	40.0[1]	Macédoine du Nord
Norway	2017-09	36.4	38.2	39.6	39.6	39.6	39.6	41.4	40.8	41.4[1]	Norvège
Oman	2019-10	...	2.4	0.0	1.2	1.2	1.2	1.2	1.2	2.3[1]	Oman
Pakistan	2018-07	...	21.3	22.2	20.7	20.6	20.6	20.6	20.2	20.2[1]	Pakistan
Palau	2016-11	0.0	0.0	0.0	0.0	0.0	12.5	12.5	12.5	12.5[1]	Palaos
Panama	2019-05	9.7	16.7	8.5	19.3	18.3	18.3	18.3	18.3	22.5[1]	Panama
Papua New Guinea	2017-07	1.8	0.9	0.9	2.7	2.7	2.7	0.0	0.0	0.0[1]	Papouasie-Nvl-Guinée
Paraguay	2018-04	2.5	10.0	12.5	15.0	15.0	13.8	13.8	15.0	16.3[1]	Paraguay
Peru	2016-04	10.8	18.3	27.5	22.3	22.3	27.7	27.7	30.0	30.0[1,7]	Pérou
Philippines	2019-05	12.4	15.3	21.0	27.2	27.2	29.5	29.5	29.5	28.0[1]	Philippines
Poland	2019-10	13.0	20.2	20.0	24.1	27.4	28.0	28.0	29.1	28.7[1]	Pologne
Portugal	2019-10	18.7	19.1	27.4	31.3	34.8	34.8	34.8	35.7	40.0[1]	Portugal
Qatar	2016-06	...	...	0.0	0.0	0.0	0.0	0.0	9.8	9.8[1]	Qatar
Republic of Korea	2016-04	3.7	13.0	14.7	16.3	16.3	17.0	17.0	17.1	17.3[1]	République de Corée
Republic of Moldova	2019-02	8.9	15.8	23.8	20.8	21.8	22.8	22.8	22.8	24.8[1]	République de Moldova
Romania	2016-12	7.3	11.4	11.4	13.7	13.7	20.7	20.7	20.7	21.9[1]	Roumanie
Russian Federation	2016-09	7.7	9.8	14.0	13.6	13.6	15.8	15.8	15.8	15.8[1]	Fédération de Russie
Rwanda	2018-09	17.1	48.8	56.3	63.8	63.8	61.3	61.3	61.3	61.3[1]	Rwanda

Proportion of seats held by women in national parliament *(continued)*
Percentage, as of January each year

Proportion de sièges occupés par les femmes au parlement national *(suite)*
Pourcentage, données disponibles en janvier de chaque année

Region, country or area[&]	Last Election date Dernière date de l'élection	2000	2005	2010	2015	2016	2017	2018	2019	2020	Région, pays ou zone[&]
Saint Kitts and Nevis	2015-02	13.3	0.0	6.7	6.7	13.3	13.3	13.3	13.3	20.0[1]	Saint-Kitts-et-Nevis
Saint Lucia	2016-06	11.1	11.1	11.1	16.7	16.7	16.7	16.7	16.7	16.7[1]	Sainte-Lucie
Saint Vincent & Grenadines	2015-12	4.8	22.7	21.7	13.0	13.0	13.0	13.0	13.0	13.0[1]	Saint-Vincent-Grenadines
Samoa	2016-03	8.2	6.1	8.2	6.1	6.1	10.0	10.0	10.0	10.0[1]	Samoa
San Marino	2019-12	13.3	16.7	16.7	16.7	16.7	26.7	26.7	25.0	31.7[1]	Saint-Marin
Sao Tome and Principe	2018-10	9.1	9.1	7.3	18.2	18.2	18.2	18.2	14.5	14.6[1]	Sao Tomé-et-Principe
Saudi Arabia	2016-12	...	0.0	0.0	19.9	19.9	19.9	19.9	19.9	19.9[1]	Arabie saoudite
Senegal	2017-07	12.1	19.2	22.7	42.7	42.7	42.7	41.8	41.8	43.0[1]	Sénégal
Serbia	2016-04	...	...	21.6	34.0	34.0	34.4	34.4	37.7	37.7[1]	Serbie
Serbia and Monten. [former]		5.1	7.9	...	...	...	...	...	...	...	Serbie-et-Monténégro [anc.]
Seychelles	2016-09	23.5	29.4	23.5	43.8	43.8	21.2	21.2	21.2	21.2[1]	Seychelles
Sierra Leone	2018-03	8.8	14.5	13.2	12.4	12.4	12.4	12.4	12.3	12.3[1]	Sierra Leone
Singapore	2015-09	4.3	16.0	23.4	25.3	23.1	23.8	23.0	23.0	24.0[1]	Singapour
Slovakia	2016-03	12.7	16.7	18.0	18.7	18.7	20.0	20.0	20.0	20.7[1]	Slovaquie
Slovenia	2018-06	7.8	12.2	14.4	36.7	36.7	36.7	36.7	24.4	27.8[1]	Slovénie
Solomon Islands	2019-04	2.0	0.0	0.0	2.0	2.0	2.0	2.0	2.0	6.1[1]	Îles Salomon
Somalia	2017-02	...	...	6.9	13.8	13.8	24.2	24.4	24.4	24.4[1]	Somalie
South Africa	2019-05	30.0	32.8	44.5	41.5	42.0	42.2	42.4	42.7	46.4[1]	Afrique du Sud
South Sudan	2016-08	...	...	...	26.5	26.5	28.5	28.5	28.5	28.5[1]	Soudan du sud
Spain	2019-11	21.6	36.0	36.6	41.1	40.0	39.1	39.1	41.1	44.0[1]	Espagne
Sri Lanka	2015-08	4.9	4.9	5.8	5.8	5.8	5.8	5.8	5.3	5.3[1]	Sri Lanka
Sudan		...	...	...	24.3	30.5	30.5	30.5	27.7	...	Soudan
Sudan [former]		8.8	9.7	18.9	...	...	...	...	...	...	Soudan [anc.]
Suriname	2015-05	15.7	19.6	25.5	11.8	25.5	25.5	25.5	29.4	31.4[1]	Suriname
Sweden	2018-09	42.7	45.3	46.4	43.6	43.6	43.6	43.6	47.3	47.0[1]	Suède
Switzerland	2019-10	22.5	25.0	29.0	30.5	32.0	32.5	32.5	32.5	41.5[1]	Suisse
Syrian Arab Republic	2016-04	10.4	12.0	12.4	12.4	12.4	13.2	13.2	13.2	12.4[1]	République arabe syrienne
Tajikistan	2015-03	2.8	12.7	17.5	16.9	19.0	19.0	19.0	19.0	19.1[1]	Tadjikistan
Thailand	2019-03	5.6	8.8	13.3	6.1	6.1	4.9	4.8	5.4	16.2[1]	Thaïlande
Timor-Leste	2018-05	...	25.3	29.2	38.5	38.5	38.5	32.3	40.0	38.5[1]	Timor-Leste
Togo	2018-12	4.9	6.2	11.1	17.6	17.6	17.6	17.6	16.5	18.7[1]	Togo
Tonga	2017-11	0.0	0.0	3.1	0.0	0.0	3.8	7.4	7.4	7.4[1]	Tonga
Trinidad and Tobago	2015-09	11.1	19.4	26.8	28.6	31.0	31.0	31.0	31.0	31.0[1]	Trinité-et-Tobago
Tunisia	2019-10	11.5	22.8	27.6	31.3	31.3	31.3	31.3	35.9	24.9[1]	Tunisie
Turkey	2018-06	4.2	4.4	9.1	14.4	14.9	14.9	14.6	17.4	17.3[1]	Turquie
Turkmenistan	2018-03	26.0	...	16.8	25.8	25.8	25.8	25.8	25.0	25.0[1]	Turkménistan
Tuvalu	2019-09	0.0	0.0	0.0	6.7	6.7	6.7	6.7	6.7	6.3[1]	Tuvalu
Uganda	2016-02	17.9	23.9	31.5	35.0	35.0	34.3	34.3	34.9	34.9[1]	Ouganda
Ukraine	2019-07	7.8	5.3	8.0	11.8	12.1	12.3	12.3	11.6	20.8[1]	Ukraine
United Arab Emirates	2019-10	0.0	0.0	22.5	17.5	22.5	20.0	22.5	22.5	50.0[1]	Émirats arabes unis
United Kingdom	2019-12	18.4	18.1	19.5	22.8	29.4	30.0	32.0	32.0	33.9[1]	Royaume-Uni
United Rep. of Tanzania	2015-10	22.2	21.4	30.7	36.0	36.6	36.4	37.2	36.9	36.9[1]	Rép.-Unie de Tanzanie
United States of America	2018-11	13.3	14.9	16.8	19.4	19.4	19.1	19.5	23.6	23.4[1,8]	États-Unis d'Amérique
Uruguay	2019-10	12.1	12.1	14.1	13.1	16.2	20.2	20.2	22.2	21.2[1]	Uruguay
Uzbekistan	2015-01	6.8	17.5	22.0	16.0	16.0	16.0	16.0	16.0	32.0[1]	Ouzbékistan
Vanuatu	2016-01	0.0	3.8	3.8	0.0	0.0	0.0	0.0	0.0	0.0[1]	Vanuatu
Venezuela (Boliv. Rep. of)	2015-12	12.1	9.7	17.5	17.0	14.4	22.2	22.2	22.2	22.2[1]	Venezuela (Rép. boliv. du)
Viet Nam	2016-05	26.0	27.3	25.8	24.3	24.3	26.7	26.7	26.7	26.7[1]	Viet Nam
Yemen	2003-04	0.7	0.3	0.3	0.3	0.0	0.0	0.0	0.3	0.3[1,9]	Yémen
Zambia	2016-08	10.1	12.0	14.0	12.7	12.7	18.0	18.0	18.0	16.8[1]	Zambie
Zimbabwe	2018-07	14.0	10.0	15.0	31.5	31.5	32.6	33.2	31.9	31.9[1]	Zimbabwe
LDC[§]		9.3	13.1	19.3	21.7	22.8	23.2	22.1	22.9	23.1[1]	PMA[§]

4

Proportion of seats held by women in national parliament *(continued)*
Percentage, as of January each year

Proportion de sièges occupés par les femmes au parlement national *(suite)*
Pourcentage, données disponibles en janvier de chaque année

Source:

Inter-Parliamentary Union (IPU), Geneva, the database on "Women in National Parliament", last accessed March 2020.

& Data prior to 2019 is reported as of February 1st of the reported year.

1 Data are as at 1 January of reporting year.
2 The statistics refer to the situation before the 2019 election, which itself was invalidated. Fresh elections are expected in May 2020.
3 The figures correspond to the results of the December 2019 elections. They do not include 9 members to be appointed by the President and 2 ex officio members (the Speaker and the Attorney General).
4 The term of all members in the 119-member Chamber of Deputies and 20 of 30 senators expired on 13 January 2020. There are currently only 10 sitting senators.
5 The figures on the National Assembly correspond to the provisional results of the November 2019 elections, excluding members yet to be appointed. Newly elected members are due to be sworn in March 2020.
6 Data as of 7 Feb 2018. Only the partial results (http://archive.ipu.org/wmn-e/arc/classif010118.htm) of most recent Napali elections were available on Feb 1. Complete results were released on 7 Feb 2018.
7 The figures correspond to the situation prior to the dissolution of Parliament in September 2019. New elections were held in January 2020 (final results are still pending).
8 Total refers to all voting members of the House of Representatives.

9 Data corresponds to the composition of the House of Representatives elected in 2003, and of the Consultative Council appointed in 2001.

Source:

Union interparlementaire, Genève, base des données des « Les femmes dans les parlements nationaux », dernier accès mars 2020.

& Les données antérieures à 2019 sont publiées au 1er février de l'année considérée.

1 Les données sont au 1er janvier de l'année de référence.
2 Les statistiques se réfèrent à la situation avant les élections de 2019, elle-même invalidée. De nouvelles élections sont attendues en mai 2020.
3 Les chiffres correspondent aux résultats des élections de décembre 2019. Ils ne comprennent pas 9 membres nommés par le président et 2 membres d'office (le président et le procureur général).
4 Le mandat de tous les membres de la Chambre des députés de 119 membres et de 20 des 30 sénateurs a expiré le 13 janvier 2020. Il n'y a actuellement que 10 sénateurs en fonction.
5 Les chiffres sur l'Assemblée nationale correspondent aux résultats provisoires des élections de novembre 2019, à l'exclusion des membres non encore nommés. Les membres nouvellement élus doivent prêter serment en mars 2020.
6 Données au 7 février 2018. Seuls les résultats partiels (http://archive.ipu.org/wmn-e/arc/classif010118.htm) des dernières élections napaliaises étaient disponibles le 1er février. Les résultats complets ont été publiés le 7 février. 2018.
7 The figures correspond to the situation prior to the dissolution of Parliament in September 2019. New elections were held in January 2020 (final results are still pending).
8 Total fait référence à tous les membres votants de la Chambre des représentants.

9 Les données correspondent à la composition de la Chambre des représentants élue en 2003 et du Conseil consultatif nommé en 2001.

5

Ratio of girls to boys in primary, secondary and tertiary education

Rapport filles/garçons dans l'enseignement primaire, secondaire et supérieur

Region, country or area	1995	2005	2010	2015	2016	2017	2018	Région, pays ou zone
Total, all countries or areas								**Total, tous pays ou zones**
Primary education	0.91	0.95	0.97	1.00	1.01	1.01	* 1.00	Enseignement primaire
Secondary education	0.88	0.95	0.97	0.99	0.99	0.99	* 0.99	Enseignement secondaire
Tertiary education	* 0.95	1.05	1.08	1.12	1.12	1.13	* 1.14	Enseignement supérieur
Northern Africa								**Afrique septentrionale**
Primary education	0.86	0.93	0.95	* 0.97	0.97	0.97	0.97	Enseignement primaire
Secondary education	0.86	* 0.99	0.98	* 0.99	0.99	1.00	* 1.00	Enseignement secondaire
Tertiary education	* 0.76	0.96	1.07	1.10	1.15	1.14	* 1.17	Enseignement supérieur
Sub-Saharan Africa								**Afrique subsaharienne**
Primary education	0.84	0.88	0.93	0.96	0.96	* 0.96	* 0.96	Enseignement primaire
Secondary education	* 0.80	0.78	0.82	0.86	* 0.87	* 0.88	* 0.88	Enseignement secondaire
Tertiary education	* 0.59	0.67	0.67	* 0.72	* 0.73	* 0.73	* 0.74	Enseignement supérieur
Northern America								**Amérique septentrionale**
Primary education	0.99	0.99	0.99	1.00	1.00	0.99	* 1.00	Enseignement primaire
Secondary education	1.01	1.01	1.01	1.01	1.00	1.00	* 1.00	Enseignement secondaire
Tertiary education	1.28	1.42	1.39	1.35	1.34	1.36	* 1.36	Enseignement supérieur
Latin America & the Caribbean								**Amérique latine et Caraïbes**
Primary education	0.97	0.97	0.97	0.98	0.98	0.98	* 0.98	Enseignement primaire
Secondary education	* 1.07	1.07	1.08	1.06	1.05	1.04	* 1.04	Enseignement secondaire
Tertiary education	* 1.07	1.21	1.29	1.29	1.30	1.30	* 1.30	Enseignement supérieur
Central Asia								**Asie centrale**
Primary education	0.98	0.99	0.99	0.99	0.99	0.99	0.99	Enseignement primaire
Secondary education	* 1.00	0.96	0.98	0.99	0.98	0.98	* 0.98	Enseignement secondaire
Tertiary education	* 0.96	1.03	1.00	1.01	0.99	0.98	1.00	Enseignement supérieur
Eastern Asia								**Asie orientale**
Primary education	0.95	* 1.00	0.99	1.00	1.00	1.01	1.01	Enseignement primaire
Secondary education	0.89	* 0.98	1.00	1.02	1.02	1.02	1.02	Enseignement secondaire
Tertiary education	* 0.64	0.86	1.00	...	1.14	1.15	1.16	Enseignement supérieur
South-eastern Asia								**Asie du Sud-Est**
Primary education	0.97	0.97	1.00	0.97	0.98	0.98	* 0.98	Enseignement primaire
Secondary education	* 0.93	1.00	1.01	1.00	1.02	1.02	* 1.03	Enseignement secondaire
Tertiary education	0.95	* 1.00	1.07	1.18	1.22	1.23	* 1.23	Enseignement supérieur
Southern Asia								**Asie méridionale**
Primary education	0.82	* 0.96	1.00	1.06	1.09	1.08	* 1.07	Enseignement primaire
Secondary education	0.67	0.86	0.93	1.00	1.00	1.00	* 1.00	Enseignement secondaire
Tertiary education	0.54	0.75	0.77	0.96	0.96	0.98	1.00	Enseignement supérieur
Western Asia								**Asie occidentale**
Primary education	0.88	0.91	0.93	* 0.94	0.94	* 0.94	* 0.94	Enseignement primaire
Secondary education	0.75	0.86	0.90	* 0.91	* 0.91	* 0.90	* 0.90	Enseignement secondaire
Tertiary education	0.77	0.90	0.94	0.97	0.96	0.96	* 0.97	Enseignement supérieur
Europe								**Europe**
Primary education	0.99	0.99	0.99	1.00	1.00	1.00	* 1.00	Enseignement primaire
Secondary education	1.02	1.00	0.99	1.00	1.00	0.99	* 0.99	Enseignement secondaire
Tertiary education	1.14	1.28	1.29	1.23	1.22	1.22	* 1.22	Enseignement supérieur
Oceania								**Océanie**
Primary education	0.97	0.98	0.97	0.97	0.97	0.97	* 0.97	Enseignement primaire
Secondary education	0.99	* 0.97	* 0.93	0.89	0.88	0.90	* 0.90	Enseignement secondaire
Tertiary education	1.06	* 1.24	* 1.35	1.42	1.42	1.41	* 1.41	Enseignement supérieur
Afghanistan								**Afghanistan**
Primary education	0.52	0.58	0.68	0.68	0.68	0.68	0.67	Enseignement primaire
Secondary education	0.38	0.33	0.50	0.56	0.57	* 0.57	0.57	Enseignement secondaire
Tertiary education	...	...	...	...	...	...	0.35	Enseignement supérieur
Albania								**Albanie**
Primary education	0.97	1.01	1.01	1.03	1.04	1.03	1.04	Enseignement primaire
Secondary education	0.99	0.97	1.01	0.96	0.97	0.99	1.01	Enseignement secondaire
Tertiary education	1.07	1.45	1.36	1.43	1.47	1.53	1.57	Enseignement supérieur
Algeria								**Algérie**
Primary education	0.88	0.93	0.94	0.95	0.95	0.95	0.96	Enseignement primaire
Secondary education	0.89	1.10	1.04	...	...	...	...	Enseignement secondaire
Tertiary education	...	1.28	1.44	1.56	1.67	1.49	1.66	Enseignement supérieur
Angola								**Angola**
Primary education	...	...	0.80	0.87	...	...	...	Enseignement primaire
Secondary education	...	...	0.68	...	0.64	...	...	Enseignement secondaire
Tertiary education	...	...	...	0.79	0.83	...	...	Enseignement supérieur

Region, country or area	1995	2005	2010	2015	2016	2017	2018	Région, pays ou zone
Anguilla								**Anguilla**
Primary education	...	1.02	0.96	...	...	...	...	Enseignement primaire
Secondary education	...	0.99	0.99	...	...	...	...	Enseignement secondaire
Tertiary education	...	3.00	...	...	...	...	...	Enseignement supérieur
Antigua and Barbuda								**Antigua-et-Barbuda**
Primary education	...	...	0.92	0.97	...	0.98	0.99	Enseignement primaire
Secondary education	...	...	1.05	1.02	...	0.97	0.96	Enseignement secondaire
Tertiary education	...	...	2.68	...	...	...	...	Enseignement supérieur
Argentina								**Argentine**
Primary education	...	0.99	0.99	1.00	1.00	1.00	...	Enseignement primaire
Secondary education	...	1.09	1.10	1.06	1.05	1.04	...	Enseignement secondaire
Tertiary education	...	1.44	1.49	1.63	1.66	1.66	...	Enseignement supérieur
Armenia								**Arménie**
Primary education	1.02	1.02	1.03	1.02	1.01	1.00	1.00	Enseignement primaire
Secondary education	...	...	0.98	1.05	...	...	1.04	Enseignement secondaire
Tertiary education	...	1.40	1.22	1.19	1.27	1.27	1.33	Enseignement supérieur
Aruba								**Aruba**
Primary education	...	0.94	0.99	...	...	...	...	Enseignement primaire
Secondary education	...	1.00	1.05	...	...	...	...	Enseignement secondaire
Tertiary education	...	1.44	1.41	2.26	1.94	...	...	Enseignement supérieur
Australia								**Australie**
Primary education	1.00	1.02	1.00	1.00	1.00	1.00	...	Enseignement primaire
Secondary education	1.00	...	...	0.87	0.87	0.89	...	Enseignement secondaire
Tertiary education	1.04	...	...	1.44	1.43	1.42	...	Enseignement supérieur
Austria								**Autriche**
Primary education	0.99	1.00	0.99	0.99	0.99	1.00	...	Enseignement primaire
Secondary education	0.94	0.95	0.96	0.96	0.96	0.96	...	Enseignement secondaire
Tertiary education	0.94	...	...	1.19	1.19	1.18	...	Enseignement supérieur
Azerbaijan								**Azerbaïdjan**
Primary education	1.12	* 0.95	* 0.99	* 0.98	* 0.99	* 1.02	* 1.01	Enseignement primaire
Secondary education	1.02	...	...	...	...	...	* 1.00	Enseignement secondaire
Tertiary education	0.88	...	* 0.99	* 1.16	* 1.18	* 1.15	* 1.15	Enseignement supérieur
Bahamas								**Bahamas**
Primary education	1.00	0.97	0.98	0.97	1.01	...	1.00	Enseignement primaire
Secondary education	1.00	0.99	1.04	1.01	1.02	1.02	1.06	Enseignement secondaire
Tertiary education	2.71	...	...	...	...	...	...	Enseignement supérieur
Bahrain								**Bahreïn**
Primary education	1.01	1.04	...	1.01	1.02	1.00	0.99	Enseignement primaire
Secondary education	1.04	1.11	1.01	0.99	1.01	1.04	1.06	Enseignement secondaire
Tertiary education	1.62	3.06	...	1.92	1.87	1.89	1.83	Enseignement supérieur
Bangladesh								**Bangladesh**
Primary education	...	1.05	* 1.06	...	...	1.07	1.07	Enseignement primaire
Secondary education	...	1.07	1.12	1.13	1.10	1.17	1.16	Enseignement secondaire
Tertiary education	...	0.52	...	...	0.70	0.70	0.71	Enseignement supérieur
Barbados								**Barbade**
Primary education	...	1.00	* 1.02	0.99	1.00	0.97	0.96	Enseignement primaire
Secondary education	...	0.99	* 1.00	1.04	1.05	1.04	1.04	Enseignement secondaire
Tertiary education	...	...	2.18	...	...	...	...	Enseignement supérieur
Belarus								**Bélarus**
Primary education	0.96	0.97	1.00	1.00	1.00	0.99	1.00	Enseignement primaire
Secondary education	...	...	0.97	0.98	0.98	0.98	0.99	Enseignement secondaire
Tertiary education	...	1.37	* 1.45	1.33	1.29	1.24	1.19	Enseignement supérieur
Belgium								**Belgique**
Primary education	0.99	1.00	1.00	1.00	1.00	1.00	...	Enseignement primaire
Secondary education	1.08	1.12	1.14	1.14	1.12	1.12	...	Enseignement secondaire
Tertiary education	1.02	1.25	1.27	1.31	1.30	1.31	...	Enseignement supérieur
Belize								**Belize**
Primary education	0.96	0.96	0.96	0.95	0.95	0.95	0.95	Enseignement primaire
Secondary education	1.03	1.03	1.08	1.03	1.02	1.05	1.04	Enseignement secondaire
Tertiary education	...	1.58	1.60	1.61	1.62	1.62	...	Enseignement supérieur
Benin								**Bénin**
Primary education	0.57	0.79	0.89	0.93	0.94	0.94	0.94	Enseignement primaire
Secondary education	...	...	...	0.71	0.76	...	...	Enseignement secondaire
Tertiary education	0.21	...	0.35	0.40	0.42	0.44	...	Enseignement supérieur

Ratio of girls to boys in primary, secondary and tertiary education *(continued)*

Rapport filles/garçons dans l'enseignement primaire, secondaire et supérieur *(suite)*

Region, country or area	1995	2005	2010	2015	2016	2017	2018	Région, pays ou zone
Bermuda								**Bermudes**
Primary education	0.99	1.05	...	0.98	...	...	...	Enseignement primaire
Secondary education	...	1.13	1.18	1.12	...	...	...	Enseignement secondaire
Tertiary education	...	...	2.06	2.31	...	1.68	1.50	Enseignement supérieur
Bhutan								**Bhoutan**
Primary education	0.78	0.97	1.02	1.01	1.00	1.00	1.00	Enseignement primaire
Secondary education	...	0.92	1.04	1.07	1.11	1.12	* 1.13	Enseignement secondaire
Tertiary education	...	0.61	0.62	...	...	...	0.99	Enseignement supérieur
Bolivia (Plurin. State of)								**Bolivie (État plurin. de)**
Primary education	0.97	1.00	0.99	0.98	0.98	0.99	0.99	Enseignement primaire
Secondary education	...	0.95	1.00	0.99	0.98	0.98	0.98	Enseignement secondaire
Botswana								**Botswana**
Primary education	1.02	0.99	...	0.98	...	...	...	Enseignement primaire
Secondary education	1.08	1.03	...	...	...	...	...	Enseignement secondaire
Tertiary education	0.83	0.86	...	1.34	1.42	1.43	...	Enseignement supérieur
Brazil								**Brésil**
Primary education	...	* 0.94	...	* 0.96	* 0.97	* 0.97	...	Enseignement primaire
Secondary education	...	* 1.10	...	* 1.06	* 1.05	* 1.03	...	Enseignement secondaire
Tertiary education	...	* 1.29	...	* 1.34	* 1.38	* 1.37	...	Enseignement supérieur
British Virgin Islands								**Îles Vierges britanniques**
Primary education	1.00	0.96	...	0.94	0.95	0.96	...	Enseignement primaire
Secondary education	...	1.12	1.02	1.09	1.11	1.11	...	Enseignement secondaire
Tertiary education	...	...	...	1.79	1.59	...	1.80	Enseignement supérieur
Brunei Darussalam								**Brunéi Darussalam**
Primary education	0.95	0.96	1.00	1.00	1.00	1.00	1.01	Enseignement primaire
Secondary education	...	0.99	1.01	1.02	1.03	1.03	1.02	Enseignement secondaire
Tertiary education	...	1.99	1.87	1.71	1.66	1.62	1.56	Enseignement supérieur
Bulgaria								**Bulgarie**
Primary education	0.99	0.99	1.00	0.99	0.99	0.99	...	Enseignement primaire
Secondary education	1.00	0.96	0.96	0.97	0.97	0.97	...	Enseignement secondaire
Tertiary education	1.60	1.16	1.32	1.28	1.24	1.24	...	Enseignement supérieur
Burkina Faso								**Burkina Faso**
Primary education	0.66	0.80	0.91	0.97	0.98	0.98	0.98	Enseignement primaire
Secondary education	...	0.71	0.76	0.92	0.95	0.97	1.00	Enseignement secondaire
Tertiary education	0.28	0.45	0.48	0.52	0.51	0.52	0.58	Enseignement supérieur
Burundi								**Burundi**
Primary education	0.80	0.86	0.99	1.03	1.02	1.02	1.01	Enseignement primaire
Secondary education	...	* 0.74	0.72	0.94	0.99	1.05	1.11	Enseignement secondaire
Tertiary education	...	* 0.38	0.54	...	0.43	0.45	...	Enseignement supérieur
Cabo Verde								**Cabo Verde**
Primary education	...	0.96	0.93	0.93	0.93	0.93	0.93	Enseignement primaire
Secondary education	...	1.13	1.19	1.12	1.10	1.10	1.10	Enseignement secondaire
Tertiary education	...	1.07	1.29	1.46	1.50	1.50	1.49	Enseignement supérieur
Cambodia								**Cambodge**
Primary education	0.82	0.93	0.94	0.99	0.97	0.98	0.98	Enseignement primaire
Tertiary education	0.19	0.46	0.60	0.82	...	0.87	0.90	Enseignement supérieur
Cameroon								**Cameroun**
Primary education	0.90	* 0.84	0.86	0.90	0.90	0.90	0.90	Enseignement primaire
Secondary education	0.69	0.79	...	0.86	0.86	...	...	Enseignement secondaire
Tertiary education	...	* 0.66	0.81	0.80	0.88	0.81	...	Enseignement supérieur
Canada								**Canada**
Primary education	0.99	0.99	1.01	1.01	1.00	1.00	...	Enseignement primaire
Secondary education	1.00	0.98	0.98	1.01	1.02	1.01	...	Enseignement secondaire
Tertiary education	1.17	...	* 1.38	* 1.34	* 1.34	* 1.34	...	Enseignement supérieur
Central African Republic								**République centrafricaine**
Primary education	...	0.70	0.73	...	0.78	...	...	Enseignement primaire
Secondary education	...	...	...	...	0.65	0.67	...	Enseignement secondaire
Tertiary education	...	...	0.32	...	...	...	...	Enseignement supérieur
Chad								**Tchad**
Primary education	0.49	0.68	0.73	0.77	0.77	...	...	Enseignement primaire
Secondary education	0.24	* 0.35	0.42	0.45	0.46	...	...	Enseignement secondaire
Tertiary education	...	0.06	* 0.17	0.29	...	...	...	Enseignement supérieur
Chile								**Chili**
Primary education	...	0.96	0.97	0.97	0.97	0.97	...	Enseignement primaire
Secondary education	...	1.01	1.03	1.01	1.01	1.00	...	Enseignement secondaire
Tertiary education	0.86	0.96	1.07	1.11	1.13	1.15	...	Enseignement supérieur

Ratio of girls to boys in primary, secondary and tertiary education *(continued)*

Rapport filles/garçons dans l'enseignement primaire, secondaire et supérieur *(suite)*

Region, country or area	1995	2005	2010	2015	2016	2017	2018	Région, pays ou zone
China [1]								**Chine [1]**
Primary education	0.95	...	0.98	1.00	1.01	1.01	1.01	Enseignement primaire
Secondary education	0.85	...	1.00	...	...	...	...	Enseignement secondaire
Tertiary education	...	0.90	1.06	1.19	1.20	1.21	1.22	Enseignement supérieur
China, Hong Kong SAR								**Chine, RAS de Hong Kong**
Primary education	1.01	...	...	1.02	1.03	1.04	1.04	Enseignement primaire
Secondary education	...	1.01	1.00	0.98	0.98	0.97	0.97	Enseignement secondaire
Tertiary education	...	1.01	* 1.00	1.13	1.15	1.12	1.11	Enseignement supérieur
China, Macao SAR								**Chine, RAS de Macao**
Primary education	...	0.94	0.98	0.98	0.99	0.99	0.99	Enseignement primaire
Secondary education	...	0.93	0.97	0.99	1.00	1.00	1.00	Enseignement secondaire
Tertiary education	...	0.67	0.96	1.30	1.33	1.31	1.35	Enseignement supérieur
Colombia								**Colombie**
Primary education	0.99	0.98	0.98	0.97	0.97	0.97	0.97	Enseignement primaire
Secondary education	1.15	1.11	1.10	1.07	1.07	1.06	1.05	Enseignement secondaire
Tertiary education	1.01	1.08	1.10	1.17	1.16	1.17	1.17	Enseignement supérieur
Comoros								**Comores**
Primary education	...	...	...	...	...	0.96	1.00	Enseignement primaire
Secondary education	...	...	...	...	...	1.06	1.07	Enseignement secondaire
Tertiary education	...	...	0.74	...	...	...	...	Enseignement supérieur
Congo								**Congo**
Primary education	0.85	0.93	0.95	...	...	...	...	Enseignement primaire
Tertiary education	...	...	...	...	...	0.67	...	Enseignement supérieur
Cook Islands								**Îles Cook**
Primary education	...	0.99	0.95	0.96	0.98	...	...	Enseignement primaire
Secondary education	...	1.05	1.10	1.06	1.04	...	...	Enseignement secondaire
Costa Rica								**Costa Rica**
Primary education	0.99	0.97	0.98	0.99	1.01	1.01	1.01	Enseignement primaire
Secondary education	1.08	1.04	1.04	1.04	1.05	1.07	1.08	Enseignement secondaire
Tertiary education	...	...	...	1.31	1.24	1.25	1.21	Enseignement supérieur
Côte d'Ivoire								**Côte d'Ivoire**
Primary education	0.73	...	...	0.88	0.90	0.91	0.93	Enseignement primaire
Secondary education	...	...	...	0.70	0.72	0.74	0.77	Enseignement secondaire
Tertiary education	0.34	...	0.51	0.65	0.68	0.69	...	Enseignement supérieur
Croatia								**Croatie**
Primary education	1.00	1.00	1.00	1.00	1.00	1.00	...	Enseignement primaire
Secondary education	1.04	1.03	1.07	1.05	1.05	1.05	...	Enseignement secondaire
Tertiary education	1.01	1.21	1.34	1.35	1.38	1.37	...	Enseignement supérieur
Cuba								**Cuba**
Primary education	0.99	0.97	0.98	0.94	0.95	0.95	0.96	Enseignement primaire
Secondary education	1.12	1.02	1.00	1.02	1.03	1.02	1.02	Enseignement secondaire
Tertiary education	1.46	* 1.69	1.64	1.41	1.41	1.69	1.58	Enseignement supérieur
Cyprus								**Chypre**
Primary education	1.00	* 1.00	* 1.00	* 1.00	* 1.00	* 1.00	...	Enseignement primaire
Secondary education	* 1.01	* 1.02	* 1.01	* 0.99	* 0.99	* 0.98	...	Enseignement secondaire
Tertiary education	* 1.27	* 1.13	* 0.90	* 1.36	* 1.21	* 1.18	...	Enseignement supérieur
Czechia								**Tchéquie**
Primary education	1.00	0.99	1.00	1.00	1.01	1.01	...	Enseignement primaire
Secondary education	1.03	1.02	1.01	1.01	1.01	1.01	...	Enseignement secondaire
Tertiary education	0.96	1.16	1.40	1.41	1.41	1.41	...	Enseignement supérieur
Dem. People's Rep. Korea								**Rép. pop. dém. de Corée**
Primary education	...	...	...	1.00	...	...	1.00	Enseignement primaire
Secondary education	...	...	...	1.01	...	...	...	Enseignement secondaire
Tertiary education	...	...	...	0.55	...	...	0.51	Enseignement supérieur
Dem. Rep. of the Congo								**Rép. dém. du Congo**
Primary education	0.69	...	0.87	0.99	...	...	...	Enseignement primaire
Secondary education	0.61	...	0.58	0.64	...	...	...	Enseignement secondaire
Tertiary education	...	...	...	...	0.56	...	...	Enseignement supérieur
Denmark								**Danemark**
Primary education	1.00	1.00	1.00	0.99	0.99	0.99	...	Enseignement primaire
Secondary education	1.03	1.04	1.01	1.05	1.03	1.01	...	Enseignement secondaire
Tertiary education	1.12	1.38	1.45	1.40	1.36	1.37	...	Enseignement supérieur
Djibouti								**Djibouti**
Primary education	0.78	0.82	...	1.07	1.07	1.06	1.02	Enseignement primaire
Secondary education	0.69	0.66	...	0.95	0.97	0.99	1.00	Enseignement secondaire
Tertiary education	...	0.72	0.75	...	...	...	...	Enseignement supérieur

Region, country or area	1995	2005	2010	2015	2016	2017	2018	Région, pays ou zone
Dominica								**Dominique**
Primary education	1.15	1.00	0.98	0.98	0.97	...	...	Enseignement primaire
Secondary education	...	1.08	1.09	0.99	...	...	...	Enseignement secondaire
Dominican Republic								**République dominicaine**
Primary education	...	* 0.95	* 0.88	* 0.91	* 0.92	* 0.93	* 0.94	Enseignement primaire
Secondary education	...	* 1.19	* 1.12	* 1.10	* 1.09	* 1.09	* 1.08	Enseignement secondaire
Tertiary education	...	...	...	* 1.83	* 1.79	* 1.79	...	Enseignement supérieur
Ecuador								**Équateur**
Primary education	1.00	1.00	1.00	1.00	1.01	1.01	1.02	Enseignement primaire
Secondary education	...	1.01	1.05	1.04	1.03	1.03	1.03	Enseignement secondaire
Tertiary education	...	...	...	1.17	...	...	...	Enseignement supérieur
Egypt								**Égypte**
Primary education	0.89	0.95	0.97	...	1.00	1.00	1.00	Enseignement primaire
Secondary education	0.88	...	0.97	...	0.98	0.98	0.99	Enseignement secondaire
Tertiary education	...	0.84	0.92	0.96	1.02	1.03	...	Enseignement supérieur
El Salvador								**El Salvador**
Primary education	0.98	0.97	0.95	0.96	0.96	0.97	0.97	Enseignement primaire
Secondary education	...	1.00	0.99	1.01	1.00	0.99	0.99	Enseignement secondaire
Tertiary education	0.97	1.12	1.11	1.11	1.12	1.12	1.13	Enseignement supérieur
Equatorial Guinea								**Guinée équatoriale**
Primary education	...	0.97	0.99	0.99	...	...	...	Enseignement primaire
Secondary education	...	0.74	...	...	...	...	...	Enseignement secondaire
Eritrea								**Érythrée**
Primary education	0.81	0.81	0.85	0.86	...	0.86	0.86	Enseignement primaire
Secondary education	0.72	0.60	0.77	0.85	...	0.90	0.91	Enseignement secondaire
Tertiary education	0.16	...	0.38	0.65	0.71	...	...	Enseignement supérieur
Estonia								**Estonie**
Primary education	0.97	0.97	0.99	1.00	1.00	1.00	...	Enseignement primaire
Secondary education	1.12	1.04	1.00	1.00	1.01	1.02	...	Enseignement secondaire
Tertiary education	1.10	1.68	1.66	1.52	1.51	1.53	...	Enseignement supérieur
Eswatini								**Eswatini**
Primary education	0.98	0.93	0.91	0.91	0.92	0.92	...	Enseignement primaire
Secondary education	...	0.96	0.95	1.00	0.99	...	...	Enseignement secondaire
Tertiary education	...	0.96	...	...	...	...	...	Enseignement supérieur
Ethiopia								**Éthiopie**
Primary education	0.60	0.84	0.92	0.91	...	...	...	Enseignement primaire
Secondary education	0.80	0.60	0.83	0.96	...	...	...	Enseignement secondaire
Tertiary education	0.26	0.32	0.43	...	...	...	...	Enseignement supérieur
Fiji								**Fidji**
Primary education	1.00	...	...	0.98	0.98	...	...	Enseignement primaire
Tertiary education	...	* 1.19	...	...	...	...	...	Enseignement supérieur
Finland								**Finlande**
Primary education	1.00	0.99	0.99	0.99	1.00	0.99	...	Enseignement primaire
Secondary education	1.15	1.05	1.05	1.10	1.10	1.10	...	Enseignement secondaire
Tertiary education	1.17	1.21	1.22	1.20	1.19	1.18	...	Enseignement supérieur
France								**France**
Primary education	0.98	* 0.99	* 0.99	* 0.99	* 0.99	* 0.99	...	Enseignement primaire
Secondary education	0.99	* 1.00	* 1.01	* 1.01	* 1.01	* 1.01	...	Enseignement secondaire
Tertiary education	1.25	* 1.25	* 1.26	* 1.24	* 1.24	* 1.24	...	Enseignement supérieur
French Guiana								**Guyane française**
Primary education	0.97	...	...	...	...	...	...	Enseignement primaire
Secondary education	1.04	...	...	...	...	...	...	Enseignement secondaire
French Polynesia								**Polynésie française**
Primary education	0.96	...	...	...	...	...	...	Enseignement primaire
Gabon								**Gabon**
Primary education	1.00	...	...	...	...	...	...	Enseignement primaire
Secondary education	0.84	...	...	...	...	...	...	Enseignement secondaire
Gambia								**Gambie**
Primary education	0.75	1.03	1.03	1.07	1.08	1.08	1.09	Enseignement primaire
Secondary education	0.56	...	* 0.96	...	...	...	...	Enseignement secondaire
Tertiary education	0.55	...	0.70	...	...	...	...	Enseignement supérieur
Georgia								**Géorgie**
Primary education	0.99	1.04	1.01	1.00	1.00	1.01	1.01	Enseignement primaire
Secondary education	0.94	1.04	...	1.03	1.02	1.01	1.01	Enseignement secondaire
Tertiary education	1.31	1.08	1.31	1.24	1.16	1.14	1.11	Enseignement supérieur

5 Ratio of girls to boys in primary, secondary and tertiary education *(continued)*

Rapport filles/garçons dans l'enseignement primaire, secondaire et supérieur *(suite)*

Region, country or area	1995	2005	2010	2015	2016	2017	2018	Région, pays ou zone
Germany								**Allemagne**
Primary education	0.99	1.00	0.99	1.00	1.00	1.00	...	Enseignement primaire
Secondary education	0.96	0.97	0.95	0.95	0.95	0.94	...	Enseignement secondaire
Tertiary education	0.80	...	...	0.98	1.00	1.01	...	Enseignement supérieur
Ghana								**Ghana**
Primary education	0.90	0.96	...	1.00	1.01	1.01	1.01	Enseignement primaire
Secondary education	0.73	* 0.84	...	0.95	0.97	0.97	0.99	Enseignement secondaire
Tertiary education	...	0.56	...	0.70	0.72	0.73	0.77	Enseignement supérieur
Gibraltar								**Gibraltar**
Primary education	...	...	...	...	0.99	1.00	...	Enseignement primaire
Secondary education	...	...	...	...	0.98	0.97	...	Enseignement secondaire
Greece								**Grèce**
Primary education	1.02	0.98	0.98	0.99	1.00	1.00	...	Enseignement primaire
Secondary education	1.01	0.95	0.97	0.93	0.94	0.94	...	Enseignement secondaire
Tertiary education	1.05	1.11	1.07	...	1.02	1.01	...	Enseignement supérieur
Grenada								**Grenade**
Primary education	0.92	0.97	0.96	0.96	0.97	0.95	0.98	Enseignement primaire
Secondary education	...	* 1.03	1.03	0.98	1.02	1.04	1.03	Enseignement secondaire
Tertiary education	...	...	...	1.15	1.27	1.22	1.25	Enseignement supérieur
Guadeloupe								**Guadeloupe**
Secondary education	1.09							Enseignement secondaire
Guatemala								**Guatemala**
Primary education	0.87	0.94	0.98	0.97	0.97	0.97	0.97	Enseignement primaire
Secondary education	...	0.92	0.94	0.94	0.95	0.95	0.95	Enseignement secondaire
Tertiary education	...	...	...	1.18	...	...	...	Enseignement supérieur
Guinea								**Guinée**
Primary education	0.51	0.80	0.82	...	0.82	...	...	Enseignement primaire
Secondary education	...	* 0.49	...	...	...	...	...	Enseignement secondaire
Tertiary education	...	0.21	0.31	...	...	...	...	Enseignement supérieur
Guinea-Bissau								**Guinée-Bissau**
Primary education	0.57	...	0.93	...	...	...	...	Enseignement primaire
Guyana								**Guyana**
Primary education	0.97	1.00	0.97	...	...	...	...	Enseignement primaire
Secondary education	...	1.02	1.04	...	...	...	...	Enseignement secondaire
Tertiary education	0.89	2.13	2.36	...	...	...	...	Enseignement supérieur
Haiti								**Haïti**
Primary education	0.95	...	...	...	...	...	...	Enseignement primaire
Honduras								**Honduras**
Primary education	1.01	1.00	1.00	0.99	1.00	1.00	...	Enseignement primaire
Secondary education	...	...	1.23	1.20	1.17	1.15	...	Enseignement secondaire
Tertiary education	...	...	1.16	1.37	1.38	1.36	1.37	Enseignement supérieur
Hungary								**Hongrie**
Primary education	0.99	0.98	0.99	1.00	1.00	0.99	...	Enseignement primaire
Secondary education	1.04	0.99	0.99	1.01	0.99	1.00	...	Enseignement secondaire
Tertiary education	1.13	1.46	1.36	1.26	1.25	1.24	...	Enseignement supérieur
Iceland								**Islande**
Primary education	1.00	0.98	1.01	1.00	1.00	1.00	...	Enseignement primaire
Secondary education	0.97	1.01	1.02	1.01	1.00	0.99	...	Enseignement secondaire
Tertiary education	1.40	1.92	1.79	1.79	1.87	1.87	...	Enseignement supérieur
India								**Inde**
Primary education	0.83	...	* 1.03	1.12	1.16	1.15	...	Enseignement primaire
Secondary education	0.65	* 0.84	0.94	1.02	1.02	* 1.02	* 1.04	Enseignement secondaire
Tertiary education	0.57	0.72	0.74	1.00	1.02	1.04	1.07	Enseignement supérieur
Indonesia								**Indonésie**
Primary education	0.97	* 0.97	1.03	0.97	0.97	0.97	0.97	Enseignement primaire
Secondary education	0.86	* 0.99	1.01	1.00	1.03	1.02	1.03	Enseignement secondaire
Tertiary education	0.63	...	0.88	1.11	1.13	1.15	1.16	Enseignement supérieur
Iran (Islamic Republic of)								**Iran (Rép. islamique d')**
Primary education	0.92	0.97	0.98	1.06	1.07	1.06	...	Enseignement primaire
Secondary education	0.84	0.96	0.94	0.94	0.95	0.96	...	Enseignement secondaire
Tertiary education	...	1.06	1.00	...	0.86	0.86	...	Enseignement supérieur
Iraq								**Iraq**
Tertiary education	...	* 0.60	...	...	...	...	...	Enseignement supérieur

Region, country or area	1995	2005	2010	2015	2016	2017	2018	Région, pays ou zone
Ireland								**Irlande**
Primary education	1.00	* 1.00	* 1.00	* 1.00	* 0.99	* 1.00	...	Enseignement primaire
Secondary education	1.06	* 1.09	* 1.06	* 1.03	* 1.03	* 0.98	...	Enseignement secondaire
Tertiary education	1.02	* 1.24	* 1.08	* 1.09	* 1.11	* 1.11	...	Enseignement supérieur
Israel								**Israël**
Primary education	...	1.01	1.00	1.01	1.01	1.01	...	Enseignement primaire
Secondary education	...	0.99	1.02	1.01	1.02	1.02	...	Enseignement secondaire
Tertiary education	...	1.33	1.29	1.38	1.40	1.41	...	Enseignement supérieur
Italy								**Italie**
Primary education	0.99	0.99	0.99	1.00	1.00	0.97	...	Enseignement primaire
Secondary education	1.00	0.99	0.99	1.00	1.00	0.99	...	Enseignement secondaire
Tertiary education	1.14	1.37	1.43	1.37	1.36	1.35	...	Enseignement supérieur
Jamaica								**Jamaïque**
Primary education	...	...	...	1.06	0.99	0.98	0.96	Enseignement primaire
Secondary education	...	1.06	1.08	1.07	1.05	1.05	1.03	Enseignement secondaire
Tertiary education	...	...	2.31	1.75	...	...	...	Enseignement supérieur
Jordan								**Jordanie**
Primary education	1.01	1.01	0.98	...	0.98	0.98	0.98	Enseignement primaire
Secondary education	...	1.03	1.04	...	...	1.03	1.03	Enseignement secondaire
Tertiary education	...	1.09	1.14	1.09	1.07	1.14	1.19	Enseignement supérieur
Kazakhstan								**Kazakhstan**
Primary education	1.01	1.00	1.01	1.00	1.00	1.02	1.02	Enseignement primaire
Secondary education	...	...	1.01	1.03	1.03	1.01	1.01	Enseignement secondaire
Tertiary education	1.29	...	1.27	1.28	1.24	1.26	1.25	Enseignement supérieur
Kenya								**Kenya**
Primary education	0.98	0.96	...	1.00	1.00	...	...	Enseignement primaire
Secondary education	...	* 0.94	...	...	...	...	...	Enseignement secondaire
Tertiary education	...	* 0.59	...	0.71	0.70	0.74	...	Enseignement supérieur
Kiribati								**Kiribati**
Primary education	1.03	1.01	...	1.02	1.02	1.07	...	Enseignement primaire
Secondary education	1.24	1.15	...	...	...	...	...	Enseignement secondaire
Kuwait								**Koweït**
Primary education	1.01	1.04	0.98	1.03	1.04	1.03	1.10	Enseignement primaire
Secondary education	1.06	* 1.09	1.02	1.06	...	...	...	Enseignement secondaire
Tertiary education	...	...	...	...	2.22	...	...	Enseignement supérieur
Kyrgyzstan								**Kirghizistan**
Primary education	1.02	0.98	0.99	0.99	0.99	0.99	0.99	Enseignement primaire
Secondary education	...	1.00	1.00	1.01	1.00	1.00	1.00	Enseignement secondaire
Tertiary education	1.26	1.26	1.30	1.31	1.28	1.24	1.30	Enseignement supérieur
Lao People's Dem. Rep.								**Rép. dém. populaire lao**
Primary education	0.81	0.87	0.91	0.95	0.95	0.96	0.96	Enseignement primaire
Secondary education	0.66	0.75	0.82	0.92	0.92	0.93	* 0.93	Enseignement secondaire
Tertiary education	0.41	0.70	0.76	0.95	0.99	1.04	1.08	Enseignement supérieur
Latvia								**Lettonie**
Primary education	0.97	* 0.98	* 0.98	* 1.00	* 1.00	* 1.00	...	Enseignement primaire
Secondary education	1.07	* 0.99	* 0.99	* 0.98	* 0.99	* 0.99	...	Enseignement secondaire
Tertiary education	...	* 1.79	* 1.75	* 1.56	* 1.53	* 1.46	...	Enseignement supérieur
Lesotho								**Lesotho**
Primary education	1.11	0.99	0.96	0.95	0.95	0.95	...	Enseignement primaire
Secondary education	...	1.26	1.39	1.35	1.35	1.35	...	Enseignement secondaire
Tertiary education	1.17	1.27	...	1.50	...	1.62	1.55	Enseignement supérieur
Liberia								**Libéria**
Primary education	...	...	...	0.90	0.99	0.99	...	Enseignement primaire
Secondary education	...	...	...	0.77	...	...	...	Enseignement secondaire
Tertiary education	...	...	0.53	...	...	...	...	Enseignement supérieur
Libya								**Libye**
Primary education	...	0.99	...	...	...	...	...	Enseignement primaire
Secondary education	...	* 1.19	...	...	...	...	...	Enseignement secondaire
Liechtenstein								**Liechtenstein**
Primary education	...	0.92	* 0.94	* 0.98	* 0.96	* 0.97	...	Enseignement primaire
Secondary education	...	0.87	* 0.85	* 0.78	* 0.78	* 0.81	...	Enseignement secondaire
Tertiary education	...	0.40	* 0.62	* 0.49	* 0.55	* 0.63	...	Enseignement supérieur
Lithuania								**Lituanie**
Primary education	0.97	* 0.99	* 0.99	* 1.00	* 1.00	* 1.00	...	Enseignement primaire
Secondary education	1.05	* 0.99	* 0.98	* 0.96	* 0.96	* 0.96	...	Enseignement secondaire
Tertiary education	1.44	* 1.56	* 1.51	* 1.44	* 1.37	* 1.37	...	Enseignement supérieur

Region, country or area	1995	2005	2010	2015	2016	2017	2018	Région, pays ou zone
Luxembourg								**Luxembourg**
Primary education	...	1.00	1.01	1.00	1.00	0.99	...	Enseignement primaire
Secondary education	1.01	1.05	1.03	1.04	1.03	1.02	...	Enseignement secondaire
Tertiary education	...	...	1.11	1.11	1.11	1.11	...	Enseignement supérieur
Madagascar								**Madagascar**
Primary education	1.04	0.96	0.98	1.00	1.00	...	1.01	Enseignement primaire
Secondary education	...	* 0.96	...	* 0.99	0.99	1.01	1.03	Enseignement secondaire
Tertiary education	0.83	0.89	0.91	0.90	0.92	0.93	0.95	Enseignement supérieur
Malawi								**Malawi**
Primary education	0.90	1.01	1.02	1.02	1.03	1.03	1.01	Enseignement primaire
Secondary education	0.67	0.79	0.88	* 0.91	0.89	0.94	0.98	Enseignement secondaire
Tertiary education	0.42	* 0.53	0.59	...	...	...	...	Enseignement supérieur
Malaysia								**Malaisie**
Primary education	1.00	1.00	1.01	1.01	1.01	1.01	...	Enseignement primaire
Secondary education	1.09	1.10	1.08	1.09	1.07	1.06	1.08	Enseignement secondaire
Tertiary education	...	1.32	1.37	1.30	1.17	1.16	1.23	Enseignement supérieur
Maldives								**Maldives**
Primary education	0.97	0.98	...	0.97	1.00	1.02	...	Enseignement primaire
Secondary education	1.05	...	...	...	...	...	...	Enseignement secondaire
Tertiary education	...	...	...	...	...	3.60	...	Enseignement supérieur
Mali								**Mali**
Primary education	0.69	0.79	0.86	0.90	0.88	0.89	0.90	Enseignement primaire
Secondary education	0.49	* 0.62	0.69	0.79	0.74	0.81	0.82	Enseignement secondaire
Tertiary education	0.18	...	0.41	0.42	0.45	0.42	...	Enseignement supérieur
Malta								**Malte**
Primary education	0.97	0.98	1.00	1.01	1.02	1.00	...	Enseignement primaire
Secondary education	0.94	0.96	0.89	1.06	1.04	1.00	...	Enseignement secondaire
Tertiary education	0.98	1.34	1.34	1.38	1.37	1.37	...	Enseignement supérieur
Marshall Islands								**Îles Marshall**
Primary education	...	1.25	...	0.98	1.00	...	...	Enseignement primaire
Secondary education	...	1.02	...	1.07	1.07	...	...	Enseignement secondaire
Martinique								**Martinique**
Primary education	0.98	...	...	...	...	...	...	Enseignement primaire
Secondary education	1.06	...	...	...	...	...	...	Enseignement secondaire
Mauritania								**Mauritanie**
Primary education	0.84	1.03	1.05	1.05	1.06	1.07	1.06	Enseignement primaire
Secondary education	0.57	0.88	* 0.85	0.93	0.97	1.00	1.02	Enseignement secondaire
Tertiary education	0.21	0.33	0.40	0.50	0.51	0.50	...	Enseignement supérieur
Mauritius								**Maurice**
Primary education	1.00	1.00	1.01	1.02	1.02	1.02	1.03	Enseignement primaire
Secondary education	...	* 0.98	* 1.05	1.04	1.05	1.07	1.06	Enseignement secondaire
Tertiary education	1.00	* 1.03	1.21	1.31	1.29	1.40	...	Enseignement supérieur
Mexico								**Mexique**
Primary education	0.97	0.98	0.99	1.00	1.00	1.00	...	Enseignement primaire
Secondary education	0.97	1.04	1.08	1.07	1.07	1.08	...	Enseignement secondaire
Tertiary education	0.83	0.98	0.98	0.98	1.01	1.02	...	Enseignement supérieur
Micronesia (Féd. States of)								**Micronésie (États féd. de)**
Primary education	...	0.97	...	0.98	...	...	...	Enseignement primaire
Secondary education	...	1.08	...	...	...	...	...	Enseignement secondaire
Mongolia								**Mongolie**
Primary education	1.03	1.00	0.98	0.98	0.98	0.98	0.98	Enseignement primaire
Secondary education	1.33	1.11	1.07	...	...	...	...	Enseignement secondaire
Tertiary education	...	1.65	1.53	1.37	1.38	1.42	1.40	Enseignement supérieur
Montenegro								**Monténégro**
Primary education	...	1.02	1.00	1.00	0.99	1.00	0.95	Enseignement primaire
Secondary education	...	1.03	1.03	1.02	1.02	1.01	1.01	Enseignement secondaire
Tertiary education	...	1.58	1.26	...	1.27	1.30	1.35	Enseignement supérieur
Montserrat								**Montserrat**
Primary education	0.97	0.93	...	...	1.03	1.18	1.10	Enseignement primaire
Secondary education	...	1.05	...	...	1.00	1.08	1.12	Enseignement secondaire
Tertiary education	...	...	6.21	...	...	...	...	Enseignement supérieur
Morocco								**Maroc**
Primary education	0.74	0.91	0.94	0.95	0.95	0.96	0.96	Enseignement primaire
Secondary education	0.74	0.85	0.87	...	...	0.89	0.92	Enseignement secondaire
Tertiary education	0.71	0.80	0.90	0.96	0.93	0.97	0.99	Enseignement supérieur

Region, country or area	1995	2005	2010	2015	2016	2017	2018	Région, pays ou zone
Mozambique								**Mozambique**
Primary education	0.71	0.83	0.89	* 0.91	0.92	0.93	0.93	Enseignement primaire
Secondary education	0.61	0.68	0.80	* 0.91	...	0.89	...	Enseignement secondaire
Tertiary education	0.30	0.48	0.65	0.72	0.78	0.80	0.81	Enseignement supérieur
Myanmar								**Myanmar**
Primary education	0.94	1.00	0.99	...	0.97	0.95	0.96	Enseignement primaire
Secondary education	...	0.96	1.05	...	1.09	1.09	1.09	Enseignement secondaire
Tertiary education	1.57	...	...	...	...	...	1.41	Enseignement supérieur
Namibia								**Namibie**
Primary education	0.98	0.98	0.96	...	...	0.96	0.97	Enseignement primaire
Secondary education	1.15	1.11	...	...	...	...	...	Enseignement secondaire
Tertiary education	1.51	0.85	...	1.73	1.73	1.98	...	Enseignement supérieur
Nauru								**Nauru**
Primary education	...	0.94	...	...	0.95	...	...	Enseignement primaire
Secondary education	...	1.03	...	...	1.02	...	...	Enseignement secondaire
Nepal								**Népal**
Primary education	0.69	0.91	1.08	1.06	1.05	1.02	...	Enseignement primaire
Secondary education	0.59	* 0.81	* 0.98	* 1.05	* 1.06	* 1.07	...	Enseignement secondaire
Tertiary education	...	0.54	0.64	0.94	0.98	1.01	1.07	Enseignement supérieur
Netherlands								**Pays-Bas**
Primary education	0.98	0.98	1.00	1.00	1.00	1.00	...	Enseignement primaire
Secondary education	0.95	0.98	0.99	1.02	1.02	1.01	...	Enseignement secondaire
Tertiary education	0.93	1.08	1.12	1.14	1.13	1.15	...	Enseignement supérieur
New Zealand								**Nouvelle-Zélande**
Primary education	1.00	0.99	1.00	1.01	1.01	1.00	...	Enseignement primaire
Secondary education	0.98	1.06	1.05	1.06	1.06	1.06	...	Enseignement secondaire
Tertiary education	1.25	...	...	1.41	1.41	1.43	...	Enseignement supérieur
Nicaragua								**Nicaragua**
Primary education	1.04	0.99	0.99	...	...	...	...	Enseignement primaire
Secondary education	...	1.16	1.13	...	...	...	...	Enseignement secondaire
Tertiary education	1.05	...	...	...	...	...	...	Enseignement supérieur
Niger								**Niger**
Primary education	0.62	0.72	0.81	0.85	0.85	0.87	...	Enseignement primaire
Secondary education	...	0.63	0.70	0.74	0.75	0.75	...	Enseignement secondaire
Tertiary education	...	0.36	0.40	0.48	0.56	0.49	0.41	Enseignement supérieur
Nigeria								**Nigéria**
Primary education	0.83	0.84	* 0.91	...	0.94	...	...	Enseignement primaire
Secondary education	...	0.83	0.87	0.92	0.90	...	...	Enseignement secondaire
Tertiary education	...	0.71	0.74	...	...	...	...	Enseignement supérieur
Niue								**Nioué**
Primary education	...	0.97	...	1.00	1.00	...	...	Enseignement primaire
Secondary education	...	1.10	...	1.22	...	...	...	Enseignement secondaire
North Macedonia								**Macédoine du Nord**
Primary education	0.99	0.98	0.99	1.00	...	1.00	...	Enseignement primaire
Secondary education	0.99	0.97	0.97	0.98	...	0.97	...	Enseignement secondaire
Tertiary education	1.23	1.38	1.16	1.25	...	1.32	...	Enseignement supérieur
Norway								**Norvège**
Primary education	1.00	1.00	1.00	1.00	1.00	1.00	...	Enseignement primaire
Secondary education	0.95	1.01	0.98	0.98	0.97	0.96	...	Enseignement secondaire
Tertiary education	1.25	1.52	1.62	1.46	1.48	1.49	...	Enseignement supérieur
Oman								**Oman**
Primary education	0.99	0.99	...	1.04	1.03	1.05	1.10	Enseignement primaire
Secondary education	0.95	0.96	...	0.98	0.94	0.94	0.92	Enseignement secondaire
Tertiary education	1.18	1.07	1.44	1.91	1.85	2.04	2.11	Enseignement supérieur
Pakistan								**Pakistan**
Primary education	...	0.77	0.85	0.86	0.85	0.86	0.84	Enseignement primaire
Secondary education	...	...	0.77	0.79	0.81	0.81	0.85	Enseignement secondaire
Tertiary education	...	0.87	...	0.87	0.87	0.87	0.87	Enseignement supérieur
Panama								**Panama**
Primary education	...	0.97	0.96	0.98	0.98	0.98	...	Enseignement primaire
Secondary education	...	1.07	1.06	1.05	1.03	1.06	...	Enseignement secondaire
Tertiary education	...	1.64	1.53	1.57	1.57	...	...	Enseignement supérieur
Papua New Guinea								**Papouasie-Nvl-Guinée**
Primary education	0.87	0.85	...	...	0.91	...	...	Enseignement primaire
Secondary education	0.68	...	...	...	0.73	...	...	Enseignement secondaire
Tertiary education	0.47	...	...	...	...	...	...	Enseignement supérieur

5 Ratio of girls to boys in primary, secondary and tertiary education *(continued)*

Rapport filles/garçons dans l'enseignement primaire, secondaire et supérieur *(suite)*

Region, country or area	1995	2005	2010	2015	2016	2017	2018	Région, pays ou zone
Paraguay								**Paraguay**
Primary education	0.98	0.98	0.97	...	...	...	...	Enseignement primaire
Secondary education	1.08	1.04	1.06	...	...	...	...	Enseignement secondaire
Tertiary education	...	1.14	1.43	...	...	...	...	Enseignement supérieur
Peru								**Pérou**
Primary education	0.98	1.00	1.00	1.00	0.99	0.97	0.97	Enseignement primaire
Secondary education	0.95	0.99	1.03	1.00	0.97	0.96	0.95	Enseignement secondaire
Tertiary education	...	1.04	...	...	1.07	1.06	...	Enseignement supérieur
Philippines								**Philippines**
Primary education	0.99	0.99	...	0.97	0.97	0.96	...	Enseignement primaire
Secondary education	...	1.12	...	1.08	1.09	1.11	...	Enseignement secondaire
Tertiary education	1.37	1.23	1.25	...	...	1.31	...	Enseignement supérieur
Poland								**Pologne**
Primary education	0.99	0.99	0.99	...	...	1.00	...	Enseignement primaire
Secondary education	1.01	0.99	0.99	0.96	0.97	0.97	...	Enseignement secondaire
Tertiary education	1.41	1.41	1.52	1.52	1.51	1.51	...	Enseignement supérieur
Portugal								**Portugal**
Primary education	0.95	0.95	0.97	0.96	0.96	0.97	...	Enseignement primaire
Secondary education	1.08	1.10	1.03	0.97	0.97	0.98	...	Enseignement secondaire
Tertiary education	1.34	1.31	1.18	1.13	1.12	1.13	...	Enseignement supérieur
Puerto Rico								**Porto Rico**
Primary education	...	...	1.04	1.00	1.00	...	...	Enseignement primaire
Secondary education	...	...	1.06	1.08	1.09	...	...	Enseignement secondaire
Tertiary education	...	...	1.48	1.44	1.46	...	...	Enseignement supérieur
Qatar								**Qatar**
Primary education	0.99	0.96	1.03	1.01	0.99	1.00	1.01	Enseignement primaire
Secondary education	0.97	0.92	0.95	...	...	...	...	Enseignement secondaire
Tertiary education	5.60	* 3.48	5.89	7.06	7.45	7.73	7.82	Enseignement supérieur
Republic of Korea								**République de Corée**
Primary education	1.03	0.99	1.00	1.00	1.00	1.00	...	Enseignement primaire
Secondary education	1.00	1.02	0.99	0.99	0.99	0.99	...	Enseignement secondaire
Tertiary education	0.57	0.64	0.74	0.78	0.79	0.79	...	Enseignement supérieur
Republic of Moldova								**République de Moldova**
Primary education	0.99	* 0.99	* 1.00	* 0.99	* 0.99	* 1.00	* 1.00	Enseignement primaire
Secondary education	1.04	* 1.04	* 1.02	* 1.01	* 1.00	* 0.99	* 0.99	Enseignement secondaire
Tertiary education	1.15	* 1.46	* 1.34	* 1.34	* 1.34	* 1.31	* 1.34	Enseignement supérieur
Réunion								**Réunion**
Secondary education	1.03	...	...	...	...	...	...	Enseignement secondaire
Romania								**Roumanie**
Primary education	1.00	0.99	0.98	0.99	0.99	0.99	...	Enseignement primaire
Secondary education	1.03	1.02	0.99	1.00	1.00	1.00	...	Enseignement secondaire
Tertiary education	0.94	1.26	1.37	1.25	1.27	1.27	...	Enseignement supérieur
Russian Federation								**Fédération de Russie**
Primary education	0.99	1.00	...	1.01	1.01	1.00	...	Enseignement primaire
Secondary education	...	0.99	...	0.98	0.98	0.98	...	Enseignement secondaire
Tertiary education	...	1.37	...	1.20	1.19	1.19	...	Enseignement supérieur
Rwanda								**Rwanda**
Primary education	...	1.01	1.03	1.01	1.00	0.99	0.99	Enseignement primaire
Secondary education	...	0.89	1.00	1.09	1.10	1.12	1.12	Enseignement secondaire
Tertiary education	...	...	0.78	0.79	0.77	0.90	0.81	Enseignement supérieur
Saint Helena								**Sainte-Hélène**
Secondary education	* 0.99	...	...	...	...	...	...	Enseignement secondaire
Saint Kitts and Nevis								**Saint-Kitts-et-Nevis**
Primary education	1.03	0.99	0.95	0.99	0.97	...	...	Enseignement primaire
Secondary education	...	* 1.11	* 0.98	0.99	1.03	...	...	Enseignement secondaire
Tertiary education	...	...	...	2.01	...	...	...	Enseignement supérieur
Saint Lucia								**Sainte-Lucie**
Primary education	...	0.96	...	0.97	0.97	0.99	1.01	Enseignement primaire
Secondary education	...	1.18	0.99	0.99	1.01	1.01	1.00	Enseignement secondaire
Tertiary education	...	2.72	2.58	1.90	1.95	2.00	1.98	Enseignement supérieur
Saint Pierre and Miquelon								**Saint-Pierre-et-Miquelon**
Secondary education	* 1.16	...	...	...	...	...	...	Enseignement secondaire
Saint Vincent & Grenadines								**Saint-Vincent-Grenadines**
Primary education	...	0.90	0.95	0.99	0.99	0.98	0.99	Enseignement primaire
Secondary education	...	1.25	1.05	1.01	1.03	1.00	1.03	Enseignement secondaire
Tertiary education	...	...	...	1.67	...	...	...	Enseignement supérieur

Region, country or area	1995	2005	2010	2015	2016	2017	2018	Région, pays ou zone
Samoa								**Samoa**
Primary education	1.03	1.01	0.99	1.00	1.01	1.00	1.00	Enseignement primaire
Secondary education	1.12	1.13	1.14	1.11	1.10	...	...	Enseignement secondaire
San Marino								**Saint-Marin**
Primary education	...	...	1.13	...	...	...	1.16	Enseignement primaire
Secondary education	...	...	1.03	...	...	...	0.89	Enseignement secondaire
Tertiary education	...	...	1.50	...	...	...	0.74	Enseignement supérieur
Sao Tome and Principe								**Sao Tomé-et-Principe**
Primary education	...	0.96	0.99	0.96	0.96	0.97	...	Enseignement primaire
Secondary education	...	1.06	1.02	1.11	1.14	1.16	...	Enseignement secondaire
Tertiary education	...	...	0.97	1.04	...	...	...	Enseignement supérieur
Saudi Arabia								**Arabie saoudite**
Primary education	...	* 0.98	0.99	1.03	0.99	1.01	1.01	Enseignement primaire
Secondary education	...	* 0.94	...	0.98	0.92	0.90	0.94	Enseignement secondaire
Tertiary education	0.91	1.48	1.15	1.01	1.01	0.99	1.05	Enseignement supérieur
Senegal								**Sénégal**
Primary education	0.77	0.96	1.06	1.12	1.12	1.16	1.13	Enseignement primaire
Secondary education	...	0.75	0.87	...	...	1.09	1.10	Enseignement secondaire
Tertiary education	...	...	* 0.58	0.59	0.59	0.60	0.68	Enseignement supérieur
Serbia								**Serbie**
Primary education	...	* 1.01	* 1.00	* 1.00	* 1.00	* 1.00	* 1.00	Enseignement primaire
Secondary education	...	* 1.03	* 1.02	* 1.01	* 1.01	* 1.01	* 1.01	Enseignement secondaire
Tertiary education	...	* 1.30	* 1.30	* 1.33	* 1.31	* 1.35	* 1.38	Enseignement supérieur
Seychelles								**Seychelles**
Primary education	1.02	0.98	1.03	1.03	1.03	1.05	1.06	Enseignement primaire
Secondary education	1.00	1.07	* 1.06	1.07	1.11	1.12	1.07	Enseignement secondaire
Tertiary education	...	...	...	2.17	1.87	2.31	2.07	Enseignement supérieur
Sierra Leone								**Sierra Leone**
Primary education	...	...	...	1.01	1.01	1.02	1.03	Enseignement primaire
Secondary education	...	...	...	0.88	0.92	0.97	...	Enseignement secondaire
Singapore								**Singapour**
Primary education	...	...	...	...	* 1.00	* 1.00	...	Enseignement primaire
Secondary education	...	...	...	...	* 0.99	* 0.99	...	Enseignement secondaire
Tertiary education	...	...	...	...	* 1.16	* 1.16	...	Enseignement supérieur
Sint Maarten (Dutch part)								**St-Martin (partie néerland.)**
Tertiary education	...	...	...	3.39	...	...	...	Enseignement supérieur
Slovakia								**Slovaquie**
Primary education	1.00	0.99	0.99	0.99	0.99	0.99	...	Enseignement primaire
Secondary education	1.05	1.01	1.01	1.01	1.01	1.01	...	Enseignement secondaire
Tertiary education	1.00	1.29	1.55	1.54	1.52	1.53	...	Enseignement supérieur
Slovenia								**Slovénie**
Primary education	1.00	0.99	1.00	1.01	1.01	1.00	...	Enseignement primaire
Secondary education	1.04	1.00	0.99	1.01	1.03	1.02	...	Enseignement secondaire
Tertiary education	1.37	1.43	1.49	1.47	1.43	1.43	...	Enseignement supérieur
Solomon Islands								**Îles Salomon**
Primary education	...	0.95	0.98	0.99	0.99	0.99	1.00	Enseignement primaire
Secondary education	...	0.83	0.86	...	...	...	...	Enseignement secondaire
South Africa								**Afrique du Sud**
Primary education	0.99	0.97	0.96	0.93	0.97	0.97	...	Enseignement primaire
Secondary education	...	1.07	1.06	0.99	1.10	1.09	...	Enseignement secondaire
Tertiary education	...	...	...	...	1.40	1.43	...	Enseignement supérieur
South Sudan								**Soudan du sud**
Primary education	...	...	...	0.71	...	...	...	Enseignement primaire
Secondary education	...	...	...	0.54	...	...	...	Enseignement secondaire
Spain								**Espagne**
Primary education	0.98	0.99	0.99	1.02	1.02	1.02	...	Enseignement primaire
Secondary education	1.09	1.07	1.03	0.99	1.00	1.01	...	Enseignement secondaire
Tertiary education	1.16	1.23	1.24	1.19	1.20	1.20	...	Enseignement supérieur
Sri Lanka								**Sri Lanka**
Primary education	0.97	0.99	0.98	0.98	0.98	0.99	0.99	Enseignement primaire
Secondary education	1.08	...	1.01	...	1.03	1.05	1.05	Enseignement secondaire
Tertiary education	...	...	1.79	1.54	1.56	1.51	1.48	Enseignement supérieur
State of Palestine								**État de Palestine**
Primary education	0.99	0.99	0.98	1.00	1.00	1.00	1.00	Enseignement primaire
Secondary education	0.97	1.05	1.08	1.10	1.10	1.10	1.10	Enseignement secondaire
Tertiary education	...	1.02	1.34	1.57	1.59	1.62	1.57	Enseignement supérieur

Region, country or area	1995	2005	2010	2015	2016	2017	2018	Région, pays ou zone
Sudan								**Soudan**
Primary education	...	0.88	0.90	0.91	0.93	0.94	...	Enseignement primaire
Secondary education	...	0.93	0.87	0.98	0.98	1.01	...	Enseignement secondaire
Tertiary education	...	1.13	1.17	1.02	...	...	...	Enseignement supérieur
Suriname								**Suriname**
Primary education	...	0.98	1.00	1.01	1.00	1.00	1.00	Enseignement primaire
Secondary education	...	1.34	1.29	1.32	...	...	...	Enseignement secondaire
Sweden								**Suède**
Primary education	1.01	1.00	0.99	1.04	1.03	1.01	...	Enseignement primaire
Secondary education	1.15	1.00	0.99	1.14	1.12	1.07	...	Enseignement secondaire
Tertiary education	1.26	1.54	1.53	1.53	1.54	1.56	...	Enseignement supérieur
Switzerland								**Suisse**
Primary education	1.00	1.00	1.00	1.00	0.99	0.99	...	Enseignement primaire
Secondary education	0.94	0.94	0.97	0.97	0.96	0.96	...	Enseignement secondaire
Tertiary education	0.60	0.87	0.99	1.03	1.02	1.03	...	Enseignement supérieur
Syrian Arab Republic								**République arabe syrienne**
Primary education	0.91	0.97	0.97	...	...	...	...	Enseignement primaire
Secondary education	0.83	0.96	1.00	...	...	...	...	Enseignement secondaire
Tertiary education	0.72	0.90	0.86	1.10	1.14	...	...	Enseignement supérieur
Tajikistan								**Tadjikistan**
Primary education	0.97	0.97	0.98	0.99	0.99	0.99	...	Enseignement primaire
Secondary education	...	0.84	0.87	...	...	...	...	Enseignement secondaire
Tertiary education	...	0.47	0.53	0.67	0.72	0.76	...	Enseignement supérieur
Thailand								**Thaïlande**
Primary education	...	0.97	0.99	0.94	1.00	1.00	1.00	Enseignement primaire
Secondary education	...	* 1.05	1.07	0.96	1.00	0.96	0.98	Enseignement secondaire
Tertiary education	...	1.12	1.28	...	1.41	...	...	Enseignement supérieur
Timor-Leste								**Timor-Leste**
Primary education	...	0.91	0.95	0.98	0.97	0.96	0.96	Enseignement primaire
Secondary education	...	0.97	0.99	1.06	1.06	1.07	1.08	Enseignement secondaire
Tertiary education	...	...	0.72	...	...	...	...	Enseignement supérieur
Togo								**Togo**
Primary education	0.68	0.85	0.90	0.95	0.95	0.95	0.96	Enseignement primaire
Secondary education	0.35	0.53	...	...	...	0.73	...	Enseignement secondaire
Tertiary education	0.15	...	...	0.43	0.43	0.45	0.51	Enseignement supérieur
Tokelau								**Tokélaou**
Primary education	...	...	...	...	0.83	...	...	Enseignement primaire
Secondary education	...	...	...	...	0.91	...	...	Enseignement secondaire
Tonga								**Tonga**
Primary education	0.99	0.97	0.98	0.99	...	...	...	Enseignement primaire
Secondary education	...	...	1.07	1.03	...	...	...	Enseignement secondaire
Trinidad and Tobago								**Trinité-et-Tobago**
Primary education	1.00	* 0.97	0.97	...	...	...	...	Enseignement primaire
Tunisia								**Tunisie**
Primary education	0.93	0.99	1.00	1.00	1.00	1.00	0.99	Enseignement primaire
Secondary education	0.91	1.10	1.10	...	1.14	...	...	Enseignement secondaire
Tertiary education	0.78	1.24	1.55	1.66	1.73	1.80	1.81	Enseignement supérieur
Turkey								**Turquie**
Primary education	0.92	0.95	0.99	0.99	0.99	0.99	...	Enseignement primaire
Secondary education	0.65	0.83	0.92	0.97	0.98	0.95	...	Enseignement secondaire
Tertiary education	0.62	...	...	...	...	...	...	Enseignement supérieur
Tuvalu								**Tuvalu**
Primary education	...	0.97	...	0.96	0.94	...	0.92	Enseignement primaire
Secondary education	...	...	...	1.21	1.17	...	1.14	Enseignement secondaire
Uganda								**Ouganda**
Primary education	0.84	0.99	1.01	1.02	1.03	1.03	...	Enseignement primaire
Tertiary education	0.48	...	0.75	...	...	...	...	Enseignement supérieur
Ukraine								**Ukraine**
Primary education	...	1.00	1.01	...	...	...	...	Enseignement primaire
Secondary education	...	* 0.93	* 0.98	...	...	...	...	Enseignement secondaire
Tertiary education	...	1.24	1.26	...	...	...	...	Enseignement supérieur
United Arab Emirates								**Émirats arabes unis**
Primary education	0.98	...	...	1.00	0.96	0.98	...	Enseignement primaire
Secondary education	1.05	...	...	...	0.96	0.92	...	Enseignement secondaire

Region, country or area	1995	2005	2010	2015	2016	2017	2018	Région, pays ou zone
United Kingdom								**Royaume-Uni**
Primary education	...	1.00	0.99	1.00	1.00	1.00	...	Enseignement primaire
Secondary education	0.99	1.03	1.00	1.03	...	1.03	...	Enseignement secondaire
Tertiary education	1.06	1.39	1.34	1.33	1.35	1.36	...	Enseignement supérieur
United Rep. of Tanzania								**Rép.-Unie de Tanzanie**
Primary education	0.99	0.97	1.02	1.05	1.05	1.03	1.03	Enseignement primaire
Secondary education	0.81	...	0.82	0.99	1.01	1.02	1.05	Enseignement secondaire
Tertiary education	0.20	* 0.49	0.82	0.54	...	...	...	Enseignement supérieur
United States of America								**États-Unis d'Amérique**
Primary education	...	* 0.99	* 0.99	* 1.00	* 1.00	* 0.99	...	Enseignement primaire
Secondary education	...	* 1.02	* 1.01	* 1.01	* 0.99	* 0.99	...	Enseignement secondaire
Tertiary education	...	* 1.42	* 1.39	* 1.36	* 1.34	* 1.36	...	Enseignement supérieur
United States Virgin Islands								**Îles Vierges américaines**
Secondary education	* 0.95	...	...	...	...	...	...	Enseignement secondaire
Uruguay								**Uruguay**
Primary education	0.99	0.97	0.97	0.98	0.98	0.98	...	Enseignement primaire
Secondary education	1.20	1.15	1.17	...	...	1.11	...	Enseignement secondaire
Tertiary education	...	1.74	...	...	...	...	...	Enseignement supérieur
Uzbekistan								**Ouzbékistan**
Primary education	0.96	1.00	0.98	0.99	0.99	0.99	0.99	Enseignement primaire
Secondary education	...	0.97	1.00	0.99	0.99	0.99	...	Enseignement secondaire
Tertiary education	...	0.69	0.68	0.63	0.65	0.61	0.70	Enseignement supérieur
Vanuatu								**Vanuatu**
Primary education	...	0.97	0.99	0.97	...	...	...	Enseignement primaire
Secondary education	...	...	1.00	1.03	...	...	...	Enseignement secondaire
Venezuela (Boliv. Rep. of)								**Venezuela (Rép. boliv. du)**
Primary education	...	0.98	0.97	0.98	0.98	0.98	...	Enseignement primaire
Secondary education	...	1.13	1.10	1.08	1.08	1.08	...	Enseignement secondaire
Viet Nam								**Viet Nam**
Primary education	1.00	0.95	0.95	1.00	1.02	1.02	1.02	Enseignement primaire
Tertiary education	...	0.72	1.02	1.01	1.24	...	...	Enseignement supérieur
Yemen								**Yémen**
Primary education	...	0.74	0.82	...	0.87	...	...	Enseignement primaire
Secondary education	...	0.49	0.62	...	0.73	...	...	Enseignement secondaire
Tertiary education	...	...	0.44	...	...	...	...	Enseignement supérieur
Zambia								**Zambie**
Primary education	0.93	0.94	1.01	1.00	1.02	1.02	...	Enseignement primaire
Zimbabwe								**Zimbabwe**
Primary education	0.98	...	...	...	...	...	...	Enseignement primaire
Secondary education	0.84	...	...	...	...	...	...	Enseignement secondaire
Tertiary education	...	...	0.73	0.84	...	...	...	Enseignement supérieur

Source:

United Nations Educational, Scientific and Cultural Organization (UNESCO), Montreal, the UNESCO Institute for Statistics (UIS) statistics database, last accessed May 2020.

Source:

Organisation des Nations Unies pour l'éducation, la science et la culture (UNESCO), Montréal, base de données statistiques de l'Institut de statistique (ISU) de l'UNESCO, dernier accès mai 2020.

1   For statistical purposes, the data for China do not include those for the Hong Kong Special Administrative Region (Hong Kong SAR), Macao Special Administrative Region (Macao SAR) and Taiwan Province of China.

1   Pour la présentation des statistiques, les données pour la Chine ne comprennent pas la région administrative spéciale de Hong Kong (RAS de Hong Kong), la région administrative spéciale de Macao (RAS de Macao) et la province chinoise de Taïwan.

6

Enrollment in primary, secondary and tertiary education levels
Number of students enrolled (thousands) and gross enrollment ratio by sex

Inscriptions aux niveaux primaire, secondaire et supérieur
Nombre d'élèves inscrits (milliers) et taux brut de scolarisation par sexe

Region, country or area / Région, pays ou zone	Year & / Année &	Primary education / Enseignement primaire Total ('000)	Gross enrollment ratio Taux brut de scolarisation M/H	F	Secondary education / Enseignement secondaire Total ('000)	Gross enrollment ratio Taux brut de scolarisation M/H	F	Tertiary education / Enseignement supérieur Total ('000)	Gross enrollment ratio Taux brut de scolarisation M/H	F
Total, all countries or areas	2005	678 921	104.5	99.7	509 254	65.8	62.3	139 578	23.8	24.9
Total, tous pays ou zones	2010	697 001	104.4	101.8	546 192	72.2	69.8	182 258	28.5	30.7
	2014	715 427	102.9	102.7	580 893	75.7	74.9	213 025	33.9	37.8
	2015	720 012	102.5	102.5	582 977	75.9	74.9	217 627	34.8	38.9
	*2018	750 739	103.8	104.1	594 663	76.0	75.1	223 672	35.6	40.6
Northern Africa	2005	23 023	96.9	89.9	* 16 897	* 69.8	* 68.9	4 586	24.1	23.2
Afrique septentrionale	2010	23 598	100.8	95.5	17 399	72.0	70.3	5 514	26.2	28.2
	2014	25 162	101.1	97.8	18 624	77.7	76.7	5 890	28.1	30.3
	2015	* 25 786	* 101.5	* 98.0	* 18 934	* 78.6	* 78.2	6 358	30.1	33.1
	2018	28 398	102.7	100.1	* 20 102	* 81.2	* 81.2	* 6 853	* 32.2	* 37.7
Sub-Saharan Africa	2005	113 380	100.8	88.9	32 059	35.7	27.9	4 091	7.1	4.8
Afrique subsaharienne	2010	135 894	102.2	94.6	44 913	43.5	35.7	5 884	9.0	6.1
	2014	154 954	103.0	97.9	54 670	46.5	40.0	* 7 508	* 10.2	* 7.2
	2015	156 719	101.0	96.8	56 880	46.9	40.5	* 7 723	* 10.3	* 7.4
	*2018	168 645	100.7	96.5	61 218	46.0	40.5	8 149	10.5	7.7
Northern America	2005	26 759	102.0	100.9	27 033	95.0	96.3	18 245	65.6	92.9
Amérique septentrionale	2010	26 565	100.6	99.7	26 809	95.1	95.9	21 859	75.2	104.8
	2014	26 792	99.9	99.7	26 895	97.5	98.6	21 279	73.5	99.9
	2015	27 094	100.5	100.5	27 063	98.3	99.3	21 097	73.8	99.9
	*2018	28 054	102.0	101.5	27 615	100.4	100.0	20 641	73.4	99.8
Latin America & the Caribbean	2005	69 078	117.8	114.3	58 894	83.8	89.9	16 091	28.1	34.0
Amérique latine et Caraïbes	2010	67 216	116.7	113.1	61 227	85.8	92.9	22 074	36.1	46.5
	2014	65 387	111.1	108.7	64 261	91.2	97.1	25 529	41.6	53.9
	2015	64 615	110.1	107.9	64 042	92.0	97.1	26 223	42.7	55.2
	*2018	64 479	110.3	108.2	63 617	94.0	97.9	27 966	45.1	58.6
Eastern Asia	2005	* 126 355	* 103.4	* 103.2	* 115 222	* 70.5	* 69.2	28 737	25.4	21.8
Asie orientale	2010	113 597	100.0	98.4	113 530	89.3	89.1	39 209	27.8	27.9
	2014	106 550	96.1	96.2	102 398	85.7	87.4	50 194	43.0	47.4
	2015	107 284	96.4	96.7	99 601	84.6	86.5	51 555	45.7	51.5
	2018	113 812	100.2	101.3	96 045	84.8	86.3	51 772	47.8	55.4
South-eastern Asia	2005	68 253	106.8	103.8	40 815	62.6	62.4	11 321	* 21.0	* 21.0
Asie du Sud-Est	2010	68 327	106.8	107.1	45 538	70.5	71.3	14 475	26.0	27.7
	2014	68 843	108.7	106.6	50 074	78.3	79.0	17 671	29.4	34.8
	2015	68 713	108.9	106.1	51 401	80.7	80.9	18 158	30.3	35.7
	*2018	68 369	108.2	105.6	55 714	81.4	83.5	18 686	30.6	37.8
Southern Asia	2005	* 181 481	* 104.8	* 100.1	120 738	54.8	47.0	16 055	11.7	8.8
Asie méridionale	2010	191 840	105.9	105.8	143 371	61.1	57.1	28 467	19.3	15.0
	2014	195 228	103.1	109.3	168 939	68.7	68.6	40 030	24.1	23.3
	2015	196 427	103.6	109.9	170 485	69.0	68.9	41 931	25.2	24.1
	2018	* 202 968	* 106.8	* 114.8	* 174 147	* 69.7	* 69.9	44 659	25.7	25.8
Western Asia	2005	24 173	105.0	95.6	19 714	79.7	68.6	5 186	28.0	25.3
Asie occidentale	2010	25 404	105.5	98.1	22 396	80.0	72.2	7 524	36.2	34.0
	2014	* 25 900	* 105.3	* 98.3	* 25 126	* 86.5	* 78.9	10 615	48.8	46.9
	2015	* 26 083	* 104.5	* 98.1	* 25 222	* 86.7	* 79.0	11 274	51.7	50.0
	*2018	25 855	99.5	93.5	26 282	88.6	80.1	12 512	57.1	55.5
Europe	2005	38 467	102.1	101.3	65 272	97.7	97.5	32 163	55.4	70.8
Europe	2010	36 752	102.1	101.6	58 635	101.2	100.5	33 705	59.7	76.8
	2014	37 919	101.0	101.2	57 922	106.9	106.6	30 629	62.8	77.0
	2015	38 365	100.5	100.7	57 466	106.9	106.5	29 646	62.5	76.8
	*2018	40 234	101.1	100.9	58 098	107.4	106.7	28 898	64.5	79.0
Oceania	2005	3 142	91.0	89.1	* 3 566	* 111.7	* 108.5	* 1 616	* 57.2	* 70.7
Océanie	2010	3 556	99.4	96.4	* 3 770	* 114.7	* 107.1	* 1 987	* 61.0	* 82.4
	2014	4 080	106.7	103.2	* 3 886	* 116.9	* 104.5	* 2 172	* 62.7	* 88.5
	2015	4 101	104.9	101.8	3 909	117.6	104.1	2 206	63.6	90.5
	*2018	4 304	104.6	101.7	3 953	113.8	102.0	2 076	61.0	86.1

6

Enrollment in primary, secondary and tertiary education levels *(continued)*
Number of students enrolled (thousands) and gross enrollment ratio by sex

Inscriptions aux niveaux primaire, secondaire et supérieur *(suite)*
Nombre d'élèves inscrits (milliers) et taux brut de scolarisation par sexe

Region, country or area Région, pays ou zone	Year & Année &	Primary education Enseignement primaire			Secondary education Enseignement secondaire			Tertiary education Enseignement supérieur		
		Total ('000)	Gross enrollment ratio Taux brut de scolarisation		Total ('000)	Gross enrollment ratio Taux brut de scolarisation		Total ('000)	Gross enrollment ratio Taux brut de scolarisation	
			M/H	F		M/H	F		M/H	F
Afghanistan Afghanistan	2004	4 430	144.6	62.6	594	28.4	5.9	28	1.8	0.5
	2005	4 319	123.1	71.8	651	27.6	9.0	...	...	...
	2009	4 946	116.4	76.5	1 716	59.4	28.6	95	6.0	1.4
	2010	5 279	118.6	80.6	2 044	66.9	33.3	...	...	...
	2014	6 218	124.2	86.7	2 603	67.1	37.3	263	12.6	3.5
	2015	6 199	122.7	83.5	2 651	65.9	36.8	...	...	...
	2018	6 545	124.2	82.9	3 064	70.1	40.0	371	14.2	4.9
Albania Albanie	2005	238	100.4	101.0	407	79.2	76.5	63	18.8	27.4
	2010	225	93.2	93.8	356	87.9	88.4	122	38.0	51.6
	2014	196	102.4	106.1	333	100.4	94.8	176	54.6	78.3
	2015	188	104.0	107.3	315	99.5	95.1	163	51.6	73.5
	2018	171	105.2	109.1	269	95.2	95.7	132	43.0	67.6
Algeria Algérie	2005	4 362	111.7	103.3	3 654	75.5	82.7	792	18.4	23.5
	2010	3 312	119.0	111.5	4 616	95.2	98.7	1 144	24.5	35.4
	2011	3 363	120.2	112.8	4 573	97.8	101.5	1 189	25.5	37.1
	2014	3 765	121.4	115.5	...	...	...	1 245	27.3	41.9
	2015	3 925	118.7	113.0	...	...	...	1 289	28.8	45.0
	2018	4 430	112.4	107.3	...	...	...	1 601	38.8	64.4
American Samoa Samoa américaines	2007	...	...	...	...	...	...	2	...	...
Andorra Andorre	2005	4	...	...	4	...	...	~0	...	...
	2008	4	...	...	4	...	...	~0	...	...
	2010	4	...	...	4	...	...	...	...	...
	2014	4	...	...	4	...	...	~0	...	...
	2015	4	...	...	4	...	...	1	...	...
	2018	4	...	...	5	...	...	1	...	...
Angola Angola	2002	...	...	...	* 462	* 16.4	* 13.6	13	* 0.9	* 0.6
	2005	...	...	...	...	...	...	48	...	...
	2006	...	...	...	...	...	...	49	...	...
	2010	4 273	117.7	94.1	850	31.3	21.3	...	...	...
	2011	5 027	146.9	92.5	885	32.3	20.7	143	9.0	3.3
	2013	...	...	...	...	...	...	219	9.9	7.8
	2015	5 621	121.1	105.9	...	...	...	221	9.4	7.4
	2016	...	...	...	2 034	61.8	39.7	253	10.2	8.5
Anguilla Anguilla	2005	1	112.5	114.5	1	96.0	94.7	~0	1.4	4.1
	2008	2	126.3	122.2	1	105.6	102.0	~0	1.6	7.6
	2010	2	124.4	118.9	1	112.1	111.0	...	...	...
	2011	2	124.2	119.0	1	114.2	114.3	...	...	...
Antigua and Barbuda Antigua-et-Barbuda	2000	13	...	...	5	* 83.0	* 76.6	...	...	...
	2010	11	117.2	107.3	8	109.9	115.7	1	9.0	24.2
	2012	10	110.7	105.4	8	101.5	117.6	2	15.3	34.3
	2014	10	108.7	103.3	8	106.7	107.3	...	...	...
	2015	10	106.8	103.2	8	107.1	109.3	...	...	...
	2018	10	105.4	104.6	8	113.3	109.1	...	...	...
Argentina Argentine	2005	4 873	115.8	114.7	3 884	88.8	96.8	2 083	52.6	75.5
	2010	4 947	117.7	116.2	4 213	95.0	104.2	2 521	58.9	87.8
	2014	4 780	111.6	111.3	4 451	102.6	109.6	2 869	62.2	100.3
	2015	4 784	111.4	111.2	4 502	103.8	110.2	2 966	64.1	104.5
	2017	4 754	109.9	109.6	4 613	106.5	111.0	3 141	67.8	112.8
Armenia Arménie	2000	180	98.0	99.3	409	87.8	96.5	93	31.5	39.3
	2005	125	94.6	96.3	370	...	...	115	32.8	46.0
	2010	102	97.7	100.7	306	105.6	103.7	146	47.6	58.0
	2014	143	96.3	97.5	245	83.7	88.4	113	43.9	50.1
	2015	145	94.3	95.8	240	84.0	88.3	106	42.4	50.5
	2018	153	92.7	92.7	235	81.7	84.8	103	47.1	62.6

Enrollment in primary, secondary and tertiary education levels *(continued)*
Number of students enrolled (thousands) and gross enrollment ratio by sex

Inscriptions aux niveaux primaire, secondaire et supérieur *(suite)*
Nombre d'élèves inscrits (milliers) et taux brut de scolarisation par sexe

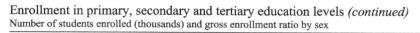

| Region, country or area Région, pays ou zone | Year & Année & | Primary education Enseignement primaire | | | Secondary education Enseignement secondaire | | | Tertiary education Enseignement supérieur | | |
| | | Total ('000) | Gross enrollment ratio Taux brut de scolarisation | | Total ('000) | Gross enrollment ratio Taux brut de scolarisation | | Total ('000) | Gross enrollment ratio Taux brut de scolarisation | |
			M/H	F		M /H	F		M/H	F
Aruba	2005	10	114.9	107.8	7	95.8	96.1	2	25.9	37.3
Aruba	2010	10	114.5	113.0	7	93.5	98.3	2	31.1	43.9
	2012	9	102.8	105.4	8	110.2	112.1	3	30.5	45.6
	2014	10	118.9	115.2	...	...	...	1	10.1	23.0
	2015	...	...	...	...	...	...	1	9.4	21.4
	2016	...	...	...	...	...	...	1	10.7	20.7
Australia	2005	1 935	102.0	103.6	...	...	...	...	...	...
Australie	2010	2 015	105.7	105.5	...	...	...	...	...	...
	2014	2 169	105.6	105.3	...	...	...	...	...	...
	2015	2 141	101.6	101.6	2 709	167.9	145.9	1 903	97.6	141.0
	2017	2 217	100.3	100.3	2 650	159.0	141.2	1 775	93.8	133.3
Austria	2005	363	100.9	100.8	781	102.8	97.8	...	...	...
Autriche	2010	328	100.4	99.1	744	100.7	96.8	385	...	...
	2014	327	101.9	101.3	697	101.5	97.7	421	72.3	86.3
	2015	328	102.4	101.5	691	102.1	98.5	426	73.8	88.0
	2017	335	103.2	103.0	687	102.5	98.3	430	78.1	92.5
Azerbaijan	2005	568	* 98.2	* 92.8	...	...	...	...	...	...
Azerbaïdjan	2010	482	* 94.2	* 93.2	...	...	...	181	* 19.4	* 19.2
	2014	518	* 106.6	* 105.5	...	...	...	195	* 21.7	* 24.8
	2015	551	* 107.4	* 105.6	...	...	...	204	* 23.6	* 27.5
	2018	635	* 99.5	* 100.0	945	* 94.4	* 94.5	201	* 25.9	* 29.7
Bahamas	2005	37	101.9	98.8	32	88.8	88.1	...	...	...
Bahamas	2010	34	89.9	88.0	34	87.6	91.2	...	...	...
	2014	32	84.1	82.3	32	80.5	82.3	...	...	...
	2015	33	87.4	85.1	26	66.1	66.7	...	...	...
	2018	30	81.6	81.2	27	67.3	71.6	...	...	...
Bahrain	2005	83	94.1	97.5	72	91.5	101.5	19	13.0	39.9
Bahreïn	2006	90	96.1	101.0	74	92.1	101.1	18	12.2	38.3
	2010	...	...	...	80	92.2	93.5	...	...	...
	2014	104	99.1	100.4	90	98.7	99.2	38	29.1	57.5
	2015	108	100.7	101.7	92	102.5	101.8	39	30.9	59.3
	2018	114	100.0	98.8	99	95.8	101.7	45	37.0	67.8
Bangladesh	2005	16 219	99.4	104.0	10 109	45.5	48.5	912	8.4	4.4
Bangladesh	2009	* 16 539	* 100.6	* 105.4	10 907	48.2	51.9	1 582	13.5	8.1
	2010	* 16 987	* 102.8	* 109.3	11 334	48.7	54.7	...	...	...
	2013	...	...	...	13 314	57.9	62.6	...	...	...
	2014	...	...	...	...	...	...	2 068	15.9	11.7
	2015	...	...	...	14 567	61.8	69.7	...	...	...
	2018	17 338	112.4	120.8	15 870	67.4	78.3	3 151	24.0	17.0
Barbados	2001	24	99.9	98.7	21	103.3	103.7	8	23.1	57.0
Barbade	2005	22	96.3	95.9	21	109.1	108.0	...	...	...
	2010	* 23	* 98.8	* 100.4	* 19	* 101.7	* 102.1	13	43.9	95.8
	2011	* 23	* 98.2	* 98.3	20	101.8	105.6	12	40.3	90.6
	2014	21	95.0	95.4	21	106.6	109.7	...	...	...
	2015	21	96.2	95.6	21	105.7	109.5	...	...	...
	2018	20	101.2	97.5	20	101.8	105.8	...	...	...
Belarus	2005	380	100.0	96.7	...	...	...	529	57.2	78.4
Bélarus	2010	358	104.5	104.3	763	109.9	106.4	569	* 65.4	* 94.6
	2014	369	98.2	98.5	649	106.5	104.5	518	78.7	105.1
	2015	387	99.1	99.2	644	106.3	104.6	477	77.2	102.6
	2018	428	100.6	100.4	649	103.1	101.7	389	80.2	95.1
Belgium	2005	739	100.7	100.2	1 200	151.1	169.1	390	54.5	67.9
Belgique	2010	732	102.0	101.8	1 203	146.9	167.3	445	60.0	75.9
	2014	774	103.7	103.6	1 210	152.3	172.7	496	63.5	82.8
	2015	783	103.2	103.1	1 218	153.6	174.7	505	64.8	84.7
	2017	815	103.9	104.0	1 187	149.7	167.8	527	69.3	90.5

6 Enrollment in primary, secondary and tertiary education levels *(continued)*
Number of students enrolled (thousands) and gross enrollment ratio by sex

Inscriptions aux niveaux primaire, secondaire et supérieur *(suite)*
Nombre d'élèves inscrits (milliers) et taux brut de scolarisation par sexe

Region, country or area Région, pays ou zone	Year & Année &	Primary education Enseignement primaire			Secondary education Enseignement secondaire			Tertiary education Enseignement supérieur		
		Total ('000)	Gross enrollment ratio Taux brut de scolarisation		Total ('000)	Gross enrollment ratio Taux brut de scolarisation		Total ('000)	Gross enrollment ratio Taux brut de scolarisation	
			M/H	F		M/H	F		M/H	F
Belize	2005	50	115.7	110.8	29	75.3	77.7	5	12.5	19.6
Belize	2010	53	114.8	110.3	33	72.4	78.2	7	16.8	26.9
	2014	52	114.2	108.9	37	77.9	81.7	9	18.1	29.9
	2015	52	115.5	110.2	38	79.6	81.7	9	17.8	28.7
	2017	52	116.0	110.4	40	81.9	86.2	9	18.8	30.5
	2018	51	114.6	108.7	40	83.7	87.1	...	...	...
Benin	2001	1 055	106.7	74.4	* 257	* 32.1	* 15.2	28	* 7.2	* 1.8
Bénin	2004	1 320	117.2	89.9	345	39.2	18.4	41	...	...
	2005	1 318	112.4	89.0	...	...	...	42	...	...
	2010	1 788	126.9	113.2	...	...	...	114	20.3	7.2
	2014	2 133	134.6	124.4	897	66.4	45.8	150	23.3	8.5
	2015	2 238	137.2	127.6	964	68.5	48.9	131	19.3	7.7
	2016	2 268	135.1	126.5	993	67.1	50.7	129	18.2	7.6
	2017	2 252	130.8	122.3	...	...	...	126	17.0	7.5
	2018	2 224	125.8	118.0	...	...	...	...	...	...
Bermuda	2005	5	95.1	100.0	5	73.9	83.6	...	...	...
Bermudes	2006	5	93.8	101.2	5	72.0	78.4	1	18.0	40.2
	2010	4	...	...	4	71.2	83.7	1	20.1	41.4
	2014	4	99.5	96.5	4	71.7	82.0	1	19.7	36.9
	2015	4	102.1	100.2	4	72.6	81.5	1	15.3	35.3
	2018	...	...	...	...	...	...	1	15.3	22.9
Bhutan	2005	99	92.2	89.9	42	46.3	42.7	4	6.2	3.7
Bhoutan	2010	110	107.0	109.4	60	62.5	64.7	5	8.8	5.5
	2013	104	106.4	107.5	69	72.7	78.6	9	12.2	9.4
	2014	102	104.8	106.2	74	79.7	85.9	...	...	...
	2015	99	103.7	104.8	74	81.3	86.8	...	...	...
	2018	92	100.1	100.2	* 76	* 84.7	* 95.7	12	15.6	15.5
Bolivia (Plurin. State of)	2005	1 513	114.7	114.9	1 038	89.0	84.9	...	...	...
Bolivie (État plurin. de)	2010	1 444	104.8	104.2	1 136	88.9	88.5	...	...	...
	2014	1 346	97.0	94.8	1 209	90.8	90.0	...	...	...
	2015	1 345	96.9	94.9	1 234	92.0	90.7	...	...	...
	2018	1 379	98.6	97.6	1 234	90.7	88.8	...	...	...
Bosnia and Herzegovina	2005	...	...	...	...	...	...	84	...	...
Bosnie-Herzégovine	2010	175	...	...	323	...	...	105	...	...
	2014	161	...	...	297	...	...	112	...	...
	2015	163	...	...	278	...	...	108	...	...
	2018	159	...	...	248	...	...	95	...	...
Botswana	2005	329	111.9	110.4	173	82.4	84.8	20	10.7	9.2
Botswana	2006	330	112.5	110.4	177	82.8	87.2	22	12.1	9.7
	2008	327	109.7	107.3	168	76.4	83.5	31	...	...
	2009	331	109.8	106.6	...	...	...	48	...	...
	2010	...	...	...	...	...	...	42	...	...
	2014	341	105.3	102.1	...	...	...	55	24.6	30.0
	2015	345	104.4	102.1	...	...	...	61	25.8	34.6
	2017	...	...	...	...	...	...	49	20.5	29.2
Brazil	2005	18 661	* 137.2	* 129.2	24 863	* 96.5	* 106.2	4 572	* 22.8	* 29.3
Brésil	2009	17 452	* 133.9	* 128.2	23 617	* 91.5	* 102.1	6 115	* 31.9	* 42.2
	2010	16 893	...	...	23 539	...	...	6 553	...	...
	2014	16 630	* 116.7	* 111.7	24 225	* 96.8	* 105.2	8 072	* 42.3	* 57.6
	2015	16 299	* 115.1	* 110.4	23 502	* 97.4	* 102.9	8 285	* 43.7	* 58.5
	2017	16 107	* 117.4	* 113.4	23 118	* 99.3	* 102.4	8 571	* 43.5	* 59.4
British Virgin Islands	2004	3	113.2	107.8	2	104.3	107.5	1	43.3	98.0
Îles Vierges britanniques	2005	3	114.8	109.8	2	110.7	123.6	...	...	...
	2009	3	109.6	108.7	2	104.1	109.7	1	56.2	89.6
	2010	3	...	...	2	107.1	109.1	...	...	...
	2014	3	113.9	108.7	2	88.1	97.5	...	...	...
	2015	3	122.3	114.5	2	89.3	96.9	1	30.2	54.2
	2017	3	131.5	125.9	2	96.3	107.1	...	...	...
	2018	...	...	...	...	...	...	~0	11.7	20.9

6

Enrollment in primary, secondary and tertiary education levels *(continued)*
Number of students enrolled (thousands) and gross enrollment ratio by sex

Inscriptions aux niveaux primaire, secondaire et supérieur *(suite)*
Nombre d'élèves inscrits (milliers) et taux brut de scolarisation par sexe

Region, country or area Région, pays ou zone	Year & Année &	Primary education Enseignement primaire			Secondary education Enseignement secondaire			Tertiary education Enseignement supérieur		
		Total ('000)	Gross enrollment ratio Taux brut de scolarisation		Total ('000)	Gross enrollment ratio Taux brut de scolarisation		Total ('000)	Gross enrollment ratio Taux brut de scolarisation	
			M/H	F		M /H	F		M/H	F
Brunei Darussalam	2005	46	112.7	108.4	44	97.3	95.8	5	9.7	19.4
Brunéi Darussalam	2010	44	106.8	106.3	49	98.9	99.5	6	10.9	20.4
	2014	41	105.5	105.5	49	98.8	100.5	11	23.7	41.1
	2015	40	105.7	105.3	47	95.5	97.5	11	23.4	39.9
	2018	39	102.7	103.6	44	92.4	94.6	11	24.8	38.7
Bulgaria	2005	290	103.9	102.8	686	91.0	87.3	238	42.1	48.9
Bulgarie	2010	260	108.5	108.2	532	92.1	88.2	287	50.0	66.1
	2014	259	97.0	96.3	519	105.9	102.3	283	60.0	75.6
	2015	262	94.7	93.7	501	103.9	100.6	279	62.0	79.1
	2017	265	89.6	89.1	486	99.5	96.8	250	63.7	78.8
Burkina Faso	2005	1 271	64.6	51.8	295	16.7	11.8	28	3.2	1.4
Burkina Faso	2010	2 048	81.6	74.3	538	24.8	18.9	51	4.8	2.3
	2014	2 594	88.5	86.2	842	32.4	28.3	81	6.8	3.3
	2015	2 707	89.5	87.2	966	35.1	32.3	84	6.6	3.5
	2018	3 206	96.9	95.3	1 281	40.7	40.7	118	8.2	4.8
Burundi	2005	1 037	87.3	74.7	* 171	* 15.0	* 11.0	17	* 3.6	* 1.4
Burundi	2010	1 850	138.0	136.4	338	27.1	19.5	29	4.2	2.3
	2014	2 047	132.1	136.5	583	42.1	36.8	51	7.8	2.5
	2015	2 072	129.0	132.8	664	45.8	42.9	...	...	...
	2017	2 126	122.9	124.8	665	48.1	50.4	62	8.4	3.8
	2018	2 171	120.7	122.2	675	45.8	51.1	...	...	...
Cabo Verde	2005	83	116.7	111.7	53	66.8	75.3	4	7.4	7.9
Cabo Verde	2010	71	115.2	107.0	62	79.6	94.3	10	15.8	20.3
	2014	67	111.6	103.2	60	89.1	101.3	13	19.5	28.5
	2015	66	109.2	101.7	59	89.6	100.0	13	18.8	27.5
	2018	64	107.5	100.5	53	83.9	92.5	12	19.0	28.3
Cambodia	2004	2 763	137.3	126.4	* 630	* 36.7	* 25.7	45	3.9	1.8
Cambodge	2005	2 695	135.6	126.0	...	...	...	57	4.7	2.1
	2008	2 341	127.6	119.7	* 930	* 48.7	* 41.6	137	12.0	6.2
	2010	2 273	127.4	120.2	...	...	...	195	17.4	10.5
	2011	2 224	126.3	117.8	...	...	...	223	18.2	11.4
	2014	2 129	120.0	113.5	...	...	...	...	...	...
	2015	2 179	117.5	116.7	...	...	...	217	14.4	11.8
	2018	2 147	108.7	106.1	...	...	...	211	14.4	12.9
Cameroon	2005	2 978	* 112.5	* 94.3	784	30.2	23.8	* 100	* 7.1	* 4.6
Cameroun	2009	3 351	113.8	98.6	1 269	44.1	36.8	174	10.1	8.0
	2010	3 510	116.0	100.2	...	...	...	220	12.3	10.0
	2014	4 143	119.8	106.7	2 000	62.1	52.8	350	18.3	14.3
	2015	4 370	122.4	109.9	2 108	63.6	54.4	372	18.8	15.1
	2016	4 481	122.2	110.0	2 207	64.6	55.4	279	13.3	11.7
	2017	4 371	116.0	104.5	...	...	...	290	14.1	11.4
	2018	4 202	108.7	98.0	...	...	...	...	...	...
Canada	*2002	...	...	...	...	...	...	1 255	50.7	68.9
Canada	2005	2 321	97.8	96.9	2 602	102.5	100.2	...	...	...
	2010	2 168	98.4	98.9	2 612	103.6	101.2	* 1 430	* 52.0	* 71.8
	2014	2 249	100.9	102.2	2 661	109.0	109.7	* 1 578	* 56.4	* 75.3
	2015	2 304	102.1	102.9	2 642	109.9	110.9	* 1 564	* 55.5	* 74.5
	2017	2 365	101.1	100.8	2 653	113.0	114.5	* 1 626	* 59.1	* 79.3
Cayman Islands	2003	...	...	...	...	...	...	1	...	...
Îles Caïmanes	2005	3	...	...	3	...	...	...	...	...
	2008	4	...	...	3	...	...	1	...	...
	2013	4	...	...	3	...	...	...	...	...
	2018	4	...	...	3	...	...	...	...	...

6 Enrollment in primary, secondary and tertiary education levels *(continued)*
Number of students enrolled (thousands) and gross enrollment ratio by sex

Inscriptions aux niveaux primaire, secondaire et supérieur *(suite)*
Nombre d'élèves inscrits (milliers) et taux brut de scolarisation par sexe

Region, country or area	Year &	Primary education Enseignement primaire			Secondary education Enseignement secondaire			Tertiary education Enseignement supérieur		
		Total ('000)	Gross enrollment ratio Taux brut de scolarisation		Total ('000)	Gross enrollment ratio Taux brut de scolarisation		Total ('000)	Gross enrollment ratio Taux brut de scolarisation	
Région, pays ou zone	Année &		M/H	F		M/H	F		M/H	F
Central African Republic	2000	...	...	...	...	...	...	6	3.2	0.6
République centrafricaine	*2001	459	91.8	63.9	70	15.7	8.3	...	...	...
	*2002	411	81.2	55.3	72	...	...	...	...	...
	2004	363	68.8	46.4	...	...	...	6	...	...
	2005	412	75.1	52.6	...	...	...	...	...	...
	2009	608	98.7	71.4	93	17.4	9.8	10	3.5	1.5
	2010	637	101.2	73.4	...	...	...	11	4.0	1.3
	2012	662	99.8	75.7	126	22.9	11.9	13	4.4	1.6
	2016	814	114.6	89.4	119	18.2	11.8	...	...	...
	2017	...	...	...	138	20.5	13.8	...	...	...
Chad	2005	1 262	85.3	57.8	* 245	* 23.2	* 8.0	12	2.7	0.2
Tchad	2010	1 727	94.6	69.1	430	31.7	13.4	* 22	* 3.6	* 0.6
	2014	2 443	115.8	87.3	509	31.7	14.3	* 42	* 5.7	* 1.1
	2015	2 270	103.7	79.4	513	30.9	13.9	42	5.0	1.5
	2016	2 213	98.2	75.5	535	30.9	14.2	...	...	...
Chile	2005	1 721	106.9	102.1	1 630	92.9	94.1	664	50.4	48.3
Chili	2010	1 547	105.2	102.2	1 518	88.7	91.4	988	65.5	70.3
	2014	1 469	102.5	99.3	1 556	100.3	101.1	1 205	78.4	87.5
	2015	1 478	102.2	99.1	1 546	101.5	102.1	1 222	80.7	89.9
	2017	1 515	102.9	99.9	1 521	101.6	102.0	1 239	82.5	94.7
China	2001	130 133	112.8	111.8	86 517	* 62.0	* 58.0	9 399	...	...
Chine	2003	...	...	...	95 625	63.9	60.3	15 186	16.9	13.9
	2005	...	...	...	...	...	...	20 601	20.0	18.1
	2010	101 019	99.8	98.0	99 218	88.3	88.0	31 047	23.5	25.0
	2014	95 107	95.8	95.8	88 692	...	...	41 924	39.4	45.8
	2015	95 958	96.2	96.4	86 127	...	...	43 367	42.3	50.2
	2018	101 873	99.7	100.8	84 322	...	...	44 935	45.9	55.9
China, Hong Kong SAR	2005	451	...	...	498	81.9	82.7	152	33.4	33.6
Chine, RAS de Hong Kong	2010	349	...	...	508	87.9	88.2	265	* 59.7	* 59.5
	2014	324	108.8	109.8	416	102.2	100.5	305	65.4	73.3
	2015	333	109.3	111.1	394	103.1	101.4	299	65.2	74.0
	2018	366	106.4	111.2	349	109.1	105.8	298	72.9	81.1
China, Macao SAR	2005	37	103.0	96.8	47	89.4	83.3	23	65.8	44.2
Chine, RAS de Macao	2010	25	95.8	94.0	38	89.2	86.4	29	56.1	54.1
	2014	23	97.8	97.0	32	94.4	92.0	30	57.0	73.0
	2015	24	100.1	98.5	30	95.2	93.8	31	62.1	80.8
	2018	30	100.7	100.1	27	101.2	100.9	33	77.4	104.5
Colombia	2005	5 298	122.6	120.4	4 297	78.7	87.2	1 224	29.5	31.9
Colombie	2010	5 085	121.3	119.3	5 080	93.0	102.3	1 674	37.5	41.3
	2014	4 543	116.4	112.7	4 828	91.4	98.7	2 221	47.7	55.2
	2015	4 479	117.0	113.4	4 794	91.5	98.1	2 294	49.3	57.4
	2018	4 304	116.2	112.8	4 821	95.0	100.1	2 408	51.1	59.7
Comoros	2003	104	120.8	99.5	38	43.5	36.5	2	3.5	2.7
Comores	2004	104	114.5	101.6	43	49.8	38.0	...	...	...
	2008	111	113.0	104.1	...	...	...	...	...	...
	2010	...	...	...	...	...	...	4	6.6	4.9
	2014	120	108.6	101.2	70	59.1	63.1	6	9.9	8.0
	2018	124	99.6	99.4	74	57.6	61.4	...	...	...
Congo	2003	510	101.0	94.9	204	46.9	32.1	* 12	* 5.4	* 2.1
Congo	2004	584	112.8	105.8	* 235	* 48.5	* 40.8	...	...	...
	2005	597	112.4	104.6	...	...	...	...	...	...
	2009	672	111.1	103.6	...	...	...	23	10.3	2.2
	2010	705	112.2	106.1	...	...	...	...	...	...
	2012	734	102.8	110.5	339	56.3	48.8	39	12.3	7.7
	2013	...	...	...	...	...	...	37	10.6	8.0
	2017	...	...	...	...	...	...	55	15.2	10.1

6

Enrollment in primary, secondary and tertiary education levels *(continued)*
Number of students enrolled (thousands) and gross enrollment ratio by sex

Inscriptions aux niveaux primaire, secondaire et supérieur *(suite)*
Nombre d'élèves inscrits (milliers) et taux brut de scolarisation par sexe

Region, country or area Région, pays ou zone	Year & Année &	Primary education Enseignement primaire			Secondary education Enseignement secondaire			Tertiary education Enseignement supérieur		
		Total ('000)	Gross enrollment ratio Taux brut de scolarisation		Total ('000)	Gross enrollment ratio Taux brut de scolarisation		Total ('000)	Gross enrollment ratio Taux brut de scolarisation	
			M/H	F		M /H	F		M/H	F
Cook Islands	2005	2	84.4	83.3	2	61.9	64.9	...	...	...
Îles Cook	2010	2	89.8	85.4	2	78.3	86.4	...	...	...
	2012	2	98.7	93.4	2	87.0	88.4	1	35.8	42.7
	2014	2	102.4	101.1	2	82.9	88.1	...	...	...
	2015	2	104.2	99.8	2	85.4	90.6	...	...	...
	2016	2	109.5	107.5	2	84.8	88.6	...	...	...
Costa Rica	2004	558	115.1	112.4	340	77.9	81.2	109	23.9	29.5
Costa Rica	2005	542	113.3	110.4	347	79.9	83.4	...	...	...
	2010	521	118.0	115.7	414	99.0	103.2	...	...	...
	2014	476	112.3	111.3	460	117.0	123.4	217	46.8	57.9
	2015	473	111.6	111.0	460	120.4	125.3	218	46.1	60.3
	2018	484	112.8	113.8	477	128.1	137.7	217	50.0	60.7
Côte d'Ivoire	*2003	2 046	80.2	63.5	...	...	...	...	...	...
Côte d'Ivoire	2009	2 383	79.5	64.1	...	...	...	* 153	* 11.0	* 5.7
	2010	...	...	...	...	...	...	144	10.2	5.2
	2014	3 177	93.0	80.6	1 418	46.1	31.8	177	10.6	6.0
	2015	3 371	96.4	84.9	1 587	49.9	35.1	193	10.7	6.9
	2017	3 772	102.9	93.8	1 898	55.6	41.3	218	11.1	7.6
	2018	3 900	103.6	96.0	2 041	57.7	44.3	...	...	...
Croatia	2005	196	103.4	103.3	400	91.7	94.8	135	40.5	49.2
Croatie	2010	167	91.9	92.0	389	96.6	103.4	150	46.3	62.1
	2014	161	101.2	100.8	370	97.0	100.5	166	57.2	78.3
	2015	162	100.6	100.6	360	96.5	101.0	162	56.7	76.7
	2017	163	96.4	96.5	340	97.1	101.8	165	57.4	78.8
Cuba	2005	895	102.6	99.6	937	92.3	93.9	472	* 46.4	* 78.5
Cuba	2010	853	102.6	100.2	809	92.1	92.4	801	72.2	118.6
	2013	772	99.9	98.3	787	91.0	91.0	373	37.2	62.1
	2014	763	102.5	97.4	830	96.4	97.7	302	...	...
	2015	746	102.3	96.5	825	96.7	99.1	261	30.2	42.5
	2018	741	104.1	99.6	795	100.4	101.9	296	32.3	51.0
Curaçao Curaçao	2013	21	164.2	157.7	11	83.8	90.8	2	13.0	29.6
Cyprus	2005	61	* 100.9	* 100.8	64	* 95.7	* 97.5	20	* 31.2	* 35.3
Chypre	2010	55	* 101.6	* 101.6	64	* 90.9	* 92.0	32	* 50.9	* 45.6
	2014	53	* 98.7	* 99.6	59	* 99.4	* 99.5	34	* 44.1	* 62.6
	2015	54	* 99.3	* 99.3	57	* 100.1	* 99.4	37	* 51.1	* 69.4
	2017	56	* 99.3	* 99.4	55	* 101.1	* 99.5	45	* 69.6	* 82.4
Czechia	2005	503	99.9	98.5	975	94.8	96.6	336	44.8	52.0
Tchéquie	2010	463	104.0	103.6	837	94.4	94.9	437	53.6	74.9
	2014	511	98.7	98.7	781	104.5	104.9	419	54.9	76.9
	2015	535	99.3	99.7	770	104.6	105.6	396	53.8	75.7
	2017	576	100.4	101.0	772	103.1	103.9	353	53.4	75.3
Dem. People's Rep. Korea	2009	1 547	99.4	99.4	...	...	...	593	40.8	20.6
Rép. pop. dém. de Corée	2011	...	...	...	...	...	...	600	...	...
	2015	1 358	94.5	94.7	2 148	92.3	93.3	565	36.1	20.0
	2018	1 508	112.8	112.8	...	...	...	526	35.5	18.2
Dem. Rep. of the Congo	2002	5 455	74.8	59.0	...	...	...	...	...	...
Rép. dém. du Congo	2009	10 244	108.1	92.8	3 399	53.1	29.8	378	10.3	3.2
	2010	10 572	106.9	93.0	3 484	52.2	30.1	...	...	...
	2013	12 601	111.8	101.3	3 996	52.9	32.8	443	9.5	4.3
	2014	13 535	115.4	104.9	4 388	56.1	34.9	...	...	...
	2015	13 763	108.4	107.6	4 619	56.3	36.0	...	...	...
	2016	...	...	...	...	...	...	465	8.5	4.7
Denmark	2005	414	98.8	98.7	465	121.9	126.5	232	67.7	93.4
Danemark	2010	403	99.5	99.7	504	119.0	120.0	241	60.4	87.4
	2014	467	101.9	100.7	554	126.7	132.1	301	67.4	95.3
	2015	469	102.1	100.8	553	127.3	133.4	314	68.7	96.3
	2017	473	101.6	100.9	534	128.4	129.8	312	68.4	93.6

6

Enrollment in primary, secondary and tertiary education levels *(continued)*
Number of students enrolled (thousands) and gross enrollment ratio by sex

Inscriptions aux niveaux primaire, secondaire et supérieur *(suite)*
Nombre d'élèves inscrits (milliers) et taux brut de scolarisation par sexe

Region, country or area Région, pays ou zone	Year & Année &	Primary education Enseignement primaire			Secondary education Enseignement secondaire			Tertiary education Enseignement supérieur		
		Total ('000)	Gross enrollment ratio Taux brut de scolarisation		Total ('000)	Gross enrollment ratio Taux brut de scolarisation		Total ('000)	Gross enrollment ratio Taux brut de scolarisation	
			M/H	F		M/H	F		M/H	F
Djibouti	2005	51	48.0	39.2	30	27.6	18.2	2	2.7	1.9
Djibouti	2009	56	58.9	58.5	44	38.5	31.1	3	4.0	3.0
	2010	...	...	...	...	...	...	3	4.1	3.1
	2011	61	64.2	69.3	51	42.1	39.4	5	6.0	4.6
	2014	64	69.4	73.0	59	47.1	45.0	...	...	...
	2015	63	67.9	72.8	59	48.0	45.3	...	...	...
	2019	69	75.4	75.1	65	51.2	52.9	...	...	...
Dominica	2005	9	91.4	91.5	7	99.2	107.6	...	...	...
Dominique	2010	8	103.6	101.8	7	85.1	93.0	...	...	...
	2014	8	115.8	116.4	6	91.4	90.0	...	...	...
	2015	8	117.1	115.2	6	94.7	93.8	...	...	...
	2016	7	116.2	113.2	...	...	...	...	...	...
Dominican Republic	2003	1 375	* 115.4	* 116.3	...	...	...	287	* 26.5	* 41.6
République dominicaine	2005	1 290	* 111.1	* 105.5	808	* 64.9	* 77.5	...	...	...
	2010	1 318	* 117.3	* 103.4	905	* 73.6	* 82.8	...	...	...
	2014	1 268	* 112.7	* 102.2	931	* 76.2	* 84.2	456	* 37.8	* 60.9
	2015	1 307	* 116.4	* 106.2	929	* 76.2	* 83.8	480	* 36.6	* 67.0
	2017	1 253	* 111.5	* 104.0	925	* 76.5	* 83.0	557	* 43.0	* 77.0
	2018	1 226	* 108.8	* 102.5	925	* 77.0	* 83.0	...	...	...
Ecuador	2005	1 998	109.9	109.9	1 053	61.6	62.5	...	...	...
Équateur	2008	2 008	106.7	108.7	...	...	...	535	36.0	41.6
	2010	2 114	112.9	113.2	1 655	90.3	94.5	...	...	...
	2012	2 089	111.8	112.7	1 823	97.1	102.1	573	34.5	45.3
	2013	2 068	111.1	111.6	1 883	99.9	104.4	586	...	...
	2014	2 094	112.7	113.1	1 942	102.6	107.2	...	...	...
	2015	1 998	107.4	107.9	1 932	102.0	106.2	669	41.5	48.4
	2018	1 932	102.4	104.1	1 892	100.1	102.8	...	...	...
Egypt	2004	* 7 928	* 97.2	* 94.1	* 8 330	* 84.0	* 79.6	2 261	31.9	25.8
Égypte	2005	9 564	98.2	93.1	...	...	...	2 352	32.7	27.5
	2010	10 542	103.7	100.7	6 846	69.8	67.9	2 646	32.8	30.0
	2014	11 128	104.0	103.7	8 208	81.0	80.6	2 544	32.8	29.3
	2015	...	...	...	...	...	...	2 869	35.7	34.3
	2017	12 161	106.0	106.3	8 938	87.4	85.9	2 914	34.6	35.8
	2018	12 643	106.1	106.5	9 137	88.5	87.3	...	...	...
El Salvador	2005	1 045	120.2	116.1	524	67.7	67.8	122	21.6	24.2
El Salvador	2010	940	117.6	112.3	577	69.3	69.0	150	24.8	27.4
	2014	777	108.5	103.9	625	76.7	77.1	176	26.5	29.1
	2015	741	104.8	100.4	600	75.0	75.6	179	26.5	29.4
	2018	663	96.3	93.3	522	71.9	71.4	191	27.5	31.1
Equatorial Guinea	2000	73	112.9	93.2	21	32.3	14.5	1	2.4	1.2
Guinée équatoriale	2005	76	91.5	88.5	26	29.9	22.1	...	...	...
	2010	85	69.8	68.9	...	...	...	...	...	...
	2012	92	69.3	69.0	...	...	...	...	...	...
	2015	93	62.0	61.6	...	...	...	...	...	...
Eritrea	2004	375	120.2	96.7	194	46.6	26.7	5	2.7	0.4
Érythrée	2005	378	124.0	100.8	217	50.4	30.2	...	...	...
	2010	286	90.2	76.9	248	58.8	45.1	12	4.7	1.8
	2014	362	86.0	73.4	270	64.9	52.9	13	5.1	2.5
	2015	362	81.7	70.4	246	56.0	47.5	11	4.2	2.7
	2016	...	...	...	...	...	...	10	3.9	2.8
	2018	350	73.6	63.1	260	49.9	45.4	...	...	...
Estonia	2005	86	100.2	97.6	124	101.0	104.7	68	50.9	85.8
Estonie	2010	73	103.8	102.2	95	105.2	105.3	69	51.6	85.9
	2014	77	98.3	97.7	78	108.7	108.1	60	58.8	88.7
	2015	80	97.1	97.1	78	111.3	110.8	55	57.7	87.5
	2017	86	97.2	97.3	83	116.2	118.9	48	55.4	84.8

Enrollment in primary, secondary and tertiary education levels *(continued)*
Number of students enrolled (thousands) and gross enrollment ratio by sex

Inscriptions aux niveaux primaire, secondaire et supérieur *(suite)*
Nombre d'élèves inscrits (milliers) et taux brut de scolarisation par sexe

| Region, country or area | Year & | Primary education Enseignement primaire | | | Secondary education Enseignement secondaire | | | Tertiary education Enseignement supérieur | | |
| | | Total ('000) | Gross enrollment ratio Taux brut de scolarisation | | Total ('000) | Gross enrollment ratio Taux brut de scolarisation | | Total ('000) | Gross enrollment ratio Taux brut de scolarisation | |
Région, pays ou zone	Année &		M/H	F		M /H	F		M/H	F
Eswatini	2005	222	116.0	107.5	71	53.9	51.8	6	5.1	4.9
Eswatini	2006	230	122.8	112.5	77	58.6	55.9	6	5.3	4.6
	2010	241	131.0	118.8	89	67.3	63.7	...	...	...
	2013	239	128.2	115.7	93	72.0	70.1	8	7.0	6.6
	2014	240	126.6	114.8	97	74.1	73.5	...	...	...
	2015	241	124.9	113.5	100	76.0	76.0	...	...	...
	2016	239	121.8	111.8	108	82.6	82.2	...	...	...
	2017	237	119.9	110.3	...	...	...	...	...	...
Ethiopia	2005	10 020	86.1	71.9	2 488	31.3	18.8	191	4.3	1.4
Éthiopie	2010	13 635	95.2	88.0	4 207	38.0	31.6	578	10.5	4.5
	2012	14 532	97.7	90.7	4 929	39.4	35.7	693	11.2	5.2
	2014	15 733	103.5	95.0	...	...	...	757	10.9	5.3
	2015	16 198	105.8	96.1	5 029	35.6	34.2	...	...	...
Fiji	2004	113	113.5	111.8	102	88.1	93.9	13	14.6	17.4
Fidji	*2005	...	...	...	...	...	...	13	14.7	17.6
	2009	101	105.6	104.0	98	82.9	90.7	...	...	...
	2012	103	106.5	106.7	97	85.7	94.3	...	...	...
	2013	105	107.8	107.8	...	...	...	...	...	...
	2015	109	107.9	105.5	...	...	...	...	...	...
	2016	110	107.6	105.2	...	...	...	...	...	...
Finland	2005	382	98.8	98.0	431	109.3	114.3	306	83.3	100.5
Finlande	2010	347	99.8	99.1	427	105.2	110.1	304	84.3	103.1
	2014	352	100.8	100.4	537	139.7	153.5	306	80.8	97.3
	2015	355	100.8	100.3	540	142.9	157.5	302	79.8	95.8
	2017	364	100.4	99.9	543	146.8	161.5	296	81.0	95.7
France	2005	4 015	* 105.1	* 104.1	6 036	* 106.6	* 107.0	2 187	* 47.9	* 60.0
France	2010	4 159	* 103.4	* 102.1	5 873	* 105.9	* 107.0	2 245	* 48.7	* 61.2
	2014	4 189	* 101.5	* 101.0	5 947	* 102.7	* 104.2	2 389	* 55.0	* 68.3
	2015	4 256	* 102.3	* 101.7	5 983	* 102.9	* 103.9	2 424	* 56.1	* 69.7
	2017	4 310	* 102.8	* 102.2	6 058	* 103.5	* 104.1	2 533	* 58.7	* 72.8
Gabon	2002	282	141.2	140.6	* 105	...	...	...	...	...
Gabon	2003	280	137.9	137.1	...	...	...	10	10.4	6.1
	2011	318	142.1	137.7	...	...	...	...	...	...
Gambia	2004	205	81.1	82.0	...	...	...	2	1.9	0.4
Gambie	2005	205	78.4	80.9	...	...	...	...	...	...
	2010	229	78.8	80.8	* 124	* 51.2	* 49.1	3	2.3	1.6
	2012	244	79.4	83.0	...	...	...	5	3.2	2.2
	2014	275	84.4	89.1	...	...	...	...	...	...
	2015	294	87.1	93.0	...	...	...	...	...	...
	2018	350	93.6	102.5	...	...	...	...	...	...
Georgia	2005	338	98.9	102.9	316	92.7	96.3	174	49.4	53.5
Géorgie	2008	311	103.6	104.6	305	97.8	100.9	130	* 34.5	* 43.5
	2009	299	103.3	104.1	342	...	...	95	25.3	32.7
	2010	289	102.7	104.1	...	...	...	106	28.4	37.0
	2014	285	104.7	103.8	282	96.0	99.1	121	37.1	47.7
	2015	289	102.7	102.8	278	98.1	100.8	128	41.6	51.6
	2018	305	98.1	99.2	280	105.3	106.8	148	57.3	63.7
	2019	...	...	...	...	...	...	151	60.2	68.1
Germany	2005	3 306	103.3	102.9	8 268	103.6	100.9	...	...	...
Allemagne	2010	3 068	103.3	102.7	7 664	106.7	101.2	...	...	...
	2014	2 863	100.7	100.4	7 201	102.0	97.3	2 912	67.0	63.9
	2015	2 879	101.7	101.6	7 113	101.1	96.4	2 978	68.4	67.0
	2017	2 955	103.9	104.2	7 029	101.4	95.2	3 092	69.8	70.7
Ghana	2005	2 930	88.3	84.7	* 1 370	* 43.5	* 36.4	120	7.5	4.2
Ghana	2009	3 659	101.1	99.5	1 812	51.7	45.7	203	10.8	6.7
	2014	4 117	104.6	104.6	2 266	66.0	62.0	402	18.3	12.4
	2015	4 342	108.4	108.3	2 440	69.6	66.1	418	18.4	12.9
	2018	4 401	103.0	104.2	2 677	71.8	70.8	444	17.7	13.6
	2019	4 550	104.1	105.6	2 851	64.6	64.5	...	...	...

Enrollment in primary, secondary and tertiary education levels *(continued)*
Number of students enrolled (thousands) and gross enrollment ratio by sex

Inscriptions aux niveaux primaire, secondaire et supérieur *(suite)*
Nombre d'élèves inscrits (milliers) et taux brut de scolarisation par sexe

Region, country or area Région, pays ou zone	Year & Année &	Primary education Enseignement primaire			Secondary education Enseignement secondaire			Tertiary education Enseignement supérieur		
		Total ('000)	Gross enrollment ratio Taux brut de scolarisation		Total ('000)	Gross enrollment ratio Taux brut de scolarisation		Total ('000)	Gross enrollment ratio Taux brut de scolarisation	
			M/H	F		M/H	F		M/H	F
Gibraltar Gibraltar	2001	2	84.6	84.3	2	98.6	100.3	...	...	...
	2009	3	110.9	112.8	2	85.2	83.2	...	...	...
	2017	3	103.4	103.7	2	119.1	115.7	...	...	...
Greece Grèce	2005	650	98.9	96.8	716	103.1	98.4	647	80.8	90.1
	2010	643	99.6	97.4	717	108.1	104.4	642	100.5	107.3
	2014	629	98.4	97.3	668	105.2	99.2	677	120.1	125.0
	2015	644	100.0	99.1	663	105.8	98.4	...	...	...
	2017	649	99.5	99.6	668	107.5	101.4	735	136.2	137.0
Grenada Grenade	2005	14	104.7	101.7	* 13	* 108.4	* 111.5	...	...	...
	2009	14	119.4	111.6	11	109.0	109.9	7	54.2	75.3
	2010	14	119.1	113.9	12	114.9	118.6	...	...	...
	2014	13	119.7	117.5	10	113.2	111.0	...	...	...
	2015	13	120.6	116.3	9	112.8	110.7	9	88.8	102.5
	2018	13	107.7	106.0	9	118.2	122.1	9	93.2	116.2
Guatemala Guatemala	2002	2 076	107.3	98.8	608	37.8	33.8	112	10.6	7.8
	2005	2 345	113.3	106.3	754	43.2	39.8	...	...	...
	2007	2 449	114.0	108.7	864	46.4	43.6	234	17.1	17.5
	2010	2 653	116.6	114.3	1 082	53.9	50.7	233	...	...
	2014	2 417	104.1	101.0	1 166	54.0	51.2	299	17.2	19.2
	2015	2 382	103.1	99.9	1 221	55.8	52.6	367	20.0	23.6
	2018	2 362	103.2	100.5	1 227	54.0	51.4	...	...	...
Guinea Guinée	2005	1 207	86.6	69.4	* 420	* 39.0	* 19.1	24	5.2	1.1
	2008	1 364	90.0	75.4	531	43.1	24.6	80	14.6	4.5
	2010	1 453	92.3	76.0	...	...	...	99	16.8	5.2
	2014	1 730	100.4	85.0	716	47.5	31.0	118	16.2	7.0
	2016	1 777	100.5	82.4	...	...	...	...	...	...
Guinea-Bissau Guinée-Bissau	2000	150	90.9	60.6	26	23.6	12.7	...	...	...
	2005	252	...	...	51	...	...	3	...	...
	2006	269	...	...	55	...	...	4	...	...
	2010	279	122.9	114.5	...	...	...	...	...	...
Guyana Guyana	2005	117	101.1	100.6	71	88.1	90.3	7	7.7	16.4
	2010	99	97.9	95.0	81	88.4	91.9	8	6.9	16.3
	2012	94	99.6	96.0	86	96.3	99.2	9	7.8	15.4
Honduras Honduras	2004	1 257	106.5	106.0	...	...	...	* 123	* 13.2	* 19.0
	2005	1 232	101.8	101.7	...	...	...	...	...	...
	2010	1 275	100.6	100.7	655	59.1	72.8	170	18.1	20.9
	2014	1 150	92.6	91.2	620	45.6	53.5	186	16.9	23.1
	2015	1 154	93.0	92.5	638	46.2	55.4	195	17.3	23.6
	2017	1 124	91.6	91.5	655	48.6	55.9	245	20.7	28.1
	2018	...	...	...	...	...	...	267	22.2	30.3
Hungary Hongrie	2005	431	99.2	97.1	960	96.7	95.8	436	53.0	77.5
	2010	388	101.2	100.5	905	97.7	96.4	389	54.1	73.8
	2014	393	102.2	101.5	858	103.9	104.5	329	45.5	58.9
	2015	396	102.5	102.2	827	102.7	103.3	308	43.5	54.7
	2017	391	101.1	100.5	808	103.4	103.6	287	43.3	53.9
Iceland Islande	2005	31	98.0	95.7	33	110.5	112.1	15	48.1	92.5
	2010	30	99.0	99.6	36	106.5	108.2	18	56.8	101.5
	2014	30	98.7	97.7	38	116.6	120.7	20	59.8	104.1
	2015	30	98.7	98.6	37	118.6	119.6	19	54.7	98.0
	2017	32	100.4	100.3	35	118.1	116.9	18	50.6	94.4
India Inde	2003	125 569	103.4	101.9	81 050	54.3	44.5	11 295	12.5	8.6
	2005	...	...	...	89 462	* 58.4	* 49.0	11 777	12.3	8.9
	2010	138 414	* 107.7	* 110.7	107 687	64.9	61.1	20 741	20.3	15.1
	2014	137 809	102.4	114.0	129 439	73.3	75.0	30 306	25.5	25.4
	2015	138 518	102.8	114.8	129 542	73.1	74.7	32 107	26.7	26.8
	2017	143 227	105.6	121.1	129 829	* 73.0	* 74.1	33 374	26.9	28.0
	2018	...	...	...	133 144	* 73.9	* 76.6	34 338	27.2	29.1

Enrollment in primary, secondary and tertiary education levels *(continued)*
Number of students enrolled (thousands) and gross enrollment ratio by sex

Inscriptions aux niveaux primaire, secondaire et supérieur *(suite)*
Nombre d'élèves inscrits (milliers) et taux brut de scolarisation par sexe

Region, country or area Région, pays ou zone	Year & Année &	Primary education Enseignement primaire			Secondary education Enseignement secondaire			Tertiary education Enseignement supérieur		
		Total ('000)	Gross enrollment ratio Taux brut de scolarisation		Total ('000)	Gross enrollment ratio Taux brut de scolarisation		Total ('000)	Gross enrollment ratio Taux brut de scolarisation	
			M/H	F		M/H	F		M/H	F
Indonesia	2004	29 142	109.7	108.1	16 354	62.1	61.6	3 551	18.5	14.7
Indonésie	2005	29 150	* 109.6	* 106.2	15 993	* 60.5	* 59.8	* 3 662	...	...
	2010	30 342	107.4	111.0	19 976	76.2	76.7	5 001	25.7	22.5
	2014	29 838	107.4	104.7	22 587	83.0	82.4	6 463	29.2	32.7
	2015	29 700	107.4	104.4	23 756	86.0	86.3	7 044	31.5	35.0
	2018	29 426	108.1	104.6	24 894	87.8	90.0	8 037	33.8	39.0
Iran (Islamic Republic of)	2005	6 207	100.9	97.5	9 066	78.6	75.8	2 126	23.1	24.5
Iran (Rép. islamique d')	2010	5 630	101.7	99.6	7 347	83.2	78.0	3 791	44.2	44.1
	2014	7 441	105.0	110.3	5 795	88.3	82.2	4 685	70.9	63.8
	2015	7 670	105.7	112.3	5 712	88.7	83.0	...	...	...
	2017	8 172	107.7	113.9	5 684	87.9	84.7	4 074	73.3	62.9
Iraq	2004	4 335	113.0	95.3	1 706	56.9	38.2	413	20.0	11.9
Iraq	*2005	...	...	...	...	...	...	425	20.1	12.0
	2007	4 864	117.8	99.1	2 038	61.4	46.0	...	...	...
Ireland	2005	454	* 103.3	* 102.9	317	* 105.2	* 114.6	187	* 52.5	* 65.3
Irlande	2010	506	* 103.2	* 103.3	336	* 114.8	* 121.7	194	* 60.8	* 65.4
	2014	536	* 101.8	* 101.3	348	* 115.3	* 118.3	204	* 71.8	* 75.9
	2015	545	* 101.4	* 101.0	355	* 115.4	* 118.7	215	* 74.0	* 80.6
	2017	559	* 101.0	* 100.7	392	* 126.3	* 124.3	225	* 73.7	* 82.0
Israel	2005	722	104.5	105.0	673	106.3	105.6	311	50.7	67.2
Israël	2010	807	105.2	105.7	708	102.0	104.5	360	57.6	74.6
	2014	862	105.0	105.4	768	102.3	103.8	377	57.3	77.1
	2015	884	105.3	106.0	785	103.2	104.2	374	55.2	76.3
	2017	917	104.4	105.4	819	104.2	106.0	377	52.8	74.5
Italy	2005	2 771	103.0	101.6	4 507	99.6	98.9	2 015	54.6	74.8
Italie	2010	2 822	103.5	102.5	4 626	103.4	102.4	1 980	54.4	77.7
	2014	2 863	101.4	100.9	4 597	102.6	102.0	1 854	51.9	72.1
	2015	2 856	100.6	100.2	4 606	102.4	102.1	1 826	51.6	70.8
	2017	2 902	103.4	100.3	4 602	101.6	100.9	1 837	53.0	71.5
Jamaica	2002	330	96.2	96.1	228	83.1	86.1	45	11.7	25.5
Jamaïque	2004	331	96.1	96.4	246	88.0	91.9	52	...	...
	2005	326	...	...	246	87.1	92.4	48	...	...
	2010	294	...	...	260	88.2	95.5	71	16.4	37.8
	2013	278	...	...	229	79.5	85.6	74	16.6	38.2
	2014	266	...	...	224	79.1	85.4	...	...	...
	2015	259	89.3	94.5	215	78.2	83.8	75	19.9	34.7
	2018	249	93.0	88.9	201	81.0	83.6	...	...	...
Japan	2014	6 715	...	...	7 227	...	...	3 862	...	...
Japon	2015	6 638	...	...	7 221	...	...	3 845	...	...
	2017	6 532	...	...	7 093	...	...	3 853	...	...
Jordan	2005	805	96.4	97.4	626	83.2	85.7	218	35.8	39.0
Jordanie	2010	820	82.7	81.1	710	78.6	81.6	247	34.8	39.6
	2012	849	77.6	75.3	724	73.2	75.2	307	38.9	44.8
	2014	980	79.9	79.1	749	68.0	70.3	...	...	...
	2015	...	...	...	...	...	...	313	35.1	38.2
	2018	1 134	82.2	80.7	790	62.1	64.2	321	31.5	37.4
Kazakhstan	2000	1 208	96.8	97.1	1 994	91.3	96.2	418	29.1	34.6
Kazakhstan	2005	1 024	102.6	102.5	...	...	...	...	...	...
	2010	958	108.5	109.1	1 818	98.2	98.8	757	40.7	51.7
	2014	1 122	112.5	112.6	1 662	105.3	108.0	727	43.2	54.5
	2015	1 196	111.5	111.7	1 679	108.5	112.2	658	40.8	52.1
	2019	1 461	103.5	105.3	1 928	112.7	113.8	685	55.4	68.4
Kenya	2005	6 076	101.5	97.1	* 2 468	* 48.3	* 45.7	* 114	* 3.7	* 2.2
Kenya	2009	7 150	105.1	102.7	3 204	59.9	53.7	168	4.7	3.3
	*2014	8 158	105.4	106.1	...	...	...	...	...	...
	2015	8 169	103.7	103.6	...	...	...	421	10.8	7.7
	2016	8 290	103.0	103.4	...	...	...	540	13.5	9.4
	2017	...	...	...	...	...	...	563	13.2	9.7

Enrollment in primary, secondary and tertiary education levels *(continued)*
Number of students enrolled (thousands) and gross enrollment ratio by sex

Inscriptions aux niveaux primaire, secondaire et supérieur *(suite)*
Nombre d'élèves inscrits (milliers) et taux brut de scolarisation par sexe

Region, country or area Région, pays ou zone	Year & Année &	Primary education Enseignement primaire			Secondary education Enseignement secondaire			Tertiary education Enseignement supérieur		
		Total ('000)	Gross enrollment ratio Taux brut de scolarisation		Total ('000)	Gross enrollment ratio Taux brut de scolarisation		Total ('000)	Gross enrollment ratio Taux brut de scolarisation	
			M/H	F		M/H	F		M/H	F
Kiribati	2005	16	111.1	112.8	12	83.1	95.3	...	...	...
Kiribati	2008	16	107.6	112.7	12	82.7	91.4	...	...	...
	2009	16	107.2	113.2	...	...	...	...	...	...
	2014	16	113.0	114.8	...	...	...	...	...	...
	2015	16	104.5	106.6	...	...	...	...	...	...
	2017	17	97.9	104.9	...	...	...	...	...	...
Kuwait	2004	158	98.2	107.4	267	99.5	105.4	* 37	* 12.2	* 28.1
Koweït	2005	203	103.0	106.9	* 244	* 104.8	* 114.7	...	...	...
	2010	214	103.2	101.2	264	97.0	98.8	...	...	...
	2014	253	102.7	104.9	* 283	* 91.6	* 96.3	106	35.4	68.9
	2015	264	101.0	104.3	302	94.9	101.0	113	36.9	76.5
	2018	280	88.1	97.2	...	...	...	116	35.8	76.1
Kyrgyzstan	2005	434	99.6	98.0	721	86.4	86.7	220	37.8	47.5
Kirghizistan	2010	391	99.8	99.1	694	87.7	87.4	261	36.6	47.8
	2014	435	106.3	105.3	651	90.5	91.2	268	39.9	52.0
	2015	451	105.8	105.0	643	90.5	91.7	265	40.6	53.0
	2018	529	107.9	107.2	675	95.1	95.0	218	36.0	46.7
Lao People's Dem. Rep.	2005	891	120.2	104.4	394	49.8	37.4	47	9.2	6.4
Rép. dém. populaire lao	2010	916	128.9	117.9	435	51.5	42.3	118	18.9	14.4
	2014	871	121.3	114.8	601	61.8	55.9	132	19.1	17.7
	2015	850	116.6	111.3	640	66.1	60.7	130	18.7	17.7
	2018	786	104.3	100.4	* 678	* 69.6	* 65.0	105	17.4	15.5
Latvia	2005	84	* 106.1	* 103.5	272	* 103.0	* 102.4	131	* 54.4	* 97.3
Lettonie	2010	114	* 103.9	* 101.9	147	* 103.5	* 102.1	113	* 50.4	* 88.4
	2014	115	* 99.9	* 99.7	122	* 115.1	* 112.2	90	* 58.7	* 83.8
	2015	117	* 99.4	* 99.4	118	* 113.5	* 111.2	86	* 58.4	* 91.1
	2017	122	* 99.3	* 99.5	117	* 111.3	* 110.2	83	* 72.0	* 105.1
Lebanon	2005	* 476	...	...	* 378	...	...	166	...	...
Liban	2010	462	...	...	383	...	...	202	...	...
	2014	481	...	...	370	...	...	229	...	...
	2015	491	...	...	382	...	...	216	...	...
	2018	509	...	...	403	...	...	231	...	...
Lesotho	2005	422	127.8	126.3	94	34.0	43.0	8	3.0	3.7
Lesotho	2006	425	131.6	129.6	96	35.3	44.8	9	3.3	3.9
	2010	389	127.4	122.1	126	47.1	65.4	...	...	...
	2014	366	119.1	114.0	131	51.2	69.4	24	9.1	12.9
	2015	362	119.6	113.7	133	51.8	69.7	22	8.2	12.2
	2017	368	124.1	117.8	136	52.8	71.3	23	8.2	13.3
	2018	...	...	...	...	...	...	22	8.0	12.4
Liberia	2000	496	133.7	98.5	136	41.4	30.3	52	25.2	14.0
Libéria	2009	605	108.0	96.5	...	...	...	...	...	...
	2010	...	...	...	...	...	...	33	12.4	6.6
	2012	...	...	...	...	...	...	44	14.7	9.2
	2014	684	101.6	93.1	223	43.5	33.6	...	...	...
	2015	684	100.3	90.2	227	42.8	32.9	...	...	...
	2017	635	85.5	84.7	...	...	...	...	...	...
Libya	2003	739	104.8	101.6	* 798	* 100.7	* 107.2	* 375	* 57.5	* 63.6
Libye	2005	714	102.7	101.5	702	* 84.5	* 100.7	...	...	...
	2006	755	111.3	106.6	733	90.2	106.0	...	...	...
Liechtenstein	2005	2	111.5	102.5	3	115.2	100.1	1	35.4	14.0
Liechtenstein	2010	2	* 108.6	* 102.3	3	* 117.6	* 100.0	1	* 44.3	* 27.4
	2014	2	* 103.1	* 102.3	3	* 127.8	* 103.3	1	* 50.8	* 24.1
	2015	2	* 106.5	* 104.8	3	* 130.7	* 101.7	1	* 44.8	* 21.9
	2017	2	* 106.3	* 102.9	3	* 129.1	* 105.1	1	* 43.6	* 27.4
Lithuania	2005	158	* 103.2	* 102.4	424	* 104.8	* 104.2	195	* 62.5	* 97.5
Lituanie	2010	122	* 101.0	* 99.8	343	* 106.0	* 104.1	201	* 69.2	* 104.6
	2014	108	* 101.7	* 101.4	277	* 110.4	* 105.8	148	* 57.4	* 84.2
	2015	108	* 102.2	* 101.9	263	* 109.8	* 105.4	141	* 57.5	* 82.7
	2017	114	* 103.9	* 103.9	243	* 110.6	* 106.0	126	* 61.4	* 84.0

6

Enrollment in primary, secondary and tertiary education levels *(continued)*
Number of students enrolled (thousands) and gross enrollment ratio by sex

Inscriptions aux niveaux primaire, secondaire et supérieur *(suite)*
Nombre d'élèves inscrits (milliers) et taux brut de scolarisation par sexe

Region, country or area Région, pays ou zone	Year & Année &	Primary education Enseignement primaire			Secondary education Enseignement secondaire			Tertiary education Enseignement supérieur		
		Total ('000)	Gross enrollment ratio Taux brut de scolarisation		Total ('000)	Gross enrollment ratio Taux brut de scolarisation		Total ('000)	Gross enrollment ratio Taux brut de scolarisation	
			M/H	F		M /H	F		M/H	F
Luxembourg Luxembourg	2003	34	99.5	99.3	35	93.6	98.7	3	11.1	13.3
	2005	35	100.7	100.9	36	92.9	97.9	...	...	...
	2010	35	97.1	98.1	43	99.8	102.8	5	17.3	19.2
	2012	35	97.0	97.3	44	98.7	102.1	6	18.2	20.7
	2014	35	97.4	97.7	47	101.6	103.9	...	...	...
	2015	36	99.0	98.9	47	100.5	104.2	7	18.8	20.8
	2017	37	102.6	102.0	48	102.6	104.8	7	18.2	20.1
Madagascar Madagascar	2005	3 598	142.0	135.8	* 621	* 21.9	* 21.0	45	2.8	2.5
	2009	4 324	151.0	147.6	* 1 022	* 31.6	29.7	68	3.7	3.3
	2010	4 242	145.0	142.4	...	...	...	74	3.8	3.5
	2014	4 611	145.4	145.0	1 494	38.7	38.0	113	5.0	4.6
	2015	4 764	147.3	147.3	* 1 536	* 38.7	* 38.3	117	5.0	4.6
	2018	4 861	142.0	143.1	1 548	36.0	37.1	144	5.5	5.2
Malawi Malawi	2005	2 868	129.9	131.0	516	31.3	24.8	6	* 0.6	* 0.3
	2010	3 417	137.3	140.2	692	36.1	31.9	10	0.9	0.5
	2011	3 564	138.9	142.3	736	37.1	33.1	12	1.0	0.6
	2014	4 097	146.0	148.8	920	42.3	38.1	...	...	...
	2015	4 205	144.9	147.9	* 962	* 42.6	* 38.9	...	...	...
	2018	4 442	141.8	143.1	1 041	40.6	39.9	...	...	...
Malaysia Malaisie	2005	3 202	100.0	100.0	2 489	76.8	84.7	697	24.1	31.9
	2010	3 234	99.3	100.2	2 616	74.5	80.2	1 061	31.4	43.0
	2014	3 178	104.0	104.8	2 846	82.1	88.8	1 128	33.9	45.4
	2015	3 108	103.5	104.1	2 801	81.4	88.7	1 302	39.8	51.7
	2017	3 085	104.6	106.0	2 745	83.1	88.0	1 249	40.5	47.1
	2018	...	...	...	2 593	78.8	85.4	1 285	40.7	49.9
Maldives Maldives	2003	66	125.2	122.6	29	63.9	71.8	~0	0.1	0.3
	2004	63	124.2	121.3	* 29	* 63.3	* 72.7	...	...	...
	2005	58	118.0	116.1	...	...	...	...	...	...
	2008	47	114.3	109.3	...	...	...	5	9.7	13.0
	2009	45	112.7	108.6	...	...	...	...	...	...
	2010	42	...	...	...	...	...	...	...	...
	2014	40	...	...	...	...	...	6	8.5	20.1
	2015	42	103.0	100.0	...	...	...	...	...	...
	2017	45	96.2	98.1	...	...	...	14	16.6	59.8
Mali Mali	2002	1 227	75.4	56.7	...	...	...	23	2.8	1.4
	2005	1 506	82.7	65.0	430	* 31.9	* 19.6	...	...	...
	2010	2 019	89.7	77.0	758	46.5	31.9	81	8.6	3.6
	2014	2 182	81.6	72.4	961	50.5	37.4	88	8.4	3.5
	2015	2 227	79.7	71.5	945	46.5	36.8	83	7.7	3.2
	2017	2 539	84.6	75.6	1 017	45.9	37.1	73	6.3	2.7
	2018	2 477	79.5	71.6	1 046	45.0	37.0	...	...	...
Malta Malte	2005	30	101.5	99.0	40	103.8	99.9	9	27.7	37.2
	2010	25	101.6	101.9	37	110.0	98.2	11	32.0	42.9
	2014	24	102.1	103.6	30	92.8	96.2	13	38.5	50.7
	2015	25	102.8	104.3	29	92.1	97.8	13	39.9	55.0
	2017	26	104.9	105.1	31	104.8	104.7	14	46.0	63.2
Marshall Islands Îles Marshall	2002	9	127.2	118.6	6	66.8	69.8	1	14.0	18.5
	2005	8	101.0	126.5	5	61.1	62.0	...	...	...
	2009	8	98.8	97.4	5	75.6	79.3	...	...	...
	2011	9	96.2	93.2	...	...	...	...	...	...
	2012	...	...	...	...	...	...	1	23.5	23.8
	2015	8	88.5	86.5	5	64.1	68.8	...	...	...
	2016	8	84.9	84.6	6	62.4	66.6	...	...	...
Mauritania Mauritanie	2005	444	92.2	95.2	93	23.8	20.8	9	4.4	1.5
	2010	531	97.5	102.0	* 110	* 22.4	* 19.1	15	6.2	2.5
	2013	569	96.7	101.4	171	31.1	29.1	19	7.5	3.3
	2014	592	97.7	103.1	179	32.1	29.3	...	...	...
	2015	633	102.0	107.0	188	32.5	30.3	21	7.4	3.7
	2017	617	93.6	99.8	204	32.5	32.6	19	6.6	3.3
	2018	655	97.1	102.8	237	36.5	37.1	...	...	...

Enrollment in primary, secondary and tertiary education levels *(continued)*
Number of students enrolled (thousands) and gross enrollment ratio by sex

Inscriptions aux niveaux primaire, secondaire et supérieur *(suite)*
Nombre d'élèves inscrits (milliers) et taux brut de scolarisation par sexe

Region, country or area Région, pays ou zone	Year & Année &	Primary education Enseignement primaire			Secondary education Enseignement secondaire			Tertiary education Enseignement supérieur		
		Total ('000)	Gross enrollment ratio Taux brut de scolarisation		Total ('000)	Gross enrollment ratio Taux brut de scolarisation		Total ('000)	Gross enrollment ratio Taux brut de scolarisation	
			M/H	F		M /H	F		M/H	F
Mauritius	2005	124	103.3	103.1	* 129	* 89.7	* 87.6	* 21	* 21.0	* 21.7
Maurice	2010	117	102.5	103.1	* 127	* 87.2	* 91.3	33	30.5	36.9
	2014	105	101.4	103.5	133	99.0	100.8	40	35.1	43.2
	2015	102	102.0	103.8	129	95.3	99.5	38	32.4	42.5
	2017	93	100.6	102.4	125	92.5	99.1	39	33.9	47.5
	2018	90	99.8	102.5	122	92.5	97.8	...	...	...
Mexico	2005	14 700	109.6	107.6	10 564	80.6	84.0	2 385	24.5	23.9
Mexique	2010	14 906	111.4	109.8	11 682	83.8	90.4	2 847	27.9	27.3
	2014	14 627	108.3	107.7	12 993	94.7	100.1	3 419	31.4	30.8
	2015	14 398	106.7	106.5	13 473	97.6	104.1	3 515	32.1	31.6
	2017	14 182	105.5	106.0	14 035	100.7	108.2	4 430	39.8	40.6
Micronesia (Fed. States of)	*2000	...	...	...	...	...	...	2	...	...
Micronésie (États féd. de)	2005	19	112.5	109.6	14	79.9	86.6	...	...	...
	2007	19	112.4	113.8	...	...	...	...	...	...
	2014	14	102.9	99.9	...	...	...	...	...	...
	2015	14	98.3	96.0	...	...	...	...	...	...
Monaco	2004	2	...	...	3	...	...	...	...	...
Monaco	2010	2	...	...	3	...	...	...	...	...
	2014	2	...	...	3	...	...	...	...	...
	2015	2	...	...	3	...	...	...	...	...
	2019	2	...	...	3	...	...	1	...	...
Mongolia	2005	251	98.0	98.0	339	85.6	95.0	124	33.8	55.9
Mongolie	2010	274	127.2	124.3	276	88.3	94.8	166	42.5	65.1
	2014	239	102.3	100.3	...	...	...	175	52.7	75.2
	2015	251	101.3	99.4	...	...	...	180	57.4	78.9
	2018	311	105.3	102.8	...	...	...	155	54.7	76.7
Montenegro	2005	38	111.8	113.7	68	93.0	96.1	11	17.2	27.2
Monténégro	2010	35	110.3	110.6	70	99.0	101.9	24	46.5	58.3
	2012	38	96.1	98.7	63	92.0	94.4	...	...	...
	2015	38	95.3	95.5	61	92.0	93.5	...	...	...
	2018	39	102.2	97.6	57	89.3	90.5	24	47.9	64.9
Montserrat	2005	1	161.2	150.6	~0	82.5	86.5	...	...	...
Montserrat	2009	~0	154.0	163.4	~0	124.0	123.7	~0	5.3	26.3
	2010	...	...	...	...	...	...	~0	4.9	30.2
	2014	~0	92.9	96.0	~0	173.5	180.4	...	...	...
	2018	~0	104.6	114.8	~0	94.5	105.9	...	...	...
Morocco	2005	4 023	110.9	100.7	1 948	54.3	46.3	368	13.1	10.5
Maroc	2010	3 945	113.0	106.3	2 393	67.6	58.8	447	15.3	13.8
	2012	4 017	113.3	108.0	2 554	75.1	64.1	606	20.2	18.7
	2014	4 030	112.4	107.4	...	...	...	789	25.8	24.9
	2015	4 039	112.3	106.6	...	...	...	877	29.0	27.8
	2018	4 323	116.1	111.5	2 871	83.7	76.6	1 056	36.2	35.7
Mozambique	2005	3 943	109.5	91.3	306	16.0	10.9	28	2.0	0.9
Mozambique	2010	5 278	119.2	105.9	672	28.0	22.5	104	5.7	3.7
	2014	* 5 705	* 112.7	* 102.5	* 1 026	* 35.2	* 31.5	157	7.3	5.1
	2015	* 5 902	* 113.8	* 103.4	* 1 073	* 35.2	* 31.9	175	7.8	5.6
	2017	6 139	112.0	103.6	1 216	37.4	33.4	201	7.9	6.3
	2018	6 563	116.8	108.4	...	...	...	214	8.1	6.5
Myanmar	2001	4 782	98.2	96.0	2 302	39.1	36.5	553	...	...
Myanmar	2005	4 948	98.1	98.2	2 589	45.1	43.5	...	...	...
	2007	5 014	...	...	2 686	46.3	46.1	508	9.0	12.2
	2010	5 126	98.6	97.6	2 852	47.1	49.2	...	...	...
	2012	...	...	...	...	...	...	634	12.2	14.9
	2014	5 177	103.3	100.3	3 191	51.3	52.3	...	...	...
	2018	5 300	114.8	109.7	4 187	65.6	71.3	932	15.6	22.0

Enrollment in primary, secondary and tertiary education levels *(continued)*
Number of students enrolled (thousands) and gross enrollment ratio by sex

Inscriptions aux niveaux primaire, secondaire et supérieur *(suite)*
Nombre d'élèves inscrits (milliers) et taux brut de scolarisation par sexe

Region, country or area Région, pays ou zone	Year & Année &	Primary education Enseignement primaire			Secondary education Enseignement secondaire			Tertiary education Enseignement supérieur		
		Total ('000)	Gross enrollment ratio Taux brut de scolarisation		Total ('000)	Gross enrollment ratio Taux brut de scolarisation		Total ('000)	Gross enrollment ratio Taux brut de scolarisation	
			M/H	F		M /H	F		M/H	F
Namibia	2005	404	114.6	112.0	148	60.3	66.7	14	7.3	6.2
Namibie	2007	410	116.0	112.6	158	61.5	70.0	...	...	...
	2008	407	115.9	112.2	...	...	...	20	8.1	10.3
	2010	407	117.5	112.9	...	...	...	...	...	...
	2013	425	123.7	118.4	...	...	...	...	...	...
	2014	...	...	...	...	...	...	47	14.8	24.5
	2015	...	...	...	...	...	...	50	15.1	26.0
	2017	476	126.5	121.8	...	...	...	56	15.3	30.3
	2018	491	126.4	122.1	...	...	...	...	...	...
Nauru	2005	2	135.9	127.2	1	48.8	50.1	...	...	...
Nauru	2008	1	93.8	93.4	1	63.9	67.9	...	...	...
	2014	2	121.3	111.6	1	86.0	83.2	...	...	...
	2016	2	129.7	123.2	1	81.9	83.6	...	...	...
Nepal	2005	4 030	119.6	109.2	2 054	* 53.1	* 43.1	187	10.2	5.5
Népal	2010	4 901	139.3	149.9	* 2 694	* 58.3	* 56.9	377	17.6	11.3
	2013	4 577	139.8	151.3	* 3 111	* 64.4	* 66.4	477	19.0	15.4
	2014	4 402	138.3	148.5	* 3 164	* 65.7	* 68.1	459	...	...
	2015	4 335	139.9	148.6	* 3 176	* 66.3	* 69.4	445	15.5	14.5
	2018	...	...	...	...	...	...	405	12.0	12.8
	2019	3 970	140.8	143.5	3 464	77.4	83.0	...	...	...
Netherlands	2005	1 278	107.9	105.5	1 411	119.5	117.2	565	56.4	61.1
Pays-Bas	2010	1 294	108.5	108.1	1 475	122.9	121.2	651	60.3	67.3
	2012	1 277	105.8	105.8	1 550	130.1	127.9	794	73.0	80.4
	2015	1 208	102.7	102.7	1 613	132.6	134.6	843	75.2	86.1
	2017	1 182	104.2	104.2	1 650	134.7	136.5	875	79.3	90.9
Netherlands Antilles [mer] Antilles néerlandaises [anc.]	2002	23	...	...	15	...	...	2	...	...
New Zealand	2005	353	100.1	99.3	526	117.1	123.6	...	...	...
Nouvelle-Zélande	2010	348	101.0	101.3	512	116.4	121.8	...	...	...
	2014	360	97.5	97.8	492	111.9	119.1	261	64.4	92.6
	2015	368	97.7	98.2	487	111.5	118.1	270	67.3	94.9
	2017	384	99.8	100.2	486	111.1	118.2	269	67.9	97.2
Nicaragua	2002	923	114.4	114.6	383	55.1	65.5	100	16.5	18.4
Nicaragua	2005	945	120.3	118.6	438	63.1	73.5	...	...	...
	2010	924	121.1	120.1	465	69.1	78.0	...	...	...
Niger	2005	1 064	56.2	40.2	182	11.9	7.4	11	1.6	0.6
Niger	2010	1 726	69.2	55.9	307	15.3	10.7	17	2.0	0.8
	2012	2 051	74.5	62.1	389	17.7	12.3	22	2.3	0.9
	2014	2 277	75.2	63.8	515	21.0	15.3	...	...	...
	2015	2 445	77.4	65.6	595	23.1	17.0	52	4.4	2.1
	2017	2 768	80.1	69.2	787	27.7	20.7	65	5.0	2.4
	2018	...	...	...	...	...	...	80	6.2	2.6
Nigeria	2005	22 115	109.8	92.6	6 398	38.1	31.7	1 392	12.3	8.7
Nigéria	2010	* 21 558	* 89.1	* 81.0	9 057	47.2	41.2	1 395	11.0	8.1
	2011	23 669	93.8	87.5	9 591	49.1	41.9	1 513	12.0	8.3
	2014	25 801	90.8	89.4	10 496	48.2	43.0	...	...	...
	2015	...	...	...	11 116	48.8	44.7	...	...	...
	2016	25 591	87.2	82.2	10 315	44.1	39.8	...	...	...
Niue	2005	~0	103.5	100.0	~0	82.9	90.8	...	...	...
Nioué	2014	~0	114.8	134.6	~0	88.2	115.6	...	...	...
	2015	~0	127.7	127.8	~0	89.5	109.4	...	...	...
	2016	~0	127.5	126.9	...	...	...	...	...	...
North Macedonia	2005	110	94.5	92.5	214	82.8	80.2	49	24.6	34.1
Macédoine du Nord	2010	111	88.0	86.7	197	83.3	81.0	62	34.7	40.4
	2014	108	91.8	91.0	171	81.8	79.3	61	34.0	42.8
	2015	109	93.7	94.0	169	82.6	81.2	64	36.7	45.9
	2017	109	97.2	97.1	161	82.5	80.3	61	36.7	48.6

Enrollment in primary, secondary and tertiary education levels *(continued)*
Number of students enrolled (thousands) and gross enrollment ratio by sex

Inscriptions aux niveaux primaire, secondaire et supérieur *(suite)*
Nombre d'élèves inscrits (milliers) et taux brut de scolarisation par sexe

Region, country or area Région, pays ou zone	Year & Année &	Primary education Enseignement primaire			Secondary education Enseignement secondaire			Tertiary education Enseignement supérieur		
		Total ('000)	Gross enrollment ratio Taux brut de scolarisation		Total ('000)	Gross enrollment ratio Taux brut de scolarisation		Total ('000)	Gross enrollment ratio Taux brut de scolarisation	
			M/H	F		M/H	F		M/H	F
Norway	2005	430	98.4	98.7	403	113.2	114.3	214	62.4	95.1
Norvège	2010	424	98.9	99.2	435	113.5	111.7	225	56.5	91.2
	2014	426	99.9	99.8	439	114.6	110.8	264	63.7	92.2
	2015	431	100.0	99.8	443	116.0	113.2	268	63.8	92.9
	2017	445	100.3	100.2	448	119.4	114.2	284	66.3	98.7
Oman	2005	312	93.2	92.1	302	89.2	86.0	48	17.9	19.1
Oman	2009	302	105.4	100.8	322	102.3	97.2	76	19.8	27.4
	2010	...	...	...	...	...	...	78	19.8	28.5
	2013	320	106.0	112.3	293	98.5	100.5	105	22.5	41.0
	2014	337	106.4	113.1	...	...	...	118	24.6	48.9
	2015	351	106.0	110.7	287	104.2	102.4	127	28.3	54.2
	2018	279	98.6	108.6	422	111.0	102.5	120	26.4	55.6
Pakistan	2005	17 258	91.5	70.3	6 852	...	...	783	5.3	4.6
Pakistan	2009	18 468	90.2	77.1	9 433	36.5	29.0	* 1 226	* 7.3	* 6.2
	2010	18 756	91.0	77.6	9 655	37.3	28.8	...	...	...
	2014	19 432	90.7	77.4	11 287	41.5	32.8	1 932	9.4	10.0
	2015	19 847	91.4	78.3	12 078	44.0	34.9	1 872	9.8	8.6
	2018	22 931	102.0	86.1	13 358	45.9	39.1	1 878	9.6	8.3
Palau	*2002	...	...	...	...	...	...	~0	25.8	54.0
Palaos	2004	2	111.2	108.7	2	90.2	90.9	...	...	...
	2005	2	...	...	2	...	...	...	...	...
	2007	2	...	...	2	...	...	...	...	...
	2013	2	119.0	107.0	2	110.6	121.7	1	43.9	66.4
	2014	2	119.6	105.2	2	110.8	122.9	...	...	...
Panama	2005	430	109.1	105.3	256	65.7	70.3	126	32.1	52.5
Panama	2010	440	107.0	103.1	284	69.2	73.5	139	35.1	53.7
	2014	427	100.3	97.9	312	72.4	77.8	145	34.5	54.8
	2015	418	97.2	94.9	317	73.9	77.9	157	36.8	58.0
	2016	409	93.8	92.4	345	80.8	83.1	161	37.3	58.6
	2017	419	95.4	93.4	323	74.1	78.3	...	...	...
Papua New Guinea	2005	532	60.1	50.9	...	...	...	...	...	...
Papouasie-Nvl-Guinée	2008	601	61.4	54.3	...	...	...	...	...	...
	2012	1 132	107.7	95.7	378	44.0	33.0	...	...	...
	2016	1 275	113.2	103.6	507	54.7	39.9	...	...	...
Paraguay	2005	934	112.1	109.7	529	64.9	67.2	156	24.0	27.4
Paraguay	2010	839	104.3	100.9	561	65.7	69.8	225	28.6	40.9
	2012	838	105.7	103.0	631	73.3	78.6	...	...	...
	2016	727	...	...	611	...	...	...	...	...
Peru	2005	4 077	113.6	113.9	2 470	82.8	81.6	908	32.2	33.4
Pérou	2006	4 026	113.7	114.1	2 540	84.4	85.1	951	32.9	35.6
	2010	3 763	109.8	110.0	2 675	91.1	93.5	...	...	...
	2014	3 496	101.0	101.2	2 671	97.7	96.3	...	...	...
	2015	3 513	100.2	100.3	2 682	97.8	97.4	...	...	...
	2017	3 544	104.9	102.1	2 775	106.8	102.5	1 896	68.7	72.7
	2018	3 593	108.8	105.1	2 780	109.3	103.6	...	...	...
Philippines	2005	13 084	106.5	105.4	6 352	78.3	87.7	2 403	24.7	30.4
Philippines	2009	13 687	108.3	107.1	6 767	80.9	87.5	2 625	25.5	31.5
	2010	...	...	...	...	...	...	2 774	26.3	32.9
	2014	14 460	114.2	111.9	7 220	83.3	90.9	3 563	31.3	40.1
	2015	14 453	113.9	110.5	7 319	84.4	91.5	...	...	...
	2017	14 040	109.4	105.5	9 007	82.0	90.6	3 589	30.8	40.4
Poland	2005	2 724	94.8	94.3	3 445	99.9	99.3	2 118	52.9	74.7
Pologne	2010	2 235	96.9	96.1	2 842	96.2	95.7	2 149	59.6	90.7
	2014	2 153	100.0	100.3	2 641	108.9	104.8	1 763	54.2	83.5
	2015	...	...	...	2 548	109.7	105.7	1 665	53.5	81.1
	2017	2 297	100.0	100.0	2 408	111.7	108.1	1 550	54.4	81.9

Enrollment in primary, secondary and tertiary education levels *(continued)*
Number of students enrolled (thousands) and gross enrollment ratio by sex

Inscriptions aux niveaux primaire, secondaire et supérieur *(suite)*
Nombre d'élèves inscrits (milliers) et taux brut de scolarisation par sexe

Region, country or area Région, pays ou zone	Year & Année &	Primary education Enseignement primaire			Secondary education Enseignement secondaire			Tertiary education Enseignement supérieur		
		Total ('000)	Gross enrollment ratio Taux brut de scolarisation		Total ('000)	Gross enrollment ratio Taux brut de scolarisation		Total ('000)	Gross enrollment ratio Taux brut de scolarisation	
			M/H	F		M /H	F		M/H	F
Portugal Portugal	2005	753	120.9	115.1	670	93.4	102.7	381	48.2	63.0
	2010	734	113.2	109.9	721	105.3	108.3	384	60.2	71.2
	2014	674	110.3	105.7	769	117.5	114.7	362	60.7	70.3
	2015	657	109.0	104.9	779	120.6	116.9	338	57.9	65.6
	2017	630	107.9	104.4	770	121.1	118.7	347	60.1	67.7
Puerto Rico Porto Rico	2010	300	95.7	99.3	291	83.6	88.3	249	72.4	106.9
	2014	259	90.3	90.6	266	84.6	91.5	241	76.9	110.1
	2015	251	89.0	89.1	279	91.0	98.4	241	79.5	114.5
	2016	228	83.2	82.8	236	78.7	85.4	233	79.8	116.2
Qatar Qatar	2005	70	108.6	103.7	56	103.9	96.1	* 10	* 8.9	* 31.2
	2010	89	100.9	104.4	69	108.3	102.7	14	4.5	26.3
	2014	117	97.9	100.3	88	...	...	25	6.2	40.3
	2015	130	102.2	103.0	96	...	...	28	6.4	45.0
	2018	154	103.3	104.4	108	...	...	34	7.0	54.9
Republic of Korea République de Corée	2005	4 032	101.5	100.7	3 796	96.1	98.2	3 210	110.8	70.9
	2010	3 306	101.7	101.8	3 959	96.6	96.1	3 270	116.7	86.8
	2014	2 736	98.4	98.3	3 579	100.1	99.6	3 318	106.2	81.9
	2015	2 722	98.9	98.7	3 397	100.3	99.7	3 268	105.3	82.0
	2017	2 682	98.2	98.0	3 072	100.6	100.0	3 136	104.8	82.8
Republic of Moldova République de Moldova	2005	184	* 98.6	* 97.2	394	* 86.2	* 90.0	130	* 29.5	* 42.9
	2010	141	* 93.7	* 93.3	308	* 87.0	* 89.0	130	* 32.7	* 43.7
	2014	138	* 93.3	* 92.9	246	* 86.8	* 87.9	116	* 35.9	* 47.3
	2015	139	* 92.9	* 91.9	233	* 85.8	* 86.5	109	* 35.3	* 47.4
	2018	140	* 90.6	* 90.6	226	* 87.3	* 86.5	87	* 34.2	* 45.7
Romania Roumanie	2005	970	110.5	109.0	2 090	81.7	83.3	739	41.1	51.9
	2010	842	100.8	99.1	1 822	98.1	97.2	1 000	54.2	74.4
	2012	807	99.5	97.6	1 714	98.0	97.0	705	44.0	55.9
	2014	...	...	...	1 609	94.6	94.2	579	42.0	52.7
	2015	947	89.8	88.5	1 563	92.9	92.9	542	41.7	52.2
	2017	928	85.7	84.6	1 502	91.1	91.4	532	43.8	55.4
Russian Federation Fédération de Russie	2005	5 309	95.1	95.3	12 433	83.3	82.5	9 003	61.3	84.2
	2009	5 015	99.1	99.6	9 614	85.4	84.1	9 330	64.2	86.8
	2014	5 726	97.4	98.0	9 061	99.9	97.7	6 996	71.5	85.8
	2015	5 983	98.7	99.5	9 385	103.4	101.0	6 592	72.7	87.6
	2017	6 574	102.8	102.3	9 905	104.7	102.1	5 887	75.0	89.1
Rwanda Rwanda	2004	1 753	128.4	128.9	204	16.6	14.9	25	3.7	2.1
	2005	1 858	132.6	134.6	219	17.7	15.7	28	...	...
	2010	2 299	146.4	150.1	426	31.6	31.6	63	6.7	5.2
	2014	2 399	138.7	142.1	587	38.3	41.9	78	8.0	6.7
	2015	2 451	138.7	140.6	568	36.3	39.4	80	8.5	6.7
	2018	2 504	134.0	132.1	658	38.5	43.3	76	7.5	6.0
Saint Kitts and Nevis Saint-Kitts-et-Nevis	2005	6	110.1	109.2	* 4	* 90.2	* 99.9	...	...	...
	2008	6	116.2	110.3	4	105.2	113.5	1	12.8	27.6
	2010	6	116.5	110.6	* 4	* 107.4	* 105.2	...	...	...
	2014	6	108.8	108.4	4	109.4	105.0	3	84.0	86.1
	2015	5	108.7	107.9	4	108.3	107.5	4	57.7	115.9
	2016	5	110.4	107.1	4	105.1	108.7	...	...	...
Saint Lucia Sainte-Lucie	2005	24	105.2	100.6	14	71.6	84.2	2	7.0	19.0
	2007	22	103.2	98.0	15	83.4	92.6	1	5.2	12.0
	2010	19	...	...	16	94.4	93.3	2	6.9	17.8
	2014	17	...	...	14	87.8	87.3	3	10.7	22.3
	2015	17	102.8	99.5	13	88.9	88.1	3	11.3	21.4
	2018	16	102.1	103.2	12	89.3	89.4	2	9.4	18.7
Saint Vincent & Grenadines Saint-Vincent-Grenadines	2005	18	124.0	112.1	10	79.6	99.4	...	...	...
	2010	14	111.9	106.2	11	105.5	110.7	...	...	...
	2014	13	111.4	109.6	10	106.1	106.5	2	15.3	33.8
	2015	13	110.7	109.7	10	107.1	107.7	2	17.8	29.8
	2018	13	114.1	112.7	10	105.9	108.7	...	...	...

6

Enrollment in primary, secondary and tertiary education levels *(continued)*
Number of students enrolled (thousands) and gross enrollment ratio by sex

Inscriptions aux niveaux primaire, secondaire et supérieur *(suite)*
Nombre d'élèves inscrits (milliers) et taux brut de scolarisation par sexe

Region, country or area Région, pays ou zone	Year & Année &	Primary education Enseignement primaire			Secondary education Enseignement secondaire			Tertiary education Enseignement supérieur		
		Total ('000)	Gross enrollment ratio Taux brut de scolarisation		Total ('000)	Gross enrollment ratio Taux brut de scolarisation		Total ('000)	Gross enrollment ratio Taux brut de scolarisation	
			M/H	F		M /H	F		M/H	F
Samoa	2000	28	95.9	97.3	22	73.7	83.9	1	7.8	7.2
Samoa	2005	31	109.0	109.8	24	78.2	88.2	...	...	...
	2010	31	111.5	109.9	26	82.3	93.6	...	...	...
	2014	31	107.7	108.0	26	88.6	99.6	...	...	...
	2015	32	106.4	106.4	26	89.3	99.1	...	...	...
	2016	33	106.6	107.9	26	88.8	98.0	...	...	...
	2018	33	110.6	110.4	...	...	...	...	...	...
San Marino	2000	1	84.0	87.5	1	44.2	47.5	1	42.8	63.9
Saint-Marin	2004	1	...	...	...	...	...	...	...	...
	2010	2	106.4	120.3	2	91.2	93.9	1	46.6	69.7
	2012	2	109.5	103.8	2	97.1	98.3	1	41.9	58.7
	2018	2	100.4	116.9	2	71.5	63.8	1	48.6	36.0
Sao Tome and Principe	2005	30	128.1	123.1	8	41.6	44.1	...	...	...
Sao Tomé-et-Principe	2010	34	117.0	116.2	10	51.2	52.3	1	4.4	4.3
	2014	34	105.8	102.0	19	* 71.5	* 78.7	2	10.4	9.1
	2015	36	107.3	103.2	22	78.2	86.9	2	13.1	13.7
	2017	37	108.5	105.0	26	82.9	95.9	...	...	...
Saudi Arabia	2005	* 3 098	* 96.4	* 95.0	* 2 610	* 90.1	* 84.8	604	23.9	35.6
Arabie saoudite	2009	3 255	106.0	103.3	* 2 997	* 100.4	* 89.0	758	27.8	35.5
	2010	3 321	107.1	106.2	...	...	...	904	34.1	39.3
	2014	3 737	120.8	117.2	...	...	...	1 497	58.5	58.1
	2015	3 494	108.7	112.1	3 320	117.9	115.0	1 528	60.7	61.4
	2018	3 299	99.2	100.3	3 108	113.2	106.8	1 620	66.3	69.9
Senegal	2005	1 444	81.4	78.5	406	25.6	19.1	* 59	...	...
Sénégal	2010	1 695	81.7	86.4	725	38.7	33.8	* 92	* 9.6	* 5.6
	2014	1 927	80.8	90.5	1 095	50.4	50.1	141	13.5	7.9
	2015	1 977	80.2	89.8	1 136	...	...	145	13.5	8.0
	2018	2 142	75.9	86.1	1 087	41.7	45.7	185	15.2	10.3
Serbia	2005	325	* 102.5	* 103.0	632	* 87.3	* 90.0	225	* 38.6	* 50.1
Serbie	2010	283	* 96.1	* 95.6	591	* 90.5	* 92.4	227	* 42.8	* 55.6
	2014	285	* 100.9	* 101.4	548	* 93.3	* 95.4	243	* 50.5	* 66.0
	2015	279	* 101.5	* 101.2	553	* 96.0	* 97.4	241	* 50.2	* 66.9
	2018	267	* 100.3	* 100.3	534	* 94.6	* 95.6	256	* 56.7	* 78.3
Seychelles	2005	9	110.1	108.1	9	79.0	84.8	...	...	...
Seychelles	2010	9	108.8	112.1	8	* 72.5	* 77.1	...	...	...
	2014	9	104.8	106.4	7	77.2	81.2	~0	3.7	9.6
	2015	9	102.8	106.0	7	78.6	84.4	1	9.2	20.0
	2018	9	97.6	103.3	7	78.8	84.2	1	11.2	23.3
Sierra Leone	2001	554	85.4	60.4	156	* 28.1	* 20.3	9	2.8	1.2
Sierra Leone	*2002	...	...	...	...	...	...	9	2.8	1.1
	2013	1 300	118.1	118.3	417	41.5	36.3	...	...	...
	2015	1 360	115.3	116.9	449	41.6	36.5	...	...	...
	2017	1 487	123.3	125.6	492	42.5	41.1	...	...	...
	2018	1 370	110.8	114.7	...	...	...	...	...	...
Singapore	2009	295	...	...	232	...	...	213	...	...
Singapour	2010	...	...	...	...	...	...	237	...	...
	2012	...	...	...	...	...	...	255	...	...
	2017	235	* 100.7	* 100.6	171	* 108.1	* 107.0	195	* 78.9	* 91.2
Sint Maarten (Dutch part)	2014	4	127.5	128.9	3	92.7	88.5	~0	3.0	8.3
St-Martin (partie néerland.)	2015	...	...	...	...	...	...	~0	2.6	9.0
Slovakia	2005	242	98.8	97.6	663	92.8	93.7	181	35.4	45.6
Slovaquie	2010	212	101.9	101.0	550	91.8	92.8	235	45.0	69.6
	2014	214	100.2	99.3	465	90.2	91.2	198	41.6	64.3
	2015	216	98.9	98.1	454	90.5	91.5	184	40.1	61.8
	2017	225	99.0	98.4	442	90.5	91.6	156	37.1	56.6
Slovenia	2005	93	101.0	100.0	181	97.4	96.9	112	65.6	93.5
Slovénie	2010	107	99.5	99.5	138	99.3	98.6	115	72.3	107.4
	2014	112	99.5	100.0	145	110.1	110.9	91	67.5	97.9
	2015	116	99.6	100.3	143	109.7	111.0	86	65.4	96.0
	2017	124	100.2	100.6	148	114.2	117.1	80	64.9	93.0

6

Enrollment in primary, secondary and tertiary education levels *(continued)*
Number of students enrolled (thousands) and gross enrollment ratio by sex

Inscriptions aux niveaux primaire, secondaire et supérieur *(suite)*
Nombre d'élèves inscrits (milliers) et taux brut de scolarisation par sexe

Region, country or area Région, pays ou zone	Year & Année &	Primary education Enseignement primaire			Secondary education Enseignement secondaire			Tertiary education Enseignement supérieur		
		Total ('000)	Gross enrollment ratio Taux brut de scolarisation		Total ('000)	Gross enrollment ratio Taux brut de scolarisation		Total ('000)	Gross enrollment ratio Taux brut de scolarisation	
			M/H	F		M /H	F		M/H	F
Solomon Islands Îles Salomon	2005	75	103.2	97.8	22	33.2	27.4	...	...	...
	2010	95	116.0	113.2	40	51.9	44.9	...	...	...
	2012	98	113.9	111.6	42	49.5	47.0	...	...	...
	2014	102	115.0	111.8	...	...	...	...	...	...
	2015	104	114.2	113.0	...	...	...	...	...	...
	2018	105	106.4	106.0	...	...	...	...	...	...
Somalia Somalie	2007	457	30.1	16.6	87	8.1	3.7	...	...	...
South Africa Afrique du Sud	2005	7 314	107.8	104.1	4 658	84.3	90.5	...	...	...
	2010	7 024	106.8	102.7	4 690	91.0	96.6	...	...	...
	2014	7 195	104.7	100.7	5 221	102.9	112.8	1 019	16.5	23.2
	2015	7 556	109.2	101.9	5 279	110.1	108.8	1 051	...	...
	2017	7 582	102.6	99.1	5 052	100.4	109.0	1 116	18.4	26.4
South Sudan Soudan du sud	2011	1 451	108.1	71.6	134	12.8	6.5	...	...	...
	2015	1 274	85.3	60.4	164	14.3	7.7	...	...	...
Spain Espagne	2005	2 485	103.7	102.3	3 108	113.7	121.2	1 809	60.5	74.2
	2010	2 721	104.4	103.6	3 185	117.6	120.7	1 879	68.1	84.2
	2014	2 961	106.5	107.9	3 288	123.3	123.4	1 982	77.8	93.5
	2015	3 010	105.6	107.2	3 313	125.3	124.6	1 964	78.3	93.2
	2017	3 042	101.9	103.6	3 333	125.2	126.9	2 010	81.1	97.0
Sri Lanka Sri Lanka	2005	1 611	99.8	99.3	...	...	...	...	...	...
	2010	1 721	100.7	98.2	2 525	96.3	97.5	262	11.7	20.9
	2013	1 767	101.9	99.4	2 606	97.2	101.8	298	14.8	22.9
	2014	1 778	102.5	100.2	...	...	...	302	16.8	21.7
	2015	1 778	102.7	100.6	...	...	...	308	15.5	23.9
	2018	1 725	100.7	99.6	2 728	98.0	102.6	301	15.8	23.4
State of Palestine État de Palestine	2005	387	88.5	88.0	657	87.6	91.8	138	40.5	41.3
	2010	403	92.2	90.4	711	82.5	89.1	197	41.1	54.9
	2014	442	98.1	97.4	709	80.5	88.4	214	35.2	54.7
	2015	450	97.5	97.5	721	81.9	89.9	221	35.3	55.6
	2018	488	98.5	98.7	765	85.2	93.9	222	34.5	54.3
Sudan Soudan	2005	3 177	67.4	59.1	1 344	40.1	37.3	364	11.5	13.0
	2010	4 024	75.6	67.8	1 687	45.5	39.4	523	14.7	17.2
	2014	4 388	75.1	69.3	1 974	47.0	42.7	632	16.4	17.4
	2015	4 518	76.4	69.8	2 060	46.0	45.3	653	16.8	17.1
	2017	4 900	79.2	74.4	2 205	46.3	47.0	...	...	...
Sudan [former] Soudan [anc.]	2000	2 567	...	...	980	...	...	* 204	...	...
	2005	3 278	...	...	* 1 370	...	...	...	...	...
	2009	4 744	...	...	1 837	...	...	...	...	...
Suriname Suriname	2002	64	104.6	103.6	42	62.5	88.1	5	9.5	15.7
	2005	66	105.8	104.2	46	58.8	78.7	...	...	...
	2010	71	114.2	113.8	50	62.6	80.7	...	...	...
	2014	70	112.4	114.3	52	62.1	85.4	...	...	...
	2015	72	115.2	116.4	55	67.1	88.6	...	...	...
	2018	68	109.0	108.7	58	...	...	...	...	...
Sweden Suède	2005	658	95.9	95.7	735	104.3	103.8	427	64.8	99.9
	2010	576	101.7	101.2	731	98.6	97.6	455	58.5	89.6
	2014	757	117.7	124.2	827	124.8	141.6	429	49.3	75.7
	2015	792	120.5	125.5	844	131.5	150.0	429	49.6	75.6
	2017	861	125.8	127.4	916	148.1	157.9	426	52.7	82.1
Switzerland Suisse	2005	524	102.5	102.1	575	98.3	92.5	200	49.1	42.5
	2010	493	103.1	102.6	605	97.5	94.6	249	53.2	52.7
	2013	484	103.7	103.5	617	100.1	97.6	280	55.9	56.6
	2014	484	103.4	103.5	...	...	...	290	56.8	57.7
	2015	490	104.3	104.0	614	103.2	99.6	294	56.9	58.5
	2017	508	105.5	104.8	609	104.7	100.2	301	58.8	60.3

Enrollment in primary, secondary and tertiary education levels *(continued)*
Number of students enrolled (thousands) and gross enrollment ratio by sex

Inscriptions aux niveaux primaire, secondaire et supérieur *(suite)*
Nombre d'élèves inscrits (milliers) et taux brut de scolarisation par sexe

Region, country or area Région, pays ou zone	Year & Année &	Primary education Enseignement primaire			Secondary education Enseignement secondaire			Tertiary education Enseignement supérieur		
		Total ('000)	Gross enrollment ratio Taux brut de scolarisation		Total ('000)	Gross enrollment ratio Taux brut de scolarisation		Total ('000)	Gross enrollment ratio Taux brut de scolarisation	
			M/H	F		M/H	F		M/H	F
Syrian Arab Republic République arabe syrienne	2005	2 252	122.1	118.6	2 389	71.2	68.2	361	19.1	17.1
	2010	2 429	118.8	114.7	2 732	72.1	72.3	574	27.7	23.9
	2013	1 547	83.1	80.2	1 857	52.7	52.4	660	32.9	32.8
	2014	...	...	...	...	...	...	792	41.1	42.1
	2015	...	...	...	...	...	...	773	40.7	44.8
	2016	...	...	...	...	...	...	697	37.5	42.8
Tajikistan Tadjikistan	2005	693	101.9	98.3	984	87.4	73.0	149	27.8	13.2
	2010	682	102.7	100.2	1 032	90.4	78.9	196	29.9	15.8
	2013	665	101.6	99.9	1 063	93.0	83.8	195	29.2	16.4
	2014	662	98.7	97.8	...	...	...	209	30.6	18.6
	2015	683	98.1	97.1	...	...	...	225	31.6	21.3
	2017	771	101.4	100.3	...	...	...	265	35.5	26.9
Thailand Thaïlande	2005	5 975	103.3	100.5	4 533	* 71.9	* 75.4	2 359	42.0	47.2
	2010	5 147	97.4	96.3	4 807	79.6	85.3	2 427	44.3	56.6
	2014	5 182	101.3	102.9	6 792	117.2	123.6	2 433	42.7	57.8
	2015	5 081	103.5	97.6	6 757	123.0	118.2	...	...	...
	2016	5 063	100.5	101.0	6 571	118.9	118.4	2 411	41.0	57.8
	2018	4 901	99.8	99.8	6 266	118.9	116.5	...	...	...
Timor-Leste Timor-Leste	2002	184	...	...	53	...	...	* 6	* 8.1	* 9.3
	2005	178	110.1	100.2	75	55.7	54.2	...	...	...
	2010	230	126.1	119.2	102	62.6	62.1	19	20.6	14.8
	2014	246	129.4	126.2	119	66.4	70.4	...	...	...
	2015	244	129.8	126.6	129	70.5	74.4	...	...	...
	2018	213	117.3	113.2	156	80.3	87.0	...	...	...
Togo Togo	2005	997	124.0	105.3	404	60.3	32.0	...	...	...
	2007	1 022	119.1	103.1	409	* 59.4	* 31.4	33	...	...
	2010	1 287	133.9	120.8	...	...	...	56	...	...
	2011	1 300	130.6	118.8	546	...	...	63	...	...
	2014	1 413	127.6	120.3	...	...	...	67	14.8	6.1
	2015	1 498	131.2	124.9	...	...	...	71	15.4	6.6
	2017	1 524	127.3	121.4	728	71.6	52.1	89	18.0	8.1
	2018	1 549	126.0	121.5	...	...	...	102	19.2	9.8
Tokelau Tokélaou	2003	~0	107.6	111.8	~0	80.0	86.7	...	...	...
	2016	~0	150.8	125.0	~0	85.5	77.8	...	...	...
Tonga Tonga	2002	17	111.7	106.7	15	105.5	116.4	1	* 4.2	* 7.1
	2003	18	118.3	112.0	16	...	...	1	4.8	8.0
	2004	17	114.3	108.6	14	...	...	...	...	...
	2005	17	113.4	110.1	...	...	...	...	...	...
	2010	17	109.4	107.3	15	100.4	107.2	...	...	...
	2014	17	116.0	115.4	15	93.3	99.9	...	...	...
	2015	17	116.7	116.0	16	99.4	102.4	...	...	...
Trinidad and Tobago Trinité-et-Tobago	2004	* 137	* 103.4	* 100.0	* 105	* 82.6	* 88.5	17	10.6	13.4
	*2005	130	100.7	97.8	...	...	...	...	...	...
	2010	131	108.0	104.4	...	...	...	...	...	...
Tunisia Tunisie	2005	1 184	112.4	110.8	1 239	80.5	88.9	327	28.4	35.2
	2010	1 030	107.4	107.0	1 164	86.2	94.5	370	27.8	43.2
	2011	1 028	107.9	107.7	1 152	88.6	95.3	362	26.8	43.8
	2014	1 089	113.3	113.4	1 020	...	...	332	26.8	44.1
	2015	1 115	114.5	114.6	1 008	...	...	323	26.6	44.1
	2016	1 139	114.8	115.1	1 047	86.9	99.3	294	24.2	41.8
	2018	1 202	115.9	114.9	...	...	...	272	22.8	41.2
Turkey Turquie	2005	6 678	105.8	100.5	6 345	91.6	76.1	2 106	...	...
	2010	6 635	102.0	100.6	7 531	87.9	80.5	3 529	...	...
	2014	5 575	106.6	106.1	10 899	104.3	101.4	5 473	...	...
	2015	5 434	103.4	102.7	10 969	104.2	101.5	6 063	...	...
	2017	4 972	93.6	92.7	11 404	108.5	103.4	7 199	...	...
Turkmenistan Turkménistan	2014	359	89.2	87.5	651	87.6	84.0	44	9.7	6.2

6

Enrollment in primary, secondary and tertiary education levels *(continued)*
Number of students enrolled (thousands) and gross enrollment ratio by sex

Inscriptions aux niveaux primaire, secondaire et supérieur *(suite)*
Nombre d'élèves inscrits (milliers) et taux brut de scolarisation par sexe

Region, country or area Région, pays ou zone	Year & Année &	Primary education Enseignement primaire			Secondary education Enseignement secondaire			Tertiary education Enseignement supérieur		
		Total ('000)	Gross enrollment ratio Taux brut de scolarisation		Total ('000)	Gross enrollment ratio Taux brut de scolarisation		Total ('000)	Gross enrollment ratio Taux brut de scolarisation	
			M/H	F		M /H	F		M/H	F
Turks and Caicos Islands	2005	2	...	...	2	...	...	...	...	...
Îles Turques-et-Caïques	2009	3	...	...	2	...	...	...	...	...
	2010	...	...	...	...	...	...	~0	...	...
	2014	3	...	...	2	...	...	...	...	...
	2015	3	...	...	2	...	...	~0	...	...
	2018	4	...	...	2	...	...	...	...	...
Tuvalu	2001	1	108.9	114.7	1	60.5	58.4	...	...	...
Tuvalu	2005	1	113.1	109.9	...	...	...	...	...	...
	2006	1	112.6	108.4	...	...	...	...	...	...
	2014	1	98.0	94.1	1	72.4	85.3	...	...	...
	2015	1	101.7	97.8	1	75.2	90.9	...	...	...
	2018	1	89.4	82.5	1	62.5	71.2	...	...	...
Uganda	2004	7 377	130.9	127.9	733	21.7	17.1	88	4.6	2.8
Ouganda	2005	7 224	123.9	122.0	...	...	...	...	...	...
	2007	7 538	121.0	120.3	1 032	27.5	21.8	...	...	...
	2010	8 375	121.5	122.4	...	...	...	121	4.7	3.5
	2013	8 459	111.1	113.0	...	...	...	...	...	...
	2014	...	...	...	...	...	...	165	5.6	4.1
	2015	8 264	101.6	103.7	...	...	...	...	...	...
	2017	8 841	101.3	104.1	...	...	...	...	...	...
Ukraine	2005	1 946	106.6	106.2	4 043	* 99.2	* 91.8	2 605	63.0	77.9
Ukraine	2010	1 540	98.5	99.1	3 133	* 96.7	* 94.4	2 635	71.3	89.5
	2014	1 685	98.0	100.1	2 714	96.9	95.0	2 146	76.8	88.8
	2015	1 537	...	...	2 370	...	...	1 776	...	...
	2018	1 677	...	...	2 377	...	...	1 615	...	...
United Arab Emirates	2005	263	...	...	...	...	...	...	...	...
Émirats arabes unis	2007	284	101.1	102.1	...	...	...	80	...	...
	2010	327	...	...	...	...	...	102	...	...
	2014	410	102.1	104.1	...	...	...	143	...	...
	2015	461	111.4	111.6	...	...	...	157	...	...
	2017	486	109.4	107.3	528	109.3	100.4	192	...	...
United Kingdom	2005	4 635	106.4	106.3	5 761	103.9	107.0	2 288	49.5	68.8
Royaume-Uni	2010	4 422	104.8	104.3	5 538	102.7	103.1	2 479	50.5	67.5
	2014	4 509	102.4	102.2	6 557	124.1	128.8	2 353	48.9	64.5
	2015	4 621	102.0	101.9	6 375	122.8	126.4	2 330	48.6	64.7
	2017	4 820	101.3	101.0	6 386	124.1	127.7	2 432	51.0	69.4
United Rep. of Tanzania	2005	7 541	107.0	103.8	...	...	...	* 52	* 2.0	* 1.0
Rép.-Unie de Tanzanie	2010	8 419	101.9	103.8	1 826	34.8	28.5	85	2.4	1.9
	2013	8 232	88.2	91.9	...	...	...	158	4.8	2.6
	2014	8 223	84.6	89.0	1 947	31.3	30.2	...	...	...
	2015	8 298	82.5	87.0	1 774	27.3	27.0	182	5.2	2.8
	2016	8 639	83.4	87.3	1 808	26.6	26.8	179	...	...
	2018	10 112	93.0	95.4	2 148	28.8	30.1	...	...	...
United States of America	*2005	...	102.4	101.3	...	94.2	95.9	...	66.9	95.2
États-Unis d'Amérique	*2010	...	100.8	99.8	...	94.3	95.4	...	77.7	108.3
	2014	24 538	* 99.8	* 99.5	24 230	* 96.4	* 97.5	19 700	* 75.4	* 102.6
	2015	24 786	* 100.3	* 100.3	24 417	* 97.2	* 98.2	19 532	* 75.8	* 102.7
	2017	25 124	* 102.2	* 101.4	24 788	* 99.2	* 98.7	19 015	* 75.0	* 102.0
United States Virgin Islands Îles Vierges américaines	2007	...	...	...	...	...	...	2	...	...
Uruguay	2005	366	115.6	112.7	323	94.2	108.5	111	33.2	57.9
Uruguay	2006	365	117.3	114.0	323	93.5	108.5	113	34.5	58.0
	2010	342	114.6	110.9	321	93.2	109.5	132	...	...
	2014	322	112.6	110.1	339	...	...	160	...	...
	2015	317	112.2	109.8	340	...	...	156	...	...
	2017	304	109.3	107.6	357	114.1	126.6	162	...	...

6

Enrollment in primary, secondary and tertiary education levels *(continued)*
Number of students enrolled (thousands) and gross enrollment ratio by sex

Inscriptions aux niveaux primaire, secondaire et supérieur *(suite)*
Nombre d'élèves inscrits (milliers) et taux brut de scolarisation par sexe

Region, country or area Région, pays ou zone	Year & Année &	Primary education Enseignement primaire			Secondary education Enseignement secondaire			Tertiary education Enseignement supérieur		
		Total ('000)	Gross enrollment ratio Taux brut de scolarisation		Total ('000)	Gross enrollment ratio Taux brut de scolarisation		Total ('000)	Gross enrollment ratio Taux brut de scolarisation	
			M/H	F		M /H	F		M/H	F
Uzbekistan	2005	2 383	97.1	97.0	4 516	90.2	87.5	266	11.9	8.2
Ouzbékistan	2010	1 971	94.7	93.1	4 449	89.8	89.9	289	11.1	7.6
	2014	2 034	99.2	97.7	4 083	92.5	91.5	260	10.0	6.2
	2015	2 135	100.6	99.2	3 964	92.4	91.3	262	10.0	6.3
	2017	2 391	104.4	102.9	3 893	93.9	92.7	281	11.4	6.9
	2018	2 485	105.0	103.4	...	...	...	300	11.8	8.2
Vanuatu	2004	39	122.4	120.0	14	45.8	39.5	* 1	* 5.9	* 3.5
Vanuatu	2005	39	119.2	116.1	...	...	...	...	...	...
	2010	42	123.0	121.9	20	59.6	59.5	...	...	...
	2013	44	120.2	116.3	...	...	...	...	...	...
	2015	46	110.7	107.8	21	53.5	54.9	...	...	...
Venezuela (Boliv. Rep. of)	2003	3 450	105.8	103.7	1 866	64.8	74.6	* 983	* 38.9	* 41.7
Venezuela (Rép. boliv. du)	2004	3 453	105.6	103.5	1 954	67.6	77.0	* 1 050	...	...
	2005	3 449	105.1	103.2	2 028	70.1	79.3	...	...	...
	2008	3 439	104.3	101.7	2 224	77.8	85.7	2 109	* 59.3	* 100.3
	2009	3 462	104.7	102.0	2 252	79.1	86.5	2 123	...	...
	2010	3 458	104.2	101.3	2 255	79.0	86.6	...	...	...
	2014	3 493	102.2	100.4	2 567	89.4	96.3	...	...	...
	2015	3 476	102.0	99.8	2 523	87.7	94.5	...	...	...
	2017	3 285	98.3	96.0	2 391	84.7	91.6	...	...	...
Viet Nam	2005	7 773	100.1	95.2	...	...	...	1 355	18.7	13.5
Viet Nam	2010	6 923	108.1	103.2	...	...	...	2 020	22.6	23.0
	2014	7 435	110.4	110.2	...	...	...	2 692	29.9	31.6
	2015	7 544	109.7	110.1	...	...	...	2 467	29.0	29.2
	2016	7 790	110.4	112.1	...	...	...	2 307	25.5	31.7
	2018	8 042	109.5	111.9	...	...	...	...	...	...
Yemen	2005	3 220	102.2	75.5	1 455	62.1	30.3	200	14.5	5.2
Yémen	2010	3 427	100.9	82.3	1 561	54.2	33.6	272	14.9	6.5
	2011	3 641	105.3	85.8	1 643	56.3	35.6	267	14.0	6.2
	2013	3 875	106.6	89.4	1 768	58.2	40.0	...	...	...
	2016	3 900	99.9	87.1	1 916	59.6	43.3	...	...	...
Zambia	2005	2 573	115.4	108.8	...	...	...	...	...	...
Zambie	2010	2 899	106.6	107.3	...	...	...	...	...	...
	2012	3 135	107.9	108.4	...	...	...	57	4.8	3.5
	2014	3 218	104.2	104.5	...	...	...	...	...	...
	2015	3 216	101.3	101.6	...	...	...	...	...	...
	2017	3 285	97.5	99.9	...	...	...	...	...	...
Zimbabwe	2003	2 362	105.4	103.2	758	42.6	37.4	...	...	...
Zimbabwe	2010	...	...	...	...	...	...	95	7.8	5.7
	2013	2 663	111.1	108.7	957	53.5	51.3	94	7.9	6.1
	2015	...	...	...	...	...	...	136	10.9	9.2

Source:

United Nations Educational, Scientific and Cultural Organization (UNESCO), Montreal, the UNESCO Institute for Statistics (UIS) statistics database, last accessed May 2020.

Source:

Organisation des Nations Unies pour l'éducation, la science et la culture (UNESCO), Montréal, base de données statistiques de l'Institut de statistique (ISU) de l'UNESCO, dernier accès mai 2020.

& Data relate to the calendar year in which the academic year ends.

& Les données se réfèrent à l'année civile durant laquelle l'année scolaire se termine.

Teaching staff at the primary, secondary and tertiary levels
Number of teachers and Pupil teacher ratio

Personnel enseignant au niveau primaire, secondaire et supérieur
Nombre d'enseignants et ratio élèves/enseignant par niveau d'enseignement

Region, country or area Région, pays ou zone	Year & Année &	Primary education Enseignant primaire		Secondary education Enseignant secondaire		Tertiary education Enseignant supérieur	
		Total Totale ('000)	Pupil-teacher ratio Ratio élèves/ enseignant	Total Totale ('000)	Pupil-teacher ratio Ratio élèves/ enseignant	Total Totale ('000)	Pupil-teacher ratio Ratio élèves/ enseignant
Total, all countries or areas	**2005**	* 26 890	* 25.2	* 28 494	* 17.9	9 229	...
Total, tous pays ou zones	**2010**	* 28 671	24.3	32 336	16.9	11 151	...
	2015	* 31 161	23.1	33 479	17.4	12 918	...
	***2018**	32 020	23.4	34 984	17.0	13 063	...
Northern Africa	2005	* 944	24.4	* 993	* 17.0	* 173	...
Afrique septentrionale	2010	* 972	24.3	* 1 162	* 15.0	* 209	...
	*2015	1 176	21.9	1 205	15.7	258	...
	2018	* 1 248	22.8	1 256	* 16.0	* 270	...
Sub-Saharan Africa	2005	* 2 576	44.0	1 172	27.4	* 179	...
Afrique subsaharienne	2010	* 3 168	42.9	* 1 868	* 24.0	* 263	...
	2015	* 4 070	38.5	* 2 669	* 21.3	* 348	...
	*2016	4 167	38.5	2 637	21.9	363	...
	*2018	4 397	38.4	2 782	22.0	...	...
Northern America	2005	* 1 865	14.4	1 774	15.2	1 386	...
Amérique septentrionale	2010	* 1 920	13.8	1 898	14.1	1 646	...
	2015	* 1 847	14.7	1 803	15.0	1 786	...
	*2018	1 945	14.4	1 848	14.9	1 759	...
Latin America & the	2005	* 2 936	23.5	3 470	17.0	* 1 225	...
Caribbean	2010	* 2 915	23.1	3 549	17.3	* 1 677	...
Amérique latine et Caraïbes	2015	* 2 975	21.7	3 906	16.4	1 824	...
	*2018	3 027	21.3	3 857	16.5	1 901	...
Central Asia	2005	* 242	19.8	793	11.4	* 102	...
Asie centrale	2010	* 226	18.8	747	11.5	113	...
	2015	* 253	19.1	784	10.2	117	...
	2018	* 264	21.3	835	* 9.4	107	...
Eastern Asia	2005	* 6 683	* 18.9	* 6 500	* 17.7	2 179	...
Asie orientale	2010	* 6 659	17.1	7 435	15.3	2 405	...
	2012	* 6 581	16.9	7 594	14.4	* 2 535	...
	2015	* 6 565	16.3	7 281	13.7	...	...
	2018	* 6 930	16.4	7 302	13.2	...	...
South-central Asia	*2005	4 826	38.6	4 949	26.2	843	...
Asie centrale et du Sud	2010	* 5 502	* 35.6	6 446	23.6	* 1 370	...
	2015	* 6 308	31.9	6 511	27.4	1 913	...
	2018	* 6 411	* 32.5	* 7 330	* 24.8	1 971	...
South-eastern Asia	2005	* 2 939	23.2	2 237	18.2	580	...
Asie du Sud-Est	2010	* 3 245	21.1	* 2 699	* 16.9	* 691	...
	2015	* 3 710	* 18.5	* 2 765	* 18.6	722	...
	*2018	3 500	19.5	3 029	18.4	778	...
Southern Asia	*2005	4 583	39.6	4 156	29.0	741	...
Asie méridionale	2010	* 5 275	* 36.4	5 699	25.2	* 1 256	...
	2015	* 6 055	32.4	5 727	29.8	1 796	...
	2018	* 6 147	* 33.0	* 6 495	* 26.8	1 864	...
Western Asia	2005	* 1 289	* 18.7	* 1 340	* 14.7	307	...
Asie occidentale	2010	* 1 444	* 17.6	* 1 592	* 14.1	373	...
	2015	* 1 583	* 16.5	* 1 788	* 14.1	483	...
	*2018	1 509	17.1	1 928	13.6	507	...
Europe	2005	* 2 673	14.4	5 836	11.2	2 275	...
Europe	2010	* 2 674	13.7	* 5 471	* 10.7	* 2 416	...
	2015	* 2 732	14.0	5 329	10.8	2 380	...
	*2018	2 849	14.1	5 434	10.7	2 384	...
Oceania	*2005	159	19.8	...	...	...	...
Océanie	*2010	175	20.3	...	...	...	...
	*2015	195	21.1	...	...	...	...
	*2017	202	21.1	...	...	...	...

7

Teaching staff at the primary, secondary and tertiary levels *(continued)*
Number of teachers and Pupil teacher ratio

Personnel enseignant au niveau primaire, secondaire et supérieur *(suite)*
Nombre d'enseignants et ratio élèves/enseignant par niveau d'enseignement

Region, country or area Région, pays ou zone	Year & Année &	Primary education Enseignant primaire		Secondary education Enseignant secondaire		Tertiary education Enseignant supérieur	
		Total Totale ('000)	Pupil-teacher ratio Ratio élèves/ enseignant	Total Totale ('000)	Pupil-teacher ratio Ratio élèves/ enseignant	Total Totale ('000)	Pupil-teacher ratio Ratio élèves/ enseignant
Afghanistan	2004	...	...	...	...	2	15.5
Afghanistan	2007	110	42.8	33	31.6	...	...
	2009	115	42.8	...	...	3	28.5
	2010	119	44.4	...	...	...	...
	2014	...	...	...	...	11	23.9
	2015	143	43.4	83	32.0	...	...
	2018	134	48.8	91	33.5	17	21.5
Albania	2001	13	21.8	22	17.0	3	13.5
Albanie	2003	12	21.5	22	17.7	...	...
	2010	11	19.7	24	14.8	...	...
	2011	11	19.9	23	15.2	10	13.8
	2015	10	18.6	23	13.5	...	...
	2018	10	17.6	24	11.2	9	14.1
Algeria	2005	171	25.4	...	...	28	27.9
Algérie	2010	142	23.3	...	...	40	28.8
	2015	165	23.8	...	...	54	24.0
	2018	182	24.3	...	...	59	27.3
American Samoa Samoa américaines	2007	...	...	...	...	~0	15.3
Andorra	2004	~0	12.7	~0	7.1	~0	3.9
Andorre	2005	~0	11.5	~0	7.8	...	...
	2008	~0	10.0	...	...	~0	5.3
	2009	~0	10.3	...	...	~0	...
	2010	~0	9.6	...	...	...	...
	2015	~0	9.9	1	8.1	~0	4.6
	2018	~0	10.5	1	8.0	~0	4.4
Angola	*2001	...	...	22	19.0	...	...
Angola	*2002	...	...	...	...	1	9.8
	2006	...	...	...	...	1	37.9
	2010	94	45.6	...	...	...	...
	2011	118	42.5	32	27.4	8	18.2
	2015	112	50.0	73	...	9	25.5
	2016	96	...	76	26.8	...	...
Anguilla	2005	~0	15.4	* ~0	* 12.5	~0	1.4
Anguilla	2007	~0	16.1	~0	10.4	~0	3.9
	2008	~0	14.1	...	...	~0	3.9
	2010	~0	14.5	...	...	...	...
	2011	~0	14.8	~0	8.5	...	...
Antigua and Barbuda	2000	1	18.7	~0	13.4	...	...
Antigua-et-Barbuda	2010	1	15.1	1	12.2	~0	6.8
	2012	1	13.8	1	11.6	~0	8.2
	2015	1	14.3	1	11.5	...	...
	2018	1	12.4	1	9.3	...	...
Argentina	2004	274	18.0	254	15.4	142	14.9
Argentine	2005	279	17.4	257	15.1	...	...
	2008	289	17.2	324	12.2	...	...
	2009	...	...	...	...	142	16.8
Armenia	2005	6	21.2	...	...	17	6.8
Arménie	2007	7	19.3	...	...	16	8.3
	2010	...	...	...	...	16	9.2
	2015	...	...	...	...	16	6.8
	2018	10	15.4	29	8.0	15	6.9
Aruba	2005	1	18.1	1	14.2	~0	9.2
Aruba	2010	1	16.8	1	13.8	~0	10.4
	2012	1	14.8	1	15.1	~0	9.9
	2015	...	...	...	...	~0	13.6
	2016	...	...	...	...	~0	8.6
Austria	2005	29	12.4	71	11.0	...	...
Autriche	2010	30	11.0	75	10.0	47	8.3
	2015	31	10.6	72	9.6	61	7.0
	2017	33	10.0	74	9.3	60	7.2

Teaching staff at the primary, secondary and tertiary levels *(continued)*
Number of teachers and Pupil teacher ratio

Personnel enseignant au niveau primaire, secondaire et supérieur *(suite)*
Nombre d'enseignants et ratio élèves/enseignant par niveau d'enseignement

Region, country or area Région, pays ou zone	Year & Année &	Primary education Enseignant primaire		Secondary education Enseignant secondaire		Tertiary education Enseignant supérieur	
		Total Totale ('000)	Pupil-teacher ratio Ratio élèves/ enseignant	Total Totale ('000)	Pupil-teacher ratio Ratio élèves/ enseignant	Total Totale ('000)	Pupil-teacher ratio Ratio élèves/ enseignant
Azerbaijan Azerbaïdjan	2005	42	13.4	...	...	...	...
	2010	44	11.0	...	...	26	7.0
	2015	41	13.5	...	...	21	9.7
	2018	41	15.4	124	7.6	20	9.9
Bahamas Bahamas	*2004	2	16.8	2	14.2	...	...
	2005	...	...	2	13.6	...	...
	2010	2	14.1	3	12.1	...	...
	2015	2	21.0	2	11.8	...	...
	2018	2	19.4	2	12.5	...	...
Bahrain Bahreïn	2003	...	...	...	...	1	22.3
	*2004	...	...	...	...	1	...
	2015	9	11.7	9	9.9	3	15.4
	2018	10	11.9	10	10.2	2	21.9
Bangladesh Bangladesh	2005	345	47.0	423	23.9	52	17.4
	2009	361	* 45.8	387	28.2	59	26.9
	2010	395	* 43.0	400	28.3	...	...
	2013	...	...	378	35.2	...	...
	2014	...	...	...	...	90	22.9
	2015	528	...	...	...	...	...
	2018	* 577	* 30.1	452	35.1	85	37.1
Barbados Barbade	*2001	1	17.0	1	17.2	1	13.5
	2005	1	15.1	* 1	* 15.9	...	...
	2006	...	...	1	14.6	...	...
	2007	2	14.5	...	...	1	14.5
	*2010	2	13.0	...	...	...	...
	2015	2	13.4	1	17.5	...	...
	2018	1	14.0	1	17.9	...	...
Belarus Bélarus	2005	24	16.0	...	...	42	12.7
	2010	24	15.0	...	...	41	14.0
	2015	22	17.6	77	8.4	33	14.6
	2018	22	19.2	76	8.6	28	13.9
Belgium Belgique	2005	64	11.5	...	...	26	15.1
	2010	66	11.0	...	...	29	15.6
	2015	70	11.2	129	9.4	29	17.6
	2017	72	11.3	132	9.0	31	17.0
Belize Belize	2005	2	23.6	* 2	* 18.7	...	...
	2010	2	22.2	2	16.8	...	...
	2015	3	20.4	2	16.3	1	14.2
	2017	3	19.6	2	16.6	1	13.9
	2018	3	19.8	2	16.7	...	...
Benin Bénin	2001	20	53.5	* 12	* 21.6	* 1	* 29.4
	2004	26	51.6	* 14	* 23.9	...	...
	2005	28	46.8	...	...	...	...
	2010	39	46.4	...	...	6	17.8
	2011	42	44.2	...	...	6	17.3
	2015	50	45.0	93	10.3	...	...
	2016	54	41.6	90	11.0	...	...
	2017	52	43.6	...	...	4	29.5
	2018	57	39.2	...	...	...	...
Bermuda Bermudes	2005	1	8.3	1	7.0	~0	...
	2010	1	7.4	1	5.4	~0	15.3
	2015	~0	10.4	1	6.3	~0	18.7
	2016	~0	...	1	...	...	...
	2018	...	...	...	...	~0	14.5
Bhutan Bhoutan	2005	3	31.1	1	28.1	...	...
	2010	4	25.9	3	21.4	1	6.7
	2012	5	24.0	3	19.9	1	7.7
	2015	2	40.0	6	12.1	...	...
	2018	3	34.7	* 7	* 10.8	1	15.6
Bolivia (Plurin. State of) Bolivie (État plurin. de)	2015	79	17.0	60	20.4	...	...
	2018	77	17.8	67	18.5	...	...

Teaching staff at the primary, secondary and tertiary levels *(continued)*
Number of teachers and Pupil teacher ratio

Personnel enseignant au niveau primaire, secondaire et supérieur *(suite)*
Nombre d'enseignants et ratio élèves/enseignant par niveau d'enseignement

Region, country or area Région, pays ou zone	Year & Année &	Primary education Enseignant primaire		Secondary education Enseignant secondaire		Tertiary education Enseignant supérieur	
		Total Totale ('000)	Pupil-teacher ratio Ratio élèves/ enseignant	Total Totale ('000)	Pupil-teacher ratio Ratio élèves/ enseignant	Total Totale ('000)	Pupil-teacher ratio Ratio élèves/ enseignant
Bosnia and Herzegovina	2010	...	...	...	...	8	12.4
Bosnie-Herzégovine	2015	9	17.2	27	10.1	10	11.3
	2018	9	16.9	27	9.1	10	9.4
Botswana	2005	13	25.6	13	13.8	...	...
Botswana	2007	13	25.2	13	13.8	...	...
	2009	13	25.5	...	...	...	...
	2012	14	23.4	...	...	2	21.8
	2015	15	23.7	...	...	...	...
	2017	...	...	...	...	3	18.3
Brazil	2005	887	21.0	1 612	15.4	293	15.6
Brésil	2010	762	22.2	1 413	16.7	345	19.0
	2015	792	20.6	1 429	16.5	429	19.3
	2017	796	20.2	1 382	16.7	446	19.2
British Virgin Islands	2004	~0	13.9	~0	9.3	~0	10.9
Îles Vierges britanniques	2005	~0	14.9	~0	9.3	...	...
	2009	~0	13.5	~0	8.7	~0	11.5
	2010	~0	13.2	~0	8.7	...	...
	2015	~0	11.7	~0	8.1	~0	9.5
	2017	~0	11.6	~0	8.7	...	...
	2018	...	...	...	...	~0	5.4
Brunei Darussalam	2005	5	10.1	4	10.1	1	8.5
Brunéi Darussalam	2009	4	12.0	5	10.5	1	9.6
	2010	4	11.3	...	...	1	8.3
	2015	4	10.0	5	8.8	1	11.9
	2018	4	9.9	5	8.3	1	12.4
Bulgaria	2005	18	16.2	57	12.0	21	11.3
Bulgarie	2010	15	17.5	44	12.1	21	13.8
	2014	15	17.7	39	13.2	23	12.3
	2016	15	17.6	39	12.6	23	11.8
	2017	17	15.2	...	...	22	11.2
Burkina Faso	2003	23	44.7	8	31.3	...	...
Burkina Faso	2005	27	47.2	...	...	2	14.1
	2010	39	52.4	18	30.3	3	17.7
	2015	64	42.2	38	25.2	5	18.3
	2018	81	39.7	55	23.1	7	17.3
Burundi	2005	21	48.7	* 7	* 22.8	1	16.1
Burundi	2010	37	50.6	11	29.9	2	16.4
	2014	47	43.7	16	37.2	2	25.2
	2015	48	43.2	19	35.8	...	...
	2017	43	49.6	24	28.0	3	19.8
	2018	51	42.5	25	26.6	...	...
Cabo Verde	2005	3	26.0	2	23.5	~0	8.1
Cabo Verde	2010	3	23.6	4	17.5	1	11.0
	2015	3	21.9	4	16.4	1	9.2
	2018	3	21.1	3	15.4	1	8.0
Cambodia	2003	49	56.2	24	23.6	2	17.4
Cambodge	2005	51	53.2	...	...	2	22.7
	2006	51	50.4	27	30.0	3	29.0
	2007	49	50.9	30	28.9	...	...
	2010	47	48.4	...	...	...	...
	2015	48	45.5	...	...	12	17.7
	2017	51	41.7	...	...	15	13.9
	2018	51	41.7	...	...	...	...
Cameroon	2005	* 62	* 47.8	* 48	* 16.2	3	* 31.5
Cameroun	2008	70	46.0	43	26.3	4	38.5
	2010	77	45.8	...	...	* 4	* 52.0
	2014	94	44.2	98	20.4	* 7	* 52.3
	2015	105	41.5	106	19.9	...	...
	2016	105	42.7	115	19.3	...	...
	2018	94	44.8	...	...	...	...

Teaching staff at the primary, secondary and tertiary levels *(continued)*
Number of teachers and Pupil teacher ratio

Personnel enseignant au niveau primaire, secondaire et supérieur *(suite)*
Nombre d'enseignants et ratio élèves/enseignant par niveau d'enseignement

Region, country or area Région, pays ou zone	Year & Année &	Primary education Enseignant primaire		Secondary education Enseignant secondaire		Tertiary education Enseignant supérieur	
		Total Totale ('000)	Pupil-teacher ratio Ratio élèves/ enseignant	Total Totale ('000)	Pupil-teacher ratio Ratio élèves/ enseignant	Total Totale ('000)	Pupil-teacher ratio Ratio élèves/ enseignant
Canada Canada	2000	141	17.4	...	...	...	...
	*2010	...	...	...	...	207	6.9
	*2015	...	...	...	...	205	7.6
	*2016	...	...	...	...	174	9.2
Cayman Islands Îles Caïmanes	2001	~0	15.2	* ~0	* 9.8	* ~0	* 18.8
	2005	~0	12.8	* ~0	* 10.3	...	...
	2008	~0	12.1	~0	8.9	~0	26.8
	2012	~0	13.3	1	5.3	...	...
	2013	~0	13.0	...	...	...	...
	2018	~0	15.7	~0	11.0	...	...
Central African Republic République centrafricaine	2000	...	...	...	...	~0	19.5
	2005	5	88.6	...	...	...	...
	2009	6	94.6	1	80.1	~0	30.7
	2010	8	84.3	2	...	...	...
	2011	8	81.3	2	66.8	~0	34.6
	2012	8	80.1	2	68.1	...	...
	2016	10	83.4	3	34.6	...	...
	2017	...	...	4	31.6	...	...
Chad Tchad	2005	20	63.2	* 7	* 33.5	1	9.5
	2009	27	61.0	13	32.3	2	8.6
	2010	28	62.2	13	32.5	...	...
	2015	41	55.5	19	27.5	2	26.4
	2016	39	56.9	20	27.1	...	...
Chile Chili	2005	66	26.1	66	24.8	...	...
	2010	66	23.4	69	21.9	...	...
	2015	80	18.4	80	19.4	...	...
	2017	85	17.8	83	18.4	...	...
China Chine	2001	5 860	22.2	4 572	18.9	* 589	* 16.0
	2003	5 779	...	5 138	18.6	* 742	* 20.5
	2005	...	...	...	...	1 404	14.7
	2010	5 997	16.8	6 417	15.5	1 557	19.9
	2011	5 939	16.8	6 431	15.2	1 607	19.5
	2015	5 889	16.3	6 234	13.8	...	...
	2018	6 202	16.4	6 360	13.3	...	...
China, Hong Kong SAR Chine, RAS de Hong Kong	2005	25	18.3	* 28	* 18.1	...	...
	2010	23	15.2	* 30	* 16.7	...	...
	2015	24	13.7	* 30	* 13.0	...	...
	2018	27	13.3	31	11.2	...	...
China, Macao SAR Chine, RAS de Macao	2005	2	23.2	2	22.4	2	15.4
	2010	2	16.1	2	16.2	2	14.4
	2015	2	14.1	3	11.4	2	15.4
	2018	2	13.5	3	9.8	2	14.4
Colombia Colombie	2005	187	28.3	164	26.2	94	13.1
	2009	181	29.3	187	26.7	* 110	* 14.2
	2010	181	28.1	187	27.1	...	...
	2015	185	24.2	181	26.5	149	15.4
	2018	185	23.3	186	25.9	162	14.8
Comoros Comores	2003	3	35.9	3	11.3	~0	13.7
	2004	3	35.0	3	13.8	...	...
	2008	4	30.2	...	...	...	...
	2010	...	...	...	...	~0	17.1
	2013	4	27.8	8	8.7	~0	25.7
	2014	...	...	8	8.6	~0	26.3
	2018	4	28.1	9	8.3	...	...
Congo Congo	2003	8	65.2	* 7	* 28.1	* 1	* 13.8
	2004	7	82.8	* 7	* 34.3	...	...
	2009	10	64.4	...	...	1	20.0
	2010	14	49.1	...	...	...	...
	2012	17	44.4	18	18.7	3	11.8
	2013	...	...	...	...	3	12.3
	2017	...	...	...	...	4	12.2

Teaching staff at the primary, secondary and tertiary levels *(continued)*
Number of teachers and Pupil teacher ratio

Personnel enseignant au niveau primaire, secondaire et supérieur *(suite)*
Nombre d'enseignants et ratio élèves/enseignant par niveau d'enseignement

Region, country or area Région, pays ou zone	Year & Année &	Primary education Enseignant primaire		Secondary education Enseignant secondaire		Tertiary education Enseignant supérieur	
		Total Totale ('000)	Pupil-teacher ratio Ratio élèves/ enseignant	Total Totale ('000)	Pupil-teacher ratio Ratio élèves/ enseignant	Total Totale ('000)	Pupil-teacher ratio Ratio élèves/ enseignant
Cook Islands	2005	~0	16.1	~0	15.6	...	...
Îles Cook	2010	~0	15.0	~0	16.2	...	...
	2015	~0	17.2	~0	13.9	~0	...
	2016	~0	17.4	~0	15.7	~0	...
Costa Rica	2002	24	22.6	15	18.8	...	...
Costa Rica	2005	25	21.3	...	...	...	...
	2010	29	17.9	27	15.5	...	...
	2015	37	12.7	33	14.0	...	...
	2018	40	12.2	38	12.4	...	...
Côte d'Ivoire	*2003	48	42.4	...	...	...	...
Côte d'Ivoire	2009	* 57	42.1	...	...	...	...
	2010	...	...	...	...	10	14.2
	2014	* 75	42.5	64	22.3	19	9.1
	2015	* 80	42.1	...	...	19	10.3
	2017	* 89	42.4	72	26.3	19	11.7
	2018	* 93	41.8	75	27.3	...	...
Croatia	2005	* 11	17.5	39	10.1	...	...
Croatie	2010	* 12	14.3	48	8.1	16	9.5
	2015	* 12	13.7	51	7.0	16	10.1
	2016	* 12	13.5	52	6.7	17	9.8
Cuba	2005	* 87	10.3	85	11.1	91	5.2
Cuba	2010	* 93	9.1	85	9.5	153	5.2
	2015	* 84	8.9	91	9.0	57	4.6
	2018	* 81	9.2	83	9.6	62	4.8
Cyprus	2005	* 3	17.7	6	11.3	1	13.8
Chypre	2010	* 4	13.8	7	9.8	3	12.6
	2015	* 5	11.9	6	10.4	3	12.7
	2017	* 5	12.0	7	8.3	3	13.9
Czechia	2005	* 31	16.2	93	10.4	24	13.8
Tchéquie	2006	* 30	15.7	92	10.5	23	15.0
	2010	* 25	18.7	76	11.0	...	...
	2013	* 26	18.9	69	11.5	16	26.0
Dem. People's Rep. Korea	2009	* 70	22.0	124	...	69	8.6
Rép. pop. dém. de Corée	2015	* 66	20.5	123	17.5	63	9.0
	2018	* 74	20.3	124	...	...	...
Dem. Rep. of the Congo	2002	* 159	34.3	...	...	...	...
Rép. dém. du Congo	2009	* 274	37.3	212	16.0	23	16.4
	2010	* 286	37.0	218	16.0	...	...
	2013	* 340	37.1	281	14.2	29	15.3
	2015	* 415	33.2	324	14.2	...	...
Denmark	2001	* 40	9.9	44	10.1	...	...
Danemark	2014	* 44	10.7	49	11.3	28	10.7
	2015	...	...	...	...	37	8.5
Djibouti	2002	...	...	1	31.9	* ~0	* 15.2
Djibouti	2004	* 1	34.5	...	...	~0	12.3
	2005	...	...	...	...	~0	17.7
	2009	* 2	34.1	1	29.7	~0	20.1
	2010	...	...	...	...	~0	20.5
	2011	* 2	35.2	2	27.9	~0	19.2
	2015	* 2	33.0	3	22.8	...	...
	2018	* 2	29.4	3	25.4	...	...
Dominica	2005	* 1	18.2	~0	15.1	...	...
Dominique	2010	* 1	16.0	1	13.2	...	...
	2015	* 1	14.0	1	10.7	...	...
	2016	* 1	13.1	1	...	...	...
Dominican Republic	2003	...	...	...	...	11	25.8
République dominicaine	2005	* 53	24.3	31	26.4	...	...
	2010	* 52	25.5	32	28.2	...	...
	2015	* 71	18.3	42	22.1	19	25.5
	2017	* 66	18.9	50	18.6	20	27.4
	2018	* 65	18.9	...	...	...	...

7   Teaching staff at the primary, secondary and tertiary levels *(continued)*
Number of teachers and Pupil teacher ratio

Personnel enseignant au niveau primaire, secondaire et supérieur *(suite)*
Nombre d'enseignants et ratio élèves/enseignant par niveau d'enseignement

Region, country or area Région, pays ou zone	Year & Année &	Primary education Enseignant primaire		Secondary education Enseignant secondaire		Tertiary education Enseignant supérieur	
		Total Totale ('000)	Pupil-teacher ratio Ratio élèves/ enseignant	Total Totale ('000)	Pupil-teacher ratio Ratio élèves/ enseignant	Total Totale ('000)	Pupil-teacher ratio Ratio élèves/ enseignant
Ecuador	2001	* 85	23.1	* 69	* 13.6	15	...
Équateur	2005	* 87	22.9	* 76	* 13.9	...	...
	2008	...	...	...	...	27	19.9
	2010	* 96	22.0	83	19.9	...	...
	2015	* 80	25.1	86	22.4	40	16.6
	2018	* 80	24.3	92	20.6	...	...
Egypt	*2004	363	21.9	488	17.1	81	28.0
Égypte	*2005	373	25.6	...	...	...	...
	2009	* 382	27.2	549	12.1	...	...
	2010	* 380	27.7	...	...	...	...
	2014	...	...	...	...	107	23.9
	2018	* 534	23.7	603	15.2	...	...
El Salvador	2005	* 24	43.2	* 18	* 28.9	8	15.2
El Salvador	2009	* 31	31.0	23	24.4	9	16.2
	2010	...	...	...	...	9	16.5
	2015	* 25	29.7	19	30.8	10	18.1
	2018	* 25	26.9	19	27.6	11	18.0
Equatorial Guinea	2000	* 2	43.4	* 1	* 23.2	~0	4.9
Guinée équatoriale	2003	* 2	32.0	...	...	...	...
	2005	...	...	1	19.2	...	...
	2010	* 3	27.2	...	...	...	...
	2015	* 4	23.2	...	...	...	...
Eritrea	2004	* 8	46.7	4	47.8	~0	10.8
Érythrée	2005	* 8	47.5	4	51.3	...	...
	2010	* 8	38.0	6	38.7	1	19.2
	2015	* 8	43.3	6	38.9	1	19.5
	2016	* 9	...	6	...	1	14.1
	2018	* 9	38.7	7	35.0	...	...
Estonia	2001	* 8	14.1	12	10.1	7	8.8
Estonie	2005	...	...	...	...	6	10.7
	2006	* 8	10.6	...	...	* 6	* 10.7
	2010	* 6	11.7	11	8.8	...	...
	2013	* 7	11.5	10	8.1	...	...
	2017	* 8	11.3	9	9.2	4	11.3
Eswatini	2005	* 7	32.9	4	16.7	~0	13.7
Eswatini	2006	* 7	33.3	4	19.3	~0	12.3
	2010	* 7	32.3	5	18.1	...	...
	2013	* 9	28.1	6	16.0	~0	17.6
	2015	* 9	27.6	6	15.8	1	...
	2016	* 9	27.3	7	15.5	...	...
	2017	* 9	26.6	...	...	...	...
Ethiopia	2000	* 87	67.3	...	...	2	27.1
Éthiopie	2005	...	...	...	...	5	39.4
	2009	* 234	57.9	82	47.4	12	34.1
	2010	* 252	54.1	98	43.1	...	...
	2011	* 260	55.1	113	40.3	...	...
	*2012	...	...	122	40.4	...	...
	2014	...	...	...	...	24	31.2
Fiji	2004	* 4	28.2	* 5	* 22.4	...	...
Fidji	2008	* 4	26.0	5	18.7	...	...
	2012	* 4	28.0	5	19.3	...	...
Finland	2005	* 25	15.5	42	10.3	19	16.4
Finlande	2010	* 25	14.0	43	9.9	15	19.7
	2014	* 26	13.3	42	12.8	16	19.3
	2017	* 27	13.7	40	13.6	15	19.8
France	2004	* 203	18.6	511	11.4	136	15.9
France	2005	* 216	18.6	528	11.4	...	...
	2010	* 234	17.8	463	12.7	...	...
	2013	* 229	18.2	457	12.9	110	21.3
Gabon	2003	* 8	36.0	...	...	...	...
Gabon	2011	* 13	24.5	...	...	...	...

Teaching staff at the primary, secondary and tertiary levels *(continued)*
Number of teachers and Pupil teacher ratio

Personnel enseignant au niveau primaire, secondaire et supérieur *(suite)*
Nombre d'enseignants et ratio élèves/enseignant par niveau d'enseignement

Region, country or area Région, pays ou zone	Year & Année &	Primary education Enseignant primaire		Secondary education Enseignant secondaire		Tertiary education Enseignant supérieur	
		Total Totale ('000)	Pupil-teacher ratio Ratio élèves/ enseignant	Total Totale ('000)	Pupil-teacher ratio Ratio élèves/ enseignant	Total Totale ('000)	Pupil-teacher ratio Ratio élèves/ enseignant
Gambia	2004	* 5	38.5	...	...	~0	11.4
Gambie	2005	* 6	36.6	...	...	...	...
	*2010	6	37.5	...	...	...	...
	2012	* 7	33.9	...	...	~0	23.2
	2015	* 8	37.1	6	...	...	...
	2018	* 10	36.1	8	...	...	...
Georgia	2003	* 17	14.5	49	9.2	29	5.5
Géorgie	2005	...	...	...	...	29	5.9
	2009	* 34	* 8.9	* 45	* 7.6	12	7.7
	2010	...	...	...	...	13	7.9
	2015	* 32	9.0	38	7.2	18	7.1
	2018	* 34	9.0	37	7.6	18	8.3
Germany	2002	* 236	14.3	590	14.3	277	...
Allemagne	2005	* 234	14.1	596	13.9	...	...
	2010	* 242	12.7	594	12.9	...	...
	2015	* 236	12.2	586	12.1	396	7.5
	2017	* 240	12.3	587	12.0	407	7.6
Ghana	2005	* 89	32.8	* 73	* 18.8	...	...
Ghana	2009	* 111	33.1	99	18.3	...	...
	*2010	121	...	112	...	...	...
	2015	* 139	31.3	147	16.6	14	28.9
	2018	* 162	27.2	167	16.0	17	26.5
Gibraltar	2001	* ~0	20.7	~0	11.7	...	...
Gibraltar	2009	* ~0	16.0	~0	5.9	...	...
	2017	* ~0	14.2	~0	15.0	...	...
Greece	2005	* 59	11.1	86	8.3	27	23.8
Grèce	2007	* 62	10.3	87	7.9	29	20.8
	2014	* 67	9.4	80	8.3	15	44.5
	2015	* 67	9.6	76	8.7	...	...
	2017	* 69	9.4	78	8.6	19	38.8
Grenada	2004	* 1	17.7	* 1	* 20.1	...	...
Grenade	2005	* 1	18.2	...	...	...	...
	2010	* 1	16.1	1	15.5	...	...
	2015	* 1	17.0	1	11.9	2	4.3
	2018	* 1	16.4	1	12.8	2	5.7
Guatemala	2002	* 69	30.1	44	13.7	4	27.7
Guatemala	*2003	...	...	...	...	4	...
	2005	* 76	31.1	48	15.8	...	...
	2010	* 99	26.9	77	14.0	...	...
	2014	* 105	23.0	92	12.7	...	...
	2018	* 117	20.3	117	10.5	...	...
Guinea	2005	* 27	44.9	12	* 34.4	...	...
Guinée	2008	* 31	44.1	16	33.3	...	...
	2010	* 34	42.2	...	...	5	19.1
	2011	* 35	44.1	19	33.1	6	17.9
	2014	* 38	45.6	...	...	6	18.7
	*2015	36	...	...	...	...	...
	2016	* 38	47.1	...	...	...	...
Guinea-Bissau	2000	* 3	44.1	* 2	* 15.0	...	...
Guinée-Bissau	2006	* 4	62.2	1	37.3	~0	147.6
	2010	* 5	51.9	...	...	...	...
Guyana	2005	* 4	28.0	* 4	* 18.0	1	12.6
Guyana	2010	* 4	24.6	4	21.4	1	10.6
	2012	* 4	23.2	4	20.3	1	13.1
Honduras	2004	* 38	32.9	17	...	* 7	* 17.1
Honduras	*2005	42	29.1	...	...	...	...
	2009	* 37	33.9	...	...	...	...
	2010	...	...	...	...	9	19.8
	2015	* 40	29.1	40	16.1	10	20.0
	2017	* 44	25.6	39	16.7	10	24.6
	2018	...	...	...	...	12	21.5

7

Teaching staff at the primary, secondary and tertiary levels *(continued)*
Number of teachers and Pupil teacher ratio

Personnel enseignant au niveau primaire, secondaire et supérieur *(suite)*
Nombre d'enseignants et ratio élèves/enseignant par niveau d'enseignement

Region, country or area Région, pays ou zone	Year & Année &	Primary education Enseignant primaire		Secondary education Enseignant secondaire		Tertiary education Enseignant supérieur	
		Total Totale ('000)	Pupil-teacher ratio Ratio élèves/ enseignant	Total Totale ('000)	Pupil-teacher ratio Ratio élèves/ enseignant	Total Totale ('000)	Pupil-teacher ratio Ratio élèves/ enseignant
Hungary	2005	* 41	10.4	97	9.9	25	17.2
Hongrie	2010	* 37	10.6	89	10.2	25	15.8
	2015	* 36	11.0	80	10.3	21	14.6
	2016	* 37	10.8	81	10.0	22	13.6
Iceland	2005	...	...	...	...	2	8.5
Islande	2010	...	...	...	...	2	8.6
	2012	* 3	9.9	...	...	2	8.7
	2015	* 3	10.1	...	...	...	...
India	2003	* 3 038	41.3	2 507	32.3	428	26.4
Inde	2004	...	...	2 586	32.7	539	22.0
	2010	...	...	4 252	25.3	...	...
	2015	* 4 399	31.5	4 093	31.7	1 322	24.3
	2017	* 4 373	32.7	4 731	27.4	1 366	24.4
	2018	...	...	4 668	28.5	1 389	24.7
Indonesia	2005	* 1 428	20.4	1 282	12.5	272	* 13.5
Indonésie	2010	* 1 596	19.0	1 641	12.2	271	18.4
	2014	* 1 802	16.6	1 460	15.5	258	25.0
	2015	...	...	...	...	231	30.5
	2018	* 1 727	17.0	1 637	15.2	295	27.3
Iran (Islamic Republic of)	2005	* 285	21.7	...	...	115	18.4
Iran (Rép. islamique d')	2009	* 278	20.5	...	...	164	20.5
	2010	...	...	...	...	174	21.8
	2014	* 287	25.9	331	17.5	288	16.3
	2015	* 286	26.8	...	...	...	...
	2017	* 286	28.5	299	19.0	276	14.8
Iraq	2004	* 211	20.5	91	18.8	19	22.1
Iraq	*2005	...	...	...	...	19	22.1
	2007	* 287	17.0	148	13.7	...	...
Ireland	2005	* 25	17.9	...	...	12	16.0
Irlande	2010	* 32	15.8	...	...	13	15.4
	2012	* 32	16.1	...	...	...	...
Israel	*2005	55	13.0	68	9.9	...	...
Israël	*2009	60	13.1	71	9.8	...	...
	2010	* 62	13.1	...	...	...	...
	2015	* 73	12.1	...	...	...	...
	2016	* 74	12.1	...	...	...	...
Italy	2005	* 264	10.5	428	10.5	94	21.4
Italie	2007	* 273	10.3	451	10.1	104	19.5
	2010	...	...	...	...	106	18.7
	2015	* 237	12.0	408	11.3	90	20.3
	2017	* 253	11.5	461	10.0	91	20.1
Jamaica	2002	...	...	* 12	* 19.3	2	22.8
Jamaïque	2004	* 12	27.5	13	19.1	...	...
	2010	...	...	18	14.3	...	...
	2015	* 12	22.0	13	16.4	...	...
	2018	* 10	24.8	12	16.7	...	...
Japan	2015	* 410	16.2	634	11.4	550[1]	7.0
Japon	2017	* 417	15.7	638	11.1	560	6.9
Jordan	2003	* 39	* 19.9	* 34	* 17.9	7	26.8
Jordanie	2005	...	...	...	...	8	26.4
	2010	...	...	...	...	10	24.6
	2014	* 58	16.9	51	14.6	...	...
	2015	...	...	...	...	14	22.5
	2017	* 53	21.0	67	11.4	23	12.5
	2018	* 61	18.5	64	12.3	...	...
Kazakhstan	2000	...	...	...	...	31	13.4
Kazakhstan	2005	* 59	17.3	...	...	...	...
	2010	* 59	16.2	...	...	49	15.5
	2015	* 74	16.2	224	7.5	51	13.0
	2018	* 72	19.6	265	7.0	38	16.5

Teaching staff at the primary, secondary and tertiary levels *(continued)*
Number of teachers and Pupil teacher ratio

Personnel enseignant au niveau primaire, secondaire et supérieur *(suite)*
Nombre d'enseignants et ratio élèves/enseignant par niveau d'enseignement

Region, country or area Région, pays ou zone	Year & Année &	Primary education Enseignant primaire		Secondary education Enseignant secondaire		Tertiary education Enseignant supérieur	
		Total Totale ('000)	Pupil-teacher ratio Ratio élèves/ enseignant	Total Totale ('000)	Pupil-teacher ratio Ratio élèves/ enseignant	Total Totale ('000)	Pupil-teacher ratio Ratio élèves/ enseignant
Kenya Kenya	*2005	145	42.0	91	27.2	...	...
	*2009	165	43.3	96	33.4	...	...
	*2015	267	30.7	199	...	...	...
	2017	...	...	...	...	21	27.0
Kiribati Kiribati	2005	* 1	24.7	1	17.0	...	...
	2008	* 1	25.0	1	17.4	...	...
	2014	* 1	26.4	...	...	...	...
	2017	* 1	25.5	...	...	...	...
Kuwait Koweït	2004	* 12	12.8	25	10.6	* 2	* 17.0
	2005	* 17	12.1	...	...	...	...
	2009	* 25	8.6	* 31	* 8.2	...	...
	2010	* 26	8.4	...	...	...	...
	2015	* 30	8.9	40	7.6	...	...
	2018	* 32	8.9	45	...	...	...
Kyrgyzstan Kirghizistan	2005	* 18	24.5	54	13.4	13	16.5
	2010	* 16	24.3	48	14.3	17	14.9
	2015	* 17	26.2	60	10.8	21	12.8
	2018	* 21	25.0	63	10.6	20	11.1
Lao People's Dem. Rep. Rép. dém. populaire lao	2005	* 28	31.5	16	24.8	2	20.7
	2010	* 32	28.8	21	20.2	5	22.5
	2015	* 35	24.2	* 34	* 18.7	12	10.6
	2018	* 35	* 22.3	* 37	* 18.2	9	11.3
Latvia Lettonie	2005	* 7	12.2	25	10.8	6	20.9
	2010	* 10	11.9	16	9.0	7	16.3
	2015	* 11	11.1	15	8.0	7	12.6
	2017	* 11	11.5	14	8.3	7	11.8
Lebanon Liban	2005	* 33	* 14.6	* 42	* 9.0	21	8.0
	2010	* 33	14.1	43	8.9	25	8.0
	2014	* 39	12.3	48	7.7	46	5.0
	2016	* 40	12.2	50	7.7	...	...
	2017	* 40	12.5	...	...	...	...
Lesotho Lesotho	2005	* 10	41.6	3	27.0	1	14.2
	2006	* 10	40.8	4	25.8	1	13.3
	2010	* 12	33.8	* 5	* 24.5	...	...
	2014	* 11	32.8	* 6	* 23.5	1	29.3
	2015	* 11	33.1	6	24.0	...	...
	2017	* 11	32.9	5	25.3	1	20.0
	2018	...	...	...	...	1	19.7
Liberia Libéria	2000	* 13	38.3	...	...	1	72.3
	*2001	...	...	...	...	1	...
	2009	* 22	27.4	...	...	...	...
	2010	...	...	...	...	1	24.4
	2012	...	...	...	...	2	21.6
	2015	* 22	30.4	12	18.4	...	...
	2017	* 28	22.3	18	...	...	...
Libya Libye	*2003	...	...	...	...	16	23.9
Liechtenstein Liechtenstein	2005	* ~0	8.6	~0	9.6	...	...
	2009	* ~0	6.5	~0	9.3	...	...
	2010	* ~0	6.1	...	...	...	...
	2015	* ~0	7.8	~0	9.9	~0	6.3
	2017	* ~0	7.8	~0	9.6	~0	7.1
Lithuania Lituanie	2005	* 11	14.1	43	9.9	13	14.9
	2010	* 10	12.8	39	8.8	14	14.3
	2015	* 8	12.9	33	7.9	13	10.8
	2017	* 8	13.5	31	7.8	12	10.4
Luxembourg Luxembourg	2005	* 3	11.3	3	10.3	...	...
	2010	* 4	9.3	5	8.5	1	5.4
	2015	* 4	8.5	5	9.4	1	8.9
	2016	* 4	8.3	5[1]	8.8	1	9.2

Teaching staff at the primary, secondary and tertiary levels *(continued)*
Number of teachers and Pupil teacher ratio

Personnel enseignant au niveau primaire, secondaire et supérieur *(suite)*
Nombre d'enseignants et ratio élèves/enseignant par niveau d'enseignement

Region, country or area Région, pays ou zone	Year & Année &	Primary education Enseignant primaire		Secondary education Enseignant secondaire		Tertiary education Enseignant supérieur	
		Total Totale ('000)	Pupil-teacher ratio Ratio élèves/ enseignant	Total Totale ('000)	Pupil-teacher ratio Ratio élèves/ enseignant	Total Totale ('000)	Pupil-teacher ratio Ratio élèves/ enseignant
Madagascar	2005	* 67	53.6	* 29	* 21.6	2	25.5
Madagascar	2009	* 90	47.9	44	* 23.5	4	16.3
	2010	* 106	40.1	...	...	4	16.6
	2014	* 111	41.7	65	23.1	6	18.8
	2015	* 116	41.2	...	...	6	18.7
	2018	* 122	39.8	80	19.3	6	24.8
Malawi	2005	...	...	...	...	1	7.5
Malawi	2010	* 43	* 79.3	* 16	* 43.2	1	11.6
	2011	* 47	* 76.1	* 17	* 42.1	1	13.6
	*2015	60	69.5	25	37.9	...	...
	2018	* 76	58.7	14	72.3	...	...
Malaysia	2005	* 190	16.9	153	16.3	45	15.4
Malaisie	2010	* 257	12.6	191	13.7	75	14.2
	2013	* 274	11.8	207	13.3	69	16.2
	2015	* 270	11.5	...	...	82	15.9
	2017	* 265	11.7	224	12.3	90	13.9
	2018	* 240	...	227	11.4	96	13.3
Maldives	2003	* 4	18.2	2	13.7	~0	1.9
Maldives	2005	* 3	20.1	...	...	...	...
	2010	* 4	11.7	...	...	...	...
	2015	* 4	10.3	...	...	...	...
	2017	* 4	10.2	...	...	1	17.4
Mali	2000	* 16	65.3	* 9	* 29.0	* 1	* 20.5
Mali	2005	* 28	54.4	...	...	...	...
	2009	* 38	50.1	* 29	* 23.4	...	...
	2010	* 40	50.4	...	...	...	...
	2015	* 52	42.7	49	19.2	...	...
	2017	* 66	38.2	58	17.4	2	30.8
	2018	* 65	37.8	...	...	...	...
Malta	2005	* 2	18.4	3	11.5	1	11.4
Malte	2008	* 2	17.5	4	10.6	1	9.8
	2010	* 2	14.3	...	...	1	9.0
	2015	* 2	13.5	4	7.8	2	8.1
	2017	* 2	12.9	4	7.1	2	8.3
Marshall Islands	2002	* 1	16.9	~0	16.7	~0	18.8
Îles Marshall	*2003	...	...	~0	14.9	...	...
	2012	...	...	...	...	~0	19.6
Mauritania	2005	* 11	40.3	3	31.0	~0	24.6
Mauritanie	2006	* 11	41.4	* 4	* 26.2	~0	28.8
	2010	* 14	37.2	...	...	~0	38.4
	2013	* 16	35.4	...	...	~0	43.0
	2015	* 18	35.8	6	33.5	...	...
	2018	* 19	34.3	9	25.9	...	...
Mauritius	2005	* 6	22.3	7	* 17.4	...	...
Maurice	2010	* 5	21.5	8	* 15.3	1	30.4
	2015	* 5	18.8	10	12.9	...	...
	2018	* 6	16.2	11	11.0	...	...
Mexico	2005	* 519	28.3	593	17.8	251	9.5
Mexique	2010	* 530	28.1	652	17.9	310	9.2
	2015	* 535	26.9	838	16.1	364	9.7
	2017	* 534	26.6	833	16.9	387	11.4
Micronesia (Fed. States of)	*2000	...	...	...	...	~0	17.1
Micronésie (États féd. de)	*2015	1	19.7	...	...	...	...
Monaco	2001	* ~0	22.3	~0	10.8	...	...
Monaco	2004	...	...	~0	11.1	...	...
	2008	...	...	1	5.8	...	...
	2015	* ~0	12.6	~0	8.1	...	...
	2016	* ~0	13.7	...	...	~0	6.9
	2017	* ~0	10.5	* ~0	* 8.5	...	...
	2018	* ~0	11.4	...	...	...	...

7 Teaching staff at the primary, secondary and tertiary levels *(continued)*
Number of teachers and Pupil teacher ratio

Personnel enseignant au niveau primaire, secondaire et supérieur *(suite)*
Nombre d'enseignants et ratio élèves/enseignant par niveau d'enseignement

Region, country or area Région, pays ou zone	Year & Année &	Primary education Enseignant primaire		Secondary education Enseignant secondaire		Tertiary education Enseignant supérieur	
		Total Totale ('000)	Pupil-teacher ratio Ratio élèves/ enseignant	Total Totale ('000)	Pupil-teacher ratio Ratio élèves/ enseignant	Total Totale ('000)	Pupil-teacher ratio Ratio élèves/ enseignant
Mongolia Mongolie	2005	* 7	34.2	15	22.4	8	15.4
	2010	* 9	30.2	19	14.5	9	18.9
	2015	* 9	28.2	21[1]	...	9	20.3
	2018	* 10	30.4	21	...	7	23.1
Montenegro Monténégro	2018	...	...	...	...	2	14.9
Montserrat Montserrat	2005	* ~0	20.4	~0	11.5	...	...
	2009	* ~0	13.1	~0	13.3	...	...
	2014	* ~0	11.0	~0	12.7	...	...
	2018	* ~0	17.0	~0	8.8	...	...
Morocco Maroc	2004	* 148	27.6	* 100	* 18.7	19	18.5
	2005	* 148	27.1	...	...	19	19.0
	2009	* 145	26.6	...	...	20	21.4
	2010	* 150	26.2	...	...	...	...
	2015	* 156	25.9	...	...	33	26.9
	2018	* 161	26.8	148	19.4	37	28.7
Mozambique Mozambique	2005	* 59	66.3	* 10	* 32.2	3	9.4
	2010	* 90	58.5	* 20	* 34.1	6	16.2
	2014	* 104	* 54.8	* 26	* 40.0	10	15.2
	*2015	108	54.7	27	39.7	...	...
	2017	* 117	52.4	33	36.5	14	14.1
	2018	* 119	55.3	...	...	14	15.2
Myanmar Myanmar	2001	* 148	32.3	75	30.8	11	52.6
	2005	* 160	30.9	78	33.1	...	...
	2007	* 172	29.1	82	32.8	11	47.6
	2010	* 182	28.2	84	34.1	...	...
	2012	...	...	...	...	25	25.3
	2014	* 188	27.6	100	31.8	...	...
	2018	* 218	24.4	154	27.2	26	35.5
Namibia Namibie	2003	* 13	31.6	6	25.2	1	13.1
	2005	* 13	30.8	6	25.1	...	...
	2007	* 14	29.9	6	24.6	...	...
	2008	* 14	29.4	...	...	1	16.4
	2010	* 14	29.8	...	...	...	...
	2015	...	...	...	...	3	16.3
	2017	...	...	11	...	3	16.6
	2018	* 20	25.1	...	...	...	...
Nauru Nauru	2005	* ~0	27.9	~0	15.4	...	...
	2007	* ~0	19.9	~0	20.9	...	...
	2008	* ~0	22.4	...	...	...	...
	2014	* ~0	39.5	~0	22.8	...	...
	2016	* ~0	40.2	~0	24.8	...	...
Nepal Népal	2003	* 110	35.7	53	34.7	...	...
	2005	* 101	39.7	...	...	7	27.2
	2007	* 113	40.0	...	...	10	25.7
	2010	* 154	31.9	* 84	* 32.0	...	...
	2013	* 179	25.6	* 107	* 29.2	8	60.0
	2015	* 188	23.1	* 111	* 28.6	...	...
	2017	* 198	20.9	* 116	* 28.8	...	...
Netherlands Pays-Bas	2005	...	...	107	13.1	45	12.7
	2010	...	...	107	13.7	52	12.6
	2015	* 104	11.6	112	14.5	63	13.5
	2017	* 100	11.8	114	14.5	69	12.7
Netherlands Antilles [former] Antilles néerlandaises [anc.]	2002	* 1	20.0	1	12.8	* ~0	* 7.6
New Zealand Nouvelle-Zélande	2005	* 22	16.3	36	14.7	...	...
	2010	* 24	14.5	35	14.5	...	...
	2015	* 25	14.5	35	13.8	16	16.7
	2017	* 26	14.9	36	13.6	17	16.0
Nicaragua Nicaragua	2002	* 26	35.2	* 11	* 33.9	7	15.3
	2005	* 28	33.6	13	33.7	...	...
	2010	* 31	30.2	15	30.8	...	...

Teaching staff at the primary, secondary and tertiary levels *(continued)*
Number of teachers and Pupil teacher ratio

Personnel enseignant au niveau primaire, secondaire et supérieur *(suite)*
Nombre d'enseignants et ratio élèves/enseignant par niveau d'enseignement

Region, country or area Région, pays ou zone	Year & Année &	Primary education Enseignant primaire		Secondary education Enseignant secondaire		Tertiary education Enseignant supérieur	
		Total Totale ('000)	Pupil-teacher ratio Ratio élèves/ enseignant	Total Totale ('000)	Pupil-teacher ratio Ratio élèves/ enseignant	Total Totale ('000)	Pupil-teacher ratio Ratio élèves/ enseignant
Niger Niger	2005	* 24	43.7	7	27.4	1	14.9
	2010	* 45	38.6	10	30.8	2	11.3
	2015	* 67	36.6	21	28.0	3	15.1
	2017	* 76	36.3	26	29.7	4	15.3
	2018	* 69	...	29	...	5	14.7
Nigeria Nigéria	2004	* 598	35.8	155	40.6	37	34.8
	2005	* 599	36.9	159	40.2	...	...
	2010	* 574	* 37.6	390	23.2	57	24.6
	2011	...	...	...	...	67	22.6
Niue Nioué	2004	* ~0	11.5	~0	8.4	...	...
	2005	...	...	~0	8.2	...	...
	2015	* ~0	17.3	~0	7.9	...	...
	2016	* ~0	15.5	...	...	...	...
North Macedonia Macédoine du Nord	2005	* 6	19.4	15	14.7	3	16.9
	2010	* 7	15.9	17	11.9	3	17.8
	2015	* 8	14.4	18	9.4	* 4	* 17.7
	2017	* 7	14.9	18	8.7	4	14.9
Norway Norvège	2001	...	...	...	...	15	12.3
	2015	* 49	8.9	51	8.6	27	9.9
	2017	* 52	8.6	52	8.6	33	8.6
Oman Oman	*2003	16	19.9	16	17.4	...	...
	2005	...	...	...	...	3	16.2
	2010	...	...	...	...	5	16.8
	2015	...	...	...	...	8	16.2
	2016	...	...	...	...	8	16.2
	2018	* 29	9.7	41	10.2	...	...
Pakistan Pakistan	2005	* 450	38.3	* 295	* 23.3	...	...
	2010	* 464	40.5	...	...	...	...
	2015	* 428	46.3	* 572	* 21.1	...	...
	2018	* 520	44.1	* 655	* 20.4	57	33.0
Palau Palaos	2000	* ~0	15.7	~0	15.1	* ~0	* 10.9
	*2002	...	...	...	...	~0	10.5
	2013	...	...	...	...	~0	8.2
Panama Panama	2005	* 18	24.2	16	15.6	11	11.0
	2010	* 19	23.5	19	15.3	15	9.2
	2015	* 19	21.9	24	13.3	15	10.6
	2016	* 19	21.4	24	14.5	14	11.5
	2017	* 19	22.0	24	13.6	...	...
Papua New Guinea Papouasie-Nvl-Guinée	*2001	14	36.2	...	...	...	...
	2012	...	...	14	27.4	...	...
	2016	* 36	35.5	15	34.3	...	...
Paraguay Paraguay	*2004	33	27.8	44	11.8	...	...
	2012	* 35	24.2	34	18.4	...	...
Peru Pérou	2002	* 171	25.1	134	18.9	56	14.8
	2005	* 177	23.0	148	16.7	...	...
	2010	* 191	19.7	167	16.0	...	...
	2015	* 195	18.0	190	14.1	...	...
	2017	* 198	17.9	190	14.6	98	19.3
	2018	* 207	17.4	196	14.2	...	...
Philippines Philippines	2005	* 373	35.1	168	37.9	* 113	* 21.3
	2009	* 435	31.4	194	34.8	...	...
	2015	* 478	30.3	279	26.2	...	...
	2017	* 483	29.1	377	23.9	151	23.7
Poland Pologne	2005	* 236	11.5	296	11.6	95	22.3
	2010	* 240	9.3	273	10.4	103	20.9
	2014	* 211	10.2	279	9.5	100	17.6
	2015	* 220	...	273	9.3	97	17.1
	2017	* 226	10.2	265	9.1	...	...
Portugal Portugal	2005	* 72	10.5	94	7.1	37	10.4
	2010	* 68	10.8	98	7.3	36	10.6
	2015	* 49	13.3	78	9.9	32	10.4
	2017	* 51	12.4	81	9.5	33	10.5

7

Teaching staff at the primary, secondary and tertiary levels *(continued)*
Number of teachers and Pupil teacher ratio

Personnel enseignant au niveau primaire, secondaire et supérieur *(suite)*
Nombre d'enseignants et ratio élèves/enseignant par niveau d'enseignement

Region, country or area Région, pays ou zone	Year & Année &	Primary education Enseignant primaire		Secondary education Enseignant secondaire		Tertiary education Enseignant supérieur	
		Total Totale ('000)	Pupil-teacher ratio Ratio élèves/ enseignant	Total Totale ('000)	Pupil-teacher ratio Ratio élèves/ enseignant	Total Totale ('000)	Pupil-teacher ratio Ratio élèves/ enseignant
Puerto Rico Porto Rico	2010	* 26	11.7	26	11.1	16	15.4
	2015	* 18	13.9	15	18.9	16	14.8
	2016	* 17	13.5	14	17.2	17	13.6
Qatar Qatar	2005	* 6	11.1	5	11.6	1	* 14.6
	2010	* 7	12.0	7	9.9	2	8.6
	2015	* 11	11.6	9	10.7	2	12.9
	2018	* 13	12.2	10	11.0	2	14.0
Republic of Korea République de Corée	2005	* 144	27.9	210	18.1	191	16.8
	2010	* 158	20.9	225	17.6	223	14.7
	2015	* 164	16.6	236	14.4	225	14.5
	2017	* 165	16.3	232	13.3	220	14.3
Republic of Moldova République de Moldova	2005	* 10	18.0	31	12.8	8	16.7
	2010	* 9	15.4	29	10.5	8	16.8
	2015	* 8	17.5	25	9.3	7	16.5
	2018	* 8	17.9	23	9.9	6	13.8
Romania Roumanie	2005	* 57	17.0	162	12.9	31	23.9
	2010	* 52	16.1	146	12.5	31	32.1
	2015	* 50	18.9	129	12.1	28	19.5
	2017	* 48	19.3	124	12.1	27	20.0
Russian Federation Fédération de Russie	2005	* 317	* 16.7	* 1 306	* 9.5	625	14.4
	2009	* 278	18.1	1 136	8.5	670	13.9
	2012	* 282	19.6	1 046	8.8	554	14.4
	2015	* 297	20.1	...	...	627	10.5
	2017	* 309	21.3	...	...	597	9.9
Rwanda Rwanda	2005	* 27	69.0	8	28.7	* 2	* 15.3
	2009	* 33	68.3	15	22.6	3	18.7
	2010	* 36	64.6	...	...	3	22.2
	2015	* 42	58.3	30	19.2	3	23.9
	2018	* 42	59.5	23	28.2	3	24.7
Saint Kitts and Nevis Saint-Kitts-et-Nevis	2005	* ~0	17.6	* ~0	* 9.9	...	...
	2010	* ~0	14.1	~0	* 9.3	...	...
	2015	* ~0	15.1	1	8.3	~0	7.6
	2016	* ~0	13.9	1	7.9	...	...
Saint Lucia Sainte-Lucie	2005	* 1	22.0	1	16.9	~0	12.6
	2010	* 1	18.5	* 1	* 15.7	~0	9.3
	2015	* 1	15.5	1	11.7	~0	10.2
	2018	* 1	14.7	1	11.1	~0	7.7
Saint Vincent & Grenadines Saint-Vincent-Grenadines	*2004	1	17.2	1	18.1	...	...
	2010	* 1	16.3	1	16.8	...	...
	2015	* 1	14.9	1	15.0	...	...
	2018	* 1	14.4	1	13.9	...	...
Samoa Samoa	2000	* 1	24.0	1	21.2	~0	7.8
	2002	* 1	27.2	1	21.0	...	...
	2010	* 1	30.2	1	21.5	...	...
San Marino Saint-Marin	2004	* ~0	6.3	...	...	...	...
	2010	* ~0	6.5	~0	14.5	...	...
	2012	* ~0	6.3	...	...	...	...
	2018	* ~0	6.9	~0	5.8	~0	5.1
Sao Tome and Principe Sao Tomé-et-Principe	2005	* 1	30.8	* ~0	* 21.7	...	...
	2009	* 1	26.2	...	...	...	...
	2010	...	...	...	...	~0	8.1
	2015	* 1	38.8	1	20.8	~0	8.0
	2016	* 1	32.2	1	24.8	...	...
	2017	* 1	31.2	...	...	...	...
Saudi Arabia Arabie saoudite	2005	* 273	* 11.3	* 234	* 11.1	27	22.5
	2009	* 285	* 11.4	* 264	* 11.3	39	19.2
	2010	* 298	11.2	...	...	50	18.2
	2015	* 321	10.9	323	10.3	77	19.8
	2018	* 239	13.8	270	11.5	85	19.0

7 Teaching staff at the primary, secondary and tertiary levels *(continued)*
Number of teachers and Pupil teacher ratio

Personnel enseignant au niveau primaire, secondaire et supérieur *(suite)*
Nombre d'enseignants et ratio élèves/enseignant par niveau d'enseignement

Region, country or area Région, pays ou zone	Year & Année &	Primary education Enseignant primaire		Secondary education Enseignant secondaire		Tertiary education Enseignant supérieur	
		Total Totale ('000)	Pupil-teacher ratio Ratio élèves/ enseignant	Total Totale ('000)	Pupil-teacher ratio Ratio élèves/ enseignant	Total Totale ('000)	Pupil-teacher ratio Ratio élèves/ enseignant
Senegal	2005	* 35	41.7	* 15	* 26.4	...	...
Sénégal	2010	* 50	33.7	...	...	...	...
	2015	* 62	32.1	56	20.4	6	25.8
	2017	* 65	32.8	57	18.9	8	20.2
	2018	* 59	36.3	...	...	7	27.9
Serbia	2010	* 17	16.4	62	9.6	15	15.3
Serbie	2015	* 18	15.2	65	8.5	11	22.5
	2018	* 19	14.3	67	7.9	12	22.1
Seychelles	2005	* 1	13.7	1	14.4	...	...
Seychelles	2010	* 1	12.5	1	12.8	...	...
	2015	* 1	13.7	1	12.0	~0	14.4
	2018	* 1	14.5	1	10.8	~0	17.5
Sierra Leone	2001	* 15	37.3	6	26.6	1	7.7
Sierra Leone	*2002	...	...	...	...	1	7.5
	2015	* 40	33.8	22	20.5	...	...
	2016	* 38	37.3	22	22.0	...	...
	2018	* 50	27.5	...	...	...	...
Singapore	2009	* 16	18.2	14	16.2	15	13.8
Singapour	2010	...	...	...	...	17	14.1
	2012	...	...	...	...	19	13.5
	2017	* 16	14.7	15	11.5	15	13.3
Sint Maarten (Dutch part)	2012	* ~0	11.3	~0	11.8	~0	3.3
St-Martin (partie néerland.)	2014	...	...	~0	7.6	~0	3.6
	2015	...	...	...	...	~0	3.6
Slovakia	2005	* 14	17.5	51	13.1	13	14.3
Slovaquie	2010	* 14	15.2	46	12.0	13	17.6
	2015	* 14	15.2	41	11.2	13	14.4
	2017	* 15	15.5	40	11.1	12	12.8
Slovenia	2005	* 6	15.1	16	11.2	4	25.1
Slovénie	2010	* 6	17.0	15	9.1	7	16.5
	2015	* 7	16.9	14	10.2	7	12.0
	2016	* 9	13.8	15	9.7	7	11.3
Solomon Islands	*2000	...	...	1	10.1	...	...
Îles Salomon	2010	* 5	19.9	1	28.1	...	...
	2012	* 5	19.1	2	25.9	...	...
	2015	* 4	25.7	2	...	...	...
	2018	* 4	25.4	...	...	...	...
Somalia Somalie	2007	* 13	35.5	5	19.3	...	...
South Africa	2005	* 233	* 31.4	142	32.9	...	...
Afrique du Sud	2009	* 212	* 33.6	187	25.0	...	...
	2010	* 238	29.5	...	...	...	...
	2015	* 249	30.3	190	27.8	...	...
	2017	...	...	183	27.6	...	...
South Sudan Soudan du sud	*2015	27	46.8	6	27.5	...	...
Spain	2005	* 181	13.8	280	11.1	145	12.5
Espagne	2010	* 219	12.4	295	10.8	155	12.1
	2015	* 228	13.2	276	12.0	157	12.5
	2017	* 232	13.1	288	11.6	167	12.0
Sri Lanka	2005	* 73	21.9	...	...	...	...
Sri Lanka	2010	* 72	23.9	...	...	...	...
	2012	* 72	24.4	150	17.3	...	...
	2015	* 77	23.2	...	...	...	...
	2018	* 79	21.7	156	17.5	10	29.8
State of Palestine	2005	* 16	24.5	25	26.6	* 5	* 30.5
État de Palestine	2010	* 14	27.8	32	22.5	7	27.2
	2015	* 19	24.0	36	19.9	8	26.1
	2018	* 20	24.5	44	17.3	8	27.9
Sudan Soudan	2015	...	...	...	...	13	49.8

7

Teaching staff at the primary, secondary and tertiary levels *(continued)*
Number of teachers and Pupil teacher ratio

Personnel enseignant au niveau primaire, secondaire et supérieur *(suite)*
Nombre d'enseignants et ratio élèves/enseignant par niveau d'enseignement

Region, country or area Région, pays ou zone	Year & Année &	Primary education Enseignant primaire		Secondary education Enseignant secondaire		Tertiary education Enseignant supérieur	
		Total Totale ('000)	Pupil-teacher ratio Ratio élèves/ enseignant	Total Totale ('000)	Pupil-teacher ratio Ratio élèves/ enseignant	Total Totale ('000)	Pupil-teacher ratio Ratio élèves/ enseignant
Sudan [former] Soudan [anc.]	*2000	...	...	...	...	4	45.5
	2005	* 113	29.0	64	* 21.5	...	...
	*2009	124	38.4	83	22.2	...	...
Suriname Suriname	2005	* 4	18.6	3	13.9	...	...
	2010	* 5	14.9	4	13.8	...	...
	2015	* 5	13.3	5	12.0	...	...
	2018	* 5	13.4	...	...	...	...
Sweden Suède	2005	* 66	10.1	76	9.7	38	11.3
	2010	* 60	9.5	75	9.7	29	15.6
	2015	* 65	12.1	66	12.9	34	12.6
	2017	* 70	12.2	70	13.1	35	12.3
Switzerland Suisse	2005	...	...	...	...	34	5.9
	2010	...	...	...	...	40	6.2
	2013	* 46	10.4	67	9.3	...	...
	2014	* 48	10.1	64	...	33	8.9
	2017	* 51	9.9	62	9.8	34	8.7
Syrian Arab Republic République arabe syrienne	2002	* 115	25.3	65	18.1	...	...
	2015	...	...	...	...	12	64.4
Tajikistan Tadjikistan	2005	* 32	21.3	60	16.4	10	14.9
	2010	* 27	25.2	60	17.1	13	14.8
	2011	* 29	23.3	68	15.4	13	14.5
	2015	* 31	22.3	...	...	13	17.6
	2017	* 35	22.3	...	...	16	16.7
Thailand Thaïlande	2002	* 326	18.6	* 173	* 24.0	64	33.6
	*2003	...	...	...	...	66	33.6
	2008	* 348	16.0	223	21.2	* 76	* 32.1
	2010	* 317	16.3	...	...	...	...
	2014	* 337	15.4	230	29.5	104	23.5
	2015	* 301	16.9	240	28.2	104	...
	2016	* 304	16.7	247	26.6	98	24.6
	2018	* 295	16.6	241	25.9	...	...
Timor-Leste Timor-Leste	2002	* 4	47.2	2	29.5	* ~0	* 51.6
	2004	* 4	50.7	3	27.6	...	...
	2005	...	...	3	23.7	...	...
	2009	* 7	29.8	...	...	1	14.0
	2010	* 8	30.2	4	23.0	...	...
	2011	* 8	31.4	4	24.3	...	...
	2018	* 8	26.9	6	26.5	...	...
Togo Togo	2005	* 30	33.6	13	30.5	~0	...
	2007	* 26	39.1	* 12	* 35.5	~0	69.2
	2010	* 32	40.6	...	...	...	...
	2011	* 32	40.9	21	26.2	2	27.1
	2015	* 34	44.2	...	...	4	18.0
	2018	* 39	40.1	...	...	5	21.3
Tokelau Tokélaou	2003	* ~0	5.8	~0	7.1	...	...
	2016	* ~0	11.9	...	...	...	...
Tonga Tonga	2000	* 1	22.1	1	14.6	* ~0	* 5.1
	2002	* 1	22.1	1	14.4	...	...
	2005	* 1	20.3	...	...	...	...
	2010	* 1	24.9	1	14.9	...	...
	2015	* 1	21.6	1	14.5	...	...
Trinidad and Tobago Trinité-et-Tobago	2004	* 8	* 17.5	...	...	2	9.7
	*2005	8	16.5	...	...	...	...
	*2009	7	17.6	...	...	...	...
Tunisia Tunisie	2005	* 59	20.0	72	17.2	17	19.6
	2010	* 60	17.1	88	13.3	21	17.4
	2011	* 59	17.4	85	13.6	22	16.8
	2012	* 61	17.1	...	...	22	15.9
	2015	* 71	15.8	...	...	...	...
	2018	* 71	16.9	87	...	...	...

7

Teaching staff at the primary, secondary and tertiary levels *(continued)*
Number of teachers and Pupil teacher ratio

Personnel enseignant au niveau primaire, secondaire et supérieur *(suite)*
Nombre d'enseignants et ratio élèves/enseignant par niveau d'enseignement

Region, country or area Région, pays ou zone	Year & Année &	Primary education Enseignant primaire		Secondary education Enseignant secondaire		Tertiary education Enseignant supérieur	
		Total Totale ('000)	Pupil-teacher ratio Ratio élèves/ enseignant	Total Totale ('000)	Pupil-teacher ratio Ratio élèves/ enseignant	Total Totale ('000)	Pupil-teacher ratio Ratio élèves/ enseignant
Turkey	2005	...	...	...	...	82	25.7
Turquie	2010	...	...	...	...	105	33.5
	2015	* 295	18.4	594	18.5	149	40.7
	2017	* 293	17.0	657	17.3	152	47.4
Turkmenistan							
Turkménistan	2014	...	...	...	...	8	5.4
Turks and Caicos Islands	2003	* ~0	15.2	~0	8.7	...	...
Îles Turques-et-Caïques	2014	* ~0	9.3	~0	8.8	...	...
	2015	...	...	~0	9.6	...	...
	2018	* ~0	17.7	~0	10.1	...	...
Tuvalu	2004	* ~0	19.2	...	...	...	...
Tuvalu	2015	* ~0	12.7	~0	6.2	...	...
	2018	* ~0	15.6	~0	8.6	...	...
Uganda	2004	* 147	50.1	40	18.5	4	21.2
Ouganda	2005	* 140	51.7	* 40	...	...	...
	2007	* 152	49.6	56	18.5	...	...
	2010	* 172	48.6	66	...	5	22.6
	2011	* 170	47.8	49	...	6	24.5
	2014	* 191	...	64	...	...	...
	2015	* 193	42.9	...	...	...	...
	2017	* 207	42.7	...	...	...	...
Ukraine	2000	* 105	19.9	389	13.4	* 146	* 12.4
Ukraine	2005	* 104	18.7	...	...	187	13.9
	2010	* 98	15.7	...	...	201	13.1
	2015	* 124	12.4	340	7.0	169	10.5
	2018	* 129	13.0	324	7.3	156	10.3
United Arab Emirates	2005	* 17	15.2	...	...	...	...
Émirats arabes unis	2009	* 20	15.6	...	...	5	18.6
	2010	* 19	16.8	...	...	...	...
	2015	* 20	23.6	...	...	9	17.8
	2016	* 19	24.5	46	9.5	9	17.0
	2017	...	...	...	...	10	18.4
United Kingdom	2005	* 265	17.5	388	14.9	122	18.7
Royaume-Uni	2008	* 244	18.3	* 375	* 14.3	134	17.4
	2010	* 252	17.5	...	...	140	17.7
	2014	* 272	16.6	414	15.8	152	15.5
	2015	...	...	412	15.5	149	15.7
	2017	* 319	15.1	384	16.6	156	15.6
United Rep. of Tanzania	2005	* 135	55.9	...	...	3	* 18.8
Rép.-Unie de Tanzanie	2010	* 166	50.8	...	...	4	18.9
	2012	* 181	45.8	...	...	5	34.4
	2014	* 191	43.1	83	23.5	...	...
	2018	* 200	50.6	103	20.9	...	...
United States of America	2005	* 1 731	...	1 635	...	1 208	...
États-Unis d'Amérique	2010	* 1 795	...	1 758	...	1 439	...
	2015	* 1 714	14.5	1 661	14.7	1 581	12.4
	2017	* 1 769	14.2	1 695	14.6	1 581	12.0
United States Virgin Islands							
Îles Vierges américaines	2007	...	...	...	...	~0	9.2
Uruguay	2005	* 18	20.2	22	14.6	12	9.3
Uruguay	2010	* 25	13.8	25	12.7	17	8.0
	2015	* 27	11.8	...	...	21	7.6
	2017	* 28	11.0	...	...	22	7.2
Uzbekistan	2005	* 119	19.9	339	13.3	20	13.3
Ouzbékistan	2010	* 111	17.8	342	13.0	23	12.5
	2015	* 112	19.0	371	10.7	24	10.7
	2017	* 113	21.2	377	10.3	24	11.7
	2018	* 116	21.5	374	...	25	11.9

Teaching staff at the primary, secondary and tertiary levels *(continued)*
Number of teachers and Pupil teacher ratio

Personnel enseignant au niveau primaire, secondaire et supérieur *(suite)*
Nombre d'enseignants et ratio élèves/enseignant par niveau d'enseignement

Region, country or area Région, pays ou zone	Year & Année &	Primary education Enseignant primaire		Secondary education Enseignant secondaire		Tertiary education Enseignant supérieur	
		Total Totale ('000)	Pupil-teacher ratio Ratio élèves/ enseignant	Total Totale ('000)	Pupil-teacher ratio Ratio élèves/ enseignant	Total Totale ('000)	Pupil-teacher ratio Ratio élèves/ enseignant
Vanuatu Vanuatu	2001	* 2	23.7	1	15.1	~0	25.0
	2002	* 2	23.2	...	...	* ~0	* 24.9
	2004	* 2	20.0	...	...	...	...
	2010	* 2	21.7	...	...	...	...
	2015	* 2	26.6	1	20.6	...	...
Venezuela (Boliv. Rep. of) Venezuela (Rép. boliv. du)	*2004	...	...	...	...	82	12.8
	*2009	...	...	...	...	165	12.9
Viet Nam Viet Nam	2005	* 361	21.6	...	...	48	28.4
	2010	* 348	19.9	...	...	70	29.0
	2015	* 392	19.2	...	...	91	27.1
	2016	* 397	19.6	...	...	94	24.6
	2018	* 397	20.3	...	...	...	...
Yemen Yémen	*2005	...	...	...	...	7	29.2
	2007	...	...	...	...	7	32.2
	2010	* 111	30.8	...	...	...	...
	*2012	122	30.3	...	...	...	...
	2016	* 145	26.9	...	...	...	...
Zambia Zambie	*2005	46	56.5	...	...	...	...
	*2010	55	53.0	...	...	...	...
	2015	* 75	42.7	...	...	...	...
	2017	* 78	42.1	...	...	...	...
Zimbabwe Zimbabwe	2003	* 61	38.6	34	22.3	...	...
	2010	...	...	...	...	4	23.2
	2013	* 73	36.4	43	22.5	6	17.0
	2015	...	...	...	...	8	17.9

Source:

United Nations Educational, Scientific and Cultural Organization
(UNESCO), Montreal, the UNESCO Institute for Statistics (UIS) statistics
database, last accessed May 2020.

& Data relate to the calendar year in which the academic year ends.

1   Data included elsewhere under another category.

Source:

Organisation des Nations Unies pour l'éducation, la science et la culture
(UNESCO), Montréal, base de données statistiques de l'Institut de
statistique (ISU) de l'UNESCO, dernier accès mai 2020.

& Les données se réfèrent à l'année civile durant laquelle l'année scolaire
se termine.

1   Données incluses ailleurs dans une autre catégorie.

Public expenditure on education
By expenditure type, level of education, total government expenditure and GDP

Dépenses publiques afférentes à l'éducation
Par type de dépenses, niveau de scolarité, dépenses publiques totales et PIB

Country or area Pays ou zone	Year Année	Percentage of total expenditure in public institutions Pourcentage des dépenses publiques totales en faveur de l'éducation			Percentage of government expenditure on education by level Pourcentage des dépenses publiques selon le niveau d'enseignement				As % of Govt. Expenditure En % des dépenses du gouvt.	As % of GDP En % du PIB
		Current expenditure Dépenses courantes	Staff Compensation Rémunération du personnel	Capital expenditure Dépenses en Capital	Pre-primary Préprimaire	Primary Primaire	Secondary Secondaire	Tertiary Tertiaire		
Afghanistan Afghanistan	2010	9.3	72.4	18.3	...	62.1	26.7	9.0	17.1	3.5
	2015	9.0	71.4	19.6	...	56.7	24.4	16.0	12.5	3.3
	*2017	...	...	...	...	44.2	22.3	...	15.7	4.1
Albania Albanie	2005	...	...	...	...	...	...	...	11.4	3.3
	2007	...	...	...	...	...	...	...	11.2	3.3
	2015	12.5	79.5	8.1	...	56.8	21.6	21.2	11.3	3.4
	2017	11.9	79.8	8.3	...	57.6	21.6	18.9	12.4	3.6
	*2018	...	...	...	...	...	...	...	8.4	2.5
Algeria Algérie	2008	...	...	...	...	...	...	27.0	11.4	4.3
American Samoa Samoa américaines	2006	...	...	6.2	...	...	...	11.2	...	14.6
Andorra Andorre	2005	...	...	...	16.9	24.1	20.6	3.9	...	1.6
	2010	30.9	36.7	1.7	14.6	28.9	20.9	3.9	...	3.1
	2013	59.4	40.0	0.6	18.2	32.1	35.2	4.6	...	2.4
	2015	63.6	...	1.3	13.2	22.1	24.9	5.5	19.5	3.3
	2018	63.8	35.6	0.5	11.9	21.4	25.3	5.6	19.3	3.2
Angola Angola	2005	...	...	...	...	36.5	55.2	8.3	8.0	2.1
	2006	...	...	24.3	13.5	31.4	42.4	8.7	7.5	2.3
	2010	...	...	...	...	...	...	8.7	...	3.4
Anguilla Anguilla	2005	6.7	80.9	...	1.9	28.5	51.3	18.3	...	3.0
	2008	* 9.8	* 69.4	* 20.8	1.6	39.4	56.1	2.8	...	2.8
Antigua and Barbuda Antigua-et-Barbuda	2002	25.7	...	3.9	2.1	28.6	35.2	6.7	11.7	3.4
	2009	21.6	73.2	5.2	0.3	41.6	48.4	7.4	6.9	2.5
Argentina Argentine	2004	11.6	87.6	0.8	8.3	36.7	37.8	17.2	15.1	3.5
	2005	...	...	...	7.9	34.2	41.7	16.2	15.8	3.9
	2010	9.9	85.9	4.2	7.4	33.1	39.7	19.9	15.0	5.0
	2015	7.2	82.0	10.8	8.1	30.0	41.3	20.5	14.0	5.8
	2017	7.0	82.1	10.9	8.8	29.6	39.5	22.1	13.3	5.5
Armenia Arménie	2005	...	...	...	...	...	...	...	13.6	2.7
	2009	...	...	...	11.3	...	...	9.4	13.5	3.8
	2010	...	...	...	...	...	...	11.7	12.4	3.2
	2014	8.5	65.5	26.0	...	...	54.5	13.6	9.4	2.2
	2015	11.6	88.5	...	11.8	19.4	...	12.7	10.7	2.8
	2017	14.6	73.0	12.4	12.0	19.4	46.9	13.0	10.4	2.7
Aruba Aruba	2005	6.1	90.7	3.2	6.8	26.7	26.8	11.5	18.9	4.7
	2009	5.7	87.0	...	...	...	...	...	21.5	5.9
	2010	...	...	...	...	...	...	...	22.1	6.9
	2015	6.9	93.1	...	5.2	23.8	30.7	25.1	22.9	6.5
	2016	7.0	93.0	...	5.7	27.5	33.2	18.4	21.4	6.2
Australia Australie	2000	24.7	68.3	7.0	1.2	34.1	38.6	23.4	13.4	4.9
	2005	...	...	...	1.0	34.6	39.7	22.2	13.6	4.9
	2010	...	...	...	1.2	36.8	36.8	22.3	14.3	5.6
	2015	27.1	65.2	7.7	3.3	31.8	30.5	28.9	14.1	5.3
	2016	...	...	...	4.4	33.0	31.3	26.8	13.8	5.3
Austria Autriche	2005	23.2	72.1	4.7	7.4	19.0	45.9	27.3	10.3	5.2
	2010	24.9	70.2	4.9	10.3	17.1	44.4	27.7	10.8	5.7
	2015	26.2	68.3	5.5	8.8	16.6	39.9	32.6	10.7	5.5
	2016	26.2	67.6	6.2	9.1	16.6	39.6	32.5	11.0	5.5
Azerbaijan Azerbaïdjan	2005	31.6	66.8	1.6	6.9	...	...	6.9	13.2	3.0
	2010	32.6	64.8	2.5	7.1	...	...	14.0	8.7	2.8
	2015	45.9	52.0	2.2	9.5	...	...	12.8	7.6	3.0
	2017	39.5	59.2	1.3	11.3	...	...	16.4	7.0	2.5
Bahamas Bahamas	*2000	...	...	...	...	...	...	...	18.9	2.2
Bahrain Bahreïn	2008	...	...	...	...	...	...	...	10.6	2.5
	2012	13.8	82.3	3.8	...	...	...	...	8.3	2.6
	2013	...	...	...	...	32.1	43.4	24.4	7.2	2.5
	2015	...	...	...	...	33.0	44.2	...	7.3	2.7
	2017	...	...	...	...	...	...	...	7.2	2.3

Public expenditure on education *(continued)*
By expenditure type, level of education, total government expenditure and GDP

Dépenses publiques afférentes à l'éducation *(suite)*
Par type de dépenses, niveau de scolarité, dépenses publiques totales et PIB

Country or area Pays ou zone	Year Année	Percentage of total expenditure in public institutions Pourcentage des dépenses publiques totales en faveur de l'éducation			Percentage of government expenditure on education by level Pourcentage des dépenses publiques selon le niveau d'enseignement				As % of Govt. Expenditure En % des dépenses du gouvt.	As % of GDP En % du PIB
		Current expenditure Dépenses courantes	Staff Comp- ensation Rémun- ération du personnel	Capital expenditure Dépenses en Capital	Pre-primary Préprimaire	Primary Primaire	Secondary Secondaire	Tertiary Tertiaire		
Bangladesh	2004	...	...	...	...	40.0	48.5	11.5	16.0	1.9
Bangladesh	2009	21.2	59.8	19.0	...	44.7	40.2	13.5	14.0	1.9
	2012	4.3	95.2	0.5	...	44.6	39.1	14.7	15.6	2.2
	*2013	...	...	...	...	...	...	...	13.8	2.0
	2016	12.9	73.0	14.2	...	...	64.3	33.3	11.4	1.5
	2018	...	...	...	...	...	...	...	14.6	2.0
Barbados	2005	16.2	79.9	4.0	* 6.3	* 27.9	31.7	31.6	17.5	5.6
Barbade	2008	14.5	78.6	6.9	0.4	36.9	29.4	30.1	15.2	4.9
	2010	10.4	83.4	6.2	...	...	29.6	32.5	17.5	6.0
	2014	47.8	48.6	3.6	...	...	22.5	39.3	17.5	6.2
	2016	50.5	45.3	4.2	...	29.6	39.3	31.1	14.1	5.1
	2017	38.5	57.1	4.4	...	...	...	28.5	12.9	4.7
Belarus	2005	30.1	65.2	4.8	17.4	...	...	25.5	12.6	5.9
Bélarus	2010	26.5	62.6	10.9	19.0	...	...	17.1	11.8	5.1
	2011	26.8	65.4	7.8	21.0	...	...	17.3	11.6	4.7
	2015	26.4	68.9	4.8	...	...	...	16.8	11.5	4.8
	2017	27.4	67.0	5.6	24.0	...	50.5	16.5	12.3	4.8
Belgium	2005	11.7	85.5	2.8	9.6	...	...	21.7	11.2	5.8
Belgique	2010	11.9	84.3	3.8	9.5	...	...	22.2	12.0	6.4
	2013	13.0	81.4	5.6	10.6	23.4	42.1	21.8	11.9	6.6
	2015	13.9	81.0	5.0	10.7	23.5	...	22.1	12.2	6.5
	2016	14.1	80.3	5.6	10.8	23.8	...	22.3	12.3	6.5
Belize	2003	* 18.3	* 62.3	* 19.3	...	...	...	...	16.1	5.2
Belize	2004	...	...	...	0.6	42.6	39.2	10.8	16.2	5.3
	2010	...	...	...	1.5	46.1	41.1	8.7	22.4	6.6
	2015	...	...	...	4.9	32.9	41.2	11.8	21.6	6.8
	2017	...	...	...	4.5	31.4	40.0	9.5	21.3	7.4
Benin	2001	15.2	56.8	28.0	* 1.2	* 55.4	* 25.1	18.3	15.3	3.2
Bénin	2005	13.3	73.0	13.7	...	* 46.0	* 32.8	21.2	18.8	3.6
	2010	6.2	85.7	8.2	2.6	52.8	28.0	15.6	26.1	5.0
	2015	22.2	69.5	8.3	4.3	49.8	23.7	22.1	17.5	4.4
	*2018	...	...	...	...	...	...	...	17.7	4.0
Bermuda	2005	...	...	...	* 7.0	* 40.7	* 52.3	...	12.1	2.0
Bermudes	2010	...	...	...	8.9	30.8	45.4	13.5	12.9	2.6
	2014	...	...	...	7.5	29.9	44.3	18.2	7.8	1.8
	2015	18.6	79.9	1.5	7.0	30.7	44.3	...	9.0	1.7
	2017	...	...	...	6.5	32.2	44.4	17.0	7.8	1.5
Bhutan	2005	...	...	...	...	22.3	50.9	14.1	22.8	7.1
Bhoutan	2010	...	...	...	...	29.9	53.9	15.1	11.0	4.0
	2014	...	...	...	...	32.0	55.7	10.3	17.8	5.9
	2015	50.1	35.9	14.0	...	...	41.5	...	26.4	7.3
	*2018	...	...	...	...	...	...	...	22.8	6.6
Botswana	2005	...	...	...	...	30.0	39.6	27.9	25.8	10.7
Botswana	2009	...	...	9.8	...	17.8	32.7	41.5	20.5	9.6
Brazil	2005	23.6	70.3	6.1	8.2	34.0	38.8	19.0	11.3	4.5
Brésil	2010	24.3	68.5	7.2	7.6	31.3	44.7	16.4	14.2	5.6
	2011	20.7	73.2	6.1	8.8	29.3	45.1	16.8	15.3	5.7
	2015	21.3	74.7	3.9	...	25.6	41.4	21.5	16.2	6.2
	2016	21.0	75.6	3.4	...	...	...	...	...	...
British Virgin Islands	*2004	2.3	90.3	7.4	...	...	...	...	...	...
Îles Vierges	2005	0.7	99.3	...	0.1	33.7	31.2	34.2	...	3.0
britanniques	2007	15.1	77.8	7.1	0.1	28.4	37.7	33.1	...	3.2
	2010	...	...	...	0.1	34.1	34.0	...	...	3.8
	2015	...	...	...	–0.0	16.6	19.0	22.1	...	5.1
	2017	...	...	...	...	29.9	35.1	35.1	...	2.4
Brunei Darussalam	2000	...	...	...	...	...	...	...	8.9	3.7
Brunéi Darussalam	2010	...	...	...	...	28.5	46.8	24.4	5.3	2.0
	2014	...	...	...	...	...	38.7	31.9	10.0	3.4
	2016	30.6	66.2	3.2	0.7	19.5	60.8	18.9	11.4	4.4
Bulgaria	2005	26.7	63.2	10.1	16.9	20.3	45.9	16.9	12.1	4.1
Bulgarie	2010	28.4	66.6	5.1	22.5	19.6	43.0	14.8	11.2	3.9
	2013	20.9	71.8	7.3	25.3	19.7	38.9	15.9	11.4	4.1

8

Public expenditure on education *(continued)*
By expenditure type, level of education, total government expenditure and GDP

Dépenses publiques afférentes à l'éducation *(suite)*
Par type de dépenses, niveau de scolarité, dépenses publiques totales et PIB

Country or area Pays ou zone	Year Année	Percentage of total expenditure in public institutions Pourcentage des dépenses publiques totales en faveur de l'éducation			Percentage of government expenditure on education by level Pourcentage des dépenses publiques selon le niveau d'enseignement				As % of Govt. Expenditure En % des dépenses du gouvt.	As % of GDP En % du PIB
		Current expenditure Dépenses courantes	Staff Compensation Rémunération du personnel	Capital expenditure Dépenses en Capital	Pre-primary Préprimaire	Primary Primaire	Secondary Secondaire	Tertiary Tertiaire		
Burkina Faso	2005	...	...	...	0.2	71.2	10.3	9.6	19.5	4.4
Burkina Faso	2007	8.0	56.7	35.3	0.6	67.0	15.7	15.2	17.9	4.6
	2010	...	...	...	...	60.3	18.0	18.8	16.2	3.9
	2015	...	...	...	0.1	57.9	22.1	13.7	18.0	4.2
	*2018	...	...	...	...	...	...	...	22.7	6.0
Burundi	2004	15.7	57.8	26.6	~0.0	50.7	29.5	18.3	9.2	3.7
Burundi	2005	...	...	...	...	51.6	33.1	15.3	11.0	3.6
	2010	23.7	68.5	7.9	~0.0	45.4	27.9	18.0	16.6	6.8
	2012	20.5	77.6	1.9	~0.0	44.0	24.2	20.6	16.4	6.2
	2013	...	...	...	~0.0	45.4	26.8	24.2	17.2	6.0
	*2015	...	...	...	...	...	...	...	24.2	6.4
	2018	...	...	...	...	...	...	...	19.9	5.0
Cabo Verde	2002	...	...	...	...	43.8	29.8	17.5	19.8	7.9
Cabo Verde	2004	3.3	80.0	16.7	...	...	...	...	20.8	7.5
	*2005	2.1	82.4	16.7	...	...	...	...	...	...
	2008	...	...	15.9	0.3	36.3	36.6	11.3	18.2	5.5
	2009	...	...	...	...	44.1	33.0	14.0	15.9	5.3
	2010	15.6	77.1	7.3	...	...	...	...	14.2	5.6
	2015	14.3	82.0	3.6	1.2	39.4	39.6	18.4	16.7	5.3
	2016	12.2	82.8	4.9	1.1	39.1	40.8	17.6	17.8	5.3
	2017	...	...	...	1.0	38.1	39.9	17.2	16.4	5.2
Cambodia	2001	...	...	...	1.1	74.4	11.2	...	11.4	1.7
Cambodge	2002	...	...	...	1.0	64.6	...	...	10.1	1.7
	2004	...	...	...	...	...	...	...	12.4	1.7
	2010	...	...	...	1.7	50.0	42.5	5.8	7.3	1.5
	2012	57.3	42.7	...	2.0	49.2	44.1	...	7.2	1.6
	2013	...	...	...	2.7	49.7	41.5	6.1	9.6	2.1
	2014	...	...	0.5	2.6	48.5	44.1	...	8.8	1.9
	2018	...	...	...	...	...	...	...	8.8	2.2
Cameroon	2005	...	...	...	...	35.1	52.0	12.6	21.4	2.9
Cameroun	2010	6.5	80.2	13.4	3.9	34.2	52.7	9.0	18.8	3.0
	2012	...	...	...	3.5	36.2	52.6	7.8	15.2	2.7
	2013	10.7	75.7	13.6	4.0	33.9	...	10.2	13.8	2.8
	*2015	...	...	...	...	...	...	...	13.2	2.8
	*2018	...	...	...	...	...	...	...	16.9	3.1
Canada	2000	25.9	70.5	3.6	3.9	...	...	...	13.0	5.4
Canada	2005	25.4	70.0	4.6	...	...	...	...	12.2	4.8
	2010	24.5	65.8	9.7	...	...	...	35.4	12.3	5.4
	2011	24.1	65.5	10.4	...	...	26.4	35.6	12.2	5.3
	2013	23.4	68.8	7.8	...	...	...	...	...	...
Cayman Islands	2005	...	...	...	1.2	49.3	49.5	...	...	2.3
Îles Caïmanes	2006	2.4	97.6	...	...	46.0	54.0	...	...	2.6
Central African	2005	...	79.2	2.2	...	...	...	...	9.7	1.7
Republic	2008	13.5	84.2	2.3	...	...	25.9	17.5	7.9	1.3
République	2010	...	...	1.1	2.3	53.3	24.0	20.5	6.5	1.1
centrafricaine	2011	...	...	...	...	...	...	27.3	7.8	1.1
Chad	2005	...	...	...	...	45.8	35.5	18.7	14.7	1.7
Tchad	2010	...	...	31.3	0.4	51.6	27.4	19.8	8.1	2.0
	2011	...	...	20.8	0.3	40.7	34.9	16.3	10.1	2.3
	2012	2.6	75.5	21.9	...	46.7	20.7	30.3	9.2	2.2
	2013	...	...	...	...	...	24.7	31.7	12.5	2.9
	*2018	...	...	...	...	...	...	...	17.2	2.2
Chile	2005	17.5	78.1	4.4	9.6	37.4	39.0	14.0	16.2	3.3
Chili	2009	18.1	78.9	3.0	12.8	36.4	35.2	15.6	17.0	4.2
	2010	...	...	...	13.4	31.7	32.5	22.3	17.8	4.2
	2015	...	...	...	13.2	25.6	29.4	25.7	19.6	4.9
	2017	...	...	...	13.8	27.9	28.5	25.2	21.3	5.4
China, Hong Kong SAR	2005	...	...	...	2.3	23.1	33.8	28.4	22.5	4.1
Chine, RAS de Hong Kong	2010	...	...	12.7	3.8	20.9	35.5	27.8	19.9	3.5
	2012	...	...	18.2	3.9	18.7	33.6	32.8	18.6	3.5
	2015	...	...	...	4.7	20.9	33.9	29.5	18.6	3.3
	2018	...	...	...	6.5	22.1	31.3	29.4	18.8	3.3

Public expenditure on education *(continued)*
By expenditure type, level of education, total government expenditure and GDP

Dépenses publiques afférentes à l'éducation *(suite)*
Par type de dépenses, niveau de scolarité, dépenses publiques totales et PIB

Country or area Pays ou zone	Year Année	Percentage of total expenditure in public institutions Pourcentage des dépenses publiques totales en faveur de l'éducation			Percentage of government expenditure on education by level Pourcentage des dépenses publiques selon le niveau d'enseignement				As % of Govt. Expenditure En % des dépenses du gouvt.	As % of GDP En % du PIB
		Current expenditure Dépenses courantes	Staff Compensation Rémunération du personnel	Capital expenditure Dépenses en Capital	Pre-primary Préprimaire	Primary Primaire	Secondary Secondaire	Tertiary Tertiaire		
China, Macao SAR	2000	...	...	...	* 7.6	* 24.8	* 25.0	28.4	...	3.3
Chine, RAS de	2003	...	...	...	...	* 24.8	...	41.1	11.7	2.8
Macao	2005	...	...	...	...	...	...	45.6	10.5	2.3
	2010	19.5	39.0	41.5	...	...	...	48.4	15.4	2.6
	2015	31.7	59.1	9.2	...	...	...	42.2	13.4	3.0
	2017	28.3	64.3	7.4	...	...	...	37.1	13.5	2.7
Colombia	2004	23.3	71.0	5.7	* 2.7	* 48.3	* 35.7	13.3	15.4	4.1
Colombie	2005	...	...	...	2.6	47.4	36.1	13.8	15.5	4.0
	2010	6.8	71.0	22.3	5.8	35.9	34.8	22.1	16.4	4.8
	2015	5.8	69.0	25.2	5.9	36.7	35.4	21.4	15.1	4.5
	2018	4.2	83.1	12.6	5.3	32.7	38.1	23.3	16.0	4.5
Comoros	2002	...	...	...	* 0.4	* 45.2	* 40.1	* 7.7	15.8	2.3
Comores	2008	...	...	...	...	61.7	23.7	14.6	29.2	4.4
	2015	4.8	95.2	...	7.1	54.6	27.7	10.4	13.3	2.5
Congo	2005	...	...	...	* 2.9	* 27.3	* 41.2	* 25.9	7.6	1.8
Congo	2010	...	...	...	4.6	31.0	53.3	10.9	24.7	6.2
	*2015	...	...	...	...	...	...	...	8.0	4.6
	*2018	...	...	...	...	...	...	...	15.6	3.6
Cook Islands	2000	...	...	...	7.1	50.6	36.5	...	6.7	2.1
Îles Cook	2013	...	...	...	11.4	40.4	40.6	7.6	8.8	3.0
	2014	15.7	84.3	...	...	...	...	9.2	11.6	3.9
	2015	16.3	82.4	1.3	...	...	...	8.9	...	3.9
	2016	34.0	63.3	2.6	...	...	...	11.5	...	4.7
Costa Rica	2004	...	...	...	7.9	45.5	27.8	18.8	20.4	4.9
Costa Rica	2010	...	...	...	5.4	41.9	31.5	18.4	22.9	6.6
	2015	...	...	...	6.0	36.8	33.7	22.3	23.4	7.1
	2018	39.9	57.5	2.6	4.5	28.7	28.7	23.1	26.1	7.0
Côte d'Ivoire	2000	...	...	...	* ~0.0	* 41.6	* 32.7	22.0	20.8	3.7
Côte d'Ivoire	2001	...	...	...	...	* 42.2	...	19.4	23.2	3.7
	2005	...	...	...	...	...	...	20.0	21.8	4.1
	2010	21.8	71.2	7.0	2.0	42.7	33.1	22.2	22.8	4.6
	*2015	21.4	72.7	5.9	3.0	41.4	34.2	21.4	21.2	4.8
	2018	14.6	80.0	5.4	3.5	47.3	35.1	14.0	18.3	4.4
Croatia	2004	30.0	65.6	4.4	9.2	...	...	18.1	7.8	3.8
Croatie	2010	23.0	70.6	6.4	13.8	...	...	18.3	8.8	4.2
	2011	21.3	74.4	4.3	14.1	...	...	22.2	8.6	4.1
	2013	27.3	69.4	3.2	...	...	...	21.9	9.6	4.6
	2015	26.3	69.3	4.4	...	...	...	...	...	...
Cuba	2005	34.3	52.6	13.2	8.3	30.3	37.7	22.1	...	10.6
Cuba	2007	46.7	50.2	3.1	8.1	30.1	36.0	25.1	...	11.9
	2010	40.5	58.6	0.9	6.8	29.0	29.1	...	...	12.8
Curaçao										
Curaçao	2013	13.9	86.1	...	9.2	27.5	33.9	5.3	...	4.9
Cyprus	2005	9.8	76.9	13.4	4.9	27.3	44.9	22.9	15.8	6.3
Chypre	2010	11.5	77.5	11.0	5.5	31.0	43.0	20.5	15.6	6.6
	2015	13.0	82.9	4.1	5.5	32.2	41.3	20.7	16.2	6.4
	2016	12.7	81.2	6.1	5.3	32.7	40.9	20.8	16.7	6.3
Czechia	2005	34.4	56.0	9.7	9.8	14.5	51.3	21.0	9.2	3.9
Tchéquie	2010	38.4	51.5	10.1	11.4	16.2	45.7	22.5	9.3	4.1
	2015	56.6	35.5	7.9	9.0	13.3	29.8	13.3	13.9	5.8
	2016	56.3	38.3	5.4	8.8	13.2	29.0	12.6	14.2	5.6
Dem. Rep. of the	2010	2.6	87.8	9.6	0.6	33.3	33.7	24.0	9.6	1.5
Congo	2013	1.7	81.4	16.9	1.0	61.6	14.4	22.0	16.2	2.1
Rép. dém. du	2015	...	...	...	...	...	...	23.8	11.7	2.2
Congo	*2017	...	...	...	...	...	...	...	14.0	1.5
Denmark	2005	20.7	74.1	5.3	8.6	23.3	36.3	28.7	15.8	8.1
Danemark	2010	18.0	74.9	7.1	11.5	23.7	34.5	27.3	15.1	8.6
	2013	20.1	73.5	6.3	13.9	24.9	32.4	26.9	15.2	8.5
	2014	19.9	73.7	6.4	...	27.2	40.0	30.7	13.8	7.6

Public expenditure on education *(continued)*
By expenditure type, level of education, total government expenditure and GDP

Dépenses publiques afférentes à l'éducation *(suite)*
Par type de dépenses, niveau de scolarité, dépenses publiques totales et PIB

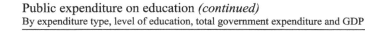

Country or area Pays ou zone	Year Année	Percentage of total expenditure in public institutions Pourcentage des dépenses publiques totales en faveur de l'éducation			Percentage of government expenditure on education by level Pourcentage des dépenses publiques selon le niveau d'enseignement				As % of Govt. Expenditure En % des dépenses du gouvt.	As % of GDP En % du PIB
		Current expenditure Dépenses courantes	Staff Compensation Rémunération du personnel	Capital expenditure Dépenses en Capital	Pre-primary Préprimaire	Primary Primaire	Secondary Secondaire	Tertiary Tertiaire		
Djibouti Djibouti	2005	...	42.2	2.7	...	...	...	...	22.7	8.4
	2007	...	38.8	4.6	...	19.0	...	...	22.5	8.4
	2010	...	...	...	...	34.1	37.3	16.5	12.3	4.5
	*2015	...	...	...	...	...	1.3	...	8.6	5.3
	*2016	...	...	...	...	42.8	0.8	...	12.0	5.8
	*2018	...	...	...	...	...	...	...	14.0	5.6
Dominica Dominique	2012	...	100.0	...	...	...	...	...	...	...
	2015	...	...	...	1.9	45.8	43.4	8.9	10.5	3.4
Dominican Republic République dominicaine	2002	16.6	76.7	6.7	2.1	62.8	...	...	12.1	1.9
	*2003	...	...	...	...	...	...	...	9.7	1.8
	2004	24.1	72.6	3.4	...	...	...	...	...	...
	2007	15.5	66.9	17.6	4.2	58.7	18.0	14.5	12.6	2.0
Ecuador Équateur	2000	16.7	78.1	5.2	...	38.3	34.6	5.2	5.0	1.2
	2010	...	...	...	21.4	32.4	10.4	35.8	13.0	4.5
	2015	...	...	...	21.1	23.3	12.1	43.5	12.6	5.0
Egypt Égypte	2005	...	...	...	...	...	...	...	15.0	4.8
	2008	...	...	...	...	...	...	...	10.9	3.8
El Salvador El Salvador	2005	27.3	66.9	5.8	* 8.5	* 51.0	* 29.1	* 11.1	* 14.7	* 3.2
	2008	37.8	51.7	10.5	9.1	38.0	22.0	...	19.4	4.5
	2010	...	...	...	7.9	42.7	30.1	12.2	16.2	4.0
	2015	19.0	67.1	6.2	7.2	40.6	31.8	7.9	16.6	3.9
	2016	25.0	68.0	7.0	9.2	47.2	35.3	8.0	16.1	3.8
	2017	...	92.0	8.0	9.9	45.6	34.9	9.4	15.6	3.7
	2018	...	...	6.7	10.3	46.2	34.0	9.2	14.9	3.6
Eritrea Érythrée	2002	8.6	31.0	60.4	...	26.0	35.4	14.9	5.6	3.5
	2004	...	...	41.7	...	23.1	21.1	31.9	5.7	3.1
	2006	22.7	57.7	19.6	...	...	...	...	5.2	2.1
Estonia Estonie	2002	28.8	56.3	15.0	5.2	28.0	40.9	19.7	15.1	5.5
	2004	...	...	9.5	6.4	25.8	46.3	17.4	14.3	4.9
	2005	...	...	...	7.4	25.3	43.7	18.9	14.3	4.8
	2010	...	...	...	7.8	24.6	40.1	21.7	13.6	5.5
	2013	28.9	57.7	13.4	7.3	30.7	29.4	28.2	12.6	4.8
	2015	26.9	64.8	8.4	...	23.9	25.9	27.0	13.0	5.1
	2016	26.5	66.4	7.1	...	25.0	25.2	27.1	13.1	5.2
Eswatini Eswatini	2005	...	...	...	~0.0	39.9	34.9	23.9	20.9	6.5
	2010	...	...	...	0.2	47.2	35.5	16.6	18.3	6.1
	2014	36.2	59.3	4.5	1.1	50.8	34.1	13.3	24.8	7.1
Ethiopia Éthiopie	*2002	...	...	...	...	...	...	...	16.2	3.6
	2010	21.0	44.8	34.1	~0.0	28.4	25.0	43.9	26.3	4.5
	2015	19.4	45.2	35.4	1.9	27.5	18.1	47.9	27.1	4.7
Fiji Fidji	2004	...	...	...	0.2	39.1	32.6	15.9	23.7	6.2
	2005	...	...	...	...	...	...	...	20.3	5.1
	2009	...	...	...	...	...	...	...	15.9	4.5
	2011	...	...	...	0.4	44.4	15.9	13.0	15.2	4.2
	2013	1.2	98.7	0.1	...	38.6	...	22.6	14.3	3.9
Finland Finlande	2005	32.1	60.9	7.0	5.5	20.8	41.9	31.8	12.2	6.0
	2010	33.6	60.3	6.1	5.8	19.9	42.4	31.8	11.9	6.5
	2015	34.7	56.5	8.8	10.8	20.2	37.5	26.7	12.4	7.1
	2016	35.5	55.7	8.8	11.0	20.5	36.9	26.5	12.3	6.9
Gabon Gabon	*2000	...	...	...	...	...	...	...	17.7	3.8
	2010	...	...	...	3.6	29.6	28.3	37.8	13.3	3.1
	2014	...	45.5	...	3.8	29.2	28.9	37.8	11.2	2.7
Gambia Gambie	2005	...	...	...	...	61.4	23.1	14.3	5.3	1.1
	2010	10.8	46.4	42.8	...	65.3	23.4	9.9	17.6	4.2
	2012	7.4	50.4	42.2	...	60.0	31.4	7.4	13.8	4.1
	2015	...	...	...	...	55.8	32.8	11.3	11.0	2.1
	*2018	...	...	...	...	...	...	...	11.2	2.4
Georgia Géorgie	2005	...	...	...	...	...	...	...	11.2	2.5
	2008	...	...	...	10.7	36.0	37.0	11.6	8.9	2.9
	*2009	...	...	...	12.3	...	...	...	9.0	3.2
	2012	...	...	...	14.4	34.3	32.1	19.2	6.7	2.0
	2017	...	...	...	...	...	...	10.1	13.0	3.8

8

Public expenditure on education *(continued)*
By expenditure type, level of education, total government expenditure and GDP

Dépenses publiques afférentes à l'éducation *(suite)*
Par type de dépenses, niveau de scolarité, dépenses publiques totales et PIB

Country or area / Pays ou zone	Year / Année	Current expenditure / Dépenses courantes	Staff Compensation / Rémunération du personnel	Capital expenditure / Dépenses en Capital	Pre-primary / Préprimaire	Primary / Primaire	Secondary / Secondaire	Tertiary / Tertiaire	As % of Govt. Expenditure / En % des dépenses du gouvt.	As % of GDP / En % du PIB
Germany / Allemagne	2010	19.8	70.6	9.6	9.1	13.5	45.5	27.2	10.3	4.9
	2015	20.2	73.0	6.8	9.5	12.9	41.9	25.9	11.0	4.8
	2016	20.2	73.1	6.7	9.5	12.9	41.3	26.0	10.9	4.8
Ghana / Ghana	2005	22.3	63.0	14.7	5.9	39.5	32.5	22.1	23.4	7.4
	2010	14.3	68.8	16.9	6.1	30.9	37.1	25.9	20.7	5.5
	2014	18.2	73.3	8.6	7.3	21.7	37.0	18.3	21.0	4.5
	*2015	...	...	...	...	...	...	...	23.8	4.5
	*2018	...	...	...	...	...	...	...	18.6	4.0
Gibraltar / Gibraltar	2017	42.3	54.2	3.5	...	...	...	...	...	...
Greece / Grèce	2005	11.0	67.3	21.7	...	...	33.9	36.1	8.7	4.0
Grenada / Grenade	2003	8.3	82.2	9.5	5.7	36.4	35.8	9.8	10.8	3.9
	2017	...	...	...	6.1	31.3	27.4	13.6	14.0	3.2
Guatemala / Guatemala	2008	9.9	65.2	11.5	10.0	59.8	12.8	10.8	23.3	3.2
	2010	...	...	0.1	11.2	55.6	14.8	11.3	19.3	2.8
	2015	20.9	75.3	3.8	17.3	49.9	12.9	13.8	24.1	3.0
	2018	27.2	65.2	7.6	13.1	55.6	13.2	13.9	23.7	2.9
Guinea / Guinée	2005	...	...	...	...	...	...	30.6	10.9	1.8
	2010	...	...	7.7	...	38.9	24.9	36.2	12.4	2.6
	2015	12.6	75.1	12.3	0.1	38.9	21.9	39.1	11.6	2.5
	2018	12.6	75.0	12.4	0.1	61.6	20.9	17.3	14.9	2.6
Guinea-Bissau / Guinée-Bissau	2010	12.5	61.5	26.0	0.7	46.7	46.7	5.0	9.1	1.9
	2013	0.9	48.3	50.8	0.8	64.4	30.4	3.9	16.2	2.1
Guyana / Guyana	2004	37.6	51.8	10.6	11.6	32.1	26.5	6.2	11.1	5.5
	2005	23.1	62.3	14.6	...	...	...	...	13.8	8.1
	2010	22.8	68.4	8.7	11.5	29.1	33.4	5.3	11.8	3.6
	2012	22.5	62.9	14.6	11.6	30.6	33.3	5.1	10.2	3.2
	2015	...	...	...	...	...	...	...	17.8	5.2
	*2018	...	...	...	...	...	...	...	16.0	5.9
Haiti / Haïti	2015	...	...	...	...	...	...	...	14.6	3.2
	2018	...	...	...	...	...	...	...	14.4	2.8
Honduras / Honduras	2013	15.6	79.7	4.7	7.3	48.9	25.3	18.5	19.9	5.9
	2015	...	...	...	...	...	...	13.7	24.6	6.4
	2018	...	...	...	...	...	...	...	23.0	6.1
Hungary / Hongrie	2005	21.0	71.6	7.4	14.2	20.1	40.4	18.9	10.8	5.3
	2010	27.1	62.5	10.4	14.4	17.8	40.3	20.1	9.7	4.8
	2015	26.3	67.4	6.3	16.8	16.4	38.1	14.3	9.1	4.6
	2016	22.1	70.5	7.4	16.3	16.2	40.2	16.1	10.1	4.7
Iceland / Islande	2005	23.6	67.9	8.5	6.7	35.0	33.6	19.1	17.8	7.4
	2010	20.8	72.6	6.6	9.6	32.4	31.2	21.5	14.6	7.0
	2015	29.7	64.8	5.5	11.5	28.6	28.1	18.9	18.2	7.5
	2016	30.4	65.1	4.5	11.3	27.9	27.3	19.9	16.8	7.5
India / Inde	2005	9.0	86.2	4.8	1.3	35.6	42.9	19.6	11.2	3.2
	2010	...	...	...	1.1	25.2	37.0	36.1	11.8	3.4
	2013	...	...	...	1.6	28.4	41.4	28.5	14.1	3.8
Indonesia / Indonésie	*2005	...	...	...	...	...	...	...	15.1	2.9
	2010	33.6	54.5	11.9	0.7	44.4	24.3	16.1	16.7	2.8
	2014	25.0	63.3	11.7	1.8	43.7	26.8	15.1	17.7	3.3
	2015	24.1	64.1	11.9	...	42.6	27.0	15.8	20.5	3.6
Iran (Islamic Republic of) / Iran (Rép. islamique d')	2002	...	...	8.2	0.9	25.9	36.3	18.5	26.3	4.5
	2005	...	...	...	1.0	22.4	34.6	15.4	22.3	4.1
	2010	...	...	...	1.0	24.7	49.2	21.4	18.8	3.7
	2014	25.9	67.6	6.5	0.2	26.9	39.7	28.0	19.7	2.8
	2015	...	...	4.2	0.2	26.7	37.9	29.4	18.6	2.8
	2018	14.8	80.3	4.9	0.4	33.1	34.4	28.2	21.1	4.0
Ireland / Irlande	2005	17.3	74.2	8.4	0.1	33.6	34.8	23.3	13.6	4.5
	2010	19.7	71.6	8.7	1.6	35.3	33.8	22.2	9.3	6.0
	2015	15.1	78.1	6.9	2.0	36.9	33.3	23.3	13.0	3.8
	2016	14.9	77.7	7.4	...	37.3	35.5	19.6	13.4	3.7

Public expenditure on education *(continued)*
By expenditure type, level of education, total government expenditure and GDP

Dépenses publiques afférentes à l'éducation *(suite)*
Par type de dépenses, niveau de scolarité, dépenses publiques totales et PIB

Country or area Pays ou zone	Year Année	Percentage of total expenditure in public institutions Pourcentage des dépenses publiques totales en faveur de l'éducation			Percentage of government expenditure on education by level Pourcentage des dépenses publiques selon le niveau d'enseignement				As % of Govt. Expenditure En % des dépenses du gouvt.	As % of GDP En % du PIB
		Current expenditure Dépenses courantes	Staff Compensation Rémunération du personnel	Capital expenditure Dépenses en Capital	Pre-primary Préprimaire	Primary Primaire	Secondary Secondaire	Tertiary Tertiaire		
Israel Israël	2005	25.1	68.8	6.1	10.7	37.5	28.9	16.6	13.2	5.8
	2010	18.7	72.9	8.4	11.0	41.2	25.7	16.9	13.7	5.5
	2015	15.5	75.3	9.2	13.6	38.7	30.6	16.2	15.5	5.9
	2016	15.2	75.4	9.4	14.2	38.9	30.8	15.2	15.5	5.8
Italy Italie	2005	20.9	71.9	7.2	10.3	24.6	46.5	17.2	9.0	4.2
	2010	20.5	74.7	4.8	10.0	25.0	42.9	18.8	8.7	4.4
	2015	18.9	76.1	5.0	11.7	25.0	42.7	18.6	8.1	4.1
	2016	22.0	74.5	3.6	11.6	23.9	...	19.1	7.8	3.8
Jamaica Jamaïque	2004	7.5	88.1	4.5	5.6	32.6	41.9	18.8	11.7	3.9
	2005	...	...	...	4.9	* 34.2	* 38.0	22.1	14.3	4.6
	2008	4.9	85.6	9.4	5.5	30.2	42.6	15.7	19.1	6.2
	2009	7.0	93.0	...	8.2	33.2	37.1	20.3	17.6	6.2
	2010	...	...	...	4.0	36.3	36.6	21.8	16.1	6.4
	2015	18.7	78.9	2.3	3.6	36.7	39.4	17.4	20.1	5.5
	2018	21.2	76.8	2.0	4.0	34.2	37.7	19.6	18.6	5.4
Japan Japon	2014	21.3	...	13.9	2.8	33.1	37.8	20.8	9.1	3.6
	2016	18.6	70.0	11.3	3.1	35.1	42.0	19.8	8.4	3.2
Jordan Jordanie	2018	11.3	78.3	10.4	0.6	42.2	34.5	22.7	11.6	3.6
Kazakhstan Kazakhstan	2005	40.6	53.2	6.2	3.8	...	...	12.3	10.3	2.3
	2009	34.2	56.8	9.0	6.8	...	...	13.1	13.0	3.1
	2010	32.8	57.8	9.4	...	...	...	...	...	...
	2015	36.6	59.9	3.5	10.9	...	65.8	15.3	12.2	2.8
	2016	33.6	62.3	4.1	11.8	...	68.6	11.6	13.8	3.0
	2018	26.8	68.7	4.5	...	0.7	...	9.4	13.9	2.8
Kenya Kenya	2004	...	...	...	1.6	62.1	23.4	12.9	26.7	6.8
	2005	...	...	...	...	...	...	...	27.5	7.3
	2006	...	...	...	0.1	54.1	21.7	15.4	25.1	7.0
	2010	...	...	...	...	...	...	...	20.6	5.5
	2015	31.6	60.9	7.5	1.8	36.3	41.8	13.1	16.7	5.3
	*2018	...	...	...	...	...	...	...	19.1	5.3
Kiribati Kiribati	2001	...	...	...	...	34.3	...	...	11.5	12.0
Kuwait Koweït	2005	17.4	74.9	7.7	9.8	19.8	36.2	32.6	13.9	4.7
	*2006	...	...	...	9.6	20.4	36.2	32.6	13.4	3.8
Kyrgyzstan Kirghizistan	2005	28.4	66.2	5.4	6.2	...	...	19.2	16.8	4.9
	2010	29.1	64.5	6.5	8.1	...	...	15.5	15.7	5.8
	2014	17.6	69.1	13.3	10.7	...	...	4.6	14.2	5.5
	2015	16.2	68.1	15.7	...	...	...	...	15.6	6.0
	2017	14.4	70.7	14.9	13.2	...	...	3.0	15.7	6.0
Lao People's Dem. Rep. Rép. dém. populaire lao	2002	...	...	...	1.9	45.0	19.0	12.6	15.3	2.8
	2005	...	...	...	1.6	62.5	...	...	14.1	2.4
	2010	16.7	65.0	18.3	6.8	46.5	29.9	16.2	7.2	1.7
	2014	12.4	72.6	15.0	6.6	40.6	38.6	13.8	11.8	2.9
Latvia Lettonie	2004	21.9	69.7	8.4	13.0	16.3	56.4	13.4	14.5	4.9
	2010	21.6	65.7	12.7	16.8	28.5	38.4	15.9	11.8	5.1
	2015	23.8	60.5	15.6	15.1	30.1	31.4	22.1	14.1	5.3
	2016	25.3	65.3	9.3	17.0	32.0	33.4	16.0	12.9	4.7
Lebanon Liban	2005	1.6	94.7	3.7	...	...	...	28.8	8.4	2.6
	2010	0.1	88.0	11.9	...	...	...	27.2	5.5	1.6
	2011	0.1	86.8	13.1	...	...	...	26.5	5.7	1.6
	2013	2.4	97.6	...	...	...	17.1	28.7	8.6	2.4
Lesotho Lesotho	2001	...	...	8.7	...	53.2	23.8	18.6	23.8	9.4
	2005	...	...	...	...	* 43.0	* 18.3	* 36.4	32.4	12.1
	2008	...	...	* 1.7	0.1	36.0	20.5	36.4	24.7	12.1
	2018	3.6	92.9	3.5	0.2	56.0	30.1	7.4	13.9	6.5
Liberia Libéria	2008	47.4	41.4	11.2	...	...	...	...	6.5	1.7
	2012	...	...	...	...	30.7	34.5	* 31.6	5.2	1.8
	*2014	...	...	...	...	...	...	...	6.9	2.3
	*2018	...	...	...	23.3	42.4	53.4	...	8.1	2.6

8

Public expenditure on education *(continued)*
By expenditure type, level of education, total government expenditure and GDP

Dépenses publiques afférentes à l'éducation *(suite)*
Par type de dépenses, niveau de scolarité, dépenses publiques totales et PIB

Country or area Pays ou zone	Year Année	Percentage of total expenditure in public institutions Pourcentage des dépenses publiques totales en faveur de l'éducation			Percentage of government expenditure on education by level Pourcentage des dépenses publiques selon le niveau d'enseignement				As % of Govt. Expenditure En % des dépenses du gouvt.	As % of GDP En % du PIB
		Current expenditure Dépenses courantes	Staff Compensation Rémunération du personnel	Capital expenditure Dépenses en Capital	Pre-primary Préprimaire	Primary Primaire	Secondary Secondaire	Tertiary Tertiaire		
Liechtenstein Liechtenstein	2004	...	...	...	6.5	29.0	42.6	13.9	...	2.4
	2007	19.3	80.7	...	6.9	30.6	47.2	9.1	...	1.9
	2008	30.2	69.8	...	7.3	31.1	52.4	...	...	2.0
	2010	18.9	68.4	12.6	...	...	...	...	...	2.6
	2011	20.7	73.9	5.4	7.1	38.6	47.4	...	...	2.6
Lithuania Lituanie	2005	20.1	73.0	6.8	12.1	14.9	50.6	21.0	14.6	4.9
	2010	19.5	72.9	7.6	12.9	16.7	44.9	23.6	12.9	5.3
	2015	20.1	67.5	12.4	13.3	16.5	36.7	27.9	12.3	4.2
	2016	21.0	72.1	6.9	15.7	18.9	38.6	20.5	12.0	4.0
Luxembourg Luxembourg	2001	11.2	71.3	17.5	...	...	...	...	9.3	3.6
	2015	14.1	76.1	9.8	14.5	31.6	40.7	13.1	9.4	4.0
Madagascar Madagascar	2005	* 24.4	* 43.8	31.8	...	57.3	18.9	10.1	18.0	3.8
	2008	31.3	58.7	10.0	0.4	53.6	22.1	15.4	16.3	2.9
	2009	...	...	...	0.3	52.3	18.2	15.4	22.6	3.2
	2012	...	...	* 4.6	0.2	47.4	19.3	15.2	20.3	2.7
	2013	29.5	67.4	3.1	...	...	...	...	14.0	2.1
	*2015	...	...	...	...	...	...	~0.0	17.0	2.6
	*2017	...	...	...	...	...	...	~0.0	...	...
	*2018	...	...	...	...	...	...	...	19.8	3.2
Malawi Malawi	2001	...	...	...	...	45.2	22.5	15.3	...	4.5
	2003	...	...	...	...	54.9	21.1	...	16.6	3.2
	2010	...	...	4.9	~0.0	34.8	24.1	29.8	12.5	3.5
	2013	14.5	71.7	13.8	~0.0	36.7	24.4	28.4	20.4	5.4
	2015	...	...	1.2	...	44.0	27.8	24.2	21.6	5.6
	2016	...	...	3.1	...	43.9	28.8	23.1	17.1	4.7
	*2018	...	...	...	...	...	...	...	15.8	4.7
Malaysia Malaisie	2004	30.2	56.8	13.1	1.1	29.6	35.1	33.4	21.0	5.9
	2009	15.7	68.8	15.5	1.2	27.7	32.8	35.9	18.5	6.0
	2010	...	...	...	1.2	28.6	33.7	34.5	18.4	5.0
	2013	25.4	65.1	9.5	3.1	32.1	34.2	30.5	19.5	5.5
	2015	28.7	65.7	5.6	3.1	33.2	...	...	19.8	5.0
	2018	21.3	72.1	6.6	3.2	34.0	41.4	21.3	19.7	4.5
Maldives Maldives	2005	...	...	...	...	54.1	...	...	13.0	5.0
	2010	20.5	78.3	1.2	12.7	42.5	25.0	7.3	12.5	4.1
	2015	43.5	55.6	1.0	11.8	39.7	24.3	12.7	12.9	4.4
	2016	38.4	60.8	0.7	10.8	36.4	21.6	20.6	11.3	4.1
Mali Mali	2005	...	...	...	...	...	...	...	16.3	3.5
	2010	40.9	54.1	5.0	0.2	25.3	53.8	20.7	16.5	3.3
	2015	34.4	61.8	3.8	0.3	45.1	33.0	20.8	18.2	3.8
	2016	38.5	57.8	3.6	0.3	39.6	37.4	21.7	13.9	3.1
	2017	...	...	3.0	0.4	44.7	37.0	17.3	16.5	3.8
Malta Malte	2004	14.5	79.9	5.6	5.2	21.1	39.8	11.0	10.6	4.5
	2010	17.5	72.4	10.1	7.4	21.6	45.7	22.8	15.7	6.5
	2015	13.7	72.7	13.6	9.7	24.3	37.5	25.3	13.2	5.2
Marshall Islands Îles Marshall	2002	* 22.6	* 75.0	* 2.4	...	45.5	38.9	14.7	14.8	8.7
	2003	...	...	...	...	...	...	...	22.5	12.2
	2006	42.8	35.8	21.4	...	...	...	...	...	...
Mauritania Mauritanie	*2004	...	...	...	...	...	...	...	8.2	2.5
	2010	...	...	...	0.5	47.5	23.2	18.8	16.0	3.6
	2013	...	...	...	...	43.2	23.3	11.6	11.4	2.9
	*2016	...	...	...	0.5	55.9	25.9	17.7	9.3	2.6
Mauritius Maurice	2005	...	...	...	1.5	27.2	44.2	11.3	17.1	4.1
	2010	...	...	13.5	1.4	27.0	52.6	9.4	14.6	3.6
	2015	...	...	...	1.2	20.6	64.1	6.8	19.5	4.9
	2018	...	...	...	1.2	22.8	62.7	6.4	19.6	4.8
Mexico Mexique	2005	11.2	85.7	3.1	10.4	39.1	30.3	17.5	21.9	4.8
	2010	10.3	85.7	3.9	10.2	36.0	30.3	19.7	18.6	5.2
	2011	10.6	85.5	3.9	10.4	35.5	30.7	18.1	18.4	5.1
	2015	11.9	85.1	3.1	...	32.5	32.3	21.5	19.0	5.2
	2016	13.3	83.4	3.3	...	32.5	32.9	21.1	17.9	4.9

Public expenditure on education *(continued)*
By expenditure type, level of education, total government expenditure and GDP

Dépenses publiques afférentes à l'éducation *(suite)*
Par type de dépenses, niveau de scolarité, dépenses publiques totales et PIB

Country or area Pays ou zone	Year Année	Percentage of total expenditure in public institutions Pourcentage des dépenses publiques totales en faveur de l'éducation			Percentage of government expenditure on education by level Pourcentage des dépenses publiques selon le niveau d'enseignement				As % of Govt. Expenditure En % des dépenses du gouvt.	As % of GDP En % du PIB
		Current expenditure Dépenses courantes	Staff Compensation Rémunération du personnel	Capital expenditure Dépenses en Capital	Pre-primary Préprimaire	Primary Primaire	Secondary Secondaire	Tertiary Tertiaire		
Micronesia (Fed. States of) Micronésie (États féd. de)	*2000	...	...	...	...	...	...	...	10.0	6.7
	2015	...	...	...	...	...	...	...	22.3	12.5
Monaco Monaco	2004	2.1	90.9	7.0	4.3	15.4	45.8	4.4	5.9	1.2
	2010	8.4	90.7	0.9	3.2	15.3	37.7	...	6.4	1.3
	2014	4.3	87.3	8.4	3.6	16.0	41.1	...	5.0	1.0
	2015	8.5	83.7	7.8	...	...	...	...	...	...
	2016	8.5	80.8	10.7	3.0	12.7	31.5	...	6.6	1.4
	2017	...	...	...	...	...	...	...	7.0	1.5
Mongolia Mongolie	2000	55.8	43.4	0.8	...	...	...	...	16.1	5.6
	2002	...	...	4.9	14.1	...	...	15.5	20.3	7.2
	2004	...	...	...	18.5	25.1	32.8	18.4	13.6	4.3
	2010	...	...	...	22.0	26.9	33.7	6.7	14.7	4.6
	2013	98.3	1.7	~0.0	22.8	22.6	35.3	16.4	15.4	4.9
	2015	98.1	1.9	...	25.7	26.4	33.7	11.4	13.5	4.2
	2017	21.8	69.3	8.9	26.3	32.2	29.2	6.4	12.6	4.1
Montserrat Montserrat	2001	* 27.5	* 41.4	* 31.2	13.6	20.6	29.5	5.5	...	4.8
	2004	...	...	...	...	20.5	...	...	...	3.8
	2009	...	...	...	...	...	...	...	...	5.1
	2018	...	60.7	10.3	5.7	13.0	22.6	17.2	...	8.3
	2019	29.0	...	...	...	...	...	...	...	...
Morocco Maroc	2008	...	...	...	~0.0	35.5	43.1	...	17.5	5.3
	2009	...	...	...	...	37.7	41.9	20.2	17.3	5.3
Mozambique Mozambique	2005	...	...	22.6	...	...	...	...	22.7	4.4
	2006	...	...	26.8	...	57.7	29.3	12.1	18.6	4.3
	2013	22.2	58.5	19.3	...	49.2	30.6	13.7	19.0	6.5
	*2018	...	...	...	...	...	...	...	17.9	5.6
Myanmar Myanmar	2011	9.3	77.2	13.4	...	50.5	23.5	19.1	5.9	0.8
	2017	22.4	57.2	20.3	0.5	36.0	39.4	11.3	10.1	2.2
	2018	...	...	...	...	39.3	41.0	14.8	10.3	2.0
	2019	18.0	56.6	25.4	...	36.3	38.4	14.6	10.5	...
Namibia Namibie	2000	19.3	73.6	7.2	0.2	58.8	27.2	12.0	21.9	7.0
	2003	...	...	...	0.5	63.1	25.8	9.1	20.3	6.3
	2008	...	* 79.9	...	0.4	47.6	18.7	9.9	24.9	6.5
	2010	22.1	77.0	0.8	...	40.0	23.5	23.1	26.1	8.3
	2014	3.5	89.1	7.4	1.3	16.9	15.3	50.6	7.6	3.1
Nauru Nauru	2002	...	...	...	...	67.5	...	...	...	...
	*2007	20.8	56.9	...	...	...	...	...	...	...
Nepal Népal	2003	...	...	...	...	* 56.5	22.1	10.3	21.3	3.1
	2005	...	...	...	...	...	...	...	22.3	3.4
	2010	18.0	69.2	12.8	1.0	55.7	30.5	12.7	16.0	3.6
	2015	24.9	64.1	11.0	2.1	53.8	33.3	10.8	17.0	3.7
	2018	...	...	...	...	...	...	...	14.1	5.2
Netherlands Pays-Bas	2005	17.5	69.8	12.7	7.7	...	...	...	12.3	5.1
	2010	18.5	69.6	11.9	6.9	...	...	...	11.7	5.5
	2015	20.8	67.8	11.4	6.6	22.3	40.9	30.1	12.2	5.3
	2016	20.6	68.5	10.8	6.4	21.2	40.5	31.9	12.8	5.5
New Zealand Nouvelle-Zélande	2005	...	...	...	3.3	...	...	...	16.3	6.3
	2010	...	...	...	6.7	...	...	...	15.7	7.0
	2015	...	...	...	7.6	23.2	37.0	25.6	16.4	6.3
	2016	...	...	...	7.5	26.1	35.6	23.7	16.8	6.4
Nicaragua Nicaragua	2002	10.7	80.1	9.2	...	...	...	...	15.7	2.4
	*2003	...	...	...	...	...	...	...	14.9	2.4
	2004	...	...	11.7	...	...	...	...	...	...
	2010	10.7	46.2	11.4	3.6	39.8	13.2	26.0	22.8	4.5
	2015	...	...	...	...	...	...	...	18.7	4.1
	2016	...	...	...	...	...	...	...	17.9	4.1
	2017	...	...	...	...	...	...	...	...	4.3

Public expenditure on education *(continued)*
By expenditure type, level of education, total government expenditure and GDP

Dépenses publiques afférentes à l'éducation *(suite)*
Par type de dépenses, niveau de scolarité, dépenses publiques totales et PIB

Country or area Pays ou zone	Year Année	Percentage of total expenditure in public institutions Pourcentage des dépenses publiques totales en faveur de l'éducation			Percentage of government expenditure on education by level Pourcentage des dépenses publiques selon le niveau d'enseignement				As % of Govt. Expenditure En % des dépenses du gouvt.	As % of GDP En % du PIB
		Current expenditure Dépenses courantes	Staff Compensation Rémunération du personnel	Capital expenditure Dépenses en Capital	Pre-primary Préprimaire	Primary Primaire	Secondary Secondaire	Tertiary Tertiaire		
Niger Niger	2003	...	...	...	...	72.6	...	...	13.8	2.4
	2010	14.2	77.9	7.9	2.4	61.0	21.3	12.6	18.1	3.7
	2015	31.8	56.3	11.9	7.6	45.8	32.2	13.5	18.5	6.0
	2017	25.8	71.8	2.4	10.8	48.1	17.6	23.3	13.2	3.5
	*2018	...	...	...	...	...	...	...	16.8	4.9
Niue Nioué	2002	...	...	...	...	28.8	50.7	...	...	...
	2016	10.3	89.7	...	5.2	37.0	56.9	...	...	...
	2017	...	...	...	5.7	33.4	60.1	...	...	...
North Macedonia Macédoine du Nord	2002	10.8	87.1	2.1	...	...	...	15.0	8.6	3.3
Norway Norvège	2005	22.4	66.9	10.7	4.1	25.0	35.7	32.4	16.5	6.9
	2010	21.3	67.4	11.3	4.9	26.7	35.3	29.6	15.2	6.7
	2015	18.1	69.7	12.3	8.8	23.7	29.4	25.9	15.7	7.6
	2016	17.9	69.7	12.4	9.3	22.8	28.6	26.7	16.0	8.0
Oman Oman	2002	...	...	14.4	...	46.8	43.2	10.0	11.1	4.3
	2005	...	...	...	...	50.5	41.8	7.6	10.1	3.5
	2009	...	...	...	...	33.0	40.2	26.9	10.9	4.2
	2013	20.7	67.6	11.7	...	...	32.1	...	11.1	5.0
	2016	14.6	66.5	18.8	...	...	...	...	...	...
Pakistan Pakistan	2005	12.3	49.2	38.5	...	...	...	...	13.8	2.3
	2007	14.8	59.1	26.1	...	...	...	...	15.4	2.6
	2010	...	...	...	...	...	...	...	11.9	2.3
	2013	...	...	24.6	...	32.7	25.1	32.2	11.5	2.5
	2015	...	...	...	...	31.1	37.4	22.8	13.2	2.7
	2017	...	...	...	...	...	...	22.1	14.5	2.9
Palau Palaos	2001	...	...	...	* 14.6	* 44.9	9.6	20.7	15.3	7.8
	*2002	...	...	...	...	...	...	...	15.5	7.6
Panama Panama	2002	11.1	67.9	21.0	2.2	32.1	29.2	28.1	17.0	4.2
	*2004	...	...	...	4.0	34.5	25.9	28.4	14.6	3.6
	2008	...	...	14.1	...	...	...	...	14.9	3.5
	2011	...	...	...	3.0	23.5	22.4	22.2	13.0	3.2
Papua New Guinea Papouasie-Nvl-Guinée	*2018	...	...	...	...	...	...	...	8.7	1.9
Paraguay Paraguay	2004	6.2	89.4	4.4	7.6	46.6	29.8	15.9	18.2	2.9
	2010	9.5	65.5	6.5	6.7	38.5	36.1	18.5	18.8	2.8
	2012	11.7	79.9	8.4	6.1	38.3	33.0	22.4	19.6	3.7
	2016	17.0	76.8	6.2	8.7	36.4	31.3	23.3	18.2	3.4
Peru Pérou	2005	9.3	81.3	9.4	8.1	35.6	31.4	10.7	14.3	2.8
	2010	14.5	64.6	20.9	12.0	39.9	34.2	13.8	13.6	2.9
	2015	28.3	49.5	22.2	16.6	36.5	30.8	16.1	17.6	4.0
	2018	21.9	61.3	16.8	16.1	33.9	34.2	15.8	17.1	3.7
Philippines Philippines	2005	11.1	85.5	3.4	0.1	52.0	26.8	13.3	12.4	2.4
	2009	18.4	73.4	8.2	1.7	55.0	29.7	12.0	13.2	2.7
Poland Pologne	2005	32.6	60.5	6.9	9.9	31.0	36.6	21.8	12.2	5.4
	2010	29.3	61.4	9.3	10.0	31.0	35.5	22.8	11.1	5.1
	2015	23.6	69.0	7.4	12.7	30.8	30.8	25.3	11.5	4.8
	2016	24.1	70.7	5.2	13.7	31.7	31.3	22.8	11.3	4.6
Portugal Portugal	2005	10.2	86.2	3.6	7.4	30.6	40.8	18.1	10.9	5.1
	2010	12.1	84.1	3.8	7.2	27.0	44.0	20.2	10.4	5.4
	2015	12.0	83.2	4.8	8.1	29.0	42.6	18.3	10.2	4.9
Puerto Rico Porto Rico	2014	37.4	58.0	4.6	7.4	22.0	24.6	36.8	...	6.1
Qatar Qatar	2005	...	...	...	...	...	...	...	13.7	4.0
	2009	...	...	...	4.4	17.6	14.7	...	14.8	3.4
	2010	...	...	...	...	...	...	...	13.8	4.5
	2014	45.5	22.7	31.9	...	...	...	...	12.7	3.6
	2017	24.9	52.7	22.4	...	...	...	...	8.6	2.9
Republic of Korea République de Corée	2016	...	...	...	9.2	31.7	38.7	20.4	...	4.6

Public expenditure on education *(continued)*
By expenditure type, level of education, total government expenditure and GDP

Dépenses publiques afférentes à l'éducation *(suite)*
Par type de dépenses, niveau de scolarité, dépenses publiques totales et PIB

Country or area / Pays ou zone	Year / Année	Percentage of total expenditure in public institutions / Pourcentage des dépenses publiques totales en faveur de l'éducation			Percentage of government expenditure on education by level / Pourcentage des dépenses publiques selon le niveau d'enseignement				As % of Govt. Expenditure / En % des dépenses du gouvt.	As % of GDP / En % du PIB
		Current expenditure / Dépenses courantes	Staff Compensation / Rémunération du personnel	Capital expenditure / Dépenses en Capital	Pre-primary / Préprimaire	Primary / Primaire	Secondary / Secondaire	Tertiary / Tertiaire		
Republic of Moldova République de Moldova	2005	...	...	...	...	...	...	...	19.3	7.2
	2010	29.1	62.6	8.2	19.5	18.0	37.3	18.0	22.3	7.6
	2014	28.6	60.8	10.6	21.0	22.7	35.7	17.2	18.8	6.3
	2015	...	52.2	7.5	...	...	...	...	...	...
	2018	23.5	64.9	11.6	24.4	23.3	36.0	11.9	17.5	5.5
Romania Roumanie	2005	34.4	59.1	6.5	9.1	* 13.8	* 44.3	23.2	10.8	3.5
	2010	27.1	62.2	10.8	10.0	16.4	35.8	28.5	9.1	3.5
	2015	31.8	62.5	5.7	10.7	13.3	41.1	21.2	9.1	3.1
	2016	25.3	68.3	6.3	10.3	12.5	39.1	23.8	9.5	3.0
Russian Federation Fédération de Russie	2005	...	...	...	13.9	...	...	21.1	12.0	3.8
	2008	...	...	...	15.0	...	...	23.1	12.0	4.1
	2013	22.5	69.3	8.2	23.7	...	...	21.9	10.9	3.8
	2015	21.9	70.9	7.2	...	...	...	21.1	10.9	3.8
	2016	19.8	74.3	5.9	...	...	...	21.6	11.0	3.7
Rwanda Rwanda	2000	...	47.3	20.3	* 0.5	* 48.2	* 16.7	* 34.7	18.8	3.9
	2001	24.4	33.8	41.8	...	...	...	...	25.3	5.4
	2010	25.1	58.7	16.1	0.2	36.7	30.7	22.7	17.5	4.9
	*2015	41.4	47.9	10.8	1.3	32.7	42.6	20.9	12.5	3.8
	*2016	44.8	42.2	13.0	7.7	34.6	52.8	...	12.3	3.5
	2018	...	...	...	1.3	28.6	38.3	19.8	10.8	3.1
Saint Kitts and Nevis Saint-Kitts-et-Nevis	2005	...	...	...	...	...	...	...	11.1	3.6
	2007	...	...	...	...	...	...	...	13.1	4.0
	2015	...	...	...	15.6	21.4	40.2	15.4	8.6	2.6
	2016	18.6	61.7	19.8	...	...	...	...	...	...
Saint Lucia Sainte-Lucie	2004	26.1	73.2	0.7	0.4	47.2	33.4	...	15.0	3.8
	2005	...	...	...	...	...	...	...	16.3	4.7
	2006	28.4	45.3	26.3	...	...	...	...	19.0	5.3
	*2010	...	...	...	1.8	42.3	45.6	4.6	14.2	3.8
	2011	...	...	...	1.5	42.3	45.1	* 5.0	13.8	3.8
	2015	...	...	11.7	1.4	34.2	43.8	...	16.5	4.4
	2018	10.1	83.7	6.2	...	35.1	40.3	...	14.4	3.7
Saint Vincent & Grenadines Saint-Vincent-Grenadines	2005	14.6	51.9	33.6	0.3	41.0	31.7	3.7	22.6	6.4
	2010	5.6	94.4	...	2.0	41.4	36.3	7.0	15.5	5.1
	2018	...	...	...	...	36.9	31.5	...	18.8	5.7
Samoa Samoa	2001	...	...	...	* 0.7	* 36.2	* 29.8	33.2	12.8	3.8
	*2002	...	...	...	...	45.8	...	...	12.8	3.8
	2008	...	...	...	...	...	...	...	16.1	5.1
	2016	...	...	...	0.9	37.0	42.8	9.2	10.5	4.1
San Marino Saint-Marin	2010	4.2	95.8	...	19.0	31.7	39.5	9.8	10.8	2.3
	2011	5.0	95.0	...	20.2	33.3	35.8	10.8	10.6	2.4
	2017	9.6	90.2	0.2	15.4	34.4	34.7	6.8	13.1	3.1
Sao Tome and Principe Sao Tomé-et-Principe	2005	...	...	...	...	...	...	...	12.1	4.9
	2010	...	...	...	...	...	...	...	19.3	9.7
	2014	...	...	...	12.0	55.8	22.6	9.6	12.3	3.7
	2015	...	...	...	...	...	...	...	11.3	3.9
	*2018	...	...	...	...	...	...	...	20.1	5.1
Saudi Arabia Arabie saoudite	2005	...	...	...	...	...	...	...	19.3	5.4
	2008	...	...	...	...	...	...	...	19.3	5.1
Senegal Sénégal	2005	...	...	...	0.9	41.8	22.4	22.0	21.8	4.1
	2010	18.3	72.6	9.1	1.1	43.2	27.9	26.8	24.0	5.2
	2015	23.6	61.7	14.7	4.0	34.2	29.3	32.1	23.8	5.5
	2016	27.2	67.8	5.0	0.5	31.3	16.7	28.1	21.3	5.1
	2018	...	...	...	0.6	31.7	16.8	32.8	21.5	4.7
Serbia Serbie	2010	22.4	75.1	2.5	0.5	45.9	23.3	29.1	10.1	4.3
	2015	19.4	78.7	1.9	0.7	45.3	22.9	30.1	8.9	3.8
	2017	36.6	58.3	5.1	...	...	...	29.9	9.3	3.7
Seychelles Seychelles	2002	23.9	66.4	9.7	* 10.5	* 32.0	* 26.1	17.4	9.2	5.2
	2003	31.8	59.3	8.9	* 8.6	* 32.8	* 28.9	...	12.0	5.4
	2006	29.8	56.7	13.5	4.1	...	...	17.9	11.0	4.8
	2014	51.7	40.9	7.4	13.3	37.4	32.3	1.1	12.1	4.1
	2016	64.5	30.2	5.2	9.0	30.6	27.1	21.6	11.7	4.4

Public expenditure on education *(continued)*
By expenditure type, level of education, total government expenditure and GDP

Dépenses publiques afférentes à l'éducation *(suite)*
Par type de dépenses, niveau de scolarité, dépenses publiques totales et PIB

Country or area Pays ou zone	Year Année	Percentage of total expenditure in public institutions Pourcentage des dépenses publiques totales en faveur de l'éducation			Percentage of government expenditure on education by level Pourcentage des dépenses publiques selon le niveau d'enseignement				As % of Govt. Expenditure En % des dépenses du gouvt.	As % of GDP En % du PIB
		Current expenditure Dépenses courantes	Staff Compensation Rémunération du personnel	Capital expenditure Dépenses en Capital	Pre-primary Préprimaire	Primary Primaire	Secondary Secondaire	Tertiary Tertiaire		
Sierra Leone Sierra Leone	*2005	...	...	...	...	...	...	...	15.5	2.8
	2010	28.3	69.1	2.5	...	50.7	26.4	19.6	12.8	2.6
	2011	24.5	74.3	1.2	...	52.6	26.3	17.9	12.4	2.7
	2014	...	...	0.5	...	43.1	23.4	30.7	15.1	2.7
	2018	...	...	...	...	31.0	20.5	46.4	32.5	7.1
Singapore Singapour	2005	...	...	...	...	...	...	...	22.3	3.2
	2010	...	...	9.2	...	20.8	25.0	35.1	18.6	3.1
	2013	...	...	8.2	...	22.0	23.0	35.3	28.8	2.9
Slovakia Slovaquie	2005	34.1	60.2	5.6	10.1	17.1	48.9	21.0	9.5	3.8
	2010	30.8	57.0	12.2	9.4	20.7	46.9	19.6	9.8	4.1
	2015	32.0	53.0	15.0	10.5	19.1	37.9	29.9	10.3	4.6
	2016	30.6	64.2	5.3	12.9	22.2	42.2	21.3	9.4	3.9
Slovenia Slovénie	2003	21.0	69.4	9.6	9.2	* 21.8	* 46.6	22.3	13.7	5.7
	2005	20.6	69.4	10.0	10.4	...	...	22.0	13.3	5.6
	2010	21.3	70.0	8.7	10.3	28.5	37.1	24.0	12.1	5.6
	2015	22.3	69.6	8.2	11.3	28.3	34.4	19.9	11.2	4.9
	2016	20.8	66.5	12.8	10.9	28.8	34.5	19.7	11.7	4.8
Solomon Islands Îles Salomon	2010	...	...	...	...	...	...	...	17.5	9.9
South Africa Afrique du Sud	2005	20.9	66.3	2.9	0.6	42.9	32.6	15.1	19.9	5.1
	2006	...	69.8	* 3.5	0.5	45.1	31.1	12.8	18.0	5.1
	2009	...	...	* 3.8	0.9	41.1	30.9	12.5	18.3	5.2
	2010	...	...	...	1.1	42.5	31.4	11.9	18.0	5.7
	2014	29.5	67.2	3.3	1.5	38.8	30.7	12.2	19.1	6.0
	2015	...	...	...	...	...	30.7	12.5	18.7	6.0
	2018	22.6	72.4	4.9	1.5	38.7	30.8	15.3	18.9	6.2
South Sudan Soudan du sud	2014	34.6	48.8	16.5	0.6	57.5	16.6	24.7	4.1	1.7
	2015	75.5	24.5	...	0.6	53.8	18.0	27.6	3.3	1.5
	2016	6.5	93.5	...	0.3	36.4	12.2	50.4	0.9	1.5
	2017	...	...	...	0.1	48.6	18.5	31.5	1.1	1.0
	*2018	...	...	...	...	...	...	...	0.9	...
Spain Espagne	2005	16.7	73.5	9.8	12.4	25.8	39.5	22.4	10.8	4.1
	2010	17.7	71.6	10.8	14.1	25.5	37.0	23.4	10.6	4.8
	2015	18.2	76.5	5.3	11.0	26.6	36.8	22.4	9.8	4.3
	2016	18.4	77.1	4.6	10.9	26.9	37.3	21.8	10.0	4.2
Sri Lanka Sri Lanka	2010	9.9	75.5	14.6	...	25.0	53.2	16.4	8.6	1.7
	2015	18.3	62.4	19.3	...	28.3	47.1	19.4	11.0	2.2
	2018	24.0	50.7	25.3	...	29.9	45.7	20.7	11.3	2.1
State of Palestine État de Palestine	2010	...	...	...	...	...	...	...	...	6.7
	2015	11.3	85.2	3.5	...	...	...	...	...	5.1
	2017	14.2	83.5	2.2	...	...	...	...	...	5.3
Sudan Soudan	2005	...	...	...	...	...	...	...	6.0	1.6
	2009	...	...	...	...	...	...	...	10.8	2.2
Sweden Suède	2005	28.4	65.0	6.6	7.8	26.2	38.2	27.5	12.8	6.6
	2010	31.3	63.1	5.6	10.2	24.3	35.6	29.0	13.3	6.6
	2015	29.6	65.3	5.1	17.0	23.3	27.1	24.9	15.5	7.5
	2016	29.6	65.5	4.9	16.8	24.1	27.4	24.1	15.7	7.7
Switzerland Suisse	2005	15.5	75.3	9.1	3.6	29.7	37.7	26.0	15.8	5.2
	2010	16.2	75.2	8.6	3.7	28.0	41.3	25.3	15.4	4.9
	2015	15.4	74.3	10.2	7.9	28.5	35.6	26.3	15.5	5.1
	2016	15.3	74.1	10.6	8.0	28.9	35.6	26.0	15.5	5.1
Syrian Arab Republic République arabe syrienne	2002	...	...	...	...	44.4	33.4	21.0	16.8	5.2
	2004	...	...	...	...	...	...	24.8	17.1	5.4
	2009	...	...	...	...	38.9	36.9	24.2	19.2	5.1
Tajikistan Tadjikistan	2005	...	...	...	3.8	...	...	7.4	15.3	3.5
	2010	...	...	...	5.0	...	...	10.1	15.3	4.0
	2015	...	...	14.0	5.3	...	...	9.9	16.4	5.2
Thailand Thaïlande	2004	...	...	...	10.4	31.0	24.0	20.6	21.5	4.0
	2005	...	...	...	13.6	...	...	21.7	20.5	3.9
	2010	45.8	50.9	3.3	5.7	40.1	28.6	16.5	16.2	3.5
	2013	45.8	49.2	5.0	5.4	41.1	29.8	15.6	19.1	4.1
	2014	31.8	62.5	5.7	...	...	...	...	...	...

Public expenditure on education *(continued)*
By expenditure type, level of education, total government expenditure and GDP

Dépenses publiques afférentes à l'éducation *(suite)*
Par type de dépenses, niveau de scolarité, dépenses publiques totales et PIB

| Country or area
Pays ou zone | Year
Année | Percentage of total expenditure in public institutions
Pourcentage des dépenses publiques totales en faveur de l'éducation | | | Percentage of government expenditure on education by level
Pourcentage des dépenses publiques selon le niveau d'enseignement | | | | As % of Govt. Expenditure
En % des dépenses du gouvt. | As % of GDP
En % du PIB |
		Current expenditure Dépenses courantes	Staff Comp-ensation Rémun-ération du personnel	Capital expenditure Dépenses en Capital	Pre-primary Préprimaire	Primary Primaire	Secondary Secondaire	Tertiary Tertiaire		
Timor-Leste Timor-Leste	2010	52.5	37.8	9.7	...	...	...	10.4	9.2	2.4
	2014	46.4	49.5	4.0	1.2	64.9	29.8	4.1	6.8	2.7
	2015	...	...	...	...	...	...	...	8.6	4.4
	*2018	...	...	...	...	...	...	...	7.9	4.1
Togo Togo	2000	20.9	69.1	10.0	...	48.6	29.3	17.4	24.4	3.9
	2005	...	...	...	...	41.8	...	...	17.7	3.2
	2010	14.7	74.7	10.6	2.6	51.7	25.6	16.7	19.6	4.1
	2015	7.0	90.5	2.5	1.6	64.5	16.3	17.3	16.7	5.1
	2016	7.1	90.5	2.4	1.6	64.1	16.0	17.9	16.0	5.0
	*2017	...	...	...	...	...	...	17.7	23.1	5.0
	*2018	...	...	...	...	...	...	...	21.8	5.4
Tonga Tonga	2004	...	...	...	...	44.4	30.1	21.7	18.1	3.9
Trinidad and Tobago Trinité-et-Tobago	2003	...	...	...	0.6	39.2	36.8	...	13.9	3.1
Tunisia Tunisie	2000	8.2	77.3	14.5	...	* 33.3	* 45.0	* 21.7	* 24.6	* 6.2
	2002	...	...	11.6	...	* 32.9	* 44.4	22.8	22.9	5.8
	2005	...	...	...	...	* 34.3	* 41.6	24.1	26.7	6.5
	2008	...	...	10.0	...	27.7	47.3	25.0	25.3	6.3
	2010	...	...	10.4	...	...	...	28.2	24.8	6.3
	2015	...	...	...	...	...	71.6	23.9	22.6	6.6
Turkey Turquie	2004	12.6	66.3	21.1	0.6	...	...	27.9	8.7	3.0
	2006	14.9	74.6	10.6	...	...	...	31.9	8.0	2.8
Turkmenistan Turkménistan	2012	...	...	33.7	28.1	...	...	9.2	20.8	3.0
Turks and Caicos Islands Îles Turques-et-Caïques	2002	9.8	61.1	29.2	* 5.0	* 21.1	31.7	22.9	...	5.1
	2003	...	...	...	...	* 21.6	28.0	37.2	...	4.7
	2005	13.7	69.5	16.8	...	* 30.0	47.7	...	...	2.5
	2015	...	...	17.6	...	36.1	41.5	22.4	14.3	3.2
	2018	6.5	74.6	18.8	16.7	19.4	39.4	24.4	12.1	2.9
Uganda Ouganda	2004	12.1	62.7	25.2	...	61.2	17.3	11.9	20.3	5.0
	2010	51.1	35.5	13.4	...	47.3	39.4	13.3	10.1	2.4
	2014	48.3	39.1	12.6	...	59.2	24.6	16.3	10.9	2.3
	*2015	...	...	...	...	...	...	...	12.1	2.8
	*2018	...	...	...	...	...	...	...	10.9	2.5
Ukraine Ukraine	2000	...	...	8.3	11.1	...	...	32.3	11.4	4.2
	2005	...	...	...	11.0	...	...	29.5	13.7	6.1
	2009	...	...	...	12.5	...	...	32.4	15.1	7.3
	2014	...	...	2.2	16.3	18.0	27.8	31.5	13.1	5.9
	2017	...	...	7.7	17.5	21.7	30.7	25.0	13.1	5.4
United Kingdom Royaume-Uni	2005	18.5	73.5	8.0	5.9	26.5	45.4	22.3	13.2	5.0
	2010	29.8	58.8	11.4	5.2	30.1	48.3	16.4	13.0	5.7
	2015	23.5	73.9	2.6	3.5	32.2	41.0	22.8	13.8	5.6
	2016	20.9	76.8	2.3	3.6	32.3	37.8	25.6	13.8	5.5
United Rep. of Tanzania Rép.-Unie de Tanzanie	2005	...	...	...	5.8	56.0	12.9	21.7	18.1	3.5
	2009	...	...	...	4.4	41.9	16.7	33.8	17.4	4.0
	2010	...	...	...	...	...	11.3	28.3	19.6	4.5
	2014	...	...	...	6.0	49.2	18.3	21.4	17.3	3.4
	*2018	...	...	...	...	...	...	...	20.6	3.7
United States of America États-Unis d'Amérique	2014	21.6	69.7	8.7	6.6	31.0	34.6	27.5	13.4	5.0
Uruguay Uruguay	2005	14.5	80.8	4.7	8.9	33.8	35.5	21.8	9.5	2.7
	2006	14.1	80.2	5.7	8.7	33.3	36.0	22.0	9.8	2.9
	2011	14.9	80.5	4.6	10.2	27.9	33.2	26.8	15.2	4.4
	2015	13.4	82.6	4.0	...	...	...	...	...	...
	2017	14.1	82.8	3.2	11.1	23.1	34.7	24.8	14.9	4.8
Uzbekistan Ouzbékistan	*2015	...	...	...	...	...	...	...	23.6	5.8
	*2017	...	...	...	...	...	...	...	23.0	5.3

Public expenditure on education *(continued)*
By expenditure type, level of education, total government expenditure and GDP

Dépenses publiques afférentes à l'éducation *(suite)*
Par type de dépenses, niveau de scolarité, dépenses publiques totales et PIB

Country or area Pays ou zone	Year Année	Percentage of total expenditure in public institutions Pourcentage des dépenses publiques totales en faveur de l'éducation			Percentage of government expenditure on education by level Pourcentage des dépenses publiques selon le niveau d'enseignement				As % of Govt. Expenditure En % des dépenses du gouvt.	As % of GDP En % du PIB
		Current expenditure Dépenses courantes	Staff Compensation Rémunération du personnel	Capital expenditure Dépenses en Capital	Pre-primary Préprimaire	Primary Primaire	Secondary Secondaire	Tertiary Tertiaire		
Vanuatu Vanuatu	2001	1.1	51.7	47.2	0.1	27.9	57.4	10.5	40.1	9.0
	2003	...	...	...	...	...	...	...	44.8	8.4
	2008	11.4	87.4	1.2	0.5	49.7	32.9	5.9	21.4	5.8
	2009	8.8	89.5	1.7	0.1	54.3	29.7	...	18.7	5.0
	2015	...	...	...	0.1	41.3	28.7	...	13.7	5.5
	2017	20.8	78.0	1.2	0.1	44.6	32.9	...	12.7	4.7
Venezuela (Boliv. Rep. of) Venezuela (Rép. boliv. du)	2009	20.2	76.9	2.9	11.6	31.5	19.0	22.6	...	6.9
Viet Nam Viet Nam	2010	32.3	42.4	25.3	13.3	30.0	42.2	14.5	17.1	5.1
	2013	31.3	46.9	21.9	15.7	29.7	39.6	15.0	18.5	5.7
	2018	...	...	...	...	...	...	...	14.5	4.2
Yemen Yémen	*2001	...	...	...	...	...	...	...	30.3	9.2
	2008	...	...	25.7	...	...	...	...	12.5	5.2
Zambia Zambie	2004	25.2	73.0	1.8	...	63.9	13.3	18.0	10.6	2.5
	2005	...	...	...	...	59.8	14.5	25.8	7.7	1.7
	2008	...	...	...	...	...	...	...	5.7	1.1
	2015	11.9	71.6	16.5	0.5	62.7	24.9	11.8	16.3	4.6
	2016	16.6	75.6	7.8	0.5	67.4	19.7	12.3	15.4	3.7
	2017	...	...	...	0.4	67.4	23.3	8.9	14.8	3.7
	*2018	...	...	...	...	...	...	...	17.0	4.7
Zimbabwe Zimbabwe	2010	...	...	...	...	51.6	25.6	22.8	8.5	1.5
	2014	...	...	...	2.0	47.8	26.9	16.8	30.0	6.1
	*2018	...	...	...	...	...	...	...	19.0	4.6

Source:

United Nations Educational, Scientific and Cultural Organization (UNESCO), Montreal, the UNESCO Institute for Statistics (UIS) statistics database, last accessed May 2020.

Source:

Organisation des Nations Unies pour l'éducation, la science et la culture (UNESCO), Montréal, base de données statistiques de l'Institut de statistique (ISU) de l'UNESCO, dernier accès mai 2020.

Health Personnel
Number of health workers and workforce density (per 1 000 population)

Le personnel de santé
Personnel de santé et densité (pour 1 000 habitants)

Country or area Pays ou zone	Year Année	Physicians Médecins		Dentists Dentistes		Pharmacists Pharmaciens		Nurses and midwives Infirmières et Sages- femmes	
		Number Nombre	Per 1 000 Pour 1 000	Number Nombre	Per 1 000 Pour 1 000	Number Nombre	Per 1 000 Pour 1 000	Number Nombre	Per 1 000 Pour 1 000
Afghanistan	2001	4 104	1.9	...	...	525	~0.0	...	...
Afghanistan	2005	...	...	...	...	900	~0.0	14 930	0.6
	2008	4 834	1.7	382	~0.0	829	~0.0	13 780	0.5
	2009	6 037	2.1	...	...	847	~0.0	17 257	0.6
	2010	6 901	2.4	...	...	814	~0.0	...	...
	2015	9 808	2.9	123	~0.0	1 712	~0.0	4 471	0.1
	2016	9 842	2.8	120	~0.0	1 675	~0.0	5 243	0.1
	2017	...	...	...	...	...	...	6 370	0.2
Albania	2003	3 699	11.9	...	...	1 100	0.4	11 238	3.6
Albanie	2004	3 699	11.9	...	...	...	...	11 136	3.6
	2005	...	...	...	...	...	...	11 136	3.6
	2006	3 626	11.8	1 035	0.3	1 173	0.4	12 746	4.2
	2010	3 640	12.4	...	...	1 324	0.4	11 846	4.0
	2013	3 709	12.8	...	...	2 441	0.8	12 455	4.3
	2016	3 511	12.2	...	...	...	...	10 534	3.6
Algeria	2002	35 368	11.1	8 861	0.3	5 413	0.2	69 749	2.2
Algérie	2005	33 952	10.2	9 022	0.3	6 104	0.2	...	...
	2007	40 857	12.0	10 621	0.3	7 417	0.2	65 919	1.9
	2014	...	...	...	...	...	...	11 139	0.3
	2017	74 000	17.9	...	...	...	...	92 000	2.2
	2018	72 604	17.2	...	...	18 807	0.4	...	1.5
Andorra	2003	244	33.3	44	0.6	68	0.9	215	2.9
Andorre	2005	255	32.3	...	...	72	0.9	266	3.4
	2009	266	31.5	...	...	78	0.9	311	3.7
	2015	260	33.3	64	0.8	79	1.0	313	4.0
Angola	2004	1 165	0.6	222	~0.0	...	...	18 485	1.0
Angola	2009	2 956	1.3	...	...	...	...	29 592	1.3
	2013	...	...	...	...	...	...	30	~0.0
	2017	6 400	2.2	...	...	...	...	...	...
	2018	...	...	...	...	...	...	...	0.4
Antigua and Barbuda	2007	144	17.1	...	...	15	0.2	277	3.3
Antigua-et-Barbuda	2008	45	5.3	...	...	...	...	...	...
	2015	...	...	...	...	...	...	422	4.5
	2017	282	29.6	...	...	...	...	429	4.5
	2018	...	...	...	...	...	...	...	4.5
Argentina	2001	121 076	32.5	35 944	1.0	21 177	0.6	16 600	0.4
Argentine	2004	122 623	31.9	35 592	0.9	...	...	18 685	0.5
	2013	166 187	39.4	...	...	...	...	179 175	4.2
	2017	175 313	39.9	...	...	...	...	114 219	2.6
Armenia	2005	7 645	25.6	...	...	95	~0.0	14 872	5.0
Arménie	2010	8 177	28.4	1 257	0.4	123	~0.0	15 076	5.2
	2014	8 425	28.9	1 138	0.4	150	0.1	15 014	5.2
	2015	8 526	29.1	...	...	143	~0.0	14 492	5.0
	2017	12 964	44.0	...	...	...	...	17 984	6.1
Australia	2001	47 875	24.9	8 200	0.4	...	...	11 649	0.6
Australie	2005	56 084	27.8	...	...	14 900	0.7	196 998	9.8
	2010	74 061	33.4	11 473	0.5	19 237	0.9	230 446	10.4
	2015	83 490	34.9	13 834	0.6	20 281	0.8	292 015	12.2
	2016	86 550	35.7	14 205	0.6	20 960	0.9	300 987	12.4
	2017	90 417	36.8	...	...	21 656	0.9	308 556	12.6
Austria	2005	35 784	43.4	...	...	5 076	0.6	50 999	6.2
Autriche	2010	40 381	48.0	4 685	0.6	5 579	0.7	56 524	6.7
	2015	44 292	51.0	4 906	0.6	6 104	0.7	60 871	7.0
	2017	45 596	51.7	5 009	0.6	6 246	0.7	62 532	7.1
	2018	...	...	...	...	6 349	0.7	...	0.3
Azerbaijan	2005	30 584	35.8	...	...	1 740	0.2	70 377	8.2
Azerbaïdjan	2010	33 085	36.6	2 467	0.3	1 831	0.2	66 401	7.4
	2014	32 756	34.5	2 601	0.3	1 897	0.2	61 157	6.4

Country or area Pays ou zone	Year Année	Physicians Médecins		Dentists Dentistes		Pharmacists Pharmaciens		Nurses and midwives Infirmières et Sages- femmes	
		Number Nombre	Per 1 000 Pour 1 000	Number Nombre	Per 1 000 Pour 1 000	Number Nombre	Per 1 000 Pour 1 000	Number Nombre	Per 1 000 Pour 1 000
Bahamas Bahamas	2008	947	27.6	79	0.2	138	0.4	1 391	4.0
	2011	830	23.1	84	0.2	202	0.6	1 458	4.1
	2017	766	20.1	102	0.3	...	...	1 241	3.3
	2018	...	...	...	...	...	...		4.6
Bahrain Bahreïn	2005	928	10.4	98	0.1	164	0.2	2 389	2.7
	2010	1 178	9.5	122	0.1	196	0.2	3 052	2.5
	2015	1 270	9.3	134	0.1	222	0.2	3 422	2.5
Bangladesh Bangladesh	2002	...	...	1 886	~0.0	7 622	0.1	...	...
	2005	42 881	3.1	2 344	~0.0	...	...	39 471	0.3
	2010	53 643	3.6	4 336	~0.0	12 172	0.1	27 005	0.2
	2015	75 915	4.9	6 520	~0.0	12 199	0.1	42 965	0.3
	2017	86 754	5.4	8 155	~0.0	25 692	0.2	50 510	0.3
	2018	93 741	5.8	...	...	29 127	0.2		0.4
Barbados Barbade	2005	489	17.7	83	0.3	251	0.9	1 311	4.7
	2017	711	24.8	88	0.3	...	...	864	3.0
	2018	...	...	...	...	...	...	...	3.1
Belarus Bélarus	2005	31 694	33.2	...	...	2 898	0.3	96 019	10.0
	2010	30 615	32.5	5 087	0.5	2 731	0.3	99 995	10.6
	2014	47 272	50.1	5 414	0.6	3 240	0.3	103 582	11.0
	2015	48 995	51.9	...	...	3 424	0.4	103 859	11.0
Belgium Belgique	2005	30 081	28.5	7 731	0.7	11 882	1.1	99 189	9.4
	2010	31 815	29.1	7 675	0.7	12 629	1.2	110 405	10.1
	2015	34 020	30.1	8 291	0.7	13 643	1.2	133 287	11.8
	2016	34 834	30.7	8 478	0.7	13 876	1.2	136 004	12.0
	2017	35 069	30.7	...	...	14 084	1.2	216 673	19.0
	2018	...	...	...	...	21 895	1.9		19.5
Belize Belize	2000	251	10.2	32	0.1	...	...	303	1.2
	2009	241	7.7	12	~0.0	112	0.4	570	1.8
	2010	...	...	12	~0.0	...	...	...	...
	2012	387	11.5	...	...	...	...	373	1.1
	2014	200	5.7	...	...	...	...	...	...
	2017	422	11.2	58	0.2	254	0.7	...	...
Benin Bénin	2004	311	0.4	11	~0.0	...	...	5 789	0.7
	2008	542	0.6	37	~0.0	20	~0.0	7 129	0.8
	2010	513	0.6	...	...	16	~0.0	4 158	0.5
	2013	1 850	1.9	...	...	1 330	0.1	5 823	0.6
	2016	523	0.5	9	~0.0	13	~0.0	8 258	0.8
	2018	908	0.8	...	...	306	~0.0		0.4
Bhutan Bhoutan	2004	118	1.9	10	~0.0	...	...	515	0.8
	2007	144	2.2	7	~0.0	10	~0.0	545	0.8
	2008	171	2.6	...	...	14	~0.0	666	1.0
	2015	251	3.5	...	...	15	~0.0	1 070	1.5
	2017	300	4.0	67	0.1	37	~0.0	1 219	1.6
	2018	320	4.2	...	...	43	0.1	...	1.9
Bolivia (Plurin. State of) Bolivie (État plurin. de)	2001	10 329	12.0	...	...	2 593	0.3	18 091	2.1
	2010	4 406	4.4	976	0.1	567	0.1	8 366	0.8
	2011	4 771	4.7	1 130	0.1	660	0.1	10 139	1.0
	2015	...	...	...	...	...	...	12 950	1.2
	2016	17 542	15.9	2 428	0.2	2 477	0.2	12 332	1.1
	2017	...	...	...	...	...	...	17 449	1.6
Bosnia and Herzegovina Bosnie-Herzégovine	2005	5 773	15.3	...	...	331	0.1	18 332	4.9
	2010	6 665	18.0	797	0.2	371	0.1	20 331	5.5
	2014	7 426	21.3	825	0.2	441	0.1	21 352	6.1
	2015	7 413	21.6	...	...	443	0.1	21 193	6.2
	2017	...	...	...	...	...	...	18 650	5.6
	2018	...	...	...	...	...	...	...	5.7

Country or area Pays ou zone	Year Année	Physicians Médecins Number Nombre	Per 1 000 Pour 1 000	Dentists Dentistes Number Nombre	Per 1 000 Pour 1 000	Pharmacists Pharmaciens Number Nombre	Per 1 000 Pour 1 000	Nurses and midwives Infirmières et Sages-femmes Number Nombre	Per 1 000 Pour 1 000
Botswana	2004	715	4.1	38	~0.0	...	...	4 753	2.7
Botswana	2005	466	2.6	...	...	...	...	4 468	2.5
	2009	693	3.6	55	~0.0	107	0.1	5 816	3.0
	2010	819	4.1	55	~0.0	...	...	5 816	2.9
	2011	819	4.1	55	~0.0	430	0.2	5 816	2.9
	2012	819	4.0	55	~0.0	...	...	5 816	2.9
	2013	...	...	...	...	...	...	1 501	0.7
	2016	1 138	5.3	91	~0.0	...	...	8 888	4.1
	2018	...	...	...	...	...	...	...	5.4
Brazil	2005	310 138	16.7	207 904	1.1	99 696	0.5	101 341	0.5
Brésil	2010	355 006	18.1	223 021	1.1	107 564	0.5	287 119	1.5
	2013	378 354	18.8	...	...	...	...	1 520 533	7.6
	2015	...	...	...	...	...	...	1 862 357	9.1
	2017	450 009	21.7	258 842	1.2	141 968	0.7	2 023 671	9.7
	2018	453 351	21.6	...	...	...	...	...	10.1
Brunei Darussalam	2005	390	10.7	73	0.2	41	0.1	2 006	5.5
Brunéi Darussalam	2010	563	14.5	86	0.2	43	0.1	2 907	7.5
	2015	739	17.8	94	0.2	71	0.2	2 756	6.6
	2017	683	16.1	...	...	...	...	2 589	6.1
	2018	...	...	...	...	...	...	...	5.9
Bulgaria	2005	28 174	36.7	...	...	...	...	34 690	4.5
Bulgarie	2010	27 963	37.7	6 389	0.9	...	...	35 033	4.7
	2014	28 801	39.8	7 054	1.0	...	...	35 180	4.9
	2015	29 038	40.3	...	...	...	...	34 671	4.8
Burkina Faso	2004	708	0.5	58	~0.0	...	...	6 557	0.5
Burkina Faso	2010	713	0.5	32	~0.0	184	~0.0	8 645	0.6
	2012	787	0.5	38	~0.0	203	~0.0	10 459	0.6
	2015	1 189	0.7	...	...	258	~0.0	12 131	0.7
	2016	1 202	0.7	...	...	235	~0.0	12 281	0.7
	2017	1 626	0.9	...	...	...	...	16 945	0.9
Burundi	2004	200	0.3	14	~0.0	...	...	1 348	0.2
Burundi	2010	418	0.5	2	~0.0	23	~0.0	5 973	0.7
	2012	498	0.5	...	...	4	~0.0	6 502	0.7
	2015	508	0.5	...	...	...	...	6 767	0.7
	2017	1 084	1.0	...	...	...	...	9 231	0.9
Cabo Verde	2010	292	5.9	4	~0.0	4	~0.0	543	1.1
Cabo Verde	2011	292	5.9	3	~0.0	3	~0.0	543	1.1
	2015	410	7.8	...	...	...	...	498	0.9
	2016	...	...	4	~0.0	4	~0.0	612	1.2
	2017	...	...	...	...	...	...	688	1.3
	2018	...	...	...	...	...	...	...	1.3
Cambodia	2000	2 047	1.7	209	~0.0	564	~0.0	11 125	0.9
Cambodge	2010	3 294	2.3	242	~0.0	548	~0.0	12 251	0.9
	2014	2 944	1.9	252	~0.0	526	~0.0	14 697	1.0
	2015	...	...	...	...	...	...	9 140	0.6
	2017	...	...	...	...	...	...	11 217	0.7
	2018	...	...	...	...	...	...	...	0.7
Cameroon	2005	1 049	0.6	26	~0.0	27	~0.0	6 705	0.4
Cameroun	2010	1 712	0.8	58	~0.0	42	~0.0	10 714	0.5
	2011	1 842	0.9	58	~0.0	162	~0.0	19 159	0.9
	2013	...	...	...	...	...	...	127	~0.0
	2016	...	2.3	88	~0.0	199	~0.0	...	...
Canada	2004	...	...	18 281	0.6	...	...	...	...
Canada	2008	...	...	19 433	0.6	...	...	...	...
	2015	...	...	22 454	0.6	...	...	353 738	9.8
	2016	84 063	23.1	23 060	0.6	40 888	1.1	359 473	9.9
	2017	...	...	...	...	...	...	365 450	9.9
	2018	...	...	...	...	...	...	...	9.9
Central African Republic	2004	331	0.8	6	~0.0	...	...	1 613	0.4
République centrafricaine	2009	205	0.5	4	~0.0	10	~0.0	1 097	0.3
	2015	324	0.7	...	...	20	~0.0	927	0.2

Le personnel de santé *(suite)*
Personnel de santé et densité (pour 1 000 habitants)

Country or area Pays ou zone	Year Année	Physicians Médecins Number Nombre	Per 1 000 Pour 1 000	Dentists Dentistes Number Nombre	Per 1 000 Pour 1 000	Pharmacists Pharmaciens Number Nombre	Per 1 000 Pour 1 000	Nurses and midwives Infirmières et Sages-femmes Number Nombre	Per 1 000 Pour 1 000
Chad	2004	345	0.4	7	~0.0	...	...	2 499	0.3
Tchad	2006	368	0.4	...	...	...	...	1 891	0.2
	2015	696	0.5	...	...	79	~0.0	3 563	0.3
	2017	651	0.4	...	...	71	~0.0	3 487	0.2
Chile	2005	15 865	9.8	12	~0.0	...	...	1 523	0.1
Chili	2009	17 382	10.3	15	~0.0	...	...	1 690	0.1
	2010	24 455	14.3	...	...	4 498	0.3	21 618	1.3
	2015	38 580	21.5	...	...	7 965	0.4	197 260	11.0
	2016	41 767	22.9	2 865	0.2	8 558	0.5	204 756	11.2
	2017	45 088	24.4	...	...	9 128	0.5	224 179	12.1
	2018	48 531	25.9	...	...	9 858	0.5	...	13.3
China	2005	1 622 684	12.1	51 012	~0.0	349 533	0.3	1 349 589	1.0
Chine	2010	2 000 000	14.5	...	...	353 916	0.3	2 048 071	1.5
	2011	2 025 873	14.6	119 000	0.1	363 993	0.3	2 244 020	1.6
	2015	2 508 408	17.7	...	...	423 294	0.3	3 241 469	2.3
	2017	2 828 999	19.8	...	...	453 000	0.3	3 804 021	2.7
Colombia	2005	62 807	14.7	37 371	0.9	...	...	28 163	0.7
Colombie	2010	71 980	15.9	44 858	1.0	...	...	39 226	0.9
	2015	93 815	19.7	46 299	1.0	...	...	55 369	1.2
	2017	103 026	21.1	...	...	...	...	62 184	1.3
	2018	108 499	21.9	...	...	...	...	...	1.3
Comoros	2005	116	1.9	17	~0.0	15	~0.0	344	0.6
Comores	2009	128	1.9	21	~0.0	18	~0.0	473	0.7
	2012	123	1.7	18	~0.0	16	~0.0	667	0.9
	2013	...	...	...	...	...	...	295	0.4
	2016	216	2.7	...	...	...	...	500	0.6
Congo	2004	756	2.2	...	...	...	...	3 672	1.0
Congo	2007	401	1.0	...	...	38	~0.0	3 492	0.9
	2010	494	1.2	...	...	...	...	1 867	0.4
	2011	723	1.7	133	~0.0	250	0.1	7 866	1.8
	2015	...	...	...	...	...	...	3 852	0.8
	2016	...	...	...	...	191	~0.0	3 717	0.7
	2018	...	...	...	...	...	...	...	0.6
Cook Islands	2001	14	7.8	10	0.5	2	0.1	52	2.9
Îles Cook	2004	20	10.6	10	0.5	...	...	80	4.2
	2009	24	12.9	4	0.2	1	0.1	116	6.2
	2014	25	14.1	22	1.3	1	0.1	116	6.6
	2015	...	...	...	...	...	...	120	6.8
	2017	...	...	...	...	...	...	107	6.1
	2018	...	...	...	...	...	...	...	6.7
Costa Rica	2000	5 204	13.1	1 467	0.4	1 144	0.3	3 653	0.9
Costa Rica	2005	...	...	...	...	...	...	6 232	1.5
	2010	10 554	23.1	...	...	...	...	8 527	1.9
	2013	5 411	11.4	599	0.1	891	0.2	10 274	2.2
	2015	6 687	13.8	...	...	3 518	0.7	12 884	2.7
	2016	6 741	13.8	...	...	3 574	0.7	14 724	3.0
	2017	14 619	29.5	49	~0.0	...	...	15 740	3.2
	2018	14 468	28.9	...	...	...	...	...	3.4
Côte d'Ivoire	2005	1 698	0.9	204	~0.0	128	~0.0	8 988	0.5
Côte d'Ivoire	2008	2 746	1.4	274	~0.0	413	~0.0	9 231	0.5
	2014	5 240	2.3	490	~0.0	2 430	0.1	14 168	0.6
	2015	...	...	...	...	...	...	10 891	0.5
	2017	...	...	...	...	...	...	13 583	0.6
	2018	...	...	...	...	...	...	...	0.6
Croatia	2005	11 100	25.4	...	...	2 480	0.6	22 974	5.2
Croatie	2010	12 304	28.4	3 158	0.7	2 851	0.7	25 000	5.8
	2015	13 430	31.7	3 614	0.9	3 042	0.7	26 210	6.2
	2016	12 624	30.0	...	...	...	...	34 184	8.1

Le personnel de santé *(suite)*
Personnel de santé et densité (pour 1 000 habitants)

Country or area Pays ou zone	Year Année	Physicians Médecins		Dentists Dentistes		Pharmacists Pharmaciens		Nurses and midwives Infirmières et Sages-femmes	
		Number Nombre	Per 1 000 Pour 1 000	Number Nombre	Per 1 000 Pour 1 000	Number Nombre	Per 1 000 Pour 1 000	Number Nombre	Per 1 000 Pour 1 000
Cuba	2002	67 079	59.9	9 955	0.9	...	...	83 880	7.5
Cuba	2005	70 594	62.7	10 554	0.9	...	...	...	...
	2010	76 506	68.2	12 144	1.1	...	...	103 014	9.2
	2014	85 563	75.7	16 630	1.5	...	...	90 765	8.0
	2015	87 982	77.7	...	...	...	...	...	...
	2017	94 059	83.0	19 064	1.7	...	...	87 637	7.7
	2018	95 487	84.2	...	...	...	...	...	7.6
Cyprus	2005	1 949	19.0	...	...	160	0.2	3 096	3.0
Chypre	2010	2 399	21.6	772	0.7	181	0.2	3 946	3.5
	2014	2 880	25.0	839	0.7	188	0.2	4 509	3.9
	2015	3 046	26.2	...	...	750	0.6	4 684	4.0
	2016	2 283	19.5	...	...	...	...	6 145	5.3
Czechia	2005	35 811	34.9	...	...	5 761	0.6	87 154	8.5
Tchéquie	2010	37 053	35.2	7 263	0.7	6 061	0.6	89 233	8.5
	2015	41 893	39.5	8 461	0.8	6 965	0.7	88 744	8.4
	2016	42 682	40.2	7 955	0.7	7 172	0.7	89 208	8.4
	2017	43 283	40.7	...	...	7 308	0.7	89 337	8.4
	2018	43 951	41.2	...	...	...	...	...	...
Dem. People's Rep. Korea	2003	74 597	31.7	3 955	0.2	7 303	0.3	93 414	4.0
Rép. pop. dém. de Corée	2008	79 931	32.9	4 314	0.2	8 622	0.4	100 768	4.1
	2012	85 470	34.5	4 615	0.2	9 215	0.4	...	...
	2014	87 839	35.1	...	...	9 404	0.4	...	...
	2017	93 667	36.8	5 595	0.2	10 094	0.4	113 135	4.4
Dem. Rep. of the Congo	2009	5 832	0.9	45	~0.0	283	~0.0	25 587	0.4
Rép. dém. du Congo	2013	6 418	0.9	...	...	...	...	61 368	0.9
	2015	...	...	...	...	...	...	72 270	0.9
	2016	5 832	0.7	...	...	404	~0.0	1 793	~0.0
	2017	...	...	...	...	...	...	73 046	0.9
	2018	...	...	...	...	...	...	...	1.1
Denmark	2005	18 072	33.3	4 634	0.9	2 499	0.5	53 284	9.8
Danemark	2010	20 670	37.2	4 485	0.8	2 628	0.5	56 091	10.1
	2015	22 332	39.3	4 205	0.7	2 931	0.5	58 260	10.2
	2016	22 902	40.1	...	...	2 979	0.5	58 938	10.3
Djibouti	2004	129	1.7	10	~0.0	...	...	296	0.4
Djibouti	2005	140	1.8	...	...	18	~0.0	450	0.6
	2006	185	2.3	...	...	16	~0.0	...	...
	2008	...	...	...	...	266	0.3	...	...
	2014	201	2.2	19	~0.0	210	0.2	655	0.7
Dominica	2001	124	17.8	...	...	18	0.3	438	6.3
Dominique	2015	...	...	...	...	...	...	477	6.7
	2017	80	11.2	5	0.1	...	...	436	6.1
	2018	...	...	...	...	...	...	...	6.4
Dominican Republic	2000	15 670	18.5	7 000	0.8	3 330	0.4	15 352	1.8
République dominicaine	2008	10 385	11.0	1 205	0.1	...	...	...	...
	2009	...	...	1 785	0.2	...	...	12 686	1.3
	2011	14 983	15.3	1 910	0.2	...	...	13 374	1.4
	2015	...	...	...	...	...	...	14 957	1.5
	2017	...	...	2 261	0.2	...	...	12 297	1.2
	2018	...	...	...	...	...	...	...	1.4
Ecuador	2003	20 020	15.0	2 213	0.2	497	~0.0	20 372	1.5
Équateur	2009	23 614	16.0	3 363	0.2	664	~0.0	27 764	1.9
	2010	31 690	21.1	...	...	...	...	24 910	1.7
	2015	33 474	20.7	8 564	0.5	672	~0.0	40 731	2.5
	2016	33 589	20.4	5 243	0.3	...	...	47 065	2.9
	2017	...	...	...	...	...	...	47 444	2.8
	2018	...	...	...	...	...	...	...	2.5

Country or area Pays ou zone	Year Année	Physicians Médecins Number Nombre	Per 1 000 Pour 1 000	Dentists Dentistes Number Nombre	Per 1 000 Pour 1 000	Pharmacists Pharmaciens Number Nombre	Per 1 000 Pour 1 000	Nurses and midwives Infirmières et Sages-femmes Number Nombre	Per 1 000 Pour 1 000
Egypt	2003	38 485	5.3	...	...	...	...	...	...
Égypte	2004	...	...	8 193	0.1	...	...	146 761	2.0
	2006	...	...	...	...	...	...	179 590	2.3
	2015	75 960	8.2	16 880	0.2	36 573	0.4	179 450	1.9
	2017	77 083	8.0	19 111	0.2	42 067	0.4	185 852	1.9
	2018	44 502	4.5	...	...	45 014	0.5	...	1.9
El Salvador	2005	10 355	17.1	4 255	0.7	2 280	0.4	...	...
El Salvador	2007	...	...	...	...	...	...	8 350	1.4
	2008	11 542	18.8	4 669	0.8	2 316	0.4	...	...
	2015	...	...	...	...	...	...	11 121	1.8
	2016	9 955	15.7	...	...	...	...	11 466	1.8
	2017	...	...	...	...	4 181	0.7	11 738	1.8
	2018	...	...	...	...	...	...	...	1.8
Equatorial Guinea	2004	153	2.1	5	~0.0	...	...	271	0.4
Guinée équatoriale	2017	507	4.0	...	...	...	...	634	0.5
Eritrea	2004	215	0.8	16	~0.0	...	...	2 505	0.9
Érythrée	2015	...	...	...	...	...	...	3 962	1.2
	2016	212	0.6	...	...	...	...	4 860	1.4
	2017	...	...	...	...	...	...	4 528	1.3
	2018	...	...	...	...	...	...	...	1.4
Estonia	2000	4 371	31.2	909	0.6	815	0.6	20 278	14.5
Estonie	2005	4 261	31.4	...	...	849	0.6	8 915	6.6
	2010	4 319	32.4	1 198	0.9	842	0.6	8 524	6.4
	2015	4 492	34.2	1 239	0.9	948	0.7	8 355	6.4
	2016	4 548	34.6	1 257	1.0	963	0.7	8 469	6.4
	2017	4 569	34.6	...	...	956	0.7	8 612	6.5
	2018	5 931	44.8	...	...	1 441	1.1	...	11.2
Eswatini	2000	...	...	3	~0.0	46	~0.0	3 345	3.3
Eswatini	2004	171	1.7	17	~0.0	...	...	6 828	6.7
	2009	173	1.6	13	~0.0	20	~0.0	1 626	1.5
	2011	109	1.0	46	~0.0	30	~0.0	1 292	1.2
	2015	...	...	...	...	...	...	3 976	3.6
	2016	366	3.3	...	...	...	...	4 200	3.8
	2017	...	...	...	...	...	...	4 431	3.9
	2018	...	...	...	...	...	...	...	4.1
Ethiopia	2003	1 936	0.3	60	~0.0	172	~0.0	15 544	0.2
Éthiopie	2005	2 453	0.3	...	...	191	~0.0	18 809	0.2
	2009	2 152	0.3	...	...	632	~0.0	21 488	0.3
	2013	...	...	...	...	...	...	6 925	0.1
	2017	10 496	1.0	...	...	...	...	88 164	0.8
	2018	8 395	0.8	...	...	3 907	~0.0	...	0.7
Fiji	2003	380	4.7	60	0.1	90	0.1	1 660	2.0
Fidji	2009	372	4.4	171	0.2	76	0.1	1 957	2.3
	2015	747	8.6	64	0.1	95	0.1	2 621	3.0
	2018	...	...	...	...	...	...	...	3.4
Finland	2002	15 077	28.9	4 658	0.9	7 000	1.3	78 402	15.0
Finlande	2005	15 731	29.9	...	...	5 425	1.0	67 837	12.9
	2010	17 521	32.7	4 234	0.8	5 944	1.1	76 500	14.3
	2014	18 526	33.9	3 925	0.7	5 941	1.1	80 150	14.7
	2015	18 257	33.3	...	...	...	...	4 768	0.9
	2016	20 956	38.1	...	...	...	...	81 022	14.7
France	2003	206 289	34.2	40 648	0.7	66 266	1.1	462 865	7.7
France	2005	210 312	34.4	...	...	70 664	1.2	496 178	8.1
	2008	212 479	34.2	41 422	0.7	74 465	1.2	527 165	8.5
	2010	212 132	33.7	...	...	73 298	1.2	566 696	9.0
	2015	207 789	32.2	42 602	0.7	70 247	1.1	682 896	10.6
	2016	209 367	32.4	43 026	0.7	70 025	1.1	704 220	10.9
	2017	211 162	32.6	...	...	69 346	1.1	723 770	11.2
	2018	212 337	32.7	...	...	69 145	1.1	...	11.5

Country or area Pays ou zone	Year Année	Physicians Médecins		Dentists Dentistes		Pharmacists Pharmaciens		Nurses and midwives Infirmières et Sages- femmes	
		Number Nombre	Per 1 000 Pour 1 000	Number Nombre	Per 1 000 Pour 1 000	Number Nombre	Per 1 000 Pour 1 000	Number Nombre	Per 1 000 Pour 1 000
Gabon Gabon	2004	395	2.9	14	~0.0	...	...	6 778	5.0
	2008	147	1.0	...	...	...	...	...	...
	2013	...	...	...	...	...	...	437	0.2
	2016	715	3.6	9	~0.0	46	~0.0	5 109	2.5
	2017	1 408	6.8	...	...	121	0.1	6 083	2.9
Gambia Gambie	2005	166	1.1	10	~0.0	11	~0.0	732	0.5
	2008	175	1.0	12	~0.0	13	~0.0	1 411	0.8
	2015	213	1.0	17	~0.0	5	~0.0	3 222	1.5
Georgia Géorgie	2005	16 068	38.2	...	...	339	0.1	17 436	4.1
	2010	18 227	44.5	1 257	0.3	353	0.1	16 191	3.9
	2015	20 143	50.1	2 469	0.6	315	0.1	16 167	4.0
	2017	24 572	61.3	...	...	496	0.1	19 468	4.9
	2018	28 501	71.2	...	...	395	0.1	...	4.7
Germany Allemagne	2005	280 012	34.3	...	...	48 058	0.6	897 000	11.0
	2010	303 645	37.6	66 427	0.8	50 604	0.6	963 000	11.9
	2015	338 129	41.3	69 863	0.9	52 568	0.6	1 056 000	12.9
	2016	344 755	41.9	70 305	0.9	52 430	0.6	1 080 000	13.1
	2017	351 195	42.5	...	...	53 480	0.6	1 094 000	13.2
Ghana Ghana	2004	3 240	1.5	104	~0.0	...	...	19 707	0.9
	2008	1 855	0.8	45	~0.0	547	~0.0	22 834	1.0
	2010	2 325	0.9	...	...	...	...	26 287	1.1
	2012	2 486	1.0	...	...	...	...	...	...
	2013	...	...	...	...	9 564	0.4	11 287	0.4
	2015	...	...	...	...	...	...	55 747	2.0
	2017	3 957	1.4	...	...	718	~0.0	68 492	2.4
	2018	...	...	...	...	...	...	...	4.2
Greece Grèce	2005	37 985	33.8	...	...	...	...	39 173	3.5
	2010	42 943	39.4	14 661	1.3	11 160	1.0	40 978	3.8
	2014	55 827	52.2	13 746	1.2	11 579	1.1	37 842	3.5
	2015	55 992	52.5	...	...	11 299	1.1	37 320	3.5
	2017	57 909	54.8	...	...	11 251	1.1	38 400	3.6
Grenada Grenade	2003	58	5.6	9	0.1	...	...	366	3.5
	2006	69	6.6	19	0.2	...	...	398	3.8
	2016	...	...	...	...	75	0.7	...	...
	2017	156	14.1	17	0.2	...	...	339	3.1
	2018	...	...	...	...	...	...	...	6.3
Guatemala Guatemala	2007	...	...	2 376	0.2	...	...	...	...
	2009	12 940	9.0	...	...	...	...	12 452	0.9
	2015	...	...	...	...	...	...	871	0.1
	2017	...	...	...	...	...	...	1 160	0.1
	2018	6 122	3.6	180	~0.0	68	~0.0	...	0.1
Guinea Guinée	2004	987	1.1	22	~0.0	...	...	4 408	0.5
	2005	940	1.0	17	~0.0	177	~0.0	...	...
	2015	977	0.9	...	...	142	~0.0	4 765	0.4
	2016	977	0.8	...	...	107	~0.0	1 453	0.1
Guinea-Bissau Guinée-Bissau	2004	188	1.4	3	~0.0	...	...	1 072	0.8
	2009	124	0.8	7	~0.0	9	~0.0	1 042	0.7
	2015	354	2.0	...	...	...	...	964	0.6
	2016	227	1.3	...	...	5	~0.0	1 058	0.6
	2018	...	...	...	...	...	...	...	0.7
Guyana Guyana	2000	366	4.9	30	~0.0	...	...	1 738	2.3
	2009	161	2.2	29	~0.0	15	~0.0	989	1.3
	2010	515	6.9	...	...	...	...	754	1.0
	2015	...	...	...	...	...	...	535	0.7
	2017	...	...	...	...	...	...	610	0.8
	2018	625	8.0	28	~0.0	7	~0.0	...	1.0
Haiti Haïti	2011	1 392	1.4	50	~0.0	85	~0.0	11 982	1.2
	2015	911	0.9	...	...	...	...	3 018	0.3
	2018	2 606	2.3	237	~0.0	336	~0.0	...	0.7

Country or area Pays ou zone	Year Année	Physicians Médecins Number Nombre	Per 1 000 Pour 1 000	Dentists Dentistes Number Nombre	Per 1 000 Pour 1 000	Pharmacists Pharmaciens Number Nombre	Per 1 000 Pour 1 000	Nurses and midwives Infirmières et Sages-femmes Number Nombre	Per 1 000 Pour 1 000
Honduras	2000	3 676	5.6	1 141	0.2	351	0.1	8 528	1.3
Honduras	2005	2 680	3.6	...	...	...	...	7 796	1.0
	2008	...	...	236	~0.0	...	...	...	...
	2010	2 454	3.0	...	...	...	...	7 151	0.9
	2013	8 657	9.8	...	...	...	...	6 220	0.7
	2015	...	...	...	...	...	...	6 109	0.7
	2017	2 913	3.1	308	~0.0	...	...	6 957	0.7
	2018	...	...	...	...	...	...	...	0.7
Hungary	2005	28 055	27.8	...	...	5 313	0.5	61 993	6.1
Hongrie	2010	28 686	28.9	5 257	0.5	5 821	0.6	63 838	6.4
	2015	30 486	31.2	5 936	0.6	7 039	0.7	65 367	6.7
	2016	31 515	32.3	6 083	0.6	7 353	0.8	64 786	6.6
	2017	32 543	33.5	...	...	7 557	0.8	66 199	6.8
	2018	33 078	34.1	...	...	7 842	0.8	...	6.9
Iceland	2005	1 072	36.3	289	1.0	...	...	4 378	14.8
Islande	2010	1 142	35.7	299	0.9	155	0.5	4 875	15.2
	2015	1 249	37.8	278	0.8	160	0.5	5 387	16.3
	2017	1 330	39.8	279	0.8	171	0.5	5 253	15.7
	2018	1 373	40.8	...	...	...	...	...	16.2
India	2003	625 400	5.6	47 318	~0.0	559 408	0.5	1 382 901	1.2
Inde	2005	660 801	5.8	55 344	~0.0	...	...	1 481 270	1.3
	2009	757 377	6.2	104 603	0.1	655 801	0.5	1 043 363	0.9
	2010	816 629	6.6	...	...	656 101	0.5	1 073 638	0.9
	2013	...	...	...	...	664 176	0.5	1 562 186	1.2
	2014	938 861	7.3	154 436	0.1	...	...	1 780 006	1.4
	2015	...	...	...	...	...	...	1 900 837	1.5
	2017	1 041 395	7.8	251 207	0.2	908 523	0.7	2 821 815	2.1
	2018	1 159 309	8.6	...	...	1 199 518	0.9	...	1.7
Indonesia	2003	29 499	1.3	5 267	~0.0	1 367	~0.0	179 959	0.8
Indonésie	2009	34 544	1.5	5 442	~0.0	2 007	~0.0	238 485	1.0
	2010	33 736	1.4	8 731	~0.0	...	...	266 348	1.1
	2015	70 735	2.7	12 740	~0.0	30 329	0.1	335 646	1.3
	2017	99 703	3.8	14 455	0.1	45 839	0.2	543 386	2.1
	2018	114 271	4.3	...	...	22 811	0.1	...	2.4
Iran (Islamic Republic of)	2005	61 870	8.9	13 210	0.2	13 900	0.2	98 020	1.4
Iran (Rép. islamique d')	2006	37 822	5.4	9 522	0.1	7 161	0.1	119 170	1.7
	2015	90 470	11.5	26 188	0.3	15 872	0.2	148 404	1.9
	2017	91 101	11.3	...	...	19 011	0.2	212 063	2.6
	2018	129 604	15.8	...	...	24 000	0.3	...	0.4
Iraq	2010	19 738	6.6	4 799	0.2	5 675	0.2	...	...
Iraq	2014	35 664	10.4	7 891	0.2	8 609	0.3	64 611	1.9
	2015	...	...	...	...	...	...	58 687	1.6
	2017	31 451	8.4	9 524	0.2	10 939	0.3	68 068	1.8
	2018	27 208	7.1	...	...	12 552	0.3	...	2.0
Ireland	2005	14 671	35.4	...	...	3 800	0.9	50 800	12.3
Irlande	2010	18 821	41.3	2 721	0.6	4 567	1.0	58 500	12.8
	2015	14 654	31.5	2 828	0.6	5 191	1.1	76 172	16.4
	2017	15 660	33.0	...	...	5 525	1.2	76 526	16.1
	2018	15 962	33.1	...	...	...	...	...	...
Israel	2005	24 512	37.5	...	...	4 500	0.7	38 115	5.8
Israël	2010	25 853	35.2	6 367	0.9	5 733	0.8	38 022	5.2
	2015	27 620	34.6	6 633	0.8	6 233	0.8	43 456	5.4
	2016	28 083	34.6	6 533	0.8	6 133	0.8	45 252	5.6
	2017	28 674	34.8	...	...	6 600	0.8	46 991	5.7
	2018	38 764	46.3	...	...	...	...	...	0.3
Italy	2005	215 739	37.0	...	...	...	...	288 412	4.9
Italie	2010	226 384	38.2	34 023	0.6	...	...	327 235	5.5
	2015	233 102	38.5	47 604	0.8	69 939	1.2	346 219	5.7
	2017	241 512	39.8	49 363	0.8	70 934	1.2	367 710	6.1
	2018	241 136	39.8	...	...	66 362	1.1	...	5.7

Le personnel de santé *(suite)*
Personnel de santé et densité (pour 1 000 habitants)

Country or area Pays ou zone	Year Année	Physicians Médecins		Dentists Dentistes		Pharmacists Pharmaciens		Nurses and midwives Infirmières et Sages-femmes	
		Number Nombre	Per 1 000 Pour 1 000	Number Nombre	Per 1 000 Pour 1 000	Number Nombre	Per 1 000 Pour 1 000	Number Nombre	Per 1 000 Pour 1 000
Jamaica Jamaïque	2003	2 253	8.3	212	0.1	...	...	4 374	1.6
	2008	1 103	4.0	46	~0.0	96	~0.0	2 930	1.1
	2015	1 199	4.2	37	~0.0	82	~0.0	4 194	1.5
	2016	1 322	4.6	45	~0.0	63	~0.0	4 669	1.6
	2017	3 815	13.1	260	0.1	...	...	4 286	1.5
	2018	...	...	...	...	...	...	...	0.8
Japan Japon	2004	270 371	21.1	95 197	0.7	...	...	25 257	0.2
	2010	283 548	22.1	98 739	0.8	197 616	1.5	1 320 623	10.3
	2014	300 075	23.4	100 994	0.8	216 077	1.7	1 475 591	11.5
	2016	308 105	24.1	101 584	0.8	230 186	1.8	1 526 797	12.0
	2018	...	...	...	...	...	...	...	12.2
Jordan Jordanie	2005	12 909	22.4	4 194	0.7	7 100	1.2	17 428	3.0
	2010	16 212	22.3	5 691	0.8	9 151	1.3	25 661	3.5
	2015	26 019	28.1	6 806	0.7	12 076	1.3	1 923	0.2
	2017	22 739	23.2	7 107	0.7	15 668	1.6	32 878	3.4
	2018	...	...	...	...	...	...	...	2.8
Kazakhstan Kazakhstan	2005	55 509	36.0	...	...	15 628	1.0	105 987	6.9
	2010	63 835	39.3	6 657	0.4	11 265	0.7	125 492	7.7
	2014	68 864	39.8	6 430	0.4	14 163	0.8	124 583	7.2
	2015	...	...	...	...	14 301	0.8	128 164	7.3
Kenya Kenya	2002	4 506	1.3	746	~0.0	...	...	...	...
	2004	...	...	...	...	...	...	16 146	0.5
	2010	7 129	1.7	898	~0.0	3 097	0.1	29 678	0.7
	2014	9 149	2.0	1 090	~0.0	2 355	0.1	43 311	0.9
	2015	...	...	...	...	...	...	41 413	0.9
	2017	...	...	...	...	...	...	53 168	1.1
	2018	8 042	1.6	...	...	964	~0.0	...	1.2
Kiribati Kiribati	2004	...	...	3	~0.0	...	...	260	2.9
	2010	41	4.0	4	~0.0	4	~0.0	404	3.9
	2013	22	2.0	7	0.1	3	~0.0	501	4.6
	2016	...	...	8	0.1	3	~0.0	...	...
	2018	...	...	...	...	...	...	...	3.8
Kuwait Koweït	2001	...	...	673	0.3	722	0.3	9 197	4.4
	2009	5 340	18.9	1 054	0.4	888	0.3	13 554	4.8
	2010	7 269	24.3	1 634	0.5	...	...	19 535	6.5
	2014	9 789	26.5	2 269	0.6	1 814	0.5	24 585	6.7
	2015	10 150	26.5	2 587	0.7	...	...	27 430	7.2
	2017	...	...	...	...	...	...	29 808	7.3
	2018	...	...	...	...	...	...	...	7.4
Kyrgyzstan Kirghizistan	2005	12 773	25.2	...	...	120	~0.0	32 167	6.3
	2010	12 685	23.4	1 022	0.2	169	~0.0	30 614	5.6
	2014	12 934	22.1	965	0.2	242	~0.0	34 743	5.9
Lao People's Dem. Rep. Rép. dém. populaire lao	2005	1 614	2.8	...	...	...	...	5 724	1.0
	2009	1 211	2.0	228	~0.0	...	...	5 322	0.9
	2010	4 880	7.8	...	...	...	...	5 357	0.9
	2014	3 286	5.0	341	0.1	1 276	0.2	8 226	1.2
	2015	...	...	...	...	...	...	7 078	1.1
	2017	2 591	3.7	...	...	1 711	0.2	8 791	1.3
	2018	...	...	...	...	...	...	...	1.0
Latvia Lettonie	2005	6 628	29.4	1 450	0.6	1 279	0.6	11 656	5.2
	2010	6 517	30.8	1 488	0.7	1 433	0.7	10 922	5.2
	2015	6 324	31.7	1 419	0.7	1 574	0.8	9 661	4.8
	2016	6 295	31.9	1 411	0.7	1 643	0.8	9 489	4.8
	2017	6 225	31.9	...	...	...	...	9 271	4.8
Lebanon Liban	2001	11 505	28.8	4 283	1.3	3 359	0.8	4 157	1.0
	2005	...	...	...	...	4 105	0.9	4 720	1.0
	2010	11 583	23.4	5 395	1.2	5 508	1.1	8 791	1.8
	2015	13 738	21.0	5 527	0.9	7 590	1.2	10 071	1.5
	2017	13 813	20.3	6 727	1.1	8 368	1.2	11 196	1.6
	2018	14 431	21.0	...	...	8 868	1.3	...	1.7

Le personnel de santé *(suite)*
Personnel de santé et densité (pour 1 000 habitants)

Country or area Pays ou zone	Year Année	Physicians Médecins Number Nombre	Per 1 000 Pour 1 000	Dentists Dentistes Number Nombre	Per 1 000 Pour 1 000	Pharmacists Pharmaciens Number Nombre	Per 1 000 Pour 1 000	Nurses and midwives Infirmières et Sages- femmes Number Nombre	Per 1 000 Pour 1 000
Lesotho	2003	89	0.4	3	~0.0	3	~0.0	1 123	0.6
Lesotho	2010	138	0.7	...	...	...	...	1 328	0.7
	2018	...	...	...	...	...	...	...	3.3
Liberia	2004	103	0.3	3	~0.0	...	...	1 035	0.3
Libéria	2010	90	0.2	23	~0.0	46	~0.0	1 805	0.5
	2015	168	0.4	...	...	...	...	453	0.1
	2018	...	...	...	...	...	...	...	0.5
Libya	2004	7 070	12.4	850	0.1	...	...	27 160	4.8
Libye	2009	12 009	19.6	3 792	0.6	2 275	0.4	42 982	7.0
	2014	13 095	20.6	4 583	0.7	3 928	0.6	43 216	6.8
	2015	12 158	18.9	4 987	0.8	3 117	0.5	...	...
	2017	13 757	20.9	5 776	0.9	3 956	0.6	42 975	6.5
Lithuania	2003	11 303	33.1	...	...	2 270	0.7	26 142	7.7
Lituanie	2005	11 034	33.0	...	...	...	...	25 265	7.6
	2010	10 666	34.1	2 456	0.8	...	...	23 722	7.6
	2015	12 605	43.0	2 644	0.9	...	...	23 172	7.9
	2016	13 681	47.4	2 787	1.0	...	...	23 020	8.0
	2017	13 731	48.3	...	...	2 803	1.0	22 705	8.0
	2018	17 796	63.5	...	...	...	...	...	9.8
Luxembourg	2005	1 190	26.0	...	...	326	0.7	5 255	11.5
Luxembourg	2010	1 406	27.7	422	0.8	374	0.7	5 786	11.4
	2015	1 656	29.2	506	0.9	397	0.7	6 990	12.3
	2017	1 781	30.1	581	1.0	416	0.7	7 206	12.2
Madagascar	2005	3 303	1.8	197	~0.0	8	~0.0	6 418	0.4
Madagascar	2010	4 130	2.0	195	~0.0	7	~0.0	4 724	0.2
	2012	3 188	1.4	181	~0.0	6	~0.0	4 858	0.2
	2013	3 523	1.5	...	...	17	~0.0	6 838	0.3
	2014	4 275	1.8	...	...	...	...	...	...
	2016	...	...	...	...	4	~0.0	...	...
	2018	...	...	...	...	...	...	...	0.1
Malawi	2004	266	0.2	...	...	...	...	7 264	0.6
Malawi	2008	257	0.2	...	...	293	~0.0	3 896	0.3
	2009	265	0.2	...	...	...	...	4 812	0.3
	2013	...	...	...	...	...	...	48	~0.0
	2016	284	0.2	...	...	...	...	5 141	0.3
	2018	649	0.4	...	...	101	~0.0	...	0.4
Malaysia	2002	17 020	7.0	2 160	0.1	2 880	0.1	43 380	1.8
Malaisie	2010	32 979	11.7	3 810	0.1	7 759	0.3	90 199	3.2
	2015	46 491	15.4	10 596	0.3	10 511	0.3	101 696	3.4
	2017	...	...	...	...	...	...	107 858	3.5
Maldives	2004	302	9.7	10	~0.0	...	...	886	2.8
Maldives	2010	525	14.4	32	0.1	247	0.7	1 868	5.1
	2015	1 313	28.9	62	0.1	199	0.4	2 990	6.6
	2016	...	...	10	~0.0	...	...	...	...
	2017	1 848	37.2	...	...	238	0.5	3 223	6.5
	2018	2 353	45.6	...	...	179	0.3	...	6.4
Mali	2004	1 053	0.9	44	~0.0	...	...	8 338	0.7
Mali	2010	1 536	1.0	35	~0.0	135	~0.0	6 715	0.4
	2012	1 711	1.1	...	...	...	...	6 027	0.4
	2013	...	...	...	...	...	...	1 961	0.1
	2016	2 506	1.4	...	...	194	~0.0	7 422	0.4
	2018	2 454	1.3	...	...	182	~0.0	...	0.4
Malta	2003	1 254	31.3	...	...	...	...	2 194	5.5
Malte	2005	...	...	...	...	...	...	2 345	5.8
	2010	892	21.5	184	0.4	301	0.7	2 838	6.9
	2015	1 240	28.6	206	0.5	558	1.3	3 629	8.4
	2018	...	...	...	...	...	...	...	9.5
Marshall Islands	2010	32	5.7	4	0.1	2	~0.0	127	2.3
Îles Marshall	2012	24	4.2	4	0.1	4	0.1	187	3.3
	2018	...	...	...	...	...	...	...	3.3

Country or area Pays ou zone	Year Année	Physicians Médecins		Dentists Dentistes		Pharmacists Pharmaciens		Nurses and midwives Infirmières et Sages- femmes	
		Number Nombre	Per 1 000 Pour 1 000	Number Nombre	Per 1 000 Pour 1 000	Number Nombre	Per 1 000 Pour 1 000	Number Nombre	Per 1 000 Pour 1 000
Mauritania	2004	313	1.1	47	~0.0	...	...	1 893	0.6
Mauritanie	2009	445	1.3	70	~0.0	77	~0.0	2 303	0.7
	2010	547	1.6	...	...	...	...	2 803	0.8
	2015	692	1.7	...	...	...	...	4 137	1.0
	2017	791	1.9	...	...	...	...	4 571	1.1
	2018	821	1.9	...	...	78	~0.0	...	0.9
Mauritius	2004	1 303	10.7	167	0.1	...	...	4 604	3.8
Maurice	2010	1 500	12.0	260	0.2	400	0.3	3 600	2.9
	2015	2 550	20.3	380	0.3	497	0.4	4 261	3.4
	2017	2 927	23.2	...	...	531	0.4	4 445	3.5
	2018	3 210	25.3	...	...	...	...	...	...
Mexico	2000	195 897	19.8	59 683	0.6	...	...	88 678	0.9
Mexique	2005	187 115	17.7	...	...	...	...	233 769	2.2
	2010	255 133	22.4	13 225	0.1	5 588	~0.0	275 171	2.4
	2015	283 275	23.3	15 915	0.1	...	...	294 585	2.4
	2016	286 675	23.2	12 754	0.1	...	...	309 577	2.5
	2017	297 307	23.8	...	...	...	...	312 893	2.5
	2018	...	...	...	...	...	...	...	2.4
Micronesia (Fed. States of)	2005	62	5.8	13	0.1	...	...	20	0.2
Micronésie (États féd. de)	2008	64	6.2	14	0.1	...	...	16	0.2
	2009	20	1.9	...	...	...	...	63	0.6
	2018	...	...	...	...	...	...	...	2.0
Monaco Monaco	2014	280	75.1	38	1.0	98	2.6	752	20.2
Mongolia	2002	6 732	27.6	315	0.1	901	0.4	8 826	3.6
Mongolie	2010	7 497	27.6	533	0.2	1 176	0.4	9 876	3.6
	2012	8 597	30.4	796	0.3	1 475	0.5	10 684	3.8
	2015	9 653	32.2	...	...	1 504	0.5	11 357	3.8
	2016	8 739	28.6	715	0.2	...	...	12 471	4.1
	2017	...	...	...	...	...	...	11 930	3.8
	2018	...	...	...	...	...	...	...	3.9
Montenegro	2005	1 203	19.5	...	...	...	...	3 309	5.4
Monténégro	2010	1 276	20.4	26	~0.0	...	...	3 298	5.3
	2015	1 490	23.8	25	~0.0	...	...	3 352	5.3
	2018	1 730	27.6	...	...	120	0.2	...	5.2
Morocco	2004	15 991	5.3	3 091	0.1	...	...	24 328	0.8
Maroc	2009	20 682	6.5	2 668	0.1	9 006	0.3	29 689	0.9
	2014	31 235	9.1	4 655	0.1	...	...	32 276	0.9
	2015	...	...	4 872	0.1	...	...	...	...
	2017	26 003	7.3	4 855	0.1	9 244	0.3	49 412	1.4
Mozambique	2004	514	0.3	16	~0.0	...	...	6 500	0.3
Mozambique	2005	...	...	...	...	...	...	6 771	0.3
	2010	1 145	0.5	60	~0.0	48	~0.0	9 507	0.4
	2013	1 452	0.6	136	~0.0	103	~0.0	19 073	0.7
	2015	1 103	0.4	...	...	194	~0.0	17 243	0.6
	2017	2 180	0.8	223	~0.0	255	~0.0	19 601	0.7
	2018	2 473	0.8	...	...	305	~0.0	...	0.7
Myanmar	2005	18 584	3.8	1 594	~0.0	...	...	36 521	0.7
Myanmar	2010	26 435	5.2	2 562	0.1	...	...	45 200	0.9
	2012	29 832	5.8	3 011	0.1	...	...	48 871	1.0
	2015	...	...	3 270	0.1	...	...	...	...
	2017	46 110	8.6	4 301	0.1	2 063	~0.0	53 671	1.0
	2018	36 363	6.8	...	...	3 965	0.1	...	1.0
Namibia	2004	598	3.1	82	~0.0	...	...	6 145	3.2
Namibie	2007	774	3.9	90	~0.0	239	0.1	5 750	2.9
	2015	...	...	...	...	...	...	4 365	1.9
	2017	1 421	5.9	...	...	...	...	4 853	2.0
	2018	1 024	4.2	...	...	598	0.2	...	2.0

Country or area Pays ou zone	Year Année	Physicians Médecins		Dentists Dentistes		Pharmacists Pharmaciens		Nurses and midwives Infirmières et Sages- femmes	
		Number Nombre	Per 1 000 Pour 1 000	Number Nombre	Per 1 000 Pour 1 000	Number Nombre	Per 1 000 Pour 1 000	Number Nombre	Per 1 000 Pour 1 000
Nauru Nauru	2004	10	10.1	1	0.1	...	...	63	6.4
	2008	10	10.1	1	0.1	...	...	69	7.0
	2009	10	10.1	1	0.1	...	...	...	...
	2010	11	11.0	...	...	...	...	...	...
	2015	14	13.5	2	0.2	2	0.2	70	6.7
	2018	...	...	...	...	...	...	...	7.7
Nepal Népal	2004	5 384	2.1	245	~0.0	...	...	11 825	0.5
	2012	13 925	5.2	...	...	1 200	~0.0	43 130	1.6
	2013	15 181	5.6	...	...	...	...	50 413	1.9
	2014	...	...	...	...	...	...	57 495	2.1
	2017	25 148	9.1	6 079	0.2	2 711	0.1	78 695	2.8
	2018	21 033	7.5	...	...	11 108	0.4	...	3.1
Netherlands Pays-Bas	2005	44 186	27.0	...	...	2 952	0.2	135 943	8.3
	2010	49 242	29.5	8 345	0.5	3 308	0.2	2 681	0.2
	2015	59 144	34.9	8 561	0.5	3 599	0.2	182 070	10.7
	2017	61 368	36.1	...	...	3 578	0.2	190 365	11.2
New Zealand Nouvelle-Zélande	2002	8 190	20.7	1 620	0.4	...	...	...	...
	2005	11 555	27.9	...	...	2 787	0.7	40 141	9.7
	2010	13 398	30.7	2 548	0.6	2 750	0.6	46 218	10.6
	2012	14 280	32.0	2 663	0.6	2 861	0.6	46 716	10.5
	2015	15 210	33.0	...	...	3 075	0.7	55 330	12.0
	2016	15 764	33.8	3 160	0.7	3 148	0.7	56 508	12.1
	2017	16 329	34.7	...	...	3 197	0.7	57 932	12.3
	2018	17 027	35.9	...	...	3 408	0.7	...	12.4
Nicaragua Nicaragua	2005	2 717	5.0	246	~0.0	...	...	6 294	1.2
	2010	4 239	7.3	258	~0.0	...	...	7 366	1.3
	2014	5 495	9.0	260	~0.0	1 141	0.2	8 323	1.4
	2015	5 795	9.3	...	...	...	...	8 505	1.4
	2017	6 318	9.9	...	...	...	...	9 912	1.6
	2018	6 320	9.8	254	~0.0	...	...	...	1.5
Niger Niger	2004	296	0.2	15	~0.0	...	...	2 818	0.2
	2009	439	0.3	17	~0.0	22	~0.0	3 231	0.2
	2015	944	0.5	...	...	50	~0.0	4 077	0.2
	2016	900	0.4	...	...	24	~0.0	5 602	0.3
Nigeria Nigéria	2005	39 210	2.8	2 113	~0.0	12 072	0.1	213 425	1.5
	2009	58 363	3.8	2 464	~0.0	14 353	0.1	166 173	1.1
	2010	...	...	8 359	0.1	11 598	0.1	215 055	1.4
	2013	65 759	3.8	...	...	...	...	176 195	1.0
	2015	...	...	...	...	20 035	0.1	...	...
	2016	83 565	4.5	...	...	...	...	326 376	1.8
	2018	74 543	3.8	...	...	24 668	0.1	...	1.2
Niue Nioué	2003	4	23.5	2	1.1	1	0.6	17	10.0
	2004	4	23.5	2	1.2	...	...	22	12.9
	2008	3	18.8	2	1.3	1	0.6	16	10.0
	2018	...	...	...	...	...	...	...	12.5
North Macedonia Macédoine du Nord	2005	4 392	21.3	...	...	...	...	7 012	3.4
	2010	5 541	26.8	1 599	0.8	...	...	8 681	4.2
	2015	5 975	28.7	1 824	0.9	...	...	7 884	3.8
Norway Norvège	2005	10 636	23.0	...	...	...	...	65 337	14.1
	2010	12 190	25.0	4 293	0.9	3 120	0.6	81 428	16.7
	2015	13 766	26.5	4 434	0.9	3 863	0.7	92 880	17.9
	2017	15 011	28.3	4 590	0.9	4 241	0.8	96 159	18.2
	2018	15 568	29.2	...	...	4 424	0.8	...	18.2
Oman Oman	2005	4 182	16.7	448	0.2	753	0.3	9 277	3.7
	2010	5 862	19.3	654	0.2	1 251	0.4	12 865	4.2
	2015	8 914	20.9	1 149	0.3	2 131	0.5	19 331	4.5
	2017	9 132	19.6	1 350	0.3	2 445	0.5	19 938	4.3
	2018	9 674	20.0	...	...	2 692	0.6	...	4.2

Le personnel de santé *(suite)*
Personnel de santé et densité (pour 1 000 habitants)

Country or area Pays ou zone	Year Année	Physicians Médecins Number Nombre	Per 1 000 Pour 1 000	Dentists Dentistes Number Nombre	Per 1 000 Pour 1 000	Pharmacists Pharmaciens Number Nombre	Per 1 000 Pour 1 000	Nurses and midwives Infirmières et Sages-femmes Number Nombre	Per 1 000 Pour 1 000
Pakistan	2004	116 298	7.4	6 452	~0.0	...	...	71 764	0.5
Pakistan	2005	126 350	7.9	...	...	...	...	...	...
	2010	144 901	8.1	10 508	0.1	...	...	100 397	0.6
	2012	160 880	8.6	...	...	24 907	0.1	82 119	0.4
	2015	184 711	9.3	16 652	0.1	...	...	94 766	0.5
	2017	208 007	10.0	...	...	33 455	0.2	124 445	0.6
	2018	208 007	9.8	...	...	33 455	0.2	...	0.7
Palau	2004	...	...	...	...	...	...	120	6.0
Palaos	2007	...	...	5	0.2	1	0.1	...	...
	2010	29	16.1	...	...	2	0.1	119	6.6
	2014	25	14.2	...	...	...	...	111	6.3
	2018	...	...	...	...	...	...	...	7.3
Panama	2005	4 488	13.5	938	0.3	...	...	6 675	2.0
Panama	2010	5 121	14.1	1 091	0.3	...	...	9 021	2.5
	2013	6 068	15.8	1 037	0.3	...	...	11 240	2.9
	2015	...	...	...	...	...	...	10 961	2.8
	2016	6 333	15.7	1 129	0.3	...	...	12 056	3.0
	2017	...	...	...	...	855	0.2	12 676	3.1
	2018	...	...	...	...	...	...	...	3.1
Papua New Guinea	2000	275	0.5	90	~0.0	...	...	2 841	0.5
Papouasie-Nvl-Guinée	2009	...	...	121	~0.0	...	...	...	...
	2010	376	0.5	...	...	...	...	3 643	0.5
	2012	...	...	...	...	354	~0.0	...	...
	2013	...	...	...	...	...	...	293	~0.0
	2017	...	...	...	...	568	0.1	1 901	0.2
	2018	602	0.7	...	...	115	~0.0	...	0.5
Paraguay	2002	6 355	11.5	2 426	0.4	845	0.2	10 261	1.9
Paraguay	2012	8 203	12.8	1 054	0.2	...	...	6 689	1.0
	2015	...	...	...	...	...	...	4 459	0.7
	2017	...	...	681	0.1	...	...	5 073	0.7
	2018	9 421	13.5	1 129	0.2	221	~0.0	...	1.7
Peru	2009	27 272	9.5	3 570	0.1	1 822	0.1	37 672	1.3
Pérou	2012	33 669	11.4	4 471	0.1	1 528	0.1	45 024	1.5
	2015	...	...	...	...	...	...	62 954	2.1
	2016	40 352	13.1	5 719	0.2	...	...	67 298	2.2
	2017	...	...	...	...	...	...	69 585	2.2
	2018	...	...	...	...	...	...	...	2.4
Philippines	2002	90 370	11.1	43 220	0.5	46 360	0.6	347 227	4.3
Philippines	2004	93 862	11.1	45 903	0.5	...	...	359 052	4.2
	2005	106 083	12.3	...	...	...	...	369 065	4.3
	2009	116 734	12.6	...	...	...	...	521 865	5.6
	2010	119 497	12.7	...	...	...	...	...	...
	2011	...	...	...	...	59 000	0.6	...	...
	2017	63 141	6.0	...	...	34 767	0.3	554 729	5.3
	2018	...	...	...	...	...	...	...	4.9
Poland	2005	81 600	21.3	...	...	22 091	0.6	215 213	5.6
Pologne	2010	83 201	21.7	12 549	0.3	25 203	0.7	223 385	5.8
	2015	88 437	23.3	12 603	0.3	28 121	0.7	219 845	5.8
	2016	91 730	24.2	13 308	0.3	29 268	0.8	218 723	5.8
	2017	90 284	23.8	...	...	29 330	0.8	216 442	5.7
	2018	...	...	...	...	...	...	...	6.9
Portugal	2005	36 779	35.0	5 056	0.5	5 735	0.5	48 155	4.6
Portugal	2010	42 126	39.8	8 105	0.8	7 674	0.7	62 433	5.9
	2014	47 473	45.6	9 125	0.9	8 379	0.8	66 340	6.4
	2015	49 236	47.5	...	...	8 711	0.8	67 730	6.5
	2017	52 718	51.2	...	...	9 340	0.9	71 758	7.0

Le personnel de santé *(suite)*
Personnel de santé et densité (pour 1 000 habitants)

Country or area Pays ou zone	Year Année	Physicians Médecins Number Nombre	Per 1 000 Pour 1 000	Dentists Dentistes Number Nombre	Per 1 000 Pour 1 000	Pharmacists Pharmaciens Number Nombre	Per 1 000 Pour 1 000	Nurses and midwives Infirmières et Sages- femmes Number Nombre	Per 1 000 Pour 1 000
Qatar	2005	2 150	24.8	690	0.8	1 100	1.3	4 880	5.6
Qatar	2006	2 313	22.6	486	0.5	1 056	1.0	6 185	6.0
	2010	6 919	37.3	...	...	...	...	10 615	5.7
	2014	4 267	17.4	1 662	0.7	2 136	0.9	13 771	5.6
	2016	7 152	26.9	2 155	0.8	2 757	1.0	16 968	6.4
	2018	6 913	24.9	...	...	2 474	0.9	...	7.3
Republic of Korea	2005	85 369	17.5	21 581	0.4	30 600	0.6	186 556	3.8
République de Corée	2010	98 293	19.8	20 936	0.4	32 152	0.6	229 819	4.6
	2015	114 322	22.5	23 540	0.5	33 206	0.7	304 142	6.0
	2017	120 630	23.6	25 300	0.5	36 980	0.7	363 821	7.1
	2018	...	...	...	...	...	...	...	7.3
Republic of Moldova	2005	9 892	23.8	...	...	1 650	0.4	23 490	5.6
République de Moldova	2010	9 728	23.8	1 641	0.4	1 779	0.4	23 079	5.6
	2013	10 198	25.0	1 751	0.4	1 901	0.5	22 358	5.5
	2015	10 110	24.8	1 778	0.4	...	...	20 368	5.0
	2017	13 018	32.1	...	...	1 644	0.4	19 988	4.9
Romania	2002	45 805	21.0	8 274	0.4	7 089	0.3	123 404	5.6
Roumanie	2005	47 388	22.1	...	...	9 259	0.4	123 392	5.8
	2010	50 778	24.8	12 959	0.6	13 534	0.7	116 921	5.7
	2013	52 828	26.2	14 248	0.7	16 231	0.8	123 520	6.1
	2016	44 670	22.6	15 965	0.8	18 385	0.9	120 604	6.1
	2017	58 583	29.8	...	...	17 833	0.9	145 226	7.4
Russian Federation	2005	333 378	23.2	...	...	9 479	0.1	1 110 948	7.7
Fédération de Russie	2010	343 345	23.9	41 481	0.3	8 344	0.1	1 100 625	7.7
	2014	580 311	40.1	41 113	0.3	7 115	~0.0	655 814	4.5
	2015	543 604	37.5	...	...	...	...	1 299 980	9.0
	2017	...	...	...	...	...	...	1 243 250	8.5
Rwanda	2009	...	...	72	~0.0	36	~0.0	6 639	0.7
Rwanda	2015	1 284	1.1	127	~0.0	114	~0.0	11 235	1.0
	2017	1 643	1.4	...	...	879	0.1	13 454	1.1
	2018	1 648	1.3	...	...	886	0.1	...	1.2
Saint Kitts and Nevis	2001	49	11.0	15	0.3	...	...	294	6.6
Saint-Kitts-et-Nevis	2015	137	26.8	20	0.4	...	...	216	4.2
Saint Lucia	2001	...	...	27	0.2	23	0.1	371	2.3
Sainte-Lucie	2004	68	4.2	7	~0.0	...	...	375	2.3
	2005	83	5.1	...	...	...	...	326	2.0
	2010	287	16.5	28	0.2	...	...	...	...
	2014	478	26.8	40	0.2	...	...	280	1.6
	2017	116	6.4	...	...	79	0.4	571	3.2
Saint Vincent & Grenadines	2001	62	5.8	21	0.2	23	0.2	476	4.4
Saint-Vincent-Grenadines	2004	101	9.3	13	0.1	...	...	504	4.6
	2010	72	6.7	...	...	...	...	282	2.6
	2015	...	...	...	...	...	...	1 037	9.5
	2017	...	...	...	...	...	...	693	6.3
	2018	...	...	...	...	...	...	...	7.0
Samoa	2003	50	2.8	10	0.1	20	0.1	310	1.7
Samoa	2005	50	2.8	...	...	...	...	...	...
	2008	85	4.6	17	0.1	16	0.1	348	1.9
	2010	64	3.4	45	0.2	...	...	286	1.5
	2013	92	4.8	12	0.1	14	0.1	...	...
	2014	...	...	...	...	...	...	357	1.9
	2016	67	3.5	29	0.1	...	...	...	...
	2018	...	...	...	...	...	...	...	2.5
San Marino Saint-Marin	2014	201	61.1	22	0.7	22	0.7	270	8.2
Sao Tome and Principe	2004	81	5.3	...	...	...	...	308	2.0
Sao Tomé-et-Principe	2015	63	3.2	...	...	...	...	442	2.2
	2017	11	0.5	...	...	...	...	2	~0.0
	2018	...	...	...	...	...	...	...	1.9

Country or area Pays ou zone	Year Année	Physicians Médecins Number Nombre	Per 1 000 Pour 1 000	Dentists Dentistes Number Nombre	Per 1 000 Pour 1 000	Pharmacists Pharmaciens Number Nombre	Per 1 000 Pour 1 000	Nurses and midwives Infirmières et Sages-femmes Number Nombre	Per 1 000 Pour 1 000
Saudi Arabia	2000	14 950	7.2	...	...	...	...	36 495	1.8
Arabie saoudite	2001	14 464	6.8	1 581	0.1	...	...	...	...
	2010	66 014	24.1	...	...	14 928	0.5	129 792	4.7
	2014	79 313	25.7	12 301	0.4	21 639	0.7	160 811	5.2
	2016	77 138	23.8	14 201	0.4	25 497	0.8	183 971	5.7
	2017	83 966	25.4	...	...	25 119	0.8	180 821	5.5
	2018	88 023	26.1	...	...	29 125	0.9	...	5.5
Senegal	2004	594	0.6	70	~0.0	...	...	3 287	0.3
Sénégal	2008	741	0.6	105	~0.0	107	~0.0	5 254	0.4
	2013	4 381	3.2	54	~0.0	806	0.1	23 504	1.7
	2015	3 023	2.1	...	...	143	~0.0	2 798	0.2
	2016	1 066	0.7	121	~0.0	170	~0.0	4 492	0.3
	2017	1 066	0.7	...	...	170	~0.0	4 822	0.3
Serbia	2005	20 786	22.6	...	...	...	...	7 937	0.9
Serbie	2010	22 316	24.8	2 530	0.3	...	...	7 919	0.9
	2015	21 840	24.6	1 901	0.2	...	...	67 618	7.6
	2016	27 563	31.1	4 555	0.5	7 178	0.8	53 881	6.1
Seychelles	2005	104	11.7	10	0.1	7	0.1	390	4.4
Seychelles	2010	100	11.0	19	0.2	4	~0.0	412	4.5
	2012	93	10.0	14	0.2	4	~0.0	419	4.5
	2016	203	21.2	20	0.2	45	0.5	773	8.1
Sierra Leone	2004	168	0.3	5	~0.0	...	...	2 510	0.5
Sierra Leone	2010	136	0.2	6	~0.0	33	~0.0	1 842	0.3
	2011	165	0.3	...	...	197	~0.0	1 828	0.3
	2014	...	...	...	...	...	...	7 052	1.0
	2016	...	...	...	...	82	~0.0	1 641	0.2
Singapore	2005	6 748	15.8	1 277	0.3	1 330	0.3	20 167	4.7
Singapour	2010	8 819	17.2	1 568	0.3	1 814	0.4	29 340	5.7
	2013	10 339	19.0	1 804	0.3	2 186	0.4	30 392	5.6
	2014	11 120	20.1	...	...	...	...	31 746	5.7
	2015	...	...	...	...	...	...	33 604	6.0
	2016	12 967	22.9	2 198	0.4	2 875	0.5	34 870	6.2
	2017	...	...	...	...	...	...	35 636	6.2
Slovakia	2003	17 663	32.7	...	...	2 535	0.5	36 569	6.8
Slovaquie	2005	16 318	30.2	...	...	...	...	34 038	6.3
	2009	17 798	33.0	2 633	0.5	...	...	34 477	6.4
	2010	18 110	33.5	...	...	...	...	34 619	6.4
	2015	18 719	34.4	2 647	0.5	...	...	32 664	6.0
	2017	18 608	34.2	...	...	...	...	1 736	0.3
Slovenia	2005	4 692	23.5	...	...	890	0.4	15 016	7.5
Slovénie	2010	4 979	24.4	1 259	0.6	1 102	0.5	16 871	8.3
	2015	5 830	28.2	1 392	0.7	1 295	0.6	18 277	8.8
	2016	6 224	30.0	1 421	0.7	1 356	0.7	20 114	9.7
	2017	6 408	30.9	...	...	1 422	0.7	20 711	10.0
Solomon Islands	2005	89	1.9	52	0.1	53	0.1	694	1.5
Îles Salomon	2008	89	1.8	...	...	...	...	...	...
	2009	...	...	...	...	...	...	1 080	2.1
	2013	107	1.9	27	~0.0	75	0.1	1 139	2.0
	2016	120	1.9	29	~0.0	74	0.1	...	...
	2018	...	...	...	...	...	...	...	2.2
Somalia	2006	300	0.3	...	...	...	...	965	0.1
Somalie	2014	309	0.2	...	...	...	...	1 502	0.1
South Africa	2004	34 829	7.4	5 577	0.1	...	...	184 459	3.9
Afrique du Sud	2005	...	...	...	...	...	...	37 085	0.8
	2010	37 599	7.3	5 296	0.1	...	...	52 370	1.0
	2015	43 277	7.8	5 985	0.1	15 784	0.3	70 300	1.3
	2016	44 949	8.0	6 333	0.1	15 267	0.3	74 842	1.3
	2017	51 616	9.1	8 586	0.2	...	...	74 556	1.3

Health Personnel *(continued)*
Number of health workers and workforce density (per 1 000 population)

Le personnel de santé *(suite)*
Personnel de santé et densité (pour 1 000 habitants)

Country or area Pays ou zone	Year Année	Physicians Médecins		Dentists Dentistes		Pharmacists Pharmaciens		Nurses and midwives Infirmières et Sages- femmes	
		Number Nombre	Per 1 000 Pour 1 000	Number Nombre	Per 1 000 Pour 1 000	Number Nombre	Per 1 000 Pour 1 000	Number Nombre	Per 1 000 Pour 1 000
Spain	2005	121 515	27.6	22 150	0.5	37 433	0.9	190 400	4.3
Espagne	2010	142 162	30.3	27 826	0.6	43 000	0.9	239 867	5.1
	2014	148 086	31.7	33 286	0.7	54 567	1.2	239 333	5.1
	2015	150 127	32.2	...	...	55 400	1.2	245 533	5.3
	2017	180 633	38.7	...	...	53 867	1.2	267 266	5.7
Sri Lanka	2005	10 198	5.2	954	~0.0	...	...	27 514	1.4
Sri Lanka	2007	11 023	5.6	1 314	0.1	886	~0.0	40 678	2.1
	2010	14 668	7.2	1 046	0.1	...	...	35 367	1.7
	2015	18 032	8.6	1 340	0.1	1 504	0.1	40 993	2.0
	2016	18 761	8.9	1 900	0.1	1 546	0.1	40 942	1.9
	2017	19 601	9.3	...	...	1 626	0.1	42 185	2.0
	2018	21 316	10.0	...	...	1 750	0.1	...	2.2
State of Palestine	2014	5 000	...	...	...	...	...	1 100	...
État de Palestine	2017	16 678	...	...	...	...	...	12 093	...
	2018	10 417	...	...	...	...	...	...	...
Sudan	2004	7 552	0.2	701	~0.0	...	...	31 496	1.0
Soudan	2008	10 813	0.3	772	~0.0	386	~0.0	32 439	1.0
	2015	15 845	4.1	8 116	0.2	17 005	0.4	32 077	0.8
	2017	10 683	2.6	...	...	1 027	~0.0	28 372	0.7
Sudan [former]	2004	7 552	2.5	...	...	...	...	...	...
Soudan [anc.]	2008	10 813	3.3	...	...	...	...	...	...
Suriname	2004	400	8.1	42	0.1	...	...	2 580	5.2
Suriname	2009	369	7.1	25	~0.0	31	0.1	1 602	3.1
	2015	585	10.5	...	...	...	...	1 167	2.1
	2017	676	11.9	...	...	...	...	1 100	1.9
	2018	697	12.1	...	...	...	...	...	2.8
Sweden	2005	31 732	35.1	...	...	6 868	0.8	102 846	11.4
Suède	2010	36 414	38.8	7 546	0.8	7 084	0.8	110 337	11.8
	2015	41 848	42.9	7 813	0.8	7 427	0.8	114 468	11.7
	2016	39 187	39.8	...	...	7 603	0.8	115 622	11.8
	2017	...	...	...	...	...	...	117 040	11.8
Switzerland	2005	28 223	38.2	...	...	4 487	0.6	96 052	13.0
Suisse	2010	29 803	38.2	4 109	0.5	4 973	0.6	116 807	15.0
	2015	34 762	41.9	4 200	0.5	5 339	0.6	139 899	16.9
	2016	35 592	42.5	4 217	0.5	5 863	0.7	145 205	17.3
	2017	36 324	43.0	...	...	5 889	0.7	148 278	17.5
Syrian Arab Republic	2005	28 247	15.4	15 725	0.9	13 218	0.7	34 604	1.9
République arabe syrienne	2010	31 194	14.6	15 984	0.8	16 554	0.8	40 053	1.9
	2014	29 025	15.5	16 585	0.9	27 715	1.5	43 210	2.3
	2016	22 485	12.9	12 532	0.7	18 614	1.1	26 908	1.5
Tajikistan	2003	12 688	19.4	...	...	680	0.1	23 320	3.6
Tadjikistan	2005	13 272	19.6	...	...	...	...	23 518	3.5
	2010	12 778	17.0	1 234	0.2	...	...	29 742	4.0
	2014	17 352	21.0	1 289	0.2	...	...	39 229	4.8
Thailand	2002	18 987	3.0	4 471	0.1	7 350	0.1	84 683	1.3
Thaïlande	2004	18 918	2.9	4 129	0.1	...	...	96 704	1.5
	2010	26 244	3.9	11 847	0.2	8 700	0.1	138 710	2.1
	2015	31 959	4.7	...	...	12 231	0.2	162 734	2.4
	2017	55 890	8.1	11 575	0.2	28 896	0.4	204 675	3.0
	2018	55 890	8.1	...	...	38 398	0.6	...	2.8
Timor-Leste	2004	...	...	2	~0.0	...	...	1 795	1.8
Timor-Leste	2010	...	...	7	~0.0	15	~0.0	1 255	1.1
	2015	831	7.0	18	~0.0	10	~0.0	1 773	1.5
	2017	933	7.5	85	0.1	254	0.2	2 165	1.7
	2018	916	7.2	...	...	...	...	...	1.7
Togo	2004	244	0.5	18	~0.0	...	...	1 937	0.4
Togo	2008	349	0.6	15	~0.0	11	~0.0	1 816	0.3
	2010	1 640	2.6	66	~0.0	...	...	9 386	1.5
	2015	361	0.5	18	~0.0	17	~0.0	2 210	0.3
	2017	230	0.3	...	...	218	~0.0	3 234	0.4
	2018	611	0.8	...	...	213	~0.0	...	0.4

Health Personnel *(continued)*
Number of health workers and workforce density (per 1 000 population)

Le personnel de santé *(suite)*
Personnel de santé et densité (pour 1 000 habitants)

Country or area Pays ou zone	Year Année	Physicians Médecins		Dentists Dentistes		Pharmacists Pharmaciens		Nurses and midwives Infirmières et Sages-femmes	
		Number Nombre	Per 1 000 Pour 1 000	Number Nombre	Per 1 000 Pour 1 000	Number Nombre	Per 1 000 Pour 1 000	Number Nombre	Per 1 000 Pour 1 000
Tonga Tonga	2001	35	3.6	33	0.3	17	0.2	341	3.5
	2002	30	3.0	...	...	...	...	350	3.5
	2003	...	...	23	0.2	...	...	...	...
	2010	58	5.6	10	0.1	4	~0.0	400	3.8
	2013	55	5.4	12	0.1	4	~0.0	408	4.0
	2018	...	...	...	...	...	...	...	4.2
Trinidad and Tobago Trinité-et-Tobago	2003	1 038	8.1	249	0.2	525	0.4	3 980	3.1
	2010	2 402	18.1	343	0.3	641	0.5	3 905	2.9
	2011	2 431	18.2	343	0.3	650	0.5	4 379	3.3
	2015	3 631	26.5	489	0.4	...	...	4 773	3.5
	2017	4 657	33.7	...	...	928	0.7	7 812	5.6
	2018	5 792	41.7	...	...	923	0.7	...	4.1
Tunisia Tunisie	2004	13 330	13.3	2 100	0.2	...	...	28 537	2.8
	2005	9 422	9.3	1 850	0.2	2 114	0.2	...	...
	2010	12 996	12.2	3 130	0.3	3 236	0.3	23 836	2.2
	2015	14 655	13.1	3 494	0.3	2 592	0.2	29 851	2.7
	2017	14 892	13.0	...	...	2 615	0.2	28 739	2.5
Turkey Turquie	2005	100 853	14.9	18 149	0.3	22 756	0.3	121 723	1.8
	2010	123 447	17.1	21 432	0.3	26 506	0.4	165 115	2.3
	2015	141 259	18.0	24 834	0.3	27 530	0.4	205 889	2.6
	2017	149 997	18.5	...	...	28 512	0.4	219 883	2.7
Turkmenistan Turkménistan	2002	32 706	71.0	876	0.2	1 240	0.3	31 271	6.8
	2005	11 905	25.0	...	...	986	0.2	23 519	4.9
	2010	11 570	22.7	586	0.1	928	0.2	22 961	4.5
	2014	12 161	22.3	631	0.1	926	0.2	24 201	4.4
Tuvalu Tuvalu	2003	...	10.3	2	0.2	...	...	...	...
	2008	...	9.7	2	0.2	...	...	...	...
	2009	...	11.5	...	...	...	...	...	...
	2014	...	9.1	5	0.5	...	...	...	...
	2018	...	...	...	...	...	...	...	4.3
Uganda Ouganda	2005	3 361	1.2	98	~0.0	162	~0.0	37 625	1.4
	2015	3 645	1.0	276	~0.0	45	~0.0	59 496	1.6
	2017	6 918	1.7	...	...	...	...	60 456	1.5
	2018	...	...	...	...	...	...	...	1.2
Ukraine Ukraine	2005	141 521	30.2	...	...	1 185	~0.0	311 390	6.6
	2010	159 495	34.8	30 147	0.7	1 818	~0.0	342 156	7.5
	2014	134 986	29.9	26 954	0.6	1 521	~0.0	300 489	6.7
United Arab Emirates Émirats arabes unis	2005	6 971	15.2	1 414	0.3	2 790	0.6	13 764	3.0
	2010	12 137	14.2	3 081	0.4	1 528	0.2	22 682	2.7
	2015	20 481	22.1	4 916	0.5	5 247	0.6	46 155	5.0
	2016	22 195	23.7	5 165	0.6	6 871	0.7	51 777	5.5
	2017	23 107	24.4	...	...	7 930	0.8	53 915	5.7
	2018	24 345	25.3	...	...	8 469	0.9	...	5.7
United Kingdom Royaume-Uni	2005	145 413	24.1	...	...	36 467	0.6	581 718	9.6
	2010	166 674	26.3	32 423	0.5	40 641	0.6	557 747	8.8
	2015	180 888	27.5	34 621	0.5	54 380	0.8	546 220	8.3
	2017	185 921	27.9	34 760	0.5	58 329	0.9	548 798	8.2
	2018	188 783	28.1	...	...	59 704	0.9	...	8.2
United Rep. of Tanzania Rép.-Unie de Tanzanie	2002	822	0.2	147	~0.0	111	~0.0	13 292	0.4
	2006	...	...	43	~0.0	...	...	9 440	0.2
	2014	3 015	0.6	104	~0.0	707	~0.0	21 552	0.4
	2016	742	0.1	...	...	...	...	...	...
	2017	...	...	...	...	...	...	31 940	0.6
United States of America États-Unis d'Amérique	2005	718 473	24.4	179 414	0.6	259 259	0.9	...	...
	2010	752 572	24.4	178 559	0.6	285 794	0.9	3 891 298	12.6
	2015	827 261	25.8	195 156	0.6	...	...	...	...
	2017	849 126	26.1	...	...	...	...	4 729 338	14.5
Uruguay Uruguay	2002	12 384	37.2	3 936	1.2	...	...	2 880	0.9
	2008	13 197	39.5	2 476	0.7	...	...	19 595	5.9
	2017	17 456	50.8	5 115	1.5	...	...	6 671	1.9

Health Personnel *(continued)*
Number of health workers and workforce density (per 1 000 population)

Le personnel de santé *(suite)*
Personnel de santé et densité (pour 1 000 habitants)

Country or area Pays ou zone	Year Année	Physicians Médecins		Dentists Dentistes		Pharmacists Pharmaciens		Nurses and midwives Infirmières et Sages- femmes	
		Number Nombre	Per 1 000 Pour 1 000	Number Nombre	Per 1 000 Pour 1 000	Number Nombre	Per 1 000 Pour 1 000	Number Nombre	Per 1 000 Pour 1 000
Uzbekistan	2005	70 564	26.7	...	...	828	~0.0	290 162	11.0
Ouzbékistan	2010	72 522	25.4	4 693	0.2	1 074	~0.0	324 493	11.4
	2014	72 237	23.7	4 520	0.1	1 243	~0.0	343 223	11.3
Vanuatu	2004	30	1.5	...	...	...	...	360	1.8
Vanuatu	2008	26	1.2	3	~0.0	2	~0.0	380	1.7
	2012	46	1.8	17	0.1	29	0.1	459	1.8
	2016	46	1.7	...	...	...	...	...	...
	2018	...	...	...	...	...	...	...	1.4
Venezuela (Boliv. Rep. of)	2001	48 000	19.5	13 680	0.5	...	...	28 000	1.1
Venezuela (Rép. boliv. du)	2018	...	...	...	...	...	...		0.9
Viet Nam	2005	51 466	6.1	...	...	15 090	0.2	69 665	0.8
Viet Nam	2010	62 458	7.1	...	...	23 494	0.3	108 435	1.2
	2015	73 797	8.0	...	...	31 535	0.3	131 858	1.4
	2016	77 539	8.3	...	...	31 719	0.3	135 432	1.4
Yemen	2004	6 739	3.5	478	~0.0	...	...	13 746	0.7
Yémen	2009	7 127	3.2	...	...	...	...	...	...
	2010	...	...	573	~0.0	1 010	~0.0	16 590	0.7
	2014	13 560	5.3	543	~0.0	2 716	0.1	22 696	0.9
	2015	...	...	...	...	...	...	19 190	0.7
	2017	...	...	...	...	...	...	21 384	0.8
	2018	...	...	...	...	...	...	...	0.8
Zambia	2004	1 499	1.3	269	~0.0	...	...	...	...
Zambie	2005	646	0.6	...	...	...	...	8 369	0.7
	2010	836	0.6	246	~0.0	317	~0.0	9 932	0.7
	2012	2 399	1.7	77	~0.0	409	~0.0	...	...
	2013	...	...	...	...	...	...	2 773	0.2
	2016	2 664	1.6	312	~0.0	1 159	0.1	3 333	0.2
	2017	...	...	...	...	...	...	21 890	1.3
	2018	20 591	11.9	...	...	771	~0.0	...	1.3
Zimbabwe	2005	1 516	1.3	...	...	...	...	...	...
Zimbabwe	2010	1 615	1.3	239	~0.0	55	~0.0	10 525	0.8
	2014	1 685	1.2	250	~0.0	193	~0.0	20 885	1.5
	2015	2 508	1.8	...	...	141	~0.0	19 099	1.4
	2017	2 646	1.9	...	...	272	~0.0	36 976	2.6
	2018	3 026	2.1	...	...	1 397	0.1	...	1.9

Source:

World Health Organisation (WHO), Geneva, WHO Global Health
Workforce statistics database, last accessed April 2020.

Source:

Organisation mondiale de la santé (OMS), Genève, base de données de
l'OMS sur les statistiques relatives aux personnels de santé, dernier accès
avril 2020.

Region, country or area[&]	2000	2005	2010	2015	2016	2017	Région, pays ou zone[&]
Afghanistan							**Afghanistan**
Current expenditure (% GDP)	...	9.9	8.6	10.1	11.0	11.8	Dépenses courantes (% du PIB)
Domestic General govt.(% expend. total)	...	3.4	2.3	2.0	2.1	2.3	Dépenses intérieures (en % du totale)
Albania							**Albanie**
Domestic General govt.(% expend. total)	8.0	9.3	15.2	14.6	15.1	14.7	Dépenses intérieures (en % du totale)
Algeria							**Algérie**
Current expenditure (% GDP)	3.5	3.2	5.1	7.0	6.6	6.4	Dépenses courantes (% du PIB)
Domestic General govt.(% expend. total)	8.8	8.3	9.5	10.7	10.7	10.7	Dépenses intérieures (en % du totale)
Andorra							**Andorre**
Current expenditure (% GDP)	9.3	8.6	9.4	10.3	10.3	10.3	Dépenses courantes (% du PIB)
Domestic General govt.(% expend. total)	13.0	11.0	10.9	15.2	14.0	14.0	Dépenses intérieures (en % du totale)
Angola							**Angola**
Current expenditure (% GDP)	1.9	2.9	2.7	2.6	2.7	2.8	Dépenses courantes (% du PIB)
Domestic General govt.(% expend. total)	2.7	4.8	4.2	4.6	5.4	5.4	Dépenses intérieures (en % du totale)
Antigua and Barbuda							**Antigua-et-Barbuda**
Current expenditure (% GDP)	* 4.5	* 5.0	* 5.2	* 4.7	* 4.4	* 4.5	Dépenses courantes (% du PIB)
Domestic General govt.(% expend. total)	* 11.0	* 11.4	* 13.1	* 9.9	* 8.9	* 9.5	Dépenses intérieures (en % du totale)
Argentina							**Argentine**
Current expenditure (% GDP)	8.5	7.6	8.6	8.8	7.5	9.1	Dépenses courantes (% du PIB)
Domestic General govt.(% expend. total)	17.8	16.0	16.7	16.5	13.5	16.1	Dépenses intérieures (en % du totale)
Armenia							**Arménie**
Current expenditure (% GDP)	4.2	5.9	9.2	10.1	10.0	10.4	Dépenses courantes (% du PIB)
Domestic General govt.(% expend. total)	3.9	7.4	6.4	6.1	6.1	5.3	Dépenses intérieures (en % du totale)
Australia							**Australie**
Current expenditure (% GDP)	* 7.6	* 8.0	* 8.4	* 9.3	* 9.2	* 9.2	Dépenses courantes (% du PIB)
Domestic General govt.(% expend. total)	* 15.2	* 16.3	* 16.3	* 17.2	* 17.5	* 17.8	Dépenses intérieures (en % du totale)
Austria							**Autriche**
Current expenditure (% GDP)	* 9.2	* 9.6	* 10.2	* 10.4	* 10.4	* 10.4	Dépenses courantes (% du PIB)
Domestic General govt.(% expend. total)	* 13.4	* 13.7	* 14.0	* 14.7	* 15.0	* 15.3	Dépenses intérieures (en % du totale)
Azerbaijan							**Azerbaïdjan**
Current expenditure (% GDP)	* 3.9	* 7.4	* 4.8	* 6.7	* 6.7	* 6.7	Dépenses courantes (% du PIB)
Domestic General govt.(% expend. total)	* 4.8	* 4.1	* 3.2	* 3.4	* 3.3	* 2.8	Dépenses intérieures (en % du totale)
Bahamas							**Bahamas**
Current expenditure (% GDP)	4.0	4.7	5.9	5.7	6.1	# 5.8	Dépenses courantes (% du PIB)
Domestic General govt.(% expend. total)	16.2	16.7	17.3	15.9	16.0	# 11.3	Dépenses intérieures (en % du totale)
Bahrain							**Bahreïn**
Current expenditure (% GDP)	3.6	3.2	3.8	5.0	4.9	4.7	Dépenses courantes (% du PIB)
Domestic General govt.(% expend. total)	10.2	8.6	8.5	8.8	8.5	8.5	Dépenses intérieures (en % du totale)
Bangladesh [1]							**Bangladesh** [1]
Current expenditure (% GDP)	* 2.0	* 2.3	2.5	2.5	* 2.3	2.3	Dépenses courantes (% du PIB)
Domestic General govt.(% expend. total)	* 5.2	* 4.4	4.4	3.4	* 3.0	3.0	Dépenses intérieures (en % du totale)
Barbados							**Barbade**
Current expenditure (% GDP)	5.3	6.8	6.8	7.0	6.9	6.8	Dépenses courantes (% du PIB)
Domestic General govt.(% expend. total)	12.3	11.8	10.4	9.1	9.3	9.1	Dépenses intérieures (en % du totale)
Belarus							**Bélarus**
Current expenditure (% GDP)	5.5	6.3	5.7	6.1	* 5.9	* 5.9	Dépenses courantes (% du PIB)
Domestic General govt.(% expend. total)	12.1	10.1	8.7	8.8	* 10.3	* 10.6	Dépenses intérieures (en % du totale)
Belgium							**Belgique**
Current expenditure (% GDP)	* 7.9	* 9.0	* 10.0	* 10.3	* 10.3	* 10.3	Dépenses courantes (% du PIB)
Domestic General govt.(% expend. total)	* 12.1	* 13.4	* 14.5	* 14.8	* 15.0	* 15.3	Dépenses intérieures (en % du totale)
Belize							**Belize**
Current expenditure (% GDP)	4.1	4.7	5.8	5.9	6.1	5.6	Dépenses courantes (% du PIB)
Domestic General govt.(% expend. total)	6.6	9.5	13.1	11.8	11.8	11.0	Dépenses intérieures (en % du totale)
Benin							**Bénin**
Current expenditure (% GDP)	4.2	4.0	4.1	4.0	3.9	3.7	Dépenses courantes (% du PIB)
Domestic General govt.(% expend. total)	5.2	4.8	5.1	3.2	3.7	4.6	Dépenses intérieures (en % du totale)
Bhutan [1]							**Bhoutan** [1]
Current expenditure (% GDP)	* 4.3	* 4.0	* 3.5	* 3.7	* 3.5	* 3.2	Dépenses courantes (% du PIB)
Domestic General govt.(% expend. total)	* 7.6	* 6.8	* 5.6	* 10.0	* 8.3	* 7.9	Dépenses intérieures (en % du totale)
Bolivia (Plurin. State of)							**Bolivie (État plurin. de)**
Current expenditure (% GDP)	4.4	5.1	5.5	6.6	6.9	6.4	Dépenses courantes (% du PIB)
Domestic General govt.(% expend. total)	8.3	8.3	9.7	9.7	11.1	11.5	Dépenses intérieures (en % du totale)

Region, country or area[&]	2000	2005	2010	2015	2016	2017	Région, pays ou zone[&]
Bosnia and Herzegovina							**Bosnie-Herzégovine**
Current expenditure (% GDP)	7.7	9.1	9.0	9.3	9.2	8.9	Dépenses courantes (% du PIB)
Domestic General govt.(% expend. total)	7.3	10.8	12.4	15.2	15.5	15.5	Dépenses intérieures (en % du totale)
Botswana							**Botswana**
Current expenditure (% GDP)	5.8	5.0	6.2	5.7	5.6	6.1	Dépenses courantes (% du PIB)
Domestic General govt.(% expend. total)	8.2	8.2	8.1	10.4	11.2	14.3	Dépenses intérieures (en % du totale)
Brazil							**Brésil**
Current expenditure (% GDP)	8.3	8.0	7.9	8.9	9.2	9.5	Dépenses courantes (% du PIB)
Domestic General govt.(% expend. total)	10.1	8.4	9.2	9.8	9.9	10.3	Dépenses intérieures (en % du totale)
Brunei Darussalam [2]							**Brunéi Darussalam** [2]
Current expenditure (% GDP)	2.5	2.2	2.3	2.4	2.5	2.4	Dépenses courantes (% du PIB)
Domestic General govt.(% expend. total)	5.7	6.4	5.8	5.9	6.2	6.2	Dépenses intérieures (en % du totale)
Bulgaria [3]							**Bulgarie** [3]
Current expenditure (% GDP)	5.9	6.9	7.1	8.2	8.2	8.1	Dépenses courantes (% du PIB)
Domestic General govt.(% expend. total)	8.5	11.2	10.9	10.3	11.9	12.0	Dépenses intérieures (en % du totale)
Burkina Faso							**Burkina Faso**
Current expenditure (% GDP)	3.3	4.4	5.9	5.8	7.0	6.9	Dépenses courantes (% du PIB)
Domestic General govt.(% expend. total)	4.8	6.0	6.0	7.2	11.0	10.0	Dépenses intérieures (en % du totale)
Burundi							**Burundi**
Current expenditure (% GDP)	* 6.2	* 8.4	* 11.3	* 6.6	* 7.5	* 7.5	Dépenses courantes (% du PIB)
Domestic General govt.(% expend. total)	* 5.9	* 6.2	* 4.9	* 9.2	* 8.5	* 8.5	Dépenses intérieures (en % du totale)
Cabo Verde							**Cabo Verde**
Current expenditure (% GDP)	4.4	4.3	4.5	4.8	4.8	5.2	Dépenses courantes (% du PIB)
Domestic General govt.(% expend. total)	7.5	8.8	7.2	10.1	10.4	9.9	Dépenses intérieures (en % du totale)
Cambodia [1,4]							**Cambodge** [1,4]
Current expenditure (% GDP)	6.5	6.9	6.9	6.2	6.1	5.9	Dépenses courantes (% du PIB)
Domestic General govt.(% expend. total)	8.6	9.9	6.5	6.4	6.0	6.1	Dépenses intérieures (en % du totale)
Cameroon							**Cameroun**
Current expenditure (% GDP)	* 4.0	* 4.1	* 4.5	* 4.7	* 4.7	* 4.7	Dépenses courantes (% du PIB)
Domestic General govt.(% expend. total)	* 4.4	* 5.2	* 5.1	* 3.3	* 3.0	* 3.1	Dépenses intérieures (en % du totale)
Canada							**Canada**
Current expenditure (% GDP)	8.3	9.1	10.7	10.5	10.7	10.6	Dépenses courantes (% du PIB)
Domestic General govt.(% expend. total)	14.8	17.1	18.3	19.6	19.5	19.3	Dépenses intérieures (en % du totale)
Central African Republic							**République centrafricaine**
Current expenditure (% GDP)	* 4.4	* 4.8	* 3.7	* 6.3	* 4.3	* 5.8	Dépenses courantes (% du PIB)
Domestic General govt.(% expend. total)	* 10.9	* 9.8	* 5.7	* 3.5	* 5.0	* 5.0	Dépenses intérieures (en % du totale)
Chad							**Tchad**
Current expenditure (% GDP)	* 5.5	* 4.8	* 4.1	* 4.5	* 5.0	* 4.5	Dépenses courantes (% du PIB)
Domestic General govt.(% expend. total)	* 11.4	* 12.4	* 3.5	* 5.2	* 5.7	* 4.7	Dépenses intérieures (en % du totale)
Chile							**Chili**
Current expenditure (% GDP)	7.0	6.6	6.8	8.3	8.5	9.0	Dépenses courantes (% du PIB)
Domestic General govt.(% expend. total)	11.0	12.9	13.7	16.0	16.7	17.7	Dépenses intérieures (en % du totale)
China							**Chine**
Current expenditure (% GDP)	* 4.5	* 4.1	* 4.2	* 4.9	* 5.0	* 5.2	Dépenses courantes (% du PIB)
Domestic General govt.(% expend. total)	* 6.1	* 7.5	* 8.8	* 9.4	* 9.1	* 9.1	Dépenses intérieures (en % du totale)
Colombia							**Colombie**
Current expenditure (% GDP)	* 5.7	* 6.1	* 7.1	* 7.3	* 7.2	* 7.2	Dépenses courantes (% du PIB)
Domestic General govt.(% expend. total)	* 14.9	* 16.8	* 17.3	* 17.2	* 18.0	* 17.5	Dépenses intérieures (en % du totale)
Comoros							**Comores**
Current expenditure (% GDP)	* 12.2	* 9.9	* 8.5	* 7.8	* 7.5	* 7.4	Dépenses courantes (% du PIB)
Domestic General govt.(% expend. total)	* 9.7	* 6.7	* 3.5	* 3.8	* 3.6	* 3.4	Dépenses intérieures (en % du totale)
Congo							**Congo**
Current expenditure (% GDP)	1.7	1.9	2.0	3.4	3.5	2.9	Dépenses courantes (% du PIB)
Domestic General govt.(% expend. total)	2.3	2.0	3.6	2.7	2.9	3.4	Dépenses intérieures (en % du totale)
Cook Islands [1]							**Îles Cook** [1]
Current expenditure (% GDP)	3.2	4.2	3.5	2.9	3.5	3.3	Dépenses courantes (% du PIB)
Domestic General govt.(% expend. total)	9.6	9.6	9.3	5.2	5.7	5.7	Dépenses intérieures (en % du totale)
Costa Rica							**Costa Rica**
Current expenditure (% GDP)	6.6	6.7	8.1	7.8	7.5	7.3	Dépenses courantes (% du PIB)
Domestic General govt.(% expend. total)	25.3	25.7	31.7	29.5	28.6	26.9	Dépenses intérieures (en % du totale)
Côte d'Ivoire							**Côte d'Ivoire**
Current expenditure (% GDP)	5.6	5.3	6.1	4.4	4.5	4.5	Dépenses courantes (% du PIB)
Domestic General govt.(% expend. total)	4.6	3.9	4.1	4.7	4.8	5.1	Dépenses intérieures (en % du totale)
Croatia							**Croatie**
Current expenditure (% GDP)	7.7	6.9	8.1	# 6.8[5]	6.8[5]	6.8[5]	Dépenses courantes (% du PIB)
Domestic General govt.(% expend. total)	14.6	12.5	14.1	# 11.7[5]	11.9[5]	12.4[5]	Dépenses intérieures (en % du totale)

Region, country or area&	2000	2005	2010	2015	2016	2017	Région, pays ou zone&
Cuba							**Cuba**
Current expenditure (% GDP)	6.6	8.8	10.7	12.8	12.2	11.7	Dépenses courantes (% du PIB)
Domestic General govt.(% expend. total)	10.8	11.7	13.9	18.2	17.3	15.9	Dépenses intérieures (en % du totale)
Cyprus							**Chypre**
Current expenditure (% GDP)	5.3	5.4	6.3	6.8	6.8	6.7	Dépenses courantes (% du PIB)
Domestic General govt.(% expend. total)	6.3	5.7	7.1	7.1	7.5	7.6	Dépenses intérieures (en % du totale)
Czechia							**Tchéquie**
Current expenditure (% GDP)	* 5.7	* 6.4	* 6.9	* 7.2	* 7.1	* 7.2	Dépenses courantes (% du PIB)
Domestic General govt.(% expend. total)	* 12.4	* 12.9	* 13.2	* 14.3	* 14.8	* 15.2	Dépenses intérieures (en % du totale)
Dem. Rep. of the Congo							**Rép. dém. du Congo**
Current expenditure (% GDP)	1.6	4.3	4.0	3.9	3.9	4.0	Dépenses courantes (% du PIB)
Domestic General govt.(% expend. total)	2.5	2.5	2.5	3.8	3.9	3.3	Dépenses intérieures (en % du totale)
Denmark							**Danemark**
Current expenditure (% GDP)	8.1	9.1	10.3	10.2	10.2	10.1	Dépenses courantes (% du PIB)
Domestic General govt.(% expend. total)	12.8	14.9	15.3	15.8	16.3	16.6	Dépenses intérieures (en % du totale)
Djibouti							**Djibouti**
Current expenditure (% GDP)	4.1	4.5	4.3	4.4	3.7	3.3	Dépenses courantes (% du PIB)
Domestic General govt.(% expend. total)	6.1	5.3	7.0	4.1	4.1	4.1	Dépenses intérieures (en % du totale)
Dominica							**Dominique**
Current expenditure (% GDP)	5.2	5.2	5.6	5.4	5.2	5.9	Dépenses courantes (% du PIB)
Domestic General govt.(% expend. total)	8.4	9.5	8.3	10.6	8.0	7.3	Dépenses intérieures (en % du totale)
Dominican Republic							**République dominicaine**
Current expenditure (% GDP)	4.9	4.4	5.6	6.0	6.1	6.1	Dépenses courantes (% du PIB)
Domestic General govt.(% expend. total)	11.8	9.2	15.9	14.0	16.0	15.6	Dépenses intérieures (en % du totale)
Ecuador							**Équateur**
Current expenditure (% GDP)	3.3	5.6	7.1	8.6	8.3	8.3	Dépenses courantes (% du PIB)
Domestic General govt.(% expend. total)	4.1	7.9	9.2	10.7	11.0	11.9	Dépenses intérieures (en % du totale)
Egypt							**Égypte**
Current expenditure (% GDP)	4.9	4.9	4.2	5.3	5.4	5.3	Dépenses courantes (% du PIB)
Domestic General govt.(% expend. total)	6.7	5.2	4.4	5.1	5.1	5.4	Dépenses intérieures (en % du totale)
El Salvador							**El Salvador**
Current expenditure (% GDP)	8.9	8.4	8.2	7.6	7.7	7.2	Dépenses courantes (% du PIB)
Domestic General govt.(% expend. total)	18.5	19.6	17.7	20.8	20.9	19.2	Dépenses intérieures (en % du totale)
Equatorial Guinea							**Guinée équatoriale**
Current expenditure (% GDP)	* 2.3	* 1.5	* 1.8	* 2.9	* 3.2	* 3.1	Dépenses courantes (% du PIB)
Domestic General govt.(% expend. total)	* 1.4	* 1.5	* 1.5	* 1.3	* 2.5	* 2.9	Dépenses intérieures (en % du totale)
Eritrea							**Érythrée**
Current expenditure (% GDP)	* 4.5	* 5.3	* 3.5	* 2.9	* 2.9	* 2.9	Dépenses courantes (% du PIB)
Domestic General govt.(% expend. total)	* 2.1	* 1.1	* 1.5	* 1.2	* 2.9	* 2.7	Dépenses intérieures (en % du totale)
Estonia							**Estonie**
Current expenditure (% GDP)	5.2	5.1	6.3	6.4	6.5	6.4	Dépenses courantes (% du PIB)
Domestic General govt.(% expend. total)	10.8	11.1	11.6	12.1	12.4	12.2	Dépenses intérieures (en % du totale)
Eswatini							**Eswatini**
Current expenditure (% GDP)	4.6	7.4	8.6	7.1	6.8	6.9	Dépenses courantes (% du PIB)
Domestic General govt.(% expend. total)	9.8	12.6	13.8	8.7	7.8	10.0	Dépenses intérieures (en % du totale)
Ethiopia							**Éthiopie**
Current expenditure (% GDP)	4.4	4.1	5.5	3.9	3.9	3.5	Dépenses courantes (% du PIB)
Domestic General govt.(% expend. total)	7.0	7.5	5.1	5.6	5.0	4.8	Dépenses intérieures (en % du totale)
Fiji							**Fidji**
Current expenditure (% GDP)	* 3.7	* 3.6	* 3.7	* 3.6	* 3.5	* 3.5	Dépenses courantes (% du PIB)
Domestic General govt.(% expend. total)	* 10.6	* 10.4	* 8.6	* 7.0	* 7.7	* 7.2	Dépenses intérieures (en % du totale)
Finland							**Finlande**
Current expenditure (% GDP)	6.8	8.0	8.9	9.7	9.4	9.2	Dépenses courantes (% du PIB)
Domestic General govt.(% expend. total)	10.6	12.5	12.5	13.2	12.9	13.0	Dépenses intérieures (en % du totale)
France							**France**
Current expenditure (% GDP)	9.6	10.2	11.2	11.5	11.5	11.3	Dépenses courantes (% du PIB)
Domestic General govt.(% expend. total)	14.6	15.1	15.1	15.5	15.6	15.5	Dépenses intérieures (en % du totale)
Gabon							**Gabon**
Current expenditure (% GDP)	2.9	2.9	2.5	2.7	3.1	2.8	Dépenses courantes (% du PIB)
Domestic General govt.(% expend. total)	5.2	5.1	6.8	7.0	9.2	9.7	Dépenses intérieures (en % du totale)
Gambia							**Gambie**
Current expenditure (% GDP)	2.7	2.8	3.4	3.1	3.0	3.3	Dépenses courantes (% du PIB)
Domestic General govt.(% expend. total)	6.9	10.4	7.8	2.8	3.1	3.1	Dépenses intérieures (en % du totale)
Georgia [6]							**Géorgie** [6]
Current expenditure (% GDP)	7.4	8.3	9.5	7.9	8.4	7.6	Dépenses courantes (% du PIB)
Domestic General govt.(% expend. total)	4.9	5.6	6.2	9.6	10.3	9.5	Dépenses intérieures (en % du totale)

Region, country or area&	2000	2005	2010	2015	2016	2017	Région, pays ou zone&
Germany							**Allemagne**
Current expenditure (% GDP)	9.8	10.2	11.0	11.1	11.1	11.2	Dépenses courantes (% du PIB)
Domestic General govt.(% expend. total)	17.2	16.8	17.6	19.5	19.6	19.9	Dépenses intérieures (en % du totale)
Ghana							**Ghana**
Current expenditure (% GDP)	2.8	3.8	4.6	4.6	3.5	3.3	Dépenses courantes (% du PIB)
Domestic General govt.(% expend. total)	6.0	10.6	11.9	8.6	6.5	6.1	Dépenses intérieures (en % du totale)
Greece							**Grèce**
Current expenditure (% GDP)	...	8.6	9.6	8.1	8.3	8.0	Dépenses courantes (% du PIB)
Domestic General govt.(% expend. total)	...	11.4	12.4	8.7	10.2	10.2	Dépenses intérieures (en % du totale)
Grenada							**Grenade**
Current expenditure (% GDP)	5.3	5.5	6.2	4.7	4.7	4.8	Dépenses courantes (% du PIB)
Domestic General govt.(% expend. total)	6.8	10.0	9.0	7.6	9.0	9.0	Dépenses intérieures (en % du totale)
Guatemala							**Guatemala**
Current expenditure (% GDP)	5.7	6.4	6.1	6.0	6.0	5.8	Dépenses courantes (% du PIB)
Domestic General govt.(% expend. total)	14.1	14.2	14.2	18.1	18.1	17.2	Dépenses intérieures (en % du totale)
Guinea							**Guinée**
Current expenditure (% GDP)	3.5	3.1	3.0	5.8	5.3	4.1	Dépenses courantes (% du PIB)
Domestic General govt.(% expend. total)	2.4	2.4	1.8	2.0	4.1	4.1	Dépenses intérieures (en % du totale)
Guinea-Bissau							**Guinée-Bissau**
Current expenditure (% GDP)	* 7.7	* 7.7	* 6.6	* 8.6	* 8.0	* 7.2	Dépenses courantes (% du PIB)
Domestic General govt.(% expend. total)	* 13.7	* 13.7	* 5.9	* 2.8	* 2.7	* 3.0	Dépenses intérieures (en % du totale)
Guyana							**Guyana**
Current expenditure (% GDP)	* 3.9	* 5.2	* 5.5	* 4.5	* 5.1	* 4.9	Dépenses courantes (% du PIB)
Domestic General govt.(% expend. total)	* 6.8	* 6.1	* 5.5	* 7.7	* 10.0	* 8.5	Dépenses intérieures (en % du totale)
Haiti							**Haïti**
Current expenditure (% GDP)	6.9	5.5	8.1	# 8.6	8.4	8.0	Dépenses courantes (% du PIB)
Domestic General govt.(% expend. total)	13.9	6.6	6.4	# 4.4	5.0	5.2	Dépenses intérieures (en % du totale)
Honduras							**Honduras**
Current expenditure (% GDP)	6.4	7.7	8.7	7.7	8.2	7.9	Dépenses courantes (% du PIB)
Domestic General govt.(% expend. total)	13.7	12.4	14.0	11.4	12.3	11.7	Dépenses intérieures (en % du totale)
Hungary							**Hongrie**
Current expenditure (% GDP)	* 6.8	* 8.0	* 7.5	* 7.0	* 7.1	* 6.9	Dépenses courantes (% du PIB)
Domestic General govt.(% expend. total)	* 9.9	* 11.4	* 10.2	* 9.4	* 10.3	* 10.1	Dépenses intérieures (en % du totale)
Iceland							**Islande**
Current expenditure (% GDP)	* 9.0	* 9.1	* 8.5	* 8.2	* 8.1	* 8.3	Dépenses courantes (% du PIB)
Domestic General govt.(% expend. total)	* 17.6	* 18.0	* 14.4	* 15.9	* 15.0	* 15.7	Dépenses intérieures (en % du totale)
India [2]							**Inde [2]**
Current expenditure (% GDP)	* 4.0	* 3.8	* 3.3	* # 3.6	* 3.5	* 3.5	Dépenses courantes (% du PIB)
Domestic General govt.(% expend. total)	* 3.3	* 3.0	* 3.1	* # 3.4	* 3.4	* 3.4	Dépenses intérieures (en % du totale)
Indonesia							**Indonésie**
Current expenditure (% GDP)	1.9	2.6	3.0	* 3.0	* 3.1	3.0	Dépenses courantes (% du PIB)
Domestic General govt.(% expend. total)	3.6	4.2	4.5	* 6.9	* 8.3	8.7	Dépenses intérieures (en % du totale)
Iran (Islamic Republic of)							**Iran (Rép. islamique d')**
Current expenditure (% GDP)	* 4.7	* 5.3	* 6.8	* 7.8	* 8.9	* 8.7	Dépenses courantes (% du PIB)
Domestic General govt.(% expend. total)	* 11.0	* 9.4	* 11.9	* 22.6	* 22.9	* 22.9	Dépenses intérieures (en % du totale)
Iraq							**Iraq**
Current expenditure (% GDP)	...	2.9	3.2	3.1	3.3	4.2	Dépenses courantes (% du PIB)
Domestic General govt.(% expend. total)	...	3.2	4.8	1.7	1.7	5.0	Dépenses intérieures (en % du totale)
Ireland							**Irlande**
Current expenditure (% GDP)	5.9	7.6	10.5	7.3	7.4	7.2	Dépenses courantes (% du PIB)
Domestic General govt.(% expend. total)	14.8	18.1	12.3	18.3	19.5	20.0	Dépenses intérieures (en % du totale)
Israel							**Israël**
Current expenditure (% GDP)	6.8	7.1	7.0	7.1	7.3	7.4	Dépenses courantes (% du PIB)
Domestic General govt.(% expend. total)	8.9	9.3	10.7	11.7	12.1	11.9	Dépenses intérieures (en % du totale)
Italy							**Italie**
Current expenditure (% GDP)	7.6	8.4	9.0	9.0	8.9	8.8	Dépenses courantes (% du PIB)
Domestic General govt.(% expend. total)	11.8	13.7	14.1	13.3	13.5	13.4	Dépenses intérieures (en % du totale)
Jamaica							**Jamaïque**
Current expenditure (% GDP)	5.8	4.4	5.0	5.7	5.7	6.0	Dépenses courantes (% du PIB)
Domestic General govt.(% expend. total)	11.8	7.6	9.0	12.9	12.8	13.3	Dépenses intérieures (en % du totale)
Japan							**Japon**
Current expenditure (% GDP)	* 7.2	* 7.8	* 9.2	* 10.9	* 10.8	* 10.9	Dépenses courantes (% du PIB)
Domestic General govt.(% expend. total)	* 15.3	* 17.8	* 18.9	* 23.2	* 23.2	* 23.6	Dépenses intérieures (en % du totale)
Jordan							**Jordanie**
Current expenditure (% GDP)	9.6	8.9	8.4	7.6	7.2	8.1	Dépenses courantes (% du PIB)
Domestic General govt.(% expend. total)	12.7	11.8	17.0	12.2	12.2	12.4	Dépenses intérieures (en % du totale)

Region, country or area[&]	2000	2005	2010	2015	2016	2017	Région, pays ou zone[&]
Kazakhstan							**Kazakhstan**
Current expenditure (% GDP)	* 4.2	* 3.9	* 2.7	* 3.0	* 3.4	* 3.1	Dépenses courantes (% du PIB)
Domestic General govt.(% expend. total)	* 9.2	* 11.4	* 8.3	* 8.4	* 9.6	* 7.9	Dépenses intérieures (en % du totale)
Kenya							**Kenya**
Current expenditure (% GDP)	4.6	5.3	6.1	# 5.2	5.0	4.8	Dépenses courantes (% du PIB)
Domestic General govt.(% expend. total)	7.1	6.9	7.3	# 7.8	8.0	8.0	Dépenses intérieures (en % du totale)
Kiribati [1,7]							**Kiribati** [1,7]
Current expenditure (% GDP)	8.6	11.5	9.2	8.0	9.3	10.8	Dépenses courantes (% du PIB)
Domestic General govt.(% expend. total)	11.4	11.4	10.3	6.7	6.5	6.9	Dépenses intérieures (en % du totale)
Kuwait							**Koweït**
Current expenditure (% GDP)	2.5	2.4	2.8	4.0	4.0	5.3	Dépenses courantes (% du PIB)
Domestic General govt.(% expend. total)	5.2	6.8	5.2	6.2	6.2	8.9	Dépenses intérieures (en % du totale)
Kyrgyzstan							**Kirghizistan**
Current expenditure (% GDP)	4.4	7.5	7.0	7.1	6.4	6.2	Dépenses courantes (% du PIB)
Domestic General govt.(% expend. total)	7.1	13.1	9.2	7.1	6.3	6.2	Dépenses intérieures (en % du totale)
Lao People's Dem. Rep. [8]							**Rép. dém. populaire lao** [8]
Current expenditure (% GDP)	4.3	3.3	2.9	# 2.5[5]	2.4[5]	2.5[5]	Dépenses courantes (% du PIB)
Domestic General govt.(% expend. total)	6.2	5.7	2.7	# 3.8[5]	3.7[5]	4.0[5]	Dépenses intérieures (en % du totale)
Latvia							**Lettonie**
Current expenditure (% GDP)	* 5.4	* 5.9	* 6.1	* 5.7	* 6.2	* 6.0	Dépenses courantes (% du PIB)
Domestic General govt.(% expend. total)	* 7.4	* 9.6	* 8.1	* 8.8	* 9.4	* 9.0	Dépenses intérieures (en % du totale)
Lebanon							**Liban**
Current expenditure (% GDP)	10.8	7.6	7.4	7.7	7.8	8.2	Dépenses courantes (% du PIB)
Domestic General govt.(% expend. total)	7.5	9.2	10.3	13.5	13.5	13.5	Dépenses intérieures (en % du totale)
Lesotho							**Lesotho**
Current expenditure (% GDP)	* 5.9	* 5.1	* 7.6	* 8.4	* 7.9	* 8.8	Dépenses courantes (% du PIB)
Domestic General govt.(% expend. total)	* 7.7	* 5.8	* 8.6	* 11.3	* 10.9	* 11.8	Dépenses intérieures (en % du totale)
Liberia							**Libéria**
Current expenditure (% GDP)	* 4.0	* 8.9	* 8.8	* 10.3	* 9.8	* 8.2	Dépenses courantes (% du PIB)
Domestic General govt.(% expend. total)	* 5.0	* 4.5	* 3.2	* 3.3	* 3.9	* 4.2	Dépenses intérieures (en % du totale)
Libya							**Libye**
Current expenditure (% GDP)	* 3.4	* 2.6	* 3.6	...	...	...	Dépenses courantes (% du PIB)
Domestic General govt.(% expend. total)	* 6.0	* 5.8	* 4.3	...	...	...	Dépenses intérieures (en % du totale)
Lithuania							**Lituanie**
Current expenditure (% GDP)	* 6.2	* 5.6	* 6.8	* 6.5	* 6.6	* 6.5	Dépenses courantes (% du PIB)
Domestic General govt.(% expend. total)	* 10.6	* 10.1	* 11.5	* 12.3	* 12.8	* 12.8	Dépenses intérieures (en % du totale)
Luxembourg							**Luxembourg**
Current expenditure (% GDP)	5.9	7.2	7.0	5.5	5.5	5.5	Dépenses courantes (% du PIB)
Domestic General govt.(% expend. total)	13.0	13.9	13.7	11.1	11.1	10.8	Dépenses intérieures (en % du totale)
Madagascar							**Madagascar**
Current expenditure (% GDP)	* 5.2	* 6.0	* 5.3	* 5.7	* 6.1	* 5.5	Dépenses courantes (% du PIB)
Domestic General govt.(% expend. total)	* 11.5	* 10.6	* 15.2	* 15.3	* 17.5	* 15.0	Dépenses intérieures (en % du totale)
Malawi							**Malawi**
Current expenditure (% GDP)	3.4	6.1	7.2	9.3	9.7	9.6	Dépenses courantes (% du PIB)
Domestic General govt.(% expend. total)	7.1	6.1	5.8	9.7	9.8	9.8	Dépenses intérieures (en % du totale)
Malaysia							**Malaisie**
Current expenditure (% GDP)	* 2.6	* 2.8	* 3.2	* 3.9	* 3.8	* 3.9	Dépenses courantes (% du PIB)
Domestic General govt.(% expend. total)	* 4.6	* 5.6	* 6.3	* 8.2	* 8.3	* 8.9	Dépenses intérieures (en % du totale)
Maldives							**Maldives**
Current expenditure (% GDP)	7.7	8.8	# * 8.5	8.7	10.2	9.0	Dépenses courantes (% du PIB)
Domestic General govt.(% expend. total)	8.8	7.7	# * 13.6	18.5	20.4	21.8	Dépenses intérieures (en % du totale)
Mali							**Mali**
Current expenditure (% GDP)	5.6	5.1	4.6	4.1	3.8	3.8	Dépenses courantes (% du PIB)
Domestic General govt.(% expend. total)	6.8	6.4	3.3	4.4	5.4	5.8	Dépenses intérieures (en % du totale)
Malta							**Malte**
Current expenditure (% GDP)	6.6	8.7	8.2	9.2	9.2	9.3	Dépenses courantes (% du PIB)
Domestic General govt.(% expend. total)	11.8	14.2	12.9	14.2	15.8	16.5	Dépenses intérieures (en % du totale)
Marshall Islands [8,9]							**Îles Marshall** [8,9]
Current expenditure (% GDP)	19.7	21.6	15.2	17.6	17.9	16.4	Dépenses courantes (% du PIB)
Domestic General govt.(% expend. total)	17.1	6.6	7.7	11.6	12.1	9.5	Dépenses intérieures (en % du totale)
Mauritania							**Mauritanie**
Current expenditure (% GDP)	4.7	4.6	3.4	4.7	4.1	4.4	Dépenses courantes (% du PIB)
Domestic General govt.(% expend. total)	2.5	3.8	4.2	5.5	5.8	6.1	Dépenses intérieures (en % du totale)
Mauritius							**Maurice**
Current expenditure (% GDP)	2.9	3.6	4.6	5.7	5.7	5.7	Dépenses courantes (% du PIB)
Domestic General govt.(% expend. total)	6.9	7.4	8.3	9.5	10.0	10.0	Dépenses intérieures (en % du totale)

Region, country or area[&]	2000	2005	2010	2015	2016	2017	Région, pays ou zone[&]
Mexico							**Mexique**
Current expenditure (% GDP)	4.4	5.8	6.0	5.8	5.6	5.5	Dépenses courantes (% du PIB)
Domestic General govt.(% expend. total)	9.9	11.1	10.5	11.2	10.8	11.0	Dépenses intérieures (en % du totale)
Micronesia (Fed. States of) [8]							**Micronésie (États féd. de)** [8]
Current expenditure (% GDP)	7.8	17.7	13.1	12.5	12.6	12.4	Dépenses courantes (% du PIB)
Domestic General govt.(% expend. total)	2.6	4.5	3.4	5.8	5.5	4.9	Dépenses intérieures (en % du totale)
Monaco							**Monaco**
Current expenditure (% GDP)	* 1.7	* 2.1	* 2.3	* 2.0	* 1.7	* 1.8	Dépenses courantes (% du PIB)
Domestic General govt.(% expend. total)	* 6.9	* 7.9	* 9.2	* 8.1	* 6.7	* 6.7	Dépenses intérieures (en % du totale)
Mongolia							**Mongolie**
Current expenditure (% GDP)	4.9	3.8	3.7	4.2	* 4.4	4.0	Dépenses courantes (% du PIB)
Domestic General govt.(% expend. total)	12.3	9.0	7.7	7.1	* 6.5	8.2	Dépenses intérieures (en % du totale)
Morocco							**Maroc**
Current expenditure (% GDP)	4.0	4.8	5.9	5.1	5.2	5.2	Dépenses courantes (% du PIB)
Domestic General govt.(% expend. total)	4.0	4.0	7.5	6.9	7.3	7.5	Dépenses intérieures (en % du totale)
Mozambique							**Mozambique**
Current expenditure (% GDP)	* 3.9	* 6.4	* 5.1	* 5.3	* 5.1	* 4.9	Dépenses courantes (% du PIB)
Domestic General govt.(% expend. total)	* 13.8	* 15.8	* 2.2	* 4.7	* 4.7	* 4.7	Dépenses intérieures (en % du totale)
Myanmar [2,10]							**Myanmar** [2,10]
Current expenditure (% GDP)	* 1.8	* 2.0	* 1.8	* 5.2	* 4.8	* 4.7	Dépenses courantes (% du PIB)
Domestic General govt.(% expend. total)	* 1.3	* 1.1	* 1.2	* 4.8	* 3.1	* 3.5	Dépenses intérieures (en % du totale)
Namibia							**Namibie**
Current expenditure (% GDP)	9.8	10.3	9.7	9.9	9.1	8.6	Dépenses courantes (% du PIB)
Domestic General govt.(% expend. total)	16.0	16.3	11.9	9.6	10.5	10.7	Dépenses intérieures (en % du totale)
Nauru [1,7,11]							**Nauru** [1,7,11]
Current expenditure (% GDP)	13.5	12.6	10.4	13.3	13.9	11.0	Dépenses courantes (% du PIB)
Domestic General govt.(% expend. total)	9.7	18.0	7.3	6.8	7.1	5.6	Dépenses intérieures (en % du totale)
Nepal [12]							**Népal** [12]
Current expenditure (% GDP)	3.6	4.5	5.0	6.2	6.3	5.6	Dépenses courantes (% du PIB)
Domestic General govt.(% expend. total)	4.3	6.3	4.8	5.1	5.3	4.5	Dépenses intérieures (en % du totale)
Netherlands							**Pays-Bas**
Current expenditure (% GDP)	* 7.7	* 9.1	* 10.2	* 10.3	* 10.3	* 10.1	Dépenses courantes (% du PIB)
Domestic General govt.(% expend. total)	* 12.6	* 14.7	* 14.3	* 15.1	* 15.3	* 15.3	Dépenses intérieures (en % du totale)
New Zealand							**Nouvelle-Zélande**
Current expenditure (% GDP)	* 7.5	* 8.3	* 9.6	* 9.3	* 9.3	* 9.2	Dépenses courantes (% du PIB)
Domestic General govt.(% expend. total)	* 14.7	* 17.4	* 17.6	* 18.9	* 19.2	* 19.3	Dépenses intérieures (en % du totale)
Nicaragua							**Nicaragua**
Current expenditure (% GDP)	5.2	6.1	7.0	8.0	8.8	8.6	Dépenses courantes (% du PIB)
Domestic General govt.(% expend. total)	10.2	11.3	13.2	17.4	19.6	18.6	Dépenses intérieures (en % du totale)
Niger							**Niger**
Current expenditure (% GDP)	7.2	8.2	6.9	7.1	6.2	7.7	Dépenses courantes (% du PIB)
Domestic General govt.(% expend. total)	8.4	12.3	8.7	4.6	5.7	9.7	Dépenses intérieures (en % du totale)
Nigeria							**Nigéria**
Current expenditure (% GDP)	3.2	4.5	3.3	3.6	3.6	3.8	Dépenses courantes (% du PIB)
Domestic General govt.(% expend. total)	2.4	6.4	2.7	5.3	5.0	4.6	Dépenses intérieures (en % du totale)
Niue [1,7,11]							**Nioué** [1,7,11]
Current expenditure (% GDP)	8.3	10.6	10.3	8.2	7.7	8.6	Dépenses courantes (% du PIB)
Domestic General govt.(% expend. total)	6.6	7.2	6.9	5.6	5.0	5.2	Dépenses intérieures (en % du totale)
North Macedonia							**Macédoine du Nord**
Current expenditure (% GDP)	8.9	7.7	6.7	6.3	6.4	6.1	Dépenses courantes (% du PIB)
Domestic General govt.(% expend. total)	14.7	13.5	12.5	12.8	13.1	12.8	Dépenses intérieures (en % du totale)
Norway							**Norvège**
Current expenditure (% GDP)	* 7.7	* 8.3	* 8.9	* 10.1	* 10.5	* 10.4	Dépenses courantes (% du PIB)
Domestic General govt.(% expend. total)	* 15.0	* 16.5	* 16.8	* 17.7	* 17.7	* 17.9	Dépenses intérieures (en % du totale)
Oman							**Oman**
Current expenditure (% GDP)	3.1	2.6	2.8	4.3	4.3	3.8	Dépenses courantes (% du PIB)
Domestic General govt.(% expend. total)	7.0	6.1	6.7	7.6	7.6	7.6	Dépenses intérieures (en % du totale)
Pakistan							**Pakistan**
Current expenditure (% GDP)	2.9	2.7	2.6	2.7	2.9	2.9	Dépenses courantes (% du PIB)
Domestic General govt.(% expend. total)	5.9	3.7	2.8	3.7	4.1	4.3	Dépenses intérieures (en % du totale)
Palau [8]							**Palaos** [8]
Current expenditure (% GDP)	* 8.9	* 9.3	* 11.6	* 10.9	* 11.8	* 12.0	Dépenses courantes (% du PIB)
Domestic General govt.(% expend. total)	* 8.2	* 8.7	* 8.5	* 11.0	* 16.5	* 17.4	Dépenses intérieures (en % du totale)
Panama							**Panama**
Current expenditure (% GDP)	7.0	6.2	7.2	6.8	7.2	7.3	Dépenses courantes (% du PIB)
Domestic General govt.(% expend. total)	19.8	16.5	19.2	19.4	21.7	20.1	Dépenses intérieures (en % du totale)

Region, country or area&	2000	2005	2010	2015	2016	2017	Région, pays ou zone&
Papua New Guinea							**Papouasie-Nvl-Guinée**
Current expenditure (% GDP)	2.0	2.5	2.1	1.9	2.5	2.5	Dépenses courantes (% du PIB)
Domestic General govt.(% expend. total)	8.3	7.8	7.1	6.0	8.0	9.2	Dépenses intérieures (en % du totale)
Paraguay							**Paraguay**
Current expenditure (% GDP)	5.5	4.1	4.6	* 6.7	* 6.7	* 6.7	Dépenses courantes (% du PIB)
Domestic General govt.(% expend. total)	6.8	5.9	9.0	* 10.9	* 11.2	* 10.5	Dépenses intérieures (en % du totale)
Peru							**Pérou**
Current expenditure (% GDP)	4.5	4.5	4.7	* 5.0	* 5.1	* 5.0	Dépenses courantes (% du PIB)
Domestic General govt.(% expend. total)	10.6	12.2	11.6	* 13.9	* 15.1	* 14.9	Dépenses intérieures (en % du totale)
Philippines							**Philippines**
Current expenditure (% GDP)	* 3.2	* 3.9	* 4.3	* 4.3	* 4.4	* 4.4	Dépenses courantes (% du PIB)
Domestic General govt.(% expend. total)	* 6.5	* 6.6	* 7.2	* 7.3	* 7.2	* 7.1	Dépenses intérieures (en % du totale)
Poland							**Pologne**
Current expenditure (% GDP)	* 5.3	* 5.8	* 6.4	* 6.4	* 6.5	* 6.5	Dépenses courantes (% du PIB)
Domestic General govt.(% expend. total)	* 8.6	* 9.0	* 10.0	* 10.6	* 11.0	* 10.9	Dépenses intérieures (en % du totale)
Portugal							**Portugal**
Current expenditure (% GDP)	8.4	9.4	9.8	9.0	9.0	9.0	Dépenses courantes (% du PIB)
Domestic General govt.(% expend. total)	13.8	14.4	13.2	12.3	13.4	13.0	Dépenses intérieures (en % du totale)
Qatar							**Qatar**
Current expenditure (% GDP)	2.0	2.6	1.8	3.1	3.0	2.6	Dépenses courantes (% du PIB)
Domestic General govt.(% expend. total)	3.9	6.6	4.1	6.3	6.3	6.3	Dépenses intérieures (en % du totale)
Republic of Korea							**République de Corée**
Current expenditure (% GDP)	* 4.0	* 4.8	* 6.2	* 7.0	* 7.3	* 7.6	Dépenses courantes (% du PIB)
Domestic General govt.(% expend. total)	* 8.1	* 9.3	* 11.8	* 12.5	* 13.1	* 13.4	Dépenses intérieures (en % du totale)
Republic of Moldova [13]							**République de Moldova** [13]
Current expenditure (% GDP)	4.9	8.0	10.1	8.6	7.5	7.0	Dépenses courantes (% du PIB)
Domestic General govt.(% expend. total)	8.5	13.6	13.6	12.2	12.1	11.6	Dépenses intérieures (en % du totale)
Romania							**Roumanie**
Current expenditure (% GDP)	* 4.2	* 5.5	* 5.8	* 4.9	* 5.0	* 5.2	Dépenses courantes (% du PIB)
Domestic General govt.(% expend. total)	* 8.7	* 13.2	* 11.5	* 10.7	* 11.3	* 12.1	Dépenses intérieures (en % du totale)
Russian Federation							**Fédération de Russie**
Current expenditure (% GDP)	5.0	4.8	5.0	5.3[14]	5.3[14]	5.3[14]	Dépenses courantes (% du PIB)
Domestic General govt.(% expend. total)	9.7	9.9	8.6	8.8[14]	8.2[14]	8.8[14]	Dépenses intérieures (en % du totale)
Rwanda							**Rwanda**
Current expenditure (% GDP)	* 4.3	* 8.8	* 8.6	# * 6.5	* 6.8	* 6.6	Dépenses courantes (% du PIB)
Domestic General govt.(% expend. total)	* 3.5	* 8.1	* 8.6	# * 7.9	* 8.9	* 8.9	Dépenses intérieures (en % du totale)
Saint Kitts and Nevis							**Saint-Kitts-et-Nevis**
Current expenditure (% GDP)	4.7	4.5	5.3	4.9	5.0	5.0	Dépenses courantes (% du PIB)
Domestic General govt.(% expend. total)	5.8	6.4	5.9	6.6	8.1	8.2	Dépenses intérieures (en % du totale)
Saint Lucia							**Sainte-Lucie**
Current expenditure (% GDP)	5.4	5.4	5.4	4.8	5.2	4.5	Dépenses courantes (% du PIB)
Domestic General govt.(% expend. total)	8.1	6.2	7.0	8.4	8.5	8.9	Dépenses intérieures (en % du totale)
Saint Vincent & Grenadines							**Saint-Vincent-Grenadines**
Current expenditure (% GDP)	4.3	4.0	4.6	4.3	4.3	4.5	Dépenses courantes (% du PIB)
Domestic General govt.(% expend. total)	11.7	9.0	8.2	9.2	9.6	9.5	Dépenses intérieures (en % du totale)
Samoa [1]							**Samoa** [1]
Current expenditure (% GDP)	4.4	4.8	5.5	5.7	5.5	5.5	Dépenses courantes (% du PIB)
Domestic General govt.(% expend. total)	11.8	10.4	10.4	11.5	11.6	11.6	Dépenses intérieures (en % du totale)
San Marino							**Saint-Marin**
Current expenditure (% GDP)	5.3	4.9	6.6	7.4	6.8	7.4	Dépenses courantes (% du PIB)
Domestic General govt.(% expend. total)	11.8	11.8	13.1	11.6	12.2	12.2	Dépenses intérieures (en % du totale)
Sao Tome and Principe							**Sao Tomé-et-Principe**
Current expenditure (% GDP)	* 10.5	* 11.5	* 6.8	* 5.4	* 6.2	* 6.2	Dépenses courantes (% du PIB)
Domestic General govt.(% expend. total)	* 31.9	* 11.5	* 4.1	* 4.9	* 8.0	* 10.8	Dépenses intérieures (en % du totale)
Saudi Arabia							**Arabie saoudite**
Current expenditure (% GDP)	4.2	3.4	3.6	6.0	5.8	...	Dépenses courantes (% du PIB)
Domestic General govt.(% expend. total)	9.2	8.8	6.8	10.1	10.1	...	Dépenses intérieures (en % du totale)
Senegal							**Sénégal**
Current expenditure (% GDP)	3.6	3.7	4.0	4.4	4.3	4.1	Dépenses courantes (% du PIB)
Domestic General govt.(% expend. total)	9.0	8.5	5.4	4.7	4.5	3.9	Dépenses intérieures (en % du totale)
Serbia [15]							**Serbie** [15]
Current expenditure (% GDP)	* 6.5	* 8.3	9.5	8.8	8.6	8.4	Dépenses courantes (% du PIB)
Domestic General govt.(% expend. total)	* 13.6	* 13.6	13.6	11.9	11.9	11.9	Dépenses intérieures (en % du totale)
Seychelles							**Seychelles**
Current expenditure (% GDP)	4.6	5.0	4.8	4.6	5.2	5.0	Dépenses courantes (% du PIB)
Domestic General govt.(% expend. total)	6.8	9.3	9.0	10.0	9.5	10.1	Dépenses intérieures (en % du totale)

Region, country or area[&]	2000	2005	2010	2015	2016	2017	Région, pays ou zone[&]
Sierra Leone							**Sierra Leone**
Current expenditure (% GDP)	11.5	11.0	10.9	20.4	16.5	13.4	Dépenses courantes (% du PIB)
Domestic General govt.(% expend. total)	12.7	9.5	6.3	7.9	7.9	7.9	Dépenses intérieures (en % du totale)
Singapore [2,16]							**Singapour** [2,16]
Current expenditure (% GDP)	3.4	3.0	* 3.2	* 4.2	* 4.4	* 4.4	Dépenses courantes (% du PIB)
Domestic General govt.(% expend. total)	6.7	6.9	* 7.5	* 11.1	* 11.9	* 12.6	Dépenses intérieures (en % du totale)
Slovakia							**Slovaquie**
Current expenditure (% GDP)	* 5.3	* 6.6	* 7.8	* 6.8	* 7.1	* 6.7	Dépenses courantes (% du PIB)
Domestic General govt.(% expend. total)	* 9.0	* 12.3	* 13.3	* 12.0	* 13.7	* 13.3	Dépenses intérieures (en % du totale)
Slovenia							**Slovénie**
Current expenditure (% GDP)	* 7.8	* 8.0	* 8.6	* 8.5	* 8.5	* 8.2	Dépenses courantes (% du PIB)
Domestic General govt.(% expend. total)	* 12.0	* 12.8	* 12.6	* 12.7	* 13.5	* 13.6	Dépenses intérieures (en % du totale)
Solomon Islands							**Îles Salomon**
Current expenditure (% GDP)	* 5.3	* 10.1	* 7.3	* 5.2	* 5.2	* 4.7	Dépenses courantes (% du PIB)
Domestic General govt.(% expend. total)	* 23.1	* 20.0	* 7.5	* 7.3	* 7.6	* 7.2	Dépenses intérieures (en % du totale)
South Africa [2]							**Afrique du Sud** [2]
Current expenditure (% GDP)	7.4	6.7	7.4	8.2	8.1	8.1	Dépenses courantes (% du PIB)
Domestic General govt.(% expend. total)	10.9	9.8	12.4	13.3	13.3	13.3	Dépenses intérieures (en % du totale)
South Sudan							**Soudan du sud**
Current expenditure (% GDP)	...	...	...	...	...	* 9.8	Dépenses courantes (% du PIB)
Domestic General govt.(% expend. total)	...	...	...	...	...	* 2.1	Dépenses intérieures (en % du totale)
Spain							**Espagne**
Current expenditure (% GDP)	6.8	7.7	9.0	9.1	9.0	8.9	Dépenses courantes (% du PIB)
Domestic General govt.(% expend. total)	12.4	14.4	14.8	14.8	15.1	15.3	Dépenses intérieures (en % du totale)
Sri Lanka							**Sri Lanka**
Current expenditure (% GDP)	4.2	4.0	3.9	# 3.9	3.9	3.8	Dépenses courantes (% du PIB)
Domestic General govt.(% expend. total)	10.1	10.1	7.8	# 8.4	8.6	8.5	Dépenses intérieures (en % du totale)
Sudan							**Soudan**
Current expenditure (% GDP)	* 3.6[17]	* 4.1[17]	* 5.1[17]	* 7.2	* 6.4	* 6.3	Dépenses courantes (% du PIB)
Domestic General govt.(% expend. total)	* 11.8[17]	* 8.1[17]	* 9.5[17]	* 18.3	* 13.1	* 8.3	Dépenses intérieures (en % du totale)
Suriname							**Suriname**
Current expenditure (% GDP)	6.3	5.6	5.0	6.2	6.3	6.2	Dépenses courantes (% du PIB)
Domestic General govt.(% expend. total)	11.6	11.9	8.6	10.5	15.1	11.8	Dépenses intérieures (en % du totale)
Sweden							**Suède**
Current expenditure (% GDP)	7.4	8.3	8.5	11.0	11.0	11.0	Dépenses courantes (% du PIB)
Domestic General govt.(% expend. total)	11.7	12.9	13.7	18.5	18.4	18.7	Dépenses intérieures (en % du totale)
Switzerland							**Suisse**
Current expenditure (% GDP)	9.8	10.8	10.7	11.9	12.2	12.3	Dépenses courantes (% du PIB)
Domestic General govt.(% expend. total)	8.2	9.7	10.1	10.6	10.6	11.0	Dépenses intérieures (en % du totale)
Syrian Arab Republic							**République arabe syrienne**
Current expenditure (% GDP)	4.3	4.1	3.3	...	...	...	Dépenses courantes (% du PIB)
Domestic General govt.(% expend. total)	5.6	7.3	5.1	...	...	...	Dépenses intérieures (en % du totale)
Tajikistan							**Tadjikistan**
Current expenditure (% GDP)	4.3	5.2	5.7	6.9	7.0	7.2	Dépenses courantes (% du PIB)
Domestic General govt.(% expend. total)	4.6	4.3	4.5	6.4	5.1	5.9	Dépenses intérieures (en % du totale)
Thailand [8]							**Thaïlande** [8]
Current expenditure (% GDP)	3.1	3.2	3.4	3.7	* 3.8	3.7	Dépenses courantes (% du PIB)
Domestic General govt.(% expend. total)	12.7	13.1	14.4	14.8	* 15.1	15.0	Dépenses intérieures (en % du totale)
Timor-Leste							**Timor-Leste**
Current expenditure (% GDP)	...	1.3	1.4	# * 3.5	* 4.0	* 3.9	Dépenses courantes (% du PIB)
Domestic General govt.(% expend. total)	...	3.6	2.7	# * 4.5	* 3.1	* 5.2	Dépenses intérieures (en % du totale)
Togo							**Togo**
Current expenditure (% GDP)	3.3	4.0	5.9	6.2	6.6	6.2	Dépenses courantes (% du PIB)
Domestic General govt.(% expend. total)	2.4	3.8	7.4	4.2	4.3	5.1	Dépenses intérieures (en % du totale)
Tonga [1]							**Tonga** [1]
Current expenditure (% GDP)	2.9	4.2	4.7	4.7	5.2	5.3	Dépenses courantes (% du PIB)
Domestic General govt.(% expend. total)	11.4	10.6	9.0	6.8	7.3	7.4	Dépenses intérieures (en % du totale)
Trinidad and Tobago							**Trinité-et-Tobago**
Current expenditure (% GDP)	4.2	4.4	5.1	6.0	6.9	7.0	Dépenses courantes (% du PIB)
Domestic General govt.(% expend. total)	6.8	8.9	8.0	8.3	9.8	11.2	Dépenses intérieures (en % du totale)
Tunisia							**Tunisie**
Current expenditure (% GDP)	5.0	5.4	5.9	7.0	7.0	7.2	Dépenses courantes (% du PIB)
Domestic General govt.(% expend. total)	10.5	11.4	13.0	13.7	13.7	13.6	Dépenses intérieures (en % du totale)
Turkey							**Turquie**
Current expenditure (% GDP)	* 4.6	* 4.9	* 5.1	* 4.1	* 4.3	* 4.2	Dépenses courantes (% du PIB)
Domestic General govt.(% expend. total)	* 7.2	* 10.3	* 10.9	* 9.7	* 9.6	* 9.7	Dépenses intérieures (en % du totale)

Region, country or area[&]	2000	2005	2010	2015	2016	2017	Région, pays ou zone[&]
Turkmenistan							**Turkménistan**
Current expenditure (% GDP)	6.9	9.6	5.0	6.3	6.6	6.9	Dépenses courantes (% du PIB)
Domestic General govt.(% expend. total)	13.3	10.3	8.7	8.7	8.7	8.7	Dépenses intérieures (en % du totale)
Tuvalu [7]							**Tuvalu [7]**
Current expenditure (% GDP)	24.2	11.4	16.4	16.7	16.9	17.1	Dépenses courantes (% du PIB)
Domestic General govt.(% expend. total)	11.9	11.6	14.8	10.9	10.0	10.0	Dépenses intérieures (en % du totale)
Uganda [18]							**Ouganda [18]**
Current expenditure (% GDP)	7.6	11.4	10.5	6.8	6.4	6.3	Dépenses courantes (% du PIB)
Domestic General govt.(% expend. total)	9.5	14.2	7.6	5.1	5.1	5.1	Dépenses intérieures (en % du totale)
Ukraine							**Ukraine**
Current expenditure (% GDP)	5.3	6.3	6.8	6.9[19]	6.8[19]	7.0[19]	Dépenses courantes (% du PIB)
Domestic General govt.(% expend. total)	7.1	8.4	7.5	6.6[19]	7.0[19]	7.4[19]	Dépenses intérieures (en % du totale)
United Arab Emirates							**Émirats arabes unis**
Current expenditure (% GDP)	2.4	2.3	3.9	3.6	3.4	3.3	Dépenses courantes (% du PIB)
Domestic General govt.(% expend. total)	7.6	8.4	8.5	7.9	7.9	7.9	Dépenses intérieures (en % du totale)
United Kingdom							**Royaume-Uni**
Current expenditure (% GDP)	6.0	7.2	8.4	9.7	9.7	9.6	Dépenses courantes (% du PIB)
Domestic General govt.(% expend. total)	13.8	14.5	15.0	18.4	18.8	18.7	Dépenses intérieures (en % du totale)
United Rep. of Tanzania [20]							**Rép.-Unie de Tanzanie [20]**
Current expenditure (% GDP)	* 3.4	* 6.4	* 5.3	* 3.6	* 4.0	* 3.6	Dépenses courantes (% du PIB)
Domestic General govt.(% expend. total)	* 6.1	* 12.6	* 7.3	* 7.3	* 9.5	* 9.5	Dépenses intérieures (en % du totale)
United States of America							**États-Unis d'Amérique**
Current expenditure (% GDP)	12.5	14.5	16.4	* 16.8	* 17.2	* 17.1	Dépenses courantes (% du PIB)
Domestic General govt.(% expend. total)	16.2	17.9	18.4	* 22.3	* 22.5	* 22.5	Dépenses intérieures (en % du totale)
Uruguay							**Uruguay**
Current expenditure (% GDP)	10.0	8.4	8.6	9.0	9.2	9.3	Dépenses courantes (% du PIB)
Domestic General govt.(% expend. total)	14.3	13.2	16.9	19.0	19.3	19.8	Dépenses intérieures (en % du totale)
Uzbekistan							**Ouzbékistan**
Current expenditure (% GDP)	* 5.4	* 5.0	* 5.6	* 6.1	* 6.3	* 6.4	Dépenses courantes (% du PIB)
Domestic General govt.(% expend. total)	* 6.1	* 6.5	* 8.0	* 10.1	* 10.1	* 10.2	Dépenses intérieures (en % du totale)
Vanuatu [21]							**Vanuatu [21]**
Current expenditure (% GDP)	3.3	3.3	3.4	4.2	3.7	3.3	Dépenses courantes (% du PIB)
Domestic General govt.(% expend. total)	9.7	11.7	6.8	4.9	5.4	5.3	Dépenses intérieures (en % du totale)
Venezuela (Boliv. Rep. of)							**Venezuela (Rép. boliv. du)**
Current expenditure (% GDP)	7.3	6.1	6.8	5.1[22]	3.2[22]	1.2[22]	Dépenses courantes (% du PIB)
Domestic General govt.(% expend. total)	11.9	8.4	8.2	4.3[22]	1.6[22]	1.4[22]	Dépenses intérieures (en % du totale)
Viet Nam							**Viet Nam**
Current expenditure (% GDP)	4.8	5.1	6.0	5.7	* 5.7	5.5	Dépenses courantes (% du PIB)
Domestic General govt.(% expend. total)	7.5	7.1	7.9	8.1	* 9.4	9.5	Dépenses intérieures (en % du totale)
Yemen							**Yémen**
Current expenditure (% GDP)	* 4.7	* 5.2	* 5.2	* 4.2	…	…	Dépenses courantes (% du PIB)
Domestic General govt.(% expend. total)	* 7.5	* 4.5	* 3.8	* 2.2	…	…	Dépenses intérieures (en % du totale)
Zambia							**Zambie**
Current expenditure (% GDP)	* 7.2	* 6.9	* 3.7	* 4.4	* 4.5	* 4.5	Dépenses courantes (% du PIB)
Domestic General govt.(% expend. total)	* 14.9	* 8.2	* 4.7	* 7.4	* 7.1	* 6.9	Dépenses intérieures (en % du totale)
Zimbabwe							**Zimbabwe**
Current expenditure (% GDP)	…	…	10.7	7.5	7.7	6.6	Dépenses courantes (% du PIB)
Domestic General govt.(% expend. total)	…	…	15.2	16.6	15.2	15.2	Dépenses intérieures (en % du totale)

Source:

World Health Organization (WHO), Geneva, WHO Global Health Expenditure database, last accessed January 2020.

& These estimates are in line with the 2011 System of Health Accounts (SHA).

1   Data refer to fiscal years beginning 1 July.

2   Data refer to fiscal years beginning 1 April.

Source:

Organisation mondiale de la santé (OMS), Genève, base de données de l'OMS sur les dépenses de santé mondiales, dernier accès janvier 2020.

& Ces estimations sont conformes au Système de comptes de la santé (SCS) de 2011.

1   Les données se réfèrent aux exercices budgétaires commençant le 1er juillet.

2   Les données se réfèrent aux exercices budgétaires commençant le 1er avril.

3	Health expenditure data do not include funds from foreign origin flowing in the health financing system.	3	Les données sur les dépenses de santé n'incluent pas les fonds d'origine étrangère qui entrent dans le système de financement de la santé.
4	2012 data are based on a health accounts study based on SHA2011. Numbers were converted to SHA 1.0 format for comparability.	4	Les données de 2012 sont basées sur une étude sur les comptes de santé basée sur SCS2011. Les nombres ont été convertis au format SCS 1.0 pour la comparabilité.
5	Data are based on SHA2011.	5	Les données sont basées sur SCS2011.
6	As a result of recent health-care reforms, public compulsory insurance has since 2008 been implemented by private insurance companies. The voucher cost of this insurance is treated as general government health expenditure.	6	L'assurance publique obligatoire est réalisée depuis 2008 par des sociétés privées dont le coût des coupons est traité comme dépense publique de santé du fait des réformes des soins de santé.
7	General government expenditure (GGE) can be larger than the Gross domestic product (GDP) because government accounts for a very large part of domestic consumption and because a large part of domestic consumption in the country is accounted for by imports.	7	Les dépenses publiques peuvent être supérieure au produit intérieur brut (PIB) parce que le gouvernement contribue très largement à la consommation intérieure et aussi une grande partie de la consommation intérieure du pays et représentée par les importations.
8	Data refer to fiscal years ending 30 September.	8	Les données se réfèrent aux exercices budgétaires finissant le 30 septembre.
9	Health expenditure indicators are high as they spend a lot on health using direct funding from the United States and also from their domestic funds. Current health expenditure is mostly government.	9	Les indicateurs de dépenses de santé sont élevés car ils dépensent beaucoup pour la santé en utilisant le financement direct de - États-Unis et aussi de leurs fonds nationaux. Dépenses de santé est principalement le gouvernement.
10	Country is still reporting data based on SHA 1.0.	10	Le pays rapporte toujours des données basées sur SCS 1.0.
11	Indicators are sensitive to external funds flowing in to the country.	11	Les indicateurs sont sensibles aux fonds externes vers le pays.
12	Data refer to fiscal years ending 15 July.	12	Les données se réfèrent aux exercices budgétaires finissant le 15 juillet.
13	Excluding the Transnistria region.	13	Non compris la région de Transnistrie.
14	From 2015 the data is adjusted by WHO in accordance with UN General Assembly Resolution A/RES/68/262.	14	À partir de 2015 les données sont ajustées conformes à la résolution A/RES/68/262.
15	Excluding Kosovo and Metohija.	15	Non compris Kosovo et Metohija.
16	Medisave is classified as Social insurance scheme, considering that it is a compulsory payment.	16	Medisave est classé comme régime d'assurance sociale, considérant qu'il s'agit d'un paiement obligatoire.
17	Including South Sudan.	17	Y compris le Sud Soudan.
18	Unlike other countries, in Uganda Fiscal Years starting on July 1 and ending in June 30 are converted to the previous year and that is a special request from the country.	18	Contrairement aux autres pays, en Ouganda, les années fiscales commençant le 1er juillet et se terminant le 30 juin sont converties en années précédentes et il s'agit d'une demande spéciale du pays.
19	Since 2014 Ukraine data does not include the Luhansk People's Republic, the Autonomous Republic of Crimea and the Donetsk People's Republic data.	19	Depuis 2014, les données de l'Ukraine ne comprennent pas les données de la République populaire de Louhansk, de la République autonome de Crimée et de la République populaire de Donetsk.
20	Tanzania mainland only, excluding Zanzibar.	20	Tanzanie continentale seulement, Zanzibar non compris.
21	Government expenditures show fluctuations due to variations in capital investment.	21	Les dépenses publiques manifestent des fluctuations du fait de variations des investissements.
22	For 2015 - 2017, WHO is using the exchange rate of United Nations to report health expenditrue indicators in USD.	22	Pour 2015-2017, l'OMS utilise le taux de change des Nations Unies pour déclarer les indicateurs de dépenses de santé en Dollars américains.

11

Intentional homicides and other crimes
By type of crime per 100 000 population and homicide victims by sex

Homicides intentionnels et autres crimes
Par type de crime pour 100 000 habitants et victimes d'homicides par sexe

Country or area Pays ou zone	Year Année	Intentional homicides Homicides volontaires			Other crimes (per 100 000 pop.) Autres infractions (pour 100 000 hab.)				
		Per 100 000 Pour 100 000	Victims (%) Victimes (%)		Assault Agression	Kidnapping Enlèvement	Theft Vol simple	Robbery Vol qualifié	Sexual Violence Violences Sexuelles
			Male Hommes	Female Femmes					
Total, all countries or areas	2005	6.3	10.1	2.4	...	...	...	...	...
Total, tous pays ou zones	2010	6.0	9.6	2.4	...	...	...	...	...
	2017	6.0	9.7	2.2	...	...	...	...	...
Africa	2005	13.0	...	...	...	...	...	...	...
Afrique	2010	12.7	...	...	...	...	...	...	...
	2017	13.0	...	...	...	...	...	...	...
Americas	2005	14.5	26.2	3.1	...	...	...	...	...
Amériques	2010	15.8	28.7	3.3	...	...	...	...	...
	2017	17.0	30.8	3.4	...	...	...	...	...
Northern America	2005	5.3	8.5	2.3	...	...	...	...	...
Amérique septentrionale	2010	4.5	7.0	2.0	...	...	...	...	...
	2017	5.0	8.0	2.2	...	...	...	...	...
Caribbean	2005	17.1	30.0	3.7	...	...	...	...	...
Caraïbes	2010	17.0	30.4	3.4	...	...	...	...	...
	2017	14.0	27.3	3.1	...	...	...	...	...
Central America	2005	16.3	28.9	3.5	...	...	...	...	...
Amérique centrale	2010	27.8	49.7	5.3	...	...	...	...	...
	2017	26.5	46.5	5.6	...	...	...	...	...
South America	2005	21.5	40.0	3.6	...	...	...	...	...
Amérique du Sud	2010	20.8	38.3	3.6	...	...	...	...	...
	2017	23.6	44.9	4.0	...	...	...	...	...
Asia	2005	2.9	4.1	1.7	...	...	...	...	...
Asie	2010	2.7	3.6	1.7	...	...	...	...	...
	2017	2.1	2.8	1.4	...	...	...	...	...
Central Asia	2005	6.5	10.2	2.8	...	...	...	...	...
Asie centrale	2010	5.6	8.7	2.7	...	...	...	...	...
	2017	2.8	5.8	1.7	...	...	...	...	...
Eastern Asia	2005	1.5	1.6	1.3	...	...	...	...	...
Asie orientale	2010	0.9	1.0	0.9	...	...	...	...	...
	2017	0.6	0.6	0.6	...	...	...	...	...
South-eastern Asia	2005	2.8	4.8	0.9	...	...	...	...	...
Asie du Sud-Est	2010	2.8	4.8	0.8	...	...	...	...	...
	2017	2.4	4.4	0.7	...	...	...	...	...
Southern Asia	2005	4.0	5.2	2.7	...	...	...	...	...
Asie méridionale	2010	4.0	4.9	3.1	...	...	...	...	...
	2017	3.2	4.1	2.8	...	...	...	...	...
Western Asia	2005	4.7	7.3	1.9	...	...	...	...	...
Asie occidentale	2010	3.8	5.8	1.5	...	...	...	...	...
	2017	3.5	6.2	1.6	...	...	...	...	...
Europe	2005	6.5	9.9	3.4	...	...	...	...	...
Europe	2010	3.5	5.1	2.0	...	...	...	...	...
	2017	3.0	4.4	1.6	...	...	...	...	...
Eastern Europe	2005	13.9	21.9	6.8	...	...	...	...	...
Europe orientale	2010	6.9	13.5	4.2	...	...	...	...	...
	2017	5.9	9.2	3.1	...	...	...	...	...
Northern Europe	2005	1.9	2.5	1.2	...	...	...	...	...
Europe septentrionale	2010	1.4	1.9	1.0	...	...	...	...	...
	2017	1.3	1.6	0.9	...	...	...	...	...
Southern Europe	2005	1.3	2.0	0.6	...	...	...	...	...
Europe méridionale	2010	1.2	1.6	0.7	...	...	...	...	...
	2017	0.8	1.1	0.5	...	...	...	...	...
Western Europe	2005	1.3	1.5	1.0	...	...	...	...	...
Europe occidentale	2010	1.1	1.3	0.9	...	...	...	...	...
	2017	1.1	1.2	0.8	...	...	...	...	...
Oceania	2005	3.1	3.9	2.3	...	...	...	...	...
Océanie	2010	3.0	3.5	2.4	...	...	...	...	...
	2017	2.8	3.8	1.8	...	...	...	...	...
Australia and New Zealand	2005	1.3	1.6	1.0	...	...	...	...	...
Australie et Nouvelle-Zélande	2010	1.0	1.2	0.9	...	...	...	...	...
	2017	0.8	1.2	0.5	...	...	...	...	...
Afghanistan	2010	3.4	...	...	...	...	...	...	...
Afghanistan	2017	6.7	12.3	0.8	...	...	...	...	...
Albania	2005	5.0	8.6	1.4	5.3	...	96.7	...	2.9
Albanie	2010	4.3	7.3	1.3	6.0	0.3	134.9	8.0	2.7
	2016	2.7	4.2	1.2	4.1	0.1	195.2	5.5	4.2
	2017	2.0	3.1	0.9	4.3	0.1	...	6.4	3.9

Intentional homicides and other crimes *(continued)*
By type of crime per 100 000 population and homicide victims by sex

Homicides intentionnels et autres crimes *(suite)*
Par type de crime pour 100 000 habitants et victimes d'homicides par sexe

Country or area Pays ou zone	Year Année	Intentional homicides Homicides volontaires Per 100 000 Pour 100 000	Victims (%) Victimes (%) Male Hommes	Female Femmes	Other crimes (per 100 000 pop.) Autres infractions (pour 100 000 hab.) Assault Agression	Kidnapping Enlèvement	Theft Vol simple	Robbery Vol qualifié	Sexual Violence Violences Sexuelles
Algeria	2005	0.6	...	...	99.3	0.3	...	...	...
Algérie	2010	0.7	...	...	115.0	0.5	141.9	51.4	10.5
	2015	1.4	2.3	0.4	123.6	1.3	124.8	65.5	8.5
American Samoa	2005	10.1	...	...	...	...	...	...	...
Samoa américaines	2010	8.9	...	...	...	...	...	...	...
	2016	5.4	...	...	...	...	...	...	...
Andorra	2004	1.3	...	...	...	...	...	...	...
Andorre	2010	0.0	0.0	0.0	116.7	0.0	1 329.8	9.5	11.9
	2015	0.0	0.0	0.0	170.5	0.0	1 341.0	10.3	14.1
Angola									
Angola	2012	4.8	...	...	...	...	...	...	...
Anguilla	2000	8.9	...	0.0	...	...	...	...	...
Anguilla	2005	0.0	...	...	...	...	...	...	...
	2009	7.5	...	0.0	...	...	...	...	...
	2010	0.0	...	...	...	...	...	...	...
	2013	7.2	...	0.0	...	...	...	...	...
	2014	28.3	...	...	...	...	...	...	...
Antigua and Barbuda	2002	6.4	10.2	3.0	...	...	...	...	...
Antigua-et-Barbuda	2005	3.7	...	...	...	...	...	...	...
	2008	18.7	27.0	11.2	...	...	...	...	...
	2010	6.8	...	...	...	...	...	...	...
	2012	11.1	...	...	...	...	...	...	...
	2017	...	...	...	...	14.7	...	...	...
Argentina	2005	5.7	...	...	365.4	...	780.8	...	...
Argentine	2008	5.9	...	...	362.4	...	709.1	...	26.5
	2010	5.8	...	...	...	...	...	...	...
	2016	6.0	...	...	328.6	...	620.9	1 004.6	28.6
	2017	5.2	8.8	1.8	323.5	...	...	922.6	32.4
Armenia	2005	1.9	3.4	0.7	6.0	0.7	82.6	...	1.7
Arménie	2010	1.9	3.4	0.7	5.4	1.4	127.4	12.4	2.9
	2016	3.0	5.1	1.0	6.3	1.7	193.4	10.5	4.0
	2017	2.4	4.3	0.7	6.2	1.2	...	7.8	3.5
Aruba	2005	6.0	10.5	1.9	...	...	...	...	...
Aruba	2010	3.9	8.3	0.0	...	...	...	...	...
	2014	1.9	4.1	0.0	...	...	...	...	...
Australia	2005	1.3	1.6	0.9	...	...	2 568.7	...	...
Australie	2010	1.0	1.2	0.8	309.9	2.8	2 154.2	66.1	85.1
	2016	0.9	1.2	0.7	292.6	2.2	2 445.6	38.8	95.0
	2017	0.8	1.2	0.5	296.8	2.0	...	39.0	101.5
Austria	2005	0.7	0.7	0.6	43.8	0.1	2 144.7	...	20.3
Autriche	2010	0.7	0.7	0.7	42.9	0.1	1 853.2	51.2	39.2
	2016	0.7	0.6	0.7	37.6	~0.0	1 640.9	35.5	50.2
	2017	0.8	0.8	0.8	...	~0.0	...	...	...
Azerbaijan	2005	2.2	...	...	1.9	0.3	25.2	...	...
Azerbaïdjan	2010	2.3	3.2	1.4	1.9	~0.0	42.8	3.3	2.3
	2016	2.1	2.5	1.8	3.4	0.1	24.7	5.0	1.1
	2017	2.0	2.5	1.6	3.8	0.1	...	4.0	1.2
Bahamas	2005	16.0	27.9	4.8	...	7.4	446.2	...	135.1
Bahamas	2010	26.5	46.5	7.7	862.8	5.1	554.7	94.6	87.0
	2012	30.5	57.3	5.3	860.4	7.7	545.3	100.8	82.1
	2017	32.0	62.6	3.1	1 008.9	2.9	...	164.9	84.0
Bahrain	2005	0.4	...	...	396.9	1.4	1 086.5	...	...
Bahreïn	2007	0.4	...	...	254.3	0.0	700.4	...	14.0
	2008	0.5	...	...	327.7	...	681.4	...	15.7
	2010	0.9	...	...	...	...	...	...	...
	2014	0.5	...	...	...	...	...	...	...
Bangladesh	2005	2.6	...	...	0.4	0.9	9.0	...	...
Bangladesh	2006	3.0	...	...	0.4	0.8	9.2	...	...
	2010	2.7	...	...	...	...	...	...	...
	2017	2.2	...	...	...	...	...	...	...
Barbados	2005	10.5	15.0	6.4	627.2	8.3	409.4	...	69.6
Barbade	2010	11.0	17.0	5.5	535.8	4.3	733.0	172.7	59.9
	2016	7.7	14.5	1.4	545.1	3.8	594.8	65.0	63.6
	2017	10.5	20.3	1.4	502.5	3.5	...	83.6	60.1
Belarus	2005	8.6	...	...	20.0	0.4	1 079.2	...	8.6
Bélarus	2010	4.3	6.1	2.7	12.3	0.2	781.1	50.3	3.9
	2014	3.6	5.1	2.3	8.8	0.3	429.7	26.1	4.8
	2017	2.5	3.3	1.9	...	0.2	...	...	...

Intentional homicides and other crimes *(continued)*
By type of crime per 100 000 population and homicide victims by sex

Homicides intentionnels et autres crimes *(suite)*
Par type de crime pour 100 000 habitants et victimes d'homicides par sexe

Country or area Pays ou zone	Year Année	Intentional homicides Homicides volontaires Per 100 000 Pour 100 000	Victims (%) Victimes (%) Male Hommes	Female Femmes	Other crimes (per 100 000 pop.) Autres infractions (pour 100 000 hab.) Assault Agression	Kidnapping Enlèvement	Theft Vol simple	Robbery Vol qualifié	Sexual Violence Violences Sexuelles
Belgium	2005	2.1	2.5	1.7	639.2	8.7	2 061.0	...	57.3
Belgique	2010	1.7	2.2	1.2	710.8	10.3	2 087.5	218.1	64.8
	2014	1.9	2.3	1.4	627.5	10.3	1 857.6	195.4	61.5
	2015	2.0	...	...	611.6	10.4	1 653.0	198.4	59.7
	2017	1.7	...	...	607.4	10.2	...	166.0	62.8
Belize	2004	28.6	46.7	10.2	...	...	...	...	...
Belize	2005	28.5	...	...	...	3.2	590.9	...	...
	2009	30.8	55.9	5.7	164.8	0.6	374.3	...	64.1
	2010	40.0	70.0	10.0	...	...	259.6	148.1	40.4
	2014	34.8	62.9	6.8	295.2	1.1	234.0	86.1	42.2
	2015	33.0	61.1	5.0	...	6.7	218.6	59.3	51.2
	2016	37.5	66.9	8.1	...	...	204.4	63.0	...
	2017	37.8	69.9	5.8	...	1.3	...	...	...
Benin									
Bénin	2017	1.1	...	...	47.7	4.7	...	1.6	...
Bermuda	2004	1.5	0.0	2.9	659.1	...	1 519.7	...	...
Bermudes	2005	3.1	6.5	0.0	...	...	...	...	...
	2010	10.9	23.0	0.0	949.2	1.5	935.4	152.3	141.5
	2016	13.0	27.2	0.0	73.0	...	2 146.0	...	142.9
	2017	8.1	17.1	0.0	58.7	0.0	...	79.4	146.0
Bhutan	2005	1.7	...	...	...	...	...	...	...
Bhoutan	2010	2.3	...	...	...	0.1	71.3	6.9	10.4
	2014	...	...	...	72.5	0.4	74.0	1.8	11.3
	2017	1.7	2.3	1.1	131.4	0.0	...	2.3	10.3
Bolivia (Plurin. State of)	2005	5.2	...	...	65.3	1.1	41.2	...	18.7
Bolivie (État plurin. de)	2008	8.5	14.1	2.8	71.9	1.3	49.6	...	26.4
	2010	12.7	...	...	84.1	0.9	50.3	124.1	39.2
	2012	11.8	...	...	71.6	1.0	50.1	138.9	46.5
	2016	6.2	8.2	4.3	73.5	1.5	...	...	...
	2017	...	...	...	...	1.1	...	...	...
Bosnia and Herzegovina	2002	2.4	3.5	1.3	...	...	...	...	...
Bosnie-Herzégovine	2005	1.9	...	...	36.4	0.2	489.2	...	...
	2010	1.5	2.5	0.5	13.6	~0.0	306.7	...	4.0
	2016	1.3	1.8	0.9	29.8	~0.0	132.6	30.0	4.2
	2017	1.3	1.9	0.6	22.4	0.0	...	19.7	4.7
Botswana	2005	16.2	...	...	...	...	...	...	...
Botswana	2010	15.2	...	...	878.6	0.2	1 495.5	120.9	...
	2014	...	...	...	806.5	0.1	1 419.6	81.3	131.6
Brazil	2005	23.4	43.6	3.8	...	...	...	...	...
Brésil	2010	22.1	41.0	3.7	365.7	0.2	706.5	552.4	23.8
	2013	26.9	50.1	4.5	329.0	0.2	887.8	503.6	28.0
	2017	30.8	58.2	4.3	284.8	0.3	...	797.3	...
British Virgin Islands	2002	4.7	...	0.0	...	...	...	...	...
Îles Vierges britanniques	2004	17.9	...	...	...	...	...	...	...
	2006	8.3	...	...	...	...	...	...	...
Brunei Darussalam	2000	1.2	1.2	1.2	...	...	...	...	...
Brunéi Darussalam	2005	0.5	...	...	145.2	0.0	329.3	...	...
	2006	0.8	...	...	121.9	0.0	307.0	...	...
	2010	0.3	...	...	...	...	...	...	...
	2013	0.5	...	...	...	...	...	...	...
Bulgaria	2005	2.6	3.9	1.3	47.6	2.5	560.9	...	13.5
Bulgarie	2010	2.0	3.3	0.7	40.9	1.6	679.9	50.3	9.4
	2016	1.1	1.6	0.6	34.5	1.0	457.6	23.3	7.7
	2017	1.5	2.0	1.0	39.6	1.4	...	21.9	9.2
Burkina Faso	2005	0.5	...	...	...	...	...	...	...
Burkina Faso	2010	0.8	...	...	...	...	...	...	...
	2017	1.3	...	...	...	...	...	...	...
Burundi	2010	4.0	...	...	3.5	0.3	...	35.0	8.1
Burundi	2014	5.7	9.5	2.1	5.6	0.8	8.2	45.7	12.9
	2016	6.1	9.9	2.3	...	...	...	...	...
Cabo Verde	2005	9.5	...	...	...	...	...	...	...
Cabo Verde	2010	7.9	...	...	829.6	1.2	760.9	623.5	41.2
	2015	8.8	14.8	2.7	801.0	1.0	792.6	1 042.3	41.9
	2017	7.1	11.9	2.2	...	1.1	...	...	...
Cambodia	2005	3.4	...	...	...	...	...	...	...
Cambodge	2010	2.3	...	...	...	...	...	...	...
	2011	1.8	...	...	...	...	...	...	...

Intentional homicides and other crimes *(continued)*
By type of crime per 100 000 population and homicide victims by sex

Homicides intentionnels et autres crimes *(suite)*
Par type de crime pour 100 000 habitants et victimes d'homicides par sexe

Country or area Pays ou zone	Year Année	Intentional homicides Homicides volontaires			Other crimes (per 100 000 pop.) Autres infractions (pour 100 000 hab.)				
		Per 100 000 Pour 100 000	Victims (%) Victimes (%) Male Hommes	Female Femmes	Assault Agression	Kidnapping Enlèvement	Theft Vol simple	Robbery Vol qualifié	Sexual Violence Violences Sexuelles
Cameroon	2003	6.0	...	...	17.8	...	70.5	...	...
Cameroun	2005	...	...	...	17.7	...	67.7	...	...
	2010	4.9	...	...	24.2	2.3	80.7	80.7	10.1
	2014	0.9	1.1	0.8	16.3	1.9	111.4	16.3	3.1
	2015	1.2	1.3	1.0	20.6	4.2	69.9	20.6	...
	2016	1.2	1.4	0.9	7.7	2.4	...	17.6	...
	2017	1.4	...	...	18.2	3.5	...	18.1	...
Canada	2005	2.1	3.0	1.1	166.2	12.1	2 039.2	...	81.9
Canada	2010	1.6	2.4	0.9	162.3	12.6	1 593.7	89.3	78.8
	2016	1.7	2.5	0.8	146.8	10.4	1 404.7	60.4	83.8
	2017	1.8	2.7	0.9	150.8	10.3	...	61.9	95.3
Cayman Islands	2005	6.1	...	0.0	...	...	...	...	...
Îles Caïmanes	2006	2.0	0.0	...	...	...	...	...	...
	2010	15.9	...	0.0	...	...	...	...	...
	2014	8.2	...	0.0	...	...	...	...	...
Central African Republic République centrafricaine	2016	20.1	29.8	10.6	...	...	...	...	...
Channel Islands	2005	0.7	...	...	...	...	...	...	...
Îles Anglo-Normandes	2010	0.0	...	...	...	...	...	...	...
Chile	2005	3.6	6.2	1.0	...	0.9	959.5	...	...
Chili	2010	3.2	5.3	1.1	130.5	1.5	1 095.8	478.6	76.2
	2016	3.4	5.8	1.0	65.9	1.9	953.0	636.4	67.3
	2017	4.2	7.4	1.1	59.4	1.6	...	633.5	69.5
China	2005	1.6	...	...	...	...	...	...	...
Chine	2010	1.0	...	...	...	...	...	...	...
	2017	0.6	...	...	...	...	...	...	...
China, Hong Kong SAR	2005	0.5	0.6	0.4	119.5	0.0	520.1	...	21.6
Chine, RAS de Hong Kong	2010	0.5	0.5	0.5	109.1	~0.0	493.0	11.2	26.4
	2013	0.9	0.8	1.0	93.4	~0.0	445.7	7.1	25.1
	2017	0.3	0.3	0.4	...	...	...	...	...
China, Macao SAR	2005	0.8	...	...	...	...	...	...	...
Chine, RAS de Macao	2010	0.4	0.8	0.0	341.3	0.4	522.7	33.1	8.4
	2016	0.2	0.3	0.0	279.5	0.0	478.3	16.0	9.5
	2017	0.3	0.0	0.6	279.8	0.0	...	17.3	10.3
Colombia	2005	42.5	79.5	6.9	71.3	1.9	161.2	...	10.8
Colombie	2010	34.2	64.2	5.3	117.5	0.6	203.0	135.9	15.1
	2016	25.7	48.1	4.2	372.8	0.4	179.7	304.4	44.4
	2017	25.0	46.5	4.3	250.6	0.4	...	244.4	63.0
Cook Islands Îles Cook	2012	3.5	...	...	...	...	...	...	...
Costa Rica	2005	7.8	12.7	2.9	...	0.3	195.1	...	...
Costa Rica	2010	11.5	20.3	2.7	173.8	0.2	442.4	943.5	142.3
	2013	8.7	15.8	1.5	173.4	0.1	691.4	1 011.3	153.5
	2017	12.2	22.0	2.3	155.5	0.2	...	1 587.5	191.2
Côte d'Ivoire Côte d'Ivoire	2008	...	...	...	51.6	...	...	...	3.7
Croatia	2005	1.6	1.9	1.2	26.3	0.5	694.3	...	14.2
Croatie	2010	1.4	1.4	1.4	22.8	0.3	313.7	28.8	9.2
	2016	1.0	1.2	0.9	18.8	~0.0	302.7	25.4	16.1
	2017	1.1	1.4	0.8	19.1	0.0	...	20.7	11.4
Cuba	2005	6.1	9.2	3.0	...	...	...	...	...
Cuba	2010	4.5	6.8	2.2	...	...	...	...	...
	2016	5.0	8.0	2.1	...	...	...	...	...
Curaçao	2005	20.0	32.8	8.7	...	...	...	...	...
Curaçao	2007	19.0	36.2	4.1	...	...	...	...	...
Cyprus	2005	1.9	3.5	0.4	12.8	1.6	116.8	...	10.9
Chypre	2010	0.7	1.3	0.2	15.5	2.4	150.0	14.0	7.1
	2016	1.1	1.4	0.9	12.4	0.1	61.7	9.0	3.7
	2017	0.6	1.2	0.0	12.2	0.8	...	9.9	2.8
Czechia	2005	1.1	1.3	0.9	211.4	0.1	1 502.5	...	18.0
Tchéquie	2010	1.0	1.0	1.0	171.5	0.1	1 198.7	38.1	12.7
	2016	0.6	0.6	0.7	47.6	0.2	676.8	15.5	13.1
	2017	0.6	0.7	0.6	44.8	0.2	...	14.9	13.3
Denmark	2005	1.0	1.3	0.7	205.0	...	3 100.7	...	...
Danemark	2010	0.8	0.7	0.8	31.6	...	4 351.1	60.7	36.2
	2016	1.0	1.2	0.8	30.3	...	3 948.7	38.3	66.4
	2017	1.2	1.8	0.7	33.2	...	...	35.6	83.7

11

Intentional homicides and other crimes *(continued)*
By type of crime per 100 000 population and homicide victims by sex

Homicides intentionnels et autres crimes *(suite)*
Par type de crime pour 100 000 habitants et victimes d'homicides par sexe

Country or area Pays ou zone	Year Année	Intentional homicides Homicides volontaires			Other crimes (per 100 000 pop.) Autres infractions (pour 100 000 hab.)				
		Per 100 000 Pour 100 000	Victims (%) Victimes (%)		Assault Agression	Kidnapping Enlèvement	Theft Vol simple	Robbery Vol qualifié	Sexual Violence Violences Sexuelles
			Male Hommes	Female Femmes					
Dominica	2001	1.4	0.0	...	...	...	...	...	...
Dominique	2002	12.9	...	0.0	...	...	...	...	...
	2005	11.3	...	...	...	...	...	...	...
	2010	21.2	...	...	...	...	...	...	...
	2011	8.5	...	0.0	...	...	...	...	...
	2017	26.6	...	...	88.7	5.6	...	101.4	0.0
Dominican Republic	2005	26.3	47.6	4.7	...	0.2	...	...	...
République dominicaine	2006	23.3	42.4	3.9	...	0.2	...	...	...
	2010	25.5	46.5	4.4	...	...	...	...	...
	2016	15.5	27.8	3.3	30.2	0.2	8.4	67.2	62.6
	2017	11.6	19.5	3.6	...	...	...	...	...
Ecuador	2005	15.3	28.2	2.4	56.1	...	43.1	...	...
Équateur	2010	17.5	31.7	3.2	30.0	...	33.4	360.4	24.3
	2016	5.8	9.5	2.2	44.3	5.9	192.7	499.5	65.0
	2017	5.8	9.2	2.4	38.9	4.7	...	457.2	80.5
Egypt	2005	0.7	1.2	0.2	...	~0.0	46.3	...	...
Égypte	2010	2.2	3.9	0.5	0.2	0.1	93.2	0.8	0.2
	2011	3.2	5.6	0.8	0.4	0.3	103.1	3.2	0.1
	2012	2.6	4.5	0.6	...	...	...	...	...
El Salvador	2005	64.1	120.6	12.6	76.5	0.1	177.1	...	...
El Salvador	2010	64.5	117.0	17.3	62.9	0.5	156.5	87.6	36.1
	2015	105.2	204.5	17.2	93.1	0.3	135.0	81.6	70.2
	2017	61.7	115.9	13.8	58.6	0.2	...	59.4	68.5
Estonia	2005	8.3	13.4	3.9	9.7	0.1	2 245.7	...	29.6
Estonie	2010	5.3	8.6	2.3	7.7	0.0	1 895.9	45.0	20.6
	2015	3.4	5.6	1.5	7.5	0.0	863.4	25.6	42.8
	2017	2.2	3.4	1.1	5.8	0.0	...	15.2	19.6
Eswatini	2004	14.2	...	...	1 421.7	9.4	2 032.3	...	...
Eswatini	2005	13.5	...	...	...	...	...	...	...
	2010	19.5	...	...	...	...	...	...	...
	2017	11.6	...	...	...	...	...	...	...
Ethiopia									
Éthiopie	2012	8.8	...	...	...	...	...	...	...
Fiji	2005	2.8	3.3	2.2	...	...	...	...	...
Fidji	2010	2.3	3.2	1.4	...	...	...	...	...
	2014	2.3	1.8	2.8	...	...	...	...	...
Finland	2005	2.3	3.3	1.3	579.3	~0.0	2 378.4	...	36.5
Finlande	2010	2.2	3.5	1.0	37.2	~0.0	1 853.0	28.1	45.0
	2016	1.3	1.9	0.8	29.0	0.1	2 082.4	30.4	58.0
	2017	1.3	1.4	1.1	28.7	~0.0	...	29.8	55.4
France	2005	1.6	...	...	243.2	3.3	1 366.3	...	39.1
France	2010	1.3	...	...	368.8	3.3	1 864.8	192.5	36.5
	2016	1.4	1.7	1.0	375.6	5.9	2 136.2	161.5	58.1
	2017	1.3	1.6	0.9	...	...	...	154.3	64.4
French Guiana	2005	22.2	...	...	...	...	...	...	...
Guyane française	2009	13.2	21.6	4.8	...	...	...	...	...
French Polynesia									
Polynésie française	2009	0.4	...	...	...	...	...	...	...
Georgia	2005	9.6	16.5	3.3	8.7	2.1	386.1	...	3.9
Géorgie	2010	4.6	8.1	1.3	3.1	0.1	277.4	15.6	4.0
	2014	2.7	3.9	1.6	5.7	...	236.9	11.7	3.2
	2016	1.0	0.3	1.6	...	...	...	...	...
Germany	2005	1.1	1.2	0.9	605.8	2.1	2 738.2	...	67.6
Allemagne	2010	1.0	1.0	1.0	176.8	6.1	1 509.4	59.6	45.2
	2016	1.2	1.2	1.1	170.4	5.8	1 570.0	52.3	45.2
	2017	1.0	1.1	0.9	165.8	5.6	...	47.0	42.1
Ghana	2005	1.8	...	...	...	...	...	...	...
Ghana	2010	1.7	...	...	...	...	...	...	...
	2017	2.1	...	...	...	...	...	...	...
Gibraltar									
Gibraltar	2010	3.0	...	...	...	...	...	...	...
Greece	2005	1.2	1.6	0.8	69.3	0.2	549.2	...	5.6
Grèce	2010	1.6	2.7	0.6	10.1	1.6	1 088.5	55.8	4.7
	2016	0.8	1.1	0.5	14.3	0.6	958.8	44.5	4.6
	2017	0.8	1.2	0.4	14.3	0.7	...	40.4	4.3
Greenland	2005	17.6	...	...	...	...	...	...	...
Groenland	2010	19.4	...	...	...	...	...	...	...
	2016	5.3	...	...	...	...	...	...	...

11 Intentional homicides and other crimes *(continued)*
By type of crime per 100 000 population and homicide victims by sex

Homicides intentionnels et autres crimes *(suite)*
Par type de crime pour 100 000 habitants et victimes d'homicides par sexe

Country or area Pays ou zone	Year Année	Intentional homicides Homicides volontaires	Victims (%) Victimes (%)		Other crimes (per 100 000 pop.) Autres infractions (pour 100 000 hab.)				
		Per 100 000 Pour 100 000	Male Hommes	Female Femmes	Assault Agression	Kidnapping Enlèvement	Theft Vol simple	Robbery Vol qualifié	Sexual Violence Violences Sexuelles
Grenada	2005	10.5	15.2	5.8	1 803.8	0.0	1 726.7	...	143.8
Grenade	2010	9.4	14.9	3.8	1 086.8	0.0	906.6	24.5	104.7
	2016	10.0	14.4	5.5	397.3	0.0	2 250.9	50.0	208.2
	2017	10.8	17.9	3.6	337.8	0.0	...	51.4	179.3
Guadeloupe	2005	5.7	11.3	0.7	...	...	...	...	...
Guadeloupe	2009	8.9	16.2	2.5	...	...	...	...	...
	2016	5.8	...	...	...	...	...	...	...
Guam	2005	4.4	...	...	...	...	...	...	...
Guam	2010	1.9	...	...	...	...	...	...	...
	2011	2.5	...	...	...	...	...	...	...
Guatemala	2005	40.8	75.0	7.8	46.5	0.4	32.9	...	2.4
Guatemala	2010	40.7	73.3	9.3	50.9	0.9	44.5	22.1	3.4
	2012	33.8	61.0	7.4	39.9	0.5	59.7	25.0	4.3
	2015	29.4	54.6	7.6	14.6	2.5	290.1	...	65.8
	2016	27.3	94.6	...	11.2	...	296.2	...	62.6
	2017	26.1	...	...	...	...	...	...	...
Guinea	2005	...	...	...	3.1	0.2	...	...	...
Guinée	2007	...	...	...	3.1	0.2	14.2	...	0.3
	2008	...	...	...	...	0.3	...	...	...
Guinea-Bissau	2014	3.8	...	...	195.9	3.6	58.9	42.1	...
Guinée-Bissau	2016	3.6	...	...	112.2	0.7	...	20.3	...
	2017	1.1	...	...	...	...	...	...	...
Guyana	2005	19.0	30.5	7.5	...	...	...	...	32.0
Guyana	2010	18.7	29.3	8.2	1 492.9	0.3	521.5	146.2	19.6
	2016	18.4	34.2	2.6	149.7	0.0	624.6	167.2	37.5
	2017	14.8	24.2	5.4	271.2	0.0	...	161.3	31.7
Haiti	2010	6.8	...	...	...	...	...	...	...
Haïti	2016	9.5	17.7	1.4	...	...	...	...	...
Holy See	2010	0.0	0.0	0.0	0.0	0.0	0.0	0.0	0.0
Saint-Siège	2015	0.0	0.0	0.0	0.0	0.0	0.0	0.0	0.0
Honduras	2005	43.1	...	...	...	...	...	...	...
Honduras	2010	75.0	141.0	9.2	...	...	53.8	...	...
	2016	55.6	101.2	10.0	14.5	0.2	33.3	180.2	16.6
	2017	41.0	73.7	8.3	21.8	0.2	...	120.8	15.5
Hungary	2005	1.6	1.8	1.4	122.3	0.1	1 251.8	...	8.5
Hongrie	2010	1.4	1.6	1.2	146.8	0.2	1 351.8	34.2	13.0
	2015	2.3	2.6	2.0	127.6	...	1 138.5	14.7	17.2
	2016	2.1	2.6	1.6	...	0.1	959.6	11.3	6.2
	2017	2.5	3.7	1.4	...	~0.0	...	8.6	6.0
Iceland	2005	1.0	2.0	0.0	...	...	1 078.3	...	97.6
Islande	2010	0.6	1.2	0.0	17.8	...	1 537.5	13.1	67.8
	2016	0.3	0.0	0.6	22.3	...	1 045.8	15.1	150.0
	2017	0.9	0.6	1.2	30.8	...	...	14.7	142.5
India	2005	3.9	5.0	2.8	23.6	2.0	23.8	...	5.4
Inde	2010	3.8	4.5	3.0	23.4	3.1	26.8	1.9	5.9
	2013	3.6	4.2	2.9	26.1	5.1	29.1	2.8	9.1
	2017	3.1	3.4	2.8	...	...	...	...	...
Indonesia	2004	0.6	...	...	...	...	...	...	...
Indonésie	2010	0.4	...	...	13.2	0.2	10.1	4.1	...
	2016	0.5	...	...	5.5	0.1	10.2	4.6	2.0
	2017	0.4	...	...	4.7	0.1	...	4.0	2.1
Iran (Islamic Republic of)	2004	2.9	...	...	...	...	159.3	...	...
Iran (Rép. islamique d')	2009	3.0	...	...	...	...	...	...	...
	2014	2.5	4.4	0.6	...	...	...	...	...
Iraq	2010	9.0	14.7	3.3	...	...	...	...	...
Iraq	2013	10.1	16.7	3.3	...	...	...	...	...
Ireland	2005	1.3	2.1	0.4	301.4	1.8	1 421.9	...	43.5
Irlande	2010	1.2	2.1	0.3	330.2	2.9	1 436.5	70.2	52.0
	2016	0.8	1.4	0.1	76.5	1.5	1 383.8	44.7	47.5
	2017	0.9	1.1	0.6	85.2	1.6	...	46.0	53.5
Isle of Man Île de Man	2016	0.0	...	...	...	...	...	...	...
Israel	2005	2.6	3.8	1.5	782.9	6.4	1 919.0	...	70.4
Israël	2010	2.0	3.2	0.9	626.3	3.6	984.8	39.6	67.5
	2011	2.0	3.1	0.9	575.3	3.5	945.8	36.7	61.1
	2017	1.5	2.4	0.6	...	...	...	...	...

Intentional homicides and other crimes *(continued)*
By type of crime per 100 000 population and homicide victims by sex

Homicides intentionnels et autres crimes *(suite)*
Par type de crime pour 100 000 habitants et victimes d'homicides par sexe

Country or area Pays ou zone	Year Année	Intentional homicides Homicides volontaires			Other crimes (per 100 000 pop.) Autres infractions (pour 100 000 hab.)				
		Per 100 000 Pour 100 000	Victims (%) Victimes (%)		Assault Agression	Kidnapping Enlèvement	Theft Vol simple	Robbery Vol qualifié	Sexual Violence Violences Sexuelles
			Male Hommes	Female Femmes					
Italy	2005	1.0	1.7	0.5	97.2	0.6	1 882.9	...	6.9
Italie	2010	0.9	1.3	0.5	109.3	0.6	1 591.3	80.9	8.1
	2015	0.8	1.1	0.4	107.2	0.5	1 725.7	57.9	7.4
	2017	0.6	0.8	0.4	108.4	0.3	...	51.4	8.4
Jamaica	2005	61.1	109.6	13.5	...	1.1	...	...	39.9
Jamaïque	2008	58.2	105.3	11.8	...	1.5	...	...	52.9
	2010	51.5	93.2	10.3	50.1	...	...	101.6	52.9
	2016	46.6	84.4	9.2	77.8	0.4	6.5	49.3	53.9
	2017	56.4	102.5	10.9	98.7	0.4		43.4	54.7
Japan	2005	0.5	0.5	0.5	47.0	0.2	719.5	...	8.4
Japon	2010	0.4	0.4	0.4	20.7	0.1	480.9	3.2	6.5
	2016	0.3	0.3	0.3	19.1	0.2	293.1	1.8	5.6
	2017	0.2	0.2	0.3	...	...	...	...	...
Jordan	2005	1.2	...	...	254.5	0.5	122.6	...	...
Jordanie	2006	1.7	...	...	261.9	0.6	149.3	...	...
	2010	1.6	2.1	1.1	...	...	168.0	...	...
	2012	2.0	3.3	0.6	...	...	167.0	...	...
	2017	1.4	2.0	0.7	...	...	...	6.1	...
Kazakhstan	2004	13.7	...	...	...	...	...	...	...
Kazakhstan	2005	...	...	...	...	0.6	409.9	...	...
	2010	8.5	13.3	4.1	9.8	0.8	369.1	66.0	2.2
	2015	4.9	7.1	2.8	5.1	0.5	1 188.9	69.4	2.7
	2017	5.1	7.9	2.4	11.3	0.4	...	52.4	11.7
Kenya	2005	3.0	...	...	34.7	0.4	33.3	...	7.1
Kenya	2010	4.6	...	...	33.5	0.2	28.5	6.8	11.5
	2016	4.8	7.1	2.6	32.0	...	2.8	5.4	12.7
	2017	4.9	8.1	1.7	31.8	0.1	...	5.4	10.9
Kiribati	2001	4.7	...	...	...	...	...	...	...
Kiribati	2010	3.9	...	...	...	...	...	...	...
	2012	7.5	...	...	...	...	...	...	...
Kosovo	2010	6.0	9.6	2.3	...	1.9	...	...	...
Kosovo	2017	2.6	3.8	1.4	...	0.9	...	...	...
Kuwait	2005	1.8	1.9	1.7	26.2	12.3	431.3	...	16.4
Koweït	2009	1.7	2.3	1.0	24.3	12.7	288.2	...	18.0
	2010	2.0	2.7	1.0	...	...	...	...	...
	2012	1.8	2.6	0.7	...	...	...	...	...
Kyrgyzstan	2005	9.7	15.3	4.1	5.2	0.5	243.1	...	...
Kirghizistan	2009	7.9	10.9	4.9	6.7	0.1	205.0	...	...
	2010	16.8	...	...	9.9	1.5	182.3	51.6	...
	2016	4.4	...	...	4.7	0.9	153.0	16.0	...
	2017	4.1	...	...	...	0.8	...	...	...
Latvia	2005	5.6	...	...	48.9	0.3	1 078.5	...	32.0
Lettonie	2010	3.3	...	...	57.9	0.4	1 210.9	50.6	10.9
	2016	3.5	3.9	3.2	33.3	0.4	738.1	33.0	11.1
	2017	4.2	4.6	3.8	33.7	0.2	...	31.0	13.4
Lebanon	2010	3.3	...	...	191.7	11.3	579.8	...	4.2
Liban	2015	3.5	...	...	118.9	15.4	383.1	42.7	3.2
	2016	3.5	...	...	111.6	...	...	...	2.8
	2017	3.6	...	...	...	...	...	...	2.2
Lesotho	2009	36.3	...	...	368.4	3.1	226.0	...	...
Lesotho	2010	38.3	...	...	...	...	...	...	...
	2015	43.6	...	...	...	...	...	...	...
Liberia	2010	3.3	...	...	...	...	...	...	...
Libéria	2012	3.3	...	...	...	...	...	...	...
Liechtenstein	2005	0.0	...	...	202.9	0.0	500.0	...	51.4
Liechtenstein	2009	0.0	0.0	0.0	250.0	0.0	538.9	...	8.3
	2010	2.8	...	0.0	213.9	0.0	483.3	5.6	16.7
	2016	0.0	0.0	0.0	186.8	0.0	515.8	10.5	23.7
	2017	2.6	0.0	...	...	...	...	...	...
Lithuania	2005	11.1	17.5	5.6	12.2	2.1	825.9	...	16.7
Lituanie	2010	7.0	10.0	4.4	7.8	2.2	849.2	87.3	16.5
	2016	5.3	8.0	3.0	7.5	0.0	690.8	46.4	7.2
	2017	4.5	6.2	3.1	6.3	0.0	...	38.2	7.9
Luxembourg	2004	0.4	0.4	0.4	...	...	...	...	...
Luxembourg	2005	0.9	...	...	...	...	...	...	...
	2010	2.0	2.0	2.0	487.2	5.3	1 420.9	74.2	41.5
	2014	0.7	0.7	0.7	131.2	9.4	1 848.5	110.8	64.7
	2017	0.3	...	...	98.8	7.8	...	76.7	61.1

11

Intentional homicides and other crimes *(continued)*
By type of crime per 100 000 population and homicide victims by sex

Homicides intentionnels et autres crimes *(suite)*
Par type de crime pour 100 000 habitants et victimes d'homicides par sexe

Country or area Pays ou zone	Year Année	Intentional homicides Homicides volontaires Per 100 000 Pour 100 000	Victims (%) Victimes (%) Male Hommes	Female Femmes	Other crimes (per 100 000 pop.) Autres infractions (pour 100 000 hab.) Assault Agression	Kidnapping Enlèvement	Theft Vol simple	Robbery Vol qualifié	Sexual Violence Violences Sexuelles
Madagascar	2010	...	...	...	16.3	0.0	0.3	14.8	3.3
Madagascar	2015	...	...	...	9.0	~0.0	0.9	7.2	4.6
Malawi	2005	1.6	...	...	...	...	...	...	...
Malawi	2010	3.6	...	...	...	...	...	...	...
	2012	1.8	...	...	...	...	...	...	...
Malaysia	2005	2.4	...	...	16.5	...	133.6	...	...
Malaisie	2006	2.2	...	...	21.8	...	141.7	...	...
	2010	1.9	...	...	...	...	...	...	...
	2013	2.1	...	...	...	...	...	...	...
Maldives	2003	1.3	...	...	...	...	...	...	...
Maldives	2004	...	...	...	...	0.3	...	...	...
	2010	1.6	...	...	403.8	7.1	1 093.2	149.5	142.9
	2013	0.7	...	...	309.9	1.9	1 606.5	175.2	137.7
	2017	...	...	...	...	6.8	...	...	...
Malta	2005	1.0	1.0	1.0	...	...	2 373.3	...	...
Malte	2010	1.0	1.5	0.5	43.5	0.0	1 876.6	47.3	22.0
	2015	0.9	0.9	0.9	42.2	0.0	1 993.8	55.8	24.0
	2017	2.1	3.6	0.5	...	0.0	...	...	...
Martinique	2005	4.8	...	...	...	...	...	...	...
Martinique	2009	2.8	4.4	1.4	...	...	...	...	...
Mauritius	2005	3.0	3.9	2.1	10.0	...	1 172.3	...	25.7
Maurice	2010	2.6	4.0	1.3	19.1	2.8	863.9	86.9	34.6
	2011	2.6	3.9	1.3	18.4	4.0	731.1	65.1	37.3
	2017	2.6	3.2	2.0	...	...	...	...	...
Mayotte									
Mayotte	2009	5.9	...	...	...	...	...	...	...
Mexico	2005	9.4	16.6	2.4	225.6	0.3	80.0	...	27.0
Mexique	2010	22.6	41.8	4.2	202.2	1.1	115.8	647.0	29.9
	2016	19.9	36.0	4.5	51.6	1.0	251.1	128.8	29.6
	2017	25.7	46.9	5.4	44.0	1.3	...	179.2	29.3
Monaco	2005	3.0	...	...	455.9	0.0	952.9	...	27.0
Monaco	2006	2.9	...	...	411.8	5.9	1 017.7	...	...
	2010	0.0	...	...	...	...	...	...	...
	2015	0.0	0.0	0.0	518.4	2.7	1 431.6	31.6	15.8
	2016	...	...	...	...	2.6	1 094.7	...	13.2
Mongolia	2005	15.8	...	...	118.4	~0.0	264.6	...	13.4
Mongolie	2010	8.8	12.8	4.9	214.0	0.0	212.4	19.1	13.3
	2016	6.0	9.6	2.5	61.9	~0.0	296.6	15.5	9.5
	2017	6.1	9.5	2.9	12.8	0.1	...	39.6	12.1
Montenegro	2005	3.6	...	...	25.2	...	250.0	...	5.7
Monténégro	2010	2.4	2.6	2.2	30.9	0.3	84.9	0.5	5.8
	2016	4.5	8.1	0.9	20.4	0.3	80.7	20.4	3.5
	2017	2.4	3.5	1.3	23.4	0.0	...	18.8	3.7
Montserrat	2004	0.0	0.0	0.0	...	...	...	...	...
Montserrat	2005	20.7	...	0.0	...	...	...	...	...
	2008	20.4	...	0.0	...	...	...	...	...
	2012	20.3	0.0	...	...	...	...	...	...
Morocco	2005	1.5	...	...	107.1	1.0	203.9	...	3.1
Maroc	2009	1.4	2.4	0.3	97.4	1.0	245.5	...	10.2
	2010	1.4	...	...	...	...	...	...	...
	2015	1.2	1.9	0.6	162.3	1.9	140.2	54.9	10.0
	2017	2.1	3.7	0.6	331.3	2.1	...	135.4	11.3
Mozambique	2005	5.3	...	...	6.2	...	27.1	...	3.9
Mozambique	2009	3.6	...	...	2.3	...	20.7	...	2.7
	2010	3.7	...	...	...	...	...	...	...
	2011	3.5	...	...	...	...	...	...	...
Myanmar	2005	1.4	...	...	...	...	...	...	...
Myanmar	2010	1.6	2.7	0.6	5.3	...	3.4	~0.0	0.5
	2013	2.4	4.1	0.8	9.7	~0.0	5.2	0.2	0.7
	2016	2.3	3.9	0.7	8.7	~0.0	5.9	0.3	...
Namibia	2004	18.5	...	...	...	...	...	...	...
Namibie	2010	14.8	...	...	...	...	...	...	...
	2012	17.7	...	...	...	...	...	...	...
Nepal	2005	3.4	...	...	4.1	0.5	2.0	...	...
Népal	2006	2.3	...	...	4.0	0.9	2.1	...	...
	2010	3.0	...	...	...	...	...	...	...
	2016	2.3	...	...	0.2	0.1	4.7	0.3	...

Intentional homicides and other crimes *(continued)*
By type of crime per 100 000 population and homicide victims by sex

Homicides intentionnels et autres crimes *(suite)*
Par type de crime pour 100 000 habitants et victimes d'homicides par sexe

Country or area Pays ou zone	Year Année	Intentional homicides Homicides volontaires			Other crimes (per 100 000 pop.) Autres infractions (pour 100 000 hab.)				
		Per 100 000 Pour 100 000	Victims (%) Victimes (%) Male Hommes	Female Femmes	Assault Agression	Kidnapping Enlèvement	Theft Vol simple	Robbery Vol qualifié	Sexual Violence Violences Sexuelles
Netherlands	2005	1.1	1.4	0.7	409.7	5.6	4 631.6	...	44.5
Pays-Bas	2010	0.9	1.1	0.6	361.3	3.9	3 968.7	96.7	57.6
	2016	0.6	0.8	0.4	29.6	2.5	1 791.8	52.9	27.9
	2017	0.8	1.1	0.5	28.1	2.3	...	47.2	28.1
New Caledonia									
Nouvelle-Calédonie	2009	3.2	...	...	...	...	...	...	...
New Zealand	2005	1.5	1.7	1.3	234.2	7.0	3 088.2	...	59.6
Nouvelle-Zélande	2010	1.0	1.0	1.0	257.7	5.2	2 676.0	57.0	66.7
	2013	1.0	1.5	0.5	198.1	4.4	2 253.0	45.0	82.7
	2017	0.7	1.0	0.5	521.6	8.1	...	79.6	125.2
Nicaragua	2005	13.4	...	...	355.5	0.2	266.8	...	...
Nicaragua	2010	13.5	24.6	2.6	315.0	0.1	179.5	488.1	62.3
	2015	8.4	14.9	2.1	...	...	...	...	...
	2016	7.2	...	...	...	...	...	...	...
Niger									
Niger	2012	4.4	...	...	...	...	...	...	...
Nigeria	2010	...	...	...	11.4	0.5	12.9	1.4	1.1
Nigéria	2013	...	...	...	9.6	0.3	14.0	1.1	1.0
	2016	34.5	...	...	...	...	...	...	...
North Macedonia	2005	2.1	3.4	0.9	...	1.2	...	...	...
Macédoine du Nord	2010	2.1	2.7	1.4	12.0	0.8	236.4	29.2	6.0
	2014	1.7	2.4	1.0	10.3	0.4	239.8	14.7	6.5
	2017	1.5	2.6	0.4	7.1	0.3	...	20.0	4.9
Norway	2005	0.7	0.7	0.7	63.9	...	2 991.8	...	42.3
Norvège	2010	0.6	0.6	0.6	59.9	...	2 592.8	34.5	50.1
	2016	0.5	0.6	0.4	41.9	...	1 990.2	15.4	105.9
	2017	0.5	0.6	0.5	39.9	...	...	14.7	106.4
Oman	2005	2.1	...	...	...	...	...	...	...
Oman	2008	1.7	...	...	75.7	0.3	200.5	...	6.7
	2010	1.6	...	...	...	...	...	...	...
	2017	0.5	0.7	0.3	1.4	0.3	...	0.7	2.8
Other non-specified areas	2001	1.4	...	...	...	...	...	...	...
Autres zones non-spécifiées	2010	0.8	...	...	...	...	...	...	...
	2015	0.8	...	...	...	...	...	...	...
Pakistan	2005	6.1	...	...	...	...	...	...	...
Pakistan	2010	7.4	...	...	19.8	10.4	27.4	10.1	1.9
	2016	4.2	...	...	14.6	8.9	19.8	6.4	1.9
	2017	4.0	...	...	13.1	8.8	...	6.0	1.8
Palau									
Palaos	2017	0.0	...	...	...	...	...	...	...
Panama	2005	10.9	19.6	2.2	...	0.5	419.8	...	23.5
Panama	2010	12.6	23.4	1.7	166.4	1.0	501.3	260.9	27.7
	2016	10.0	17.8	2.2	62.2	0.6	395.9	191.3	80.4
	2017	9.7	17.1	2.2	81.4	0.6	...	242.8	114.0
Papua New Guinea	2005	9.3	...	...	...	...	...	...	...
Papouasie-Nvl-Guinée	2010	9.8	...	...	...	...	...	...	...
Paraguay	2005	15.2	...	...	38.4	~0.0	...	...	...
Paraguay	2010	11.9	21.0	2.4	31.2	~0.0	499.1	219.0	54.3
	2016	9.9	17.8	1.7	9.8	~0.0	625.3	328.7	71.8
	2017	7.9	13.9	1.7	3.1	0.4	...	28.8	...
Peru	2005	...	...	...	52.8	1.8	188.2	...	...
Pérou	2010	...	...	...	65.6	1.6	192.3	195.7	18.2
	2016	7.9	12.5	3.3	73.5	0.8	306.9	248.1	29.3
	2017	7.9	14.3	1.6	82.8	0.6	...	222.9	31.1
Philippines	2005	7.5	...	...	...	0.1	12.9	...	...
Philippines	2010	9.2	15.7	2.6	...	~0.0	77.6	38.4	2.3
	2012	8.7	15.1	2.3	...	~0.0	44.9	27.8	1.8
	2016	11.0	...	...	...	...	47.9	20.5	...
	2017	8.4	...	...	...	...	...	15.3	...
Poland	2005	1.4	2.2	0.7	...	0.1	726.8	...	...
Pologne	2010	1.0	1.4	0.6	28.7	0.1	532.0	50.5	8.1
	2015	0.8	1.0	0.6	18.3	0.6	381.8	26.8	7.2
	2016	0.7	1.0	0.4	20.1	...	332.7	25.4	8.3
	2017	0.8	1.0	0.5	19.2	...	...	21.4	8.5
Portugal	2005	1.3	2.0	0.6	373.2	4.2	873.8	...	15.4
Portugal	2010	1.2	1.6	0.8	8.1	4.7	1 088.8	192.9	20.2
	2014	0.9	0.9	0.9	5.2	3.6	1 005.6	149.7	22.4
	2016	0.6	...	...	5.1	2.9	753.2	128.9	23.9
	2017	0.7	...	...	5.7	2.8	...	115.5	24.7

Intentional homicides and other crimes *(continued)*
By type of crime per 100 000 population and homicide victims by sex

Homicides intentionnels et autres crimes *(suite)*
Par type de crime pour 100 000 habitants et victimes d'homicides par sexe

Country or area Pays ou zone	Year Année	Intentional homicides Homicides volontaires			Other crimes (per 100 000 pop.) Autres infractions (pour 100 000 hab.)				
		Per 100 000 Pour 100 000	Victims (%) Victimes (%) Male Hommes	Female Femmes	Assault Agression	Kidnapping Enlèvement	Theft Vol simple	Robbery Vol qualifié	Sexual Violence Violences Sexuelles
Puerto Rico	2005	22.7	43.6	3.5	...	...	...	...	...
Porto Rico	2010	28.8	56.2	3.4	75.8	...	747.9	182.0	...
	2016	21.4	41.3	3.3	109.5	1.4	705.5	99.1	...
	2017	23.0	45.9	2.2	100.4	0.9	...	91.0	37.7
Qatar	2004	0.7	0.8	0.4	39.6	0.8	97.5	...	...
Qatar	2005	0.7	0.3	1.4	...	...	103.7	...	...
	2006	0.5	0.6	0.3	...	...	102.0	...	...
	2010	0.2	0.3	0.0	...	...	...	...	...
	2014	0.4	0.4	0.3	...	...	...	...	...
Republic of Korea	2005	0.8	...	...	...	...	387.6	...	...
République de Corée	2010	1.0	...	...	590.1	0.4	543.8	8.9	36.8
	2016	0.7	0.6	0.8	98.1	0.2	398.2	2.3	43.5
	2017	0.6	0.6	0.6	87.3	0.1	...	1.9	47.2
Republic of Moldova	2005	7.1	9.8	4.6	9.5	0.4	276.7	...	9.4
République de Moldova	2010	6.5	8.3	4.8	10.2	0.9	334.0	4.5	13.6
	2014	4.3	7.4	1.5	7.9	2.2	410.7	3.1	15.9
	2017	3.5	5.4	1.7	...	...	...	...	...
Réunion	2005	3.2	4.5	1.8	...	...	...	...	...
Réunion	2009	1.8	2.3	1.4	...	...	...	...	...
Romania	2005	2.0	2.7	1.4	41.6	1.3	201.7	...	...
Roumanie	2010	1.3	1.8	0.9	60.1	1.6	238.5	12.1	7.3
	2016	1.5	2.2	0.9	1.5	1.7	465.2	15.6	9.0
	2017	1.3	1.7	0.9	1.4	1.6	...	16.1	7.8
Russian Federation	2005	24.8	40.1	11.5	40.3	0.8	1 094.9	...	12.9
Fédération de Russie	2010	11.6	18.5	5.7	21.2	0.4	772.5	114.7	10.6
	2016	10.9	17.4	5.3	17.3	0.2	506.7	7.9	11.1
	2017	9.1	14.5	4.5	16.0	0.2	...	6.3	11.6
Rwanda	2010	2.9	...	...	20.0	0.1	...	20.6	...
Rwanda	2013	3.3	...	...	30.5	0.2	...	25.6	16.0
	2015	2.6	...	...	...	...	...	...	...
Saint Helena	2005	0.0	...	...	...	...	...	...	...
Sainte-Hélène	2009	0.0	...	...	...	...	...	...	...
Saint Kitts and Nevis	2004	23.7	...	0.0	...	...	...	...	...
Saint-Kitts-et-Nevis	2005	17.1	...	...	...	...	...	...	...
	2010	42.8	...	...	316.3	4.1	1 087.8	177.6	126.5
	2011	68.8	...	...	279.6	6.1	1 002.0	134.7	130.6
	2012	36.1	...	...	...	...	...	...	...
Saint Lucia	2004	22.9	41.7	4.7	...	...	...	...	...
Sainte-Lucie	2005	25.1	...	...	...	...	...	...	...
	2010	25.3	44.9	6.2	...	...	...	...	...
	2017	29.3	55.0	4.4	...	...	...	...	...
Saint Martin (French part) St-Martin (partie française)	2016	27.7	...	...	...	...	...	...	...
Saint Pierre and Miquelon	2006	0.0	0.0	0.0	...	...	...	...	...
Saint-Pierre-et-Miquelon	2009	15.8	...	...	...	...	...	...	...
Saint Vincent & Grenadines	2005	23.9	34.6	13.0	1 148.6	1.8	1 773.4	...	104.6
Saint-Vincent-Grenadines	2010	23.1	39.9	5.6	1 212.0	1.8	1 760.2	108.3	155.6
	2012	25.8	...	...	1 029.6	3.7	1 947.2	148.1	162.0
	2016	36.5	64.6	7.4	753.2	8.2	...	72.5	99.1
Samoa	2010	8.6	...	...	...	...	...	...	...
Samoa	2013	3.1	...	...	...	...	...	...	...
San Marino	2005	0.0	0.0	0.0	...	...	...	...	...
Saint-Marin	2010	0.0	0.0	0.0	...	...	...	...	...
	2011	0.0	0.0	0.0	...	...	...	...	...
Sao Tome and Principe	2004	...	...	...	0.7	...	...	...	...
Sao Tomé-et-Principe	2010	3.3	0.0	0.0	0.0	0.0	8.9	0.6	0.0
	2011	3.3	0.0	0.0	2.2	0.0	10.8	0.5	0.0
Saudi Arabia	2005	1.2	...	...	...	...	...	...	...
Arabie saoudite	2007	1.1	...	...	...	...	...	...	...
	2015	1.5	...	...	1.4	...	...	...	0.1
	2017	1.3	2.0	0.3	5.6	1.8	...	9.3	...
Senegal	2005	...	...	...	2.5	...	...	...	...
Sénégal	2010	...	...	...	2.4	...	19.7	19.7	...
	2015	0.3	...	...	...	~0.0	17.2	17.2	1.7
	2016	...	...	...	...	...	...	...	0.9
Serbia	2005	1.6	2.3	1.0	17.6	0.3	182.4	...	5.8
Serbie	2010	1.4	2.0	0.9	15.5	0.2	177.0	40.3	5.5
	2016	1.4	1.9	0.9	15.1	0.1	253.5	27.4	3.2
	2017	1.1	1.5	0.6	14.5	0.1	...	20.7	3.5

11

Intentional homicides and other crimes *(continued)*
By type of crime per 100 000 population and homicide victims by sex

Homicides intentionnels et autres crimes *(suite)*
Par type de crime pour 100 000 habitants et victimes d'homicides par sexe

Country or area Pays ou zone	Year Année	Intentional homicides Homicides volontaires			Other crimes (per 100 000 pop.) Autres infractions (pour 100 000 hab.)				
		Per 100 000 Pour 100 000	Victims (%) Victims (%) Male Hommes	Female Femmes	Assault Agression	Kidnapping Enlèvement	Theft Vol simple	Robbery Vol qualifié	Sexual Violence Violences Sexuelles
Seychelles	2004	11.4	18.8	4.1	...	...	...	...	...
Seychelles	2010	9.9	16.4	2.9	...	...	...	...	...
	2014	17.0	27.9	5.4	...	...	...	...	...
	2016	12.5	...	...	...	...	...	...	...
Sierra Leone	2005	1.8	...	...	...	...	...	...	...
Sierra Leone	2008	3.0	...	...	324.0	...	171.3	...	10.2
	2010	2.5	...	...	...	...	...	...	...
	2015	1.7	...	...	...	...	...	...	...
Singapore	2005	0.5	...	...	14.2	0.0	496.2	...	...
Singapour	2010	0.4	0.6	0.1	8.4	0.0	356.2	10.1	30.8
	2011	0.3	0.4	0.2	7.7	0.0	327.7	7.5	29.4
	2016	0.3	0.4	0.3	8.7	...	241.7	1.7	25.3
	2017	0.2	0.2	0.2	7.4	...	...	1.2	30.6
Slovakia	2005	1.7	2.3	1.2	72.2	0.3	350.0	...	...
Slovaquie	2010	1.5	1.9	1.1	44.9	0.1	452.7	22.0	10.4
	2016	1.0	1.4	0.7	30.6	1.9	291.6	9.7	12.1
	2017	1.5	2.2	0.8	30.1	1.7	...	8.6	12.9
Slovenia	2005	1.0	1.0	1.0	115.5	0.2	1 478.2	...	15.6
Slovénie	2010	0.7	0.7	0.8	106.8	0.2	1 415.1	22.7	18.4
	2016	0.5	0.8	0.2	71.9	0.1	1 031.6	10.9	17.2
	2017	0.9	1.0	0.9	67.3	~0.0	...	11.5	20.6
Solomon Islands	2005	5.5	...	...	...	...	218.9	...	43.4
Îles Salomon	2008	3.8	...	...	...	...	174.6	...	24.3
South Africa	2005	38.7	...	...	...	...	...	...	...
Afrique du Sud	2010	31.0	52.0	10.6	...	...	...	...	...
	2017	35.7	62.0	10.1	293.6	9.6	...	331.7	87.9
South Sudan									
Soudan du sud	2012	14.9	...	...	...	...	...	...	...
Spain	2005	1.2	1.8	0.6	392.6	0.5	...	...	...
Espagne	2010	0.9	1.1	0.7	53.4	0.3	308.2	179.9	21.2
	2016	0.6	0.8	0.5	37.2	0.2	349.7	151.5	23.3
	2017	0.7	0.8	0.5	38.8	0.1	...	143.2	25.1
Sri Lanka	2004	7.1	...	...	109.2	4.5	135.7	...	...
Sri Lanka	2005	6.2	...	...	...	...	...	...	...
	2010	3.8	6.0	1.6	318.9	1.0	62.6	31.8	4.4
	2016	2.5	4.0	1.2	17.0	1.4	29.3	16.4	27.6
	2017	2.3	3.9	0.8	...	1.2	...	...	...
State of Palestine	2005	2.3	...	...	183.7	5.6	122.4	...	...
État de Palestine	2010	0.8	1.1	0.5	7.1	0.5	67.6	70.1	4.4
	2012	0.6	1.0	0.2	8.2	0.3	45.9	47.1	2.8
	2013	0.6	...	...	...	...	...	86.2	3.1
	2017	0.7	1.2	0.2	...	...	...	...	...
Sudan									
Soudan	2008	5.1	...	...	...	...	...	...	...
Suriname	2004	9.3	...	...	...	...	2 752.4	...	...
Suriname	2005	13.8	...	...	...	...	...	...	...
	2008	8.3	12.7	3.9	...	...	...	...	...
	2016	7.3	8.8	5.7	70.1	...	...	...	...
	2017	5.4	...	...	63.2	...	...	...	...
Sweden	2005	0.9	1.2	0.7	803.7	...	4 921.2	...	129.6
Suède	2010	1.0	1.4	0.6	59.6	...	3 918.7	98.2	150.4
	2016	1.1	1.6	0.6	50.4	...	3 816.6	87.0	179.8
	2017	1.1	1.7	0.5	47.3	...	...	87.3	190.6
Switzerland	2005	1.0	1.0	1.0	109.6	3.3	1 928.0	...	...
Suisse	2010	0.7	0.7	0.7	6.2	0.0	2 065.3	56.4	31.9
	2016	0.5	0.5	0.6	6.8	~0.0	1 714.5	22.4	32.7
	2017	0.5	0.6	0.5	6.9	~0.0	...	20.6	30.7
Syrian Arab Republic	2004	2.4	...	...	35.7	0.8	64.8	...	...
République arabe syrienne	2005	2.3	...	...	33.5	0.2	...	...	...
	2008	2.6	...	...	2.7	0.1	31.5	...	0.4
	2010	2.2	...	...	...	...	...	...	...
Tajikistan	2005	2.3	...	...	...	...	52.4	...	...
Tadjikistan	2010	2.4	4.2	0.6	72.9	1.9	47.3	3.3	2.6
	2011	1.6	2.8	0.4	48.5	2.2	47.7	3.7	2.6

11

Intentional homicides and other crimes *(continued)*
By type of crime per 100 000 population and homicide victims by sex

Homicides intentionnels et autres crimes *(suite)*
Par type de crime pour 100 000 habitants et victimes d'homicides par sexe

Country or area Pays ou zone	Year Année	Intentional homicides Homicides volontaires			Other crimes (per 100 000 pop.) Autres infractions (pour 100 000 hab.)				
		Per 100 000 Pour 100 000	Victims (%) Victimes (%) Male Hommes	Female Femmes	Assault Agression	Kidnapping Enlèvement	Theft Vol simple	Robbery Vol qualifié	Sexual Violence Violences Sexuelles
Thailand	2005	7.3	13.0	1.9	43.2	~0.0	93.1	...	...
Thaïlande	2010	5.4	9.7	1.3	13.6	~0.0	80.9	2.7	2.9
	2014	3.9	6.7	1.2	18.5	~0.0	58.3	2.1	1.8
	2015	3.5	...	...	19.9	0.4	57.3	2.2	5.9
	2016	3.2	...	...	...	2.2	47.9	1.5	5.5
	2017	2.6	...	...	...	...	...	...	...
Timor-Leste	2005	4.6	...	...	...	...	...	...	...
Timor-Leste	2010	3.6	...	...	...	...	...	...	...
	2015	4.1	...	...	...	0.4	...	...	4.6
	2017	...	...	...	...	0.3	...	1.9	10.7
Tonga	2005	4.0	7.9	0.0	...	...	...	...	...
Tonga	2010	1.0	1.9	0.0	...	...	...	...	...
	2012	1.0	0.0	1.9	...	...	...	...	...
Trinidad and Tobago	2005	29.8	53.9	6.0	61.8	4.5	212.2	...	61.9
Trinité-et-Tobago	2010	35.6	63.9	7.9	46.4	0.5	307.9	385.8	57.8
	2015	30.6	57.7	4.2	43.8	0.3	136.5	180.2	50.7
Tunisia	2005	2.6	...	...	...	...	...	...	...
Tunisie	2010	2.7	...	...	...	...	...	...	...
	2012	3.1	...	...	...	...	...	...	...
Turkey	2005	4.9	8.1	1.8	155.7	12.9	152.8	...	4.4
Turquie	2010	4.2	6.8	1.7	305.4	18.8	248.3	11.9	5.8
	2014	...	...	...	102.8	42.7	277.4	55.2	54.0
	2016	3.3	5.7	1.1	87.6	...	212.9	34.0	42.9
	2017	3.1	5.2	1.0	...	...	...	...	...
Turkmenistan	2004	4.4	...	...	...	2.7	...	...	...
Turkménistan	2005	4.3	...	...	1.9	...	35.0	...	...
	2006	4.2	...	...	1.7	...	29.8	...	...
Turks and Caicos Islands	2002	8.6	...	0.0	...	...	...	...	...
Îles Turques-et-Caïques	2005	0.0	...	...	...	...	...	...	...
	2009	6.3	...	0.0	...	...	...	...	...
	2014	5.7	...	0.0	...	...	...	...	...
Tuvalu	2005	0.0	...	...	...	...	...	...	...
Tuvalu	2010	9.5	...	...	...	...	...	...	...
	2012	18.6	...	...	...	...	...	...	...
Uganda	2005	9.0	...	...	126.8	...	198.9	...	50.9
Ouganda	2010	9.7	16.1	3.6	70.9	0.5	72.3	18.6	26.7
	2016	11.3	18.3	4.5	17.7	2.4	109.8	18.3	49.3
	2017	11.5	19.3	4.0	13.9	...	...	16.6	...
Ukraine	2005	6.5	9.5	3.8	14.3	0.4	398.1	...	4.1
Ukraine	2010	4.3	6.6	2.4	8.8	0.6	556.3	50.9	2.9
	2017	6.2	11.1	1.9	3.6	1.3	...	47.5	1.9
United Arab Emirates	2004	0.7	...	...	...	12.4	271.3	...	...
Émirats arabes unis	2005	1.2	...	...	15.6	18.8	...	...	...
	2006	0.7	...	...	14.3	18.3	...	...	...
	2010	0.8	0.8	0.8	...	...	...	...	...
	2015	0.6	0.8	0.4	3.5	0.9	67.1	8.9	4.1
	2016	0.7	...	...	3.7	0.8	51.3	11.0	4.8
	2017	0.5	...	...	2.4	0.7	...	16.5	...
United Kingdom	2005	1.4	1.8	1.0	...	...	...	...	...
Royaume-Uni	2010	1.2	1.5	0.9	...	...	...	...	...
	2017	1.2	1.7	0.7	...	...	...	...	...
United Rep. of Tanzania	2004	7.8	...	...	...	...	...	...	...
Rép.-Unie de Tanzanie	2010	8.8	15.1	2.5	...	0.0	...	26.9	~0.0
	2015	7.3	12.0	2.6	4.6	0.0	0.4	18.2	0.1
	2016	6.5	...	...	...	...	...	...	...
United States of America	2005	5.7	9.1	2.4	292.3	...	2 299.5	...	...
États-Unis d'Amérique	2010	4.8	7.5	2.1	253.0	...	2 007.9	119.4	...
	2016	5.4	8.6	2.3	248.6	...	1 745.6	103.0	...
	2017	5.3	8.5	2.2	249.4	...	...	98.3	...
United States Virgin Islands	2005	34.3	65.3	5.4	...	...	...	...	...
Îles Vierges américaines	2010	52.8	96.5	12.7	...	...	...	...	...
	2012	49.3	99.2	3.6	...	...	...	...	...
Uruguay	2003	5.9	...	...	...	0.1	2 906.3	...	...
Uruguay	2004	6.0	...	...	...	...	3 182.5	...	...
	2005	5.7	...	...	...	...	...	...	...
	2010	6.1	10.1	2.4	15.5	...	2 836.2	411.7	...
	2016	7.8	13.7	2.4	16.6	0.8	3 224.3	548.9	46.6
	2017	8.3	13.7	3.1	12.5	1.1	...	522.5	61.4

11

Intentional homicides and other crimes *(continued)*
By type of crime per 100 000 population and homicide victims by sex

Homicides intentionnels et autres crimes *(suite)*
Par type de crime pour 100 000 habitants et victimes d'homicides par sexe

Country or area Pays ou zone	Year Année	Intentional homicides Homicides volontaires			Other crimes (per 100 000 pop.) Autres infractions (pour 100 000 hab.)				
		Per 100 000 Pour 100 000	Victims (%) Victimes (%) Male Hommes	Female Femmes	Assault Agression	Kidnapping Enlèvement	Theft Vol simple	Robbery Vol qualifié	Sexual Violence Violences Sexuelles
Uzbekistan	2005	3.4	...	...	...	...	...	...	...
Ouzbékistan	2008	3.0	...	...	...	...	...	...	...
	2017	1.1	...	...	4.4	0.1	...	2.6	...
Venezuela (Boliv. Rep. of)	2005	37.7	71.1	4.2	...	...	...	...	...
Venezuela (Rép. boliv. du)	2010	46.0	86.6	5.5	...	...	...	...	...
	2017	49.9	93.9	5.3	...	1.0	...	...	...
Viet Nam	2005	1.3	...	...	...	...	...	...	...
Viet Nam	2010	1.5	...	...	...	...	...	...	...
	2011	1.5	...	...	...	...	...	...	...
Yemen	2005	4.7	...	...	...	0.5	...	...	0.0
Yémen	2009	4.4	...	...	0.1	0.2	...	...	0.3
	2010	4.7	...	...	...	...	...	...	...
	2013	6.8	...	...	...	...	...	...	...
Zambia	2000	7.7	...	...	...	...	...	...	...
Zambie	2010	6.0	...	...	...	...	...	...	...
	2015	5.4	...	...	...	...	...	...	...
Zimbabwe	2005	11.2	...	...	766.0	0.4	915.0	...	...
Zimbabwe	2008	...	...	...	414.0	1.8	738.7	...	...
	2010	5.6	...	...	...	...	...	...	...
	2012	7.5	...	...	...	...	...	...	...

Source:

United Nations Office on Drugs and Crime (UNODC), Vienna, UNODC Statistics database, last accessed June 2020.

Source:

Office des Nations Unies contre la drogue et le crime (ONUDC), Vienne, base de données statistiques de l'ONUDC, dernier accès juin 2020.

Part Two

Economic activity

Deuxième partie

Activité économique

12

Gross domestic product and gross domestic product per capita
In millions of US dollars at current and constant 2015 prices; per capita US dollars; real rates of growth

Produit intérieur brut et produit intérieur brut par habitant
En millions de dollars É.-U. aux prix courants et constants de 2015; par habitant en dollars É.U.; taux de croissance réels

Country or area	1985	1995	2005	2010	2015	2017	2018	Pays ou zone
Total, all countries or areas								**Total, tous pays ou zones**
GDP at current prices	13 567 238	31 128 273	47 605 038	66 231 829	74 882 648	80 789 198	85 693 322	PIB aux prix courants
GDP per capita	2 787	5 420	7 279	9 523	10 149	10 706	11 232	PIB par habitant
GDP at constant prices	30 053 963	40 241 007	56 369 520	64 699 161	74 882 648	79 428 816	81 894 343	PIB aux prix constants
Growth rates	3.5	3.1	4.1	4.4	3.0	3.3	3.1	Taux de croissance
Africa								**Afrique**
GDP at current prices	551 052	584 724	1 127 604	1 968 455	2 306 279	2 234 233	2 365 243	PIB aux prix courants
GDP per capita	1 006	816	1 233	1 897	1 953	1 798	1 856	PIB par habitant
GDP at constant prices	824 665	997 744	1 545 861	2 022 419	2 306 279	2 429 754	2 507 127	PIB aux prix constants
Growth rates	3.7	2.7	6.2	5.6	2.6	3.5	3.2	Taux de croissance
Northern Africa								**Afrique septentrionale**
GDP at current prices	142 506	207 392	373 106	648 727	729 675	661 194	666 216	PIB aux prix courants
GDP per capita	1 115	1 285	1 928	3 204	3 267	2 847	2 814	PIB par habitant
GDP at constant prices	310 883	390 995	603 915	764 170	729 675	791 873	820 016	PIB aux prix constants
Growth rates	6.2	1.6	6.1	4.7	1.8	5.2	3.6	Taux de croissance
Sub-Saharan Africa								**Afrique subsaharienne**
GDP at current prices	408 546	377 332	754 498	1 319 729	1 576 604	1 573 039	1 699 027	PIB aux prix courants
GDP per capita	973	680	1 046	1 580	1 647	1 557	1 638	PIB par habitant
GDP at constant prices	513 783	606 749	941 946	1 258 249	1 576 604	1 637 881	1 687 111	PIB aux prix constants
Growth rates	2.2	3.3	6.3	6.1	3.0	2.7	3.0	Taux de croissance
Eastern Africa								**Afrique orientale**
GDP at current prices	65 430	69 248	112 227	217 860	321 979	364 121	393 669	PIB aux prix courants
GDP per capita	399	318	391	644	829	888	934	PIB par habitant
GDP at constant prices	80 025	107 766	160 962	241 179	321 979	357 338	378 773	PIB aux prix constants
Growth rates	2.0	4.6	6.5	7.9	5.9	5.7	6.0	Taux de croissance
Middle Africa								**Afrique centrale**
GDP at current prices	35 267	36 081	99 548	189 046	237 287	245 959	250 276	PIB aux prix courants
GDP per capita	579	431	889	1 436	1 539	1 499	1 480	PIB par habitant
GDP at constant prices	95 450	84 253	138 981	190 569	237 287	236 854	239 286	PIB aux prix constants
Growth rates	1.7	6.8	9.2	5.0	1.4	0.7	1.0	Taux de croissance
Southern Africa								**Afrique australe**
GDP at current prices	62 927	166 991	279 562	406 242	350 025	387 003	408 569	PIB aux prix courants
GDP per capita	1 693	3 526	5 116	6 958	5 557	5 969	6 215	PIB par habitant
GDP at constant prices	163 500	190 538	265 307	310 496	350 025	357 086	360 440	PIB aux prix constants
Growth rates	-1.0	3.3	5.2	3.3	1.2	1.4	0.9	Taux de croissance
Western Africa								**Afrique occidentale**
GDP at current prices	244 922	105 012	263 162	506 581	667 313	575 956	646 513	PIB aux prix courants
GDP per capita	1 551	511	982	1 650	1 897	1 552	1 696	PIB par habitant
GDP at constant prices	174 808	224 192	376 696	516 005	667 313	686 602	708 613	PIB aux prix constants
Growth rates	5.6	1.5	6.0	7.5	3.0	2.6	3.2	Taux de croissance
Americas								**Amériques**
GDP at current prices	5 491 293	10 217 194	17 076 573	21 963 119	25 283 842	26 950 282	27 867 704	PIB aux prix courants
GDP per capita	8 227	13 160	19 326	23 530	25 807	27 033	27 722	PIB par habitant
GDP at constant prices	11 528 292	15 229 447	21 064 130	22 674 522	25 283 842	26 066 617	26 678 785	PIB aux prix constants
Growth rates	3.9	2.4	3.7	3.3	2.1	2.1	2.3	Taux de croissance
Northern America								**Amérique septentrionale**
GDP at current prices	4 707 044	8 249 550	14 216 498	16 617 674	19 789 297	21 178 707	22 302 188	PIB aux prix courants
GDP per capita	17 672	28 017	43 438	48 408	55 428	58 515	61 221	PIB par habitant
GDP at constant prices	9 103 173	12 093 185	16 945 467	17 742 296	19 789 297	20 591 117	21 176 700	PIB aux prix constants
Growth rates	4.2	2.7	3.5	2.6	2.7	2.4	2.8	Taux de croissance
Latin America & the Caribbean								**Amérique latine et Caraïbes**
GDP at current prices	784 249	1 967 644	2 860 075	5 345 445	5 494 545	5 771 575	5 565 516	PIB aux prix courants
GDP per capita	1 955	4 083	5 141	9 058	8 824	9 089	8 683	PIB par habitant
GDP at constant prices	2 425 119	3 136 262	4 118 663	4 932 225	5 494 545	5 475 500	5 502 085	PIB aux prix constants
Growth rates	2.8	1.1	4.5	5.9	0.1	0.8	0.5	Taux de croissance
Caribbean								**Caraïbes**
GDP at current prices	69 866	120 339	222 633	290 518	344 059	361 872	371 468	PIB aux prix courants
GDP per capita	2 257	3 415	5 741	7 219	8 257	8 606	8 800	PIB par habitant
GDP at constant prices	167 403	200 446	288 259	316 529	344 059	349 364	352 687	PIB aux prix constants
Growth rates	0.8	4.0	3.5	1.7	2.5	0.6	1.0	Taux de croissance
Central America								**Amérique centrale**
GDP at current prices	255 437	412 218	972 212	1 210 271	1 402 101	1 418 016	1 492 059	PIB aux prix courants
GDP per capita	2 497	3 310	6 661	7 680	8 299	8 181	8 503	PIB par habitant
GDP at constant prices	639 761	781 343	1 091 438	1 198 377	1 402 101	1 479 236	1 510 651	PIB aux prix constants
Growth rates	2.6	-5.0	2.6	4.9	3.4	2.3	2.1	Taux de croissance

12

Gross domestic product and gross domestic product per capita *(continued)*
In millions of US dollars at current and constant 2015 prices; per capita US dollars; real rates of growth

Produit intérieur brut et produit intérieur brut par habitant *(suite)*
En millions de dollars É.-U. aux prix courants et constants de 2015; par habitant en dollars É.U.; taux de croissance réels

Country or area	1985	1995	2005	2010	2015	2017	2018	Pays ou zone
South America								**Amérique du Sud**
GDP at current prices	458 946	1 435 087	1 665 230	3 844 656	3 748 385	3 991 688	3 701 989	PIB aux prix courants
GDP per capita	1 713	4 455	4 481	9 800	9 096	9 512	8 746	PIB par habitant
GDP at constant prices	1 617 955	2 154 473	2 738 967	3 417 319	3 748 385	3 646 900	3 638 747	PIB aux prix constants
Growth rates	3.1	3.2	5.4	6.6	-1.3	0.3	-0.2	Taux de croissance
Asia								**Asie**
GDP at current prices	2 895 273	9 223 411	12 390 608	20 957 643	26 659 277	29 581 856	31 839 880	PIB aux prix courants
GDP per capita	1 013	2 641	3 115	4 979	6 014	6 547	6 982	PIB par habitant
GDP at constant prices	5 885 861	9 968 287	15 612 925	20 702 029	26 659 277	29 371 092	30 705 850	PIB aux prix constants
Growth rates	4.8	5.6	6.3	7.7	4.8	5.0	4.5	Taux de croissance
Central Asia								**Asie centrale**
GDP at current prices	...	41 639	93 163	227 976	316 820	278 742	286 205	PIB aux prix courants
GDP per capita	...	783	1 594	3 630	4 626	3 933	3 972	PIB par habitant
GDP at constant prices	...	95 531	166 895	234 785	316 820	341 747	357 750	PIB aux prix constants
Growth rates	...	-6.5	9.0	7.5	3.5	4.5	4.7	Taux de croissance
Eastern Asia								**Asie orientale**
GDP at current prices	1 925 557	7 191 368	8 559 951	13 653 535	17 788 106	19 639 200	21 355 820	PIB aux prix courants
GDP per capita	1 502	4 910	5 473	8 508	10 813	11 833	12 816	PIB par habitant
GDP at constant prices	3 877 707	6 575 515	10 241 459	13 773 543	17 788 106	19 580 596	20 509 684	PIB aux prix constants
Growth rates	6.7	5.6	6.2	8.1	4.8	5.2	4.7	Taux de croissance
South-eastern Asia								**Asie du Sud-Est**
GDP at current prices	243 806	703 487	958 893	1 980 866	2 466 781	2 783 869	2 974 090	PIB aux prix courants
GDP per capita	608	1 449	1 709	3 318	3 889	4 293	4 539	PIB par habitant
GDP at constant prices	508 894	1 015 740	1 486 959	1 931 292	2 466 781	2 718 112	2 854 817	PIB aux prix constants
Growth rates	0.5	7.8	5.7	7.9	4.7	5.2	5.0	Taux de croissance
Southern Asia								**Asie méridionale**
GDP at current prices	377 583	625 199	1 270 195	2 542 992	3 129 879	3 777 179	3 949 688	PIB aux prix courants
GDP per capita	356	473	800	1 485	1 712	2 016	2 083	PIB par habitant
GDP at constant prices	690 868	1 056 379	1 809 954	2 429 083	3 129 879	3 612 418	3 797 623	PIB aux prix constants
Growth rates	4.4	6.1	6.8	7.1	6.2	6.5	5.1	Taux de croissance
Western Asia								**Asie occidentale**
GDP at current prices	348 327	661 719	1 508 407	2 552 273	2 957 691	3 102 866	3 274 077	PIB aux prix courants
GDP per capita	3 021	3 975	7 348	10 994	11 493	11 648	12 095	PIB par habitant
GDP at constant prices	808 392	1 225 123	1 907 657	2 333 326	2 957 691	3 118 219	3 185 976	PIB aux prix constants
Growth rates	-0.8	4.1	6.5	5.7	3.8	2.3	2.2	Taux de croissance
Europe								**Europe**
GDP at current prices	4 415 160	10 629 668	16 109 894	19 860 115	19 160 796	20 353 840	21 908 725	PIB aux prix courants
GDP per capita	5 738	14 593	22 040	26 905	25 724	27 238	29 279	PIB par habitant
GDP at constant prices	11 227 196	13 257 217	17 026 804	18 023 697	19 160 796	20 008 574	20 418 094	PIB aux prix constants
Growth rates	2.5	2.2	2.5	2.3	1.9	2.5	2.0	Taux de croissance
Eastern Europe								**Europe orientale**
GDP at current prices	1 124 318	794 157	1 628 298	2 864 772	2 627 186	3 007 953	3 262 795	PIB aux prix courants
GDP per capita	3 025	2 566	5 473	9 715	8 924	10 229	11 106	PIB par habitant
GDP at constant prices	1 895 221	1 415 852	2 031 043	2 397 833	2 627 186	2 749 564	2 838 699	PIB aux prix constants
Growth rates	1.6	-0.8	5.6	3.3	-~0.0	3.1	3.2	Taux de croissance
Northern Europe								**Europe septentrionale**
GDP at current prices	810 631	2 171 076	3 992 198	4 286 874	4 755 722	4 654 690	5 005 288	PIB aux prix courants
GDP per capita	9 802	23 366	41 573	42 823	46 073	44 595	47 699	PIB par habitant
GDP at constant prices	2 312 441	2 992 871	4 136 040	4 276 924	4 755 722	4 979 553	5 082 089	PIB aux prix constants
Growth rates	4.0	3.8	3.3	2.3	3.6	2.5	2.1	Taux de croissance
Southern Europe								**Europe méridionale**
GDP at current prices	780 801	2 126 468	3 606 698	4 302 127	3 619 794	3 919 151	4 209 516	PIB aux prix courants
GDP per capita	5 504	14 736	24 102	28 122	23 654	25 655	27 585	PIB par habitant
GDP at constant prices	2 349 476	2 890 431	3 682 240	3 729 942	3 619 794	3 777 668	3 838 931	PIB aux prix constants
Growth rates	2.5	3.0	1.8	0.7	1.9	2.3	1.6	Taux de croissance
Western Europe								**Europe occidentale**
GDP at current prices	1 699 410	5 537 967	6 882 700	8 406 342	8 158 094	8 772 046	9 431 125	PIB aux prix courants
GDP per capita	9 809	30 469	36 654	44 198	42 003	44 740	47 885	PIB par habitant
GDP at constant prices	4 670 059	5 958 063	7 177 481	7 618 998	8 158 094	8 501 790	8 658 375	PIB aux prix constants
Growth rates	2.2	1.9	1.5	2.9	1.5	2.4	1.8	Taux de croissance
Oceania								**Océanie**
GDP at current prices	214 459	473 276	900 360	1 482 497	1 472 455	1 668 987	1 711 770	PIB aux prix courants
GDP per capita	8 596	16 249	26 959	40 519	37 211	40 992	41 469	PIB par habitant
GDP at constant prices	587 948	788 310	1 119 799	1 276 494	1 472 455	1 552 779	1 584 487	PIB aux prix constants
Growth rates	3.7	3.9	2.9	2.4	3.1	2.9	2.0	Taux de croissance
Australia and New Zealand								**Australie et Nouvelle-Zélande**
GDP at current prices	206 320	454 246	875 660	1 446 047	1 426 321	1 621 521	1 661 791	PIB aux prix courants
GDP per capita	10 898	20 964	36 015	54 517	49 964	55 367	56 063	PIB par habitant
GDP at constant prices	570 424	761 461	1 087 350	1 237 950	1 426 321	1 505 885	1 537 022	PIB aux prix constants
Growth rates	3.7	4.0	2.9	2.3	3.0	3.0	2.1	Taux de croissance

Gross domestic product and gross domestic product per capita *(continued)*
In millions of US dollars at current and constant 2015 prices; per capita US dollars; real rates of growth

Produit intérieur brut et produit intérieur brut par habitant *(suite)*
En millions de dollars É.-U. aux prix courants et constants de 2015; par habitant en dollars É.U.; taux de croissance réels

Country or area	1985	1995	2005	2010	2015	2017	2018	Pays ou zone
Melanesia								**Mélanésie**
GDP at current prices	5 971	13 533	17 353	28 167	38 235	38 897	40 948	PIB aux prix courants
GDP per capita	1 116	2 025	2 108	3 066	3 778	3 699	3 821	PIB par habitant
GDP at constant prices	12 693	20 614	24 548	30 826	38 235	38 594	38 989	PIB aux prix constants
Growth rates	2.3	0.3	3.6	8.2	4.9	0.4	1.0	Taux de croissance
Micronesia								**Micronésie**
GDP at current prices	257	544	714	864	1 050	1 176	1 185	PIB aux prix courants
GDP per capita	1 222	2 066	2 519	2 978	3 441	3 769	3 755	PIB par habitant
GDP at constant prices	694	884	909	903	1 050	1 089	1 102	PIB aux prix constants
Growth rates	3.3	6.1	1.7	2.5	5.8	1.7	1.2	Taux de croissance
Polynesia								**Polynésie**
GDP at current prices	1 911	4 953	6 632	7 419	6 848	7 392	7 846	PIB aux prix courants
GDP per capita	4 184	9 664	11 666	12 675	11 488	12 273	12 947	PIB par habitant
GDP at constant prices	4 137	5 352	6 992	6 815	6 848	7 211	7 374	PIB aux prix constants
Growth rates	5.4	0.9	1.6	-1.7	2.3	3.0	2.3	Taux de croissance
Afghanistan								**Afghanistan**
GDP at current prices	3 322	3 236	6 622	16 078	20 608	21 516	20 514	PIB aux prix courants
GDP per capita	278	179	258	551	599	593	552	PIB par habitant
GDP at constant prices	11 447	6 916	10 106	15 861	20 608	22 865	22 485	PIB aux prix constants
Growth rates	0.3	49.9	9.9	3.2	-1.8	7.1	-1.7	Taux de croissance
Albania								**Albanie**
GDP at current prices	2 324	2 393	8 052	11 927	11 387	13 025	15 059	PIB aux prix courants
GDP per capita	783	769	2 609	4 046	3 939	4 516	5 224	PIB par habitant
GDP at constant prices	5 164	4 739	8 057	10 420	11 387	12 214	12 710	PIB aux prix constants
Growth rates	1.8	13.3	5.5	3.7	2.2	3.8	4.1	Taux de croissance
Algeria								**Algérie**
GDP at current prices	57 866	41 971	103 198	161 207	165 979	167 390	173 757	PIB aux prix courants
GDP per capita	2 580	1 459	3 113	4 481	4 178	4 044	4 115	PIB par habitant
GDP at constant prices	77 474	81 507	124 381	140 977	165 979	173 517	175 946	PIB aux prix constants
Growth rates	3.7	3.8	5.9	3.6	3.7	1.3	1.4	Taux de croissance
Andorra								**Andorre**
GDP at current prices	439	1 491	3 256	3 355	2 812	3 021	3 238	PIB aux prix courants
GDP per capita	9 837	23 359	41 281	39 734	36 041	39 231	42 052	PIB par habitant
GDP at constant prices	1 382	1 856	3 323	2 896	2 812	2 914	2 962	PIB aux prix constants
Growth rates	2.3	2.8	7.4	-5.4	0.8	1.7	1.6	Taux de croissance
Angola								**Angola**
GDP at current prices	9 109	6 642	36 971	83 799	116 194	122 124	105 902	PIB aux prix courants
GDP per capita	914	476	1 902	3 588	4 167	4 096	3 437	PIB par habitant
GDP at constant prices	30 426	29 857	62 251	93 159	116 194	113 029	111 673	PIB aux prix constants
Growth rates	3.5	15.0	15.0	4.9	0.9	-0.1	-1.2	Taux de croissance
Anguilla								**Anguilla**
GDP at current prices	27	104	229	268	331	281	293	PIB aux prix courants
GDP per capita	3 720	10 515	18 398	19 938	23 148	19 281	19 891	PIB par habitant
GDP at constant prices	73	170	301	315	331	301	286	PIB aux prix constants
Growth rates	12.9	-2.3	13.1	-4.5	3.1	-7.7	-5.0	Taux de croissance
Antigua and Barbuda								**Antigua-et-Barbuda**
GDP at current prices	245	577	1 023	1 149	1 337	1 468	1 611	PIB aux prix courants
GDP per capita	3 962	8 407	12 557	13 049	14 286	15 383	16 727	PIB par habitant
GDP at constant prices	540	825	1 232	1 231	1 337	1 455	1 562	PIB aux prix constants
Growth rates	7.7	-4.4	6.5	-7.8	3.8	3.1	7.4	Taux de croissance
Argentina								**Argentine**
GDP at current prices	95 530	279 701	200 622	426 487	644 903	642 696	518 475	PIB aux prix courants
GDP per capita	3 162	8 031	5 158	10 429	14 971	14 628	11 688	PIB par habitant
GDP at constant prices	287 082	377 768	472 004	599 349	644 903	648 339	632 036	PIB aux prix constants
Growth rates	-7.0	-2.8	8.9	10.1	2.7	2.7	-2.5	Taux de croissance
Armenia								**Arménie**
GDP at current prices	...	1 372	5 226	9 875	10 553	11 527	12 433	PIB aux prix courants
GDP per capita	...	426	1 753	3 432	3 607	3 915	4 212	PIB par habitant
GDP at constant prices	...	3 036	7 048	8 517	10 553	11 367	11 963	PIB aux prix constants
Growth rates	...	6.9	13.9	2.2	3.2	7.5	5.2	Taux de croissance
Aruba								**Aruba**
GDP at current prices	431	1 384	2 443	2 502	2 920	3 056	3 203	PIB aux prix courants
GDP per capita	6 834	17 229	24 419	24 607	27 980	29 006	30 262	PIB par habitant
GDP at constant prices	960	2 286	2 998	2 671	2 920	3 038	3 066	PIB aux prix constants
Growth rates	9.1	2.5	1.2	-3.3	5.7	2.0	0.9	Taux de croissance
Australia								**Australie**
GDP at current prices	182 212	391 094	760 940	1 299 463	1 248 854	1 416 105	1 453 871	PIB aux prix courants
GDP per capita	11 633	21 736	37 710	58 654	52 182	57 601	58 393	PIB par habitant
GDP at constant prices	485 389	660 759	945 527	1 085 036	1 248 854	1 314 343	1 340 067	PIB aux prix constants
Growth rates	4.0	3.9	2.8	2.5	2.8	2.8	2.0	Taux de croissance

Gross domestic product and gross domestic product per capita *(continued)*
In millions of US dollars at current and constant 2015 prices; per capita US dollars; real rates of growth

Produit intérieur brut et produit intérieur brut par habitant *(suite)*
En millions de dollars É.-U. aux prix courants et constants de 2015; par habitant en dollars É.U.; taux de croissance réels

Country or area	1985	1995	2005	2010	2015	2017	2018	Pays ou zone
Austria								**Autriche**
GDP at current prices	69 388	241 054	315 967	391 893	381 818	418 316	455 508	PIB aux prix courants
GDP per capita	9 112	30 169	38 282	46 599	43 995	47 429	51 230	PIB par habitant
GDP at constant prices	207 166	268 468	339 519	362 278	381 818	399 422	409 087	PIB aux prix constants
Growth rates	2.5	2.7	2.2	1.8	1.0	2.5	2.4	Taux de croissance
Azerbaijan								**Azerbaïdjan**
GDP at current prices	...	3 081	13 245	52 906	53 076	40 867	46 939	PIB aux prix courants
GDP per capita	...	396	1 551	5 857	5 516	4 151	4 718	PIB par habitant
GDP at constant prices	...	8 616	22 443	47 989	53 076	51 305	52 030	PIB aux prix constants
Growth rates	...	-11.8	28.0	4.8	1.1	-0.3	1.4	Taux de croissance
Bahamas								**Bahamas**
GDP at current prices	3 306	5 165	9 836	10 096	11 752	12 150	12 425	PIB aux prix courants
GDP per capita	14 095	18 433	30 278	28 444	31 406	31 828	32 218	PIB par habitant
GDP at constant prices	7 415	8 313	11 657	11 521	11 752	11 813	11 998	PIB aux prix constants
Growth rates	4.8	4.4	3.4	1.5	0.6	0.1	1.6	Taux de croissance
Bahrain								**Bahreïn**
GDP at current prices	4 475	6 787	15 969	25 713	31 126	35 433	37 876	PIB aux prix courants
GDP per capita	10 669	12 040	17 959	20 722	22 689	23 715	24 134	PIB par habitant
GDP at constant prices	8 029	12 279	19 842	26 003	31 126	33 431	34 277	PIB aux prix constants
Growth rates	-16.1	1.9	6.8	4.3	2.9	3.7	2.5	Taux de croissance
Bangladesh								**Bangladesh**
GDP at current prices	19 169	37 866	57 628	114 508	194 466	245 633	269 628	PIB aux prix courants
GDP per capita	211	329	414	776	1 245	1 538	1 671	PIB par habitant
GDP at constant prices	42 200	63 504	106 644	143 127	194 466	223 472	241 045	PIB aux prix constants
Growth rates	3.0	4.9	6.0	5.6	6.6	7.3	7.9	Taux de croissance
Barbados								**Barbade**
GDP at current prices	1 439	2 297	3 936	4 530	4 715	4 978	5 087	PIB aux prix courants
GDP per capita	5 617	8 637	14 242	16 056	16 525	17 392	17 746	PIB par habitant
GDP at constant prices	3 559	3 809	4 779	4 713	4 715	4 869	4 850	PIB aux prix constants
Growth rates	1.1	2.0	4.0	-2.3	2.4	0.6	-0.4	Taux de croissance
Belarus								**Bélarus**
GDP at current prices	...	14 324	31 232	57 232	56 455	54 725	59 662	PIB aux prix courants
GDP per capita	...	1 421	3 266	6 075	5 981	5 791	6 312	PIB par habitant
GDP at constant prices	...	19 207	37 454	53 219	56 455	56 465	58 182	PIB aux prix constants
Growth rates	...	-10.4	9.4	7.8	-3.8	2.5	3.0	Taux de croissance
Belgium								**Belgique**
GDP at current prices	86 266	288 029	385 561	480 952	462 150	504 250	543 026	PIB aux prix courants
GDP per capita	8 699	28 276	36 557	43 968	40 942	44 156	47 293	PIB par habitant
GDP at constant prices	251 992	317 484	402 524	433 266	462 150	478 348	485 324	PIB aux prix constants
Growth rates	1.7	2.4	2.3	2.9	2.0	2.0	1.5	Taux de croissance
Belize								**Belize**
GDP at current prices	232	620	1 102	1 377	1 724	1 837	1 871	PIB aux prix courants
GDP per capita	1 405	2 996	3 883	4 271	4 776	4 888	4 885	PIB par habitant
GDP at constant prices	425	792	1 359	1 529	1 724	1 757	1 794	PIB aux prix constants
Growth rates	1.0	0.6	1.9	3.0	2.8	1.9	2.1	Taux de croissance
Benin								**Bénin**
GDP at current prices	1 130	2 345	4 804	6 970	8 454	9 269	10 412	PIB aux prix courants
GDP per capita	264	397	602	758	799	829	907	PIB par habitant
GDP at constant prices	2 417	3 460	5 359	6 470	8 454	9 395	10 009	PIB aux prix constants
Growth rates	7.5	10.1	1.7	2.1	6.5	5.8	6.5	Taux de croissance
Bermuda								**Bermudes**
GDP at current prices	1 428	2 557	4 868	5 853	5 891	6 269	6 351	PIB aux prix courants
GDP per capita	23 963	40 301	73 474	89 510	92 487	99 437	101 208	PIB par habitant
GDP at constant prices	4 186	4 800	6 561	6 575	5 891	6 032	6 007	PIB aux prix constants
Growth rates	4.2	5.4	1.7	-2.5	0.4	2.5	-0.4	Taux de croissance
Bhutan								**Bhoutan**
GDP at current prices	172	289	819	1 585	2 060	2 528	2 658	PIB aux prix courants
GDP per capita	371	541	1 262	2 313	2 830	3 391	3 524	PIB par habitant
GDP at constant prices	213	488	1 003	1 577	2 060	2 328	2 463	PIB aux prix constants
Growth rates	5.7	6.8	7.1	11.7	6.6	4.6	5.8	Taux de croissance
Bolivia (Plurin. State of)								**Bolivie (État plurin. de)**
GDP at current prices	4 124	6 715	9 549	19 650	33 000	37 509	40 288	PIB aux prix courants
GDP per capita	667	881	1 034	1 955	3 036	3 351	3 549	PIB par habitant
GDP at constant prices	10 704	14 637	20 184	25 267	33 000	35 851	37 365	PIB aux prix constants
Growth rates	-1.0	4.7	4.4	4.1	4.9	4.2	4.2	Taux de croissance
Bosnia and Herzegovina								**Bosnie-Herzégovine**
GDP at current prices	...	2 034	11 223	17 176	16 212	18 081	19 782	PIB aux prix courants
GDP per capita	...	531	2 981	4 635	4 727	5 395	5 951	PIB par habitant
GDP at constant prices	...	3 753	13 180	15 172	16 212	17 251	17 693	PIB aux prix constants
Growth rates	...	20.8	3.9	0.9	3.1	3.2	2.6	Taux de croissance

12
Gross domestic product and gross domestic product per capita *(continued)*
In millions of US dollars at current and constant 2015 prices; per capita US dollars; real rates of growth

Produit intérieur brut et produit intérieur brut par habitant *(suite)*
En millions de dollars É.-U. aux prix courants et constants de 2015; par habitant en dollars É.U.; taux de croissance réels

Country or area	1985	1995	2005	2010	2015	2017	2018	Pays ou zone
Botswana								**Botswana**
GDP at current prices	838	4 731	9 931	12 787	14 421	17 406	18 615	PIB aux prix courants
GDP per capita	783	3 220	5 520	6 435	6 800	7 893	8 258	PIB par habitant
GDP at constant prices	2 551	5 938	9 137	11 420	14 421	15 479	16 168	PIB aux prix constants
Growth rates	9.2	7.0	4.6	8.6	-1.7	2.9	4.5	Taux de croissance
Brazil								**Brésil**
GDP at current prices	187 460	778 053	891 634	2 208 838	1 802 212	2 053 602	1 868 613	PIB aux prix courants
GDP per capita	1 386	4 802	4 790	11 286	8 814	9 881	8 921	PIB par habitant
GDP at constant prices	850 377	1 080 249	1 368 459	1 703 150	1 802 212	1 761 180	1 780 863	PIB aux prix constants
Growth rates	7.8	4.2	3.2	7.5	-3.5	1.1	1.1	Taux de croissance
British Virgin Islands								**Îles Vierges britanniques**
GDP at current prices	53	453	994	1 021	1 174	1 364	1 446	PIB aux prix courants
GDP per capita	3 772	23 475	42 997	36 732	40 283	46 122	48 511	PIB par habitant
GDP at constant prices	132	735	1 206	1 148	1 174	1 288	1 328	PIB aux prix constants
Growth rates	1.4	23.6	14.3	-0.1	0.8	2.4	3.1	Taux de croissance
Brunei Darussalam								**Brunéi Darussalam**
GDP at current prices	4 425	5 245	10 561	13 707	12 930	12 128	13 567	PIB aux prix courants
GDP per capita	19 717	17 655	28 926	35 269	31 164	28 572	31 627	PIB par habitant
GDP at constant prices	9 949	10 623	12 575	12 995	12 930	12 777	12 784	PIB aux prix constants
Growth rates	-1.5	4.5	0.4	2.6	-0.4	1.3	0.1	Taux de croissance
Bulgaria								**Bulgarie**
GDP at current prices	16 483	18 992	29 869	50 364	50 631	58 952	66 199	PIB aux prix courants
GDP per capita	1 837	2 267	3 886	6 783	7 032	8 300	9 388	PIB par habitant
GDP at constant prices	34 456	33 151	39 544	46 370	50 631	54 404	56 082	PIB aux prix constants
Growth rates	2.7	4.8	7.2	0.6	4.0	3.5	3.1	Taux de croissance
Burkina Faso								**Burkina Faso**
GDP at current prices	1 764	2 704	6 144	10 100	11 823	14 170	16 200	PIB aux prix courants
GDP per capita	228	268	458	647	653	738	820	PIB par habitant
GDP at constant prices	2 656	3 723	6 950	9 082	11 823	13 299	14 206	PIB aux prix constants
Growth rates	13.1	5.7	8.7	8.4	3.9	6.2	6.8	Taux de croissance
Burundi								**Burundi**
GDP at current prices	1 171[1]	1 000	1 117	2 032	2 811	3 217	3 285	PIB aux prix courants
GDP per capita	247[1]	167	152	234	277	297	294	PIB par habitant
GDP at constant prices	1 708	1 827	1 905	2 376	2 811	3 023	3 027	PIB aux prix constants
Growth rates	11.7	-7.0	0.9	5.1	-0.4	4.2	0.1	Taux de croissance
Cabo Verde								**Cabo Verde**
GDP at current prices	157	558	1 105	1 664	1 596	1 770	1 977	PIB aux prix courants
GDP per capita	503	1 444	2 387	3 378	3 042	3 293	3 635	PIB par habitant
GDP at constant prices	383	597	1 160	1 483	1 596	1 733	1 821	PIB aux prix constants
Growth rates	8.6	7.5	6.5	1.5	1.0	3.7	5.1	Taux de croissance
Cambodia								**Cambodge**
GDP at current prices	1 059	3 309	6 293	11 242	18 050	22 177	24 572	PIB aux prix courants
GDP per capita	137	311	474	786	1 163	1 385	1 512	PIB par habitant
GDP at constant prices	2 070	4 185	9 237	12 760	18 050	20 674	22 224	PIB aux prix constants
Growth rates	4.7	5.9	13.2	6.0	7.0	7.2	7.5	Taux de croissance
Cameroon								**Cameroun**
GDP at current prices	9 597	9 641	17 944	26 144	30 905	35 009	38 694	PIB aux prix courants
GDP per capita	953	709	1 012	1 285	1 326	1 425	1 534	PIB par habitant
GDP at constant prices	17 682	13 204	20 281	24 077	30 905	33 490	34 850	PIB aux prix constants
Growth rates	2.4	3.5	2.0	3.4	5.7	3.5	4.1	Taux de croissance
Canada								**Canada**
GDP at current prices	366 185	605 923	1 173 143	1 617 266	1 556 127	1 650 187	1 712 562	PIB aux prix courants
GDP per capita	14 224	20 776	36 473	47 361	43 194	44 925	46 192	PIB par habitant
GDP at constant prices	771 472	955 088	1 320 888	1 398 719	1 556 127	1 620 218	1 650 656	PIB aux prix constants
Growth rates	4.7	2.7	3.2	3.1	0.7	3.0	1.9	Taux de croissance
Cayman Islands								**Îles Caïmanes**
GDP at current prices	548	1 709	4 010	4 277	4 785	5 225	5 485	PIB aux prix courants
GDP per capita	28 176	53 127	81 399	75 461	77 518	82 440	85 474	PIB par habitant
GDP at constant prices	1 331	2 665	4 502	4 370	4 785	5 083	5 249	PIB aux prix constants
Growth rates	3.5	4.8	6.5	-2.7	2.8	3.0	3.3	Taux de croissance
Central African Republic								**République centrafricaine**
GDP at current prices	905	1 167	1 413	2 034	1 632	1 997	2 243	PIB aux prix courants
GDP per capita	356	362	350	464	363	435	481	PIB par habitant
GDP at constant prices	1 625	1 814	1 965	2 319	1 632	1 780	1 857	PIB aux prix constants
Growth rates	3.3	5.2	2.4	3.6	4.8	4.3	4.3	Taux de croissance
Chad								**Tchad**
GDP at current prices	987	1 643	6 681	10 971	11 690	10 394	11 387	PIB aux prix courants
GDP per capita	194	234	662	918	828	692	736	PIB par habitant
GDP at constant prices	2 082	2 894	6 593	9 709	11 690	11 104	11 375	PIB aux prix constants
Growth rates	7.9	1.4	7.9	15.0	4.6	-2.4	2.4	Taux de croissance

Gross domestic product and gross domestic product per capita *(continued)*
In millions of US dollars at current and constant 2015 prices; per capita US dollars; real rates of growth

Produit intérieur brut et produit intérieur brut par habitant *(suite)*
En millions de dollars É.-U. aux prix courants et constants de 2015; par habitant en dollars É.U.; taux de croissance réels

Country or area	1985	1995	2005	2010	2015	2017	2018	Pays ou zone
Chile								**Chili**
GDP at current prices	18 985	75 099	122 965	218 538	243 919	277 746	298 231	PIB aux prix courants
GDP per capita	1 549	5 222	7 599	12 808	13 574	15 037	15 923	PIB par habitant
GDP at constant prices	52 229	109 700	167 485	201 494	243 919	251 166	261 275	PIB aux prix constants
Growth rates	2.0	10.6	6.2	5.8	2.3	1.3	4.0	Taux de croissance
China [2]								**Chine** [2]
GDP at current prices	309 839	734 485	2 285 961	6 087 192	11 015 562	12 143 572	13 608 152	PIB aux prix courants
GDP per capita	288	592	1 718	4 447	7 830	8 546	9 532	PIB par habitant
GDP at constant prices	701 601	1 832 275	4 422 624	7 541 001	11 015 562	12 551 829	13 376 104	PIB aux prix constants
Growth rates	13.4	11.0	11.4	10.4	6.9	6.8	6.6	Taux de croissance
China, Hong Kong SAR								**Chine, RAS de Hong Kong**
GDP at current prices	35 700	144 652	181 569	228 639	309 386	341 685	362 682	PIB aux prix courants
GDP per capita	6 752	23 775	26 821	32 821	43 054	46 766	49 199	PIB par habitant
GDP at constant prices	83 953	157 720	220 758	267 552	309 386	328 288	338 145	PIB aux prix constants
Growth rates	0.8	2.4	7.4	6.8	2.4	3.8	3.0	Taux de croissance
China, Macao SAR								**Chine, RAS de Macao**
GDP at current prices	1 349	6 996	12 092	28 124	45 362	50 559	54 545	PIB aux prix courants
GDP per capita	4 758	18 147	25 043	52 253	75 341	81 209	86 355	PIB par habitant
GDP at constant prices	6 998	13 880	23 282	39 621	45 362	49 337	51 660	PIB aux prix constants
Growth rates	0.7	3.3	8.1	25.3	-21.6	9.7	4.7	Taux de croissance
Colombia								**Colombie**
GDP at current prices	48 856	109 250	145 181	286 104	293 482	311 790	330 228	PIB aux prix courants
GDP per capita	1 631	3 000	3 404	6 327	6 176	6 375	6 650	PIB par habitant
GDP at constant prices	96 595	150 006	187 555	233 341	293 482	303 657	311 728	PIB aux prix constants
Growth rates	3.1	5.2	4.7	4.3	3.0	1.4	2.7	Taux de croissance
Comoros								**Comores**
GDP at current prices	240	483	787	907	988	1 065	1 166	PIB aux prix courants
GDP per capita	675	1 016	1 287	1 315	1 271	1 309	1 401	PIB par habitant
GDP at constant prices	531	626	761	760	988	1 065	1 097	PIB aux prix constants
Growth rates	2.0	3.6	2.8	4.8	2.0	3.0	3.0	Taux de croissance
Congo								**Congo**
GDP at current prices	2 339	2 207	6 350	13 678	11 092	10 979	14 173	PIB aux prix courants
GDP per capita	1 138	815	1 753	3 200	2 284	2 148	2 703	PIB par habitant
GDP at constant prices	5 403	5 391	7 412	10 774	11 092	10 447	10 554	PIB aux prix constants
Growth rates	-1.2	4.0	7.6	15.0	-13.2	-3.1	1.0	Taux de croissance
Cook Islands								**Îles Cook**
GDP at current prices	31	116	199	241	302	346	363	PIB aux prix courants
GDP per capita	1 749	6 052	10 443	13 093	17 183	19 741	20 705	PIB par habitant
GDP at constant prices	145	207	265	266	302	347	367	PIB aux prix constants
Growth rates	8.8	-4.4	-1.1	-4.9	5.7	9.5	5.7	Taux de croissance
Costa Rica								**Costa Rica**
GDP at current prices	4 989	11 507	19 952	37 269	54 776	58 175	60 126	PIB aux prix courants
GDP per capita	1 823	3 246	4 656	8 142	11 299	11 753	12 027	PIB par habitant
GDP at constant prices	14 924	24 296	36 203	45 676	54 776	59 042	60 615	PIB aux prix constants
Growth rates	0.7	4.1	3.9	5.0	3.6	3.4	2.7	Taux de croissance
Côte d'Ivoire								**Côte d'Ivoire**
GDP at current prices	6 978[1]	11 105[1]	17 085	24 885	33 119	38 148	43 028	PIB aux prix courants
GDP per capita	704[1]	782[1]	931	1 212	1 426	1 561	1 716	PIB par habitant
GDP at constant prices	14 751	18 367	21 747	24 269	33 119	38 514	41 377	PIB aux prix constants
Growth rates	4.5	7.1	1.7	2.0	8.8	7.7	7.4	Taux de croissance
Croatia								**Croatie**
GDP at current prices	...	22 418	45 386	59 808	49 531	55 319	60 991	PIB aux prix courants
GDP per capita	...	4 856	10 367	13 818	11 701	13 225	14 674	PIB par habitant
GDP at constant prices	...	33 054	48 654	49 938	49 531	52 865	54 290	PIB aux prix constants
Growth rates	...	6.8	4.3	-1.5	2.4	3.1	2.7	Taux de croissance
Cuba								**Cuba**
GDP at current prices	22 921	30 428	42 644	64 328	87 206	96 851	100 023	PIB aux prix courants
GDP per capita	2 270	2 795	3 787	5 730	7 700	8 541	8 822	PIB par habitant
GDP at constant prices	53 332	36 619	58 415	75 943	87 206	89 239	91 246	PIB aux prix constants
Growth rates	1.6	2.5	11.2	2.4	4.4	1.8	2.2	Taux de croissance
Curaçao								**Curaçao**
GDP at current prices	...	...	2 345	2 951	3 152	3 117	3 128	PIB aux prix courants
GDP per capita	...	...	18 018	19 782	19 718	19 239	19 219	PIB par habitant
GDP at constant prices	...	...	3 011	3 190	3 152	3 067	3 000	PIB aux prix constants
Growth rates	...	...	...	0.1	0.3	-1.7	-2.2	Taux de croissance
Cyprus [3]								**Chypre** [3]
GDP at current prices	2 711	9 933	18 694	25 707	19 771	22 638	24 963	PIB aux prix courants
GDP per capita	5 011	15 265	25 311	30 993	23 323	26 484	28 968	PIB par habitant
GDP at constant prices	6 982	12 621	18 869	21 514	19 771	22 025	22 920	PIB aux prix constants
Growth rates	4.7	9.9	4.9	2.0	3.4	4.4	4.1	Taux de croissance

Gross domestic product and gross domestic product per capita *(continued)*
In millions of US dollars at current and constant 2015 prices; per capita US dollars; real rates of growth

Produit intérieur brut et produit intérieur brut par habitant *(suite)*
En millions de dollars É.-U. aux prix courants et constants de 2015; par habitant en dollars É.U.; taux de croissance réels

Country or area	1985	1995	2005	2010	2015	2017	2018	Pays ou zone
Czechia								**Tchéquie**
GDP at current prices	...	59 774	136 281	207 478	186 830	215 914	245 226	PIB aux prix courants
GDP per capita	...	5 771	13 285	19 691	17 623	20 291	22 992	PIB par habitant
GDP at constant prices	...	115 197	152 384	171 904	186 830	199 740	205 647	PIB aux prix constants
Growth rates	...	6.2	6.5	2.3	5.3	4.4	3.0	Taux de croissance
Dem. People's Rep. Korea								**Rép. pop. dém. de Corée**
GDP at current prices	12 075	4 849	13 031	13 945	16 283	17 365	17 487	PIB aux prix courants
GDP per capita	722	222	548	571	650	686	688	PIB par habitant
GDP at constant prices	18 300	14 702	15 882	15 794	16 283	16 324	15 646	PIB aux prix constants
Growth rates	3.7	-4.4	3.8	-0.5	-1.1	-3.5	-4.1	Taux de croissance
Dem. Rep. of the Congo								**Rép. dém. du Congo**
GDP at current prices	7 524	8 947	11 965	21 566	37 918	37 642	47 146	PIB aux prix courants
GDP per capita	252	215	218	334	497	462	561	PIB par habitant
GDP at constant prices	29 507	20 182	19 924	26 094	37 918	40 264	42 593	PIB aux prix constants
Growth rates	0.5	0.7	6.1	7.1	6.9	3.7	5.8	Taux de croissance
Denmark								**Danemark**
GDP at current prices	62 659	185 008	264 467	321 995	302 673	329 417	355 675	PIB aux prix courants
GDP per capita	12 252	35 356	48 779	57 967	53 206	57 467	61 834	PIB par habitant
GDP at constant prices	188 102	226 659	280 921	283 894	302 673	318 861	326 486	PIB aux prix constants
Growth rates	4.0	3.0	2.3	1.9	2.3	2.0	2.4	Taux de croissance
Djibouti								**Djibouti**
GDP at current prices	355	510	709	1 244	2 445	2 767	2 923	PIB aux prix courants
GDP per capita	835	808	905	1 480	2 676	2 931	3 049	PIB par habitant
GDP at constant prices	666	764	927	1 466	2 445	2 747	2 903	PIB aux prix constants
Growth rates	-0.2	5.6	3.6	11.7	7.7	5.1	5.6	Taux de croissance
Dominica								**Dominique**
GDP at current prices	117	260	370	494	541	520	551	PIB aux prix courants
GDP per capita	1 596	3 653	5 247	6 967	7 598	7 275	7 691	PIB par habitant
GDP at constant prices	274	388	466	535	541	514	526	PIB aux prix constants
Growth rates	1.3	2.0	-0.3	-2.8	-2.6	-7.2	2.3	Taux de croissance
Dominican Republic								**République dominicaine**
GDP at current prices	5 618	15 747	35 510	53 160	68 802	76 011	81 299	PIB aux prix courants
GDP per capita	869	2 014	3 903	5 483	6 692	7 230	7 650	PIB par habitant
GDP at constant prices	16 054	23 894	39 669	53 754	68 802	76 690	82 021	PIB aux prix constants
Growth rates	-2.1	5.5	9.3	8.3	7.0	4.6	7.0	Taux de croissance
Ecuador								**Équateur**
GDP at current prices	17 141	24 421	41 507	69 555	99 290	104 296	108 398	PIB aux prix courants
GDP per capita	1 891	2 132	3 002	4 634	6 124	6 214	6 345	PIB par habitant
GDP at constant prices	38 173	50 574	67 646	79 915	99 290	100 395	101 778	PIB aux prix constants
Growth rates	3.9	2.3	5.3	3.5	0.1	2.4	1.4	Taux de croissance
Egypt								**Égypte**
GDP at current prices	23 784	65 758	94 456	214 630	317 745	195 135	249 751	PIB aux prix courants
GDP per capita	483	1 055	1 251	2 593	3 437	2 023	2 538	PIB par habitant
GDP at constant prices	81 876	133 430	206 216	278 268	317 745	345 419	363 775	PIB aux prix constants
Growth rates	6.8	4.6	4.5	5.1	4.4	4.2	5.3	Taux de croissance
El Salvador								**El Salvador**
GDP at current prices	1 892	8 922	14 698	18 448	23 438	24 928	26 057	PIB aux prix courants
GDP per capita	383	1 585	2 429	2 983	3 706	3 902	4 058	PIB par habitant
GDP at constant prices	10 258	15 188	19 830	21 277	23 438	24 579	25 203	PIB aux prix constants
Growth rates	2.0	6.4	3.6	1.4	2.4	2.3	2.5	Taux de croissance
Equatorial Guinea								**Guinée équatoriale**
GDP at current prices	88	215	8 520	16 299	13 176	12 518	13 324	PIB aux prix courants
GDP per capita	251	433	11 367	17 272	11 275	9 919	10 179	PIB par habitant
GDP at constant prices	460	741	9 886	13 048	13 176	11 658	11 111	PIB aux prix constants
Growth rates	12.9	11.7	8.9	-8.9	-9.1	-3.2	-4.7	Taux de croissance
Eritrea								**Érythrée**
GDP at current prices	...	640	1 098	2 117	4 442	5 928	6 855	PIB aux prix courants
GDP per capita	...	290	389	668	1 329	1 737	1 985	PIB par habitant
GDP at constant prices	...	3 012	3 595	3 458	4 442	4 751	4 950	PIB aux prix constants
Growth rates	...	20.9	1.5	2.2	2.6	5.0	4.2	Taux de croissance
Estonia								**Estonie**
GDP at current prices	...	4 471	14 096	19 697	23 049	26 859	30 747	PIB aux prix courants
GDP per capita	...	3 120	10 398	14 786	17 523	20 357	23 242	PIB par habitant
GDP at constant prices	...	10 293	19 881	19 572	23 049	25 015	26 206	PIB aux prix constants
Growth rates	...	4.6	9.5	2.7	1.8	5.7	4.8	Taux de croissance
Eswatini								**Eswatini**
GDP at current prices	539	1 902	3 178	4 439	4 073	4 446	4 711	PIB aux prix courants
GDP per capita	771	2 052	3 084	4 168	3 690	3 953	4 146	PIB par habitant
GDP at constant prices	1 134	2 223	2 996	3 525	4 073	4 209	4 308	PIB aux prix constants
Growth rates	1.9	4.8	6.0	3.8	2.3	2.0	2.4	Taux de croissance

Gross domestic product and gross domestic product per capita *(continued)*
In millions of US dollars at current and constant 2015 prices; per capita US dollars; real rates of growth

Produit intérieur brut et produit intérieur brut par habitant *(suite)*
En millions de dollars É.-U. aux prix courants et constants de 2015; par habitant en dollars É.U.; taux de croissance réels

Country or area	1985	1995	2005	2010	2015	2017	2018	Pays ou zone
Ethiopia								**Éthiopie**
GDP at current prices	...	7 587	12 164	26 311	63 079	76 785	80 292	PIB aux prix courants
GDP per capita	...	133	159	300	626	722	735	PIB par habitant
GDP at constant prices	...	13 323	22 745	38 120	63 079	74 297	79 356	PIB aux prix constants
Growth rates	...	6.1	11.8	12.6	10.4	9.5	6.8	Taux de croissance
Fiji								**Fidji**
GDP at current prices	1 143	1 993	2 981	3 141	4 682	5 353	5 537	PIB aux prix courants
GDP per capita	1 605	2 571	3 628	3 653	5 391	6 101	6 267	PIB par habitant
GDP at constant prices	2 167	2 996	3 751	3 884	4 682	5 060	5 239	PIB aux prix constants
Growth rates	-3.9	2.5	0.7	3.0	4.7	5.4	3.5	Taux de croissance
Finland								**Finlande**
GDP at current prices	55 875	134 186	204 804	249 181	234 585	255 065	276 878	PIB aux prix courants
GDP per capita	11 377	26 213	38 944	46 439	42 799	46 280	50 136	PIB par habitant
GDP at constant prices	132 025	152 798	223 132	233 659	234 585	248 097	252 244	PIB aux prix constants
Growth rates	3.5	4.2	2.8	3.2	0.6	3.1	1.7	Taux de croissance
France [4]								**France** [4]
GDP at current prices	553 143	1 600 997	2 196 071	2 642 610	2 438 208	2 592 689	2 778 892	PIB aux prix courants
GDP per capita	9 763	26 904	34 807	40 685	36 612	38 684	41 358	PIB par habitant
GDP at constant prices	1 406 339	1 770 422	2 223 897	2 316 636	2 438 208	2 520 630	2 564 108	PIB aux prix constants
Growth rates	1.6	2.1	1.7	1.9	1.1	2.3	1.7	Taux de croissance
French Polynesia								**Polynésie française**
GDP at current prices	1 716	4 421	5 703	6 081	5 324	5 686	6 100	PIB aux prix courants
GDP per capita	9 694	20 271	22 037	22 821	19 492	20 594	21 968	PIB par habitant
GDP at constant prices	3 322	4 370	5 619	5 386	5 324	5 525	5 662	PIB aux prix constants
Growth rates	5.4	0.5	1.4	-2.5	1.8	2.4	2.5	Taux de croissance
Gabon								**Gabon**
GDP at current prices	4 639	5 519	9 579	14 359	14 372	14 929	16 994	PIB aux prix courants
GDP per capita	5 609	5 087	6 889	8 841	7 379	7 230	8 019	PIB par habitant
GDP at constant prices	8 120	10 024	10 471	11 139	14 372	14 745	14 928	PIB aux prix constants
Growth rates	-2.3	5.0	1.1	7.1	3.9	0.5	1.2	Taux de croissance
Gambia								**Gambie**
GDP at current prices	1 087	1 306	1 028	1 543	1 378	1 505	1 633	PIB aux prix courants
GDP per capita	1 439	1 157	666	861	661	680	716	PIB par habitant
GDP at constant prices	585	770	1 098	1 351	1 378	1 473	1 569	PIB aux prix constants
Growth rates	3.4	0.9	-2.4	5.9	4.1	4.8	6.5	Taux de croissance
Georgia								**Géorgie**
GDP at current prices	...	2 844	6 744	12 243	14 954	16 243	17 600	PIB aux prix courants
GDP per capita	...	571	1 602	2 987	3 716	4 052	4 397	PIB par habitant
GDP at constant prices	...	4 807	9 089	11 739	14 954	16 134	16 915	PIB aux prix constants
Growth rates	...	2.6	9.6	6.2	3.0	4.8	4.8	Taux de croissance
Germany								**Allemagne**
GDP at current prices	732 522	2 585 619	2 845 732	3 396 354	3 360 550	3 665 804	3 949 549	PIB aux prix courants
GDP per capita	9 429	31 867	34 873	42 020	41 089	44 349	47 514	PIB par habitant
GDP at constant prices	1 987 683	2 578 886	2 907 212	3 082 969	3 360 550	3 520 176	3 573 945	PIB aux prix constants
Growth rates	2.3	1.5	0.7	4.2	1.7	2.5	1.5	Taux de croissance
Ghana								**Ghana**
GDP at current prices	8 748	13 714	22 765	42 587	49 182	58 995	65 535	PIB aux prix courants
GDP per capita	684	806	1 044	1 719	1 766	2 026	2 202	PIB par habitant
GDP at constant prices	10 407	16 211	25 960	34 971	49 182	55 020	58 467	PIB aux prix constants
Growth rates	5.1	4.0	6.2	7.9	2.2	8.1	6.3	Taux de croissance
Greece								**Grèce**
GDP at current prices	47 816	136 886	247 777	299 362	196 591	203 589	218 139	PIB aux prix courants
GDP per capita	4 797	12 739	22 074	27 496	18 442	19 262	20 731	PIB par habitant
GDP at constant prices	149 297	168 931	244 480	240 488	196 591	199 169	203 022	PIB aux prix constants
Growth rates	2.5	2.1	0.6	-5.5	-0.4	1.5	1.9	Taux de croissance
Greenland								**Groenland**
GDP at current prices	451	1 321	1 850	2 503	2 499	2 827	3 052	PIB aux prix courants
GDP per capita	8 482	23 671	32 481	44 196	44 329	50 046	53 950	PIB par habitant
GDP at constant prices	1 390	1 545	2 088	2 458	2 499	2 628	2 713	PIB aux prix constants
Growth rates	3.7	3.7	5.0	1.7	-2.5	0.5	3.2	Taux de croissance
Grenada								**Grenade**
GDP at current prices	136	278	695	771	997	1 126	1 169	PIB aux prix courants
GDP per capita	1 359	2 774	6 644	7 258	9 097	10 153	10 486	PIB par habitant
GDP at constant prices	361	522	896	856	997	1 080	1 125	PIB aux prix constants
Growth rates	8.1	2.1	13.3	-0.5	6.4	4.4	4.1	Taux de croissance
Guatemala								**Guatemala**
GDP at current prices	9 967	13 066	27 211	41 338	63 767	75 620	78 461	PIB aux prix courants
GDP per capita	1 210	1 255	2 078	2 825	3 924	4 471	4 549	PIB par habitant
GDP at constant prices	22 021	31 351	44 171	52 849	63 767	67 554	69 679	PIB aux prix constants
Growth rates	-0.6	5.0	3.3	2.9	4.1	2.8	3.1	Taux de croissance

12
Gross domestic product and gross domestic product per capita *(continued)*
In millions of US dollars at current and constant 2015 prices; per capita US dollars; real rates of growth

Produit intérieur brut et produit intérieur brut par habitant *(suite)*
En millions de dollars É.-U. aux prix courants et constants de 2015; par habitant en dollars É.U.; taux de croissance réels

Country or area	1985	1995	2005	2010	2015	2017	2018	Pays ou zone
Guinea								**Guinée**
GDP at current prices	2 850	5 260	4 063	6 853	8 794	9 915	11 640	PIB aux prix courants
GDP per capita	521	724	446	672	769	822	938	PIB par habitant
GDP at constant prices	2 841	4 225	6 114	7 026	8 794	11 049	11 686	PIB aux prix constants
Growth rates	5.0	4.7	3.0	4.8	3.8	13.4	5.8	Taux de croissance
Guinea-Bissau								**Guinée-Bissau**
GDP at current prices	415	800	587	849	1 047	1 350	1 459	PIB aux prix courants
GDP per capita	476	735	436	558	603	739	778	PIB par habitant
GDP at constant prices	481	676	756	891	1 047	1 179	1 224	PIB aux prix constants
Growth rates	4.3	4.0	4.3	4.6	6.1	5.9	3.8	Taux de croissance
Guyana								**Guyana**
GDP at current prices	737	991	1 315	2 259	3 179	3 555	3 818	PIB aux prix courants
GDP per capita	956	1 302	1 763	3 015	4 143	4 586	4 901	PIB par habitant
GDP at constant prices	1 392	1 741	2 063	2 553	3 179	3 357	3 472	PIB aux prix constants
Growth rates	2.4	5.0	-2.0	4.1	3.1	2.2	3.4	Taux de croissance
Haiti								**Haïti**
GDP at current prices	2 665	2 696	4 047	6 708	8 355	8 521	9 287	PIB aux prix courants
GDP per capita	421	348	440	674	781	776	835	PIB par habitant
GDP at constant prices	7 033	6 204	6 835	7 095	8 355	8 576	8 703	PIB aux prix constants
Growth rates	0.6	9.9	1.8	-5.5	1.2	1.2	1.5	Taux de croissance
Honduras								**Honduras**
GDP at current prices	4 342	4 724	9 757	15 839	20 980	23 101	23 970	PIB aux prix courants
GDP per capita	1 014	828	1 308	1 904	2 302	2 450	2 500	PIB par habitant
GDP at constant prices	7 302	10 138	14 776	17 639	20 980	22 840	23 696	PIB aux prix constants
Growth rates	4.2	4.1	6.1	3.7	3.8	4.8	3.7	Taux de croissance
Hungary								**Hongrie**
GDP at current prices	23 713	46 439	112 981	131 136	124 530	141 511	157 883	PIB aux prix courants
GDP per capita	2 244	4 487	11 202	13 209	12 736	14 544	16 264	PIB par habitant
GDP at constant prices	87 176	79 383	113 674	112 514	124 530	132 771	139 534	PIB aux prix constants
Growth rates	-0.3	1.5	4.2	0.7	3.8	4.3	5.1	Taux de croissance
Iceland								**Islande**
GDP at current prices	2 940	7 018	16 813	13 684	17 389	24 493	25 882	PIB aux prix courants
GDP per capita	12 169	26 223	56 996	42 718	52 655	73 246	76 867	PIB par habitant
GDP at constant prices	7 485	8 866	14 318	15 132	17 389	19 395	20 289	PIB aux prix constants
Growth rates	3.3	0.1	6.3	-3.4	4.7	4.6	4.6	Taux de croissance
India								**Inde**
GDP at current prices	230 043	371 783	823 612	1 669 620	2 146 759	2 625 091	2 779 352	PIB aux prix courants
GDP per capita	293	386	718	1 353	1 639	1 961	2 055	PIB par habitant
GDP at constant prices	355 589	608 291	1 116 782	1 567 418	2 146 759	2 488 587	2 658 094	PIB aux prix constants
Growth rates	5.3	7.6	7.9	8.5	8.0	7.2	6.8	Taux de croissance
Indonesia								**Indonésie**
GDP at current prices	102 171	236 456	304 372	755 094	860 854	1 015 423	1 042 173	PIB aux prix courants
GDP per capita	617	1 196	1 345	3 122	3 332	3 837	3 893	PIB par habitant
GDP at constant prices	186 991	380 896	497 632	657 835	860 854	950 000	999 127	PIB aux prix constants
Growth rates	2.5	8.2	5.7	6.2	4.9	5.1	5.2	Taux de croissance
Iran (Islamic Republic of)								**Iran (Rép. islamique d')**
GDP at current prices	76 257	114 364	226 452	491 099	393 436	460 976	473 091	PIB aux prix courants
GDP per capita	1 611	1 861	3 246	6 658	5 012	5 714	5 783	PIB par habitant
GDP at constant prices	182 365	214 751	330 405	401 979	393 436	462 895	440 468	PIB aux prix constants
Growth rates	1.9	2.4	3.2	5.8	-1.3	3.8	-4.8	Taux de croissance
Iraq								**Iraq**
GDP at current prices	16 878	4 863	49 955	138 517	166 774	190 644	212 272	PIB aux prix courants
GDP per capita	1 085	241	1 856	4 657	4 688	5 077	5 523	PIB par habitant
GDP at constant prices	53 746	32 111	94 053	120 516	166 774	182 617	180 864	PIB aux prix constants
Growth rates	-~0.0	-18.3	1.7	6.4	4.7	-3.8	-1.0	Taux de croissance
Ireland								**Irlande**
GDP at current prices	21 296	69 225	211 644	222 149	291 500	335 663	382 674	PIB aux prix courants
GDP per capita	6 065	19 271	51 107	48 757	62 655	70 617	79 415	PIB par habitant
GDP at constant prices	64 325	101 533	206 041	210 479	291 500	326 837	353 540	PIB aux prix constants
Growth rates	3.1	9.6	5.7	1.8	25.2	8.1	8.2	Taux de croissance
Israel								**Israël**
GDP at current prices	27 448	100 385	142 529	233 996	299 813	353 253	370 588	PIB aux prix courants
GDP per capita	6 802	19 043	21 829	31 852	37 578	42 851	44 215	PIB par habitant
GDP at constant prices	82 155	143 799	203 985	252 233	299 813	322 896	334 007	PIB aux prix constants
Growth rates	4.0	8.7	4.1	5.6	2.3	3.6	3.4	Taux de croissance
Italy								**Italie**
GDP at current prices	452 198	1 174 699	1 857 478	2 134 018	1 835 899	1 961 806	2 084 882	PIB aux prix courants
GDP per capita	7 942	20 546	31 871	35 972	30 306	32 334	34 389	PIB par habitant
GDP at constant prices	1 337 817	1 662 885	1 927 161	1 899 562	1 835 899	1 891 303	1 905 948	PIB aux prix constants
Growth rates	2.8	2.8	0.8	1.7	0.8	1.7	0.8	Taux de croissance

12

Gross domestic product and gross domestic product per capita *(continued)*
In millions of US dollars at current and constant 2015 prices; per capita US dollars; real rates of growth

Produit intérieur brut et produit intérieur brut par habitant *(suite)*
En millions de dollars É.-U. aux prix courants et constants de 2015; par habitant en dollars É.U.; taux de croissance réels

Country or area	1985	1995	2005	2010	2015	2017	2018	Pays ou zone
Jamaica								**Jamaïque**
GDP at current prices	2 605	6 578	11 244	13 221	14 196	14 806	15 714	PIB aux prix courants
GDP per capita	1 115	2 596	4 104	4 704	4 911	5 069	5 354	PIB par habitant
GDP at constant prices	8 897	13 067	14 087	13 748	14 196	14 536	14 818	PIB aux prix constants
Growth rates	-4.6	1.0	0.9	-1.5	0.9	1.0	1.9	Taux de croissance
Japan								**Japon**
GDP at current prices	1 398 893	5 449 118	4 755 410	5 700 098	4 389 476	4 859 951	4 971 323	PIB aux prix courants
GDP per capita	11 477	43 122	37 057	44 344	34 297	38 116	39 082	PIB par habitant
GDP at constant prices	2 712 502	3 711 588	4 157 594	4 177 964	4 389 476	4 501 390	4 536 881	PIB aux prix constants
Growth rates	5.2	2.7	1.7	4.2	1.2	1.9	0.8	Taux de croissance
Jordan								**Jordanie**
GDP at current prices	5 173	6 802	12 720	26 520	37 923	40 709	42 231	PIB aux prix courants
GDP per capita	1 784	1 482	2 206	3 652	4 092	4 160	4 238	PIB par habitant
GDP at constant prices	11 763	15 523	24 754	33 281	37 923	39 526	40 294	PIB aux prix constants
Growth rates	-2.7	6.2	8.1	2.7	2.6	2.1	1.9	Taux de croissance
Kazakhstan								**Kazakhstan**
GDP at current prices	...	20 562	57 124	148 047	184 388	166 806	179 340	PIB aux prix courants
GDP per capita	...	1 298	3 709	9 109	10 493	9 226	9 790	PIB par habitant
GDP at constant prices	...	57 792	107 064	144 702	184 388	193 983	201 936	PIB aux prix constants
Growth rates	...	-8.2	9.7	7.3	1.2	4.1	4.1	Taux de croissance
Kenya								**Kenya**
GDP at current prices	9 110	13 428	21 506	40 000	64 008	78 757	87 906	PIB aux prix courants
GDP per capita	458	484	587	952	1 337	1 568	1 710	PIB par habitant
GDP at constant prices	20 226	28 779	38 361	48 918	64 008	71 066	75 557	PIB aux prix constants
Growth rates	4.3	4.4	5.9	8.4	5.7	4.9	6.3	Taux de croissance
Kiribati								**Kiribati**
GDP at current prices	30	56	112	156	169	186	189	PIB aux prix courants
GDP per capita	468	720	1 215	1 517	1 525	1 626	1 627	PIB par habitant
GDP at constant prices	94	110	140	139	169	178	183	PIB aux prix constants
Growth rates	-4.6	-0.6	5.0	-0.9	10.3	4.3	2.3	Taux de croissance
Kosovo								**Kosovo**
GDP at current prices	...	5 304	3 680	5 830	6 440	7 246	7 943	PIB aux prix courants
GDP per capita	...	2 351	2 099	3 430	3 615	4 049	4 453	PIB par habitant
GDP at constant prices	...	3 979	4 285	5 506	6 440	6 986	7 252	PIB aux prix constants
Growth rates	...	8.1	3.9	3.3	4.1	4.2	3.8	Taux de croissance
Kuwait								**Koweït**
GDP at current prices	21 446	26 554	80 798	115 416	114 585	119 534	141 698	PIB aux prix courants
GDP per capita	12 359	16 535	35 591	38 576	29 874	29 470	34 249	PIB par habitant
GDP at constant prices	34 951	54 453	90 480	95 861	114 585	113 832	115 244	PIB aux prix constants
Growth rates	-4.3	1.4	10.6	-2.4	0.6	-3.5	1.2	Taux de croissance
Kyrgyzstan								**Kirghizistan**
GDP at current prices	...	1 492	2 460	4 794	6 678	7 703	8 093	PIB aux prix courants
GDP per capita	...	327	485	884	1 121	1 244	1 284	PIB par habitant
GDP at constant prices	...	2 678	4 237	5 263	6 678	7 298	7 550	PIB aux prix constants
Growth rates	...	-5.4	-0.2	-0.5	3.9	4.7	3.5	Taux de croissance
Lao People's Dem. Rep.								**Rép. dém. populaire lao**
GDP at current prices	626	1 852	2 946	7 313	14 390	16 853	17 954	PIB aux prix courants
GDP per capita	170	382	512	1 170	2 135	2 424	2 542	PIB par habitant
GDP at constant prices	2 188	3 644	6 743	9 899	14 390	16 463	17 491	PIB aux prix constants
Growth rates	5.1	7.5	6.8	8.1	7.3	6.9	6.2	Taux de croissance
Latvia								**Lettonie**
GDP at current prices	...	5 390	16 909	23 804	27 090	30 273	34 426	PIB aux prix courants
GDP per capita	...	2 149	7 508	11 234	13 561	15 516	17 852	PIB par habitant
GDP at constant prices	...	12 199	23 320	22 729	27 090	28 615	29 937	PIB aux prix constants
Growth rates	...	-0.8	10.7	-4.5	3.3	3.8	4.6	Taux de croissance
Lebanon								**Liban**
GDP at current prices	2 275	11 506	21 490	38 420	49 974	53 394	56 409	PIB aux prix courants
GDP per capita	858	3 261	4 574	7 757	7 650	7 830	8 224	PIB par habitant
GDP at constant prices	24 259	24 538	31 789	45 918	49 974	51 057	51 184	PIB aux prix constants
Growth rates	24.3	6.5	2.7	8.0	0.4	0.6	0.3	Taux de croissance
Lesotho								**Lesotho**
GDP at current prices	297	955	1 560	2 386	2 465	2 579	2 631	PIB aux prix courants
GDP per capita	195	503	781	1 196	1 197	1 233	1 248	PIB par habitant
GDP at constant prices	689	1 144	1 613	2 037	2 465	2 530	2 560	PIB aux prix constants
Growth rates	9.4	4.6	2.7	6.1	1.6	-0.9	1.2	Taux de croissance
Liberia								**Libéria**
GDP at current prices	1 076	209	706	1 292	2 075	2 145	2 122	PIB aux prix courants
GDP per capita	502	102	219	332	464	456	440	PIB par habitant
GDP at constant prices	1 450	211	802	1 566	2 075	2 092	2 117	PIB aux prix constants
Growth rates	-2.0	-4.3	5.3	7.3	...	2.5	1.2	Taux de croissance

12 Gross domestic product and gross domestic product per capita *(continued)*
In millions of US dollars at current and constant 2015 prices; per capita US dollars; real rates of growth

Produit intérieur brut et produit intérieur brut par habitant *(suite)*
En millions de dollars É.-U. aux prix courants et constants de 2015; par habitant en dollars É.U.; taux de croissance réels

Country or area	1985	1995	2005	2010	2015	2017	2018	Pays ou zone
Libya								**Libye**
GDP at current prices	29 887	28 292	45 451	80 942	17 666	25 120	34 377	PIB aux prix courants
GDP per capita	7 715	5 717	7 838	13 060	2 752	3 817	5 147	PIB par habitant
GDP at constant prices	86 944	84 872	117 127	155 910	17 666	24 310	28 657	PIB aux prix constants
Growth rates	8.3	-2.2	10.3	4.3	-45.5	64.0	17.9	Taux de croissance
Liechtenstein								**Liechtenstein**
GDP at current prices	681	2 695	4 046	5 621	6 269	6 553	6 796	PIB aux prix courants
GDP per capita	24 967	87 281	116 560	156 167	167 294	173 358	179 258	PIB par habitant
GDP at constant prices	2 597	3 677	5 370	5 980	6 269	6 699	6 835	PIB aux prix constants
Growth rates	7.0	1.9	4.8	7.4	~0.0	4.4	2.0	Taux de croissance
Lithuania								**Lituanie**
GDP at current prices	...	6 702	26 141	37 034	41 392	47 751	53 455	PIB aux prix courants
GDP per capita	...	1 848	7 817	11 856	14 118	16 782	19 083	PIB par habitant
GDP at constant prices	...	17 916	32 475	34 377	41 392	44 253	45 866	PIB aux prix constants
Growth rates	...	3.3	7.7	1.5	2.0	4.2	3.6	Taux de croissance
Luxembourg								**Luxembourg**
GDP at current prices	4 738	21 588	37 346	53 212	57 744	64 182	70 920	PIB aux prix courants
GDP per capita	12 915	52 894	81 571	104 772	101 889	108 432	117 370	PIB par habitant
GDP at constant prices	16 533	28 778	44 415	50 117	57 744	61 474	63 386	PIB aux prix constants
Growth rates	2.8	1.4	3.2	4.9	4.3	1.8	3.1	Taux de croissance
Madagascar								**Madagascar**
GDP at current prices	2 748	3 668	5 849	9 983	11 323	13 176	13 851	PIB aux prix courants
GDP per capita	273	272	319	472	467	515	527	PIB par habitant
GDP at constant prices	5 671	6 387	8 628	9 925	11 323	12 238	12 797	PIB aux prix constants
Growth rates	1.2	1.7	4.6	0.6	3.1	3.9	4.6	Taux de croissance
Malawi								**Malawi**
GDP at current prices	2 028	2 474	3 656	6 960	6 431	6 348	7 196	PIB aux prix courants
GDP per capita	279	251	290	479	384	359	397	PIB par habitant
GDP at constant prices	2 305	2 779	3 702	5 294	6 431	6 949	7 227	PIB aux prix constants
Growth rates	4.7	9.0	3.3	6.9	3.3	5.2	4.0	Taux de croissance
Malaysia								**Malaisie**
GDP at current prices	31 200	88 833	143 534	255 018	301 355	318 955	358 579	PIB aux prix courants
GDP per capita	2 000	4 336	5 587	9 041	9 955	10 254	11 373	PIB par habitant
GDP at constant prices	54 088	117 335	186 898	232 654	301 355	332 838	348 619	PIB aux prix constants
Growth rates	-1.1	9.8	5.3	7.4	5.1	5.7	4.7	Taux de croissance
Maldives								**Maldives**
GDP at current prices	166	566	1 163	2 588	4 109	4 736	5 327	PIB aux prix courants
GDP per capita	876	2 228	3 640	7 077	9 033	9 541	10 331	PIB par habitant
GDP at constant prices	617	1 408	2 106	3 117	4 109	4 667	4 989	PIB aux prix constants
Growth rates	13.0	7.1	-13.1	7.3	2.9	6.8	6.9	Taux de croissance
Mali								**Mali**
GDP at current prices	1 260	2 837	6 245	10 679	13 095	15 376	17 172	PIB aux prix courants
GDP per capita	161	296	489	710	751	831	900	PIB par habitant
GDP at constant prices	1 004	2 173	5 323	8 803	13 095	15 215	16 231	PIB aux prix constants
Growth rates	8.5	37.2	10.4	10.9	7.6	6.8	6.7	Taux de croissance
Malta								**Malte**
GDP at current prices	1 156	3 697	6 393	8 741	10 702	12 780	14 549	PIB aux prix courants
GDP per capita	3 339	9 810	15 799	21 100	24 685	29 184	33 123	PIB par habitant
GDP at constant prices	2 961	5 212	7 412	8 192	10 702	12 072	12 863	PIB aux prix constants
Growth rates	2.6	6.3	3.8	3.5	10.7	6.7	6.6	Taux de croissance
Marshall Islands								**Îles Marshall**
GDP at current prices	44	121	140	168	181	208	214	PIB aux prix courants
GDP per capita	1 155	2 405	2 539	2 986	3 159	3 578	3 667	PIB par habitant
GDP at constant prices	85	163	158	172	181	193	198	PIB aux prix constants
Growth rates	-6.3	8.2	3.6	7.1	-0.6	4.5	2.6	Taux de croissance
Mauritania								**Mauritanie**
GDP at current prices	1 395	2 161	2 808	5 450	6 321	7 063	7 620	PIB aux prix courants
GDP per capita	784	934	929	1 560	1 562	1 649	1 730	PIB par habitant
GDP at constant prices	1 813	2 382	3 459	4 717	6 321	6 858	7 105	PIB aux prix constants
Growth rates	3.4	-2.4	9.0	6.9	4.1	3.6	3.6	Taux de croissance
Mauritius								**Maurice**
GDP at current prices	1 152	4 273	6 775	10 004	11 692	13 259	14 220	PIB aux prix courants
GDP per capita	1 134	3 786	5 544	8 016	9 284	10 486	11 222	PIB par habitant
GDP at constant prices	2 742	5 013	7 758	9 775	11 692	12 604	13 080	PIB aux prix constants
Growth rates	6.9	4.4	1.8	4.4	3.6	3.8	3.8	Taux de croissance
Mexico								**Mexique**
GDP at current prices	224 593	360 073	877 477	1 057 801	1 170 567	1 158 229	1 223 401	PIB aux prix courants
GDP per capita	2 956	3 928	8 278	9 271	9 606	9 282	9 695	PIB par habitant
GDP at constant prices	566 506	677 038	940 516	1 012 355	1 170 567	1 229 702	1 254 236	PIB aux prix constants
Growth rates	2.8	-6.3	2.3	5.1	3.3	2.1	2.0	Taux de croissance

Gross domestic product and gross domestic product per capita *(continued)*
In millions of US dollars at current and constant 2015 prices; per capita US dollars; real rates of growth

Produit intérieur brut et produit intérieur brut par habitant *(suite)*
En millions de dollars É.-U. aux prix courants et constants de 2015; par habitant en dollars É.U.; taux de croissance réels

Country or area	1985	1995	2005	2010	2015	2017	2018	Pays ou zone
Micronesia (Fed. States of)								**Micronésie (États féd. de)**
GDP at current prices	108	222	251	297	315	363	371	PIB aux prix courants
GDP per capita	1 262	2 063	2 362	2 884	2 894	3 253	3 296	PIB par habitant
GDP at constant prices	205	311	320	316	315	325	329	PIB aux prix constants
Growth rates	16.6	4.2	2.1	2.1	4.9	2.4	1.4	Taux de croissance
Monaco								**Monaco**
GDP at current prices	1 059	3 070	4 203	5 362	6 259	6 431	7 188	PIB aux prix courants
GDP per capita	36 728	99 960	124 190	150 577	165 945	167 516	185 835	PIB par habitant
GDP at constant prices	2 626	3 306	4 142	4 542	6 259	6 253	6 633	PIB aux prix constants
Growth rates	1.6	2.1	1.6	-1.4	4.9	-3.4	6.1	Taux de croissance
Mongolia								**Mongolie**
GDP at current prices	1 216	1 678	2 926	7 189	11 750	11 434	13 010	PIB aux prix courants
GDP per capita	633	730	1 158	2 643	3 919	3 672	4 104	PIB par habitant
GDP at constant prices	3 204	3 358	5 284	7 232	11 750	12 613	13 460	PIB aux prix constants
Growth rates	5.7	6.3	7.3	6.4	2.4	5.2	6.7	Taux de croissance
Montenegro								**Monténégro**
GDP at current prices	...	1 215	2 279	4 139	4 053	4 857	5 507	PIB aux prix courants
GDP per capita	...	1 958	3 697	6 630	6 465	7 739	8 772	PIB par habitant
GDP at constant prices	...	1 794	3 078	3 704	4 053	4 369	4 591	PIB aux prix constants
Growth rates	...	14.3	4.2	2.7	3.4	4.7	5.1	Taux de croissance
Montserrat								**Montserrat**
GDP at current prices	44	69	49	56	61	60	64	PIB aux prix courants
GDP per capita	4 040	6 991	10 108	11 331	12 358	12 030	12 754	PIB par habitant
GDP at constant prices	97	109	51	53	61	60	62	PIB aux prix constants
Growth rates	5.9	-8.8	3.1	-2.8	-1.9	-2.8	3.7	Taux de croissance
Morocco [5]								**Maroc** [5]
GDP at current prices	15 111	38 728	62 545	93 217	101 179	109 714	117 921	PIB aux prix courants
GDP per capita	672	1 435	2 054	2 882	2 919	3 083	3 273	PIB par habitant
GDP at constant prices	30 612	39 780	61 195	81 274	101 179	110 465	114 546	PIB aux prix constants
Growth rates	6.3	-6.6	3.0	4.0	4.9	5.8	3.7	Taux de croissance
Mozambique								**Mozambique**
GDP at current prices	8 875	2 817	8 459	11 121	15 951	13 219	14 717	PIB aux prix courants
GDP per capita	695	182	413	473	590	461	499	PIB par habitant
GDP at constant prices	2 134	2 998	7 913	11 324	15 951	17 181	17 770	PIB aux prix constants
Growth rates	-8.8	2.2	8.7	6.7	6.7	3.7	3.4	Taux de croissance
Myanmar								**Myanmar**
GDP at current prices	6 607	7 763	11 931	41 445	62 543	66 491	72 745	PIB aux prix courants
GDP per capita	174	177	244	819	1 187	1 246	1 354	PIB par habitant
GDP at constant prices	7 967	9 497	25 907	44 050	62 543	70 685	75 067	PIB aux prix constants
Growth rates	2.9	6.9	13.6	10.2	7.0	6.8	6.2	Taux de croissance
Namibia								**Namibie**
GDP at current prices	1 606	3 942	7 121	11 282	11 651	13 566	14 519	PIB aux prix courants
GDP per capita	1 340	2 422	3 674	5 325	5 033	5 646	5 930	PIB par habitant
GDP at constant prices	3 468	4 755	7 189	8 855	11 651	11 679	11 671	PIB aux prix constants
Growth rates	0.5	3.9	2.5	6.0	6.1	-0.9	-0.1	Taux de croissance
Nauru								**Nauru**
GDP at current prices	33	35	26	59	104	134	127	PIB aux prix courants
GDP per capita	3 887	3 280	2 670	5 925	10 050	12 654	11 876	PIB par habitant
GDP at constant prices	162	71	31	45	104	120	115	PIB aux prix constants
Growth rates	-2.8	-7.9	-12.1	13.6	2.8	4.0	-4.0	Taux de croissance
Nepal								**Népal**
GDP at current prices	2 741	4 534	8 259	16 281	20 801	25 587	27 830	PIB aux prix courants
GDP per capita	163	210	321	603	770	926	991	PIB par habitant
GDP at constant prices	5 584	8 989	13 546	16 833	20 801	22 644	24 152	PIB aux prix constants
Growth rates	6.1	3.5	3.5	4.8	3.3	8.2	6.7	Taux de croissance
Netherlands								**Pays-Bas**
GDP at current prices	143 847	452 287	685 076	846 555	765 265	833 870	914 105	PIB aux prix courants
GDP per capita	9 911	29 240	41 857	50 744	45 179	48 990	53 583	PIB par habitant
GDP at constant prices	394 307	520 709	688 450	737 269	765 265	804 802	825 706	PIB aux prix constants
Growth rates	2.6	3.1	2.1	1.3	2.0	2.9	2.6	Taux de croissance
Netherlands Antilles [former]								**Antilles néerlandaises [anc.]**
GDP at current prices	1 190	2 571	3 053	3 848	...	...	...	PIB aux prix courants
GDP per capita	7 020	14 690	18 663	20 985	...	...	...	PIB par habitant
GDP at constant prices	3 089	3 861	3 913	4 219	...	...	...	PIB aux prix constants
Growth rates	-2.1	1.6	1.1	-0.3	...	...	...	Taux de croissance
New Caledonia								**Nouvelle-Calédonie**
GDP at current prices	855	3 628	6 236	9 355	8 772	9 459	10 174	PIB aux prix courants
GDP per capita	5 480	18 772	26 375	36 900	32 363	34 129	36 335	PIB par habitant
GDP at constant prices	2 791	5 208	6 519	7 907	8 772	9 104	9 251	PIB aux prix constants
Growth rates	4.5	5.9	3.6	6.9	0.6	1.6	1.6	Taux de croissance

12

Gross domestic product and gross domestic product per capita *(continued)*
In millions of US dollars at current and constant 2015 prices; per capita US dollars; real rates of growth

Produit intérieur brut et produit intérieur brut par habitant *(suite)*
En millions de dollars É.-U. aux prix courants et constants de 2015; par habitant en dollars É.U.; taux de croissance réels

Country or area	1985	1995	2005	2010	2015	2017	2018	Pays ou zone
New Zealand								**Nouvelle-Zélande**
GDP at current prices	24 108	63 151	114 721	146 584	177 468	205 416	207 921	PIB aux prix courants
GDP per capita	7 376	17 184	27 741	33 543	38 458	43 687	43 836	PIB par habitant
GDP at constant prices	85 035	100 702	141 823	152 914	177 468	191 542	196 955	PIB aux prix constants
Growth rates	1.6	4.6	3.3	1.0	4.2	4.0	2.8	Taux de croissance
Nicaragua								**Nicaragua**
GDP at current prices	3 605	4 118	6 300	8 759	12 757	13 844	13 118	PIB aux prix courants
GDP per capita	965	885	1 158	1 504	2 050	2 168	2 029	PIB par habitant
GDP at constant prices	6 211	5 733	8 555	9 779	12 757	13 962	13 430	PIB aux prix constants
Growth rates	-4.1	5.9	4.3	4.4	4.8	4.7	-3.8	Taux de croissance
Niger								**Niger**
GDP at current prices	2 040	2 380	4 489	7 620	9 659	11 170	12 821	PIB aux prix courants
GDP per capita	295	251	330	463	483	517	571	PIB par habitant
GDP at constant prices	3 494	3 806	5 557	7 149	9 659	10 719	11 470	PIB aux prix constants
Growth rates	7.7	3.3	7.4	8.4	4.3	5.0	7.0	Taux de croissance
Nigeria								**Nigéria**
GDP at current prices	210 154	50 486	176 134	363 360	494 583	375 770	421 821	PIB aux prix courants
GDP per capita	2 515	468	1 268	2 292	2 730	1 969	2 154	PIB par habitant
GDP at constant prices	121 696	155 089	274 839	387 074	494 583	490 549	500 010	PIB aux prix constants
Growth rates	5.9	-0.1	6.4	8.0	2.7	0.8	1.9	Taux de croissance
North Macedonia								**Macédoine du Nord**
GDP at current prices	...	4 707	6 259	9 407	10 065	11 307	12 629	PIB aux prix courants
GDP per capita	...	2 373	3 038	4 543	4 840	5 431	6 063	PIB par habitant
GDP at constant prices	...	5 748	7 335	8 919	10 065	10 463	10 808	PIB aux prix constants
Growth rates	...	-1.1	4.7	3.4	3.9	1.1	3.3	Taux de croissance
Norway								**Norvège**
GDP at current prices	65 417	152 031	308 884	428 757	385 802	398 394	434 167	PIB aux prix courants
GDP per capita	15 751	34 814	66 680	87 754	74 195	75 221	81 336	PIB par habitant
GDP at constant prices	193 994	253 494	337 670	354 112	385 802	398 995	404 140	PIB aux prix constants
Growth rates	5.6	4.2	2.6	0.7	2.0	2.3	1.3	Taux de croissance
Oman								**Oman**
GDP at current prices	10 281	13 650	31 082	56 913	65 481	79 277	92 111	PIB aux prix courants
GDP per capita	6 861	6 193	12 377	18 713	15 345	16 991	19 073	PIB par habitant
GDP at constant prices	20 586	31 524	38 809	49 883	65 481	66 866	68 261	PIB aux prix constants
Growth rates	14.5	4.8	2.5	1.7	5.1	1.8	2.1	Taux de croissance
Pakistan								**Pakistan**
GDP at current prices	38 840	77 266	117 708	174 508	267 035	303 092	282 346	PIB aux prix courants
GDP per capita	421	624	734	973	1 339	1 458	1 330	PIB par habitant
GDP at constant prices	74 537	123 848	185 487	219 392	267 035	297 858	314 031	PIB aux prix constants
Growth rates	7.6	5.0	7.7	1.6	4.7	5.7	5.4	Taux de croissance
Palau								**Palaos**
GDP at current prices	41	110	184	183	280	286	284	PIB aux prix courants
GDP per capita	3 044	6 432	9 326	10 220	15 872	16 078	15 859	PIB par habitant
GDP at constant prices	149	229	262	232	280	273	277	PIB aux prix constants
Growth rates	5.4	16.6	0.2	0.3	10.1	-3.5	1.7	Taux de croissance
Panama								**Panama**
GDP at current prices	5 817	9 188	15 714	29 440	54 092	62 284	65 055	PIB aux prix courants
GDP per capita	2 621	3 354	4 719	8 082	13 630	15 166	15 575	PIB par habitant
GDP at constant prices	12 114	16 806	26 026	37 273	54 092	59 799	61 998	PIB aux prix constants
Growth rates	5.1	1.8	7.2	5.8	5.7	5.3	3.7	Taux de croissance
Papua New Guinea								**Papouasie-Nvl-Guinée**
GDP at current prices	3 682	7 274	7 312	14 251	22 962	22 006	23 077	PIB aux prix courants
GDP per capita	902	1 402	1 126	1 949	2 832	2 608	2 681	PIB par habitant
GDP at constant prices	7 021	11 323	13 080	17 432	22 962	22 475	22 475	PIB aux prix constants
Growth rates	3.6	-3.3	3.9	10.1	6.9	-1.5	~0.0	Taux de croissance
Paraguay								**Paraguay**
GDP at current prices	5 200[6]	10 440[6]	11 306	27 239	36 164	39 009	40 307	PIB aux prix courants
GDP per capita	1 414[6]	2 186[6]	1 941	4 360	5 407	5 681	5 795	PIB par habitant
GDP at constant prices	12 398[6]	17 720[6]	22 846	29 762	36 164	39 594	41 178	PIB aux prix constants
Growth rates	4.0[6]	5.4[6]	2.1	11.1	3.1	5.0	4.0	Taux de croissance
Peru								**Pérou**
GDP at current prices	14 529	53 371	76 080	147 528	189 757	210 716	222 237	PIB aux prix courants
GDP per capita	735	2 196	2 730	5 082	6 228	6 701	6 947	PIB par habitant
GDP at constant prices	65 761	76 897	107 742	150 257	189 757	202 233	210 274	PIB aux prix constants
Growth rates	2.1	7.4	6.3	8.3	3.3	2.5	4.0	Taux de croissance
Philippines								**Philippines**
GDP at current prices	34 052	82 121	103 072	199 591	292 774	313 620	330 910	PIB aux prix courants
GDP per capita	627	1 177	1 194	2 124	2 867	2 982	3 103	PIB par habitant
GDP at constant prices	82 536	115 779	172 628	219 635	292 774	333 825	354 668	PIB aux prix constants
Growth rates	-7.3	4.7	4.8	7.6	6.1	6.7	6.2	Taux de croissance

12 Gross domestic product and gross domestic product per capita *(continued)*
In millions of US dollars at current and constant 2015 prices; per capita US dollars; real rates of growth

Produit intérieur brut et produit intérieur brut par habitant *(suite)*
En millions de dollars É.-U. aux prix courants et constants de 2015; par habitant en dollars É.U.; taux de croissance réels

Country or area	1985	1995	2005	2010	2015	2017	2018	Pays ou zone
Poland								**Pologne**
GDP at current prices	73 333	142 138	306 127	479 321	477 581	526 376	585 661	PIB aux prix courants
GDP per capita	1 975	3 696	7 979	12 505	12 557	13 869	15 444	PIB par habitant
GDP at constant prices	198 463	216 668	325 994	411 450	477 581	516 518	543 108	PIB aux prix constants
Growth rates	3.6	7.0	3.5	3.6	3.8	4.9	5.1	Taux de croissance
Portugal								**Portugal**
GDP at current prices	27 115	118 120	197 175	237 881	199 314	221 358	240 792	PIB aux prix courants
GDP per capita	2 731	11 705	18 763	22 450	19 223	21 515	23 478	PIB par habitant
GDP at constant prices	110 367	158 239	201 835	207 893	199 314	210 469	215 607	PIB aux prix constants
Growth rates	2.8	4.3	0.8	1.7	1.8	3.5	2.4	Taux de croissance
Puerto Rico								**Porto Rico**
GDP at current prices	20 574	43 246	83 915	98 381	103 376	104 250	101 131	PIB aux prix courants
GDP per capita	6 305	12 122	23 105	27 482	30 571	32 952	33 271	PIB par habitant
GDP at constant prices	53 129	85 278	113 935	106 406	103 376	99 357	94 483	PIB aux prix constants
Growth rates	2.1	4.5	-2.0	-0.4	-1.0	-2.7	-4.9	Taux de croissance
Qatar								**Qatar**
GDP at current prices	6 153	8 138	44 530	125 122	161 740	166 929	191 362	PIB aux prix courants
GDP per capita	16 591	15 850	51 456	67 403	63 039	61 264	68 794	PIB par habitant
GDP at constant prices	15 330	21 086	53 065	121 472	161 740	167 797	170 303	PIB aux prix constants
Growth rates	-2.1	2.4	7.5	16.7	3.7	1.6	1.5	Taux de croissance
Republic of Korea								**République de Corée**
GDP at current prices	102 870	570 531	934 901	1 144 067	1 465 773	1 623 901	1 720 489	PIB aux prix courants
GDP per capita	2 521	12 597	19 197	23 091	28 841	31 781	33 622	PIB par habitant
GDP at constant prices	248 139	611 553	1 021 193	1 261 202	1 465 773	1 556 646	1 598 129	PIB aux prix constants
Growth rates	7.7	9.6	4.3	6.8	2.8	3.2	2.7	Taux de croissance
Republic of Moldova								**République de Moldova**
GDP at current prices	...	2 121	3 587	6 975	7 745	9 670	11 309	PIB aux prix courants
GDP per capita	...	489	862	1 707	1 903	2 382	2 791	PIB par habitant
GDP at constant prices	...	4 432	5 507	6 452	7 745	8 466	8 701	PIB aux prix constants
Growth rates	...	-1.4	7.5	7.1	-0.3	4.7	2.8	Taux de croissance
Romania								**Roumanie**
GDP at current prices	50 742	37 657	98 454	166 225	177 895	211 696	239 552	PIB aux prix courants
GDP per capita	2 199	1 640	4 597	8 120	8 928	10 771	12 281	PIB par habitant
GDP at constant prices	125 287	102 743	133 644	153 653	177 895	199 694	207 589	PIB aux prix constants
Growth rates	-0.1	7.1	4.7	-3.9	3.9	7.1	4.0	Taux de croissance
Russian Federation								**Fédération de Russie**
GDP at current prices	...	402 295	771 495	1 539 845	1 366 031	1 581 443	1 660 514	PIB aux prix courants
GDP per capita	...	2 714	5 370	10 732	9 422	10 867	11 394	PIB par habitant
GDP at constant prices	...	727 598	1 060 642	1 262 284	1 366 031	1 392 871	1 424 278	PIB aux prix constants
Growth rates	...	-4.1	6.4	4.5	-2.3	1.6	2.3	Taux de croissance
Rwanda								**Rwanda**
GDP at current prices	1 813	1 230	2 581	5 772	8 278	9 136	9 510	PIB aux prix courants
GDP per capita	295	211	292	575	728	763	773	PIB par habitant
GDP at constant prices	2 336	1 581	3 860	5 752	8 278	9 308	10 111	PIB aux prix constants
Growth rates	4.4	33.5	9.4	7.3	8.9	6.1	8.6	Taux de croissance
Saint Kitts and Nevis								**Saint-Kitts-et-Nevis**
GDP at current prices	111	313	547	760	923	997	1 011	PIB aux prix courants
GDP per capita	2 651	7 451	11 678	15 509	18 029	19 155	19 275	PIB par habitant
GDP at constant prices	302	522	780	819	923	930	958	PIB aux prix constants
Growth rates	8.6	5.4	9.7	-0.6	1.0	-2.0	2.9	Taux de croissance
Saint Lucia								**Sainte-Lucie**
GDP at current prices	249	617	935	1 400	1 659	1 817	1 922	PIB aux prix courants
GDP per capita	1 973	4 204	5 724	8 044	9 262	10 040	10 566	PIB par habitant
GDP at constant prices	624	1 053	1 306	1 606	1 659	1 755	1 770	PIB aux prix constants
Growth rates	7.5	1.1	-1.7	0.4	0.2	2.6	0.9	Taux de croissance
Saint Vincent & Grenadines								**Saint-Vincent-Grenadines**
GDP at current prices	133	312	551	681	755	792	811	PIB aux prix courants
GDP per capita	1 276	2 890	5 071	6 293	6 921	7 213	7 361	PIB par habitant
GDP at constant prices	310	459	670	716	755	777	794	PIB aux prix constants
Growth rates	6.2	7.5	2.5	-3.3	1.3	1.0	2.2	Taux de croissance
Samoa								**Samoa**
GDP at current prices	88	202	447	692	787	825	833	PIB aux prix courants
GDP per capita	548	1 185	2 486	3 722	4 066	4 221	4 250	PIB par habitant
GDP at constant prices	407	442	703	741	787	811	816	PIB aux prix constants
Growth rates	3.9	6.0	5.1	2.4	6.7	-0.6	0.7	Taux de croissance
San Marino								**Saint-Marin**
GDP at current prices	320	1 020	2 027	2 139	1 419	1 529	1 638	PIB aux prix courants
GDP per capita	14 029	39 330	69 139	68 505	42 643	45 399	48 473	PIB par habitant
GDP at constant prices	878	1 332	2 070	1 881	1 419	1 462	1 479	PIB aux prix constants
Growth rates	2.8	9.3	2.3	-4.6	-6.2	0.6	1.1	Taux de croissance

Gross domestic product and gross domestic product per capita *(continued)*
In millions of US dollars at current and constant 2015 prices; per capita US dollars; real rates of growth

Produit intérieur brut et produit intérieur brut par habitant *(suite)*
En millions de dollars É.-U. aux prix courants et constants de 2015; par habitant en dollars É.U.; taux de croissance réels

Country or area	1985	1995	2005	2010	2015	2017	2018	Pays ou zone
Sao Tome and Principe								**Sao Tomé-et-Principe**
GDP at current prices	79	99	126	197	308	365	411	PIB aux prix courants
GDP per capita	750	749	801	1 095	1 545	1 765	1 948	PIB par habitant
GDP at constant prices	144	146	197	250	308	337	345	PIB aux prix constants
Growth rates	9.3	2.0	7.1	4.6	3.6	4.6	2.2	Taux de croissance
Saudi Arabia								**Arabie saoudite**
GDP at current prices	103 894	143 152	328 461	528 207	654 270	688 586	782 483	PIB aux prix courants
GDP per capita	7 919	7 680	13 792	19 263	20 628	20 802	23 217	PIB par habitant
GDP at constant prices	200 048	336 810	444 967	509 172	654 270	660 268	674 893	PIB aux prix constants
Growth rates	-9.8	0.2	5.6	5.0	4.1	-0.7	2.2	Taux de croissance
Senegal								**Sénégal**
GDP at current prices	3 632	6 306	11 267	16 725	17 761	20 940	23 809	PIB aux prix courants
GDP per capita	561	726	1 016	1 319	1 218	1 358	1 502	PIB par habitant
GDP at constant prices	6 174	7 748	12 270	14 596	17 761	20 242	21 614	PIB aux prix constants
Growth rates	3.8	4.7	5.6	4.2	6.4	7.1	6.8	Taux de croissance
Serbia								**Serbie**
GDP at current prices	...	21 822[7]	26 252	39 460	37 160	44 120	50 597	PIB aux prix courants
GDP per capita	...	2 208[7]	3 528	5 412	5 237	6 267	7 209	PIB par habitant
GDP at constant prices	...	22 236[7]	31 993	36 491	37 160	42 593	44 464	PIB aux prix constants
Growth rates	...	5.7[7]	5.5	0.6	0.8	2.0	4.4	Taux de croissance
Seychelles								**Seychelles**
GDP at current prices	204	614	919	970	1 377	1 503	1 590	PIB aux prix courants
GDP per capita	2 925	8 011	10 368	10 628	14 503	15 590	16 378	PIB par habitant
GDP at constant prices	438	666	876	1 084	1 377	1 502	1 620	PIB aux prix constants
Growth rates	10.3	-0.6	9.0	5.9	4.9	4.3	7.9	Taux de croissance
Sierra Leone								**Sierra Leone**
GDP at current prices	1 376	1 179	1 650	2 578	4 248	3 739	4 101	PIB aux prix courants
GDP per capita	362	274	292	402	592	499	536	PIB par habitant
GDP at constant prices	2 798	2 512	2 679	3 457	4 248	4 688	4 905	PIB aux prix constants
Growth rates	2.3	-10.0	4.5	5.3	-20.5	3.8	4.6	Taux de croissance
Singapore								**Singapour**
GDP at current prices	18 555	87 892	127 418	236 420	306 254	336 679	361 115	PIB aux prix courants
GDP per capita	6 858	24 927	29 870	46 075	54 765	58 983	62 721	PIB par habitant
GDP at constant prices	46 541	106 460	177 762	246 179	306 254	327 341	337 919	PIB aux prix constants
Growth rates	-0.7	7.0	7.5	15.2	2.5	3.9	3.2	Taux de croissance
Sint Maarten (Dutch part)								**St-Martin (partie néerland.)**
GDP at current prices	...	...	708	896	1 066	1 043	980	PIB aux prix courants
GDP per capita	...	...	21 175	26 238	26 682	25 166	23 367	PIB par habitant
GDP at constant prices	...	...	911	1 014	1 066	1 020	933	PIB aux prix constants
Growth rates	...	...	...	1.1	0.5	-4.8	-8.5	Taux de croissance
Slovakia								**Slovaquie**
GDP at current prices	...	20 042	49 033	90 184	88 457	95 477	105 956	PIB aux prix courants
GDP per capita	...	3 728	9 082	16 687	16 274	17 526	19 431	PIB par habitant
GDP at constant prices	...	40 408	61 339	77 833	88 457	93 082	96 837	PIB aux prix constants
Growth rates	...	5.8	6.6	5.7	4.8	3.0	4.0	Taux de croissance
Slovenia								**Slovénie**
GDP at current prices	...	21 354	36 204	48 161	43 090	48 562	54 034	PIB aux prix courants
GDP per capita	...	10 724	18 148	23 570	20 804	23 388	26 005	PIB par habitant
GDP at constant prices	...	26 407	38 472	42 210	43 090	46 583	48 501	PIB aux prix constants
Growth rates	...	4.1[7]	3.8	1.3	2.2	4.8	4.1	Taux de croissance
Solomon Islands								**Îles Salomon**
GDP at current prices	160	365	429	720	1 059	1 199	1 271	PIB aux prix courants
GDP per capita	591	1 015	914	1 363	1 756	1 885	1 947	PIB par habitant
GDP at constant prices	378	637	644	898	1 059	1 134	1 177	PIB aux prix constants
Growth rates	2.8	10.0	12.8	10.6	2.5	3.7	3.9	Taux de croissance
Somalia								**Somalie**
GDP at current prices	810	1 122	2 316	1 093	1 455	1 497	1 494	PIB aux prix courants
GDP per capita	122	150	222	91	105	103	100	PIB par habitant
GDP at constant prices	1 194	865	1 115	1 265	1 455	1 560	1 609	PIB aux prix constants
Growth rates	9.5	...	3.0	2.6	2.7	2.3	3.1	Taux de croissance
South Africa								**Afrique du Sud**
GDP at current prices	59 648	155 461	257 772	375 348	317 416	349 007	368 094	PIB aux prix courants
GDP per capita	1 825	3 752	5 384	7 329	5 731	6 122	6 369	PIB par habitant
GDP at constant prices	155 659	176 477	244 372	284 658	317 416	323 190	325 734	PIB aux prix constants
Growth rates	-1.2	3.1	5.3	3.0	1.2	1.4	0.8	Taux de croissance
South Sudan								**Soudan du sud**
GDP at current prices	...	...	...	14 986	13 216	7 621	8 207	PIB aux prix courants
GDP per capita	...	...	...	1 576	1 233	698	748	PIB par habitant
GDP at constant prices	...	...	...	16 090	13 216	13 169	13 616	PIB aux prix constants
Growth rates	...	...	...	-0.9	3.4	-0.7	3.4	Taux de croissance

12

Gross domestic product and gross domestic product per capita *(continued)*
In millions of US dollars at current and constant 2015 prices; per capita US dollars; real rates of growth

Produit intérieur brut et produit intérieur brut par habitant *(suite)*
En millions de dollars É.-U. aux prix courants et constants de 2015; par habitant en dollars É.U.; taux de croissance réels

Country or area	1985	1995	2005	2010	2015	2017	2018	Pays ou zone
Spain								**Espagne**
GDP at current prices	180 796	614 612	1 153 257	1 420 722	1 195 119	1 312 552	1 419 735	PIB aux prix courants
GDP per capita	4 668	15 447	26 199	30 273	25 607	28 138	30 406	PIB par habitant
GDP at constant prices	591 502	794 244	1 140 904	1 196 671	1 195 119	1 266 955	1 296 741	PIB aux prix constants
Growth rates	2.3	2.8	3.7	0.2	3.8	2.9	2.4	Taux de croissance
Sri Lanka								**Sri Lanka**
GDP at current prices	6 873	15 293	27 932	56 726	80 604	88 020	88 942	PIB aux prix courants
GDP per capita	425	838	1 429	2 800	3 855	4 166	4 190	PIB par habitant
GDP at constant prices	18 316	28 184	43 875	59 780	80 604	87 101	89 896	PIB aux prix constants
Growth rates	5.0	5.5	6.2	8.0	5.0	3.4	3.2	Taux de croissance
State of Palestine								**État de Palestine**
GDP at current prices	1 005	3 490	5 126	9 682	13 972	16 128	16 277	PIB aux prix courants
GDP per capita	571	1 333	1 433	2 387	3 085	3 397	3 347	PIB par habitant
GDP at constant prices	2 635	5 986	8 740	11 082	13 972	15 427	15 616	PIB aux prix constants
Growth rates	-0.6	7.1	11.3	5.8	3.7	1.4	1.2	Taux de croissance
Sudan								**Soudan**
GDP at current prices	...	...	...	54 678	83 934	124 022	50 515	PIB aux prix courants
GDP per capita	...	...	...	1 583	2 158	3 039	1 208	PIB par habitant
GDP at constant prices	...	...	...	67 787	83 934	93 660	91 487	PIB aux prix constants
Growth rates	...	...	...	8.5	3.7	7.4	-2.3	Taux de croissance
Sudan [former]								**Soudan [anc.]**
GDP at current prices	6 624	12 847	35 183	69 665	...	...	...	PIB aux prix courants
GDP per capita	295	440	914	1 581	...	...	...	PIB par habitant
GDP at constant prices	19 863	31 661	62 907	83 876	...	...	...	PIB aux prix constants
Growth rates	5.4	6.0	9.0	6.6	...	...	...	Taux de croissance
Suriname								**Suriname**
GDP at current prices	1 196	844	2 193	4 368	4 787	3 210	3 458	PIB aux prix courants
GDP per capita	3 246	1 911	4 391	8 256	8 562	5 627	6 004	PIB par habitant
GDP at constant prices	2 536	2 507	3 523	4 419	4 787	4 601	4 722	PIB aux prix constants
Growth rates	14.0	~0.0	3.9	5.2	-3.4	1.8	2.6	Taux de croissance
Sweden								**Suède**
GDP at current prices	113 189	265 394	389 753	495 329	503 651	540 545	556 086	PIB aux prix courants
GDP per capita	13 543	30 034	43 121	52 750	51 577	54 574	55 767	PIB par habitant
GDP at constant prices	260 811	303 820	413 186	453 486	503 651	528 244	539 999	PIB aux prix constants
Growth rates	2.2	4.0	2.9	6.2	4.4	2.4	2.2	Taux de croissance
Switzerland								**Suisse**
GDP at current prices	107 765	342 626	408 697	583 783	679 832	679 950	705 141	PIB aux prix courants
GDP per capita	16 746	48 978	55 328	74 761	81 939	80 412	82 709	PIB par habitant
GDP at constant prices	400 817	466 333	561 953	625 941	679 832	703 988	723 351	PIB aux prix constants
Growth rates	3.7	0.5	3.1	3.0	1.3	1.8	2.8	Taux de croissance
Syrian Arab Republic								**République arabe syrienne**
GDP at current prices	10 044	13 539	28 397	60 465	19 090	13 182	16 628	PIB aux prix courants
GDP per capita	943	944	1 547	2 830	1 061	771	981	PIB par habitant
GDP at constant prices	15 358	21 609	33 045	41 986	19 090	18 815	19 271	PIB aux prix constants
Growth rates	6.1	7.0	6.2	3.4	-6.1	2.6	2.4	Taux de croissance
Tajikistan								**Tadjikistan**
GDP at current prices	...	1 218	2 312	5 642	7 855	7 158	7 523	PIB aux prix courants
GDP per capita	...	211	341	750	929	806	827	PIB par habitant
GDP at constant prices	...	2 699	4 288	5 872	7 855	8 993	9 635	PIB aux prix constants
Growth rates	...	-12.4	6.7	6.5	6.0	7.1	7.1	Taux de croissance
Thailand								**Thaïlande**
GDP at current prices	40 313	169 279	189 318	341 105	401 296	455 275	504 992	PIB aux prix courants
GDP per capita	775	2 847	2 894	5 076	5 840	6 578	7 274	PIB par habitant
GDP at constant prices	87 037	213 636	288 645	346 968	401 296	431 456	449 271	PIB aux prix constants
Growth rates	4.6	8.1	4.2	7.5	3.1	4.0	4.1	Taux de croissance
Timor-Leste								**Timor-Leste**
GDP at current prices	...	438	1 814	3 999	3 093	2 487	2 581	PIB aux prix courants
GDP per capita	...	519	1 823	3 657	2 585	2 001	2 036	PIB par habitant
GDP at constant prices	...	1 177	2 184	3 325	3 093	2 829	2 909	PIB aux prix constants
Growth rates	...	9.5	35.9	-1.2	20.6	-9.2	2.8	Taux de croissance
Togo								**Togo**
GDP at current prices	860	1 663	2 281	3 426	4 178	4 632	5 165	PIB aux prix courants
GDP per capita	264	393	406	534	570	602	655	PIB par habitant
GDP at constant prices	1 858	2 241	2 623	3 101	4 178	4 578	4 803	PIB aux prix constants
Growth rates	3.7	6.8	-4.7	6.1	5.7	3.8	4.9	Taux de croissance
Tonga								**Tonga**
GDP at current prices	73	203	262	374	400	492	504	PIB aux prix courants
GDP per capita	779	2 118	2 592	3 595	3 973	4 828	4 886	PIB par habitant
GDP at constant prices	254	312	378	393	400	489	487	PIB aux prix constants
Growth rates	6.6	4.0	1.6	3.6	-2.9	11.0	-0.4	Taux de croissance

Gross domestic product and gross domestic product per capita *(continued)*
In millions of US dollars at current and constant 2015 prices; per capita US dollars; real rates of growth

Produit intérieur brut et produit intérieur brut par habitant *(suite)*
En millions de dollars É.-U. aux prix courants et constants de 2015; par habitant en dollars É.U.; taux de croissance réels

Country or area	1985	1995	2005	2010	2015	2017	2018	Pays ou zone
Trinidad and Tobago								**Trinité-et-Tobago**
GDP at current prices	7 396	5 344	16 025	22 182	25 063	22 475	23 808	PIB aux prix courants
GDP per capita	6 320	4 261	12 360	16 702	18 290	16 238	17 130	PIB par habitant
GDP at constant prices	9 779	9 356	19 864	24 059	25 063	22 942	22 885	PIB aux prix constants
Growth rates	-4.1	4.0	6.2	3.3	1.8	-2.3	-0.2	Taux de croissance
Tunisia								**Tunisie**
GDP at current prices	9 234	19 795	32 272	44 051	43 173	39 813	39 895	PIB aux prix courants
GDP per capita	1 260	2 169	3 193	4 142	3 862	3 482	3 450	PIB par habitant
GDP at constant prices	14 114	19 746	32 089	39 954	43 173	44 501	45 606	PIB aux prix constants
Growth rates	5.7	2.3	4.0	3.0	1.2	1.9	2.5	Taux de croissance
Turkey								**Turquie**
GDP at current prices	92 554	233 085	501 423	771 877	859 794	852 669	771 355	PIB aux prix courants
GDP per capita	1 884	3 985	7 384	10 672	10 949	10 512	9 368	PIB par habitant
GDP at constant prices	219 498	336 906	520 147	610 067	859 794	953 448	980 400	PIB aux prix constants
Growth rates	4.2	7.2	9.0	8.5	6.1	7.5	2.8	Taux de croissance
Turkmenistan								**Turkménistan**
GDP at current prices	...	2 190	14 181	22 583	36 052	37 915	40 749	PIB aux prix courants
GDP per capita	...	520	2 983	4 439	6 478	6 585	6 965	PIB par habitant
GDP at constant prices	...	8 368	13 348	21 868	36 052	40 764	43 272	PIB aux prix constants
Growth rates	...	-7.2	13.0	9.2	6.5	6.5	6.2	Taux de croissance
Turks and Caicos Islands								**Îles Turques-et-Caïques**
GDP at current prices	58	191	579	687	894	963	1 022	PIB aux prix courants
GDP per capita	5 856	11 748	20 534	21 028	24 833	25 934	27 142	PIB par habitant
GDP at constant prices	114	311	698	765	894	973	1 024	PIB aux prix constants
Growth rates	10.7	7.3	14.4	1.0	5.9	4.3	5.3	Taux de croissance
Tuvalu								**Tuvalu**
GDP at current prices	4	12	22	31	35	44	46	PIB aux prix courants
GDP per capita	428	1 265	2 168	2 982	3 157	3 862	4 001	PIB par habitant
GDP at constant prices	9	20	27	29	35	39	42	PIB aux prix constants
Growth rates	-1.8	-5.0	-4.1	-3.3	9.2	5.9	7.0	Taux de croissance
Uganda								**Ouganda**
GDP at current prices	4 743	7 148	11 158	19 683	25 098	27 208	30 098	PIB aux prix courants
GDP per capita	326	350	403	607	657	661	704	PIB par habitant
GDP at constant prices	3 607	6 831	13 435	19 845	25 098	27 002	29 393	PIB aux prix constants
Growth rates	-0.3	9.4	10.0	8.2	5.7	4.9	8.9	Taux de croissance
Ukraine								**Ukraine**
GDP at current prices	...	50 376	89 239	136 012[8]	91 031[8]	112 190[8]	130 832[8]	PIB aux prix courants
GDP per capita	...	990	1 903[8]	2 970[8]	2 026[8]	2 522[8]	2 957[8]	PIB par habitant
GDP at constant prices	...	77 064	100 863	102 154[8]	91 031[8]	95 553[8]	98 740[8]	PIB aux prix constants
Growth rates	...	-12.2	3.1	0.3[8]	-9.8[8]	2.5[8]	3.3[8]	Taux de croissance
United Arab Emirates								**Émirats arabes unis**
GDP at current prices	41 134	66 603	182 978	289 787	358 135	377 701	414 179	PIB aux prix courants
GDP per capita	30 109	27 578	39 880	33 893	38 663	39 812	43 005	PIB par habitant
GDP at constant prices	99 780	139 064	247 156	278 380	358 135	370 909	377 312	PIB aux prix constants
Growth rates	-2.4	8.2	4.9	1.6	5.1	0.5	1.7	Taux de croissance
United Kingdom								**Royaume-Uni**
GDP at current prices	489 256	1 341 652	2 538 688	2 475 244	2 928 591	2 666 229	2 855 297	PIB aux prix courants
GDP per capita	8 673	23 159	42 109	39 005	44 467	39 957	42 526	PIB par habitant
GDP at constant prices	1 465 699	1 905 295	2 585 096	2 649 483	2 928 591	3 041 240	3 083 382	PIB aux prix constants
Growth rates	4.2	3.6	3.2	1.9	2.4	1.9	1.4	Taux de croissance
United Rep. of Tanzania [9]								**Rép.-Unie de Tanzanie** [9]
GDP at current prices	11 074 074	7 198	17 174	31 553	47 379	53 276	57 145	PIB aux prix courants
GDP per capita	512	249	459	732	947	1 003	1 044	PIB par habitant
GDP at constant prices	10 123	14 882	25 697	34 515	47 379	54 061	57 819	PIB aux prix constants
Growth rates	4.6	3.6	7.4	6.4	6.2	6.8	7.0	Taux de croissance
United States of America								**États-Unis d'Amérique**
GDP at current prices	4 338 979	7 639 749	13 036 637	14 992 052	18 224 780	19 519 424	20 580 223	PIB aux prix courants
GDP per capita	18 042	28 811	44 193	48 516	56 797	60 044	62 918	PIB par habitant
GDP at constant prices	8 326 125	11 131 752	15 615 930	16 334 544	18 224 780	18 962 238	19 517 324	PIB aux prix constants
Growth rates	4.2	2.7	3.5	2.6	2.9	2.4	2.9	Taux de croissance
Uruguay								**Uruguay**
GDP at current prices	5 226	21 312	17 363	40 285	53 274	59 530	59 597	PIB aux prix courants
GDP per capita	1 735	6 610	5 227	11 992	15 614	17 322	17 278	PIB par habitant
GDP at constant prices	20 501	30 066	33 781	45 125	53 274	55 578	56 479	PIB aux prix constants
Growth rates	1.5	-1.5	7.5	7.8	0.4	2.6	1.6	Taux de croissance
Uzbekistan								**Ouzbékistan**
GDP at current prices	...	16 177	17 085	46 909	81 847	59 160	50 500	PIB aux prix courants
GDP per capita	...	710	646	1 645	2 646	1 851	1 555	PIB par habitant
GDP at constant prices	...	23 994	37 958	57 080	81 847	90 710	95 356	PIB aux prix constants
Growth rates	...	-0.9	7.0	8.5	7.4	4.5	5.1	Taux de croissance

Gross domestic product and gross domestic product per capita *(continued)*
In millions of US dollars at current and constant 2015 prices; per capita US dollars; real rates of growth

Produit intérieur brut et produit intérieur brut par habitant *(suite)*
En millions de dollars É.-U. aux prix courants et constants de 2015; par habitant en dollars É.U.; taux de croissance réels

Country or area	1985	1995	2005	2010	2015	2017	2018	Pays ou zone
Vanuatu								**Vanuatu**
GDP at current prices	133	273	395	701	760	880	889	PIB aux prix courants
GDP per capita	1 020	1 621	1 887	2 967	2 802	3 082	3 037	PIB par habitant
GDP at constant prices	336	450	554	706	760	821	847	PIB aux prix constants
Growth rates	1.1	4.7	5.3	1.6	0.2	4.4	3.2	Taux de croissance
Venezuela (Boliv. Rep. of)								**Venezuela (Rép. boliv. du)**
GDP at current prices	59 963	74 889	145 514	393 806	344 417	248 029	208 338	PIB aux prix courants
GDP per capita	3 462	3 415	5 505	13 847	11 449	8 436	7 212	PIB par habitant
GDP at constant prices	180 206	242 607	285 679	342 687	344 417	240 949	197 578	PIB aux prix constants
Growth rates	0.2	4.0	10.3	-1.5	-6.2	-15.7	-18.0	Taux de croissance
Viet Nam								**Viet Nam**
GDP at current prices	4 798	20 736	57 633	115 932	193 241	223 780	244 901	PIB aux prix courants
GDP per capita	79	277	687	1 318	2 085	2 366	2 563	PIB par habitant
GDP at constant prices	29 528	53 684	106 748	144 994	193 241	219 225	234 736	PIB aux prix constants
Growth rates	5.6	9.5	7.5	6.4	6.7	6.8	7.1	Taux de croissance
Yemen								**Yémen**
GDP at current prices	...	5 935	19 041	30 907	26 660	24 152	26 672	PIB aux prix courants
GDP per capita	...	398	947	1 335	1 006	868	936	PIB par habitant
GDP at constant prices	...	20 356	39 376	47 713	26 660	20 498	20 223	PIB aux prix constants
Growth rates	...	16.7	5.1	3.3	-30.5	-10.0	-1.3	Taux de croissance
Zambia								**Zambie**
GDP at current prices	2 772	3 807	8 332	20 265	20 859	25 868	27 283	PIB aux prix courants
GDP per capita	400	419	703	1 489	1 314	1 535	1 572	PIB par habitant
GDP at constant prices	6 260	6 623	10 687	16 222	20 859	22 405	23 319	PIB aux prix constants
Growth rates	-~0.0	2.9	7.2	10.3	2.9	3.5	4.1	Taux de croissance
Zanzibar								**Zanzibar**
GDP at current prices	...	186	438	817	1 184	1 448	1 618	PIB aux prix courants
GDP per capita	...	235	408	652	821	944	1 024	PIB par habitant
GDP at constant prices	...	350	682	889	1 184	1 349	1 444	PIB aux prix constants
Growth rates	...	3.5	4.9	4.3	6.2	7.7	7.1	Taux de croissance
Zimbabwe								**Zimbabwe**
GDP at current prices	8 720	11 063	7 189	12 042	19 963	22 041	24 312	PIB aux prix courants
GDP per capita	982	970	595	948	1 445	1 548	1 684	PIB par habitant
GDP at constant prices	7 881	10 458	8 316	14 100	19 963	21 060	22 077	PIB aux prix constants
Growth rates	6.9	0.2	-4.1	19.7	1.8	4.7	4.8	Taux de croissance

Source:

United Nations Statistics Division, New York, National Accounts Statistics: Analysis of Main Aggregates (AMA) database, last accessed June 2020.

Source:

Organisation des Nations Unies, Division de statistique, New York, base de données des statistiques des comptes nationaux : Analyse des principaux agrégats, denier accès juin 2020.

1 Data compiled in accordance with the System of National Accounts 1968 (1968 SNA).
2 For statistical purposes, the data for China do not include those for the Hong Kong Special Administrative Region (Hong Kong SAR), Macao Special Administrative Region (Macao SAR) and Taiwan Province of China.
3 Excluding northern Cyprus.
4 Including French Guiana, Guadeloupe, Martinique and Réunion.
5 Including Western Sahara.
6 Does not incorporate export of binational hydroelectric power at market prices.
7 Including Kosovo and Metohija.
8 The Government of Ukraine has informed the United Nations that it is not in a position to provide statistical data concerning the Autonomous Republic of Crimea and the city of Sevastopol.
9 Tanzania mainland only, excluding Zanzibar.

1 Données compilées selon le Système de comptabilité nationale de 1968 (SCN 1968).
2 Pour la présentation des statistiques, les données pour la Chine ne comprennent pas la région administrative spéciale de Hong Kong (RAS de Hong Kong), la région administrative spéciale de Macao (RAS de Macao) et la province chinoise de Taïwan.
3 Chypre du nord non compris.
4 Y compris Guadeloupe, Guyane française, Martinique et Réunion.
5 Y compris les données de Sahara occidental.
6 Ne comprend pas l'exportation d'énergie hydroélectrique binationale aux prix du marché.
7 Y compris Kosovo et Metohija.
8 Le Gouvernement ukrainien a informé l'Organisation des Nations Unies qu'il n'est pas en mesure de fournir des données statistiques concernant la République autonome de Crimée et Sébastopol.
9 Tanzanie continentale seulement, Zanzibar non compris.

Country or area &	1985	1995	2005	2010	2015	2017	2018	Pays ou zone &
Afghanistan								**Afghanistan**
Agriculture	51.2	65.7	35.2	28.8	22.7	24.8	21.4	Agriculture
Industry	24.9	10.5	26.0	21.3	22.7	22.0	24.5	Industrie
Services	23.9	23.8	38.8	49.8	54.7	53.2	54.1	Services
Albania [1]								**Albanie** [1]
Agriculture	38.7	54.3	21.5	20.7	22.5	21.8	21.0	Agriculture
Industry [2]	43.1	26.5	28.7	28.7	24.8	23.3	24.3	Industrie [2]
Services [3,4]	18.3	19.2	49.8	50.7	52.7	54.9	54.7	Services [3,4]
Algeria								**Algérie**
Agriculture	8.4	10.4	8.0	8.6	12.1	12.4	12.4	Agriculture
Industry	49.8	47.9	59.7	51.4	37.3	38.9	41.0	Industrie
Services	41.9	41.7	32.3	40.0	50.6	48.7	46.6	Services
Andorra [1]								**Andorre** [1]
Agriculture	0.5	0.5	0.4	0.5	0.5	0.5	0.5	Agriculture
Industry [2]	18.3	18.8	17.3	14.6	10.8	11.1	11.0	Industrie [2]
Services [3,4]	81.2	80.7	82.3	84.8	88.6	88.4	88.5	Services [3,4]
Angola								**Angola**
Agriculture	13.6	7.4	5.0	6.2	9.1	10.1	9.7	Agriculture
Industry	43.4	67.4	59.7	52.1	42.1	42.6	42.5	Industrie
Services	43.0	25.2	35.3	41.7	48.8	47.3	47.8	Services
Anguilla								**Anguilla**
Agriculture	5.6	3.3	2.7	2.0	2.3	2.4	3.5	Agriculture
Industry	16.6	14.5	19.3	15.8	15.3	11.0	14.6	Industrie
Services	77.8	82.2	78.0	82.2	82.4	86.6	81.9	Services
Antigua and Barbuda								**Antigua-et-Barbuda**
Agriculture	2.2	1.9	2.0	1.8	1.8	2.0	2.0	Agriculture
Industry	11.4	14.4	16.3	18.3	18.7	21.7	23.8	Industrie
Services	86.4	83.7	81.7	79.9	79.5	76.2	74.2	Services
Argentina								**Argentine**
Agriculture	7.4	5.3	9.3	8.5	6.1	6.5	7.2	Agriculture
Industry	37.7	26.0	33.7	30.1	27.5	25.9	27.2	Industrie
Services	54.9	68.7	57.0	61.4	66.3	67.6	65.6	Services
Armenia [1]								**Arménie** [1]
Agriculture	...	40.3	19.9	17.8	18.9	16.4	15.0	Agriculture
Industry	...	28.4	43.8	34.7	28.2	28.2	27.4	Industrie
Services [3,4]	...	31.3	36.3	47.4	52.9	55.4	57.6	Services [3,4]
Aruba								**Aruba**
Agriculture [5]	0.0	0.0	0.0	0.0	0.0	0.0	0.0	Agriculture [5]
Industry [2]	11.9	11.8	15.1	12.0	13.7	13.6	13.7	Industrie [2]
Services [3,4]	88.1	88.1	84.9	88.0	86.3	86.4	86.2	Services [3,4]
Australia [1]								**Australie** [1]
Agriculture	4.5	3.7	3.0	2.4	2.6	2.8	2.8	Agriculture
Industry [2]	35.5	28.4	27.8	28.3	24.0	25.8	25.0	Industrie [2]
Services [3,4]	60.1	67.9	69.2	69.3	73.4	71.5	72.3	Services [3,4]
Austria [1]								**Autriche** [1]
Agriculture	3.6	2.4	1.4	1.4	1.3	1.3	1.3	Agriculture
Industry [2]	34.5	32.1	30.5	28.7	28.2	28.6	28.8	Industrie [2]
Services [3,4]	61.9	65.5	68.1	69.9	70.5	70.1	69.9	Services [3,4]
Azerbaijan [1]								**Azerbaïdjan** [1]
Agriculture	...	26.6	9.8	5.9	6.8	6.0	5.7	Agriculture
Industry [2]	...	33.3	62.9	64.1	49.3	53.5	56.6	Industrie [2]
Services [3,4]	...	40.2	27.3	30.0	43.9	40.5	37.7	Services [3,4]
Bahamas [1]								**Bahamas** [1]
Agriculture	2.2	1.9	1.1	1.2	0.9	0.9	1.0	Agriculture
Industry [2]	13.9	11.3	11.5	12.3	13.1	15.8	14.8	Industrie [2]
Services [3,4]	84.0	86.8	87.4	86.6	86.0	83.3	84.2	Services [3,4]
Bahrain [6]								**Bahreïn** [6]
Agriculture	0.8	0.7	0.3	0.3	0.3	0.3	0.3	Agriculture
Industry	38.9	36.1	42.8	45.5	40.7	41.7	43.7	Industrie
Services	60.2	63.2	56.9	54.2	59.0	58.0	56.0	Services
Bangladesh								**Bangladesh**
Agriculture	35.7	26.4	20.1	17.8	15.3	14.2	13.8	Agriculture
Industry	21.5	24.6	27.2	26.1	27.8	29.3	30.2	Industrie
Services	42.8	49.1	52.6	56.0	57.0	56.5	56.0	Services

Gross value added by kind of economic activity *(continued)*
Percentage distribution, current prices

Valeur ajoutée brute par type d'activité économique *(suite)*
Répartition en pourcentage, aux prix courants

Country or area [&]	1985	1995	2005	2010	2015	2017	2018	Pays ou zone [&]
Barbados								**Barbade**
Agriculture	4.3	3.5	1.8	1.5	1.5	1.5	1.5	Agriculture
Industry	22.7	16.5	16.6	15.8	15.4	14.7	14.9	Industrie
Services	73.0	80.0	81.6	82.7	83.1	83.8	83.6	Services
Belarus [1]								**Bélarus [1]**
Agriculture	…	16.8	9.7	10.1	7.2	8.7	7.5	Agriculture
Industry [2]	…	37.5	43.8	40.3	37.7	36.4	36.8	Industrie [2]
Services [3,4]	…	45.6	46.5	49.5	55.1	54.9	55.7	Services [3,4]
Belgium [1]								**Belgique [1]**
Agriculture	2.6	1.4	0.9	0.9	0.8	0.7	0.6	Agriculture
Industry [2]	31.3	28.9	25.3	23.4	22.0	21.7	21.4	Industrie [2]
Services [3,4]	66.1	69.7	73.8	75.7	77.3	77.6	78.0	Services [3,4]
Belize								**Belize**
Agriculture	17.8	17.4	14.9	12.8	14.7	12.9	11.0	Agriculture
Industry	21.4	20.3	16.7	21.0	16.3	15.6	13.7	Industrie
Services	60.7	62.3	68.4	66.2	69.0	71.5	75.3	Services
Benin								**Bénin**
Agriculture	32.4	23.7	27.1	25.4	22.7	25.4	24.5	Agriculture
Industry	15.5	32.5	30.3	24.7	24.4	23.7	23.4	Industrie
Services	52.0	43.8	42.5	49.9	52.9	50.9	52.0	Services
Bermuda								**Bermudes**
Agriculture	0.8	0.8	0.8	0.7	0.7	0.7	0.7	Agriculture
Industry [7]	10.4	10.4	9.7	7.1	5.5	5.6	5.6	Industrie [7]
Services	88.9	88.8	89.5	92.2	93.9	93.6	93.7	Services
Bhutan								**Bhoutan**
Agriculture	42.3	33.2	23.2	17.5	17.5	18.3	17.7	Agriculture
Industry	21.4	33.5	37.3	44.6	43.2	42.7	43.1	Industrie
Services	36.4	33.3	39.5	37.9	39.3	39.1	39.2	Services
Bolivia (Plurin. State of)								**Bolivie (État plurin. de)**
Agriculture	28.7	16.4	13.9	12.4	12.6	13.4	13.2	Agriculture
Industry	28.5	32.1	30.9	35.8	31.0	30.4	30.2	Industrie
Services	42.8	51.5	55.2	51.8	56.5	56.2	56.5	Services
Bosnia and Herzegovina [1]								**Bosnie-Herzégovine [1]**
Agriculture	…	22.0	9.8	8.0	7.3	6.6	7.0	Agriculture
Industry	…	31.8	25.3[2]	26.4[2]	26.5[2]	28.0[2]	27.7[2]	Industrie
Services	…	46.2	64.9[3,4]	65.6[3,4]	66.2[3,4]	65.4[3,4]	65.3[3,4]	Services
Botswana								**Botswana**
Agriculture	7.4	4.9	2.0	2.8	2.4	2.2	2.2	Agriculture
Industry	54.3	46.5	47.6	35.7	33.2	32.8	32.3	Industrie
Services	38.3	48.6	50.3	61.6	64.4	65.0	65.5	Services
Brazil [1]								**Brésil [1]**
Agriculture	11.0	5.5	5.5	4.8	5.0	5.4	5.1	Agriculture
Industry	42.2	26.0[2]	28.5[2]	27.4[2]	22.5[2]	21.3[2]	21.6[2]	Industrie
Services	46.7	68.5[3,4]	66.0[3,4]	67.8[3,4]	72.5[3,4]	73.3[3,4]	73.3[3,4]	Services
British Virgin Islands [1]								**Îles Vierges britanniques [1]**
Agriculture	0.7	0.3	0.2	0.1	0.1	0.1	0.1	Agriculture
Industry [2]	4.4	6.5	5.5	4.8	6.7	6.7	7.0	Industrie [2]
Services [3,4]	95.0	93.3	94.3	95.0	93.1	93.2	92.9	Services [3,4]
Brunei Darussalam [1]								**Brunéi Darussalam [1]**
Agriculture	0.4	1.1	0.9	0.7	1.1	1.1	1.0	Agriculture
Industry [2]	78.5	53.4	72.0	67.4	60.2	58.7	62.2	Industrie [2]
Services [3,4]	21.1	45.5	27.1	31.9	38.7	40.2	36.7	Services [3,4]
Bulgaria [1]								**Bulgarie [1]**
Agriculture	13.0	10.0	8.6	4.6	4.7	4.7	3.9	Agriculture
Industry [2]	53.9	19.3	28.6	26.8	27.4	28.1	25.8	Industrie [2]
Services [3,4]	33.0	70.7	62.9	68.6	67.9	67.2	70.3	Services [3,4]
Burkina Faso								**Burkina Faso**
Agriculture	28.3	28.3	29.3	26.2	24.9	23.8	24.3	Agriculture
Industry	26.6	23.9	22.0	28.2	26.7	27.7	26.5	Industrie
Services	45.2	47.8	48.7	45.6	48.4	48.5	49.2	Services
Burundi								**Burundi**
Agriculture	55.8[8]	48.2	43.0	40.7	37.5	39.7	38.5	Agriculture
Industry	16.9[8]	19.2	17.8	16.3	16.4	17.6	17.4	Industrie
Services	27.2[8]	32.6	39.1	43.0	46.2	42.6	44.1	Services

Country or area [&]	1985	1995	2005	2010	2015	2017	2018	Pays ou zone [&]
Cabo Verde [1]								**Cabo Verde [1]**
Agriculture	17.3	15.6	11.7	9.2	10.0	7.8	6.2	Agriculture
Industry [2]	25.5	29.9	22.8	20.8	20.7	21.1	22.6	Industrie [2]
Services [3,4]	57.2	54.5	65.5	70.1	69.3	71.1	71.3	Services [3,4]
Cambodia								**Cambodge**
Agriculture	47.0	51.4	32.4	36.0	28.2	24.9	23.5	Agriculture
Industry	13.6	12.9	26.4	23.3	29.4	32.8	34.4	Industrie
Services	39.4	35.7	41.2	40.7	42.3	42.3	42.1	Services
Cameroon [1]								**Cameroun [1]**
Agriculture	14.8	17.5	15.2	15.1	16.1	15.7	15.7	Agriculture
Industry [2]	31.2	28.6	30.3	29.1	27.4	27.5	28.1	Industrie [2]
Services [3,4]	54.0	53.8	54.6	55.8	56.6	56.8	56.2	Services [3,4]
Canada [1]								**Canada [1]**
Agriculture	3.5	2.9	2.0	1.6	2.0	1.9	2.0	Agriculture
Industry	35.1	30.7	31.1	27.9[2]	25.9[2]	26.4[2]	25.6[2]	Industrie
Services	61.4	66.4	66.8	70.5[3,4]	72.1[3,4]	71.7[3,4]	72.4[3,4]	Services
Cayman Islands [1]								**Îles Caïmanes [1]**
Agriculture	0.3	0.3	0.3	0.3	0.4	0.4	0.4	Agriculture
Industry [2]	11.2	10.2	10.1	7.4	7.4	7.6	7.6	Industrie [2]
Services [4]	88.6	89.5	89.6	92.2[3]	92.2[3]	91.9[3]	92.0[3]	Services [4]
Central African Republic								**République centrafricaine**
Agriculture	35.7	36.1	45.0	41.2	31.4	31.1	31.5	Agriculture
Industry	22.2	26.9	18.6	24.0	26.0	25.8	25.8	Industrie
Services	42.1	37.0	36.5	34.8	42.6	43.0	42.8	Services
Chad								**Tchad**
Agriculture	31.7	27.7	26.0	35.9	29.5	34.0	30.6	Agriculture
Industry	14.9	15.0	35.1	36.7	31.7	20.1	19.2	Industrie
Services	53.4	57.3	38.9	27.4	38.8	45.8	50.2	Services
Chile [1]								**Chili [1]**
Agriculture	5.9	5.9	4.5	3.9	4.0	4.2	4.0	Agriculture
Industry [2]	37.3	41.4	40.3	38.8	32.6	32.4	32.8	Industrie [2]
Services [3,4]	56.7	52.7	55.2	57.3	63.4	63.4	63.3	Services [3,4]
China [9,10]								**Chine [9,10]**
Agriculture	28.2	19.8	12.0	9.6	8.7	7.9	7.5	Agriculture
Industry	42.8	46.9	47.2	46.7	41.3	40.7	40.8	Industrie
Services [11]	29.0	33.3	40.9	43.7	50.0	51.5	51.7	Services [11]
China, Hong Kong SAR [1]								**Chine, RAS de Hong Kong [1]**
Agriculture [7,12]	0.6	0.2	0.1	0.1	0.1	0.1	0.1	Agriculture [7,12]
Industry [7,13]	26.8	14.1	8.7	7.0	7.3	7.5	7.3	Industrie [7,13]
Services [11,14]	72.6	85.7	91.3	93.0	92.7	92.4	92.6	Services [11,14]
China, Macao SAR								**Chine, RAS de Macao**
Industry [7,13]	21.7	14.8	14.9	7.4	10.5	6.9	8.8	Industrie [7,13]
Services	78.3	85.2	85.1	92.6	89.5	93.1	91.2	Services
Colombia								**Colombie**
Agriculture	12.1	9.2	8.3	7.0	6.6	7.0	6.9	Agriculture
Industry [2]	31.8	29.9	33.2	34.3	31.5	29.5	29.3	Industrie [2]
Services [3,4]	56.1	60.9	58.6	58.7	61.9	63.4	63.8	Services [3,4]
Comoros								**Comores**
Agriculture	26.5	31.9	37.3	31.6	31.1	32.6	31.5	Agriculture
Industry	17.5	11.7	10.9	12.2	11.8	13.1	12.4	Industrie
Services	56.0	56.3	51.8	56.1	57.1	54.3	56.1	Services
Congo								**Congo**
Agriculture	7.8	10.2	5.5	4.1	7.6	9.3	10.3	Agriculture
Industry	40.6	34.3	59.7	68.4	48.1	42.2	41.5	Industrie
Services	51.6	55.5	34.8	27.6	44.4	48.5	48.1	Services
Cook Islands [6]								**Îles Cook [6]**
Agriculture	5.1	5.1	4.9	3.4	3.2	3.3	3.1	Agriculture
Industry [2]	8.6	7.3	9.0	7.9	11.3	8.6	7.8	Industrie [2]
Services [3,4]	86.3	87.7	86.1	88.7	85.4	88.1	89.1	Services [3,4]
Costa Rica [1]								**Costa Rica [1]**
Agriculture	14.4	14.0	9.6	7.2	5.4	5.4	5.0	Agriculture
Industry [2]	33.5	29.2	26.9	25.4	21.2	20.6	21.1	Industrie [2]
Services [3,4]	52.1	56.8	63.6	67.4	73.4	73.9	73.9	Services [3,4]

Country or area [&]	1985	1995	2005	2010	2015	2017	2018	Pays ou zone [&]
Côte d'Ivoire								**Côte d'Ivoire**
Agriculture	28.1[8]	26.6[8]	24.3	26.0	24.9	23.7	21.7	Agriculture
Industry	20.5[8]	22.3[8]	24.5	23.8	28.2	27.1	27.7	Industrie
Services	51.4	51.1	51.3	50.2	46.9	49.2	50.5	Services
Croatia [1]								**Croatie** [1]
Agriculture	...	6.9	4.6	4.4	3.6	3.6	3.5	Agriculture
Industry [2]	...	32.3	29.0	26.1	25.8	25.2	24.8	Industrie [2]
Services [3,4]	...	60.8	66.3	69.5	70.6	71.2	71.7	Services [3,4]
Cuba								**Cuba**
Agriculture	9.5	6.4	4.4	3.7	3.9	3.8	3.8	Agriculture
Industry	20.7	25.9	21.8	23.1	22.6	24.6	25.2	Industrie
Services	69.9	67.7	73.8	73.2	73.5	71.6	71.0	Services
Curaçao								**Curaçao**
Agriculture [15]	...	...	0.6	0.5	0.5	0.4	0.4	Agriculture [15]
Industry	...	...	16.4	16.2	20.2	20.2	18.5	Industrie
Services	...	...	83.0	83.3	79.3	79.4	81.1	Services
Cyprus [1,16]								**Chypre** [1,16]
Agriculture	7.6	5.2	3.1	2.3	2.1	2.3	2.3	Agriculture
Industry [2]	27.0	22.0	20.5	16.4	11.6	13.1	14.1	Industrie [2]
Services [3,4]	65.4	72.8	76.4	81.2	86.3	84.6	83.6	Services [3,4]
Czechia [1]								**Tchéquie** [1]
Agriculture	...	4.4	2.4	1.7	2.5	2.3	2.2	Agriculture
Industry [2]	...	38.9	37.7	36.8	37.8	37.0	35.8	Industrie [2]
Services [3,4]	...	56.7	59.8	61.5	59.7	60.7	62.0	Services [3,4]
Dem. People's Rep. Korea								**Rép. pop. dém. de Corée**
Agriculture	28.3	27.6	25.0	20.8	21.6	22.8	23.3	Agriculture
Industry	48.5	42.0	42.8	48.2	46.2	45.5	43.7	Industrie
Services	52.2	50.6	60.6	53.3	54.5	53.4	53.7	Services
Dem. Rep. of the Congo								**Rép. dém. du Congo**
Agriculture	31.8	57.0	22.3	22.4	19.7	20.8	20.0	Agriculture
Industry	31.0	17.0	32.9	40.5	44.8	43.5	46.0	Industrie
Services [17]	32.5	29.8	41.0	38.9	38.4	38.3	37.5	Services [17]
Denmark [1]								**Danemark** [1]
Agriculture	4.9	3.3	1.3	1.4	1.1	1.6	1.2	Agriculture
Industry [2]	26.5	25.5	26.2	22.8	23.0	23.6	24.4	Industrie [2]
Services [3,4]	75.4	84.4	95.5	102.1	107.9	106.3	107.5	Services [3,4]
Djibouti								**Djibouti**
Agriculture	4.4	3.2	3.6	2.8	1.3	1.5	1.4	Agriculture
Industry	20.9	15.3	16.2	16.1	12.1	12.4	11.8	Industrie
Services	66.8	72.5	60.2	60.3	58.3	58.0	62.9	Services
Dominica								**Dominique**
Agriculture	22.7	13.7	13.2	13.8	16.7	15.8	13.8	Agriculture
Industry	13.7	16.0	15.0	14.4	14.0	13.0	19.7	Industrie
Services	67.6	66.1	72.7	71.8	68.5	71.1	60.7	Services
Dominican Republic [1]								**République dominicaine** [1]
Agriculture	13.4	10.7	7.7	6.5	6.0	6.1	6.0	Agriculture
Industry [2]	41.9	35.1	32.5	29.9	30.3	29.2	30.3	Industrie [2]
Services [3,4]	39.6	50.3	55.9	54.7	56.3	56.9	56.2	Services [3,4]
Ecuador [1]								**Équateur** [1]
Agriculture	19.6	22.6	10.0	10.2	10.2	10.0	9.9	Agriculture
Industry [2]	30.7	28.0	33.4	36.3	34.4	34.9	34.9	Industrie [2]
Services [3,4]	56.7	58.2	57.7	57.2	58.2	59.8	60.6	Services [3,4]
Egypt [18]								**Égypte** [18]
Agriculture	18.4	16.8	14.4	14.0	11.3	11.7	11.5	Agriculture
Industry	31.8	32.7	36.9	37.5	36.2	34.3	35.9	Industrie
Services	53.8	49.5	49.2	47.8	53.8	54.4	52.6	Services
El Salvador [1]								**El Salvador** [1]
Agriculture	18.4	12.6	6.8	7.6	6.1	5.5	5.4	Agriculture
Industry [2]	20.8	27.9	26.8	27.5	27.8	27.7	28.0	Industrie [2]
Services [3,4]	75.1	60.1	48.8	52.8	56.2	56.4	56.8	Services [3,4]
Equatorial Guinea								**Guinée équatoriale**
Agriculture	14.5	12.5	1.5	1.1	1.9	2.3	2.3	Agriculture
Industry	20.6	35.8	81.3	74.3	59.0	55.7	57.1	Industrie
Services	17.7	60.3	37.5	43.4	55.7	58.6	56.7	Services

Country or area [&]	1985	1995	2005	2010	2015	2017	2018	Pays ou zone [&]
Eritrea								**Érythrée**
Agriculture	...	20.9	24.2	19.1	17.2	17.2	17.3	Agriculture
Industry	...	16.8	21.9	23.1	23.5	23.5	23.5	Industrie
Services	...	51.2	54.5	54.4	55.6	55.6	55.0	Services
Estonia [1]								**Estonie** [1]
Agriculture	...	4.7	3.7	3.6	3.3	2.7	3.1	Agriculture
Industry [2]	...	31.0	29.7	27.6	27.3	27.7	27.7	Industrie [2]
Services [3,4]	25.3	61.1	58.2	62.0	61.5	62.1	62.3	Services [3,4]
Eswatini [1]								**Eswatini** [1]
Agriculture	14.5	7.9	11.3	10.4	9.8	8.7	9.0	Agriculture
Industry [2]	24.8	41.2	40.9	38.7	37.4	35.1	34.6	Industrie [2]
Services [3,4]	35.5	45.6	47.2	53.2	57.3	55.9	55.8	Services [3,4]
Ethiopia								**Éthiopie**
Agriculture	...	55.0	45.2	45.3	38.8	35.9	32.8	Agriculture
Industry	...	9.8	13.1	10.4	17.5	25.1	28.7	Industrie
Services	...	18.1	21.5	21.3	19.3	18.8	18.8	Services
Fiji [1]								**Fidji** [1]
Agriculture	16.4	16.4	12.8	10.2	10.2	13.3	13.4	Agriculture
Industry [2]	16.1	17.8	17.9	19.9	19.6	19.9	19.4	Industrie [2]
Services [3,4]	73.2	66.6	61.3	60.7	59.9	56.9	58.8	Services [3,4]
Finland [1]								**Finlande** [1]
Agriculture	7.8	4.3	2.6	2.8	2.6	2.7	2.8	Agriculture
Industry [2]	35.1	33.7	33.5	29.9	27.0	28.1	28.4	Industrie [2]
Services [3,4]	63.7	73.1	68.4	74.7	48.9	47.8	47.5	Services [3,4]
France [1,19]								**France** [1,19]
Agriculture	3.7	2.7	1.9	1.8	1.8	1.7	1.8	Agriculture
Industry [2]	28.8	24.9	21.8	19.8	19.8	19.3	19.0	Industrie [2]
Services [3,4]	68.3	74.7	78.6	78.3	79.5	79.5	79.8	Services [3,4]
French Polynesia								**Polynésie française**
Agriculture	4.7	5.2	3.4	2.5	3.1	3.1	3.1	Agriculture
Industry	21.0	12.5	12.7	12.3	11.8	11.8	11.8	Industrie
Services	62.8	71.1	68.9	72.2	72.9	76.0	74.2	Services
Gabon								**Gabon**
Agriculture	5.0	7.3	5.2	4.2	4.7	5.6	5.2	Agriculture
Industry	58.5	54.5	62.6	59.6	51.9	48.1	49.5	Industrie
Services	76.9	72.6	60.6	64.5	73.7	76.1	79.2	Services
Gambia [1]								**Gambie** [1]
Agriculture	25.6	23.0	34.0	37.4	24.3	22.7	21.6	Agriculture
Industry [2]	9.1	12.7	12.2	10.4	18.8	19.4	16.9	Industrie [2]
Services [3,4]	13.6	51.6	45.5	45.3	41.3	40.9	42.4	Services [3,4]
Georgia								**Géorgie**
Agriculture	...	48.5	18.8	9.6	8.8	7.2	7.8	Agriculture
Industry [2]	...	12.0	22.3	19.1	21.5	23.3	22.9	Industrie [2]
Services [3,4]	...	23.3	48.9	60.4	63.9	62.8	62.2	Services [3,4]
Germany [1]								**Allemagne** [1]
Agriculture	1.7	1.1	0.8	0.9	0.8	0.9	0.9	Agriculture
Industry [2]	39.3	32.9	29.1	29.9	30.1	30.5	30.5	Industrie [2]
Services [3,4]	64.6	65.9	71.9	72.4	72.8	75.2	76.9	Services [3,4]
Ghana [1]								**Ghana** [1]
Agriculture	34.1	30.6	29.1	28.9	22.1	21.2	19.7	Agriculture
Industry [2]	30.7	35.0	33.2	28.2	34.6	32.7	34.0	Industrie [2]
Services [3,4]	41.1	45.3	44.6	48.3	46.3	46.6	44.5	Services [3,4]
Greece [1]								**Grèce** [1]
Agriculture	10.2	8.1	4.8	3.3	4.3	4.2	4.3	Agriculture
Industry [2]	27.0	21.6	19.8	15.7	16.1	17.2	17.5	Industrie [2]
Services [3,4]	56.2	64.1	69.1	75.2	76.2	74.1	74.7	Services [3,4]
Greenland								**Groenland**
Agriculture	17.5	17.5	17.5	13.8	17.6	19.9	18.6	Agriculture
Industry	15.5	15.5	16.8	18.6	17.6	17.7	18.4	Industrie
Services	73.8	84.3	69.2	69.5	66.7	66.1	67.1	Services
Grenada								**Grenade**
Agriculture	16.1	9.5	3.4	5.2	8.6	6.4	6.3	Agriculture
Industry	16.3	18.6	26.1	16.8	14.2	15.1	16.2	Industrie
Services	59.0	53.3	70.5	83.3	85.4	89.3	88.9	Services

Country or area [&]	1985	1995	2005	2010	2015	2017	2018	Pays ou zone [&]
Guatemala								**Guatemala**
Agriculture	27.2	25.4	13.1	11.4	10.8	10.3	10.2	Agriculture
Industry	20.7	20.7	28.6	28.0	27.2	25.9	25.2	Industrie
Services	68.3	66.4	62.6	57.0	56.8	52.2	53.4	Services
Guinea								**Guinée**
Agriculture	18.3	25.7	14.9	18.6	20.1	19.5	19.5	Agriculture
Industry	31.9	27.2	34.9	34.3	28.6	34.6	32.7	Industrie
Services	40.7	33.0	42.7	44.1	46.1	42.2	44.4	Services
Guinea-Bissau								**Guinée-Bissau**
Agriculture	46.5	55.1	45.4	46.2	49.0	52.1	49.9	Agriculture
Industry	15.6	12.2	14.7	13.5	12.8	13.3	13.3	Industrie
Services	31.5	26.6	39.2	42.5	38.5	37.1	38.1	Services
Guyana								**Guyana**
Agriculture	20.0	37.1	25.7	17.6	18.9	14.8	14.7	Agriculture
Industry	31.6	33.3	28.7	34.5	32.9	38.2	38.4	Industrie
Services	46.1	39.6	55.4	60.4	64.1	64.7	64.4	Services
Haiti								**Haïti**
Agriculture	33.3	24.3	18.9	25.7	17.3	18.6	18.6	Agriculture
Industry	24.7	31.4	36.7	27.4	34.7	32.1	31.7	Industrie
Services	47.4	41.3	36.4	32.6	33.2	32.3	32.6	Services
Honduras								**Honduras**
Agriculture	20.4	20.4	13.1	11.9	12.6	13.4	12.3	Agriculture
Industry	23.8	29.9	27.6	26.2	26.5	27.5	28.0	Industrie
Services	47.2	47.9	56.8	61.3	59.4	58.1	58.9	Services
Hungary [1]								**Hongrie** [1]
Agriculture	16.0	8.5	4.3	3.6	4.5	4.5	4.2	Agriculture
Industry [2]	42.3	30.5	31.5	29.9	31.4	30.3	30.1	Industrie [2]
Services [3,4]	47.2	66.1	63.8	63.3	64.3	67.1	66.5	Services [3,4]
Iceland [1]								**Islande** [1]
Agriculture	11.3	11.0	5.7	7.1	6.0	4.2	5.2	Agriculture
Industry [2]	34.1	28.4	24.9	24.1	22.3	22.6	22.4	Industrie [2]
Services [3,4]	45.1	50.4	65.6	65.9	70.1	70.5	66.0	Services [3,4]
India [1]								**Inde** [1]
Agriculture	32.6	27.4	19.2	18.4	17.7	17.2	16.1	Agriculture
Industry [2]	29.9	31.7	32.2	33.1	30.0	29.3	29.6	Industrie [2]
Services [3,4]	51.4	53.3	56.5	56.0	55.7	57.1	62.0	Services [3,4]
Indonesia [1]								**Indonésie** [1]
Agriculture	19.8	14.2	12.1	14.3	13.9	13.7	13.3	Agriculture
Industry [2]	33.1	38.3	43.1	43.9	41.4	41.0	41.4	Industrie [2]
Services [3,4]	42.7	42.3	38.4	38.9	43.1	42.2	42.7	Services [3,4]
Iran (Islamic Republic of)								**Iran (Rép. islamique d')**
Agriculture	13.1	12.4	6.2	6.4	10.6	9.6	10.0	Agriculture
Industry	31.4	38.7	47.7	43.4	33.2	35.3	34.3	Industrie
Services	50.0	41.3	39.8	42.2	53.7	50.7	50.5	Services
Iraq								**Iraq**
Agriculture	13.9	12.3	6.9	5.1	4.2	2.9	1.9	Agriculture
Industry	42.2[20,21]	66.0	63.3	55.4	45.0	50.0	55.3	Industrie
Services	50.6[22]	29.7	38.9	51.5	51.2	52.4	48.4	Services
Ireland [1]								**Irlande** [1]
Agriculture	9.1	6.2	1.2	1.0	1.0	1.3	1.0	Agriculture
Industry [2]	30.6	32.1	34.3	25.6	41.0	38.3	39.3	Industrie [2]
Services [3,4]	58.9	58.2	65.5	69.9	60.1	60.8	60.0	Services [3,4]
Israel [1]								**Israël** [1]
Agriculture	4.3	2.0	1.8	1.7	1.3	1.3	1.3	Agriculture
Industry [2]	28.6	28.0	24.1	23.6	22.5	21.5	21.5	Industrie [2]
Services [3,4]	69.8	76.2	75.6	77.1	76.5	78.2	78.2	Services [3,4]
Italy [1]								**Italie** [1]
Agriculture	4.7	3.3	2.3	2.0	2.3	2.2	2.2	Agriculture
Industry [2]	33.1	29.2	25.8	24.3	23.2	23.7	23.9	Industrie [2]
Services [3,4]	72.8	75.3	81.1	81.3	81.4	79.3	78.8	Services [3,4]
Jamaica								**Jamaïque**
Agriculture	5.4	9.2	5.7	5.9	7.2	7.7	7.7	Agriculture
Industry	28.4	29.4	23.9	20.0	22.0	22.6	23.5	Industrie
Services	53.4	53.8	63.2	68.6	66.1	65.8	65.7	Services

13 Gross value added by kind of economic activity *(continued)*
Percentage distribution, current prices

Valeur ajoutée brute par type d'activité économique *(suite)*
Répartition en pourcentage, aux prix courants

Country or area &	1985	1995	2005	2010	2015	2017	2018	Pays ou zone &
Japan [1,6]								**Japon [1,6]**
Agriculture	2.9	1.7	1.1	1.1	1.1	1.2	1.1	Agriculture
Industry [2]	39.5	34.7	30.1	28.5	29.2	29.3	28.5	Industrie [2]
Services [3,4]	61.1	58.8	62.6	63.7	62.4	62.1	62.8	Services [3,4]
Jordan [1]								**Jordanie [1]**
Agriculture	7.0	5.8	4.0	4.5	5.4	5.8	5.9	Agriculture
Industry [2]	27.3	28.3	28.2	31.0	29.9	29.1	29.0	Industrie [2]
Services [3,4]	39.1	74.8	72.5	70.4	76.3	75.8	75.8	Services [3,4]
Kazakhstan [1]								**Kazakhstan [1]**
Agriculture	...	12.9	6.6	4.7	5.0	4.8	4.7	Agriculture
Industry [2]	...	30.2	39.2	41.9	32.5	34.3	35.9	Industrie [2]
Services [3,4]	...	42.9	47.7	47.5	50.6	48.9	48.2	Services [3,4]
Kenya [1]								**Kenya [1]**
Agriculture	28.7	27.6	23.2	27.1	32.2	37.2	36.7	Agriculture
Industry [2]	25.2	20.9	22.3	20.3	18.5	18.0	17.6	Industrie [2]
Services [3,4]	51.1	57.0	55.3	50.7	45.1	41.5	41.8	Services [3,4]
Kiribati [18]								**Kiribati [18]**
Agriculture	44.0	26.9	21.8	24.2	22.6	24.0	24.0	Agriculture
Industry	9.4	9.1	9.3	11.9	15.7	15.4	15.6	Industrie
Services	29.2	59.4	65.6	66.8	69.9	69.9	70.5	Services
Kosovo [1]								**Kosovo [1]**
Agriculture	...	7.2	17.2	16.2	12.6	11.4	8.9	Agriculture
Industry [2]	...	32.6	26.6	28.4	29.1	31.8	32.6	Industrie [2]
Services [3,4]	...	55.5	49.6	45.0	46.5	44.3	43.6	Services [3,4]
Kuwait								**Koweït**
Agriculture	0.6	0.4	0.3	0.4	0.5	0.5	0.4	Agriculture
Industry	56.4	52.8	60.2	58.2	48.7	48.7	54.7	Industrie
Services	30.1	51.6	58.3	59.0	71.1	69.0	65.0	Services
Kyrgyzstan [1]								**Kirghizistan [1]**
Agriculture	...	43.1	31.3	18.8	15.4	13.9	13.1	Agriculture
Industry [2]	...	21.8	22.1	28.2	27.5	30.4	30.9	Industrie [2]
Services [3,4]	...	37.0	40.1	45.6	46.0	45.3	45.8	Services [3,4]
Lao People's Dem. Rep. [1]								**Rép. dém. populaire lao [1]**
Agriculture	39.1	42.8	29.1	23.6	19.7	18.3	17.7	Agriculture
Industry [2]	16.2	15.7	26.2	30.9	31.0	34.9	35.5	Industrie [2]
Services [3,4]	23.1	48.7	57.7	57.4	59.2	58.2	57.3	Services [3,4]
Latvia [1]								**Lettonie [1]**
Agriculture	...	8.6	4.1	4.5	4.0	4.0	4.1	Agriculture
Industry [2]	...	30.2	22.8	23.1	22.1	22.0	22.5	Industrie [2]
Services [3,4]	...	51.7	60.2	66.8	68.4	67.2	66.9	Services [3,4]
Lebanon [1]								**Liban [1]**
Agriculture	3.7	5.7	4.0	4.3	3.7	3.1	3.3	Agriculture
Industry [2]	23.5	32.3	16.7	15.7	16.6	15.7	16.3	Industrie [2]
Services [3,4]	74.2	61.1	74.8	72.7	73.5	76.0	73.8	Services [3,4]
Lesotho [1]								**Lesotho [1]**
Agriculture	16.8	9.2	6.2	5.6	5.6	5.7	6.0	Agriculture
Industry	15.7	32.4	37.7	32.9	34.8	34.3	34.0	Industrie
Services [3,4]	63.5	50.1	49.8	52.2	52.9	52.1	53.2	Services [3,4]
Liberia								**Libéria**
Agriculture	35.9	80.5	68.8	70.2	70.0	74.1	72.5	Agriculture
Industry	24.7	5.2	9.8	11.9	9.9	7.9	9.4	Industrie
Services	36.3	21.1	17.5	15.9	16.5	15.6	15.6	Services
Libya								**Libye**
Agriculture	3.5	6.7	2.2	2.5	0.9	0.9	0.9	Agriculture
Industry	58.8	40.3	75.7	74.0	67.1	67.1	67.1	Industrie
Services	54.0	62.8	23.7	24.6	33.0	34.2	33.4	Services
Liechtenstein [1]								**Liechtenstein [1]**
Agriculture	2.4	1.5	0.2	0.1	0.1	0.1	0.1	Agriculture
Industry [2]	32.6	30.1	45.5	45.2	43.6	46.6	44.5	Industrie [2]
Services [3,4]	38.4	70.2	77.4	79.6	81.9	78.2	81.5	Services [3,4]
Lithuania [1]								**Lituanie [1]**
Agriculture [23]	...	11.1	4.8	3.4	3.8	3.9	3.2	Agriculture [23]
Industry [2,23]	...	31.5	32.7	29.1	29.6	28.8	28.4	Industrie [2,23]
Services [3,4]	...	54.1	52.0	56.4	54.8	54.9	55.8	Services [3,4]

13 Gross value added by kind of economic activity *(continued)*
Percentage distribution, current prices

Valeur ajoutée brute par type d'activité économique *(suite)*
Répartition en pourcentage, aux prix courants

Country or area &	1985	1995	2005	2010	2015	2017	2018	Pays ou zone &
Luxembourg [1]								**Luxembourg [1]**
Agriculture	2.0	1.0	0.4	0.3	0.2	0.3	0.3	Agriculture
Industry [2]	28.1	21.2	16.5	12.7	12.2	12.4	13.0	Industrie [2]
Services [3,4]	73.4	82.6	88.6	89.5	89.7	90.0	87.6	Services [3,4]
Madagascar								**Madagascar**
Agriculture	39.4	38.0	32.3	30.3	27.0	25.7	25.2	Agriculture
Industry	13.6	14.5	18.2	18.8	19.9	21.0	24.4	Industrie
Services	28.6	37.1	40.0	50.4	56.3	56.3	55.3	Services
Malawi [1]								**Malawi [1]**
Agriculture	50.0	31.9	37.1	31.9	32.4	32.0	31.0	Agriculture
Industry [2]	28.1	21.9	16.8	16.4	16.4	15.9	15.9	Industrie [2]
Services [3,4]	31.7	50.5	49.0	51.2	50.9	52.1	53.6	Services [3,4]
Malaysia								**Malaisie**
Agriculture	20.3	12.7	8.4	10.2	8.4	8.7	7.6	Agriculture
Industry	39.2	40.5[2,6]	46.9[2,6]	40.9[2,6]	38.9[2,6]	38.7[2,6]	38.8[2,6]	Industrie
Services	60.0	72.2[3,4,6]	64.6[3,4,6]	71.6[3,4,6]	71.3[3,4,6]	68.6[3,4,6]	68.1[3,4,6]	Services
Maldives [1]								**Maldives [1]**
Agriculture	10.7	7.5	8.7	6.1	6.3	6.2	6.5	Agriculture
Industry [2]	8.2	9.8	13.2	10.2	12.1	12.7	15.0	Industrie [2]
Services [3,4]	63.0	54.6	56.9	54.6	53.1	55.3	52.8	Services [3,4]
Mali								**Mali**
Agriculture	36.1	38.8	34.4	34.9	40.2	39.8	39.9	Agriculture
Industry	14.7	18.0	25.9	25.3	19.5	19.6	20.5	Industrie
Services	65.8	58.2	49.7	48.5	51.8	50.7	49.2	Services
Malta [1]								**Malte [1]**
Agriculture	4.4	2.8	2.2	1.7	1.2	0.9	1.0	Agriculture
Industry [2]	33.3	28.5	23.0	19.0	13.3	12.7	12.7	Industrie [2]
Services [3,4]	49.8	60.2	73.7	76.9	83.5	82.7	84.6	Services [3,4]
Marshall Islands								**Îles Marshall**
Agriculture	9.7	10.5	9.0	15.4	14.4	16.4	15.7	Agriculture
Industry	12.5	14.0	10.0	12.4	10.3	13.5	12.1	Industrie
Services	68.2	63.8	76.1	65.3	71.5	66.8	68.7	Services
Mauritania								**Mauritanie**
Agriculture	27.6	34.1	22.8	17.8	22.4	23.4	24.1	Agriculture
Industry	30.8	28.4	30.5	42.2	25.3	29.5	26.8	Industrie
Services	51.8	51.9	54.1	50.9	57.6	55.3	56.8	Services
Mauritius								**Maurice**
Agriculture [1]	14.8	9.8	5.7	4.1	3.6	3.5	3.2	Agriculture [1]
Industry	32.2	31.3	26.6	25.3[2]	21.7[2]	20.0[2]	20.1[2]	Industrie
Services	58.7	58.0	64.9	69.6[3,4]	76.0[3,4]	77.5[3,4]	77.3[3,4]	Services
Mexico [1]								**Mexique [1]**
Agriculture	7.3	4.6	3.2	3.4	3.4	3.6	3.5	Agriculture
Industry [2]	44.3	34.2	34.3	33.7	31.8	32.5	31.9	Industrie [2]
Services [3,4]	40.0	54.2	56.8	56.4	55.1	53.4	54.6	Services [3,4]
Micronesia (Fed. States of)								**Micronésie (États féd. de)**
Agriculture	24.5	24.9	24.2	26.7	27.7	27.5	28.0	Agriculture
Industry	7.4	7.2	5.7	7.8	6.5	6.5	6.5	Industrie
Services	97.2	97.1	97.0	79.6	75.2	77.4	76.5	Services
Monaco [1,6]								**Monaco [1,6]**
Industry	12.8	12.8	12.2	12.9	17.6	12.8	13.1	Industrie
Services	78.9	62.6	63.1	76.5	73.9	75.2	74.6	Services
Mongolia [1]								**Mongolie [1]**
Agriculture	9.9	28.5	17.8	13.1	14.5	11.4	12.2	Agriculture
Industry [2]	32.5	33.8	37.4	37.0	33.8	42.1	42.8	Industrie [2]
Services [3,4]	16.5	41.1	48.2	57.0	63.5	61.3	59.5	Services [3,4]
Montenegro [1]								**Monténégro [1]**
Agriculture	...	12.1	10.3	9.2	9.8	8.4	8.2	Agriculture
Industry [2]	...	25.3	22.1	20.5	17.4	18.2	19.5	Industrie [2]
Services [3,4]	...	73.5	59.9	52.5	57.1	55.9	55.6	Services [3,4]
Montserrat								**Montserrat**
Agriculture	4.0	4.9	0.9	1.1	1.4	1.4	1.4	Agriculture
Industry	17.7	12.3	16.7	13.3	12.4	11.8	13.4	Industrie
Services	60.6	65.5	83.2	91.2	86.5	88.1	86.5	Services

13 Gross value added by kind of economic activity *(continued)*
Percentage distribution, current prices

Valeur ajoutée brute par type d'activité économique *(suite)*
Répartition en pourcentage, aux prix courants

Country or area &	1985	1995	2005	2010	2015	2017	2018	Pays ou zone &
Morocco [24]								**Maroc [24]**
Agriculture	17.4	15.1	13.1	14.4	14.3	14.0	13.9	Agriculture
Industry	32.8	29.6	28.9	28.6	29.5	29.6	29.4	Industrie
Services	55.2	68.2	64.5	64.0	64.3	60.7	60.8	Services
Mozambique [1]								**Mozambique [1]**
Agriculture	47.5	37.7	27.2	29.8	25.9	27.8	27.4	Agriculture
Industry	13.2	15.7[2]	21.3[2]	18.3[2]	20.5[2]	26.7[2]	27.2[2]	Industrie
Services	38.8	38.3[3,4]	57.2[3,4]	57.5[3,4]	60.0[3,4]	56.7[3,4]	55.6[3,4]	Services
Myanmar [6]								**Myanmar [6]**
Agriculture	48.2	60.0	46.7	36.9	26.8	23.3	26.3	Agriculture
Industry	13.1	9.9	17.5	26.5	34.5	36.3	34.7	Industrie
Services [17]	24.9	20.4	23.3	23.6	25.9	25.4	23.6	Services [17]
Namibia								**Namibie**
Agriculture	7.9	10.5	11.4	9.2	6.3	7.4	7.6	Agriculture
Industry	39.7	24.2	27.3	29.8	30.5	30.5	31.1	Industrie
Services	71.9	84.9	83.8	65.7	81.9	86.3	84.8	Services
Nauru [6]								**Nauru [6]**
Agriculture	6.0	6.4	7.8	4.2	2.4	2.4	2.4	Agriculture
Industry	32.9	27.7	-6.5	43.6	40.7	35.2	37.5	Industrie
Services	49.7	54.3	80.1	52.8	43.8	42.4	42.3	Services
Nepal								**Népal**
Agriculture	49.0	38.9	35.2	35.4	31.7	29.6	28.1	Agriculture
Industry	11.5	17.7	17.1	15.1	14.8	14.5	14.9	Industrie
Services	37.8	41.4	47.7	48.5	53.4	58.4	59.4	Services
Netherlands [1]								**Pays-Bas [1]**
Agriculture	4.1	3.4	2.1	2.0	1.9	2.1	1.8	Agriculture
Industry [2]	32.1	26.5	23.6	21.9	20.2	19.8	20.0	Industrie [2]
Services [3,4]	70.6	75.9	69.5	72.1	72.3	71.8	71.9	Services [3,4]
Netherlands Antilles [former]								**Antilles néerlandaises [anc.]**
Agriculture	1.1	0.9	0.8	0.6	...	...	...	Agriculture
Industry	20.5	18.4	15.6	15.7	...	...	...	Industrie
Services	71.0	71.8	80.6	78.1	22.7	23.1	23.1	Services
New Caledonia								**Nouvelle-Calédonie**
Agriculture	1.8	1.8	1.7	1.5	2.1	2.0	2.0	Agriculture
Industry	25.9	22.0	26.6	28.3	23.9	24.9	24.6	Industrie
Services [17]	68.1	71.2	73.6	70.5	75.3	74.1	74.6	Services [17]
New Zealand [1]								**Nouvelle-Zélande [1]**
Agriculture	7.4	7.0	4.9	7.1	4.9	6.4	5.8	Agriculture
Industry [2]	34.1	27.8	25.8	23.0	23.2	22.3	22.5	Industrie [2]
Services [3,4]	58.2	67.7	70.1	73.0	73.1	73.9	72.2	Services [3,4]
Nicaragua								**Nicaragua**
Agriculture	14.9	22.4	17.8	18.7	17.8	16.7	16.9	Agriculture
Industry	33.7	22.0	22.9	24.2	28.5	27.7	28.2	Industrie
Services	50.3	57.5	60.2	56.5	53.2	54.2	54.6	Services
Niger [1]								**Niger [1]**
Agriculture	32.9	32.0	41.2	39.2	34.9	38.0	40.7	Agriculture
Industry [2]	23.8	16.9	14.0	19.8	23.1	21.4	19.2	Industrie [2]
Services [3,4]	45.2	44.8	43.1	47.7	53.6	51.0	49.4	Services [3,4]
Nigeria [1]								**Nigéria [1]**
Agriculture	18.4	25.7	26.4	23.9	20.9	21.1	21.4	Agriculture
Industry [2]	33.8	36.9	28.5	25.3	20.4	22.6	26.0	Industrie [2]
Services [3,4]	24.2	34.3	46.4	44.1	50.2	51.5	50.7	Services [3,4]
North Macedonia [1]								**Macédoine du Nord [1]**
Agriculture	...	12.5	11.3	11.7	11.1	9.1	8.4	Agriculture
Industry [2]	...	24.7	23.7	24.4	27.4	28.0	27.4	Industrie [2]
Services	22.7	68.0[3,4]	61.1[3,4]	60.3[3,4]	55.9[3,4]	54.6[3,4]	54.8[3,4]	Services
Norway [1]								**Norvège [1]**
Agriculture	3.2	3.0	1.6	1.8	1.7	2.2	2.3	Agriculture
Industry [2]	40.6	33.2	42.6	39.0	34.8	33.6	39.0	Industrie [2]
Services [3,4]	44.1	54.1	50.1	53.7	59.8	59.0	54.4	Services [3,4]
Oman								**Oman**
Agriculture	2.3	2.9	1.6	1.4	2.2	2.1	2.2	Agriculture
Industry	63.3	49.7	62.1	62.6	45.7	52.3	48.6	Industrie
Services	53.4	65.0	56.2	56.0	68.6	64.4	66.1	Services

Gross value added by kind of economic activity *(continued)*
Percentage distribution, current prices

Valeur ajoutée brute par type d'activité économique *(suite)*
Répartition en pourcentage, aux prix courants

Country or area [&]	1985	1995	2005	2010	2015	2017	2018	Pays ou zone [&]
Pakistan [1]								**Pakistan** [1]
Agriculture	30.5	28.1	24.5	24.3	25.1	24.4	24.0	Agriculture
Industry [2]	16.7	17.9	21.2	20.6	20.1	19.1	19.3	Industrie [2]
Services [3,4]	41.6	59.4	53.9	57.0	67.6	67.5	66.7	Services [3,4]
Palau [1]								**Palaos** [1]
Agriculture	16.7	8.1	4.2	4.2	3.3	3.6	3.5	Agriculture
Industry [2]	25.4	11.1	15.2	11.0	8.3	9.0	8.8	Industrie [2]
Services [3,4]	65.2	74.6	81.2	88.7	80.6	79.4	81.6	Services [3,4]
Panama								**Panama**
Agriculture	7.0	7.1	6.6	3.8	2.9	2.4	2.3	Agriculture
Industry	21.9	19.6	16.1	20.1	28.7	30.5	30.2	Industrie
Services	72.2	69.8	62.6	55.2	50.1	49.9	50.4	Services
Papua New Guinea								**Papouasie-Nvl-Guinée**
Agriculture	18.6	22.0	22.7	20.2	19.6	19.3	19.5	Agriculture
Industry	14.4	23.0	34.0	34.2	29.9	31.3	30.5	Industrie
Services	60.1	49.6	46.3	50.8	53.9	53.4	53.5	Services
Paraguay								**Paraguay**
Agriculture	15.1	13.2	11.6	14.0	10.2	11.1	11.0	Agriculture
Industry	34.9[25]	37.2[25]	44.5	37.3	37.4	37.2	37.2	Industrie
Services	57.7	57.7	45.4	49.3	56.8	55.5	55.6	Services
Peru [1]								**Pérou** [1]
Agriculture	8.7	8.9	7.5	7.5	7.7	7.3	7.5	Agriculture
Industry [2]	45.4	32.3	37.7	39.1	33.2	33.9	33.9	Industrie [2]
Services [3,4]	40.4	49.8	57.3	55.0	59.2	59.4	59.5	Services [3,4]
Philippines [1]								**Philippines** [1]
Agriculture	21.2	18.8	12.7	12.3	10.3	9.7	9.3	Agriculture
Industry [2,10]	38.0	35.0	33.8	32.6	30.9	30.5	30.8	Industrie [2,10]
Services [3,4,10]	33.3	52.9	57.5	58.9	61.9	63.3	63.9	Services [3,4,10]
Poland [1]								**Pologne** [1]
Agriculture	14.6	5.6	3.3	2.9	2.5	3.1	2.4	Agriculture
Industry [2]	51.4	37.4	32.8	33.9	33.9	32.3	32.7	Industrie [2]
Services [3,4]	50.1	55.1	60.3	60.3	62.4	62.8	62.9	Services [3,4]
Portugal [1]								**Portugal** [1]
Agriculture	13.3	5.4	2.7	2.2	2.4	2.4	2.4	Agriculture
Industry [2]	26.8	28.2	24.7	22.7	22.3	22.1	22.2	Industrie [2]
Services [3,4]	47.4	57.0	60.8	61.7	60.2	60.8	60.9	Services [3,4]
Puerto Rico [6]								**Porto Rico** [6]
Agriculture	2.5	1.0	0.6	0.8	0.8	0.8	0.8	Agriculture
Industry	45.3	47.6	47.3	50.7	51.1	51.0	49.9	Industrie
Services	41.4	46.5	45.8	46.4	49.6	48.7	48.4	Services
Qatar [1]								**Qatar** [1]
Agriculture	1.0	1.0	0.1	0.1	0.2	0.2	0.2	Agriculture
Industry [2,6]	57.8	53.0	74.6	67.5	55.4	54.6	58.8	Industrie [2,6]
Services [3,4,6]	56.8	54.6	37.7	40.8	48.8	49.7	46.6	Services [3,4,6]
Republic of Korea [1]								**République de Corée** [1]
Agriculture	12.7	5.7	2.9	2.4	2.2	2.0	2.0	Agriculture
Industry [2]	37.7	40.0	37.7	37.5	37.2	38.0	37.3	Industrie [2]
Services [3,4]	26.5	47.9	63.2	67.6	69.5	70.9	72.1	Services [3,4]
Republic of Moldova [1]								**République de Moldova** [1]
Agriculture	...	30.2	17.7	13.0	13.2	13.3	11.8	Agriculture
Industry [2]	...	35.2	25.9	23.7	26.0	25.3	26.6	Industrie [2]
Services	11.9	38.0[3,4]	57.8[3,4]	54.1[3,4]	58.0[3,4]	58.5[3,4]	57.8[3,4]	Services
Romania [1]								**Roumanie** [1]
Agriculture	15.5	19.2	9.6	5.6	4.8	4.8	4.8	Agriculture
Industry [2]	54.0	38.4	36.4	42.4	34.1	31.9	32.0	Industrie [2]
Services [3,4]	18.6	58.3	58.5	64.0	61.1	61.9	61.4	Services [3,4]
Russian Federation								**Fédération de Russie**
Agriculture	...	7.1	4.9	3.8	4.3	3.9	3.5	Agriculture
Industry	...	39.5	38.2	34.8	33.3	33.7	35.9	Industrie
Services	8.3	32.1	40.1	48.3	53.6	52.0	52.4	Services
Rwanda [1]								**Rwanda** [1]
Agriculture	50.7	42.9	39.3	30.2	30.1	33.3	31.2	Agriculture
Industry [2]	19.2	13.7	13.8	15.8	18.3	16.9	17.4	Industrie [2]
Services [3,4]	48.4	62.6	59.2	65.5	63.4	61.5	62.8	Services [3,4]

Country or area [&]	1985	1995	2005	2010	2015	2017	2018	Pays ou zone [&]
Saint Kitts and Nevis								**Saint-Kitts-et-Nevis**
Agriculture	5.4	3.2	1.8	1.4	1.1	1.2	1.2	Agriculture
Industry	18.1	22.8	24.0	25.2	26.1	29.6	27.7	Industrie
Services	90.2	87.0	88.2	86.8	87.8	86.8	87.3	Services
Saint Lucia								**Sainte-Lucie**
Agriculture	12.0	7.5	3.5	2.5	2.1	1.7	1.8	Agriculture
Industry	16.0	16.2	18.7	13.7	13.0	13.2	11.6	Industrie
Services	57.6	59.4	74.0	86.0	85.3	85.3	88.7	Services
Saint Vincent & Grenadines								**Saint-Vincent-Grenadines**
Agriculture	15.1	11.2	6.2	7.1	7.3	8.2	8.6	Agriculture
Industry	19.6	20.9	18.6	19.2	18.0	17.8	17.8	Industrie
Services	57.9	54.0	60.8	73.3	77.3	76.7	78.0	Services
Samoa								**Samoa**
Agriculture [6]	24.7	22.3	13.7	9.1	8.9	10.3	9.4	Agriculture [6]
Industry [2]	20.3[6]	20.2[6]	22.4[6]	18.1[10]	18.1[10]	15.9[10]	14.6[10]	Industrie [2]
Services [1,3,4]	50.4	51.6	48.7	48.6	48.9	50.7	51.2	Services [1,3,4]
San Marino [1]								**Saint-Marin** [1]
Agriculture	0.1	0.1	0.1	0.1	0.0	0.0	0.0	Agriculture
Industry [2]	40.9	40.8	38.2	35.6	34.4	34.5	34.7	Industrie [2]
Services [3,4]	74.9	74.6	84.2	91.4	89.4	87.4	86.8	Services [3,4]
Sao Tome and Principe								**Sao Tomé-et-Principe**
Agriculture	27.6	26.4	18.3	11.8	12.2	12.0	11.3	Agriculture
Industry	17.9	19.6	14.9	18.2	15.7	15.7	15.4	Industrie
Services	30.5	28.3	33.4	37.4	46.7	46.3	46.1	Services
Saudi Arabia [1]								**Arabie saoudite** [1]
Agriculture	3.6	5.9	3.2	2.6	2.6	2.5	2.2	Agriculture
Industry [2]	41.2	48.9	61.8	58.2	45.3	45.9	49.6	Industrie [2]
Services [3,4]	63.9	55.9	50.6	50.4	60.0	59.7	57.4	Services [3,4]
Senegal [1]								**Sénégal** [1]
Agriculture	17.3	18.3	16.0	16.6	16.0	16.7	17.3	Agriculture
Industry [2]	27.1	28.9	26.3	25.6	26.4	25.9	25.7	Industrie [2]
Services [3,4]	33.6	43.8	54.1	55.7	56.4	55.3	55.4	Services [3,4]
Serbia [1]								**Serbie** [1]
Agriculture	...	20.9	12.0	10.2	8.2	7.3	7.7	Agriculture
Industry [2]	...	35.5	29.3	28.4	31.4	31.4	30.8	Industrie [2]
Services [3,4]	...	59.3	72.0	79.1	78.2	77.4	79.2	Services [3,4]
Seychelles [1]								**Seychelles** [1]
Agriculture	6.7	5.9	3.8	2.7	2.4	2.3	2.4	Agriculture
Industry [2]	9.2	13.5	19.4	16.5	14.0	14.1	13.4	Industrie [2]
Services [3,4]	67.5	69.1	57.9	55.4	55.4	54.8	53.2	Services [3,4]
Sierra Leone								**Sierra Leone**
Agriculture	41.0	48.1	51.0	55.2	60.5	62.0	61.0	Agriculture
Industry	20.4	9.1	11.6	8.1	4.6	5.3	5.5	Industrie
Services	44.1	55.5	54.6	54.3	51.3	51.4	51.9	Services
Singapore [1]								**Singapour** [1]
Agriculture	1.0	0.2	0.1	0.0	0.0	0.0	0.0	Agriculture
Industry [2,7]	33.4	33.8	32.4	27.6	25.6	24.8	26.1	Industrie [2,7]
Services [3,4]	35.9	36.5	70.3	76.3	82.1	79.1	80.1	Services [3,4]
Sint Maarten (Dutch part)								**St-Martin (partie néerland.)**
Agriculture	...	...	0.3	0.1	0.1	0.1	0.1	Agriculture
Industry	...	...	16.4	13.4	9.8	10.8	9.9	Industrie
Services	...	19.9	73.8	74.3	76.3	77.0	76.8	Services
Slovakia [1]								**Slovaquie** [1]
Agriculture	...	2.6	1.8	1.8	2.9	2.7	2.6	Agriculture
Industry [2]	...	32.0	36.1	33.9	33.9	32.3	33.6	Industrie [2]
Services [3,4]	...	67.0	58.7	63.3	63.3	66.0	64.5	Services [3,4]
Slovenia [1]								**Slovénie** [1]
Agriculture	...	4.7	2.8	2.2	2.4	2.1	2.4	Agriculture
Industry [2]	...	34.5	33.9	30.4	32.4	32.7	32.7	Industrie [2]
Services [3,4]	...	55.3	62.2	69.0	68.6	67.9	67.8	Services [3,4]
Solomon Islands								**Îles Salomon**
Agriculture	50.4	44.7	30.4	28.7	25.0	25.6	25.4	Agriculture
Industry	8.3	14.4	7.5	13.3	15.5	15.2	15.2	Industrie
Services	42.6	45.3	60.3	52.3	51.6	51.6	51.5	Services

13 Gross value added by kind of economic activity *(continued)*

Percentage distribution, current prices

Valeur ajoutée brute par type d'activité économique *(suite)*

Répartition en pourcentage, aux prix courants

Country or area [&]	1985	1995	2005	2010	2015	2017	2018	Pays ou zone [&]
Somalia								**Somalie**
Agriculture	66.1	60.1	60.1	60.2	60.2	60.2	60.2	Agriculture
Industry	7.6	7.3	7.4	7.4	7.4	7.4	7.4	Industrie
Services	30.2	36.7	37.3	36.5	37.7	37.3	37.3	Services
South Africa								**Afrique du Sud**
Agriculture	5.1	3.8	2.7	2.6	2.3	2.6	2.4	Agriculture
Industry	42.8	33.9	30.3	30.2	29.1	29.3	29.0	Industrie
Services	31.4	37.9	42.0	56.6	64.8	61.7	61.8	Services
South Sudan [1]								**Soudan du sud [1]**
Agriculture	...	...	...	5.1	4.2	2.9	1.9	Agriculture
Industry	...	...	...	55.4	45.0	50.0	55.3	Industrie
Services	...	...	...	52.4	56.5	56.2	52.1	Services
Spain [1]								**Espagne [1]**
Agriculture	5.7	4.2	3.1	2.6	3.0	3.1	3.1	Agriculture
Industry [2]	34.8	30.6	30.3	25.2	22.1	22.2	22.1	Industrie [2]
Services [3,4]	58.6	62.1	67.5	71.7	74.8	73.5	73.9	Services [3,4]
Sri Lanka [1]								**Sri Lanka [1]**
Agriculture	22.2	16.6	8.8	9.5	8.8	8.6	8.6	Agriculture
Industry	31.8[2]	32.8[2]	31.0[2]	29.7[2]	29.3[2]	30.1[2]	29.4	Industrie
Services [3,4]	44.1	55.2	65.1	64.8	63.5	63.9	64.6	Services [3,4]
State of Palestine [1]								**État de Palestine [1]**
Agriculture	21.0	20.1	10.3	10.6	8.7	8.3	8.5	Agriculture
Industry [2]	27.4	28.3	24.0	21.8	19.2	22.6	22.3	Industrie [2]
Services [3,4]	35.0	35.4	47.3	66.0	71.9	71.8	72.9	Services [3,4]
Sudan								**Soudan**
Agriculture	...	...	...	42.6	32.9	26.4	24.8	Agriculture
Industry	...	...	...	14.0	13.0	17.1	14.0	Industrie
Services	...	...	...	40.3	23.0	22.1	23.9	Services
Sudan [former]								**Soudan [anc.]**
Agriculture	36.7	37.1	34.5	34.6	...	...	...	Agriculture
Industry	13.2	9.9	21.7	22.9	...	...	...	Industrie
Services	40.7	47.6	44.7	47.9	...	...	...	Services
Suriname								**Suriname**
Agriculture [18]	8.6	29.9	11.3	10.2	10.0	12.3	12.3	Agriculture [18]
Industry	28.5[18]	27.5	37.4	37.9	28.0	35.9	34.5	Industrie
Services	61.7[18]	32.4	46.0	46.9	50.9	49.3	51.8	Services
Sweden [1]								**Suède [1]**
Agriculture	5.9	3.3	1.4	1.9	1.6	1.6	1.6	Agriculture
Industry [26]	32.5	30.5	28.1	27.0	24.8	24.9	25.5	Industrie [26]
Services [3,4]	66.3	69.2	71.2	72.1	72.3	73.1	72.5	Services [3,4]
Switzerland [1]								**Suisse [1]**
Agriculture	2.4	1.5	0.9	0.7	0.7	0.7	0.7	Agriculture
Industry [2]	32.6	30.1	27.0	26.6	25.9	25.5	25.8	Industrie [2]
Services [3,4]	70.4	81.6	78.0	78.6	80.8	81.0	80.9	Services [3,4]
Syrian Arab Republic [10]								**République arabe syrienne [10]**
Agriculture	21.0	28.2	20.3	19.7	20.7	20.6	20.6	Agriculture
Industry	21.9	18.1	31.2	30.7	30.0	30.1	30.1	Industrie
Services	25.0	24.3	44.5	52.7	48.1	47.1	45.6	Services
Tajikistan								**Tadjikistan**
Agriculture	...	31.6	23.8	21.8	24.7	23.7	20.9	Agriculture
Industry	...	48.4	30.7	27.9	27.5	30.1	30.1	Industrie
Services	...	40.2	44.6	39.9	43.8	45.3	50.8	Services
Thailand [1,6]								**Thaïlande [1,6]**
Agriculture	15.8	9.1	9.2	10.5	8.9	8.3	8.3	Agriculture
Industry [2]	31.8	37.3	38.5	39.9	36.2	35.2	35.6	Industrie [2]
Services	21.0	38.5[3,4]	33.6[3,4]	31.0[3,4]	38.9[3,4]	41.0[3,4]	38.9[3,4]	Services
Timor-Leste [1]								**Timor-Leste [1]**
Agriculture	...	20.6	7.4	5.7	8.9	10.4	10.0	Agriculture
Industry	...	47.8	76.1[2]	79.1[2]	57.9[2]	45.6[2]	49.6[2]	Industrie
Services	...	35.4	34.3[3,4]	33.6[3,4]	43.6[3,4]	50.8[3,4]	47.9[3,4]	Services
Togo								**Togo**
Agriculture	30.9	34.2	34.0	33.8	28.2	27.1	27.7	Agriculture
Industry [27]	25.7	27.5	16.5	16.0	18.0	17.5	18.4	Industrie [27]
Services [28]	45.2	39.7	44.8	47.1	58.3	61.8	61.1	Services [28]

Gross value added by kind of economic activity *(continued)*
Percentage distribution, current prices

Valeur ajoutée brute par type d'activité économique *(suite)*
Répartition en pourcentage, aux prix courants

Country or area [&]	1985	1995	2005	2010	2015	2017	2018	Pays ou zone [&]
Tonga								**Tonga**
Agriculture	37.8	22.1	20.2	18.2	22.6	21.9	22.0	Agriculture
Industry	14.9	22.0	19.1	19.9	20.9	21.5	21.0	Industrie
Services	47.2	64.5	60.4	65.6	62.6	60.0	57.8	Services
Trinidad and Tobago [1]								**Trinité-et-Tobago** [1]
Agriculture	5.0	3.3	0.9	0.7	1.1	1.2	1.1	Agriculture
Industry [2]	41.9	42.9	56.7	52.3	40.1	40.0	42.8	Industrie [2]
Services [3,4]	51.4	52.6	50.2	50.0	53.2	55.5	54.0	Services [3,4]
Tunisia [18]								**Tunisie** [18]
Agriculture	14.4	10.5	10.0	8.1	10.9	10.3	10.4	Agriculture
Industry	34.7	29.6	28.8	31.1	26.6	24.7	25.7	Industrie
Services	59.4	62.2	63.7	59.8	64.3	66.3	66.4	Services
Turkey [1]								**Turquie** [1]
Agriculture	16.2	12.4	10.6	10.3	7.8	6.9	6.5	Agriculture
Industry [2]	34.1	38.3	29.0	28.0	31.7	33.0	32.9	Industrie [2]
Services [3,4]	21.5	30.3	43.1	43.3	42.3	41.4	41.0	Services [3,4]
Turkmenistan								**Turkménistan**
Agriculture	...	16.9	18.8	11.5	9.4	8.9	9.1	Agriculture
Industry	...	65.3	37.6	60.0	57.8	60.2	59.8	Industrie
Services	...	56.6	74.2	65.1	76.0	70.8	73.5	Services
Turks and Caicos Islands								**Îles Turques-et-Caïques**
Agriculture	1.3	1.3	1.2	0.6	0.6	0.6	0.6	Agriculture
Industry	16.3	16.4	19.7	12.4	10.5	10.2	11.4	Industrie
Services	54.1	50.9	54.3	57.5	50.7	49.7	52.0	Services
Tuvalu								**Tuvalu**
Agriculture	10.8	24.0	22.2	27.3	21.4	20.0	21.9	Agriculture
Industry	13.5	14.0	8.3	5.7[29]	12.7[29]	17.8[29]	12.5[29]	Industrie
Services	80.6	77.2	75.7	75.5	72.8	67.1	69.9	Services
Uganda [1]								**Ouganda** [1]
Agriculture	50.2	40.2	28.7	26.3	25.8	27.0	23.6	Agriculture
Industry [2]	9.5	17.0	22.2	20.5	22.2	21.7	22.9	Industrie [2]
Services [3]	21.3	45.0[4]	55.2[4]	57.0[4]	56.8[4]	58.4[4]	58.1[4]	Services [3]
Ukraine [1]								**Ukraine** [1]
Agriculture	...	14.5	10.0	8.4	14.2	12.1	12.0	Agriculture
Industry [2,30]	...	41.8	34.1	29.3	25.6	27.7	27.5	Industrie [2,30]
Services [3,4]	...	50.3	51.7	55.4	55.4	55.0	53.9	Services [3,4]
United Arab Emirates								**Émirats arabes unis**
Agriculture	0.9	1.6	1.3	0.8	0.7	0.8	0.7	Agriculture
Industry	60.8	47.5	54.0	52.5	43.9	43.0	46.8	Industrie
Services	39.2	46.3	46.0	48.3	54.8	56.8	55.2	Services
United Kingdom [1]								**Royaume-Uni** [1]
Agriculture	1.4	1.5	0.6	0.7	0.7	0.7	0.7	Agriculture
Industry [2]	34.8	27.4	22.4	21.0	20.3	19.7	19.6	Industrie [2]
Services [3,4]	68.6	73.0	77.0	78.3	79.9	80.2	79.9	Services [3,4]
United Rep. of Tanzania [1,31]								**Rép.-Unie de Tanzanie** [1,31]
Agriculture	27.6	29.2	26.3	27.6	29.2	31.3	30.7	Agriculture
Services [4]	53.1	37.4	44.8	48.3	46.8	42.8	44.1	Services [4]
United States of America [1,10]								**États-Unis d'Amérique** [1,10]
Agriculture	1.6	1.2	1.0	1.0	1.0	0.9	0.8	Agriculture
Industry [2]	28.3	24.3	21.5	19.7	18.8	18.6	18.9	Industrie [2]
Services [3,4]	63.3	73.0	76.7	78.4	75.9	77.0	76.5	Services [3,4]
Uruguay								**Uruguay**
Agriculture	12.5	8.1	9.8	8.0	6.7	5.6	6.2	Agriculture
Industry	30.8	25.9	26.6	27.3	28.0	27.2	26.9	Industrie
Services	55.9	42.9	40.0	41.7	44.8	45.8	45.9	Services
Uzbekistan								**Ouzbékistan**
Agriculture [1]	...	47.2	45.3	32.9	33.6	33.5	31.7	Agriculture [1]
Industry [2]	...	22.5	20.9	25.9	25.9	27.5	31.3	Industrie [2]
Services [3,4]	...	43.6	47.4	53.0	54.2	56.2	55.2	Services [3,4]
Vanuatu [1]								**Vanuatu** [1]
Agriculture	32.6	30.5	24.1	21.9	23.1	23.1	22.8	Agriculture
Industry [2]	5.9	9.1	8.5	13.0	11.5	11.0	11.2	Industrie [2]
Services [3,4]	49.7	49.1	52.7	53.7	67.5	60.7	63.0	Services [3,4]

Country or area [&]	1985	1995	2005	2010	2015	2017	2018	Pays ou zone [&]
Venezuela (Boliv. Rep. of)								**Venezuela (Rép. boliv. du)**
Agriculture	6.4	5.9	4.0	5.7	6.3	5.7	5.9	Agriculture
Industry	51.9	47.1	56.9	51.0	30.5	36.5	35.4	Industrie
Services	41.6	51.6	41.8	39.8	48.3	48.3	48.4	Services
Viet Nam [1]								**Viet Nam [1]**
Agriculture [6]	39.0	24.5	19.3	21.0	18.9	17.0	16.2	Agriculture [6]
Industry [2]	21.4[6]	26.1[6]	38.1[6]	36.7	37.0	37.1	38.1	Industrie [2]
Services [3,4,6]	26.2	54.8	51.6	55.3	57.8	61.7	61.6	Services [3,4,6]
Yemen								**Yémen**
Agriculture	...	17.3	9.6	12.1	18.2	19.1	19.3	Agriculture
Industry	...	27.4	43.8	38.7	20.1	20.2	20.6	Industrie
Services	...	28.3	17.9	18.5	28.9	24.9	24.3	Services
Zambia [1]								**Zambie [1]**
Agriculture	13.3	15.1	15.5	10.0	5.3	4.3	3.0	Agriculture
Industry	50.8	36.8	28.6	34.1[2]	35.3[2]	39.9[2]	35.5[2]	Industrie
Services	19.1	53.1	55.2	59.4[3,4]	56.9[3,4]	53.5[3,4]	56.3[3,4]	Services
Zanzibar [1]								**Zanzibar [1]**
Agriculture	...	21.3	23.0	24.7	24.2	23.7	23.2	Agriculture
Industry [2]	...	22.5	17.5	19.5	20.2	21.5	19.5	Industrie [2]
Services [3,4]	...	65.9	51.0	63.6	58.4	60.9	59.7	Services [3,4]
Zimbabwe								**Zimbabwe**
Agriculture	17.7	11.5	10.7	10.9	9.3	9.2	9.2	Agriculture
Industry	23.7	23.8	36.7	23.5	25.0	23.7	22.9	Industrie
Services	26.0	26.2	30.7	25.4	32.9	33.0	33.9	Services

Source:

United Nations Statistics Division, New York, National Accounts Statistics: Analysis of Main Aggregates (AMA) database, last accessed June 2020.

[&] Table is in ISIC Rev. 3 unless otherwise indicated.

Source:

Organisation des Nations Unies, Division de statistique, New York, base de données des statistiques des comptes nationaux : Analyse des principaux agrégats, denier accès juin 2020.

[&] Sauf indication contraire la classification utilisée dans ce tableau est la CITI Rev. 3.

1	Data classified according to ISIC Rev. 4.
2	Excludes publishing activities. Includes irrigation and canals.
3	Excludes repair of personal and household goods.
4	Excludes computer and related activities and radio/TV activities.
5	Including mining and quarrying.
6	At producers' prices.
7	Excluding mining and quarrying.
8	Data compiled in accordance with the System of National Accounts 1968 (1968 SNA).
9	For statistical purposes, the data for China do not include those for the Hong Kong Special Administrative Region (Hong Kong SAR), Macao Special Administrative Region (Macao SAR) and Taiwan Province of China.
10	Including taxes less subsidies on production and imports.
11	Excludes repair of motor vehicles and motorcycles, personal and household goods.
12	Excluding hunting and forestry.
13	Includes waste management.
14	Excluding waste management.
15	Includes mining and handicrafts.
16	Excluding northern Cyprus.
17	Excludes hotels and restaurants.
18	At factor cost.
19	Including French Guiana, Guadeloupe, Martinique and Réunion.
20	Gas distribution is included in Wholesale and retail trade.

1	Classifiées selon la CITI, Rév. 4.
2	Exclut les activités d'édition. Comprend l'irrigation et les canaux.
3	Exclut la réparation des biens personnels et ménagers.
4	Exclut l'Informatique et activités connexes et les activités de radio et de television.
5	Y compris les industries extractives.
6	Aux prix à la production.
7	Non compris les industries extractives.
8	Données compilées selon le Système de comptabilité nationale de 1968 (SCN 1968).
9	Pour la présentation des statistiques, les données pour la Chine ne comprennent pas la région administrative spéciale de Hong Kong (RAS de Hong Kong), la région administrative spéciale de Macao (RAS de Macao) et la province chinoise de Taïwan.
10	Y compris les impôts moins les subventions sur la production et les importations.
11	Non compris les réparations de véhicules à moteur et de motocycles, et d'articles personnels et ménagers.
12	Non compris la chasse et la sylviculture.
13	Y compris la gestion des déchets.
14	Gestion des déchets non-compris.
15	Y compris l'extraction et l'artisanat.
16	Chypre du nord non compris.
17	Non compris les hôtels et restaurants.
18	Au coût des facteurs.
19	Y compris Guadeloupe, Guyane française, Martinique et Réunion.
20	La distribution de gaz est incluse dans le commerce de gros et de detail.

Gross value added by kind of economic activity *(continued)*
Percentage distribution, current prices

Valeur ajoutée brute par type d'activité économique *(suite)*
Répartition en pourcentage, aux prix courants

21	Agricultural services and related activities such as cotton ginning and pressing are included in Manufacturing.
22	Distribution of petroleum products is included in Services.
23	Includes publishing activities and landscaping care.
24	Including Western Sahara.
25	Does not incorporate value added generated by binational hydroelectric plants.
26	Excludes irrigation canals and landscaping care.
27	Construction refers to buildings and public works.
28	Refers to trade only.
29	Includes electricity, gas and water.
30	The Government of Ukraine has informed the United Nations that it is not in a position to provide statistical data concerning the Autonomous Republic of Crimea and the city of Sevastopol.
31	Tanzania mainland only, excluding Zanzibar.

21	Les services agricoles et les activités connexes (par exemple l'égrenage du coton, tressage) figurent sous l'industrie manufacturière.
22	La distribution du gaz est inclue dans la catégorie Services.
23	Y compris les activités d'édition et l'aménagement paysager.
24	Y compris les données de Sahara occidental.
25	Ne comprend pas la valeur ajoutée produite par les centrales hydroélectriques binationales.
26	Exclut les canaux d'irrigation et l'aménagement paysager.
27	Construction se rapporte aux bâtiments et travaux publics.
28	Se rapporte seulement au commerce
29	Y compris l'électricité, le gaz, et l'eau.
30	Le Gouvernement ukrainien a informé l'Organisation des Nations Unies qu'il n'est pas en mesure de fournir des données statistiques concernant la République autonome de Crimée et Sébastopol.
31	Tanzanie continentale seulement, Zanzibar non compris.

Balance of payments summary
Millions of US dollars

Résumé de la balance des paiements
Millions de dollars É.-U.

Country or area&	1985	1995	2010	2015	2017	2018	2019	Pays ou zone&
Afghanistan								**Afghanistan**
Current account	-243	...	-578	-4 193	-3 294	-3 897	-3 799	Compte des transac. cour.
Capital account	...	...	1 897	1 318	1 306	1 314	824	Compte de capital
Financial account	-75	...	1 091	-260	446	477	133	Compte financier
Albania								**Albanie**
Current account	-36	-12	-1 356	-980	-982	-1 010	-1 165	Compte des transac. cour.
Capital account	...	389	113	139	139	122	85	Compte de capital
Financial account	-30	432	-797	-682	-1 082	-915	-1 010	Compte financier
Algeria								**Algérie**
Current account	1 015	...	12 220	-27 038	-22 059	...	...	Compte des transac. cour.
Capital account	...	...	4	~0	1	...	...	Compte de capital
Financial account	1 141	...	10 921	-27 202	-22 015	...	...	Compte financier
Angola								**Angola**
Current account	195	-295	7 506	-10 273	-633	7 403	5 137	Compte des transac. cour.
Capital account	...	...	1	6	3	3	2	Compte de capital
Financial account	-460	-314	7 219	-11 466	-748	7 246	4 186	Compte financier
Anguilla								**Anguilla**
Current account	...	-10	-51	-89	-22	-136	...	Compte des transac. cour.
Capital account	...	1	4	1	2	3	...	Compte de capital
Financial account	...	4	-35	-36	-37	-145	...	Compte financier
Antigua and Barbuda								**Antigua-et-Barbuda**
Current account	-23	-1	-167	29	-130	-113	...	Compte des transac. cour.
Capital account	...	4	17	47	26	20	...	Compte de capital
Financial account	-23	24	-158	93	-45	-120	...	Compte financier
Argentina								**Argentine**
Current account	-952	-5 118	-1 623	-17 622	-31 163	-27 276	-3 462	Compte des transac. cour.
Capital account	...	14	78	52	173	83	127	Compte de capital
Financial account	-1 484	-7 777	-3 803	-18 497	-31 297	-28 079	-4 058	Compte financier
Armenia								**Arménie**
Current account	...	-221	-1 261	-287	-344	-1 165	-1 118	Compte des transac. cour.
Capital account	...	8	99	65	46	125	54	Compte de capital
Financial account	...	-198	-1 275	-347	-527	-683	-559	Compte financier
Aruba								**Aruba**
Current account	...	~0	-460	111	30	-3	...	Compte des transac. cour.
Capital account	...	0	4	0	...	...	...	Compte de capital
Financial account	...	1	-446	112	17	-6	...	Compte financier
Australia								**Australie**
Current account	...	-18 669	-44 714	-56 959	-35 781	-29 264	7 122	Compte des transac. cour.
Capital account	...	-300	-287	-456	-388	-361	-544	Compte de capital
Financial account	...	-18 866	-44 105	-58 333	-40 653	-35 228	5 523	Compte financier
Austria								**Autriche**
Current account	...	...	11 472	6 634	6 419	10 799	11 714	Compte des transac. cour.
Capital account	...	...	268	-1 988	-320	-284	-122	Compte de capital
Financial account	...	...	4 753	4 493	9 180	12 400	13 194	Compte financier
Azerbaijan								**Azerbaïdjan**
Current account	...	-401	15 040	-222	1 685	6 051	4 365	Compte des transac. cour.
Capital account	...	-2	...	-44	100	1	-19	Compte de capital
Financial account	...	-342	14 065	-2 352	2 173	6 699	5 008	Compte financier
Bahamas								**Bahamas**
Current account	-3	-146	-814	-1 203	-1 509	-1 505	...	Compte des transac. cour.
Financial account	30	-107	-1 097	-347	-1 094	-845	...	Compte financier
Bahrain								**Bahreïn**
Current account	39	237	770	-752	-1 600	-2 435	...	Compte des transac. cour.
Capital account	...	157	50	253	604	795	...	Compte de capital
Financial account	834	1 896	927	1 118	-70	3 144	...	Compte financier
Bangladesh								**Bangladesh**
Current account	-455	-824	2 109	2 580	-5 985	-7 593	-3 087	Compte des transac. cour.
Capital account	...	...	603	442	293	291	233	Compte de capital
Financial account	-523	-691	-1 745	2 272	-6 186	-8 693	-4 551	Compte financier
Barbados								**Barbade**
Current account	-5	1	-272	-99	...	...	...	Compte des transac. cour.
Capital account	-2	-3	-4	-7	...	...	...	Compte de capital
Financial account	16	-17	-599	-231	...	...	...	Compte financier

Balance of payments summary *(continued)*
Millions of US dollars

Résumé de la balance des paiements *(suite)*
Millions de dollars É.-U.

Country or area&	1985	1995	2010	2015	2017	2018	2019	Pays ou zone&
Belarus								**Bélarus**
Current account	...	-458	-8 280	-1 831	-952	24	-1 166	Compte des transac. cour.
Capital account	...	7	...	5	2	20	35	Compte de capital
Financial account	...	-282	-7 578	-1 322	-366	223	-651	Compte financier
Belgium								**Belgique**
Current account	...	...	7 338	6 363	6 180	-7 348	-6 512	Compte des transac. cour.
Capital account	...	...	-247	63	614	154	704	Compte de capital
Financial account	...	...	1 305	8 201	3 791	-8 999	-5 848	Compte financier
Belize								**Belize**
Current account	9	-17	-46	-175	-131	-155	...	Compte des transac. cour.
Capital account	...	...	5	9	16	24	...	Compte de capital
Financial account	-7	5	-22	-148	-119	-126	...	Compte financier
Benin								**Bénin**
Current account	-39	-167	-531	-679	-531	-649	...	Compte des transac. cour.
Capital account	...	88	122	125	196	197	...	Compte de capital
Financial account	-23	-79	-375	-669	-687	-717	...	Compte financier
Bermuda								**Bermudes**
Current account	...	...	696	943	940	958	...	Compte des transac. cour.
Financial account	...	...	714	760	824	956	...	Compte financier
Bhutan								**Bhoutan**
Current account	...	...	-323	-548	-540	-498	-564	Compte des transac. cour.
Capital account	...	...	150	226	186	166	125	Compte de capital
Financial account	...	...	-105	-348	-263	-186	-112	Compte financier
Bolivia (Plurin. State of)								**Bolivie (État plurin. de)**
Current account	-285	-303	874	-1 936	-1 849	-1 819	-1 362	Compte des transac. cour.
Capital account	...	...	...	47	7	10	6	Compte de capital
Financial account	-92	-413	64	-2 822	-2 551	-3 001	-2 577	Compte financier
Bosnia and Herzegovina								**Bosnie-Herzégovine**
Current account	...	...	-1 031	-822	-785	-751	-710	Compte des transac. cour.
Capital account	...	...	264	207	197	190	181	Compte de capital
Financial account	...	...	-647	-504	-449	-416	-312	Compte financier
Botswana								**Botswana**
Current account	82	300	-804	318	929	345	...	Compte des transac. cour.
Capital account	0	12	...	...	...	...	...	Compte de capital
Financial account	131	240	-871	462	666	-376	...	Compte financier
Brazil								**Brésil**
Current account	-280	-18 136	-79 014	-54 472	-15 015	-41 540	-49 452	Compte des transac. cour.
Capital account	...	...	242	461	379	440	369	Compte de capital
Financial account	-803	-16 337	-69 970	-56 152	-9 931	-42 412	-51 511	Compte financier
Brunei Darussalam								**Brunéi Darussalam**
Current account	...	...	5 016	2 157	1 984	940	894	Compte des transac. cour.
Financial account	...	...	4 918	4 508	1 171	42	303	Compte financier
Bulgaria								**Bulgarie**
Current account	-136	-26	-965	61	2 122	3 492	2 742	Compte des transac. cour.
Capital account	...	...	398	1 557	605	701	998	Compte de capital
Financial account	463	118	861	3 969	2 704	3 815	2 864	Compte financier
Burkina Faso								**Burkina Faso**
Current account	...	...	-182	-895	-896	-665	...	Compte des transac. cour.
Capital account	...	...	181	260	298	317	...	Compte de capital
Financial account	...	...	16	-626	-595	-365	...	Compte financier
Burundi								**Burundi**
Current account	-41	10	-301	-373	-373	-363	...	Compte des transac. cour.
Capital account	...	...	78	56	168	118	...	Compte de capital
Financial account	-50	16	-226	-329	-175	-215	...	Compte financier
Cabo Verde								**Cabo Verde**
Current account	-9	-62	-223	-51	-140	-97	-4	Compte des transac. cour.
Capital account	...	21	38	19	16	15	10	Compte de capital
Financial account	-4	-76	-270	-81	-105	-149	7	Compte financier
Cambodia								**Cambodge**
Current account	...	-186	-981	-1 598	-1 800	-2 992	-4 207	Compte des transac. cour.
Capital account	...	92	434	265	279	293	168	Compte de capital
Financial account	...	-82	-788	-1 846	-1 762	-2 237	-3 718	Compte financier
Cameroon								**Cameroun**
Current account	-562	90	-857	-1 174	-950	-1 409	...	Compte des transac. cour.
Capital account	...	20	147	22	120	159	...	Compte de capital
Financial account	-453	-16	-521	-1 126	-1 121	-1 402	...	Compte financier

Résumé de la balance des paiements *(suite)*
Millions de dollars É.-U.

Country or area[&]	1985	1995	2010	2015	2017	2018	2019	Pays ou zone[&]
Canada								**Canada**
Current account	-5 839	-5 061	-58 163	-54 696	-46 428	-42 993	-34 193	Compte des transac. cour.
Capital account	-1	-433	-121	-86	-58	-60	-67	Compte de capital
Financial account	-9 987	-1 621	-58 302	-52 308	-41 554	-35 509	-27 711	Compte financier
Cayman Islands								**Îles Caïmanes**
Current account	...	...	...	...	-998	...	...	Compte des transac. cour.
Capital account	...	...	...	...	-2	...	...	Compte de capital
Financial account	...	...	...	...	319	...	...	Compte financier
Central African Republic								**République centrafricaine**
Current account	-49	...	...	...	...	...	...	Compte des transac. cour.
Financial account	-56	...	...	...	...	...	...	Compte financier
Chad								**Tchad**
Current account	-87	...	...	...	...	...	...	Compte des transac. cour.
Financial account	-93	...	...	...	...	...	...	Compte financier
Chile								**Chili**
Current account	-1 413	-1 350	3 069	-5 647	-5 965	-9 157	...	Compte des transac. cour.
Capital account	...	...	6 240	675	67	42	...	Compte de capital
Financial account	-1 483	-1 218	8 480	-5 202	-4 685	-8 035	...	Compte financier
China [1]								**Chine** [1]
Current account	-11 417	1 618	237 810	304 164	195 117	25 499	141 335	Compte des transac. cour.
Capital account	...	...	4 630	316	-91	-569	-327	Compte de capital
Financial account	-11 411	-16 205	189 424	91 521	-18 011	-153 806	-57 043	Compte financier
China, Hong Kong SAR								**Chine, RAS de Hong Kong**
Current account	...	...	16 012	10 264	15 621	13 514	22 740	Compte des transac. cour.
Capital account	...	...	-571	-28	-83	-201	-84	Compte de capital
Financial account	...	...	10 867	16 568	9 706	22 139	31 454	Compte financier
China, Macao SAR								**Chine, RAS de Macao**
Current account	...	...	11 089	11 484	16 402	19 060	...	Compte des transac. cour.
Capital account	...	...	19	-8	-45	-13	...	Compte de capital
Financial account	...	...	6 809	5 159	14 474	12 229	...	Compte financier
Colombia								**Colombie**
Current account	-1 809	-4 516	-8 732	-18 564	-10 241	-13 047	-13 800	Compte des transac. cour.
Financial account	-2 082	-4 564	-9 344	-18 241	-9 559	-12 416	-13 103	Compte financier
Comoros								**Comores**
Current account	-14	-19	-39	-2	-23	-28	...	Compte des transac. cour.
Capital account	...	...	71	31	48	32	...	Compte de capital
Financial account	-12	-21	35	31	25	2	...	Compte financier
Congo								**Congo**
Current account	-161	-625	900	-4 629	...	...	...	Compte des transac. cour.
Capital account	...	45	2 667	70	...	...	...	Compte de capital
Financial account	-120	-635	3 314	-4 147	...	...	...	Compte financier
Costa Rica								**Costa Rica**
Current account	-126	-358	-1 214	-1 921	-1 961	-1 999	-1 545	Compte des transac. cour.
Capital account	...	...	54	31	41	31	32	Compte de capital
Financial account	17	-301	-1 642	-2 611	-2 145	-1 909	-1 276	Compte financier
Côte d'Ivoire								**Côte d'Ivoire**
Current account	...	...	465	-201	-1 049	-2 077	...	Compte des transac. cour.
Capital account	...	...	1 179	265	193	152	...	Compte de capital
Financial account	...	...	1 591	11	-778	-2 012	...	Compte financier
Croatia								**Croatie**
Current account	...	-1 442	-1 485	1 595	2 103	1 028	1 456	Compte des transac. cour.
Capital account	...	...	77	370	606	856	1 207	Compte de capital
Financial account	...	-1 102	-862	1 987	2 794	2 112	2 687	Compte financier
Curaçao								**Curaçao**
Current account	...	...	...	-519	-681	-898	...	Compte des transac. cour.
Capital account	...	...	...	~0	~0	4	...	Compte de capital
Financial account	...	...	...	-483	-652	-880	...	Compte financier
Cyprus								**Chypre**
Current account	-180	-205	-2 799	-84	-1 133	-1 067	-1 655	Compte des transac. cour.
Capital account	...	...	72	6	97	151	37	Compte de capital
Financial account	-142	-150	-3 015	379	-194	-579	-1 078	Compte financier
Czechia								**Tchéquie**
Current account	...	-1 374	-7 351	461	3 148	1 190	-866	Compte des transac. cour.
Capital account	...	6	1 953	4 130	1 830	625	610	Compte de capital
Financial account	...	-771	-6 445	7 080	4 795	2 908	1 568	Compte financier

14

Balance of payments summary *(continued)*
Millions of US dollars

Résumé de la balance des paiements *(suite)*
Millions de dollars É.-U.

Country or area[&]	1985	1995	2010	2015	2017	2018	2019	Pays ou zone[&]
Dem. Rep. of the Congo								**Rép. dém. du Congo**
Current account	...	...	-2 174	-1 484	-1 241	-2 169	...	Compte des transac. cour.
Capital account	...	...	10 084	252	465	245	...	Compte de capital
Financial account	...	...	9 059	-1 241	-844	-1 738	...	Compte financier
Denmark								**Danemark**
Current account	-2 767	1 855	21 051	24 953	25 683	24 781	27 581	Compte des transac. cour.
Capital account	...	...	84	-1 057	150	36	177	Compte de capital
Financial account	-3 071	2 929	-1 005	17 814	23 183	12 903	27 976	Compte financier
Djibouti								**Djibouti**
Current account	...	78	50	714	-132	541	...	Compte des transac. cour.
Capital account	...	5	55	48	26	70	...	Compte de capital
Financial account	...	-5	-17	-380	-342	-411	...	Compte financier
Dominica								**Dominique**
Current account	-6	-40	-80	-41	-66	-225	...	Compte des transac. cour.
Capital account	...	22	30	55	462	123	...	Compte de capital
Financial account	-7	-34	-54	24	389	-114	...	Compte financier
Dominican Republic								**République dominicaine**
Current account	-108	-183	-4 024	-1 280	-133	-1 160	-1 205	Compte des transac. cour.
Capital account	...	1	4	2 089	2	2	1	Compte de capital
Financial account	48	-107	-4 983	-737	-1 396	-1 863	-1 364	Compte financier
Ecuador								**Équateur**
Current account	76	-1 000	-1 582	-2 221	-151	-1 335	-79	Compte des transac. cour.
Capital account	...	2 078	105	-49	125	-175	84	Compte de capital
Financial account	244	645	-1 581	-2 232	-407	-1 696	84	Compte financier
Egypt								**Égypte**
Current account	-1 816	-254	-4 504	-17 243	-7 940	-7 698	-10 222	Compte des transac. cour.
Capital account	...	...	-39	-148	-156	-133	-170	Compte de capital
Financial account	-1 231	18	-6 688	-22 162	-15 007	-11 440	-15 034	Compte financier
El Salvador								**El Salvador**
Current account	-29	-262	-533	-754	-465	-1 226	-558	Compte des transac. cour.
Capital account	...	...	232	65	85	203	224	Compte de capital
Financial account	-6	-290	-264	-765	-552	-1 243	-198	Compte financier
Equatorial Guinea								**Guinée équatoriale**
Current account	...	-123	...	...	...	...	...	Compte des transac. cour.
Capital account	...	53	...	...	...	...	...	Compte de capital
Financial account	...	-60	...	...	...	...	...	Compte financier
Eritrea								**Érythrée**
Current account	...	-31	...	...	...	...	...	Compte des transac. cour.
Financial account	...	-72	...	...	...	...	...	Compte financier
Estonia								**Estonie**
Current account	...	-158	340	403	723	612	690	Compte des transac. cour.
Capital account	...	-1	670	470	268	428	298	Compte de capital
Financial account	...	-150	1 033	1 056	928	929	1 042	Compte financier
Eswatini								**Eswatini**
Current account	-38	-30	-388	533	273	61	196	Compte des transac. cour.
Capital account	...	-~0	14	-2	6	-2	-1	Compte de capital
Financial account	-27	49	-318	179	318	2	125	Compte financier
Ethiopia								**Éthiopie**
Current account	106	39	-635	-7 567	-5 929	-4 611	...	Compte des transac. cour.
Capital account	...	11	...	...	...	...	...	Compte de capital
Financial account	-63	-72	-3 262	-7 638	-6 334	-6 755	...	Compte financier
Faroe Islands								**Îles Féroé**
Current account	...	...	144	...	...	...	...	Compte des transac. cour.
Fiji								**Fidji**
Current account	19	-113	-149	-164	-358	-469	-696	Compte des transac. cour.
Capital account	...	116	3	3	4	5	3	Compte de capital
Financial account	-2	5	221	-88	-337	-797	-488	Compte financier
Finland								**Finlande**
Current account	-806	5 231	2 792	-1 683	-1 748	-4 570	-2 060	Compte des transac. cour.
Capital account	...	66	234	174	202	229	197	Compte de capital
Financial account	-849	3 913	4 364	-7 784	-11 088	-14 436	-1 593	Compte financier
France								**France**
Current account	-35	10 840	-22 031	-9 130	-16 470	-19 014	-18 549	Compte des transac. cour.
Capital account	...	442	1 636	-1 110	350	2 441	2 177	Compte de capital
Financial account	256	8 230	774	-1 229	-33 650	-34 336	-62 010	Compte financier

14 Balance of payments summary *(continued)*
Millions of US dollars

Résumé de la balance des paiements *(suite)*
Millions de dollars É.-U.

Country or area[&]	1985	1995	2010	2015	2017	2018	2019	Pays ou zone[&]
French Polynesia								**Polynésie française**
Current account	...	...	-18	291	...	...	...	Compte des transac. cour.
Capital account	...	...	-1	~0	...	...	...	Compte de capital
Financial account	...	...	-119	315	...	...	...	Compte financier
Gabon								**Gabon**
Current account	-162	515	2 453	141	...	...	...	Compte des transac. cour.
Capital account	...	5	1	4	...	...	...	Compte de capital
Financial account	-225	287	1 121	585	...	...	...	Compte financier
Gambia								**Gambie**
Current account	8	-8	17	-99	-111	-79	...	Compte des transac. cour.
Capital account	...	...	38	19	55	33	...	Compte de capital
Financial account	-4	-22	36	-16	-117	-113	...	Compte financier
Georgia								**Géorgie**
Current account	...	...	-1 199	-1 767	-1 308	-1 193	-901	Compte des transac. cour.
Capital account	...	...	198	58	83	76	47	Compte de capital
Financial account	...	...	-1 076	-1 781	-1 235	-1 155	-904	Compte financier
Germany								**Allemagne**
Current account	17 994	-32 191	196 172	288 621	287 218	293 073	274 847	Compte des transac. cour.
Capital account	-741	-3 120	1 615	-19	-3 535	759	-339	Compte de capital
Financial account	20 714	-37 877	123 715	259 482	319 882	281 073	228 555	Compte financier
Ghana								**Ghana**
Current account	-134	-144	-2 747	-2 824	-2 003	-2 044	...	Compte des transac. cour.
Capital account	...	...	338	474	241	258	...	Compte de capital
Financial account	-71	-276	-3 586	-2 732	-1 777	-2 058	...	Compte financier
Greece								**Grèce**
Current account	-3 276	-2 864	-30 263	-1 611	-3 606	-6 249	-2 928	Compte des transac. cour.
Capital account	...	...	2 776	2 193	1 042	419	759	Compte de capital
Financial account	-3 320	-3 185	-28 104	1 624	-1 940	-4 870	-504	Compte financier
Grenada								**Grenade**
Current account	3	-42	-204	-122	-135	-116	...	Compte des transac. cour.
Capital account	...	9	36	32	67	62	...	Compte de capital
Financial account	1	-1	-141	-58	-66	-69	...	Compte financier
Guatemala								**Guatemala**
Current account	-246	-572	-767	-774	804	595	1 854	Compte des transac. cour.
Capital account	...	62	12	2	~0	1	~0	Compte de capital
Financial account	-203	-647	-521	-1 112	406	391	1 170	Compte financier
Guinea								**Guinée**
Current account	...	-216	-327	-1 020	519	-191	...	Compte des transac. cour.
Capital account	...	45	47	231	146	140	...	Compte de capital
Financial account	...	-137	-241	-777	678	-38	...	Compte financier
Guinea-Bissau								**Guinée-Bissau**
Current account	-76	-35	-71	21	4	-54	...	Compte des transac. cour.
Capital account	31	49	980	60	104	42	...	Compte de capital
Financial account	-55	3	907	68	95	-22	...	Compte financier
Guyana								**Guyana**
Current account	-97	-135	-246	-39	-391	-1 072	...	Compte des transac. cour.
Capital account	...	11	65	70	13	13	...	Compte de capital
Financial account	-101	-113	-317	-127	-387	-1 207	...	Compte financier
Haiti								**Haïti**
Current account	-95	-87	-102	-271	-265	-343	...	Compte des transac. cour.
Capital account	...	50	1 474	22	28	34	...	Compte de capital
Financial account	-48	88	1 738	-399	-422	-365	...	Compte financier
Honduras								**Honduras**
Current account	-220	-201	-804	-980	-176	-1 284	-163	Compte des transac. cour.
Capital account	...	17	48	34	45	16	22	Compte de capital
Financial account	-259	-139	-896	-1 086	-775	-1 010	-403	Compte financier
Hungary								**Hongrie**
Current account	-455	-1 712	342	2 926	3 272	139	-1 247	Compte des transac. cour.
Capital account	...	60	2 382	5 686	1 203	3 538	2 923	Compte de capital
Financial account	-530	301	1 353	7 280	1 947	1 187	-644	Compte financier
Iceland								**Islande**
Current account	-115	13	-881	894	929	792	1 404	Compte des transac. cour.
Capital account	...	-4	-11	-11	-13	-16	-15	Compte de capital
Financial account	-168	-33	-680	874	464	1 512	1 704	Compte financier

14

Balance of payments summary *(continued)*
Millions of US dollars

Résumé de la balance des paiements *(suite)*
Millions de dollars É.-U.

Country or area[&]	1985	1995	2010	2015	2017	2018	2019	Pays ou zone[&]
India								**Inde**
Current account	-4 141	-5 563	-54 516	-22 457	-38 168	-65 599	-26 894	Compte des transac. cour.
Capital account	...	...	50	37	37	-123	-1 156	Compte de capital
Financial account	-3 641	-4 593	-55 470	-23 593	-39 559	-64 011	-27 376	Compte financier
Indonesia								**Indonésie**
Current account	-1 923	-6 431	5 144	-17 519	-16 196	-30 633	-30 387	Compte des transac. cour.
Capital account	...	...	50	17	46	97	39	Compte de capital
Financial account	-1 272	-8 686	3 866	-17 941	-17 101	-32 255	-31 976	Compte financier
Iran (Islamic Republic of)								**Iran (Rép. islamique d')**
Current account	-476	3 358	...	...	...	...	...	Compte des transac. cour.
Financial account	11	3 641	...	...	...	...	...	Compte financier
Iraq								**Iraq**
Current account	...	...	6 488	-2 762	14 892	34 370	15 675	Compte des transac. cour.
Capital account	...	...	25	-2	-1	-6	-11	Compte de capital
Financial account	...	...	-2 637	-16 953	6 288	22 145	11 722	Compte financier
Ireland								**Irlande**
Current account	...	...	2 320	31 682	3 398	40 901	-36 374	Compte des transac. cour.
Capital account	...	...	-827	-1 450	-28 537	-60 574	-38 644	Compte de capital
Financial account	...	...	-8 432	36 265	-10 393	-14 131	-73 785	Compte financier
Israel								**Israël**
Current account	988	-4 790	8 091	15 429	8 192	9 277	14 051	Compte des transac. cour.
Capital account	151	285	336	332	341	364	393	Compte de capital
Financial account	22	-3 831	8 475	15 130	10 057	1 675	2 607	Compte financier
Italy								**Italie**
Current account	-4 088	25 096	-70 819	25 379	51 397	51 525	58 933	Compte des transac. cour.
Capital account	222	1 721	106	6 821	1 033	-783	-2 124	Compte de capital
Financial account	-7 735	5 625	-106 235	42 228	54 937	35 379	51 277	Compte financier
Jamaica								**Jamaïque**
Current account	-271	-99	-934	-430	-386	-288	...	Compte des transac. cour.
Capital account	...	21	4	1 466	7	20	...	Compte de capital
Financial account	-285	-81	-785	132	-1 432	-1 350	...	Compte financier
Japan								**Japon**
Current account	...	...	220 888	136 472	203 169	176 098	184 540	Compte des transac. cour.
Capital account	...	...	-4 964	-2 253	-2 499	-1 923	-3 809	Compte de capital
Financial account	...	...	252 662	180 933	167 732	181 853	221 802	Compte financier
Jordan								**Jordanie**
Current account	-260	-259	-1 882	-3 406	-4 301	-2 850	...	Compte des transac. cour.
Capital account	...	...	~0	113	42	34	...	Compte de capital
Financial account	-290	-401	-1 117	-2 617	-3 239	-3 879	...	Compte financier
Kazakhstan								**Kazakhstan**
Current account	...	-213	1 386	-6 012	-5 102	-223	-6 498	Compte des transac. cour.
Capital account	...	...	7 898	132	347	203	127	Compte de capital
Financial account	...	-864	15 338	-10 424	-6 844	1 056	-5 031	Compte financier
Kenya								**Kenya**
Current account	-115	-1 578	-2 369	-4 289	-5 018	...	...	Compte des transac. cour.
Capital account	0	124	240	262	184	...	...	Compte de capital
Financial account	-82	252	-1 987	-4 199	-4 741	...	...	Compte financier
Kiribati								**Kiribati**
Current account	-2	...	~0	56	71	77	...	Compte des transac. cour.
Capital account	7	...	13	33	32	26	...	Compte de capital
Financial account	~0	...	2	84	101	101	...	Compte financier
Kosovo								**Kosovo**
Current account	...	...	-678	-547	-378	-600	-459	Compte des transac. cour.
Capital account	...	...	28	28	-13	-13	-10	Compte de capital
Financial account	...	...	-419	-342	-288	-396	-192	Compte financier
Kuwait								**Koweït**
Current account	4 798	5 016	36 989	8 584	7 757	24 049	...	Compte des transac. cour.
Capital account	...	-194	2 096	-288	-448	-242	...	Compte de capital
Financial account	2 879	-298	46 187	11 542	27 493	26 728	...	Compte financier
Kyrgyzstan								**Kirghizistan**
Current account	...	-235	-475	-1 052	-536	-962	...	Compte des transac. cour.
Capital account	...	2	-11	79	131	335	...	Compte de capital
Financial account	...	-341	-394	-779	-390	-383	...	Compte financier

14 Balance of payments summary *(continued)*
Millions of US dollars

Résumé de la balance des paiements *(suite)*
Millions de dollars É.-U.

Country or area[&]	1985	1995	2010	2015	2017	2018	2019	Pays ou zone[&]
Lao People's Dem. Rep.								**Rép. dém. populaire lao**
Current account	-114	-237	29	-2 268	-1 260	-1 430	...	Compte des transac. cour.
Capital account	...	...	...	36	22	12	...	Compte de capital
Financial account	-75	-131	-374	-2 748	-1 962	-2 349	...	Compte financier
Latvia								**Lettonie**
Current account	...	-16	435	-241	300	-211	-176	Compte des transac. cour.
Capital account	...	...	471	749	195	613	659	Compte de capital
Financial account	...	-669	966	603	441	1 022	507	Compte financier
Lebanon								**Liban**
Current account	...	...	-7 552	-8 542	-12 134	-12 445	...	Compte des transac. cour.
Capital account	...	...	39	1 801	1 648	1 540	...	Compte de capital
Financial account	...	...	-457	-8 722	-8 857	-5 626	...	Compte financier
Lesotho								**Lesotho**
Current account	142	-165	-158	-78	-115	-4	-80	Compte des transac. cour.
Capital account	8	296	108	37	39	37	86	Compte de capital
Financial account	170	254	-18	-217	-61	115	45	Compte financier
Liberia								**Libéria**
Current account	1	...	-853	171	-566	-674	...	Compte des transac. cour.
Capital account	...	...	2 136	100	65	465	...	Compte de capital
Financial account	6	...	-1 488	-463	-676	-272	...	Compte financier
Libya								**Libye**
Current account	1 906	1 672	16 801	-9 346	4 426	11 276	...	Compte des transac. cour.
Financial account	1 578	1 908	14 509	-7 214	3 636	10 053	...	Compte financier
Lithuania								**Lituanie**
Current account	...	-614	72	-1 015	463	818	2 298	Compte des transac. cour.
Capital account	...	-39	1 412	1 237	575	781	928	Compte de capital
Financial account	...	-366	961	814	1 497	1 321	2 271	Compte financier
Luxembourg								**Luxembourg**
Current account	...	...	3 584	2 949	3 336	3 333	3 095	Compte des transac. cour.
Capital account	...	...	-263	-292	-245	930	-128	Compte de capital
Financial account	...	...	3 297	2 675	3 093	4 262	3 008	Compte financier
Madagascar								**Madagascar**
Current account	-184	-276	-917	-281	-65	80	...	Compte des transac. cour.
Capital account	...	40	75	130	234	240	...	Compte de capital
Financial account	-173	-132	-734	-38	170	206	...	Compte financier
Malawi								**Malawi**
Current account	-126	-78	-969	-930	-1 414	-1 427	...	Compte des transac. cour.
Capital account	...	...	710	228	871	733	...	Compte de capital
Financial account	-21	-162	-6	-825	-199	-476	...	Compte financier
Malaysia								**Malaisie**
Current account	-600	-8 644	25 644	9 068	8 960	7 590	...	Compte des transac. cour.
Capital account	...	...	-34	-309	-6	-23	...	Compte de capital
Financial account	-781	-9 405	5 924	70	4 990	-2 685	...	Compte financier
Maldives								**Maldives**
Current account	-6	-18	-196	-302	-1 026	-1 388	...	Compte des transac. cour.
Capital account	...	...	9	10	...	...	...	Compte de capital
Financial account	6	-50	-71	-530	-792	-1 675	...	Compte financier
Mali								**Mali**
Current account	-210	-284	-1 190	-697	-1 210	-836	...	Compte des transac. cour.
Capital account	81	130	252	342	258	239	...	Compte de capital
Financial account	-147	-167	-907	-312	-876	-548	...	Compte financier
Malta								**Malte**
Current account	-26	-380	-420	301	1 350	1 621	1 436	Compte des transac. cour.
Capital account	...	13	171	296	85	133	129	Compte de capital
Financial account	-42	-346	-64	162	1 374	668	491	Compte financier
Marshall Islands								**Îles Marshall**
Current account	...	...	-14	-7	13	53	...	Compte des transac. cour.
Capital account	...	...	19	8	15	11	...	Compte de capital
Financial account	...	...	19	29	58	-42	...	Compte financier
Mauritania								**Mauritanie**
Current account	-116	22	...	-956	-709	-973	...	Compte des transac. cour.
Capital account	...	...	...	31	11	19	...	Compte de capital
Financial account	-122	4	...	-1 058	-753	-817	...	Compte financier
Mauritius								**Maurice**
Current account	-30	-22	-1 006	-417	-612	-816	...	Compte des transac. cour.
Financial account	22	84	-856	-533	-465	-899	...	Compte financier

14 Balance of payments summary *(continued)*
Millions of US dollars

Résumé de la balance des paiements *(suite)*
Millions de dollars É.-U.

Country or area[&]	1985	1995	2010	2015	2017	2018	2019	Pays ou zone[&]
Mexico								**Mexique**
Current account	800	-1 576	-4 872	-31 011	-20 495	-23 004	-2 444	Compte des transac. cour.
Capital account	...	...	-167	-102	150	-65	-56	Compte de capital
Financial account	-2 117	-5 824	-27 651	-36 915	-34 168	-32 997	-11 311	Compte financier
Micronesia (Fed. States of)								**Micronésie (États féd. de)**
Current account	...	...	-25	...	...	...	...	Compte des transac. cour.
Capital account	...	...	64	...	...	...	...	Compte de capital
Financial account	...	...	29	...	...	...	...	Compte financier
Mongolia								**Mongolie**
Current account	-814	39	-885	-948	-1 155	-1 903	-2 162	Compte des transac. cour.
Capital account	...	...	152	116	78	88	161	Compte de capital
Financial account	-730	49	-794	-1 056	-1 133	-1 979	-2 225	Compte financier
Montenegro								**Monténégro**
Current account	...	...	-852	-443	-761	-943	-837	Compte des transac. cour.
Capital account	...	...	-1	~0	~0	...	~0	Compte de capital
Financial account	...	...	-848	-328	-755	-822	-990	Compte financier
Montserrat								**Montserrat**
Current account	...	-2	-19	-1	-6	-1	...	Compte des transac. cour.
Capital account	...	7	13	14	6	2	...	Compte de capital
Financial account	...	-1	-6	4	-11	7	...	Compte financier
Morocco								**Maroc**
Current account	-891	-1 186	-3 925	-2 161	-3 677	-6 205	-4 915	Compte des transac. cour.
Capital account	...	...	...	1	...	...	...	Compte de capital
Financial account	-847	-801	-4 092	-1 484	-2 843	-4 933	-3 472	Compte financier
Mozambique								**Mozambique**
Current account	...	...	-1 679	-5 968	-2 586	-4 501	...	Compte des transac. cour.
Capital account	...	...	357	288	203	164	...	Compte de capital
Financial account	...	...	-1 267	-5 655	-2 318	-4 332	...	Compte financier
Myanmar								**Myanmar**
Current account	-205	-258	1 574	-2 838	-4 504	-2 137	...	Compte des transac. cour.
Capital account	...	...	...	...	1	~0	...	Compte de capital
Financial account	-164	-275	-559	-3 975	-4 784	-1 911	...	Compte financier
Namibia								**Namibie**
Current account	...	176	-389	-1 559	-510	-387	-284	Compte des transac. cour.
Capital account	...	40	187	107	183	131	114	Compte de capital
Financial account	...	229	-490	-1 319	-314	-184	-132	Compte financier
Nauru								**Nauru**
Current account	...	...	24	-17	14	8	...	Compte des transac. cour.
Capital account	...	...	4	3	9	6	...	Compte de capital
Financial account	...	...	27	-24	19	11	...	Compte financier
Nepal								**Népal**
Current account	-122	-356	-128	2 447	-1 033	-2 775	...	Compte des transac. cour.
Capital account	...	...	185	162	149	134	...	Compte de capital
Financial account	-119	-354	-123	2 512	-280	-1 665	...	Compte financier
Netherlands								**Pays-Bas**
Current account	4 248	25 773	61 803	48 501	90 174	99 065	92 805	Compte des transac. cour.
Capital account	-39	-497	-4 122	-3 760	-332	-599	-244	Compte de capital
Financial account	3 144	16 928	51 354	45 413	85 652	104 998	101 295	Compte financier
Netherlands Antilles [former]								**Antilles néerlandaises [anc.]**
Current account	403	128	...	...	...	...	...	Compte des transac. cour.
Capital account	...	63	...	...	...	...	...	Compte de capital
New Caledonia								**Nouvelle-Calédonie**
Current account	...	...	-1 360	-1 119	...	...	...	Compte des transac. cour.
Capital account	...	...	2	3	...	...	...	Compte de capital
Financial account	...	...	-1 279	-1 121	...	...	...	Compte financier
New Zealand								**Nouvelle-Zélande**
Current account	...	...	-3 429	-4 655	-5 561	-7 709	-5 966	Compte des transac. cour.
Capital account	...	...	5 232	227	181	-28	49	Compte de capital
Financial account	...	...	1 626	1 439	-1 342	-1 390	-3 962	Compte financier
Nicaragua								**Nicaragua**
Current account	-771	-722	-780	-1 145	-675	83	...	Compte des transac. cour.
Capital account	45	1 707	264	375	178	111	...	Compte de capital
Financial account	-913	1 127	-351	-1 269	-839	-198	...	Compte financier

14 Balance of payments summary *(continued)*
Millions of US dollars

Résumé de la balance des paiements *(suite)*
Millions de dollars É.-U.

Country or area&	1985	1995	2010	2015	2017	2018	2019	Pays ou zone&
Niger								**Niger**
Current account	-64	-152	-1 137	-1 486	-1 274	-1 625	...	Compte des transac. cour.
Capital account	...	65	196	294	408	624	...	Compte de capital
Financial account	-37	28	-926	-1 208	-876	-1 015	...	Compte financier
Nigeria								**Nigéria**
Current account	2 604	-802	13 111	-15 439	10 399	5 334	...	Compte des transac. cour.
Capital account	...	-14	...	...	...	...	...	Compte de capital
Financial account	2 469	-848	-1 802	5 335	3 998	-907	...	Compte financier
North Macedonia								**Macédoine du Nord**
Current account	...	...	-198	-193	-97	-26	-353	Compte des transac. cour.
Capital account	...	...	4	8	20	13	5	Compte de capital
Financial account	...	...	-193	-187	-89	-3	-272	Compte financier
Norway								**Norvège**
Current account	3 030	5 233	50 258	31 106	18 212	31 138	16 065	Compte des transac. cour.
Capital account	...	-170	-164	-118	-96	-173	-148	Compte de capital
Financial account	1 954	1 116	43 365	9 664	7 834	30 524	10 890	Compte financier
Oman								**Oman**
Current account	-10	-801	4 634	-10 954	-10 981	-4 347	...	Compte des transac. cour.
Capital account	...	...	-65	543	260	279	...	Compte de capital
Financial account	-336	-413	5 926	-10 860	-11 467	-4 814	...	Compte financier
Pakistan								**Pakistan**
Current account	-1 067	-3 349	-1 354	-2 803	-16 180	-18 859	-7 143	Compte des transac. cour.
Capital account	9	...	109	274	436	323	294	Compte de capital
Financial account	-1 027	-3 653	-2 433	-2 881	-16 072	-18 916	-6 519	Compte financier
Palau								**Palaos**
Current account	...	...	-19	-24	-52	...	...	Compte des transac. cour.
Capital account	...	...	30	21	14	...	...	Compte de capital
Financial account	...	...	6	29	-33	...	...	Compte financier
Panama								**Panama**
Current account	75	-471	-3 113	-4 848	-3 692	-5 355	-3 500	Compte des transac. cour.
Capital account	...	9	43	27	25	23	22	Compte de capital
Financial account	-46	-447	-2 803	-6 480	-5 798	-6 359	-5 229	Compte financier
Papua New Guinea								**Papouasie-Nvl-Guinée**
Current account	-122	674	-642	4 407	5 348	5 451	...	Compte des transac. cour.
Capital account	0	...	37	1	9	8	...	Compte de capital
Financial account	-125	587	-1 815	4 920	5 136	4 075	...	Compte financier
Paraguay								**Paraguay**
Current account	-252	-217	49	-145	1 214	-71	-447	Compte des transac. cour.
Capital account	...	11	40	154	166	153	151	Compte de capital
Financial account	-178	-964	-82	198	607	-1 017	-687	Compte financier
Peru								**Pérou**
Current account	102	-4 625	-3 564	-9 526	-2 669	-3 594	...	Compte des transac. cour.
Capital account	32	93	26	6	18	6	...	Compte de capital
Financial account	-1 394	-4 280	-1 850	-10 308	-1 400	-5 144	...	Compte financier
Philippines								**Philippines**
Current account	-36	-1 980	7 179	7 266	-2 143	-8 773	-464	Compte des transac. cour.
Capital account	...	...	88	84	69	65	70	Compte de capital
Financial account	510	-4 074	3 753	4 916	-3 662	-11 638	1 581	Compte financier
Poland								**Pologne**
Current account	-982	854	-25 843	-2 626	100	-5 820	2 776	Compte des transac. cour.
Capital account	...	285	8 611	11 331	6 795	12 148	11 803	Compte de capital
Financial account	-864	575	-31 020	720	-2 754	1 891	9 872	Compte financier
Portugal								**Portugal**
Current account	380	-132	-24 407	471	3 051	917	-236	Compte des transac. cour.
Capital account	...	...	3 314	2 485	1 906	2 388	2 291	Compte de capital
Financial account	127	-3 325	-20 791	2 702	4 891	3 567	2 613	Compte financier
Qatar								**Qatar**
Current account	...	...	...	13 751	6 426	16 652	4 229	Compte des transac. cour.
Capital account	...	...	...	-737	-468	-240	-143	Compte de capital
Financial account	...	...	...	13 433	7 109	15 332	3 269	Compte financier
Republic of Korea								**République de Corée**
Current account	-2 079	-10 230	27 951	105 119	75 231	77 467	59 971	Compte des transac. cour.
Capital account	...	...	-63	-60	-27	317	-64	Compte de capital
Financial account	-3 660	-11 380	21 449	102 465	84 425	76 934	60 950	Compte financier

14 Balance of payments summary *(continued)*
Millions of US dollars

Résumé de la balance des paiements *(suite)*
Millions de dollars É.-U.

Country or area[&]	1985	1995	2010	2015	2017	2018	2019	Pays ou zone[&]
Republic of Moldova								**République de Moldova**
Current account	...	-85	-481	-463	-555	-1 211	-1 159	Compte des transac. cour.
Capital account	...	...	5	55	-21	-36	-52	Compte de capital
Financial account	...	-103	-402	-464	-508	-1 186	-1 206	Compte financier
Romania								**Roumanie**
Current account	1 381	-1 774	-8 478	-1 015	-5 906	-10 503	-11 384	Compte des transac. cour.
Capital account	...	242	259	4 336	2 565	2 928	3 188	Compte de capital
Financial account	1 263	-1 076	-7 548	2 491	-3 485	-6 037	-5 986	Compte financier
Russian Federation								**Fédération de Russie**
Current account	...	7 438	67 452	67 777	32 430	113 733	64 607	Compte des transac. cour.
Capital account	...	786	-41	-309	-192	-1 104	-692	Compte de capital
Financial account	...	-7 560	58 278	70 326	34 800	116 057	61 905	Compte financier
Rwanda								**Rwanda**
Current account	...	...	-427	-1 267	-690	-746	...	Compte des transac. cour.
Capital account	...	...	286	300	190	245	...	Compte de capital
Financial account	...	...	-351	-803	-568	-540	...	Compte financier
Saint Kitts and Nevis								**Saint-Kitts-et-Nevis**
Current account	-7	-45	-139	-80	-110	-72	...	Compte des transac. cour.
Capital account	...	6	56	50	44	64	...	Compte de capital
Financial account	-7	-23	-109	-77	-108	-60	...	Compte financier
Saint Lucia								**Sainte-Lucie**
Current account	-13	-36	-203	38	27	103	...	Compte des transac. cour.
Capital account	...	12	42	14	16	38	...	Compte de capital
Financial account	-11	-25	-136	63	10	84	...	Compte financier
Saint Vincent & Grenadines								**Saint-Vincent-Grenadines**
Current account	4	-40	-208	-116	-95	-99	...	Compte des transac. cour.
Capital account	...	5	52	12	76	9	...	Compte de capital
Financial account	6	-35	-148	-126	-53	-69	...	Compte financier
Samoa								**Samoa**
Current account	2	9	-44	-13	-11	20	...	Compte des transac. cour.
Capital account	...	...	31	44	42	31	...	Compte de capital
Financial account	6	8	-21	26	54	1	...	Compte financier
Sao Tome and Principe								**Sao Tomé-et-Principe**
Current account	-16	...	-88	-69	-73	-75	...	Compte des transac. cour.
Capital account	...	...	42	32	30	30	...	Compte de capital
Financial account	-10	...	-61	-23	-45	-66	...	Compte financier
Saudi Arabia								**Arabie saoudite**
Current account	-12 932	-5 318	66 751	-56 724	10 464	70 606	49 842	Compte des transac. cour.
Capital account	...	...	...	-1 062	-1 848	-2 329	-1 733	Compte de capital
Financial account	-12 931	-5 318	32 598	-72 516	6 917	67 611	46 402	Compte financier
Senegal								**Sénégal**
Current account	-360	-244	-589	-945	-1 526	-2 215	...	Compte des transac. cour.
Capital account	88	209	302	343	385	441	...	Compte de capital
Financial account	-269	-55	-305	-584	-1 102	-1 792	...	Compte financier
Serbia								**Serbie**
Current account	...	...	-2 692	-1 370	-2 323	-2 459	-3 536	Compte des transac. cour.
Capital account	...	...	-1	-19	6	-7	-125	Compte de capital
Financial account	...	...	-2 078	-1 024	-1 865	-2 074	-3 432	Compte financier
Seychelles								**Seychelles**
Current account	-19	1	-214	-256	-295	-283	-278	Compte des transac. cour.
Capital account	...	1	275	37	52	50	48	Compte de capital
Financial account	-17	-26	138	-218	-262	-225	-226	Compte financier
Sierra Leone								**Sierra Leone**
Current account	3	-118	-585	-1 003	-526	-646	...	Compte des transac. cour.
Capital account	...	...	118	127	148	66	...	Compte de capital
Financial account	-6	-97	-445	-421	-313	-342	...	Compte financier
Singapore								**Singapour**
Current account	-4	14 486	54 996	57 574	55 600	64 114	63 139	Compte des transac. cour.
Financial account	639	14 175	59 639	53 463	58 414	61 671	61 288	Compte financier
Sint Maarten (Dutch part)								**St-Martin (partie néerland.)**
Current account	...	...	...	18	47	64	...	Compte des transac. cour.
Capital account	...	...	...	-~0	...	17	...	Compte de capital
Financial account	...	...	...	53	74	161	...	Compte financier

14

Balance of payments summary *(continued)*
Millions of US dollars

Résumé de la balance des paiements *(suite)*
Millions de dollars É.-U.

Country or area&	1985	1995	2010	2015	2017	2018	2019	Pays ou zone&
Slovakia								**Slovaquie**
Current account	...	390	-4 210	-1 849	-1 834	-2 760	-3 019	Compte des transac. cour.
Capital account	...	46	1 392	2 854	113	1 422	1 053	Compte de capital
Financial account	...	580	-3 140	-435	-3 087	-2 277	-1 724	Compte financier
Slovenia								**Slovénie**
Current account	...	-75	-357	1 645	2 988	3 073	3 525	Compte des transac. cour.
Capital account	...	-6	72	455	-360	-263	-188	Compte de capital
Financial account	...	-276	-1 417	1 976	2 332	3 014	2 553	Compte financier
Solomon Islands								**Îles Salomon**
Current account	-28	8	-144	-36	-63	-48	-142	Compte des transac. cour.
Capital account	...	1	50	55	60	60	73	Compte de capital
Financial account	-29	8	-116	20	-12	54	-50	Compte financier
South Africa								**Afrique du Sud**
Current account	2 261	-2 493	-5 492	-14 568	-8 913	-13 384	-10 667	Compte des transac. cour.
Capital account	...	...	31	19	18	18	17	Compte de capital
Financial account	1 350	-3 385	-7 508	-16 253	-8 198	-10 995	-8 151	Compte financier
South Sudan								**Soudan du sud**
Current account	...	...	...	-500	282	-316	...	Compte des transac. cour.
Capital account	...	...	...	75	117	153	...	Compte de capital
Financial account	...	...	...	-321	-71	559	...	Compte financier
Spain								**Espagne**
Current account	2 785	-1 967	-52 250	24 108	35 611	27 307	27 724	Compte des transac. cour.
Capital account	...	5 861	5 338	7 698	3 261	6 681	4 545	Compte de capital
Financial account	942	261	-42 448	31 545	37 925	36 318	37 745	Compte financier
Sri Lanka								**Sri Lanka**
Current account	-418	-770	-1 075	-1 883	-2 309	-2 814	...	Compte des transac. cour.
Capital account	...	116	150	46	11	14	...	Compte de capital
Financial account	-461	-491	-1 778	-2 312	-2 123	-3 328	...	Compte financier
State of Palestine								**État de Palestine**
Current account	...	-984	-1 307	-2 066	-1 564	-1 659	...	Compte des transac. cour.
Capital account	...	262	828	491	397	389	...	Compte de capital
Financial account	...	-557	-201	-1 960	-998	-1 414	...	Compte financier
Sudan								**Soudan**
Current account	154	-500	-1 725	-5 461	-4 611	-4 679	...	Compte des transac. cour.
Capital account	...	...	378	250	152	163	...	Compte de capital
Financial account	5	-481	-1 633	-5 118	-3 401	-2 981	...	Compte financier
Suriname								**Suriname**
Current account	...	...	651	-786	61	-118	-411	Compte des transac. cour.
Capital account	...	...	54	1	...	-~0	-3	Compte de capital
Financial account	...	...	537	-1 036	-91	-150	-730	Compte financier
Sweden								**Suède**
Current account	-1 010	4 940	29 196	20 695	16 685	9 665	20 783	Compte des transac. cour.
Capital account	...	...	-681	-981	-376	-15	-133	Compte de capital
Financial account	-1 758	3 388	34 610	7 342	22 000	7 107	18 025	Compte financier
Switzerland								**Suisse**
Current account	6 039	20 703	85 822	76 602	43 629	57 857	86 167	Compte des transac. cour.
Capital account	...	-462	-4 437	-30 265	1 155	5 265	-8 539	Compte de capital
Financial account	8 500	11 260	104 973	44 057	35 430	72 550	36 568	Compte financier
Syrian Arab Republic								**République arabe syrienne**
Current account	-958	263	-367	...	...	...	...	Compte des transac. cour.
Capital account	...	20	50	...	...	...	...	Compte de capital
Financial account	-974	318	824	...	...	...	...	Compte financier
Tajikistan								**Tadjikistan**
Current account	...	...	-581	-477	159	-380	-185	Compte des transac. cour.
Capital account	...	...	69	144	135	176	166	Compte de capital
Financial account	...	...	-245	-485	151	-469	-185	Compte financier
Thailand								**Thaïlande**
Current account	-1 537	-13 582	11 486	27 753	43 952	28 457	37 911	Compte des transac. cour.
Capital account	...	...	245	~0	-141	-611	4	Compte de capital
Financial account	-1 434	-14 778	7 751	22 658	38 454	22 212	26 509	Compte financier
Timor-Leste								**Timor-Leste**
Current account	...	...	1 671	225	-339	-191	134	Compte des transac. cour.
Capital account	...	...	31	29	34	52	26	Compte de capital
Financial account	...	...	1 703	191	-212	-107	65	Compte financier

Balance of payments summary *(continued)*
Millions of US dollars

Résumé de la balance des paiements *(suite)*
Millions de dollars É.-U.

Country or area&	1985	1995	2010	2015	2017	2018	2019	Pays ou zone&
Togo								**Togo**
Current account	-27	-122	-200	-461	-97	-185	...	Compte des transac. cour.
Capital account	...	3	1 389	270	244	316	...	Compte de capital
Financial account	-28	-139	1 192	-182	166	123	...	Compte financier
Tonga								**Tonga**
Current account	-2	...	-87	-44	-29	-27	-8	Compte des transac. cour.
Capital account	...	...	72	23	54	49	36	Compte de capital
Financial account	-1	...	120	3	28	-6	16	Compte financier
Trinidad and Tobago								**Trinité-et-Tobago**
Current account	-48	294	4 172	1 744	1 208	1 386	...	Compte des transac. cour.
Capital account	...	...	...	...	1	2	...	Compte de capital
Financial account	-322	298	4 199	-1 069	-660	-937	...	Compte financier
Tunisia								**Tunisie**
Current account	-581	-774	-2 104	-3 850	-4 080	-4 429	...	Compte des transac. cour.
Capital account	...	47	82	225	184	128	...	Compte de capital
Financial account	-607	-861	-1 927	-3 619	-3 511	-3 736	...	Compte financier
Turkey								**Turquie**
Current account	-1 013	-2 338	-44 620	-27 314	-40 584	-20 745	8 691	Compte des transac. cour.
Capital account	...	...	-51	-21	15	62	34	Compte de capital
Financial account	-1 849	17	-45 128	-21 211	-46 837	-10 903	557	Compte financier
Turks and Caicos Islands								**Îles Turques-et-Caïques**
Current account	...	...	...	154	35	173	...	Compte des transac. cour.
Capital account	...	...	...	...	17	...	...	Compte de capital
Financial account	...	...	...	440	30	107	...	Compte financier
Tuvalu								**Tuvalu**
Current account	...	...	-14	...	...	...	...	Compte des transac. cour.
Capital account	...	...	9	...	...	...	...	Compte de capital
Financial account	...	...	-~0	...	...	...	...	Compte financier
Uganda								**Ouganda**
Current account	5	-281	-1 610	-1 671	-1 488	-2 302	-2 333	Compte des transac. cour.
Capital account	...	48	...	108	122	95	87	Compte de capital
Financial account	-48	-204	-1 113	-1 267	-876	-1 956	-1 625	Compte financier
Ukraine								**Ukraine**
Current account	...	-1 152	-3 016	1 616	-2 442	-4 367	-1 322	Compte des transac. cour.
Capital account	...	6	188	456	-4	37	38	Compte de capital
Financial account	...	-1 098	-1 463	1 677	-1 969	-2 622	-39	Compte financier
United Kingdom								**Royaume-Uni**
Current account	3 314	-13 436	-78 779	-143 589	-93 031	-110 231	-106 886	Compte des transac. cour.
Capital account	...	486	-1 130	-3 022	-2 036	-3 321	-1 015	Compte de capital
Financial account	4 358	-4 522	-104 495	-159 089	-104 181	-110 817	-130 116	Compte financier
United Rep. of Tanzania								**Rép.-Unie de Tanzanie**
Current account	-375	-590	-2 211	-3 978	-1 814	-1 890	...	Compte des transac. cour.
Capital account	...	191	538	380	377	221	...	Compte de capital
Financial account	-415	-369	-2 712	-2 894	-508	-2 514	...	Compte financier
United States of America								**États-Unis d'Amérique**
Current account	-124 455	-113 561	-431 271	-407 769	-439 642	-490 991	-498 350	Compte des transac. cour.
Capital account	...	-222	-158	-43	18 950	3 235	-10	Compte de capital
Financial account	-104 677	-82 815	-446 430	-325 959	-357 589	-445 455	-395 910	Compte financier
Uruguay								**Uruguay**
Current account	-98	-213	-731	-491	420	54	419	Compte des transac. cour.
Capital account	...	...	...	175	5	44	52	Compte de capital
Financial account	141	-194	-1 418	-739	1 586	-143	854	Compte financier
Uzbekistan								**Ouzbékistan**
Current account	...	...	...	1 071	1 476	-3 594	-3 246	Compte des transac. cour.
Capital account	...	...	...	...	100	143	254	Compte de capital
Financial account	...	...	...	-919	-827	-2 975	-6 451	Compte financier
Vanuatu								**Vanuatu**
Current account	-10	-18	-42	-4	-56	85	...	Compte des transac. cour.
Capital account	10	31	21	83	49	40	...	Compte de capital
Financial account	-5	-20	-149	198	217	526	...	Compte financier
Venezuela (Boliv. Rep. of)								**Venezuela (Rép. boliv. du)**
Current account	3 327	2 014	5 585	-16 051	...	...	...	Compte des transac. cour.
Capital account	...	...	-211	-3 980	...	...	...	Compte de capital
Financial account	2 328	1 520	1 644	-22 296	...	...	...	Compte financier

14   Balance of payments summary *(continued)*
Millions of US dollars

Résumé de la balance des paiements *(suite)*
Millions de dollars É.-U.

Country or area[&]	1985	1995	2010	2015	2017	2018	2019	Pays ou zone[&]
Viet Nam								**Viet Nam**
Current account	...	...	-4 276	-2 041	-1 649	5 899	...	Compte des transac. cour.
Financial account	...	...	-7 966	-6 999	-7 483	-2 431	...	Compte financier
Yemen								**Yémen**
Current account	...	...	-1 054	-3 026	...	...	...	Compte des transac. cour.
Capital account	...	...	88	...	...	...	...	Compte de capital
Financial account	...	...	-900	-2 365	...	...	...	Compte financier
Zambia								**Zambie**
Current account	-395	...	1 525	-768	-435	-342	242	Compte des transac. cour.
Capital account	...	...	150	81	58	66	97	Compte de capital
Financial account	-544	...	1 646	-724	-354	-252	364	Compte financier
Zimbabwe								**Zimbabwe**
Current account	-64	...	-1 444	-1 678	-308	...	...	Compte des transac. cour.
Capital account	0	0	231	398	278	0	0	Compte de capital
Financial account	-38	...	-411	-1 642	-384	...	...	Compte financier
Euro Area								**Zone euro**
Current account	...	...	-41 234	322 471	399 750	425 196	357 792	Compte des transac. cour.
Capital account	...	...	14 579	20 361	-22 309	-39 332	-22 359	Compte de capital
Financial account	...	...	-24 180	309 129	390 935	441 416	314 940	Compte financier

Source:

International Monetary Fund (IMF), Washington, D.C., Balance of
Payment (BOP) Statistics database, last accessed June 2020.

Source:

Fonds monétaire international (FMI), Washington, D.C., base de données
des statistiques Balance des Paiements (BDP), dernier accès juin 2020.

[&] Financial account includes reserves and related items.

[&] Compte financier inclut les réserves et les éléments connexes.

1   For statistical purposes, the data for China do not include those for
the Hong Kong Special Administrative Region (Hong Kong SAR),
Macao Special Administrative Region (Macao SAR) and Taiwan
Province of China.

1   Pour la présentation des statistiques, les données pour la Chine ne
comprennent pas la région administrative spéciale de Hong Kong
(RAS de Hong Kong), la région administrative spéciale de Macao
(RAS de Macao) et la province chinoise de Taïwan.

Country or area	National currency Monnaie nationale	1995	2005	2010	2015	2016	2017	2018	2019	Pays ou zone
Afghanistan										**Afghanistan**
End of period	Afghani (AFN)	47.5	50.4	45.3	68.1	66.8	69.5	75.0	78.4	Fin de période
Period average		36.6	49.5	46.5	61.1	67.9	68.0	72.1	77.7	Moy. sur période
Åland Islands										**Îles d'Åland**
End of period	Euro (EUR)	...	0.8	0.7	0.9	0.9	0.8	0.9	0.9	Fin de période
Period average		...	0.8	0.8	0.9	0.9	0.9	0.8	0.9	Moy. sur période
Albania										**Albanie**
End of period	Lek (ALL)	94.2	103.6	104.0	125.8	128.2	111.1	107.8	108.6	Fin de période
Period average		92.7	99.9	103.9	126.0	124.1	119.1	108.0	109.9	Moy. sur période
Algeria										**Algérie**
End of period	Algerian Dinar (DZD),	52.2	73.4	74.9	107.1	110.5	114.9	118.3	119.2	Fin de période
Period average	dinar algérien (DZD)	47.7	73.3	74.4	100.7	109.4	111.0	116.6	119.4	Moy. sur période
Andorra										**Andorre**
End of period	Euro (EUR)	...	0.8	0.7	0.9	0.9	0.8	0.9	0.9	Fin de période
Period average		...	0.8	0.8	0.9	0.9	0.9	0.8	0.9	Moy. sur période
Angola										**Angola**
End of period	Kwanza (AOA)	~0.0	80.8	92.6	135.3	165.9	165.9	308.6	482.2	Fin de période
Period average		~0.0	87.2	91.9	120.1	163.7	165.9	252.9	364.8	Moy. sur période
Anguilla										**Anguilla**
End of period	E. Caribbean Dollar (XCD),	2.7	2.7	2.7	2.7	2.7	2.7	2.7	2.7	Fin de période
Period average	dollar des Caraïb. (XCD) [1]	2.7	2.7	2.7	2.7	2.7	2.7	2.7	2.7	Moy. sur période
Antigua and Barbuda										**Antigua-et-Barbuda**
End of period	E. Caribbean Dollar (XCD),	2.7	2.7	2.7	2.7	2.7	2.7	2.7	2.7	Fin de période
Period average	dollar des Caraïb. (XCD) [1]	2.7	2.7	2.7	2.7	2.7	2.7	2.7	2.7	Moy. sur période
Argentina										**Argentine**
End of period	Argentine Peso (ARS),	1.0	3.0	4.0	13.1	15.9	18.6	37.6	59.8	Fin de période
Period average	peso argentin (ARS)	1.0	2.9	3.9	9.2	14.8	16.6	28.1	48.1	Moy. sur période
Armenia										**Arménie**
End of period	Armenian Dram (AMD),	402.0	450.2	363.4	483.8	483.9	484.1	483.8	479.7	Fin de période
Period average	dram arménien (AMD)	405.9	457.7	373.7	477.9	480.5	482.7	483.0	480.4	Moy. sur période
Aruba										**Aruba**
End of period	Aruban Florin (AWG),	1.8	1.8	1.8	1.8	1.8	1.8	1.8	1.8	Fin de période
Period average	florin de Aruba (AWG)	1.8	1.8	1.8	1.8	1.8	1.8	1.8	1.8	Moy. sur période
Australia										**Australie**
End of period	Australian Dollar (AUD),	1.3	1.4	1.0	1.4	1.4	1.3	1.4	1.4	Fin de période
Period average	dollar australien (AUD)	1.3	1.3	1.1	1.3	1.3	1.3	1.3	1.4	Moy. sur période
Austria										**Autriche**
End of period	Euro (EUR)	...	0.8	0.7	0.9	0.9	0.8	0.9	0.9	Fin de période
Period average		...	0.8	0.8	0.9	0.9	0.9	0.8	0.9	Moy. sur période
Azerbaijan										**Azerbaïdjan**
End of period	Azerbaijan manat (AZN),	0.9	0.9	0.8	1.6	1.8	1.7	1.7	1.7	Fin de période
Period average	manat azerbaïdjanais (AZN)	0.9	0.9	0.8	1.0	1.6	1.7	1.7	1.7	Moy. sur période
Bahamas										**Bahamas**
End of period	Bahamian Dollar (BSD),	1.0	1.0	1.0	1.0	1.0	1.0	1.0	1.0	Fin de période
Period average	dollar des Bahamas (BSD)	1.0	1.0	1.0	1.0	1.0	1.0	1.0	1.0	Moy. sur période
Bahrain										**Bahreïn**
End of period	Bahraini Dinar (BHD),	0.4	0.4	0.4	0.4	0.4	0.4	0.4	0.4	Fin de période
Period average	dinar de Bahreïn (BHD)	0.4	0.4	0.4	0.4	0.4	0.4	0.4	0.4	Moy. sur période
Bangladesh										**Bangladesh**
End of period	Taka (BDT)	40.8	66.2	70.7	78.5	78.7	82.7	83.9	84.9	Fin de période
Period average		40.3	64.3	69.6	77.9	78.5	80.4	83.5	84.5	Moy. sur période
Barbados										**Barbade**
End of period	Barbados Dollar (BBD),	2.0	2.0	2.0	2.0	2.0	2.0	2.0	2.0	Fin de période
Period average	dollar de la Barbade (BBD)	2.0	2.0	2.0	2.0	2.0	2.0	2.0	2.0	Moy. sur période
Belarus										**Bélarus**
End of period	Belarusian Ruble (BYN),	0.0	0.2	0.3	1.9	2.0	2.0	2.2	2.1	Fin de période
Period average	rouble bélarussien (BYN)	~0.0	0.2	0.3	1.6	2.0	1.9	2.0	2.1	Moy. sur période
Belgium										**Belgique**
End of period	Euro (EUR)	...	0.8	0.7	0.9	0.9	0.8	0.9	0.9	Fin de période
Period average		...	0.8	0.8	0.9	0.9	0.9	0.8	0.9	Moy. sur période
Belize										**Belize**
End of period	Belize Dollar (BZD),	2.0	2.0	2.0	2.0	2.0	2.0	2.0	2.0	Fin de période
Period average	dollar du Belize (BZD)	2.0	2.0	2.0	2.0	2.0	2.0	2.0	2.0	Moy. sur période

Country or area	National currency Monnaie nationale	1995	2005	2010	2015	2016	2017	2018	2019	Pays ou zone
Benin										**Bénin**
End of period	CFA Franc, BCEAO (XOF),	490.0	556.0	490.9	602.5	622.3	546.9	572.9	583.9	Fin de période
Period average	franc CFA, BCEAO (XOF) [2]	499.1	527.3	494.8	591.2	592.6	580.7	555.4	586.0	Moy. sur période
Bermuda										**Bermudes**
End of period	Bermudian Dollar (BMD),	1.0	1.0	1.0	1.0	1.0	1.0	1.0	1.0	Fin de période
Period average	dollar des Bermudes (BMD)	1.0	1.0	1.0	1.0	1.0	1.0	1.0	1.0	Moy. sur période
Bhutan										**Bhoutan**
End of period	Ngultrum (BTN)	35.2	45.1	44.8	66.3	68.0	63.9	69.8	71.3	Fin de période
Period average		32.4	44.1	45.7	64.2	67.2	65.1	68.4	70.4	Moy. sur période
Bolivia (Plurin. State of)										**Bolivie (État plurin. de)**
End of period	Boliviano (BOB)	4.9	8.0	7.0	6.9	6.9	6.9	6.9	6.9	Fin de période
Period average		4.8	8.1	7.0	6.9	6.9	6.9	6.9	6.9	Moy. sur période
Bosnia and Herzegovina										**Bosnie-Herzégovine**
End of period	Convertible Mark (BAM),	...	1.7	1.5	1.8	1.9	1.6	1.7	1.7	Fin de période
Period average	marka convertible (BAM)	...	1.6	1.5	1.8	1.8	1.7	1.7	1.7	Moy. sur période
Botswana										**Botswana**
End of period	Pula (BWP)	2.8	5.5	6.4	11.2	10.6	9.9	10.7	10.6	Fin de période
Period average		2.8	5.1	6.8	10.1	10.9	10.3	10.2	10.8	Moy. sur période
Bouvet Island										**Île Bouvet**
End of period	Norwegian Krone (NOK),	6.3	6.8	5.9	8.8	8.6	8.2	8.7	8.8	Fin de période
Period average	couronne norvégienne (NOK)	6.3	6.4	6.0	8.1	8.4	8.3	8.1	8.8	Moy. sur période
Brazil										**Brésil**
End of period	Brazilian Real (BRL),	1.0	2.3	1.7	3.9	3.3	3.3	3.9	4.0	Fin de période
Period average	real brésilien (BRL)	0.9	2.4	1.8	3.3	3.5	3.2	3.7	3.9	Moy. sur période
Brunei Darussalam										**Brunéi Darussalam**
End of period	Brunei Dollar (BND),	1.4	1.7	1.3	1.4	1.4	1.3	1.4	1.3	Fin de période
Period average	dollar du Brunéi (BND)	1.4	1.7	1.4	1.4	1.4	1.4	1.3	1.4	Moy. sur période
Bulgaria										**Bulgarie**
End of period	Bulgarian Lev (BGN),	0.1	1.7	1.5	1.8	1.9	1.6	1.7	1.7	Fin de période
Period average	lev bulgare (BGN)	0.1	1.6	1.5	1.8	1.8	1.7	1.7	1.7	Moy. sur période
Burkina Faso										**Burkina Faso**
End of period	CFA Franc, BCEAO (XOF),	490.0	556.0	490.9	602.5	622.3	546.9	572.9	583.9	Fin de période
Period average	franc CFA, BCEAO (XOF) [2]	499.1	527.3	494.8	591.2	592.6	580.7	555.4	585.9	Moy. sur période
Burundi										**Burundi**
End of period	Burundi Franc (BIF),	277.9	997.8	1 232.5	1 617.1	1 688.6	1 766.7	1 808.3	1 881.6	Fin de période
Period average	franc burundais (BIF)	249.8	1 081.6	1 230.7	1 571.9	1 654.6	1 729.1	1 782.9	1 845.6	Moy. sur période
Cabo Verde										**Cabo Verde**
End of period	Cabo Verde Escudo (CVE),	77.5	93.2	83.0	100.9	105.5	92.4	96.3	98.5	Fin de période
Period average	escudo du Cabo Verde (CVE)	76.9	88.6	83.3	99.4	99.7	97.8	93.4	98.5	Moy. sur période
Cambodia										**Cambodge**
End of period	Riel (KHR)	2 526.0	4 112.0	4 051.0	4 051.5	4 044.5	4 041.5	4 033.0	4 084.0	Fin de période
Period average		2 450.8	4 092.5	4 184.9	4 067.8	4 058.7	4 050.6	4 051.2	4 061.1	Moy. sur période
Cameroon										**Cameroun**
End of period	CFA Franc, BEAC (XAF),	490.0	556.0	490.9	602.5	622.3	546.9	572.9	583.9	Fin de période
Period average	franc CFA, BEAC (XAF) [3]	499.1	527.3	494.8	591.2	592.6	580.7	555.4	585.9	Moy. sur période
Canada										**Canada**
End of period	Canadian Dollar (CAD),	1.4	1.2	1.0	1.4	1.3	1.3	1.4	1.3	Fin de période
Period average	dollar canadien (CAD)	1.4	1.2	1.0	1.3	1.3	1.3	1.3	1.3	Moy. sur période
Cayman Islands										**Îles Caïmanes**
End of period	Cayman Islands Dollar (KYD),	0.8	0.8	0.8	0.8	0.8	0.8	0.8	0.8	Fin de période
Period average	dollar des Îles Caïmanes (KYD)	0.8	0.8	0.8	0.8	0.8	0.8	0.8	0.8	Moy. sur période
Central African Republic										**République centrafricaine**
End of period	CFA Franc, BEAC (XAF),	490.0	556.0	490.9	602.5	622.3	546.9	572.9	583.9	Fin de période
Period average	franc CFA, BEAC (XAF) [3]	499.1	527.3	494.8	591.2	592.6	580.7	555.4	585.9	Moy. sur période
Chad										**Tchad**
End of period	CFA Franc, BEAC (XAF),	490.0	556.0	490.9	602.5	622.3	546.9	572.9	583.9	Fin de période
Period average	franc CFA, BEAC (XAF) [3]	499.1	527.3	494.8	591.2	592.6	580.7	555.4	585.9	Moy. sur période
Channel Islands										**Îles Anglo-Normandes**
End of period	Pound Sterling (GBP),	0.6	0.6	0.6	0.7	0.8	0.7	0.8	0.8	Fin de période
Period average	livre sterling (GBP)	0.6	0.6	0.6	0.7	0.7	0.8	0.7	0.8	Moy. sur période
Chile										**Chili**
End of period	Chilean Peso (CLP),	407.1	514.2	468.4	707.3	667.3	615.2	695.7	744.6	Fin de période
Period average	peso chilien (CLP)	396.8	559.8	510.2	654.1	677.0	648.8	641.3	702.9	Moy. sur période

Country or area	National currency Monnaie nationale	1995	2005	2010	2015	2016	2017	2018	2019	Pays ou zone
China [4]										**Chine** [4]
End of period	Yuan Renminbi (CNY),	8.3	8.1	6.6	6.5	6.9	6.5	6.9	7.0	Fin de période
Period average	yuan (CNY)	8.4	8.2	6.8	6.2	6.6	6.8	6.6	6.9	Moy. sur période
China, Hong Kong SAR										**Chine, RAS de Hong Kong**
End of period	Hong Kong Dollar (HKD),	7.7	7.8	7.8	7.8	7.8	7.8	7.8	7.8	Fin de période
Period average	dollar de Hong Kong (HKD)	7.7	7.8	7.8	7.8	7.8	7.8	7.8	7.8	Moy. sur période
China, Macao SAR										**Chine, RAS de Macao**
End of period	Pataca (MOP)	8.0	8.0	8.0	8.0	8.0	8.1	8.1	8.0	Fin de période
Period average		8.0	8.0	8.0	8.0	8.0	8.0	8.1	8.1	Moy. sur période
Christmas Island										**Île Christmas**
End of period	Australian dollar (AUD),	1.3	1.4	1.0	1.4	1.4	1.3	1.4	1.4	Fin de période
Period average	dollar australien (AUD)	1.3	1.3	1.1	1.3	1.3	1.3	1.3	1.4	Moy. sur période
Cocos (Keeling) Islands										**Îles des Cocos (Keeling)**
End of period	Australian dollar (AUD),	1.3	1.4	1.0	1.4	1.4	1.3	1.4	1.4	Fin de période
Period average	dollar australien (AUD)	1.3	1.3	1.1	1.3	1.3	1.3	1.3	1.4	Moy. sur période
Colombia										**Colombie**
End of period	Colombian Peso (COP),	987.7	2 284.2	1 989.9	3 149.5	3 000.7	2 971.6	3 275.0	3 294.1	Fin de période
Period average	peso colombien (COP)	912.8	2 320.8	1 898.6	2 741.9	3 054.1	2 951.3	2 955.7	3 280.8	Moy. sur période
Comoros										**Comores**
End of period	Comorian Franc (KMF),	367.5	417.0	368.2	451.9	466.7	410.2	429.7	437.9	Fin de période
Period average	franc comorien (KMF)	374.4	395.4	371.1	443.4	444.5	435.5	416.6	439.5	Moy. sur période
Congo										**Congo**
End of period	CFA Franc, BEAC (XAF),	490.0	556.0	490.9	602.5	622.3	546.9	572.9	583.9	Fin de période
Period average	franc CFA, BEAC (XAF) [3]	499.1	527.3	494.8	591.2	592.6	580.7	555.4	585.9	Moy. sur période
Cook Islands										**Îles Cook**
End of period	New Zealand Dollar (NZD),	1.5	1.5	1.3	1.5	1.4	1.4	1.5	1.5	Fin de période
Period average	dollar néo-zélandais (NZD)	1.5	1.4	1.4	1.4	1.4	1.4	1.4	1.5	Moy. sur période
Costa Rica										**Costa Rica**
End of period	Costa Rican Colon (CRC),	194.9	496.7	513.0	538.4	554.6	569.5	608.1	573.3	Fin de période
Period average	colon costaricien (CRC)	179.7	477.8	525.8	534.6	544.7	567.5	577.0	587.3	Moy. sur période
Côte d'Ivoire										**Côte d'Ivoire**
End of period	CFA Franc, BCEAO (XOF),	490.0	556.0	490.9	602.5	622.3	546.9	572.9	583.9	Fin de période
Period average	franc CFA, BCEAO (XOF) [2]	499.1	527.3	494.8	591.2	592.6	580.7	555.4	585.9	Moy. sur période
Croatia										**Croatie**
End of period	Kuna (HRK)	5.3	6.2	5.6	7.0	7.2	6.3	6.5	6.6	Fin de période
Period average		5.2	5.9	5.5	6.9	6.8	6.6	6.3	6.6	Moy. sur période
Cuba [5]										**Cuba** [5]
End of period	Cuban Peso (CUP), peso cubain (CUP) [6]	...	...	...	1.0	1.0	1.0	1.0	1.0	Fin de période
Curaçao										**Curaçao**
End of period	Neth. Ant. Guilder (ANG),	...	...	1.8	1.8	1.8	1.8	1.8	1.8	Fin de période
Period average	florin des Ant. néer. (ANG) [7]	...	...	...	1.8	1.8	1.8	1.8	1.8	Moy. sur période
Cyprus										**Chypre**
End of period	Euro (EUR)	...	0.8	0.7	0.9	0.9	0.8	0.9	0.9	Fin de période
Period average		...	0.8	0.8	0.9	0.9	0.9	0.8	0.9	Moy. sur période
Czechia										**Tchéquie**
End of period	Czech Koruna (CZK),	26.6	24.6	18.8	24.8	25.6	21.3	22.5	22.6	Fin de période
Period average	couronne tchèque (CZK)	26.5	24.0	19.1	24.6	24.4	23.4	21.7	22.9	Moy. sur période
Dem. People's Rep. Korea [5]										**Rép. pop. dém. de Corée** [5]
End of period	North Korean Won (KPW), won nord-coréen (KPW)	...	...	...	109.0	110.9	105.0	106.8	107.7	Fin de période
Dem. Rep. of the Congo										**Rép. dém. du Congo**
End of period	Congolese Franc (CDF),	0.1	431.3	915.1	926.8	1 215.6	1 592.2	1 635.6	1 672.9	Fin de période
Period average	franc congolais (CDF)	0.1	473.9	905.9	926.0	1 010.3	1 464.4	1 622.5	1 647.8	Moy. sur période
Denmark										**Danemark**
End of period	Danish Krone (DKK),	5.5	6.3	5.6	6.8	7.1	6.2	6.5	6.7	Fin de période
Period average	couronne danoise (DKK)	5.6	6.0	5.6	6.7	6.7	6.6	6.3	6.7	Moy. sur période
Djibouti										**Djibouti**
End of period	Djibouti Franc (DJF),	177.7	177.7	177.7	177.7	177.7	177.7	177.7	177.7	Fin de période
Period average	franc Djibouti (DJF)	177.7	177.7	177.7	177.7	177.7	177.7	177.7	177.7	Moy. sur période
Dominica										**Dominique**
End of period	E. Caribbean Dollar (XCD),	2.7	2.7	2.7	2.7	2.7	2.7	2.7	2.7	Fin de période
Period average	dollar des Caraïb. (XCD) [1]	2.7	2.7	2.7	2.7	2.7	2.7	2.7	2.7	Moy. sur période

Country or area	National currency Monnaie nationale	1995	2005	2010	2015	2016	2017	2018	2019	Pays ou zone
Dominican Republic										**République dominicaine**
End of period	Dominican Peso (DOP),	12.9	34.5	37.5	45.6	46.7	48.3	50.3	53.0	Fin de période
Period average	peso dominicain (DOP)	12.9	30.3	36.8	45.0	46.1	47.5	49.5	51.3	Moy. sur période
Ecuador										**Équateur**
End of period	US Dollar (USD),	...	1.0	1.0	1.0	1.0	1.0	1.0	1.0	Fin de période
Period average	dollar des É.-U. (USD)	...	1.0	1.0	1.0	1.0	1.0	1.0	1.0	Moy. sur période
Egypt										**Égypte**
End of period	Egyptian Pound (EGP),	3.4	5.7	5.8	7.8	18.1	17.7	17.9	16.0	Fin de période
Period average	livre égyptienne (EGP)	3.4	5.8	5.6	7.7	10.0	17.8	17.8	16.8	Moy. sur période
El Salvador										**El Salvador**
End of period	US Dollar (USD),	...	1.0	1.0	1.0	1.0	1.0	1.0	1.0	Fin de période
Period average	dollar des É.-U. (USD)	...	1.0	1.0	1.0	1.0	1.0	1.0	1.0	Moy. sur période
Equatorial Guinea										**Guinée équatoriale**
End of period	CFA Franc, BEAC (XAF),	490.0	556.0	490.9	602.5	622.3	546.9	572.9	583.9	Fin de période
Period average	franc CFA, BEAC (XAF) [3]	499.1	527.3	494.8	591.2	592.6	580.7	555.4	585.9	Moy. sur période
Eritrea										**Érythrée**
End of period	Nakfa (ERN)	6.3	15.4	15.4	15.4	15.1	15.1	15.1	15.1	Fin de période
		6.2	15.4	15.4	15.4	15.4	15.1	15.1	15.1	Moy. sur période
Estonia										**Estonie**
End of period	Euro (EUR)	...	...	...	0.9	0.9	0.8	0.9	0.9	Fin de période
Period average		...	...	...	0.9	0.9	0.9	0.8	0.9	Moy. sur période
Eswatini										**Eswatini**
End of period	Lilangeni (SZL)	3.6	6.3	6.6	15.5	13.7	12.3	14.4	14.1	Fin de période
Period average		3.6	6.4	7.3	12.8	14.7	13.3	13.2	14.5	Moy. sur période
Ethiopia										**Éthiopie**
End of period	Ethiopian Birr (ETB),	6.3	8.7	16.6	21.1	22.4	27.2	28.0	31.8	Fin de période
Period average	birr éthiopien (ETB)	6.2	8.7	14.4	20.6	21.7	23.9	27.4	29.1	Moy. sur période
Falkland Islands (Malvinas)										**Îles Falkland (Malvinas)**
End of period	Falkland Islands Pound (FKP),	0.6	0.6	0.6	0.7	0.8	0.7	0.8	0.8	Fin de période
Period average	livre de Îles Falkland (FKP)	0.6	0.6	0.6	0.7	0.7	0.8	0.7	0.8	Moy. sur période
Faroe Islands										**Îles Féroé**
End of period	Danish Krone (DKK),	5.5	6.3	5.6	6.8	7.1	6.2	6.5	6.7	Fin de période
Period average	couronne danoise (DKK)	5.6	6.0	5.6	6.7	6.7	6.6	6.3	6.7	Moy. sur période
Fiji										**Fidji**
End of period	Fiji Dollar (FJD),	1.4	1.7	1.8	2.1	2.1	2.1	2.1	2.1	Fin de période
Period average	dollar des Fidji (FJD)	1.4	1.7	1.9	2.1	2.1	2.1	2.1	2.2	Moy. sur période
Finland										**Finlande**
End of period	Euro (EUR)	...	0.8	0.7	0.9	0.9	0.8	0.9	0.9	Fin de période
Period average		...	0.8	0.8	0.9	0.9	0.9	0.8	0.9	Moy. sur période
France										**France**
End of period	Euro (EUR)	...	0.8	0.7	0.9	0.9	0.8	0.9	0.9	Fin de période
Period average		...	0.8	0.8	0.9	0.9	0.9	0.8	0.9	Moy. sur période
French Guiana										**Guyane française**
End of period	Euro (EUR)	...	0.8	0.7	0.9	0.9	0.8	0.9	0.9	Fin de période
Period average		...	0.8	0.8	0.9	0.9	0.9	0.8	0.9	Moy. sur période
French Polynesia										**Polynésie française**
End of period	CFP Franc (XPF),	89.1	101.2	89.3	109.6	113.2	99.5	104.2	106.2	Fin de période
Period average	franc CFP (XPF) [8]	90.8	95.9	90.0	107.6	107.8	105.6	101.0	106.6	Moy. sur période
French Southern Territories										**Terres australes françaises**
End of period	Euro (EUR)	...	0.8	0.7	0.9	0.9	0.8	0.9	0.9	Fin de période
Period average		...	0.8	0.8	0.9	0.9	0.9	0.8	0.9	Moy. sur période
Gabon										**Gabon**
End of period	CFA Franc, BEAC (XAF),	490.0	556.0	490.9	602.5	622.3	546.9	572.9	583.9	Fin de période
Period average	franc CFA, BEAC (XAF) [3]	499.1	527.3	494.8	591.2	592.6	580.7	555.4	585.9	Moy. sur période
Gambia										**Gambie**
End of period	Dalasi (GMD)	9.6	28.1	28.4	39.8	43.9	47.6	49.5	...	Fin de période
Period average		9.5	28.6	28.0	42.5	43.4	46.6	48.2	...	Moy. sur période
Georgia										**Géorgie**
End of period	Lari (GEL)	1.2	1.8	1.8	2.4	2.6	2.6	2.7	2.9	Fin de période
Period average		...	1.8	1.8	2.3	2.4	2.5	2.5	2.8	Moy. sur période
Ghana										**Ghana**
End of period	Ghana Cedi (GHS),	0.1	0.9	1.5	3.8	4.2	4.4	4.8	5.5	Fin de période
Period average	cedi ghanéen (GHS)	0.1	0.9	1.4	3.7	3.9	4.4	4.6	5.2	Moy. sur période

Country or area	National currency Monnaie nationale	1995	2005	2010	2015	2016	2017	2018	2019	Pays ou zone
Gibraltar										**Gibraltar**
End of period	Gibraltar Pound (GIP),	0.6	0.6	0.6	0.7	0.8	0.7	0.8	0.8	Fin de période
Period average	livre de Gibraltar (GIP)	0.6	0.6	0.6	0.7	0.7	0.8	0.7	0.8	Moy. sur période
Greece										**Grèce**
End of period	Euro (EUR)	...	0.8	0.7	0.9	0.9	0.8	0.9	0.9	Fin de période
Period average		...	0.8	0.8	0.9	0.9	0.9	0.8	0.9	Moy. sur période
Greenland										**Groenland**
End of period	Danish Krone (DKK),	5.5	6.3	5.6	6.8	7.1	6.2	6.5	6.7	Fin de période
Period average	couronne danoise (DKK)	5.6	6.0	5.6	6.7	6.7	6.6	6.3	6.7	Moy. sur période
Grenada										**Grenade**
End of period	E. Caribbean Dollar (XCD),	2.7	2.7	2.7	2.7	2.7	2.7	2.7	2.7	Fin de période
Period average	dollar des Caraïb. (XCD) [1]	2.7	2.7	2.7	2.7	2.7	2.7	2.7	2.7	Moy. sur période
Guadeloupe										**Guadeloupe**
End of period	Euro (EUR)	...	0.8	0.7	0.9	0.9	0.8	0.9	0.9	Fin de période
Period average		...	0.8	0.8	0.9	0.9	0.9	0.8	0.9	Moy. sur période
Guatemala										**Guatemala**
End of period	Quetzal (GTQ)	6.0	7.6	8.0	7.7	7.5	7.3	7.7	7.7	Fin de période
Period average		5.8	7.6	8.1	7.7	7.6	7.3	7.5	7.7	Moy. sur période
Guernsey										**Guernesey**
End of period	Pound Sterling (GBP),	0.6	0.6	0.6	0.7	0.8	0.7	0.8	0.8	Fin de période
Period average	livre sterling (GBP)	0.6	0.6	0.6	0.7	0.7	0.8	0.7	0.8	Moy. sur période
Guinea										**Guinée**
End of period	Guinean Franc (GNF),	998.0	4 500.0	6 083.9	8 003.7	9 225.3	9 006.4	9 084.8	9 400.8	Fin de période
Period average	franc guinéen (GNF)	991.4	3 644.3	5 726.1	7 485.5	8 967.9	9 088.3	9 011.1	9 183.9	Moy. sur période
Guinea-Bissau										**Guinée-Bissau**
End of period	CFA Franc, BCEAO (XOF),	490.0	556.0	490.9	602.5	622.3	546.9	572.9	583.9	Fin de période
Period average	franc CFA, BCEAO (XOF) [2]	499.1	527.3	494.8	591.2	592.6	580.7	555.4	585.9	Moy. sur période
Guyana										**Guyana**
End of period	Guyana Dollar (GYD),	140.5	200.3	203.5	206.5	206.5	206.5	208.5	208.5	Fin de période
Period average	dollar guyanien (GYD)	142.0	199.9	203.6	206.5	206.5	206.5	207.7	208.5	Moy. sur période
Haiti										**Haïti**
End of period	Gourde (HTG)	16.2	43.0	39.9	56.7	67.4	63.7	77.2	92.0	Fin de période
Period average		15.1	40.4	39.8	50.7	63.3	64.8	68.0	88.8	Moy. sur période
Heard Is. and McDonald Is.										**Île Heard-et-Îles MacDonald**
End of period	Australian Dollar (AUD),	1.3	1.4	1.0	1.4	1.4	1.3	1.4	1.4	Fin de période
Period average	dollar australien (AUD)	1.3	1.3	1.1	1.3	1.3	1.3	1.3	1.4	Moy. sur période
Holy See										**Saint-Siège**
End of period	Euro (EUR)	...	0.8	0.7	0.9	0.9	0.8	0.9	0.9	Fin de période
Period average		...	0.8	0.8	0.9	0.9	0.9	0.8	0.9	Moy. sur période
Honduras										**Honduras**
End of period	Lempira (HNL)	10.3	18.9	18.9	22.4	23.5	23.6	24.3	24.6	Fin de période
Period average		...	18.8	18.9	21.9	22.8	23.5	23.9	24.5	Moy. sur période
Hungary										**Hongrie**
End of period	Forint (HUF)	139.5	213.6	208.7	286.6	293.7	258.8	280.9	294.7	Fin de période
Period average		125.7	199.6	207.9	279.3	281.5	274.4	270.2	290.7	Moy. sur période
Iceland										**Islande**
End of period	Iceland Krona (ISK),	65.2	63.0	115.1	129.6	112.8	104.4	116.3	121.1	Fin de période
Period average	couronne islandaise (ISK)	64.7	63.0	122.2	131.9	120.8	106.8	108.3	122.6	Moy. sur période
India										**Inde**
End of period	Indian Rupee (INR),	35.2	45.1	44.8	66.3	68.0	63.9	69.8	71.3	Fin de période
Period average	roupie indienne (INR)	32.4	44.1	45.7	64.2	67.2	65.1	68.4	70.4	Moy. sur période
Indonesia										**Indonésie**
End of period	Rupiah (IDR)	2 308.0	9 830.0	8 991.0	13 795.0	13 436.0	13 548.0	14 481.0	13 901.0	Fin de période
Period average		2 248.6	9 704.7	9 090.4	13 389.4	13 308.3	13 380.8	14 236.9	14 147.7	Moy. sur période
Iran (Islamic Republic of)										**Iran (Rép. islamique d')**
End of period	Iranian Rial (IRR),	1 747.5	9 091.0	10 353.0	30 130.0	32 376.0	36 074.0	42 000.0	42 000.0	Fin de période
Period average	rial iranien (IRR)	1 748.4	8 964.0	10 254.2	29 011.5	30 914.9	33 226.3	40 864.3	42 000.0	Moy. sur période
Iraq										**Iraq**
End of period	Iraqi Dinar (IQD),	1 938.7	1 487.0	1 170.0	1 182.0	1 182.0	1 184.0	1 182.0	1 182.0	Fin de période
Period average	dinar iraquien (IQD)	2 002.4	1 472.0	1 170.0	1 167.3	1 182.0	1 184.0	1 182.8	1 182.0	Moy. sur période
Ireland										**Irlande**
End of period	Euro (EUR)	...	0.8	0.7	0.9	0.9	0.8	0.9	0.9	Fin de période
Period average		...	0.8	0.8	0.9	0.9	0.9	0.8	0.9	Moy. sur période

Country or area	National currency Monnaie nationale	1995	2005	2010	2015	2016	2017	2018	2019	Pays ou zone
Isle of Man										**Île de Man**
End of period	Pound Sterling (GBP),	0.6	0.6	0.6	0.7	0.8	0.7	0.8	0.8	Fin de période
Period average	livre sterling (GBP)	0.6	0.6	0.6	0.7	0.7	0.8	0.7	0.8	Moy. sur période
Israel										**Israël**
End of period	New Israeli Sheqel (ILS),	3.1	4.6	3.5	3.9	3.8	3.5	3.7	3.5	Fin de période
Period average	nouv. shekel israélien (ILS)	3.0	4.5	3.7	3.9	3.8	3.6	3.6	3.6	Moy. sur période
Italy										**Italie**
End of period	Euro (EUR)	...	0.8	0.7	0.9	0.9	0.8	0.9	0.9	Fin de période
Period average		...	0.8	0.8	0.9	0.9	0.9	0.8	0.9	Moy. sur période
Jamaica										**Jamaïque**
End of period	Jamaican Dollar (JMD),	39.6	64.4	85.6	120.0	127.8	124.3	126.8	131.2	Fin de période
Period average	dollar jamaïcain (JMD)	35.1	62.3	87.2	117.0	125.1	128.0	128.9	133.3	Moy. sur période
Japan										**Japon**
End of period	Yen (JPY)	102.8	118.0	81.5	120.5	116.8	112.9	110.8	109.1	Fin de période
Period average		94.1	110.2	87.8	121.0	108.8	112.2	110.4	109.0	Moy. sur période
Jersey										**Jersey**
End of period	Pound Sterling (GBP),	0.6	0.6	0.6	0.7	0.8	0.7	0.8	0.8	Fin de période
Period average	livre sterling (GBP)	0.6	0.6	0.6	0.7	0.7	0.8	0.7	0.8	Moy. sur période
Jordan										**Jordanie**
End of period	Jordanian Dinar (JOD),	0.7	0.7	0.7	0.7	0.7	0.7	0.7	0.7	Fin de période
Period average	dinar jordanien (JOD)	0.7	0.7	0.7	0.7	0.7	0.7	0.7	0.7	Moy. sur période
Kazakhstan										**Kazakhstan**
End of period	Tenge (KZT)	64.0	134.0	147.5	340.0	333.3	332.3	384.2	382.6	Fin de période
Period average		61.0	132.9	147.4	221.7	342.2	326.0	344.7	382.7	Moy. sur période
Kenya										**Kenya**
End of period	Kenyan Shilling (KES),	55.9	72.4	80.8	102.3	102.5	103.2	101.8	101.3	Fin de période
Period average	shilling kényan (KES)	51.4	75.6	79.2	98.2	101.5	103.4	101.3	102.0	Moy. sur période
Kiribati										**Kiribati**
End of period	Australian Dollar (AUD),	1.3	1.4	1.0	1.4	1.4	1.3	1.4	1.4	Fin de période
Period average	dollar australien (AUD)	1.3	1.3	1.1	1.3	1.3	1.3	1.3	1.4	Moy. sur période
Kosovo										**Kosovo**
End of period	Euro (EUR)	...	0.8	0.7	0.9	0.9	0.8	0.9	0.9	Fin de période
Period average		...	0.8	0.8	0.9	0.9	0.9	0.8	0.9	Moy. sur période
Kuwait										**Koweït**
End of period	Kuwaiti Dinar (KWD),	0.3	0.3	0.3	0.3	0.3	0.3	0.3	0.3	Fin de période
Period average	dinar koweïtien (KWD)	0.3	0.3	0.3	0.3	0.3	0.3	0.3	0.3	Moy. sur période
Kyrgyzstan										**Kirghizistan**
End of period	Som (KGS)	11.2	41.3	47.1	75.9	69.2	68.8	69.9	69.6	Fin de période
Period average		10.8	41.0	46.0	64.5	69.9	68.9	68.8	69.8	Moy. sur période
Lao People's Dem. Rep.										**Rép. dém. populaire lao**
End of period	Lao Kip (LAK)	923.0	10 743.0	8 058.0	8 148.0	8 184.0	8 293.0	8 530.0	8 861.0	Fin de période
Period average		804.7	10 655.2	8 254.2	8 127.6	8 124.4	8 244.8	8 401.3	8 679.4	Moy. sur période
Latvia										**Lettonie**
End of period	Euro (EUR)	...	0.8	0.7	0.9	0.9	0.8	0.9	0.9	Fin de période
Period average		...	0.8	0.8	0.9	0.9	0.9	0.8	0.9	Moy. sur période
Lebanon										**Liban**
End of period	Lebanese Pound (LBP),	1 596.0	1 507.5	1 507.5	1 507.5	1 507.5	1 507.5	1 507.5	1 507.5	Fin de période
Period average	livre libanaise (LBP)	1 621.4	1 507.5	1 507.5	1 507.5	1 507.5	1 507.5	1 507.5	1 507.5	Moy. sur période
Lesotho										**Lesotho**
End of period	Loti (LSL)	3.6	6.3	6.6	15.5	13.7	12.3	14.4	14.1	Fin de période
Period average		3.6	6.4	7.3	12.8	14.7	13.3	13.2	14.5	Moy. sur période
Liberia										**Libéria**
End of period	Liberian Dollar (LRD),	43.8	56.5	71.5	88.5	102.5	125.5	157.6	187.9	Fin de période
Period average	dollar libérien (LRD)	49.8	57.1	71.4	86.2	94.4	112.7	144.1	186.4	Moy. sur période
Libya										**Libye**
End of period	Libyan Dinar (LYD),	0.4	1.4	1.3	1.4	1.4	1.4	1.4	1.4	Fin de période
Period average	dinar libyen (LYD)	0.4	1.3	1.3	1.4	1.4	1.4	1.4	1.4	Moy. sur période
Liechtenstein										**Liechtenstein**
End of period	Swiss Franc (CHF),	1.2	1.3	0.9	1.0	1.0	1.0	1.0	1.0	Fin de période
Period average	franc suisse (CHF)	1.2	1.2	1.0	1.0	1.0	1.0	1.0	1.0	Moy. sur période
Lithuania										**Lituanie**
End of period	Euro (EUR)	...	0.8	0.7	0.9	0.9	0.8	0.9	0.9	Fin de période
Period average		...	0.8	0.8	0.9	0.9	0.9	0.8	0.9	Moy. sur période

Country or area	National currency Monnaie nationale	1995	2005	2010	2015	2016	2017	2018	2019	Pays ou zone
Luxembourg										**Luxembourg**
End of period	Euro (EUR)	...	0.8	0.7	0.9	0.9	0.8	0.9	0.9	Fin de période
Period average		...	0.8	0.8	0.9	0.9	0.9	0.8	0.9	Moy. sur période
Madagascar										**Madagascar**
End of period	Malagasy Ariary (MGA),	684.6	2 159.8	2 146.1	3 199.2	3 347.9	3 230.2	3 470.2	3 627.3	Fin de période
Period average	ariary malgache (MGA)	853.1	2 003.0	2 090.0	2 933.5	3 176.5	3 116.1	3 334.8	3 618.3	Moy. sur période
Malawi										**Malawi**
End of period	Malawi Kwacha (MWK),	15.3	123.8	150.8	672.7	728.6	732.0	733.7	...	Fin de période
Period average	kwacha malawien (MWK)	15.3	118.4	150.5	499.6	718.0	730.3	732.3	...	Moy. sur période
Malaysia										**Malaisie**
End of period	Malaysian Ringgit (MYR),	2.5	3.8	3.1	4.3	4.5	4.1	4.1	4.1	Fin de période
Period average	ringgit malaisien (MYR)	2.5	3.8	3.2	3.9	4.1	4.3	4.0	4.1	Moy. sur période
Maldives										**Maldives**
End of period	Rufiyaa (MVR)	11.8	12.8	12.8	15.4	15.4	15.4	15.4	15.4	Fin de période
Period average		11.8	12.8	12.8	15.4	15.4	15.4	15.4	15.4	Moy. sur période
Mali										**Mali**
End of period	CFA Franc, BCEAO (XOF),	490.0	556.0	490.9	602.5	622.3	546.9	572.9	583.9	Fin de période
Period average	franc CFA, BCEAO (XOF) [2]	499.1	527.3	494.8	591.2	592.6	580.7	555.4	585.9	Moy. sur période
Malta										**Malte**
End of period	Euro (EUR)	...	0.8	0.7	0.9	0.9	0.8	0.9	0.9	Fin de période
Period average		...	0.8	0.8	0.9	0.9	0.9	0.8	0.9	Moy. sur période
Martinique										**Martinique**
End of period	Euro (EUR)	...	0.8	0.7	0.9	0.9	0.8	0.9	0.9	Fin de période
Period average		...	0.8	0.8	0.9	0.9	0.9	0.8	0.9	Moy. sur période
Mauritania										**Mauritanie**
End of period	Ouguiya (MRU)	13.7	27.1	28.2	33.9	35.6	35.3	36.4	37.3	Fin de période
Period average		13.0	26.6	27.6	32.5	35.2	35.8	35.7	36.7	Moy. sur période
Mauritius										**Maurice**
End of period	Mauritius Rupee (MUR),	17.7	30.7	30.4	35.9	36.0	33.5	34.2	36.6	Fin de période
Period average	roupie mauricienne (MUR)	17.4	29.5	30.8	35.1	35.5	34.5	33.9	35.5	Moy. sur période
Mayotte										**Mayotte**
End of period	Euro (EUR)	...	0.8	0.7	0.9	0.9	0.8	0.9	0.9	Fin de période
Period average		...	0.8	0.8	0.9	0.9	0.9	0.8	0.9	Moy. sur période
Mexico										**Mexique**
End of period	Mexican Peso (MXN),	7.6	10.8	12.4	17.2	20.7	19.8	19.7	18.8	Fin de période
Period average	peso mexicain (MXN)	6.4	10.9	12.6	15.8	18.7	18.9	19.2	19.3	Moy. sur période
Monaco										**Monaco**
End of period	Euro (EUR)	...	0.8	0.7	0.9	0.9	0.8	0.9	0.9	Fin de période
Period average		...	0.8	0.8	0.9	0.9	0.9	0.8	0.9	Moy. sur période
Mongolia										**Mongolie**
End of period	Tugrik (MNT)	473.6	1 221.0	1 256.5	1 996.0	2 489.5	2 427.1	2 643.7	2 734.3	Fin de période
Period average		448.6	1 205.2	1 357.1	1 970.3	2 140.3	2 439.8	2 472.5	2 663.5	Moy. sur période
Montenegro										**Monténégro**
End of period	Euro (EUR)	...	0.8	0.7	0.9	0.9	0.8	0.9	0.9	Fin de période
Period average		...	0.8	0.8	0.9	0.9	0.9	0.8	0.9	Moy. sur période
Montserrat										**Montserrat**
End of period	E. Caribbean Dollar (XCD),	2.7	2.7	2.7	2.7	2.7	2.7	2.7	2.7	Fin de période
Period average	dollar des Caraïb. (XCD) [1]	2.7	2.7	2.7	2.7	2.7	2.7	2.7	2.7	Moy. sur période
Morocco										**Maroc**
End of period	Moroccan Dirham (MAD),	8.5	9.2	8.4	9.9	10.1	9.3	9.6	9.6	Fin de période
Period average	dirham marocain (MAD)	8.5	8.9	8.4	9.8	9.8	9.7	9.4	9.6	Moy. sur période
Mozambique										**Mozambique**
End of period	Mozambique Metical (MZN),	10.9	24.2	32.6	45.9	71.4	59.0	61.5	61.5	Fin de période
Period average	metical de Mozambique (MZN)	9.0	23.1	34.0	40.0	63.1	63.6	60.3	62.5	Moy. sur période
Myanmar										**Myanmar**
End of period	Kyat (MMK)	5.8	6.0	5.6	1 304.0	1 357.5	1 362.0	1 550.0	1 465.5	Fin de période
Period average		5.7	5.8	5.6	1 162.6	1 234.9	1 360.4	1 429.8	1 518.3	Moy. sur période
Namibia										**Namibie**
End of period	Namibia Dollar (NAD),	3.6	6.3	6.6	15.5	13.6	12.4	14.4	14.1	Fin de période
Period average	dollar namibien (NAD)	3.6	6.4	7.3	12.9	14.7	13.3	13.2	14.4	Moy. sur période
Nauru										**Nauru**
End of period	Australian Dollar (AUD),	1.3	1.4	1.0	1.4	1.4	1.3	1.4	1.4	Fin de période
Period average	dollar australien (AUD)	1.3	1.3	1.1	1.3	1.3	1.3	1.3	1.4	Moy. sur période

Country or area	National currency Monnaie nationale	1995	2005	2010	2015	2016	2017	2018	2019	Pays ou zone
Nepal										**Népal**
End of period	Nepalese Rupee (NPR),	56.0	74.1	71.7	107.3	108.0	103.0	115.0	113.3	Fin de période
Period average	roupie népalaise (NPR)	51.9	71.4	73.3	102.4	107.4	104.5	108.9	112.6	Moy. sur période
Netherlands										**Pays-Bas**
End of period	Euro (EUR)	...	0.8	0.7	0.9	0.9	0.8	0.9	0.9	Fin de période
Period average		...	0.8	0.8	0.9	0.9	0.9	0.8	0.9	Moy. sur période
New Caledonia										**Nouvelle-Calédonie**
End of period	CFP Franc (XPF),	89.1	101.2	89.3	109.6	113.2	99.5	104.2	106.2	Fin de période
Period average	franc CFP (XPF) [8]	90.8	95.9	90.0	107.6	107.8	105.6	101.0	106.6	Moy. sur période
New Zealand										**Nouvelle-Zélande**
End of period	New Zealand Dollar (NZD),	1.5	1.5	1.3	1.5	1.4	1.4	1.5	1.5	Fin de période
Period average	dollar néo-zélandais (NZD)	1.5	1.4	1.4	1.4	1.4	1.4	1.4	1.5	Moy. sur période
Nicaragua										**Nicaragua**
End of period	Cordoba Oro (NIO)	8.0	17.1	21.9	27.9	29.3	30.8	32.3	33.8	Fin de période
Period average		7.5	16.7	21.4	27.3	28.6	30.1	31.6	33.1	Moy. sur période
Niger										**Niger**
End of period	CFA Franc, BCEAO (XOF),	490.0	556.0	490.9	602.5	622.3	546.9	572.9	583.9	Fin de période
Period average	franc CFA, BCEAO (XOF) [2]	499.1	527.3	494.8	591.2	592.6	580.7	555.4	585.9	Moy. sur période
Nigeria										**Nigéria**
End of period	Naira (NGN)	21.9	129.0	150.7	197.0	305.0	306.0	307.0	307.0	Fin de période
Period average		21.9	131.3	150.3	192.4	253.5	305.8	306.1	306.9	Moy. sur période
Niue										**Nioué**
End of period	New Zealand Dollar (NZD),	1.5	1.5	1.3	1.5	1.4	1.4	1.5	1.5	Fin de période
Period average	dollar néo-zélandais (NZD)	1.5	1.4	1.4	1.4	1.4	1.4	1.4	1.5	Moy. sur période
Norfolk Island										**Île Norfolk**
End of period	Australian dollar (AUD),	1.3	1.4	1.0	1.4	1.4	1.3	1.4	1.4	Fin de période
Period average	dollar australien (AUD)	1.3	1.3	1.1	1.3	1.3	1.3	1.3	1.4	Moy. sur période
North Macedonia										**Macédoine du Nord**
End of period	Denar (MKD)	38.0	51.9	46.3	56.4	58.3	51.3	53.7	55.0	Fin de période
Period average		37.9	49.3	46.5	55.5	55.7	54.7	52.1	54.9	Moy. sur période
Norway										**Norvège**
End of period	Norwegian Krone (NOK),	6.3	6.8	5.9	8.8	8.6	8.2	8.7	8.8	Fin de période
Period average	couronne norvégienne (NOK)	6.3	6.4	6.0	8.1	8.4	8.3	8.1	8.8	Moy. sur période
Oman										**Oman**
End of period	Rial Omani (OMR),	0.4	0.4	0.4	0.4	0.4	0.4	0.4	0.4	Fin de période
Period average	rial omanais (OMR)	0.4	0.4	0.4	0.4	0.4	0.4	0.4	0.4	Moy. sur période
Other non-specified areas										**Autres zones non-spécifiées**
End of period	New Taiwan Dollar (TWD),	27.3	32.9	30.4	33.1	32.3	29.8	30.7	30.1	Fin de période
Period average	nouv. dollar de Taïwan (TWD)	26.5	32.2	31.6	31.9	32.3	30.4	30.2	30.9	Moy. sur période
Pakistan										**Pakistan**
End of period	Pakistan Rupee (PKR),	34.3	59.8	85.7	104.9	104.8	110.4	138.8	154.9	Fin de période
Period average	roupie pakistanaise (PKR)	31.6	59.5	85.2	102.8	104.8	105.5	121.8	150.0	Moy. sur période
Panama										**Panama**
End of period	Balboa (PAB)	1.0	1.0	1.0	1.0	1.0	1.0	1.0	1.0	Fin de période
Period average		1.0	1.0	1.0	1.0	1.0	1.0	1.0	1.0	Moy. sur période
Papua New Guinea										**Papouasie-Nvl-Guinée**
End of period	Kina (PGK)	1.3	3.1	2.6	3.0	3.2	3.2	3.4	3.4	Fin de période
Period average		1.3	3.1	2.7	2.8	3.1	3.2	3.3	3.4	Moy. sur période
Paraguay										**Paraguay**
End of period	Guarani (PYG),	1 979.7	6 120.0	4 565.3	5 806.9	5 766.9	5 590.5	5 960.5	6 453.1	Fin de période
Period average	guaraní (PYG)	1 963.0	6 177.9	4 758.4	5 204.9	5 670.5	5 618.9	5 732.1	6 240.7	Moy. sur période
Peru										**Pérou**
End of period	Sol (PEN)	2.3	3.4	2.8	3.4	3.4	3.2	3.4	3.3	Fin de période
Period average		2.3	3.3	2.8	3.2	3.4	3.3	3.3	3.3	Moy. sur période
Philippines										**Philippines**
End of period	Philippine Piso (PHP),	26.2	53.1	43.9	47.2	49.8	49.9	52.7	50.7	Fin de période
Period average	piso philippin (PHP)	25.7	55.1	45.1	45.5	47.5	50.4	52.7	51.8	Moy. sur période
Pitcairn										**Pitcairn**
End of period	New Zealand dollar (NZD),	1.5	1.5	1.3	1.5	1.4	1.4	1.5	1.5	Fin de période
Period average	dollar néo-zélandais (NZD)	1.5	1.4	1.4	1.4	1.4	1.4	1.4	1.5	Moy. sur période
Poland										**Pologne**
End of period	Zloty (PLN)	2.5	3.3	3.0	3.9	4.2	3.5	3.8	3.8	Fin de période
Period average		2.4	3.2	3.0	3.8	3.9	3.8	3.6	3.8	Moy. sur période

Country or area	National currency Monnaie nationale	1995	2005	2010	2015	2016	2017	2018	2019	Pays ou zone
Portugal										**Portugal**
End of period	Euro (EUR)	...	0.8	0.7	0.9	0.9	0.8	0.9	0.9	Fin de période
Period average		...	0.8	0.8	0.9	0.9	0.9	0.8	0.9	Moy. sur période
Qatar										**Qatar**
End of period	Qatari Rial (QAR),	3.6	3.6	3.6	3.6	3.6	3.6	3.6	3.6	Fin de période
Period average	riyal qatari (QAR)	3.6	3.6	3.6	3.6	3.6	3.6	3.6	3.6	Moy. sur période
Republic of Korea										**République de Corée**
End of period	South Korean Won (KRW),	774.7	1 011.6	1 134.8	1 172.5	1 207.7	1 070.5	1 118.1	1 157.8	Fin de période
Period average	won sud-coréen (KRW)	771.3	1 024.1	1 156.1	1 131.2	1 160.4	1 130.4	1 100.5	1 165.4	Moy. sur période
Republic of Moldova										**République de Moldova**
End of period	Moldovan Leu (MDL),	4.5	12.8	12.2	19.7	20.0	17.1	17.1	17.2	Fin de période
Period average	leu moldove (MDL)	4.5	12.6	12.4	18.8	19.9	18.5	16.8	17.6	Moy. sur période
Réunion										**Réunion**
End of period	Euro (EUR)	...	0.8	0.7	0.9	0.9	0.8	0.9	0.9	Fin de période
Period average		...	0.8	0.8	0.9	0.9	0.9	0.8	0.9	Moy. sur période
Romania										**Roumanie**
End of period	Romanian Leu (RON),	0.3	3.1	3.2	4.1	4.3	3.9	4.1	4.3	Fin de période
Period average	leu roumain (RON)	0.2	2.9	3.2	4.0	4.1	4.1	3.9	4.2	Moy. sur période
Russian Federation										**Fédération de Russie**
End of period	Russian Ruble (RUB),	4.6	28.8	30.5	72.9	60.7	57.6	69.5	61.9	Fin de période
Period average	ruble russe (RUB)	...	28.3	30.4	60.9	67.1	58.3	62.7	64.7	Moy. sur période
Rwanda										**Rwanda**
End of period	Rwanda Franc (RWF),	299.8	553.7	594.5	747.4	819.8	843.3	879.1	922.5	Fin de période
Period average	franc rwandais (RWF)	262.2	557.8	583.1	719.9	787.3	831.6	861.1	899.4	Moy. sur période
Saint Barthélemy										**Saint-Barthélemy**
End of period	Euro (EUR)	...	0.8	0.7	0.9	0.9	0.8	0.9	0.9	Fin de période
Period average		...	0.8	0.8	0.9	0.9	0.9	0.8	0.9	Moy. sur période
Saint Helena										**Sainte-Hélène**
End of period	Saint Helena Pound (SHP),	0.6	0.6	0.6	0.7	0.8	0.7	0.8	0.8	Fin de période
Period average	livre de Sainte-Hélène (SHP)	0.6	0.6	0.6	0.7	0.7	0.8	0.7	0.8	Moy. sur période
Saint Kitts and Nevis										**Saint-Kitts-et-Nevis**
End of period	E. Caribbean Dollar (XCD),	2.7	2.7	2.7	2.7	2.7	2.7	2.7	2.7	Fin de période
Period average	dollar des Caraïb. (XCD) [1]	2.7	2.7	2.7	2.7	2.7	2.7	2.7	2.7	Moy. sur période
Saint Lucia										**Sainte-Lucie**
End of period	E. Caribbean Dollar (XCD),	2.7	2.7	2.7	2.7	2.7	2.7	2.7	2.7	Fin de période
Period average	dollar des Caraïb. (XCD) [1]	2.7	2.7	2.7	2.7	2.7	2.7	2.7	2.7	Moy. sur période
Saint Martin (French part)										**St-Martin (partie française)**
End of period	Euro (EUR)	...	0.8	0.7	0.9	0.9	0.8	0.9	0.9	Fin de période
Period average		...	0.8	0.8	0.9	0.9	0.9	0.8	0.9	Moy. sur période
Saint Pierre and Miquelon										**Saint-Pierre-et-Miquelon**
End of period	Euro (EUR)	...	0.8	0.7	0.9	0.9	0.8	0.9	0.9	Fin de période
Period average		...	0.8	0.8	0.9	0.9	0.9	0.8	0.9	Moy. sur période
Saint Vincent & Grenadines										**Saint-Vincent-Grenadines**
End of period	E. Caribbean Dollar (XCD),	2.7	2.7	2.7	2.7	2.7	2.7	2.7	2.7	Fin de période
Period average	dollar des Caraïb. (XCD) [1]	2.7	2.7	2.7	2.7	2.7	2.7	2.7	2.7	Moy. sur période
Samoa										**Samoa**
End of period	Tala (WST)	2.5	2.8	2.3	2.6	2.6	2.5	2.6	2.6	Fin de période
Period average		2.5	2.7	2.5	2.6	2.6	2.6	2.6	2.6	Moy. sur période
San Marino										**Saint-Marin**
End of period	Euro (EUR)	...	0.8	0.7	0.9	0.9	0.8	0.9	0.9	Fin de période
Period average		...	0.8	0.8	0.9	0.9	0.9	0.8	0.9	Moy. sur période
Sao Tome and Principe										**Sao Tomé-et-Principe**
End of period	Dobra (STN)	1.8	11.9	18.3	22.4	23.4	20.5	21.4	21.9	Fin de période
Period average		1.4	10.6	18.5	22.1	22.1	21.7	20.8	21.9	Moy. sur période
Saudi Arabia										**Arabie saoudite**
End of period	Saudi Riyal (SAR),	3.8	3.8	3.8	3.8	3.8	3.8	3.8	3.8	Fin de période
Period average	rial saoudien (SAR)	3.8	3.8	3.8	3.8	3.8	3.8	3.8	3.8	Moy. sur période
Senegal										**Sénégal**
End of period	CFA Franc, BCEAO (XOF),	490.0	556.0	490.9	602.5	622.3	546.9	572.9	583.9	Fin de période
Period average	franc CFA, BCEAO (XOF) [2]	499.1	527.3	494.8	591.2	592.6	580.7	555.4	585.9	Moy. sur période
Serbia										**Serbie**
End of period	Serbian Dinar (RSD	...	72.2	79.3	111.2	117.1	99.1	103.4	104.9	Fin de période
Period average	dinar de Serbie (RSD)	...	66.7	77.7	108.8	111.3	107.8	100.2	105.2	Moy. sur période

Country or area	National currency Monnaie nationale	1995	2005	2010	2015	2016	2017	2018	2019	Pays ou zone
Seychelles										**Seychelles**
End of period	Seychelles Rupee (SCR),	4.9	5.5	12.1	13.2	13.5	13.8	14.0	14.1	Fin de période
Period average	roupie seychelloise (SCR)	4.8	5.5	12.1	13.3	13.3	13.6	13.9	14.0	Moy. sur période
Sierra Leone										**Sierra Leone**
End of period	Leone (SLL)	943.4	2 932.5	4 198.0	5 639.1	7 195.4	7 537.0	8 396.1	9 716.7	Fin de période
Period average		755.2	2 889.6	3 978.1	5 080.7	6 290.3	7 384.4	7 931.6	9 010.2	Moy. sur période
Singapore										**Singapour**
End of period	Singapore Dollar (SGD),	1.4	1.7	1.3	1.4	1.4	1.3	1.4	1.3	Fin de période
Period average	dollar singapourien (SGD)	1.4	1.7	1.4	1.4	1.4	1.4	1.3	1.4	Moy. sur période
Sint Maarten (Dutch part)										**St-Martin (partie néerland.)**
End of period	Neth. Ant. Guilder (ANG),	...	...	1.8	1.8	1.8	1.8	1.8		Fin de période
Period average	florin des Ant. néer. (ANG) [7]	...	...	...	1.8	1.8	1.8	1.8	...	Moy. sur période
Slovakia										**Slovaquie**
End of period	Euro (EUR)	...	0.8	0.7	0.9	0.9	0.8	0.9	0.9	Fin de période
Period average		...	0.8	0.8	0.9	0.9	0.9	0.8	0.9	Moy. sur période
Slovenia										**Slovénie**
End of period	Euro (EUR)	...	0.8	0.7	0.9	0.9	0.8	0.9	0.9	Fin de période
Period average		...	0.8	0.8	0.9	0.9	0.9	0.8	0.9	Moy. sur période
Solomon Islands										**Îles Salomon**
End of period	Solomon Is. Dollar (SBD),	3.5	7.6	8.1	8.1	8.2	7.9	8.1	8.2	Fin de période
Period average	dollar des Îl. Salomon (SBD) [9]	3.4	7.5	8.1	7.9	7.9	7.9	8.0	8.2	Moy. sur période
Somalia										**Somalie**
End of period	Somali Shilling (SOS),	...	...	30 900.0	22 285.0	24 005.0	23 605.0	...	...	Fin de période
Period average	shilling somalien (SOS)	...	...	31 269.7	22 254.2	23 061.8	23 098.0	...	...	Moy. sur période
South Africa										**Afrique du Sud**
End of period	Rand (ZAR)	3.6	6.3	6.6	15.5	13.7	12.3	14.4	14.0	Fin de période
Period average		3.6	6.4	7.3	12.8	14.7	13.3	13.2	14.4	Moy. sur période
South Georgia & Sandwich Is.										**Géorgie du S.-Îles Sandwich**
End of period	Pound Sterling (GBP),	0.6	0.6	0.6	0.7	0.8	0.7	0.8	0.8	Fin de période
Period average	livre sterling (GBP)	0.6	0.6	0.6	0.7	0.7	0.8	0.7	0.8	Moy. sur période
South Sudan										**Soudan du sud**
End of period	S. Sudanese Pound (SSP),	...	...	...	16.6	83.9	127.9	154.0	161.1	Fin de période
Period average	livre s.-soudanaise (SSP) [10]	...	...	...	3.6	46.7	113.6	141.4	158.0	Moy. sur période
Spain										**Espagne**
End of period	Euro (EUR)	...	0.8	0.7	0.9	0.9	0.8	0.9	0.9	Fin de période
Period average		...	0.8	0.8	0.9	0.9	0.9	0.8	0.9	Moy. sur période
Sri Lanka										**Sri Lanka**
End of period	Sri Lanka Rupee (LKR),	54.0	102.1	111.0	144.1	149.8	152.9	182.3	181.6	Fin de période
Period average	roupie sri-lankaise (LKR)	51.3	100.5	113.1	135.9	145.6	152.4	162.5	178.7	Moy. sur période
Sudan										**Soudan**
End of period	Sudanese Pound (SDG),	0.5	2.3	2.5	6.1	6.6	6.7	47.5	...	Fin de période
Period average	livre soudanaise (SDG)	0.6	2.4	2.3	6.0	6.2	6.7	24.3	...	Moy. sur période
Suriname										**Suriname**
End of period	Surinam Dollar (SRD),	0.4	2.7	2.7	4.0	7.4	7.5	7.5	7.5	Fin de période
Period average	dollar surinamais (SRD)	0.4	2.7	2.7	3.4	6.2	7.5	7.5	7.5	Moy. sur période
Svalbard and Jan Mayen Is.										**Îles Svalbard-et-Jan Mayen**
End of period	Norwegian Krone (NOK),	6.3	6.8	5.9	8.8	8.6	8.2	8.7	8.8	Fin de période
Period average	couronne norvégienne (NOK)	6.3	6.4	6.0	8.1	8.4	8.3	8.1	8.8	Moy. sur période
Sweden										**Suède**
End of period	Swedish Krona (SEK),	6.7	8.0	6.7	8.4	9.1	8.2	9.0	9.3	Fin de période
Period average	couronne suédoise (SEK)	7.1	7.5	7.2	8.4	8.6	8.5	8.7	9.5	Moy. sur période
Switzerland										**Suisse**
End of period	Swiss Franc (CHF),	1.2	1.3	0.9	1.0	1.0	1.0	1.0	1.0	Fin de période
Period average	franc suisse (CHF)	1.2	1.2	1.0	1.0	1.0	1.0	1.0	1.0	Moy. sur période
Syrian Arab Republic [5]										**République arabe syrienne [5]**
End of period	Syrian Pound (SYP), livre syrienne (SYP)	...	...	46.6	338.0	514.9	434.0	434.0	700.0	Fin de période
Tajikistan										**Tadjikistan**
End of period	Somoni (TJS)	0.3	3.2	4.4	7.0	7.9	8.8	9.4	9.7	Fin de période
Period average		0.1	3.1	4.4	6.2	7.8	8.5	9.2	9.5	Moy. sur période
Thailand										**Thaïlande**
End of period	Baht (THB)	25.2	41.0	30.2	36.1	35.8	32.7	32.4	30.2	Fin de période
Period average		24.9	40.2	31.7	34.2	35.3	33.9	32.3	31.0	Moy. sur période

Country or area	National currency Monnaie nationale	1995	2005	2010	2015	2016	2017	2018	2019	Pays ou zone
Togo										**Togo**
End of period	CFA Franc, BCEAO (XOF),	490.0	556.0	490.9	602.5	622.3	546.9	572.9	583.9	Fin de période
Period average	franc CFA, BCEAO (XOF) [2]	499.1	527.3	494.8	591.2	592.6	580.7	555.4	585.9	Moy. sur période
Tokelau										**Tokélaou**
End of period	New Zealand Dollar (NZD	1.5	1.5	1.3	1.5	1.4	1.4	1.5	1.5	Fin de période
Period average .	dollar néo-zélandais (NZD)	1.5	1.4	1.4	1.4	1.4	1.4	1.4	1.5	Moy. sur période
Tonga										**Tonga**
End of period	Pa'anga (TOP)	1.3	2.1	1.8	2.2	2.2	2.2	2.3	2.3	Fin de période
Period average		1.3	1.9	1.9	2.1	2.2	2.2	2.2	2.3	Moy. sur période
Trinidad and Tobago										**Trinité-et-Tobago**
End of period	TT Dollar (TTD),	6.0	6.3	6.4	6.4	6.8	6.8	6.8	6.8	Fin de période
Period average	dollar de la T-et-T (TTD) [11]	5.9	6.3	6.4	6.4	6.7	6.8	6.8	6.8	Moy. sur période
Tunisia										**Tunisie**
End of period	Tunisian Dinar (TND),	1.0	1.4	1.4	2.0	2.3	2.5	3.0	2.8	Fin de période
Period average	dinar tunisien (TND)	0.9	1.3	1.4	2.0	2.1	2.4	2.6	2.9	Moy. sur période
Turkey										**Turquie**
End of period	Turkish Lira (TRY),	0.1	1.3	1.5	2.9	3.5	3.8	5.3	5.9	Fin de période
Period average	livre turque (TRY)	~0.0	1.3	1.5	2.7	3.0	3.6	4.8	5.7	Moy. sur période
Turkmenistan [5]										**Turkménistan [5]**
End of period	Turkmen. Manat (TMT), manat turkmène (TMT) [12]	...	...	3.5	3.5	3.5	3.5	3.5	3.5	Fin de période
Tuvalu										**Tuvalu**
End of period	Australian Dollar (AUD),	1.3	1.4	1.0	1.4	1.4	1.3	1.4	1.4	Fin de période
Period average	dollar australien (AUD)	1.3	1.3	1.1	1.3	1.3	1.3	1.3	1.4	Moy. sur période
Uganda										**Ouganda**
End of period	Uganda Shilling (UGX),	1 009.5	1 816.9	2 308.3	3 377.0	3 610.5	3 635.1	3 713.4	3 665.2	Fin de période
Period average	shilling ougandais (UGX)	968.9	1 780.5	2 177.6	3 240.6	3 420.1	3 611.2	3 727.1	3 704.0	Moy. sur période
Ukraine [13]										**Ukraine [13]**
End of period	Hryvnia (UAH)	1.8	5.1	8.0	24.0	27.2	28.1	27.7	23.7	Fin de période
Period average		1.5	5.1	7.9	21.8	25.6	26.6	27.2	25.8	Moy. sur période
United Arab Emirates										**Émirats arabes unis**
End of period	UAE Dirham (AED),	3.7	3.7	3.7	3.7	3.7	3.7	3.7	3.7	Fin de période
Period average	dirham des É.A.U. (AED) [14]	3.7	3.7	3.7	3.7	3.7	3.7	3.7	3.7	Moy. sur période
United Kingdom										**Royaume-Uni**
End of period	Pound Sterling (GBP),	0.6	0.6	0.6	0.7	0.8	0.7	0.8	0.8	Fin de période
Period average	livre sterling (GBP)	0.6	0.6	0.6	0.7	0.7	0.8	0.7	0.8	Moy. sur période
United Rep. of Tanzania										**Rép.-Unie de Tanzanie**
End of period	Tanzanian Shilling (TZS),	550.4	1 165.5	1 453.5	2 148.5	2 172.6	2 230.1	2 281.2	2 287.9	Fin de période
Period average	shilling tanzanien (TZS)	574.8	1 128.9	1 395.6	1 991.4	2 177.1	2 228.9	2 263.8	2 288.2	Moy. sur période
Uruguay										**Uruguay**
End of period	Peso Uruguayo (UYU),	7.1	24.1	20.1	29.9	29.3	28.8	32.4	37.3	Fin de période
Period average	peso uruguayen (UYU)	6.3	24.5	20.1	27.3	30.2	28.7	30.7	35.3	Moy. sur période
Uzbekistan [5]										**Ouzbékistan [5]**
End of period	Uzbekistan Sum (UZS), sum ouzbek (UZS)	...	...	1 640.0	2 780.1	3 218.0	8 125.0	8 345.0	9 502.0	Fin de période
Vanuatu										**Vanuatu**
End of period	Vatu (VUV)	113.7	112.3	93.2	110.5	112.3	107.5	112.6	114.3	Fin de période
Period average		112.1	109.2	96.9	109.0	108.5	107.8	110.2	114.3	Moy. sur période
Venezuela (Boliv. Rep. of)										**Venezuela (Rép. boliv. du)**
End of period	Bolívar (VEF), bolivar (VEF)	0.3	2.1	2.6	6.3	10.0	10.0	...	...	Fin de période
Period average		0.2	2.1	2.6	6.3	9.3	10.0	...	...	Moy. sur période
Viet Nam										**Viet Nam**
End of period	Dong (VND)	11 015.0	15 916.0	18 932.0	21 890.0	22 159.0	22 425.0	22 825.0	23 155.0	Fin de période
Period average		11 038.3	15 858.9	18 612.9	21 697.6	21 935.0	22 370.1	22 602.1	23 050.2	Moy. sur période
Wallis and Futuna Islands										**Îles Wallis-et-Futuna**
End of period	CFP Franc (XPF),	89.1	101.2	89.3	109.6	113.2	99.5	104.2	106.2	Fin de période
Period average	franc CFP (XPF) [8]	90.8	96.0	90.1	107.6	107.9	105.9	101.1	106.6	Moy. sur période
Western Sahara										**Sahara occidental**
End of period	Moroccan Dirham (MAD),	8.5	9.2	8.4	9.9	10.1	9.3	9.6	9.6	Fin de période
Period average	dirham marocain (MAD)	8.5	8.9	8.4	9.8	9.8	9.7	9.4	9.6	Moy. sur période
Zambia										**Zambie**
End of period	Zambian Kwacha (ZMW),	1.0	3.5	4.8	11.0	9.9	9.9	11.9	14.1	Fin de période
Period average	kwacha zambien (ZMW)	0.9	4.5	4.8	8.6	10.3	9.5	10.5	12.9	Moy. sur période

Country or area	National currency Monnaie nationale	1995	2005	2010	2015	2016	2017	2018	2019	Pays ou zone
Zimbabwe										**Zimbabwe**
End of period	Zimbabwe Dollar (ZWL),	~0.0	80.8	...	...	...	...	...	16.8	Fin de période
Period average	dollar du Zimbabwe (ZWL)	~0.0	22.4	...	...	...	...	...	...	Moy. sur période
Euro Area										**Zone euro**
End of period	Euro (EUR)	...	0.8	0.7	0.9	0.9	0.8	0.9	0.9	Fin de période
Period average		...	0.8	0.8	0.9	0.9	0.9	0.8	0.9	Moy. sur période

Source:

International Monetary Fund (IMF), Washington, D.C., the database on International Financial Statistics supplemented by operational rates of exchange for United Nations programmes, last accessed June 2020.

1	East Caribbean Dollar.
2	African Financial Community (CFA) Franc, Central Bank of West African States (BCEAO).
3	African Financial Community (CFA) Franc, Bank of Central African States (BEAC).
4	For statistical purposes, the data for China do not include those for the Hong Kong Special Administrative Region (Hong Kong SAR), Macao Special Administrative Region (Macao SAR) and Taiwan Province of China.
5	UN operational exchange rate.
6	The national currency of Cuba is the Cuban Peso (CUP). The convertible peso (CUC) is used by foreigners and tourists in Cuba.
7	Netherlands Antillean Guilder.
8	Communauté financière du Pacifique (CFP) Franc.
9	Solomon Islands Dollar.
10	South Sudanese Pound.
11	Trinidad and Tobago Dollar.
12	Turkmenistan New Manat.
13	The Government of Ukraine has informed the United Nations that it is not in a position to provide statistical data concerning the Autonomous Republic of Crimea and the city of Sevastopol.
14	United Arab Emirates Dirham.

Source:

Fonds monétaire international (FMI), Washington, D.C., base de données des Statistiques Financières Internationales, complétée par les taux de change opérationnels de la Trésorerie de l'ONU, dernier accès juin 2020.

1	dollar des Caraïbes orientales.
2	franc Communauté financière africaine (CFA), Banque centrale des États de l'Afrique de l'Ouest (BCEAO).
3	franc Communauté financière africaine (CFA), Banque des États de l'Afrique centrale (BEAC).
4	Pour la présentation des statistiques, les données pour la Chine ne comprennent pas la région administrative spéciale de Hong Kong (RAS de Hong Kong), la région administrative spéciale de Macao (RAS de Macao) et la province chinoise de Taïwan.
5	Taux de change opérationnel des Nations Unies.
6	La monnaie nationale du Cuba est le Peso Cubain (CUP). Le Peso Cubain Convertible (CUC) est utilisé par les touristes et les étrangers à Cuba.
7	florin des Antilles néerlandaises.
8	franc Communauté financière du Pacifique (CFP).
9	dollar des Îles Salomon.
10	livre sud-soudanaise.
11	dollar de la Trinité-et-Tobago.
12	nouveau manat turkmène.
13	Le Gouvernement ukrainien a informé l'Organisation des Nations Unies qu'il n'est pas en mesure de fournir des données statistiques concernant la République autonome de Crimée et Sébastopol.
14	dirham des Émirats arabes unis.

16
Labour force participation rate and unemployment rate
Labour force (LF) participation rate and unemployment rate by sex (percent)

Taux d'activité et taux de chômage
Taux d'activité et taux de chômage par sexe (pourcentage)

Region, country or area & Région, pays ou zone &	Year Année	Male and Female Hommes et femmes LF particip. rate Taux d'activité	Male and Female Hommes et femmes Unemployment rate Taux de Chômage	Male Hommes LF particip. rate Taux d'activité	Male Hommes Unemployment rate Taux de Chômage	Female Femmes LF particip. rate Taux d'activité	Female Femmes Unemployment rate Taux de Chômage
Total, all countries or areas	*2005	63.8	5.9	77.3	5.7	50.3	6.2
Total, tous pays ou zones	*2010	62.5	5.9	76.1	5.8	48.8	6.1
	*2015	61.4	5.6	75.0	5.5	47.7	5.8
	*2020	60.5	5.4	74.0	5.3	47.0	5.6
Africa	*2005	64.8	7.1	75.1	6.7	54.9	7.6
Afrique	*2010	64.6	6.5	74.6	5.8	54.8	7.4
	*2015	63.3	6.7	72.8	6.1	54.0	7.3
	*2020	63.1	6.8	72.0	6.2	54.4	7.5
Northern Africa	*2005	47.0	12.8	72.5	10.7	21.6	19.9
Afrique septentrionale	*2010	47.8	10.6	73.1	7.5	22.8	20.1
	*2015	46.7	13.1	71.0	10.2	22.6	22.2
	*2020	45.7	11.9	69.3	8.9	22.2	21.0
Sub-Saharan Africa	*2005	70.3	5.9	75.9	5.5	64.8	6.3
Afrique subsaharienne	*2010	69.5	5.7	75.0	5.4	64.1	6.1
	*2015	67.9	5.4	73.3	5.0	62.7	5.9
	*2020	67.6	5.9	72.7	5.6	62.7	6.2
Eastern Africa	*2005	78.3	3.9	83.6	3.6	73.2	4.2
Afrique orientale	*2010	78.4	4.0	83.6	3.6	73.3	4.4
	*2015	77.7	3.3	82.9	3.0	72.7	3.7
	*2020	77.4	3.2	82.0	2.9	72.9	3.6
Middle Africa	*2005	73.7	3.9	76.4	4.3	71.1	3.5
Afrique centrale	*2010	70.3	5.4	73.8	5.2	66.8	5.6
	*2015	69.1	5.0	72.8	5.1	65.6	4.8
	*2020	68.7	4.8	72.2	5.0	65.3	4.5
Southern Africa	*2005	55.9	28.7	64.5	23.4	47.8	35.6
Afrique australe	*2010	53.4	24.5	61.2	22.5	46.0	27.0
	*2015	56.4	24.7	63.4	22.7	49.7	27.1
	*2020	56.9	27.5	63.5	25.6	50.7	29.8
Western Africa	*2005	63.9	4.5	70.3	4.5	57.5	4.5
Afrique occidentale	*2010	63.3	4.4	69.5	4.2	57.1	4.6
	*2015	59.1	4.6	65.2	4.1	53.1	5.1
	*2020	58.4	6.0	64.3	5.5	52.5	6.5
Americas	*2005	64.6	6.8	76.2	6.0	53.5	8.0
Amériques	*2010	63.9	7.9	74.8	7.5	53.6	8.6
	*2015	63.3	6.2	73.9	5.7	53.1	6.9
	*2020	63.3	6.6	73.4	5.9	53.6	7.5
Northern America	*2005	65.2	5.3	72.2	5.3	58.5	5.2
Amérique septentrionale	*2010	63.9	9.5	70.1	10.3	58.0	8.5
	*2015	62.4	5.5	68.6	5.6	56.4	5.3
	*2020	62.1	4.0	68.1	4.1	56.4	4.0
Latin America & the Caribbean	*2005	64.1	7.9	78.8	6.5	50.2	10.1
Amérique latine et Caraïbes	*2010	64.0	7.0	77.9	5.8	50.8	8.7
	*2015	63.8	6.7	77.2	5.8	51.1	8.0
	*2020	64.0	8.1	76.6	6.9	52.0	9.8
Caribbean	*2005	57.3	7.8	69.7	6.4	45.4	9.9
Caraïbes	*2010	58.2	8.5	69.7	7.2	47.1	10.2
	*2015	59.4	8.5	70.1	6.8	49.2	10.8
	*2020	59.9	7.3	70.2	5.8	50.1	9.4
Central America	*2005	61.1	3.9	81.8	3.7	42.0	4.3
Amérique centrale	*2010	61.1	5.2	80.3	5.1	43.4	5.3
	*2015	61.4	4.4	79.8	4.1	44.2	4.9
	*2020	61.6	4.1	79.6	3.7	44.9	4.7
South America	*2005	66.0	9.3	78.7	7.5	53.8	11.8
Amérique du Sud	*2010	65.6	7.4	77.9	5.9	53.9	9.6
	*2015	65.2	7.4	76.9	6.3	54.0	8.8
	*2020	65.3	9.7	76.1	8.4	55.0	11.5
Central Asia	*2005	62.6	7.9	72.7	7.7	53.2	8.1
Asie centrale	*2010	63.1	6.1	73.6	6.1	53.2	6.1
	*2015	63.6	5.7	74.4	5.7	53.3	5.6
	*2020	62.7	5.9	74.2	6.0	51.8	5.8

16 Labour force participation rate and unemployment rate *(continued)*
Labour force (LF) participation rate and unemployment rate by sex (percent)

Taux d'activité et taux de chômage *(suite)*
Taux d'activité et taux de chômage par sexe (pourcentage)

Region, country or area & Région, pays ou zone &	Year Année	Male and Female Hommes et femmes		Male Hommes		Female Femmes	
		LF particip. rate Taux d'activité	Unemployment rate Taux de Chômage	LF particip. rate Taux d'activité	Unemployment rate Taux de Chômage	LF particip. rate Taux d'activité	Unemployment rate Taux de Chômage
Eastern Asia	*2005	71.9	4.5	79.1	4.9	64.4	3.9
Asie orientale	*2010	69.8	4.5	77.5	5.0	62.0	3.9
	*2015	68.7	4.5	76.3	4.9	61.0	3.9
	*2020	66.9	4.2	74.5	4.6	59.0	3.6
South-eastern Asia	*2005	67.5	4.4	81.0	4.1	54.4	4.9
Asie du Sud-Est	*2010	68.7	3.2	81.1	3.1	56.5	3.4
	*2015	68.3	2.9	80.5	3.0	56.2	2.8
	*2020	67.5	3.1	79.3	3.1	56.0	3.0
Southern Asia	*2005	57.2	5.3	82.6	5.2	30.3	5.9
Asie méridionale	*2010	53.9	5.2	80.2	5.2	26.0	5.5
	*2015	51.6	5.4	78.1	5.2	23.7	6.2
	*2020	50.7	5.4	76.9	5.3	23.1	5.8
Western Asia [1]	*2005	48.3	8.1	75.0	7.1	16.7	13.1
Asie occidentale [1]	*2010	49.8	7.2	76.0	5.9	16.9	14.0
	*2015	51.4	7.5	77.6	5.6	18.6	17.0
	*2020	51.3	8.0	77.7	6.1	18.0	18.6
Caucasus [2]	*2005	50.1	10.4	69.8	10.3	31.8	10.6
Caucase [2]	*2010	51.8	10.7	69.7	10.4	35.0	11.1
	*2015	54.4	9.9	71.4	9.1	38.5	11.1
	*2020	55.6	11.5	71.9	10.8	40.1	12.7
Eastern Europe	*2005	57.8	8.7	65.1	8.8	51.6	8.6
Europe orientale	*2010	58.8	8.0	66.7	8.5	52.0	7.4
	*2015	59.2	6.6	67.7	6.9	52.0	6.2
	*2020	58.5	4.7	67.0	5.0	51.3	4.5
Northern Europe	*2005	62.0	...	68.9	...	55.6	...
Europe septentrionale	*2010	62.0	...	68.1	...	56.3	...
	*2015	62.3	...	67.8	...	57.1	...
	*2020	62.7	...	67.6	...	57.9	...
Southern Europe	*2005	53.3	10.4	64.4	8.4	42.8	13.1
Europe méridionale	*2010	53.4	14.3	62.7	13.5	44.7	15.4
	*2015	53.2	17.2	61.4	16.2	45.6	18.5
	*2020	53.1	11.3	60.9	9.9	45.9	13.0
Western Europe	*2005	58.0	9.1	65.7	8.9	50.8	9.4
Europe occidentale	*2010	58.8	7.2	65.4	7.3	52.6	7.2
	*2015	58.9	6.9	64.6	7.2	53.5	6.6
	*2020	59.0	5.0	64.3	5.1	53.9	4.8
Oceania	*2005	64.3	4.5	71.2	4.5	57.5	4.6
Océanie	*2010	63.0	5.0	69.1	5.0	56.9	5.1
	*2015	62.5	5.5	67.8	5.5	57.2	5.4
	*2020	62.5	4.8	67.2	4.8	57.9	4.7
Afghanistan	*2005	48.5	11.4	78.8	10.8	15.8	14.9
Afghanistan	*2010	47.4	11.5	78.4	10.9	14.9	14.8
	*2015	48.4	11.4	76.2	10.7	18.8	14.4
	*2020	48.9	11.2	74.6	10.4	21.8	14.1
Albania	*2005	57.5	16.5	67.1	16.1	47.9	16.9
Albanie	*2010	54.3	14.1	62.9	12.8	45.8	15.9
	*2015	55.0	17.1	63.8	17.1	46.1	17.1
	*2020	55.6	12.8	64.4	13.3	46.6	12.2
Algeria	*2005	42.5	15.3	71.8	14.8	12.8	18.0
Algérie	*2010	42.3	10.0	70.0	8.1	14.4	19.1
	*2015	41.5	11.2	67.4	10.0	15.2	16.7
	*2020	41.0	11.5	67.0	9.6	14.6	20.5
American Samoa [3]	2000	52.9	5.1	58.8	4.9	41.2	6.0
Samoa américaines [3]	#2005	59.9	...	...	...	...	...
	2010	52.8	# 9.2	...	...	...	...
Angola	*2005	77.1	3.8	78.8	4.7	75.5	2.9
Angola	*2010	77.3	9.4	78.9	8.0	75.8	10.9
	*2015	77.6	7.3	79.1	6.9	76.1	7.7
	*2020	77.4	6.8	78.8	6.9	76.1	6.6
Anguilla							
Anguilla	2002	72.3	7.8	77.2	6.3	67.2	9.5

16 Labour force participation rate and unemployment rate *(continued)*
Labour force (LF) participation rate and unemployment rate by sex (percent)

Taux d'activité et taux de chômage *(suite)*
Taux d'activité et taux de chômage par sexe (pourcentage)

Region, country or area & Région, pays ou zone &	Year Année	Male and Female Hommes et femmes		Male Hommes		Female Femmes	
		LF particip. rate Taux d'activité	Unemployment rate Taux de Chômage	LF particip. rate Taux d'activité	Unemployment rate Taux de Chômage	LF particip. rate Taux d'activité	Unemployment rate Taux de Chômage
Antigua and Barbuda Antigua-et-Barbuda	2001	71.7	8.4	78.4	8.0	65.9	8.8
Argentina	*2005	62.0	11.5	75.5	10.0	49.6	13.6
Argentine	*2010	60.4	7.7	74.0	6.7	48.0	9.2
	*2015	60.0	7.8	73.0	7.0	48.0	8.9
	*2020	61.2	10.4	72.7	9.7	50.6	11.5
Armenia	*2005	52.6	10.4	61.7	9.6	45.0	11.3
Arménie	*2010	56.5	19.0	67.8	17.1	47.2	21.3
	*2015	57.1	18.3	66.8	17.4	49.0	19.3
	*2020	55.5	16.6	65.8	15.9	47.0	17.5
Aruba	2001	...	6.9	...	6.5	...	7.4
Aruba	#2010[4]	63.9[5]	10.6	68.9[5]	10.8	59.5[5]	10.4
	#2011	63.8	...	69.6	...	58.8	...
Australia	*2005	64.6	5.0	72.2	4.9	57.1	5.2
Australie	*2010	65.6	5.2	72.5	5.1	58.8	5.4
	*2015	65.2	6.1	71.2	6.0	59.2	6.1
	*2020	65.4	5.3	70.7	5.3	60.2	5.4
Austria	*2005	58.1	5.6	66.1	5.4	50.7	5.9
Autriche	*2010	60.0	4.8	66.9	5.0	53.5	4.6
	*2015	60.1	5.7	66.0	6.1	54.5	5.3
	*2020	60.6	4.8	66.4	4.8	55.0	4.7
Azerbaijan	*2005	62.8	7.3	68.4	7.3	57.7	7.4
Azerbaïdjan	*2010	63.8	5.6	67.5	4.4	60.2	6.9
	*2015	65.5	5.0	68.7	4.1	62.5	5.9
	*2020	66.1	6.0	69.3	5.2	63.1	6.8
Bahamas	*2005	74.7	10.2	81.0	9.3	68.8	11.2
Bahamas	*2010	74.6	14.8	81.6	14.6	68.1	15.1
	*2015	74.8	12.0	81.7	11.1	68.4	13.0
	*2020	74.5	11.3	81.5	10.7	68.0	11.9
Bahrain	*2005	68.6	1.0	86.2	0.3	38.9	3.6
Bahreïn	*2010	72.2	1.1	87.4	0.4	43.8	3.7
	*2015	71.6	1.1	87.0	0.4	43.8	3.8
	*2020	73.6	0.8	87.2	0.2	45.0	3.2
Bangladesh	*2005	57.5	4.3	85.6	3.4	27.9	7.1
Bangladesh	*2010	56.9	3.4	83.2	3.0	29.9	4.4
	*2015	56.6	4.4	80.4	3.2	32.4	7.5
	*2020	59.0	4.2	81.3	3.4	36.4	6.0
Barbados	*2005	68.9	9.1	74.8	7.5	63.6	10.8
Barbade	*2010	67.4	10.7	72.4	10.9	62.9	10.5
	*2015	65.4	11.4	69.5	12.4	61.6	10.3
	*2020	64.9	10.9	68.7	10.5	61.4	11.4
Belarus	*2005	60.9	8.5	67.3	10.0	55.4	6.8
Bélarus	*2010	63.0	6.1	69.6	7.5	57.5	4.7
	*2015	64.3	5.9	71.0	7.5	58.6	4.3
	*2020	63.7	4.6	71.3	5.9	57.3	3.4
Belgium	*2005	53.2	8.4	61.3	7.6	45.5	9.5
Belgique	*2010	54.0	8.3	60.8	8.1	47.5	8.5
	*2015	53.5	8.5	59.1	9.1	48.0	7.8
	*2020	53.4	5.7	58.4	6.0	48.5	5.3
Belize	*2005	63.9	10.9	81.9	7.4	45.8	17.2
Belize	*2010	63.3	8.5	80.4	5.9	46.4	13.0
	*2015	64.0	7.6	80.0	5.4	48.4	11.1
	*2020	65.2	6.4	80.6	4.3	50.2	9.5
Benin	*2005	71.9	0.8	76.6	1.0	67.3	0.6
Bénin	*2010	71.1	1.0	73.0	0.9	69.2	1.2
	*2015	70.8	2.6	73.3	2.4	68.4	2.8
	*2020	71.0	2.0	73.0	2.0	69.0	2.1
Bermuda [3]	2000	...	2.7	...	3.1	...	2.3
Bermudes [3]	#2009	82.0	4.5	86.0	6.0	79.0	3.0
	2010	84.0	...	87.0	...	81.0	...
	2012[6]	76.1	8.4	80.0	8.7	72.6	8.2
	2013[6]	...	6.7	...	...	...	...

Labour force participation rate and unemployment rate *(continued)*
Labour force (LF) participation rate and unemployment rate by sex (percent)

Taux d'activité et taux de chômage *(suite)*
Taux d'activité et taux de chômage par sexe (pourcentage)

Region, country or area & Région, pays ou zone &	Year Année	Male and Female Hommes et femmes		Male Hommes		Female Femmes	
		LF particip. rate Taux d'activité	Unemployment rate Taux de Chômage	LF particip. rate Taux d'activité	Unemployment rate Taux de Chômage	LF particip. rate Taux d'activité	Unemployment rate Taux de Chômage
Bhutan	*2005	70.6	3.1	75.3	2.9	65.2	3.3
Bhoutan	*2010	68.3	3.3	72.5	2.8	63.5	4.1
	*2015	65.9	2.5	72.6	1.9	58.2	3.3
	*2020	67.0	2.4	73.8	1.8	59.0	3.3
Bolivia (Plurin. State of)	*2005	72.7	2.8	82.8	2.3	62.6	3.6
Bolivie (État plurin. de)	*2010	72.0	2.6	82.1	2.2	62.0	3.1
	*2015	67.0	3.1	79.7	2.6	54.4	3.8
	*2020	71.7	3.5	80.4	3.1	63.0	3.8
Bosnia and Herzegovina	*2005	44.0	30.5	57.2	28.2	31.6	34.3
Bosnie-Herzégovine	*2010	45.9	27.3	58.2	25.7	34.3	29.9
	*2015	46.9	27.7	58.2	25.8	36.3	30.7
	*2020	46.1	18.4	57.7	16.6	35.2	21.3
Botswana	*2005	62.5	19.8	71.0	17.7	54.7	22.2
Botswana	*2010	60.1	17.9	66.9	14.7	53.8	21.5
	*2015	70.9	17.8	77.7	14.8	64.9	20.8
	*2020	71.0	18.7	77.0	15.9	65.5	21.8
Brazil	*2005	66.4	9.6	78.2	7.4	55.1	12.5
Brésil	*2010	64.7	7.7	76.5	5.6	53.5	10.6
	*2015	64.1	8.4	75.3	7.2	53.3	10.1
	*2020	63.7	12.0	73.9	10.2	54.1	14.3
Brunei Darussalam	*2005	67.1	5.7	77.6	4.7	56.2	7.0
Brunéi Darussalam	*2010	66.4	6.7	75.3	5.9	57.0	8.0
	*2015	65.9	7.9	73.1	7.3	58.0	8.8
	*2020	64.4	9.0	70.7	8.3	57.6	10.0
Bulgaria	*2005	50.4	10.1	56.4	10.3	44.7	9.8
Bulgarie	*2010	53.4	10.3	59.5	10.9	47.7	9.6
	*2015	54.2	9.1	60.1	9.8	48.6	8.4
	*2020	55.2	3.9	61.9	4.2	49.1	3.5
Burkina Faso	*2005	74.2	4.0	86.8	3.5	62.4	4.6
Burkina Faso	*2010	70.4	4.7	81.7	3.6	59.7	6.2
	*2015	66.7	6.4	75.4	4.0	58.3	9.4
	*2020	66.3	6.4	74.7	4.0	58.2	9.5
Burundi	*2005	80.4	1.8	79.2	2.4	81.6	1.3
Burundi	*2010	78.8	1.8	77.3	2.3	80.2	1.3
	*2015	78.6	1.6	77.1	2.0	80.0	1.1
	*2020	79.1	1.4	77.8	1.9	80.4	1.0
Cabo Verde	*2005	57.6	10.6	71.5	10.4	45.0	11.0
Cabo Verde	*2010	58.6	10.7	70.2	10.4	47.1	11.1
	*2015	59.9	11.9	68.7	11.6	51.2	12.4
	*2020	60.6	12.3	67.6	13.0	53.6	11.5
Cambodia	*2005	81.0	1.4	86.9	1.2	75.7	1.5
Cambodge	*2010	85.2	0.8	89.1	0.8	81.8	0.8
	*2015	80.3	0.4	86.9	0.3	74.3	0.5
	*2020	82.4	0.7	89.0	0.6	76.3	0.9
Cameroon	*2005	81.8	4.4	85.4	4.2	78.2	4.6
Cameroun	*2010	76.0	4.1	81.4	3.4	70.6	4.9
	*2015	76.3	3.5	81.6	3.1	71.1	4.0
	*2020	75.9	3.4	81.0	3.0	70.9	3.9
Canada	*2005	66.7	6.8	72.6	7.0	60.9	6.5
Canada	*2010	66.6	8.1	71.5	8.8	61.9	7.2
	*2015	65.6	6.9	70.5	7.5	60.9	6.3
	*2020	64.9	5.4	69.2	5.7	60.7	5.1
Cayman Islands	2005	...	3.5	...	...	...	...
Îles Caïmanes	#2009	84.2[5]	6.0	88.0[5]	7.0	80.6[5]	5.0
	2010	81.8	6.7	...	...	...	...
	2013	83.1	6.3	85.6	6.7	80.6	5.8
Central African Republic	*2005	72.4	3.9	80.0	4.0	65.1	3.8
République centrafricaine	*2010	72.6	3.9	80.4	4.0	65.0	3.8
	*2015	72.8	3.9	81.2	3.9	64.7	3.8
	*2020	71.9	3.7	79.8	3.8	64.4	3.6

16

Labour force participation rate and unemployment rate *(continued)*
Labour force (LF) participation rate and unemployment rate by sex (percent)

Taux d'activité et taux de chômage *(suite)*
Taux d'activité et taux de chômage par sexe (pourcentage)

Region, country or area & Région, pays ou zone &	Year Année	Male and Female Hommes et femmes		Male Hommes		Female Femmes	
		LF particip. rate Taux d'activité	Unemployment rate Taux de Chômage	LF particip. rate Taux d'activité	Unemployment rate Taux de Chômage	LF particip. rate Taux d'activité	Unemployment rate Taux de Chômage
Chad	*2005	71.9	1.3	80.0	1.6	63.9	0.8
Tchad	*2010	71.5	1.6	79.3	1.9	63.8	1.2
	*2015	70.9	1.8	78.2	2.1	63.8	1.6
	*2020	70.7	1.9	77.5	2.1	63.9	1.8
Channel Islands	*2005	59.3	8.0	69.0	8.1	50.1	7.9
Îles Anglo-Normandes	*2010	59.1	8.4	67.8	8.3	50.8	8.6
	*2015	58.9	8.1	67.1	7.9	51.0	8.3
	*2020	58.0	7.5	65.6	7.4	50.6	7.7
Chile	*2005	57.3	9.3	74.0	7.6	41.4	12.3
Chili	*2010	60.4	8.4	74.6	7.4	46.9	9.9
	*2015	62.1	6.5	74.7	6.1	50.1	7.1
	*2020	62.8	7.1	74.1	6.6	52.0	7.8
China [7]	*2005	73.6	4.5	80.0	5.0	66.9	3.9
Chine [7]	*2010	71.3	4.5	78.3	5.0	64.0	3.9
	*2015	69.8	4.6	76.9	5.1	62.5	4.0
	*2020	67.5	4.4	74.8	4.8	59.8	3.8
China, Hong Kong SAR	*2005	60.9	5.6	71.1	6.5	51.7	4.4
Chine, RAS de Hong Kong	*2010	59.2	4.3	68.1	5.0	51.4	3.5
	*2015	60.8	3.3	68.5	3.4	54.3	3.2
	*2020	59.7	4.3	67.0	4.9	53.7	3.6
China, Macao SAR	*2005	64.4	4.1	72.5	4.4	57.3	3.8
Chine, RAS de Macao	*2010	70.8	2.8	76.9	3.6	65.3	2.1
	*2015	71.6	1.8	77.2	2.0	66.6	1.6
	*2020	70.2	2.5	76.3	3.0	64.6	2.0
Colombia	*2005	66.3	11.9	81.2	9.1	52.5	15.9
Colombie	*2010	68.2	11.0	81.6	8.6	55.7	14.2
	*2015	69.9	8.3	82.0	6.4	58.5	10.8
	*2020	68.9	9.7	81.0	7.5	57.5	12.7
Comoros	*2005	41.8	4.5	50.2	4.3	33.3	4.9
Comores	*2010	42.1	4.6	49.7	4.3	34.5	4.9
	*2015	42.8	4.5	49.8	4.2	35.7	4.9
	*2020	43.4	4.4	50.0	4.1	36.8	4.8
Congo	*2005	68.9	19.8	70.9	18.5	66.9	21.1
Congo	*2010	69.6	14.0	71.5	12.4	67.7	15.6
	*2015	69.8	9.9	71.9	9.1	67.7	10.8
	*2020	69.3	9.3	71.2	8.7	67.4	9.9
Cook Islands	2001[8]	74.5	...	75.5	...	63.0	...
Îles Cook	#2006[5]	70.2	6.9	76.1	6.7	64.2	7.3
	2011[5]	71.0	8.2	76.6	8.2	65.4	8.1
Costa Rica	*2005	62.5	6.6	80.4	5.0	44.7	9.3
Costa Rica	*2010	60.8	7.2	76.5	6.0	45.3	9.1
	*2015	62.0	9.0	75.6	7.6	48.4	11.2
	*2020	62.0	12.7	75.9	10.7	48.2	15.9
Côte d'Ivoire	*2005	62.9	5.5	76.7	5.6	48.0	5.4
Côte d'Ivoire	*2010	60.3	6.7	72.1	6.8	47.8	6.6
	*2015	57.7	3.1	67.3	2.5	47.8	4.0
	*2020	56.9	3.4	65.4	3.2	48.3	3.8
Croatia	*2005	53.3	12.6	61.1	11.6	46.2	13.8
Croatie	*2010	52.7	11.6	59.8	11.0	46.2	12.3
	*2015	52.5	16.2	59.2	15.6	46.6	16.9
	*2020	51.0	7.1	57.2	6.1	45.3	8.3
Cuba	*2005	52.5	2.0	67.1	1.8	38.3	2.2
Cuba	*2010	55.1	2.5	68.4	2.4	42.0	2.7
	*2015	54.2	2.4	67.1	2.3	41.6	2.6
	*2020	53.4	1.6	66.7	1.5	40.5	1.7
Curaçao	2005	59.4	18.2	65.4	17.1	54.8	19.2
Curaçao	2008	59.0	10.3	66.5	8.0	53.2	12.5
	#2009[6]	...	9.6	...	7.8	...	11.2
	2013[6]	...	13.0	...	10.5	...	15.4

16

Labour force participation rate and unemployment rate *(continued)*
Labour force (LF) participation rate and unemployment rate by sex (percent)

Taux d'activité et taux de chômage *(suite)*
Taux d'activité et taux de chômage par sexe (pourcentage)

Region, country or area & Région, pays ou zone &	Year Année	Male and Female Hommes et femmes		Male Hommes		Female Femmes	
		LF particip. rate Taux d'activité	Unemployment rate Taux de Chômage	LF particip. rate Taux d'activité	Unemployment rate Taux de Chômage	LF particip. rate Taux d'activité	Unemployment rate Taux de Chômage
Cyprus Chypre	*2005	63.0	5.3	72.7	4.4	53.2	6.5
	*2010	64.1	6.3	70.6	6.1	57.6	6.4
	*2015	62.6	14.9	67.4	15.0	57.9	14.8
	*2020	62.9	7.2	68.0	6.4	57.8	8.3
Czechia Tchéquie	*2005	59.5	7.9	68.9	6.5	50.8	9.8
	*2010	58.4	7.3	68.0	6.4	49.2	8.5
	*2015	59.6	5.1	68.3	4.2	51.4	6.1
	*2020	60.3	1.9	68.2	1.6	52.8	2.3
Dem. People's Rep. Korea Rép. pop. dém. de Corée	*2005	81.5	2.9	88.6	3.3	74.9	2.5
	*2010	80.9	2.9	88.0	3.3	74.2	2.5
	*2015	80.5	2.9	87.7	3.3	73.7	2.5
	*2020	80.3	2.8	87.7	3.1	73.3	2.4
Dem. Rep. of the Congo Rép. dém. du Congo	*2005	71.6	2.9	72.8	3.5	70.5	2.2
	*2010	66.3	4.0	68.7	4.7	63.9	3.2
	*2015	63.9	4.4	66.8	5.2	61.1	3.6
	*2020	63.2	4.3	66.1	5.0	60.4	3.4
Denmark Danemark	*2005	65.9	4.8	71.4	4.4	60.5	5.3
	*2010	64.4	7.5	69.1	8.4	59.8	6.5
	*2015	62.0	6.2	66.4	5.9	57.7	6.4
	*2020	62.1	4.9	66.2	4.6	58.2	5.1
Djibouti Djibouti	*2005	60.6	10.6	74.1	10.7	47.1	10.6
	*2010	60.8	10.7	71.0	10.7	49.6	10.7
	*2015	60.5	10.6	69.5	10.4	50.4	10.8
	*2020	60.3	10.3	68.8	10.3	50.8	10.4
Dominica Dominique	2001	57.7	11.0	70.2	12.0	45.0	9.5
Dominican Republic République dominicaine	*2005	57.5	6.6	74.8	4.9	40.2	9.8
	*2010	58.1	5.2	73.8	4.1	42.4	7.1
	*2015	63.7	7.6	78.0	5.5	49.6	10.9
	*2020	64.4	5.9	77.4	4.2	51.6	8.4
Ecuador Équateur	*2005	68.2	3.8	83.9	3.2	52.6	4.7
	*2010	65.1	4.1	80.5	3.5	49.9	5.0
	*2015	66.5	3.6	81.0	3.0	52.1	4.5
	*2020	68.1	4.2	81.0	3.6	55.3	5.2
Egypt Égypte	*2005	46.6	11.2	73.0	7.3	20.3	25.1
	*2010	49.1	8.8	75.6	4.8	22.6	22.1
	*2015	47.9	13.1	73.3	9.4	22.5	24.9
	*2020	46.5	10.1	70.9	6.6	22.1	21.4
El Salvador El Salvador	*2005	60.9	7.2	79.0	8.9	45.5	4.8
	*2010	59.9	4.9	76.6	5.4	46.0	4.2
	*2015	58.8	4.0	75.3	4.4	45.2	3.5
	*2020	59.2	4.2	75.9	4.7	45.5	3.6
Equatorial Guinea Guinée équatoriale	*2005	60.4	6.7	67.1	6.9	52.3	6.4
	*2010	61.8	6.7	67.7	6.8	54.0	6.5
	*2015	62.4	6.6	67.8	6.8	54.9	6.4
	*2020	62.3	6.5	67.5	6.6	55.0	6.3
Eritrea Érythrée	*2005	75.1	5.4	80.3	5.5	70.0	5.2
	*2010	77.1	5.4	83.0	5.6	71.4	5.2
	*2015	78.8	5.3	86.1	5.5	71.6	5.2
	*2020	78.3	5.2	85.3	5.3	71.4	5.0
Estonia Estonie	*2005	58.6	8.0	64.7	9.2	53.5	6.9
	*2010	60.5	16.7	67.1	19.3	55.0	14.1
	*2015	62.2	6.2	69.5	6.2	56.0	6.1
	*2020	63.3	5.4	70.7	5.6	56.8	5.2
Eswatini Eswatini	*2005	50.8	27.6	58.0	24.7	44.8	30.6
	*2010	50.9	26.9	57.4	24.6	45.5	29.4
	*2015	51.4	23.5	56.4	21.9	47.0	25.1
	*2020	52.7	22.0	56.9	20.5	48.6	23.6
Ethiopia Éthiopie	*2005	82.1	2.5	90.1	1.8	74.4	3.3
	*2010	81.2	2.3	88.9	1.7	73.8	3.1
	*2015	80.1	2.2	87.1	1.6	73.3	2.9
	*2020	79.6	2.1	85.8	1.5	73.6	2.8

16

Labour force participation rate and unemployment rate *(continued)*
Labour force (LF) participation rate and unemployment rate by sex (percent)

Taux d'activité et taux de chômage *(suite)*
Taux d'activité et taux de chômage par sexe (pourcentage)

Region, country or area & Région, pays ou zone &	Year Année	Male and Female Hommes et femmes		Male Hommes		Female Femmes	
		LF particip. rate Taux d'activité	Unemployment rate Taux de Chômage	LF particip. rate Taux d'activité	Unemployment rate Taux de Chômage	LF particip. rate Taux d'activité	Unemployment rate Taux de Chômage
Falkland Islands (Malvinas) [9] Îles Falkland (Malvinas) [9]	2013	# 81.9	1.2	# 86.0	1.1	# 77.2	1.4
Faroe Islands Îles Féroé	2005[3] 2010[6,10] 2013[6,10]	... 81.7 82.9	3.2 # 6.4 4.0	... 85.3 86.0	2.6 # 5.1 3.4	... 77.5 79.4	3.9 # 8.0 4.9
Fiji Fidji	*2005 *2010 *2015 *2020	57.0 61.5 58.8 57.6	3.9 4.3 4.4 4.1	78.4 79.2 77.0 76.2	3.3 4.1 3.8 3.5	34.9 43.1 40.1 38.6	5.2 4.8 5.5 5.3
Finland Finlande	*2005 *2010 *2015 *2020	60.6 59.8 58.8 58.9	8.4 8.4 9.4 6.7	64.8 63.9 62.3 62.5	8.2 9.1 9.9 7.0	56.6 56.0 55.5 55.3	8.6 7.6 8.8 6.3
France France	*2005 *2010 *2015 *2020	55.9 56.1 55.5 54.9	8.5 8.9 10.4 8.3	62.5 61.9 60.6 59.6	7.8 8.7 10.8 8.5	49.9 50.8 50.8 50.7	9.3 9.1 9.9 8.2
French Guiana [6] Guyane française [6]	2005 2010 #2013	42.1 48.9 53.4	24.8 21.0 21.3	48.2 54.9 58.8	22.8 17.8 16.7	36.3 43.2 48.4	27.0 25.1 26.3
French Polynesia Polynésie française	*2005 *2010 *2015 *2020	56.8 56.6 55.6 53.8	12.4 14.3 13.8 11.9	65.7 64.2 62.4 60.1	11.5 14.0 13.0 11.0	47.5 48.6 48.6 47.4	13.7 14.8 14.7 13.1
Gabon Gabon	*2005 *2010 *2015 *2020	47.7 49.5 51.3 53.1	16.9 20.4 20.3 20.2	57.5 58.4 59.7 61.9	12.8 14.7 14.5 14.3	38.0 40.2 42.5 43.8	23.0 29.0 28.7 28.7
Gambia Gambie	*2005 *2010 *2015 *2020	58.3 58.6 59.0 59.6	9.4 9.4 9.3 9.1	68.7 68.0 67.8 68.1	7.0 6.9 6.8 6.6	48.4 49.7 50.6 51.4	12.5 12.6 12.6 12.3
Georgia Géorgie	*2005 *2010 *2015 *2020	64.1 66.3 69.3 68.3	13.8 20.2 16.5 14.7	73.6 77.7 80.9 80.9	14.8 22.4 18.7 16.1	55.9 56.4 59.1 57.4	12.7 17.5 13.9 13.1
Germany Allemagne	*2005 *2010 *2015 *2020	58.5 59.4 60.1 60.8	11.2 7.0 4.6 3.0	66.7 66.5 66.1 66.5	11.4 7.4 5.0 3.3	50.7 52.8 54.3 55.3	10.9 6.5 4.2 2.7
Ghana Ghana	*2005 *2010 *2015 *2020	71.9 70.1 68.0 67.7	5.5 5.3 6.8 4.5	74.2 73.3 72.5 71.8	5.3 4.9 7.0 4.4	69.7 66.9 63.5 63.5	5.7 5.8 6.6 4.7
Gibraltar Gibraltar	2001	68.4	...	78.8	...	57.5	...
Greece Grèce	*2005 *2010 *2015 *2020	53.7 53.4 52.2 51.4	10.0 12.7 24.9 15.5	65.0 63.2 59.9 59.3	6.3 10.0 21.8 11.8	42.8 44.1 44.8 43.9	15.5 16.4 28.9 20.2
Greenland Groenland	2005 2006 #2013[11,12]	... ...	9.3 8.4 9.7	... ...	10.4 10.0 9.6	... ...	8.0 6.7 9.8
Grenada Grenade	2001	...	10.2	...	9.6	...	10.9
Guadeloupe [6] Guadeloupe [6]	2005 2010 #2013	41.8 41.6 52.7	25.9 23.8 26.1	46.8 44.2 56.5	22.4 21.4 23.8	37.7 39.5 49.6	29.5 26.0 28.3
Guam Guam	*2005 *2010 *2015 *2020	68.1 66.7 65.3 64.2	7.0 8.2 6.9 5.7	79.8 78.4 77.0 76.2	6.5 7.4 7.0 5.7	56.1 54.7 53.4 52.2	7.8 9.4 6.8 5.7

16

Labour force participation rate and unemployment rate *(continued)*
Labour force (LF) participation rate and unemployment rate by sex (percent)

Taux d'activité et taux de chômage *(suite)*
Taux d'activité et taux de chômage par sexe (pourcentage)

Region, country or area & Région, pays ou zone &	Year Année	Male and Female Hommes et femmes		Male Hommes		Female Femmes	
		LF particip. rate Taux d'activité	Unemployment rate Taux de Chômage	LF particip. rate Taux d'activité	Unemployment rate Taux de Chômage	LF particip. rate Taux d'activité	Unemployment rate Taux de Chômage
Guatemala Guatemala	*2005	62.5	3.0	85.3	2.8	41.6	3.4
	*2010	61.5	3.5	84.3	3.3	40.5	3.8
	*2015	61.4	2.5	85.5	2.0	39.1	3.5
	*2020	62.4	2.5	86.4	2.1	39.9	3.4
Guinea Guinée	*2005	63.5	4.5	64.9	5.6	62.4	3.5
	*2010	63.0	4.5	63.6	5.6	62.5	3.5
	*2015	62.3	4.4	62.0	5.6	62.6	3.5
	*2020	61.6	4.3	60.3	5.5	62.8	3.3
Guinea-Bissau Guinée-Bissau	*2005	71.7	2.6	79.4	2.9	64.8	2.4
	*2010	71.5	2.7	78.7	2.9	65.1	2.4
	*2015	71.9	2.6	78.8	2.8	65.6	2.4
	*2020	72.0	2.5	78.6	2.7	65.9	2.2
Guyana Guyana	*2005	56.4	11.1	77.0	9.5	36.0	14.4
	*2010	56.3	11.5	73.8	9.6	39.3	14.8
	*2015	56.2	12.0	70.1	10.0	42.4	15.3
	*2020	56.2	11.8	68.4	9.6	44.1	15.2
Haiti Haïti	*2005	64.4	14.4	70.1	12.5	59.1	16.5
	*2010	65.3	15.4	71.6	13.0	59.3	18.1
	*2015	66.5	14.0	72.0	11.2	61.2	17.0
	*2020	67.4	13.9	72.9	11.4	62.1	16.7
Honduras Honduras	*2005	63.9	4.9	85.5	4.1	43.0	6.5
	*2010	64.4	4.1	84.8	3.4	44.5	5.4
	*2015	66.6	6.2	85.3	4.5	48.3	9.0
	*2020	68.8	5.2	85.8	4.3	52.1	6.8
Hungary Hongrie	*2005	50.2	7.2	58.4	7.0	42.9	7.4
	*2010	50.5	11.2	58.2	11.6	43.8	10.7
	*2015	54.8	6.8	63.4	6.6	47.3	7.0
	*2020	56.4	3.5	65.3	3.4	48.5	3.5
Iceland Islande	*2005	75.8	2.6	80.7	2.6	70.9	2.5
	*2010	74.9	7.6	79.1	8.3	70.6	6.7
	*2015	77.0	4.0	81.0	3.9	73.1	4.1
	*2020	74.8	3.2	78.9	3.3	70.6	3.2
India Inde	*2005	58.2	5.6	82.9	5.6	31.8	5.6
	*2010	54.0	5.6	80.5	5.6	25.7	5.7
	*2015	50.8	5.6	77.9	5.6	21.7	5.6
	*2020	49.2	5.4	76.0	5.4	20.3	5.3
Indonesia Indonésie	*2005	63.9	8.0	82.4	6.8	45.5	10.1
	*2010	67.2	5.6	83.2	5.1	51.2	6.4
	*2015	66.5	4.5	82.4	4.6	50.6	4.4
	*2020	67.5	4.8	81.8	4.9	53.2	4.7
Iran (Islamic Republic of) Iran (Rép. islamique d')	*2005	47.5	12.1	74.6	10.6	19.5	18.2
	*2010	42.9	13.5	69.9	11.9	15.7	20.7
	*2015	42.4	11.1	69.7	9.3	14.8	19.5
	*2020	44.3	11.2	71.1	9.3	17.3	19.0
Iraq Iraq	*2005	42.3	9.0	73.3	9.2	11.5	7.6
	*2010	42.1	8.4	72.3	8.0	12.0	10.5
	*2015	44.0	10.7	73.8	8.5	14.1	22.2
	*2020	43.1	12.8	74.3	10.0	11.8	30.5
Ireland Irlande	*2005	65.1	4.3	75.9	4.6	54.6	4.0
	*2010	63.0	14.5	70.5	17.1	55.6	11.4
	*2015	62.2	9.9	69.5	10.7	55.1	8.9
	*2020	61.8	5.2	67.9	5.5	55.8	4.8
Isle of Man Île de Man	2001	63.3	1.6	71.4	1.7	55.7	1.5
	2006	62.8	2.4	69.9	2.8	56.3	2.0
	#2011[3]	63.3	3.3[11]	69.3	3.8[11]	57.5	2.8[11]
	#2013[13]	...	2.6	...	3.4	...	1.7
Israel Israël	*2005	61.7	11.3	68.8	11.1	55.1	11.6
	*2010	63.0	8.5	69.4	8.9	57.0	8.0
	*2015	64.1	5.3	69.5	5.1	59.0	5.4
	*2020	64.0	3.8	68.5	3.8	59.7	3.8

16

Labour force participation rate and unemployment rate *(continued)*
Labour force (LF) participation rate and unemployment rate by sex (percent)

Taux d'activité et taux de chômage *(suite)*
Taux d'activité et taux de chômage par sexe (pourcentage)

Region, country or area & Région, pays ou zone &	Year Année	Male and Female Hommes et femmes		Male Hommes		Female Femmes	
		LF particip. rate Taux d'activité	Unemployment rate Taux de Chômage	LF particip. rate Taux d'activité	Unemployment rate Taux de Chômage	LF particip. rate Taux d'activité	Unemployment rate Taux de Chômage
Italy Italie	*2005	49.0	7.7	61.0	6.2	37.8	10.1
	*2010	48.0	8.4	59.0	7.5	37.9	9.6
	*2015	48.7	11.9	58.7	11.3	39.5	12.7
	*2020	49.4	9.8	58.7	9.1	40.7	10.9
Jamaica Jamaïque	*2005	64.7	11.3	73.7	7.6	56.1	15.8
	*2010	63.2	12.4	71.1	9.2	55.6	16.3
	*2015	64.3	13.5	71.5	9.9	57.4	17.9
	*2020	66.2	8.0	72.6	5.7	60.0	10.6
Japan Japon	*2005	60.6	4.4	73.5	4.6	48.4	4.2
	*2010	60.1	5.1	72.1	5.4	48.7	4.6
	*2015	60.0	3.4	70.8	3.6	49.9	3.1
	*2020	61.6	2.3	71.0	2.4	52.7	2.2
Jordan Jordanie	*2005	40.9	14.8	67.6	12.9	12.2	26.1
	*2010	41.8	12.5	67.2	10.5	15.3	21.8
	*2015	39.3	13.1	63.9	11.0	14.0	22.7
	*2020	39.2	14.6	63.5	12.8	14.4	23.0
Kazakhstan Kazakhstan	*2005	69.5	8.1	75.3	6.7	64.4	9.6
	*2010	70.4	5.8	75.9	4.9	65.4	6.6
	*2015	70.9	4.9	77.0	4.4	65.4	5.5
	*2020	68.3	4.6	75.1	3.9	62.2	5.3
Kenya Kenya	*2005	65.1	2.8	70.1	2.7	60.3	3.0
	*2010	70.6	2.8	75.1	2.6	66.4	3.1
	*2015	74.4	2.8	77.9	2.6	71.0	3.0
	*2020	74.9	2.7	77.5	2.5	72.3	2.8
Kiribati Kiribati	2005	# 26.4[14]	14.7[15]	# 32.8[14]	12.3[15]	# 20.4[14]	18.2[15]
	2010	# 59.3[14]	30.6[15]	66.8[14]	27.6[15]	52.3[14]	34.1[15]
Kosovo [13] Kosovo [13]	2005	48.7	41.4	68.3	32.9	29.7	60.5
	2009	47.7	# 45.4	66.9	# 56.4	28.7	# 40.7
	#2012	37.1	30.9	55.5	28.1	17.9	40.0
	#2013	40.6	...	60.2	...	21.1	...
Kuwait Koweït	*2005	67.0	1.6	82.6	1.0	41.8	3.3
	*2010	69.4	1.8	84.7	1.4	46.6	2.9
	*2015	72.6	2.2	87.2	1.3	50.0	4.7
	*2020	73.4	2.3	87.3	1.2	49.3	5.6
Kyrgyzstan Kirghizistan	*2005	64.9	8.1	76.1	7.4	54.1	9.1
	*2010	64.1	8.6	76.6	7.7	52.2	9.9
	*2015	62.4	7.6	75.5	6.5	49.9	9.0
	*2020	59.6	6.6	75.7	5.9	44.5	7.9
Lao People's Dem. Rep. Rép. dém. populaire lao	*2005	78.8	1.4	79.8	1.4	77.9	1.4
	*2010	78.1	0.7	79.4	0.8	76.8	0.7
	*2015	78.5	0.7	80.2	0.7	76.8	0.6
	*2020	78.5	0.6	80.2	0.7	76.8	0.6
Latvia Lettonie	*2005	57.3	10.0	65.6	10.1	50.4	10.0
	*2010	59.0	19.5	65.3	22.7	53.9	16.3
	*2015	60.1	9.9	67.5	11.1	54.0	8.6
	*2020	61.0	6.5	67.9	7.1	55.3	6.0
Lebanon Liban	*2005	47.6	8.3	72.5	7.9	21.2	9.7
	*2010	46.8	6.4	69.8	5.1	22.8	10.6
	*2015	46.9	6.4	71.4	5.1	22.6	10.4
	*2020	47.0	6.3	71.3	5.1	22.9	9.8
Lesotho Lesotho	*2005	70.5	30.8	77.9	25.1	63.8	37.1
	*2010	68.2	26.8	76.5	22.1	60.6	32.2
	*2015	67.7	24.4	76.0	20.8	59.8	28.7
	*2020	67.9	22.8	76.1	20.1	60.1	26.1
Liberia Libéria	*2005	75.1	2.2	80.6	2.2	69.8	2.3
	*2010	75.6	2.3	81.1	2.3	70.1	2.3
	*2015	75.1	2.1	80.1	2.3	70.2	1.8
	*2020	76.3	2.7	80.6	3.2	72.1	2.2
Libya Libye	*2005	46.7	18.9	60.7	15.9	31.8	25.1
	*2010	48.6	19.0	62.9	15.8	33.6	25.2
	*2015	49.5	18.9	64.8	15.5	34.0	25.3
	*2020	49.6	18.6	65.3	15.5	33.8	24.7

16

Labour force participation rate and unemployment rate *(continued)*
Labour force (LF) participation rate and unemployment rate by sex (percent)

Taux d'activité et taux de chômage *(suite)*
Taux d'activité et taux de chômage par sexe (pourcentage)

Region, country or area & Région, pays ou zone &	Year Année	Male and Female Hommes et femmes		Male Hommes		Female Femmes	
		LF particip. rate Taux d'activité	Unemployment rate Taux de Chômage	LF particip. rate Taux d'activité	Unemployment rate Taux de Chômage	LF particip. rate Taux d'activité	Unemployment rate Taux de Chômage
Liechtenstein Liechtenstein	2005	63.0	...	73.7	...	52.8	...
	2010	61.6	2.6[13]	70.9	2.3[13]	52.6	3.1[13]
	2013	61.9	2.6[13]	70.6	2.3[13]	53.5	3.1[13]
Lithuania Lituanie	*2005	56.2	8.3	62.9	8.1	50.6	8.5
	*2010	57.0	17.8	62.3	21.2	52.6	14.5
	*2015	59.3	9.1	65.0	10.1	54.6	8.2
	*2020	61.4	6.3	67.6	6.5	56.2	6.1
Luxembourg Luxembourg	*2005	54.8	4.5	64.7	3.5	45.4	5.8
	*2010	57.0	4.4	65.4	3.8	48.8	5.1
	*2015	59.4	6.7	65.2	6.1	53.6	7.4
	*2020	59.5	5.2	63.7	4.7	55.1	5.8
Madagascar Madagascar	*2005	86.6	2.6	89.2	1.8	84.2	3.5
	*2010	89.1	4.3	91.0	3.3	87.1	5.3
	*2015	86.5	1.8	89.6	1.8	83.5	1.8
	*2020	86.2	1.8	89.0	1.7	83.5	2.0
Malawi Malawi	*2005	77.4	5.9	80.6	4.9	74.4	6.9
	*2010	77.6	5.9	82.1	4.9	73.3	7.0
	*2015	77.3	5.9	82.2	4.9	72.7	6.8
	*2020	76.8	5.7	81.3	4.8	72.6	6.7
Malaysia Malaisie	*2005	61.1	3.5	77.4	3.4	44.0	3.7
	*2010	60.4	3.3	76.2	3.2	43.5	3.4
	*2015	64.4	3.1	77.6	2.9	50.5	3.4
	*2020	64.4	3.4	77.2	3.1	50.9	3.8
Maldives Maldives	*2005	57.7	2.9	73.3	2.6	40.4	3.7
	*2010	62.3	4.1	77.1	3.7	44.1	5.1
	*2015	68.2	5.7	82.4	5.6	45.1	5.8
	*2020	70.5	6.4	85.2	6.4	41.7	6.5
Mali Mali	*2005	70.3	9.8	80.8	8.2	60.2	11.8
	*2010	70.9	8.1	81.9	5.9	60.3	10.9
	*2015	71.1	7.7	81.2	6.9	61.3	8.8
	*2020	70.8	7.3	80.6	6.8	61.2	8.1
Malta Malte	*2005	48.3	6.9	67.7	6.3	29.5	8.4
	*2010	50.0	6.9	66.5	6.7	34.0	7.1
	*2015	54.6	5.4	67.0	5.4	42.2	5.4
	*2020	56.3	3.4	66.8	3.2	45.9	3.6
Marshall Islands Îles Marshall	2006[3]	44.6	...	...	...	...	...
	#2011	...	4.7	...	4.9	...	4.5
Martinique [6] Martinique [6]	2005	43.6	18.7	48.5	16.9	39.6	20.4
	2010	45.9	21.0	49.1	19.7	43.3	22.2
	#2013	53.1	22.8	53.8	22.8	52.6	22.8
Mauritania Mauritanie	*2005	48.0	9.8	68.1	8.6	28.6	12.6
	*2010	46.1	9.8	64.5	8.7	28.1	12.4
	*2015	45.7	9.8	63.1	8.7	28.4	12.2
	*2020	45.9	9.6	63.0	8.4	28.9	12.2
Mauritius Maurice	*2005	58.9	9.5	77.1	5.8	41.3	16.3
	*2010	58.3	7.7	74.1	4.5	43.1	12.9
	*2015	59.3	7.4	73.4	5.3	45.7	10.7
	*2020	58.1	6.7	71.7	4.4	45.1	10.1
Mexico Mexique	*2005	60.6	3.6	81.4	3.4	41.3	3.9
	*2010	60.7	5.3	79.7	5.4	43.1	5.2
	*2015	60.8	4.3	79.0	4.2	43.9	4.5
	*2020	60.7	3.7	78.3	3.4	44.3	4.1
Monaco [16] Monaco [16]	2000	45.7	3.6	57.3	2.5	35.1	5.2
Mongolia Mongolie	*2005	59.1	7.1	64.8	7.3	53.6	6.9
	*2010	59.0	6.6	65.1	7.1	53.1	5.9
	*2015	60.3	4.9	67.2	5.4	53.8	4.3
	*2020	59.4	6.0	66.1	6.2	53.1	5.7
Montenegro Monténégro	*2005	48.1	30.3	55.5	26.2	41.2	35.6
	*2010	48.4	19.7	55.8	18.8	41.5	20.7
	*2015	52.9	17.5	59.4	17.7	46.6	17.3
	*2020	54.5	14.8	62.7	14.6	46.6	15.0

Labour force participation rate and unemployment rate *(continued)*
Labour force (LF) participation rate and unemployment rate by sex (percent)

Taux d'activité et taux de chômage *(suite)*
Taux d'activité et taux de chômage par sexe (pourcentage)

Region, country or area & Région, pays ou zone &	Year Année	Male and Female Hommes et femmes		Male Hommes		Female Femmes	
		LF particip. rate Taux d'activité	Unemployment rate Taux de Chômage	LF particip. rate Taux d'activité	Unemployment rate Taux de Chômage	LF particip. rate Taux d'activité	Unemployment rate Taux de Chômage
Montserrat	#2001	85.2	9.5	89.2	...	80.6	...
Montserrat	2011	...	5.6	...	7.7	...	3.3
Morocco	*2005	50.3	11.0	75.8	10.8	26.3	11.6
Maroc	*2010	49.8	9.1	75.5	9.0	25.5	9.5
	*2015	47.2	9.5	72.5	9.1	23.0	10.4
	*2020	45.2	9.0	69.9	8.5	21.4	10.4
Mozambique	*2005	84.9	3.0	83.1	3.8	86.6	2.4
Mozambique	*2010	82.4	3.3	82.0	3.6	82.8	3.0
	*2015	78.8	3.4	80.0	3.2	77.8	3.7
	*2020	78.0	3.2	79.0	3.0	77.1	3.4
Myanmar	*2005	69.3	0.8	83.8	0.7	56.3	0.9
Myanmar	*2010	67.2	0.8	82.3	0.7	53.6	0.9
	*2015	65.6	0.8	80.7	0.7	51.9	0.9
	*2020	61.5	1.7	77.2	1.3	47.3	2.3
Namibia	*2005	56.0	22.0	62.6	19.6	50.1	24.6
Namibie	*2010	57.5	22.1	63.0	20.3	52.6	24.0
	*2015	60.7	20.9	65.4	19.1	56.4	22.8
	*2020	60.0	20.6	63.7	20.4	56.6	20.8
Nauru	2002[3]	78.0	22.7	86.8	17.1	69.6	29.6
Nauru	2011	64.0	# 23.0	78.9	# 21.4	49.3	# 25.5
Nepal	*2005	84.5	1.6	89.2	1.8	80.1	1.3
Népal	*2010	83.3	1.5	87.4	1.8	79.5	1.3
	*2015	83.2	1.5	85.3	1.8	81.5	1.3
	*2020	83.9	1.5	85.2	1.7	82.9	1.3
Netherlands	*2005	62.9	5.9	71.2	5.0	54.9	6.9
Pays-Bas	*2010	64.4	5.0	71.0	4.5	58.0	5.6
	*2015	64.1	6.9	70.1	6.5	58.2	7.3
	*2020	63.4	3.0	68.7	2.8	58.1	3.1
Netherlands Antilles [former] [6,14,17]	#2009	56.3	...	61.1	...	52.6	...
Antilles néerlandaises [anc.] [6,14,17]	2011	57.9	...	62.2	...	54.5	...
New Caledonia	*2005	65.8	15.4	71.1	13.0	60.6	18.2
Nouvelle-Calédonie	*2010	66.1	14.4	71.1	12.4	61.0	16.8
	*2015	63.8	14.1	68.8	13.2	58.7	15.3
	*2020	62.8	12.8	68.2	11.6	57.5	14.2
New Zealand	*2005	67.2	3.8	74.7	3.5	60.1	4.2
Nouvelle-Zélande	*2010	67.2	6.6	73.8	6.2	61.0	6.9
	*2015	68.3	5.4	74.1	4.9	62.8	5.9
	*2020	69.8	4.0	75.2	3.7	64.7	4.4
Nicaragua	*2005	62.5	5.4	82.2	5.1	44.1	5.8
Nicaragua	*2010	64.4	7.8	83.0	7.3	47.1	8.7
	*2015	66.2	4.7	84.2	4.2	49.4	5.4
	*2020	66.5	7.4	84.2	7.4	49.9	7.4
Niger	*2005	79.6	3.1	90.9	3.4	68.8	2.7
Niger	*2010	79.6	0.6	91.0	0.6	68.6	0.5
	*2015	72.5	0.5	84.3	0.6	61.0	0.4
	*2020	71.8	0.5	83.5	0.6	60.3	0.4
Nigeria	*2005	59.7	3.7	64.2	3.8	55.2	3.7
Nigéria	*2010	59.9	3.8	64.5	3.8	55.3	3.8
	*2015	53.9	4.3	58.9	3.7	48.9	5.1
	*2020	52.7	8.0	57.8	7.4	47.6	8.7
Niue	2001	75.5	2.2	76.7	2.3	74.8	2.1
Nioué	#2002	...	9.7	...	...	...	...
North Macedonia	*2005	53.9	37.3	66.0	36.5	42.1	38.4
Macédoine du Nord	*2010	55.6	32.0	68.6	31.9	42.8	32.2
	*2015	55.5	26.1	67.7	26.7	43.5	25.1
	*2020	55.0	16.4	67.2	17.1	43.0	15.4
Northern Mariana Islands [3]	2003	81.8	4.6	82.5	5.0	81.3	4.3
Îles Mariannes du Nord [3]	2005	...	6.5	...	7.3	...	5.8
	#2010	72.3	11.2	77.6	9.7	66.6	13.0

16 Labour force participation rate and unemployment rate *(continued)*
Labour force (LF) participation rate and unemployment rate by sex (percent)

Taux d'activité et taux de chômage *(suite)*
Taux d'activité et taux de chômage par sexe (pourcentage)

Region, country or area & Région, pays ou zone &	Year Année	Male and Female Hommes et femmes		Male Hommes		Female Femmes	
		LF particip. rate Taux d'activité	Unemployment rate Taux de Chômage	LF particip. rate Taux d'activité	Unemployment rate Taux de Chômage	LF particip. rate Taux d'activité	Unemployment rate Taux de Chômage
Norway Norvège	*2005	65.4	4.4	70.3	4.6	60.7	4.2
	*2010	65.7	3.5	69.6	4.0	61.8	2.9
	*2015	64.9	4.3	68.4	4.6	61.3	4.0
	*2020	63.7	3.3	67.0	3.4	60.3	3.2
Oman Oman	*2005	55.8	5.0	77.4	4.2	24.7	8.4
	*2010	62.0	5.0	82.2	3.9	27.0	10.7
	*2015	70.4	3.6	88.3	2.2	30.3	13.2
	*2020	72.7	2.6	90.4	1.1	31.0	12.4
Pakistan Pakistan	*2005	51.3	0.6	82.4	0.7	18.4	0.4
	*2010	51.6	0.7	79.9	0.7	21.7	0.6
	*2015	53.0	3.6	80.8	2.8	23.9	6.2
	*2020	52.7	4.5	81.7	4.2	22.2	5.3
Palau [3] Palaos [3]	2005	67.5	4.2	75.4	3.7	58.1	4.9
Panama Panama	*2005	64.6	3.7	81.1	2.9	48.0	4.9
	*2010	63.5	3.7	80.0	2.9	47.1	5.1
	*2015	64.9	3.0	79.2	2.4	50.7	3.9
	*2020	66.5	3.8	79.8	3.1	53.4	5.0
Papua New Guinea Papouasie-Nvl-Guinée	*2005	61.1	2.4	62.5	3.2	59.6	1.6
	*2010	48.3	2.0	49.3	2.7	47.2	1.3
	*2015	47.4	2.6	48.2	3.7	46.6	1.4
	*2020	47.0	2.5	47.9	3.5	46.1	1.4
Paraguay Paraguay	*2005	70.9	4.8	85.3	3.9	56.1	6.3
	*2010	69.0	4.6	83.8	3.6	53.9	6.1
	*2015	69.6	4.6	82.9	4.3	55.9	5.0
	*2020	72.2	4.8	84.5	4.1	59.4	5.9
Peru Pérou	*2005	72.7	4.9	81.4	4.9	64.1	4.9
	*2010	78.9	3.5	85.9	3.2	72.1	3.8
	*2015	75.7	3.0	83.8	3.0	67.9	3.0
	*2020	78.0	3.2	85.5	3.0	70.6	3.4
Philippines Philippines	*2005	61.9	3.8	76.4	3.5	47.6	4.2
	*2010	62.2	3.6	76.0	3.5	48.5	3.8
	*2015	62.2	3.1	75.3	3.0	49.3	3.2
	*2020	59.7	2.2	73.2	2.0	46.2	2.4
Poland Pologne	*2005	55.1	17.8	63.0	16.6	47.8	19.1
	*2010	55.9	9.6	64.3	9.3	48.3	10.0
	*2015	56.6	7.5	65.2	7.3	48.8	7.7
	*2020	56.4	3.0	65.1	3.0	48.3	3.1
Portugal Portugal	*2005	62.0	7.6	69.3	6.7	55.3	8.6
	*2010	61.1	10.8	66.9	9.8	55.8	11.9
	*2015	58.6	12.4	64.2	12.2	53.8	12.8
	*2020	58.4	5.9	63.6	5.3	53.9	6.6
Puerto Rico Porto Rico	*2005	47.3	11.4	59.0	12.2	36.8	10.1
	*2010	44.6	16.1	54.9	18.7	35.5	12.6
	*2015	40.8	12.0	50.1	13.7	32.5	9.7
	*2020	38.4	8.4	46.9	9.9	30.9	6.4
Qatar Qatar	*2005	80.3	1.1	93.9	0.7	45.7	3.5
	*2010	87.4	0.5	96.3	0.1	51.4	2.8
	*2015	87.9	0.2	95.2	0.1	58.9	0.9
	*2020	87.0	0.1	95.1	~0.0	56.8	0.4
Republic of Korea République de Corée	*2005	62.1	3.7	74.0	3.9	50.4	3.4
	*2010	60.8	3.7	72.2	4.0	49.5	3.3
	*2015	62.6	3.6	73.3	3.6	51.9	3.5
	*2020	62.9	4.6	73.1	4.8	52.8	4.3
Republic of Moldova République de Moldova	*2005	48.4	7.3	50.8	8.6	46.3	6.0
	*2010	41.7	7.5	45.2	9.1	38.6	5.7
	*2015	44.1	3.7	47.3	4.5	41.3	2.9
	*2020	42.7	5.4	45.8	6.6	40.0	4.1
Réunion [6] Réunion [6]	2005	50.1	30.1	60.3	27.6	41.1	33.3
	2010	52.1	28.9	59.9	28.0	45.3	30.0
	#2013	54.9	28.9	61.3	28.3	49.1	29.7

16

Labour force participation rate and unemployment rate *(continued)*
Labour force (LF) participation rate and unemployment rate by sex (percent)

Taux d'activité et taux de chômage *(suite)*
Taux d'activité et taux de chômage par sexe (pourcentage)

Region, country or area & Région, pays ou zone &	Year Année	Male and Female Hommes et femmes		Male Hommes		Female Femmes	
		LF particip. rate Taux d'activité	Unemployment rate Taux de Chômage	LF particip. rate Taux d'activité	Unemployment rate Taux de Chômage	LF particip. rate Taux d'activité	Unemployment rate Taux de Chômage
Romania	*2005	53.5	7.2	61.1	7.8	46.3	6.4
Roumanie	*2010	54.9	7.0	64.3	7.6	46.3	6.2
	*2015	54.5	6.8	64.4	7.5	45.2	5.9
	*2020	54.3	3.9	64.4	4.4	44.9	3.4
Russian Federation	*2005	60.9	7.1	67.8	7.3	55.2	6.9
Fédération de Russie	*2010	62.5	7.4	70.3	7.9	55.9	6.8
	*2015	62.6	5.6	71.2	5.8	55.5	5.3
	*2020	61.4	4.4	69.8	4.5	54.4	4.3
Rwanda	*2005	84.9	0.9	85.6	1.1	84.2	0.8
Rwanda	*2010	84.5	1.1	84.9	1.1	84.1	1.0
	*2015	83.9	1.1	84.0	1.1	83.9	1.2
	*2020	83.6	1.0	83.3	1.0	84.0	1.1
Saint Helena	2005	...	5.2	...	...	...	...
Sainte-Hélène	2010	...	2.0	...	...	...	...
Saint Kitts and Nevis							
Saint-Kitts-et-Nevis	2001	# 68.8	5.1	# 62.8	4.3	# 74.9	5.9
Saint Lucia	*2005	65.8	18.7	75.3	15.2	56.8	23.1
Sainte-Lucie	*2010	65.8	17.1	74.9	16.1	57.0	18.4
	*2015	66.7	24.1	75.2	21.4	58.5	27.5
	*2020	67.2	20.2	74.9	17.9	59.7	22.9
Saint Vincent & Grenadines	*2005	66.6	20.1	80.0	21.5	52.8	17.8
Saint-Vincent-Grenadines	*2010	65.9	19.4	78.4	21.0	52.9	17.1
	*2015	65.7	19.3	77.6	20.8	53.4	17.1
	*2020	65.8	18.9	76.9	20.4	54.5	16.7
Samoa	*2005	44.7	5.2	56.5	4.6	32.1	6.3
Samoa	*2010	44.2	5.6	56.0	5.1	31.6	6.5
	*2015	44.5	8.7	56.5	7.8	31.7	10.3
	*2020	43.5	8.4	55.2	7.6	31.0	9.8
San Marino	2003	66.2	...	79.2	...	53.8	...
Saint-Marin	2010	...	4.4	...	2.1	...	7.3
	#2014[4]	...	6.6	...	4.3	...	9.5
Sao Tome and Principe	*2005	56.2	16.5	73.6	11.3	39.6	25.7
Sao Tomé-et-Principe	*2010	58.7	14.7	76.2	9.8	41.5	23.5
	*2015	58.8	13.5	76.1	9.1	41.7	21.4
	*2020	57.5	13.7	74.1	9.4	41.2	21.3
Saudi Arabia	*2005	50.5	6.1	74.0	4.7	17.7	14.2
Arabie saoudite	*2010	51.3	5.6	74.6	3.5	18.3	17.5
	*2015	56.1	5.6	79.5	2.5	22.2	21.7
	*2020	56.2	5.9	78.7	2.8	22.3	22.5
Senegal	*2005	50.8	8.9	69.4	7.1	33.9	12.3
Sénégal	*2010	48.5	10.4	64.4	8.2	34.3	14.0
	*2015	45.7	6.8	58.0	6.4	34.7	7.3
	*2020	45.7	6.7	57.5	5.9	35.1	7.8
Serbia	*2005	54.7	20.9	64.6	16.8	45.5	26.2
Serbie	*2010	50.8	19.2	59.2	18.5	42.9	20.2
	*2015	52.1	17.7	60.4	16.8	44.2	18.8
	*2020	54.7	12.7	62.6	11.7	47.3	14.1
Seychelles	2005	72.1	5.5	...	6.1	...	4.9
Seychelles	#2011[6,18]	65.0	4.1	68.3	3.8	61.9	4.5
Sierra Leone	*2005	64.5	3.5	65.5	4.6	63.6	2.4
Sierra Leone	*2010	60.7	4.2	61.6	5.0	59.8	3.3
	*2015	58.2	4.6	59.3	5.5	57.1	3.8
	*2020	57.8	4.4	58.4	5.2	57.2	3.6
Singapore	*2005	65.6	5.6	77.8	5.3	53.3	6.1
Singapour	*2010	68.8	4.1	78.7	3.9	58.1	4.4
	*2015	71.4	3.8	79.4	3.7	62.6	4.0
	*2020	70.4	4.4	78.2	4.3	61.8	4.5
Slovakia	*2005	59.6	16.3	68.6	15.5	51.3	17.2
Slovaquie	*2010	58.8	14.4	67.6	14.2	50.6	14.6
	*2015	59.6	11.5	67.8	10.3	52.0	12.9
	*2020	59.3	5.1	67.1	4.6	52.0	5.7

16 Labour force participation rate and unemployment rate *(continued)*
Labour force (LF) participation rate and unemployment rate by sex (percent)

Taux d'activité et taux de chômage *(suite)*
Taux d'activité et taux de chômage par sexe (pourcentage)

Region, country or area & Région, pays ou zone &	Year Année	Male and Female Hommes et femmes		Male Hommes		Female Femmes	
		LF particip. rate Taux d'activité	Unemployment rate Taux de Chômage	LF particip. rate Taux d'activité	Unemployment rate Taux de Chômage	LF particip. rate Taux d'activité	Unemployment rate Taux de Chômage
Slovenia Slovénie	*2005	59.2	6.5	66.0	6.1	52.8	7.0
	*2010	59.2	7.2	65.5	7.4	53.1	7.0
	*2015	57.4	9.0	62.9	8.1	52.0	10.0
	*2020	57.8	3.8	62.8	3.7	53.0	3.9
Solomon Islands Îles Salomon	*2005	84.5	2.0	86.1	2.2	82.9	1.9
	*2010	84.4	1.7	86.0	1.7	82.7	1.7
	*2015	83.9	0.7	85.6	0.7	82.3	0.7
	*2020	83.8	0.5	85.5	0.5	82.1	0.6
Somalia Somalie	*2005	48.5	11.7	76.1	11.8	21.1	11.2
	*2010	47.4	11.7	74.8	11.8	20.5	11.4
	*2015	47.1	11.6	73.6	11.7	21.2	11.4
	*2020	47.4	11.4	73.7	11.5	21.8	11.1
South Africa Afrique du Sud	*2005	55.2	29.3	63.9	23.6	46.9	36.6
	*2010	52.5	24.7	60.4	22.9	44.9	27.0
	*2015	55.4	25.2	62.5	23.2	48.6	27.5
	*2020	56.0	28.5	62.7	26.5	49.7	30.8
South Sudan Soudan du sud	*2005	73.8	12.6	77.1	11.6	70.6	13.8
	*2010	73.3	12.7	76.0	11.6	70.6	13.8
	*2015	72.6	12.6	74.6	11.4	70.7	13.8
	*2020	72.4	12.3	73.8	11.1	71.0	13.4
Spain Espagne	*2005	56.9	9.2	68.0	7.1	46.1	12.0
	*2010	59.3	19.9	67.2	19.6	51.7	20.2
	*2015	58.5	22.1	64.7	20.8	52.6	23.6
	*2020	57.2	13.0	63.0	10.8	51.6	15.6
Sri Lanka Sri Lanka	*2005	56.4	7.7	76.8	5.6	36.9	11.9
	*2010	54.6	4.8	76.5	3.5	34.4	7.5
	*2015	54.8	4.5	75.8	3.0	35.7	7.5
	*2020	53.7	4.2	74.3	2.9	35.3	6.6
State of Palestine État de Palestine	*2005	38.9	20.0	64.5	20.7	12.7	16.7
	*2010	39.5	21.4	64.7	21.4	13.8	21.6
	*2015	43.7	23.0	69.2	20.2	17.6	34.3
	*2020	44.1	26.1	69.8	22.4	17.9	40.6
Sudan Soudan	*2005	50.5	15.3	73.1	13.4	28.2	20.2
	*2010	49.4	15.2	71.3	10.5	28.1	26.8
	*2015	48.7	17.3	69.2	11.9	28.6	30.0
	*2020	48.4	16.6	68.1	12.0	29.1	27.2
Suriname Suriname	*2005	50.8	9.3	65.1	5.8	36.6	15.4
	*2010	51.5	7.2	64.2	3.7	38.9	12.8
	*2015	51.6	7.2	64.0	4.5	39.3	11.7
	*2020	51.0	7.5	63.4	4.6	38.8	12.1
Sweden Suède	*2005	62.9	7.5	67.0	7.6	58.8	7.4
	*2010	63.2	8.6	67.4	8.7	59.0	8.5
	*2015	64.0	7.4	67.4	7.6	60.7	7.3
	*2020	64.6	6.7	67.7	7.1	61.5	6.3
Switzerland Suisse	*2005	67.0	4.4	75.1	3.9	59.5	5.1
	*2010	67.0	4.8	74.3	4.5	59.9	5.2
	*2015	68.2	4.8	74.2	4.7	62.4	4.9
	*2020	68.1	4.9	73.5	4.7	62.9	5.0
Syrian Arab Republic République arabe syrienne	*2005	46.6	8.9	76.2	6.0	16.2	22.9
	*2010	43.0	8.6	72.8	6.2	13.1	22.0
	*2015	43.9	8.5	73.6	6.1	14.1	21.2
	*2020	44.0	8.5	74.0	6.1	14.3	20.5
Tajikistan Tadjikistan	*2005	42.4	13.0	54.5	13.6	30.3	11.8
	*2010	43.0	11.6	56.2	12.2	29.9	10.5
	*2015	42.2	11.5	52.9	12.2	31.4	10.4
	*2020	42.1	11.0	52.9	11.7	31.3	9.8
Thailand Thaïlande	*2005	72.5	1.4	80.9	1.5	64.6	1.2
	*2010	71.7	0.6	80.1	0.6	63.9	0.6
	*2015	69.1	0.6	77.7	0.6	60.9	0.6
	*2020	67.0	0.8	75.8	0.8	58.9	0.8

16

Labour force participation rate and unemployment rate *(continued)*
Labour force (LF) participation rate and unemployment rate by sex (percent)

Taux d'activité et taux de chômage *(suite)*
Taux d'activité et taux de chômage par sexe (pourcentage)

Region, country or area & Région, pays ou zone &	Year Année	Male and Female Hommes et femmes		Male Hommes		Female Femmes	
		LF particip. rate Taux d'activité	Unemployment rate Taux de Chômage	LF particip. rate Taux d'activité	Unemployment rate Taux de Chômage	LF particip. rate Taux d'activité	Unemployment rate Taux de Chômage
Timor-Leste	*2005	68.7	3.3	74.3	2.7	63.0	3.9
Timor-Leste	*2010	65.7	3.3	70.7	2.7	60.6	4.0
	*2015	66.6	4.5	71.9	3.3	61.2	5.8
	*2020	67.3	4.6	72.7	3.2	61.9	6.3
Togo	*2005	80.7	4.4	80.7	4.5	80.7	4.3
Togo	*2010	79.1	2.4	80.7	2.7	77.6	2.1
	*2015	78.3	2.2	79.9	2.7	76.6	1.7
	*2020	77.5	2.0	78.9	2.5	76.1	1.5
Tonga	*2005	60.3	2.1	75.4	1.3	45.7	3.5
Tonga	*2010	60.0	1.2	75.3	0.6	45.4	2.1
	*2015	60.0	1.1	74.8	0.5	45.8	2.1
	*2020	59.8	1.2	74.3	0.6	45.8	2.1
Trinidad and Tobago	*2005	64.7	3.1	76.1	2.6	53.5	3.8
Trinité-et-Tobago	*2010	62.3	3.8	73.9	3.4	51.1	4.3
	*2015	61.8	2.2	73.2	1.9	50.8	2.6
	*2020	59.5	2.8	69.6	2.6	49.8	3.0
Tunisia	*2005	45.1	12.9	67.5	12.1	23.3	15.2
Tunisie	*2010	46.7	13.1	69.6	10.9	24.5	19.0
	*2015	46.9	15.2	70.1	12.6	24.7	22.4
	*2020	45.9	16.2	69.2	13.8	23.6	22.8
Turkey	*2005	46.0	10.6	70.1	10.4	23.3	11.2
Turquie	*2010	47.7	10.7	69.6	10.4	27.0	11.4
	*2015	51.0	10.2	71.6	9.2	31.5	12.6
	*2020	52.7	12.9	72.4	11.7	33.9	15.4
Turkmenistan	*2005	62.6	7.3	75.0	8.9	50.9	5.0
Turkménistan	*2010	63.3	4.0	76.2	5.2	51.1	2.3
	*2015	64.6	4.0	78.2	5.2	51.7	2.2
	*2020	64.4	4.1	78.2	5.3	51.3	2.3
Turks and Caicos Islands	#2005	62.0	...	...	...	...	...
Îles Turques-et-Caïques	#2008	64.0	8.3	...	...	...	...
Tuvalu							
Tuvalu	2005	58.2	6.5	69.6	4.9	47.9	8.6
Uganda	*2005	70.6	1.9	76.5	1.7	65.1	2.1
Ouganda	*2010	71.0	3.6	76.3	3.0	66.1	4.3
	*2015	70.8	1.9	75.3	1.4	66.7	2.4
	*2020	70.4	1.9	73.9	1.5	67.1	2.3
Ukraine	*2005	55.1	7.2	62.9	7.5	48.6	6.8
Ukraine	*2010	55.0	8.1	63.0	9.3	48.4	6.8
	*2015	54.7	9.1	63.6	10.1	47.4	8.1
	*2020	53.9	8.9	62.8	9.9	46.5	7.9
United Arab Emirates	*2005	78.6	3.1	92.6	2.6	37.3	7.2
Émirats arabes unis	*2010	83.8	2.5	94.7	2.1	44.3	5.9
	*2015	83.0	1.9	94.7	1.4	50.6	4.7
	*2020	82.2	2.5	93.6	1.7	52.5	6.0
United Kingdom	*2005	61.8	4.8	69.2	5.1	54.7	4.3
Royaume-Uni	*2010	61.9	7.8	68.6	8.6	55.5	6.9
	*2015	62.4	5.3	68.3	5.5	56.7	5.1
	*2020	62.8	4.1	68.1	4.3	57.7	3.9
United Rep. of Tanzania	*2005	88.4	3.3	90.0	2.4	86.7	4.3
Rép.-Unie de Tanzanie	*2010	86.7	3.0	89.2	2.5	84.2	3.5
	*2015	83.8	2.1	87.9	1.6	79.9	2.7
	*2020	83.3	2.0	87.2	1.6	79.4	2.4
United States of America	*2005	65.0	5.1	72.2	5.1	58.2	5.1
États-Unis d'Amérique	*2010	63.6	9.6	69.9	10.5	57.5	8.6
	*2015	62.0	5.3	68.4	5.4	55.8	5.2
	*2020	61.8	3.9	67.9	3.9	55.9	3.8
United States Virgin Islands	*2005	64.3	9.1	69.4	8.2	59.8	9.9
Îles Vierges américaines	*2010	63.3	10.0	67.6	9.4	59.4	10.6
	*2015	61.4	9.5	64.2	8.8	58.9	10.2
	*2020	60.1	8.8	62.4	8.3	58.1	9.2

16

Labour force participation rate and unemployment rate *(continued)*
Labour force (LF) participation rate and unemployment rate by sex (percent)

Taux d'activité et taux de chômage *(suite)*
Taux d'activité et taux de chômage par sexe (pourcentage)

Region, country or area & Région, pays ou zone &	Year Année	Male and Female Hommes et femmes		Male Hommes		Female Femmes	
		LF particip. rate Taux d'activité	Unemployment rate Taux de Chômage	LF particip. rate Taux d'activité	Unemployment rate Taux de Chômage	LF particip. rate Taux d'activité	Unemployment rate Taux de Chômage
Uruguay Uruguay	*2005	62.5	12.0	73.7	9.5	52.3	15.3
	*2010	65.5	7.2	76.8	5.3	55.3	9.5
	*2015	65.0	7.5	75.2	6.4	55.7	8.9
	*2020	64.1	8.8	73.4	7.0	55.7	10.9
Uzbekistan Ouzbékistan	*2005	62.5	6.9	74.3	7.1	51.3	6.6
	*2010	63.3	5.4	75.4	5.5	51.6	5.1
	*2015	64.7	5.2	77.4	5.3	52.3	4.9
	*2020	65.0	6.1	78.1	6.3	52.3	5.8
Vanuatu Vanuatu	*2005	69.6	4.6	78.3	4.2	60.7	5.1
	*2010	69.7	4.6	78.9	4.2	60.6	5.2
	*2015	70.0	4.6	79.0	4.2	60.9	5.1
	*2020	69.8	4.4	78.7	4.0	60.9	4.9
Venezuela (Boliv. Rep. of) Venezuela (Rép. boliv. du)	*2005	64.2	10.7	79.2	10.0	49.4	11.6
	*2010	63.8	7.1	78.4	7.2	49.5	7.0
	*2015	62.8	7.4	76.8	6.8	49.2	8.5
	*2020	59.3	9.4	74.3	9.2	45.2	9.6
Viet Nam Viet Nam	*2005	76.1	2.1	80.8	2.0	71.7	2.3
	*2010	76.3	1.1	81.4	1.2	71.4	1.1
	*2015	78.2	2.1	83.3	2.2	73.3	2.0
	*2020	77.3	2.0	82.2	2.1	72.6	2.0
Western Sahara Sahara occidental	*2005	52.9	9.7	78.9	8.4	22.7	14.7
	*2010	53.8	9.7	79.3	8.4	24.3	14.7
	*2015	54.2	9.6	79.6	8.4	25.2	14.3
	*2020	54.2	9.4	79.3	8.1	26.1	14.0
Yemen Yémen	*2005	42.1	12.2	69.9	11.9	14.4	13.4
	*2010	39.4	12.9	68.8	12.0	10.0	19.6
	*2015	37.2	13.4	68.4	12.4	6.0	25.3
	*2020	38.0	12.8	70.2	11.9	5.7	24.5
Zambia Zambie	*2005	79.6	15.9	85.9	16.7	73.6	15.1
	*2010	76.7	13.2	82.5	13.1	71.1	13.3
	*2015	75.2	10.1	80.3	9.6	70.3	10.7
	*2020	74.6	11.4	79.0	10.9	70.4	12.0
Zimbabwe Zimbabwe	*2005	82.2	4.5	88.2	4.3	77.1	4.6
	*2010	82.4	5.2	88.5	4.6	77.3	5.8
	*2015	83.0	5.3	89.2	4.7	77.8	5.9
	*2020	83.1	5.0	89.0	4.4	78.2	5.5
European Union (EU) Union européenne (UE)	*2005	56.7	9.0	65.2	8.3	48.7	9.7
	*2010	57.2	9.5	64.8	9.6	50.1	9.5
	*2015	57.4	9.4	64.2	9.3	51.0	9.5
	*2020	57.5	6.1	64.0	5.9	51.4	6.4

Source:

International Labour Organization (ILO), Geneva, Key Indicators of the Labour Market (KILM 9th edition) and the ILOSTAT database, last accessed January 2020.

& Population aged 15 years and over, unless otherwise footnoted.

1 Data excludes Armenia, Azerbaijan, Cyprus, Georgia, Israel and Turkey.
2 Caucasus refers to Armenia, Azerbaijan, Cyprus, Georgia, Israel and Turkey.
3 Population aged 16 years and over.
4 Population aged 14 years and over.
5 Resident population (de jure).
6 Excluding the institutional population.

Source:

Organisation internationale du Travail (OIT), Genève, Indicateurs Clés du Marché du Travail (ICMT 9e édition) et ILOSTAT base de données, dernier accès janvier 2020.

& Sauf indication contraire, population âgée de 15 ans et plus.

1 Les données excluent l'Arménie, l'Azerbaïdjan, Chypre, la Géorgie, l'Israël et la Turquie.
2 Le Caucase se rapporte à l'Arménie, l'Azerbaïdjan, Chypre, la Géorgie, l'Israël et la Turquie.
3 Population âgée de 16 ans et plus.
4 Population âgée de 14 ans et plus.
5 Population résidente (de droit).
6 Non compris la population dans les institutions.

16

Labour force participation rate and unemployment rate *(continued)*
Labour force (LF) participation rate and unemployment rate by sex (percent)

Taux d'activité et taux de chômage *(suite)*
Taux d'activité et taux de chômage par sexe (pourcentage)

7	For statistical purposes, the data for China do not include those for the Hong Kong Special Administrative Region (Hong Kong SAR), Macao Special Administrative Region (Macao SAR) and Taiwan Province of China.
8	Population aged 15 to 69 years.
9	Population aged 16 to 65 years.
10	Population aged 15 to 74 years.
11	Nationals, residents.
12	Population aged 18 to 64 years.
13	Population aged 15 to 64 years.
14	Persons present (de facto).
15	De facto population.
16	Population aged 17 years and over.
17	Main city or metropolitan area.
18	Excluding some areas.

7	Pour la présentation des statistiques, les données pour la Chine ne comprennent pas la région administrative spéciale de Hong Kong (RAS de Hong Kong), la région administrative spéciale de Macao (RAS de Macao) et la province chinoise de Taïwan.
8	Population âgée de 15 à 69 ans.
9	Population âgée de 16 à 65 ans.
10	Population âgée de 15 à 74 ans.
11	Ressortissants, résidents.
12	Population âgée de 18 à 64 ans.
13	Population âgée de 15 à 64 ans.
14	Personnes présentes (de facto).
15	Population de fait.
16	Population âgée de 17 ans et plus.
17	Ville principale ou zone métropolitaine.
18	Certaines régions sont exclues.

17 Employment by economic activity
Percentage of persons employed by sex and ISIC 4 categories; agriculture (agr.), industry (ind.) and services (ser.)

Emploi par activité économique
Personnes employées par sexe et branches de la CITI rév. 4; agriculture (agr.), industrie (ind.) et services (ser.), pourcentage

Region, country or area [+] Région, pays ou zone [+]	Year Année	Male and Female Hommes et femmes			Male Hommes			Female Femmes		
		Agr.	Ind.	Ser.	Agr.	Ind.	Ser.	Agr.	Ind.	Ser.
Total, all countries or areas	***2005**	**37.0**	**21.2**	**41.8**	**37.3**	**24.2**	**38.6**	**36.5**	**16.7**	**46.8**
Total, tous pays ou zones	***2010**	**33.0**	**22.6**	**44.4**	**33.5**	**26.2**	**40.3**	**32.3**	**16.9**	**50.8**
	***2015**	**28.9**	**23.2**	**48.0**	**29.6**	**27.3**	**43.1**	**27.7**	**16.7**	**55.6**
	***2020**	**26.5**	**23.1**	**50.4**	**27.2**	**27.6**	**45.2**	**25.4**	**16.0**	**58.6**
Africa	*2005	56.6	11.6	31.8	53.1	14.5	32.4	61.4	7.7	30.9
Afrique	*2010	53.4	12.2	34.3	50.4	15.6	34.0	57.5	7.7	34.8
	*2015	50.4	13.0	36.7	48.3	16.6	35.2	53.2	8.2	38.6
	*2020	48.7	13.3	38.1	47.1	17.1	35.9	50.8	8.3	41.0
Northern Africa	*2005	33.3	21.5	45.2	29.7	24.0	46.3	46.4	12.2	41.4
Afrique septentrionale	*2010	29.2	24.5	46.3	25.5	28.1	46.4	42.8	11.4	45.7
	*2015	26.7	24.6	48.7	23.2	28.4	48.4	39.2	11.2	49.6
	*2020	24.8	25.6	49.6	21.7	29.6	48.7	36.0	11.2	52.9
Sub-Saharan Africa	*2005	61.0	9.7	29.2	59.5	11.9	28.6	62.7	7.3	30.0
Afrique subsaharienne	*2010	58.1	9.9	32.1	57.5	12.0	30.5	58.8	7.4	33.8
	*2015	54.5	10.9	34.5	54.7	13.5	31.8	54.4	7.9	37.7
	*2020	52.6	11.2	36.2	53.2	14.0	32.7	51.9	8.0	40.0
Eastern Africa	*2005	73.2	6.8	20.0	70.3	8.6	21.1	76.3	4.8	18.9
Afrique orientale	*2010	69.7	7.4	22.9	67.4	9.6	23.0	72.2	5.1	22.8
	*2015	66.2	8.1	25.6	64.9	10.7	24.4	67.6	5.4	27.0
	*2020	63.7	8.7	27.6	63.0	11.6	25.5	64.5	5.5	30.0
Southern Africa	*2005	8.9	26.3	64.8	10.3	34.0	55.8	6.8	14.8	78.5
Afrique australe	*2010	6.9	24.5	68.6	7.9	32.6	59.5	5.5	13.7	80.8
	*2015	7.3	24.1	68.6	8.5	33.1	58.4	5.7	12.4	81.9
	*2020	6.6	23.0	70.4	7.9	31.8	60.3	5.0	12.0	83.0
Western Africa	*2005	52.1	11.4	36.4	55.8	11.6	32.7	47.8	11.3	40.9
Afrique occidentale	*2010	48.2	11.2	40.6	53.0	11.2	35.8	42.5	11.2	46.4
	*2015	42.6	13.3	44.2	48.4	13.5	38.1	35.4	13.0	51.7
	*2020	39.9	13.9	46.2	46.2	14.4	39.5	32.2	13.4	54.4
Americas	*2005	11.2	22.0	66.8	14.8	29.0	56.2	6.2	12.3	81.5
Amériques	*2010	10.0	20.9	69.1	13.7	28.2	58.1	5.1	11.0	83.9
	*2015	9.1	20.9	70.0	12.5	28.4	59.0	4.5	10.8	84.6
	*2020	9.0	20.0	71.0	12.3	27.3	60.4	4.5	10.4	85.1
Northern America	*2005	1.5	22.3	76.2	2.0	32.5	65.5	0.8	10.3	88.9
Amérique septentrionale	*2010	1.5	19.7	78.8	2.1	29.6	68.4	0.8	8.5	90.8
	*2015	1.5	19.9	78.7	2.0	29.3	68.6	0.8	8.8	90.4
	*2020	1.3	19.7	79.0	1.8	29.2	68.9	0.7	8.5	90.7
Latin America & the Caribbean	*2005	18.0	21.7	60.3	22.8	26.8	50.4	10.6	13.9	75.5
Amérique latine et Caraïbes	*2010	15.4	21.6	63.0	20.2	27.4	52.4	8.2	12.9	78.9
	*2015	13.9	21.6	64.6	18.4	27.9	53.6	7.2	12.3	80.6
	*2020	13.7	20.3	66.1	18.2	26.3	55.5	7.1	11.7	81.2
Caribbean	*2005	19.6	17.3	63.1	26.2	22.3	51.5	9.4	9.8	80.9
Caraïbes	*2010	18.3	15.5	66.2	25.2	20.6	54.3	8.2	8.2	83.6
	*2015	17.1	15.3	67.6	24.0	20.6	55.4	7.3	7.7	85.0
	*2020	16.0	15.3	68.7	22.8	21.2	56.0	6.6	7.1	86.3
Central America	*2005	18.2	25.6	56.2	24.9	29.1	46.0	6.0	19.2	74.8
Amérique centrale	*2010	17.5	23.3	59.2	24.6	27.1	48.3	5.3	16.8	77.9
	*2015	16.7	23.7	59.6	23.8	27.8	48.4	4.7	16.7	78.6
	*2020	16.0	24.2	59.8	22.9	28.5	48.6	4.6	16.9	78.5
South America	*2005	17.8	20.7	61.5	21.7	26.3	52.0	12.2	12.6	75.3
Amérique du Sud	*2010	14.4	21.5	64.1	18.0	28.2	53.8	9.1	12.0	78.8
	*2015	12.5	21.3	66.1	15.8	28.6	55.6	8.0	11.2	80.8
	*2020	12.5	19.2	68.3	15.8	25.8	58.5	8.1	10.3	81.7
Central Asia	*2005	35.8	21.5	42.6	35.6	27.2	37.3	36.2	14.3	49.5
Asie centrale	*2010	31.2	23.4	45.3	30.8	29.9	39.3	31.8	14.9	53.3
	*2015	25.4	25.3	49.3	24.8	32.8	42.3	26.2	15.3	58.5
	*2020	22.0	26.9	51.1	21.9	34.7	43.5	22.3	16.3	61.4
Eastern Asia	*2005	40.3	24.2	35.5	42.4	24.8	32.8	37.6	23.5	38.9
Asie orientale	*2010	33.2	28.2	38.6	35.1	29.7	35.1	30.8	26.2	43.0
	*2015	26.1	28.5	45.4	28.0	31.1	41.0	23.6	25.3	51.1
	*2020	22.6	27.5	49.8	24.3	30.7	45.0	20.5	23.5	56.0

17

Employment by economic activity *(continued)*
Percentage of persons employed by sex and ISIC 4 categories; agriculture (agr.), industry (ind.) and services (ser.)

Emploi par activité économique *(suite)*
Personnes employées par sexe et branches de la CITI rév. 4; agriculture (agr.), industrie (ind.) et services (ser.), pourcentage

Region, country or area [+] Région, pays ou zone [+]	Year Année	Male and Female Hommes et femmes			Male Hommes			Female Femmes		
		Agr.	Ind.	Ser.	Agr.	Ind.	Ser.	Agr.	Ind.	Ser.
South-eastern Asia	*2005	44.5	18.9	36.7	45.0	20.7	34.3	43.7	16.2	40.1
Asie du Sud-Est	*2010	40.5	19.2	40.3	41.3	21.8	37.0	39.4	15.6	45.0
	*2015	35.2	21.3	43.5	36.1	24.6	39.3	33.9	16.6	49.5
	*2020	29.8	22.9	47.3	31.4	26.6	42.0	27.6	17.9	54.5
Southern Asia	*2005	53.5	18.8	27.7	47.9	20.5	31.6	69.8	13.8	16.4
Asie méridionale	*2010	49.4	21.5	29.1	44.2	23.5	32.3	66.6	14.9	18.5
	*2015	44.3	23.7	32.1	39.8	25.6	34.6	60.2	16.9	23.0
	*2020	40.0	25.5	34.5	35.8	27.7	36.6	55.0	17.8	27.2
Western Asia [1]	*2005	15.1	23.4	61.5	14.6	26.0	59.4	17.7	8.7	73.6
Asie occidentale [1]	*2010	10.8	27.2	62.0	11.0	30.2	58.8	9.6	8.6	81.8
	*2015	10.6	26.2	63.2	11.0	29.4	59.6	8.1	7.4	84.4
	*2020	9.0	25.8	65.1	9.4	28.8	61.8	6.7	6.8	86.5
Caucasus [2]	*2005	27.3	22.7	50.0	21.5	27.5	51.0	39.2	12.9	48.0
Caucase [2]	*2010	24.9	22.8	52.3	19.2	28.5	52.3	35.6	12.0	52.4
	*2015	21.9	23.5	54.6	17.4	29.7	52.9	30.0	12.4	57.6
	*2020	19.6	23.0	57.4	16.1	29.3	54.6	25.5	12.2	62.3
Eastern Europe	*2005	14.2	29.7	56.1	15.7	38.1	46.1	12.6	20.5	66.9
Europe orientale	*2010	11.7	28.6	59.7	13.2	38.5	48.4	10.1	17.8	72.1
	*2015	9.8	28.1	62.0	11.4	38.4	50.2	8.1	16.7	75.2
	*2020	8.4	28.2	63.4	10.1	38.6	51.3	6.6	16.5	76.9
Northern Europe	*2005	2.8	23.1	74.1	3.8	34.0	62.2	1.6	10.5	87.9
Europe septentrionale	*2010	2.2	19.9	78.0	3.1	30.2	66.7	1.2	8.3	90.6
	*2015	2.1	19.3	78.7	2.9	29.1	68.1	1.1	8.3	90.6
	*2020	1.7	18.5	79.8	2.5	28.1	69.5	0.9	7.8	91.3
Southern Europe	*2005	8.5	29.3	62.3	8.7	38.5	52.8	8.2	15.4	76.4
Europe méridionale	*2010	7.6	25.8	66.6	8.2	35.5	56.3	6.8	12.7	80.5
	*2015	6.9	23.5	69.6	8.1	32.2	59.6	5.4	12.1	82.5
	*2020	6.1	23.4	70.5	7.3	32.2	60.5	4.5	12.1	83.3
Western Europe	*2005	3.1	26.3	70.6	3.8	36.9	59.2	2.2	13.4	84.4
Europe occidentale	*2010	2.4	24.7	72.9	3.0	35.8	61.2	1.7	11.7	86.6
	*2015	2.1	23.6	74.2	2.7	34.6	62.7	1.5	11.2	87.3
	*2020	1.8	22.9	75.3	2.4	33.5	64.2	1.2	10.9	87.9
Afghanistan	*2005	62.2	11.5	26.2	59.4	11.5	29.1	78.5	11.5	10.0
Afghanistan	*2010	54.7	14.4	30.9	51.5	14.1	34.4	73.0	16.3	10.8
	*2015	47.1	17.0	35.8	42.4	16.0	41.7	68.5	21.9	9.6
	*2020	42.4	18.3	39.4	36.4	16.5	47.1	64.8	24.8	10.3
Albania	*2005	47.2	15.8	37.0	38.6	21.4	40.0	59.2	7.9	32.9
Albanie	2010	42.1	20.6	37.3	34.3	27.7	38.1	53.1	10.6	36.3
	2015	41.4	18.6	40.0	36.8	22.0	41.2	47.8	13.9	38.3
	*2020	36.1	20.2	43.7	33.3	23.2	43.6	40.0	16.2	43.8
Algeria	*2005	18.4	26.4	55.2	20.1	26.4	53.5	8.6	26.1	65.3
Algérie	*2010	11.9	30.1	58.0	13.3	31.2	55.5	3.5	24.3	72.2
	*2015	10.3	31.0	58.7	11.7	32.4	55.9	3.6	24.2	72.3
	*2020	9.7	30.7	59.6	10.9	32.0	57.1	3.5	23.3	73.2
American Samoa [3,4]	2000	3.1	41.7	51.9	...	...	...	...	...	...
Samoa américaines [3,4]	#2010	3.0	23.2	73.8	...	...	...	...	...	...
Angola	*2005	38.2	8.9	53.0	30.3	16.0	53.7	46.1	1.7	52.2
Angola	*2010	48.9	7.8	43.3	42.6	14.3	43.2	55.5	1.2	43.3
	*2015	50.6	8.6	40.8	43.8	16.0	40.2	57.5	1.2	41.4
	*2020	50.2	8.1	41.7	44.2	15.2	40.6	56.0	1.1	42.9
Anguilla [4] Anguilla [4]	#2001	2.9	18.9	76.7	4.8	32.1	61.7	0.7	3.7	93.9
Antigua and Barbuda [4]	2005	2.8	15.6	81.6	4.4	26.1	69.5	1.2	5.0	93.8
Antigua-et-Barbuda [4]	2008	2.8	15.6	81.6	4.4	26.1	69.5	1.2	5.0	93.8
Argentina	2005	1.3	23.3	75.5	1.7	32.0	66.4	0.7	10.7	88.6
Argentine	2010	1.3	23.3	75.4	1.9	32.9	65.2	0.4	9.4	90.2
	*2015	0.3	23.7	76.1	0.4	34.2	65.4	0.1	8.7	91.3
	*2020	0.1	21.0	78.9	0.1	30.2	69.7	~0.0	8.6	91.3
Armenia	*2005	38.3	18.2	43.6	32.6	26.8	40.6	45.0	8.0	47.0
Arménie	2010	38.6	17.4	44.0	31.6	26.7	41.7	47.3	5.8	46.9
	2015	35.3	15.9	48.8	31.2	23.1	45.6	40.1	7.5	52.4
	*2020	28.9	17.5	53.6	26.3	24.5	49.1	31.9	9.2	58.9

Employment by economic activity *(continued)*
Percentage of persons employed by sex and ISIC 4 categories; agriculture (agr.), industry (ind.) and services (ser.)

Emploi par activité économique *(suite)*
Personnes employées par sexe et branches de la CITI rév. 4; agriculture (agr.), industrie (ind.) et services (ser.), pourcentage

Region, country or area [+] Région, pays ou zone [+]	Year Année	Male and Female Hommes et femmes			Male Hommes			Female Femmes		
		Agr.	Ind.	Ser.	Agr.	Ind.	Ser.	Agr.	Ind.	Ser.
Aruba [4] Aruba [4]	#2000	0.5	16.4	82.3	0.8	26.7	71.6	0.2	4.5	94.7
	#2010[5]	0.6	14.5	84.4	1.0	24.4	74.1	0.3	4.5	94.8
	#2011	0.6	14.0	85.1	0.8	24.4	74.4	0.4	3.3	96.1
Australia Australie	2005	3.6	21.1	75.3	4.5	30.6	64.9	2.5	9.3	88.2
	2010	3.2	21.0	75.8	4.0	31.1	64.9	2.3	8.6	89.1
	2015	2.6	19.4	78.0	3.3	29.3	67.3	1.9	7.7	90.5
	*2020	2.5	19.8	77.7	3.3	30.0	66.7	1.6	8.0	90.4
Austria Autriche	2005	5.3	27.6	67.2	5.3	39.7	55.1	5.3	12.9	81.8
	2010	5.2	24.9	69.9	5.4	36.5	58.1	5.0	11.5	83.5
	2015	4.5	25.8	69.7	4.8	37.8	57.4	4.2	12.1	83.7
	*2020	3.5	25.0	71.5	3.9	36.7	59.4	3.1	11.6	85.4
Azerbaijan Azerbaïdjan	2005	39.3	12.1	48.6	41.1	15.2	43.7	37.4	8.7	54.0
	2010	38.2	13.7	48.1	32.4	20.8	46.8	44.5	6.1	49.4
	2015	36.4	14.1	49.6	31.0	21.8	47.2	42.1	5.9	52.1
	*2020	35.5	15.0	49.5	30.4	23.2	46.3	40.9	6.1	52.9
Bahamas Bahamas	2005	3.5	17.8	78.7	6.3	29.3	64.3	0.3	5.1	94.6
	*2010	2.8	16.1	81.1	4.8	27.5	67.7	0.5	3.6	95.9
	*2015	2.4	14.7	82.9	4.2	25.0	70.8	0.4	3.1	96.6
	*2020	2.1	14.0	83.9	3.7	23.9	72.4	0.3	2.9	96.8
Bahrain Bahreïn	*2005	1.3	30.9	67.8	1.7	36.2	62.2	0.1	10.2	89.7
	2010	1.1	35.7	63.2	1.4	42.6	56.0	0.1	9.0	90.9
	2015	1.1	35.2	63.8	1.4	42.1	56.5	0.1	9.2	90.7
	*2020	1.0	35.1	64.0	1.2	41.4	57.4	~0.0	8.6	91.4
Bangladesh Bangladesh	*2005	51.1	13.9	35.0	45.4	14.6	40.1	70.6	11.5	17.9
	2010	47.3	17.6	35.1	41.0	19.2	39.8	65.6	13.0	21.4
	*2015	43.5	19.9	36.6	35.7	21.7	42.6	64.0	15.4	20.6
	*2020	37.7	21.6	40.6	29.7	23.1	47.2	56.5	18.3	25.2
Barbados Barbade	*2005	3.5	17.1	79.4	4.4	25.8	69.8	2.6	7.7	89.8
	2010	2.8	18.8	78.4	3.8	28.6	67.6	1.9	8.7	89.4
	2015	2.9	19.4	77.8	4.2	29.0	66.8	1.6	9.7	88.8
	*2020	2.6	18.9	78.5	3.6	28.5	67.9	1.5	9.0	89.5
Belarus Bélarus	*2005	12.8	31.5	55.6	16.5	40.7	42.8	9.2	22.4	68.4
	*2010	11.0	32.2	56.8	14.2	42.7	43.2	8.0	21.8	70.2
	2015	9.7	31.1	59.2	12.8	42.0	45.1	6.6	20.3	73.0
	*2020	10.8	30.2	59.0	14.3	41.8	43.9	7.1	18.5	74.3
Belgium Belgique	2005	2.0	24.7	73.3	2.5	34.9	62.6	1.5	11.3	87.2
	2010	1.4	23.4	75.3	1.7	34.3	64.0	0.9	10.1	89.0
	2015	1.2	21.4	77.4	1.6	32.8	65.7	0.7	8.4	90.9
	*2020	0.9	20.6	78.4	1.2	31.3	67.4	0.6	8.3	91.1
Belize Belize	2005	19.6	17.9	62.6	27.7	21.7	50.6	3.2	10.3	86.5
	*2010	18.9	16.5	64.5	27.0	20.4	52.5	3.9	9.3	86.8
	2015	18.1	15.4	66.5	25.9	19.7	54.4	4.6	8.0	87.4
	*2020	16.6	15.7	67.7	23.8	19.6	56.6	4.6	9.3	86.0
Benin Bénin	*2005	46.1	19.5	34.4	52.5	19.9	27.6	39.2	19.0	41.8
	*2010	44.0	18.7	37.3	51.1	19.9	29.0	36.8	17.6	45.7
	*2015	41.2	18.6	40.2	48.8	20.4	30.8	33.3	16.8	49.9
	*2020	38.0	19.1	42.9	46.1	21.6	32.3	29.6	16.5	53.9
Bermuda Bermudes	2004[6]	1.7	12.1	86.2	3.0	20.5	76.6	0.3	3.1	96.6
	#2010[3,4]	1.4	12.9	85.7	2.4	22.6	75.0	0.4	3.2	96.4
	#2012[4,7]	1.7	9.6	88.7	3.0	16.5	80.5	0.3	2.6	97.1
	#2013[3,4,8]	1.6	10.3	87.6	...	...	...	...	...	...
Bhutan Bhoutan	*2005	62.0	9.4	28.6	54.6	11.9	33.6	71.8	6.2	22.0
	2010	59.6	6.6	33.8	54.9	6.6	38.6	65.9	6.7	27.4
	2015	58.0	9.7	32.4	52.3	9.9	37.8	66.3	9.2	24.5
	*2020	54.6	11.1	34.3	49.0	11.5	39.5	62.9	10.4	26.6
Bolivia (Plurin. State of) Bolivie (État plurin. de)	2005	38.6	19.4	42.0	38.3	25.9	35.8	39.0	10.7	50.3
	*2010	30.0	20.7	49.3	29.5	28.3	42.1	30.6	10.6	58.8
	2015	27.8	22.5	49.6	27.5	30.4	42.1	28.3	11.0	60.7
	*2020	30.4	19.4	50.3	30.5	26.6	42.9	30.2	10.1	59.7
Bosnia and Herzegovina Bosnie-Herzégovine	*2005	21.2	30.4	48.4	20.3	37.1	42.6	22.8	17.8	59.4
	2010	19.7	30.9	49.4	17.9	39.4	42.7	22.8	16.3	60.9
	*2015	17.5	30.6	51.9	17.4	39.0	43.6	17.7	17.1	65.2
	*2020	15.1	32.3	52.6	15.1	41.1	43.9	15.1	17.9	67.0

17

Employment by economic activity *(continued)*
Percentage of persons employed by sex and ISIC 4 categories; agriculture (agr.), industry (ind.) and services (ser.)

Emploi par activité économique *(suite)*
Personnes employées par sexe et branches de la CITI rév. 4; agriculture (agr.), industrie (ind.) et services (ser.), pourcentage

Region, country or area [+] Région, pays ou zone [+]	Year Année	Male and Female Hommes et femmes			Male Hommes			Female Femmes		
		Agr.	Ind.	Ser.	Agr.	Ind.	Ser.	Agr.	Ind.	Ser.
Botswana	*2005	22.6	20.5	56.9	28.8	25.9	45.3	14.9	13.7	71.4
Botswana	*2010	24.6	18.2	57.1	28.6	24.5	46.8	19.6	10.3	70.0
	*2015	22.3	18.3	59.5	26.3	25.6	48.1	17.6	10.0	72.4
	*2020	20.4	18.1	61.5	24.3	25.7	50.0	16.0	9.4	74.6
Brazil	2005	16.6	22.0	61.4	20.5	27.9	51.6	11.1	13.4	75.5
Brésil	*2010	12.6	22.5	64.8	16.6	29.4	54.0	7.0	12.6	80.4
	2015	10.2	22.2	67.6	13.9	29.8	56.3	5.0	11.7	83.3
	*2020	9.1	19.6	71.3	12.9	26.5	60.7	4.0	10.3	85.7
British Virgin Islands [4] Îles Vierges britanniques [4]	2010	0.5	11.1	87.4	...	...	...	...	...	...
Brunei Darussalam	*2005	0.9	20.6	78.5	1.0	27.7	71.3	0.8	10.2	89.1
Brunéi Darussalam	*2010	0.7	19.3	80.0	0.8	25.4	73.8	0.6	10.5	89.0
	*2015	0.7	17.8	81.5	1.0	23.1	76.0	0.5	10.3	89.3
	*2020	1.3	15.8	82.8	2.0	20.9	77.1	0.5	8.9	90.6
Bulgaria	2005	8.9	34.2	56.8	10.7	38.9	50.4	6.8	28.8	64.3
Bulgarie	2010	6.8	33.0	60.2	8.2	40.7	51.0	5.2	24.1	70.7
	2015	6.9	29.9	63.2	9.1	36.2	54.7	4.3	22.7	72.9
	*2020	6.3	30.1	63.7	8.2	37.0	54.8	4.0	22.1	73.9
Burkina Faso	*2005	67.4	11.7	20.9	73.9	9.4	16.7	58.9	14.7	26.4
Burkina Faso	*2010	48.2	20.9	31.0	55.6	18.8	25.6	38.3	23.6	38.1
	*2015	29.1	32.0	38.9	35.6	31.3	33.1	20.7	32.8	46.5
	*2020	24.7	33.9	41.4	30.7	34.1	35.2	16.6	33.8	49.6
Burundi	*2005	92.3	1.9	5.8	87.6	3.3	9.1	96.6	0.6	2.8
Burundi	*2010	92.1	1.8	6.1	87.5	3.2	9.3	96.3	0.5	3.2
	*2015	92.0	1.6	6.4	87.5	2.9	9.6	96.1	0.4	3.4
	*2020	92.0	1.4	6.5	87.8	2.6	9.7	96.0	0.4	3.7
Cabo Verde	*2005	19.4	20.6	60.0	24.1	26.3	49.6	12.5	12.4	75.1
Cabo Verde	*2010	16.2	22.2	61.5	20.4	28.8	50.8	10.1	12.4	77.5
	*2015	14.6	21.6	63.8	19.0	28.7	52.3	8.6	12.0	79.4
	*2020	11.1	22.1	66.8	15.2	31.0	53.8	6.1	11.0	82.9
Cambodia	*2005	62.0	13.2	24.8	61.3	12.7	26.0	62.7	13.7	23.6
Cambodge	*2010	57.3	16.0	26.7	56.9	15.6	27.5	57.7	16.4	25.9
	2015	42.5	24.9	32.6	40.5	25.5	34.0	44.6	24.3	31.1
	*2020	31.2	29.6	39.2	29.2	31.3	39.5	33.2	27.8	38.9
Cameroon	*2005	62.0	10.7	27.3	56.9	12.9	30.2	67.5	8.4	24.1
Cameroun	*2010	55.1	12.2	32.8	49.7	14.2	36.0	61.2	9.8	29.0
	*2015	46.5	14.3	39.1	41.8	17.5	40.7	51.9	10.8	37.3
	*2020	42.9	15.1	42.1	39.0	18.3	42.6	47.2	11.3	41.4
Canada	2005	2.1	22.7	75.2	2.8	33.1	64.2	1.4	10.8	87.8
Canada	2010	1.8	20.2	78.0	2.4	30.7	66.9	1.1	8.5	90.3
	2015	1.6	19.9	78.4	2.2	30.2	67.6	1.0	8.6	90.4
	*2020	1.4	19.4	79.2	1.9	29.4	68.7	0.9	8.3	90.8
Cayman Islands	2005[4]	1.7	22.2	75.5	2.6	39.3	57.3	0.6	3.3	95.7
Îles Caïmanes	#2010	0.6	14.9	84.2	1.1	26.2	72.5	0.1	3.2	96.4
	#2013	0.8	15.5	83.6	1.5	29.0	69.5	0.2	2.0	97.7
Central African Republic	*2005	80.0	6.0	13.9	76.2	8.5	15.4	84.6	3.2	12.2
République centrafricaine	*2010	78.8	6.2	15.1	75.0	8.7	16.3	83.2	3.2	13.7
	*2015	78.5	5.3	16.2	74.9	7.5	17.5	82.8	2.7	14.5
	*2020	77.1	5.4	17.5	73.8	7.7	18.5	81.0	2.7	16.3
Chad	*2005	79.9	2.3	17.8	79.0	3.7	17.3	81.0	0.7	18.3
Tchad	*2010	78.5	2.4	19.1	78.3	3.8	18.0	78.8	0.7	20.5
	*2015	77.0	2.4	20.7	77.7	3.8	18.5	76.1	0.7	23.3
	*2020	76.3	2.1	21.6	77.8	3.4	18.8	74.5	0.6	25.0
Channel Islands	*2005	5.4	29.2	65.3	6.7	39.6	53.8	3.8	15.8	80.4
Îles Anglo-Normandes	*2010	4.7	26.7	68.6	6.0	37.1	57.0	3.1	13.5	83.4
	*2015	4.0	24.9	71.1	5.3	35.2	59.6	2.5	11.8	85.7
	*2020	3.5	22.9	73.6	4.7	33.0	62.3	2.0	10.2	87.8
Chile	2005	13.2	23.0	63.9	17.3	29.3	53.4	5.9	11.6	82.5
Chili	2010	10.6	23.0	66.4	14.1	31.1	54.8	5.1	10.3	84.6
	2015	9.4	23.3	67.3	12.7	31.7	55.6	4.5	11.2	84.2
	*2020	8.8	22.0	69.2	11.7	30.8	57.5	4.8	9.9	85.3

Employment by economic activity *(continued)*
Percentage of persons employed by sex and ISIC 4 categories; agriculture (agr.), industry (ind.) and services (ser.)

Emploi par activité économique *(suite)*
Personnes employées par sexe et branches de la CITI rév. 4; agriculture (agr.), industrie (ind.) et services (ser.), pourcentage

Region, country or area [+] Région, pays ou zone [+]	Year Année	Male and Female Hommes et femmes			Male Hommes			Female Femmes		
		Agr.	Ind.	Ser.	Agr.	Ind.	Ser.	Agr.	Ind.	Ser.
China [9] Chine [9]	*2005	44.8	23.8	31.4	47.8	23.2	29.0	41.1	24.5	34.4
	*2010	36.7	28.7	34.6	39.2	29.3	31.5	33.5	27.9	38.5
	*2015	28.6	29.2	42.2	31.0	30.8	38.1	25.5	27.1	47.4
	*2020	24.7	28.2	47.1	26.8	30.6	42.6	22.1	25.1	52.8
China, Hong Kong SAR Chine, RAS de Hong Kong	2005	0.3	15.1	84.7	0.3	22.1	77.5	0.2	6.5	93.3
	*2010	0.2	12.8	87.0	0.3	19.9	79.8	0.2	4.8	95.0
	*2015	0.2	12.0	87.8	0.3	19.5	80.3	0.1	4.2	95.7
	*2020	0.2	11.5	88.3	0.2	19.1	80.7	0.1	3.9	96.0
China, Macao SAR Chine, RAS de Macao	2005	0.4	24.9	74.7	0.6	38.7	60.7	0.1	9.7	90.1
	2010	0.4	13.7	85.9	0.7	22.8	76.5	0.1	4.1	95.8
	2015	0.4	15.8	83.8	0.7	26.7	72.6	0.1	4.4	95.5
	*2020	0.4	9.5	90.1	0.6	16.1	83.3	0.1	2.5	97.4
Colombia Colombie	*2005	20.6	18.9	60.4	29.8	20.6	49.6	6.4	16.4	77.2
	2010	18.4	20.0	61.6	26.2	22.8	50.9	7.0	15.9	77.1
	2015	16.0	19.8	64.2	22.4	24.1	53.6	7.2	14.0	78.8
	*2020	16.5	20.0	63.5	22.7	23.8	53.4	7.6	14.6	77.7
Comoros Comores	*2005	55.4	14.2	30.4	50.6	15.6	33.8	62.8	12.0	25.2
	*2010	53.7	13.7	32.6	49.2	15.4	35.3	60.3	11.1	28.6
	*2015	51.8	13.4	34.8	47.6	15.5	36.9	57.7	10.4	31.9
	*2020	49.9	13.0	37.0	46.1	15.5	38.4	55.2	9.7	35.1
Congo Congo	2005	40.0	23.4	36.6	38.8	23.2	38.0	41.2	23.7	35.2
	*2010	37.4	23.3	39.2	36.6	23.7	39.8	38.3	23.0	38.7
	*2015	35.0	23.0	42.0	34.7	23.9	41.5	35.3	22.1	42.6
	*2020	33.8	21.7	44.5	34.4	22.5	43.1	33.1	21.0	45.9
Cook Islands [10] Îles Cook [10]	2011	4.3	11.7	84.0	6.4	17.7	75.9	1.8	5.0	93.3
Costa Rica Costa Rica	2005	15.2	21.6	63.1	20.9	26.5	52.7	4.8	12.6	82.6
	*2010	11.4	20.0	68.6	15.9	25.1	59.0	3.6	11.2	85.2
	2015	12.3	19.2	68.5	17.4	25.1	57.6	4.2	9.6	86.2
	*2020	11.9	19.8	68.3	16.6	25.2	58.2	4.1	10.8	85.0
Côte d'Ivoire Côte d'Ivoire	*2005	49.3	11.7	39.0	51.6	11.8	36.6	45.3	11.5	43.2
	*2010	47.3	11.4	41.4	50.4	11.5	38.1	42.3	11.1	46.6
	*2015	43.6	12.1	44.4	48.4	13.1	38.5	36.4	10.5	53.1
	*2020	39.3	13.4	47.3	45.7	15.4	38.9	30.3	10.8	59.0
Croatia Croatie	2005	17.3	28.6	54.1	16.0	37.2	46.8	18.9	18.1	63.0
	2010	14.3	27.5	58.3	13.2	38.0	48.8	15.5	14.9	69.6
	2015	9.2	26.7	64.1	10.8	36.7	52.5	7.4	15.0	77.5
	*2020	5.8	27.5	66.8	6.8	38.2	55.0	4.5	14.9	80.7
Cuba Cuba	*2005	21.1	18.1	60.8	27.6	21.4	51.0	9.8	12.6	77.6
	2010	18.6	17.1	64.3	24.9	20.5	54.5	8.5	11.5	79.9
	*2015	18.6	17.1	64.3	25.2	21.0	53.7	8.1	10.9	81.0
	*2020	17.3	16.8	65.9	23.6	21.0	55.4	7.2	10.1	82.7
Curaçao [4] Curaçao [4]	2000	1.1	18.0	80.9	2.0	28.6	69.4	0.2	5.6	94.2
	2005	0.9	15.3	83.8	...	...	...	...	...	...
	2008	1.1	17.6	81.3	...	...	...	...	...	...
Cyprus Chypre	2005	4.7	24.0	71.2	5.6	33.7	60.7	3.4	10.4	86.2
	2010	3.8	20.4	75.8	4.9	29.7	65.5	2.5	9.2	88.3
	2015	4.0	16.2	79.8	5.7	24.8	69.5	2.1	6.3	91.6
	*2020	2.0	16.3	81.7	2.9	24.8	72.3	0.9	6.1	93.0
Czechia Tchéquie	2005	4.0	39.5	56.5	4.9	49.4	45.7	2.8	26.5	70.7
	2010	3.1	38.0	58.9	4.0	49.0	47.0	1.9	23.2	74.9
	2015	2.9	38.0	59.0	3.9	49.1	47.0	1.6	23.7	74.6
	*2020	2.6	37.1	60.2	3.5	48.2	48.4	1.6	23.4	74.9
Dem. People's Rep. Korea Rép. pop. dém. de Corée	*2005	54.4	16.7	28.9	44.8	23.9	31.4	64.9	9.0	26.2
	*2010	53.5	15.4	31.1	44.5	22.1	33.4	63.4	8.1	28.5
	*2015	52.0	14.5	33.5	43.7	20.9	35.4	61.2	7.5	31.4
	*2020	51.1	13.2	35.7	43.6	19.1	37.3	59.4	6.8	33.8
Dem. Rep. of the Congo Rép. dém. du Congo	2005	71.9	8.2	19.9	63.7	13.2	23.1	79.9	3.3	16.8
	*2010	70.0	8.6	21.4	62.4	13.8	23.8	77.9	3.3	18.9
	*2015	67.0	9.5	23.5	59.7	15.3	25.0	74.7	3.5	21.8
	*2020	65.1	9.8	25.1	58.4	15.8	25.9	72.2	3.5	24.3

Employment by economic activity *(continued)*
Percentage of persons employed by sex and ISIC 4 categories; agriculture (agr.), industry (ind.) and services (ser.)

Emploi par activité économique *(suite)*
Personnes employées par sexe et branches de la CITI rév. 4; agriculture (agr.), industrie (ind.) et services (ser.), pourcentage

Region, country or area [+] / Région, pays ou zone [+]	Year / Année	Male and Female Hommes et femmes			Male Hommes			Female Femmes		
		Agr.	Ind.	Ser.	Agr.	Ind.	Ser.	Agr.	Ind.	Ser.
Denmark Danemark	2005	3.2	23.9	72.9	4.6	33.9	61.6	1.6	12.4	86.0
	2010	2.4	19.6	78.0	3.9	29.1	67.1	0.9	9.2	89.9
	2015	2.5	19.3	78.2	3.8	27.8	68.4	1.1	9.7	89.3
	*2020	2.1	18.3	79.6	3.2	27.1	69.7	0.9	8.4	90.7
Djibouti Djibouti	*2005	43.4	11.4	45.2	43.7	14.0	42.3	42.9	7.4	49.7
	*2010	40.7	11.5	47.8	41.6	14.3	44.1	39.4	7.1	53.5
	*2015	36.5	12.3	51.2	37.6	15.6	46.8	34.7	7.3	58.0
	*2020	32.4	13.3	54.3	33.8	17.0	49.2	30.2	7.6	62.2
Dominica [6] Dominique [6]	#2001	21.0	20.0	58.8	29.4	26.8	43.9	8.3	9.7	81.5
Dominican Republic République dominicaine	2005	13.7	22.6	63.7	19.3	26.4	54.3	2.6	15.1	82.3
	2010	12.4	18.5	69.1	18.2	23.4	58.4	2.2	9.7	88.2
	2015	10.0	18.5	71.5	15.3	23.7	61.0	1.4	9.9	88.7
	*2020	8.8	19.9	71.3	13.7	26.8	59.5	1.3	9.3	89.4
Ecuador Équateur	2005	30.3	17.6	52.1	33.5	22.3	44.2	25.3	10.1	64.6
	2010	27.9	18.5	53.6	32.2	23.1	44.7	20.9	11.1	68.0
	2015	26.2	19.7	54.1	28.5	25.1	46.4	22.6	11.2	66.3
	*2020	29.4	18.2	52.5	31.4	23.3	45.4	26.5	10.6	62.9
Egypt Égypte	2005	30.9	21.5	47.5	27.4	25.2	47.3	46.7	4.9	48.4
	2010	28.3	25.4	46.3	24.7	30.1	45.2	42.9	5.9	51.2
	2015	25.8	25.1	49.1	22.2	30.0	47.8	40.2	5.6	54.2
	*2020	23.3	28.2	48.6	20.3	33.7	46.1	34.9	7.2	58.0
El Salvador El Salvador	2005	20.0	22.2	57.8	30.7	23.7	45.6	4.8	20.1	75.1
	2010	20.8	21.4	57.9	32.0	23.5	44.6	5.4	18.4	76.2
	2015	18.1	22.2	59.7	28.5	24.1	47.4	3.9	19.5	76.6
	*2020	16.0	22.1	62.0	25.3	25.6	49.0	3.3	17.2	79.5
Equatorial Guinea Guinée équatoriale	*2005	45.2	19.0	35.8	42.3	25.7	32.0	49.7	8.7	41.6
	*2010	41.7	22.9	35.4	39.0	29.3	31.6	46.1	12.3	41.6
	*2015	42.0	20.9	37.1	40.2	26.8	33.0	45.0	11.0	44.0
	*2020	42.5	18.5	38.9	42.5	23.4	34.2	42.6	10.2	47.2
Eritrea Érythrée	*2005	65.2	10.0	24.7	60.2	13.8	26.0	70.8	5.9	23.4
	*2010	64.7	9.1	26.3	60.0	12.6	27.4	69.9	5.1	25.0
	*2015	63.1	8.5	28.5	58.7	11.8	29.5	68.1	4.7	27.2
	*2020	60.8	8.5	30.7	56.8	11.8	31.3	65.4	4.5	30.0
Estonia Estonie	2005	5.2	34.1	60.7	7.2	44.1	48.8	3.2	24.2	72.6
	2010	4.2	30.3	65.5	5.7	43.1	51.2	2.8	18.0	79.2
	2015	3.9	30.7	65.4	5.2	43.2	51.6	2.5	17.5	80.0
	*2020	3.1	29.4	67.6	4.5	41.0	54.5	1.5	16.8	81.7
Eswatini Eswatini	*2005	17.0	25.8	57.2	18.5	24.8	56.7	15.3	27.0	57.8
	*2010	15.2	25.3	59.5	16.9	25.2	58.0	13.5	25.4	61.1
	*2015	13.5	24.6	61.8	15.2	25.4	59.4	11.7	23.9	64.5
	*2020	12.3	23.5	64.2	14.1	24.7	61.2	10.2	22.2	67.6
Ethiopia Éthiopie	2005	78.1	7.4	14.5	82.1	5.9	12.0	73.4	9.1	17.5
	*2010	74.0	8.0	18.0	78.9	7.2	13.9	68.1	9.0	22.9
	*2015	69.1	9.1	21.8	75.6	9.0	15.4	61.5	9.2	29.4
	*2020	65.6	10.4	24.0	72.6	10.8	16.5	57.4	9.8	32.7
Faroe Islands [3,6] Îles Féroé [3,6]	2005	11.1	22.2	66.7	20.0	33.3	53.3	8.3	8.3	83.3
Fiji Fidji	*2005	46.0	14.9	39.0	46.3	16.1	37.5	45.4	12.1	42.6
	*2010	43.9	14.4	41.7	44.7	15.8	39.5	42.4	11.7	45.9
	*2015	39.4	13.2	47.4	39.8	15.6	44.6	38.7	8.5	52.8
	*2020	35.7	13.3	51.0	36.6	15.7	47.7	33.9	8.4	57.7
Finland Finlande	2005	4.8	25.8	69.4	6.6	38.3	55.1	2.9	12.3	84.8
	2010	4.4	23.3	72.3	6.0	35.9	58.1	2.8	9.9	87.3
	2015	4.2	21.7	74.1	6.1	34.0	59.9	2.2	8.7	89.1
	*2020	3.5	22.0	74.5	5.0	34.4	60.6	1.9	8.7	89.4
France France	2005	3.6	23.8	72.6	4.8	33.8	61.4	2.3	12.1	85.6
	2010	2.9	22.3	74.8	3.9	33.1	63.0	1.8	10.2	88.1
	2015	2.7	20.4	76.9	3.8	30.5	65.7	1.7	9.4	88.9
	*2020	2.4	19.9	77.7	3.4	29.7	66.9	1.3	9.3	89.3
French Guiana [8,11] Guyane française [8,11]	2010	...	14.1	51.5	...	...	...	...	...	...
	2012	...	14.9	58.3	...	...	...	...	...	...

17

Employment by economic activity *(continued)*
Percentage of persons employed by sex and ISIC 4 categories; agriculture (agr.), industry (ind.) and services (ser.)

Emploi par activité économique *(suite)*
Personnes employées par sexe et branches de la CITI rév. 4; agriculture (agr.), industrie (ind.) et services (ser.), pourcentage

Region, country or area [+] Région, pays ou zone [+]	Year Année	Male and Female Hommes et femmes			Male Hommes			Female Femmes		
		Agr.	Ind.	Ser.	Agr.	Ind.	Ser.	Agr.	Ind.	Ser.
French Polynesia	*2005	9.3	17.6	73.1	11.8	24.4	63.7	5.5	7.4	87.1
Polynésie française	*2010	8.7	16.4	74.9	11.2	23.7	65.1	5.2	6.2	88.6
	*2015	7.7	15.1	77.1	10.2	22.4	67.4	4.5	5.5	90.1
	*2020	6.8	14.6	78.6	9.1	21.9	69.0	3.7	4.9	91.4
Gabon	*2005	39.0	9.9	51.0	28.5	14.4	57.1	56.9	2.4	40.7
Gabon	*2010	37.2	10.2	52.6	27.6	14.5	57.8	54.4	2.5	43.1
	*2015	34.9	10.6	54.5	25.6	15.1	59.4	51.4	2.6	45.9
	*2020	32.4	10.8	56.9	24.0	15.2	60.8	47.3	2.8	49.9
Gambia	*2005	33.7	16.5	49.8	27.4	24.6	48.0	42.7	4.9	52.4
Gambie	*2010	31.0	16.4	52.6	25.6	24.8	49.6	38.5	4.6	56.8
	*2015	29.2	15.8	54.9	24.3	24.4	51.4	36.0	4.2	59.8
	*2020	26.6	15.8	57.7	22.5	24.5	53.1	32.1	4.0	63.9
Georgia	2005	54.3	9.3	36.4	51.8	13.7	34.5	57.2	4.4	38.4
Géorgie	2010	48.1	10.6	41.3	46.4	16.3	37.3	50.0	4.2	45.8
	2015	44.0	11.0	44.9	41.3	16.3	42.4	47.1	5.1	47.8
	*2020	41.3	14.2	44.5	39.3	21.3	39.4	43.7	5.8	50.5
Germany	2005	2.4	29.8	67.8	2.9	41.1	56.0	1.7	16.0	82.3
Allemagne	2010	1.6	28.3	70.0	2.0	40.2	57.8	1.2	14.3	84.5
	2015	1.4	27.7	70.9	1.8	39.7	58.5	1.0	13.9	85.2
	*2020	1.2	26.8	72.1	1.5	38.3	60.2	0.8	13.5	85.7
Ghana	*2005	55.0	14.2	30.9	58.9	14.1	27.0	50.8	14.3	35.0
Ghana	*2010	50.2	13.7	36.1	54.0	14.9	31.1	46.0	12.2	41.7
	2015	35.2	18.7	46.1	41.9	17.4	40.8	27.4	20.2	52.3
	*2020	28.5	22.2	49.4	34.7	20.6	44.7	21.3	24.1	54.7
Greece	2005	12.2	22.4	65.5	11.3	30.0	58.7	13.5	9.9	76.6
Grèce	2010	12.4	19.6	68.0	12.3	27.6	60.1	12.6	7.8	79.6
	2015	12.9	14.9	72.2	13.3	19.9	66.8	12.4	8.0	79.7
	*2020	11.7	15.2	73.1	12.2	20.5	67.3	11.0	7.6	81.4
Greenland [11,12]										
Groenland [11,12]	2011	4.6	12.6	82.5	8.1	20.3	71.3	0.3	3.3	96.2
Guadeloupe [8,11]	2010	...	13.8	64.4	...	...	...	...	...	...
Guadeloupe [8,11]	2012	3.3	13.5	65.5	...	...	...	...	...	...
Guam	*2005	0.4	14.2	85.4	0.6	21.3	78.1	0.1	3.6	96.3
Guam	2010	0.3	15.1	84.6	0.5	22.7	76.9	0.1	3.8	96.1
	*2015	0.3	14.8	84.9	0.4	22.5	77.1	0.1	3.7	96.3
	*2020	0.2	14.3	85.5	0.3	21.6	78.0	0.1	3.5	96.5
Guatemala	*2005	34.7	21.4	43.9	45.5	22.0	32.5	14.5	20.3	65.1
Guatemala	2010	33.5	22.0	44.5	43.9	21.0	35.1	13.5	24.0	62.5
	2015	31.9	18.9	49.2	42.6	19.5	38.0	9.8	17.7	72.5
	*2020	31.3	18.4	50.3	41.8	19.4	38.9	9.7	16.5	73.8
Guernsey										
Guernesey	2013	1.5	13.6	84.8	1.0	12.2	40.9	0.5	1.4	44.3
Guinea	*2005	69.3	5.4	25.3	65.2	9.5	25.3	72.8	1.9	25.2
Guinée	*2010	67.5	5.3	27.2	64.2	9.4	26.4	70.2	1.9	27.9
	*2015	64.9	5.4	29.7	62.6	9.7	27.7	66.8	1.9	31.3
	*2020	61.3	6.2	32.5	59.6	11.2	29.2	62.6	2.1	35.3
Guinea-Bissau	*2005	72.2	7.4	20.4	68.2	9.9	21.9	76.5	4.8	18.7
Guinée-Bissau	*2010	71.0	7.1	21.8	67.5	9.6	22.8	74.8	4.4	20.8
	*2015	69.7	6.9	23.4	66.9	9.4	23.8	72.8	4.2	23.0
	*2020	67.8	7.0	25.2	65.6	9.6	24.8	70.2	4.2	25.6
Guyana	*2005	22.4	24.2	53.4	28.7	29.9	41.4	8.2	11.5	80.3
Guyana	*2010	20.6	23.5	55.9	26.6	30.4	43.0	9.2	10.0	80.8
	*2015	18.0	23.2	58.7	23.3	31.5	45.2	8.9	8.9	82.2
	*2020	16.8	22.9	60.3	21.7	31.9	46.4	8.8	8.1	83.2
Haiti	*2005	35.5	6.9	57.6	49.2	10.6	40.2	19.6	2.6	77.8
Haïti	*2010	33.6	6.5	59.9	47.3	10.1	42.6	16.9	2.2	80.8
	*2015	30.3	7.1	62.6	43.6	11.3	45.1	14.5	2.1	83.4
	*2020	28.3	6.6	65.0	41.5	10.7	47.8	12.7	1.9	85.5
Honduras	2005	33.1	23.5	43.4	45.7	22.8	31.5	8.4	24.9	66.7
Honduras	2010	36.5	19.1	44.5	49.5	19.0	31.5	11.9	19.1	69.0
	2015	28.7	21.8	49.5	40.5	22.3	37.2	7.5	20.9	71.6
	*2020	30.1	19.7	50.2	42.4	21.1	36.6	9.8	17.4	72.8

Employment by economic activity *(continued)*
Percentage of persons employed by sex and ISIC 4 categories; agriculture (agr.), industry (ind.) and services (ser.)

Emploi par activité économique *(suite)*
Personnes employées par sexe et branches de la CITI rév. 4; agriculture (agr.), industrie (ind.) et services (ser.), pourcentage

Region, country or area [+] Région, pays ou zone [+]	Year Année	Male and Female Hommes et femmes			Male Hommes			Female Femmes		
		Agr.	Ind.	Ser.	Agr.	Ind.	Ser.	Agr.	Ind.	Ser.
Hungary	2005	4.9	32.5	62.7	6.7	41.9	51.4	2.6	21.2	76.2
Hongrie	2010	4.5	30.7	64.8	6.5	40.2	53.4	2.3	19.8	77.9
	2015	4.9	30.3	64.8	6.8	39.9	53.3	2.6	18.9	78.4
	*2020	4.6	32.8	62.6	6.3	43.5	50.2	2.5	20.0	77.5
Iceland	2005	6.5	21.7	71.8	9.6	31.5	58.9	3.1	10.6	86.3
Islande	2010	5.6	18.4	76.0	8.6	28.1	63.3	2.2	7.8	90.0
	2015	4.2	17.8	77.9	6.5	27.7	65.8	1.7	6.9	91.3
	*2020	3.8	16.1	80.1	6.1	24.4	69.5	1.3	6.8	91.9
India	2005	56.0	18.8	25.2	50.6	20.7	28.8	71.1	13.7	15.3
Inde	2010	51.5	21.8	26.7	46.9	23.7	29.4	67.0	15.5	17.5
	*2015	45.7	24.1	30.3	42.4	25.7	31.9	58.4	17.7	24.0
	*2020	41.5	26.2	32.3	38.5	28.2	33.3	53.6	17.9	28.5
Indonesia	2005	44.0	18.8	37.2	43.8	20.3	35.9	44.4	15.9	39.7
Indonésie	2010	39.1	18.7	42.2	39.6	20.9	39.5	38.4	14.9	46.7
	2015	33.0	22.0	44.9	33.3	25.9	40.8	32.6	15.8	51.6
	*2020	27.7	22.7	49.6	29.2	26.3	44.6	25.5	17.1	57.4
Iran (Islamic Republic of)	2005	24.8	30.4	44.9	22.7	30.8	46.5	33.6	28.4	38.0
Iran (Rép. islamique d')	2010	19.2	32.2	48.6	17.5	33.8	48.8	28.0	24.4	47.6
	2015	18.0	32.5	49.4	17.1	34.1	48.7	22.8	23.8	53.4
	*2020	17.8	30.3	51.9	17.2	31.6	51.1	20.5	24.3	55.2
Iraq	*2005	24.9	20.9	54.2	25.0	22.1	52.9	24.1	13.7	62.2
Iraq	*2010	21.9	21.7	56.4	22.0	23.1	54.9	21.3	12.8	65.9
	*2015	19.4	22.8	57.9	19.4	24.5	56.1	19.3	11.8	68.9
	*2020	17.8	22.4	59.9	17.9	23.8	58.4	17.2	10.7	72.1
Ireland	2005	5.9	27.6	66.5	9.3	39.2	51.5	1.3	11.9	86.8
Irlande	2010	5.8	18.1	76.2	9.1	26.3	64.6	1.9	8.7	89.4
	2015	5.3	18.1	76.6	8.5	26.2	65.3	1.6	8.5	89.9
	*2020	4.5	18.5	77.0	7.2	27.4	65.5	1.3	8.2	90.5
Isle of Man [4]	2001	1.4	16.1	82.5	2.2	25.0	72.9	0.5	5.5	94.0
Île de Man [4]	2006	1.9	14.8	83.3	2.9	24.0	73.0	0.7	3.9	95.4
Israel	2005	2.0	21.6	76.4	2.8	30.2	67.1	1.1	11.3	87.5
Israël	*2010	1.3	19.1	79.6	1.8	27.8	70.4	0.7	9.2	90.1
	2015	1.0	17.6	81.4	1.4	26.1	72.6	0.6	8.0	91.4
	*2020	0.9	16.8	82.3	1.3	25.1	73.6	0.5	7.6	91.9
Italy	2005	4.2	30.7	65.1	4.8	39.2	56.0	3.3	17.4	79.3
Italie	2010	3.8	28.6	67.6	4.5	38.5	57.0	2.7	14.1	83.1
	2015	3.8	26.6	69.6	4.7	36.1	59.2	2.4	13.3	84.3
	*2020	3.6	25.6	70.8	4.6	35.0	60.4	2.2	12.7	85.1
Jamaica	2005	18.1	17.8	64.1	25.1	26.9	48.0	8.4	5.2	86.3
Jamaïque	*2010	17.8	16.2	66.0	25.0	23.7	51.2	8.1	6.1	85.8
	2015	17.7	14.9	67.3	25.1	21.9	53.0	7.9	5.7	86.4
	*2020	15.7	16.2	68.1	21.6	24.5	53.9	8.4	6.0	85.6
Japan	2005	4.5	28.0	67.6	4.4	35.2	60.4	4.6	17.6	77.9
Japon	2010	4.1	25.6	70.4	4.2	33.3	62.5	3.9	14.8	81.3
	2015	3.6	25.0	71.4	3.9	32.9	63.2	3.2	14.5	82.3
	*2020	3.4	24.1	72.6	3.7	32.2	64.1	2.9	13.8	83.3
Jordan	*2005	4.0	25.9	70.1	4.4	27.2	68.5	1.3	17.0	81.7
Jordanie	*2010	3.5	26.4	70.1	4.0	28.3	67.7	1.2	16.3	82.5
	*2015	3.3	25.4	71.3	3.7	27.4	68.9	1.1	14.4	84.5
	*2020	3.0	24.4	72.6	3.4	26.6	69.9	0.9	12.9	86.2
Kazakhstan	2005	32.4	18.0	49.6	33.4	24.6	42.0	31.3	10.9	57.8
Kazakhstan	2010	28.3	18.7	53.0	29.1	25.6	45.3	27.4	11.4	61.2
	2015	18.0	20.6	61.4	18.9	29.0	52.1	17.1	11.5	71.4
	*2020	15.4	20.5	64.1	16.8	29.0	54.2	13.9	11.2	74.9
Kenya	2005	61.1	6.7	32.2	54.8	10.6	34.6	68.1	2.3	29.6
Kenya	*2010	60.3	6.3	33.4	54.1	10.3	35.6	67.1	1.8	31.0
	*2015	57.3	6.7	36.0	51.3	11.3	37.4	63.8	1.9	34.4
	*2020	53.8	7.4	38.7	48.0	12.6	39.3	59.8	2.0	38.1
Kiribati	2005[6]	7.1	8.4	81.1	8.7	10.9	77.3	4.7	4.5	87.8
Kiribati	2010	22.1	16.1	61.8	32.1	9.1	58.8	9.0	25.3	65.7
Kosovo [11,13]										
Kosovo [11,13]	2012	4.6	28.4	67.1	4.3	33.3	62.3	5.4	10.1	84.7

17

Employment by economic activity *(continued)*
Percentage of persons employed by sex and ISIC 4 categories; agriculture (agr.), industry (ind.) and services (ser.)

Emploi par activité économique *(suite)*
Personnes employées par sexe et branches de la CITI rév. 4; agriculture (agr.), industrie (ind.) et services (ser.), pourcentage

Region, country or area [+] Région, pays ou zone [+]	Year Année	Male and Female Hommes et femmes			Male Hommes			Female Femmes		
		Agr.	Ind.	Ser.	Agr.	Ind.	Ser.	Agr.	Ind.	Ser.
Kuwait	2005	2.7	20.7	76.6	3.5	26.4	70.1	~0.0	2.2	97.8
Koweït	*2010	2.5	24.5	73.0	3.4	32.1	64.5	~0.0	3.6	96.3
	*2015	2.2	24.8	73.0	3.0	32.4	64.5	~0.0	3.5	96.4
	*2020	2.0	24.4	73.7	2.6	31.0	66.5	~0.0	3.3	96.7
Kyrgyzstan	2005	38.5	17.6	43.9	39.3	22.9	37.8	37.3	10.3	52.4
Kirghizistan	*2010	32.3	21.0	46.7	32.7	27.9	39.4	31.8	11.1	57.1
	2015	29.3	20.9	49.8	27.5	27.7	44.7	31.9	10.8	57.3
	*2020	20.4	24.7	54.9	21.0	30.8	48.1	19.3	14.7	66.0
Lao People's Dem. Rep.	*2005	77.3	6.0	16.7	74.3	7.2	18.6	80.3	4.9	14.9
Rép. dém. populaire lao	2010	71.5	8.3	20.2	69.3	10.0	20.7	73.6	6.7	19.7
	*2015	65.9	10.6	23.5	64.0	13.0	23.1	67.8	8.1	24.1
	*2020	61.7	12.2	26.2	59.9	15.2	24.9	63.5	9.0	27.5
Latvia	2005	12.1	26.5	61.5	15.9	35.2	48.9	8.0	17.2	74.8
Lettonie	2010	8.6	23.1	68.3	11.8	33.5	54.7	5.7	13.6	80.7
	2015	7.9	23.6	68.4	10.9	34.7	54.5	5.0	12.7	82.2
	*2020	6.5	23.7	69.8	9.3	34.8	55.9	3.7	12.7	83.5
Lebanon	*2005	17.4	24.3	58.3	17.0	25.9	57.0	18.8	18.3	62.9
Liban	*2010	14.7	25.2	60.1	14.2	27.4	58.4	16.4	17.6	66.0
	*2015	14.4	23.5	62.1	14.0	25.9	60.1	15.6	15.4	69.0
	*2020	13.4	22.3	64.3	13.2	24.8	61.9	14.0	14.0	72.0
Lesotho	*2005	13.9	41.1	45.0	20.5	45.8	33.7	5.3	35.0	59.7
Lesotho	*2010	11.3	42.4	46.3	16.6	48.6	34.7	4.2	34.1	61.7
	*2015	9.4	42.9	47.7	13.9	50.4	35.7	3.4	32.9	63.8
	*2020	8.4	41.9	49.6	12.7	50.4	36.9	2.9	30.8	66.4
Liberia	*2005	50.8	10.3	39.0	49.6	14.6	35.8	52.1	5.4	42.5
Libéria	2010	47.3	10.8	41.9	47.2	15.5	37.3	47.5	5.4	47.1
	*2015	44.2	11.0	44.9	45.0	16.0	39.0	43.3	5.3	51.4
	*2020	43.0	10.1	46.9	44.8	14.9	40.3	41.1	4.9	54.0
Libya	*2005	21.6	27.0	51.4	18.8	32.0	49.1	28.0	15.3	56.7
Libye	*2010	19.1	27.5	53.4	16.5	33.3	50.2	24.9	14.7	60.4
	*2015	20.3	22.3	57.4	18.6	27.0	54.4	24.0	12.0	64.0
	*2020	18.8	21.7	59.5	17.4	26.5	56.1	21.6	11.3	67.1
Lithuania	2005	14.3	29.1	56.7	16.9	37.0	46.0	11.5	20.8	67.7
Lituanie	2010	8.8	24.6	66.6	11.4	33.4	55.2	6.5	16.6	76.9
	2015	9.1	25.1	65.9	11.6	34.0	54.4	6.6	16.5	76.9
	*2020	6.6	25.9	67.4	9.0	35.5	55.4	4.3	16.4	79.4
Luxembourg	2005	1.7	17.3	81.0	2.2	25.5	72.3	1.1	5.8	93.1
Luxembourg	2010	1.1	13.3	85.6	1.4	19.8	78.8	0.7	4.8	94.5
	2015	1.0	12.5	86.4	1.3	19.1	79.6	0.7	4.4	94.9
	*2020	1.0	11.5	87.5	1.4	17.9	80.7	0.5	4.0	95.5
Madagascar	2005	82.0	3.4	14.6	81.5	5.1	13.4	82.5	1.6	15.9
Madagascar	*2010	73.4	6.0	20.6	75.0	6.7	18.3	71.6	5.3	23.1
	*2015	66.4	8.4	25.1	69.5	8.7	21.8	63.2	8.2	28.6
	*2020	63.8	9.1	27.1	67.6	9.5	23.0	59.9	8.6	31.5
Malawi	*2005	52.1	13.5	34.4	50.1	16.1	33.8	54.1	10.9	35.0
Malawi	*2010	48.1	14.2	37.7	46.8	17.3	35.9	49.5	11.0	39.6
	*2015	45.6	14.0	40.4	45.2	17.3	37.6	46.0	10.6	43.5
	*2020	43.2	13.8	43.0	43.6	17.2	39.2	42.7	10.1	47.1
Malaysia	2005	14.6	29.7	55.6	17.1	32.6	50.3	10.1	24.4	65.5
Malaisie	2010	14.2	27.7	58.0	17.1	31.6	51.3	8.9	20.5	70.7
	2015	12.5	27.5	60.0	15.3	32.5	52.2	7.9	19.3	72.8
	*2020	10.1	26.8	63.1	12.5	31.7	55.8	6.1	19.0	74.9
Maldives	*2005	16.8	22.7	60.5	21.3	17.8	60.8	7.5	32.5	59.9
Maldives	*2010	12.8	20.9	66.4	16.4	17.9	65.7	4.6	27.5	67.9
	*2015	9.8	19.1	71.2	12.2	17.7	70.1	2.5	23.2	74.3
	*2020	8.2	18.3	73.4	9.8	17.7	72.5	1.9	20.8	77.3
Mali	*2005	70.4	9.1	20.5	70.0	9.9	20.0	70.9	7.9	21.2
Mali	*2010	68.6	8.8	22.5	68.6	9.8	21.6	68.6	7.5	23.9
	2015	62.3	8.3	29.5	62.5	10.0	27.5	61.9	6.0	32.0
	*2020	62.3	7.6	30.2	62.2	9.4	28.4	62.4	5.2	32.4
Malta	2005	2.1	29.8	68.1	2.8	35.6	61.7	0.6	16.8	82.6
Malte	2010	1.3	25.5	73.1	1.9	31.9	66.2	0.3	13.2	86.5
	2015	1.5	20.0	78.5	2.1	27.4	70.6	0.5	8.4	91.0
	*2020	0.9	18.0	81.0	1.4	24.6	74.0	0.3	8.5	91.2

Employment by economic activity *(continued)*
Percentage of persons employed by sex and ISIC 4 categories; agriculture (agr.), industry (ind.) and services (ser.)

Emploi par activité économique *(suite)*
Personnes employées par sexe et branches de la CITI rév. 4; agriculture (agr.), industrie (ind.) et services (ser.), pourcentage

Region, country or area [+] Région, pays ou zone [+]	Year Année	Male and Female Hommes et femmes			Male Hommes			Female Femmes		
		Agr.	Ind.	Ser.	Agr.	Ind.	Ser.	Agr.	Ind.	Ser.
Marshall Islands [4] Îles Marshall [4]	#2010	11.0	9.4	79.6	...	...	...	...	...	...
Martinique [8,11] Martinique [8,11]	2010	4.1	11.9	65.3	...	...	...	...	...	...
	2012	3.9	11.8	69.0	...	...	...	...	...	...
Mauritania Mauritanie	*2005	59.7	11.5	28.8	59.0	12.5	28.5	61.4	9.3	29.3
	*2010	56.9	11.9	31.2	56.6	12.9	30.5	57.8	9.4	32.8
	*2015	53.8	12.5	33.7	53.8	13.7	32.5	53.7	9.7	36.6
	*2020	50.6	13.1	36.3	51.1	14.5	34.4	49.5	10.1	40.4
Mauritius Maurice	2005	10.0	32.4	57.5	10.5	34.2	55.3	9.0	28.9	62.2
	2010	8.6	28.7	62.7	9.2	32.7	58.1	7.6	21.5	70.9
	*2015	6.9	26.6	66.5	7.6	31.9	60.5	5.7	17.8	76.4
	*2020	5.9	25.1	69.0	6.6	31.0	62.4	4.9	15.5	79.7
Mexico Mexique	*2005	15.0	27.1	57.9	20.5	31.4	48.1	5.0	19.3	75.7
	2010	13.9	24.4	61.7	19.8	29.1	51.1	3.9	16.3	79.8
	2015	13.4	25.2	61.4	19.2	30.1	50.6	3.7	16.8	79.4
	*2020	12.4	26.2	61.4	17.9	31.4	50.8	3.4	17.6	79.0
Mongolia Mongolie	2005	39.9	16.8	43.3	42.8	18.7	38.6	36.5	14.6	48.9
	2010	33.5	16.2	50.2	34.7	20.2	45.1	32.2	11.6	56.2
	2015	28.5	20.3	51.3	29.7	26.5	43.8	27.0	12.9	60.1
	*2020	26.9	19.5	53.6	29.3	25.9	44.8	24.1	11.9	64.0
Montenegro Monténégro	2005	8.6	19.2	72.1	8.5	26.2	65.3	8.8	9.2	82.0
	*2010	6.2	18.7	75.1	7.0	26.0	67.0	5.1	9.3	85.6
	2015	7.7	17.5	74.8	7.4	25.3	67.4	8.2	8.0	83.8
	*2020	7.8	19.2	73.0	8.3	28.1	63.6	7.1	7.7	85.1
Morocco Maroc	2005	45.5	19.5	22.6	39.7	20.8	39.5	61.5	15.9	22.6
	*2010	40.5	21.5	38.0	33.1	24.6	42.3	61.3	12.9	25.8
	*2015	37.2	21.7	41.1	30.6	24.8	44.6	57.5	12.2	30.3
	*2020	34.1	21.8	44.0	28.2	24.7	47.1	53.2	12.5	34.3
Mozambique Mozambique	*2005	79.5	3.8	16.7	67.8	7.9	24.2	89.0	0.5	10.5
	*2010	76.4	5.3	18.3	64.9	10.3	24.8	86.4	1.0	12.6
	2015	72.1	7.7	20.1	61.3	13.4	25.4	82.1	2.6	15.3
	*2020	69.9	8.6	21.5	59.3	14.6	26.1	79.8	3.0	17.2
Myanmar Myanmar	*2005	57.1	16.3	26.6	58.8	16.8	24.3	54.7	15.5	29.7
	*2010	53.5	17.7	28.8	54.7	18.9	26.4	52.0	16.0	32.1
	2015	51.7	16.8	31.5	52.8	18.4	28.8	50.1	14.5	35.4
	*2020	48.1	16.3	35.6	51.7	17.0	31.3	42.9	15.2	41.9
Namibia Namibie	*2005	29.7	14.6	55.8	33.3	19.5	47.3	25.4	8.7	65.9
	*2010	28.1	13.9	57.9	29.6	21.0	49.5	26.5	6.0	67.5
	*2015	24.5	17.0	58.5	25.2	27.0	47.8	23.8	6.0	70.2
	*2020	21.8	16.4	61.8	23.7	24.6	51.7	19.9	7.9	72.2
Nepal Népal	*2005	72.6	12.3	15.1	63.1	17.9	18.9	82.5	6.4	11.1
	*2010	70.2	13.3	16.5	60.2	19.6	20.2	80.3	6.9	12.8
	*2015	67.3	14.3	18.5	55.2	22.4	22.4	76.9	7.8	15.3
	*2020	64.5	15.3	20.2	52.3	24.1	23.7	74.4	8.3	17.3
Netherlands Pays-Bas	2005	3.7	21.0	75.3	4.7	30.7	64.5	2.4	8.6	89.0
	2010	3.1	17.7	79.2	4.1	26.9	69.0	1.8	6.7	91.5
	2015	2.3	16.4	81.2	3.0	25.2	71.8	1.5	6.0	92.4
	*2020	2.0	15.8	82.2	2.7	24.2	73.2	1.2	6.1	92.7
New Caledonia Nouvelle-Calédonie	2005	3.1	21.3	75.6	4.2	31.9	63.8	1.6	8.0	90.4
	*2010	2.6	22.0	75.5	3.6	33.3	63.1	1.3	8.0	90.7
	*2015	2.2	21.6	76.2	3.1	33.2	63.7	1.0	7.5	91.5
	*2020	1.9	20.7	77.5	2.7	32.0	65.3	0.8	6.7	92.4
New Zealand Nouvelle-Zélande	2005	7.2	22.2	70.7	9.0	32.1	58.9	5.0	10.5	84.5
	2010	6.7	20.6	72.6	8.8	30.1	61.0	4.3	9.7	86.0
	2015	6.1	21.6	72.3	8.0	31.9	60.1	4.0	10.0	86.0
	*2020	5.6	19.4	75.1	7.3	28.8	63.9	3.6	9.0	87.5
Nicaragua Nicaragua	2005	28.9	19.7	51.4	40.7	20.1	39.2	8.1	19.0	72.9
	*2010	29.4	18.4	52.2	42.8	19.4	37.8	7.0	16.7	76.3
	*2015	31.0	17.6	51.4	44.6	19.9	35.5	9.0	13.9	77.1
	*2020	30.6	15.6	53.8	44.7	18.0	37.2	8.2	11.7	80.1
Niger Niger	*2005	77.7	7.9	14.4	80.7	4.4	14.9	74.1	12.2	13.7
	*2010	77.1	7.5	15.4	80.2	4.3	15.5	73.1	11.5	15.3
	*2015	75.9	7.4	16.7	79.3	4.5	16.2	71.3	11.3	17.4
	*2020	74.8	7.2	18.0	78.8	4.4	16.8	69.5	11.0	19.6

Employment by economic activity *(continued)*
Percentage of persons employed by sex and ISIC 4 categories; agriculture (agr.), industry (ind.) and services (ser.)

Emploi par activité économique *(suite)*
Personnes employées par sexe et branches de la CITI rév. 4; agriculture (agr.), industrie (ind.) et services (ser.), pourcentage

Region, country or area [+] Région, pays ou zone [+]	Year Année	Male and Female Hommes et femmes			Male Hommes			Female Femmes		
		Agr.	Ind.	Ser.	Agr.	Ind.	Ser.	Agr.	Ind.	Ser.
Nigeria	*2005	45.0	11.4	43.6	50.3	11.4	38.4	38.8	11.5	49.8
Nigéria	*2010	41.4	10.3	48.4	48.3	9.6	42.1	33.2	11.0	55.8
	*2015	36.9	12.2	50.9	45.3	11.8	43.0	26.5	12.6	60.8
	*2020	34.7	12.2	53.1	43.8	11.8	44.4	23.3	12.8	63.9
Niue [4]	2001	9.0	20.4	70.1	11.4	28.7	59.4	5.8	8.7	85.1
Nioué [4]	#2002	4.8	9.3	85.9	...	...	...	...	...	...
North Macedonia	*2005	20.8	32.9	46.3	20.7	35.0	44.4	20.9	29.7	49.3
Macédoine du Nord	*2010	18.6	30.3	51.1	18.8	32.9	48.4	18.4	26.2	55.4
	2015	17.9	30.5	51.6	18.1	34.5	47.4	17.5	24.5	58.0
	*2020	15.1	31.4	53.5	15.7	34.7	49.6	14.1	26.5	59.4
Northern Mariana Islands [3,6]										
Îles Mariannes du Nord [3,6]	#2000	1.5	47.2	45.8	...	...	...	...	...	...
Norway	2005	3.3	20.9	75.8	4.8	32.3	62.9	1.6	8.0	90.4
Norvège	2010	2.5	19.7	77.8	3.9	31.2	64.9	1.0	7.0	92.0
	2015	2.0	20.1	77.9	3.0	31.7	65.3	0.9	7.2	91.9
	*2020	2.0	19.1	78.9	2.9	30.1	67.0	1.0	6.7	92.3
Oman	*2005	7.9	18.9	73.2	9.1	20.3	70.6	2.6	11.9	85.5
Oman	2010	5.2	36.9	58.0	6.0	42.3	51.7	0.5	6.0	93.5
	*2015	4.9	33.6	61.4	5.5	37.6	56.9	0.4	4.6	94.9
	*2020	4.4	32.8	62.7	5.0	36.5	58.5	0.3	4.1	95.5
Pakistan	2005	43.1	20.3	36.6	38.0	21.4	40.6	67.3	15.1	17.7
Pakistan	2010	43.4	21.4	35.2	35.5	24.0	40.6	74.1	11.5	14.4
	2015	41.0	24.0	35.0	32.6	26.6	40.8	72.1	14.5	13.4
	*2020	35.9	25.8	38.3	28.7	28.0	43.3	64.0	17.3	18.6
Palau [3]	2000[6]	7.1	13.8	79.1	9.6	20.7	69.7	3.1	2.6	94.4
Palaos [3]	2008[4]	2.4	11.8	85.9	...	...	...	...	...	...
Panama	2005	15.7	17.2	67.1	22.2	21.8	55.9	4.3	9.1	86.5
Panama	2010	17.4	18.7	63.9	23.1	23.9	53.0	7.5	9.7	82.8
	2015	14.7	18.7	66.6	19.0	24.5	56.4	7.9	9.5	82.6
	*2020	13.7	18.8	67.5	17.7	24.8	57.5	7.8	9.7	82.5
Papua New Guinea	*2005	71.0	3.7	25.3	67.7	5.9	26.5	74.4	1.5	24.1
Papouasie-Nvl-Guinée	*2010	66.4	4.8	28.8	63.3	7.6	29.1	69.6	1.9	28.5
	*2015	61.3	6.4	32.3	58.4	10.1	31.5	64.3	2.5	33.2
	*2020	57.8	6.7	35.5	55.8	10.5	33.7	59.8	2.7	37.5
Paraguay	2005	32.0	15.8	52.2	38.1	19.9	42.0	22.3	9.2	68.5
Paraguay	2010	25.6	19.2	55.2	30.2	25.6	44.2	18.1	8.7	73.2
	2015	19.7	19.7	60.6	23.4	26.3	50.3	14.0	9.6	76.4
	*2020	19.9	17.9	62.1	23.7	24.8	51.5	14.4	7.7	77.9
Peru	2005	34.8	14.1	51.1	36.6	18.2	45.2	32.6	8.9	58.5
Pérou	2010	27.7	16.9	55.4	28.7	22.7	48.7	26.6	10.1	63.3
	2015	28.3	16.6	55.2	29.3	22.9	47.8	27.1	9.0	63.9
	*2020	27.2	15.3	57.5	28.5	21.0	50.5	25.7	8.5	65.9
Philippines	*2005	35.4	15.6	49.0	42.9	18.3	38.8	23.4	11.3	65.3
Philippines	*2010	32.8	15.5	51.6	40.1	18.8	41.2	21.5	10.5	68.0
	2015	29.2	16.2	54.6	35.9	20.3	43.8	19.0	10.0	71.0
	*2020	22.5	19.8	57.6	28.4	26.2	45.4	13.2	9.8	77.0
Poland	2005	17.4	29.2	53.4	18.0	39.0	43.1	16.6	17.1	66.3
Pologne	2010	13.1	30.3	56.6	13.4	41.8	44.8	12.7	16.1	71.2
	2015	11.5	30.5	57.9	12.5	41.9	45.6	10.4	16.4	73.2
	*2020	8.9	32.0	59.1	9.9	43.9	46.2	7.7	17.2	75.1
Portugal	2005	12.1	30.4	57.6	11.2	40.6	48.3	13.1	18.4	68.5
Portugal	2010	11.2	27.3	61.5	11.5	37.5	51.0	10.9	16.0	73.1
	2015	7.5	24.3	68.1	9.6	33.0	57.4	5.4	15.2	79.4
	*2020	5.7	24.6	69.8	7.6	33.7	58.7	3.7	15.0	81.4
Puerto Rico	2005	2.1	19.0	78.9	3.3	24.9	71.8	0.4	10.9	88.8
Porto Rico	*2010	1.4	17.4	81.3	2.1	23.6	74.3	0.4	9.4	90.2
	*2015	1.2	16.3	82.5	1.8	22.3	75.9	0.3	8.4	91.2
	*2020	1.0	15.5	83.5	1.6	21.5	76.9	0.3	7.9	91.8
Qatar	*2005	2.9	41.1	56.0	3.4	48.1	48.5	0.1	3.6	96.3
Qatar	*2010	1.5	56.4	42.1	1.6	63.0	35.4	~0.0	5.2	94.8
	2015	1.2	54.1	44.6	1.4	61.6	37.0	~0.0	5.9	94.1
	*2020	1.2	54.4	44.5	1.4	62.0	36.6	~0.0	6.4	93.6

Employment by economic activity *(continued)*
Percentage of persons employed by sex and ISIC 4 categories; agriculture (agr.), industry (ind.) and services (ser.)

Emploi par activité économique *(suite)*
Personnes employées par sexe et branches de la CITI rév. 4; agriculture (agr.), industrie (ind.) et services (ser.), pourcentage

Region, country or area [+] Région, pays ou zone [+]	Year Année	Male and Female Hommes et femmes			Male Hommes			Female Femmes		
		Agr.	Ind.	Ser.	Agr.	Ind.	Ser.	Agr.	Ind.	Ser.
Republic of Korea	2005	7.9	26.9	65.2	7.3	34.0	58.7	8.9	16.6	74.5
République de Corée	2010	6.6	25.0	68.4	6.4	32.5	61.1	6.9	14.4	78.8
	2015	5.1	25.2	69.7	5.1	33.4	61.5	5.1	13.7	81.2
	*2020	4.8	25.0	70.2	5.0	33.6	61.4	4.5	13.2	82.3
Republic of Moldova	2005	40.7	16.0	43.3	41.1	20.8	38.1	40.2	11.5	48.4
République de Moldova	2010	27.5	18.7	53.8	30.5	24.9	44.6	24.4	12.3	63.2
	2015	34.2	17.8	48.0	38.5	23.8	37.6	29.7	11.8	58.5
	*2020	35.4	17.1	47.5	38.7	22.4	38.9	32.1	11.8	56.1
Réunion [8]	2010[11]	4.2	14.1	67.1	...	...	...	...	...	...
Réunion [8]	#2012	4.3	12.7	81.7	6.3	20.0	72.0	2.1	4.1	93.0
Romania	2005	32.3	30.5	37.3	31.7	35.1	33.2	33.1	24.8	42.2
Roumanie	2010	31.0	28.3	40.7	29.9	35.0	35.1	32.4	19.9	47.7
	2015	25.6	28.5	46.0	25.6	35.0	39.5	25.6	20.0	54.4
	*2020	21.3	30.1	48.6	21.4	36.8	41.8	21.1	21.4	57.5
Russian Federation	2005	10.1	29.6	60.3	12.3	37.8	49.9	7.9	21.0	71.0
Fédération de Russie	2010	7.7	27.8	64.5	9.8	37.5	52.7	5.6	17.7	76.8
	2015	6.7	27.3	66.0	8.2	37.9	53.9	5.1	16.1	78.8
	*2020	5.6	26.6	67.8	7.3	37.1	55.5	3.8	15.5	80.8
Rwanda	*2005	85.2	3.6	11.2	78.5	6.3	15.2	91.6	1.0	7.4
Rwanda	*2010	79.5	5.7	14.8	70.5	9.8	19.7	88.0	1.8	10.2
	*2015	66.7	8.3	25.0	56.3	14.1	29.6	76.5	2.7	20.7
	*2020	61.7	9.1	29.2	52.0	15.7	32.3	70.7	2.9	26.4
Saint Helena [4,14] Sainte-Hélène [4,14]	2008	7.3	20.0	72.7	11.8	33.9	54.3	1.7	2.9	95.4
Saint Kitts and Nevis [6] Saint-Kitts-et-Nevis [6]	#2001	0.2	48.8	42.1	0.4	51.6	34.7	0.1	45.5	50.6
Saint Lucia	*2005	20.5	19.3	60.2	25.3	25.6	49.1	14.0	10.5	75.5
Sainte-Lucie	*2010	19.8	18.6	61.7	24.4	26.7	48.9	13.8	8.0	78.2
	*2015	18.5	17.9	63.7	23.1	25.8	51.0	12.2	7.2	80.6
	*2020	17.0	18.3	64.7	21.5	27.1	51.4	11.2	7.1	81.7
Saint Vincent & Grenadines	*2005	14.3	20.6	65.0	19.2	29.4	51.4	7.1	7.8	85.1
Saint-Vincent-Grenadines	*2010	12.9	20.5	66.6	17.5	29.5	53.0	6.1	7.3	86.5
	*2015	11.7	20.0	68.4	16.1	29.1	54.8	5.2	6.8	87.9
	*2020	10.5	19.9	69.5	14.8	29.5	55.7	4.6	6.7	88.7
Samoa	*2005	37.9	22.4	39.8	51.8	15.6	32.6	11.2	35.3	53.5
Samoa	*2010	34.5	23.1	42.4	48.0	16.5	35.5	8.7	35.8	55.5
	*2015	32.3	22.6	45.1	45.1	16.8	38.2	7.4	34.0	58.6
	*2020	29.9	23.3	46.9	41.9	18.2	40.0	6.4	33.2	60.3
San Marino	2005[4]	0.5	39.3	60.2	0.6	50.4	49.1	0.3	23.4	76.3
Saint-Marin	#2010	0.3	34.3	65.4	0.4	45.6	54.0	0.2	18.7	81.1
Sao Tome and Principe	2005	27.9	17.2	54.9	33.7	23.5	42.7	15.6	3.8	80.6
Sao Tomé-et-Principe	*2010	24.3	17.8	57.9	29.8	24.5	45.8	12.7	3.6	83.7
	*2015	21.1	18.3	60.5	26.3	25.5	48.2	10.4	3.5	86.2
	*2020	18.7	18.5	62.9	23.7	25.9	50.5	8.5	3.3	88.2
Saudi Arabia	*2005	4.1	20.4	75.4	4.7	23.4	71.9	0.4	1.0	98.5
Arabie saoudite	*2010	4.2	21.1	74.7	4.8	24.0	71.2	0.2	1.5	98.3
	2015	6.1	22.7	71.2	7.0	26.0	67.0	0.5	1.6	97.9
	*2020	2.3	24.8	72.9	2.6	28.2	69.2	0.3	2.1	97.6
Senegal	*2005	42.3	12.7	45.0	43.7	15.7	40.6	39.5	6.9	53.6
Sénégal	*2010	38.2	12.8	49.0	40.3	16.3	43.4	34.5	6.4	59.1
	2015	33.3	13.0	53.7	36.4	17.8	45.8	28.7	5.8	65.6
	*2020	29.4	13.6	56.9	32.9	19.0	48.1	24.3	5.5	70.3
Serbia	2005	23.3	27.6	49.1	23.3	34.3	42.4	23.3	17.5	59.2
Serbie	2010	22.3	25.6	52.1	23.3	32.8	43.8	21.0	16.0	63.0
	2015	19.4	24.5	56.1	21.8	30.2	48.1	16.3	16.9	66.8
	*2020	15.1	27.4	57.6	16.9	33.9	49.2	12.7	18.9	68.3
Seychelles [8,15] Seychelles [8,15]	2011	3.6	17.9	78.2	6.4	25.3	68.1	0.7	10.4	88.5
Sierra Leone	*2005	68.1	6.2	25.8	65.9	10.1	24.0	70.2	2.3	27.5
Sierra Leone	*2010	63.9	5.3	30.8	64.2	9.0	26.8	63.6	1.6	34.9
	*2015	57.9	5.8	36.3	60.3	10.2	29.5	55.6	1.3	43.1
	*2020	54.4	6.5	39.1	57.5	11.7	30.8	51.3	1.4	47.3

17

Employment by economic activity *(continued)*
Percentage of persons employed by sex and ISIC 4 categories; agriculture (agr.), industry (ind.) and services (ser.)

Emploi par activité économique *(suite)*
Personnes employées par sexe et branches de la CITI rév. 4; agriculture (agr.), industrie (ind.) et services (ser.), pourcentage

Region, country or area [+] Région, pays ou zone [+]	Year Année	Male and Female Hommes et femmes			Male Hommes			Female Femmes		
		Agr.	Ind.	Ser.	Agr.	Ind.	Ser.	Agr.	Ind.	Ser.
Singapore Singapour	2005	1.1	22.5	76.4	1.4	25.9	72.7	0.5	17.6	81.9
	*2010	0.9	21.6	77.5	1.2	25.8	72.9	0.4	15.2	84.3
	*2015	0.8	17.3	81.9	1.1	20.9	78.0	0.4	12.2	87.4
	*2020	0.7	15.2	84.1	1.0	18.6	80.4	0.3	10.4	89.3
Slovakia Slovaquie	2005	4.8	38.8	56.4	6.4	49.6	43.9	2.6	25.2	72.1
	2010	3.2	37.1	59.7	4.4	50.0	45.5	1.8	21.1	77.1
	2015	3.2	36.1	60.7	4.7	48.4	46.9	1.3	20.8	77.9
	*2020	2.1	36.1	61.8	3.0	49.2	47.8	1.0	20.1	78.9
Slovenia Slovénie	2005	9.1	37.1	53.8	9.1	46.9	44.0	9.1	25.4	65.5
	2010	8.8	32.6	58.6	9.1	42.7	48.2	8.5	20.5	71.0
	2015	7.1	32.0	60.9	7.1	43.4	49.5	7.1	18.2	74.7
	*2020	5.1	33.5	61.5	5.6	44.8	49.6	4.5	20.2	75.3
Solomon Islands Îles Salomon	*2005	48.4	7.3	44.3	47.5	11.1	41.4	49.4	3.2	47.4
	*2010	44.8	8.2	47.0	44.1	12.6	43.3	45.6	3.6	50.8
	*2015	39.9	9.4	50.7	39.5	14.4	46.1	40.4	4.1	55.5
	*2020	37.1	9.6	53.4	37.2	14.6	48.2	36.9	4.2	58.9
Somalia Somalie	*2005	84.2	4.4	11.4	82.7	5.1	12.2	89.3	2.1	8.6
	*2010	83.8	4.1	12.1	82.5	4.7	12.8	88.5	1.9	9.6
	*2015	83.4	3.8	12.8	82.2	4.4	13.4	87.7	1.7	10.6
	*2020	83.0	3.5	13.4	81.9	4.1	14.0	86.8	1.6	11.6
South Africa Afrique du Sud	*2005	7.1	26.4	66.6	8.1	34.4	57.4	5.4	13.8	80.8
	2010	4.9	24.4	70.7	5.7	32.8	61.6	3.8	13.0	83.2
	2015	5.6	23.8	70.6	6.7	33.1	60.2	4.2	11.7	84.0
	*2020	5.0	22.7	72.3	6.1	31.7	62.2	3.6	11.3	85.1
South Sudan Soudan du sud	*2005	56.8	17.5	25.7	40.8	24.0	35.3	74.3	10.4	15.3
	*2010	56.4	16.8	26.8	40.5	23.4	36.1	73.6	9.7	16.7
	*2015	56.8	15.2	28.0	41.1	21.4	37.5	73.5	8.5	17.9
	*2020	56.1	14.1	29.7	40.6	20.0	39.4	72.5	8.0	19.5
Spain Espagne	2005	5.3	29.6	65.1	6.5	41.1	52.5	3.5	12.4	84.1
	2010	4.2	23.0	72.8	5.6	33.6	60.8	2.4	9.6	88.0
	2015	4.1	19.9	76.0	5.8	29.2	65.0	2.1	8.7	89.2
	*2020	4.0	20.2	75.8	5.6	29.4	65.0	2.0	8.9	89.1
Sri Lanka Sri Lanka	*2005	37.3	24.2	38.5	35.1	24.1	40.8	41.9	24.4	33.6
	2010	31.8	25.5	42.6	29.5	25.4	45.1	36.8	25.8	37.4
	2015	28.7	25.8	45.6	26.8	25.9	47.2	32.3	25.4	42.2
	*2020	23.7	30.4	45.9	22.3	31.4	46.3	26.5	28.4	45.0
State of Palestine État de Palestine	2005	15.0	26.1	58.9	11.4	29.6	59.0	32.9	8.6	58.5
	2010	11.8	24.7	63.5	9.8	28.2	62.0	21.3	7.9	70.8
	2015	8.7	28.7	62.6	7.8	32.2	60.0	13.1	11.6	75.3
	*2020	5.9	31.7	62.4	5.8	36.0	58.2	6.4	9.6	84.0
Sudan Soudan	*2005	49.4	13.0	37.7	44.0	16.4	39.6	64.3	3.4	32.3
	*2010	45.6	14.7	39.8	40.4	18.3	41.3	61.1	3.8	35.1
	*2015	41.5	16.8	41.7	36.1	21.0	42.9	57.6	4.4	38.1
	*2020	39.7	15.9	44.4	34.8	20.0	45.2	53.5	4.3	42.2
Suriname Suriname	*2005	8.4	24.1	67.5	10.3	32.0	57.8	4.7	8.5	86.8
	*2010	7.6	24.3	68.1	9.4	33.2	57.4	4.4	8.1	87.5
	*2015	7.4	23.9	68.7	9.3	33.2	57.5	4.1	7.5	88.4
	*2020	7.4	23.5	69.1	9.4	32.9	57.7	4.0	7.1	88.9
Sweden Suède	2005	2.3	22.0	75.6	3.5	33.6	62.9	1.1	9.3	89.6
	2010	2.1	19.9	78.0	3.1	30.9	66.0	1.0	7.6	91.4
	2015	2.0	18.3	79.7	3.0	28.7	68.3	1.0	6.9	92.1
	*2020	1.6	17.7	80.7	2.3	27.7	69.9	0.8	6.8	92.3
Switzerland Suisse	2005	3.9	22.5	73.6	4.8	32.0	63.2	2.8	11.0	86.2
	2010	3.5	22.4	74.1	4.1	32.3	63.6	2.7	10.7	86.6
	2015	3.4	20.8	75.8	3.9	30.0	66.1	2.9	10.1	87.0
	*2020	2.9	20.0	77.2	3.3	29.1	67.6	2.4	9.5	88.1
Syrian Arab Republic République arabe syrienne	*2005	22.6	27.5	49.9	20.1	30.8	49.1	37.2	8.2	54.6
	*2010	14.5	31.0	54.4	14.4	34.3	51.3	15.2	9.2	75.5
	*2015	12.0	28.3	59.7	12.3	31.5	56.2	10.1	8.3	81.6
	*2020	10.5	26.5	63.0	10.9	29.6	59.4	7.9	7.7	84.4
Tajikistan Tadjikistan	*2005	55.5	17.2	27.3	44.1	24.4	31.4	75.3	4.5	20.2
	*2010	52.4	15.6	31.9	43.3	21.3	35.4	69.2	5.2	25.6
	*2015	48.3	15.6	36.1	38.6	21.2	40.1	64.3	6.2	29.5
	*2020	44.2	16.0	39.9	34.9	21.1	43.9	59.4	7.4	33.2

Employment by economic activity *(continued)*
Percentage of persons employed by sex and ISIC 4 categories; agriculture (agr.), industry (ind.) and services (ser.)

Emploi par activité économique *(suite)*
Personnes employées par sexe et branches de la CITI rév. 4; agriculture (agr.), industrie (ind.) et services (ser.), pourcentage

Region, country or area [+] Région, pays ou zone [+]	Year Année	Male and Female Hommes et femmes			Male Hommes			Female Femmes		
		Agr.	Ind.	Ser.	Agr.	Ind.	Ser.	Agr.	Ind.	Ser.
Thailand	2005	38.7	22.4	38.9	40.3	22.5	37.1	36.7	22.2	41.1
Thaïlande	2010	38.2	20.6	41.1	40.1	22.7	37.2	36.1	18.2	45.7
	2015	32.3	23.7	44.0	34.3	26.1	39.5	29.8	20.8	49.4
	*2020	31.2	22.5	46.3	33.6	25.0	41.4	28.2	19.6	52.2
Timor-Leste	*2005	55.7	8.2	36.1	55.0	9.8	35.2	56.5	6.3	37.3
Timor-Leste	2010	50.8	9.3	39.9	50.8	11.4	37.8	50.9	6.7	42.4
	*2015	47.4	10.0	42.6	48.8	12.0	39.2	45.7	7.6	46.7
	*2020	43.7	9.8	46.4	46.5	11.5	42.0	40.3	7.8	51.9
Togo	*2005	46.7	12.6	40.7	47.3	11.1	41.6	46.2	13.9	39.8
Togo	*2010	44.0	12.4	43.6	45.1	11.3	43.6	42.9	13.4	43.7
	*2015	40.2	12.8	47.0	41.8	12.2	46.0	38.7	13.3	48.0
	*2020	37.2	12.9	49.9	39.3	12.7	48.0	35.0	13.1	51.9
Tonga	*2005	30.4	30.2	39.4	46.9	13.9	39.3	3.7	56.8	39.5
Tonga	*2010	27.9	29.7	42.3	43.3	14.2	42.5	3.1	54.9	42.1
	*2015	26.3	28.9	44.8	41.2	14.3	44.6	2.8	52.1	45.1
	*2020	23.7	29.2	47.1	37.2	15.3	47.5	2.3	51.3	46.4
Trinidad and Tobago	2005	4.3	31.1	64.5	6.2	41.8	52.0	1.7	16.2	82.1
Trinité-et-Tobago	*2010	3.8	29.8	66.5	5.1	40.8	54.2	1.9	14.2	83.9
	2015	3.4	27.9	68.6	4.9	38.6	56.5	1.4	13.0	85.7
	*2020	2.9	26.6	70.5	4.1	37.2	58.7	1.3	12.4	86.3
Tunisia	2005	18.5	32.4	49.1	17.8	31.7	50.6	20.8	34.7	44.6
Tunisie	2010	17.9	33.4	48.6	17.2	33.6	49.1	20.1	32.8	47.1
	*2015	14.5	33.3	52.2	15.5	33.2	51.2	11.3	33.5	55.2
	*2020	12.7	32.5	54.8	13.8	32.4	53.7	9.2	32.6	58.1
Turkey	2005	25.7	26.3	48.0	18.5	29.7	51.8	46.2	16.7	37.1
Turquie	2010	23.7	26.2	50.1	17.4	30.4	52.2	39.2	16.0	44.8
	2015	20.4	27.2	52.4	15.7	32.1	52.2	31.0	16.2	52.7
	*2020	18.0	26.1	55.9	14.6	31.1	54.4	25.3	15.5	59.2
Turkmenistan	*2005	28.1	36.3	35.6	30.6	36.3	33.0	24.7	36.2	39.1
Turkménistan	*2010	24.8	39.2	36.0	26.2	40.7	33.1	22.9	37.1	40.1
	*2015	21.9	41.2	36.9	22.6	43.7	33.7	20.8	37.8	41.4
	*2020	19.5	42.6	37.9	20.0	45.7	34.3	18.8	38.3	43.0
Turks and Caicos Islands [4]	2005	1.4	16.8	70.9	...	...	...	...	...	...
Îles Turques-et-Caïques [4]	#2008	1.2	23.1	74.0	...	...	...	...	...	...
Uganda	*2005	68.4	7.7	24.0	62.2	10.0	27.7	75.1	5.1	19.8
Ouganda	*2010	66.8	7.8	25.4	61.7	10.5	27.9	72.4	4.9	22.8
	*2015	72.6	6.8	20.6	68.0	9.9	22.1	77.5	3.5	19.0
	*2020	72.4	6.6	20.9	68.3	9.9	21.8	76.8	3.2	20.0
Ukraine	*2005	22.1	26.3	51.6	22.5	35.5	42.0	21.8	16.3	61.9
Ukraine	2010	20.3	25.7	54.0	21.0	35.5	43.5	19.6	15.4	65.0
	2015	15.3	24.7	60.1	17.2	34.6	48.1	13.1	13.9	73.0
	*2020	14.1	24.8	61.1	16.2	34.8	49.0	11.8	13.7	74.5
United Arab Emirates	*2005	5.1	34.9	60.0	5.8	38.1	56.1	~0.0	9.7	90.2
Émirats arabes unis	*2010	3.4	37.2	59.4	3.8	40.9	55.3	~0.0	7.5	92.5
	*2015	2.0	35.7	62.4	2.4	41.1	56.5	~0.0	6.2	93.8
	*2020	1.4	34.2	64.4	1.6	40.1	58.2	~0.0	5.4	94.6
United Kingdom	2005	1.4	22.2	76.4	1.9	33.1	65.0	0.7	9.4	89.9
Royaume-Uni	2010	1.2	19.2	79.6	1.7	29.4	68.8	0.6	7.4	92.0
	2015	1.1	18.7	80.2	1.6	28.2	70.2	0.6	7.7	91.7
	*2020	1.0	17.7	81.3	1.4	26.9	71.7	0.6	7.2	92.2
United Rep. of Tanzania	*2005	74.5	4.8	20.6	71.0	7.1	21.9	78.2	2.5	19.2
Rép.-Unie de Tanzanie	*2010	70.4	5.8	23.8	67.0	8.4	24.6	74.0	3.0	23.0
	*2015	67.5	6.4	26.1	65.0	9.4	25.6	70.2	3.1	26.7
	*2020	64.9	6.8	28.3	63.0	10.2	26.8	66.9	3.1	30.0
United States of America	2005	1.4	22.3	76.3	2.0	32.4	65.6	0.8	10.3	89.0
États-Unis d'Amérique	2010	1.4	19.6	78.9	2.0	29.4	68.5	0.7	8.5	90.8
	2015	1.4	19.9	78.7	2.0	29.2	68.8	0.8	8.8	90.4
	*2020	1.3	19.7	79.0	1.8	29.2	69.0	0.7	8.6	90.7
United States Virgin Islands	*2005	4.8	24.5	70.7	8.0	38.2	53.8	1.4	9.7	89.0
Îles Vierges américaines	*2010	4.2	23.2	72.6	7.1	37.3	55.6	1.1	8.9	90.0
	*2015	3.7	20.3	76.0	6.5	32.9	60.5	1.0	8.0	91.1
	*2020	3.2	19.6	77.2	5.7	32.4	61.9	0.8	7.5	91.7

17

Employment by economic activity *(continued)*
Percentage of persons employed by sex and ISIC 4 categories; agriculture (agr.), industry (ind.) and services (ser.)

Emploi par activité économique *(suite)*
Personnes employées par sexe et branches de la CITI rév. 4; agriculture (agr.), industrie (ind.) et services (ser.), pourcentage

Region, country or area [+] Région, pays ou zone [+]	Year Année	Male and Female Hommes et femmes			Male Hommes			Female Femmes		
		Agr.	Ind.	Ser.	Agr.	Ind.	Ser.	Agr.	Ind.	Ser.
Uruguay Uruguay	*2005	10.9	21.2	67.9	15.2	27.4	57.3	5.1	12.7	82.2
	2010	11.6	21.4	67.0	16.5	28.8	54.7	5.1	11.8	83.1
	2015	8.8	20.5	70.7	12.3	29.0	58.7	4.5	9.7	85.8
	*2020	7.9	18.7	73.4	11.5	27.1	61.4	3.5	8.2	88.3
Uzbekistan Ouzbékistan	*2005	36.2	22.9	40.9	35.6	28.5	35.9	37.0	15.1	47.8
	*2010	30.9	25.4	43.6	30.1	32.5	37.4	32.1	15.6	52.3
	*2015	26.7	27.7	45.6	25.9	35.8	38.3	27.8	16.2	56.1
	*2020	23.3	29.9	46.8	22.9	38.6	38.5	23.9	17.4	58.7
Vanuatu Vanuatu	*2005	64.0	5.9	30.2	62.7	8.7	28.6	65.6	2.1	32.2
	*2010	60.2	6.9	32.9	59.1	10.3	30.6	61.7	2.4	35.9
	*2015	58.3	6.1	35.6	58.5	9.1	32.4	58.1	2.2	39.7
	*2020	55.3	6.3	38.4	56.1	9.4	34.6	54.2	2.3	43.5
Venezuela (Boliv. Rep. of) Venezuela (Rép. boliv. du)	2005	10.3	20.6	69.1	15.4	26.6	58.1	2.2	11.2	86.7
	*2010	8.3	21.8	69.9	12.6	29.0	58.4	1.6	10.6	87.8
	*2015	7.4	20.3	72.3	11.4	27.3	61.3	1.2	9.6	89.1
	*2020	8.4	16.1	75.5	13.1	21.5	65.4	1.1	7.7	91.2
Viet Nam Viet Nam	*2005	54.8	18.8	26.4	52.8	22.4	24.7	56.9	14.8	28.3
	2010	48.7	21.7	29.6	46.4	25.7	27.8	51.2	17.3	31.6
	2015	44.0	22.7	33.2	42.7	25.9	31.4	45.4	19.3	35.2
	*2020	36.2	28.4	35.4	35.0	32.7	32.3	37.5	23.7	38.8
Western Sahara Sahara occidental	*2005	27.2	22.7	50.2	24.7	25.2	50.1	37.8	11.7	50.4
	*2010	24.4	24.0	51.5	22.0	27.0	51.1	34.3	12.2	53.5
	*2015	21.9	25.1	53.0	19.6	28.4	52.0	30.8	12.6	56.7
	*2020	19.8	25.7	54.5	17.7	29.2	53.1	27.4	12.8	59.8
Yemen Yémen	*2005	29.8	16.9	53.3	27.8	18.2	53.9	39.6	10.1	50.3
	2010	24.1	19.0	56.9	23.5	19.7	56.8	28.4	14.1	57.5
	*2015	29.2	12.8	58.0	27.7	12.9	59.5	49.3	12.3	38.4
	*2020	28.6	10.0	61.4	27.4	9.9	62.7	46.0	10.9	43.2
Zambia Zambie	2005	72.3	7.1	20.6	65.6	10.8	23.6	79.5	3.1	17.4
	*2010	64.3	8.8	26.9	57.1	13.6	29.3	72.2	3.5	24.3
	*2015	51.7	10.7	37.7	45.9	16.4	37.7	58.0	4.3	37.7
	*2020	48.5	10.8	40.7	43.7	16.7	39.6	53.6	4.4	41.9
Zimbabwe Zimbabwe	*2005	64.5	9.6	25.9	57.1	15.7	27.1	71.9	3.5	24.7
	*2010	65.5	9.2	25.2	59.3	15.5	25.2	71.6	3.1	25.3
	*2015	67.2	7.1	25.7	62.9	12.3	24.9	71.4	2.1	26.5
	*2020	66.3	6.5	27.2	62.9	11.3	25.8	69.6	1.9	28.5
European Union (EU) Union européenne (UE)	*2005	6.2	27.6	66.2	6.9	37.7	55.4	5.3	14.8	79.9
	*2010	5.2	25.2	69.6	5.9	35.8	58.3	4.3	12.5	83.2
	*2015	4.5	24.1	71.4	5.5	34.2	60.4	3.4	12.1	84.5
	*2020	3.8	23.7	72.5	4.7	33.7	61.6	2.7	11.9	85.4

Source:

International Labour Organization (ILO), Geneva, Key Indicators of the Labour Market (KILM 9th edition) and the ILOSTAT database, last accessed January 2020.

+ Ages 15 years and over unless indicated otherwise. Table is in ISIC Rev. 4 unless otherwise indicated.

1 Data excludes Armenia, Azerbaijan, Cyprus, Georgia, Israel and Turkey.
2 Caucasus refers to Armenia, Azerbaijan, Cyprus, Georgia, Israel and Turkey.
3 Population aged 16 years and over.
4 Data classified according to ISIC Rev. 3.
5 Population aged 14 years and over.
6 Data classified according to ISIC Rev. 2.
7 Population aged 13 years and over.

Source:

Organisation internationale du Travail (OIT), Genève, Indicateurs Clés du Marché du Travail (ICMT 9e édition) et ILOSTAT base de données, dernier accès janvier 2020.

+ Sauf indication contraire, Age 15 ans et plus. Sauf indication contraire, la classification utilisée dans ce tableau est la CITI Rév. 4.

1 Les données excluent l'Arménie, l'Azerbaïdjan, Chypre, la Géorgie, l'Israël et la Turquie.
2 Le Caucase se rapportent à l'Arménie, l'Azerbaïdjan, Chypre, la Géorgie, l'Israël et la Turquie.
3 Population âgée de 16 ans et plus.
4 Données classifiées selon la CITI, Rév. 3.
5 Population âgée de 14 ans et plus.
6 Données classifiées selon la CITI, Rév. 2.
7 Population âgée de 13 ans et plus.

17

Employment by economic activity *(continued)*
Percentage of persons employed by sex and ISIC 4 categories; agriculture (agr.), industry (ind.) and services (ser.)

Emploi par activité économique *(suite)*
Personnes employées par sexe et branches de la CITI rév. 4; agriculture (agr.), industrie (ind.) et services (ser.), pourcentage

8	Excluding the institutional population.	8	Non compris la population dans les institutions.
9	For statistical purposes, the data for China do not include those for the Hong Kong Special Administrative Region (Hong Kong SAR), Macao Special Administrative Region (Macao SAR) and Taiwan Province of China.	9	Pour la présentation des statistiques, les données pour la Chine ne comprennent pas la région administrative spéciale de Hong Kong (RAS de Hong Kong), la région administrative spéciale de Macao (RAS de Macao) et la province chinoise de Taïwan.
10	Resident population (de jure).	10	Population résidente (de droit).
11	Population aged 15 to 64 years.	11	Population âgée de 15 à 64 ans.
12	Nationals, residents.	12	Ressortissants, résidents.
13	Civilians only.	13	Civils uniquement.
14	Population aged 15 to 69 years.	14	Population âgée de 15 à 69 ans.
15	Excluding some areas.	15	Certaines régions sont exclues.

18 Consumer price indices

General and food (Index base: 2010 = 100)

Indices des prix à la consommation

Généraux et alimentation (Indices base: 2010 = 100)

Country or area	2000	2005	2010	2015	2017	2018	2019	Pays ou zone
Afghanistan								**Afghanistan**
General	...	71.6	100.0	132.9	145.6	...	...	Généraux
Food	...	...	...	* 100.8	* 113.9	...	...	Alimentation
Åland Islands								**Îles d'Åland**
General	* 85.6[1]	* 90.8[1]	# 100.0	108.6	111.1	112.5	113.3	Généraux
Food	83.4[1]	* 90.3[1]	100.0	114.3	113.7	115.6	117.6	Alimentation
Albania [1]								**Albanie** [1]
General	74.1	86.7	100.0	111.4	115.1	117.4	119.1	Généraux
Food	...	82.8	100.0	118.8	127.3	130.8	134.6	Alimentation
Algeria [2]								**Algérie** [2]
General	70.4	81.8	100.0	126.7	142.4	148.5[1]	151.4[1]	Généraux
Food [1]	...	...	100.0	131.3	142.5	147.3	146.5	Alimentation [1]
Andorra [1]								**Andorre** [1]
General	...	89.6	100.0	103.3	105.5	105.8	105.8	Généraux
Food	...	92.0	100.0	108.2	112.3	114.5	115.8	Alimentation
Angola [3]								**Angola** [3]
General	* 2.9	* 53.7	* 100.0	* 161.1	* 280.8	* 337.5	...	Généraux
Food	...	* 45.5	* 100.0	* 167.3	* 286.6	...	...	Alimentation
Anguilla								**Anguilla**
General	69.1	81.9	# 0.0	105.1	105.9	...	...	Généraux
Food [1]	...	...	100.0	111.4	112.3	113.4	116.0	Alimentation [1]
Antigua and Barbuda								**Antigua-et-Barbuda**
General	81.1	89.5	100.0	110.3	112.5	113.8	...	Généraux
Argentina [4]								**Argentine** [4]
General	...	...	...	...	112.9	151.6	232.8	Généraux
Food	...	...	...	...	111.7	148.2	234.8	Alimentation
Armenia								**Arménie**
General	* 65.0	* 76.4	* # 100.0	* 124.8	* 124.2	* 127.3	* 129.2	Généraux
Food [1]	...	...	* 100.0	* 127.1	* 127.9	...	...	Alimentation [1]
Aruba [1]								**Aruba** [1]
General	* 72.0	84.1	100.0	103.4	101.4	105.1	109.5	Généraux
Food	...	73.6	100.0	111.9	119.4	133.0	150.1	Alimentation
Australia [1,5]								**Australie** [1,5]
General	74.4	86.3	# 100.0	112.0	115.7	117.9	119.8	Généraux
Food	...	...	100.0	107.6	109.2	110.3	112.9	Alimentation
Austria								**Autriche**
General	82.6	91.4	100.0	110.7	114.0	116.3	118.1	Généraux
Food	79.1	88.1	100.0	114.4	118.0	119.7	121.0	Alimentation
Azerbaijan								**Azerbaïdjan**
General	# 49.0	61.1	100.0	117.7	149.5	152.9	156.9	Généraux
Food [6]	...	...	100.0	119.6	159.8	163.0	166.7	Alimentation [6]
Bahamas								**Bahamas**
General	* 80.0	* 88.2	* 100.0	* 109.6	* 110.9	* 113.4	...	Généraux
Food [7,8]	...	...	...	106.5	...	...	...	Alimentation [7,8]
Bahrain [1]								**Bahreïn** [1]
General	83.4	87.5	100.0	110.6	115.2	117.6	118.8	Généraux
Food	...	...	100.0	114.5	117.1	119.6	122.4	Alimentation
Bangladesh								**Bangladesh**
General	53.9	69.2	100.0[1]	144.6[1]	161.2[1]	170.2[1]	179.7[1]	Généraux
Food [9]	...	...	...	230.3	257.9	273.9	289.2	Alimentation [9]
Barbados								**Barbade**
General	...	...	100.0[1,10]	167.6[11,12]	177.6[11,12]	184.1[11,12]	191.7[11,12]	Généraux
Food [11,12]	...	...	...	200.7	230.9	234.6	248.6	Alimentation [11,12]
Belarus								**Bélarus**
General	* 16.0	* 61.7	* 100.0	387.0	459.0	480.1	508.1	Généraux
Food	...	...	100.0	389.9	...	471.0	501.7	Alimentation
Belgium								**Belgique**
General	81.4[1]	90.4[1]	100.0[1]	108.6[1]	112.8[1]	115.5	117.1	Généraux
Food	76.6	86.3	100.0	110.4	114.3	116.8	117.7	Alimentation
Belize [1]								**Belize** [1]
General	77.9	88.3	100.0	103.8	105.7	106.0	106.2	Généraux
Food [6]	76.6	82.7	100.0	104.8	103.6	103.1	103.8	Alimentation [6]
Benin								**Bénin**
General [13]	* 73.3	* 84.3	* 100.0	* 109.8	* 109.0	* 110.1	...	Généraux [13]
Food [1]	...	...	* 100.0	* 113.0	* 112.5	...	...	Alimentation [1]

Country or area	2000	2005	2010	2015	2017	2018	2019	Pays ou zone
Bhutan								**Bhoutan**
General	80.6	74.8	100.0	146.2	158.4	162.7	167.2	Généraux
Food [14]	...	...	...	* 121.5	* 135.8	...	...	Alimentation [14]
Bolivia (Plurin. State of) [1]								**Bolivie (État plurin. de) [1]**
General	62.6	73.0	100.0	133.7	142.4	145.6	148.3	Généraux
Food	...	...	100.0	145.8	159.0	163.0	168.5	Alimentation
Bosnia and Herzegovina								**Bosnie-Herzégovine**
General	...	85.0	100.0	103.7	102.9	104.3	104.9	Généraux
Food	...	* 81.4	* 100.0	* 104.1	...	...	...	Alimentation
Botswana [1]								**Botswana [1]**
General	44.0	64.3	100.0	132.9	141.1	145.7	149.7	Généraux
Food	...	56.1	100.0	126.9	134.8	134.1	136.0	Alimentation
Brazil [1]								**Brésil [1]**
General	52.5	79.5	100.0	138.4	155.7	161.4	167.4	Généraux
Food [15]	...	...	100.0	154.4	175.3	176.8	185.4	Alimentation [15]
Brunei Darussalam								**Brunéi Darussalam**
General	95.0	# 95.5	100.0	99.9	98.4	99.4	99.0	Généraux
Food	...	...	* 100.0	* 100.7	* 100.0	...	...	Alimentation
Bulgaria [1]								**Bulgarie [1]**
General	56.1	72.7	100.0	106.6	107.9	111.0	114.4	Généraux
Food	61.8	72.4	100.0	112.5	116.7	119.2	125.4	Alimentation
Burkina Faso [16]								**Burkina Faso [16]**
General	74.9	86.9	100.0	108.0	108.1	110.1	106.6	Généraux
Food [17]	...	...	...	...	* 117.6	...	...	Alimentation [17]
Burundi								**Burundi**
General [18]	41.9	61.3	100.0	154.0	188.7	183.4	...	Généraux [18]
Food	* 40.8	* 57.7	* 100.0	* 147.1	* 195.4	...	...	Alimentation
Cabo Verde [1]								**Cabo Verde [1]**
General	78.7	82.6	100.0	108.6	107.9	109.3	110.5	Généraux
Food	...	...	100.0	109.0	108.1	108.6	110.1	Alimentation
Cambodia [19]								**Cambodge [19]**
General	59.0	67.8	100.0	117.5	124.6	127.6	...	Généraux
Food [20]	...	...	...	...	* 206.7	...	...	Alimentation [20]
Cameroon								**Cameroun**
General [21]	* 77.6	* 85.7	* 100.0	* 112.9	* 114.6	* 115.8	...	Généraux
Food [21]	...	...	...	* 109.8	* 111.0	...	...	Alimentation [21]
Canada [1]								**Canada [1]**
General	81.9	91.9	100.0	108.7	112.0	114.5	116.8	Généraux
Food	75.8	86.5	100.0	114.2	115.9	118.1	122.1	Alimentation
Cayman Islands [1]								**Îles Caïmanes [1]**
General	...	...	100.0	103.6	105.0	108.4	...	Généraux
Food	...	...	100.0	115.8	116.9	122.1	...	Alimentation
Central African Republic [22]								**République centrafricaine [22]**
General	* 72.6	* 80.9	* 100.0	* 186.9	...	...	...	Généraux
Chad [23]								**Tchad [23]**
General	* 72.2	* 85.6	* 100.0	* 115.9	...	...	...	Généraux
Chile								**Chili**
General	...	...	101.4[24]	108.9[25]	115.5[25]	118.3[25]	102.4[26]	Généraux
Food	...	...	102.2[24]	114.6[25]	121.4[25]	125.1[25]	102.5[26]	Alimentation
China								**Chine**
General	...	...	100.0	114.9	103.6[27]	105.8[27]	108.8[27]	Généraux
Food	...	...	100.0	129.4	103.0[6,27]	104.9[6,27]	114.6[6,27]	Alimentation
China, Hong Kong SAR								**Chine, RAS de Hong Kong**
General	95.9	89.5	100.0	123.0	127.8	130.8	134.6	Généraux
Food	...	...	100.0	127.9	135.1	139.7	146.5	Alimentation
China, Macao SAR								**Chine, RAS de Macao**
General	80.5	79.7	100.0	131.3[1]	136.1[1]	140.2[1]	144.0[1]	Généraux
Food [1]	...	...	100.0	139.2	145.5	149.5	155.2	Alimentation [1]
Colombia [1]								**Colombie [1]**
General	58.2	79.7	100.0	117.6	132.0	136.2	140.9	Généraux
Food	...	...	100.0	121.5	138.3	139.5	146.3	Alimentation
Comoros								**Comores**
General	69.1	84.4	100.0	...	...	...	...	Généraux
Food [1]	...	...	* 100.0	...	...	...	...	Alimentation [1]
Congo [28]								**Congo [28]**
General	* 75.8	* 83.1	* 100.0	* 116.4	* 120.7	...	...	Généraux

Country or area	2000	2005	2010	2015	2017	2018	2019	Pays ou zone
Cook Islands [1,29]								**Îles Cook** [1,29]
General	...	...	100.0	111.6	111.2	111.3	...	Généraux
Food	...	...	100.0	111.7	113.5	114.0	...	Alimentation
Costa Rica [1,30]								**Costa Rica** [1,30]
General	37.4	# 63.5	100.0	121.5	123.5	126.2	128.8	Généraux
Food	...	...	100.0	122.1	123.2	125.2	126.2	Alimentation
Côte d'Ivoire [31]								**Côte d'Ivoire** [31]
General	* 75.2	* 88.1	* 100.0	* 110.9	* 112.5	* 112.9	* 111.9	Généraux
Food [1,32]	* 66.3	* 75.5	* 100.0	* 111.9	* 115.7	...	...	Alimentation [1,32]
Croatia								**Croatie**
General	# 75.8	85.8	100.0	107.4	107.4	109.0	109.8	Généraux
Food	...		116.6[33]	109.3	112.0	113.1	113.0	Alimentation
Curaçao [1]								**Curaçao** [1]
General	76.9	84.3	100.0	108.1	109.8	112.6	115.6	Généraux
Food [34]	...	...	100.0	124.8	128.9	134.6	142.7	Alimentation [34]
Cyprus [1,35]								**Chypre** [1,35]
General	77.4	88.6	100.0	101.7	100.8	102.3	102.5	Généraux
Food	...	...	100.0	103.6	102.8	103.6	104.2	Alimentation
Czechia								**Tchéquie**
General	77.8	87.0	100.0	107.5	110.9	113.3	116.5	Généraux
Food [1]	86.5	89.9	100.0	118.4	123.4	125.1	128.6	Alimentation [1]
Dem. Rep. of the Congo								**Rép. dém. du Congo**
General	6.8	58.6	100.0	130.1	...	...	...	Généraux
Food	...	...	...	* 122.0	...	...	...	Alimentation
Denmark [1]								**Danemark** [1]
General	81.7	90.0	100.0	107.1	108.6	109.5	110.3	Généraux
Food	...	86.4	100.0	109.1	112.2	112.3	113.8	Alimentation
Djibouti								**Djibouti**
General	70.1	77.8	100.0	112.5	116.2	116.4	120.3	Généraux
Dominica								**Dominique**
General	80.4	86.2	100.0	102.4	102.9	103.9	...	Généraux
Food [36]	...	...	...	* 110.9	* 111.1	...	...	Alimentation [36]
Dominican Republic [1]								**République dominicaine** [1]
General	31.8	73.4	100.0	122.5	128.5	133.1	135.5	Généraux
Food	32.1	74.6	100.0	133.0	139.0	144.0	149.4	Alimentation
Ecuador								**Équateur**
General	45.6	80.2	100.0	121.5	124.1	123.8	124.1	Généraux
Food [1]	...	70.7	100.0	125.2	129.0	126.9	127.0	Alimentation [1]
Egypt								**Égypte**
General [37]	45.1	57.8	100.0	156.8	231.1	264.4[1]	288.6[1]	Généraux [37]
Food [38]	...	...	...	194.1	* 313.9	355.7	...	Alimentation [38]
El Salvador								**El Salvador**
General [37]	71.4	84.2	100.0	108.2	109.9	111.1	111.2	Généraux [37]
Food [39]	...	...	...	...	* 119.4	...	...	Alimentation [39]
Equatorial Guinea								**Guinée équatoriale**
General	56.0	77.5	# 100.0	118.6	121.2	122.8	124.3	Généraux
Food [1]	...	...	* 100.0	* 123.4	* 120.3	...	...	Alimentation [1]
Estonia								**Estonie**
General	66.5	79.1	100.0	111.5	115.5	119.4	122.1	Généraux
Food [1]	65.2	77.1	100.0	118.0	124.8	128.6	132.4	Alimentation [1]
Eswatini								**Eswatini**
General	50.3	69.5	100.0	135.4	155.1	162.6	...	Généraux
Food [14]	...	...	...	* 113.6	* 140.0	...	...	Alimentation [14]
Ethiopia								**Éthiopie**
General	* 37.6	* # 44.8	* 100.0	* 211.4	* 249.1	...	...	Généraux
Food [1]	...	43.0	100.0	222.9	267.1	...	...	Alimentation [1]
Fiji [1]								**Fidji** [1]
General	70.1	* 80.8	100.0	116.4	124.9	130.0	132.3	Généraux
Food	...	...	100.0	127.5	132.3	136.9	143.6	Alimentation
Finland								**Finlande**
General	86.1[1]	91.2[1]	100.0[1]	108.8[1]	110.0[1]	111.2	112.3	Généraux
Food	82.5[1]	90.3[1]	100.0[1]	115.7[1]	113.3[1]	115.5	116.9	Alimentation
France [1,40]								**France** [1,40]
General	84.4	92.8	100.0	105.6	106.8	108.9	110.0	Généraux
Food [41]	82.0	91.5	100.0	105.7	107.3	109.7	112.2	Alimentation [41]

18 Consumer price indices *(continued)*
General and food (Index base: 2010 = 100)

Indices des prix à la consommation *(suite)*
Généraux et alimentation (Indices base: 2010 = 100)

Country or area	2000	2005	2010	2015	2017	2018	2019	Pays ou zone
French Guiana [1]								**Guyane française** [1]
General	...	...	100.0	105.4	0.0	107.3	108.3	Généraux
Food [34]	...	...	100.0	109.7	0.0	111.7	113.8	Alimentation [34]
Gabon								**Gabon**
General [42]	* 81.6	* 88.7	* 100.0	* 109.0	* 114.2	* 119.7	* 122.2	Généraux [42]
Food [1]	...	...	* 100.0	* 115.9	...	...	...	Alimentation [1]
Gambia								**Gambie**
General [43]	51.0	81.1	100.0	130.7	151.4	161.3	172.7	Généraux [43]
Food [44]	...	...	...	* 186.0	...	...	...	Alimentation [44]
Georgia [45]								**Géorgie** [45]
General	54.9	70.0	100.0	114.7	124.2	127.4	131.1	Généraux
Food	...	...	100.0	120.5	130.8	133.7	...	Alimentation
Germany								**Allemagne**
General	85.7	92.5	100.0	106.9	109.3	111.4	105.2[27]	Généraux
Food	84.9	89.1	100.0	112.3	116.4	119.2	107.2[27]	Alimentation
Ghana								**Ghana**
General	21.1	52.9	100.0	176.0	232.3	255.1	...	Généraux
Food [46]	...	...	...	* 123.2	* 143.6	* 154.8	...	Alimentation [46]
Greece [1]								**Grèce** [1]
General	72.2	85.3	100.0	100.8	101.1	101.7	101.9	Généraux
Food	73.9	86.9	100.0	104.8	104.9	105.3	105.2	Alimentation
Grenada								**Grenade**
General	73.5	82.9	100.0	103.9	106.6	107.4	...	Généraux
Food [1]	...	* 74.0	* 100.0	* 110.5	* 108.6	...	...	Alimentation [1]
Guadeloupe [1]								**Guadeloupe** [1]
General	...	...	100.0	106.1	106.9	108.2	109.3	Généraux
Food [34]	...	...	100.0	109.3	112.1	114.8	116.4	Alimentation [34]
Guam [1]								**Guam** [1]
General	...	...	100.0	106.3	115.5	118.5	119.6[47]	Généraux
Food [15,48]	...	...	100.0	125.2	121.4	127.2	128.2[47]	Alimentation [15,48]
Guatemala								**Guatemala**
General	# 51.9	74.6	# 100.0	121.8	132.8	137.8	142.9	Généraux
Food [49]	...	...	...	147.0	176.0	188.7	203.5	Alimentation [49]
Guinea								**Guinée**
General [50]	...	42.2	100.0	185.6	218.7	240.2	262.9	Généraux [50]
Food [1]	...	...	* 100.0	* 204.5	* 256.4	...	...	Alimentation [1]
Guinea-Bissau [51]								**Guinée-Bissau** [51]
General	78.4	84.2	100.0	108.4	111.7	...	...	Généraux
Food [17,52]	...	...	...	...	117.6	...	...	Alimentation [17,52]
Guyana [53]								**Guyana** [53]
General	* 56.4	* 72.4	* 100.0	* 109.4	* 112.4	* 113.8	* 116.2	Généraux
Haiti								**Haïti**
General	26.9	66.8	100.0	139.0	181.5	...	...	Généraux
Food [54]	...	...	100.0	142.2	186.3	...	...	Alimentation [54]
Honduras								**Honduras**
General	* 48.1	* 72.0	* 100.0	* 129.3	* 138.1	* 144.1	* 150.3	Généraux
Food [1]	* 51.5	* 70.8	* 100.0	* 126.6	* 129.8	...	...	Alimentation [1]
Hungary								**Hongrie**
General	57.9	76.9	100.0	111.4	114.5	117.7	121.6	Généraux
Food	...	...	100.0	116.6	120.6	125.6	132.4	Alimentation
Iceland								**Islande**
General	54.7	67.1	100.0	117.8	122.0	125.3	129.0	Généraux
Food	61.7	65.9	100.0	119.6	118.3	121.3	125.8	Alimentation
India								**Inde**
General [55]	54.3	66.0	100.0	148.6	159.8	167.6	180.4	Généraux [55]
Food [46]	...	...	...	127.7	136.9	139.2	144.2	Alimentation [46]
Indonesia								**Indonésie**
General	44.0	68.7	100.0	132.3	142.2	146.7	151.2	Généraux
Food [34,46]	...	...	...	128.0	139.9	145.6	147.7	Alimentation [34,46]
Iran (Islamic Republic of) [56]								**Iran (Rép. islamique d')** [56]
General	...	...	...	91.6	106.2	125.3	175.4	Généraux
Food	...	...	...	91.5	109.7	135.3	210.4	Alimentation
Iraq								**Iraq**
General	18.2	58.6	100.0	118.5	119.4	119.9	...	Généraux
Food [1]	...	...	100.0	112.8	...	...	...	Alimentation [1]

Country or area	2000	2005	2010	2015	2017	2018	2019	Pays ou zone
Ireland [1]								**Irlande** [1]
General	78.4	93.1	100.0	104.7	105.1	105.6	106.6	Généraux
Food	88.3	97.7	100.0	98.3	95.0	93.1	92.5	Alimentation
Israel								**Israël**
General	80.9	87.8	100.0	106.7	106.4	107.2	108.1	Généraux
Food	72.1	79.3	100.0	108.8	108.0	109.1	111.3	Alimentation
Italy								**Italie**
General	80.7[1]	91.0[1]	100.0	107.5	108.7[1]	109.9[1]	110.6[1]	Généraux
Food	78.2[1]	88.9[1]	100.0	108.8	111.1[1]	112.4[1]	113.3[1]	Alimentation
Jamaica [1]								**Jamaïque** [1]
General	33.8	56.0	100.0	141.1	150.8	156.4	162.5	Généraux
Food	31.6	51.7	100.0	157.2	170.7	177.7	188.9	Alimentation
Japan [1]								**Japon** [1]
General	102.7	100.4	100.0	103.6	104.0	105.0	105.5	Généraux
Food [15]	98.4	96.8	100.0	106.6	110.6	110.7	111.2	Alimentation [15]
Jordan								**Jordanie**
General	66.1	74.5	100.0	116.4	119.3	124.7	125.0	Généraux
Food	...	...	100.0	115.2	110.8	114.4	114.4	Alimentation
Kazakhstan								**Kazakhstan**
General	43.8	61.5	100.0	137.8	169.3	...	...	Généraux
Food [1]	...	* 58.6	* 100.0	* 136.8	* 167.7	...	...	Alimentation [1]
Kenya								**Kenya**
General	38.1	55.5	100.0	150.2	172.4	180.5	...	Généraux
Food [1]	...	...	* 100.0	* 172.1	* 214.8	...	...	Alimentation [1]
Kiribati								**Kiribati**
General	...	...	* 100.0	* 99.5	...	...	...	Généraux
Food [1]	...	...	* 100.0	* 94.1	...	...	...	Alimentation [1]
Kuwait								**Koweït**
General	* # 69.9	* 76.1	* 100.0	* 118.1	* 124.6	* 125.2	...	Généraux
Food	...	...	* 100.0	* 124.7	* 126.7	...	108.8[25]	Alimentation
Kyrgyzstan								**Kirghizistan**
General	49.0	59.8	100.0	146.4	151.6	153.9	155.7	Généraux
Food	...	55.9	100.0	141.7	135.8	132.9	134.6	Alimentation
Lao People's Dem. Rep.								**Rép. dém. populaire lao**
General	* 48.1	* # 78.5	* # 100.0	* 125.8	* 128.9	* 131.5	...	Généraux
Food [1]	...	...	* 100.0	* 146.6	* 152.7	...	...	Alimentation [1]
Latvia								**Lettonie**
General	59.2	72.1	100.0	107.6	110.9	113.7	116.9	Généraux
Food	53.0	69.1	100.0	110.7	118.1	118.8	122.3	Alimentation
Lebanon								**Liban**
General	...	...	* 100.0	* 115.0	* 119.0	* 126.2	...	Généraux
Food [1]	...	...	* 100.0	* 118.5	* 121.3	...	...	Alimentation [1]
Lesotho								**Lesotho**
General	50.7	71.0	100.0	127.0	141.5	148.2	155.9	Généraux
Food [1]	...	* 61.9	* 100.0	* 138.4	* 165.5	...	...	Alimentation [1]
Liberia								**Libéria**
General	...	61.8	100.0	147.6	180.6	223.1	...	Généraux
Food	...	...	* 100.0	* 162.5	* 186.5	...	...	Alimentation
Libya								**Libye**
General	98.8	79.8	100.0	...	...	...	...	Généraux
Lithuania [1]								**Lituanie** [1]
General	74.4	77.7	100.0	107.6	112.6	115.7	118.4	Généraux
Food	68.7	72.2	100.0	113.3	118.8	120.5	124.0	Alimentation
Luxembourg [1]								**Luxembourg** [1]
General	80.1	89.7	100.0	109.2	111.5	113.1	115.1	Généraux
Food	76.3	87.7	100.0	110.5	115.3	117.9	119.5	Alimentation
Madagascar								**Madagascar**
General	# 37.7	62.9	100.0	139.5	108.6[57,58]	117.9[57,58]	124.6[57,58]	Généraux
Food [57]	...	...	...	140.4[1,54]	109.3[58]	121.1[58]	127.0[58]	Alimentation [57]
Malawi								**Malawi**
General	* 32.4	* 64.2	* 100.0	* 250.6	* 340.2	* 382.5	...	Généraux
Food [46]	...	...	...	* 185.1	* 262.4	...	...	Alimentation [46]
Malaysia								**Malaisie**
General	80.5	87.7	100.0	112.8	119.6	120.7	121.5	Généraux
Food	...	...	100.0	119.4	129.2	130.9	133.0	Alimentation

Country or area	2000	2005	2010	2015	2017	2018	2019	Pays ou zone
Maldives								**Maldives**
General	* 71.1	* # 73.3	* 100.0	* 132.0	* 136.4	* 136.3	...	Généraux
Food [1]	...	...	* 100.0	* 153.0	* 163.3	...	...	Alimentation [1]
Mali [59]								**Mali** [59]
General	76.4	85.9	100.0	110.3	110.2	...	...	Généraux
Food [1,52]	...	...	* 100.0	* 112.9	* 112.0	...	...	Alimentation [1,52]
Malta								**Malte**
General	78.8	88.9	100.0	108.2	110.3	111.6	113.5	Généraux
Food [4]	...	...	...	...	* 99.8	...	...	Alimentation [4]
Martinique [1]								**Martinique** [1]
General	...	...	100.0	106.3	106.7	108.0	109.3	Généraux
Food [34]	...	...	100.0	110.3	113.0	114.3	116.0	Alimentation [34]
Mauritania [60]								**Mauritanie** [60]
General	...	...	...	...	104.8	108.0	110.5	Généraux
Food	...	...	...	...	107.2	111.7	114.7	Alimentation
Mauritius [1]								**Maurice** [1]
General	56.9	72.9	100.0	119.8	125.4	129.4	130.0	Généraux
Food	...	...	100.0	120.8	126.6	134.0	134.9	Alimentation
Mexico [1]								**Mexique** [1]
General	63.3	80.5	100.0	119.4	130.2	136.6	141.5	Généraux
Food [54]	57.5	74.4	100.0	129.9	144.4	151.3	158.1	Alimentation [54]
Micronesia (Fed. States of)								**Micronésie (États féd. de)**
General	72.4	77.6	100.0	112.7	112.1	...	...	Généraux
Mongolia								**Mongolie**
General	41.6[1]	57.3[1]	100.0[1]	163.8[1]	172.0[1]	# 112.3[27]	120.4[27]	Généraux
Food	...	...	100.0[1]	161.4[1]	164.3[1]	# 110.1[27]	121.9[27]	Alimentation
Montenegro								**Monténégro**
General	...	82.2	100.0	111.0	113.4[1]	116.3[1]	116.7[1]	Généraux
Food	...	...	100.0	114.3	115.4[1]	115.8[1]	119.5[1]	Alimentation
Montserrat								**Montserrat**
General	...	* 86.8	* 100.0	* 107.9	* 108.9	* 110.3	...	Généraux
Food [60]	...	...	...	* 99.1	* 98.6	...	...	Alimentation [60]
Morocco [1]								**Maroc** [1]
General	83.6	89.7	100.0	106.2	108.8	110.7	111.1	Généraux
Food	...	...	100.0	107.4	110.5	111.6	110.2	Alimentation
Mozambique [1]								**Mozambique** [1]
General	...	...	100.0	126.3	170.7	177.4	182.3	Généraux
Food	...	...	100.0	134.4	199.0	199.0	205.5	Alimentation
Myanmar								**Myanmar**
General	15.0	44.5	100.0	129.3	144.6	154.5	...	Généraux
Food [46]	...	...	...	* 127.9	* 145.9	...	...	Alimentation [46]
Namibia [1]								**Namibie** [1]
General	...	71.4	100.0	128.9	145.9	152.3	158.0	Généraux
Food	...	63.0	100.0	139.4	162.9	168.2	175.4	Alimentation
Nepal [61]								**Népal** [61]
General	...	...	...	103.7	116.9	121.7	128.4	Généraux
Food	...	...	...	104.4	114.8	117.1	123.7	Alimentation
Netherlands								**Pays-Bas**
General	82.0	92.7	100.0	109.3	111.0	112.9	115.9	Généraux
Food [1]	85.7	91.3	100.0	107.4	111.3	112.2	116.8	Alimentation [1]
New Caledonia [1]								**Nouvelle-Calédonie** [1]
General	...	...	100.0	106.3	...	109.9	110.2	Généraux
Food	...	...	100.0	110.6	...	113.9	110.7	Alimentation
New Zealand [1]								**Nouvelle-Zélande** [1]
General	77.0	87.0	100.0	107.9	110.7	112.4	114.2	Généraux
Food	...	...	100.0	106.0	107.7	107.5	108.7	Alimentation
Nicaragua								**Nicaragua**
General	# 45.7	62.9	100.0	136.9	147.2	154.4	162.7	Généraux
Food [1]	...	57.0	100.0	146.5	149.5	155.8	162.9	Alimentation [1]
Niger [52]								**Niger** [52]
General	...	...	...	107.3[17,62]	110.1[17,62]	# 104.1[60]	101.5[60]	Généraux
Food	...	...	...	122.4[17,62]	121.8[17,62]	# 102.2[60]	97.5[60]	Alimentation
Nigeria [63]								**Nigéria** [63]
General	29.6	61.4	100.0	158.9	214.2	240.1	267.5	Généraux
Food [1]	...	...	100.0	161.3	221.3	253.0	287.5	Alimentation [1]

Country or area	2000	2005	2010	2015	2017	2018	2019	Pays ou zone
North Macedonia								**Macédoine du Nord**
General	79.9	86.8	100.0	109.7	110.9	112.6	113.4	Généraux
Food [1]	...	83.1	100.0	111.6	110.1	111.1	112.8	Alimentation [1]
Norway								**Norvège**
General	81.9	89.3	100.0	108.6	114.6	117.7	120.3	Généraux
Food	85.6	88.3	100.0	108.4	111.2	114.0	115.2	Alimentation
Oman								**Oman**
General	74.8	76.0	100.0	109.4	112.4	113.4	113.5	Généraux
Food [1]	...	...	* 100.0	* 110.8	* 110.1	...	...	Alimentation [1]
Pakistan								**Pakistan**
General	43.1	55.3	# 100.0	145.3	156.9	164.9	182.3	Généraux
Food [1]	...	...	100.0	143.0	151.3	154.6	169.8	Alimentation [1]
Palau								**Palaos**
General	...	80.5	100.0	117.9	118.2	...	...	Généraux
Food [1]	...	* 73.6	* 100.0	* 116.4	* 115.1	...	...	Alimentation [1]
Panama								**Panama**
General [37]	77.3	81.3	100.0	119.6	121.6	122.5	122.1	Généraux [37]
Food [1]	...	* 74.0	* 100.0	* 122.6	* 123.6	...	...	Alimentation [1]
Papua New Guinea								**Papouasie-Nvl-Guinée**
General	52.9	77.1	# 100.0	127.8	143.7	150.5	...	Généraux
Food [1]	...	...	* 100.0	* 106.4	...	...	...	Alimentation [1]
Paraguay [1,64]								**Paraguay [1,64]**
General	47.3	71.4	100.0	124.8	134.6	140.0	143.8	Généraux
Food	36.1	58.2	100.0	125.8	140.8	146.3	148.0	Alimentation
Peru [10]								**Pérou [10]**
General	79.2	87.1	100.0	117.8	125.4	127.1	129.8	Généraux
Food [15,33,48]	...	...	...	...	163.1	...	...	Alimentation [15,33,48]
Philippines [46]								**Philippines [46]**
General	...	...	...	107.0	111.5	117.3	120.2	Généraux
Food	...	...	...	110.5	115.7	123.6	126.2	Alimentation
Poland [1]								**Pologne [1]**
General	...	...	100.0	108.1	109.6	111.5	113.9	Généraux
Food	...	...	100.0	109.1	114.9	117.9	123.8	Alimentation
Portugal [1]								**Portugal [1]**
General [65]	78.5	91.8	100.0	107.0	109.2	110.3	110.6	Généraux [65]
Food	85.6	95.1	100.0	107.0	109.2	110.0	110.4	Alimentation
Puerto Rico [1]								**Porto Rico [1]**
General	...	...	100.0	105.2	106.7	...	...	Généraux
Food [15]	...	...	100.0	111.1	112.4	...	...	Alimentation [15]
Qatar [25]								**Qatar [25]**
General	...	...	...	105.2	108.5	108.8	108.1	Généraux
Food	...	...	...	101.1	101.1	101.1	101.0	Alimentation
Republic of Korea [1]								**République de Corée [1]**
General	73.1	86.2	100.0	109.8	113.1	114.8	115.2	Généraux
Food	62.9	80.8	100.0	115.6	122.3	125.9	125.7	Alimentation
Republic of Moldova [66,67]								**République de Moldova [66,67]**
General	...	...	100.0	135.8	153.9	158.7	166.3	Généraux
Food [15]	...	...	100.0	137.1	159.1	167.8	180.8	Alimentation [15]
Réunion [1]								**Réunion [1]**
General	...	...	100.0	104.7	105.3	107.2	107.7	Généraux
Food [34]	...	...	100.0	110.5	111.8	115.4	116.4	Alimentation [34]
Romania								**Roumanie**
General	32.0	74.1	# 100.0	# 114.2	113.9	119.2[1]	123.8[1]	Généraux
Food	...	...	...	131.0[15,33]	99.8[27]	103.6[27]	108.5[27]	Alimentation
Russian Federation								**Fédération de Russie**
General	30.8	61.4	100.0	151.5	168.2	173.0	180.7	Généraux
Food	...	58.4	100.0	161.7	175.6	178.5	188.6	Alimentation
Rwanda [1,37]								**Rwanda [1,37]**
General	...	...	100.0	122.1	135.4	137.2	140.5	Généraux
Food	...	...	100.0	132.2	160.4	156.1	160.1	Alimentation
Saint Kitts and Nevis [1]								**Saint-Kitts-et-Nevis [1]**
General	...	...	100.0	105.7	105.7	104.6	...	Généraux
Food	...	...	100.0	102.2	95.7	98.0	...	Alimentation
Saint Lucia								**Sainte-Lucie**
General [1]	...	...	100.0	111.4	108.0	110.1	...	Généraux [1]
Food [68]	...	...	...	102.4	97.6	101.2	...	Alimentation [68]

Country or area	2000	2005	2010	2015	2017	2018	2019	Pays ou zone
Saint Vincent & Grenadines								**Saint-Vincent-Grenadines**
General	* 74.1	* 81.5	* # 100.0	* 105.1	* 107.2	* 109.7	...	Généraux
Food [1]	...	...	* 100.0	* 109.5	* 111.5	...	...	Alimentation [1]
Samoa [65]								**Samoa** [65]
General	* 57.4	* 76.4	* 100.0	* 108.4	* 111.7	* 116.4	* 117.6	Généraux
San Marino [49]								**Saint-Marin** [49]
General	...	...	...	107.7	109.5	111.4	112.5	Généraux
Food	...	...	...	121.3	126.7	133.2	138.2	Alimentation
Sao Tome and Principe								**Sao Tomé-et-Principe**
General	22.3	39.2	100.0	154.0	171.6	185.1	...	Généraux
Food [60]	...	...	...	...	* 111.9	...	...	Alimentation [60]
Saudi Arabia [1]								**Arabie saoudite** [1]
General	...	81.4	100.0	114.4	115.7	118.6	117.1	Généraux
Food	...	73.0	100.0	118.6	116.2	123.6	125.1	Alimentation
Senegal [69]								**Sénégal** [69]
General	...	...	100.0[1]	105.3[1]	108.9[1]	103.7[60]	...	Généraux
Food	...	...	100.0[1]	110.9[1]	117.2[1]	108.2[60]	...	Alimentation
Serbia								**Serbie**
General	19.8	65.2	100.0	133.0	138.7	141.4	144.0	Généraux
Food			100.0	133.2	137.2	139.7	143.3	Alimentation
Seychelles [1]								**Seychelles** [1]
General	47.1	54.1	100.0	120.9	123.1	127.7	130.0	Généraux
Food [70]	...	...	100.0	116.7	117.7	117.9	116.9	Alimentation [70]
Sierra Leone [1]								**Sierra Leone** [1]
General	...	...	100.0	134.1	175.8	204.0	234.2	Généraux
Food	...	...	100.0	137.8	185.3	218.0	237.0	Alimentation
Singapore								**Singapour**
General	85.2	88.0	100.0	113.2	113.3	113.8	114.4	Généraux
Food [1]	82.0	85.6	100.0	112.9	116.9	118.6	120.4	Alimentation [1]
Slovakia								**Slovaquie**
General	65.4	86.8	100.0	108.7	109.6	112.3	115.3	Généraux
Food	77.9	89.6	100.0	113.2	114.4	118.8	123.6	Alimentation
Slovenia								**Slovénie**
General	66.5	86.8	100.0	105.9	107.4	109.3	111.1	Généraux
Food	66.7	81.3	100.0	113.2	116.8	119.9	121.8	Alimentation
Solomon Islands								**Îles Salomon**
General	44.6	65.8	100.0	125.3	126.5	130.9	...	Généraux
Food [71]	...	...	...	* 552.5	* 551.6	...	...	Alimentation [71]
South Africa [1]								**Afrique du Sud** [1]
General	59.9	74.3	100.0[37]	130.1[37]	145.7[37]	152.4[37]	158.7[37]	Généraux
Food	48.6	67.1	100.0[37]	137.2[37]	162.2[37]	168.0[37]	173.8[37]	Alimentation
South Sudan								**Soudan du sud**
General	...	...	100.0	331.9	4 583.7	...	...	Généraux
Food [1]	...	...	* 100.0	* 349.4	* 4 574.0	...	...	Alimentation [1]
Spain [1]								**Espagne** [1]
General	75.9	* 89.0	100.0	106.5	108.4	110.2	111.0	Généraux
Food	71.9	89.2	100.0	108.2	111.1	112.9	114.1	Alimentation
Sri Lanka								**Sri Lanka**
General	36.5[1,72]	# 58.3[1,72]	100.0[1,72]	109.5[25]	122.6[25]	125.2[25]	129.6[25]	Généraux
Food	...		100.0[1,72]	110.7[25]	127.0[25]	126.8[25]	127.6[25]	Alimentation
State of Palestine								**État de Palestine**
General	67.4	80.7	100.0	111.0	111.0	110.8	112.5[1]	Généraux
Food	63.4	71.8	100.0	107.8	105.2	104.4	107.9[1]	Alimentation
Sudan								**Soudan**
General	* 41.7	* 60.0	* 100.0	* 349.8	...	...	...	Généraux
Food [73]	...	...	...	* 501.5	...	...	...	Alimentation [73]
Suriname [1]								**Suriname** [1]
General	29.0	69.0	100.0	139.2	264.1	282.8[74]	294.8	Généraux
Food	...	...	100.0	141.8	264.7	289.5[74]	304.2	Alimentation
Sweden								**Suède**
General	86.2	92.7	100.0	103.6	106.5	108.6	110.5	Généraux
Food [1]	82.7	87.2	100.0	107.9	111.4	114.0	117.2	Alimentation [1]
Switzerland [1]								**Suisse** [1]
General	* 91.7	95.7	100.0	98.2	98.3	99.2	99.5	Généraux
Food	92.7	97.8	100.0	97.1	97.9	99.1	99.2	Alimentation

Country or area	2000	2005	2010	2015	2017	2018	2019	Pays ou zone
Syrian Arab Republic								**République arabe syrienne**
General	...	...	100.0	448.8	...	...	...	Généraux
Food	...	...	100.0	512.1	...	...	...	Alimentation
Tajikistan [1]								**Tadjikistan** [1]
General	...	...	100.0	140.2	159.5	165.7	178.6	Généraux
Food [15]	...	...	100.0	146.8	168.6	173.1	192.2	Alimentation [15]
Thailand [1]								**Thaïlande** [1]
General	77.4	86.6	100.0	110.3	111.3	112.5	113.3	Généraux
Food	...	...	100.0	123.0	124.9	125.5	128.4	Alimentation
Timor-Leste								**Timor-Leste**
General	...	* 74.4	* 100.0	* 142.8	* 141.6	* 145.4	...	Généraux
Food [14]	...	...	...	* 105.7	* 104.4	...	...	Alimentation [14]
Togo								**Togo**
General	74.5	84.7	100.0	111.2	111.5	112.5	...	Généraux
Food [1,52,75]	* 73.9	* 81.5	* 100.0	* 106.6	* 105.4	...	...	Alimentation [1,52,75]
Tonga								**Tonga**
General	* 47.7	* 76.7	* 100.0	* 109.9	...	...	...	Généraux
Food [1]	...	* 75.7	* 100.0	* 116.3	...	...	...	Alimentation [1]
Trinidad and Tobago [11]								**Trinité-et-Tobago** [11]
General	51.1	64.6	100.0	133.6	140.3	141.8	...	Généraux
Food [1]	...	* 39.9	* 100.0	* 170.9	* 189.0	...	...	Alimentation [1]
Tunisia								**Tunisie**
General	* # 71.7	* 81.6	* # 100.0	* 126.7	* 138.4	...	...	Généraux
Food	...	...	100.0	100.0[27]	108.5[27]	116.4[27]	124.4[27]	Alimentation
Turkey								**Turquie**
General	* 20.6	* # 65.9	* 100.0	* 146.1	175.0	202.1	233.5	Généraux
Food	19.6[1]	60.2[1]	100.0	157.3	187.5	219.9	264.5	Alimentation
Uganda [76]								**Ouganda** [76]
General	...	...	...	150.8	167.9	172.3	177.3	Généraux
Food	...	...	...	160.7	186.8	184.6	184.2	Alimentation
Ukraine								**Ukraine**
General	34.8	51.2	100.0	180.5	235.3	261.1	281.9	Généraux
Food	...	...	100.0	166.6	204.9	227.8	246.0	Alimentation
United Arab Emirates								**Émirats arabes unis**
General	...	...	# 100.0	109.3	113.3	116.8	114.5	Généraux
Food [1]	...	...	* 100.0	* 118.3	* 121.0	...	...	Alimentation [1]
United Kingdom [1]								**Royaume-Uni** [1]
General	81.3	87.4	100.0	111.9	115.6	118.4	120.6	Généraux
Food	72.6	78.5	100.0	109.8	109.5	111.8	113.4	Alimentation
United Rep. of Tanzania [77]								**Rép.-Unie de Tanzanie** [77]
General	51.7	66.3	100.0	# 158.0	175.0	181.2	187.4	Généraux
Food [78]	...	...	...	* 96.6	* 113.3	...	...	Alimentation [78]
United States of America [37]								**États-Unis d'Amérique** [37]
General	79.0	89.6	100.0	108.7	112.4	115.2	117.2	Généraux
Food [1]	77.8	87.9	100.0	112.2	110.5	111.0	112.0	Alimentation [1]
Uruguay [1]								**Uruguay** [1]
General	43.5	70.5	100.0	150.1	174.8	188.1	202.9	Généraux
Food	38.6	64.3	100.0	158.8	179.0	193.9	210.9	Alimentation
Uzbekistan [1,58]								**Ouzbékistan** [1,58]
General	...	...	...	...	113.8	133.9	153.3	Généraux
Food	...	...	...	...	117.9	141.4	165.6	Alimentation
Vanuatu								**Vanuatu**
General	75.1	83.9	100.0	107.1	111.4[1,47]	114.0[1,47]	117.1[1,47]	Généraux
Food [1]	...	...	* 100.0	* 109.2	120.1[47]	125.1[47]	131.8[47]	Alimentation [1]
Venezuela (Boliv. Rep. of) [1]								**Venezuela (Rép. boliv. du)** [1]
General	...	...	100.0	772.0	14.7[79]	9 654.7[79]	1 931.5[80]	Généraux
Food	...	...	100.0	1 487.2	46.6[79]	35 197.2[79]	6 268.9[80]	Alimentation
Viet Nam								**Viet Nam**
General	# 48.1	59.9	100.0	144.6	153.6	159.1	163.5	Généraux
Food [60]	...	...	...	...	* 103.0	...	...	Alimentation [60]
Yemen								**Yémen**
General	* 34.2	* # 60.0	* 100.0	...	...	...	...	Généraux
Zambia								**Zambie**
General	23.8	59.9	# 100.0	144.0	180.9	194.5	212.3	Généraux
Food [24]	...	...	...	* 151.2	* 193.9	...	...	Alimentation [24]

Country or area	2000	2005	2010	2015	2017	2018	2019	Pays ou zone
Zimbabwe								**Zimbabwe**
General	...	...	100.0	106.2	105.5	...	...	Généraux
Food [1]	...	...	* 100.0	* 103.6	* 102.7	...	...	Alimentation [1]

Source:

United Nations Statistics Division (UNSD), New York, Monthly Bulletin of Statistics (MBS), last accessed June 2020.

Source:

Organisation des Nations Unies (ONU), Division de statistique, New York, Bulletin mensuel de statistique (BMS), dernier accès juin 2020.

1	Calculated by the UN Statistics Division from national indices.	1	Les indices ont été calculés par la Division de statistique de l'ONU à partir des indices nationaux.
2	Algiers	2	Alger
3	Luanda	3	Luanda
4	Index base: December 2016=100.	4	Indices base: 2016 décembre=100.
5	Weighted average of index values computed for the 8 capital cities.	5	Moyenne pondérée des données d'index calculées pour les 8 capitales.
6	Including tobacco.	6	Y compris le tabac.
7	New Providence	7	Nouvelle Providence
8	Index base: November 2014=100.	8	Indices base: 2014 novembre=100.
9	Base: July 2005-June 2006=100.	9	Base: juillet 2005-juin 2006 = 100.
10	Metropolitan Lima.	10	Lima métropolitaine.
11	Data refer to the Retail Price Index.	11	Les données se rapporte à l'index des prix en détail.
12	Index base: July 2001=100.	12	Indices base: 2001 juillet=100.
13	For Cotonou only.	13	Pour Cotonou seulement.
14	Index base: December 2012=100.	14	Indices base: 2012 décembre=100.
15	Including alcoholic beverages.	15	Y compris les boissons alcoolisées.
16	Ouagadougou	16	Ouagadougou
17	Index base: 2008=100.	17	Indices base: 2008=100.
18	Bujumbura	18	Bujumbura
19	Phnom Penh	19	Phnom Penh
20	Index Base: October to December 2006=100.	20	Indices base: octobre au décembre 2006=100.
21	Base: 2011=100.	21	Base : 2011=100.
22	Bangui	22	Bangui
23	N'Djamena	23	N'Djamena
24	Base: 2009=100.	24	Base : 2009=100.
25	Index base: 2013=100.	25	Indices base: 2013=100.
26	Base: 2018=100.	26	Base: 2018=100.
27	Index base: 2015=100.	27	Indices base: 2015=100.
28	Brazzaville	28	Brazzaville
29	Rarotonga	29	Rarotonga
30	Central area.	30	Région centrale.
31	Abidjan	31	Abidjan
32	The index pertains to African families.	32	l'indice se rapporte aux familles africaines.
33	Index base: 2005=100.	33	Indices base: 2005=100.
34	Data refers to food only.	34	Les données ne concernent que les denrées alimentaires.
35	Data refer to government controlled areas.	35	Les données se rapportent aux zones contrôlées par le Gouvernement.
36	Index base: June 2010=100.	36	Indices base: 2010 juin=100.
37	Urban areas.	37	Zones urbaines.
38	Index base: January 2010=100.	38	Indices base: 2010 janvier=100.
39	Index base: December 2009=100.	39	Indices base: 2009 décembre=100.
40	Including French overseas departments and territories.	40	Y compris les départements et territoires français d'outremer.
41	All households.	41	Tous ménages.
42	Libreville and Owendo.	42	Libreville et Owendo.
43	Banjul, Kombo St. Mary	43	Banjul, Kombo St. Mary
44	Index base: August 2004=100.	44	Indices base: 2004 août=100.
45	Data refer to 5 cities only.	45	Les données se réfère à 5 villes seulement.
46	Base: 2012=100.	46	Base: 2012=100.
47	Monthly average for quarter or index for quarter.	47	Moyenne mensuelle pour le trimestre ou indice pour le trimestre.
48	Including food and beverages consumed away from home.	48	Y compris les aliments et de boissons loin de la maison.
49	Index base: December 2010=100.	49	Indices base: 2000 décembre=100.
50	Conakry	50	Conakry
51	Bissau	51	Bissau
52	WAEMU harmonized consumer price index.	52	UEMOA harmonisé l'indice des prix à la consommation.

53	Georgetown	53	Georgetown
54	Including alcoholic beverages and tobacco.	54	Y compris les boissons alcoolisées et le tabac.
55	Industrial workers.	55	Ouvriers industriels.
56	Index base: fiscal (solar) year 2016 (21 March 2016 - 20 March 2017)=100.	56	Indices base: année fiscale (solaire) 2016 (21 mars 2016 - 20 mars 2017) = 100.
57	Data refer to 7 cities only.	57	Les données se réfère à 7 villes seulement.
58	Base: 2016 = 100	58	Base: 2016 = 100
59	Bamako	59	Bamako
60	Index base: 2014=100.	60	Indices base: 2014=100.
61	Index base: 2014/2015=100.	61	Indices base: 2014/2015=100.
62	Niamey	62	Niamey
63	Rural and urban areas.	63	Régions rurales et urbaines.
64	For Greater Asuncion only.	64	Pour le Grand Asuncion uniquement.
65	Excluding rent.	65	Sans le loyer.
66	Excluding the left side of the river Nistru and the municipality of Bender.	66	La rive gauche de la rivière Nistru et la municipalité de Bender sont exclues.
67	Data refer to 8 cities only.	67	Les données se réfère à 8 villes seulement.
68	Base: January 2018=100.	68	Base : janvier 2018=100.
69	Data refer to the national index.	69	Les données se rapporte à l'indice national.
70	Excluding fresh fish.	70	Non compris le poisson frais.
71	Honiara	71	Honiara
72	Colombo	72	Colombo
73	Index base: 2007=100.	73	Indices base: 2007=100.
74	Average for 10 months excluding data for May and June.	74	Moyenne sur 10 mois à l'exclusion des données de mai et juin.
75	For Lome only.	75	Pour Lome seulement.
76	Index base: 1 July 2009 - 30 June 2010=100.	76	Indices base: 1 juillet 2009 - 30 juin 2010=100.
77	For Tanganyika only.	77	Pour Tanganyika uniquement.
78	Index base: December 2015=100.	78	Indices base: 2015 décembre=100.
79	Figures in thousands.	79	Données en milliers.
80	Figures in millions.	80	Chiffres en millions.

Total imports, exports and balance of trade
Imports CIF, exports FOB and balance: millions of US dollars

Total des importations, des exportations et balance commerciale
Importations CAF, exportations FAB et balance: en millions de dollars É.-U.

Region, country or area &	Sys.ᵗ	1995	2005	2010	2015	2017	2018	2019	Région, pays ou zone &
Total, all countries or areas									**Total, tous pays ou zones**
Imports		5 099 057	10 577 013	15 275 115	16 465 359	17 732 818	19 497 788	18 964 357	Importations
Exports		5 050 238	10 373 445	15 102 218	16 361 680	17 482 322	19 132 377	18 723 356	Exportations
Balance		-48 819	-203 568	-172 897	-103 679	-250 496	-365 411	-241 001	Balance
Africa									**Afrique**
Imports		114 352	246 228	468 435	548 215	503 716	558 798	578 284	Importations
Exports		103 460	306 656	496 594	403 742	399 178	449 136	457 061	Exportations
Balance		-10 892	60 428	28 159	-144 473	-104 538	-109 662	-121 223	Balance
Northern Africa									**Afrique septentrionale**
Imports		45 062	87 571	181 147	205 559	194 494	217 461	212 061	Importations
Exports		33 043	114 104	165 544	108 845	107 963	119 903	114 636	Exportations
Balance		-12 019	26 533	-15 603	-96 714	-86 531	-97 558	-97 425	Balance
Sub-Saharan Africa									**Afrique subsaharienne**
Imports		69 290	158 657	287 288	342 656	309 222	341 337	366 222	Importations
Exports		70 417	192 552	331 050	294 897	291 214	329 233	342 425	Exportations
Balance		1 127	33 895	43 762	-47 759	-18 007	-12 104	-23 798	Balance
Eastern Africa									**Afrique orientale**
Imports		17 980	31 243	62 688	94 004	86 779	94 643	90 934	Importations
Exports		9 499	16 297	31 652	40 728	41 773	43 433	42 498	Exportations
Balance		-8 481	-14 945	-31 036	-53 276	-45 006	-51 210	-48 436	Balance
Middle Africa									**Afrique centrale**
Imports		5 412	18 680	43 623	56 177	39 968	37 499	39 026	Importations
Exports		10 954	48 958	90 717	70 050	60 249	66 875	67 001	Exportations
Balance		5 542	30 278	47 094	13 873	20 281	29 376	27 975	Balance
Southern Africa									**Afrique australe**
Imports		26 745	63 786	97 723	104 173	98 871	110 164	105 685	Importations
Exports		28 214	56 076	95 232	93 648	101 888	109 637	103 238	Exportations
Balance		1 470	-7 711	-2 491	-10 525	3 017	-526	-2 447	Balance
Western Africa									**Afrique occidentale**
Imports		19 153	44 948	83 254	88 302	83 604	99 032	130 577	Importations
Exports		21 750	71 221	113 448	90 470	87 305	109 288	129 687	Exportations
Balance		2 597	26 273	30 194	2 168	3 701	10 256	-889	Balance
Americas									**Amériques**
Imports		1 178 848	2 557 150	3 230 657	3 739 612	3 819 999	4 154 892	4 076 214	Importations
Exports		997 709	1 835 325	2 551 125	2 827 588	2 935 423	3 155 227	3 134 354	Exportations
Balance		-181 139	-721 825	-679 532	-912 024	-884 575	-999 665	-941 860	Balance
Northern America									**Amérique septentrionale**
Imports		936 343	2 048 668	2 362 932	2 736 654	2 843 151	3 076 681	3 026 538	Importations
Exports		774 525	1 265 374	1 665 220	1 911 491	1 967 271	2 117 280	2 092 331	Exportations
Balance		-161 818	-783 295	-697 713	-825 163	-875 880	-959 401	-934 208	Balance
Latin America & the Caribbean									**Amérique latine et Caraïbes**
Imports		242 505	508 481	867 725	1 002 958	976 848	1 078 211	1 049 676	Importations
Exports		223 184	569 951	885 906	916 097	968 152	1 037 947	1 042 023	Exportations
Balance		-19 321	61 470	18 181	-86 861	-8 696	-40 264	-7 653	Balance
Caribbean									**Caraïbes**
Imports		20 945	36 923	53 245	58 007	55 920	56 330	51 914	Importations
Exports		8 346	21 331	24 874	26 475	23 117	25 201	27 958	Exportations
Balance		-12 598	-15 592	-28 371	-31 533	-32 803	-31 128	-23 956	Balance
Central America									**Amérique centrale**
Imports		87 084	259 847	366 171	464 286	492 975	543 175	547 594	Importations
Exports		87 067	233 506	336 529	426 846	459 253	489 275	510 072	Exportations
Balance		-17	-26 340	-29 642	-37 441	-33 722	-53 900	-37 523	Balance
South America									**Amérique du Sud**
Imports		134 476	211 711	448 308	480 665	427 953	478 706	450 167	Importations
Exports		127 771	315 113	524 502	462 776	485 782	523 471	503 993	Exportations
Balance		-6 706	103 402	76 194	-17 888	57 829	44 764	53 826	Balance
Asia									**Asie**
Imports		1 500 432	3 172 210	5 459 724	6 214 435	6 735 575	7 467 017	7 174 349	Importations
Exports		1 557 385	3 569 857	5 896 164	6 831 778	7 241 499	7 921 669	7 707 847	Exportations
Balance		56 953	397 647	436 440	617 343	505 923	454 652	533 498	Balance
Central Asia									**Asie centrale**
Imports		9 375	25 644	40 985	53 082	51 575	61 759	71 667	Importations
Exports		10 782	36 890	74 961	64 827	65 351	79 323	81 196	Exportations
Balance		1 407	11 246	33 976	11 746	13 776	17 564	9 529	Balance

19

Total imports, exports and balance of trade *(continued)*
Imports CIF, exports FOB and balance: millions of US dollars

Total des importations, des exportations et balance commerciale *(suite)*
Importations CAF, exportations FAB et balance: en millions de dollars É.-U.

Region, country or area &	Sys.[1]	1995	2005	2010	2015	2017	2018	2019	Région, pays ou zone &
Eastern Asia									**Asie orientale**
Imports		804 190	1 744 378	2 967 424	3 317 929	3 599 760	4 066 746	3 894 237	Importations
Exports		894 718	1 937 757	3 219 271	3 942 643	4 093 595	4 415 573	4 284 884	Exportations
Balance		90 528	193 379	251 847	624 714	493 836	348 827	390 648	Balance
South-eastern Asia									**Asie du Sud-Est**
Imports		353 943	584 010	953 410	1 100 730	1 258 343	1 425 052	1 373 529	Importations
Exports		320 454	655 071	1 054 178	1 172 850	1 315 914	1 444 759	1 409 910	Exportations
Balance		-33 489	71 061	100 767	72 119	57 571	19 707	36 381	Balance
Southern Asia									**Asie méridionale**
Imports		74 082	229 179	497 340	560 507	642 975	710 552	650 524	Importations
Exports		65 912	193 182	354 892	394 653	467 407	470 274	413 627	Exportations
Balance		-8 171	-35 997	-142 448	-165 854	-175 568	-240 278	-236 897	Balance
Western Asia									**Asie occidentale**
Imports		155 335	407 407	749 249	953 678	923 313	916 713	898 246	Importations
Exports		154 177	557 564	919 156	976 785	981 568	1 175 996	1 165 271	Exportations
Balance		-1 159	150 158	169 907	23 107	58 254	259 283	267 025	Balance
Europe									**Europe**
Imports		2 228 669	4 439 990	5 868 691	5 711 583	6 388 329	7 019 435	6 852 851	Importations
Exports		2 320 042	4 527 059	5 904 975	6 063 469	6 623 146	7 297 159	7 100 768	Exportations
Balance		91 373	87 068	36 284	351 886	234 817	277 724	247 918	Balance
Eastern Europe									**Europe orientale**
Imports		161 835	490 657	868 649	847 926	1 035 150	1 140 326	1 120 392	Importations
Exports		176 871	594 285	994 605	1 023 967	1 156 912	1 330 866	1 286 023	Exportations
Balance		15 036	103 628	125 955	176 042	121 762	190 540	165 631	Balance
Northern Europe									**Europe septentrionale**
Imports		470 870	937 990	1 122 240	1 132 508	1 204 117	1 300 473	1 289 321	Importations
Exports		494 552	913 599	1 045 978	1 045 828	1 067 727	1 203 746	1 157 774	Exportations
Balance		23 682	-24 391	-76 262	-86 680	-136 390	-96 727	-131 546	Balance
Southern Europe									**Europe méridionale**
Imports		400 631	861 881	1 039 442	925 085	1 042 232	1 185 212	1 134 330	Importations
Exports		372 435	660 817	830 354	886 303	997 212	1 104 363	1 070 693	Exportations
Balance		-28 196	-201 064	-209 088	-38 782	-45 021	-80 849	-63 637	Balance
Western Europe									**Europe occidentale**
Imports		1 195 333	2 149 462	2 838 360	2 806 064	3 106 829	3 393 424	3 308 808	Importations
Exports		1 276 184	2 358 357	3 034 038	3 107 370	3 401 295	3 658 184	3 586 278	Exportations
Balance		80 851	208 895	195 679	301 306	294 467	264 759	277 470	Balance
Oceania									**Océanie**
Imports		76 756	161 435	247 608	251 514	285 199	297 646	282 660	Importations
Exports		71 642	134 548	253 360	235 103	283 076	309 186	323 326	Exportations
Balance		-5 114	-26 888	5 752	-16 410	-2 123	11 541	40 666	Balance
Australia and New Zealand									**Australie et Nouvelle-Zélande**
Imports		71 338	151 453	232 319	236 642	268 914	279 271	263 753	Importations
Exports		66 374	127 740	243 502	222 149	268 225	292 597	305 917	Exportations
Balance		-4 965	-23 714	11 183	-14 493	-689	13 326	42 164	Balance
Melanesia									**Mélanésie**
Imports		3 432	5 397	9 665	7 968	8 476	9 367	9 368	Importations
Exports		4 039	5 199	8 112	10 998	12 774	14 466	15 271	Exportations
Balance		607	-197	-1 553	3 030	4 298	5 099	5 903	Balance
Micronesia									**Micronésie**
Imports		897	2 379	3 292	4 627	5 371	5 924	6 536	Importations
Exports		1 028	1 295	1 508	1 737	1 838	1 893	1 949	Exportations
Balance		131	-1 084	-1 783	-2 891	-3 533	-4 031	-4 587	Balance
Polynesia									**Polynésie**
Imports		1 089	2 206	2 333	2 277	2 439	3 084	3 004	Importations
Exports		201	314	238	219	240	230	189	Exportations
Balance		-887	-1 893	-2 095	-2 058	-2 199	-2 853	-2 815	Balance
Afghanistan									**Afghanistan**
Imports	G	...	...	5 154	7 723	* 7 384	7 407	* 8 370	Importations
Exports	G	...	...	388	571	* 700	885	* 1 038	Exportations
Balance	G	...	...	-4 766	-7 151	* -6 684	-6 522	* -7 332	Balance
Albania [1]									**Albanie** [1]
Imports	G	* 713	2 614	4 603	4 320	5 294	5 941	* 5 908	Importations
Exports	G	* 202	658	1 550	1 930	2 301	2 876	* 2 720	Exportations
Balance	G	* -511	-1 956	-3 053	-2 391	-2 993	-3 065	* -3 189	Balance

19

Total imports, exports and balance of trade *(continued)*
Imports CIF, exports FOB and balance: millions of US dollars

Total des importations, des exportations et balance commerciale *(suite)*
Importations CAF, exportations FAB et balance: en millions de dollars É.-U.

Region, country or area &	Sys.[1]	1995	2005	2010	2015	2017	2018	2019	Région, pays ou zone &
Algeria									**Algérie**
Imports	S	10 782	20 357	41 000	51 803	46 053	* 46 934	* 45 140	Importations
Exports	S	9 357	46 002	57 051	34 796	35 191	* 40 711	* 34 571	Exportations
Balance	S	-1 426	25 645	16 051	-17 007	-10 862	* -6 224	* -10 569	Balance
Andorra									**Andorre**
Imports	S	1 025	* 1 796	1 541	1 294	1 478	1 609	* 1 538	Importations
Exports	S	48	143	92	90	118	129	* 124	Exportations
Balance	S	-978	* -1 653	-1 448	-1 204	-1 360	-1 480	* -1 414	Balance
Angola									**Angola**
Imports	S	* 1 466	* 8 321	18 143	21 549	15 462	16 036	* 21 340	Importations
Exports	S	* 3 592	* 23 835	52 612	33 925	34 905	42 097	* 50 822	Exportations
Balance	S	* 2 126	* 15 514	34 469	12 376	19 443	26 060	* 29 482	Balance
Anguilla									**Anguilla**
Imports	S	* 53	* 133	* 149	* 204	* 183	* 292	* 283	Importations
Exports	S	* 1	* 7	* 12	* 11	* 3	* 5	* 12	Exportations
Balance	S	* -52	* -126	* -137	* -193	* -180	* -287	* -270	Balance
Antigua and Barbuda									**Antigua-et-Barbuda**
Imports	G	* 344	525	501	465	630	569	568	Importations
Exports	G	* 53	121	35	26	62	26	37	Exportations
Balance	G	* -291	-405	-466	-439	-567	-543	-531	Balance
Argentina									**Argentine**
Imports	S	20 122	28 689	56 792	60 203	66 899	65 441	49 125	Importations
Exports	S	20 963	40 106	68 174	56 784	58 384	61 558	65 114	Exportations
Balance	S	841	11 418	11 382	-3 419	-8 515	-3 883	15 989	Balance
Armenia									**Arménie**
Imports	S	* 674	1 692	3 782	3 257	3 893	4 850	5 053	Importations
Exports	S	* 271	937	1 011	1 483	2 145	2 383	2 612	Exportations
Balance	S	* -403	-755	-2 770	-1 774	-1 748	-2 467	-2 441	Balance
Aruba									**Aruba**
Imports	S	* 566	1 030	1 071	1 165	1 195	1 258	* 1 353	Importations
Exports	S	* 15	106	125	80	89	70	* 84	Exportations
Balance	S	* -551	-924	-947	-1 085	-1 106	-1 188	* -1 270	Balance
Australia [2]									**Australie** [2]
Imports	G	* 57 381	125 221	201 703	200 114	228 785	235 535	221 481	Importations
Exports	G	* 52 628	106 011	212 109	187 792	230 175	252 758	266 377	Exportations
Balance	G	* -4 752	-19 210	10 405	-12 322	1 390	17 223	44 896	Balance
Austria									**Autriche**
Imports	S	* 66 331	119 950	150 593	147 928	166 475	184 195	176 596	Importations
Exports	S	* 53 460	117 722	144 882	145 276	159 971	176 992	171 532	Exportations
Balance	S	* -12 871	-2 228	-5 711	-2 652	-6 505	-7 203	-5 064	Balance
Azerbaijan									**Azerbaïdjan**
Imports	G	* 666	4 211	6 597	9 214	8 768	11 460	13 649	Importations
Exports	G	* 637	4 347	21 278	12 646	15 306	19 489	19 636	Exportations
Balance	G	* -30	136	14 682	3 432	6 538	8 029	5 986	Balance
Bahamas									**Bahamas**
Imports	G	* 1 243	2 567	2 862	3 161	* 3 428	* 3 743	* 4 087	Importations
Exports	G	* 176	271	620	443	* 469	* 482	* 494	Exportations
Balance	G	* -1 067	-2 296	-2 242	-2 719	* -2 959	* -3 262	* -3 593	Balance
Bahrain									**Bahreïn**
Imports	G	3 679	9 339	16 002	16 390	17 391	20 598	* 18 680	Importations
Exports	G	3 475	10 239	16 059	13 882	12 485	14 348	* 14 355	Exportations
Balance	G	-204	899	58	-2 508	-4 906	-6 250	* -4 325	Balance
Bangladesh									**Bangladesh**
Imports	G	5 438	12 631	30 504	48 059	* 47 743	* 56 216	* 66 060	Importations
Exports	G	3 407	9 332	19 231	31 734	* 31 367	* 32 778	* 34 186	Exportations
Balance	G	-2 031	-3 299	-11 273	-16 325	* -16 376	* -23 438	* -31 874	Balance
Barbados									**Barbade**
Imports	G	766	1 672	1 196	1 618	1 600	1 600	* 1 618	Importations
Exports	G	238	361	314	483	485	458	* 462	Exportations
Balance	G	-528	-1 311	-883	-1 135	-1 114	-1 142	* -1 157	Balance
Belarus									**Bélarus**
Imports	G	* 5 382	16 699	34 884	30 291	34 235	38 409	* 39 317	Importations
Exports	G	* 4 623	15 977	25 283	26 660	29 240	33 726	* 32 764	Exportations
Balance	G	* -759	-722	-9 601	-3 631	-4 995	-4 683	* -6 553	Balance

19

Total imports, exports and balance of trade *(continued)*
Imports CIF, exports FOB and balance: millions of US dollars

Total des importations, des exportations et balance commerciale *(suite)*
Importations CAF, exportations FAB et balance: en millions de dollars É.-U.

Region, country or area &	Sys.[1]	1995	2005	2010	2015	2017	2018	2019	Région, pays ou zone &
Belgium									**Belgique**
Imports	S	...	319 085	391 256	371 025	409 025	454 714	426 489	Importations
Exports	S	...	335 692	407 596	397 739	430 092	468 643	445 214	Exportations
Balance	S	...	16 606	16 340	26 714	21 068	13 929	18 725	Balance
Belize									**Belize**
Imports	G	259	439	700	996	913	958	986	Importations
Exports	G	162	208	282	314	278	241	245	Exportations
Balance	G	-97	-231	-418	-682	-636	-717	-741	Balance
Benin									**Bénin**
Imports	S	* 745	899	2 134	2 475	3 060	3 278	* 3 967	Importations
Exports	S	* 415	288	534	626	726	952	* 1 706	Exportations
Balance	S	* -329	-611	-1 600	-1 849	-2 334	-2 326	* -2 261	Balance
Bermuda									**Bermudes**
Imports	G	633	988	970	929	1 078	1 070	* 1 204	Importations
Exports	G	63	* 49	* 15	9	12	23	* 23	Exportations
Balance	G	-570	-939	-955	-920	-1 066	-1 047	* -1 181	Balance
Bhutan									**Bhoutan**
Imports	G	* 113	387	854	* 1 062	* 1 030	* 1 052	* 1 049	Importations
Exports	G	* 103	258	413	* 549	* 573	* 622	* 659	Exportations
Balance	G	* -9	-129	-440	* -512	* -457	* -430	* -390	Balance
Bolivia (Plurin. State of)									**Bolivie (État plurin. de)**
Imports	G	1 396	2 343	5 604	9 843	9 302	10 045	* 9 783	Importations
Exports	G	1 181	2 797	7 051	8 923	8 338	9 065	* 8 988	Exportations
Balance	G	-215	454	1 448	-920	-964	-980	* -795	Balance
Bosnia and Herzegovina									**Bosnie-Herzégovine**
Imports	S	* 1 068	7 054	9 223	8 994	10 474	11 630	11 159	Importations
Exports	S	* 152	2 388	4 803	5 099	6 368	7 182	6 578	Exportations
Balance	S	* -917	-4 665	-4 420	-3 895	-4 106	-4 447	-4 581	Balance
Botswana									**Botswana**
Imports	G	...	3 162	5 657	8 048	5 329	5 921	6 559	Importations
Exports	G	...	4 431	4 693	6 330	5 955	6 122	5 238	Exportations
Balance	G	...	1 268	-964	-1 718	625	201	-1 320	Balance
Brazil [2]									**Brésil** [2]
Imports	G	53 734	73 600	181 768	171 446	150 749	181 230	177 348	Importations
Exports	G	46 505	118 529	201 915	191 127	217 739	239 888	225 383	Exportations
Balance	G	-7 229	44 928	20 147	19 681	66 990	58 657	48 036	Balance
British Virgin Islands									**Îles Vierges britanniques**
Imports	G	* 122	* 227	* 313	* 430	* 486	* 520	* 538	Importations
Exports	G	* 11	* ~0	* ~0	* ~0	* ~0	* 0	* 0	Exportations
Balance	G	* -110	* -226	* -313	* -430	* -486	* -520	* -538	Balance
Brunei Darussalam									**Brunéi Darussalam**
Imports	S	2 078	* 1 447	2 539	3 229	3 085	4 164	5 103	Importations
Exports	S	2 379	* 6 242	8 908	6 353	5 571	6 574	7 039	Exportations
Balance	S	301	* 4 794	6 369	3 124	2 486	2 410	1 936	Balance
Bulgaria									**Bulgarie**
Imports	S	5 469	18 162	25 360	29 265	34 264	37 928	* 37 902	Importations
Exports	S	5 220	11 739	20 608	25 779	31 588	33 787	* 33 638	Exportations
Balance	S	-249	-6 423	-4 752	-3 486	-2 675	-4 141	* -4 264	Balance
Burkina Faso									**Burkina Faso**
Imports	G	484	1 161	2 048	2 980	3 717	4 296	* 5 193	Importations
Exports	G	171	332	1 288	2 177	2 790	3 283	* 2 927	Exportations
Balance	G	-313	-828	-760	-802	-927	-1 013	* -2 266	Balance
Burundi									**Burundi**
Imports	S	270	258	404	561	783	794	* 792	Importations
Exports	S	179	114	118	114	149	169	* 155	Exportations
Balance	S	-92	-144	-286	-447	-634	-624	* -637	Balance
Cabo Verde									**Cabo Verde**
Imports	G	* 252	438	731	603	794	815	* 941	Importations
Exports	G	* 9	89	220	67	50	75	* 76	Exportations
Balance	G	* -243	-349	-511	-537	-744	-739	* -865	Balance
Cambodia									**Cambodge**
Imports	S	* 217	2 552	4 903	10 669	14 283	17 489	* 21 413	Importations
Exports	S	* 76	3 019	5 590	8 542	11 278	12 700	* 14 276	Exportations
Balance	S	* -142	467	688	-2 126	-3 005	-4 789	* -7 138	Balance

Total des importations, des exportations et balance commerciale *(suite)*
Importations CAF, exportations FAB et balance: en millions de dollars É.-U.

Region, country or area &	Sys.ᵗ	1995	2005	2010	2015	2017	2018	2019	Région, pays ou zone &
Cameroon									**Cameroun**
Imports	S	1 079	2 800	5 133	6 037	5 184	* 4 450	* 3 262	Importations
Exports	S	1 539	2 849	3 878	4 053	3 264	* 2 649	* 1 750	Exportations
Balance	S	460	49	-1 255	-1 984	-1 919	* -1 801	* -1 512	Balance
Canada ²									**Canada ²**
Imports	G	164 371	314 444	392 109	419 375	433 045	459 948	453 234	Importations
Exports	G	191 118	360 552	386 580	408 697	420 074	450 382	446 148	Exportations
Balance	G	26 747	46 108	-5 529	-10 677	-12 971	-9 565	-7 085	Balance
Cayman Islands									**Îles Caïmanes**
Imports	G	* 390	* 1 191	* 828	915	* 1 051	* 1 270	* 1 393	Importations
Exports	G	* 4	* 52	* 24	* 65	* 39	* 39	* 39	Exportations
Balance	G	* -386	* -1 138	* -804	-851	* -1 013	* -1 232	* -1 354	Balance
Central African Republic									**République centrafricaine**
Imports	S	265	185	210	457	419	* 359	* 89	Importations
Exports	S	120	111	90	97	197	* 231	* 324	Exportations
Balance	S	-146	-75	-120	-360	-222	* -128	* 236	Balance
Chad									**Tchad**
Imports	S	* 214	* 953	* 2 507	* 2 200	* 845	* 523	* 319	Importations
Exports	S	* 243	* 3 095	* 3 410	* 2 900	* 1 344	* 915	* 613	Exportations
Balance	S	* 28	* 2 142	* 904	* 700	* 500	* 392	* 294	Balance
Chile									**Chili**
Imports	S	14 903	32 927	59 007	62 387	65 257	74 187	69 591	Importations
Exports	S	15 901	41 973	71 106	62 033	68 858	75 482	69 681	Exportations
Balance	S	998	9 046	12 099	-354	3 601	1 294	90	Balance
China ³									**Chine ³**
Imports	S	* 131 353	659 953	1 396 000	1 679 560	1 843 790	2 134 980	* 2 070 150	Importations
Exports	S	148 616	761 953	1 577 760	2 273 470	2 263 370	2 494 230	* 2 491 820	Exportations
Balance	S	* 17 263	102 001	181 762	593 904	419 578	359 248	* 421 672	Balance
China, Hong Kong SAR									**Chine, RAS de Hong Kong**
Imports	G	196 072	300 160	441 369	559 306	589 317	627 327	578 590	Importations
Exports	G	173 871	292 119	400 692	510 553	549 861	569 106	535 711	Exportations
Balance	G	-22 201	-8 042	-40 677	-48 753	-39 456	-58 221	-42 879	Balance
China, Macao SAR									**Chine, RAS de Macao**
Imports	G	2 025	4 514	5 629	10 603	* 9 449	12 069	12 024	Importations
Exports	G	2 025	2 474	870	1 339	* 1 406	1 161	1 024	Exportations
Balance	G	-1	-2 040	-4 760	-9 264	* -8 043	-10 908	-11 000	Balance
Colombia									**Colombie**
Imports	G	13 883	21 204	40 683	54 036	46 050	51 231	52 696	Importations
Exports	G	10 201	21 190	39 820	35 691	37 766	41 832	39 489	Exportations
Balance	G	-3 682	-14	-863	-18 345	-8 284	-9 399	-13 207	Balance
Comoros									**Comores**
Imports	S	62	85	181	173	209	230	201	Importations
Exports	S	11	4	14	15	38	46	49	Exportations
Balance	S	-51	-81	-167	-158	-171	-183	-152	Balance
Congo									**Congo**
Imports	S	556	* 1 342	4 369	10 550	4 560	3 486	2 242	Importations
Exports	S	1 090	* 4 744	6 918	8 623	8 252	11 155	5 576	Exportations
Balance	S	534	* 3 402	2 548	-1 927	3 692	7 669	3 334	Balance
Cook Islands									**Îles Cook**
Imports	G	* 49	81	91	* 109	* 130	* 134	* 123	Importations
Exports	G	* 5	5	5	* 14	* 21	* 17	* 6	Exportations
Balance	G	* -44	-76	-85	* -95	* -109	* -117	* -117	Balance
Costa Rica									**Costa Rica**
Imports	S	3 205	9 173	13 920	15 504	16 352	16 563	* 16 106	Importations
Exports	S	2 702	7 151	9 045	9 578	11 297	11 252	* 11 449	Exportations
Balance	S	-504	-2 023	-4 875	-5 926	-5 056	-5 311	* -4 656	Balance
Côte d'Ivoire									**Côte d'Ivoire**
Imports	S	2 472	5 865	7 849	10 406	9 614	10 970	10 483	Importations
Exports	S	* 3 736	7 248	10 284	12 560	12 446	11 821	12 718	Exportations
Balance	S	1 264	1 383	2 434	2 154	2 832	851	2 235	Balance
Croatia									**Croatie**
Imports	G	7 509	18 560	20 067	20 580	24 513	28 113	28 004	Importations
Exports	G	4 633	8 773	11 811	12 844	15 732	17 210	17 063	Exportations
Balance	G	-2 877	-9 788	-8 256	-7 737	-8 780	-10 903	-10 941	Balance

19 Total imports, exports and balance of trade *(continued)*
Imports CIF, exports FOB and balance: millions of US dollars

Total des importations, des exportations et balance commerciale *(suite)*
Importations CAF, exportations FAB et balance: en millions de dollars É.-U.

Region, country or area &	Sys.[1]	1995	2005	2010	2015	2017	2018	2019	Région, pays ou zone &
Cuba									**Cuba**
Imports	S	* 2 874	8 084	* 11 488	* 12 638	* 9 734	* 8 543	* 7 498	Importations
Exports	S	* 1 491	2 319	* 4 914	* 3 618	* 1 731	* 1 197	* 828	Exportations
Balance	S	* -1 384	-5 766	* -6 574	* -9 020	* -8 004	* -7 346	* -6 670	Balance
Cyprus									**Chypre**
Imports	G	3 694	6 382	8 645	7 133	9 308	10 813	9 219	Importations
Exports	G	1 231	1 546	1 506	3 367	3 360	5 065	3 528	Exportations
Balance	G	-2 463	-4 836	-7 138	-3 766	-5 948	-5 747	-5 691	Balance
Czechia									**Tchéquie**
Imports	S	25 303	76 527	125 691	140 716	162 899	184 924	178 552	Importations
Exports	S	21 686	78 209	132 141	157 194	182 231	202 522	198 852	Exportations
Balance	S	-3 618	1 681	6 450	16 478	19 332	17 598	20 300	Balance
Dem. People's Rep. Korea									**Rép. pop. dém. de Corée**
Imports	G	* 3 122	* 1 466	* 1 957	* 2 604	* 2 920	* 3 092	* 3 273	Importations
Exports	G	* 1 739	* 787	* 882	* 987	* 1 033	* 1 056	* 1 080	Exportations
Balance	G	* -1 382	* -679	* -1 075	* -1 617	* -1 887	* -2 036	* -2 194	Balance
Dem. Rep. of the Congo									**Rép. dém. du Congo**
Imports	S	* 869	* 2 268	* 4 500	* 6 200	* 5 655	* 5 401	* 5 159	Importations
Exports	S	* 1 562	* 2 190	* 5 300	* 5 800	* 4 491	* 3 951	* 3 477	Exportations
Balance	S	* 693	* -78	* 800	* -400	* -1 165	* -1 450	* -1 682	Balance
Denmark									**Danemark**
Imports	S	43 142	72 716	82 724	85 327	92 118	101 676	97 196	Importations
Exports	S	48 789	82 278	96 217	94 619	101 434	108 564	109 942	Exportations
Balance	S	5 648	9 562	13 492	9 291	9 317	6 889	12 746	Balance
Djibouti									**Djibouti**
Imports	G	* 176	* 277	* 603	* 890	* 1 094	* 1 212	* 1 344	Importations
Exports	G	* 13	* 39	* 470	* 132	* 137	* 140	* 143	Exportations
Balance	G	* -163	* -238	* -133	* -758	* -956	* -1 072	* -1 201	Balance
Dominica									**Dominique**
Imports	S	117	165	225	* 214	* 198	* 302	* 304	Importations
Exports	S	45	42	34	* 30	* 21	* 10	* 18	Exportations
Balance	S	-72	-124	-190	* -184	* -177	* -292	* -286	Balance
Dominican Republic [2]									**République dominicaine [2]**
Imports	G	* 3 155	6 804	15 138	17 348	19 524	* 22 291	* 20 599	Importations
Exports	G	* 872	6 183	4 767	8 384	8 856	* 9 544	* 11 117	Exportations
Balance	G	* -2 283	-621	-10 371	-8 964	-10 669	* -12 747	* -9 482	Balance
Ecuador									**Équateur**
Imports	G	4 195	9 609	20 591	21 387	19 844	23 020	* 22 425	Importations
Exports	G	4 361	9 869	17 490	18 331	19 092	21 606	* 22 245	Exportations
Balance	G	166	261	-3 101	-3 057	-752	-1 414	* -180	Balance
Egypt [4]									**Égypte [4]**
Imports	G	11 739	19 812	53 003	73 975	66 764	82 445	78 658	Importations
Exports	G	3 444	10 646	26 332	21 852	26 434	29 483	30 633	Exportations
Balance	G	-8 295	-9 166	-26 672	-52 123	-40 330	-52 961	-48 025	Balance
El Salvador									**El Salvador**
Imports	S	2 628	6 809	8 416	10 293	10 572	11 830	12 018	Importations
Exports	S	985	3 436	4 499	5 509	5 760	5 905	5 943	Exportations
Balance	S	-1 642	-3 373	-3 917	-4 784	-4 811	-5 925	-6 074	Balance
Equatorial Guinea									**Guinée équatoriale**
Imports	G	* 50	* 1 309	* 5 679	* 6 010	* 4 890	* 4 402	* 3 902	Importations
Exports	G	* 86	* 7 062	* 9 964	* 9 570	* 6 200	* 4 980	* 3 939	Exportations
Balance	G	* 36	* 5 753	* 4 285	* 3 560	* 1 310	* 578	* 37	Balance
Eritrea									**Érythrée**
Imports	G	* 432	* 503	* 1 187	* 2 801	* 4 027	* 4 781	* 5 677	Importations
Exports	G	* 73	* 11	* 13	* 15	* 17	* 17	* 18	Exportations
Balance	G	* -359	* -493	* -1 175	* -2 786	* -4 011	* -4 764	* -5 659	Balance
Estonia [5]									**Estonie [5]**
Imports	S	2 546	11 018	13 197	15 732	17 373	19 827	18 659	Importations
Exports	S	1 840	8 247	12 811	13 908	15 388	17 854	16 811	Exportations
Balance	S	-706	-2 770	-385	-1 824	-1 985	-1 973	-1 848	Balance
Eswatini									**Eswatini**
Imports	G	...	1 656	* 1 710	1 508	1 612	1 858	1 832	Importations
Exports	G	...	1 278	* 1 557	1 820	1 801	1 842	2 002	Exportations
Balance	G	...	-378	* -153	312	189	-15	169	Balance

19

Total imports, exports and balance of trade *(continued)*
Imports CIF, exports FOB and balance: millions of US dollars

Total des importations, des exportations et balance commerciale *(suite)*
Importations CAF, exportations FAB et balance: en millions de dollars É.-U.

Region, country or area &	Sys.¹	1995	2005	2010	2015	2017	2018	2019	Région, pays ou zone &
Ethiopia									**Éthiopie**
Imports	G	1 141	4 095	8 602	17 686	15 759	14 986	* 9 675	Importations
Exports	G	422	926	2 330	2 024	2 306	1 549	* 938	Exportations
Balance	G	-719	-3 169	-6 272	-15 662	-13 453	-13 437	* -8 737	Balance
Falkland Islands (Malvinas)									**Îles Falkland (Malvinas)**
Imports	G	* 27	* 8	* 50	* 21	* 13	* 10	* 8	Importations
Exports	G	* 4	* 11	* 9	* 4	* 3	* 2	* 2	Exportations
Balance	G	* -23	* 2	* -41	* -17	* -10	* -8	* -6	Balance
Faroe Islands									**Îles Féroé**
Imports	G	* 314	747	* 780	* 911	* 1 066	* 1 161	* 1 264	Importations
Exports	G	* 362	602	* 839	* 1 024	* 1 405	* 1 655	* 1 950	Exportations
Balance	G	* 48	-145	* 59	* 113	* 338	* 494	* 686	Balance
Fiji									**Fidji**
Imports	G	* 891	1 607	1 808	2 081	2 420	2 720	* 2 650	Importations
Exports	G	* 619	702	841	895	956	1 041	* 1 137	Exportations
Balance	G	* -273	-906	-967	-1 186	-1 464	-1 679	* -1 513	Balance
Finland									**Finlande**
Imports	G	29 520	58 473	68 767	60 174	70 100	78 352	* 73 335	Importations
Exports	G	40 409	65 238	70 117	59 682	67 281	75 258	* 72 802	Exportations
Balance	G	10 889	6 766	1 349	-492	-2 820	-3 094	* -533	Balance
France									**France**
Imports	S	273 387	475 857	599 172	563 398	613 133	659 375	651 164	Importations
Exports	S	277 079	434 354	511 651	493 941	523 385	568 536	569 757	Exportations
Balance	S	3 692	-41 503	-87 520	-69 457	-89 748	-90 839	-81 407	Balance
French Guiana									**Guyane française**
Imports	S	783	...	...	...	...	...	...	Importations
Exports	S	158	...	...	...	...	...	...	Exportations
Balance	S	-625	...	...	...	...	...	...	Balance
French Polynesia									**Polynésie française**
Imports	S	* 848	1 702	1 726	1 527	* 1 638	* 2 236	* 2 102	Importations
Exports	S	* 173	210	153	130	* 153	* 148	* 133	Exportations
Balance	S	* -675	-1 491	-1 573	-1 397	* -1 485	* -2 089	* -1 969	Balance
Gabon									**Gabon**
Imports	S	* 884	1 451	* 2 969	* 3 033	* 2 806	* 2 693	* 2 548	Importations
Exports	S	* 2 718	5 068	* 8 539	* 5 074	* 1 585	* 884	* 486	Exportations
Balance	S	* 1 834	3 617	* 5 570	* 2 040	* -1 221	* -1 809	* -2 062	Balance
Gambia ⁶									**Gambie** ⁶
Imports	G	215	260	284	402	549	601	494	Importations
Exports	G	19	7	68	90	22	9	25	Exportations
Balance	G	-196	-252	-215	-312	-527	-592	-469	Balance
Georgia									**Géorgie**
Imports	G	396	2 490	5 236	7 281	7 943	9 136	9 098	Importations
Exports	G	152	865	1 677	2 205	2 736	3 356	3 764	Exportations
Balance	G	-245	-1 624	-3 558	-5 077	-5 208	-5 781	-5 333	Balance
Germany									**Allemagne**
Imports	S	464 145	779 819	1 060 670	1 057 540	1 167 750	1 292 730	1 240 700	Importations
Exports	S	518 224	977 132	1 267 740	1 328 500	1 446 640	1 562 420	1 493 090	Exportations
Balance	S	54 079	197 313	207 071	270 964	278 889	269 693	252 398	Balance
Ghana ⁷									**Ghana** ⁷
Imports	G	* 1 897	4 878	8 057	14 687	12 718	11 880	10 440	Importations
Exports	G	* 1 755	3 060	5 233	13 756	14 359	17 100	16 768	Exportations
Balance	G	* -142	-1 819	-2 824	-932	1 640	5 219	6 328	Balance
Gibraltar									**Gibraltar**
Imports		* 408	* 501	* 627	* 737	* 969	* 1 101	* 1 052	Importations
Exports		* 114	* 195	* 259	* 295	* 368	* 416	* 436	Exportations
Balance		* -294	* -306	* -368	* -442	* -602	* -685	* -615	Balance
Greece									**Grèce**
Imports	S	25 805	54 894	66 453	47 264	55 301	65 141	62 198	Importations
Exports	S	* 10 896	17 434	27 586	28 289	32 155	39 491	37 886	Exportations
Balance	S	-14 909	-37 459	-38 867	-18 975	-23 146	-25 651	-24 313	Balance
Greenland									**Groenland**
Imports	G	421	700	847	667	760	829	* 738	Importations
Exports	G	364	402	389	406	596	641	* 771	Exportations
Balance	G	-57	-297	-458	-261	-164	-188	* 32	Balance

Total imports, exports and balance of trade *(continued)*
Imports CIF, exports FOB and balance: millions of US dollars

Total des importations, des exportations et balance commerciale *(suite)*
Importations CAF, exportations FAB et balance: en millions de dollars É.-U.

Region, country or area &	Sys.[1]	1995	2005	2010	2015	2017	2018	2019	Région, pays ou zone &
Grenada									**Grenade**
Imports	S	129	334	* 306	* 372	* 420	* 467	* 470	Importations
Exports	S	22	28	* 25	* 33	* 25	* 31	* 32	Exportations
Balance	S	-107	-306	* -281	* -339	* -395	* -436	* -438	Balance
Guadeloupe									**Guadeloupe**
Imports	S	1 901	...	...	...	...	...	...	Importations
Exports	S	162	...	...	...	...	...	...	Exportations
Balance	S	-1 739	...	...	...	...	...	...	Balance
Guatemala									**Guatemala**
Imports	S	3 292	10 500	13 830	17 637	18 378	* 19 613	19 871	Importations
Exports	S	1 936	5 381	8 460	10 677	11 011	* 10 773	11 289	Exportations
Balance	S	-1 357	-5 119	-5 370	-6 960	-7 367	* -8 839	-8 581	Balance
Guinea									**Guinée**
Imports	S	819	1 648	* 1 402	2 139	* 2 065	* 2 049	* 2 032	Importations
Exports	S	702	796	* 1 471	1 574	* 1 942	* 2 152	* 2 384	Exportations
Balance	S	-117	-852	* 69	-565	* -123	* 103	* 351	Balance
Guinea-Bissau									**Guinée-Bissau**
Imports	G	* 134	112	* 197	* 221	* 204	* 196	* 188	Importations
Exports	G	* 45	23	* 120	* 548	* 1 430	* 2 310	* 3 731	Exportations
Balance	G	* -89	-88	* -77	* 327	* 1 226	* 2 114	* 3 544	Balance
Guyana									**Guyana**
Imports	S	* 472	778	1 452	1 484	1 762	3 998	* 3 467	Importations
Exports	S	* 455	539	901	1 169	1 790	1 487	* 1 405	Exportations
Balance	S	* -17	-239	-551	-315	28	-2 511	* -2 062	Balance
Haiti									**Haïti**
Imports	G	650	* 1 449	* 3 147	* 3 523	* 3 463	* 3 539	* 3 118	Importations
Exports	G	35	* 470	* 579	* 1 018	* 939	* 901	* 746	Exportations
Balance	G	-615	* -979	* -2 568	* -2 505	* -2 524	* -2 638	* -2 372	Balance
Honduras									**Honduras**
Imports	S	1 728	4 419	6 895	8 381	8 612	* 9 333	* 10 059	Importations
Exports	S	656	1 294	3 104	4 201	4 970	* 4 762	* 4 161	Exportations
Balance	S	-1 072	-3 125	-3 791	-4 179	-3 642	* -4 571	* -5 898	Balance
Hungary									**Hongrie**
Imports	S	15 186	65 920	87 432	90 761	104 284	117 382	116 556	Importations
Exports	S	12 452	62 272	94 749	100 297	113 382	123 958	121 995	Exportations
Balance	S	-2 734	-3 648	7 317	9 536	9 098	6 576	5 439	Balance
Iceland									**Islande**
Imports	G	1 751	4 979	3 914	5 285	6 971	7 686	6 579	Importations
Exports	G	1 803	3 091	4 603	4 722	4 883	5 561	5 228	Exportations
Balance	G	51	-1 888	689	-563	-2 088	-2 125	-1 351	Balance
India									**Inde**
Imports	G	36 592	140 862	350 029	390 745	444 052	507 616	478 884	Importations
Exports	G	31 699	100 353	220 408	264 381	294 364	322 492	323 251	Exportations
Balance	G	-4 893	-40 509	-129 621	-126 364	-149 688	-185 124	-155 633	Balance
Indonesia [8]									**Indonésie** [8]
Imports	S	40 629	57 701	135 663	142 695	156 925	188 711	170 727	Importations
Exports	S	45 418	85 660	157 779	150 366	168 810	180 215	167 003	Exportations
Balance	S	4 789	27 959	22 116	7 671	11 885	-8 496	-3 724	Balance
Iran (Islamic Republic of) [9,10]									**Iran (Rép. islamique d')** [9,10]
Imports	S	* 13 882	* 38 869	54 697	* 41 453	51 612	* 43 014	* 20 502	Importations
Exports	S	* 18 360	60 012	83 785	* 64 084	105 844	* 76 724	* 17 394	Exportations
Balance	S	* 4 478	* 21 143	29 088	* 22 631	54 232	* 33 710	* -3 108	Balance
Iraq									**Iraq**
Imports	S	* 445	* 12 861	43 915	32 665	* 40 393	* 35 583	* 31 372	Importations
Exports	S	* 555	19 773	52 483	49 403	* 24 266	* 8 402	* 4 658	Exportations
Balance	S	* 110	* 6 912	8 568	16 738	* -16 126	* -27 181	* -26 714	Balance
Ireland									**Irlande**
Imports	G	32 321	70 284	64 601	77 795	88 828	106 931	101 473	Importations
Exports	G	43 789	110 003	120 645	124 731	138 072	167 018	170 743	Exportations
Balance	G	11 468	39 719	56 045	46 935	49 244	60 087	69 270	Balance
Israel									**Israël**
Imports	S	* 28 328	45 032	59 194	62 068	69 116	76 584	76 579	Importations
Exports	S	* 19 046	42 771	58 413	64 062	61 150	61 906	58 488	Exportations
Balance	S	* -9 282	-2 262	-781	1 994	-7 966	-14 678	-18 090	Balance

19

Total imports, exports and balance of trade *(continued)*
Imports CIF, exports FOB and balance: millions of US dollars

Total des importations, des exportations et balance commerciale *(suite)*
Importations CAF, exportations FAB et balance: en millions de dollars É.-U.

Region, country or area &	Sys.ᵗ	1995	2005	2010	2015	2017	2018	2019	Région, pays ou zone &
Italy									**Italie**
Imports	S	200 320	384 836	486 984	410 933	453 583	503 581	473 562	Importations
Exports	S	230 441	372 957	446 840	456 989	507 430	549 907	532 684	Exportations
Balance	S	30 122	-11 878	-40 145	46 055	53 847	46 326	59 121	Balance
Jamaica									**Jamaïque**
Imports	G	2 773	4 885	5 225	4 993	5 818	* 6 521	6 339	Importations
Exports	G	1 424	1 514	1 328	1 263	1 310	* 1 824	1 586	Exportations
Balance	G	-1 349	-3 370	-3 898	-3 730	-4 508	* -4 697	-4 753	Balance
Japan									**Japon**
Imports	G	336 094	515 866	694 059	625 568	671 474	748 218	720 895	Importations
Exports	G	442 937	594 941	769 774	624 874	698 097	738 201	705 640	Exportations
Balance	G	106 843	79 074	75 715	-695	26 623	-10 016	-15 255	Balance
Jordan									**Jordanie**
Imports	G	3 696	10 455	15 262	20 475	20 407	20 310	* 19 669	Importations
Exports	G	1 769	4 284	7 023	7 833	7 469	7 750	* 8 146	Exportations
Balance	G	-1 928	-6 170	-8 239	-12 642	-12 938	-12 560	* -11 523	Balance
Kazakhstan									**Kazakhstan**
Imports	G	3 805	17 333	24 024	30 567	29 599	33 658	38 357	Importations
Exports	G	5 227	27 846	57 244	45 954	48 503	61 109	57 723	Exportations
Balance	G	1 422	10 513	33 220	15 387	18 903	27 451	19 366	Balance
Kenya									**Kenya**
Imports	G	2 818	5 846	12 093	* 16 097	16 690	17 377	* 19 845	Importations
Exports	G	1 826	3 420	5 169	* 5 908	5 747	6 050	* 6 526	Exportations
Balance	G	-992	-2 426	-6 924	* -10 189	-10 943	-11 326	* -13 319	Balance
Kiribati									**Kiribati**
Imports	G	34	74	73	111	* 185	* 356	* 554	Importations
Exports	G	7	4	4	10	* 12	* 10	* 10	Exportations
Balance	G	-27	-70	-69	-101	* -173	* -347	* -544	Balance
Kuwait									**Koweït**
Imports	S	7 790	* 15 801	22 691	30 957	33 598	35 867	* 40 063	Importations
Exports	S	12 944	* 44 869	62 698	54 121	54 992	71 941	* 81 282	Exportations
Balance	S	5 155	* 29 068	40 007	23 164	21 394	36 075	* 41 219	Balance
Kyrgyzstan									**Kirghizistan**
Imports	S	522	1 108	3 223	4 068	4 487	5 292	* 5 906	Importations
Exports	S	412	672	1 488	1 441	1 757	1 835	* 2 517	Exportations
Balance	S	-110	-436	-1 734	-2 627	-2 730	-3 457	* -3 390	Balance
Lao People's Dem. Rep.									**Rép. dém. populaire lao**
Imports	S	* 588	* 874	1 837	3 778	5 160	5 848	5 797	Importations
Exports	S	* 311	* 552	1 909	2 985	4 910	5 815	5 809	Exportations
Balance	S	* -277	* -322	72	-793	-250	-33	12	Balance
Latvia									**Lettonie**
Imports	S	1 818	8 770	11 143	14 096	16 053	18 613	17 768	Importations
Exports	S	1 305	5 303	8 851	11 650	13 190	15 065	14 447	Exportations
Balance	S	-513	-3 468	-2 292	-2 446	-2 863	-3 548	-3 320	Balance
Lebanon									**Liban**
Imports	G	* 7 295	9 327	17 970	18 600	19 587	19 983	* 18 472	Importations
Exports	G	* 826	1 879	4 254	2 953	2 844	2 953	* 3 154	Exportations
Balance	G	* -6 469	-7 448	-13 716	-15 646	-16 742	-17 030	* -15 317	Balance
Lesotho									**Lesotho**
Imports	G	...	* 1 410	1 277	1 410	2 066	* 1 459	* 1 171	Importations
Exports	G	...	* 650	503	604	673	* 507	* 345	Exportations
Balance	G	...	* -760	-773	-806	-1 392	* -952	* -826	Balance
Liberia									**Libéria**
Imports	S	* 358	* 309	* 710	* 901	* 662	* 576	* 345	Importations
Exports	S	* 452	* 130	222	* 626	* 699	* 782	* 841	Exportations
Balance	S	* 94	* -179	* -488	* -275	* 38	* 207	* 496	Balance
Libya									**Libye**
Imports	G	* 4 912	* 6 058	17 674	* 12 999	* 5 743	* 3 786	* 2 450	Importations
Exports	G	* 9 363	* 31 272	36 440	* 10 200	* 2 273	* 1 064	* 489	Exportations
Balance	G	* 4 451	* 25 215	18 766	* -2 799	* -3 470	* -2 722	* -1 961	Balance
Lithuania									**Lituanie**
Imports	G	3 649	15 704	23 378	28 176	30 979	36 501	35 612	Importations
Exports	G	2 706	12 070	20 814	25 411	29 350	33 335	33 123	Exportations
Balance	G	-943	-3 634	-2 564	-2 765	-1 629	-3 167	-2 489	Balance

19 Total imports, exports and balance of trade *(continued)*
Imports CIF, exports FOB and balance: millions of US dollars

Total des importations, des exportations et balance commerciale *(suite)*
Importations CAF, exportations FAB et balance: en millions de dollars É.-U.

Region, country or area &	Sys.[t]	1995	2005	2010	2015	2017	2018	2019	Région, pays ou zone &
Luxembourg									**Luxembourg**
Imports	S	...	17 586	20 400	19 296	21 071	23 119	* 23 057	Importations
Exports	S	...	12 715	13 911	12 626	13 959	15 148	* 15 433	Exportations
Balance	S	...	-4 871	-6 489	-6 671	-7 112	-7 970	* -7 623	Balance
Madagascar									**Madagascar**
Imports	S	550	1 686	2 546	2 961	3 658	4 082	3 603	Importations
Exports	S	360	836	1 082	2 164	2 852	3 133	2 689	Exportations
Balance	S	-190	-850	-1 464	-796	-806	-949	-914	Balance
Malawi									**Malawi**
Imports	G	500	1 165	2 173	2 312	2 547	* 1 549	* 360	Importations
Exports	G	433	495	1 066	1 080	884	* 836	* 819	Exportations
Balance	G	-67	-670	-1 107	-1 232	-1 663	* -712	* 459	Balance
Malaysia									**Malaisie**
Imports	G	77 046	114 290	164 586	176 175	194 720	217 358	204 906	Importations
Exports	G	73 778	141 624	198 791	200 211	217 723	247 324	238 089	Exportations
Balance	G	-3 267	27 334	34 204	24 036	23 002	29 965	33 183	Balance
Maldives									**Maldives**
Imports	G	268	745	1 095	1 897	2 360	2 961	* 2 883	Importations
Exports	G	50	154	74	144	199	182	* 163	Exportations
Balance	G	-218	-591	-1 021	-1 753	-2 160	-2 779	* -2 720	Balance
Mali									**Mali**
Imports	S	* 774	1 544	4 704	* 3 169	4 337	* 5 618	* 8 277	Importations
Exports	S	* 443	1 075	1 996	* 2 530	1 903	* 1 268	* 879	Exportations
Balance	S	* -331	-468	-2 707	* -639	-2 434	* -4 351	* -7 397	Balance
Malta									**Malte**
Imports	G	2 942	3 865	5 732	6 788	6 828	7 204	8 211	Importations
Exports	G	1 913	2 431	3 717	3 915	4 078	3 869	4 143	Exportations
Balance	G	-1 029	-1 435	-2 015	-2 873	-2 750	-3 336	-4 068	Balance
Marshall Islands									**Îles Marshall**
Imports	G	* 75	* 68	* 76	* 84	* 88	* 90	* 71	Importations
Exports	G	* 23	* 11	* 17	* 25	* 30	* 32	* 34	Exportations
Balance	G	* -52	* -57	* -60	* -59	* -58	* -57	* -37	Balance
Martinique									**Martinique**
Imports	S	1 970	...	...	...	...	...	...	Importations
Exports	S	242	...	...	...	...	...	...	Exportations
Balance	S	-1 728	...	...	...	...	...	...	Balance
Mauritania									**Mauritanie**
Imports	S	* 326	1 342	1 708	* 3 677	3 522	* 3 402	* 3 525	Importations
Exports	S	* 550	556	1 819	* 1 522	1 989	* 2 127	* 2 301	Exportations
Balance	S	* 225	-786	111	* -2 156	-1 533	* -1 275	* -1 224	Balance
Mauritius									**Maurice**
Imports	G	2 000	3 160	4 402	4 458	5 269	5 669	5 601	Importations
Exports	G	1 538	2 144	1 850	2 481	2 103	1 988	1 876	Exportations
Balance	G	-462	-1 016	-2 553	-1 977	-3 167	-3 682	-3 725	Balance
Mayotte									**Mayotte**
Imports	G	...	309	...	...	...	...	...	Importations
Exports	G	...	6	...	...	...	...	...	Exportations
Balance	G	...	-303	...	...	...	...	...	Balance
Mexico [2]									**Mexique** [2]
Imports	G	72 453	221 819	301 482	395 234	420 395	464 294	467 293	Importations
Exports	G	79 541	214 207	298 305	380 550	409 396	450 655	472 273	Exportations
Balance	G	7 088	-7 612	-3 177	-14 684	-10 998	-13 639	4 980	Balance
Micronesia (Fed. States of)									**Micronésie (États féd. de)**
Imports	S	* 100	128	168	* 67	* 23	* 14	* 8	Importations
Exports	S	* 43	13	23	* 11	* 3	* 2	* 1	Exportations
Balance	S	* -56	-115	-145	* -56	* -20	* -12	* -7	Balance
Mongolia									**Mongolie**
Imports	G	* 415	1 183	* 3 200	3 797	4 337	5 875	* 6 039	Importations
Exports	G	* 473	1 064	* 2 908	4 669	6 201	7 012	* 7 433	Exportations
Balance	G	* 58	-118	* -291	873	1 863	1 137	* 1 394	Balance
Montenegro									**Monténégro**
Imports	S	...	...	2 182	2 050	2 611	3 003	* 2 903	Importations
Exports	S	...	...	437	353	421	466	* 459	Exportations
Balance	S	...	...	-1 745	-1 697	-2 190	-2 537	* -2 444	Balance

19 Total imports, exports and balance of trade *(continued)*
Imports CIF, exports FOB and balance: millions of US dollars

Total des importations, des exportations et balance commerciale *(suite)*
Importations CAF, exportations FAB et balance: en millions de dollars É.-U.

Region, country or area &	Sys.¹	1995	2005	2010	2015	2017	2018	2019	Région, pays ou zone &
Montserrat									**Montserrat**
Imports	S	* 51	30	* 29	* 39	* 31	* 34	* 35	Importations
Exports	S	* 2	1	1	* 3	* 6	* 5	* 6	Exportations
Balance	S	* -49	-28	* -28	* -36	* -25	* -29	* -28	Balance
Morocco									**Maroc**
Imports	S	8 540	20 803	35 379	38 146	45 039	51 299	51 075	Importations
Exports	S	4 719	11 185	17 765	22 337	25 624	29 360	29 328	Exportations
Balance	S	-3 822	-9 618	-17 614	-15 809	-19 415	-21 939	-21 747	Balance
Mozambique									**Mozambique**
Imports	S	727	2 408	3 564	* 7 852	5 702	6 786	* 8 270	Importations
Exports	S	174	1 745	2 243	* 3 649	4 719	5 196	* 5 878	Exportations
Balance	S	-553	-663	-1 321	* -4 203	-983	-1 590	* -2 392	Balance
Myanmar									**Myanmar**
Imports	G	* 1 346	* 1 907	4 866	16 913	19 253	19 345	18 578	Importations
Exports	G	* 860	* 3 776	8 873	11 432	13 879	16 672	17 997	Exportations
Balance	G	* -487	* 1 869	4 008	-5 481	-5 375	-2 674	-581	Balance
Namibia									**Namibie**
Imports	G	...	2 525	5 980	7 697	6 778	8 289	8 086	Importations
Exports	G	...	2 726	5 848	4 628	5 229	7 488	6 258	Exportations
Balance	G	...	201	-131	-3 069	-1 549	-801	-1 828	Balance
Nepal ¹¹									**Népal** ¹¹
Imports	G	* 1 330	* 2 282	5 116	6 612	10 038	* 9 502	* 4 737	Importations
Exports	G	* 345	* 863	874	660	741	* 684	* 588	Exportations
Balance	G	* -985	* -1 419	-4 242	-5 952	-9 297	* -8 818	* -4 149	Balance
Netherlands									**Pays-Bas**
Imports	S	157 929	310 591	439 987	393 728	461 870	500 631	514 513	Importations
Exports	S	177 626	349 813	492 646	437 329	527 937	555 921	577 617	Exportations
Balance	S	19 697	39 222	52 659	43 601	66 067	55 291	63 103	Balance
Netherlands Antilles [former]									**Antilles néerlandaises [anc.]**
Imports	S	* 1 830	894	* 2 687	...	...	...	...	Importations
Exports	S	* 1 354	91	* 811	...	...	...	...	Exportations
Balance	S	* -476	-803	* -1 876	...	...	...	...	Balance
New Caledonia									**Nouvelle-Calédonie**
Imports	S	* 840	1 774	3 303	2 529	* 2 515	* 2 814	* 2 951	Importations
Exports	S	* 570	1 114	1 268	1 239	* 1 460	* 1 932	* 1 674	Exportations
Balance	S	* -270	-660	-2 036	-1 291	* -1 055	* -882	* -1 277	Balance
New Zealand									**Nouvelle-Zélande**
Imports	G	13 958	26 232	30 616	36 528	40 128	43 736	42 271	Importations
Exports	G	13 745	21 729	31 393	34 357	38 050	39 839	39 540	Exportations
Balance	G	-212	-4 504	777	-2 171	-2 078	-3 897	-2 731	Balance
Nicaragua									**Nicaragua**
Imports	G	1 009	2 536	4 191	5 866	7 704	7 351	* 8 426	Importations
Exports	G	509	866	1 848	4 667	4 926	5 014	* 3 998	Exportations
Balance	G	-500	-1 670	-2 343	-1 199	-2 778	-2 337	* -4 429	Balance
Niger									**Niger**
Imports	S	345	736	2 273	2 458	* 1 620	* 1 314	* 1 127	Importations
Exports	S	273	486	479	790	* 641	* 342	* 232	Exportations
Balance	S	-71	-250	-1 794	-1 669	* -979	* -972	* -895	Balance
Nigeria									**Nigéria**
Imports	G	* 8 221	* 21 314	44 235	* 34 912	31 270	43 012	* 72 765	Importations
Exports	G	* 12 342	* 55 145	86 568	* 50 108	44 466	62 400	* 79 964	Exportations
Balance	G	* 4 121	* 33 831	42 333	* 15 196	13 196	19 388	* 7 199	Balance
North Macedonia									**Macédoine du Nord**
Imports	S	1 719	3 228	5 474	6 427	7 719	9 052	9 470	Importations
Exports	S	1 204	2 041	3 351	4 530	5 670	6 906	7 186	Exportations
Balance	S	-515	-1 187	-2 123	-1 897	-2 049	-2 145	-2 284	Balance
Northern Mariana Islands									**Îles Mariannes du Nord**
Imports	G	* 628	* 1 952	* 2 867	* 4 215	* 4 917	* 5 310	* 5 734	Importations
Exports	G	* 941	* 1 254	* 1 453	* 1 685	* 1 787	* 1 841	* 1 895	Exportations
Balance	G	* 313	* -699	* -1 414	* -2 530	* -3 130	* -3 470	* -3 838	Balance
Norway									**Norvège**
Imports	G	32 706	55 488	77 330	76 399	85 526	87 440	86 145	Importations
Exports	G	41 740	103 759	130 657	103 785	101 976	122 636	104 030	Exportations
Balance	G	9 034	48 271	53 327	27 386	16 450	35 196	17 885	Balance

19

Total imports, exports and balance of trade *(continued)*
Imports CIF, exports FOB and balance: millions of US dollars

Total des importations, des exportations et balance commerciale *(suite)*
Importations CAF, exportations FAB et balance: en millions de dollars É.-U.

Region, country or area &	Sys.[t]	1995	2005	2010	2015	2017	2018	2019	Région, pays ou zone &
Oman									**Oman**
Imports	G	4 249	8 970	19 775	29 007	26 435	25 770	* 23 383	Importations
Exports	G	5 917	18 692	36 600	35 686	32 904	41 761	* 38 723	Exportations
Balance	G	1 669	9 722	16 825	6 679	6 469	15 991	* 15 340	Balance
Other non-specified areas									**Autres zones non-spécifiées**
Imports		103 506	181 592	251 315	228 508	259 609	286 195	* 286 145	Importations
Exports		111 343	189 393	273 706	280 019	317 663	335 744	* 352 959	Exportations
Balance		7 838	7 801	22 391	51 511	58 054	49 549	* 66 814	Balance
Pakistan									**Pakistan**
Imports	G	11 704	25 097	37 537	43 990	57 440	60 163	50 047	Importations
Exports	G	8 158	16 050	21 413	22 089	21 878	23 631	23 759	Exportations
Balance	G	-3 546	-9 046	-16 124	-21 901	-35 562	-36 532	-26 288	Balance
Palau [2]									**Palaos** [2]
Imports	S	* 60	* 156	107	150	158	154	* 169	Importations
Exports	S	* 14	* 14	* 12	6	6	9	* 8	Exportations
Balance	S	* -47	* -143	-96	-144	-151	-146	* -161	Balance
Panama [12]									**Panama** [12]
Imports	S	2 511	4 152	16 737	10 375	* 10 049	* 13 233	* 12 836	Importations
Exports	S	577	963	10 987	11 348	* 11 615	* 672	* 713	Exportations
Balance	S	-1 933	-3 189	-5 751	973	* 1 566	* -12 561	* -12 123	Balance
Papua New Guinea									**Papouasie-Nvl-Guinée**
Imports	G	* 1 451	* 1 728	* 3 950	* 2 537	* 2 598	* 2 882	* 3 130	Importations
Exports	G	* 2 653	* 3 276	* 5 742	* 8 425	* 9 798	* 10 861	* 11 798	Exportations
Balance	G	* 1 202	* 1 548	* 1 792	* 5 888	* 7 200	* 7 980	* 8 669	Balance
Paraguay									**Paraguay**
Imports	S	3 136	3 274	10 033	10 291	11 873	13 334	* 12 360	Importations
Exports	S	919	3 153	6 517	8 328	8 680	9 042	* 12 425	Exportations
Balance	S	-2 217	-121	-3 517	-1 964	-3 194	-4 292	* 64	Balance
Peru									**Pérou**
Imports	S	7 584	12 502	29 966	38 026	39 764	43 123	42 376	Importations
Exports	S	5 440	17 114	35 807	33 667	44 238	47 894	46 132	Exportations
Balance	S	-2 144	4 612	5 842	-4 359	4 474	4 771	3 755	Balance
Philippines									**Philippines**
Imports	G	28 487	49 487	58 468	70 153	101 889	115 038	117 247	Importations
Exports	G	17 447	41 255	51 498	58 648	68 713	67 488	70 927	Exportations
Balance	G	-11 040	-8 233	-6 970	-11 505	-33 177	-47 550	-46 321	Balance
Poland									**Pologne**
Imports	S	29 019	101 539	174 128	189 696	217 979	267 700	246 654	Importations
Exports	S	22 862	89 378	157 065	194 461	221 308	261 815	251 865	Exportations
Balance	S	-6 157	-12 161	-17 063	4 765	3 329	-5 885	5 211	Balance
Portugal									**Portugal**
Imports	S	33 565	63 904	77 682	66 909	78 746	95 629	89 929	Importations
Exports	S	23 370	38 672	49 414	55 045	62 117	74 136	67 012	Exportations
Balance	S	-10 195	-25 232	-28 268	-11 864	-16 629	-21 493	-22 917	Balance
Qatar									**Qatar**
Imports	S	3 398	10 061	23 240	32 610	29 896	31 696	29 178	Importations
Exports	S	3 557	25 762	74 964	77 971	67 498	84 288	72 935	Exportations
Balance	S	159	15 702	51 725	45 361	37 602	52 593	43 757	Balance
Republic of Korea									**République de Corée**
Imports	G	135 109	261 236	425 208	436 487	478 469	535 183	503 263	Importations
Exports	G	* 125 056	284 418	466 381	526 753	573 627	604 807	542 172	Exportations
Balance	G	-10 052	23 183	41 173	90 266	95 158	69 624	38 909	Balance
Republic of Moldova									**République de Moldova**
Imports	G	841	2 292	3 855	3 987	4 831	5 764	5 842	Importations
Exports	G	746	1 091	1 541	1 967	2 425	2 707	2 779	Exportations
Balance	G	-95	-1 201	-2 314	-2 020	-2 406	-3 057	-3 063	Balance
Réunion									**Réunion**
Imports	S	2 711	...	...	...	...	...	...	Importations
Exports	S	209	...	...	...	...	...	...	Exportations
Balance	S	-2 502	...	...	...	...	...	...	Balance
Romania									**Roumanie**
Imports	S	10 278	40 463	62 007	69 858	85 318	97 878	96 644	Importations
Exports	S	7 910	27 730	49 413	60 605	70 627	80 078	77 299	Exportations
Balance	S	-2 368	-12 733	-12 593	-9 253	-14 691	-17 800	-19 346	Balance

19

Total imports, exports and balance of trade *(continued)*
Imports CIF, exports FOB and balance: millions of US dollars

Total des importations, des exportations et balance commerciale *(suite)*
Importations CAF, exportations FAB et balance: en millions de dollars É.-U.

Region, country or area &	Sys.ᵗ	1995	2005	2010	2015	2017	2018	2019	Région, pays ou zone &
Russian Federation [13]									**Fédération de Russie** [13]
Imports	G	* 46 710	98 707	228 912	182 782	259 967	240 226	247 161	Importations
Exports	G	* 79 869	241 452	397 068	343 908	379 207	451 495	426 720	Exportations
Balance	G	* 33 159	142 744	168 156	161 126	119 240	211 269	179 559	Balance
Rwanda									**Rwanda**
Imports	G	* 241	374	1 405	1 858	* 1 963	* 3 256	3 214	Importations
Exports	G	* 8	150	242	579	* 820	* 1 121	992	Exportations
Balance	G	* -233	-224	-1 163	-1 279	* -1 143	* -2 135	-2 221	Balance
Saint Helena									**Sainte-Hélène**
Imports	G	* 13	* 12	* 20	* 41	* 55	* 63	* 71	Importations
Exports	G	* 1	* 1	* ~0	* ~0	* ~0	* ~0	* ~0	Exportations
Balance	G	* -12	* -12	* -20	* -40	* -55	* -63	* -71	Balance
Saint Kitts and Nevis									**Saint-Kitts-et-Nevis**
Imports	S	132	210	270	297	309	* 335	* 338	Importations
Exports	S	19	34	32	32	33	* 36	* 63	Exportations
Balance	S	-113	-176	-238	-265	-276	* -299	* -275	Balance
Saint Lucia									**Sainte-Lucie**
Imports	S	* 306	486	647	583	664	* 668	* 598	Importations
Exports	S	* 109	64	215	181	142	* 69	* 55	Exportations
Balance	S	* -197	-422	-432	-403	-522	* -598	* -543	Balance
Saint Pierre and Miquelon									**Saint-Pierre-et-Miquelon**
Imports	S	* 96	* 216	* 747	* 2 259	* 2 991	* 3 402	* 3 870	Importations
Exports	S	* 16	* 31	* 137	* 533	* 780	* 931	* 1 112	Exportations
Balance	S	* -80	* -185	* -610	* -1 726	* -2 211	* -2 471	* -2 758	Balance
Saint Vincent & Grenadines									**Saint-Vincent-Grenadines**
Imports	S	134	240	379	334	330	354	* 335	Importations
Exports	S	59	40	42	47	42	44	* 37	Exportations
Balance	S	-75	-201	-338	-287	-288	-310	* -298	Balance
Samoa									**Samoa**
Imports	S	* 95	239	310	371	356	363	* 390	Importations
Exports	S	* 9	87	70	59	44	46	* 32	Exportations
Balance	S	* -86	-151	-240	-312	-312	-317	* -358	Balance
Sao Tome and Principe									**Sao Tomé-et-Principe**
Imports	S	* 29	50	112	142	147	148	* 165	Importations
Exports	S	* 5	3	6	9	11	12	* 14	Exportations
Balance	S	* -24	-46	-106	-133	-136	-136	* -151	Balance
Saudi Arabia									**Arabie saoudite**
Imports	S	28 085	57 233	103 622	174 786	134 519	135 211	* 136 472	Importations
Exports	S	49 030	180 278	250 577	203 689	221 835	294 536	* 259 208	Exportations
Balance	S	20 944	123 045	146 955	28 903	87 316	159 324	* 122 736	Balance
Senegal									**Sénégal**
Imports	G	* 1 413	3 498	4 777	5 595	6 729	8 071	8 143	Importations
Exports	G	* 412	1 471	2 086	2 612	2 989	3 623	4 175	Exportations
Balance	G	* -1 001	-2 027	-2 691	-2 984	-3 740	-4 448	-3 969	Balance
Serbia [14]									**Serbie** [14]
Imports	S	...	...	16 735	18 210	22 146	25 883	26 730	Importations
Exports	S	...	...	9 795	13 379	16 959	19 239	19 630	Exportations
Balance	S	...	...	-6 940	-4 831	-5 187	-6 644	-7 100	Balance
Serbia and Monten. [former]									**Serbie-et-Monténégro [anc.]**
Imports	S	* 2 666	* 11 393	...	...	...	...	...	Importations
Exports	S	* 1 531	* 4 430	...	...	...	...	...	Exportations
Balance	S	* -1 135	* -6 963	...	...	...	...	...	Balance
Seychelles									**Seychelles**
Imports	G	255	675	1 180	975	1 348	1 137	1 438	Importations
Exports	G	53	340	418	474	592	847	824	Exportations
Balance	G	-202	-335	-763	-501	-757	-290	-614	Balance
Sierra Leone									**Sierra Leone**
Imports	S	* 131	341	* 776	1 759	1 074	* 985	* 741	Importations
Exports	S	* 42	154	* 319	93	103	* 20	* 44	Exportations
Balance	S	* -89	-187	* -457	-1 666	-971	* -965	* -697	Balance
Singapore									**Singapour**
Imports	G	124 503	200 724	313 071	308 122	327 710	370 504	358 975	Importations
Exports	G	118 263	230 344	353 240	357 941	373 255	411 743	390 332	Exportations
Balance	G	-6 240	29 619	40 169	49 820	45 545	41 240	31 357	Balance

19

Total imports, exports and balance of trade *(continued)*
Imports CIF, exports FOB and balance: millions of US dollars

Total des importations, des exportations et balance commerciale *(suite)*
Importations CAF, exportations FAB et balance: en millions de dollars É.-U.

Region, country or area &	Sys.[t]	1995	2005	2010	2015	2017	2018	2019	Région, pays ou zone &
Slovakia									**Slovaquie**
Imports	S	8 162	34 226	65 644	73 053	81 935	92 929	90 979	Importations
Exports	S	8 374	* 32 210	65 306	74 970	83 475	93 444	90 050	Exportations
Balance	S	212	-2 016	-338	1 916	1 540	515	-930	Balance
Slovenia									**Slovénie**
Imports	S	9 492	19 626	26 592	25 870	31 149	36 267	38 179	Importations
Exports	S	8 316	17 896	24 435	26 587	31 894	36 471	37 557	Exportations
Balance	S	-1 176	-1 730	-2 157	717	744	204	-622	Balance
Solomon Islands									**Îles Salomon**
Imports	S	* 154	139	328	466	572	601	* 348	Importations
Exports	S	* 168	70	215	400	500	569	* 611	Exportations
Balance	S	* 14	-68	-112	-65	-72	-32	* 263	Balance
Somalia									**Somalie**
Imports	G	* 38	* 469	* 496	* 525	* 537	* 543	* 549	Importations
Exports	G	* 38	* 379	* 568	* 853	* 1 003	* 1 087	* 1 179	Exportations
Balance	G	* --0	* -90	* 72	* 328	* 466	* 545	* 630	Balance
South Africa [2]									**Afrique du Sud** [2]
Imports	G	...	55 033	83 100	85 510	83 086	92 637	88 037	Importations
Exports	G	...	46 991	82 631	80 265	88 229	93 677	89 396	Exportations
Balance	G	...	-8 042	-469	-5 244	5 144	1 040	1 358	Balance
South Sudan									**Soudan du sud**
Imports	G	...	...	...	* 635	* 886	* 1 048	* 1 238	Importations
Exports	G	...	...	...	* 3 103	* 1 840	* 1 417	* 1 091	Exportations
Balance	G	...	...	...	* 2 468	* 953	* 369	* -147	Balance
Spain									**Espagne**
Imports	S	113 399	289 611	315 547	304 708	341 421	391 057	375 485	Importations
Exports	S	89 616	192 798	246 265	276 959	311 601	346 064	337 215	Exportations
Balance	S	-23 783	-96 812	-69 282	-27 750	-29 821	-44 992	-38 270	Balance
Sri Lanka									**Sri Lanka**
Imports	G	* 4 756	8 307	12 354	18 967	21 316	* 22 622	* 17 992	Importations
Exports	G	* 3 790	6 160	8 304	10 440	11 741	* 12 276	* 12 589	Exportations
Balance	G	* -966	-2 147	-4 050	-8 528	-9 575	* -10 346	* -5 403	Balance
State of Palestine									**État de Palestine**
Imports	S	...	2 668	3 959	5 225	5 854	6 540	* 6 608	Importations
Exports	S	...	335	576	958	1 065	1 156	* 1 124	Exportations
Balance	S	...	-2 332	-3 383	-4 268	-4 789	-5 384	* -5 484	Balance
Sudan [15]									**Soudan** [15]
Imports	G	...	...	...	8 413	10 277	10 484	* 12 286	Importations
Exports	G	...	...	...	5 588	4 241	3 619	* 4 127	Exportations
Balance	G	...	...	...	-2 826	-6 036	-6 864	* -8 159	Balance
Sudan [former]									**Soudan [anc.]**
Imports	G	1 185	7 367	11 875	...	...	...	...	Importations
Exports	G	685	4 506	11 529	...	...	...	...	Exportations
Balance	G	-500	-2 861	-346	...	...	...	...	Balance
Suriname									**Suriname**
Imports	G	583	1 050	1 397	1 904	1 209	1 527	1 711	Importations
Exports	G	483	997	2 026	1 814	1 441	1 503	1 461	Exportations
Balance	G	-100	-53	628	-90	232	-24	-250	Balance
Sweden									**Suède**
Imports	G	61 647	111 351	148 788	138 361	154 195	170 592	158 710	Importations
Exports	G	77 436	130 264	158 411	140 001	152 902	165 959	160 538	Exportations
Balance	G	15 790	18 912	9 622	1 641	-1 293	-4 633	1 828	Balance
Switzerland									**Suisse**
Imports	S	80 152	126 574	176 281	253 152	267 501	278 666	276 292	Importations
Exports	S	81 641	130 930	195 609	291 959	299 309	310 524	313 630	Exportations
Balance	S	1 489	4 356	19 329	38 807	31 807	31 859	37 338	Balance
Syrian Arab Republic									**République arabe syrienne**
Imports	S	* 4 645	7 898	17 562	* 3 206	* 1 773	* 1 319	* 980	Importations
Exports	S	* 3 561	6 450	11 353	* 1 688	* 949	* 712	* 534	Exportations
Balance	S	* -1 084	-1 448	-6 209	* -1 518	* -824	* -607	* -447	Balance
Tajikistan									**Tadjikistan**
Imports	G	* 809	* 1 329	* 2 659	* 3 435	* 2 775	* 2 774	* 2 773	Importations
Exports	G	* 748	* 905	* 1 206	* 891	* 1 198	* 1 573	* 2 065	Exportations
Balance	G	* -61	* -424	* -1 453	* -2 544	* -1 577	* -1 201	* -708	Balance

Total imports, exports and balance of trade *(continued)*
Imports CIF, exports FOB and balance: millions of US dollars

Total des importations, des exportations et balance commerciale *(suite)*
Importations CAF, exportations FAB et balance: en millions de dollars É.-U.

Region, country or area &	Sys.¹	1995	2005	2010	2015	2017	2018	2019	Région, pays ou zone &
Thailand									**Thaïlande**
Imports	S	70 781	118 164	182 393	202 642	221 514	249 174	216 805	Importations
Exports	S	56 439	110 110	195 312	214 309	236 634	252 485	233 674	Exportations
Balance	S	-14 341	-8 054	12 918	11 667	15 120	3 312	16 870	Balance
Timor-Leste									**Timor-Leste**
Imports	S	* 112	102	* 246	* 578	588	* 552	* 536	Importations
Exports	S	* 34	43	* 42	* 45	24	* 45	* 154	Exportations
Balance	S	* -78	-58	* -205	* -533	-564	* -507	* -382	Balance
Togo									**Togo**
Imports	S	556	593	1 350	1 877	1 615	1 907	1 844	Importations
Exports	S	383	360	741	792	749	1 024	917	Exportations
Balance	S	-174	-233	-609	-1 085	-866	-883	-927	Balance
Tokelau									**Tokélaou**
Imports	G	* 1	* 1	* 1	* 1	* 1	* 1	* 1	Importations
Exports	G	* ~0	* ~0	* ~0	* ~0	* ~0	* ~0	* ~0	Exportations
Balance	G	* -~0	* -1	* -1	* -1	* -1	* -1	* -1	Balance
Tonga									**Tonga**
Imports	G	* 77	120	159	* 208	* 246	* 277	* 311	Importations
Exports	G	* 15	10	8	* 15	* 19	* 17	* 15	Exportations
Balance	G	* -63	-110	-151	* -193	* -226	* -260	* -296	Balance
Trinidad and Tobago									**Trinité-et-Tobago**
Imports	S	* 1 386	5 694	6 480	9 298	* 6 425	* 3 540	* 1 951	Importations
Exports	S	* 2 007	9 611	10 982	10 756	* 8 863	* 10 454	* 12 336	Exportations
Balance	S	* 622	3 918	4 502	1 458	* 2 439	* 6 914	* 10 385	Balance
Tunisia									**Tunisie**
Imports	G	* 7 903	13 174	22 215	20 223	20 618	* 22 513	* 22 453	Importations
Exports	G	* 5 475	10 494	16 427	14 073	14 200	* 15 666	* 15 489	Exportations
Balance	G	* -2 428	-2 681	-5 789	-6 149	-6 418	* -6 848	* -6 964	Balance
Turkey									**Turquie**
Imports	S	35 707	116 774	185 544	207 207	233 800	223 039	210 343	Importations
Exports	S	21 599	73 476	113 883	143 850	156 993	168 023	180 839	Exportations
Balance	S	-14 109	-43 298	-71 661	-63 356	-76 807	-55 016	-29 505	Balance
Turkmenistan									**Turkménistan**
Imports	G	* 1 364	* 2 217	* 2 400	* 2 596	* 2 679	* 2 721	* 2 764	Importations
Exports	G	* 677	* 3 009	* 3 335	* 3 670	* 3 813	* 3 887	* 3 962	Exportations
Balance	G	* -687	* 792	* 935	* 1 074	* 1 135	* 1 166	* 1 198	Balance
Turks and Caicos Islands									**Îles Turques-et-Caïques**
Imports	G	* 51	304	* 302	* 410	* 433	* 484	* 488	Importations
Exports	G	* 5	15	* 16	* 5	* 2	* 6	* 5	Exportations
Balance	G	* -46	-289	* -286	* -405	* -430	* -478	* -482	Balance
Tuvalu									**Tuvalu**
Imports	G	* 6	13	* 12	* 12	* 12	* 12	* 12	Importations
Exports	G	* ~0	~0	* ~0	* ~0	* ~0	* ~0	* ~0	Exportations
Balance	G	* -6	-13	* -12	* -12	* -12	* -12	* -12	Balance
Uganda									**Ouganda**
Imports	G	1 038	2 054	4 664	5 528	5 596	6 729	* 7 686	Importations
Exports	G	575	813	1 619	2 267	2 901	3 087	* 3 597	Exportations
Balance	G	-462	-1 241	-3 046	-3 261	-2 694	-3 642	* -4 089	Balance
Ukraine ¹⁶									**Ukraine** ¹⁶
Imports	G	* 15 484	36 122	60 737	37 516	49 439	57 187	* 60 783	Importations
Exports	G	* 13 128	34 228	51 430	38 127	43 428	47 335	* 50 060	Exportations
Balance	G	* -2 356	-1 894	-9 307	611	-6 011	-9 852	* -10 723	Balance
United Arab Emirates									**Émirats arabes unis**
Imports	G	* 20 776	80 814	187 001	287 025	257 687	244 646	* 244 712	Importations
Exports	G	* 27 691	115 453	198 362	300 479	313 559	387 910	* 412 260	Exportations
Balance	G	* 6 915	34 639	11 361	13 454	55 872	143 264	* 167 549	Balance
United Kingdom									**Royaume-Uni**
Imports	G	261 456	528 461	627 618	630 251	640 908	671 694	692 580	Importations
Exports	G	234 372	392 744	422 014	466 296	441 847	490 840	468 160	Exportations
Balance	G	-27 084	-135 717	-205 603	-163 955	-199 060	-180 854	-224 421	Balance
United Rep. of Tanzania									**Rép.-Unie de Tanzanie**
Imports	G	1 653	3 247	8 013	14 706	7 765	8 554	* 9 434	Importations
Exports	G	685	1 672	4 051	5 854	4 178	3 669	* 4 414	Exportations
Balance	G	-968	-1 575	-3 962	-8 852	-3 587	-4 884	* -5 020	Balance

Total imports, exports and balance of trade *(continued)*
Imports CIF, exports FOB and balance: millions of US dollars

Total des importations, des exportations et balance commerciale *(suite)*
Importations CAF, exportations FAB et balance: en millions de dollars É.-U.

Region, country or area &	Sys.[t]	1995	2005	2010	2015	2017	2018	2019	Région, pays ou zone &
United States of America									**États-Unis d'Amérique**
Imports	G	770 821	1 732 320	1 968 260	2 313 420	2 405 280	2 611 430	2 567 490	Importations
Exports	G	582 965	904 339	1 278 100	1 501 850	1 545 810	1 665 300	1 644 280	Exportations
Balance	G	-187 857	-827 981	-690 161	-811 579	-859 467	-946 130	-923 216	Balance
Uruguay									**Uruguay**
Imports	G	2 866	3 879	8 622	9 489	8 458	8 893	* 8 226	Importations
Exports	G	2 106	3 422	6 724	7 670	7 889	7 498	* 7 886	Exportations
Balance	G	-760	-457	-1 898	-1 820	-568	-1 395	* -340	Balance
Uzbekistan									**Ouzbékistan**
Imports	G	* 2 874	* 3 657	* 8 680	* 12 416	12 035	17 314	21 867	Importations
Exports	G	* 3 718	* 4 458	* 11 688	* 12 871	10 079	10 919	14 930	Exportations
Balance	G	* 844	* 801	* 3 008	* 455	-1 955	-6 395	-6 938	Balance
Vanuatu									**Vanuatu**
Imports	G	* 95	* 149	276	* 354	* 371	* 350	* 289	Importations
Exports	G	* 28	* 38	46	* 39	* 61	* 62	* 51	Exportations
Balance	G	* -67	* -111	-230	* -316	* -310	* -288	* -238	Balance
Venezuela (Boliv. Rep. of)									**Venezuela (Rép. boliv. du)**
Imports	G	10 791	21 848	32 343	* 40 146	* 6 771	* 2 667	* 1 051	Importations
Exports	G	19 093	55 413	66 963	* 37 236	* 11 563	* 6 614	* 3 783	Exportations
Balance	G	8 302	33 565	34 620	* -2 910	* 4 792	* 3 947	* 2 732	Balance
Viet Nam									**Viet Nam**
Imports	G	* 8 155	36 761	84 839	165 776	213 215	236 869	253 442	Importations
Exports	G	* 5 449	32 447	72 237	162 017	215 119	243 699	264 610	Exportations
Balance	G	* -2 706	-4 314	-12 602	-3 759	1 903	6 830	11 168	Balance
Wallis and Futuna Islands									**Îles Wallis-et-Futuna**
Imports	S	* 13	51	* 35	* 49	* 57	* 61	* 65	Importations
Exports	S	* ~0	* 1	* 1	* 1	* 1	* 1	* 1	Exportations
Balance	S	* -13	-50	* -34	* -48	* -55	* -59	* -63	Balance
Yemen									**Yémen**
Imports	S	* 1 812	5 400	9 255	6 573	* 2 945	3 309	4 716	Importations
Exports	S	* 1 917	5 608	6 437	510	* 10	15	24	Exportations
Balance	S	* 105	208	-2 818	-6 063	* -2 936	-3 294	-4 692	Balance
Zambia									**Zambie**
Imports	S	708	2 558	5 321	7 934	7 982	9 462	7 221	Importations
Exports	S	1 055	1 810	7 200	6 607	8 007	9 043	7 029	Exportations
Balance	S	347	-748	1 879	-1 328	25	-419	-192	Balance
Zimbabwe									**Zimbabwe**
Imports	G	2 659	2 072	5 852	6 053	4 962	6 450	4 787	Importations
Exports	G	1 846	1 394	3 199	3 411	3 480	4 037	4 279	Exportations
Balance	G	-813	-679	-2 653	-2 642	-1 482	-2 413	-508	Balance

Source:

United Nations Statistics Division, New York, Commodity Trade Statistics Database (UN COMTRADE), last accessed June 2020.

Source:

Organisation des Nations Unies, Division de statistique, New York, Comtrade base de données de l'ONU, dernier accès juin 2020.

& Systems of trade: Two systems of recording trade, the General trade system (G) and the Special trade system (S), are in common use. They differ mainly in the way warehoused and re-exported goods are recorded. See the Technical notes for an explanation of the trade systems.

& Systèmes de commerce : Deux systèmes d'enregistrement du commerce sont couramment utilisés, le Commerce général (G) et le Commerce spécial (S). Ils ne diffèrent que par la façon dont sont enregistrées les marchandises entreposées et les marchandises réexportées. Voir les Notes techniques pour une explication des Systèmes de commerce.

1	In 2014, the reported share of non-standard HS codes was relatively high.	
2	Imports FOB.	
3	For statistical purposes, the data for China do not include those for the Hong Kong Special Administrative Region (Hong Kong SAR), Macao Special Administrative Region (Macao SAR) and Taiwan Province of China.	
4	Special trade system up to 2007.	
5	General Extra-EU/Special Intra-EU	

1   En 2014, la part déclarée de codes SH non standard était relativement élevée.
2   Importations FAB.
3   Pour la présentation des statistiques, les données pour la Chine ne comprennent pas la région administrative spéciale de Hong Kong (RAS de Hong Kong), la région administrative spéciale de Macao (RAS de Macao) et la province chinoise de Taïwan.
4   Système commercial spécial jusqu'en 2007.
5   Extra-UE Général / intra-UE spécial

19

Total imports, exports and balance of trade *(continued)*
Imports CIF, exports FOB and balance: millions of US dollars

Total des importations, des exportations et balance commerciale *(suite)*
Importations CAF, exportations FAB et balance: en millions de dollars É.-U.

6	As of 2009, merchandise trade includes re-exports.	6	Depuis 2009, le commerce des marchandises comprend les réexportations.
7	Since 2011, Ghana have been exporting crude petroleum & natural gas in relatively larger quantities.	7	Depuis 2011, le Ghana exporte du pétrole brut et du gaz naturel en quantités relativement plus importantes.
8	Merchandise imports data follows special trade system up to 2007.	8	Les données sur les importations de marchandises suivent un système commercial spécial jusqu'en 2007.
9	Data include oil and gas. The value of oil exports and total exports are rough estimates based on information published in various petroleum industry journals.	9	Les données comprennent le pétrole et le gaz. La valeur des exportations de pétrole et des exportations totales sont des évaluations grossières basées sur l'information publiée à divers journaux d'industrie de pétrole.
10	Year ending 20 March of the year stated.	10	Année finissant le 20 mars de l'année indiquée.
11	Merchandise trade data up to 2009 reported by fiscal year and beginning 2010 reported by calendar year.	11	Données sur le commerce des marchandises jusqu'en 2009 déclarées par exercice et début 2010 déclarées par année civile.
12	From 2004 to 2011 merchandise data including Zona Libre de Colon.	12	De 2004 à 2011 données sur les marchandises, y compris la Zona Libre de Colon.
13	Russian data provided by the Russian Federation. Includes statistical data for the Autonomous Republic of Crimea and the city of Sevastopol, Ukraine, temporarily occupied by the Russian Federation.	13	Données russes fournies par la Fédération de Russie. Comprend des données statistiques pour la République autonome de Crimée et la ville de Sébastopol, Ukraine, temporairement occupée par la Fédération de Russie.
14	Special trade system up to 2008.	14	Système commercial spécial jusqu'en 2008.
15	Data up to 2011 refer to former Sudan (including South Sudan) and data beginning 2012 is attributed to Sudan without South Sudan.	15	Les données jusqu'en 2011 se réfèrent à l'ancien Soudan (y compris le Soudan du Sud) et les données commençant en 2012 sont attribuées au Soudan sans le Soudan du Sud.
16	The Government of Ukraine has informed the United Nations that it is not in a position to provide statistical data concerning the Autonomous Republic of Crimea and the city of Sevastopol.	16	Le Gouvernement ukrainien a informé l'Organisation des Nations Unies qu'il n'est pas en mesure de fournir des données statistiques concernant la République autonome de Crimée et Sébastopol.

Major trading partner
Three largest trade partners as a percentage of total international merchandise trade in US dollars, as at 2019

Partenaire commercial principal
Trois principaux partenaires commerciaux en pourcentage du total de commerce international de marchandises en dollars américains, en 2019

Country or area / Major trading partner	Percentage of exports 2010	2015	2019	Major trading partner	Percentage of imports 2010	2015	2019	Pays ou zone
Afghanistan								**Afghanistan**
Partner 1 Pakistan	39.0	39.7	* 42.9	Iran, Iran (Rép. islamique d')	7.5	23.4	* 17.1	Partenaire 1
Partner 2 India, Inde	16.8	33.1	* 40.6	China, Chine	13.7	13.5	* 15.7	Partenaire 2
Partner 3 China, Chine	3.0	1.8	* 3.2	Pakistan	11.6	17.4	* 14.7	Partenaire 3
Albania								**Albanie**
Partner 1 Italy, Italie	50.8	50.9	* 48.0	Italy, Italie	28.2	30.3	* 27.3	Partenaire 1
Partner 2 Serbia, Serbie	8.3	9.9	* 11.3	Turkey, Turquie	5.7	8.0	* 8.4	Partenaire 2
Partner 3 Spain, Espagne	3.4	5.2	* 7.8	China, Chine	6.3	8.6	* 8.4	Partenaire 3
Algeria								**Algérie**
Partner 1 Italy, Italie	15.4	15.1	* 16.0	China, Chine	11.2	15.9	* 18.1	Partenaire 1
Partner 2 France	6.6	13.2	* 12.6	France	14.9	10.5	* 9.3	Partenaire 2
Partner 3 Spain, Espagne	10.4	17.7	* 11.7	Italy, Italie	10.0	9.4	* 8.2	Partenaire 3
Andorra								**Andorre**
Partner 1 Spain, Espagne	67.4	57.5	* 61.7	Spain, Espagne	59.9	64.0	* 64.2	Partenaire 1
Partner 2 France	16.8	19.5	* 18.3	France	17.6	15.9	* 13.2	Partenaire 2
Partner 3 Norway, Norvège	4.3	3.7	* 3.7	China, Chine	4.1	3.8	* 3.6	Partenaire 3
Angola								**Angola**
Partner 1 China, Chine	39.8	42.2	* 58.2	China, Chine	10.1	15.4	* 14.5	Partenaire 1
Partner 2 India, Inde	9.7	7.9	* 9.0	Portugal	14.4	12.9	* 13.6	Partenaire 2
Partner 3 United States, États-Unis	18.9	3.7	* 3.5	Singapore, Singapour	0.8	9.7	* 9.6	Partenaire 3
Anguilla								**Anguilla**
Partner 1 Chile, Chili	...	* 0.4	* 55.4	United States, États-Unis	* 55.0	* 61.1	* 49.5	Partenaire 1
Partner 2 Malta, Malte	...	...	* 26.6	Chile, Chili	* 0.1	* 0.2	* 39.2	Partenaire 2
Partner 3 United States, États-Unis	* 22.0	* 44.9	* 5.3	Japan, Japon	* 1.2	* 3.7	* 2.1	Partenaire 3
Antigua and Barbuda								**Antigua-et-Barbuda**
Partner 1 United Arab Emirates, Émirats arabes unis	...	0.2	52.7	United States, États-Unis	34.5	* 55.5	48.2	Partenaire 1
Partner 2 United States, États-Unis	29.7	30.1	9.8	China, Chine	8.4	* 5.2	7.4	Partenaire 2
Partner 3 Netherlands, Pays-Bas	0.8	0.9	7.6	Japan, Japon	2.7	3.4	4.4	Partenaire 3
Argentina								**Argentine**
Partner 1 Brazil, Brésil	21.2	17.8	15.9	Brazil, Brésil	* 32.5	21.7	20.5	Partenaire 1
Partner 2 China, Chine	8.5	9.1	10.5	China, Chine	* 13.5	19.6	18.8	Partenaire 2
Partner 3 United States, États-Unis	5.4	6.7	6.3	United States, États-Unis	* 11.8	13.7	12.8	Partenaire 3
Armenia								**Arménie**
Partner 1 Russian Federation, Fédération de Russie	17.5	15.2	27.2	Russian Federation, Fédération de Russie	22.0	30.4	29.2	Partenaire 1
Partner 2 Switzerland, Suisse	1.7	2.8	17.5	China, Chine	10.6	9.7	14.7	Partenaire 2
Partner 3 Bulgaria, Bulgarie	15.5	5.3	7.9	Iran, Iran (Rép. islamique d')	5.8	6.1	6.4	Partenaire 3
Aruba								**Aruba**
Partner 1 Areas nes, Zones nsa [1]	3.0	14.2	* 52.2	United States, États-Unis	50.0	* 54.4	* 54.0	Partenaire 1
Partner 2 Colombia, Colombie	27.2	* 27.4	* 21.0	Areas nes, Zones nsa [1]	2.0	13.9	* 23.5	Partenaire 2
Partner 3 United States, États-Unis	* 6.2	* 6.9	* 17.9	Netherlands, Pays-Bas	11.3	* 10.4	* 10.9	Partenaire 3
Australia								**Australie**
Partner 1 China, Chine	* 25.4	* 31.9	38.7	China, Chine	* 18.7	* 23.0	25.7	Partenaire 1
Partner 2 Japan, Japon	* 18.5	* 15.9	14.8	United States, États-Unis	* 12.4	* 12.9	11.8	Partenaire 2
Partner 3 Rep. of Korea, République de Corée	* 8.6	* 7.2	6.6	Japan, Japon	* 8.7	* 7.5	7.0	Partenaire 3
Austria								**Autriche**
Partner 1 Germany, Allemagne	* 31.0	* 29.5	29.2	Germany, Allemagne	* 38.7	* 36.4	34.7	Partenaire 1
Partner 2 United States, États-Unis	* 4.4	* 6.7	6.6	Italy, Italie	* 6.6	* 6.0	6.6	Partenaire 2
Partner 3 Italy, Italie	* 7.7	* 6.2	6.3	China, Chine	* 4.7	* 5.9	6.2	Partenaire 3
Azerbaijan								**Azerbaïdjan**
Partner 1 Italy, Italie	* 33.1	* 17.8	28.7	Russian Federation, Fédération de Russie	17.4	15.6	16.8	Partenaire 1
Partner 2 Turkey, Turquie	* 0.8	* 11.7	14.6	Turkey, Turquie	11.7	12.6	12.1	Partenaire 2
Partner 3 Israel, Israël	8.2	6.3	6.8	China, Chine	8.9	5.6	10.5	Partenaire 3
Bahamas								**Bahamas**
Partner 1 United States, États-Unis	76.0	* 83.1	* 27.6	United States, États-Unis	* 90.9	81.9	* 29.2	Partenaire 1
Partner 2 Poland, Pologne	...	...	* 26.7	Rep. of Korea, République de Corée	...	0.3	* 24.6	Partenaire 2
Partner 3 Germany, Allemagne	~0.0	* 0.1	* 7.2	Japan, Japon	0.5	1.1	* 11.3	Partenaire 3
Bahrain								**Bahreïn**
Partner 1 Areas nes, Zones nsa [1]	~0.0	* ~0.0	* 48.1	Saudi Arabia, Arabie saoudite	3.0	28.7	* 33.1	Partenaire 1
Partner 2 Saudi Arabia, Arabie saoudite	7.2	66.9	* 13.3	China, Chine	7.4	9.6	* 9.1	Partenaire 2
Partner 3 United Arab Emirates, Émirats arabes unis	* 2.7	* 6.9	* 6.1	United Arab Emirates, Émirats arabes unis	2.3	6.9	* 6.4	Partenaire 3

20 Major trading partner *(continued)*
Three largest trade partners as a percentage of total international merchandise trade in US dollars, as at 2019

Partenaire commercial principal *(suite)*
Trois principaux partenaires commerciaux en pourcentage du total de commerce international de marchandises en dollars américains, en 2019

Country or area / Major trading partner		Percentage of exports			Major trading partner	Percentage of imports			Pays ou zone
		2010	2015	2019		2010	2015	2019	
Bangladesh									**Bangladesh**
Partner 1	United States, États-Unis	* 24.3	* 19.3	* 14.9	China, Chine	17.5	21.5	* 30.5	Partenaire 1
Partner 2	Germany, Allemagne	* 13.8	* 14.7	* 14.4	India, Inde	11.5	12.2	* 14.2	Partenaire 2
Partner 3	United Kingdom, Royaume-Uni	* 8.9	* 11.0	* 8.4	Singapore, Singapour	5.4	9.2	* 5.3	Partenaire 3
Barbados									**Barbade**
Partner 1	Areas nes, Zones nsa [1]	...	15.7	* 23.8	United States, États-Unis	43.9	39.2	* 39.5	Partenaire 1
Partner 2	United States, États-Unis	24.9	32.6	* 22.7	Trinidad and Tobago, Trinité-et-Tobago	7.2	15.8	* 17.9	Partenaire 2
Partner 3	Trinidad and Tobago, Trinité-et-Tobago	8.4	8.2	* 6.9	China, Chine	4.8	5.7	* 5.9	Partenaire 3
Belarus									**Bélarus**
Partner 1	Russian Federation, Fédération de Russie	39.4	38.6	* 38.2	Russian Federation, Fédération de Russie	55.8	55.8	* 58.4	Partenaire 1
Partner 2	Ukraine	10.1	9.4	* 12.0	China, Chine	4.6	7.7	* 7.8	Partenaire 2
Partner 3	United Kingdom, Royaume-Uni	3.7	11.0	* 9.1	Germany, Allemagne	6.8	4.6	* 4.7	Partenaire 3
Belgium									**Belgique**
Partner 1	Germany, Allemagne	18.6	16.8	17.9	Netherlands, Pays-Bas	18.6	16.7	17.4	Partenaire 1
Partner 2	France	16.6	15.4	14.1	Germany, Allemagne	16.1	12.7	13.2	Partenaire 2
Partner 3	Netherlands, Pays-Bas	11.9	11.4	12.1	France	11.0	9.5	9.7	Partenaire 3
Belize									**Belize**
Partner 1	United Kingdom, Royaume-Uni	26.1	26.1	33.5	United States, États-Unis	47.9	34.4	44.2	Partenaire 1
Partner 2	United States, États-Unis	49.1	38.9	25.4	China, Chine	9.7	10.1	13.6	Partenaire 2
Partner 3	Ireland, Irlande	...	4.6	6.4	Mexico, Mexique	10.0	10.8	10.9	Partenaire 3
Benin									**Bénin**
Partner 1	Bangladesh	0.6	7.4	* 22.7	Thailand, Thaïlande	8.6	7.7	* 14.0	Partenaire 1
Partner 2	India, Inde	4.6	13.0	* 18.3	India, Inde	* 0.9	9.8	* 12.1	Partenaire 2
Partner 3	Viet Nam	2.1	7.5	* 10.0	Togo	7.9	8.5	* 9.3	Partenaire 3
Bermuda									**Bermudes**
Partner 1	United States, États-Unis	* 68.9	80.8	* 62.6	United States, États-Unis	71.7	65.7	* 69.4	Partenaire 1
Partner 2	Areas nes, Zones nsa [1]	* 5.5	0.2	* 18.4	Canada	8.0	14.7	* 9.1	Partenaire 2
Partner 3	United Kingdom, Royaume-Uni	* 8.2	12.1	* 6.2	United Kingdom, Royaume-Uni	3.7	3.9	* 3.5	Partenaire 3
Bhutan									**Bhoutan**
Partner 1	India, Inde	82.4	* 71.9	* 92.3	India, Inde	75.1	* 73.1	* 84.3	Partenaire 1
Partner 2	Italy, Italie	0.1	* 1.4	* 2.1	Thailand, Thaïlande	2.5	* 2.2	* 5.0	Partenaire 2
Partner 3	Nepal, Népal	0.2	* 1.1	* 1.4	France	0.5	* 0.1	* 2.3	Partenaire 3
Bolivia (Plurin. State of)									**Bolivie (État plurin. de)**
Partner 1	Brazil, Brésil	* 34.2	27.5	* 19.0	China, Chine	11.7	18.1	* 20.7	Partenaire 1
Partner 2	Argentina, Argentine	8.2	16.8	* 16.0	Brazil, Brésil	* 18.0	16.4	* 16.1	Partenaire 2
Partner 3	India, Inde	0.1	2.2	* 8.0	Argentina, Argentine	12.7	11.8	* 11.6	Partenaire 3
Bosnia and Herzegovina									**Bosnie-Herzégovine**
Partner 1	Germany, Allemagne	* 15.8	* 16.8	14.6	Germany, Allemagne	10.5	12.1	12.0	Partenaire 1
Partner 2	Croatia, Croatie	* 15.3	* 10.5	12.2	Italy, Italie	8.9	11.1	12.0	Partenaire 2
Partner 3	Serbia, Serbie	* 14.2	* 9.4	11.4	Serbia, Serbie	10.5	10.9	11.1	Partenaire 3
Botswana									**Botswana**
Partner 1	India, Inde	0.9	12.4	21.6	South Africa, Afrique du Sud	72.8	65.3	57.9	Partenaire 1
Partner 2	Belgium, Belgique	3.3	19.8	19.6	Namibia, Namibie	1.2	14.5	7.9	Partenaire 2
Partner 3	United Arab Emirates, Émirats arabes unis	0.1	5.3	18.2	Canada	0.1	6.3	6.9	Partenaire 3
Brazil									**Brésil**
Partner 1	China, Chine	15.2	18.6	28.1	China, Chine	14.1	17.9	19.9	Partenaire 1
Partner 2	United States, États-Unis	10.0	13.5	13.2	United States, États-Unis	15.0	15.6	17.2	Partenaire 2
Partner 3	Netherlands, Pays-Bas	5.1	5.3	4.5	Argentina, Argentine	7.9	6.0	6.0	Partenaire 3
British Virgin Islands									**Îles Vierges britanniques**
Partner 1	Indonesia, Indonésie	* 4.0	* 13.5	* 14.6	United States, États-Unis	* 9.9	* 35.7	* 50.4	Partenaire 1
Partner 2	India, Inde	* 0.5	* 0.5	* 13.2	Areas nes, Zones nsa [1]	...	...	* 32.8	Partenaire 2
Partner 3	United States, États-Unis	* 14.1	* 12.9	* 8.6	Russian Federation, Fédération de Russie	* 6.2	* 8.5	* 2.4	Partenaire 3
Brunei Darussalam									**Brunéi Darussalam**
Partner 1	Japan, Japon	43.5	36.3	31.4	China, Chine	7.8	10.4	13.2	Partenaire 1
Partner 2	Singapore, Singapour	2.8	3.5	13.7	Singapore, Singapour	19.1	14.1	12.5	Partenaire 2
Partner 3	Australia, Australie	10.3	3.5	10.2	Malaysia, Malaisie	23.6	21.2	11.9	Partenaire 3
Bulgaria									**Bulgarie**
Partner 1	Germany, Allemagne	10.6	* 13.3	* 14.6	Germany, Allemagne	11.7	12.9	* 12.4	Partenaire 1
Partner 2	Italy, Italie	* 9.7	* 9.2	* 8.5	Russian Federation, Fédération de Russie	16.1	12.0	* 9.7	Partenaire 2
Partner 3	Romania, Roumanie	* 9.2	* 9.0	* 8.4	Italy, Italie	7.4	7.6	* 7.5	Partenaire 3

Major trading partner *(continued)*
Three largest trade partners as a percentage of total international merchandise trade in US dollars, as at 2019

Partenaire commercial principal *(suite)*
Trois principaux partenaires commerciaux en pourcentage du total de commerce international de marchandises en dollars américains, en 2019

Country or area	Major trading partner	Percentage of exports			Major trading partner	Percentage of imports			Pays ou zone
		2010	2015	2019		2010	2015	2019	
Burkina Faso									**Burkina Faso**
Partner 1	Switzerland, Suisse	63.5	50.6	* 52.7 China, Chine		9.7	11.1	* 12.6	Partenaire 1
Partner 2	India, Inde	0.1	10.3	* 15.4 Ivory Coast, Côte d'Ivoire		16.0	8.4	* 11.5	Partenaire 2
Partner 3	Singapore, Singapour	4.9	10.0	* 7.7 France		10.3	9.0	* 7.2	Partenaire 3
Burundi									**Burundi**
Partner 1	United Arab Emirates, Émirats arabes unis	8.8	12.7	* 29.7 Saudi Arabia, Arabie saoudite		0.6	6.3	* 17.2	Partenaire 1
Partner 2	Dem. Rep. of Congo, Rép. Dém. du Congo	6.2	24.8	* 11.2 China, Chine		12.0	12.6	* 13.0	Partenaire 2
Partner 3	Pakistan	...	...	* 7.8 United Arab Emirates, Émirats arabes unis		4.6	4.9	* 8.8	Partenaire 3
Cabo Verde									**Cabo Verde**
Partner 1	Spain, Espagne	* 32.2	69.0	* 65.0 Portugal		* 45.5	* 43.6	* 43.2	Partenaire 1
Partner 2	Portugal	* 24.4	14.1	* 15.2 Spain, Espagne		6.8	* 7.3	* 14.5	Partenaire 2
Partner 3	Italy, Italie	* ~0.0	2.0	* 13.3 Belgium, Belgique		1.8	* 2.7	* 7.4	Partenaire 3
Cambodia									**Cambodge**
Partner 1	United States, États-Unis	34.1	25.0	* 24.0 China, Chine		24.2	36.8	* 35.1	Partenaire 1
Partner 2	Germany, Allemagne	2.0	8.8	* 8.6 Thailand, Thaïlande		14.1	14.6	* 18.4	Partenaire 2
Partner 3	Japan, Japon	1.6	6.7	* 8.5 Viet Nam		9.9	8.7	* 12.7	Partenaire 3
Cameroon									**Cameroun**
Partner 1	Italy, Italie	9.7	4.6	* 13.9 China, Chine		10.6	19.4	* 17.2	Partenaire 1
Partner 2	China, Chine	8.5	12.5	* 12.1 France		14.6	10.3	* 9.8	Partenaire 2
Partner 3	France	6.3	5.2	* 10.5 Thailand, Thaïlande		3.0	4.0	* 5.7	Partenaire 3
Canada									**Canada**
Partner 1	United States, États-Unis	74.9	76.7	75.4 United States, États-Unis		50.4	53.2	50.7	Partenaire 1
Partner 2	China, Chine	3.3	3.9	3.9 China, Chine		11.0	12.2	12.5	Partenaire 2
Partner 3	United Kingdom, Royaume-Uni	4.1	3.1	3.3 Mexico, Mexique		5.5	5.8	6.1	Partenaire 3
Cayman Islands									**Îles Caïmanes**
Partner 1	Netherlands, Pays-Bas	* ~0.0	* 0.2	* 79.5 Netherlands, Pays-Bas		* 5.2	0.2	* 49.2	Partenaire 1
Partner 2	Spain, Espagne	* 59.9	* 0.6	* 11.0 United States, États-Unis		* 11.7	85.4	* 24.8	Partenaire 2
Partner 3	United States, États-Unis	* 1.0	* 13.5	* 3.3 Italy, Italie		* 2.6	0.2	* 7.3	Partenaire 3
Central African Republic									**République centrafricaine**
Partner 1	France	16.0	63.6	* 61.1 France		24.1	21.1	* 26.1	Partenaire 1
Partner 2	Benin, Bénin	...	...	* 9.9 Cameroon, Cameroun		7.1	6.6	* 12.1	Partenaire 2
Partner 3	China, Chine	8.0	6.9	* 7.0 Belgium, Belgique		3.1	3.4	* 8.1	Partenaire 3
Chad									**Tchad**
Partner 1	India, Inde	* ~0.0	* 15.4	* 29.8 China, Chine		* 22.5	* 13.2	* 20.3	Partenaire 1
Partner 2	United Arab Emirates, Émirats arabes unis	* 0.1	* 3.0	* 16.1 United Arab Emirates, Émirats arabes unis		* 1.9	* 10.2	* 13.1	Partenaire 2
Partner 3	United States, États-Unis	* 68.0	* 56.7	* 15.9 France		* 12.2	* 15.5	* 10.6	Partenaire 3
Chile									**Chili**
Partner 1	China, Chine	24.4	26.1	32.4 China, Chine		* 16.8	23.4	23.8	Partenaire 1
Partner 2	United States, États-Unis	* 9.9	* 13.2	13.6 United States, États-Unis		* 17.7	18.9	19.3	Partenaire 2
Partner 3	Japan, Japon	10.9	8.5	9.1 Brazil, Brésil		* 8.3	7.8	8.1	Partenaire 3
China									**Chine**
Partner 1	United States, États-Unis	18.0	18.0	* 19.2 Rep. of Korea, République de Corée		9.9	10.4	* 9.6	Partenaire 1
Partner 2	China,Hong Kong SAR, Chine, RAS Hong Kong	13.8	14.5	* 12.1 Japan, Japon		12.7	8.5	* 8.4	Partenaire 2
Partner 3	Japan, Japon	7.7	6.0	* 5.9 Other Asia, nes, Asie nsa		8.3	8.5	* 8.3	Partenaire 3
China, Hong Kong SAR									**Chine, RAS de Hong Kong**
Partner 1	China, Chine	52.5	56.3	55.3 China, Chine		44.7	46.7	45.7	Partenaire 1
Partner 2	United States, États-Unis	10.7	8.7	7.3 Other Asia, nes, Asie nsa		6.6	6.5	7.3	Partenaire 2
Partner 3	India, Inde	2.5	2.6	2.9 Singapore, Singapour		7.0	6.2	6.5	Partenaire 3
China, Macao SAR									**Chine, RAS de Macao**
Partner 1	China,Hong Kong SAR, Chine, RAS Hong Kong	9.6	42.2	84.8 China, Chine		29.1	13.6	33.1	Partenaire 1
Partner 2	China, Chine	5.5	11.5	10.4 Italy, Italie		4.4	0.3	10.2	Partenaire 2
Partner 3	United States, États-Unis	7.2	0.2	1.6 France		9.0	0.3	10.0	Partenaire 3
Colombia									**Colombie**
Partner 1	United States, États-Unis	* 43.1	* 28.2	31.1 United States, États-Unis		25.9	* 28.9	25.4	Partenaire 1
Partner 2	China, Chine	* 4.9	* 6.3	11.6 China, Chine		13.5	* 18.6	20.8	Partenaire 2
Partner 3	Panama	* 2.4	* 6.7	6.0 Mexico, Mexique		9.5	* 7.1	7.4	Partenaire 3
Comoros									**Comores**
Partner 1	France	22.0	22.1	45.8 United Arab Emirates, Émirats arabes unis		28.8	22.9	21.7	Partenaire 1
Partner 2	India, Inde	5.2	15.4	18.9 France		20.6	20.1	15.2	Partenaire 2
Partner 3	Germany, Allemagne	3.6	12.0	10.0 Pakistan		11.8	19.1	15.1	Partenaire 3

20

Major trading partner *(continued)*
Three largest trade partners as a percentage of total international merchandise trade in US dollars, as at 2019

Partenaire commercial principal *(suite)*
Trois principaux partenaires commerciaux en pourcentage du total de commerce international de marchandises en dollars américains, en 2019

Country or area / Major trading partner	Percentage of exports 2010	2015	2019	Major trading partner	Percentage of imports 2010	2015	2019	Pays ou zone
Congo								**Congo**
Partner 1 — China, Chine	20.9	16.0	59.8	France	12.2	6.3	15.0	Partenaire 1
Partner 2 — India, Inde	1.0	1.4	13.2	China, Chine	3.5	10.0	11.4	Partenaire 2
Partner 3 — Netherlands, Pays-Bas	2.8	0.7	4.1	Belgium, Belgique	3.7	0.9	10.3	Partenaire 3
Cook Islands								**Îles Cook**
Partner 1 — Japan, Japon	49.7	* 44.8	* 36.2	New Zealand, Nouvelle-Zélande	76.4	* 47.6	* 48.5	Partenaire 1
Partner 2 — Thailand, Thaïlande	...	* 9.6	* 19.9	Italy, Italie	~0.0	* 1.9	* 14.3	Partenaire 2
Partner 3 — France	...	* 0.9	* 15.9	Fiji, Fidji	9.4	* 8.3	* 9.6	Partenaire 3
Costa Rica								**Costa Rica**
Partner 1 — United States, États-Unis	37.4	40.8	* 41.1	United States, États-Unis	46.8	* 39.8	* 39.1	Partenaire 1
Partner 2 — Netherlands, Pays-Bas	7.0	4.6	* 6.0	China, Chine	7.1	* 12.6	* 13.7	Partenaire 2
Partner 3 — Belgium, Belgique	3.4	4.5	* 6.0	Mexico, Mexique	6.4	* 7.4	* 7.0	Partenaire 3
Côte d'Ivoire								**Côte d'Ivoire**
Partner 1 — Netherlands, Pays-Bas	14.2	* 11.4	10.7	China, Chine	* 7.0	11.6	17.2	Partenaire 1
Partner 2 — United States, États-Unis	* 10.3	7.7	6.0	Nigeria, Nigéria	* 26.3	13.9	13.5	Partenaire 2
Partner 3 — France	* 7.0	5.5	5.9	France	* 11.9	* 12.5	10.7	Partenaire 3
Croatia								**Croatie**
Partner 1 — Italy, Italie	18.7	13.4	14.0	Germany, Allemagne	12.5	15.5	15.5	Partenaire 1
Partner 2 — Germany, Allemagne	10.3	11.3	13.2	Italy, Italie	15.2	13.2	13.9	Partenaire 2
Partner 3 — Slovenia, Slovénie	7.8	12.3	10.8	Slovenia, Slovénie	5.8	10.7	11.5	Partenaire 3
Cuba								**Cuba**
Partner 1 — China, Chine	* 27.2	* 17.8	* 28.0	China, Chine	* 18.6	* 26.2	* 17.4	Partenaire 1
Partner 2 — Canada	* 22.6	* 22.0	* 25.8	Spain, Espagne	* 13.6	* 14.9	* 16.4	Partenaire 2
Partner 3 — Spain, Espagne	* 6.1	* 7.5	* 7.9	Mexico, Mexique	* 5.3	* 4.9	* 5.7	Partenaire 3
Cyprus								**Chypre**
Partner 1 — Netherlands, Pays-Bas	* 2.2	4.0	12.9	Greece, Grèce	18.7	20.3	20.3	Partenaire 1
Partner 2 — Libya, Libye	0.7	0.1	10.0	Italy, Italie	9.3	6.6	10.3	Partenaire 2
Partner 3 — Greece, Grèce	* 21.5	6.6	7.5	United Kingdom, Royaume-Uni	8.3	8.4	7.1	Partenaire 3
Czechia								**Tchéquie**
Partner 1 — Germany, Allemagne	33.1	32.2	31.8	Germany, Allemagne	26.4	26.0	24.7	Partenaire 1
Partner 2 — Slovakia, Slovaquie	8.2	9.0	7.6	China, Chine	12.1	13.5	15.8	Partenaire 2
Partner 3 — Poland, Pologne	6.0	5.9	6.0	Poland, Pologne	6.1	7.9	7.5	Partenaire 3
Dem. People's Rep. Korea								**Rép. pop. dém. de Corée**
Partner 1 — China, Chine	* 55.8	* 82.3	* 56.2	China, Chine	* 62.8	* 84.5	* 94.9	Partenaire 1
Partner 2 — Suriname	* 0.4	* 0.2	* 5.5	Russian Federation, Fédération de Russie	* 1.3	* 2.2	* 1.9	Partenaire 2
Partner 3 — Mali	* ~0.0	* ~0.0	* 5.2	Brazil, Brésil	* 0.6	* 0.1	* 0.9	Partenaire 3
Dem. Rep. of the Congo								**Rép. dém. du Congo**
Partner 1 — China, Chine	* 43.3	* 44.8	* 58.5	China, Chine	* 10.7	* 22.1	* 22.6	Partenaire 1
Partner 2 — United Arab Emirates, Émirats arabes unis	* 2.2	* 2.7	* 9.0	South Africa, Afrique du Sud	* 19.3	* 16.0	* 13.5	Partenaire 2
Partner 3 — Saudi Arabia, Arabie saoudite	* 3.4	* 10.3	* 5.6	Zambia, Zambie	* 7.6	* 8.2	* 11.5	Partenaire 3
Denmark								**Danemark**
Partner 1 — Undisclosed, Non divulgués [2]	1.4	2.0	17.6	Germany, Allemagne	20.7	20.5	21.6	Partenaire 1
Partner 2 — Germany, Allemagne	* 17.8	* 19.7	13.4	Sweden, Suède	13.3	12.3	12.0	Partenaire 2
Partner 3 — Sweden, Suède	* 15.0	* 14.8	9.8	Netherlands, Pays-Bas	7.1	8.0	7.8	Partenaire 3
Djibouti								**Djibouti**
Partner 1 — Saudi Arabia, Arabie saoudite	* 0.8	* 22.8	* 32.3	China, Chine	* 3.2	* 46.9	* 35.2	Partenaire 1
Partner 2 — United States, États-Unis	* 0.4	* 25.8	* 20.4	United Arab Emirates, Émirats arabes unis	* 18.5	* 7.5	* 21.5	Partenaire 2
Partner 3 — India, Inde	* 0.1	* 1.2	* 14.0	India, Inde	* 3.2	* 4.8	* 6.7	Partenaire 3
Dominica								**Dominique**
Partner 1 — Saudi Arabia, Arabie saoudite	...	* 10.3	* 40.4	United States, États-Unis	41.8	* 30.3	* 63.4	Partenaire 1
Partner 2 — Belarus, Bélarus	...	* ~0.0	* 8.3	China, Chine	4.0	* 13.9	* 6.3	Partenaire 2
Partner 3 — Sri Lanka	...	* 0.1	* 3.8	Italy, Italie	0.2	* 0.3	* 5.0	Partenaire 3
Dominican Republic								**République dominicaine**
Partner 1 — United States, États-Unis	57.7	53.6	* 53.3	United States, États-Unis	39.0	* 41.3	* 44.4	Partenaire 1
Partner 2 — Haiti, Haïti	16.8	12.1	* 9.6	China, Chine	10.7	13.4	* 13.2	Partenaire 2
Partner 3 — Canada	0.5	8.4	* 8.9	Mexico, Mexique	6.0	4.6	* 4.6	Partenaire 3
Ecuador								**Équateur**
Partner 1 — United States, États-Unis	* 34.7	39.4	* 30.9	United States, États-Unis	* 27.9	* 23.8	* 21.8	Partenaire 1
Partner 2 — Peru, Pérou	* 7.6	* 5.1	* 7.5	China, Chine	7.8	* 19.0	* 18.9	Partenaire 2
Partner 3 — China, Chine	1.9	3.9	* 6.9	Colombia, Colombie	* 9.8	* 7.6	* 7.9	Partenaire 3

20

Major trading partner *(continued)*
Three largest trade partners as a percentage of total international merchandise trade in US dollars, as at 2019

Partenaire commercial principal *(suite)*
Trois principaux partenaires commerciaux en pourcentage du total de commerce international de marchandises en dollars américains, en 2019

Country or area / Major trading partner		Percentage of exports			Major trading partner	Percentage of imports			Pays ou zone
		2010	2015	2019		2010	2015	2019	
Egypt									**Égypte**
Partner 1	United States, États-Unis	5.9	5.6	7.2	China, Chine	9.2	13.1	15.3	Partenaire 1
Partner 2	United Arab Emirates, Émirats arabes unis	2.3	5.1	6.8	United States, États-Unis	9.4	5.9	6.6	Partenaire 2
Partner 3	Turkey, Turquie	3.7	5.8	5.7	Saudi Arabia, Arabie saoudite	4.0	4.0	6.6	Partenaire 3
El Salvador									**El Salvador**
Partner 1	United States, États-Unis	48.4	46.9	42.2	United States, États-Unis	33.0	33.8	30.4	Partenaire 1
Partner 2	Guatemala	14.0	13.6	16.0	China, Chine	10.4	13.6	14.3	Partenaire 2
Partner 3	Honduras	12.9	14.0	15.9	Guatemala	8.7	9.9	10.6	Partenaire 3
Equatorial Guinea									**Guinée équatoriale**
Partner 1	China, Chine	* 6.2	* 17.6	* 38.7	United States, États-Unis	* 5.3	* 9.3	* 21.1	Partenaire 1
Partner 2	India, Inde	* 1.3	* 6.3	* 18.0	Spain, Espagne	* 5.8	* 16.7	* 18.6	Partenaire 2
Partner 3	Spain, Espagne	* 10.0	* 9.5	* 10.5	China, Chine	* 8.9	* 15.0	* 14.2	Partenaire 3
Eritrea									**Érythrée**
Partner 1	China, Chine	* 5.8	* 38.8	* 53.6	Egypt, Égypte	* 10.9	* 12.1	* 30.5	Partenaire 1
Partner 2	United Arab Emirates, Émirats arabes unis	* 13.4	* 4.5	* 24.4	United Arab Emirates, Émirats arabes unis	* 14.2	* 13.0	* 22.1	Partenaire 2
Partner 3	Rep. of Korea, République de Corée	* 0.1	* 3.0	* 20.5	China, Chine	* 7.6	* 32.9	* 11.2	Partenaire 3
Estonia									**Estonie**
Partner 1	Finland, Finlande	15.3	14.5	15.6	Germany, Allemagne	10.6	9.7	9.8	Partenaire 1
Partner 2	Sweden, Suède	14.0	17.3	10.0	Russian Federation, Fédération de Russie	10.5	9.8	9.6	Partenaire 2
Partner 3	Latvia, Lettonie	8.0	9.5	8.7	Finland, Finlande	11.5	9.9	8.6	Partenaire 3
Eswatini									**Eswatini**
Partner 1	South Africa, Afrique du Sud	* 50.1	62.7	66.6	South Africa, Afrique du Sud	* 81.2	79.2	73.0	Partenaire 1
Partner 2	Kenya	* 2.5	3.9	6.3	China, Chine	* 1.4	4.1	7.2	Partenaire 2
Partner 3	Nigeria, Nigéria	* 2.4	4.6	5.0	Mozambique	* 0.1	0.1	2.4	Partenaire 3
Ethiopia									**Éthiopie**
Partner 1	China, Chine	10.4	15.2	* 8.9	China, Chine	24.0	35.7	* 28.3	Partenaire 1
Partner 2	Saudi Arabia, Arabie saoudite	6.3	8.2	* 8.9	United States, États-Unis	5.6	5.4	* 10.7	Partenaire 2
Partner 3	United States, États-Unis	4.4	9.8	* 7.8	India, Inde	7.2	6.8	* 8.6	Partenaire 3
Falkland Islands (Malvinas)									**Îles Falkland (Malvinas)**
Partner 1	Spain, Espagne	* 79.7	* 70.8	* 77.3	United Kingdom, Royaume-Uni	* 77.7	* 78.1	* 78.9	Partenaire 1
Partner 2	United States, États-Unis	* 3.1	* 7.1	* 6.1	Netherlands, Pays-Bas	* 9.1	* 0.5	* 15.5	Partenaire 2
Partner 3	Morocco, Maroc	...	* 0.1	* 2.9	Spain, Espagne	* 1.2	* 1.2	* 1.3	Partenaire 3
Faroe Islands									**Îles Féroé**
Partner 1	United Kingdom, Royaume-Uni	* 17.3	* 18.3	* 20.1	Denmark, Danemark	* 30.4	* 45.3	* 55.0	Partenaire 1
Partner 2	Russian Federation, Fédération de Russie	* 4.0	* 22.2	* 20.0	Germany, Allemagne	* 6.1	* 4.8	* 12.7	Partenaire 2
Partner 3	Denmark, Danemark	* 11.0	* 13.5	* 11.8	Norway, Norvège	* 18.1	* 10.3	* 7.6	Partenaire 3
Fiji									**Fidji**
Partner 1	United States, États-Unis	11.4	15.7	* 17.9	Singapore, Singapour	33.1	19.0	* 20.8	Partenaire 1
Partner 2	Australia, Australie	21.1	* 15.1	* 12.9	China, Chine	6.1	14.6	* 16.3	Partenaire 2
Partner 3	Japan, Japon	7.2	3.9	* 7.4	Australia, Australie	20.3	15.4	* 15.7	Partenaire 3
Finland									**Finlande**
Partner 1	Germany, Allemagne	* 9.5	* 13.6	* 14.8	Germany, Allemagne	* 13.2	* 15.0	* 15.2	Partenaire 1
Partner 2	Sweden, Suède	* 11.4	* 10.1	* 10.2	Russian Federation, Fédération de Russie	* 17.7	* 11.0	* 13.9	Partenaire 2
Partner 3	Netherlands, Pays-Bas	* 6.6	* 6.4	* 6.5	Sweden, Suède	* 10.0	* 11.3	* 10.8	Partenaire 3
France									**France**
Partner 1	Germany, Allemagne	16.2	16.0	13.8	Germany, Allemagne	17.3	17.1	17.7	Partenaire 1
Partner 2	United States, États-Unis	5.7	7.3	8.3	Belgium, Belgique	7.8	7.2	9.8	Partenaire 2
Partner 3	Italy, Italie	8.1	7.2	7.4	Italy, Italie	7.5	7.4	8.1	Partenaire 3
French Polynesia									**Polynésie française**
Partner 1	Japan, Japon	20.1	26.1	* 38.6	United States, États-Unis	10.1	10.4	* 33.0	Partenaire 1
Partner 2	United States, États-Unis	11.6	18.0	* 30.6	France	28.1	25.6	* 31.8	Partenaire 2
Partner 3	France	13.2	13.9	* 13.6	New Zealand, Nouvelle-Zélande	8.1	7.5	* 6.0	Partenaire 3
Gabon									**Gabon**
Partner 1	China, Chine	* 8.0	* 18.2	* 51.6	France	* 32.9	* 18.4	* 21.7	Partenaire 1
Partner 2	Singapore, Singapour	* 0.4	* 0.4	* 6.8	China, Chine	* 4.9	* 20.5	* 16.4	Partenaire 2
Partner 3	Rep. of Korea, République de Corée	* 1.6	* 6.4	* 5.8	Belgium, Belgique	* 15.7	* 3.4	* 6.1	Partenaire 3
Gambia									**Gambie**
Partner 1	Mali	3.4	47.9	48.5	Ivory Coast, Côte d'Ivoire	19.4	18.0	14.5	Partenaire 1
Partner 2	Guinea-Bissau, Guinée-Bissau	3.1	2.0	18.9	India, Inde	4.4	3.0	12.1	Partenaire 2
Partner 3	China, Chine	2.0	2.9	13.5	China, Chine	8.7	7.0	10.6	Partenaire 3

20

Major trading partner *(continued)*
Three largest trade partners as a percentage of total international merchandise trade in US dollars, as at 2019

Partenaire commercial principal *(suite)*
Trois principaux partenaires commerciaux en pourcentage du total de commerce international de marchandises en dollars américains, en 2019

Country or area / Major trading partner		Percentage of exports			Major trading partner	Percentage of imports			Pays ou zone
		2010	2015	2019		2010	2015	2019	
Georgia									**Géorgie**
Partner 1	Azerbaijan, Azerbaïdjan	* 15.3	10.9	13.2	Turkey, Turquie	16.9	18.2	17.7	Partenaire 1
Partner 2	Russian Federation, Fédération de Russie	* 2.7	7.4	13.2	Russian Federation, Fédération de Russie	* 4.6	8.6	10.7	Partenaire 2
Partner 3	Armenia, Arménie	9.8	8.2	11.0	China, Chine	6.4	8.1	9.4	Partenaire 3
Germany									**Allemagne**
Partner 1	United States, États-Unis	6.9	* 9.5	8.9	China, Chine	9.8	9.8	10.0	Partenaire 1
Partner 2	France	* 9.5	* 8.8	8.0	Netherlands, Pays-Bas	7.7	* 8.3	7.9	Partenaire 2
Partner 3	China, Chine	5.6	* 6.0	7.3	United States, États-Unis	5.8	6.5	6.6	Partenaire 3
Ghana									**Ghana**
Partner 1	China, Chine	1.0	8.1	16.7	China, Chine	13.2	16.9	18.2	Partenaire 1
Partner 2	Switzerland, Suisse	4.1	9.9	14.7	United States, États-Unis	13.7	* 8.2	9.4	Partenaire 2
Partner 3	India, Inde	0.9	17.1	14.2	United Kingdom, Royaume-Uni	4.8	* 5.4	6.6	Partenaire 3
Gibraltar									**Gibraltar**
Partner 1	Mauritania, Mauritanie	* ~0.0	...	* 39.7	Areas nes, Zones nsa [1]	* 15.0	...	* 32.8	Partenaire 1
Partner 2	Poland, Pologne	* 1.3	* 3.9	* 18.3	Netherlands, Pays-Bas	* 9.4	* 6.9	* 15.0	Partenaire 2
Partner 3	Netherlands, Pays-Bas	* 0.1	* 0.5	* 15.3	United States, États-Unis	* 22.7	* 20.1	* 12.9	Partenaire 3
Greece									**Grèce**
Partner 1	Italy, Italie	* 9.2	11.4	10.8	Germany, Allemagne	10.7	10.6	10.6	Partenaire 1
Partner 2	Germany, Allemagne	* 9.3	7.3	6.7	Iraq	1.3	7.0	8.2	Partenaire 2
Partner 3	Turkey, Turquie	* 6.0	6.7	5.8	Italy, Italie	9.7	7.9	7.9	Partenaire 3
Greenland									**Groenland**
Partner 1	Denmark, Danemark	89.2	79.1	* 85.3	Denmark, Danemark	* 57.7	* 63.7	* 54.2	Partenaire 1
Partner 2	Areas nes, Zones nsa [1]	2.2	6.2	* 7.7	Sweden, Suède	* 21.6	* 15.6	* 17.1	Partenaire 2
Partner 3	Latvia, Lettonie	...	...	* 3.7	Spain, Espagne	0.2	* 0.2	* 11.5	Partenaire 3
Grenada									**Grenade**
Partner 1	United States, États-Unis	* 24.5	* 22.7	* 38.7	United States, États-Unis	* 31.9	* 35.7	* 37.9	Partenaire 1
Partner 2	Saint Lucia, Sainte-Lucie	* 12.8	* 10.5	* 7.6	Canada	* 2.5	* 1.9	* 22.1	Partenaire 2
Partner 3	St.Vincent & Grenadines, St.Vincent & Grenadines	* 3.2	* 2.5	* 5.8	China, Chine	* 3.4	* 3.9	* 4.2	Partenaire 3
Guatemala									**Guatemala**
Partner 1	United States, États-Unis	38.8	35.0	34.1	United States, États-Unis	37.1	37.1	37.1	Partenaire 1
Partner 2	El Salvador	11.7	11.6	12.3	China, Chine	7.1	10.6	11.2	Partenaire 2
Partner 3	Honduras	8.3	8.5	8.9	Mexico, Mexique	11.2	11.6	11.0	Partenaire 3
Guinea									**Guinée**
Partner 1	United Arab Emirates, Émirats arabes unis	* 2.2	9.9	* 35.8	China, Chine	* 19.7	14.9	* 32.3	Partenaire 1
Partner 2	China, Chine	* 2.6	1.8	* 33.8	India, Inde	* 3.7	10.9	* 8.4	Partenaire 2
Partner 3	India, Inde	* 16.8	16.4	* 6.1	Netherlands, Pays-Bas	* 15.2	13.4	* 6.2	Partenaire 3
Guinea-Bissau									**Guinée-Bissau**
Partner 1	India, Inde	* 79.0	* 67.5	* 49.9	Portugal	* 24.3	* 27.6	* 31.1	Partenaire 1
Partner 2	Belgium, Belgique	* ~0.0	* ~0.0	* 28.3	Senegal, Sénégal	* 21.4	* 22.7	* 19.9	Partenaire 2
Partner 3	Ivory Coast, Côte d'Ivoire	* 1.2	* 0.9	* 8.5	China, Chine	* 4.0	* 5.9	* 9.1	Partenaire 3
Guyana									**Guyana**
Partner 1	Canada	39.6	25.7	* 26.9	United States, États-Unis	27.7	25.9	* 57.0	Partenaire 1
Partner 2	United States, États-Unis	10.2	25.6	* 15.4	Trinidad and Tobago, Trinité-et-Tobago	22.0	23.2	* 18.2	Partenaire 2
Partner 3	Panama	0.1	1.3	* 10.9	China, Chine	5.8	7.6	* 5.5	Partenaire 3
Haiti									**Haïti**
Partner 1	United States, États-Unis	* 81.0	* 83.2	* 78.0	United States, États-Unis	* 35.2	* 31.4	* 31.0	Partenaire 1
Partner 2	Canada	* 3.6	* 2.6	* 6.5	Dominican Rep., République dominicaine	* 23.3	* 27.9	* 26.9	Partenaire 2
Partner 3	Dominican Rep., République dominicaine	* 2.3	* 4.4	* 3.2	China, Chine	* 7.4	* 12.0	* 15.5	Partenaire 3
Honduras									**Honduras**
Partner 1	United States, États-Unis	* 38.9	44.2	* 40.2	United States, États-Unis	38.5	35.0	* 34.7	Partenaire 1
Partner 2	Germany, Allemagne	7.5	8.0	* 7.9	China, Chine	7.7	15.4	* 15.0	Partenaire 2
Partner 3	Belgium, Belgique	4.3	2.7	* 7.0	Guatemala	8.9	8.0	* 8.6	Partenaire 3
Hungary									**Hongrie**
Partner 1	Germany, Allemagne	26.2	27.3	27.7	Germany, Allemagne	21.2	26.2	25.3	Partenaire 1
Partner 2	Italy, Italie	5.3	4.7	5.2	China, Chine	7.1	5.3	6.1	Partenaire 2
Partner 3	Slovakia, Slovaquie	5.1	5.0	5.2	Austria, Autriche	5.7	6.6	6.1	Partenaire 3
Iceland									**Islande**
Partner 1	Netherlands, Pays-Bas	34.0	26.1	26.3	Norway, Norvège	9.1	10.1	11.3	Partenaire 1
Partner 2	United Kingdom, Royaume-Uni	10.1	11.6	10.4	United States, États-Unis	7.9	7.9	8.5	Partenaire 2
Partner 3	Spain, Espagne	4.7	11.5	9.5	Germany, Allemagne	7.5	8.6	8.3	Partenaire 3

Partenaire commercial principal *(suite)*
Trois principaux partenaires commerciaux en pourcentage du total de commerce international de marchandises en dollars américains, en 2019

Country or area / Major trading partner		Percentage of exports 2010	2015	2019	Major trading partner	Percentage of imports 2010	2015	2019	Pays ou zone
India									**Inde**
Partner 1	United States, États-Unis	11.2	15.2	16.8	China, Chine	11.8	15.5	14.3	Partenaire 1
Partner 2	United Arab Emirates, Émirats arabes unis	12.3	11.3	9.1	United States, États-Unis	5.5	5.9	7.3	Partenaire 2
Partner 3	China, Chine	7.9	3.6	5.3	United Arab Emirates, Émirats arabes unis	8.8	5.2	6.3	Partenaire 3
Indonesia									**Indonésie**
Partner 1	China, Chine	9.9	10.0	16.7	China, Chine	15.1	20.6	26.3	Partenaire 1
Partner 2	United States, États-Unis	9.1	10.8	10.6	Singapore, Singapour	14.9	12.6	10.1	Partenaire 2
Partner 3	Japan, Japon	16.3	12.0	9.5	Japan, Japon	12.5	9.3	9.2	Partenaire 3
Iran (Islamic Republic of)									**Iran (Rép. islamique d')**
Partner 1	Other Asia, nes, Asie nsa	43.5	* 39.0	* 42.4	China, Chine	10.4	* 25.0	* 25.4	Partenaire 1
Partner 2	Other Europe, nes, Europe nsa	18.9	* 8.8	* 14.0	United Arab Emirates, Émirats arabes unis	28.6	* 13.3	* 15.8	Partenaire 2
Partner 3	China, Chine	5.3	* 10.1	* 8.6	Rep. of Korea, République de Corée	6.7	* 8.1	* 7.1	Partenaire 3
Iraq									**Iraq**
Partner 1	India, Inde	* 14.5	* 21.1	* 24.9	Areas nes, Zones nsa [1]	68.2	68.2	* 68.2	Partenaire 1
Partner 2	China, Chine	* 12.5	* 23.8	* 24.6	United Arab Emirates, Émirats arabes unis	* 4.3	* 4.9	* 7.8	Partenaire 2
Partner 3	Rep. of Korea, République de Corée	* 8.8	* 11.7	* 9.0	Turkey, Turquie	* 5.7	* 6.2	* 6.7	Partenaire 3
Ireland									**Irlande**
Partner 1	United States, États-Unis	* 23.8	* 24.5	30.8	United Kingdom, Royaume-Uni	* 28.8	* 24.1	22.5	Partenaire 1
Partner 2	United Kingdom, Royaume-Uni	* 14.0	* 12.1	10.3	United States, États-Unis	* 15.4	* 15.6	15.5	Partenaire 2
Partner 3	Belgium, Belgique	* 14.9	* 12.9	10.2	France	* 8.2	* 12.4	13.6	Partenaire 3
Israel									**Israël**
Partner 1	United States, États-Unis	* 33.2	* 31.8	27.3	United States, États-Unis	* 11.2	13.0	16.7	Partenaire 1
Partner 2	United Kingdom, Royaume-Uni	* 3.9	* 6.4	8.5	China, Chine	* 8.0	* 9.3	13.4	Partenaire 2
Partner 3	China, Chine	* 3.5	* 5.1	7.6	Germany, Allemagne	6.2	6.1	6.3	Partenaire 3
Italy									**Italie**
Partner 1	Germany, Allemagne	13.9	13.0	12.2	Germany, Allemagne	16.0	15.5	16.5	Partenaire 1
Partner 2	France	11.5	10.2	10.5	France	8.7	8.7	8.7	Partenaire 2
Partner 3	United States, États-Unis	6.2	9.0	9.6	China, Chine	7.8	7.6	7.5	Partenaire 3
Jamaica									**Jamaïque**
Partner 1	United States, États-Unis	49.6	37.0	38.8	United States, États-Unis	37.4	38.5	45.2	Partenaire 1
Partner 2	Netherlands, Pays-Bas	5.1	8.7	13.8	China, Chine	4.6	8.2	7.8	Partenaire 2
Partner 3	Canada	12.3	14.5	8.8	Colombia, Colombie	1.1	2.1	5.2	Partenaire 3
Japan									**Japon**
Partner 1	United States, États-Unis	15.6	20.2	19.9	China, Chine	22.1	25.7	23.5	Partenaire 1
Partner 2	China, Chine	19.4	17.5	19.1	United States, États-Unis	10.0	10.9	11.3	Partenaire 2
Partner 3	Rep. of Korea, République de Corée	8.1	7.0	6.6	Australia, Australie	6.5	5.6	6.3	Partenaire 3
Jordan									**Jordanie**
Partner 1	United States, États-Unis	* 13.2	* 18.5	* 22.8	Saudi Arabia, Arabie saoudite	* 19.8	* 15.0	* 16.6	Partenaire 1
Partner 2	Saudi Arabia, Arabie saoudite	* 9.6	* 15.1	* 9.9	China, Chine	10.8	12.9	* 13.6	Partenaire 2
Partner 3	Iraq	* 16.0	* 9.5	* 9.1	United States, États-Unis	5.6	6.2	* 8.7	Partenaire 3
Kazakhstan									**Kazakhstan**
Partner 1	Italy, Italie	16.7	17.7	14.5	Russian Federation, Fédération de Russie	22.8	34.4	36.7	Partenaire 1
Partner 2	China, Chine	17.7	11.9	13.6	China, Chine	16.5	16.6	17.1	Partenaire 2
Partner 3	Russian Federation, Fédération de Russie	5.3	9.9	9.7	Rep. of Korea, République de Corée	2.2	2.0	8.9	Partenaire 3
Kenya									**Kenya**
Partner 1	Uganda, Ouganda	12.7	* 10.4	* 10.1	China, Chine	12.6	* 22.6	* 21.1	Partenaire 1
Partner 2	Pakistan	4.4	* 10.8	* 9.7	India, Inde	10.8	* 9.9	* 10.5	Partenaire 2
Partner 3	United States, États-Unis	5.5	* 8.0	* 7.7	Saudi Arabia, Arabie saoudite	3.4	* 6.6	* 9.8	Partenaire 3
Kiribati									**Kiribati**
Partner 1	Thailand, Thaïlande	...	...	* 54.7	Fiji, Fidji	26.8	21.1	* 21.3	Partenaire 1
Partner 2	Philippines	...	...	* 17.1	China, Chine	5.4	11.6	* 18.2	Partenaire 2
Partner 3	Rep. of Korea, République de Corée	...	0.1	* 9.6	Australia, Australie	28.1	20.0	* 13.6	Partenaire 3
Kuwait									**Koweït**
Partner 1	Areas nes, Zones nsa [1]	...	~0.0	* 90.9	China, Chine	12.5	16.4	* 16.7	Partenaire 1
Partner 2	India, Inde	* 11.9	* 9.7	* 1.6	United States, États-Unis	11.4	9.2	* 8.7	Partenaire 2
Partner 3	China, Chine	* 8.4	* 11.7	* 1.3	United Arab Emirates, Émirats arabes unis	4.5	9.4	* 8.6	Partenaire 3
Kyrgyzstan									**Kirghizistan**
Partner 1	United Kingdom, Royaume-Uni	0.6	0.1	* 36.5	China, Chine	20.7	25.3	* 36.7	Partenaire 1
Partner 2	Russian Federation, Fédération de Russie	17.3	10.9	* 19.4	Russian Federation, Fédération de Russie	33.6	31.3	* 28.5	Partenaire 2
Partner 3	Kazakhstan	12.2	15.8	* 14.7	Kazakhstan	12.0	16.7	* 11.4	Partenaire 3

20 Major trading partner (continued)
Three largest trade partners as a percentage of total international merchandise trade in US dollars, as at 2019

Partenaire commercial principal (suite)
Trois principaux partenaires commerciaux en pourcentage du total de commerce international de marchandises en dollars américains, en 2019

Country or area / Major trading partner	Percentage of exports 2010	2015	2019	Major trading partner	Percentage of imports 2010	2015	2019	Pays ou zone
Lao People's Dem. Rep.								**Rép. dém. populaire lao**
Partner 1	Thailand, Thaïlande	53.5	33.8	41.4 Thailand, Thaïlande	71.8	58.8	50.3	Partenaire 1
Partner 2	China, Chine	11.7	34.8	28.8 China, Chine	9.8	18.9	29.0	Partenaire 2
Partner 3	Viet Nam	6.5	18.0	18.2 Viet Nam	6.6	13.9	7.8	Partenaire 3
Latvia								**Lettonie**
Partner 1	Lithuania, Lituanie	16.2	20.3	17.1 Lithuania, Lituanie	17.1	17.1	17.6	Partenaire 1
Partner 2	Estonia, Estonie	13.5	11.5	11.7 Germany, Allemagne	11.5	11.0	10.9	Partenaire 2
Partner 3	Russian Federation, Fédération de Russie	10.6	8.0	9.2 Poland, Pologne	7.9	10.8	9.4	Partenaire 3
Lebanon								**Liban**
Partner 1	United Arab Emirates, Émirats arabes unis	* 9.8	* 10.6	* 15.5 China, Chine	9.1	11.2	* 10.3	Partenaire 1
Partner 2	Saudi Arabia, Arabie saoudite	* 5.8	12.1	* 7.2 Greece, Grèce	1.4	4.2	* 8.5	Partenaire 2
Partner 3	Syria, République arabe syrienne	* 5.2	* 7.0	* 7.0 Italy, Italie	7.8	6.9	* 8.0	Partenaire 3
Lesotho								**Lesotho**
Partner 1	South Africa, Afrique du Sud	74.9	* 30.7	* 49.2 South Africa, Afrique du Sud	78.9	74.7	* 70.7	Partenaire 1
Partner 2	United States, États-Unis	21.4	* 28.8	* 45.5 China, Chine	2.6	5.2	* 14.8	Partenaire 2
Partner 3	Eswatini	0.2	* 0.3	* 1.7 Other Asia, nes, Asie nsa	5.3	8.3	* 5.3	Partenaire 3
Liberia								**Libéria**
Partner 1	Areas nes, Zones nsa [1]	...	* 20.0	* 20.0 Areas nes, Zones nsa [1]	...	...	* 59.9	Partenaire 1
Partner 2	Switzerland, Suisse	* 0.5	* 2.6	* 13.5 China, Chine	* 29.6	* 31.6	* 16.5	Partenaire 2
Partner 3	France	* 1.0	* 4.9	* 8.6 India, Inde	* 2.2	* 6.5	* 4.5	Partenaire 3
Libya								**Libye**
Partner 1	Italy, Italie	42.3	* 34.2	* 18.6 Turkey, Turquie	10.6	* 11.1	* 14.1	Partenaire 1
Partner 2	China, Chine	9.4	* 8.6	* 16.2 United Arab Emirates, Émirats arabes unis	0.6	* 10.4	* 10.5	Partenaire 2
Partner 3	Germany, Allemagne	2.6	* 12.0	* 15.5 China, Chine	9.8	* 14.7	* 9.8	Partenaire 3
Lithuania								**Lituanie**
Partner 1	Russian Federation, Fédération de Russie	15.6	13.7	14.0 Russian Federation, Fédération de Russie	32.7	16.3	14.7	Partenaire 1
Partner 2	Latvia, Lettonie	9.5	9.9	9.5 Poland, Pologne	8.8	10.3	11.9	Partenaire 2
Partner 3	Poland, Pologne	7.7	9.7	7.9 Germany, Allemagne	10.9	11.5	11.6	Partenaire 3
Luxembourg								**Luxembourg**
Partner 1	Germany, Allemagne	28.4	27.1	* 26.3 Belgium, Belgique	* 24.9	22.7	* 25.5	Partenaire 1
Partner 2	France	16.2	14.0	* 14.7 Germany, Allemagne	* 25.6	24.0	* 23.3	Partenaire 2
Partner 3	Belgium, Belgique	12.6	12.7	* 11.8 France	* 14.9	11.9	* 12.5	Partenaire 3
Madagascar								**Madagascar**
Partner 1	France	* 33.1	* 20.2	20.2 China, Chine	12.2	18.2	19.1	Partenaire 1
Partner 2	United States, États-Unis	* 4.2	* 10.8	19.8 France	14.4	* 6.2	14.1	Partenaire 2
Partner 3	China, Chine	* 5.2	* 6.6	6.3 United Arab Emirates, Émirats arabes unis	2.9	* 6.4	10.0	Partenaire 3
Malawi								**Malawi**
Partner 1	Belgium, Belgique	12.4	10.6	* 22.0 South Africa, Afrique du Sud	30.1	18.1	* 17.8	Partenaire 1
Partner 2	South Africa, Afrique du Sud	5.8	7.4	* 7.8 China, Chine	9.1	13.1	* 14.7	Partenaire 2
Partner 3	United Rep. of Tanzania, Rép.-Unie de Tanzanie	0.7	1.9	* 7.7 India, Inde	7.6	10.3	* 10.9	Partenaire 3
Malaysia								**Malaisie**
Partner 1	China, Chine	12.6	13.0	14.2 China, Chine	12.6	18.9	20.7	Partenaire 1
Partner 2	Singapore, Singapour	13.4	13.9	13.9 Singapore, Singapour	11.4	12.0	10.5	Partenaire 2
Partner 3	United States, États-Unis	9.5	9.5	9.7 United States, États-Unis	10.7	8.1	8.1	Partenaire 3
Maldives								**Maldives**
Partner 1	Thailand, Thaïlande	29.9	25.4	* 36.3 United Arab Emirates, Émirats arabes unis	18.8	16.7	* 18.1	Partenaire 1
Partner 2	Germany, Allemagne	2.8	7.0	* 12.7 China, Chine	2.9	7.8	* 16.5	Partenaire 2
Partner 3	United Kingdom, Royaume-Uni	9.5	5.7	* 9.2 Singapore, Singapour	17.9	17.1	* 12.5	Partenaire 3
Mali								**Mali**
Partner 1	South Africa, Afrique du Sud	57.1	* 47.0	* 41.0 Senegal, Sénégal	13.6	* 19.5	* 20.5	Partenaire 1
Partner 2	Switzerland, Suisse	12.1	* 15.0	* 21.4 China, Chine	9.9	* 15.6	* 15.2	Partenaire 2
Partner 3	Burkina Faso	2.2	* 3.9	* 6.1 Ivory Coast, Côte d'Ivoire	7.9	* 9.8	* 9.7	Partenaire 3
Malta								**Malte**
Partner 1	Germany, Allemagne	* 10.4	* 9.6	13.4 United Kingdom, Royaume-Uni	8.3	* 6.8	18.5	Partenaire 1
Partner 2	Italy, Italie	* 5.4	* 4.0	7.7 Italy, Italie	24.6	* 21.3	16.9	Partenaire 2
Partner 3	France	* 9.8	* 6.8	7.3 Germany, Allemagne	6.8	6.2	6.6	Partenaire 3
Marshall Islands								**Îles Marshall**
Partner 1	Thailand, Thaïlande	* 33.6	* 14.0	* 18.8 Areas nes, Zones nsa [1]	...	...	* 77.4	Partenaire 1
Partner 2	Malaysia, Malaisie	...	* 6.8	* 18.2 China, Chine	* 24.3	* 29.6	* 10.2	Partenaire 2
Partner 3	China, Chine	* 4.5	* 15.9	* 17.3 Brazil, Brésil	* 0.3	* 0.5	* 3.8	Partenaire 3

20 Major trading partner *(continued)*
Three largest trade partners as a percentage of total international merchandise trade in US dollars, as at 2019

Partenaire commercial principal *(suite)*
Trois principaux partenaires commerciaux en pourcentage du total de commerce international de marchandises en dollars américains, en 2019

Country or area	Major trading partner	Percentage of exports			Major trading partner	Percentage of imports			Pays ou zone
		2010	2015	2019		2010	2015	2019	
Mauritania									**Mauritanie**
Partner 1	China, Chine	39.4	* 36.9	* 35.1	Rep. of Korea, République de Corée	0.1	* 0.1	* 18.1	Partenaire 1
Partner 2	Switzerland, Suisse	13.1	* 13.5	* 15.4	United Arab Emirates, Émirats arabes unis	12.1	* 11.9	* 8.9	Partenaire 2
Partner 3	Spain, Espagne	7.2	* 8.9	* 11.6	Norway, Norvège	~0.0	* 0.2	* 7.8	Partenaire 3
Mauritius									**Maurice**
Partner 1	France	16.2	11.9	12.6	China, Chine	13.3	18.2	16.7	Partenaire 1
Partner 2	United Kingdom, Royaume-Uni	23.7	13.1	11.1	India, Inde	22.3	18.1	13.9	Partenaire 2
Partner 3	United States, États-Unis	10.9	10.6	10.8	South Africa, Afrique du Sud	8.4	6.5	8.1	Partenaire 3
Mexico									**Mexique**
Partner 1	United States, États-Unis	80.1	* 81.3	76.0	United States, États-Unis	48.2	47.4	44.1	Partenaire 1
Partner 2	Areas nes, Zones nsa [1]	0.1	0.4	6.2	China, Chine	15.1	17.7	17.8	Partenaire 2
Partner 3	Canada	3.6	* 2.8	3.0	Japan, Japon	5.0	4.4	3.8	Partenaire 3
Micronesia (Fed. States of)									**Micronésie (États féd. de)**
Partner 1	Thailand, Thaïlande	* 30.6	* 50.3	* 68.3	United States, États-Unis	48.7	* 23.8	* 36.2	Partenaire 1
Partner 2	China, Chine	* 3.8	* 5.6	* 14.4	China, Chine	2.7	* 7.2	* 14.8	Partenaire 2
Partner 3	Japan, Japon	* 10.4	* 18.7	* 9.4	Japan, Japon	8.7	* 12.6	* 14.4	Partenaire 3
Mongolia									**Mongolie**
Partner 1	China, Chine	* 81.8	83.5	* 92.8	China, Chine	* 41.5	35.8	* 33.5	Partenaire 1
Partner 2	United Kingdom, Royaume-Uni	* 2.1	7.2	* 2.5	Russian Federation, Fédération de Russie	* 26.8	26.9	* 29.1	Partenaire 2
Partner 3	Russian Federation, Fédération de Russie	* 2.5	1.6	* 1.2	Japan, Japon	* 4.6	7.2	* 9.6	Partenaire 3
Montenegro									**Monténégro**
Partner 1	Serbia, Serbie	* 28.2	* 22.1	* 23.6	Serbia, Serbie	26.2	28.1	* 19.3	Partenaire 1
Partner 2	Hungary, Hongrie	8.8	0.9	* 11.7	China, Chine	5.4	10.3	* 10.1	Partenaire 2
Partner 3	Areas nes, Zones nsa [1]	0.1	9.5	* 8.6	Germany, Allemagne	7.1	6.3	* 9.2	Partenaire 3
Montserrat									**Montserrat**
Partner 1	United States, États-Unis	28.5	* 48.4	* 19.5	United States, États-Unis	* 68.5	* 37.0	* 74.3	Partenaire 1
Partner 2	Antigua and Barbuda, Antigua-et-Barbuda	2.5	* 0.8	* 17.2	United Kingdom, Royaume-Uni	* 5.6	* 3.6	* 5.1	Partenaire 2
Partner 3	France	25.9	* 6.5	* 13.9	Egypt, Égypte	...	* 0.1	* 2.9	Partenaire 3
Morocco									**Maroc**
Partner 1	Spain, Espagne	* 17.0	* 22.5	24.1	Spain, Espagne	10.6	14.4	15.6	Partenaire 1
Partner 2	France	22.5	* 20.6	21.6	France	15.6	12.4	12.2	Partenaire 2
Partner 3	Italy, Italie	4.5	* 4.4	4.7	China, Chine	8.4	8.2	10.1	Partenaire 3
Mozambique									**Mozambique**
Partner 1	India, Inde	* 1.4	* 20.2	* 27.6	South Africa, Afrique du Sud	34.4	* 30.0	* 26.1	Partenaire 1
Partner 2	Netherlands, Pays-Bas	* 52.7	* 20.9	* 21.2	China, Chine	3.6	* 7.9	* 11.8	Partenaire 2
Partner 3	South Africa, Afrique du Sud	* 20.8	* 21.0	* 17.2	United Arab Emirates, Émirats arabes unis	1.3	* 7.2	* 7.6	Partenaire 3
Myanmar									**Myanmar**
Partner 1	China, Chine	2.9	39.5	31.7	China, Chine	19.8	38.0	34.7	Partenaire 1
Partner 2	Thailand, Thaïlande	35.8	29.3	17.9	Singapore, Singapour	23.1	21.6	18.2	Partenaire 2
Partner 3	Japan, Japon	2.5	3.8	7.9	Thailand, Thaïlande	9.6	11.6	11.7	Partenaire 3
Namibia									**Namibie**
Partner 1	China, Chine	2.9	3.4	24.0	South Africa, Afrique du Sud	* 72.4	63.7	43.2	Partenaire 1
Partner 2	South Africa, Afrique du Sud	29.0	* 19.5	16.2	Zambia, Zambie	1.3	2.1	14.9	Partenaire 2
Partner 3	Botswana	0.7	22.3	9.8	China, Chine	3.4	6.4	3.9	Partenaire 3
Nepal									**Népal**
Partner 1	India, Inde	65.3	63.5	* 56.7	India, Inde	63.6	60.6	* 65.0	Partenaire 1
Partner 2	United States, États-Unis	6.3	10.7	* 11.2	China, Chine	11.0	13.9	* 12.6	Partenaire 2
Partner 3	Turkey, Turquie	1.0	1.9	* 6.4	Areas nes, Zones nsa [1]	...	...	* 2.0	Partenaire 3
Netherlands									**Pays-Bas**
Partner 1	Germany, Allemagne	22.2	22.5	22.2	Germany, Allemagne	15.5	18.0	17.1	Partenaire 1
Partner 2	Belgium, Belgique	9.9	10.7	10.1	Belgium, Belgique	8.4	10.6	9.9	Partenaire 2
Partner 3	France	8.1	7.9	7.8	China, Chine	9.3	9.1	9.4	Partenaire 3
New Caledonia									**Nouvelle-Calédonie**
Partner 1	China, Chine	3.5	35.7	* 57.2	France	22.3	25.7	* 42.4	Partenaire 1
Partner 2	Rep. of Korea, République de Corée	11.6	15.1	* 13.4	Australia, Australie	* 9.7	5.7	* 12.9	Partenaire 2
Partner 3	Japan, Japon	18.8	15.9	* 11.6	Singapore, Singapour	12.9	8.2	* 11.6	Partenaire 3
New Zealand									**Nouvelle-Zélande**
Partner 1	China, Chine	11.1	17.6	27.9	China, Chine	16.0	19.6	20.2	Partenaire 1
Partner 2	Australia, Australie	23.0	17.0	14.5	Australia, Australie	18.2	11.9	11.5	Partenaire 2
Partner 3	United States, États-Unis	8.6	11.8	9.4	United States, États-Unis	10.4	11.8	10.0	Partenaire 3

20

Major trading partner *(continued)*
Three largest trade partners as a percentage of total international merchandise trade in US dollars, as at 2019

Partenaire commercial principal *(suite)*
Trois principaux partenaires commerciaux en pourcentage du total de commerce international de marchandises en dollars américains, en 2019

Country or area / Major trading partner		Percentage of exports			Major trading partner	Percentage of imports			Pays ou zone
		2010	2015	2019		2010	2015	2019	
Nicaragua									**Nicaragua**
Partner 1	United States, États-Unis	32.8	53.7	* 61.1	United States, États-Unis	20.7	18.0	* 27.8	Partenaire 1
Partner 2	El Salvador	10.7	5.6	* 5.7	China, Chine	8.7	14.4	* 13.2	Partenaire 2
Partner 3	Mexico, Mexique	2.8	11.1	* 5.6	Mexico, Mexique	7.7	10.4	* 10.1	Partenaire 3
Niger									**Niger**
Partner 1	United Arab Emirates, Émirats arabes unis	~0.0	0.2	* 32.9	Nigeria, Nigéria	3.9	3.7	* 10.0	Partenaire 1
Partner 2	Mali	0.1	2.9	* 21.6	France	11.0	31.7	* 10.0	Partenaire 2
Partner 3	China, Chine	* 7.8	1.0	* 18.5	China, Chine	43.8	23.0	* 8.1	Partenaire 3
Nigeria									**Nigéria**
Partner 1	India, Inde	10.5	* 18.0	* 15.9	China, Chine	16.6	* 19.7	* 19.4	Partenaire 1
Partner 2	Netherlands, Pays-Bas	4.5	* 7.8	* 10.7	Netherlands, Pays-Bas	0.8	* 11.7	* 11.4	Partenaire 2
Partner 3	Spain, Espagne	3.3	* 9.2	* 10.1	Rep. of Korea, République de Corée	1.3	* 1.1	* 10.8	Partenaire 3
North Macedonia									**Macédoine du Nord**
Partner 1	Germany, Allemagne	21.3	44.0	48.7	United Kingdom, Royaume-Uni	5.2	9.7	11.5	Partenaire 1
Partner 2	Serbia, Serbie	21.2	8.9	8.5	Germany, Allemagne	11.2	12.6	11.4	Partenaire 2
Partner 3	Bulgaria, Bulgarie	8.8	6.0	4.9	Greece, Grèce	8.2	7.8	8.1	Partenaire 3
Northern Mariana Islands									**Îles Mariannes du Nord**
Partner 1	Areas nes, Zones nsa [1]	* 91.1	* 91.1	* 91.1	Areas nes, Zones nsa [1]	* 66.2	* 66.1	* 66.1	Partenaire 1
Partner 2	Rep. of Korea, République de Corée	* 0.6	* 0.7	* 6.6	China, Hong Kong SAR, Chine, RAS Hong Kong	* 11.4	* 10.2	* 14.8	Partenaire 2
Partner 3	Peru, Pérou	* ~0.0	* ~0.0	* 0.4	Singapore, Singapour	* 5.6	* 2.9	* 4.7	Partenaire 3
Norway									**Norvège**
Partner 1	United Kingdom, Royaume-Uni	27.5	20.1	20.1	Sweden, Suède	14.0	11.5	11.7	Partenaire 1
Partner 2	Germany, Allemagne	11.1	17.8	14.5	Germany, Allemagne	12.3	11.3	10.8	Partenaire 2
Partner 3	Netherlands, Pays-Bas	11.9	11.0	11.1	China, Chine	8.5	10.5	10.2	Partenaire 3
Oman									**Oman**
Partner 1	Areas nes, Zones nsa [1]	16.8	3.4	* 65.3	United Arab Emirates, Émirats arabes unis	28.4	13.6	* 45.9	Partenaire 1
Partner 2	United Arab Emirates, Émirats arabes unis	11.6	* 11.8	* 6.9	China, Chine	4.8	12.9	* 5.9	Partenaire 2
Partner 3	Qatar	0.5	* 0.8	* 4.3	India, Inde	4.5	7.2	* 4.4	Partenaire 3
Other non-specified areas									**Autres zones non-spécifiées**
Partner 1	China, Chine	28.0	25.4	* 28.8	China, Chine	14.3	19.3	* 18.8	Partenaire 1
Partner 2	China, Hong Kong SAR, Chine, RAS Hong Kong	13.8	13.6	* 12.4	Japan, Japon	20.7	16.9	* 15.4	Partenaire 2
Partner 3	United States, États-Unis	11.5	12.2	* 11.8	United States, États-Unis	10.2	11.6	* 12.2	Partenaire 3
Pakistan									**Pakistan**
Partner 1	United States, États-Unis	17.2	16.6	17.0	China, Chine	14.0	25.0	24.8	Partenaire 1
Partner 2	China, Chine	6.7	8.8	8.6	United Arab Emirates, Émirats arabes unis	14.0	13.0	12.6	Partenaire 2
Partner 3	United Kingdom, Royaume-Uni	5.2	7.1	7.1	United States, États-Unis	4.3	4.4	5.2	Partenaire 3
Palau									**Palaos**
Partner 1	Japan, Japon	* 82.5	* 6.0	* 77.2	United States, États-Unis	34.9	37.7	* 34.8	Partenaire 1
Partner 2	Areas nes, Zones nsa [1]	...	32.0	* 8.9	Singapore, Singapour	17.9	14.8	* 17.0	Partenaire 2
Partner 3	Panama	...	~0.0	* 4.7	Rep. of Korea, République de Corée	2.0	6.1	* 10.3	Partenaire 3
Panama									**Panama**
Partner 1	Ecuador, Équateur	* 4.1	* 3.6	* 21.5	United States, États-Unis	20.5	* 9.3	* 18.8	Partenaire 1
Partner 2	Guatemala	* 3.9	* 4.3	* 13.2	China, Chine	24.9	* 34.1	* 16.9	Partenaire 2
Partner 3	United States, États-Unis	* 19.8	* 21.8	* 9.2	Japan, Japon	3.0	* 1.5	* 14.8	Partenaire 3
Papua New Guinea									**Papouasie-Nvl-Guinée**
Partner 1	Australia, Australie	* 42.8	* 23.3	* 25.4	Australia, Australie	* 39.5	* 25.2	* 37.8	Partenaire 1
Partner 2	China, Chine	* 6.4	* 18.4	* 24.2	China, Chine	* 7.3	* 20.1	* 16.9	Partenaire 2
Partner 3	Japan, Japon	* 7.0	* 28.0	* 23.3	Singapore, Singapour	* 11.1	* 12.0	* 12.8	Partenaire 3
Paraguay									**Paraguay**
Partner 1	Brazil, Brésil	33.7	31.5	31.1	China, Chine	34.2	23.5	* 28.2	Partenaire 1
Partner 2	Argentina, Argentine	8.5	6.9	24.1	Brazil, Brésil	24.1	24.8	* 22.3	Partenaire 2
Partner 3	Russian Federation, Fédération de Russie	6.6	9.1	* 8.7	Argentina, Argentine	11.9	10.8	* 10.0	Partenaire 3
Peru									**Pérou**
Partner 1	China, Chine	15.2	22.0	29.4	China, Chine	17.2	22.8	24.2	Partenaire 1
Partner 2	United States, États-Unis	17.1	15.1	12.5	United States, États-Unis	19.4	20.6	20.8	Partenaire 2
Partner 3	Canada	9.3	7.2	5.2	Brazil, Brésil	7.3	5.1	5.7	Partenaire 3
Philippines									**Philippines**
Partner 1	United States, États-Unis	14.7	15.0	16.3	China, Chine	8.5	16.4	22.8	Partenaire 1
Partner 2	Japan, Japon	15.2	21.1	15.1	Japan, Japon	12.5	9.6	9.6	Partenaire 2
Partner 3	China, Chine	11.1	10.9	13.8	Rep. of Korea, République de Corée	6.9	6.5	7.5	Partenaire 3

20 Major trading partner *(continued)*
Three largest trade partners as a percentage of total international merchandise trade in US dollars, as at 2019

Partenaire commercial principal *(suite)*
Trois principaux partenaires commerciaux en pourcentage du total de commerce international de marchandises en dollars américains, en 2019

Country or area	Major trading partner	Percentage of exports 2010	2015	2019	Major trading partner	Percentage of imports 2010	2015	2019	Pays ou zone
Poland									**Pologne**
Partner 1	Germany, Allemagne	26.0	26.9	27.5	Germany, Allemagne	21.7	22.6	21.4	Partenaire 1
Partner 2	Czechia, Tchéquie	5.9	6.5	6.2	China, Chine	9.5	* 11.8	12.3	Partenaire 2
Partner 3	United Kingdom, Royaume-Uni	6.3	6.8	6.0	Russian Federation, Fédération de Russie	10.5	7.6	6.5	Partenaire 3
Portugal									**Portugal**
Partner 1	Spain, Espagne	27.0	24.8	24.9	Spain, Espagne	32.0	33.0	30.4	Partenaire 1
Partner 2	France	12.0	12.2	13.0	Germany, Allemagne	13.9	12.8	13.3	Partenaire 2
Partner 3	Germany, Allemagne	13.0	11.9	12.0	France	7.2	7.4	9.8	Partenaire 3
Qatar									**Qatar**
Partner 1	Japan, Japon	28.7	20.8	18.6	United States, États-Unis	11.8	11.0	18.7	Partenaire 1
Partner 2	Rep. of Korea, République de Corée	16.0	17.3	15.6	China, Chine	9.1	11.5	11.9	Partenaire 2
Partner 3	China, Chine	3.0	6.7	12.4	Germany, Allemagne	7.2	7.5	7.1	Partenaire 3
Republic of Korea									**République de Corée**
Partner 1	China, Chine	25.1	26.0	25.1	China, Chine	16.8	20.7	21.3	Partenaire 1
Partner 2	United States, États-Unis	10.7	13.3	13.6	United States, États-Unis	9.5	10.1	12.3	Partenaire 2
Partner 3	Viet Nam	2.1	5.3	8.9	Japan, Japon	15.1	10.5	9.5	Partenaire 3
Republic of Moldova									**République de Moldova**
Partner 1	Romania, Roumanie	16.0	22.7	27.5	Romania, Roumanie	10.0	* 13.9	14.4	Partenaire 1
Partner 2	Italy, Italie	9.6	* 10.0	9.6	Russian Federation, Fédération de Russie	15.2	* 13.4	11.9	Partenaire 2
Partner 3	Russian Federation, Fédération de Russie	26.2	* 12.2	9.0	China, Chine	8.3	9.2	10.3	Partenaire 3
Romania									**Roumanie**
Partner 1	Germany, Allemagne	18.1	19.8	22.4	Germany, Allemagne	16.7	19.8	20.2	Partenaire 1
Partner 2	Italy, Italie	13.8	12.4	11.3	Italy, Italie	11.6	10.9	9.1	Partenaire 2
Partner 3	France	8.3	6.8	6.9	Hungary, Hongrie	8.7	7.9	7.0	Partenaire 3
Russian Federation [3]									**Fédération de Russie** [3]
Partner 1	China, Chine	* 5.0	* 8.3	13.4	China, Chine	17.0	19.3	21.9	Partenaire 1
Partner 2	Netherlands, Pays-Bas	13.4	11.7	10.5	Germany, Allemagne	11.6	10.5	10.2	Partenaire 2
Partner 3	Germany, Allemagne	4.0	4.7	6.6	Belarus, Bélarus	4.3	4.4	5.5	Partenaire 3
Rwanda									**Rwanda**
Partner 1	Dem. Rep. of Congo, Rép. Dém. du Congo	7.5	32.2	38.0	China, Chine	15.0	19.3	22.5	Partenaire 1
Partner 2	United Arab Emirates, Émirats arabes unis	0.2	6.9	13.5	India, Inde	5.5	9.8	10.1	Partenaire 2
Partner 3	Burundi	2.1	2.8	9.6	United Arab Emirates, Émirats arabes unis	5.1	5.1	8.7	Partenaire 3
Saint Helena									**Sainte-Hélène**
Partner 1	United States, États-Unis	* 34.5	* 37.5	* 50.5	United Kingdom, Royaume-Uni	* 45.9	* 46.4	* 65.0	Partenaire 1
Partner 2	Japan, Japon	* 21.7	* 10.8	* 12.2	South Africa, Afrique du Sud	* 14.1	* 20.5	* 21.2	Partenaire 2
Partner 3	Rep. of Korea, République de Corée	* 0.1	* ~0.0	* 10.2	Brazil, Brésil	...	* ~0.0	* 3.0	Partenaire 3
Saint Kitts and Nevis									**Saint-Kitts-et-Nevis**
Partner 1	United States, États-Unis	* 74.2	* 65.9	* 68.7	United States, États-Unis	68.0	60.0	* 67.0	Partenaire 1
Partner 2	Saint Lucia, Sainte-Lucie	* 3.5	* 3.9	* 6.8	Trinidad and Tobago, Trinité-et-Tobago	6.5	7.3	* 4.4	Partenaire 2
Partner 3	Trinidad and Tobago, Trinité-et-Tobago	1.9	5.8	* 6.5	Canada	2.0	* 2.6	* 2.7	Partenaire 3
Saint Lucia									**Sainte-Lucie**
Partner 1	United States, États-Unis	57.8	47.5	* 32.2	United States, États-Unis	42.0	* 44.4	* 43.8	Partenaire 1
Partner 2	Trinidad and Tobago, Trinité-et-Tobago	19.1	7.6	* 7.9	Trinidad and Tobago, Trinité-et-Tobago	21.0	* 19.7	* 15.0	Partenaire 2
Partner 3	Areas nes, Zones nsa [1]	...	8.5	* 7.9	Areas nes, Zones nsa [1]	...	2.0	* 6.0	Partenaire 3
Saint Pierre and Miquelon									**Saint-Pierre-et-Miquelon**
Partner 1	Canada	* 21.4	* 45.0	* 75.4	France	* 62.5	* 63.0	* 68.4	Partenaire 1
Partner 2	France	* 14.6	* 19.0	* 9.1	Canada	* 33.1	* 30.7	* 23.2	Partenaire 2
Partner 3	Belgium, Belgique	...	* 3.4	* 5.3	Netherlands, Pays-Bas	* 0.8	* 1.5	* 2.7	Partenaire 3
Saint Vincent & Grenadines									**Saint-Vincent-Grenadines**
Partner 1	Dominica, Dominique	6.5	9.0	* 17.9	United States, États-Unis	33.0	38.0	* 38.6	Partenaire 1
Partner 2	Barbados, Barbade	11.3	16.5	* 15.0	Trinidad and Tobago, Trinité-et-Tobago	27.1	17.6	* 17.9	Partenaire 2
Partner 3	Antigua and Barbuda, Antigua-et-Barbuda	7.4	13.8	* 12.5	United Kingdom, Royaume-Uni	5.7	7.1	* 7.3	Partenaire 3
Samoa									**Samoa**
Partner 1	American Samoa, Samoa américaines	4.5	18.3	* 26.7	New Zealand, Nouvelle-Zélande	30.7	26.0	* 24.9	Partenaire 1
Partner 2	New Zealand, Nouvelle-Zélande	9.3	15.0	* 17.7	Singapore, Singapour	5.9	15.5	* 18.4	Partenaire 2
Partner 3	Tokelau, Tokélaou	~0.0	2.8	* 13.8	China, Chine	6.1	14.8	* 11.9	Partenaire 3
Sao Tome and Principe									**Sao Tomé-et-Principe**
Partner 1	Netherlands, Pays-Bas	15.9	36.1	* 37.8	Portugal	* 62.4	58.6	* 53.7	Partenaire 1
Partner 2	Portugal	42.7	5.1	* 24.1	Angola	15.6	21.0	* 23.2	Partenaire 2
Partner 3	Belgium, Belgique	21.2	24.6	* 17.7	China, Chine	2.2	3.2	* 5.8	Partenaire 3

20 Major trading partner *(continued)*
Three largest trade partners as a percentage of total international merchandise trade in US dollars, as at 2019

Partenaire commercial principal *(suite)*
Trois principaux partenaires commerciaux en pourcentage du total de commerce international de marchandises en dollars américains, en 2019

Country or area	Major trading partner	Percentage of exports			Major trading partner	Percentage of imports			Pays ou zone
		2010	2015	2019		2010	2015	2019	
Saudi Arabia									**Arabie saoudite**
Partner 1	Areas nes, Zones nsa [1]	6.2	5.6	* 78.6	China, Chine	11.9	14.1	* 16.5	Partenaire 1
Partner 2	China, Chine	1.4	2.8	* 3.3	United States, États-Unis	13.4	13.7	* 13.3	Partenaire 2
Partner 3	United Arab Emirates, Émirats arabes unis	1.5	3.5	* 2.8	United Arab Emirates, Émirats arabes unis	3.6	5.1	* 8.9	Partenaire 3
Senegal									**Sénégal**
Partner 1	Mali	* 26.1	* 17.0	23.0	France	19.7	16.4	16.8	Partenaire 1
Partner 2	Switzerland, Suisse	* 7.9	8.6	14.7	China, Chine	8.3	9.7	10.7	Partenaire 2
Partner 3	India, Inde	10.0	5.4	8.7	Belgium, Belgique	2.0	3.0	6.9	Partenaire 3
Serbia									**Serbie**
Partner 1	Germany, Allemagne	10.3	12.5	12.6	Germany, Allemagne	10.6	12.4	12.9	Partenaire 1
Partner 2	Italy, Italie	11.4	16.2	10.1	Russian Federation, Fédération de Russie	12.9	9.6	9.7	Partenaire 2
Partner 3	Bosnia Herzegovina, Bosnie-Herzégovine	11.1	8.8	7.7	China, Chine	7.2	8.5	9.4	Partenaire 3
Seychelles									**Seychelles**
Partner 1	United Arab Emirates, Émirats arabes unis	37.9	* 30.3	36.7	United Arab Emirates, Émirats arabes unis	48.0	26.1	22.2	Partenaire 1
Partner 2	United Kingdom, Royaume-Uni	18.6	17.8	14.8	Qatar	~0.0	~0.0	13.9	Partenaire 2
Partner 3	British Virgin Islands, Îles Vierges britanniques	...	...	12.6	France	5.0	7.9	7.9	Partenaire 3
Sierra Leone									**Sierra Leone**
Partner 1	Netherlands, Pays-Bas	* 6.3	16.9	* 23.0	China, Chine	* 12.1	11.5	* 16.8	Partenaire 1
Partner 2	China, Chine	* 3.0	1.2	* 13.0	India, Inde	* 5.4	2.6	* 7.8	Partenaire 2
Partner 3	Ivory Coast, Côte d'Ivoire	* 0.2	...	* 12.2	Turkey, Turquie	* 3.0	0.6	* 7.2	Partenaire 3
Singapore									**Singapour**
Partner 1	China, Chine	10.3	14.4	13.2	China, Chine	10.8	13.7	13.7	Partenaire 1
Partner 2	China, Hong Kong SAR, Chine, RAS Hong Kong	11.7	11.5	11.4	United States, États-Unis	11.4	10.9	12.2	Partenaire 2
Partner 3	Malaysia, Malaisie	12.0	10.8	10.5	Malaysia, Malaisie	11.6	10.7	11.6	Partenaire 3
Slovakia									**Slovaquie**
Partner 1	Germany, Allemagne	19.1	22.3	22.3	Germany, Allemagne	15.8	15.8	16.4	Partenaire 1
Partner 2	Czechia, Tchéquie	13.9	12.2	11.0	Czechia, Tchéquie	10.1	11.1	10.1	Partenaire 2
Partner 3	Poland, Pologne	7.3	8.3	7.5	Other Europe, nes, Europe nsa	14.1	8.7	8.6	Partenaire 3
Slovenia									**Slovénie**
Partner 1	Germany, Allemagne	19.6	20.8	18.9	Germany, Allemagne	16.1	17.3	14.5	Partenaire 1
Partner 2	Italy, Italie	12.1	11.3	11.5	Italy, Italie	15.7	14.7	12.6	Partenaire 2
Partner 3	Croatia, Croatie	6.7	7.8	8.6	Switzerland, Suisse	1.9	1.9	9.3	Partenaire 3
Solomon Islands									**Îles Salomon**
Partner 1	China, Chine	49.1	58.0	* 66.8	Australia, Australie	32.4	28.9	* 18.2	Partenaire 1
Partner 2	Italy, Italie	3.1	6.9	* 7.2	Singapore, Singapour	24.1	17.1	* 16.3	Partenaire 2
Partner 3	India, Inde	~0.0	7.2	* 5.1	China, Chine	12.9	10.5	* 14.9	Partenaire 3
Somalia									**Somalie**
Partner 1	United Arab Emirates, Émirats arabes unis	* 21.4	* 17.6	* 29.4	United Arab Emirates, Émirats arabes unis	* 22.8	* 24.1	* 29.1	Partenaire 1
Partner 2	Oman	* 19.0	* 20.6	* 25.6	China, Chine	* 5.7	* 13.1	* 17.0	Partenaire 2
Partner 3	Saudi Arabia, Arabie saoudite	* 35.7	* 45.9	* 14.6	India, Inde	* 5.6	* 18.4	* 16.4	Partenaire 3
South Africa									**Afrique du Sud**
Partner 1	China, Chine	9.9	* 12.7	10.7	China, Chine	13.8	18.3	18.5	Partenaire 1
Partner 2	Germany, Allemagne	6.7	* 6.3	8.0	Germany, Allemagne	10.9	11.2	9.9	Partenaire 2
Partner 3	United States, États-Unis	8.7	* 7.8	7.0	United States, États-Unis	7.2	7.0	6.6	Partenaire 3
South Sudan									**Soudan du sud**
Partner 1	China, Chine	...	* 99.7	* 89.9	Uganda, Ouganda	...	* 30.1	* 41.4	Partenaire 1
Partner 2	United States, États-Unis	...	* ~0.0	* 4.1	United Arab Emirates, Émirats arabes unis	...	* 0.2	* 17.5	Partenaire 2
Partner 3	United Arab Emirates, Émirats arabes unis	...	...	* 2.8	Kenya	...	* 19.3	* 13.8	Partenaire 3
Spain									**Espagne**
Partner 1	France	18.2	15.4	14.6	Germany, Allemagne	11.7	13.1	11.9	Partenaire 1
Partner 2	Germany, Allemagne	11.0	12.0	10.3	France	10.7	10.9	10.0	Partenaire 2
Partner 3	Italy, Italie	9.0	7.7	7.7	China, Chine	7.9	8.6	8.7	Partenaire 3
Sri Lanka									**Sri Lanka**
Partner 1	United States, États-Unis	21.9	26.8	* 24.9	India, Inde	20.6	22.5	* 21.1	Partenaire 1
Partner 2	United Kingdom, Royaume-Uni	12.4	9.8	* 8.9	China, Chine	10.0	19.7	* 19.7	Partenaire 2
Partner 3	India, Inde	5.7	* 6.9	* 6.7	United Arab Emirates, Émirats arabes unis	2.7	5.7	* 7.3	Partenaire 3
State of Palestine									**État de Palestine**
Partner 1	Israel, Israël	84.9	83.9	* 83.7	Israel, Israël	72.6	58.3	* 55.3	Partenaire 1
Partner 2	Jordan, Jordanie	5.4	6.3	* 6.4	Turkey, Turquie	4.5	7.3	* 10.1	Partenaire 2
Partner 3	United Arab Emirates, Émirats arabes unis	2.0	2.0	* 2.3	China, Chine	4.6	7.0	* 6.5	Partenaire 3

20 Major trading partner *(continued)*
Three largest trade partners as a percentage of total international merchandise trade in US dollars, as at 2019

Partenaire commercial principal *(suite)*
Trois principaux partenaires commerciaux en pourcentage du total de commerce international de marchandises en dollars américains, en 2019

Country or area / Major trading partner		Percentage of exports			Major trading partner	Percentage of imports			Pays ou zone
		2010	2015	2019		2010	2015	2019	
Sudan									**Soudan**
Partner 1	United Arab Emirates, Émirats arabes unis	...	14.4	* 27.5	China, Chine	...	22.8	* 17.4	Partenaire 1
Partner 2	China, Chine	...	56.4	* 20.3	Russian Federation, Fédération de Russie	...	1.2	* 15.1	Partenaire 2
Partner 3	Saudi Arabia, Arabie saoudite	...	14.4	* 16.3	Saudi Arabia, Arabie saoudite	...	4.7	* 10.2	Partenaire 3
Suriname									**Suriname**
Partner 1	Areas nes, Zones nsa [1]	~0.0	57.8	39.5	United States, États-Unis	24.6	* 21.2	21.7	Partenaire 1
Partner 2	United Arab Emirates, Émirats arabes unis	13.7	22.9	36.7	Areas nes, Zones nsa [1]	~0.0	28.1	14.6	Partenaire 2
Partner 3	Belgium, Belgique	10.1	* 8.3	8.2	Netherlands, Pays-Bas	17.5	* 9.3	12.0	Partenaire 3
Sweden									**Suède**
Partner 1	Norway, Norvège	10.0	10.2	10.6	Germany, Allemagne	18.0	17.9	17.8	Partenaire 1
Partner 2	Germany, Allemagne	10.5	11.2	10.3	Netherlands, Pays-Bas	6.2	8.3	9.4	Partenaire 2
Partner 3	United States, États-Unis	7.4	7.8	7.6	Norway, Norvège	8.7	8.2	9.1	Partenaire 3
Switzerland									**Suisse**
Partner 1	Germany, Allemagne	19.3	14.2	15.3	Germany, Allemagne	31.9	20.6	20.8	Partenaire 1
Partner 2	United States, États-Unis	10.1	10.6	14.0	Italy, Italie	10.2	7.7	8.1	Partenaire 2
Partner 3	United Kingdom, Royaume-Uni	5.9	4.7	9.0	United States, États-Unis	5.4	8.0	6.8	Partenaire 3
Syrian Arab Republic									**République arabe syrienne**
Partner 1	Turkey, Turquie	5.5	* 5.9	* 15.6	Turkey, Turquie	9.5	* 27.6	* 25.0	Partenaire 1
Partner 2	Saudi Arabia, Arabie saoudite	4.8	* 11.3	* 14.2	China, Chine	8.8	* 18.5	* 18.4	Partenaire 2
Partner 3	Egypt, Égypte	* 3.4	* 18.2	* 12.5	United Arab Emirates, Émirats arabes unis	1.3	* 4.1	* 18.3	Partenaire 3
Tajikistan									**Tadjikistan**
Partner 1	Turkey, Turquie	* 23.1	* 20.5	* 19.2	China, Chine	* 43.4	* 46.8	* 35.7	Partenaire 1
Partner 2	Switzerland, Suisse	* ~0.0	* 14.2	* 16.9	Russian Federation, Fédération de Russie	* 21.2	* 19.8	* 23.9	Partenaire 2
Partner 3	Uzbekistan, Ouzbékistan	...	* 5.1	* 14.0	Kazakhstan	* 8.2	* 10.9	* 16.4	Partenaire 3
Thailand									**Thaïlande**
Partner 1	United States, États-Unis	10.4	11.2	12.7	China, Chine	13.3	20.3	21.1	Partenaire 1
Partner 2	China, Chine	11.0	11.1	12.0	Japan, Japon	20.8	15.4	14.0	Partenaire 2
Partner 3	Japan, Japon	10.5	9.4	9.9	United States, États-Unis	5.9	6.9	7.4	Partenaire 3
Timor-Leste									**Timor-Leste**
Partner 1	Indonesia, Indonésie	* 0.9	* 25.4	* 25.4	Indonesia, Indonésie	* 19.3	* 31.9	* 31.9	Partenaire 1
Partner 2	United States, États-Unis	...	* 22.3	* 22.3	China, Chine	* 4.7	* 15.1	* 15.1	Partenaire 2
Partner 3	Germany, Allemagne	* 10.5	* 13.6	* 13.6	Singapore, Singapour	...	* 13.1	* 13.1	Partenaire 3
Togo									**Togo**
Partner 1	Burkina Faso	* 9.2	13.7	14.4	China, Chine	15.8	19.7	21.8	Partenaire 1
Partner 2	Benin, Bénin	* 4.6	12.6	12.0	France	12.5	8.7	8.1	Partenaire 2
Partner 3	India, Inde	* 8.1	8.3	11.7	United States, États-Unis	2.3	2.7	6.6	Partenaire 3
Tokelau									**Tokélaou**
Partner 1	Singapore, Singapour	...	* 4.1	* 22.3	Samoa	* 0.1	* 27.8	* 35.2	Partenaire 1
Partner 2	United States, États-Unis	* 11.9	* 7.7	* 10.0	Ireland, Irlande	* 5.9	* 7.5	* 16.5	Partenaire 2
Partner 3	Burkina Faso	* 0.1	...	* 7.9	Philippines	...	...	* 13.2	Partenaire 3
Tonga									**Tonga**
Partner 1	United States, États-Unis	16.2	* 28.1	* 37.9	Fiji, Fidji	10.1	* 26.8	* 27.9	Partenaire 1
Partner 2	Rep. of Korea, République de Corée	0.6	* 14.2	* 17.3	New Zealand, Nouvelle-Zélande	31.9	* 26.5	* 23.3	Partenaire 2
Partner 3	Australia, Australie	3.9	* 8.6	* 13.7	China, Chine	5.3	* 15.6	* 12.2	Partenaire 3
Trinidad and Tobago									**Trinité-et-Tobago**
Partner 1	United States, États-Unis	48.1	41.7	* 34.1	United States, États-Unis	28.0	32.0	* 49.5	Partenaire 1
Partner 2	Spain, Espagne	2.0	* 3.0	* 6.5	China, Chine	5.8	7.1	* 6.1	Partenaire 2
Partner 3	Guyana, Guyane	* 2.4	* 2.0	* 5.9	Netherlands, Pays-Bas	0.6	0.8	* 4.4	Partenaire 3
Tunisia									**Tunisie**
Partner 1	France	* 28.7	* 29.3	* 30.6	Italy, Italie	17.6	14.9	* 15.6	Partenaire 1
Partner 2	Italy, Italie	19.9	* 18.5	* 16.5	France	* 18.9	17.8	* 15.1	Partenaire 2
Partner 3	Germany, Allemagne	* 8.5	* 10.5	* 11.6	China, Chine	6.1	8.4	* 9.0	Partenaire 3
Turkey									**Turquie**
Partner 1	Germany, Allemagne	* 10.1	* 9.3	9.2	Russian Federation, Fédération de Russie	11.6	9.8	11.0	Partenaire 1
Partner 2	United Kingdom, Royaume-Uni	* 6.4	* 7.3	6.2	Germany, Allemagne	* 9.5	10.3	9.2	Partenaire 2
Partner 3	Iraq	* 5.3	* 5.9	5.7	China, Chine	9.3	12.0	9.1	Partenaire 3
Turkmenistan									**Turkménistan**
Partner 1	China, Chine	* 39.0	* 77.0	* 76.4	Turkey, Turquie	* 23.4	* 28.9	* 24.1	Partenaire 1
Partner 2	Afghanistan	* 4.4	* 6.2	* 4.2	Russian Federation, Fédération de Russie	* 14.8	* 13.1	* 17.5	Partenaire 2
Partner 3	Uzbekistan, Ouzbékistan	...	* 1.1	* 3.9	China, Chine	* 10.8	* 12.7	* 10.2	Partenaire 3

20 Major trading partner *(continued)*
Three largest trade partners as a percentage of total international merchandise trade in US dollars, as at 2019

Partenaire commercial principal *(suite)*
Trois principaux partenaires commerciaux en pourcentage du total de commerce international de marchandises en dollars américains, en 2019

Country or area / Major trading partner	Percentage of exports			Major trading partner	Percentage of imports			Pays ou zone
	2010	2015	2019		2010	2015	2019	
Turks and Caicos Islands								**Îles Turques-et-Caïques**
Partner 1 United States, États-Unis	* 99.1	* 33.2	* 29.8	United States, États-Unis	* 98.3	* 86.0	* 82.0	Partenaire 1
Partner 2 Sudan, Soudan	...	* 0.7	* 20.8	Italy, Italie	...	* 0.4	* 2.6	Partenaire 2
Partner 3 Zambia, Zambie	...	* 0.2	* 9.2	Brazil, Brésil	...	* 1.0	* 2.5	Partenaire 3
Tuvalu								**Tuvalu**
Partner 1 Thailand, Thaïlande	* 75.2	* 87.3	* 41.9	Fiji, Fidji	* 10.0	* 13.0	* 26.7	Partenaire 1
Partner 2 Indonesia, Indonésie	* 7.0	* ~0.0	* 33.1	Singapore, Singapour	...	* 22.2	* 24.2	Partenaire 2
Partner 3 Ecuador, Équateur	...	...	* 12.4	Japan, Japon	* 61.0	* 25.3	* 22.4	Partenaire 3
Uganda								**Ouganda**
Partner 1 Kenya	11.8	18.8	* 18.8	China, Chine	8.9	15.8	* 17.6	Partenaire 1
Partner 2 United Arab Emirates, Émirats arabes unis	7.5	3.6	* 18.2	India, Inde	14.7	20.9	* 12.1	Partenaire 2
Partner 3 South Sudan, Soudan du sud	...	11.7	* 11.5	United Arab Emirates, Émirats arabes unis	8.4	7.3	* 11.7	Partenaire 3
Ukraine [4]								**Ukraine** [4]
Partner 1 Russian Federation, Fédération de Russie	* 26.1	12.7	* 7.7	Russian Federation, Fédération de Russie	36.5	20.0	* 14.1	Partenaire 1
Partner 2 Poland, Pologne	* 3.5	5.2	* 6.9	China, Chine	7.7	10.1	* 13.3	Partenaire 2
Partner 3 Italy, Italie	* 4.7	5.2	* 5.6	Germany, Allemagne	7.6	10.6	* 10.5	Partenaire 3
United Arab Emirates								**Émirats arabes unis**
Partner 1 Areas nes, Zones nsa [1]	26.4	44.9	* 55.2	China, Chine	* 7.3	* 8.0	* 15.5	Partenaire 1
Partner 2 Saudi Arabia, Arabie saoudite	1.3	* 2.2	* 5.6	India, Inde	* 12.2	* 6.2	* 9.4	Partenaire 2
Partner 3 India, Inde	* 11.0	* 5.1	* 3.3	United States, États-Unis	* 6.0	* 6.7	* 8.6	Partenaire 3
United Kingdom								**Royaume-Uni**
Partner 1 United States, États-Unis	13.9	14.9	15.7	Germany, Allemagne	12.2	15.0	12.4	Partenaire 1
Partner 2 Germany, Allemagne	10.6	10.0	9.9	United States, États-Unis	9.0	9.2	9.7	Partenaire 2
Partner 3 France	7.5	5.8	6.7	China, Chine	9.8	10.0	9.5	Partenaire 3
United Rep. of Tanzania								**Rép.-Unie de Tanzanie**
Partner 1 Rwanda	2.9	0.7	* 18.7	China, Chine	10.9	12.6	* 20.7	Partenaire 1
Partner 2 Kenya	8.0	13.6	* 9.2	India, Inde	11.2	8.6	* 14.3	Partenaire 2
Partner 3 Dem. Rep. of Congo, Rép. Dém. du Congo	3.9	3.4	* 8.5	United Arab Emirates, Émirats arabes unis	8.4	5.7	* 10.2	Partenaire 3
United States of America								**États-Unis d'Amérique**
Partner 1 Canada	19.5	18.7	17.8	China, Chine	19.5	21.8	18.4	Partenaire 1
Partner 2 Mexico, Mexique	12.8	15.7	15.6	Mexico, Mexique	11.8	12.9	14.1	Partenaire 2
Partner 3 China, Chine	7.2	7.7	6.5	Canada	14.2	13.1	12.7	Partenaire 3
Uruguay								**Uruguay**
Partner 1 China, Chine	* 10.4	* 20.4	* 20.0	China, Chine	13.0	18.4	* 18.9	Partenaire 1
Partner 2 Brazil, Brésil	* 23.4	* 15.4	* 15.1	Brazil, Brésil	18.3	17.1	* 18.4	Partenaire 2
Partner 3 United States, États-Unis	* 2.9	* 6.9	* 6.1	Argentina, Argentine	17.0	13.0	* 12.4	Partenaire 3
Uzbekistan								**Ouzbékistan**
Partner 1 Areas nes, Zones nsa [1]	...	* 2.1	44.0	China, Chine	* 14.2	* 22.5	23.1	Partenaire 1
Partner 2 Russian Federation, Fédération de Russie	* 22.5	* 14.4	13.6	Russian Federation, Fédération de Russie	* 20.0	* 21.3	18.2	Partenaire 2
Partner 3 China, Chine	* 19.3	* 13.0	11.8	Rep. of Korea, République de Corée	* 17.3	* 9.6	11.5	Partenaire 3
Vanuatu								**Vanuatu**
Partner 1 Mauritania, Mauritanie	...	* 19.3	* 32.3	China, Chine	9.9	* 19.3	* 21.3	Partenaire 1
Partner 2 Japan, Japon	4.5	* 6.3	* 25.5	Australia, Australie	30.9	* 13.8	* 19.3	Partenaire 2
Partner 3 Thailand, Thaïlande	~0.0	* 1.6	* 10.6	Fiji, Fidji	7.9	* 8.2	* 11.2	Partenaire 3
Venezuela (Boliv. Rep. of)								**Venezuela (Rép. boliv. du)**
Partner 1 China, Chine	* 5.8	* 17.7	* 34.3	United States, États-Unis	30.5	* 29.2	* 23.5	Partenaire 1
Partner 2 India, Inde	* ~0.0	* 17.4	* 27.4	China, Chine	11.1	* 18.6	* 21.2	Partenaire 2
Partner 3 United States, États-Unis	* 7.6	* 42.5	* 9.7	Brazil, Brésil	9.8	* 10.5	* 7.8	Partenaire 3
Viet Nam								**Viet Nam**
Partner 1 United States, États-Unis	19.7	20.7	23.2	China, Chine	23.8	* 29.8	29.8	Partenaire 1
Partner 2 China, Chine	10.7	10.6	15.7	Rep. of Korea, République de Corée	11.5	* 16.6	18.5	Partenaire 2
Partner 3 Japan, Japon	10.7	8.7	7.7	Japan, Japon	10.6	* 8.7	7.7	Partenaire 3
Wallis and Futuna Islands								**Îles Wallis-et-Futuna**
Partner 1 Singapore, Singapour	...	* 0.9	* 45.8	France	* 23.0	* 27.6	* 38.4	Partenaire 1
Partner 2 France	* 1.6	* 13.0	* 33.7	Fiji, Fidji	* 13.4	* 21.4	* 22.3	Partenaire 2
Partner 3 Belgium, Belgique	* 0.1	...	* 9.1	Areas nes, Zones nsa [1]	* 12.6	* 12.5	* 12.4	Partenaire 3
Yemen								**Yémen**
Partner 1 Egypt, Égypte	* 0.6	3.1	49.6	United Arab Emirates, Émirats arabes unis	* 11.7	* 11.5	24.0	Partenaire 1
Partner 2 Turkey, Turquie	~0.0	* ~0.0	28.0	China, Chine	* 7.9	* 10.8	10.4	Partenaire 2
Partner 3 Oman	* 0.2	17.0	10.5	Saudi Arabia, Arabie saoudite	6.1	8.6	6.5	Partenaire 3

Major trading partner *(continued)*
Three largest trade partners as a percentage of total international merchandise trade in US dollars, as at 2019

Partenaire commercial principal *(suite)*
Trois principaux partenaires commerciaux en pourcentage du total de commerce international de marchandises en dollars américains, en 2019

Country or area	Major trading partner	Percentage of exports			Major trading partner	Percentage of imports			Pays ou zone
		2010	2015	2019		2010	2015	2019	
Zambia									**Zambie**
Partner 1	Switzerland, Suisse	51.0	42.1	41.3	South Africa, Afrique du Sud	34.4	32.9	30.8	Partenaire 1
Partner 2	China, Chine	20.2	15.0	21.4	China, Chine	5.4	8.7	14.1	Partenaire 2
Partner 3	Dem. Rep. of Congo, Rép. Dém. du Congo	4.6	8.0	12.8	United Arab Emirates, Émirats arabes unis	2.2	2.2	10.3	Partenaire 3
Zimbabwe									**Zimbabwe**
Partner 1	South Africa, Afrique du Sud	54.2	* 67.6	49.2	South Africa, Afrique du Sud	48.0	38.4	38.7	Partenaire 1
Partner 2	United Arab Emirates, Émirats arabes unis	10.3	4.3	19.5	Singapore, Singapour	0.3	22.1	25.2	Partenaire 2
Partner 3	Areas nes, Zones nsa [1]	...	~0.0	16.7	China, Chine	5.5	7.7	8.6	Partenaire 3

Source:

United Nations Statistics Division, New York, Commodity Trade Statistics Database (UN COMTRADE), last accessed June 2020.

Source:

Organisation des Nations Unies, Division de statistique, New York, Comtrade base de données de l'ONU, dernier accès juin 2020.

1 Areas not elsewhere specified.
2 Undisclosed (Special categories).
3 Russian data provided by the Russian Federation. Includes statistical data for the Autonomous Republic of Crimea and the city of Sevastopol, Ukraine, temporarily occupied by the Russian Federation.
4 The Government of Ukraine has informed the United Nations that it is not in a position to provide statistical data concerning the Autonomous Republic of Crimea and the city of Sevastopol.

1 Zones non spécifiées ailleurs.
2 Pays non divulgués.
3 Données russes fournies par la Fédération de Russie. Comprend des données statistiques pour la République autonome de Crimée et la ville de Sébastopol, Ukraine, temporairement occupée par la Fédération de Russie.
4 Le Gouvernement ukrainien a informé l'Organisation des Nations Unies qu'il n'est pas en mesure de fournir des données statistiques concernant la République autonome de Crimée et Sébastopol.

Part Three

Energy, environment and infrastructure

Troisième partie

Energie, environnement et infrastructures

Production, trade and supply of energy
Petajoules and gigajoules per capita

Production, commerce et fourniture d'énergie
pétajoules et gigajoules par habitant

Region, country or area	1990	1995	2000	2005	2010	2015	2016	2017	Région, pays ou zone
Total, all countries or areas									**Total, tous pays ou zones**
Primary Energy Prod.	361 763	381 604	412 860	477 404	530 934	570 508	570 167	581 665	Prod. d'énergie primaire
Net imports	-8 317	-8 718	-10 452	-13 321	-12 898	-17 407	-21 798	-20 029	Importations nettes
Changes in stocks	4 119	220	-2 989	-305	73	2 553	-4 567	-1 762	Variations des stocks
Total supply	349 326	372 667	405 396	464 387	517 963	550 548	552 936	563 396	Approv. total
Supply per capita	62	65	66	71	74	75	74	75	Approv. par habitant
Africa									**Afrique**
Primary Energy Prod.	28 052	32 236	37 241	44 734	47 153	44 265	43 763	45 629	Prod. d'énergie primaire
Net imports	-12 208	-13 018	-16 261	-20 515	-19 197	-13 434	-12 283	-13 019	Importations nettes
Changes in stocks	-11	321	-33	3	20	-29	-76	46	Variations des stocks
Total supply	15 856	18 896	21 012	24 215	27 936	30 859	31 556	32 562	Approv. total
Supply per capita	25	26	26	27	27	26	26	26	Approv. par habitant
North America									**Amérique du Nord**
Primary Energy Prod.	90 168	93 936	96 711	98 775	101 199	114 922	110 326	114 222	Prod. d'énergie primaire
Net imports	7 976	9 286	15 882	20 421	13 008	1 746	2 137	-2 128	Importations nettes
Changes in stocks	1 783	-919	-2 233	-143	-597	2 072	-1 153	-1 405	Variations des stocks
Total supply	96 361	104 141	114 826	119 340	114 805	114 597	113 617	113 499	Approv. total
Supply per capita	225	228	236	232	211	201	197	195	Approv. par habitant
South America									**Amérique du Sud**
Primary Energy Prod.	16 266	20 324	24 088	26 619	29 335	31 960	31 955	31 442	Prod. d'énergie primaire
Net imports	-3 742	-5 769	-7 308	-8 048	-7 268	-7 807	-7 925	-8 167	Importations nettes
Changes in stocks	86	-8	-15	-325	-87	41	-214	-883	Variations des stocks
Total supply	12 437	14 563	16 794	18 897	22 155	24 112	24 243	24 158	Approv. total
Supply per capita	42	45	48	51	56	58	58	57	Approv. par habitant
Asia									**Asie**
Primary Energy Prod.	106 953	132 959	149 311	192 294	236 089	261 124	264 678	268 302	Prod. d'énergie primaire
Net imports	-11 491	-8 882	-9 642	-9 480	305	8 688	4 952	10 816	Importations nettes
Changes in stocks	1 714	612	-736	-385	1 644	238	-2 148	71	Variations des stocks
Total supply	93 749	123 466	140 404	183 199	234 751	269 575	271 779	279 048	Approv. total
Supply per capita	30	36	38	46	56	61	61	62	Approv. par habitant
Europe									**Europe**
Primary Energy Prod.	112 935	93 488	94 859	102 725	102 627	101 198	102 151	104 101	Prod. d'énergie primaire
Net imports	13 900	13 449	12 263	10 832	7 975	3 789	2 102	3 670	Importations nettes
Changes in stocks	344	110	261	583	-1 187	168	-832	261	Variations des stocks
Total supply	126 491	106 827	106 861	112 975	111 790	104 818	105 085	107 510	Approv. total
Supply per capita	116	147	147	155	155	141	141	144	Approv. par habitant
Oceania									**Océanie**
Primary Energy Prod.	7 389	8 661	10 649	12 256	14 530	17 039	17 294	17 969	Prod. d'énergie primaire
Net imports	-2 753	-3 784	-5 383	-6 530	-7 723	-10 387	-10 782	-11 202	Importations nettes
Changes in stocks	203	103	-233	-37	281	64	-145	148	Variations des stocks
Total supply	4 432	4 775	5 499	5 762	6 527	6 587	6 657	6 619	Approv. total
Supply per capita	163	164	177	172	178	167	166	163	Approv. par habitant
Afghanistan									**Afghanistan**
Primary Energy Prod.	19	16	18	23	41	60	70	82	Prod. d'énergie primaire
Net imports	* 28	* 13	* 8	* 14	95	* 76	* 51	* 41	Importations nettes
Changes in stocks	* 0	* 0	* 0	...	...	...	...	...	Variations des stocks
Total supply	* 46	* 29	25	36	136	135	121	123	Approv. total
Supply per capita	* 4	* 1	1	1	5	4	3	3	Approv. par habitant
Albania									**Albanie**
Primary Energy Prod.	99	43	34	48	69	87	82	69	Prod. d'énergie primaire
Net imports	* 15	4	31	43	* 22	9	15	36	Importations nettes
Changes in stocks	* 23	0	...	0	0	6	5	6	Variations des stocks
Total supply	92	47	65	91	91	91	91	100	Approv. total
Supply per capita	28	15	21	29	31	31	31	34	Approv. par habitant
Algeria									**Algérie**
Primary Energy Prod.	4 380	4 748	6 556	7 534	6 200	5 883	6 283	6 285	Prod. d'énergie primaire
Net imports	* -3 263	* -3 485	* -5 414	-5 952	-4 551	-3 692	* -4 082	* -3 986	Importations nettes
Changes in stocks	* 41	-8	-27	0	9	-33	-3	12	Variations des stocks
Total supply	1 075	1 270	1 170	1 583	1 641	2 224	2 203	2 289	Approv. total
Supply per capita	43	45	38	48	45	56	54	55	Approv. par habitant
Andorra									**Andorre**
Primary Energy Prod.	* 0	* 0	* 0	0	1	1	1	* 1	Prod. d'énergie primaire
Net imports	* 6	* 7	* 9	* 10	* 9	* 8	* 8	* 8	Importations nettes
Total supply	* 7	7	9	10	10	9	9	9	Approv. total
Supply per capita	* 130	111	138	130	114	113	116	117	Approv. par habitant
Angola									**Angola**
Primary Energy Prod.	1 198	1 582	1 782	2 888	4 016	4 089	4 017	3 820	Prod. d'énergie primaire
Net imports	* -960	-1 224	-1 475	-2 565	-3 547	* -3 536	* -3 442	-3 191	Importations nettes
Changes in stocks	...	17	21	5	1	1	* 4	10	Variations des stocks
Total supply	238	340	287	318	469	552	571	618	Approv. total
Supply per capita	23	28	21	19	20	20	20	21	Approv. par habitant
Anguilla									**Anguilla**
Primary Energy Prod.	* 0	* 0	* 0	* 0	* 0	* 0	* 0	* 0	Prod. d'énergie primaire
Net imports	* 1	* 1	* 1	* 2	* 2	* 2	* 2	* 2	Importations nettes
Total supply	* 1	* 1	* 1	* 2	* 2	* 2	* 2	* 2	Approv. total
Supply per capita	* 87	* 94	* 117	* 132	* 155	* 151	* 149	* 136	Approv. par habitant
Antigua and Barbuda									**Antigua-et-Barbuda**
Primary Energy Prod.	...	...	...	...	...	0	0	0	Prod. d'énergie primaire
Net imports	* 4	* 3	* 4	* 6	* 6	* 7	* 7	* 7	Importations nettes
Total supply	* 3	* 3	* 4	* 5	* 6	* 7	* 7	* 7	Approv. total
Supply per capita	* 53	* 49	* 56	* 65	* 69	* 69	* 70	* 69	Approv. par habitant

Region, country or area	1990	1995	2000	2005	2010	2015	2016	2017	Région, pays ou zone
Argentina									**Argentine**
Primary Energy Prod.	2 064	2 722	3 413	3 609	3 343	3 072	3 122	3 035	Prod. d'énergie primaire
Net imports	-144	-535	-866	-683	-21	371	316	354	Importations nettes
Changes in stocks	-8	-6	-17	8	16	9	-1	4	Variations des stocks
Total supply	1 928	2 194	2 564	2 919	3 307	3 435	3 439	3 385	Approv. total
Supply per capita	59	63	69	75	80	79	78	76	Approv. par habitant
Armenia									**Arménie**
Primary Energy Prod.	...	10	27	36	52	45	43	45	Prod. d'énergie primaire
Net imports	...	59	57	69	* 70	* 84	87	94	Importations nettes
Changes in stocks	...	...	...	...	* 3	1	0	1	Variations des stocks
Total supply	...	68	84	105	* 119	127	129	137	Approv. total
Supply per capita	...	21	27	34	* 41	44	44	47	Approv. par habitant
Aruba									**Aruba**
Primary Energy Prod.	0	0	* 5	* 5	* 5	* 1	* 1	* 1	Prod. d'énergie primaire
Net imports	* 7	* 10	* 49	* 54	* 51	* 12	* 12	* 13	Importations nettes
Changes in stocks	0	...	...	...	...	...	...	...	Variations des stocks
Total supply	* 7	* 10	* 54	58	* 56	* 13	* 13	* 13	Approv. total
Supply per capita	* 108	* 121	* 594	576	* 550	* 122	* 120	* 123	Approv. par habitant
Australia [2]									**Australie** [2]
Primary Energy Prod.	6 616	7 825	9 779	11 491	13 646	16 014	16 281	16 963	Prod. d'énergie primaire
Net imports	-2 697	-3 759	-5 432	-6 728	-7 941	-10 605	-11 027	-11 446	Importations nettes
Changes in stocks	203	104	-221	-29	265	78	-143	164	Variations des stocks
Total supply	3 714	3 962	4 567	4 790	5 441	5 331	5 397	5 353	Approv. total
Supply per capita	217	219	238	235	246	224	224	219	Approv. par habitant
Austria									**Autriche**
Primary Energy Prod.	341	368	410	406	483	497	506	507	Prod. d'énergie primaire
Net imports	714	741	778	1 004	893	820	854	901	Importations nettes
Changes in stocks	14	-14	-10	3	-35	-48	-15	4	Variations des stocks
Total supply	1 041	1 123	1 198	1 407	1 409	1 366	1 375	1 404	Approv. total
Supply per capita	136	142	150	171	168	157	158	161	Approv. par habitant
Azerbaijan									**Azerbaïdjan**
Primary Energy Prod.	...	628	803	1 155	2 759	2 474	2 429	2 308	Prod. d'énergie primaire
Net imports	...	-91	-319	-547	-2 239	-1 891	-1 842	-1 685	Importations nettes
Changes in stocks	...	0	-2	35	34	-22	-13	21	Variations des stocks
Total supply	...	536	485	573	486	605	599	602	Approv. total
Supply per capita	...	69	60	67	54	63	62	61	Approv. par habitant
Bahamas									**Bahamas**
Primary Energy Prod.	...	...	...	0	0	0	0	0	Prod. d'énergie primaire
Net imports	* 35	* 22	* 26	* 27	* 34	* 19	* 13	* 23	Importations nettes
Changes in stocks	* 9	* -1	* -1	* 0	...	* -10	* -13	* -5	Variations des stocks
Total supply	* 26	* 24	* 27	* 26	35	* 29	26	29	Approv. total
Supply per capita	* 100	* 86	* 91	* 83	96	* 76	66	72	Approv. par habitant
Bahrain									**Bahreïn**
Primary Energy Prod.	294	341	706	672	849	957	940	942	Prod. d'énergie primaire
Net imports	* -87	* -94	-382	-353	-339	-380	-378	-378	Importations nettes
Changes in stocks	* -6	-10	-6	-28	-3	-4	6	-15	Variations des stocks
Total supply	213	257	331	348	513	580	557	580	Approv. total
Supply per capita	433	459	518	480	413	423	390	389	Approv. par habitant
Bangladesh									**Bangladesh**
Primary Energy Prod.	681	792	857	1 027	1 304	1 509	1 601	1 605	Prod. d'énergie primaire
Net imports	84	123	139	165	163	274	246	302	Importations nettes
Changes in stocks	-3	-4	-3	1	-26	-7	-16	-18	Variations des stocks
Total supply	769	918	998	1 191	1 493	1 790	1 864	1 925	Approv. total
Supply per capita	7	8	8	8	10	11	11	12	Approv. par habitant
Barbados									**Barbade**
Primary Energy Prod.	5	5	6	4	4	3	3	2	Prod. d'énergie primaire
Net imports	9	8	10	* 12	* 16	* 15	* 16	* 14	Importations nettes
Changes in stocks	-1	0	-1	0	0	1	1	1	Variations des stocks
Total supply	16	12	16	17	20	17	17	16	Approv. total
Supply per capita	62	47	59	64	72	59	60	55	Approv. par habitant
Belarus									**Bélarus**
Primary Energy Prod.	...	139	143	155	167	163	166	180	Prod. d'énergie primaire
Net imports	...	908	885	962	980	891	867	900	Importations nettes
Changes in stocks	...	9	-2	-4	-4	-13	-27	-1	Variations des stocks
Total supply	...	1 038	1 029	1 121	1 152	1 067	1 060	1 081	Approv. total
Supply per capita	...	101	102	114	122	112	112	114	Approv. par habitant
Belgium									**Belgique**
Primary Energy Prod.	544	495	570	577	646	445	637	626	Prod. d'énergie primaire
Net imports	1 451	1 765	1 827	1 861	1 867	1 780	1 655	1 621	Importations nettes
Changes in stocks	-4	29	-21	18	18	40	-19	-52	Variations des stocks
Total supply	1 999	2 231	2 418	2 421	2 496	2 185	2 311	2 301	Approv. total
Supply per capita	201	221	238	232	228	194	203	201	Approv. par habitant
Belize									**Belize**
Primary Energy Prod.	4	4	5	4	14	9	9	9	Prod. d'énergie primaire
Net imports	4	6	6	* 7	-2	6	6	7	Importations nettes
Changes in stocks	...	...	...	...	0	0	0	* 0	Variations des stocks
Total supply	8	10	11	11	13	16	15	16	Approv. total
Supply per capita	44	44	44	39	40	44	42	43	Approv. par habitant
Benin									**Bénin**
Primary Energy Prod.	74	79	62	70	86	114	105	114	Prod. d'énergie primaire
Net imports	* 1	* 10	20	37	67	77	91	97	Importations nettes
Changes in stocks	0	0	0	2	0	-2	2	-1	Variations des stocks
Total supply	74	89	83	105	153	194	193	213	Approv. total
Supply per capita	16	16	13	14	17	18	18	19	Approv. par habitant

Production, trade and supply of energy *(continued)*
Petajoules and gigajoules per capita

Production, commerce et fourniture d'énergie *(suite)*
pétajoules et gigajoules par habitant

Region, country or area	1990	1995	2000	2005	2010	2015	2016	2017	Région, pays ou zone
Bermuda									**Bermudes**
Primary Energy Prod.	...	...	...	...	* 1	* 1	* 1	* 1	Prod. d'énergie primaire
Net imports	* 7	* 7	* 7	* 7	* 9	* 7	* 8	* 9	Importations nettes
Changes in stocks	...	...	...	...	...	-1	0	* 1	Variations des stocks
Total supply	* 7	* 8	* 7	* 8	* 9	8	9	9	Approv. total
Supply per capita	* 118	* 123	* 115	* 124	* 138	130	149	151	Approv. par habitant
Bhutan									**Bhoutan**
Primary Energy Prod.	41	43	46	53	73	77	79	79	Prod. d'énergie primaire
Net imports	* -3	* -4	* -2	-5	-16	* -13	* -13	* -12	Importations nettes
Total supply	37	39	44	48	57	64	66	67	Approv. total
Supply per capita	67	76	77	73	78	81	83	83	Approv. par habitant
Bolivia (Plurin. State of)									**Bolivie (État plurin. de)**
Primary Energy Prod.	203	241	280	582	658	954	915	878	Prod. d'énergie primaire
Net imports	-97	-85	-78	-366	-398	-608	-553	-507	Importations nettes
Changes in stocks	0	1	-2	0	-1	1	-2	-2	Variations des stocks
Total supply	106	155	205	216	261	345	363	371	Approv. total
Supply per capita	16	21	25	24	26	32	33	34	Approv. par habitant
Bonaire, St. Eustatius & Saba									**Bonaire, St-Eustache et Saba**
Primary Energy Prod.	...	...	...	...	...	0	0	0	Prod. d'énergie primaire
Net imports	...	...	...	...	...	* 5	* 5	* 6	Importations nettes
Total supply	...	...	...	...	...	* 5	* 5	* 5	Approv. total
Supply per capita	...	...	...	...	...	* 214	* 215	* 214	Approv. par habitant
Bosnia and Herzegovina									**Bosnie-Herzégovine**
Primary Energy Prod.	...	33	126	152	182	173	199	194	Prod. d'énergie primaire
Net imports	...	29	52	54	84	88	88	95	Importations nettes
Changes in stocks	...	...	-1	-1	-3	11	4	11	Variations des stocks
Total supply	...	62	179	206	269	250	282	278	Approv. total
Supply per capita	...	19	48	54	72	71	80	79	Approv. par habitant
Botswana									**Botswana**
Primary Energy Prod.	24	27	28	29	30	56	51	59	Prod. d'énergie primaire
Net imports	15	17	29	36	45	* 36	41	41	Importations nettes
Changes in stocks	0	...	...	0	0	* 11	* 0	...	Variations des stocks
Total supply	39	44	57	65	74	80	92	99	Approv. total
Supply per capita	28	28	32	35	37	36	41	43	Approv. par habitant
Brazil									**Brésil**
Primary Energy Prod.	4 490	5 038	6 308	8 344	10 127	11 969	12 666	13 066	Prod. d'énergie primaire
Net imports	1 555	1 918	1 713	900	859	799	45	-148	Importations nettes
Changes in stocks	86	-106	1	-8	-6	-17	33	18	Variations des stocks
Total supply	5 960	7 062	8 020	9 252	10 992	12 786	12 677	12 900	Approv. total
Supply per capita	40	44	46	50	56	62	61	62	Approv. par habitant
British Virgin Islands									**Îles Vierges britanniques**
Primary Energy Prod.	0	0	0	0	0	0	0	0	Prod. d'énergie primaire
Net imports	* 1	* 2	* 2	* 3	* 3	* 3	* 3	* 2	Importations nettes
Total supply	* 1	* 2	* 2	* 3	* 3	* 3	* 3	* 2	Approv. total
Supply per capita	* 58	* 84	* 87	* 115	* 103	* 99	* 97	* 77	Approv. par habitant
Brunei Darussalam									**Brunéi Darussalam**
Primary Energy Prod.	668	752	813	848	775	673	633	652	Prod. d'énergie primaire
Net imports	* -594	-683	-744	-772	-648	-560	-512	-505	Importations nettes
Changes in stocks	* -33	-1	-4	-1	-7	0	-3	-5	Variations des stocks
Total supply	107	71	73	76	136	114	124	153	Approv. total
Supply per capita	424	246	224	210	349	273	293	356	Approv. par habitant
Bulgaria									**Bulgarie**
Primary Energy Prod.	407	428	410	444	442	505	473	491	Prod. d'énergie primaire
Net imports	730	546	358	384	291	275	285	299	Importations nettes
Changes in stocks	-44	7	-5	2	-9	6	1	9	Variations des stocks
Total supply	1 181	966	773	826	741	775	757	781	Approv. total
Supply per capita	134	116	97	107	100	108	106	110	Approv. par habitant
Burkina Faso									**Burkina Faso**
Primary Energy Prod.	85	96	69	98	118	126	128	129	Prod. d'énergie primaire
Net imports	* 9	10	12	16	26	51	42	52	Importations nettes
Changes in stocks	* 0	1	-1	* 0	* -2	* 4	-6	* -4	Variations des stocks
Total supply	93	104	83	114	145	172	176	185	Approv. total
Supply per capita	10	10	7	8	9	10	9	10	Approv. par habitant
Burundi									**Burundi**
Primary Energy Prod.	* 49	* 49	51	* 53	* 54	56	56	56	Prod. d'énergie primaire
Net imports	* 4	* 4	* 5	3	5	6	7	* 8	Importations nettes
Changes in stocks	0	0	0	0	0	0	0	0	Variations des stocks
Total supply	* 52	* 53	55	* 56	* 58	62	63	63	Approv. total
Supply per capita	* 9	* 9	9	* 8	* 7	6	6	6	Approv. par habitant
Cabo Verde									**Cabo Verde**
Primary Energy Prod.	1	1	1	1	1	* 2	* 2	* 2	Prod. d'énergie primaire
Net imports	* 1	* 2	* 4	* 6	7	* 7	* 8	* 9	Importations nettes
Changes in stocks	0	...	...	...	...	...	...	...	Variations des stocks
Total supply	* 2	* 3	* 5	8	9	* 9	* 9	* 10	Approv. total
Supply per capita	* 7	* 7	* 10	16	18	* 16	* 17	* 18	Approv. par habitant
Cambodia									**Cambodge**
Primary Energy Prod.	103	98	114	105	152	184	191	198	Prod. d'énergie primaire
Net imports	* 18	22	28	39	72	111	126	139	Importations nettes
Changes in stocks	...	...	...	...	...	...	...	-2	Variations des stocks
Total supply	121	119	142	144	223	295	318	339	Approv. total
Supply per capita	13	11	11	11	16	19	20	21	Approv. par habitant
Cameroon									**Cameroun**
Primary Energy Prod.	501	457	532	442	351	493	498	472	Prod. d'énergie primaire
Net imports	* -326	* -219	-268	-152	-73	-112	-108	-85	Importations nettes
Changes in stocks	* 0	* 2	0	-5	-13	-1	0	0	Variations des stocks
Total supply	176	237	264	295	291	381	391	388	Approv. total
Supply per capita	14	17	17	17	15	17	17	16	Approv. par habitant

Region, country or area	1990	1995	2000	2005	2010	2015	2016	2017	Région, pays ou zone
Canada									**Canada**
Primary Energy Prod.	11 567	14 725	15 688	16 819	16 662	19 754	20 075	21 327	Prod. d'énergie primaire
Net imports	-2 558	-5 089	-5 433	-5 531	-6 102	-7 935	-8 324	-9 135	Importations nettes
Changes in stocks	170	-146	-351	-131	-308	61	-7	103	Variations des stocks
Total supply	8 838	9 782	10 605	11 420	10 869	11 757	11 758	12 088	Approv. total
Supply per capita	319	334	346	354	318	327	324	330	Approv. par habitant
Cayman Islands									**Îles Caïmanes**
Net imports	4	* 6	* 7	* 7	8	8	7	8	Importations nettes
Total supply	4	* 5	* 7	7	8	8	8	8	Approv. total
Supply per capita	138	* 159	* 165	130	144	133	129	135	Approv. par habitant
Central African Republic									**République centrafricaine**
Primary Energy Prod.	28	28	19	19	19	19	19	19	Prod. d'énergie primaire
Net imports	* 3	* 3	* 4	* 3	* 4	* 5	* 5	* 4	Importations nettes
Changes in stocks	0	* 0	* 0	...	...	...	...	...	Variations des stocks
Total supply	31	31	22	22	23	23	23	23	Approv. total
Supply per capita	11	9	6	5	5	5	5	5	Approv. par habitant
Chad									**Tchad**
Primary Energy Prod.	43	48	55	433	324	375	347	318	Prod. d'énergie primaire
Net imports	* 5	* 6	* 7	* -362	* -245	* -297	* -263	* -233	Importations nettes
Changes in stocks	0	0	...	...	...	...	...	...	Variations des stocks
Total supply	48	54	62	71	80	79	84	85	Approv. total
Supply per capita	8	8	7	7	7	6	6	6	Approv. par habitant
Chile									**Chili**
Primary Energy Prod.	328	346	359	391	386	541	525	543	Prod. d'énergie primaire
Net imports	289	444	730	800	894	974	1 064	1 063	Importations nettes
Changes in stocks	24	10	8	3	-6	4	6	4	Variations des stocks
Total supply	593	780	1 082	1 187	1 286	1 510	1 582	1 603	Approv. total
Supply per capita	45	54	70	73	76	85	88	89	Approv. par habitant
China [3]									**Chine** [3]
Primary Energy Prod.	32 727	39 692	40 783	63 831	88 642	100 864	95 802	99 218	Prod. d'énergie primaire
Net imports	-1 370	* -397	* 1 426	4 251	14 225	18 874	21 705	24 290	Importations nettes
Changes in stocks	959	132	-251	-752	1 248	-187	-2 375	-91	Variations des stocks
Total supply	30 398	39 163	42 461	68 833	101 618	119 926	119 882	123 598	Approv. total
Supply per capita	27	32	33	53	75	86	85	88	Approv. par habitant
China, Hong Kong SAR									**Chine, RAS de Hong Kong**
Net imports	321	382	571	578	672	634	643	585	Importations nettes
Changes in stocks	5	* -16	1	-2	129	59	53	-2	Variations des stocks
Total supply	316	398	570	579	544	576	590	587	Approv. total
Supply per capita	54	65	84	85	77	79	81	80	Approv. par habitant
China, Macao SAR									**Chine, RAS de Macao**
Primary Energy Prod.	...	...	...	* 3	* 4	* 5	* 5	* 6	Prod. d'énergie primaire
Net imports	15	18	23	26	* 29	41	40	43	Importations nettes
Changes in stocks	0	0	0	0	0	1	0	1	Variations des stocks
Total supply	15	18	24	29	32	45	46	48	Approv. total
Supply per capita	40	45	55	61	60	74	74	78	Approv. par habitant
Colombia									**Colombie**
Primary Energy Prod.	1 882	2 419	3 046	3 335	4 486	5 367	5 208	5 171	Prod. d'énergie primaire
Net imports	* -891	-1 267	-1 987	-2 139	* -3 081	* -3 799	* -3 658	-4 325	Importations nettes
Changes in stocks	7	48	-43	16	3	44	-219	-832	Variations des stocks
Total supply	983	1 104	1 103	1 180	1 402	1 524	1 770	1 677	Approv. total
Supply per capita	30	30	28	27	31	32	36	34	Approv. par habitant
Comoros									**Comores**
Primary Energy Prod.	1	2	2	2	2	3	3	3	Prod. d'énergie primaire
Net imports	* 1	* 1	* 1	* 2	* 2	* 3	* 3	* 4	Importations nettes
Total supply	2	3	3	* 4	* 5	5	* 6	* 6	Approv. total
Supply per capita	5	6	6	* 6	* 7	7	* 7	* 8	Approv. par habitant
Congo									**Congo**
Primary Energy Prod.	361	415	604	563	724	609	604	686	Prod. d'énergie primaire
Net imports	* -325	* -375	-569	-518	-649	-490	-480	-562	Importations nettes
Changes in stocks	0	0	...	0	6	0	0	...	Variations des stocks
Total supply	36	40	35	45	70	119	124	124	Approv. total
Supply per capita	15	15	11	13	16	24	24	24	Approv. par habitant
Cook Islands									**Îles Cook**
Primary Energy Prod.	...	...	...	...	...	* 0	* 0	* 0	Prod. d'énergie primaire
Net imports	* 1	* 1	* 1	* 1	* 1	* 1	* 1	* 1	Importations nettes
Total supply	* 0	* 1	* 1	1	* 1	* 1	* 1	* 1	Approv. total
Supply per capita	* 28	* 30	* 36	39	* 39	* 49	* 51	* 56	Approv. par habitant
Costa Rica									**Costa Rica**
Primary Energy Prod.	30	46	67	93	104	110	108	102	Prod. d'énergie primaire
Net imports	40	65	70	85	99	* 98	* 105	113	Importations nettes
Changes in stocks	1	0	-1	0	0	0	-1	2	Variations des stocks
Total supply	68	110	137	177	203	207	213	212	Approv. total
Supply per capita	22	32	35	41	45	43	44	43	Approv. par habitant
Côte d'Ivoire									**Côte d'Ivoire**
Primary Energy Prod.	179	178	242	451	467	526	456	438	Prod. d'énergie primaire
Net imports	* 26	* 68	* 28	-27	-40	10	2	* 20	Importations nettes
Changes in stocks	* 1	* 0	* -8	* 5	3	-6	0	-1	Variations des stocks
Total supply	204	245	278	418	425	543	457	458	Approv. total
Supply per capita	16	17	17	23	21	24	19	19	Approv. par habitant
Croatia									**Croatie**
Primary Energy Prod.	...	209	178	199	215	184	185	176	Prod. d'énergie primaire
Net imports	...	115	166	212	180	168	169	192	Importations nettes
Changes in stocks	...	-2	-4	4	5	2	1	3	Variations des stocks
Total supply	...	325	349	407	390	350	353	364	Approv. total
Supply per capita	...	70	77	92	90	83	84	87	Approv. par habitant

Production, trade and supply of energy *(continued)*
Petajoules and gigajoules per capita

Production, commerce et fourniture d'énergie *(suite)*
pétajoules et gigajoules par habitant

Region, country or area	1990	1995	2000	2005	2010	2015	2016	2017	Région, pays ou zone
Cuba									**Cuba**
Primary Energy Prod.	238	170	241	205	200	212	193	195	Prod. d'énergie primaire
Net imports	* 404	286	232	* 207	* 304	* 244	* 242	* 209	Importations nettes
Changes in stocks	-5	4	10	...	...	...	...	...	Variations des stocks
Total supply	647	452	462	412	505	457	434	404	Approv. total
Supply per capita	61	41	42	37	45	40	38	35	Approv. par habitant
Curaçao									**Curaçao**
Primary Energy Prod.	...	...	...	...	...	1	1	1	Prod. d'énergie primaire
Net imports	...	...	...	...	...	91	79	75	Importations nettes
Total supply	...	...	...	...	...	92	80	76	Approv. total
Supply per capita	...	...	...	...	...	582	502	473	Approv. par habitant
Cyprus									**Chypre**
Primary Energy Prod.	0	2	2	2	4	5	5	6	Prod. d'énergie primaire
Net imports	57	72	88	94	104	83	86	89	Importations nettes
Changes in stocks	-1	2	0	3	5	3	1	1	Variations des stocks
Total supply	58	71	90	94	103	85	91	94	Approv. total
Supply per capita	75	83	95	91	93	73	78	79	Approv. par habitant
Czechia									**Tchéquie**
Primary Energy Prod.	...	1 368	1 290	1 388	1 340	1 207	1 144	1 157	Prod. d'énergie primaire
Net imports	...	363	407	525	476	554	565	668	Importations nettes
Changes in stocks	...	-30	-49	16	-77	4	-34	8	Variations des stocks
Total supply	...	1 760	1 746	1 898	1 892	1 758	1 742	1 818	Approv. total
Supply per capita	...	171	170	186	180	166	164	171	Approv. par habitant
Dem. People's Rep. Korea									**Rép. pop. dém. de Corée**
Primary Energy Prod.	1 211	838	787	923	699	788	891	646	Prod. d'énergie primaire
Net imports	181	83	41	-28	-77	-457	-518	* -67	Importations nettes
Changes in stocks	...	...	2	...	...	...	...	* 272	Variations des stocks
Total supply	1 391	921	826	896	622	332	374	307	Approv. total
Supply per capita	69	42	36	38	25	13	15	12	Approv. par habitant
Dem. Rep. of the Congo									**Rép. dém. du Congo**
Primary Energy Prod.	499	629	677	740	856	1 218	1 256	1 264	Prod. d'énergie primaire
Net imports	-11	-34	-43	-42	-24	-8	-17	-18	Importations nettes
Changes in stocks	0	0	-1	0	0	...	...	...	Variations des stocks
Total supply	489	595	635	698	831	1 209	1 240	1 246	Approv. total
Supply per capita	13	14	13	12	13	16	16	15	Approv. par habitant
Denmark [4]									**Danemark [4]**
Primary Energy Prod.	422	653	1 161	1 311	977	668	632	655	Prod. d'énergie primaire
Net imports	297	211	-400	-506	-206	28	37	35	Importations nettes
Changes in stocks	-7	56	-18	14	-45	21	-25	-30	Variations des stocks
Total supply	726	809	779	791	815	674	694	720	Approv. total
Supply per capita	141	155	146	146	147	118	122	126	Approv. par habitant
Djibouti									**Djibouti**
Primary Energy Prod.	2	2	3	3	3	4	4	4	Prod. d'énergie primaire
Net imports	* 5	* 5	* 5	* 6	* 7	* 6	* 7	* 5	Importations nettes
Changes in stocks	0	...	...	...	* 0	1	* 1	* 0	Variations des stocks
Total supply	* 6	* 7	8	* 9	11	9	10	9	Approv. total
Supply per capita	* 12	* 11	11	* 11	13	9	10	9	Approv. par habitant
Dominica									**Dominique**
Primary Energy Prod.	0	0	0	0	0	0	0	0	Prod. d'énergie primaire
Net imports	* 1	* 1	* 1	* 2	* 2	* 2	* 3	* 2	Importations nettes
Changes in stocks	...	* 0	...	...	0	* 0	* 0	* 0	Variations des stocks
Total supply	* 1	1	2	* 2	3	* 3	* 3	* 2	Approv. total
Supply per capita	* 14	19	24	* 31	36	* 36	* 37	* 33	Approv. par habitant
Dominican Republic									**République dominicaine**
Primary Energy Prod.	22	20	24	28	27	23	26	32	Prod. d'énergie primaire
Net imports	122	212	259	* 232	271	303	323	312	Importations nettes
Changes in stocks	1	0	0	2	0	1	0	-1	Variations des stocks
Total supply	143	232	283	259	298	325	349	344	Approv. total
Supply per capita	20	29	33	28	30	31	33	32	Approv. par habitant
Ecuador									**Équateur**
Primary Energy Prod.	683	915	959	1 246	1 110	1 260	1 288	1 263	Prod. d'énergie primaire
Net imports	-428	* -577	-612	-772	-608	-676	-705	-674	Importations nettes
Changes in stocks	0	...	20	4	-20	-20	-15	-26	Variations des stocks
Total supply	255	339	328	470	521	603	597	615	Approv. total
Supply per capita	25	30	27	35	35	37	36	37	Approv. par habitant
Egypt									**Égypte**
Primary Energy Prod.	2 376	2 684	2 773	3 383	3 692	3 051	3 105	3 418	Prod. d'énergie primaire
Net imports	* -1 084	* -709	-449	-645	-511	399	650	595	Importations nettes
Changes in stocks	* 21	369	36	-4	-60	-1	-1	2	Variations des stocks
Total supply	1 271	1 605	2 288	2 742	3 242	3 450	3 756	4 012	Approv. total
Supply per capita	22	26	34	37	39	37	39	41	Approv. par habitant
El Salvador									**El Salvador**
Primary Energy Prod.	59	70	56	75	95	85	85	89	Prod. d'énergie primaire
Net imports	32	67	77	82	81	93	92	86	Importations nettes
Changes in stocks	-1	1	0	-3	-2	0	0	...	Variations des stocks
Total supply	92	136	134	159	178	179	177	175	Approv. total
Supply per capita	17	24	22	26	29	28	28	27	Approv. par habitant
Equatorial Guinea									**Guinée équatoriale**
Primary Energy Prod.	4	18	250	869	896	791	812	740	Prod. d'énergie primaire
Net imports	* 1	* -12	-240	* -798	* -807	* -723	* -784	* -721	Importations nettes
Changes in stocks	...	* 1	* 0	2	* 7	* 4	* -26	* -30	Variations des stocks
Total supply	5	5	10	68	82	64	53	49	Approv. total
Supply per capita	13	12	18	112	86	54	44	39	Approv. par habitant

Region, country or area	1990	1995	2000	2005	2010	2015	2016	2017	Région, pays ou zone
Eritrea									**Erythrée**
Primary Energy Prod.	...	31	21	21	24	27	27	28	Prod. d'énergie primaire
Net imports	...	11	9	10	7	8	9	9	Importations nettes
Changes in stocks	...	...	0	-2	0	...	...	...	Variations des stocks
Total supply	...	42	30	32	31	35	36	37	Approv. total
Supply per capita	...	13	8	7	10	10	11	11	Approv. par habitant
Estonia									**Estonie**
Primary Energy Prod.	...	139	129	163	206	234	208	242	Prod. d'énergie primaire
Net imports	...	74	66	58	31	13	10	-1	Importations nettes
Changes in stocks	...	-3	-1	0	-2	15	-24	-1	Variations des stocks
Total supply	...	217	196	220	238	232	242	243	Approv. total
Supply per capita	...	151	143	164	179	176	184	185	Approv. par habitant
Eswatini									**Eswatini**
Primary Energy Prod.	* 23	* 24	34	36	33	36	33	* 37	Prod. d'énergie primaire
Net imports	* 8	* 10	* 7	3	* 11	* 12	10	* 6	Importations nettes
Changes in stocks	...	...	...	* 0	* 0	...	* 0	* -1	Variations des stocks
Total supply	* 32	* 34	41	40	43	48	44	* 44	Approv. total
Supply per capita	* 37	* 35	39	36	41	43	39	* 39	Approv. par habitant
Ethiopia									**Éthiopie**
Primary Energy Prod.	...	885	977	1 070	1 212	1 330	1 356	1 371	Prod. d'énergie primaire
Net imports	...	31	43	60	82	133	147	163	Importations nettes
Changes in stocks	...	* -2	-2	-3	1	1	0	...	Variations des stocks
Total supply	...	918	1 022	1 132	1 293	1 462	1 504	1 534	Approv. total
Supply per capita	...	16	16	15	15	15	15	15	Approv. par habitant
Falkland Islands (Malvinas)									**Îles Falkland (Malvinas)**
Primary Energy Prod.	0	* 0	* 0	* 0	* 0	* 0	* 0	0	Prod. d'énergie primaire
Net imports	0	* 0	* 0	* 1	* 1	0	0	0	Importations nettes
Total supply	1	* 1	* 1	* 1	* 1	1	1	1	Approv. total
Supply per capita	271	* 239	* 178	* 235	* 260	197	195	183	Approv. par habitant
Faroe Islands									**Îles Féroé**
Primary Energy Prod.	0	0	0	0	0	1	1	1	Prod. d'énergie primaire
Net imports	* 11	* 9	* 10	* 11	* 9	* 9	* 9	* 9	Importations nettes
Total supply	10	* 8	* 10	* 10	* 9	* 9	* 9	* 10	Approv. total
Supply per capita	217	* 191	* 216	* 216	* 184	* 185	* 187	* 210	Approv. par habitant
Fiji									**Fidji**
Primary Energy Prod.	12	13	10	9	5	7	6	7	Prod. d'énergie primaire
Net imports	9	* 11	* 11	* 16	* 16	* 29	* 28	* 27	Importations nettes
Changes in stocks	-1	...	...	* 0	...	* 0	0	* 0	Variations des stocks
Total supply	23	* 23	22	24	21	37	33	* 34	Approv. total
Supply per capita	31	* 30	27	29	25	41	37	* 38	Approv. par habitant
Finland									**Finlande**
Primary Energy Prod.	504	549	623	701	728	732	736	753	Prod. d'énergie primaire
Net imports	708	632	731	766	725	622	616	585	Importations nettes
Changes in stocks	27	-26	2	27	-78	4	-56	-47	Variations des stocks
Total supply	1 186	1 208	1 353	1 440	1 530	1 350	1 408	1 385	Approv. total
Supply per capita	238	236	262	275	285	246	256	251	Approv. par habitant
France [5]									**France [5]**
Primary Energy Prod.	4 652	5 314	5 427	5 695	5 651	5 761[6]	5 458[6]	5 388[6]	Prod. d'énergie primaire
Net imports	4 801	4 619	5 259	5 688	5 195	4 684[6]	4 763[6]	4 882[6]	Importations nettes
Changes in stocks	71	10	148	49	-112	-27[6]	-75[6]	-8[6]	Variations des stocks
Total supply	9 381	9 924	10 537	11 333	10 958	10 472[6]	10 294[6]	10 278[6]	Approv. total
Supply per capita	165	171	178	186	174	157[6]	154[6]	153[6]	Approv. par habitant
French Guiana [1]									**Guyane française [1]**
Primary Energy Prod.	0	1	2	2	3	...	...	...	Prod. d'énergie primaire
Net imports	* 9	* 8	6	* 8	* 9	...	...	...	Importations nettes
Total supply	9	9	8	10	* 12	...	...	...	Approv. total
French Polynesia									**Polynésie française**
Primary Energy Prod.	0	0	1	1	1	* 1	* 1	* 1	Prod. d'énergie primaire
Net imports	* 6	* 6	* 8	* 11	* 11	* 10	* 11	* 11	Importations nettes
Total supply	* 7	7	9	12	12	12	11	11	Approv. total
Supply per capita	* 34	32	37	46	46	42	40	40	Approv. par habitant
Gabon									**Gabon**
Primary Energy Prod.	609	822	609	615	590	562	557	494	Prod. d'énergie primaire
Net imports	-509	-765	-572	-545	-526	-451	-445	-386	Importations nettes
Changes in stocks	50	2	-25	-3	-29	...	...	...	Variations des stocks
Total supply	50	56	62	72	93	112	113	109	Approv. total
Supply per capita	54	52	50	53	57	58	57	54	Approv. par habitant
Gambia									**Gambie**
Primary Energy Prod.	4	5	6	6	6	7	7	7	Prod. d'énergie primaire
Net imports	* 3	* 3	* 4	* 5	* 6	* 7	* 7	* 7	Importations nettes
Changes in stocks	0	...	...	...	...	...	...	...	Variations des stocks
Total supply	7	8	9	10	12	* 14	* 14	* 14	Approv. total
Supply per capita	7	7	7	7	7	* 7	* 7	* 7	Approv. par habitant
Georgia									**Géorgie**
Primary Energy Prod.	...	50	55	53	58	58	60	58	Prod. d'énergie primaire
Net imports	...	37	65	82	82	141	143	146	Importations nettes
Changes in stocks	...	0	0	0	0	1	0	-1	Variations des stocks
Total supply	...	88	120	135	140	198	203	204	Approv. total
Supply per capita	...	17	25	30	33	50	52	52	Approv. par habitant
Germany									**Allemagne**
Primary Energy Prod.	...	6 050	5 643	5 721	5 387	5 016	4 843	4 801	Prod. d'énergie primaire
Net imports	...	7 896	8 254	8 428	8 100	7 871	8 099	8 162	Importations nettes
Changes in stocks	...	-137	-184	46	-179	-16	-29	-36	Variations des stocks
Total supply	...	14 083	14 081	14 102	13 666	12 904	12 971	12 999	Approv. total
Supply per capita	...	172	171	171	169	158	158	158	Approv. par habitant

Region, country or area	1990	1995	2000	2005	2010	2015	2016	2017	Région, pays ou zone
Ghana									**Ghana**
Primary Energy Prod.	138	211	192	164	148	372	336	519	Prod. d'énergie primaire
Net imports	* 49	* 66	79	87	120	-31	18	-189	Importations nettes
Changes in stocks	0	...	...	...	0	1	14	16	Variations des stocks
Total supply	187	277	271	251	267	339	340	315	Approv. total
Supply per capita	13	16	14	12	11	12	12	11	Approv. par habitant
Gibraltar									**Gibraltar**
Net imports	3	5	6	7	8	9	10	11	Importations nettes
Changes in stocks	0	...	...	...	...	...	...	...	Variations des stocks
Total supply	2	4	5	6	7	9	10	11	Approv. total
Supply per capita	90	162	197	219	220	262	285	309	Approv. par habitant
Greece									**Grèce**
Primary Energy Prod.	385	389	418	432	395	354	281	301	Prod. d'énergie primaire
Net imports	499	569	725	820	749	654	658	653	Importations nettes
Changes in stocks	-10	8	12	-15	-11	43	6	-11	Variations des stocks
Total supply	895	950	1 131	1 265	1 155	965	933	966	Approv. total
Supply per capita	88	89	103	113	101	86	83	87	Approv. par habitant
Greenland									**Groenland**
Primary Energy Prod.	* 0	1	1	1	1	2	2	1	Prod. d'énergie primaire
Net imports	* 5	* 5	* 7	9	10	8	7	7	Importations nettes
Changes in stocks	...	...	...	* 1	1	1	0	0	Variations des stocks
Total supply	5	5	7	9	11	9	9	9	Approv. total
Supply per capita	90	95	127	165	186	155	153	156	Approv. par habitant
Grenada									**Grenade**
Primary Energy Prod.	0	0	0	0	0	0	0	0	Prod. d'énergie primaire
Net imports	* 2	* 2	* 3	3	4	4	4	4	Importations nettes
Changes in stocks	0	0	0	0	0	0	0	0	Variations des stocks
Total supply	2	2	3	3	4	4	4	4	Approv. total
Supply per capita	17	23	29	33	38	38	39	40	Approv. par habitant
Guadeloupe [1]									**Guadeloupe** [1]
Primary Energy Prod.	1	* 2	* 2	5	* 2	...	...	...	Prod. d'énergie primaire
Net imports	* 16	* 19	* 24	* 28	* 30	...	...	...	Importations nettes
Total supply	18	21	26	33	* 32	...	...	...	Approv. total
Guam									**Guam**
Primary Energy Prod.	...	...	...	...	...	0	0	0	Prod. d'énergie primaire
Net imports	...	...	...	...	...	0	0	0	Importations nettes
Total supply	...	...	...	...	...	0	0	0	Approv. total
Supply per capita	...	...	...	...	...	0	1	1	Approv. par habitant
Guatemala									**Guatemala**
Primary Energy Prod.	143	178	229	255	279	289	354	343	Prod. d'énergie primaire
Net imports	52	75	75	112	110	186	186	191	Importations nettes
Changes in stocks	0	* 1	-4	6	0	22	9	4	Variations des stocks
Total supply	195	252	307	361	388	453	531	530	Approv. total
Supply per capita	22	25	27	28	27	28	32	31	Approv. par habitant
Guernsey									**Guernesey**
Net imports	...	...	...	1	1	1	1	1	Importations nettes
Total supply	...	...	...	1	1	1	1	1	Approv. total
Supply per capita	...	...	...	17	14	13	17	18	Approv. par habitant
Guinea									**Guinée**
Primary Energy Prod.	91	110	107	109	112	114	114	115	Prod. d'énergie primaire
Net imports	* 14	* 16	* 21	* 26	* 36	* 37	* 40	* 42	Importations nettes
Changes in stocks	0	...	...	...	...	...	...	...	Variations des stocks
Total supply	105	126	128	135	147	150	154	156	Approv. total
Supply per capita	18	17	15	15	14	12	12	12	Approv. par habitant
Guinea-Bissau									**Guinée-Bissau**
Primary Energy Prod.	17	18	20	22	24	25	26	26	Prod. d'énergie primaire
Net imports	* 3	* 4	* 3	* 4	* 5	* 4	* 5	* 5	Importations nettes
Total supply	20	21	23	26	28	30	31	31	Approv. total
Supply per capita	20	19	19	19	18	17	17	17	Approv. par habitant
Guyana									**Guyana**
Primary Energy Prod.	13	9	9	9	8	7	7	7	Prod. d'énergie primaire
Net imports	16	21	21	20	23	27	30	30	Importations nettes
Changes in stocks	...	-2	-3	-3	-3	0	0	0	Variations des stocks
Total supply	28	31	34	32	34	35	37	37	Approv. total
Supply per capita	39	43	46	43	46	45	48	47	Approv. par habitant
Haiti									**Haïti**
Primary Energy Prod.	88	94	104	115	131	139	141	142	Prod. d'énergie primaire
Net imports	13	12	20	28	28	44	45	45	Importations nettes
Changes in stocks	0	...	...	...	...	0	...	...	Variations des stocks
Total supply	101	107	123	142	159	183	185	188	Approv. total
Supply per capita	14	14	14	15	16	17	17	17	Approv. par habitant
Honduras									**Honduras**
Primary Energy Prod.	69	70	64	78	93	118	120	126	Prod. d'énergie primaire
Net imports	29	50	61	91	98	99	110	127	Importations nettes
Changes in stocks	0	1	0	-4	-2	-31	-12	0	Variations des stocks
Total supply	98	119	125	172	193	247	242	252	Approv. total
Supply per capita	20	21	20	25	24	28	27	27	Approv. par habitant
Hungary									**Hongrie**
Primary Energy Prod.	612	580	485	432	495	471	479	472	Prod. d'énergie primaire
Net imports	586	513	571	727	623	561	593	691	Importations nettes
Changes in stocks	-2	11	10	8	9	-21	-1	49	Variations des stocks
Total supply	1 200	1 083	1 046	1 153	1 109	1 053	1 072	1 115	Approv. total
Supply per capita	116	105	102	114	112	108	110	115	Approv. par habitant

Production, trade and supply of energy *(continued)*
Petajoules and gigajoules per capita

Production, commerce et fourniture d'énergie *(suite)*
pétajoules et gigajoules par habitant

Region, country or area	1990	1995	2000	2005	2010	2015	2016	2017	Région, pays ou zone
Iceland									**Islande**
Primary Energy Prod.	59	63	109	127	252	285	302	299	Prod. d'énergie primaire
Net imports	28	27	31	31	26	29	30	27	Importations nettes
Changes in stocks	0	0	2	1	-1	1	0	-1	Variations des stocks
Total supply	87	90	139	158	278	313	331	327	Approv. total
Supply per capita	341	338	494	534	869	949	996	977	Approv. par habitant
India									**Inde**
Primary Energy Prod.	12 283	14 212	15 763	18 212	22 888	22 818	23 219	23 410	Prod. d'énergie primaire
Net imports	1 196	* 2 010	3 890	4 689	6 558	* 13 296	* 13 368	* 14 421	Importations nettes
Changes in stocks	45	* -41	-155	194	252	48	-214	-252	Variations des stocks
Total supply	13 435	16 262	19 808	22 706	29 193	36 066	36 802	38 083	Approv. total
Supply per capita	15	17	19	20	24	28	28	28	Approv. par habitant
Indonesia									**Indonésie**
Primary Energy Prod.	6 735[7]	8 320[7]	8 129[7]	11 351	16 863	18 140	19 030	19 187	Prod. d'énergie primaire
Net imports	* -2 753[7]	* -3 634[7]	* -3 577[7]	-4 243	-8 531	-8 660	-8 906	-9 194	Importations nettes
Changes in stocks	223[7]	100[7]	-417[7]	21	2	-30	-119	* 35	Variations des stocks
Total supply	3 759[7]	4 587[7]	4 970[7]	7 087	8 331	9 511	10 244	9 959	Approv. total
Supply per capita	20[7]	23[7]	23[7]	31	34	37	39	38	Approv. par habitant
Iran (Islamic Republic of)									**Iran (Rép. islamique d')**
Primary Energy Prod.	7 454	9 302	11 121	13 006	14 283	13 637	16 412	17 740	Prod. d'énergie primaire
Net imports	-4 634	-5 415	-5 787	* -5 682	-5 634	-3 640	-6 293	-6 948	Importations nettes
Changes in stocks	0	0	-52	103	69	7	-160	-195	Variations des stocks
Total supply	2 819	3 887	5 386	7 221	8 579	9 989	10 278	10 987	Approv. total
Supply per capita	51	65	82	104	115	126	128	135	Approv. par habitant
Iraq									**Iraq**
Primary Energy Prod.	4 411	1 265	5 482	4 147	5 274	7 565	9 667	9 881	Prod. d'énergie primaire
Net imports	* -3 656	-193	-4 487	-2 656	-3 835	-5 719	-7 225	-7 346	Importations nettes
Changes in stocks	* 169	0	0	3	1	-152	133	15	Variations des stocks
Total supply	586	1 072	995	1 488	1 437	1 997	2 309	2 521	Approv. total
Supply per capita	34	53	42	54	47	55	62	66	Approv. par habitant
Ireland									**Irlande**
Primary Energy Prod.	145	172	90	70	78	81	176	204	Prod. d'énergie primaire
Net imports	282	305	488	551	524	491	394	368	Importations nettes
Changes in stocks	10	28	-2	2	-8	14	-16	-2	Variations des stocks
Total supply	417	448	580	618	610	557	586	574	Approv. total
Supply per capita	118	124	153	149	132	119	124	121	Approv. par habitant
Isle of Man									**Île de Man**
Primary Energy Prod.	...	...	...	* 0	* 0	* 0	* 0	* 0	Prod. d'énergie primaire
Net imports	...	...	...	0	4	4	5	4	Importations nettes
Total supply	...	...	...	1	4	4	5	4	Approv. total
Supply per capita	...	...	...	9	50	49	55	53	Approv. par habitant
Israel									**Israël**
Primary Energy Prod.	18	23	27	87	162	308	347	375	Prod. d'énergie primaire
Net imports	452	628	723	690	810	657	585	618	Importations nettes
Changes in stocks	-12	-1	-17	5	0	14	-30	29	Variations des stocks
Total supply	482	652	767	773	972	951	962	965	Approv. total
Supply per capita	107	122	128	117	131	118	117	116	Approv. par habitant
Italy [8]									**Italie** [8]
Primary Energy Prod.	1 072	1 235	1 183	1 269	1 384	1 509	1 400	1 421	Prod. d'énergie primaire
Net imports	5 375	5 481	6 239	6 509	6 009	4 888	4 873	4 992	Importations nettes
Changes in stocks	80	3	190	-70	69	-5	-62	-24	Variations des stocks
Total supply	6 366	6 714	7 230	7 847	7 324	6 402	6 334	6 437	Approv. total
Supply per capita	112	118	127	134	123	108	107	108	Approv. par habitant
Jamaica									**Jamaïque**
Primary Energy Prod.	13	9	11	15	5	7	6	* 6	Prod. d'énergie primaire
Net imports	* 97	* 118	144	140	103	109	109	108	Importations nettes
Changes in stocks	-2	-3	7	1	-2	1	-1	2	Variations des stocks
Total supply	113	130	148	152	110	113	116	111	Approv. total
Supply per capita	48	53	57	57	39	39	40	38	Approv. par habitant
Japan [9]									**Japon** [9]
Primary Energy Prod.	3 118	4 076	4 402	4 313	4 228	1 345	1 460	1 727	Prod. d'énergie primaire
Net imports	15 398	16 736	17 496	17 720	16 765	16 670	16 290	16 337	Importations nettes
Changes in stocks	149	56	166	101	-6	-58	-74	-52	Variations des stocks
Total supply	18 367	20 756	21 732	21 932	20 997	18 073	17 824	18 116	Approv. total
Supply per capita	150	167	173	174	163	141	140	142	Approv. par habitant
Jersey									**Jersey**
Primary Energy Prod.	...	...	...	* 0	* 0	* 1	* 1	* 1	Prod. d'énergie primaire
Net imports	...	1	1	2	2	2	2	2	Importations nettes
Total supply	...	1	1	3	3	3	3	3	Approv. total
Supply per capita	...	9	17	28	28	29	29	29	Approv. par habitant
Jordan									**Jordanie**
Primary Energy Prod.	6	10	10	10	9	8	10	11	Prod. d'énergie primaire
Net imports	136	160	190	285	300	359	355	381	Importations nettes
Changes in stocks	4	-2	-5	7	5	5	4	8	Variations des stocks
Total supply	138	172	205	289	303	361	361	384	Approv. total
Supply per capita	40	39	42	54	42	39	38	40	Approv. par habitant
Kazakhstan									**Kazakhstan**
Primary Energy Prod.	...	2 663	3 367	5 131	6 770	6 629	6 647	7 359	Prod. d'énergie primaire
Net imports	...	-477	* -1 828	-2 771	* -3 318	* -3 603	* -3 446	* -3 981	Importations nettes
Changes in stocks	...	...	-12	8	88	19	13	42	Variations des stocks
Total supply	...	2 185	1 551	2 352	3 363	3 006	3 188	3 335	Approv. total
Supply per capita	...	137	104	155	205	169	177	183	Approv. par habitant
Kenya									**Kenya**
Primary Energy Prod.	367	420	* 487	* 580	* 650	761	736	738	Prod. d'énergie primaire
Net imports	* 71	98	141	109	137	189	202	194	Importations nettes
Changes in stocks	0	...	...	4	-5	-4	0	0	Variations des stocks
Total supply	439	518	* 627	* 686	* 793	953	938	932	Approv. total
Supply per capita	19	19	* 20	* 19	* 19	20	19	19	Approv. par habitant

Region, country or area	1990	1995	2000	2005	2010	2015	2016	2017	Région, pays ou zone
Kiribati									**Kiribati**
Primary Energy Prod.	* 0	* 0	* 0	0	* 1	* 1	* 1	* 1	Prod. d'énergie primaire
Net imports	* 0	* 0	1	* 1	1	* 1	* 1	* 1	Importations nettes
Total supply	* 1	* 1	1	* 1	1	* 1	* 1	* 1	Approv. total
Supply per capita	* 11	* 11	11	* 14	13	* 12	* 13	* 12	Approv. par habitant
Kosovo									**Kosovo**
Primary Energy Prod.	...	...	46	59	78	76	84	75	Prod. d'énergie primaire
Net imports	...	...	17	23	25	29	27	33	Importations nettes
Changes in stocks	...	...	-1	0	-2	-1	-2	0	Variations des stocks
Total supply	...	...	65	82	105	106	113	108	Approv. total
Supply per capita	...	...	38	48	59	59	62	59	Approv. par habitant
Kuwait [10]									**Koweït** [10]
Primary Energy Prod.	2 799	4 802	4 748	6 080	5 557	7 004	7 271	6 919	Prod. d'énergie primaire
Net imports	* -2 090	-3 968	-3 941	-4 915	-4 229	-5 622	-5 806	-5 420	Importations nettes
Changes in stocks	* 142	-1	-17	31	-22	-70	-68	-85	Variations des stocks
Total supply	566	835	824	1 133	1 350	1 452	1 532	1 584	Approv. total
Supply per capita	271	513	424	500	450	369	378	383	Approv. par habitant
Kyrgyzstan									**Kirghizistan**
Primary Energy Prod.	...	53	60	61	53	75	77	88	Prod. d'énergie primaire
Net imports	...	51	38	53	63	103	81	79	Importations nettes
Changes in stocks	...	3	-2	0	1	12	-4	5	Variations des stocks
Total supply	...	101	101	114	115	167	162	162	Approv. total
Supply per capita	...	22	20	23	21	29	27	27	Approv. par habitant
Lao People's Dem. Rep.									**Rép. dém. populaire lao**
Primary Energy Prod.	54	56	57	64	98	162	267	276	Prod. d'énergie primaire
Net imports	* 5	* 7	* 1	* 5	* 3	* 7	* -23	* -41	Importations nettes
Changes in stocks	...	...	...	...	...	...	* 34	* -1	Variations des stocks
Total supply	60	63	58	68	100	169	209	237	Approv. total
Supply per capita	14	13	11	12	16	25	31	35	Approv. par habitant
Latvia									**Lettonie**
Primary Energy Prod.	...	60	59	78	83	98	102	108	Prod. d'énergie primaire
Net imports	...	134	99	116	78	84	76	72	Importations nettes
Changes in stocks	...	1	-4	5	-28	3	-1	-4	Variations des stocks
Total supply	...	193	161	190	189	179	179	185	Approv. total
Supply per capita	...	77	67	82	89	90	91	95	Approv. par habitant
Lebanon									**Liban**
Primary Energy Prod.	5	8	7	10	9	8	7	* 8	Prod. d'énergie primaire
Net imports	* 108	166	198	197	253	* 330	* 340	* 361	Importations nettes
Changes in stocks	...	...	-1	-1	...	...	...	...	Variations des stocks
Total supply	* 113	174	207	206	262	337	348	369	Approv. total
Supply per capita	* 38	50	55	51	53	52	52	54	Approv. par habitant
Lesotho									**Lesotho**
Primary Energy Prod.	19	22	28	25	27	* 20	* 19	18	Prod. d'énergie primaire
Net imports	* 17	* 19	* 20	* 22	* 25	* 26	* 27	* 30	Importations nettes
Total supply	36	41	48	47	52	* 47	* 46	* 48	Approv. total
Supply per capita	22	23	24	23	25	* 22	* 21	* 21	Approv. par habitant
Liberia									**Libéria**
Primary Energy Prod.	32	25	43	53	64	76	79	81	Prod. d'énergie primaire
Net imports	* 7	* 7	* 6	* 9	* 11	* 16	* 19	* 17	Importations nettes
Total supply	38	31	49	62	75	92	97	97	Approv. total
Supply per capita	18	15	17	19	19	20	21	21	Approv. par habitant
Libya									**Libye**
Primary Energy Prod.	3 020	3 190	3 117	4 062	4 294	1 314	1 208	2 233	Prod. d'énergie primaire
Net imports	-2 676	-2 538	-2 433	-3 335	-3 365	-683	-644	-1 677	Importations nettes
Changes in stocks	-124	...	...	...	69	...	...	...	Variations des stocks
Total supply	468	653	685	727	860	630	562	555	Approv. total
Supply per capita	108	137	131	126	139	101	89	87	Approv. par habitant
Liechtenstein									**Liechtenstein**
Primary Energy Prod.	0	0	0	0	* 1	* 1	* 1	* 1	Prod. d'énergie primaire
Net imports	1	1	2	2	2	2	2	2	Importations nettes
Total supply	1	2	2	3	3	3	3	3	Approv. total
Supply per capita	45	55	65	77	92	88	88	89	Approv. par habitant
Lithuania									**Lituanie**
Primary Energy Prod.	...	160	141	169	64	77	78	86	Prod. d'énergie primaire
Net imports	...	226	169	198	231	221	222	224	Importations nettes
Changes in stocks	...	22	15	3	3	4	0	-3	Variations des stocks
Total supply	...	363	295	365	292	293	299	313	Approv. total
Supply per capita	...	100	84	107	94	100	103	108	Approv. par habitant
Luxembourg									**Luxembourg**
Primary Energy Prod.	1	2	3	5	5	6	7	8	Prod. d'énergie primaire
Net imports	143	130	140	179	173	150	149	151	Importations nettes
Changes in stocks	0	-1	2	-1	-1	-1	0	0	Variations des stocks
Total supply	143	133	142	185	179	158	156	160	Approv. total
Supply per capita	376	327	325	405	352	279	272	274	Approv. par habitant
Madagascar									**Madagascar**
Primary Energy Prod.	86	107	* 127	* 145	* 174	209	263	272	Prod. d'énergie primaire
Net imports	* 13	* 18	* 26	* 24	* 25	* 45	* 45	50	Importations nettes
Changes in stocks	* 0	0	0	0	-1	* 0	* 0	* 0	Variations des stocks
Total supply	99	126	* 153	* 168	* 201	254	307	322	Approv. total
Supply per capita	9	10	* 10	* 9	* 9	10	12	13	Approv. par habitant
Malawi									**Malawi**
Primary Energy Prod.	56	55	56	60	64	68	68	68	Prod. d'énergie primaire
Net imports	* 8	* 11	* 9	* 11	* 12	* 13	* 15	* 17	Importations nettes
Total supply	64	65	65	70	76	80	82	84	Approv. total
Supply per capita	7	7	6	5	5	5	5	5	Approv. par habitant

Region, country or area	1990	1995	2000	2005	2010	2015	2016	2017	Région, pays ou zone
Malaysia									**Malaisie**
Primary Energy Prod.	1 794	2 791	3 082	3 770	3 450	3 748	3 787	3 830	Prod. d'énergie primaire
Net imports	-1 019	* -1 069	-1 115	-1 003	* -495	-365	-310	-343	Importations nettes
Changes in stocks	3	* 14	8	21	* -10	-41	-51	4	Variations des stocks
Total supply	773	1 708	1 959	2 745	2 965	3 424	3 527	3 482	Approv. total
Supply per capita	42	82	84	105	105	111	113	110	Approv. par habitant
Maldives									**Maldives**
Primary Energy Prod.	0	0	0	0	0	0	0	0	Prod. d'énergie primaire
Net imports	* 3	* 4	* 6	* 9	* 13	* 19	* 21	* 21	Importations nettes
Total supply	* 2	4	6	9	13	19	21	22	Approv. total
Supply per capita	* 11	14	24	30	37	41	44	43	Approv. par habitant
Mali									**Mali**
Primary Energy Prod.	37	42	45	49	52	56	57	57	Prod. d'énergie primaire
Net imports	* 5	* 6	* 11	* 12	* 26	* 38	* 38	* 38	Importations nettes
Total supply	43	49	57	61	79	94	95	96	Approv. total
Supply per capita	5	5	5	5	5	5	5	5	Approv. par habitant
Malta									**Malte**
Primary Energy Prod.	...	...	...	0	0	1	1	1	Prod. d'énergie primaire
Net imports	29	31	28	37	35	25	26	33	Importations nettes
Changes in stocks	0	1	0	0	-1	-2	2	5	Variations des stocks
Total supply	29	30	29	37	35	27	25	29	Approv. total
Supply per capita	79	77	72	91	85	63	58	66	Approv. par habitant
Marshall Islands									**Îles Marshall**
Primary Energy Prod.	...	* 0	* 0	* 0	* 0	* 0	* 0	* 0	Prod. d'énergie primaire
Net imports	...	* 1	* 1	* 2	* 2	* 2	* 2	* 2	Importations nettes
Total supply	...	* 1	* 2	* 2	* 2	* 2	* 2	* 2	Approv. total
Supply per capita	...	* 28	* 30	* 35	* 41	* 42	* 42	* 43	Approv. par habitant
Martinique [1]									**Martinique** [1]
Primary Energy Prod.	0	0	* 0	* 1	* 1	...	...	...	Prod. d'énergie primaire
Net imports	* 21	* 22	* 22	* 29	* 28	...	...	...	Importations nettes
Changes in stocks	0	...	...	...	...	...	...	...	Variations des stocks
Total supply	21	* 22	* 23	30	29	...	...	...	Approv. total
Mauritania									**Mauritanie**
Primary Energy Prod.	11	12	13	15	34	30	31	30	Prod. d'énergie primaire
Net imports	* 13	* 14	16	21	7	* 30	* 28	* 43	Importations nettes
Changes in stocks	0	...	...	0	* -3	...	...	...	Variations des stocks
Total supply	* 23	* 26	29	36	45	* 60	* 59	73	Approv. total
Supply per capita	* 11	* 11	11	12	12	* 14	* 14	17	Approv. par habitant
Mauritius									**Maurice**
Primary Energy Prod.	13	15	13	12	11	12	11	10	Prod. d'énergie primaire
Net imports	21	28	34	44	49	57	* 63	82	Importations nettes
Changes in stocks	1	2	-3	-1	-2	3	6	22	Variations des stocks
Total supply	33	41	49	57	63	67	67	69	Approv. total
Supply per capita	31	36	41	45	50	53	53	55	Approv. par habitant
Mayotte [1]									**Mayotte** [1]
Primary Energy Prod.	* 0	0	0	0	0	...	...	...	Prod. d'énergie primaire
Net imports	* 1	* 1	* 2	* 3	4	...	...	...	Importations nettes
Changes in stocks	...	...	...	...	0	...	...	...	Variations des stocks
Mexico									**Mexique**
Primary Energy Prod.	8 187	8 540	9 600	11 031	9 403	8 031	7 644	6 989	Prod. d'énergie primaire
Net imports	-3 001	-3 031	-3 196	-3 491	-1 842	-250	187	670	Importations nettes
Changes in stocks	7	-7	91	-19	5	-49	6	37	Variations des stocks
Total supply	5 179	5 516	6 314	7 559	7 557	7 830	7 826	7 622	Approv. total
Supply per capita	61	60	63	71	64	62	61	59	Approv. par habitant
Micronesia (Fed. States of)									**Micronésie (États féd. de)**
Primary Energy Prod.	...	* 0	0	0	0	0	0	0	Prod. d'énergie primaire
Net imports	...	* 2	* 2	* 2	* 2	3	* 3	* 3	Importations nettes
Total supply	...	* 2	* 2	2	2	2	* 2	* 2	Approv. total
Supply per capita	...	* 16	* 18	16	15	20	* 21	* 20	Approv. par habitant
Mongolia									**Mongolie**
Primary Energy Prod.	82	72	66	138	655	654	959	1 311	Prod. d'énergie primaire
Net imports	33	* 17	21	-35	-449	-365	-667	-790	Importations nettes
Changes in stocks	...	...	...	-1	41	17	-3	126	Variations des stocks
Total supply	116	89	87	104	164	272	294	395	Approv. total
Supply per capita	53	39	36	41	61	91	97	128	Approv. par habitant
Montenegro									**Monténégro**
Primary Energy Prod.	...	...	...	25	35	30	28	27	Prod. d'énergie primaire
Net imports	...	...	...	16	14	12	14	17	Importations nettes
Changes in stocks	...	...	...	...	...	0	1	0	Variations des stocks
Total supply	...	...	...	42	48	42	41	43	Approv. total
Supply per capita	...	...	...	67	77	67	65	68	Approv. par habitant
Montserrat									**Montserrat**
Net imports	* 0	* 1	* 0	* 1	* 1	* 1	* 0	* 0	Importations nettes
Changes in stocks	...	...	...	...	0	0	0	0	Variations des stocks
Total supply	* 0	* 0	* 0	* 1	1	1	0	0	Approv. total
Supply per capita	* 41	* 48	* 75	* 93	175	149	81	72	Approv. par habitant
Morocco									**Maroc**
Primary Energy Prod.	82	83	73	74	84	62	90	89	Prod. d'énergie primaire
Net imports	* 262	* 351	* 402	* 530	* 687	752	743	780	Importations nettes
Changes in stocks	-2	10	-2	0	10	15	3	1	Variations des stocks
Total supply	345	423	478	606	762	799	831	869	Approv. total
Supply per capita	14	16	17	20	23	23	23	24	Approv. par habitant
Mozambique									**Mozambique**
Primary Energy Prod.	236	248	302	429	398	718	626	831	Prod. d'énergie primaire
Net imports	* 12	16	-11	-65	-94	* -230	* -253	-373	Importations nettes
Changes in stocks	0	0	0	-1	0	* 43	* -64	7	Variations des stocks
Total supply	248	264	292	364	305	444	437	452	Approv. total
Supply per capita	18	17	16	18	13	16	15	15	Approv. par habitant

Region, country or area	1990	1995	2000	2005	2010	2015	2016	2017	Région, pays ou zone
Myanmar									**Myanmar**
Primary Energy Prod.	446	464	648	926	969	1 176	1 207	1 186	Prod. d'énergie primaire
Net imports	6	27	-113	-307	-305	-296	-326	* -334	Importations nettes
Changes in stocks	2	-7	-3	1	2	32	10	-2	Variations des stocks
Total supply	449	498	538	618	662	848	872	854	Approv. total
Supply per capita	11	12	12	13	13	16	16	16	Approv. par habitant
Namibia									**Namibie**
Primary Energy Prod.	...	14	16	17	17	20	20	21	Prod. d'énergie primaire
Net imports	...	24	26	37	48	57	62	61	Importations nettes
Changes in stocks	...	...	...	...	0	...	...	...	Variations des stocks
Total supply	...	38	42	54	65	78	82	82	Approv. total
Supply per capita	...	23	22	26	30	32	33	32	Approv. par habitant
Nauru									**Nauru**
Primary Energy Prod.	...	...	...	...	* 0	* 0	0	0	Prod. d'énergie primaire
Net imports	* 2	* 2	* 2	* 1	* 1	* 1	* 1	* 1	Importations nettes
Changes in stocks	...	...	...	...	* 0	0	0	...	Variations des stocks
Total supply	* 2	* 1	* 1	* 1	1	* 1	* 1	* 1	Approv. total
Supply per capita	* 188	* 148	* 119	* 84	58	* 63	* 55	* 55	Approv. par habitant
Nepal									**Népal**
Primary Energy Prod.	146	271	310	349	384	424	430	438	Prod. d'énergie primaire
Net imports	9	29	39	39	62	75	114	132	Importations nettes
Changes in stocks	-1	-1	...	...	...	0	0	...	Variations des stocks
Total supply	156	301	349	388	446	499	544	571	Approv. total
Supply per capita	8	14	14	14	16	17	19	19	Approv. par habitant
Netherlands [11]									**Pays-Bas** [11]
Primary Energy Prod.	2 535	2 800	2 448	2 614	2 979	2 006	1 929	1 748	Prod. d'énergie primaire
Net imports	221	171	757	740	451	1 108	1 042	1 287	Importations nettes
Changes in stocks	-16	-72	98	38	-13	126	-80	-50	Variations des stocks
Total supply	2 771	3 043	3 106	3 316	3 443	2 989	3 052	3 085	Approv. total
Supply per capita	186	197	196	203	206	176	180	181	Approv. par habitant
Netherlands Antilles [former]									**Antilles néerlandaises [anc.]**
Primary Energy Prod.	0	0	0	0	0	...	...	...	Prod. d'énergie primaire
Net imports	* 71	* 94	83	84	68	...	...	...	Importations nettes
Changes in stocks	* -11	...	...	...	...	...	...	...	Variations des stocks
Total supply	82	* 95	83	84	69	...	...	...	Approv. total
Supply per capita	432	* 500	464	452	344	...	...	...	Approv. par habitant
New Caledonia									**Nouvelle-Calédonie**
Primary Energy Prod.	2	1	2	1	1	2	1	2	Prod. d'énergie primaire
Net imports	* 20	* 26	* 28	* 36	* 47	61	67	65	Importations nettes
Changes in stocks	...	...	...	...	2	1	0	-1	Variations des stocks
Total supply	21	27	30	37	46	61	67	68	Approv. total
Supply per capita	126	140	142	161	184	228	247	246	Approv. par habitant
New Zealand									**Nouvelle-Zélande**
Primary Energy Prod.	503	553	632	574	775	780	766	758	Prod. d'énergie primaire
Net imports	59	90	104	165	77	156	185	181	Importations nettes
Changes in stocks	1	-3	-12	-8	12	-16	1	-16	Variations des stocks
Total supply	561	646	749	748	839	952	950	955	Approv. total
Supply per capita	165	176	194	181	192	206	204	203	Approv. par habitant
Nicaragua									**Nicaragua**
Primary Energy Prod.	59	66	56	62	66	92	93	93	Prod. d'énergie primaire
Net imports	28	37	49	57	56	71	72	74	Importations nettes
Changes in stocks	0	0	-1	0	-3	0	-2	0	Variations des stocks
Total supply	86	102	107	119	125	163	167	167	Approv. total
Supply per capita	21	22	21	22	22	27	27	27	Approv. par habitant
Niger									**Niger**
Primary Energy Prod.	54	65	74	* 70	56	100	105	* 98	Prod. d'énergie primaire
Net imports	* 5	* 5	* 7	* 7	13	* -4	-9	* -11	Importations nettes
Changes in stocks	0	0	0	0	0	* 1	* 0	* 2	Variations des stocks
Total supply	60	70	81	* 77	70	94	97	* 85	Approv. total
Supply per capita	8	8	7	* 6	4	5	5	* 4	Approv. par habitant
Nigeria									**Nigéria**
Primary Energy Prod.	6 091	6 856	8 247	9 734	10 591	10 677	10 058	10 402	Prod. d'énergie primaire
Net imports	-3 312	-3 804	-4 595	-5 344	-5 283	-4 700	-3 758	-3 808	Importations nettes
Changes in stocks	-2	...	10	-10	-17	-88	45	26	Variations des stocks
Total supply	2 780	3 052	3 642	4 401	5 325	6 065	6 255	6 568	Approv. total
Supply per capita	29	28	29	31	34	33	34	34	Approv. par habitant
Niue									**Nioué**
Primary Energy Prod.	0	0	0	0	0	0	* 0	* 0	Prod. d'énergie primaire
Net imports	* 0	* 0	* 0	* 0	0	0	* 0	* 0	Importations nettes
Total supply	* 0	* 0	* 0	0	0	0	* 0	* 0	Approv. total
Supply per capita	* 34	* 34	* 42	42	52	63	* 61	* 60	Approv. par habitant
North Macedonia									**Macédoine du Nord**
Primary Energy Prod.	...	112	118	108	68	58	51	53	Prod. d'énergie primaire
Net imports	...	43	48	52	53	58	66	65	Importations nettes
Changes in stocks	...	5	-4	-4	-1	0	1	-2	Variations des stocks
Total supply	...	151	169	163	121	116	116	119	Approv. total
Supply per capita	...	77	84	80	58	56	56	57	Approv. par habitant
Norway [12]									**Norvège** [12]
Primary Energy Prod.	4 977	7 543	9 340	9 371	8 734	8 629	8 721	8 923	Prod. d'énergie primaire
Net imports	-4 024	-6 561	-8 251	-8 242	-7 475	-7 418	-7 573	-7 735	Importations nettes
Changes in stocks	77	20	15	15	2	9	12	-47	Variations des stocks
Total supply	875	962	1 074	1 114	1 257	1 202	1 135	1 235	Approv. total
Supply per capita	206	221	239	241	257	231	216	233	Approv. par habitant

Region, country or area	1990	1995	2000	2005	2010	2015	2016	2017	Région, pays ou zone
Oman									**Oman**
Primary Energy Prod.	1 531	1 931	2 359	2 356	2 793	3 228	3 310	3 242	Prod. d'énergie primaire
Net imports	* -1 392	* -1 710	-2 079	-1 912	-2 022	-2 178	-2 284	-2 139	Importations nettes
Changes in stocks	-14	-15	-38	0	-7	3	7	0	Variations des stocks
Total supply	153	236	319	445	778	1 048	1 020	1 102	Approv. total
Supply per capita	82	106	141	183	256	249	230	238	Approv. par habitant
Other non-specified areas									**Autres zones non-spécifiées**
Primary Energy Prod.	456	453	489	518	538	511	451	350	Prod. d'énergie primaire
Net imports	1 649	2 327	3 060	3 760	4 078	4 090	4 138	4 260	Importations nettes
Changes in stocks	100	117	41	42	-7	47	11	10	Variations des stocks
Total supply	2 005	2 663	3 509	4 236	4 624	4 554	4 579	4 600	Approv. total
Supply per capita	98	125	158	186	200	194	194	195	Approv. par habitant
Pakistan									**Pakistan**
Primary Energy Prod.	906	1 192	1 403	2 020	2 040	2 174	* 2 122	* 2 175	Prod. d'énergie primaire
Net imports	385	529	680	633	843	1 284	1 663	* 2 102	Importations nettes
Changes in stocks	...	...	0	10	2	13	2	* -3	Variations des stocks
Total supply	1 290	1 722	2 082	2 642	2 880	3 445	3 784	4 280	Approv. total
Supply per capita	12	14	14	17	17	18	20	22	Approv. par habitant
Palau									**Palaos**
Primary Energy Prod.	...	...	...	...	...	...	0	0	Prod. d'énergie primaire
Net imports	...	* 2	* 3	* 3	* 3	* 3	* 3	* 3	Importations nettes
Total supply	...	* 3	* 3	* 3	3	* 3	* 3	* 3	Approv. total
Supply per capita	...	* 158	* 152	* 156	161	* 174	* 175	* 182	Approv. par habitant
Panama									**Panama**
Primary Energy Prod.	24	22	28	32	26	36	39	42	Prod. d'énergie primaire
Net imports	40	49	75	88	98	113	125	135	Importations nettes
Changes in stocks	4	1	-1	0	-20	-21	-5	-20	Variations des stocks
Total supply	60	71	105	120	144	171	169	197	Approv. total
Supply per capita	25	26	35	37	39	43	42	48	Approv. par habitant
Papua New Guinea									**Papouasie-Nvl-Guinée**
Primary Energy Prod.	251	263	220	174	95	228	233	232	Prod. d'énergie primaire
Net imports	* -162	* -171	* -121	* -48	* 47	* -61	* -66	* -63	Importations nettes
Changes in stocks	0	* 3	* 0	0	2	1	-3	1	Variations des stocks
Total supply	88	89	99	126	141	166	170	168	Approv. total
Supply per capita	21	19	18	21	20	21	21	20	Approv. par habitant
Paraguay									**Paraguay**
Primary Energy Prod.	* 145	194	276	285	324	324	350	338	Prod. d'énergie primaire
Net imports	* -60	-80	-122	-109	-98	-68	-76	-55	Importations nettes
Changes in stocks	* 0	-4	2	-1	-4	0	3	-5	Variations des stocks
Total supply	* 84	118	153	178	231	255	271	288	Approv. total
Supply per capita	* 20	25	29	30	37	38	40	42	Approv. par habitant
Peru									**Pérou**
Primary Energy Prod.	439	414	391	455	810	938	957	912	Prod. d'énergie primaire
Net imports	-22	73	130	108	-15	-29	-19	10	Importations nettes
Changes in stocks	-3	23	7	-3	-13	19	-14	-38	Variations des stocks
Total supply	421	464	514	565	808	890	953	960	Approv. total
Supply per capita	19	19	20	20	27	28	30	30	Approv. par habitant
Philippines									**Philippines**
Primary Energy Prod.	540	533	695	762	924	999	1 106	1 098	Prod. d'énergie primaire
Net imports	512	759	860	* 697	718	1 066	1 082	1 187	Importations nettes
Changes in stocks	13	28	4	-10	11	14	5	-35	Variations des stocks
Total supply	1 039	1 264	1 551	1 469	1 631	2 050	2 183	2 321	Approv. total
Supply per capita	17	18	20	17	17	20	21	22	Approv. par habitant
Poland									**Pologne**
Primary Energy Prod.	4 350	4 162	3 319	3 281	2 809	2 843	2 791	2 690	Prod. d'énergie primaire
Net imports	85	50	441	692	1 355	1 193	1 288	1 672	Importations nettes
Changes in stocks	43	-36	-24	82	-93	32	-111	-22	Variations des stocks
Total supply	4 393	4 249	3 784	3 891	4 256	4 004	4 190	4 384	Approv. total
Supply per capita	115	111	99	102	111	105	110	115	Approv. par habitant
Portugal [13]									**Portugal** [13]
Primary Energy Prod.	142	139	161	151	242	224	254	220	Prod. d'énergie primaire
Net imports	579	719	870	974	726	703	654	741	Importations nettes
Changes in stocks	19	12	0	16	-15	7	-6	10	Variations des stocks
Total supply	703	846	1 031	1 109	983	920	913	951	Approv. total
Supply per capita	71	84	100	105	92	88	88	92	Approv. par habitant
Puerto Rico									**Porto Rico**
Primary Energy Prod.	* 1	0	1	0	0	1	1	* 1	Prod. d'énergie primaire
Net imports	...	...	12	24	27	52	59	49	Importations nettes
Total supply	* 1	0	13	24	27	53	61	50	Approv. total
Supply per capita	* 0	0	3	6	8	16	18	16	Approv. par habitant
Qatar									**Qatar**
Primary Energy Prod.	1 009	1 364	2 449	3 718	7 428	9 316	9 518	9 387	Prod. d'énergie primaire
Net imports	-832	-811	-1 921	-2 991	-6 261	-7 378	-7 638	-7 604	Importations nettes
Changes in stocks	-22	0	-56	-1	3	110	118	-15	Variations des stocks
Total supply	199	553	584	728	1 165	1 828	1 762	1 798	Approv. total
Supply per capita	420	1 102	988	886	655	737	686	681	Approv. par habitant
Republic of Korea									**République de Corée**
Primary Energy Prod.	941	878	1 428	1 781	1 863	2 125	2 125	2 028	Prod. d'énergie primaire
Net imports	2 857	5 358	6 555	6 863	8 752	9 371	9 704	9 835	Importations nettes
Changes in stocks	-70	115	71	-179	117	68	-1	42	Variations des stocks
Total supply	3 868	6 121	7 912	8 822	10 498	11 428	11 829	11 821	Approv. total
Supply per capita	90	137	172	188	212	226	233	232	Approv. par habitant
Republic of Moldova [14]									**République de Moldova** [14]
Primary Energy Prod.	...	4	3	4	8	31	33	37	Prod. d'énergie primaire
Net imports	...	* 184	* 64	* 85	69	69	71	78	Importations nettes
Changes in stocks	...	2	0	0	-2	0	0	0	Variations des stocks
Total supply	...	186	66	89	80	100	104	114	Approv. total
Supply per capita	...	43	16	24	20	25	26	28	Approv. par habitant

Region, country or area	1990	1995	2000	2005	2010	2015	2016	2017	Région, pays ou zone
Réunion [1]									**Réunion** [1]
Primary Energy Prod.	8	9	7	7	8	...	...	...	Prod. d'énergie primaire
Net imports	* 16	* 23	* 36	* 44	* 50	...	...	...	Importations nettes
Changes in stocks	0	0	1	1	0	...	...	...	Variations des stocks
Total supply	24	31	42	49	58	...	...	...	Approv. total
Romania									**Roumanie**
Primary Energy Prod.	1 695	1 335	1 194	1 173	1 155	1 116	1 045	1 071	Prod. d'énergie primaire
Net imports	937	591	331	446	311	217	286	319	Importations nettes
Changes in stocks	11	2	-8	-7	-7	-7	-5	-11	Variations des stocks
Total supply	2 621	1 925	1 532	1 626	1 474	1 341	1 336	1 401	Approv. total
Supply per capita	113	85	69	75	72	67	68	71	Approv. par habitant
Russian Federation									**Fédération de Russie**
Primary Energy Prod.	...	40 589	41 030	50 506	53 679	56 024	57 191	59 485	Prod. d'énergie primaire
Net imports	...	-13 397	-14 842	-22 870	-24 601	* -26 106	* -27 622	* -27 620	Importations nettes
Changes in stocks	...	472	195	298	147	75	53	684	Variations des stocks
Total supply	...	26 720	25 994	27 338	28 932	29 843	29 516	31 182	Approv. total
Supply per capita	...	180	177	190	202	207	205	217	Approv. par habitant
Rwanda									**Rwanda**
Primary Energy Prod.	28	48	46	63	76	* 85	* 86	* 86	Prod. d'énergie primaire
Net imports	* 8	* 7	* 8	* 7	* 8	* 13	* 13	* 13	Importations nettes
Changes in stocks	...	...	...	0	...	...	...	...	Variations des stocks
Total supply	35	54	54	71	84	* 98	* 99	* 99	Approv. total
Supply per capita	5	10	7	8	8	* 8	* 8	* 8	Approv. par habitant
Saint Helena									**Sainte-Hélène**
Primary Energy Prod.	* 0	0	0	0	0	0	0	0	Prod. d'énergie primaire
Net imports	0	* 0	0	0	0	* 0	* 0	* 0	Importations nettes
Total supply	0	* 0	0	0	0	* 0	* 0	* 0	Approv. total
Supply per capita	17	* 35	36	33	30	* 25	* 25	* 26	Approv. par habitant
Saint Kitts and Nevis									**Saint-Kitts-et-Nevis**
Primary Energy Prod.	1	1	1	1	0	* 0	0	0	Prod. d'énergie primaire
Net imports	* 2	* 2	* 3	* 3	3	* 4	* 4	* 4	Importations nettes
Total supply	* 2	* 2	* 3	* 3	3	* 3	* 3	* 3	Approv. total
Supply per capita	* 53	* 56	* 63	* 67	62	* 62	* 63	* 63	Approv. par habitant
Saint Lucia									**Sainte-Lucie**
Primary Energy Prod.	0	0	0	0	0	0	0	0	Prod. d'énergie primaire
Net imports	2	* 4	* 5	* 5	* 7	* 5	* 5	* 5	Importations nettes
Changes in stocks	...	...	...	...	* 1	...	...	...	Variations des stocks
Total supply	2	5	5	5	5	5	5	5	Approv. total
Supply per capita	18	31	33	30	31	30	28	29	Approv. par habitant
Saint Pierre and Miquelon									**Saint-Pierre-et-Miquelon**
Primary Energy Prod.	...	...	* 0	0	0	0	0	0	Prod. d'énergie primaire
Net imports	2	1	* 1	* 1	* 1	* 1	* 1	* 1	Importations nettes
Total supply	1	1	* 1	* 1	* 1	* 1	* 1	1	Approv. total
Supply per capita	206	164	* 125	* 149	* 160	* 171	* 171	171	Approv. par habitant
Saint Vincent & Grenadines									**Saint-Vincent-Grenadines**
Primary Energy Prod.	0	0	0	0	0	0	0	0	Prod. d'énergie primaire
Net imports	* 1	* 2	2	* 3	* 3	* 3	* 4	* 4	Importations nettes
Total supply	* 1	* 2	2	* 3	3	3	4	* 4	Approv. total
Supply per capita	* 12	* 19	21	* 31	31	29	35	* 35	Approv. par habitant
Samoa									**Samoa**
Primary Energy Prod.	1	1	1	1	1	1	1	1	Prod. d'énergie primaire
Net imports	* 2	* 2	* 2	* 3	* 3	4	* 3	* 3	Importations nettes
Changes in stocks	...	...	...	...	0	* 1	* 0	...	Variations des stocks
Total supply	* 3	* 3	* 3	* 3	* 4	5	* 5	* 5	Approv. total
Supply per capita	* 16	* 16	* 18	* 19	* 21	24	* 24	* 25	Approv. par habitant
Sao Tome and Principe									**Sao Tomé-et-Principe**
Primary Energy Prod.	1	1	1	1	1	1	1	1	Prod. d'énergie primaire
Net imports	* 1	* 1	* 1	* 1	2	* 2	* 2	* 2	Importations nettes
Total supply	* 1	1	* 2	* 2	2	* 3	* 3	* 3	Approv. total
Supply per capita	* 12	12	* 12	* 13	14	* 14	* 14	* 14	Approv. par habitant
Saudi Arabia [10]									**Arabie saoudite** [10]
Primary Energy Prod.	16 769	19 932	20 284	24 162	22 115	27 184	28 132	27 155	Prod. d'énergie primaire
Net imports	* -13 721	-16 427	-15 797	-18 116	-14 727	-17 294	-18 986	-18 251	Importations nettes
Changes in stocks	* 172	-12	0	0	-319	161	511	-43	Variations des stocks
Total supply	2 875	3 516	4 487	6 047	7 707	9 728	8 635	8 946	Approv. total
Supply per capita	178	190	224	252	281	308	268	272	Approv. par habitant
Senegal									**Sénégal**
Primary Energy Prod.	40	44	50	52	86	78	66	67	Prod. d'énergie primaire
Net imports	* 41	* 43	* 47	65	74	104	102	96	Importations nettes
Changes in stocks	0	0	1	3	-4	-4	-7	* -5	Variations des stocks
Total supply	* 81	* 87	97	114	165	187	175	168	Approv. total
Supply per capita	* 11	* 10	10	11	13	12	11	11	Approv. par habitant
Serbia [15]									**Serbie** [15]
Primary Energy Prod.	...	...	...	431	440	449	446	438	Prod. d'énergie primaire
Net imports	...	...	...	243	212	164	181	211	Importations nettes
Changes in stocks	...	...	...	2	4	1	-6	3	Variations des stocks
Total supply	...	...	...	672	648	612	633	647	Approv. total
Supply per capita	...	...	...	82	89	87	90	93	Approv. par habitant
Serbia and Monten. [former]									**Serbie-et-Monténégro [anc.]**
Primary Energy Prod.	...	497	479	...	...	...	...	...	Prod. d'énergie primaire
Net imports	...	* 25	77	...	...	...	...	...	Importations nettes
Total supply	...	522	556	...	...	...	...	...	Approv. total
Supply per capita	...	48	61	...	...	...	...	...	Approv. par habitant

Region, country or area	1990	1995	2000	2005	2010	2015	2016	2017	Région, pays ou zone
Seychelles									**Seychelles**
Primary Energy Prod.	0	0	0	0	0	0	0	0	Prod. d'énergie primaire
Net imports	1	* 4	* 9	* 10	6	* 6	* 8	* 9	Importations nettes
Changes in stocks	* 0	0	* 0	...	...	...	...	...	Variations des stocks
Total supply	2	* 3	8	10	6	7	8	8	Approv. total
Supply per capita	31	* 39	102	115	67	72	88	86	Approv. par habitant
Sierra Leone									**Sierra Leone**
Primary Energy Prod.	43	42	49	50	52	54	54	55	Prod. d'énergie primaire
Net imports	* 8	* 4	* 6	* 7	* 8	* 13	* 13	* 14	Importations nettes
Changes in stocks	0	...	...	...	...	...	...	...	Variations des stocks
Total supply	51	46	55	56	60	67	68	68	Approv. total
Supply per capita	13	12	13	11	9	9	9	9	Approv. par habitant
Singapore									**Singapour**
Primary Energy Prod.	1	4	4	8	25	28	28	28	Prod. d'énergie primaire
Net imports	493	641	783	* 860	* 1 028	* 1 248	* 926	* 1 167	Importations nettes
Changes in stocks	-163	2	27	-31	-25	40	-17	* 27	Variations des stocks
Total supply	658	644	761	899	1 079	1 236	971	1 166	Approv. total
Supply per capita	218	185	194	211	213	223	173	204	Approv. par habitant
Sint Maarten (Dutch part)									**St-Martin (partie néerland.)**
Net imports	...	...	...	...	...	* 12	* 12	* 12	Importations nettes
Total supply	...	...	...	...	...	* 12	* 12	* 12	Approv. total
Supply per capita	...	...	...	...	...	* 305	* 302	* 292	Approv. par habitant
Slovakia									**Slovaquie**
Primary Energy Prod.	...	210	263	265	250	265	266	265	Prod. d'énergie primaire
Net imports	...	510	480	514	473	405	410	464	Importations nettes
Changes in stocks	...	-22	4	4	-12	-4	-9	13	Variations des stocks
Total supply	...	742	740	776	736	675	686	717	Approv. total
Supply per capita	...	138	137	143	136	124	126	132	Approv. par habitant
Slovenia									**Slovénie**
Primary Energy Prod.	...	124	129	146	157	142	144	153	Prod. d'énergie primaire
Net imports	...	129	141	160	149	133	133	140	Importations nettes
Changes in stocks	...	-1	2	0	0	0	0	3	Variations des stocks
Total supply	...	254	269	306	306	275	278	289	Approv. total
Supply per capita	...	129	135	153	150	133	134	139	Approv. par habitant
Solomon Islands									**Îles Salomon**
Primary Energy Prod.	* 3	* 3	* 3	* 3	* 3	* 3	* 3	* 3	Prod. d'énergie primaire
Net imports	* 2	* 3	* 4	* 4	* 5	* 5	* 5	* 5	Importations nettes
Total supply	* 5	* 6	* 6	* 7	* 8	8	* 7	* 7	Approv. total
Supply per capita	* 17	* 17	* 16	* 16	* 15	13	* 12	* 12	Approv. par habitant
Somalia									**Somalie**
Primary Energy Prod.	58	69	85	103	124	129	136	139	Prod. d'énergie primaire
Net imports	* 10	* 8	* 5	* 4	* 1	* 9	* 9	* 9	Importations nettes
Changes in stocks	* 0	* 0	...	...	...	...	...	...	Variations des stocks
Total supply	68	77	90	107	126	138	145	148	Approv. total
Supply per capita	10	12	12	13	10	10	10	10	Approv. par habitant
South Africa									**Afrique du Sud**
Primary Energy Prod.	4 767	5 691	6 048	6 366	6 569	6 595	6 635	6 653	Prod. d'énergie primaire
Net imports	* -587	-1 009	-1 171	-1 183	-624	-882	-813	-752	Importations nettes
Changes in stocks	0	-68	-41	0	59	-5	-5	-9	Variations des stocks
Total supply	4 179	4 750	4 917	5 183	5 887	5 719	5 828	5 910	Approv. total
Supply per capita	114	115	110	108	114	103	104	104	Approv. par habitant
South Sudan									**Soudan du sud**
Primary Energy Prod.	...	...	...	...	...	321	257	238	Prod. d'énergie primaire
Net imports	...	...	...	...	...	-286	-225	-210	Importations nettes
Total supply	...	...	...	...	...	35	32	28	Approv. total
Supply per capita	...	...	...	...	...	3	3	3	Approv. par habitant
Spain [16]									**Espagne** [16]
Primary Energy Prod.	1 443	1 313	1 314	1 256	1 419	1 367	1 392	1 368	Prod. d'énergie primaire
Net imports	2 325	2 968	3 832	4 759	4 008	3 521	3 469	3 796	Importations nettes
Changes in stocks	6	69	52	78	73	-40	-103	-61	Variations des stocks
Total supply	3 762	4 211	5 094	5 936	5 354	4 927	4 964	5 227	Approv. total
Supply per capita	97	107	126	137	114	106	107	113	Approv. par habitant
Sri Lanka									**Sri Lanka**
Primary Energy Prod.	135	146	156	163	184	181	169	167	Prod. d'énergie primaire
Net imports	54	80	144	161	170	217	249	261	Importations nettes
Changes in stocks	2	-1	4	1	-7	-36	-49	-33	Variations des stocks
Total supply	187	225	296	324	360	433	467	461	Approv. total
Supply per capita	11	12	16	16	18	21	22	22	Approv. par habitant
State of Palestine									**État de Palestine**
Primary Energy Prod.	* 4	* 5	* 5	8	9	9	10	10	Prod. d'énergie primaire
Net imports	* 16	* 18	33	49	45	63	67	68	Importations nettes
Changes in stocks	...	...	...	0	0	0	0	...	Variations des stocks
Total supply	* 20	* 22	38	58	54	72	77	78	Approv. total
Supply per capita	...	* 8	12	16	13	16	16	16	Approv. par habitant
Sudan									**Soudan**
Primary Energy Prod.	...	...	...	...	...	457	432	412	Prod. d'énergie primaire
Net imports	...	...	...	...	...	* 41	* 58	* 121	Importations nettes
Changes in stocks	...	...	...	...	...	...	0	...	Variations des stocks
Total supply	...	...	...	...	...	498	491	532	Approv. total
Supply per capita	...	...	...	...	...	13	12	13	Approv. par habitant
Sudan [former]									**Soudan [anc.]**
Primary Energy Prod.	379	448	851	1 145	1 473	...	...	...	Prod. d'énergie primaire
Net imports	* 73	* 59	-287	-480	-762	...	...	...	Importations nettes
Changes in stocks	* 1	1	8	12	...	...	...	...	Variations des stocks
Total supply	451	506	556	654	711	...	...	...	Approv. total
Supply per capita	17	17	16	17	16	...	...	...	Approv. par habitant

Production, trade and supply of energy *(continued)*
Petajoules and gigajoules per capita

Production, commerce et fourniture d'énergie *(suite)*
pétajoules et gigajoules par habitant

Region, country or area	1990	1995	2000	2005	2010	2015	2016	2017	Région, pays ou zone
Suriname									**Suriname**
Primary Energy Prod.	15	17	33	32	43	40	39	39	Prod. d'énergie primaire
Net imports	* 15	* 16	* 1	* -4	* -4	* 2	* -1	* 0	Importations nettes
Changes in stocks	0	0	...	...	0	0	0	...	Variations des stocks
Total supply	29	34	36	26	40	43	37	40	Approv. total
Supply per capita	72	78	76	53	76	78	67	71	Approv. par habitant
Sweden									**Suède**
Primary Energy Prod.	1 235	1 312	1 257	1 426	1 354	1 400	1 439	1 491	Prod. d'énergie primaire
Net imports	724	745	720	740	721	506	592	450	Importations nettes
Changes in stocks	-5	-29	9	32	-33	52	-10	-93	Variations des stocks
Total supply	1 965	2 086	1 968	2 135	2 109	1 854	2 041	2 033	Approv. total
Supply per capita	230	236	222	236	225	190	207	205	Approv. par habitant
Switzerland [17]									**Suisse** [17]
Primary Energy Prod.	425	464	496	452	515	495	467	460	Prod. d'énergie primaire
Net imports	584	521	524	628	564	499	517	523	Importations nettes
Changes in stocks	-5	-14	-18	6	-2	-15	3	-6	Variations des stocks
Total supply	1 014	999	1 037	1 074	1 080	1 010	982	988	Approv. total
Supply per capita	151	142	144	144	137	121	116	116	Approv. par habitant
Syrian Arab Republic									**République arabe syrienne**
Primary Energy Prod.	1 036	1 403	1 417	1 171	1 165	196	177	172	Prod. d'énergie primaire
Net imports	* -554	-813	-690	-431	-233	223	240	202	Importations nettes
Changes in stocks	6	* 5	...	1	20	...	...	...	Variations des stocks
Total supply	476	585	729	740	911	419	418	374	Approv. total
Supply per capita	39	41	46	40	43	22	23	20	Approv. par habitant
Tajikistan									**Tadjikistan**
Primary Energy Prod.	...	106	103	115	115	* 131	144	* 157	Prod. d'énergie primaire
Net imports	...	40	38	33	29	35	34	30	Importations nettes
Total supply	...	146	141	148	143	167	178	187	Approv. total
Supply per capita	...	25	23	23	19	19	20	21	Approv. par habitant
Thailand									**Thaïlande**
Primary Energy Prod.	1 089	1 322	1 700	2 144	2 952	3 161	3 312	3 150	Prod. d'énergie primaire
Net imports	* 681	* 1 289	* 1 308	* 1 869	* 2 027	2 509	2 537	2 656	Importations nettes
Changes in stocks	4	-25	-67	-54	33	9	36	29	Variations des stocks
Total supply	1 766	2 635	3 075	4 067	4 945	5 662	5 812	5 777	Approv. total
Supply per capita	31	44	49	61	74	82	84	84	Approv. par habitant
Timor-Leste									**Timor-Leste**
Primary Energy Prod.	...	...	...	201	186	* 147	121	54	Prod. d'énergie primaire
Net imports	...	...	...	* -196	* -182	* -139	* -113	* -47	Importations nettes
Total supply	...	...	...	* 4	* 4	* 8	* 8	* 8	Approv. total
Supply per capita	...	...	...	* 4	* 4	* 6	* 6	* 6	Approv. par habitant
Togo									**Togo**
Primary Energy Prod.	44	57	74	84	99	113	117	120	Prod. d'énergie primaire
Net imports	* 11	* 15	* 16	15	29	28	33	34	Importations nettes
Changes in stocks	0	0	0	-1	-2	-2	...	...	Variations des stocks
Total supply	55	71	89	99	130	143	150	154	Approv. total
Supply per capita	15	17	19	18	20	19	20	20	Approv. par habitant
Tonga									**Tonga**
Primary Energy Prod.	0	0	0	0	0	0	0	0	Prod. d'énergie primaire
Net imports	1	1	1	* 2	* 2	* 2	* 2	* 2	Importations nettes
Changes in stocks	...	...	...	...	...	* 0	* 0	0	Variations des stocks
Total supply	1	1	1	* 2	2	2	2	2	Approv. total
Supply per capita	12	14	15	* 16	16	16	17	20	Approv. par habitant
Trinidad and Tobago									**Trinité-et-Tobago**
Primary Energy Prod.	529	511	799	1 464	1 786	1 557	1 370	1 367	Prod. d'énergie primaire
Net imports	-271	-264	-378	-777	-954	-753	-649	-654	Importations nettes
Changes in stocks	6	-5	1	11	-1	7	14	10	Variations des stocks
Total supply	251	251	420	676	833	797	707	703	Approv. total
Supply per capita	206	199	325	514	627	586	518	514	Approv. par habitant
Tunisia									**Tunisie**
Primary Energy Prod.	222	205	253	274	341	260	252	230	Prod. d'énergie primaire
Net imports	* -27	* 6	47	71	79	198	210	239	Importations nettes
Changes in stocks	3	-9	7	-4	-7	7	1	-5	Variations des stocks
Total supply	192	220	293	349	427	452	460	473	Approv. total
Supply per capita	23	25	31	35	40	40	40	41	Approv. par habitant
Turkey									**Turquie**
Primary Energy Prod.	1 081	1 109	1 082	1 001	1 355	1 317	1 495	1 527	Prod. d'énergie primaire
Net imports	1 162	1 514	2 097	2 500	3 097	4 162	4 254	4 691	Importations nettes
Changes in stocks	32	44	-4	-27	10	89	33	80	Variations des stocks
Total supply	2 211	2 578	3 182	3 529	4 442	5 390	5 715	6 138	Approv. total
Supply per capita	41	44	50	52	61	69	72	76	Approv. par habitant
Turkmenistan									**Turkménistan**
Primary Energy Prod.	...	1 376	1 928	2 584	1 982	3 407	3 230	3 223	Prod. d'énergie primaire
Net imports	...	-802	-1 303	-1 779	-1 030	-2 248	-2 073	-2 065	Importations nettes
Total supply	...	574	625	805	951	1 160	1 158	1 158	Approv. total
Supply per capita	...	137	139	170	187	208	204	201	Approv. par habitant
Turks and Caicos Islands									**Îles Turques-et-Caïques**
Primary Energy Prod.	0	0	0	0	0	0	0	0	Prod. d'énergie primaire
Net imports	* 0	* 1	* 1	* 2	* 3	* 3	* 3	* 3	Importations nettes
Total supply	* 0	* 1	* 1	* 2	* 3	* 3	* 3	* 3	Approv. total
Supply per capita	* 34	* 43	* 52	* 57	* 84	* 84	* 86	* 91	Approv. par habitant
Tuvalu									**Tuvalu**
Primary Energy Prod.	...	...	...	...	...	0	* 0	* 0	Prod. d'énergie primaire
Net imports	* 0	* 0	* 0	* 0	0	* 0	* 0	* 0	Importations nettes
Total supply	* 0	* 0	* 0	* 0	0	* 0	* 0	* 0	Approv. total
Supply per capita	* 8	* 9	* 10	* 13	12	* 13	* 13	* 13	Approv. par habitant

Region, country or area	1990	1995	2000	2005	2010	2015	2016	2017	Région, pays ou zone
Uganda									**Ouganda**
Primary Energy Prod.	271	300	302	390	477	595	618	* 625	Prod. d'énergie primaire
Net imports	* 9	* 12	* 17	* 26	* 46	60	63	69	Importations nettes
Changes in stocks	0	...	...	...	...	...	...	...	Variations des stocks
Total supply	281	312	319	417	523	655	680	* 693	Approv. total
Supply per capita	16	15	13	15	15	16	16	* 16	Approv. par habitant
Ukraine									**Ukraine**
Primary Energy Prod.	...	3 661	3 231	3 328	3 238	2 552[18]	2 754[18]	2 431[18]	Prod. d'énergie primaire
Net imports	...	3 411	2 343	2 458	1 762	1 268[18]	* 1 187[18]	* 1 402[18]	Importations nettes
Changes in stocks	...	0	0	-86	-490	66[18]	-19[18]	93[18]	Variations des stocks
Total supply	...	7 073	5 574	5 872	5 491	3 753[18]	3 960[18]	3 739[18]	Approv. total
Supply per capita	...	138	114	125	120	84[18]	89[18]	85[18]	Approv. par habitant
United Arab Emirates									**Émirats arabes unis**
Primary Energy Prod.	5 177	5 661	6 571	7 293	7 496	10 235	10 544	9 692	Prod. d'énergie primaire
Net imports	* -4 375	* -4 533	-4 853	-5 450	* -4 860	* -6 253	* -6 777	-6 560	Importations nettes
Changes in stocks	12	21	...	...	...	...	* 2	91	Variations des stocks
Total supply	791	1 108	1 719	1 842	2 635	3 981	3 765	3 042	Approv. total
Supply per capita	437	472	567	453	319	435	406	324	Approv. par habitant
United Kingdom [19]									**Royaume-Uni [19]**
Primary Energy Prod.	8 702	10 773	11 400	8 589	6 217	4 936	5 019	5 023	Prod. d'énergie primaire
Net imports	-174	-2 003	-2 221	729	2 038	2 484	2 287	2 203	Importations nettes
Changes in stocks	-84	-267	-139	0	-255	-172	-187	-128	Variations des stocks
Total supply	8 612	9 037	9 317	9 318	8 511	7 592	7 492	7 353	Approv. total
Supply per capita	151	156	158	155	134	116	114	111	Approv. par habitant
United Rep. of Tanzania									**Rép.-Unie de Tanzanie**
Primary Energy Prod.	315	434	535	591	654	725	738	755	Prod. d'énergie primaire
Net imports	* 27	* 30	30	57	66	102	102	99	Importations nettes
Changes in stocks	0	...	...	...	...	...	...	...	Variations des stocks
Total supply	341	463	564	649	719	828	839	855	Approv. total
Supply per capita	13	15	17	17	16	15	15	15	Approv. par habitant
United States of America [20]									**États-Unis d'Amérique [20]**
Primary Energy Prod.	69 129	69 400	69 723	68 480	72 292	84 453	80 055	83 352	Prod. d'énergie primaire
Net imports	12 755	16 483	23 551	28 783	20 343	9 053	9 254	5 336	Importations nettes
Changes in stocks	1 605	-766	-1 983	-9	-265	2 088	-1 142	-1 539	Variations des stocks
Total supply	80 280	86 648	95 257	97 271	92 899	91 418	90 451	90 228	Approv. total
Supply per capita	317	325	337	328	301	286	281	278	Approv. par habitant
United States Virgin Islands									**Îles Vierges américaines**
Primary Energy Prod.	...	...	...	...	...	* 0	* 0	* 0	Prod. d'énergie primaire
Total supply	...	...	...	...	...	* 0	* 0	* 0	Approv. total
Supply per capita	...	...	...	...	...	* 1	* 1	* 1	Approv. par habitant
Uruguay									**Uruguay**
Primary Energy Prod.	51	45	46	45	89	126	131	136	Prod. d'énergie primaire
Net imports	44	66	70	75	85	89	83	77	Importations nettes
Changes in stocks	-2	4	-2	-5	1	3	-3	-5	Variations des stocks
Total supply	96	107	119	126	173	213	217	217	Approv. total
Supply per capita	31	33	36	38	51	62	63	63	Approv. par habitant
Uzbekistan									**Ouzbékistan**
Primary Energy Prod.	...	2 045	2 307	2 446	2 309	2 120	2 176	2 205	Prod. d'énergie primaire
Net imports	...	* -177	* -183	* -399	* -502	* -382	* -374	* -328	Importations nettes
Changes in stocks	...	88	...	...	...	-2	3	-3	Variations des stocks
Total supply	...	1 780	2 124	2 046	1 806	1 740	1 799	1 880	Approv. total
Supply per capita	...	78	86	79	63	56	57	59	Approv. par habitant
Vanuatu									**Vanuatu**
Primary Energy Prod.	* 0	* 1	1	1	1	1	1	1	Prod. d'énergie primaire
Net imports	* 1	* 1	* 1	* 1	* 2	* 2	* 3	* 3	Importations nettes
Changes in stocks	...	...	...	...	* 0	0	0	...	Variations des stocks
Total supply	1	1	* 2	2	3	3	3	3	Approv. total
Supply per capita	8	9	* 11	8	11	11	11	11	Approv. par habitant
Venezuela (Boliv. Rep. of)									**Venezuela (Rép. boliv. du)**
Primary Energy Prod.	5 953	7 962	8 965	8 283	7 948	7 361	6 748	6 055	Prod. d'énergie primaire
Net imports	-4 027	-5 772	-6 320	-5 883	* -4 914	-4 891	-4 453	-3 992	Importations nettes
Changes in stocks	-18	24	15	-336	-54	-2	-2	-1	Variations des stocks
Total supply	1 944	2 167	2 629	2 737	3 087	2 472	2 297	2 064	Approv. total
Supply per capita	99	98	108	103	106	79	73	65	Approv. par habitant
Viet Nam									**Viet Nam**
Primary Energy Prod.	787	1 136	1 733	2 612	2 747	3 082	2 894	2 812	Prod. d'énergie primaire
Net imports	-3	-207	-421	-786	-409	25	206	251	Importations nettes
Changes in stocks	-7	20	50	70	5	* 74	* 66	83	Variations des stocks
Total supply	791	908	1 262	1 756	2 334	3 033	3 034	2 980	Approv. total
Supply per capita	12	12	16	21	26	32	32	31	Approv. par habitant
Wallis and Futuna Islands									**Îles Wallis-et-Futuna**
Primary Energy Prod.	...	...	...	...	* 0	* 0	* 0	* 0	Prod. d'énergie primaire
Net imports	...	...	...	0	0	0	0	* 0	Importations nettes
Total supply	...	...	...	0	0	0	0	* 0	Approv. total
Supply per capita	...	...	...	26	27	28	30	* 30	Approv. par habitant
Yemen									**Yémen**
Primary Energy Prod.	...	713	908	844	804	173	66	77	Prod. d'énergie primaire
Net imports	...	-571	-712	-529	-477	7	* 79	* 66	Importations nettes
Changes in stocks	...	0	0	40	...	...	...	...	Variations des stocks
Total supply	...	142	197	274	326	180	145	142	Approv. total
Supply per capita	...	9	11	13	14	7	5	5	Approv. par habitant
Zambia									**Zambie**
Primary Energy Prod.	207	224	248	280	319	389	421	448	Prod. d'énergie primaire
Net imports	* 14	* 19	13	25	29	45	50	53	Importations nettes
Changes in stocks	...	-1	1	0	0	...	...	...	Variations des stocks
Total supply	222	244	260	305	348	433	471	501	Approv. total
Supply per capita	28	27	25	27	25	27	28	29	Approv. par habitant

Region, country or area	1990	1995	2000	2005	2010	2015	2016	2017	Région, pays ou zone
Zimbabwe									**Zimbabwe**
Primary Energy Prod.	375	362	379	379	369	450	381	427	Prod. d'énergie primaire
Net imports	* 30	64	53	36	26	47	48	50	Importations nettes
Changes in stocks	0	5	-5	1	...	24	-39	4	Variations des stocks
Total supply	405	422	438	414	395	473	467	474	Approv. total
Supply per capita	39	36	35	33	31	34	33	33	Approv. par habitant

Source:

United Nations Statistics Division, New York, Energy Statistics Yearbook 2017, last accessed February 2020.

Source:

Organisation des Nations Unies, Division de statistique, New York, Annuaire des statistiques de l'énergie 2017, dernier accès février 2020.

1   Data after 2010 are included in France.
2   Excluding overseas territories.
3   For statistical purposes, the data for China do not include those for the Hong Kong Special Administrative Region (Hong Kong SAR), Macao Special Administrative Region (Macao SAR) and Taiwan Province of China.
4   Excluding the Faroe Islands and Greenland.
5   Including Monaco.
6   From 2011 onwards, data include Monaco and the overseas departments (Guadeloupe, French Guiana, Martinique, Mayotte and Réunion), excluding the overseas collectivities: New Caledonia, French Polynesia, Saint Barthélemy, Saint Martin, St. Pierre and Miquelon, and Wallis and Futuna.
7   Data include Timor-Leste.
8   Data include San Marino and the Holy See.
9   Data include Okinawa.
10   The data for crude oil Prod. include 50 per cent of the output of the Neutral Zone.
11   Data exclude Suriname and the Netherlands Antilles (former)

12   Including Svalbard and Jan Mayen Islands.
13   Data includes the Azores and Madeira.
14   Excluding the Transnistria region.
15   Excluding Kosovo.
16   Data include the Canary Islands.
17   Including Liechtenstein.
18   The Government of Ukraine has informed the United Nations that it is not in a position to provide statistical data concerning the Autonomous Republic of Crimea and the city of Sevastopol.
19   Shipments of coal and oil to Jersey, Guernsey and the isle of Man from the United Kingdom are not classed as exports. Supplies of coal and oil to these islands are, therefore, included as part of UK supply. Exports of natural gas to the Isle of Man included with the exports to Ireland.

20   Oil and coal trade statistics include overseas territories.

1   Les données après 2010 sont incluses en France.
2   Non compris les départements d'outre-mer.
3   Pour la présentation des statistiques, les données pour la Chine ne comprennent pas la région administrative spéciale de Hong Kong (RAS de Hong Kong), la région administrative spéciale de Macao (RAS de Macao) et la province chinoise de Taïwan.
4   Non compris les Îles Féroé et le Groenland.
5   Y compris Monaco.
6   À partir de 2011, les données incluent Monaco et les départements d'outre-mer (Guadeloupe, Guyane française, Martinique, Mayotte et Réunion), à l'exclusion des collectivités d'outre-mer: Nouvelle-Calédonie, Polynésie française, Saint-Barthélemy, Saint-Martin, Saint-Pierre et Miquelon, Wallis et Futuna.
7   Les données comprennent Timor-Leste.
8   Les données comprennent Saint-Marin et le Saint-Siège.
9   Les données incluent Okinawa.
10   Les données relatives à la Prod. de pétrole brut comprennent 50 pour cent de la Prod. de la Zone Neutre.
11   Les données excluent le Suriname et les Antilles néerlandaises (anciennement)

12   Y compris les îles Svalbard-et-Jan Mayen.
13   Les données comprennent Azores et Madère.
14   Non compris la région de Transnistrie.
15   Non compris Kosovo.
16   Les données comprennent les îles Canaries.
17   Y compris Liechtenstein.
18   Le Gouvernement ukrainien a informé l'Organisation des Nations Unies qu'il n'est pas en mesure de fournir des données statistiques concernant la République autonome de Crimée et Sébastopol.
19   Les livraisons de charbon et de pétrole du Royaume-Uni à Jersey, Guernesey et à l'île de Man ne sont pas considérées comme des exportations ; l'Approv. de charbon et pétrole à ces îles fait donc partie de l'Approv. du Royaume-Uni. Les exportations de gaz naturel vers l'île de Man sont inclues dans les exportations vers l'Irlande.

20   Les données sur le pétrole et le charbon incluent les territoires d'outre-mer.

22

Land
Thousand hectares and percent of total land

Terres
Milliers d'hectares et pourcentage de la superficie totale

Region, country or area Région, pays ou zone	Year Année	Area – Superficie ('000 hectares)				Area – Superficie (Percent of total)[&]			Sites protected for terrestrial biodiversity Sites pour la bio. terre. dans aires protég. (%)[&&]
		Total land Superficie totale	Arable land Terres arables	Permanent crops Cultures permanentes	Forest cover Superficie forestière	Arable land Terres arables	Permanent crops Cultures Permanentes	Forest cover Superficie forestière	
Total, all countries or areas	2005	12 997 688	1 356 869	145 681	4 032 743	10.4	1.1	31.0	36.22
Total, tous pays ou zones	2010	12 995 615	1 347 681	158 259	4 015 673	10.4	1.2	30.9	40.85
	2017	13 002 855	1 390 699	167 877	3 999 134	10.7	1.3	30.8	43.53
	2019	...	...	...	...	...	...	...	43.72
Africa	2005	2 964 823	215 651	30 854	654 679	7.3	1.0	22.1	...
Afrique	2010	2 964 894	225 759	33 511	638 282	7.6	1.1	21.5	...
	2017	2 964 921	240 668	35 324	624 103	8.1	1.2	21.0	...
Northern Africa	2005	838 039	41 430	5 310	36 954	4.9	0.6	4.4	18.76
Afrique septentrionale	2010	838 039	42 525	5 806	36 813	5.1	0.7	4.4	21.98
	2017	838 039	42 228	6 414	28 836	5.0	0.8	3.4	34.93
	2019	...	...	...	...	...	...	...	34.93
Sub-Saharan Africa	2005	2 126 784[1]	174 221[1]	25 544[1]	617 725[1]	8.2	1.2	29.0	34.16
Afrique subsaharienne	2010	2 126 855[1]	183 234[1]	27 706[1]	601 469[1]	8.6	1.3	28.3	39.18
	2017	2 126 882[1]	198 440[1]	28 910[1]	595 267[1]	9.3	1.4	28.0	40.87
	2019	...	...	...	...	...	...	...	41.02
Eastern Africa	2005	605 629	55 770	6 913	203 745	9.2	1.1	33.6	...
Afrique orientale	2010	605 700	62 228	7 604	196 249	10.3	1.3	32.4	...
	2017	605 727	66 555	8 375	197 308	11.0	1.4	32.6	...
Middle Africa	2005	649 682	22 745	2 762	310 491	3.5	0.4	47.8	...
Afrique centrale	2010	649 682	24 061	3 250	306 378	3.7	0.5	47.2	...
	2017	649 682	30 899	3 830	303 251	4.8	0.6	46.7	...
Southern Africa	2005	265 067	14 730	406	29 429	5.6	0.2	11.1	...
Afrique australe	2010	265 067	14 089	460	28 489	5.3	0.2	10.7	...
	2017	265 067	13 647	444	27 635	5.1	0.2	10.4	...
Western Africa	2005	606 406	80 976	15 463	74 060	13.4	2.5	12.2	...
Afrique occidentale	2010	606 406	82 855	16 392	70 353	13.7	2.7	11.6	...
	2017	606 406	87 339	16 261	67 073	14.4	2.7	11.1	...
Americas	2005	3 867 815	342 591	26 731	1 616 564	8.9	0.7	41.8	...
Amériques	2010	3 866 368	339 016	26 398	1 602 412	8.8	0.7	41.4	...
	2017	3 866 108	346 817	25 260	1 592 663	9.0	0.7	41.2	...
Northern America	2005	1 853 824	205 890	2 865	652 337	11.1	0.2	35.2	34.38
Amérique septentrionale	2010	1 852 374	195 507	2 777	656 026	10.6	0.1	35.4	39.59
	2017	1 852 374	196 017	2 774	657 168	10.6	0.1	35.5	41.38
	2019	...	...	...	...	...	...	...	41.38
Latin America & the Caribbean	2005	2 013 990[1]	2 013 990[1]	23 866[1]	964 227[1]	6.8	6.8	47.9	30.63
Amérique latine et Caraïbes	2010	2 013 993[1]	2 013 993[1]	23 621[1]	946 386[1]	7.1	7.1	47.0	34.93
	2017	2 013 733[1]	2 013 733[1]	22 486[1]	935 495[1]	7.5	7.5	46.5	37.71
	2019	...	...	...	...	...	...	...	38.04
Caribbean	2005	22 598	5 699	1 324	6 340	25.2	5.9	28.1	...
Caraïbes	2010	22 598	5 592	1 304	6 744	24.7	5.8	29.8	...
	2017	22 356	5 080	1 490	7 194	22.7	6.7	32.2	...
Central America	2005	245 227	29 276	4 837	89 276	11.9	2.0	36.4	...
Amérique centrale	2010	245 227	26 816	5 157	87 508	10.9	2.1	35.7	...
	2017	245 205	28 919	5 584	86 290	11.8	2.3	35.2	...
South America	2005	1 746 165	101 727	17 705	868 611	5.8	1.0	49.7	...
Amérique du Sud	2010	1 746 168	111 102	17 160	852 133	6.4	1.0	48.8	...
	2017	1 746 172	116 801	15 412	842 011	6.7	0.9	48.2	...
Asia	2005	3 102 282	492 109	70 539	580 868	15.9	2.3	18.7	...
Asie	2010	3 102 070	480 510	81 199	589 405	15.5	2.6	19.0	...
	2017	3 108 877	497 947	90 612	593 362	16.0	2.9	19.1	...
Central Asia	2005	392 679	37 010	714	12 038	9.4	0.2	3.1	11.55
Asie centrale	2010	392 679	36 819	743	11 799	9.4	0.2	3.0	12.14
	2017	392 562	37 369	808	11 705	9.5	0.2	3.0	12.57
	2019	...	...	...	...	...	...	...	12.57
Eastern Asia	2005	1 156 002	121 906	13 296	241 841	10.5	1.2	20.9	22.05
Asie orientale	2010	1 156 042	116 625	15 468	250 504	10.1	1.3	21.7	23.95
	2017	1 156 444	127 966	16 948	257 047	11.1	1.5	22.2	25.92
	2019	...	...	...	...	...	...	...	26.20

Land *(continued)*
Thousand hectares and percent of total land

Terres *(suite)*
Milliers d'hectares et pourcentage de la superficie totale

Region, country or area Région, pays ou zone	Year Année	Area – Superficie ('000 hectares)				Area – Superficie (Percent of total)&			Sites protected for terrestrial biodiversity Sites pour la bio. terre. dans aires protég. (%)&&
		Total land Superficie totale	Arable land Terres arables	Permanent crops Cultures permanentes	Forest cover Superficie forestière	Arable land Terres arables	Permanent crops Cultures Permanentes	Forest cover Superficie forestière	
South-eastern Asia Asie du Sud-Est	2005	434 076	65 540	36 521	217 123	15.1	8.4	50.0	26.34
	2010	434 067	68 117	42 500	214 594	15.7	9.8	49.4	30.68
	2017	440 616	73 222	48 764	210 759	16.6	11.1	47.8	35.54
	2019	...	...	...	...	...	...	...	35.58
Southern Asia Asie méridionale	2005	640 034	225 413	14 631	91 519	35.2	2.3	14.3	24.72
	2010	640 034	220 858	16 865	93 406	34.5	2.6	14.6	25.69
	2017	640 036	221 274	17 905	94 087	34.6	2.8	14.7	28.08
	2019	...	...	...	...	...	...	...	28.08
Western Asia Asie occidentale	2005	479 491	42 240	5 377	18 347	8.8	1.1	3.8	10.43
	2010	479 248	38 091	5 623	19 103	7.9	1.2	4.0	15.15
	2017	479 219	38 117	6 188	19 764	8.0	1.3	4.1	16.90
	2019	...	...	...	...	...	...	...	16.99
Europe Europe	2005	2 214 115	279 192	16 138	1 004 147	12.6	0.7	45.4	56.74
	2010	2 213 629	275 894	15 431	1 013 572	12.5	0.7	45.8	62.97
	2017	2 213 324	273 390	15 154	1 015 482	12.4	0.7	45.9	65.31
	2019	...	...	...	...	...	...	...	65.59
Eastern Europe Europe orientale	2005	1 805 641	195 108	4 505	852 968	10.8	0.2	47.2	...
	2010	1 805 269	193 590	4 275	859 827	10.7	0.2	47.6	...
	2017	1 805 343	192 991	4 032	860 425	10.7	0.2	47.7	...
Northern Europe Europe septentrionale	2005	170 310	18 785	135	74 437	11.0	0.1	43.7	...
	2010	170 245	19 212	111	74 570	11.3	0.1	43.8	...
	2017	169 779	18 729	133	74 735	11.0	0.1	44.0	...
Southern Europe Europe méridionale	2005	129 659	31 212	10 045	43 296	24.1	7.7	33.4	...
	2010	129 634	29 255	9 685	45 100	22.6	7.5	34.8	...
	2017	129 651	27 769	9 636	45 639	21.4	7.4	35.2	...
Western Europe Europe occidentale	2005	108 505	34 086	1 453	33 446	31.4	1.3	30.8	...
	2010	108 481	33 837	1 359	34 076	31.2	1.3	31.4	...
	2017	108 551	33 901	1 353	34 684	31.2	1.2	32.0	...
Oceania Océanie	2005	848 655	27 326	1 419	176 485	3.2	0.2	20.8	24.51
	2010	848 655	26 502	1 720	172 002	3.1	0.2	20.3	29.72
	2017	849 627	31 877	1 528	173 524	3.8	0.2	20.4	33.74
	2019	...	...	...	...	...	...	...	33.74
Australia and New Zealand Australie et Nouvelle-Zélande	2005	794 565	26 827	403	137 824	3.4	0.1	17.3	40.85
	2010	794 565	25 949	589	133 362	3.3	0.1	16.8	46.48
	2017	795 537	31 322	397	134 903	3.9	~0.0	17.0	52.98
	2019	...	...	...	...	...	...	...	52.99
Melanesia Mélanésie	2005	52 959	453	873	38 103	0.9	1.6	71.9	...
	2010	52 959	511	994	38 058	1.0	1.9	71.9	...
	2017	52 959	511	994	38 040	1.0	1.9	71.8	...
Micronesia Micronésie	2005	317	11	70	185	3.3	22.2	58.4	...
	2010	317	9	69	185	2.8	21.9	58.2	...
	2017	317	9	68	184	2.8	21.4	58.0	...
Polynesia Polynésie	2005	814	36	73	372	4.4	9.0	45.8	...
	2010	814	33	68	397	4.1	8.3	48.8	...
	2017	814	35	69	396	4.2	8.5	48.7	...
Afghanistan Afghanistan	2005	* 65 286	7 805	105	* 1 350	* 12.0	* 0.2	* 2.1	0.00
	2010	* 65 286	7 793	118	* 1 350	* 11.9	* 0.2	* 2.1	5.74
	2017	* 65 286	7 699	211	* 1 350	* 11.8	* 0.3	* 2.1	5.74
	2019	...	...	...	...	...	...	...	5.74
Albania Albanie	2005	2 740	538	121	* 782	19.6	4.4	* 28.6	31.71
	2010	2 740	626	70	* 776	22.8	2.6	* 28.3	47.22
	2017	2 740	607	84	* 772	22.1	3.1	* 28.2	55.94
	2019	...	...	...	...	...	...	...	57.18
Algeria Algérie	2005	238 174	7 511	852	1 536	3.2	0.4	0.6	16.63
	2010	238 174	7 502	909	1 918	3.1	0.4	0.8	16.63
	2017	238 174	7 471	1 013	* 1 956	3.1	0.4	* 0.8	16.63
	2019	...	...	...	...	...	...	...	16.63
American Samoa Samoa américaines	2005	20	* 3	* 2	* 18	* 16.5	* 8.5	* 89.4	71.12
	2010	20	* 3	* 2	* 18	* 15.0	* 9.5	* 88.6	71.12
	2017	20	* 3	* 2	* 18	* 15.0	* 9.5	* 87.7	71.12
	2019	...	...	...	...	...	...	...	71.12

Land *(continued)*
Thousand hectares and percent of total land

Terres *(suite)*
Milliers d'hectares et pourcentage de la superficie totale

Region, country or area / Région, pays ou zone	Year / Année	Area – Superficie ('000 hectares)				Area – Superficie (Percent of total)&			Sites protected for terrestrial biodiversity / Sites pour la bio. terre. dans aires protég. (%)&&
		Total land / Superficie totale	Arable land / Terres arables	Permanent crops / Cultures permanentes	Forest cover / Superficie forestière	Arable land / Terres arables	Permanent crops / Cultures Permanentes	Forest cover / Superficie forestière	
Andorra	2005	47	1	...	* 16	1.7	...	* 34.0	17.89
Andorre	2010	47	1	...	* 16	1.6	...	* 34.0	17.89
	2017	47	1	...	* 16	1.7	...	* 34.0	26.08
	2019	...	...	...	...	...	...	...	26.08
Angola	2005	124 670	* 3 300	* 290	59 104	* 2.6	* 0.2	47.4	28.05
Angola	2010	124 670	* 4 100	* 290	58 480	* 3.3	* 0.2	46.9	28.05
	2017	124 670	* 4 900	* 315	* 57 856	* 3.9	* 0.3	* 46.4	28.05
	2019	...	...	...	...	...	...	...	28.05
Anguilla	2005	9	...	...	* 6	...	...	* 61.1	6.67
Anguilla	2010	9	...	...	* 6	...	...	* 61.1	6.67
	2017	9	...	...	* 6	...	...	* 61.1	6.67
	2019	...	...	...	...	...	...	...	6.77
Antigua and Barbuda	2005	44	* 4	* 1	* 10	* 9.1	* 2.3	* 22.3	8.22
Antigua-et-Barbuda	2010	44	* 4	* 1	* 10	* 9.1	* 2.3	* 22.3	8.22
	2017	44	* 4	* 1	* 10	* 9.1	* 2.3	* 22.3	8.22
	2019	...	...	...	...	...	...	...	8.22
Argentina	2005	* 273 669	* 32 898	* 1 000	30 186	* 12.0	* 0.4	* 11.0	27.21
Argentine	2010	* 273 669	* 37 981	* 1 000	28 596	* 13.9	* 0.4	* 10.4	29.46
	2017	* 273 669	* 39 200	* 1 000	* 27 112	* 14.3	* 0.4	* 9.9	31.08
	2019	...	...	...	...	...	...	...	31.80
Armenia	2005	2 847	* 455	50	332	* 16.0	1.8	11.7	15.02
Arménie	2010	2 847	449	55	331	15.8	1.9	11.6	21.55
	2017	* 2 847	446	59	* 332	* 15.7	* 2.1	* 11.7	21.55
	2019	...	...	...	...	...	...	...	21.55
Aruba	2005	18	* 2	...	* ~0	* 11.1	...	* 2.3	37.15
Aruba	2010	18	* 2	...	* ~0	* 11.1	...	* 2.3	37.15
	2017	18	* 2	...	* ~0	* 11.1	...	* 2.3	37.15
	2019	...	...	...	...	...	...	...	37.15
Australia	2005	768 230	* 26 402	* 340	127 641	* 3.4	* ~0.0	16.6	39.54
Australie	2010	768 230	25 450	518	123 211	3.3	0.1	16.0	46.84
	2017	769 202	30 752	322	* 124 751	4.0	~0.0	* 16.2	55.68
	2019	...	...	...	...	...	...	...	55.68
Austria	2005	* 8 258	1 381	66	3 851	* 16.7	* 0.8	* 46.6	62.53
Autriche	2010	8 257	1 364	65	3 860	16.5	0.8	46.7	66.27
	2017	* 8 252	1 329	67	* 3 869	* 16.1	* 0.8	* 46.9	67.33
	2019	...	...	...	...	...	...	...	67.34
Azerbaijan	2005	8 266	1 843	222	* 877	22.3	2.7	* 10.6	29.46
Azerbaïdjan	2010	8 266	1 884	227	* 1 008	22.8	2.8	* 12.2	36.61
	2017	8 266	2 095	247	* 1 139	25.3	3.0	* 13.8	36.61
	2019	...	...	...	...	...	...	...	36.61
Bahamas	2005	* 1 001	* 7	* 4	* 515	* 0.7	* 0.4	* 51.4	12.38
Bahamas	2010	* 1 001	* 9	* 4	* 515	* 0.9	* 0.4	* 51.4	12.45
	2017	* 1 001	* 8	* 4	* 515	* 0.8	* 0.4	* 51.4	29.21
	2019	...	...	...	...	...	...	...	29.21
Bahrain	2005	74	* 2	* 3	* ~0	* 2.0	* 4.3	* 0.6	0.00
Bahreïn	2010	76	* 2	* 3	* 1	* 2.1	* 3.9	* 0.7	0.00
	2017	78	* 2	* 3	* 1	* 2.1	* 3.8	* 0.8	0.00
	2019	...	...	...	...	...	...	...	0.00
Bangladesh	2005	13 017	* 7 911	* 800	1 455	* 60.8	* 6.1	11.2	33.55
Bangladesh	2010	* 13 017	* 7 791	* 850	1 442	* 59.9	* 6.5	* 11.1	43.63
	2017	* 13 017	* 7 697	* 890	* 1 429	* 59.1	* 6.8	* 11.0	43.65
	2019	...	...	...	...	...	...	...	43.65
Barbados	2005	43	* 13	* 1	6	* 30.2	* 2.3	14.7	0.16
Barbade	2010	43	* 12	* 1	6	* 27.9	* 2.3	14.7	0.16
	2017	43	* 7	* 1	* 6	* 16.3	* 2.3	* 14.7	0.16
	2019	...	...	...	...	...	...	...	0.16
Belarus	2005	20 283	5 542	118	8 436	27.3	0.6	41.6	37.17
Bélarus	2010	20 290	5 535	122	8 534	27.3	0.6	42.1	37.17
	2017	20 299	5 727	114	* 8 634	28.2	0.6	* 42.5	47.08
	2019	...	...	...	...	...	...	...	47.08

Region, country or area Région, pays ou zone	Year Année	Area – Superficie ('000 hectares)				Area – Superficie (Percent of total)[&]			Sites protected for terrestrial biodiversity Sites pour la bio. terre. dans aires protég. (%)[&&]
		Total land Superficie totale	Arable land Terres arables	Permanent crops Cultures permanentes	Forest cover Superficie forestière	Arable land Terres arables	Permanent crops Cultures Permanentes	Forest cover Superficie forestière	
Belgium Belgique	2005	3 028	843	21	674	27.8	0.7	22.3	80.26
	2010	3 028	834	22	681	27.5	0.7	22.5	80.28
	2017	* 3 028	836	23	* 683	* 27.6	* 0.8	* 22.6	83.65
	2019	...	...	...	...	...	...	...	84.15
Belize Belize	2005	2 281	* 70	* 32	* 1 417	* 3.1	* 1.4	* 62.1	39.33
	2010	* 2 281	* 75	* 32	* 1 391	* 3.3	* 1.4	* 61.0	39.35
	2017	* 2 281	* 90	* 32	* 1 366	* 3.9	* 1.4	* 59.9	41.52
	2019	...	...	...	...	...	...	...	41.52
Benin Bénin	2005	* 11 276	* 2 654	* 280	4 811	* 23.5	* 2.5	* 42.7	66.66
	2010	* 11 276	* 2 500	* 600	4 561	* 22.2	* 5.3	* 40.4	66.66
	2017	* 11 276	* 2 800	* 600	* 4 311	* 24.8	* 5.3	* 38.2	66.66
	2019	...	...	...	...	...	...	...	66.66
Bermuda Bermudes	2005	5	~0	...	* 1	7.4	...	* 18.5	51.98
	2010	5	~0	...	* 1	5.6	...	* 18.5	51.98
	2017	5	* ~0	...	* 1	* 5.6	...	* 18.5	51.98
	2019	...	...	...	...	...	...	...	51.98
Bhutan Bhoutan	2005	3 812	* 167	* 19	2 656	* 4.4	* 0.5	69.7	43.32
	2010	3 812	101	12	2 705	2.6	0.3	71.0	45.77
	2017	* 3 814	* 100	6	* 2 755	* 2.6	* 0.1	* 72.2	47.33
	2019	...	...	...	...	...	...	...	47.33
Bolivia (Plurin. State of) Bolivie (État plurin. de)	2005	108 330	3 806	199	58 734	3.5	0.2	54.2	46.56
	2010	* 108 330	* 4 297	* 219	56 209	* 4.0	* 0.2	* 51.9	48.28
	2017	* 108 330	* 4 241	247	* 54 764	* 3.9	* 0.2	* 50.6	48.28
	2019	...	...	...	...	...	...	...	48.28
Bonaire, St. Eustatius & Saba Bonaire, St-Eustache et Saba	2005	...	...	...	...	...	...	...	39.26
	2010	...	...	...	...	...	...	...	39.26
	2019	...	...	...	...	...	...	...	39.26
Bosnia and Herzegovina Bosnie-Herzégovine	2005	5 120	1 025	95	* 2 185	20.0	1.9	* 42.7	0.00
	2010	5 120	1 004	105	* 2 185	19.6	2.1	* 42.7	18.18
	2017	5 120	1 060	107	* 2 185	20.7	2.1	* 42.7	18.18
	2019	...	...	...	...	...	...	...	18.18
Botswana Botswana	2005	* 56 673	* 240	2	11 943	* 0.4	* ~0.0	* 21.1	51.09
	2010	* 56 673	259	* 2	11 351	* 0.5	* ~0.0	* 20.0	51.09
	2017	* 56 673	* 258	* 2	* 10 840	* 0.5	* ~0.0	* 19.1	51.09
	2019	...	...	...	...	...	...	...	51.09
Brazil Brésil	2005	* 835 814	* 48 333	* 11 302	506 734	* 5.8	* 1.4	* 60.6	37.49
	2010	* 835 814	* 51 254	* 10 335	498 458	* 6.1	* 1.2	* 59.6	41.96
	2017	* 835 814	55 384	7 982	* 493 538	* 6.6	* 1.0	* 59.0	42.69
	2019	...	...	...	...	...	...	...	42.76
British Virgin Islands Îles Vierges britanniques	2005	15	* 1	* 1	* 4	* 6.7	* 6.7	* 24.4	10.52
	2010	15	* 1	* 1	* 4	* 6.7	* 6.7	* 24.3	10.52
	2017	15	* 1	* 1	* 4	* 6.7	* 6.7	* 24.1	10.52
	2019	...	...	...	...	...	...	...	10.52
Brunei Darussalam Brunéi Darussalam	2005	527	* 2	* 5	* 389	* 0.4	* 0.9	* 73.8	41.66
	2010	* 527	* 4	* 6	* 380	* 0.8	* 1.1	* 72.1	41.66
	2017	* 527	* 5	* 6	* 380	* 0.9	* 1.1	* 72.1	41.66
	2019	...	...	...	...	...	...	...	41.66
Bulgaria Bulgarie	2005	10 864	3 173	188	3 651	29.2	1.7	33.6	27.79
	2010	* 10 856	3 186	164	3 737	* 29.3	* 1.5	* 34.4	87.50
	2017	* 10 856	3 489	148	* 3 823	* 32.1	* 1.4	* 35.2	87.50
	2019	...	...	...	...	...	...	...	87.50
Burkina Faso Burkina Faso	2005	* 27 360	* 4 900	* 70	5 949	* 17.9	* 0.3	* 21.7	66.71
	2010	* 27 360	* 6 000	* 80	5 649	* 21.9	* 0.3	* 20.6	66.71
	2017	* 27 360	* 6 000	* 100	* 5 350	* 21.9	* 0.4	* 19.6	66.71
	2019	...	...	...	...	...	...	...	66.71
Burundi Burundi	2005	* 2 568	* 956	* 380	181	* 37.2	* 14.8	* 7.0	56.83
	2010	* 2 568	* 950	* 400	253	* 37.0	* 15.6	* 9.9	56.83
	2017	* 2 568	* 1 200	* 350	* 276	* 46.7	* 13.6	* 10.7	56.83
	2019	...	...	...	...	...	...	...	56.83

Land *(continued)*
Thousand hectares and percent of total land

Terres *(suite)*
Milliers d'hectares et pourcentage de la superficie totale

Region, country or area Région, pays ou zone	Year Année	Area – Superficie ('000 hectares)				Area – Superficie (Percent of total)&			Sites protected for terrestrial biodiversity Sites pour la bio. terre. dans aires protég. (%)&&
		Total land Superficie totale	Arable land Terres arables	Permanent crops Cultures permanentes	Forest cover Superficie forestière	Arable land Terres arables	Permanent crops Cultures Permanentes	Forest cover Superficie forestière	
Cabo Verde Cabo Verde	2005	403	* 48	* 2	84	* 11.9	* 0.5	20.7	9.42
	2010	403	* 50	* 3	85	* 12.4	* 0.7	21.1	9.42
	2017	403	* 50	* 4	* 90	* 12.4	* 1.0	* 22.3	12.03
	2019	...	...	...	...	...	...	...	12.03
Cambodia Cambodge	2005	17 652	* 3 700	156	10 731	* 21.0	0.9	60.8	38.12
	2010	* 17 652	* 3 800	* 155	10 094	* 21.5	* 0.9	* 57.2	39.54
	2017	* 17 652	* 3 911	* 155	* 9 457	* 22.2	* 0.9	* 53.6	39.54
	2019	...	...	...	...	...	...	...	39.54
Cameroon Cameroun	2005	47 271	5 963	* 1 250	21 016	12.6	* 2.6	44.5	20.10
	2010	* 47 271	* 6 200	* 1 500	19 916	* 13.1	* 3.2	* 42.1	24.69
	2017	* 47 271	* 6 200	* 1 550	* 18 816	* 13.1	* 3.3	* 39.8	35.33
	2019	...	...	...	...	...	...	...	35.33
Canada Canada	2005	896 559	* 39 616	* 165	347 576	* 4.4	* ~0.0	38.8	21.51
	2010	896 559	* 37 687	* 177	347 302	* 4.2	* ~0.0	38.7	26.02
	2017	896 559	38 178	174	* 347 069	4.3	~0.0	* 38.7	28.14
	2019	...	...	...	...	...	...	...	28.14
Cayman Islands Îles Caïmanes	2005	24	* ~0	* 1	* 13	* 0.8	* 2.1	* 52.9	31.62
	2010	24	* ~0	* 1	* 13	* 0.8	* 2.1	* 52.9	31.66
	2017	24	* ~0	* 1	* 13	* 0.8	* 2.1	* 52.9	32.49
	2019	...	...	...	...	...	...	...	32.49
Central African Republic République centrafricaine	2005	62 298	* 1 930	* 85	22 326	* 3.1	* 0.1	35.8	74.24
	2010	62 298	* 1 800	* 80	22 248	* 2.9	* 0.1	35.7	74.24
	2017	62 298	* 1 800	* 80	* 22 170	* 2.9	* 0.1	* 35.6	74.24
	2019	...	...	...	...	...	...	...	74.24
Chad Tchad	2005	125 920	* 3 900	* 30	6 141	* 3.1	* ~0.0	4.9	67.31
	2010	125 920	* 4 200	* 35	5 508	* 3.3	* ~0.0	4.4	67.31
	2017	* 125 920	* 5 200	* 38	* 4 875	* 4.1	* ~0.0	* 3.9	67.31
	2019	...	...	...	...	...	...	...	67.31
Channel Islands Îles Anglo-Normandes	2005	20	* 4	...	* 1	* 19.2	...	* 4.0	...
	2010	20	* 4	...	* 1	* 21.8	...	* 4.0	...
	2017	20	* 4	...	* 1	* 19.3	...	* 4.0	...
Chile Chili	2005	74 353	* 1 450	* 435	16 042	* 2.0	* 0.6	21.6	27.45
	2010	74 353	* 1 271	* 457	16 231	* 1.7	* 0.6	21.8	29.62
	2017	* 74 353	* 1 282	* 450	* 17 735	* 1.7	* 0.6	* 23.9	32.17
	2019	...	...	...	...	...	...	...	34.22
China Chine	2005	942 470	112 858	12 581	193 044	12.0	1.3	20.5	6.39
	2010	942 470	107 822	14 716	200 610	11.4	1.6	21.3	8.56
	2017	942 470	119 491	16 206	208 321	12.7	1.7	22.1	9.55
	2019	...	...	...	...	...	...	...	9.93
China, Hong Kong SAR Chine, RAS de Hong Kong	2005	105	* 5	* 1	...	* 4.8	* 1.0	...	48.93
	2010	* 105	* 4	* 1	...	* 3.3	* 1.0	...	48.93
	2017	* 105	* 3	* 1	...	* 3.0	* 1.0	...	48.93
	2019	...	...	...	...	...	...	...	48.93
China, Macao SAR Chine, RAS de Macao	2005	3	...	...	...	...	...	...	0.00
	2010	3	...	...	...	...	...	...	0.00
	2017	3	...	...	...	...	...	...	0.00
	2019	...	...	...	...	...	...	...	0.00
Colombia Colombie	2005	110 950	* 2 026	* 1 587	60 201	* 1.8	* 1.4	54.3	25.32
	2010	110 950	* 1 763	* 1 590	58 635	* 1.6	* 1.4	52.8	32.98
	2017	110 950	1 781	2 038	* 58 502	1.6	1.8	* 52.7	42.89
	2019	...	...	...	...	...	...	...	42.89
Comoros Comores	2005	186	* 65	* 53	* 42	* 34.9	* 28.5	* 22.6	8.33
	2010	186	* 65	* 53	* 39	* 34.9	* 28.5	* 21.0	8.33
	2017	186	* 66	* 50	* 37	* 35.5	* 26.9	* 19.9	8.33
	2019	...	...	...	...	...	...	...	8.33
Congo Congo	2005	* 34 150	* 490	* 57	22 471	* 1.4	* 0.2	* 65.8	46.38
	2010	* 34 150	* 510	* 66	22 411	* 1.5	* 0.2	* 65.6	49.01
	2017	* 34 150	* 550	* 78	* 22 334	* 1.6	* 0.2	* 65.4	56.48
	2019	...	...	...	...	...	...	...	56.48

Region, country or area Région, pays ou zone	Year Année	Area – Superficie ('000 hectares)				Area – Superficie (Percent of total)&			Sites protected for terrestrial biodiversity Sites pour la bio. terre. dans aires protég. (%)&&
		Total land Superficie totale	Arable land Terres arables	Permanent crops Cultures permanentes	Forest cover Superficie forestière	Arable land Terres arables	Permanent crops Cultures Permanentes	Forest cover Superficie forestière	
Cook Islands	2005	24	* 1	* 1	15	* 5.2	* 6.2	62.9	0.00
Îles Cook	2010	24	* 1	* 1	15	* 2.9	* 2.7	62.9	0.00
	2017	24	* 1	* 1	* 15	* 4.2	* 2.1	* 62.9	5.73
	2019	...	...	...	...	...	...	...	5.73
Costa Rica	2005	* 5 106	* 210	* 280	2 491	* 4.1	* 5.5	* 48.8	39.67
Costa Rica	2010	* 5 106	* 225	* 315	2 605	* 4.4	* 6.2	* 51.0	39.75
	2017	* 5 106	* 251	319	* 2 756	* 4.9	* 6.2	* 54.0	39.79
	2019	...	...	...	...	...	...	...	39.79
Côte d'Ivoire	2005	* 31 800	* 2 800	* 4 200	* 10 405	* 8.8	* 13.2	* 32.7	69.18
Côte d'Ivoire	2010	* 31 800	* 2 900	* 4 500	* 10 403	* 9.1	* 14.2	* 32.7	69.18
	2017	* 31 800	* 3 500	* 4 500	* 10 401	* 11.0	* 14.2	* 32.7	71.19
	2019	...	...	...	...	...	...	...	71.19
Croatia	2005	5 596	873	73	1 903	15.6	1.3	34.0	22.65
Croatie	2010	5 596	904	84	1 920	16.2	1.5	34.3	24.39
	2017	5 659	817	72	* 1 922	14.4	1.3	* 34.0	76.49
	2019	...	...	...	...	...	...	...	76.49
Cuba	2005	10 644	* 3 672	425	2 697	* 34.5	4.0	25.3	29.46
Cuba	2010	* 10 644	* 3 384	* 420	2 932	* 31.8	* 3.9	* 27.5	51.24
	2017	* 10 402	* 2 906	653	* 3 200	* 27.9	* 6.3	* 30.8	54.48
	2019	...	...	...	...	...	...	...	54.48
Curaçao	2005	...	...	...	...	...	...	...	6.07
Curaçao	2010	...	...	...	...	...	...	...	6.07
	2019	...	...	...	...	...	...	...	44.79
Cyprus	2005	924	123	43	173	13.3	4.7	18.7	23.87
Chypre	2010	924	83	30	173	8.9	3.2	18.7	61.91
	2017	* 924	96	27	* 173	* 10.3	* 2.9	* 18.7	74.06
	2019	...	...	...	...	...	...	...	74.06
Czechia	2005	7 726	3 209	77	2 647	41.5	1.0	34.3	89.44
Tchéquie	2010	7 724	3 171	77	2 657	41.1	1.0	34.4	94.73
	2017	7 721	2 498	45	* 2 667	32.4	0.6	* 34.5	94.73
	2019	...	...	...	...	...	...	...	94.73
Dem. People's Rep. Korea	2005	* 12 041	* 2 350	* 200	* 6 299	* 19.5	* 1.7	* 52.3	0.00
Rép. pop. dém. de Corée	2010	* 12 041	* 2 400	* 230	* 5 666	* 19.9	* 1.9	* 47.1	0.00
	2017	* 12 041	* 2 350	* 230	* 5 031	* 19.5	* 1.9	* 41.8	0.00
	2019	...	...	...	...	...	...	...	0.00
Dem. Rep. of the Congo	2005	* 226 705	* 6 700	* 750	155 692	* 3.0	* 0.3	* 68.7	49.89
Rép. dém. du Congo	2010	* 226 705	* 6 800	* 1 000	154 135	* 3.0	* 0.4	* 68.0	52.66
	2017	* 226 705	* 11 800	* 1 500	* 152 578	* 5.2	* 0.7	* 67.3	52.66
	2019	...	...	...	...	...	...	...	52.66
Denmark	2005	4 243	2 332	7	558	55.0	0.2	13.1	86.04
Danemark	2010	4 243	2 421	5	587	57.1	0.1	13.8	86.17
	2017	4 000	2 370	26	* 612	59.3	0.7	* 15.3	86.20
	2019	...	...	...	...	...	...	...	86.20
Djibouti	2005	* 2 318	* 1	...	* 6	* ~0.0	...	* 0.2	0.00
Djibouti	2010	* 2 318	2	...	* 6	* 0.1	...	* 0.2	0.00
	2017	* 2 318	* 2	...	* 6	* 0.1	...	* 0.2	0.81
	2019	...	...	...	...	...	...	...	0.81
Dominica	2005	75	* 5	* 15	* 46	* 6.7	* 20.0	* 61.3	40.00
Dominique	2010	75	* 6	* 17	* 45	* 8.0	* 22.7	* 59.5	40.00
	2017	75	* 6	* 17	* 43	* 8.0	* 22.7	* 57.8	40.00
	2019	...	...	...	...	...	...	...	40.00
Dominican Republic	2005	4 831	* 820	* 400	1 652	* 17.0	* 8.3	34.2	75.95
République dominicaine	2010	4 831	* 800	* 400	1 817	* 16.6	* 8.3	37.6	76.65
	2017	* 4 831	* 800	* 355	* 1 983	* 16.6	* 7.3	* 41.0	81.08
	2019	...	...	...	...	...	...	...	81.08
Ecuador	2005	24 836	1 296	1 214	13 335	5.2	4.9	53.7	22.85
Équateur	2010	24 836	1 186	1 391	12 942	4.8	5.6	52.1	25.90
	2017	24 836	1 033	1 431	* 12 548	4.2	5.8	* 50.5	29.97
	2019	...	...	...	...	...	...	...	30.23

Region, country or area / Région, pays ou zone	Year / Année	Area – Superficie ('000 hectares) Total land / Superficie totale	Arable land / Terres arables	Permanent crops / Cultures permanentes	Forest cover / Superficie forestière	Area – Superficie (Percent of total)& Arable land / Terres arables	Permanent crops / Cultures Permanentes	Forest cover / Superficie forestière	Sites protected for terrestrial biodiversity / Sites pour la bio. terre. dans aires protég. (%)&&
Egypt	2005	99 545	* 2 563	960	67	* 2.6	1.0	0.1	37.13
Égypte	2010	* 99 545	2 873	798	70	* 2.9	* 0.8	* 0.1	39.41
	2017	* 99 545	* 2 787	* 947	* 73	* 2.8	* 1.0	* 0.1	39.41
	2019	...	...	...	...	...	...	...	39.41
El Salvador	2005	* 2 072	* 702	227	309	* 33.9	* 11.0	* 14.9	10.38
El Salvador	2010	* 2 072	* 673	* 225	287	* 32.5	* 10.9	* 13.9	23.51
	2017	* 2 072	* 722	* 210	* 265	* 34.8	* 10.1	* 12.8	25.02
	2019	...	...	...	...	...	...	...	25.02
Equatorial Guinea	2005	2 805	* 130	* 90	1 685	* 4.6	* 3.2	60.1	100.00
Guinée équatoriale	2010	2 805	* 120	* 70	1 626	* 4.3	* 2.5	58.0	100.00
	2017	2 805	* 120	* 60	* 1 568	* 4.3	* 2.1	* 55.9	100.00
	2019	...	...	...	...	...	...	...	100.00
Eritrea	2005	* 10 100	* 620	* 2	* 1 554	* 6.1	* ~0.0	* 15.4	13.34
Érythrée	2010	* 10 100	* 690	* 2	* 1 532	* 6.8	* ~0.0	* 15.2	13.34
	2017	* 10 100	* 690	* 2	* 1 510	* 6.8	* ~0.0	* 15.0	13.34
	2019	...	...	...	...	...	...	...	13.34
Estonia	2005	4 239	592	11	2 252	14.0	0.3	53.1	94.74
Estonie	2010	4 239	645	7	2 234	15.2	0.2	52.7	94.76
	2017	4 347	684	4	* 2 232	15.7	0.1	* 51.3	94.86
	2019	...	...	...	...	...	...	...	94.87
Eswatini	2005	* 1 720	* 178	* 14	541	* 10.3	* 0.8	* 31.5	29.98
Eswatini	2010	* 1 720	* 175	* 15	563	* 10.2	* 0.9	* 32.7	29.98
	2017	* 1 720	* 175	* 15	* 586	* 10.2	* 0.9	* 34.1	30.57
	2019	...	...	...	...	...	...	...	30.57
Ethiopia	2005	* 100 000	12 823	768	13 000	* 12.8	* 0.8	* 13.0	17.61
Éthiopie	2010	* 100 000	14 565	1 118	12 296	* 14.6	* 1.1	* 12.3	18.10
	2017	* 100 000	15 969	1 571	* 12 499	* 16.0	* 1.6	* 12.5	18.10
	2019	...	...	...	...	...	...	...	18.10
Falkland Islands (Malvinas)	2005	1 217	...	...	* 0	...	...	* 0.0	10.90
Îles Falkland (Malvinas)	2010	1 217	...	...	* 0	...	...	* 0.0	10.90
	2017	1 217	...	...	* 0	...	...	* 0.0	10.90
	2019	...	...	...	...	...	...	...	10.90
Faroe Islands	2005	140	* 3	...	* ~0	* 2.1	...	* 0.1	0.00
Îles Féroé	2010	140	* 3	...	* ~0	* 2.1	...	* 0.1	0.00
	2017	140	* 3	...	* ~0	* 2.1	...	* 0.1	15.79
	2019	...	...	...	...	...	...	...	15.79
Fiji	2005	* 1 827	* 170	* 83	997	* 9.3	* 4.5	* 54.6	7.58
Fidji	2010	* 1 827	* 165	* 85	993	* 9.0	* 4.7	* 54.3	11.18
	2017	* 1 827	* 165	* 85	* 1 017	* 9.0	* 4.7	* 55.7	11.18
	2019	...	...	...	...	...	...	...	11.18
Finland	2005	30 459	2 237	4	22 143	7.3	~0.0	72.7	71.15
Finlande	2010	30 390	2 255	4	22 218	7.4	~0.0	73.1	71.31
	2017	30 392	2 242	3	* 22 218	7.4	~0.0	* 73.1	71.80
	2019	...	...	...	...	...	...	...	71.80
France	2005	* 54 756	18 378	1 111	15 861	* 33.6	* 2.0	* 29.0	59.39
France	2010	* 54 756	18 301	1 011	16 424	* 33.4	* 1.8	* 30.0	72.97
	2017	* 54 756	18 464	999	* 16 989	33.7	* 1.8	* 31.0	76.62
	2019	...	...	...	...	...	...	...	80.35
French Guiana	2005	* 8 274	12	4	8 168	* 0.1	* ~0.0	* 98.7	64.28
Guyane française	2010	* 8 277	12	4	8 138	* 0.1	* ~0.0	* 98.3	80.97
	2017	* 8 281	13	6	* 8 130	* 0.2	* 0.1	* 98.2	83.15
	2019	...	...	...	...	...	...	...	83.15
French Polynesia	2005	* 366	* 3	* 22	* 130	* 0.8	* 6.0	* 35.5	0.00
Polynésie française	2010	* 366	* 3	* 22	* 155	* 0.7	* 6.0	* 42.3	0.00
	2017	* 366	* 3	* 23	* 155	* 0.7	* 6.3	* 42.3	0.00
	2019	...	...	...	...	...	...	...	0.00
Gabon	2005	25 767	* 325	* 170	22 000	* 1.3	* 0.7	85.4	61.17
Gabon	2010	25 767	* 325	* 170	22 000	* 1.3	* 0.7	85.4	61.17
	2017	25 767	* 325	* 170	* 23 000	* 1.3	* 0.7	* 89.3	61.67
	2019	...	...	...	...	...	...	...	61.67

Region, country or area / Région, pays ou zone	Year / Année	Area – Superficie ('000 hectares)				Area – Superficie (Percent of total)&			Sites protected for terrestrial biodiversity / Sites pour la bio. terre. dans aires protég. (%)&&
		Total land / Superficie totale	Arable land / Terres arables	Permanent crops / Cultures permanentes	Forest cover / Superficie forestière	Arable land / Terres arables	Permanent crops / Cultures Permanentes	Forest cover / Superficie forestière	
Gambia	2005	1 012	* 325	* 5	471	* 32.1	* 0.5	46.5	34.59
Gambie	2010	1 012	450	* 5	480	44.5	* 0.5	47.4	34.59
	2017	* 1 012	* 440	* 5	* 488	* 43.5	* 0.5	* 48.2	34.59
	2019	...	...	...	...	...	...	...	34.59
Georgia	2005	6 949	* 470	* 110	2 773	* 6.8	* 1.6	39.9	27.22
Géorgie	2010	* 6 949	395	* 125	2 822	* 5.7	* 1.8	* 40.6	34.39
	2017	6 949	* 324	121	* 2 822	* 4.7	1.7	* 40.6	40.32
	2019	...	...	...	...	...	...	...	40.32
Germany	2005	34 876	11 904	198	11 384	34.1	0.6	32.6	71.73
Allemagne	2010	34 857	11 846	199	11 409	34.0	0.6	32.7	77.90
	2017	34 937	11 772	199	* 11 419	33.7	0.6	* 32.7	78.83
	2019	...	...	...	...	...	...	...	78.83
Ghana	2005	* 22 754	* 4 000	* 2 800	9 053	* 17.6	* 12.3	* 39.8	80.56
Ghana	2010	22 754	* 4 620	* 2 700	9 195	* 20.3	* 11.9	40.4	80.56
	2017	* 22 754	* 4 700	* 2 700	* 9 337	* 20.7	* 11.9	* 41.0	80.56
	2019	...	...	...	...	...	...	...	80.56
Gibraltar	2005	1	...	...	* 0	...	...	* 0.0	...
Gibraltar	2010	1	...	...	* 0	...	...	* 0.0	...
	2017	1	...	...	* 0	...	...	* 0.0	...
Greece	2005	* 12 890	2 639	1 136	* 3 752	* 20.5	* 8.8	* 29.1	71.28
Grèce	2010	* 12 890	2 567	1 137	* 3 903	* 19.9	* 8.8	* 30.3	86.05
	2017	* 12 890	2 138	1 082	* 4 054	* 16.6	* 8.4	* 31.5	86.05
	2019	...	...	...	...	...	...	...	86.05
Greenland	2005	41 045	...	...	* ~0	...	...	* ~0.0	26.08
Groenland	2010	41 045	...	...	* ~0	...	...	* ~0.0	26.31
	2017	41 045	...	...	* ~0	...	...	* ~0.0	26.31
	2019	...	...	...	...	...	...	...	26.31
Grenada	2005	34	* 2	* 4	* 17	* 5.9	* 11.8	* 50.0	34.45
Grenade	2010	34	* 3	* 4	* 17	* 8.8	* 11.8	* 50.0	34.45
	2017	34	* 3	* 4	* 17	* 8.8	* 11.8	* 50.0	34.45
	2019	...	...	...	...	...	...	...	34.45
Guadeloupe	2005	169	19	4	* 74	11.2	2.4	* 43.8	57.44
Guadeloupe	2010	* 169	21	3	* 73	* 12.4	* 2.0	* 43.1	82.28
	2017	* 169	23	3	* 73	* 13.7	* 1.7	* 43.0	82.38
	2019	...	...	...	...	...	...	...	82.38
Guam	2005	54	* 2	* 10	* 25	* 3.7	* 18.5	* 46.3	40.17
Guam	2010	54	* 1	* 9	* 25	* 1.9	* 16.7	* 46.3	40.17
	2017	54	* 1	* 9	* 25	* 1.9	* 16.7	* 46.3	40.17
	2019	...	...	...	...	...	...	...	40.17
Guatemala	2005	10 716	1 400	841	3 938	13.1	7.8	36.7	21.91
Guatemala	2010	* 10 716	* 1 196	* 970	3 722	* 11.2	* 9.1	* 34.7	25.33
	2017	* 10 716	* 862	* 1 183	* 3 540	* 8.0	* 11.0	* 33.0	29.98
	2019	...	...	...	...	...	...	...	29.98
Guinea	2005	* 24 572	* 2 741	* 680	6 724	* 11.2	* 2.8	* 27.4	71.15
Guinée	2010	* 24 572	* 2 900	* 700	6 544	* 11.8	* 2.8	* 26.6	71.15
	2017	* 24 572	* 3 100	* 700	* 6 364	* 12.6	* 2.8	* 25.9	71.15
	2019	...	...	...	...	...	...	...	71.15
Guinea-Bissau	2005	* 2 812	* 280	* 250	* 2 072	* 10.0	* 8.9	* 73.7	52.19
Guinée-Bissau	2010	* 2 812	* 300	* 250	* 2 022	* 10.7	* 8.9	* 71.9	52.19
	2017	* 2 812	* 300	* 250	* 1 972	* 10.7	* 8.9	* 70.1	52.57
	2019	...	...	...	...	...	...	...	52.57
Guyana	2005	* 19 685	* 420	* 28	16 602	* 2.1	* 0.1	* 84.3	...
Guyana	2010	* 19 685	* 420	* 28	16 576	* 2.1	* 0.1	* 84.2	...
	*2017	19 685	420	50	16 526	2.1	0.3	84.0	...
Haiti	2005	* 2 756	* 900	* 280	105	* 32.7	* 10.2	* 3.8	24.28
Haïti	2010	* 2 756	* 1 100	* 280	101	* 39.9	* 10.2	* 3.7	24.28
	2017	* 2 756	* 1 070	* 280	* 97	* 38.8	* 10.2	* 3.5	41.01
	2019	...	...	...	...	...	...	...	41.01

Land *(continued)*
Thousand hectares and percent of total land

Terres *(suite)*
Milliers d'hectares et pourcentage de la superficie totale

Region, country or area Région, pays ou zone	Year Année	Area – Superficie ('000 hectares)				Area – Superficie (Percent of total)&			Sites protected for terre-strial biodiversity Sites pour la bio. terre. dans aires protég. (%)&&
		Total land Superficie totale	Arable land Terres arables	Permanent crops Cultures permanentes	Forest cover Superficie forestière	Arable land Terres arables	Permanent crops Cultures Permanentes	Forest cover Superficie forestière	
Honduras Honduras	2005	* 11 189	* 1 050	* 400	5 792	* 9.4	* 3.6	* 51.8	56.85
	2010	* 11 189	* 1 020	* 480	5 192	* 9.1	* 4.3	* 46.4	57.05
	2017	* 11 189	* 1 020	* 700	* 4 592	* 9.1	* 6.3	* 41.0	59.02
	2019	...	...	...	...	...	...	...	59.02
Hungary Hongrie	2005	8 961	4 601	205	1 983	51.3	2.3	22.1	82.50
	2010	9 053	4 392	188	2 046	48.5	2.1	22.6	82.53
	2017	9 126	4 323	176	* 2 069	47.4	1.9	* 22.7	82.53
	2019	...	...	...	...	...	...	...	82.53
Iceland Islande	2005	10 025	129	...	37	1.3	...	0.4	14.97
	2010	10 025	123	...	43	1.2	...	0.4	16.70
	2017	* 10 025	121	...	* 49	* 1.2	...	* 0.5	19.08
	2019	...	...	...	...	...	...	...	19.08
India Inde	2005	297 319	* 159 444	* 10 230	67 709	* 53.6	* 3.4	22.8	17.70
	2010	* 297 319	* 157 009	* 12 225	69 790	* 52.8	* 4.1	* 23.5	17.75
	2017	* 297 319	* 156 463	* 13 000	* 70 682	* 52.6	* 4.4	* 23.8	21.02
	2019	...	...	...	...	...	...	...	21.02
Indonesia Indonésie	2005	181 157	* 22 946	* 17 900	97 857	* 12.7	* 9.9	54.0	10.64
	2010	* 181 157	* 23 600	* 21 000	94 432	* 13.0	* 11.6	* 52.1	17.35
	2017	187 752	* 26 300	* 25 000	* 91 010	* 14.0	* 13.3	* 48.5	26.01
	2019	...	...	...	...	...	...	...	26.11
Iran (Islamic Republic of) Iran (Rép. islamique d')	2005	162 876	16 533	1 574	10 692	10.2	1.0	6.6	43.60
	2010	162 876	15 390	1 672	10 692	9.4	1.0	6.6	43.60
	2017	* 162 876	* 14 687	* 1 790	* 10 692	* 9.0	* 1.1	* 6.6	43.60
	2019	...	...	...	...	...	...	...	43.60
Iraq Iraq	2005	* 43 737	* 5 200	* 190	* 825	* 11.9	* 0.4	* 1.9	1.61
	2010	* 43 432	* 4 000	* 220	* 825	* 9.2	* 0.5	* 1.9	2.96
	2017	* 43 413	* 5 000	* 400	* 825	* 11.5	* 0.9	* 1.9	5.85
	2019	...	...	...	...	...	...	...	5.85
Ireland Irlande	2005	6 889	1 184	3	695	17.2	~0.0	10.1	83.02
	2010	6 889	1 011	2	726	14.7	~0.0	10.5	85.37
	2017	6 889	441	1	* 754	6.4	~0.0	* 10.9	85.97
	2019	...	...	...	...	...	...	...	85.97
Isle of Man Île de Man	2005	57	18	...	* 3	31.2	...	* 6.1	...
	2010	57	25	...	* 3	44.5	...	* 6.1	...
	2017	57	* 23	...	* 3	* 40.4	...	* 6.1	...
Israel Israël	2005	2 164	* 311	70	155	* 14.4	3.2	7.2	18.30
	2010	2 164	* 294	77	154	* 13.6	3.6	7.1	20.27
	2017	2 164	* 387	96	* 165	* 17.9	4.4	* 7.6	20.33
	2019	...	...	...	...	...	...	...	20.33
Italy Italie	2005	29 414	7 780	2 554	8 759	26.5	8.7	29.8	73.94
	2010	* 29 414	7 042	2 588	9 028	* 23.9	* 8.8	* 30.7	77.34
	2017	* 29 414	6 736	2 482	* 9 297	* 22.9	* 8.4	* 31.6	77.35
	2019	...	...	...	...	...	...	...	77.35
Jamaica Jamaïque	2005	* 1 083	* 128	* 110	339	* 11.8	* 10.2	* 31.3	29.44
	2010	* 1 083	* 120	* 95	337	* 11.1	* 8.8	* 31.1	29.44
	2017	* 1 083	* 120	* 95	* 335	* 11.1	* 8.8	* 31.0	29.46
	2019	...	...	...	...	...	...	...	29.46
Japan Japon	2005	* 36 450	4 360	332	24 935	* 12.0	* 0.9	* 68.4	60.36
	2010	* 36 455	4 282	311	24 966	* 11.7	* 0.9	* 68.5	60.87
	2017	* 36 456	4 161	283	* 24 958	* 11.4	* 0.8	* 68.5	64.83
	2019	...	...	...	...	...	...	...	64.83
Jordan Jordanie	2005	8 824	185	86	* 98	2.1	1.0	* 1.1	7.08
	2010	8 878	178	83	* 98	2.0	0.9	* 1.1	7.33
	2017	8 878	187	78	* 98	2.1	0.9	* 1.1	10.23
	2019	...	...	...	...	...	...	...	13.48
Kazakhstan Kazakhstan	2005	* 269 970	* 28 562	116	* 3 337	* 10.6	* ~0.0	* 1.2	9.16
	2010	* 269 970	28 684	116	* 3 309	* 10.6	* ~0.0	* 1.2	10.41
	2017	* 269 970	* 29 395	* 132	* 3 309	* 10.9	* ~0.0	* 1.2	11.15
	2019	...	...	...	...	...	...	...	11.15

Region, country or area Région, pays ou zone	Year Année	Area – Superficie ('000 hectares)				Area – Superficie (Percent of total)&			Sites protected for terre-strial biodiversity Sites pour la bio. terre. dans aires protég. (%)&&
		Total land Superficie totale	Arable land Terres arables	Permanent crops Cultures permanentes	Forest cover Superficie forestière	Arable land Terres arables	Permanent crops Cultures Permanentes	Forest cover Superficie forestière	
Kenya	2005	* 56 914	* 5 264	438	4 047	* 9.2	* 0.8	* 7.1	33.24
Kenya	2010	* 56 914	* 5 500	* 520	4 230	* 9.7	* 0.9	* 7.4	34.36
	2017	* 56 914	* 5 800	* 530	* 4 413	* 10.2	* 0.9	* 7.8	34.52
	2019	...	...	...	...	...	...	...	34.52
Kiribati	2005	81	* 2	* 32	* 12	* 2.5	* 39.5	* 15.0	0.00
Kiribati	2010	* 81	* 2	* 32	* 12	* 2.5	* 39.5	* 15.0	40.00
	2017	* 81	* 2	* 32	* 12	* 2.5	* 39.5	* 15.0	40.00
	2019	...	...	...	...	...	...	...	40.00
Kuwait	2005	1 782	* 11	3	* 6	* 0.6	0.2	* 0.3	30.96
Koweït	2010	1 782	* 10	* 6	* 6	* 0.6	* 0.3	* 0.4	30.96
	2017	* 1 782	* 9	7	* 6	* 0.5	* 0.4	* 0.4	51.65
	2019	...	...	...	...	...	...	...	51.65
Kyrgyzstan	2005	* 19 180	1 284	72	869	* 6.7	* 0.4	* 4.5	25.75
Kirghizistan	2010	* 19 180	1 276	74	677	* 6.7	* 0.4	* 3.5	25.75
	2017	* 19 180	1 288	76	* 637	* 6.7	* 0.4	* 3.3	25.75
	2019	...	...	...	...	...	...	...	25.75
Lao People's Dem. Rep.	2005	23 080	* 1 150	* 85	16 870	* 5.0	* 0.4	73.1	44.04
Rép. dém. populaire lao	2010	* 23 080	* 1 400	* 130	17 816	* 6.1	* 0.6	* 77.2	44.04
	2017	* 23 080	* 1 555	* 169	* 18 761	* 6.7	* 0.7	* 81.3	44.04
	2019	...	...	...	...	...	...	...	44.04
Latvia	2005	6 220	1 092	13	3 297	17.6	0.2	53.0	90.95
Lettonie	2010	6 224	1 173	7	3 354	18.8	0.1	53.9	97.22
	2017	6 211	1 290	8	* 3 356	20.8	0.1	* 54.0	97.22
	2019	...	...	...	...	...	...	...	97.22
Lebanon	2005	* 1 023	* 142	141	137	* 13.9	* 13.8	* 13.3	11.42
Liban	2010	* 1 023	114	126	137	* 11.1	* 12.3	* 13.4	11.42
	2017	* 1 023	* 132	* 126	* 137	* 12.9	* 12.3	* 13.4	12.34
	2019	...	...	...	...	...	...	...	12.34
Lesotho	2005	3 036	323	* 4	43	10.6	* 0.1	1.4	16.43
Lesotho	2010	* 3 036	322	* 4	44	* 10.6	* 0.1	* 1.4	16.43
	2017	* 3 036	414	* 4	* 49	13.6	* 0.1	* 1.6	16.43
	2019	...	...	...	...	...	...	...	16.43
Liberia	2005	9 632	* 400	* 215	4 479	* 4.2	* 2.2	46.5	15.79
Libéria	2010	9 632	* 480	* 180	4 329	* 5.0	* 1.9	44.9	15.79
	2017	9 632	* 500	* 210	* 4 179	* 5.2	* 2.2	* 43.4	15.79
	2019	...	...	...	...	...	...	...	15.79
Libya	2005	175 954	* 1 750	* 335	* 217	* 1.0	* 0.2	* 0.1	0.00
Libye	2010	175 954	* 1 716	* 335	* 217	* 1.0	* 0.2	* 0.1	0.00
	2017	* 175 954	* 1 720	* 330	* 217	* 1.0	* 0.2	* 0.1	0.00
	2019	...	...	...	...	...	...	...	0.00
Liechtenstein	2005	16	* 4	...	* 7	* 24.4	...	* 43.1	80.82
Liechtenstein	2010	16	* 3	...	* 7	* 20.6	...	* 43.1	80.82
	2017	16	* 2	...	* 7	* 13.5	...	* 43.1	80.82
	2019	...	...	...	...	...	...	...	80.82
Lithuania	2005	6 268	1 907	40	2 121	30.4	0.6	33.8	90.18
Lituanie	2010	6 268	2 127	31	2 170	33.9	0.5	34.6	91.06
	2017	6 264	2 104	36	* 2 180	33.6	0.6	* 34.8	91.06
	2019	...	...	...	...	...	...	...	91.06
Luxembourg	2005	243	60	2	* 87	24.7	0.8	* 35.7	78.13
Luxembourg	2010	243	62	2	* 87	25.5	0.6	* 35.7	78.13
	2017	243	62	2	* 87	25.5	0.6	* 35.7	81.86
	2019	...	...	...	...	...	...	...	81.87
Madagascar	2005	* 58 154	* 3 000	* 600	12 838	* 5.2	* 1.0	* 22.1	20.43
Madagascar	2010	* 58 154	* 3 000	* 600	12 553	* 5.2	* 1.0	* 21.6	22.44
	2017	* 58 180	* 3 000	* 600	* 12 473	* 5.2	* 1.0	* 21.4	25.04
	2019	...	...	...	...	...	...	...	25.04
Malawi	2005	9 428	* 3 200	* 130	3 402	* 33.9	* 1.4	36.1	73.72
Malawi	2010	9 428	* 3 700	* 135	3 237	* 39.2	* 1.4	34.3	73.72
	2017	* 9 428	* 3 600	* 200	* 3 147	* 38.2	* 2.1	* 33.4	73.72
	2019	...	...	...	...	...	...	...	73.72

Region, country or area Région, pays ou zone	Year Année	Area – Superficie ('000 hectares)				Area – Superficie (Percent of total)&			Sites protected for terre-strial biodiversity Sites pour la bio. terre. dans aires protég. (%)&&
		Total land Superficie totale	Arable land Terres arables	Permanent crops Cultures permanentes	Forest cover Superficie forestière	Arable land Terres arables	Permanent crops Cultures Permanentes	Forest cover Superficie forestière	
Malaysia	2005	* 32 855	* 949	* 5 900	20 890	* 2.9	* 18.0	* 63.6	28.51
Malaisie	2010	* 32 855	* 854	* 6 250	22 124	* 2.6	* 19.0	* 67.3	28.51
	2017	* 32 855	* 845	* 7 460	* 22 195	* 2.6	* 22.7	* 67.6	28.51
	2019	...	...	...	...	...	...	...	28.51
Maldives	2005	30	* 3	* 5	* 1	* 10.0	* 16.7	* 3.3	0.00
Maldives	2010	30	* 4	* 3	* 1	* 13.0	* 10.0	* 3.3	0.00
	2017	30	* 4	* 3	* 1	* 13.0	* 10.0	* 3.3	0.00
	2019	...	...	...	...	...	...	...	0.00
Mali	2005	122 019	* 5 603	* 150	5 505	* 4.6	* 0.1	4.5	8.06
Mali	2010	* 122 019	* 6 261	* 150	5 110	* 5.1	* 0.1	* 4.2	8.06
	2017	* 122 019	* 6 411	* 150	* 4 715	* 5.3	* 0.1	* 3.9	8.06
	2019	...	...	...	...	...	...	...	8.06
Malta	2005	32	8	1	* ~0	25.6	3.4	* 1.1	72.48
Malte	2010	32	9	1	* ~0	28.4	3.9	* 1.1	77.46
	2017	32	9	1	* ~0	28.3	4.1	* 1.1	84.49
	2019	...	...	...	...	...	...	...	84.49
Marshall Islands	2005	18	2	8	* 13	11.1	44.4	* 70.2	7.20
Îles Marshall	2010	18	* 2	* 8	* 13	* 11.1	* 44.4	* 70.2	8.40
	2017	18	* 2	* 6	* 13	* 11.1	* 35.0	* 70.2	10.11
	2019	...	...	...	...	...	...	...	10.11
Martinique	2005	* 106	10	8	49	* 9.4	* 7.5	* 45.8	52.59
Martinique	2010	* 106	10	7	49	* 9.6	* 7.0	* 45.8	97.18
	2017	* 106	9	5	* 49	* 8.9	* 5.2	* 45.8	99.70
	2019	...	...	...	...	...	...	...	99.70
Mauritania	2005	103 070	* 400	* 11	267	* 0.4	* ~0.0	0.3	11.17
Mauritanie	2010	103 070	* 450	* 11	242	* 0.4	* ~0.0	0.2	11.17
	2017	103 070	* 400	* 11	* 225	* 0.4	* ~0.0	* 0.2	11.17
	2019	...	...	...	...	...	...	...	11.17
Mauritius	2005	203	* 85	* 4	38	* 41.9	* 2.0	18.8	8.96
Maurice	2010	203	* 80	* 4	38	* 39.4	* 2.0	18.9	9.02
	2017	203	* 75	* 4	* 39	* 36.9	* 2.0	* 19.0	9.64
	2019	...	...	...	...	...	...	...	9.64
Mayotte	2005	37	* 10	* 10	* 8	* 26.7	* 26.7	* 20.7	31.72
Mayotte	2010	37	* 17	3	* 7	* 44.4	9.1	* 18.2	64.05
	2017	37	17	3	* 6	46.1	7.3	* 15.6	64.27
	2019	...	...	...	...	...	...	...	64.27
Mexico	2005	194 395	* 23 296	2 607	67 083	* 12.0	1.3	34.5	27.75
Mexique	2010	194 395	* 21 527	2 651	66 498	* 11.1	1.4	34.2	34.01
	2017	194 395	* 23 905	2 669	* 66 040	* 12.3	1.4	* 34.0	37.03
	2019	...	...	...	...	...	...	...	37.07
Micronesia (Fed. States of)	2005	70	* 3	* 17	* 64	* 3.6	* 24.3	* 91.4	0.02
Micronésie (États féd. de)	2010	70	* 2	* 17	* 64	* 2.9	* 24.3	* 91.6	0.02
	2017	70	* 2	* 17	* 64	* 2.9	* 24.3	* 91.8	0.02
	2019	...	...	...	...	...	...	...	0.02
Mongolia	2005	* 155 356	* 695	* 2	11 308	* 0.4	* ~0.0	* 7.3	34.52
Mongolie	2010	* 155 356	* 614	* 3	13 039	* 0.4	* ~0.0	* 8.4	37.16
	2017	155 726	* 567	* 5	* 12 553	* 0.4	* ~0.0	* 8.1	41.73
	2019	...	...	...	...	...	...	...	41.73
Montenegro	2005	...	...	...	...	...	...	...	11.11
Monténégro	2010	* 1 345	172	16	827	* 12.8	* 1.2	* 61.5	11.11
	2017	* 1 345	9	5	* 827	* 0.7	* 0.4	* 61.5	11.11
	2019	...	...	...	...	...	...	...	11.11
Montserrat	2005	10	* 2	...	* 3	* 20.0	...	* 25.0	0.00
Montserrat	2010	10	* 2	...	* 3	* 20.0	...	* 25.0	0.00
	2017	10	* 2	...	* 3	* 20.0	...	* 25.0	30.63
	2019	...	...	...	...	...	...	...	30.63
Morocco	2005	* 44 630	8 122	867	5 401	* 18.2	* 1.9	* 12.1	17.86
Maroc	2010	* 44 630	7 729	1 259	5 672	* 17.3	* 2.8	* 12.7	20.71
	2017	* 44 630	* 7 816	* 1 570	* 5 632	* 17.5	* 3.5	* 12.6	53.81
	2019	...	...	...	...	...	...	...	53.81

Region, country or area Région, pays ou zone	Year Année	Area – Superficie ('000 hectares)				Area – Superficie (Percent of total)&			Sites protected for terre- strial biodiversity Sites pour la bio. terre. dans aires protég. (%)&&
		Total land Superficie totale	Arable land Terres arables	Permanent crops Cultures permanentes	Forest cover Superficie forestière	Arable land Terres arables	Permanent crops Cultures Permanentes	Forest cover Superficie forestière	
Mozambique Mozambique	2005	78 638	* 5 000	* 250	40 079	* 6.4	* 0.3	51.0	17.36
	2010	78 638	* 5 650	* 300	38 972	* 7.2	* 0.4	49.6	17.36
	2017	78 638	* 5 650	* 300	* 37 940	* 7.2	* 0.4	* 48.2	21.71
	2019	...	...	...	...	...	...	...	21.71
Myanmar Myanmar	2005	65 336	10 059	896	33 321	15.4	1.4	51.0	20.29
	2010	65 326	10 811	1 406	31 773	16.5	2.2	48.6	21.85
	2017	65 279	11 062	* 1 510	* 29 041	16.9	* 2.3	* 44.5	24.95
	2019	...	...	...	...	...	...	...	24.95
Namibia Namibie	2005	* 82 329	* 814	* 6	7 661	* 1.0	* ~0.0	* 9.3	42.06
	2010	* 82 329	* 800	* 9	7 290	* 1.0	* ~0.0	* 8.9	83.33
	2017	* 82 329	* 800	* 10	* 6 919	* 1.0	* ~0.0	* 8.4	86.09
	2019	...	...	...	...	...	...	...	86.09
Nauru Nauru	2005	2	...	* ~0	* 0	...	* 20.0	* 0.0	0.00
	2010	2	...	* ~0	* 0	...	* 20.0	* 0.0	0.00
	2017	2	...	* ~0	* 0	...	* 20.0	* 0.0	0.00
	2019	...	...	...	...	...	...	...	0.00
Nepal Népal	2005	14 335	* 2 280	* 133	3 636	* 15.9	* 0.9	25.4	43.68
	2010	14 335	* 2 180	* 152	3 636	* 15.2	* 1.1	25.4	50.65
	2017	14 335	* 2 114	* 212	* 3 636	* 14.7	* 1.5	* 25.4	50.66
	2019	...	...	...	...	...	...	...	50.66
Netherlands Pays-Bas	2005	3 376	1 111	32	365	32.9	0.9	10.8	95.12
	2010	3 373	1 023	36	373	30.3	1.1	11.1	97.21
	2017	* 3 367	1 037	38	* 376	* 30.8	* 1.1	* 11.2	97.36
	2019	...	...	...	...	...	...	...	97.90
Netherlands Antilles [former] Antilles néerlandaises [anc.]	2005	80	* 8	...	* 1	* 10.0	...	* 1.5	...
	2010	80	* 8	...	* 1	* 10.0	...	* 1.5	...
	2017	80	* 8	...	* 1	* 10.0	...	* 1.5	
New Caledonia Nouvelle-Calédonie	2005	* 1 828	* 7	* 4	* 839	* 0.4	* 0.2	* 45.9	9.11
	2010	1 828	* 7	* 4	* 839	* 0.4	* 0.2	* 45.9	26.56
	2017	* 1 828	* 6	* 4	* 839	* 0.3	* 0.2	* 45.9	36.39
	2019	...	...	...	...	...	...	...	36.39
New Zealand Nouvelle-Zélande	2005	26 331	425	63	10 183	1.6	0.2	38.7	44.22
	2010	26 331	499	71	10 151	1.9	0.3	38.6	45.72
	2017	* 26 331	* 570	* 75	* 10 152	* 2.2	* 0.3	* 38.6	46.41
	2019	...	...	...	...	...	...	...	46.44
Nicaragua Nicaragua	2005	12 034	* 2 000	* 290	3 464	* 16.6	* 2.4	28.8	70.41
	2010	12 034	* 1 531	* 295	3 114	* 12.7	* 2.5	25.9	70.41
	2017	12 034	* 1 504	* 286	* 3 114	* 12.5	* 2.4	* 25.9	70.41
	2019	...	...	...	...	...	...	...	70.41
Niger Niger	2005	* 126 670	* 14 123	* 60	1 266	* 11.1	* ~0.0	* 1.0	24.91
	2010	* 126 670	* 15 100	* 100	1 204	* 11.9	* 0.1	* 1.0	24.91
	2017	* 126 670	* 17 700	* 118	* 1 142	* 14.0	* 0.1	* 0.9	33.11
	2019	...	...	...	...	...	...	...	33.11
Nigeria Nigéria	2005	* 91 077	* 36 000	* 6 400	11 089	* 39.5	* 7.0	* 12.2	64.32
	2010	* 91 077	* 33 000	* 6 700	9 041	* 36.2	* 7.4	* 9.9	80.41
	2017	* 91 077	* 34 000	* 6 500	* 6 993	* 37.3	* 7.1	* 7.7	80.41
	2019	...	...	...	...	...	...	...	80.41
Niue Nioué	2005	26	* 1	* 3	* 19	* 3.8	* 10.8	* 73.5	0.00
	2010	26	* 1	* 3	* 19	* 3.8	* 11.5	* 71.5	0.00
	2017	26	* 1	* 3	* 18	* 3.8	* 11.5	* 69.6	0.00
	2019	...	...	...	...	...	...	...	0.00
Norfolk Island Île Norfolk	2005	4	...	...	* ~0	...	...	* 11.5	...
	2010	4	...	...	* ~0	...	...	* 11.5	...
	2017	4	...	...	* ~0	...	...	* 11.5	...
North Macedonia Macédoine du Nord	2005	2 543	448	39	* 975	17.6	1.5	* 38.3	25.77
	2010	2 522	414	35	* 998	16.4	1.4	* 39.6	26.00
	2017	2 522	417	40	* 998	16.5	1.6	* 39.6	26.00
	2019	...	...	...	...	...	...	...	26.00

Land *(continued)*
Thousand hectares and percent of total land

Terres *(suite)*
Milliers d'hectares et pourcentage de la superficie totale

| Region, country or area Région, pays ou zone | Year Année | Area – Superficie ('000 hectares) | | | | Area – Superficie (Percent of total)& | | | Sites protected for terrestrial biodiversity Sites pour la bio. terre. dans aires protég. (%)&& |
		Total land Superficie totale	Arable land Terres arables	Permanent crops Cultures permanentes	Forest cover Superficie forestière	Arable land Terres arables	Permanent crops Cultures Permanentes	Forest cover Superficie forestière	
Northern Mariana Islands Îles Mariannes du Nord	2005	46	* 1	* 1	* 31	* 2.2	* 2.2	* 67.7	7.00
	2010	46	* 1	* 1	* 30	* 2.2	* 2.2	* 65.9	40.59
	2017	46	* 1	* 1	* 29	* 2.2	* 2.2	* 64.1	40.59
	2019	...	...	...	...	...	...	...	40.59
Norway Norvège	2005	36 524	862	5	12 092	2.4	~0.0	33.1	52.17
	2010	36 524	826	5	12 102	2.3	~0.0	33.1	54.42
	2017	36 511	801	3	* 12 112	2.2	~0.0	* 33.2	57.02
	2019	...	...	...	...	...	...	...	57.72
Oman Oman	2005	30 950	28	37	2	0.1	0.1	~0.0	8.50
	2010	30 950	34	38	2	0.1	0.1	~0.0	8.50
	2017	30 950	69	32	* 2	0.2	0.1	* ~0.0	11.81
	2019	...	...	...	...	...	...	...	11.81
Other non-specified areas Autres zones non-spécifiées	*2005	3 541	603	230	...	17.0	6.5	...	...
	*2010	3 541	598	215	...	16.9	6.1	...	...
	*2017	3 541	588	205	...	16.6	5.8	...	...
Pakistan Pakistan	2005	77 088	30 170	795	* 1 902	39.1	1.0	* 2.5	34.79
	2010	* 77 088	29 390	852	* 1 687	* 38.1	* 1.1	* 2.2	34.79
	2017	* 77 088	31 210	793	* 1 472	* 40.5	* 1.0	* 1.9	34.79
	2019	...	...	...	...	...	...	...	34.79
Palau Palaos	2005	* 46	* 1	* 2	40	* 2.2	* 4.3	* 87.6	27.87
	2010	* 46	* 1	* 2	40	* 2.2	* 4.3	* 87.6	44.01
	2017	* 46	* 1	* 2	* 40	* 2.2	* 4.3	* 87.6	44.01
	2019	...	...	...	...	...	...	...	44.01
Panama Panama	2005	7 434	* 548	* 160	4 782	* 7.4	* 2.2	64.3	34.35
	2010	* 7 434	569	189	4 699	* 7.7	* 2.5	* 63.2	34.35
	2017	7 412	* 565	* 185	* 4 617	* 7.6	* 2.5	* 62.3	34.35
	2019	...	...	...	...	...	...	...	34.35
Papua New Guinea Papouasie-Nvl-Guinée	2005	* 45 286	* 240	* 600	33 586	* 0.5	* 1.3	* 74.2	6.88
	2010	* 45 286	* 300	* 700	33 573	* 0.7	* 1.5	* 74.1	6.88
	2017	* 45 286	* 300	* 700	* 33 559	* 0.7	* 1.5	* 74.1	6.88
	2019	...	...	...	...	...	...	...	6.88
Paraguay Paraguay	2005	* 39 730	* 3 460	* 100	18 475	* 8.7	* 0.3	* 46.5	30.41
	2010	* 39 730	* 4 145	* 85	16 950	* 10.4	* 0.2	* 42.7	36.16
	2017	* 39 730	* 4 864	* 85	* 15 323	* 12.2	* 0.2	* 38.6	36.25
	2019	...	...	...	...	...	...	...	36.25
Peru Pérou	2005	* 128 000	* 3 930	* 1 090	75 528	* 3.1	* 0.9	* 59.0	21.58
	2010	* 128 000	* 4 085	* 1 307	74 811	* 3.2	* 1.0	* 58.4	26.49
	2017	* 128 000	* 3 488	* 1 379	* 73 973	* 2.7	* 1.1	* 57.8	28.24
	2019	...	...	...	...	...	...	...	29.09
Philippines Philippines	2005	29 817	* 5 005	* 4 850	7 074	* 16.8	* 16.3	23.7	37.26
	2010	29 817	* 5 300	* 5 300	6 840	* 17.8	* 17.8	22.9	39.86
	2017	* 29 817	* 5 590	* 5 350	* 8 040	* 18.7	* 17.9	* 27.0	40.13
	2019	...	...	...	...	...	...	...	40.13
Pitcairn Pitcairn	2005	5	...	...	* 4	...	...	* 74.5	...
	2010	5	...	...	* 4	...	...	* 74.5	...
	2017	5	...	...	* 4	...	...	* 74.5	...
Poland Pologne	2005	30 633	12 141	378	9 200	39.6	1.2	30.0	70.40
	2010	30 628	10 829	390	9 329	35.4	1.3	30.5	86.50
	2017	30 619	10 907	384	* 9 435	35.6	1.3	* 30.8	87.34
	2019	...	...	...	...	...	...	...	87.35
Portugal Portugal	2005	* 9 147	1 305	749	3 296	* 14.3	* 8.2	* 36.0	58.05
	2010	* 9 159	1 148	714	3 239	* 12.5	* 7.8	* 35.4	70.64
	2017	* 9 161	941	768	* 3 182	* 10.3	* 8.4	* 34.7	73.11
	2019	...	...	...	...	...	...	...	73.27
Puerto Rico Porto Rico	2005	887	* 66	* 37	463	* 7.5	* 4.2	52.2	32.83
	2010	* 887	* 70	* 37	479	* 7.9	* 4.2	* 54.0	32.83
	2017	* 887	* 70	* 37	* 496	* 7.9	* 4.2	* 55.9	32.83
	2019	...	...	...	...	...	...	...	32.83

Region, country or area Région, pays ou zone	Year Année	Area – Superficie ('000 hectares)				Area – Superficie (Percent of total)&			Sites protected for terrestrial biodiversity Sites pour la bio. terre. dans aires protég. (%)&&
		Total land Superficie totale	Arable land Terres arables	Permanent crops Cultures permanentes	Forest cover Superficie forestière	Arable land Terres arables	Permanent crops Cultures Permanentes	Forest cover Superficie forestière	
Qatar	2005	1 161	* 12	3	* 0	* 1.0	0.2	* 0.0	39.97
Qatar	2010	1 161	* 14	3	* 0	* 1.2	0.2	* 0.0	39.97
	2017	1 149	* 14	3	* 0	* 1.2	0.3	* 0.0	39.97
	2019	...	...	...	...	...	...	...	39.97
Republic of Korea	2005	9 685	1 643	181	6 255	17.0	1.9	64.6	26.40
République de Corée	2010	* 9 720	* 1 507	208	6 222	* 15.5	* 2.1	* 64.0	33.79
	2017	* 9 751	* 1 397	224	* 6 184	* 14.3	* 2.3	* 63.4	36.52
	2019	...	...	...	...	...	...	...	37.48
Republic of Moldova	2005	3 289	1 833	302	* 363	55.7	9.2	* 11.0	0.00
République de Moldova	2010	3 285	1 813	299	* 386	55.2	9.1	* 11.8	0.00
	2017	3 289	1 738	237	* 409	52.8	7.2	* 12.4	0.00
	2019	...	...	...	...	...	...	...	0.00
Réunion	2005	* 250	35	3	85	* 14.0	* 1.2	* 34.0	0.86
Réunion	2010	* 250	35	3	88	* 14.1	* 1.2	* 35.2	47.09
	2017	* 251	34	3	* 88	* 13.6	* 1.2	* 35.1	47.09
	2019	...	...	...	...	...	...	...	47.09
Romania	2005	22 998	8 985	510	6 391	39.1	2.2	27.8	17.17
Roumanie	2010	23 005	9 146	463	6 515	39.8	2.0	28.3	65.03
	2017	23 008	8 543	415	* 6 861	37.1	1.8	* 29.8	76.02
	2019	...	...	...	...	...	...	...	76.02
Russian Federation Fédération de Russie	2005	1 638 139 *	121 781	1 800	808 790	7.4	0.1	49.4	24.96
	2010	1 637 687 *	* 121 649	* 1 650	815 136	* 7.4	* 0.1	* 49.8	25.09
	2017	1 637 687	* 121 649	* 1 600	* 814 931	* 7.4	* 0.1	* 49.8	25.12
	2019	...	...	...	...	...	...	...	25.12
Rwanda	2005	* 2 467	* 1 083	* 250	385	* 43.9	* 10.1	* 15.6	51.69
Rwanda	2010	* 2 467	* 1 124	* 250	446	* 45.6	* 10.1	* 18.1	51.69
	2017	* 2 467	* 1 152	* 250	* 480	* 46.7	* 10.1	* 19.5	51.69
	2019	...	...	...	...	...	...	...	51.69
Saint Helena	2005	39	* 4	...	* 2	* 10.3	...	* 5.1	...
Sainte-Hélène	*2010	39	4	...	2	10.3	...	5.1	...
	*2017	39	4	...	2	10.3	...	5.1	...
Saint Kitts and Nevis	2005	26	4	~0	11	15.3	0.1	42.3	0.00
Saint-Kitts-et-Nevis	2010	26	5	~0	11	17.3	0.4	42.3	22.35
	2017	26	* 5	* ~0	* 11	* 19.2	* 0.4	* 42.3	56.82
	2019	...	...	...	...	...	...	...	56.82
Saint Lucia	2005	* 61	* 2	* 8	21	* 3.6	* 12.6	* 34.3	32.57
Sainte-Lucie	2010	* 61	* 3	* 7	21	* 4.9	* 11.5	* 33.8	45.56
	2017	* 61	* 3	* 7	* 20	* 4.9	* 11.5	* 33.3	45.56
	2019	...	...	...	...	...	...	...	45.56
Saint Pierre and Miquelon	2005	* 23	* 3	...	3	* 13.0	...	* 13.0	...
Saint-Pierre-et-Miquelon	2010	* 23	* 3	...	3	* 13.0	...	* 12.6	...
	*2017	23	2	...	3	8.7	...	12.2	
Saint Vincent & Grenadines	2005	39	* 5	* 3	* 26	* 12.8	* 7.7	* 66.7	42.97
Saint-Vincent-Grenadines	2010	39	* 5	* 3	* 27	* 12.8	* 7.7	* 69.2	42.97
	2017	39	* 5	* 3	* 27	* 12.8	* 7.7	* 69.2	42.97
	2019	...	...	...	...	...	...	...	42.97
Samoa	2005	* 283	* 11	* 27	* 171	* 3.9	* 9.5	* 60.4	8.33
Samoa	2010	* 283	* 8	* 22	* 171	* 2.8	* 7.8	* 60.4	8.33
	2017	* 283	* 8	* 22	* 171	* 2.8	* 7.8	* 60.4	13.69
	2019	...	...	...	...	...	...	...	13.69
San Marino	2005	6	* 1	...	* 0	* 16.7	...	* 0.0	...
Saint-Marin	2010	6	* 1	...	* 0	* 16.7	...	* 0.0	...
	2017	6	* 1	...	* 0	* 16.7	...	* 0.0	...
Sao Tome and Principe	2005	* 96	* 7	* 40	56	* 7.3	* 41.7	* 58.3	0.00
Sao Tomé-et-Principe	2010	* 96	* 6	* 39	54	* 6.3	* 40.6	* 55.8	79.55
	2017	* 96	* 4	* 39	* 54	* 4.2	* 40.6	* 55.8	79.55
	2019	...	...	...	...	...	...	...	79.55

Land *(continued)*
Thousand hectares and percent of total land

Terres *(suite)*
Milliers d'hectares et pourcentage de la superficie totale

Region, country or area / Région, pays ou zone	Year / Année	Area – Superficie ('000 hectares)				Area – Superficie (Percent of total)&			Sites protected for terrestrial biodiversity / Sites pour la bio. terre. dans aires protég. (%)&&
		Total land Superficie totale	Arable land Terres arables	Permanent crops Cultures permanentes	Forest cover Superficie forestière	Arable land Terres arables	Permanent crops Cultures Permanentes	Forest cover Superficie forestière	
Saudi Arabia	2005	214 969	* 3 500	217	* 977	* 1.6	0.1	* 0.5	21.98
Arabie saoudite	2010	214 969	* 3 180	226	* 977	* 1.5	0.1	* 0.5	21.98
	2017	214 969	* 3 466	146	* 977	* 1.6	0.1	* 0.5	21.98
	2019	...	...	...	...	...	...	...	21.98
Senegal	2005	* 19 253	* 3 126	* 50	8 673	* 16.2	* 0.3	* 45.0	31.49
Sénégal	2010	* 19 253	* 3 800	* 58	8 473	* 19.7	* 0.3	* 44.0	31.49
	2017	* 19 253	* 3 200	* 78	* 8 273	* 16.6	* 0.4	* 43.0	37.83
	2019	...	...	...	...	...	...	...	37.83
Serbia	2005	...	...	...	...	...	...	...	20.82
Serbie	2010	* 8 746	2 654	190	2 713	* 30.3	* 2.2	* 31.0	22.32
	2017	* 8 746	2 595	208	* 2 720	* 29.7	* 2.4	* 31.1	26.13
	2019	...	...	...	...	...	...	...	26.13
Serbia and Monten. [former] Serbie-et-Monténégro [anc.]	2005	* 10 200	* 3 505	* 317	3 102	* 34.4	* 3.1	30.4	...
Seychelles	2005	46	* 1	* 3	41	* 2.2	* 6.5	88.4	28.57
Seychelles	2010	* 46	* 1	* 2	41	* 2.0	* 3.3	* 88.4	28.57
	2017	* 46	* ~0	* 1	* 41	* 0.3	* 3.0	* 88.4	28.57
	2019	...	...	...	...	...	...	...	28.57
Sierra Leone	2005	* 7 218	* 1 472	* 140	2 824	* 20.4	* 1.9	* 39.1	46.13
Sierra Leone	2010	* 7 218	* 1 580	* 150	2 726	* 21.9	* 2.1	* 37.8	55.11
	2017	* 7 218	* 1 584	* 165	* 3 044	* 21.9	* 2.3	* 42.2	57.26
	2019	...	...	...	...	...	...	...	57.26
Singapore	2005	* 69	* 1	* ~0	16	* 1.0	* 0.1	* 23.7	21.14
Singapour	2010	* 70	* 1	* ~0	16	* 0.9	* 0.1	* 23.3	21.14
	2017	* 71	* 1	* ~0	* 16	* 0.8	* 0.1	* 23.1	21.14
	2019	...	...	...	...	...	...	...	21.14
Sint Maarten (Dutch part)	2005	...	...	...	...	...	...	...	5.10
St-Martin (partie néerland.)	2010	...	...	...	...	...	...	...	5.10
	2019	...	...	...	...	...	...	...	5.10
Slovakia	2005	4 810	1 391	26	1 932	28.9	0.5	40.2	77.60
Slovaquie	2010	4 809	1 392	25	1 939	28.9	0.5	40.3	77.60
	2017	4 808	1 343	18	* 1 940	27.9	0.4	* 40.3	85.79
	2019	...	...	...	...	...	...	...	85.79
Slovenia	2005	2 014	176	28	1 243	8.7	1.4	61.7	86.10
Slovénie	2010	2 015	185	52	1 247	9.2	2.6	61.9	86.11
	2017	2 013	184	54	* 1 248	9.1	2.7	* 62.0	88.70
	2019	...	...	...	...	...	...	...	88.70
Solomon Islands	2005	* 2 799	* 16	* 65	* 2 241	* 0.6	* 2.3	* 80.1	3.37
Îles Salomon	2010	* 2 799	* 19	* 80	* 2 213	* 0.7	* 2.9	* 79.1	4.43
	2017	* 2 799	* 20	* 80	* 2 185	* 0.7	* 2.9	* 78.1	4.43
	2019	...	...	...	...	...	...	...	4.43
Somalia	2005	* 62 734	* 1 350	* 27	7 131	* 2.2	* ~0.0	* 11.4	0.00
Somalie	2010	* 62 734	* 1 100	* 28	6 747	* 1.8	* ~0.0	* 10.8	0.00
	2017	* 62 734	* 1 100	* 25	* 6 363	* 1.8	* ~0.0	* 10.1	0.00
	2019	...	...	...	...	...	...	...	0.00
South Africa	2005	121 309	* 13 175	* 380	9 241	* 10.9	* 0.3	7.6	28.31
Afrique du Sud	2010	121 309	12 533	430	9 241	10.3	0.4	7.6	28.96
	2017	* 121 309	* 12 000	* 413	* 9 241	* 9.9	* 0.3	* 7.6	31.17
	2019	...	...	...	...	...	...	...	32.51
South Sudan	2005	...	...	...	...	...	...	...	29.85
Soudan du sud	2010	...	...	...	...	...	...	...	33.60
	2017	...	...	...	* 7 157	...	...	...	33.60
	2019	...	...	...	...	...	...	...	33.60
Spain	2005	49 909	12 913	4 931	17 282	25.9	9.9	34.6	52.75
Espagne	2010	50 001	12 528	4 693	18 247	25.1	9.4	36.5	54.62
	2017	49 955	12 254	4 731	* 18 418	24.5	9.5	* 36.9	57.59
	2019	...	...	...	...	...	...	...	57.59
Sri Lanka	2005	6 271	* 1 100	* 970	2 118	* 17.5	* 15.5	33.8	36.85
Sri Lanka	2010	6 271	* 1 200	* 980	2 103	* 19.1	* 15.6	33.5	41.11
	2017	6 271	* 1 300	* 1 000	* 2 070	* 20.7	* 15.9	* 33.0	43.69
	2019	...	...	...	...	...	...	...	43.69

Land *(continued)*
Thousand hectares and percent of total land

Terres *(suite)*
Milliers d'hectares et pourcentage de la superficie totale

Region, country or area Région, pays ou zone	Year Année	Area – Superficie ('000 hectares)				Area – Superficie (Percent of total)&			Sites protected for terre-strial biodiversity Sites pour la bio. terre. dans aires protég. (%)&&
		Total land Superficie totale	Arable land Terres arables	Permanent crops Cultures permanentes	Forest cover Superficie forestière	Arable land Terres arables	Permanent crops Cultures Permanentes	Forest cover Superficie forestière	
State of Palestine État de Palestine	2005	602	* 99	115	* 9	* 16.4	19.1	* 1.5	12.49
	2010	602	44	54	9	7.3	9.0	* 1.5	16.83
	2017	602	* 51	* 96	* 9	* 8.4	* 16.0	* 1.5	24.39
	2019	...	...	...	...	...	...	...	24.40
Sudan Soudan	2005	...	...	...	...	...	...	...	9.09
	2010	...	...	...	...	...	...	...	9.09
	2017	...	* 19 823	* 168	* 19 210	...	...	...	17.81
	2019	...	...	...	...	...	...	...	17.81
Sudan [former] Soudan [anc.]	2005	237 600	18 750	* 130	28 111	7.9	* 0.1	11.8	...
	2010	237 600	19 878	142	27 239	8.4	0.1	11.5	...
Suriname Suriname	2005	* 15 600	49	* 6	15 371	* 0.3	* ~0.0	* 98.5	51.19
	2010	* 15 600	55	6	15 351	* 0.4	* ~0.0	* 98.4	51.19
	2017	* 15 600	* 65	* 6	* 15 332	* 0.4	* ~0.0	* 98.3	51.19
	2019	...	...	...	...	...	...	...	51.19
Sweden Suède	2005	41 034	* 2 698	* 5	28 218	* 6.6	* ~0.0	68.8	54.99
	2010	41 034	* 2 629	* 5	28 073	* 6.4	* ~0.0	68.4	57.24
	2017	40 731	* 2 563	* 5	* 28 073	* 6.3	* ~0.0	* 68.9	58.75
	2019	...	...	...	...	...	...	...	59.03
Switzerland Suisse	2005	3 952	406	23	1 217	10.3	0.6	30.8	28.74
	2010	3 952	405	24	1 235	10.2	0.6	31.3	35.29
	2017	3 952	398	25	* 1 254	10.1	0.6	* 31.7	35.48
	2019	...	...	...	...	...	...	...	35.48
Syrian Arab Republic République arabe syrienne	2005	18 357	4 675	887	* 461	25.5	4.8	* 2.5	0.00
	2010	18 363	4 687	1 009	* 491	25.5	5.5	* 2.7	0.00
	2017	* 18 363	* 4 662	* 1 071	* 491	* 25.4	* 5.8	* 2.7	0.00
	2019	...	...	...	...	...	...	...	0.00
Tajikistan Tadjikistan	2005	13 996	* 757	117	410	* 5.4	0.8	2.9	15.77
	2010	* 13 996	* 747	* 134	410	* 5.3	* 1.0	* 2.9	15.77
	2017	* 13 879	* 720	148	* 412	* 5.2	* 1.1	* 3.0	16.81
	2019	...	...	...	...	...	...	...	16.81
Thailand Thaïlande	2005	* 51 089	* 15 200	* 3 610	16 100	* 29.8	* 7.1	* 31.5	67.01
	2010	* 51 089	* 15 760	* 4 500	16 249	* 30.8	* 8.8	* 31.8	70.73
	2017	* 51 089	* 16 810	* 4 500	* 16 399	* 32.9	* 8.8	* 32.1	70.73
	2019	...	...	...	...	...	...	...	70.73
Timor-Leste Timor-Leste	2005	1 487	* 170	* 65	* 798	* 11.4	* 4.4	* 53.7	14.46
	2010	* 1 487	* 150	* 72	* 742	* 10.1	* 4.8	* 49.9	34.01
	2017	* 1 487	* 155	* 75	* 686	* 10.4	* 5.0	* 46.1	39.49
	2019	...	...	...	...	...	...	...	39.49
Togo Togo	2005	* 5 439	* 2 100	* 150	386	* 38.6	* 2.8	* 7.1	75.00
	2010	* 5 439	* 2 460	* 205	287	* 45.2	* 3.8	* 5.3	75.00
	2017	* 5 439	* 2 650	* 170	* 188	* 48.7	* 3.1	* 3.5	75.00
	2019	...	...	...	...	...	...	...	75.00
Tokelau Tokélaou	2005	1	...	* 1	* 0	...	* 60.0	* 0.0	0.00
	2010	1	...	* 1	* 0	...	* 60.0	* 0.0	0.00
	2017	1	...	* 1	* 0	...	* 60.0	* 0.0	0.00
	2019	...	...	...	...	...	...	...	0.00
Tonga Tonga	2005	* 72	* 15	* 11	9	* 20.8	* 15.3	* 12.5	25.12
	2010	72	* 17	* 11	9	* 23.6	* 15.3	12.5	26.07
	2017	72	* 18	* 11	* 9	* 25.0	* 15.3	* 12.5	26.07
	2019	...	...	...	...	...	...	...	26.07
Trinidad and Tobago Trinité-et-Tobago	2005	513	* 25	* 22	230	* 4.9	* 4.3	44.8	32.00
	2010	513	* 25	* 22	226	* 4.9	* 4.3	44.1	32.00
	2017	513	* 25	* 22	* 234	* 4.9	* 4.3	* 45.7	32.00
	2019	...	...	...	...	...	...	...	32.00
Tunisia Tunisie	2005	15 536	2 730	2 166	915	17.6	13.9	5.9	16.80
	2010	15 536	2 823	2 363	990	18.2	15.2	6.4	24.82
	2017	* 15 536	2 607	2 386	* 1 041	* 16.8	* 15.4	* 6.7	40.09
	2019	...	...	...	...	...	...	...	40.09

Region, country or area Région, pays ou zone	Year Année	Area – Superficie ('000 hectares)				Area – Superficie (Percent of total)&			Sites protected for terre-strial biodiversity Sites pour la bio. terre. dans aires protég. (%)&&
		Total land Superficie totale	Arable land Terres arables	Permanent crops Cultures permanentes	Forest cover Superficie forestière	Arable land Terres arables	Permanent crops Cultures Permanentes	Forest cover Superficie forestière	
Turkey	2005	76 963	23 830	2 776	10 662	31.0	3.6	13.9	2.28
Turquie	2010	76 963	21 384	3 011	11 203	27.8	3.9	14.6	2.28
	2017	76 963	20 036	3 348	* 11 715	26.0	4.4	* 15.2	2.34
	2019	...	...	...	...	...	...	...	2.34
Turkmenistan	2005	* 46 993	* 2 040	* 60	* 4 127	* 4.3	* 0.1	* 8.8	14.04
Turkménistan	2010	* 46 993	* 1 940	* 60	* 4 127	* 4.1	* 0.1	* 8.8	14.04
	2017	* 46 993	* 1 940	* 60	* 4 127	* 4.1	* 0.1	* 8.8	14.04
	2019	...	...	...	...	...	...	...	14.04
Turks and Caicos Islands	2005	95	* 1	...	* 34	* 1.1	...	* 36.2	27.94
Îles Turques-et-Caïques	2010	95	* 1	...	* 34	* 1.1	...	* 36.2	27.94
	2017	95	* 1	...	* 34	* 1.1	...	* 36.2	27.94
	2019	...	...	...	...	...	...	...	27.94
Tuvalu	2005	3	...	* 2	* 1	...	* 56.7	* 33.3	...
Tuvalu	2010	3	...	* 2	* 1	...	* 60.0	* 33.3	...
	2017	3	...	* 2	* 1	...	* 60.0	* 33.3	...
Uganda	2005	19 981	* 5 950	* 2 200	3 429	* 29.8	* 11.0	17.2	64.37
Ouganda	2010	20 052	* 6 750	* 2 200	2 753	* 33.7	* 11.0	13.7	70.61
	2017	* 20 052	* 6 900	* 2 200	* 2 077	* 34.4	* 11.0	* 10.4	70.61
	2019	...	...	...	...	...	...	...	70.61
Ukraine	2005	57 938	32 452	901	9 575	56.0	1.6	16.5	21.28
Ukraine	2010	57 932	32 477	897	9 548	56.1	1.5	16.5	21.35
	2017	57 930	32 774	895	* 9 657	56.6	1.5	* 16.7	21.72
	2019	...	...	...	...	...	...	...	21.72
United Arab Emirates	2005	7 102	* 68	189	* 312	* 1.0	2.7	* 4.4	...
Émirats arabes unis	2010	7 102	51	42	* 317	0.7	0.6	* 4.5	...
	2017	7 102	45	39	* 323	0.6	0.6	* 4.5	...
United Kingdom	2005	24 193	5 729	47	3 021	23.7	0.2	12.5	78.46
Royaume-Uni	2010	24 193	5 970	46	3 059	24.7	0.2	12.6	80.76
	2017	24 193	6 083	48	* 3 144	25.1	0.2	* 13.0	82.67
	2019	...	...	...	...	...	...	...	82.76
United Rep. of Tanzania	2005	88 580	* 9 700	* 1 660	49 920	* 11.0	* 1.9	56.4	60.24
Rép.-Unie de Tanzanie	2010	* 88 580	* 11 600	* 1 850	47 920	* 13.1	* 2.1	* 54.1	62.95
	2017	* 88 580	* 13 500	* 2 150	* 46 060	* 15.2	* 2.4	* 52.0	62.95
	2019	...	...	...	...	...	...	...	62.95
United States of America	2005	916 192	* 166 271	* 2 700	304 757	* 18.1	* 0.3	33.3	43.27
États-Unis d'Amérique	2010	914 742	* 157 817	* 2 600	308 720	* 17.3	* 0.3	33.7	49.43
	2017	* 914 742	* 157 837	* 2 600	* 310 095	* 17.3	* 0.3	* 33.9	51.21
	2019	...	...	...	...	...	...	...	51.21
United States Virgin Islands	2005	35	* 2	* 1	19	* 5.7	* 2.9	53.5	39.88
Îles Vierges américaines	2010	35	* 1	* 1	18	* 2.9	* 2.9	51.9	39.88
	2017	35	* 1	* 1	* 18	* 2.9	* 2.9	* 50.3	39.88
	2019	...	...	...	...	...	...	...	39.88
Uruguay	2005	17 502	* 1 392	* 40	1 522	* 8.0	* 0.2	8.7	10.37
Uruguay	2010	17 502	* 2 033	38	1 731	* 11.6	0.2	9.9	20.72
	2017	17 502	* 2 430	* 39	* 1 845	* 13.9	* 0.2	* 10.5	20.80
	2019	...	...	...	...	...	...	...	20.80
Uzbekistan	2005	42 540	* 4 367	* 349	3 295	* 10.3	* 0.8	7.7	10.11
Ouzbékistan	2010	* 42 540	* 4 172	* 359	3 276	* 9.8	* 0.8	* 7.7	10.11
	2017	* 42 540	4 026	392	* 3 220	* 9.5	* 0.9	* 7.6	10.11
	2019	...	...	...	...	...	...	...	10.11
Vanuatu	2005	* 1 219	* 20	* 121	* 440	* 1.6	* 9.9	* 36.1	2.84
Vanuatu	2010	* 1 219	* 20	* 125	* 440	* 1.6	* 10.3	* 36.1	2.84
	2017	* 1 219	* 20	* 125	* 440	* 1.6	* 10.3	* 36.1	2.84
	2019	...	...	...	...	...	...	...	2.84
Venezuela (Boliv. Rep. of)	2005	* 88 205	* 2 655	* 700	47 713	* 3.0	* 0.8	* 54.1	52.54
Venezuela (Rép. boliv. du)	2010	* 88 205	* 2 600	* 700	47 505	* 2.9	* 0.8	* 53.9	52.54
	2017	* 88 205	* 2 600	* 700	* 46 683	* 2.9	* 0.8	* 52.9	52.54
	2019	...	...	...	...	...	...	...	52.54

Region, country or area / Région, pays ou zone	Year / Année	Area – Superficie ('000 hectares)				Area – Superficie (Percent of total)&			Sites protected for terrestrial biodiversity / Sites pour la bio. terre. dans aires protég. (%)&&
		Total land / Superficie totale	Arable land / Terres arables	Permanent crops / Cultures permanentes	Forest cover / Superficie forestière	Arable land / Terres arables	Permanent crops / Cultures Permanentes	Forest cover / Superficie forestière	
Viet Nam	2005	* 31 007	6 358	3 054	13 077	* 20.5	* 9.8	* 42.2	27.59
Viet Nam	2010	* 31 007	6 437	3 681	14 128	* 20.8	* 11.9	* 45.6	30.30
	2017	* 31 007	6 988	4 539	* 14 773	* 22.5	* 14.6	* 47.6	39.16
	2019	...	...	...	...	...	...	...	39.16
Wallis and Futuna Islands	2005	14	* 1	* 5	6	* 7.1	* 35.7	41.5	...
Îles Wallis-et-Futuna	2010	14	* 1	* 5	6	* 7.1	* 35.7	41.6	...
	2017	14	* 1	* 5	* 6	* 7.1	* 35.7	* 41.6	...
Western Sahara	2005	26 600	* 4	...	* 707	* ~0.0	...	* 2.7	...
Sahara occidental	2010	26 600	* 4	...	* 707	* ~0.0	...	* 2.7	...
	2017	26 600	* 4	...	* 707	* ~0.0	...	* 2.7	...
Yemen	2005	52 797	* 1 287	236	* 549	* 2.4	0.4	* 1.0	0.00
Yémen	2010	* 52 797	* 1 291	288	* 549	* 2.4	* 0.5	* 1.0	19.44
	2017	* 52 797	* 1 098	* 290	* 549	* 2.1	* 0.5	* 1.0	19.44
	2019	...	...	...	...	...	...	...	19.44
Zambia	2005	74 339	* 2 727	* 35	50 301	* 3.7	* ~0.0	67.7	45.48
Zambie	2010	* 74 339	* 3 400	* 36	49 468	* 4.6	* ~0.0	* 66.5	45.48
	2017	* 74 339	* 3 800	* 36	* 48 635	* 5.1	* ~0.0	* 65.4	45.48
	2019	...	...	...	...	...	...	...	45.48
Zimbabwe	2005	* 38 685	* 3 900	* 100	17 259	* 10.1	* 0.3	* 44.6	76.11
Zimbabwe	2010	* 38 685	* 4 000	* 100	15 624	* 10.3	* 0.3	* 40.4	76.11
	2017	* 38 685	* 4 000	* 100	* 14 062	* 10.3	* 0.3	* 36.4	81.22
	2019	...	...	...	...	...	...	...	81.22

Source:

Food and Agriculture Organization of the United Nations (FAO), Rome, FAOSTAT data last accessed January 2020.
United Nations Environment Programme (UNEP) World Conservation Monitoring Centre (WCMC) and World Conservation Union (IUCN) and BirdLife International, Cambridge, Sustainable Development Goals database, March 2020.

& Figures calculated by the United Nations Statistics Division. && Based on spatial overlap between polygons for Key Biodiversity Areas from the World Database of Key Biodiveristy Areas and polygons for protected areas from the World Database on Protected Areas.

1 Calculated by the UN Statistics Division.

Source:

Organisation des Nations Unies pour l'alimentation et l'agriculture (FAO), Rome, base de données FAOSTAT, dernier accès janvier 2020.
Le Programme des Nations Unies pour l'environnement (PNUE) Le Centre mondial de surveillance de la conservation (CMSC) et l'Union mondiale pour la nature (IUCN) et BirdLife International, Cambridge, base de données sur les Objectifs de développement durable (ODD), mars 2020.

& Chiffres calculés par la Division de statistique des Nations Unies. && basées sur un chevauchement spatial entre les zones clés pour la biodiversité de la base de données mondiale pour les zones clés pour la biodiversité et les polygones pour les zones protégées de la base de données mondiale sur les zones protégées.

1 Calculés par la Division de statistique des Nations Unies.

23

Threatened species
Number of species by taxonomic group

Espèces menacées
Nombre d'espèces menacées par groupe taxonomique

Country or area &	2004	2010	2016	2017	2018	2019	2020	Pays ou zone &
Afghanistan								**Afghanistan**
Vertebrates	31	31	35	35	34	33	33	Vertébrés
Invertebrates	1	1	2	2	2	2	2	Invertébrés
Plants	1	2	5	5	5	5	5	Plantes
Total	33	34	42	42	41	40	40	Total
Åland Islands								**Îles d'Åland**
Vertebrates	...	...	...	...	...	...	0	Vertébrés
Invertebrates	...	...	...	...	...	...	0	Invertébrés
Plants	...	...	...	...	...	...	1	Plantes
Total	...	...	...	...	...	...	1	Total
Albania								**Albanie**
Vertebrates	33	53	63	62	62	61	64	Vertébrés
Invertebrates	4	47	62	68	71	71	73	Invertébrés
Plants	0	0	0	0	4	5	5	Plantes
Total	37	100	125	130	137	137	142	Total
Algeria								**Algérie**
Vertebrates	36	69	78	79	80	81	85	Vertébrés
Invertebrates	12	21	29	38	40	40	42	Invertébrés
Plants	2	15	18	18	23	24	28	Plantes
Total	50	105	125	135	143	145	155	Total
American Samoa								**Samoa américaines**
Vertebrates	18	21	27	27	27	29	32	Vertébrés
Invertebrates	5	57	64	64	64	65	65	Invertébrés
Plants	1	1	1	1	1	1	2	Plantes
Total	24	79	92	92	92	95	99	Total
Andorra								**Andorre**
Vertebrates	1	4	5	5	6	6	6	Vertébrés
Invertebrates	4	4	7	8	8	8	8	Invertébrés
Plants	0	0	0	0	0	1	1	Plantes
Total	5	8	12	13	14	15	15	Total
Angola								**Angola**
Vertebrates	44	77	99	103	108	111	117	Vertébrés
Invertebrates	6	7	9	9	11	11	11	Invertébrés
Plants	26	33	34	34	35	36	43	Plantes
Total	76	117	142	146	154	158	171	Total
Anguilla								**Anguilla**
Vertebrates	15	20	38	38	40	43	47	Vertébrés
Invertebrates	0	10	10	10	10	10	10	Invertébrés
Plants	3	3	4	4	4	4	3	Plantes
Total	18	33	52	52	54	57	60	Total
Antarctica								**Antarctique**
Vertebrates	8	6	6	6	6	6	6	Vertébrés
Invertebrates	0	0	0	0	0	0	0	Invertébrés
Plants	0	0	0	0	0	0	0	Plantes
Total	8	6	6	6	6	6	6	Total
Antigua and Barbuda								**Antigua-et-Barbuda**
Vertebrates	18	23	38	40	41	44	47	Vertébrés
Invertebrates	0	11	11	11	11	11	11	Invertébrés
Plants	4	4	4	4	4	4	3	Plantes
Total	22	38	53	55	56	59	61	Total
Areas n.e.s								**Zones n.s.a**
Vertebrates	1	1	3	3	5	7	...	Vertébrés
Invertebrates	0	0	1	1	1	1	...	Invertébrés
Plants	0	0	0	0	0	...	...	Plantes
Total	1	1	4	4	6	8	...	Total
Argentina								**Argentine**
Vertebrates	134	157	172	172	186	190	194	Vertébrés
Invertebrates	10	12	14	14	14	14	15	Invertébrés
Plants	42	44	70	70	70	75	76	Plantes
Total	186	213	256	256	270	279	285	Total
Armenia								**Arménie**
Vertebrates	27	29	34	34	33	34	34	Vertébrés
Invertebrates	7	6	9	9	9	9	9	Invertébrés
Plants	1	1	71	71	73	76	76	Plantes
Total	35	36	114	114	115	119	119	Total

Country or area [&]	2004	2010	2016	2017	2018	2019	2020	Pays ou zone [&]
Aruba								**Aruba**
Vertebrates	17	20	28	28	28	33	37	Vertébrés
Invertebrates	1	1	2	2	2	2	2	Invertébrés
Plants	0	1	2	2	2	3	5	Plantes
Total	18	22	32	32	32	38	44	Total
Australia								**Australie**
Vertebrates	282[1]	297[1]	319[1]	323[1]	358[1]	363	433	Vertébrés
Invertebrates	283[1]	489[1]	514[1]	531[1]	534[1]	545	548	Invertébrés
Plants	56[1]	67[1]	# 93[1]	94[1]	106[1]	108	327	Plantes
Total	621[1]	853[1]	926[1]	948[1]	998[1]	1 016	1 308	Total
Austria								**Autriche**
Vertebrates	20	23	27	26	28	28	28	Vertébrés
Invertebrates	44	55	69	71	74	74	74	Invertébrés
Plants	3	4	# 21	21	25	68	83	Plantes
Total	67	82	117	118	127	170	185	Total
Azerbaijan								**Azerbaïdjan**
Vertebrates	32	41	47	48	47	49	49	Vertébrés
Invertebrates	6	4	7	7	7	7	7	Invertébrés
Plants	0	0	42	42	43	45	46	Plantes
Total	38	45	96	97	97	101	102	Total
Bahamas								**Bahamas**
Vertebrates	36	44	65	66	71	71	72	Vertébrés
Invertebrates	1	11	12	12	12	12	12	Invertébrés
Plants	5	7	8	8	7	12	12	Plantes
Total	42	62	85	86	90	95	96	Total
Bahrain								**Bahreïn**
Vertebrates	18	19	23	23	27	33	34	Vertébrés
Invertebrates	0	13	13	13	13	13	13	Invertébrés
Plants	0	0	0	0	0	0	0	Plantes
Total	18	32	36	36	40	46	47	Total
Bangladesh								**Bangladesh**
Vertebrates	73	104	120	123	125	128	133	Vertébrés
Invertebrates	0	2	7	7	7	7	7	Invertébrés
Plants	12	16	21	21	22	23	25	Plantes
Total	85	122	148	151	154	158	165	Total
Barbados								**Barbade**
Vertebrates	18	24	39	42	43	44	48	Vertébrés
Invertebrates	0	10	11	11	11	11	11	Invertébrés
Plants	2	2	3	3	3	3	3	Plantes
Total	20	36	53	56	57	58	62	Total
Belarus								**Bélarus**
Vertebrates	10	10	14	15	15	15	15	Vertébrés
Invertebrates	8	6	9	9	10	10	10	Invertébrés
Plants	0	0	1	1	1	3	5	Plantes
Total	18	16	24	25	26	28	30	Total
Belgium								**Belgique**
Vertebrates	25	15	23	22	23	23	25	Vertébrés
Invertebrates	11	11	14	14	15	15	15	Invertébrés
Plants	0	1	# 1	1	1	17	26	Plantes
Total	36	27	38	37	39	55	66	Total
Belize								**Belize**
Vertebrates	36	48	70	69	69	73	78	Vertébrés
Invertebrates	1	12	12	12	12	12	12	Invertébrés
Plants	30	32	36	36	43	46	53	Plantes
Total	67	92	118	117	124	131	143	Total
Benin								**Bénin**
Vertebrates	17	47	66	68	70	77	82	Vertébrés
Invertebrates	0	1	3	3	3	3	3	Invertébrés
Plants	14	14	17	17	19	21	21	Plantes
Total	31	62	86	88	92	101	106	Total
Bermuda								**Bermudes**
Vertebrates	18	18	35	36	36	39	42	Vertébrés
Invertebrates	25	28	28	28	28	28	30	Invertébrés
Plants	4	4	8	8	8	8	8	Plantes
Total	47	50	71	72	72	75	80	Total

Country or area [&]	2004	2010	2016	2017	2018	2019	2020	Pays ou zone [&]
Bhutan								**Bhoutan**
Vertebrates	40	50	54	52	51	55	55	Vertébrés
Invertebrates	1	1	1	1	1	1	1	Invertébrés
Plants	7	8	18	18	43	43	45	Plantes
Total	48	59	73	71	95	99	101	Total
Bolivia (Plurin. State of)								**Bolivie (État plurin. de)**
Vertebrates	79	90	124	124	129	129	131	Vertébrés
Invertebrates	1	1	3	3	3	3	3	Invertébrés
Plants	70	72	104	104	104	112	162	Plantes
Total	150	163	231	231	236	244	296	Total
Bonaire, St. Eustatius & Saba								**Bonaire, St-Eustache et Saba**
Vertebrates	...	...	42	42	42	44	50	Vertébrés
Invertebrates	...	...	11	11	11	11	11	Invertébrés
Plants	...	...	3	3	3	3	6	Plantes
Total	...	...	56	56	56	58	67	Total
Bosnia and Herzegovina								**Bosnie-Herzégovine**
Vertebrates	29	44	51	51	50	50	55	Vertébrés
Invertebrates	10	22	36	39	42	42	43	Invertébrés
Plants	1	1	1	1	3	6	6	Plantes
Total	40	67	88	91	95	98	104	Total
Botswana								**Botswana**
Vertebrates	15	18	24	26	28	30	30	Vertébrés
Invertebrates	0	0	0	0	0	0	0	Invertébrés
Plants	0	0	2	2	2	3	3	Plantes
Total	15	18	26	28	30	33	33	Total
Bouvet Island								**Île Bouvet**
Vertebrates	1	2	3	3	3	3	2	Vertébrés
Invertebrates	0	0	0	0	0	0	0	Invertébrés
Plants	0	0	0	0	0	0	0	Plantes
Total	1	2	3	3	3	3	2	Total
Brazil								**Brésil**
Vertebrates	282[2]	341[2]	397	403	407	411	416	Vertébrés
Invertebrates	34	45	55	55	55	64	66	Invertébrés
Plants	381	387	521	532	538	582	596	Plantes
Total	697	773	973	990	1 000	1 057	1 078	Total
British Indian Ocean Terr.								**Terr. brit. de l'océan Indien**
Vertebrates	6	10	14	15	15	18	21	Vertébrés
Invertebrates	0	65	69	69	69	69	69	Invertébrés
Plants	1	1	1	1	1	1	1	Plantes
Total	7	76	84	85	85	88	91	Total
British Virgin Islands								**Îles Vierges britanniques**
Vertebrates	20	23	41	47	48	52	55	Vertébrés
Invertebrates	0	10	10	10	10	10	10	Invertébrés
Plants	10	10	10	10	20	20	23	Plantes
Total	30	43	61	67	78	82	88	Total
Brunei Darussalam								**Brunéi Darussalam**
Vertebrates	49	70	80	81	82	93	97	Vertébrés
Invertebrates	0	1	8	8	9	12	18	Invertébrés
Plants	99	99	104	104	116	131	160	Plantes
Total	148	170	192	193	207	236	275	Total
Bulgaria								**Bulgarie**
Vertebrates	35	39	49	50	49	49	49	Vertébrés
Invertebrates	9	27	38	48	57	57	57	Invertébrés
Plants	0	0	6	6	9	18	21	Plantes
Total	44	66	93	104	115	124	127	Total
Burkina Faso								**Burkina Faso**
Vertebrates	9	20	27	27	26	28	30	Vertébrés
Invertebrates	0	1	1	1	1	1	1	Invertébrés
Plants	2	3	3	3	3	4	5	Plantes
Total	11	24	31	31	30	33	36	Total
Burundi								**Burundi**
Vertebrates	22	43	44	46	46	46	48	Vertébrés
Invertebrates	4	7	7	7	7	6	6	Invertébrés
Plants	2	2	8	8	89	110	134	Plantes
Total	28	52	59	61	142	162	188	Total

Country or area [&]	2004	2010	2016	2017	2018	2019	2020	Pays ou zone [&]
Cabo Verde								**Cabo Verde**
Vertebrates	21	28	49	49	51	53	55	Vertébrés
Invertebrates	0	0	13	13	13	13	13	Invertébrés
Plants	2	3	3	3	51	51	51	Plantes
Total	23	31	65	65	115	117	119	Total
Cambodia								**Cambodge**
Vertebrates	72	107	137	141	145	154	160	Vertébrés
Invertebrates	0	67	79	79	79	79	79	Invertébrés
Plants	31	30	36	35	37	39	41	Plantes
Total	103	204	252	255	261	272	280	Total
Cameroon								**Cameroun**
Vertebrates	146	222	255	258	263	268	272	Vertébrés
Invertebrates	4	24	27	27	25	25	26	Invertébrés
Plants	334	378	490	490	544	559	592	Plantes
Total	484	624	772	775	832	852	890	Total
Canada								**Canada**
Vertebrates	62	63	79	81	86	93	95	Vertébrés
Invertebrates	11	12	25	27	37	38	38	Invertébrés
Plants	1	2	# 14	14	25	37	40	Plantes
Total	74	77	118	122	148	168	173	Total
Cayman Islands								**Îles Caïmanes**
Vertebrates	16	21	38	41	41	45	47	Vertébrés
Invertebrates	1	11	11	11	11	11	13	Invertébrés
Plants	2	2	22	22	22	23	23	Plantes
Total	19	34	71	74	74	79	83	Total
Central African Republic								**République centrafricaine**
Vertebrates	15	19	33	36	38	40	44	Vertébrés
Invertebrates	0	0	0	0	0	0	0	Invertébrés
Plants	15	17	24	24	25	26	29	Plantes
Total	30	36	57	60	63	66	73	Total
Chad								**Tchad**
Vertebrates	18	24	31	33	36	38	38	Vertébrés
Invertebrates	1	4	4	4	4	4	4	Invertébrés
Plants	2	2	6	6	6	6	6	Plantes
Total	21	30	41	43	46	48	48	Total
Chile								**Chili**
Vertebrates	83	95	111	112	132	135	140	Vertébrés
Invertebrates	0	9	13	13	13	13	13	Invertébrés
Plants	40	41	72	72	72	76	87	Plantes
Total	123	145	196	197	217	224	240	Total
China [3]								**Chine** [3]
Vertebrates	326	374	428	430	431	441	451	Vertébrés
Invertebrates	4	32	76	76	76	79	84	Invertébrés
Plants	443	453	# 575	574	588	604	637	Plantes
Total	773	859	1 079	1 080	1 095	1 124	1 172	Total
China, Hong Kong SAR								**Chine, RAS de Hong Kong**
Vertebrates	32	37	46	47	49	51	63	Vertébrés
Invertebrates	1	6	8	8	8	9	9	Invertébrés
Plants	6	6	9	9	8	10	11	Plantes
Total	39	49	63	64	65	70	83	Total
China, Macao SAR								**Chine, RAS de Macao**
Vertebrates	5	9	10	10	10	15	25	Vertébrés
Invertebrates	0	0	1	1	1	1	1	Invertébrés
Plants	0	0	0	0	0	0	0	Plantes
Total	5	9	11	11	11	16	26	Total
Christmas Island								**Île Christmas**
Vertebrates	12	16	20	20	18	22	26	Vertébrés
Invertebrates	0	16	18	18	19	19	19	Invertébrés
Plants	1	1	1	1	1	1	1	Plantes
Total	13	33	39	39	38	42	46	Total
Cocos (Keeling) Islands								**Îles des Cocos (Keeling)**
Vertebrates	5	11	12	13	13	17	20	Vertébrés
Invertebrates	0	17	20	20	20	20	20	Invertébrés
Plants	0	0	0	0	0	0	0	Plantes
Total	5	28	32	33	33	37	40	Total

Country or area &	2004	2010	2016	2017	2018	2019	2020	Pays ou zone &
Colombia								**Colombie**
Vertebrates	371	424	518	525	537	581	615	Vertébrés
Invertebrates	0	30	52	52	53	55	56	Invertébrés
Plants	222	227	257	258	261	280	354	Plantes
Total	593	681	827	835	851	916	1 025	Total
Comoros								**Comores**
Vertebrates	18	21	29	33	34	37	41	Vertébrés
Invertebrates	4	63	73	74	76	77	77	Invertébrés
Plants	5	5	7	7	9	9	9	Plantes
Total	27	89	109	114	119	123	127	Total
Congo								**Congo**
Vertebrates	29	61	81	82	86	86	92	Vertébrés
Invertebrates	1	5	7	7	7	7	7	Invertébrés
Plants	35	37	45	45	47	47	56	Plantes
Total	65	103	133	134	140	140	155	Total
Cook Islands								**Îles Cook**
Vertebrates	22	27	31	32	32	32	34	Vertébrés
Invertebrates	0	25	32	32	32	32	32	Invertébrés
Plants	1	1	11	11	11	11	11	Plantes
Total	23	53	74	75	75	75	77	Total
Costa Rica								**Costa Rica**
Vertebrates	112	142	166	169	171	176	181	Vertébrés
Invertebrates	9	27	31	31	31	31	31	Invertébrés
Plants	110	116	140	140	144	144	151	Plantes
Total	231	285	337	340	346	351	363	Total
Côte d'Ivoire								**Côte d'Ivoire**
Vertebrates	61	100	127	130	133	134	140	Vertébrés
Invertebrates	1	4	6	6	7	7	7	Invertébrés
Plants	105	106	112	113	117	129	133	Plantes
Total	167	210	245	249	257	270	280	Total
Croatia								**Croatie**
Vertebrates	46	77	93	94	93	93	97	Vertébrés
Invertebrates	11	21	68	73	79	79	80	Invertébrés
Plants	0	3	# 9	9	9	25	35	Plantes
Total	57	101	170	176	181	197	212	Total
Cuba								**Cuba**
Vertebrates	106	123	138	137	146	151	155	Vertébrés
Invertebrates	3	15	23	23	23	23	23	Invertébrés
Plants	163	166	179	179	179	180	179	Plantes
Total	272	304	340	339	348	354	357	Total
Curaçao								**Curaçao**
Vertebrates	...	...	36	38	38	39	43	Vertébrés
Invertebrates	...	...	11	11	11	11	11	Invertébrés
Plants	...	...	2	2	2	2	4	Plantes
Total	...	...	49	51	51	52	58	Total
Cyprus								**Chypre**
Vertebrates	24	31	41	42	42	44	44	Vertébrés
Invertebrates	0	4	12	12	15	15	16	Invertébrés
Plants	1	8	18	18	21	24	24	Plantes
Total	25	43	71	72	78	83	84	Total
Czechia								**Tchéquie**
Vertebrates	22	10	14	14	14	14	14	Vertébrés
Invertebrates	19	19	24	24	29	29	29	Invertébrés
Plants	4	4	# 15	15	31	51	61	Plantes
Total	45	33	53	53	74	94	104	Total
Dem. People's Rep. Korea								**Rép. pop. dém. de Corée**
Vertebrates	40	44	57	58	60	63	66	Vertébrés
Invertebrates	1	2	3	3	3	3	3	Invertébrés
Plants	3	6	17	17	17	17	19	Plantes
Total	44	52	77	78	80	83	88	Total
Dem. Rep. of the Congo								**Rép. dém. du Congo**
Vertebrates	84	162	183	182	187	188	203	Vertébrés
Invertebrates	22	51	53	53	55	54	54	Invertébrés
Plants	65	83	113	114	148	185	240	Plantes
Total	171	296	349	349	390	427	497	Total

Country or area [&]	2004	2010	2016	2017	2018	2019	2020	Pays ou zone [&]
Denmark								**Danemark**
Vertebrates	21	18	27	28	29	30	31	Vertébrés
Invertebrates	11	12	15	15	16	16	16	Invertébrés
Plants	3	3	# 4	4	4	21	30	Plantes
Total	35	33	46	47	49	67	77	Total
Djibouti								**Djibouti**
Vertebrates	19	29	38	38	43	49	50	Vertébrés
Invertebrates	0	50	57	57	57	57	57	Invertébrés
Plants	2	2	3	3	3	3	3	Plantes
Total	21	81	98	98	103	109	110	Total
Dominica								**Dominique**
Vertebrates	22	27	42	44	44	47	51	Vertébrés
Invertebrates	0	11	11	11	11	11	11	Invertébrés
Plants	11	10	11	11	11	12	12	Plantes
Total	33	48	64	66	66	70	74	Total
Dominican Republic								**République dominicaine**
Vertebrates	72	80	95	126	130	133	136	Vertébrés
Invertebrates	2	16	16	16	16	18	19	Invertébrés
Plants	30	30	42	42	45	49	48	Plantes
Total	104	126	153	184	191	200	203	Total
Ecuador								**Équateur**
Vertebrates	288	356	417	426	434	441	470	Vertébrés
Invertebrates	48	62	70	70	70	70	70	Invertébrés
Plants	1 815	1 837	# 1 866	1 862	1 864	1 882	1 961	Plantes
Total	2 151	2 255	2 353	2 358	2 368	2 393	2 501	Total
Egypt								**Égypte**
Vertebrates	43	73	96	97	99	105	107	Vertébrés
Invertebrates	1	46	56	56	56	56	57	Invertébrés
Plants	2	2	3	3	8	8	8	Plantes
Total	46	121	155	156	163	169	172	Total
El Salvador								**El Salvador**
Vertebrates	23	39	47	47	47	50	55	Vertébrés
Invertebrates	1	6	10	10	10	10	10	Invertébrés
Plants	25	27	29	29	30	33	42	Plantes
Total	49	72	86	86	87	93	107	Total
Equatorial Guinea								**Guinée équatoriale**
Vertebrates	38	60	85	85	86	88	94	Vertébrés
Invertebrates	2	2	5	5	4	4	4	Invertébrés
Plants	61	68	88	87	95	98	107	Plantes
Total	101	130	178	177	185	190	205	Total
Eritrea								**Érythrée**
Vertebrates	31	44	58	59	67	74	79	Vertébrés
Invertebrates	0	50	58	58	58	58	58	Invertébrés
Plants	3	3	4	5	5	6	6	Plantes
Total	34	97	120	122	130	138	143	Total
Estonia								**Estonie**
Vertebrates	8	8	14	15	15	15	15	Vertébrés
Invertebrates	4	3	6	6	7	7	7	Invertébrés
Plants	0	0	# 2	2	2	17	26	Plantes
Total	12	11	22	23	24	39	48	Total
Eswatini								**Eswatini**
Vertebrates	12	18	25	23	26	28	28	Vertébrés
Invertebrates	0	0	0	0	0	0	0	Invertébrés
Plants	11	11	11	11	12	13	13	Plantes
Total	23	29	36	34	38	41	41	Total
Ethiopia								**Éthiopie**
Vertebrates	65	79	92	90	95	99	101	Vertébrés
Invertebrates	6	15	15	15	15	15	15	Invertébrés
Plants	22	26	41	43	47	64	64	Plantes
Total	93	120	148	148	157	178	180	Total
Falkland Islands (Malvinas)								**Îles Falkland (Malvinas)**
Vertebrates	21	18	18	18	17	17	18	Vertébrés
Invertebrates	0	0	0	0	0	0	0	Invertébrés
Plants	5	5	5	5	5	6	6	Plantes
Total	26	23	23	23	22	23	24	Total

Country or area &	2004	2010	2016	2017	2018	2019	2020	Pays ou zone &
Faroe Islands								**Îles Féroé**
Vertebrates	11	13	20	20	22	23	24	Vertébrés
Invertebrates	0	0	0	0	0	0	0	Invertébrés
Plants	0	0	# 1	1	1	4	5	Plantes
Total	11	13	21	21	23	27	29	Total
Fiji								**Fidji**
Vertebrates	33	37	52	55	55	57	62	Vertébrés
Invertebrates	2	90	165	165	165	165	172	Invertébrés
Plants	66	65	65	71	78	78	87	Plantes
Total	101	192	282	291	298	300	321	Total
Finland								**Finlande**
Vertebrates	14	10	17	18	19	19	19	Vertébrés
Invertebrates	10	7	10	10	10	10	10	Invertébrés
Plants	1	1	# 8	8	8	21	32	Plantes
Total	25	18	35	36	37	50	61	Total
France								**France**
Vertebrates	53	62	80	82	84	84	88	Vertébrés
Invertebrates	65	91	137	153	160	160	162	Invertébrés
Plants	2	15	# 43	43	55	98	116	Plantes
Total	120	168	260	278	299	342	366	Total
French Guiana								**Guyane française**
Vertebrates	33	40	55	55	56	59	59	Vertébrés
Invertebrates	0	0	0	0	0	0	0	Invertébrés
Plants	16	16	18	18	18	18	20	Plantes
Total	49	56	73	73	74	77	79	Total
French Polynesia								**Polynésie française**
Vertebrates	46	54	63	66	66	67	68	Vertébrés
Invertebrates	29	59	65	62	62	62	65	Invertébrés
Plants	47	47	47	47	48	48	48	Plantes
Total	122	160	175	175	176	177	181	Total
French Southern Territories								**Terres australes françaises**
Vertebrates	17	21	24	25	25	28	28	Vertébrés
Invertebrates	0	0	0	0	0	0	0	Invertébrés
Plants	0	0	0	0	0	1	1	Plantes
Total	17	21	24	25	25	29	29	Total
Gabon								**Gabon**
Vertebrates	31	84	105	105	107	106	110	Vertébrés
Invertebrates	1	0	3	3	4	4	4	Invertébrés
Plants	107	120	162	162	172	181	215	Plantes
Total	139	204	270	270	283	291	329	Total
Gambia								**Gambie**
Vertebrates	17	39	60	60	63	68	78	Vertébrés
Invertebrates	0	0	2	2	2	2	2	Invertébrés
Plants	4	4	5	5	5	6	7	Plantes
Total	21	43	67	67	70	76	87	Total
Georgia								**Géorgie**
Vertebrates	33	37	42	43	42	42	42	Vertébrés
Invertebrates	10	9	15	15	15	15	15	Invertébrés
Plants	0	0	# 62	62	63	68	69	Plantes
Total	43	46	119	120	120	125	126	Total
Germany								**Allemagne**
Vertebrates	35	33	39	40	40	41	42	Vertébrés
Invertebrates	31	34	57	57	61	61	61	Invertébrés
Plants	12	12	# 24	19	43	83	97	Plantes
Total	78	79	120	116	144	185	200	Total
Ghana								**Ghana**
Vertebrates	43	83	112	114	118	120	128	Vertébrés
Invertebrates	0	1	5	5	5	5	5	Invertébrés
Plants	117	118	119	119	118	121	122	Plantes
Total	160	202	236	238	241	246	255	Total
Gibraltar								**Gibraltar**
Vertebrates	16	20	28	26	28	27	29	Vertébrés
Invertebrates	2	2	5	5	5	5	6	Invertébrés
Plants	0	0	0	0	1	1	1	Plantes
Total	18	22	33	31	34	33	36	Total

Country or area &	2004	2010	2016	2017	2018	2019	2020	Pays ou zone &
Greece								**Grèce**
Vertebrates	62	107	120	121	123	124	127	Vertébrés
Invertebrates	11	36	181	192	308	308	309	Invertébrés
Plants	2	13	# 60	61	71	80	84	Plantes
Total	75	156	361	374	502	512	520	Total
Greenland								**Groenland**
Vertebrates	11	13	21	22	24	24	24	Vertébrés
Invertebrates	0	0	0	0	0	0	0	Invertébrés
Plants	1	1	1	1	1	1	3	Plantes
Total	12	14	22	23	25	25	27	Total
Grenada								**Grenade**
Vertebrates	20	24	40	41	42	43	47	Vertébrés
Invertebrates	0	10	10	10	10	10	10	Invertébrés
Plants	3	3	3	3	3	3	3	Plantes
Total	23	37	53	54	55	56	60	Total
Guadeloupe [4]								**Guadeloupe [4]**
Vertebrates	25	30	45	48	50	53	57	Vertébrés
Invertebrates	1	16	16	16	16	16	16	Invertébrés
Plants	7	8	9	9	9	10	10	Plantes
Total	33	54	70	73	75	79	83	Total
Guam								**Guam**
Vertebrates	16	24	34	35	35	38	42	Vertébrés
Invertebrates	5	6	60	60	60	60	60	Invertébrés
Plants	3	4	4	4	4	5	5	Plantes
Total	24	34	98	99	99	103	107	Total
Guatemala								**Guatemala**
Vertebrates	115	140	176	176	175	185	189	Vertébrés
Invertebrates	8	8	13	13	13	13	13	Invertébrés
Plants	85	82	102	101	113	123	150	Plantes
Total	208	230	291	290	301	321	352	Total
Guernsey								**Guernesey**
Vertebrates	...	2	5	5	5	6	12	Vertébrés
Invertebrates	...	0	0	0	0	0	0	Invertébrés
Plants	...	0	0	0	0	0	0	Plantes
Total	...	2	5	5	5	6	12	Total
Guinea								**Guinée**
Vertebrates	42	107	132	134	138	144	168	Vertébrés
Invertebrates	3	5	7	7	8	8	8	Invertébrés
Plants	22	22	44	44	69	175	189	Plantes
Total	67	134	183	185	215	327	365	Total
Guinea-Bissau								**Guinée-Bissau**
Vertebrates	17	48	69	70	73	75	80	Vertébrés
Invertebrates	1	0	2	2	2	2	2	Invertébrés
Plants	4	4	5	5	5	10	10	Plantes
Total	22	52	76	77	80	87	92	Total
Guyana								**Guyana**
Vertebrates	41	46	65	67	73	83	86	Vertébrés
Invertebrates	1	1	1	1	1	1	1	Invertébrés
Plants	23	22	26	26	26	33	35	Plantes
Total	65	69	92	94	100	117	122	Total
Haiti								**Haïti**
Vertebrates	86	94	113	149	153	155	161	Vertébrés
Invertebrates	2	14	14	14	14	14	14	Invertébrés
Plants	28	29	42	42	80	94	94	Plantes
Total	116	137	169	205	247	263	269	Total
Heard Is. and McDonald Is.								**Île Heard-et-Îles MacDonald**
Vertebrates	12	12	12	12	12	12	12	Vertébrés
Invertebrates	0	0	0	0	0	0	0	Invertébrés
Plants	0	0	0	0	0	0	0	Plantes
Total	12	12	12	12	12	12	12	Total
Holy See								**Saint-Siège**
Vertebrates	...	1	1	1	1	1	1	Vertébrés
Invertebrates	...	0	0	0	0	0	0	Invertébrés
Plants	...	0	0	0	0	0	0	Plantes
Total	...	1	1	1	1	1	1	Total

Country or area &	2004	2010	2016	2017	2018	2019	2020	Pays ou zone &
Honduras								**Honduras**
Vertebrates	93	110	156	157	157	163	181	Vertébrés
Invertebrates	2	17	21	21	21	21	21	Invertébrés
Plants	111	113	123	123	131	134	140	Plantes
Total	206	240	300	301	309	318	342	Total
Hungary								**Hongrie**
Vertebrates	25	20	25	26	26	27	27	Vertébrés
Invertebrates	25	26	35	29	34	33	33	Invertébrés
Plants	1	1	# 12	11	45	59	63	Plantes
Total	51	47	72	66	105	119	123	Total
Iceland								**Islande**
Vertebrates	15	17	26	27	29	29	30	Vertébrés
Invertebrates	0	0	0	0	0	0	0	Invertébrés
Plants	0	0	0	0	0	2	6	Plantes
Total	15	17	26	27	29	31	36	Total
India								**Inde**
Vertebrates	283	390	528	530	540	546	550	Vertébrés
Invertebrates	23	113	135	135	135	136	138	Invertébrés
Plants	246	255	388	387	392	399	430	Plantes
Total	552	758	1 051	1 052	1 067	1 081	1 118	Total
Indonesia								**Indonésie**
Vertebrates	419	503	540	564	572	627	663	Vertébrés
Invertebrates	31	246	290	290	287	336	364	Invertébrés
Plants	383	393	427	427	436	509	627	Plantes
Total	833	1 142	1 257	1 281	1 295	1 472	1 654	Total
Iran (Islamic Republic of)								**Iran (Rép. islamique d')**
Vertebrates	65	82	105	106	111	118	125	Vertébrés
Invertebrates	3	19	24	24	24	24	24	Invertébrés
Plants	1	1	3	4	5	10	12	Plantes
Total	69	102	132	134	140	152	161	Total
Iraq								**Iraq**
Vertebrates	33	45	54	53	54	58	59	Vertébrés
Invertebrates	2	15	17	17	17	17	17	Invertébrés
Plants	0	0	1	2	2	3	4	Plantes
Total	35	60	72	72	73	78	80	Total
Ireland								**Irlande**
Vertebrates	18	24	40	41	42	44	46	Vertébrés
Invertebrates	3	2	6	6	6	6	6	Invertébrés
Plants	1	1	# 3	3	5	21	27	Plantes
Total	22	27	49	50	53	71	79	Total
Isle of Man								**Île de Man**
Vertebrates	...	2	3	3	3	2	5	Vertébrés
Invertebrates	...	0	0	0	0	0	0	Invertébrés
Plants	...	0	0	0	0	1	1	Plantes
Total	...	2	3	3	3	3	6	Total
Israel								**Israël**
Vertebrates	47	73	89	90	91	103	105	Vertébrés
Invertebrates	10	58	74	74	74	74	74	Invertébrés
Plants	0	0	9	10	23	28	28	Plantes
Total	57	131	172	174	188	205	207	Total
Italy								**Italie**
Vertebrates	53	70	85	87	89	91	95	Vertébrés
Invertebrates	58	77	141	194	222	222	223	Invertébrés
Plants	3	27	# 79	78	109	145	164	Plantes
Total	114	174	305	359	420	458	482	Total
Jamaica								**Jamaïque**
Vertebrates	54	58	71	82	87	91	94	Vertébrés
Invertebrates	5	15	15	15	15	15	15	Invertébrés
Plants	208	209	214	214	214	215	214	Plantes
Total	267	282	300	311	316	321	323	Total
Japan								**Japon**
Vertebrates	148	158	180	184	198	223	228	Vertébrés
Invertebrates	45	157	171	171	174	176	177	Invertébrés
Plants	12	15	# 46	49	50	60	65	Plantes
Total	205	330	397	404	422	459	470	Total

Country or area [&]	2004	2010	2016	2017	2018	2019	2020	Pays ou zone [&]
Jersey								**Jersey**
Vertebrates	...	2	5	5	5	6	12	Vertébrés
Invertebrates	...	0	1	1	1	1	1	Invertébrés
Plants	...	0	0	0	0	0	1	Plantes
Total	...	2	6	6	6	7	14	Total
Jordan								**Jordanie**
Vertebrates	27	41	47	47	48	55	52	Vertébrés
Invertebrates	3	48	61	61	61	61	61	Invertébrés
Plants	0	1	5	5	8	8	8	Plantes
Total	30	90	113	113	117	124	121	Total
Kazakhstan								**Kazakhstan**
Vertebrates	48	53	57	59	59	59	59	Vertébrés
Invertebrates	4	4	7	7	7	7	7	Invertébrés
Plants	1	16	16	16	14	15	15	Plantes
Total	53	73	80	82	80	81	81	Total
Kenya								**Kenya**
Vertebrates	99	137	162	162	169	176	179	Vertébrés
Invertebrates	27	72	84	86	87	92	93	Invertébrés
Plants	103	129	222	232	234	248	277	Plantes
Total	229	338	468	480	490	516	549	Total
Kiribati								**Kiribati**
Vertebrates	10	17	21	23	23	24	27	Vertébrés
Invertebrates	1	73	81	81	81	81	81	Invertébrés
Plants	0	0	0	0	0	0	0	Plantes
Total	11	90	102	104	104	105	108	Total
Kuwait								**Koweït**
Vertebrates	20	28	36	36	39	43	44	Vertébrés
Invertebrates	0	13	13	13	13	13	13	Invertébrés
Plants	0	0	0	0	0	0	0	Plantes
Total	20	41	49	49	52	56	57	Total
Kyrgyzstan								**Kirghizistan**
Vertebrates	12	23	26	26	26	26	26	Vertébrés
Invertebrates	3	3	4	4	4	4	4	Invertébrés
Plants	1	14	14	14	13	13	13	Plantes
Total	16	40	44	44	43	43	43	Total
Lao People's Dem. Rep.								**Rép. dém. populaire lao**
Vertebrates	72	107	153	147	149	164	166	Vertébrés
Invertebrates	0	3	21	21	21	21	21	Invertébrés
Plants	19	22	41	41	54	58	63	Plantes
Total	91	132	215	209	224	243	250	Total
Latvia								**Lettonie**
Vertebrates	15	9	16	17	18	18	18	Vertébrés
Invertebrates	8	9	12	12	12	12	12	Invertébrés
Plants	0	0	# 1	1	1	5	10	Plantes
Total	23	18	29	30	31	35	40	Total
Lebanon								**Liban**
Vertebrates	25	44	58	58	57	57	61	Vertébrés
Invertebrates	1	5	16	17	18	18	19	Invertébrés
Plants	0	1	10	12	24	29	29	Plantes
Total	26	50	84	87	99	104	109	Total
Lesotho								**Lesotho**
Vertebrates	11	10	11	11	13	13	13	Vertébrés
Invertebrates	1	2	3	3	3	3	2	Invertébrés
Plants	1	4	4	4	4	4	4	Plantes
Total	13	16	18	18	20	20	19	Total
Liberia								**Libéria**
Vertebrates	45	91	108	109	112	114	122	Vertébrés
Invertebrates	3	9	11	11	10	10	10	Invertébrés
Plants	46	47	52	52	53	83	86	Plantes
Total	94	147	171	172	175	207	218	Total
Libya								**Libye**
Vertebrates	24	42	55	56	56	57	62	Vertébrés
Invertebrates	0	0	4	4	4	4	5	Invertébrés
Plants	1	2	3	3	5	8	8	Plantes
Total	25	44	62	63	65	69	75	Total

Country or area &	2004	2010	2016	2017	2018	2019	2020	Pays ou zone &
Liechtenstein								**Liechtenstein**
Vertebrates	3	0	2	2	2	2	2	Vertébrés
Invertebrates	5	2	4	4	6	6	6	Invertébrés
Plants	0	0	0	0	0	4	5	Plantes
Total	8	2	6	6	8	12	13	Total
Lithuania								**Lituanie**
Vertebrates	12	12	17	17	18	18	18	Vertébrés
Invertebrates	5	5	7	7	8	8	8	Invertébrés
Plants	0	0	# 2	2	2	9	15	Plantes
Total	17	17	26	26	28	35	41	Total
Luxembourg								**Luxembourg**
Vertebrates	6	1	4	4	4	4	4	Vertébrés
Invertebrates	4	4	7	7	7	7	7	Invertébrés
Plants	0	0	0	0	0	5	5	Plantes
Total	10	5	11	11	11	16	16	Total
Madagascar								**Madagascar**
Vertebrates	222	283	527	543	551	554	556	Vertébrés
Invertebrates	32	100	110	172	194	195	195	Invertébrés
Plants	276	280	607	609	871	1 624	2 159	Plantes
Total	530	663	1 244	1 324	1 616	2 373	2 910	Total
Malawi								**Malawi**
Vertebrates	25	127	135	136	136	74	74	Vertébrés
Invertebrates	11	17	16	16	14	14	14	Invertébrés
Plants	14	14	24	24	26	37	42	Plantes
Total	50	158	175	176	176	125	130	Total
Malaysia								**Malaisie**
Vertebrates	190	246	282	288	280	343	351	Vertébrés
Invertebrates	19	242	262	264	265	282	314	Invertébrés
Plants	683	692	721	720	712	813	997	Plantes
Total	892	1 180	1 265	1 272	1 257	1 438	1 662	Total
Maldives								**Maldives**
Vertebrates	12	20	29	29	29	33	35	Vertébrés
Invertebrates	0	39	46	46	46	46	45	Invertébrés
Plants	0	0	0	0	0	0	0	Plantes
Total	12	59	75	75	75	79	80	Total
Mali								**Mali**
Vertebrates	19	23	34	34	35	37	37	Vertébrés
Invertebrates	0	0	0	0	0	0	0	Invertébrés
Plants	6	6	8	8	11	24	25	Plantes
Total	25	29	42	42	46	61	62	Total
Malta								**Malte**
Vertebrates	22	20	30	30	30	31	38	Vertébrés
Invertebrates	3	3	5	5	5	5	6	Invertébrés
Plants	0	3	4	4	4	4	5	Plantes
Total	25	26	39	39	39	40	49	Total
Marshall Islands								**Îles Marshall**
Vertebrates	12	17	25	28	28	28	31	Vertébrés
Invertebrates	1	67	73	73	73	73	73	Invertébrés
Plants	0	0	0	0	0	0	0	Plantes
Total	13	84	98	101	101	101	104	Total
Martinique								**Martinique**
Vertebrates	20	22	33	37	37	45	51	Vertébrés
Invertebrates	1	1	2	2	2	2	2	Invertébrés
Plants	8	8	9	9	9	9	9	Plantes
Total	29	31	44	48	48	56	62	Total
Mauritania								**Mauritanie**
Vertebrates	25	57	80	83	85	86	91	Vertébrés
Invertebrates	1	1	3	3	3	3	3	Invertébrés
Plants	0	0	0	0	0	0	0	Plantes
Total	26	58	83	86	88	89	94	Total
Mauritius								**Maurice**
Vertebrates	28	36	45	47	48	54	56	Vertébrés
Invertebrates	32	98	118	120	120	121	124	Invertébrés
Plants	87	88	90	90	91	91	92	Plantes
Total	147	222	253	257	259	266	272	Total

Country or area &	2004	2010	2016	2017	2018	2019	2020	Pays ou zone &
Mayotte								**Mayotte**
Vertebrates	6	9	18	18	19	22	26	Vertébrés
Invertebrates	1	60	69	70	70	72	72	Invertébrés
Plants	0	0	0	0	3	4	4	Plantes
Total	7	69	87	88	92	98	102	Total
Mexico								**Mexique**
Vertebrates	446	609	648	655	657	736	751	Vertébrés
Invertebrates	41	79	102	106	106	113	114	Invertébrés
Plants	261	255	402	401	450	529	791	Plantes
Total	748	943	1 152	1 162	1 213	1 378	1 656	Total
Micronesia (Fed. States of)								**Micronésie (États féd. de)**
Vertebrates	22	35	48	49	50	49	49	Vertébrés
Invertebrates	4	108	115	114	114	114	116	Invertébrés
Plants	4	5	4	4	4	5	5	Plantes
Total	30	148	167	167	168	168	170	Total
Monaco								**Monaco**
Vertebrates	9	11	17	18	18	19	28	Vertébrés
Invertebrates	0	0	3	3	3	3	4	Invertébrés
Plants	0	0	0	0	1	2	2	Plantes
Total	9	11	20	21	22	24	34	Total
Mongolia								**Mongolie**
Vertebrates	36	33	37	38	37	37	37	Vertébrés
Invertebrates	3	3	3	3	3	3	3	Invertébrés
Plants	0	0	0	0	0	2	3	Plantes
Total	39	36	40	41	40	42	43	Total
Montenegro								**Monténégro**
Vertebrates	...	44	57	57	56	55	60	Vertébrés
Invertebrates	...	28	35	39	42	42	43	Invertébrés
Plants	...	0	2	2	3	7	10	Plantes
Total	...	72	94	98	101	104	113	Total
Montserrat								**Montserrat**
Vertebrates	18	21	36	38	39	42	44	Vertébrés
Invertebrates	0	11	11	11	11	11	11	Invertébrés
Plants	3	3	6	6	6	6	7	Plantes
Total	21	35	53	55	56	59	62	Total
Morocco								**Maroc**
Vertebrates	40	86	101	103	105	103	106	Vertébrés
Invertebrates	8	40	60	66	69	69	71	Invertébrés
Plants	2	31	# 38	38	49	55	61	Plantes
Total	50	157	199	207	223	227	238	Total
Mozambique								**Mozambique**
Vertebrates	64	98	127	129	132	142	153	Vertébrés
Invertebrates	5	59	67	67	67	65	65	Invertébrés
Plants	46	52	84	113	122	170	208	Plantes
Total	115	209	278	309	321	377	426	Total
Myanmar								**Myanmar**
Vertebrates	107	143	178	183	187	197	200	Vertébrés
Invertebrates	2	64	77	77	77	77	77	Invertébrés
Plants	38	42	61	61	61	63	80	Plantes
Total	147	249	316	321	325	337	357	Total
Namibia								**Namibie**
Vertebrates	44	66	81	84	85	84	85	Vertébrés
Invertebrates	1	0	4	4	4	4	4	Invertébrés
Plants	24	26	28	27	27	27	28	Plantes
Total	69	92	113	115	116	115	117	Total
Nauru								**Nauru**
Vertebrates	5	12	14	14	14	15	18	Vertébrés
Invertebrates	0	62	68	68	68	68	68	Invertébrés
Plants	0	0	0	0	0	0	0	Plantes
Total	5	74	82	82	82	83	86	Total
Nepal								**Népal**
Vertebrates	69	83	87	84	84	85	86	Vertébrés
Invertebrates	1	3	3	3	3	3	3	Invertébrés
Plants	7	7	17	17	17	19	20	Plantes
Total	77	93	107	104	104	107	109	Total

Country or area &	2004	2010	2016	2017	2018	2019	2020	Pays ou zone &
Netherlands								**Pays-Bas**
Vertebrates	27	18	26	27	28	29	31	Vertébrés
Invertebrates	7	6	10	10	11	11	11	Invertébrés
Plants	0	0	# 3	3	4	19	29	Plantes
Total	34	24	39	40	43	59	71	Total
Netherlands Antilles [former]								**Antilles néerlandaises [anc.]**
Vertebrates	26	24	...	...	...	...	...	Vertébrés
Invertebrates	0	11	...	...	...	...	...	Invertébrés
Plants	2	3	...	...	...	...	...	Plantes
Total	28	38	...	...	...	...	...	Total
New Caledonia								**Nouvelle-Calédonie**
Vertebrates	34	61	114	116	117	118	120	Vertébrés
Invertebrates	11	97	125	125	125	125	129	Invertébrés
Plants	217	257	286	285	350	350	510	Plantes
Total	262	415	525	526	592	593	759	Total
New Zealand								**Nouvelle-Zélande**
Vertebrates	114	117	128	130	131	162	166	Vertébrés
Invertebrates	14	15	46	46	61	61	61	Invertébrés
Plants	21	21	# 23	23	24	24	34	Plantes
Total	149	153	197	199	216	247	261	Total
Nicaragua								**Nicaragua**
Vertebrates	49	61	78	78	79	84	89	Vertébrés
Invertebrates	2	17	20	20	20	20	20	Invertébrés
Plants	39	43	46	46	50	49	52	Plantes
Total	90	121	144	144	149	153	161	Total
Niger								**Niger**
Vertebrates	12	22	29	30	32	32	32	Vertébrés
Invertebrates	1	2	1	1	1	1	1	Invertébrés
Plants	2	2	3	3	3	4	4	Plantes
Total	15	26	33	34	36	37	37	Total
Nigeria								**Nigéria**
Vertebrates	61	113	145	148	148	151	156	Vertébrés
Invertebrates	1	12	17	17	13	13	13	Invertébrés
Plants	170	172	197	196	203	208	211	Plantes
Total	232	297	359	361	364	372	380	Total
Niue								**Nioué**
Vertebrates	12	20	22	22	22	23	25	Vertébrés
Invertebrates	0	23	30	30	30	30	30	Invertébrés
Plants	0	0	0	0	0	0	1	Plantes
Total	12	43	52	52	52	53	56	Total
Norfolk Island								**Île Norfolk**
Vertebrates	21	19	18	19	19	21	25	Vertébrés
Invertebrates	12	21	23	23	23	23	23	Invertébrés
Plants	1	1	1	2	2	2	2	Plantes
Total	34	41	42	44	44	46	50	Total
North Macedonia								**Macédoine du Nord**
Vertebrates	24	31	34	35	34	34	34	Vertébrés
Invertebrates	5	59	70	75	86	86	86	Invertébrés
Plants	0	0	0	0	5	7	13	Plantes
Total	29	90	104	110	125	127	133	Total
Northern Mariana Islands								**Îles Mariannes du Nord**
Vertebrates	22	29	39	40	40	39	42	Vertébrés
Invertebrates	2	51	57	57	...	57	57	Invertébrés
Plants	4	5	5	5	5	6	6	Plantes
Total	28	85	101	102	102	102	105	Total
Norway								**Norvège**
Vertebrates	22	27	38	40	42	43	44	Vertébrés
Invertebrates	9	7	10	10	10	10	10	Invertébrés
Plants	2	2	# 14	14	21	51	61	Plantes
Total	33	36	62	64	73	104	115	Total
Oman								**Oman**
Vertebrates	48	47	62	62	68	71	75	Vertébrés
Invertebrates	1	26	31	31	31	31	31	Invertébrés
Plants	6	6	6	6	6	6	6	Plantes
Total	55	79	99	99	105	108	112	Total

Country or area [&]	2004	2010	2016	2017	2018	2019	2020	Pays ou zone [&]
Other non-specified areas								**Autres zones non-spécifiées**
Vertebrates	79	104	123	123	129	134	144	Vertébrés
Invertebrates	0	122	128	128	128	129	129	Invertébrés
Plants	78	78	# 85	86	85	87	89	Plantes
Total	157	304	336	337	342	350	362	Total
Pakistan								**Pakistan**
Vertebrates	70	92	110	110	115	118	124	Vertébrés
Invertebrates	0	15	18	18	18	18	18	Invertébrés
Plants	2	2	12	12	12	12	13	Plantes
Total	72	109	140	140	145	148	155	Total
Palau								**Palaos**
Vertebrates	13	22	31	32	34	35	36	Vertébrés
Invertebrates	5	102	146	146	146	146	148	Invertébrés
Plants	3	4	4	4	4	5	5	Plantes
Total	21	128	181	182	184	186	189	Total
Panama								**Panama**
Vertebrates	113	125	151	153	154	161	170	Vertébrés
Invertebrates	2	20	22	22	22	22	22	Invertébrés
Plants	195	202	208	208	211	211	208	Plantes
Total	310	347	381	383	387	394	400	Total
Papua New Guinea								**Papouasie-Nvl-Guinée**
Vertebrates	141	139	155	160	161	166	173	Vertébrés
Invertebrates	12	171	181	181	180	178	183	Invertébrés
Plants	142	143	152	152	158	186	229	Plantes
Total	295	453	488	493	499	530	585	Total
Paraguay								**Paraguay**
Vertebrates	40	38	40	40	43	44	46	Vertébrés
Invertebrates	0	0	0	0	0	0	1	Invertébrés
Plants	10	10	19	19	19	20	20	Plantes
Total	50	48	59	59	62	64	67	Total
Peru								**Pérou**
Vertebrates	232	274	351	351	377	384	396	Vertébrés
Invertebrates	2	3	8	8	8	9	9	Invertébrés
Plants	274	274	334	326	328	351	414	Plantes
Total	508	551	693	685	713	744	819	Total
Philippines								**Philippines**
Vertebrates	225	262	302	306	302	284	293	Vertébrés
Invertebrates	19	213	237	238	238	240	323	Invertébrés
Plants	212	222	239	239	245	259	268	Plantes
Total	456	697	778	783	785	783	884	Total
Pitcairn								**Pitcairn**
Vertebrates	15	20	21	21	21	19	21	Vertébrés
Invertebrates	5	15	16	16	16	16	16	Invertébrés
Plants	7	7	7	7	7	7	7	Plantes
Total	27	42	44	44	44	42	44	Total
Poland								**Pologne**
Vertebrates	27	17	23	23	24	23	23	Vertébrés
Invertebrates	15	16	22	22	28	28	28	Invertébrés
Plants	4	4	# 13	13	14	32	44	Plantes
Total	46	37	58	58	66	83	95	Total
Portugal								**Portugal**
Vertebrates	51	71	92	94	98	101	106	Vertébrés
Invertebrates	82	79	97	103	197	205	205	Invertébrés
Plants	15	21	# 83	84	104	150	154	Plantes
Total	148	171	272	281	399	456	465	Total
Puerto Rico								**Porto Rico**
Vertebrates	44	49	69	69	72	76	79	Vertébrés
Invertebrates	1	1	0	0	0	0	0	Invertébrés
Plants	52	53	57	57	63	65	67	Plantes
Total	97	103	126	126	135	141	146	Total
Qatar								**Qatar**
Vertebrates	12	19	26	26	32	37	37	Vertébrés
Invertebrates	0	13	13	13	13	13	13	Invertébrés
Plants	0	0	0	0	0	0	0	Plantes
Total	12	32	39	39	45	50	50	Total

Country or area &	2004	2010	2016	2017	2018	2019	2020	Pays ou zone &
Republic of Korea								**République de Corée**
Vertebrates	54	58	72	74	78	82	90	Vertébrés
Invertebrates	1	3	5	5	8	8	8	Invertébrés
Plants	0	3	# 32	32	32	35	38	Plantes
Total	55	64	109	111	118	125	136	Total
Republic of Moldova								**République de Moldova**
Vertebrates	22	24	26	27	26	25	25	Vertébrés
Invertebrates	5	3	5	6	6	6	6	Invertébrés
Plants	0	0	2	2	2	2	2	Plantes
Total	27	27	33	35	34	33	33	Total
Réunion								**Réunion**
Vertebrates	18	16	24	24	24	29	35	Vertébrés
Invertebrates	16	73	87	89	89	89	89	Invertébrés
Plants	14	15	17	17	18	19	21	Plantes
Total	48	104	128	130	131	137	145	Total
Romania								**Roumanie**
Vertebrates	40	39	49	50	50	51	51	Vertébrés
Invertebrates	22	24	38	49	68	67	67	Invertébrés
Plants	1	1	5	5	7	20	22	Plantes
Total	63	64	92	104	125	138	140	Total
Russian Federation								**Fédération de Russie**
Vertebrates	114	93	134	136	139	139	141	Vertébrés
Invertebrates	30	25	36	39	39	38	38	Invertébrés
Plants	7	8	# 60	60	60	90	100	Plantes
Total	151	126	230	235	238	267	279	Total
Rwanda								**Rwanda**
Vertebrates	30	49	51	50	52	52	52	Vertébrés
Invertebrates	4	2	2	4	4	4	4	Invertébrés
Plants	3	4	8	8	41	71	112	Plantes
Total	37	55	61	62	97	127	168	Total
Saint Barthélemy								**Saint-Barthélemy**
Vertebrates	...	4	18	18	19	28	31	Vertébrés
Invertebrates	...	11	11	11	11	11	11	Invertébrés
Plants	...	2	2	2	2	2	2	Plantes
Total	...	17	31	31	32	41	44	Total
Saint Helena [5]								**Sainte-Hélène** [5]
Vertebrates	32	31	39	41	41	42	45	Vertébrés
Invertebrates	2	2	15	15	33	68	83	Invertébrés
Plants	26	27	44	44	44	45	45	Plantes
Total	60	60	98	100	118	155	173	Total
Tristan da Cunha								**Tristan da Cunha**
Vertebrates	...	...	...	...	...	42	...	Vertébrés
Invertebrates	...	...	...	...	...	69	...	Invertébrés
Plants	...	...	...	...	...	45	...	Plantes
Total	...	...	...	...	...	156	...	Total
Saint Kitts and Nevis								**Saint-Kitts-et-Nevis**
Vertebrates	17	24	39	40	40	43	45	Vertébrés
Invertebrates	0	10	10	10	10	10	10	Invertébrés
Plants	2	2	2	2	2	2	2	Plantes
Total	19	36	51	52	52	55	57	Total
Saint Lucia								**Sainte-Lucie**
Vertebrates	23	29	43	45	45	48	50	Vertébrés
Invertebrates	0	11	11	11	11	11	11	Invertébrés
Plants	6	6	6	6	6	8	8	Plantes
Total	29	46	60	62	62	67	69	Total
Saint Martin (French part)								**St-Martin (partie française)**
Vertebrates	...	4	37	39	40	43	46	Vertébrés
Invertebrates	...	11	10	10	10	10	10	Invertébrés
Plants	...	2	3	3	3	3	3	Plantes
Total	...	17	50	52	53	56	59	Total
Saint Pierre and Miquelon								**Saint-Pierre-et-Miquelon**
Vertebrates	2	4	11	12	14	16	19	Vertébrés
Invertebrates	0	0	0	0	0	0	0	Invertébrés
Plants	0	0	0	0	0	0	0	Plantes
Total	2	4	11	12	14	16	19	Total

Country or area &	2004	2010	2016	2017	2018	2019	2020	Pays ou zone &
Saint Vincent & Grenadines								**Saint-Vincent-Grenadines**
Vertebrates	20	24	41	43	44	45	50	Vertébrés
Invertebrates	0	10	10	10	10	10	10	Invertébrés
Plants	4	4	5	5	5	6	5	Plantes
Total	24	38	56	58	59	61	65	Total
Samoa								**Samoa**
Vertebrates	15	23	29	29	29	30	33	Vertébrés
Invertebrates	1	53	62	62	62	63	64	Invertébrés
Plants	2	2	2	2	2	2	3	Plantes
Total	18	78	93	93	93	95	100	Total
San Marino								**Saint-Marin**
Vertebrates	...	0	0	0	0	0	1	Vertébrés
Invertebrates	...	0	1	1	1	1	1	Invertébrés
Plants	...	0	0	0	0	0	0	Plantes
Total	...	0	1	1	1	1	2	Total
Sao Tome and Principe								**Sao Tomé-et-Principe**
Vertebrates	24	33	51	52	51	51	55	Vertébrés
Invertebrates	2	2	5	5	4	4	4	Invertébrés
Plants	35	35	38	37	49	49	49	Plantes
Total	61	70	94	94	104	104	108	Total
Saudi Arabia								**Arabie saoudite**
Vertebrates	37	47	66	68	69	77	80	Vertébrés
Invertebrates	1	53	59	59	59	60	60	Invertébrés
Plants	3	3	3	4	4	4	4	Plantes
Total	41	103	128	131	132	141	144	Total
Senegal								**Sénégal**
Vertebrates	40	72	95	98	101	106	109	Vertébrés
Invertebrates	0	1	13	13	13	13	13	Invertébrés
Plants	7	9	12	12	13	20	23	Plantes
Total	47	82	120	123	127	139	145	Total
Serbia								**Serbie**
Vertebrates	...	29	35	35	35	35	35	Vertébrés
Invertebrates	...	16	24	30	35	35	35	Invertébrés
Plants	...	1	# 6	6	7	14	16	Plantes
Total	...	46	65	71	77	84	86	Total
Serbia and Monten. [former]								**Serbie-et-Monténégro [anc.]**
Vertebrates	42	...	...	...	...	...	...	Vertébrés
Invertebrates	19	...	...	...	...	...	...	Invertébrés
Plants	1	...	...	...	...	...	...	Plantes
Total	62	...	...	...	...	...	...	Total
Seychelles								**Seychelles**
Vertebrates	35	45	55	57	58	64	68	Vertébrés
Invertebrates	4	100	319	320	320	321	321	Invertébrés
Plants	45	45	62	62	61	61	62	Plantes
Total	84	190	436	439	439	446	451	Total
Sierra Leone								**Sierra Leone**
Vertebrates	35	77	103	103	105	110	111	Vertébrés
Invertebrates	4	6	8	8	8	8	8	Invertébrés
Plants	47	48	65	66	71	111	117	Plantes
Total	86	131	176	177	184	229	236	Total
Singapore								**Singapour**
Vertebrates	30	58	63	63	67	77	83	Vertébrés
Invertebrates	1	162	173	173	173	173	177	Invertébrés
Plants	54	57	58	57	60	62	66	Plantes
Total	85	277	294	293	300	312	326	Total
Sint Maarten (Dutch part)								**St-Martin (partie néerland.)**
Vertebrates	...	...	37	39	40	43	46	Vertébrés
Invertebrates	...	...	10	10	10	10	10	Invertébrés
Plants	...	...	2	2	3	2	2	Plantes
Total	...	...	49	51	53	55	58	Total
Slovakia								**Slovaquie**
Vertebrates	27	15	19	20	21	21	21	Vertébrés
Invertebrates	19	17	22	24	32	32	32	Invertébrés
Plants	2	2	# 10	10	28	54	63	Plantes
Total	48	34	51	54	81	107	116	Total

23

Country or area &	2004	2010	2016	2017	2018	2019	2020	Pays ou zone &
Slovenia								**Slovénie**
Vertebrates	32	36	50	51	53	53	58	Vertébrés
Invertebrates	42	59	77	81	83	83	84	Invertébrés
Plants	0	0	# 11	11	11	26	33	Plantes
Total	74	95	138	143	147	162	175	Total
Solomon Islands								**Îles Salomon**
Vertebrates	52	63	75	77	75	77	82	Vertébrés
Invertebrates	6	141	151	151	151	150	150	Invertébrés
Plants	16	16	17	17	16	16	24	Plantes
Total	74	220	243	245	242	243	256	Total
Somalia								**Somalie**
Vertebrates	46	56	66	67	71	76	84	Vertébrés
Invertebrates	1	51	62	62	62	62	62	Invertébrés
Plants	17	21	43	46	46	49	53	Plantes
Total	64	128	171	175	179	187	199	Total
South Africa								**Afrique du Sud**
Vertebrates	155	185	219	233	248	242	247	Vertébrés
Invertebrates	127	159	202	202	208	208	196	Invertébrés
Plants	75	97	116	146	151	153	154	Plantes
Total	357	441	537	581	607	603	597	Total
South Georgia & Sandwich Is.								**Géorgie du S.-Îles Sandwich**
Vertebrates	12	10	9	9	9	9	9	Vertébrés
Invertebrates	0	0	0	0	0	0	0	Invertébrés
Plants	0	0	0	0	0	0	0	Plantes
Total	12	10	9	9	9	9	9	Total
South Sudan								**Soudan du sud**
Vertebrates	...	...	30	34	36	39	42	Vertébrés
Invertebrates	...	...	0	0	1	1	1	Invertébrés
Plants	...	...	15	15	16	17	18	Plantes
Total	...	...	45	49	53	57	61	Total
Spain								**Espagne**
Vertebrates	76	118	135	138	142	142	143	Vertébrés
Invertebrates	63	67	236	258	288	288	290	Invertébrés
Plants	14	55	# 221	221	251	306	319	Plantes
Total	153	240	592	617	681	736	752	Total
Sri Lanka								**Sri Lanka**
Vertebrates	112	149	167	167	172	175	213	Vertébrés
Invertebrates	2	120	130	130	130	129	130	Invertébrés
Plants	280	283	291	290	294	298	298	Plantes
Total	394	552	588	587	596	602	641	Total
State of Palestine								**État de Palestine**
Vertebrates	4	16	23	24	26	25	25	Vertébrés
Invertebrates	0	2	4	4	4	4	4	Invertébrés
Plants	0	0	3	3	6	10	10	Plantes
Total	4	18	30	31	36	39	39	Total
Sudan								**Soudan**
Vertebrates	36	49	63	67	73	82	89	Vertébrés
Invertebrates	2	45	50	50	50	50	50	Invertébrés
Plants	17	18	16	16	17	19	19	Plantes
Total	55	112	129	133	140	151	158	Total
Suriname								**Suriname**
Vertebrates	32	38	55	55	57	57	58	Vertébrés
Invertebrates	0	1	1	1	1	1	1	Invertébrés
Plants	27	26	27	27	27	28	29	Plantes
Total	59	65	83	83	85	86	88	Total
Svalbard and Jan Mayen Is.								**Îles Svalbard-et-Jan Mayen**
Vertebrates	9	3	7	7	9	10	10	Vertébrés
Invertebrates	0	0	0	0	0	0	0	Invertébrés
Plants	0	0	0	0	0	1	1	Plantes
Total	9	3	7	7	9	11	11	Total
Sweden								**Suède**
Vertebrates	20	15	24	25	27	28	29	Vertébrés
Invertebrates	13	11	15	15	16	16	16	Invertébrés
Plants	3	3	# 14	14	15	41	53	Plantes
Total	36	29	53	54	58	85	98	Total

Country or area [&]	2004	2010	2016	2017	2018	2019	2020	Pays ou zone [&]
Switzerland								**Suisse**
Vertebrates	17	14	18	20	22	22	22	Vertébrés
Invertebrates	30	28	43	44	47	47	47	Invertébrés
Plants	2	3	# 10	10	10	43	59	Plantes
Total	49	45	71	74	79	112	128	Total
Syrian Arab Republic								**République arabe syrienne**
Vertebrates	26	68	94	94	91	91	92	Vertébrés
Invertebrates	3	7	20	20	22	22	23	Invertébrés
Plants	0	3	13	18	26	31	32	Plantes
Total	29	78	127	132	139	144	147	Total
Tajikistan								**Tadjikistan**
Vertebrates	20	24	29	30	32	32	32	Vertébrés
Invertebrates	2	2	3	3	3	3	3	Invertébrés
Plants	2	14	12	12	12	13	13	Plantes
Total	24	40	44	45	47	48	48	Total
Thailand								**Thaïlande**
Vertebrates	136	201	245	248	255	275	279	Vertébrés
Invertebrates	1	185	211	211	211	212	213	Invertébrés
Plants	84	91	150	152	155	168	182	Plantes
Total	221	477	606	611	621	655	674	Total
Timor-Leste								**Timor-Leste**
Vertebrates	11	18	20	22	24	31	35	Vertébrés
Invertebrates	0	0	1	1	1	1	1	Invertébrés
Plants	0	0	1	1	1	3	5	Plantes
Total	11	18	22	24	26	35	41	Total
Togo								**Togo**
Vertebrates	22	43	63	65	70	74	78	Vertébrés
Invertebrates	0	1	3	3	3	3	3	Invertébrés
Plants	10	10	12	12	12	13	13	Plantes
Total	32	54	78	80	85	90	94	Total
Tokelau								**Tokélaou**
Vertebrates	6	10	14	14	14	16	19	Vertébrés
Invertebrates	0	31	35	35	35	35	35	Invertébrés
Plants	0	0	0	0	0	0	0	Plantes
Total	6	41	49	49	49	51	54	Total
Tonga								**Tonga**
Vertebrates	11	19	26	28	28	28	32	Vertébrés
Invertebrates	2	35	47	47	47	47	51	Invertébrés
Plants	3	4	4	4	5	5	7	Plantes
Total	16	58	77	79	80	80	90	Total
Trinidad and Tobago								**Trinité-et-Tobago**
Vertebrates	32	37	56	57	58	60	66	Vertébrés
Invertebrates	0	10	10	10	10	10	10	Invertébrés
Plants	1	1	2	2	50	51	50	Plantes
Total	33	48	68	69	118	121	126	Total
Tunisia								**Tunisie**
Vertebrates	31	57	70	70	71	71	74	Vertébrés
Invertebrates	5	11	17	19	20	20	21	Invertébrés
Plants	0	7	7	7	10	10	12	Plantes
Total	36	75	94	96	101	101	107	Total
Turkey								**Turquie**
Vertebrates	76	130	199	199	201	208	209	Vertébrés
Invertebrates	13	15	78	82	85	86	88	Invertébrés
Plants	3	5	# 105	107	114	132	138	Plantes
Total	92	150	382	388	400	426	435	Total
Turkmenistan								**Turkménistan**
Vertebrates	35	37	42	43	46	48	48	Vertébrés
Invertebrates	5	5	7	7	7	7	7	Invertébrés
Plants	0	3	4	4	4	4	4	Plantes
Total	40	45	53	54	57	59	59	Total
Turks and Caicos Islands								**Îles Turques-et-Caïques**
Vertebrates	18	22	37	41	42	44	47	Vertébrés
Invertebrates	0	10	10	10	10	10	10	Invertébrés
Plants	2	2	9	9	9	9	8	Plantes
Total	20	34	56	60	61	63	65	Total

Country or area &	2004	2010	2016	2017	2018	2019	2020	Pays ou zone &
Tuvalu								**Tuvalu**
Vertebrates	7	14	17	18	18	20	21	Vertébrés
Invertebrates	1	71	78	78	78	78	78	Invertébrés
Plants	0	0	0	0	0	0	0	Plantes
Total	8	85	95	96	96	98	99	Total
Uganda								**Ouganda**
Vertebrates	77	110	116	119	124	126	128	Vertébrés
Invertebrates	19	15	19	24	30	30	31	Invertébrés
Plants	38	41	52	53	64	83	107	Plantes
Total	134	166	187	196	218	239	266	Total
Ukraine								**Ukraine**
Vertebrates	40	45	52	53	53	53	53	Vertébrés
Invertebrates	14	15	23	31	38	38	38	Invertébrés
Plants	1	1	# 19	18	23	36	41	Plantes
Total	55	61	94	102	114	127	132	Total
United Arab Emirates								**Émirats arabes unis**
Vertebrates	23	32	41	41	45	49	54	Vertébrés
Invertebrates	0	16	15	15	15	15	15	Invertébrés
Plants	0	0	0	0	0	0	0	Plantes
Total	23	48	56	56	60	64	69	Total
United Kingdom								**Royaume-Uni**
Vertebrates	32	48	61	62	64	66	67	Vertébrés
Invertebrates	10	11	18	18	19	20	20	Invertébrés
Plants	13	14	# 22	22	48	78	89	Plantes
Total	55	73	101	102	131	164	176	Total
United Rep. of Tanzania								**Rép.-Unie de Tanzanie**
Vertebrates	144	313	355	355	360	366	386	Vertébrés
Invertebrates	33	80	129	125	129	147	147	Invertébrés
Plants	239	298	602	602	632	661	726	Plantes
Total	416	691	1 086	1 082	1 121	1 174	1 259	Total
U.S. Minor Outlying islands								**Îles min. éloignées des É-U**
Vertebrates	15	23	25	26	26	24	26	Vertébrés
Invertebrates	0	44	47	47	47	47	47	Invertébrés
Plants	0	0	0	0	0	0	0	Plantes
Total	15	67	72	73	73	71	73	Total
United States of America								**États-Unis d'Amérique**
Vertebrates	342	376	454	456	462	479	482	Vertébrés
Invertebrates	561	531	578	580	580	581	586	Invertébrés
Plants	240	245	# 447	477	498	556	587	Plantes
Total	1 143	1 152	1 479	1 513	1 540	1 616	1 655	Total
United States Virgin Islands								**Îles Vierges américaines**
Vertebrates	22	21	42	46	46	50	54	Vertébrés
Invertebrates	0	0	0	0	0	0	0	Invertébrés
Plants	9	12	12	12	17	17	20	Plantes
Total	31	33	54	58	63	67	74	Total
Uruguay								**Uruguay**
Vertebrates	48	78	82	82	85	86	92	Vertébrés
Invertebrates	1	1	2	2	2	2	2	Invertébrés
Plants	1	1	22	22	22	22	22	Plantes
Total	50	80	106	106	109	110	116	Total
Uzbekistan								**Ouzbékistan**
Vertebrates	29	34	39	39	43	43	43	Vertébrés
Invertebrates	1	1	3	3	3	3	3	Invertébrés
Plants	1	15	17	17	16	16	16	Plantes
Total	31	50	59	59	62	62	62	Total
Vanuatu								**Vanuatu**
Vertebrates	19	32	37	36	38	39	42	Vertébrés
Invertebrates	0	79	92	91	91	91	91	Invertébrés
Plants	10	10	10	10	10	10	11	Plantes
Total	29	121	139	137	139	140	144	Total
Venezuela (Boliv. Rep. of)								**Venezuela (Rép. boliv. du)**
Vertebrates	151	179	212	220	228	231	251	Vertébrés
Invertebrates	1	21	26	26	26	26	26	Invertébrés
Plants	67	70	82	82	81	90	102	Plantes
Total	219	270	320	328	335	347	379	Total

Country or area [&]	2004	2010	2016	2017	2018	2019	2020	Pays ou zone [&]
Viet Nam								**Viet Nam**
Vertebrates	144	186	260	260	278	310	322	Vertébrés
Invertebrates	0	92	152	152	152	154	156	Invertébrés
Plants	145	146	204	204	231	236	260	Plantes
Total	289	424	616	616	661	700	738	Total
Wallis and Futuna Islands								**Îles Wallis-et-Futuna**
Vertebrates	12	16	24	24	24	24	27	Vertébrés
Invertebrates	0	57	65	64	64	64	64	Invertébrés
Plants	1	1	1	1	1	1	1	Plantes
Total	13	74	90	89	89	89	92	Total
Western Sahara								**Sahara occidental**
Vertebrates	18	38	44	46	48	47	55	Vertébrés
Invertebrates	1	1	3	3	3	3	3	Invertébrés
Plants	0	0	0	0	0	0	0	Plantes
Total	19	39	47	49	51	50	58	Total
Yemen								**Yémen**
Vertebrates	34	48	67	68	72	78	82	Vertébrés
Invertebrates	2	62	68	68	68	68	68	Invertébrés
Plants	159	159	162	162	163	163	163	Plantes
Total	195	269	297	298	303	309	313	Total
Zambia								**Zambie**
Vertebrates	24	44	51	53	54	56	61	Vertébrés
Invertebrates	7	14	14	14	15	14	14	Invertébrés
Plants	8	9	20	21	22	28	32	Plantes
Total	39	67	85	88	91	98	107	Total
Zimbabwe								**Zimbabwe**
Vertebrates	24	34	39	41	42	43	43	Vertébrés
Invertebrates	2	5	5	5	7	8	8	Invertébrés
Plants	17	16	17	43	46	52	71	Plantes
Total	43	55	61	89	95	103	122	Total

Source:

World Conservation Union (IUCN), Gland and Cambridge, IUCN Red List of Threatened Species publication, last accessed June 2020.

Source:

Union internationale pour la conservation de la nature et de ses ressources (UICN), Gland et Cambridge, Liste rouge des espèces menacées publiée par l'UICN, dernier accès juin 2020.

[&] Vertebrates consists of mammals, birds, reptiles, amphibians and fish. Invertebrates consists of molluscs and other invertebrates. Plants consists of plants, and since 2016, fungi and protists. Reptiles, fishes, molluscs, other invertebrates, plants, fungi & protists: please note that for these groups, there are still many species that have not yet been assessed for the IUCN Red List and therefore their status is not known (i.e. these groups have not yet been completely assessed). Therefore the figures presented below for these groups should be interpreted as the number of species known to be threatened within those species that have been assessed to date, and not as the overall total number of threatened species for each group.

[&] Les vertébrés se composent de mammifères, oiseaux, reptiles, amphibiens et poissons; les invertébrés se composent de mollusques et autres invertébrés. A partir de 2016, les plantes incluent aussi les champignons et les protistes. Veuillez noter que beaucoup d'espèces tels que les reptiles, les poissons, les mollusques et autres invertébrés, les plantes, les champignons et les protistes n'ont pas été encore évaluées dans le cadre de la Liste rouge de l'UICN , donc leur statut est inconnu pour le moment (c.-à-d. ces groupes ne sont que partiellement évalués). En conséquence, les données présentées ci-dessous pour chaque groupe doivent être interprétées comme le nombre d'espèces connues et menacées parmi les espèces évaluées à ce jour, et non comme le nombre total d'espèces menacées dans chaque groupe.

1   Excluding overseas territories.
2   The figures for Amphibians displayed here are those that were agreed at the GAA Brazil workshop in April 2003; the "consistent Red List Categories" were not yet accepted by the Brazilian experts.

3   For statistical purposes, the data for China do not include those for the Hong Kong Special Administrative Region (Hong Kong SAR), Macao Special Administrative Region (Macao SAR) and Taiwan Province of China.
4   Excluding the north islands, Saint Barthélemy and Saint Martin (French part).
5   Including Ascension and Tristan da Cunha.

1   Non compris les départements d'outre-mer.
2   Les chiffres concernant les amphibiens sont ceux qui ont été convenus lors de l'atelier de l'Évaluation mondiale des amphibiens du Brésil en avril 2003 ; les "catégories conformes à la Liste rouge" n'ont pas encore été acceptées par les experts brésiliens.
3   Pour la présentation des statistiques, les données pour la Chine ne comprennent pas la région administrative spéciale de Hong Kong (RAS de Hong Kong), la région administrative spéciale de Macao (RAS de Macao) et la province chinoise de Taïwan.
4   Les îles du Nord, Saint-Barthélemy et Saint-Martin (partie française) sont exclues.
5   Y compris Ascension et Tristan da Cunha.

CO2 emission estimates
From fossil fuel combustion (thousand metric tons of carbon dioxide) and per capita

Estimation des émissions de CO2
Dues à la combustion de combustibles fossils (milliers de tonnes de dioxyde de carbone) et par habitant

Country or area[&]	1975	1985	1995	2005	2010	2015	2016	2017	Pays ou zone[&]
Albania									**Albanie**
Thousand metric tons	4 338	6 930	1 849	3 825	3 930	3 825	3 674	4 342	Milliers de tonnes
Metric tons per capita	1.8	2.3	0.6	1.3	1.3	1.3	1.3	1.5	Tonnes par habitant
Algeria									**Algérie**
Thousand metric tons	13 553	42 073	55 337	77 474	95 535	130 427	127 640	130 494	Milliers de tonnes
Metric tons per capita	0.8	1.9	1.9	2.3	2.6	3.3	3.1	3.2	Tonnes par habitant
Angola									**Angola**
Thousand metric tons	1 956	2 818	3 914	6 147	15 152	21 532	21 458	18 021	Milliers de tonnes
Metric tons per capita	0.3	0.3	0.3	0.3	0.6	0.8	0.7	0.6	Tonnes par habitant
Argentina									**Argentine**
Thousand metric tons	85 232	87 779	117 328	149 476	173 769	190 385	190 512	183 375	Milliers de tonnes
Metric tons per capita	3.3	2.9	3.4	3.8	4.2	4.4	4.3	4.1	Tonnes par habitant
Armenia									**Arménie**
Thousand metric tons	...	...	3 368	4 130	4 048	4 702	4 833	5 166	Milliers de tonnes
Metric tons per capita	...	...	1.0	1.4	1.4	1.6	1.7	1.8	Tonnes par habitant
Australia [1]									**Australie** [1]
Thousand metric tons	179 467	220 128	285 324	365 515	383 619	373 847	381 879	384 584	Milliers de tonnes
Metric tons per capita	12.8	13.9	15.7	17.9	17.4	15.7	15.8	15.6	Tonnes par habitant
Austria									**Autriche**
Thousand metric tons	49 489	52 649	59 549	74 764	68 571	62 221	62 049	64 872	Milliers de tonnes
Metric tons per capita	6.5	7.0	7.5	9.1	8.2	7.2	7.1	7.4	Tonnes par habitant
Azerbaijan									**Azerbaïdjan**
Thousand metric tons	...	...	32 372	29 018	23 532	30 806	31 409	30 806	Milliers de tonnes
Metric tons per capita	...	...	4.2	3.5	2.6	3.2	3.2	3.1	Tonnes par habitant
Bahrain									**Bahreïn**
Thousand metric tons	5 230	9 100	13 458	20 565	25 552	30 073	29 639	29 814	Milliers de tonnes
Metric tons per capita	19.6	21.7	23.9	23.1	20.6	21.9	20.8	20.0	Tonnes par habitant
Bangladesh [2]									**Bangladesh** [2]
Thousand metric tons	4 410	7 705	16 485	31 960	49 900	70 895	72 944	78 270	Milliers de tonnes
Metric tons per capita	0.1	0.1	0.1	0.2	0.3	0.4	0.4	0.5	Tonnes par habitant
Belarus									**Bélarus**
Thousand metric tons	...	...	56 958	55 014	59 498	52 618	53 063	54 070	Milliers de tonnes
Metric tons per capita	...	...	5.6	5.7	6.3	5.5	5.6	5.7	Tonnes par habitant
Belgium									**Belgique**
Thousand metric tons	115 557	100 992	111 314	107 677	103 891	92 790	91 932	90 368	Milliers de tonnes
Metric tons per capita	11.8	10.2	11.0	10.3	9.5	8.3	8.1	8.0	Tonnes par habitant
Benin									**Bénin**
Thousand metric tons	463	473	222	2 678	4 573	5 262	6 603	6 763	Milliers de tonnes
Metric tons per capita	0.1	0.1	~0.0	0.3	0.5	0.5	0.6	0.6	Tonnes par habitant
Bolivia (Plurin. State of)									**Bolivie (État plurin. de)**
Thousand metric tons	3 224	4 314	6 894	8 976	13 638	18 100	20 126	21 899	Milliers de tonnes
Metric tons per capita	0.6	0.7	0.9	1.0	1.4	1.7	1.8	2.0	Tonnes par habitant
Bosnia and Herzegovina									**Bosnie-Herzégovine**
Thousand metric tons	...	...	3 280	15 858	20 483	19 306	22 019	22 328	Milliers de tonnes
Metric tons per capita	...	...	0.9	4.2	5.5	5.5	6.3	6.4	Tonnes par habitant
Botswana									**Botswana**
Thousand metric tons	...	1 501	3 190	4 279	3 271	7 069	6 980	7 717	Milliers de tonnes
Metric tons per capita	...	1.3	2.0	2.3	1.6	3.2	3.1	3.4	Tonnes par habitant
Brazil									**Brésil**
Thousand metric tons	129 628	156 328	228 000	311 624	372 004	453 634	418 524	427 633	Milliers de tonnes
Metric tons per capita	1.2	1.2	1.4	1.7	1.9	2.2	2.0	2.0	Tonnes par habitant
Brunei Darussalam									**Brunéi Darussalam**
Thousand metric tons	1 408	2 946	4 503	4 823	6 862	5 978	6 412	6 710	Milliers de tonnes
Metric tons per capita	8.7	13.1	15.2	13.2	17.6	14.3	15.2	15.6	Tonnes par habitant
Bulgaria									**Bulgarie**
Thousand metric tons	73 315	82 206	52 737	46 473	44 362	43 715	40 549	42 820	Milliers de tonnes
Metric tons per capita	8.4	9.2	6.3	6.1	6.0	6.1	5.7	6.1	Tonnes par habitant
Cambodia									**Cambodge**
Thousand metric tons	...	...	1 471	2 639	4 622	8 012	9 287	10 763	Milliers de tonnes
Metric tons per capita	...	...	0.1	0.2	0.3	0.5	0.6	0.7	Tonnes par habitant
Cameroon									**Cameroun**
Thousand metric tons	1 019	2 378	2 459	2 936	5 051	5 945	6 104	6 153	Milliers de tonnes
Metric tons per capita	0.1	0.2	0.2	0.2	0.3	0.3	0.3	0.3	Tonnes par habitant

CO2 emission estimates *(continued)*
From fossil fuel combustion (thousand metric tons of carbon dioxide) and per capita

Estimation des émissions de CO2 *(suite)*
Dues à la combustion de combustibles fossils (milliers de tonnes de dioxyde de carbone) et par habitant

Country or area[&]	1975	1985	1995	2005	2010	2015	2016	2017	Pays ou zone[&]
Canada									**Canada**
Thousand metric tons	377 106	393 880	448 986	540 431	528 619	557 661	548 095	547 799	Milliers de tonnes
Metric tons per capita	16.3	15.2	15.3	16.8	15.5	15.6	15.2	15.0	Tonnes par habitant
Chile									**Chili**
Thousand metric tons	17 112	19 631	37 075	54 435	68 605	81 092	85 246	86 087	Milliers de tonnes
Metric tons per capita	1.6	1.6	2.6	3.3	4.0	4.5	4.7	4.6	Tonnes par habitant
China [3]									**Chine** [3]
Thousand metric tons	1 029 319	1 626 027	2 900 265	5 407 518	7 832 717	9 101 376	9 064 429	9 257 934	Milliers de tonnes
Metric tons per capita	1.1	1.5	2.4	4.1	5.9	6.6	6.6	6.7	Tonnes par habitant
China, Hong Kong SAR									**Chine, RAS de Hong Kong**
Thousand metric tons	10 897	22 306	36 527	41 332	41 997	43 917	44 729	44 035	Milliers de tonnes
Metric tons per capita	2.4	4.1	5.9	6.1	6.0	6.0	6.1	6.0	Tonnes par habitant
Colombia									**Colombie**
Thousand metric tons	28 297	39 473	54 458	53 585	60 224	77 610	87 721	75 292	Milliers de tonnes
Metric tons per capita	1.1	1.3	1.5	1.2	1.3	1.6	1.8	1.5	Tonnes par habitant
Congo									**Congo**
Thousand metric tons	606	760	537	844	1 833	3 165	2 978	2 847	Milliers de tonnes
Metric tons per capita	0.4	0.4	0.2	0.2	0.4	0.6	0.6	0.5	Tonnes par habitant
Costa Rica									**Costa Rica**
Thousand metric tons	1 738	1 949	4 439	5 463	6 622	6 940	7 488	7 584	Milliers de tonnes
Metric tons per capita	0.8	0.7	1.3	1.3	1.5	1.4	1.5	1.5	Tonnes par habitant
Côte d'Ivoire									**Côte d'Ivoire**
Thousand metric tons	3 038	3 047	3 262	5 813	6 245	9 544	9 587	10 234	Milliers de tonnes
Metric tons per capita	0.5	0.3	0.2	0.3	0.3	0.4	0.4	0.4	Tonnes par habitant
Croatia									**Croatie**
Thousand metric tons	...	...	14 774	19 917	18 249	15 513	15 859	16 193	Milliers de tonnes
Metric tons per capita	...	...	3.2	4.5	4.1	3.7	3.8	3.9	Tonnes par habitant
Cuba									**Cuba**
Thousand metric tons	24 185	32 179	22 449	25 051	29 509	26 842	27 791	26 216	Milliers de tonnes
Metric tons per capita	2.6	3.2	2.1	2.2	2.6	2.3	2.4	2.3	Tonnes par habitant
Curaçao									**Curaçao**
Thousand metric tons	...	...	...	...	...	4 691	4 151	3 748	Milliers de tonnes
Metric tons per capita	...	...	...	...	...	29.7	25.9	23.3	Tonnes par habitant
Cyprus [4]									**Chypre** [4]
Thousand metric tons	1 658	2 765	5 048	7 048	7 261	5 901	6 269	6 368	Milliers de tonnes
Metric tons per capita	3.3	5.1	7.8	9.6	8.9	7.0	7.4	7.4	Tonnes par habitant
Czechia									**Tchéquie**
Thousand metric tons	154 982[5]	175 254[5]	123 175	118 370	112 460	99 425	101 157	101 683	Milliers de tonnes
Metric tons per capita	15.4[5]	17.0[5]	11.9	11.6	10.7	9.4	9.6	9.6	Tonnes par habitant
Dem. People's Rep. Korea									**Rép. pop. dém. de Corée**
Thousand metric tons	78 599	129 448	76 532	75 340	49 293	22 546	25 427	19 580	Milliers de tonnes
Metric tons per capita	4.8	6.9	3.5	3.2	2.0	0.9	1.0	0.8	Tonnes par habitant
Dem. Rep. of the Congo									**Rép. dém. du Congo**
Thousand metric tons	2 621	3 254	1 143	1 282	1 869	2 735	1 979	2 202	Milliers de tonnes
Metric tons per capita	0.1	0.1	~0.0	~0.0	~0.0	~0.0	~0.0	~0.0	Tonnes par habitant
Denmark [6]									**Danemark** [6]
Thousand metric tons	52 646	61 032	58 385	48 495	47 254	31 948	33 487	31 264	Milliers de tonnes
Metric tons per capita	10.4	11.9	11.2	8.9	8.5	5.6	5.8	5.4	Tonnes par habitant
Dominican Republic									**République dominicaine**
Thousand metric tons	5 213	6 234	11 221	17 522	19 022	21 520	22 534	21 430	Milliers de tonnes
Metric tons per capita	1.0	1.0	1.4	1.9	1.9	2.0	2.1	2.0	Tonnes par habitant
Ecuador									**Équateur**
Thousand metric tons	5 936	11 666	16 691	23 927	32 750	37 357	35 393	34 299	Milliers de tonnes
Metric tons per capita	0.9	1.3	1.5	1.7	2.2	2.3	2.2	2.1	Tonnes par habitant
Egypt [2]									**Égypte** [2]
Thousand metric tons	25 581	64 474	81 466	145 028	176 436	199 545	204 113	209 219	Milliers de tonnes
Metric tons per capita	0.7	1.3	1.3	1.9	2.1	2.1	2.1	2.1	Tonnes par habitant
El Salvador									**El Salvador**
Thousand metric tons	1 930	1 641	4 573	6 253	5 826	6 389	6 372	5 736	Milliers de tonnes
Metric tons per capita	0.5	0.3	0.8	1.0	0.9	1.0	1.0	0.9	Tonnes par habitant
Eritrea									**Érythrée**
Thousand metric tons	...	...	776	578	480	590	600	632	Milliers de tonnes
Metric tons per capita	...	...	0.3	0.1	0.1	0.1	0.1	0.1	Tonnes par habitant

CO2 emission estimates *(continued)*
From fossil fuel combustion (thousand metric tons of carbon dioxide) and per capita

Estimation des émissions de CO2 *(suite)*
Dues à la combustion de combustibles fossils (milliers de tonnes de dioxyde de carbone) et par habitant

Country or area[&]	1975	1985	1995	2005	2010	2015	2016	2017	Pays ou zone[&]
Estonia									**Estonie**
Thousand metric tons	...	...	15 889	16 748	18 564	15 148	15 461	15 972	Milliers de tonnes
Metric tons per capita	...	...	11.0	12.3	13.9	11.5	11.7	12.1	Tonnes par habitant
Ethiopia									**Éthiopie**
Thousand metric tons	1 178[7]	1 386[7]	2 326	4 482	5 899	10 060	11 843	13 060	Milliers de tonnes
Metric tons per capita [7]	~0.0	~0.0	~0.0	0.1	0.1	0.1	0.1	0.1	Tonnes par habitant [7]
Finland									**Finlande**
Thousand metric tons	44 189	48 285	55 715	54 918	62 001	42 366	45 127	42 598	Milliers de tonnes
Metric tons per capita	9.4	9.9	10.9	10.5	11.6	7.7	8.2	7.7	Tonnes par habitant
France [8]									**France [8]**
Thousand metric tons	423 108	351 798	343 648	371 893	340 218	299 641	301 696	306 124	Milliers de tonnes
Metric tons per capita	7.8	6.2	5.8	5.9	5.2	4.5[9]	4.5[9]	4.6[9]	Tonnes par habitant
Gabon									**Gabon**
Thousand metric tons	757	1 682	1 315	1 733	2 660	3 253	3 357	3 368	Milliers de tonnes
Metric tons per capita	1.2	2.0	1.2	1.2	1.6	1.7	1.7	1.7	Tonnes par habitant
Georgia									**Géorgie**
Thousand metric tons	...	...	8 137	4 066	4 995	8 383	8 809	8 720	Milliers de tonnes
Metric tons per capita	...	...	1.7	1.0	1.3	2.3	2.4	2.3	Tonnes par habitant
Germany									**Allemagne**
Thousand metric tons	973 366	1 004 256	856 597	786 664	758 803	729 684	734 487	718 794	Milliers de tonnes
Metric tons per capita	12.4	12.9	10.5	9.7	9.5	8.9	8.9	8.7	Tonnes par habitant
Ghana									**Ghana**
Thousand metric tons	2 306	2 067	3 184	6 307	10 420	14 089	12 968	13 780	Milliers de tonnes
Metric tons per capita	0.2	0.2	0.2	0.3	0.4	0.5	0.5	0.5	Tonnes par habitant
Gibraltar									**Gibraltar**
Thousand metric tons	62	90	281	406	474	590	646	704	Milliers de tonnes
Metric tons per capita	2.4	3.2	9.7	13.1	15.3	17.3	19.0	20.7	Tonnes par habitant
Greece									**Grèce**
Thousand metric tons	34 100	54 480	76 478	95 156	83 369	64 543	63 077	63 213	Milliers de tonnes
Metric tons per capita	3.7	5.4	7.2	8.7	7.5	6.0	5.9	5.9	Tonnes par habitant
Guatemala									**Guatemala**
Thousand metric tons	3 016	3 184	5 859	10 622	10 273	15 164	16 261	15 703	Milliers de tonnes
Metric tons per capita	0.5	0.4	0.6	0.8	0.7	0.9	1.0	0.9	Tonnes par habitant
Haiti									**Haïti**
Thousand metric tons	413	796	902	1 981	2 095	3 209	3 250	3 293	Milliers de tonnes
Metric tons per capita	0.1	0.1	0.1	0.2	0.2	0.3	0.3	0.3	Tonnes par habitant
Honduras									**Honduras**
Thousand metric tons	1 328	1 672	3 575	7 193	7 535	9 559	9 132	9 427	Milliers de tonnes
Metric tons per capita	0.4	0.4	0.6	1.0	0.9	1.1	1.0	1.0	Tonnes par habitant
Hungary									**Hongrie**
Thousand metric tons	70 173	79 755	56 245	54 722	47 145	42 708	43 778	45 784	Milliers de tonnes
Metric tons per capita	6.7	7.5	5.4	5.4	4.7	4.3	4.5	4.7	Tonnes par habitant
Iceland									**Islande**
Thousand metric tons	1 614	1 628	1 964	2 235	1 949	2 057	2 065	2 173	Milliers de tonnes
Metric tons per capita	7.4	6.8	7.4	7.6	6.1	6.2	6.2	6.3	Tonnes par habitant
India									**Inde**
Thousand metric tons	217 194	376 237	703 332	1 073 701	1 583 431	2 026 705	2 057 682	2 161 567	Milliers de tonnes
Metric tons per capita	0.4	0.5	0.7	0.9	1.3	1.5	1.6	1.6	Tonnes par habitant
Indonesia									**Indonésie**
Thousand metric tons	37 840	84 233	204 207	317 824	357 646	459 139	454 267	496 406	Milliers de tonnes
Metric tons per capita	0.3	0.5	1.0	1.4	1.5	1.8	1.7	1.9	Tonnes par habitant
Iran (Islamic Republic of) [10]									**Iran (Rép. islamique d') [10]**
Thousand metric tons	68 033	145 048	244 570	417 781	498 608	553 301	554 410	567 123	Milliers de tonnes
Metric tons per capita	2.1	3.1	4.0	5.9	6.7	7.0	6.9	7.0	Tonnes par habitant
Iraq									**Iraq**
Thousand metric tons	15 539	37 974	95 145	73 176	103 577	130 762	140 337	139 878	Milliers de tonnes
Metric tons per capita	1.3	2.4	4.7	2.7	3.4	3.6	3.8	3.7	Tonnes par habitant
Ireland									**Irlande**
Thousand metric tons	21 149	26 453	32 637	44 420	39 517	35 342	36 863	35 720	Milliers de tonnes
Metric tons per capita	6.7	7.5	9.1	10.7	8.7	7.5	7.8	7.4	Tonnes par habitant
Israel									**Israël**
Thousand metric tons	16 410	24 311	44 874	58 797	68 438	63 928	63 082	63 766	Milliers de tonnes
Metric tons per capita	4.8	5.7	8.1	8.4	9.0	7.6	7.4	7.3	Tonnes par habitant

24

CO2 emission estimates *(continued)*
From fossil fuel combustion (thousand metric tons of carbon dioxide) and per capita

Estimation des émissions de CO2 *(suite)*
Dues à la combustion de combustibles fossils (milliers de tonnes de dioxyde de carbone) et par habitant

Country or area[&]	1975	1985	1995	2005	2010	2015	2016	2017	Pays ou zone[&]
Italy [11]									**Italie [11]**
Thousand metric tons	317 060	342 047	401 105	456 432	391 992	329 662	325 657	321 481	Milliers de tonnes
Metric tons per capita	5.7	6.0	7.1	7.8	6.6	5.4	5.4	5.3	Tonnes par habitant
Jamaica									**Jamaïque**
Thousand metric tons	7 448	4 669	8 417	10 282	6 931	6 993	7 525	6 972	Milliers de tonnes
Metric tons per capita	3.7	2.0	3.3	3.7	2.5	2.4	2.6	2.4	Tonnes par habitant
Japan [12]									**Japon [12]**
Thousand metric tons	849 910	866 234	1 118 247	1 166 814	1 127 152	1 155 667	1 146 888	1 132 435	Milliers de tonnes
Metric tons per capita	7.6	7.2	8.9	9.1	8.8	9.1	9.0	8.9	Tonnes par habitant
Jordan									**Jordanie**
Thousand metric tons	2 151	7 475	12 194	17 922	18 801	23 785	23 835	25 550	Milliers de tonnes
Metric tons per capita	1.0	2.6	2.7	3.1	2.6	2.6	2.5	2.6	Tonnes par habitant
Kazakhstan									**Kazakhstan**
Thousand metric tons	...	...	170 519	156 902	221 101	245 763	254 928	255 768	Milliers de tonnes
Metric tons per capita	...	...	10.8	10.4	13.5	14.0	14.3	14.2	Tonnes par habitant
Kenya									**Kenya**
Thousand metric tons	3 461	4 593	5 729	7 483	11 210	14 722	16 266	16 265	Milliers de tonnes
Metric tons per capita	0.3	0.2	0.2	0.2	0.3	0.3	0.3	0.3	Tonnes par habitant
Kosovo									**Kosovo**
Thousand metric tons	...	...	...	6 639	8 696	8 606	9 080	8 169	Milliers de tonnes
Metric tons per capita	...	...	...	3.9	4.9	4.8	5.0	4.5	Tonnes par habitant
Kuwait									**Koweït**
Thousand metric tons	15 107	36 749	32 352	64 750	77 004	91 639	93 179	89 421	Milliers de tonnes
Metric tons per capita	14.7	21.1	20.1	28.4	25.7	23.3	23.0	21.6	Tonnes par habitant
Kyrgyzstan									**Kirghizistan**
Thousand metric tons	...	...	4 459	4 892	6 040	9 897	9 299	8 909	Milliers de tonnes
Metric tons per capita	...	...	1.0	0.9	1.1	1.7	1.5	1.4	Tonnes par habitant
Latvia									**Lettonie**
Thousand metric tons	...	...	8 903	7 581	8 088	6 846	6 799	6 680	Milliers de tonnes
Metric tons per capita	...	...	3.6	3.4	3.9	3.5	3.5	3.4	Tonnes par habitant
Lebanon									**Liban**
Thousand metric tons	5 709	6 614	12 830	14 524	18 293	24 619	25 461	26 931	Milliers de tonnes
Metric tons per capita	2.2	2.5	4.2	3.6	4.2	4.2	4.2	4.4	Tonnes par habitant
Libya									**Libye**
Thousand metric tons	8 671	21 244	32 954	43 101	48 182	42 726	41 056	41 528	Milliers de tonnes
Metric tons per capita	3.3	5.5	6.7	7.4	7.8	6.9	6.5	6.5	Tonnes par habitant
Lithuania									**Lituanie**
Thousand metric tons	...	...	13 434	12 444	12 315	10 550	10 750	10 811	Milliers de tonnes
Metric tons per capita	...	...	3.7	3.7	4.0	3.6	3.7	3.8	Tonnes par habitant
Luxembourg									**Luxembourg**
Thousand metric tons	12 739	10 335	8 226	11 493	10 664	8 805	8 502	8 631	Milliers de tonnes
Metric tons per capita	35.5	28.2	20.1	24.7	21.0	15.5	14.6	14.5	Tonnes par habitant
Malaysia									**Malaisie**
Thousand metric tons	16 217	32 911	79 590	155 843	189 861	220 438	216 236	211 047	Milliers de tonnes
Metric tons per capita	1.3	2.1	3.9	6.1	6.8	7.2	6.9	6.7	Tonnes par habitant
Malta									**Malte**
Thousand metric tons	651	1 158	2 379	2 622	2 581	1 649	1 354	1 516	Milliers de tonnes
Metric tons per capita	2.1	3.4	6.3	6.5	6.2	3.7	3.0	3.3	Tonnes par habitant
Mauritius									**Maurice**
Thousand metric tons	422	612	1 551	2 962	3 662	3 968	4 042	4 182	Milliers de tonnes
Metric tons per capita	0.5	0.6	1.4	2.4	2.9	3.1	3.2	3.3	Tonnes par habitant
Mexico									**Mexique**
Thousand metric tons	134 558	241 154	291 336	412 385	440 460	442 417	446 176	445 992	Milliers de tonnes
Metric tons per capita	2.2	3.1	3.1	3.9	3.9	3.7	3.7	3.6	Tonnes par habitant
Mongolia									**Mongolie**
Thousand metric tons	...	11 762	10 235	10 985	14 140	17 119	17 981	19 276	Milliers de tonnes
Metric tons per capita	...	6.1	4.5	4.3	5.2	5.8	5.9	6.3	Tonnes par habitant
Montenegro									**Monténégro**
Thousand metric tons	...	...	...	2 005	2 584	2 358	2 113	2 206	Milliers de tonnes
Metric tons per capita	...	...	...	3.3	4.2	3.8	3.4	3.5	Tonnes par habitant
Morocco									**Maroc**
Thousand metric tons	9 662	16 273	26 074	39 216	46 397	55 371	55 300	58 150	Milliers de tonnes
Metric tons per capita	0.5	0.7	1.0	1.3	1.4	1.6	1.6	1.6	Tonnes par habitant

24

CO2 emission estimates *(continued)*
From fossil fuel combustion (thousand metric tons of carbon dioxide) and per capita

Estimation des émissions de CO2 *(suite)*
Dues à la combustion de combustibles fossiles (milliers de tonnes de dioxyde de carbone) et par habitant

Country or area&	1975	1985	1995	2005	2010	2015	2016	2017	Pays ou zone&
Mozambique									**Mozambique**
Thousand metric tons	2 376	1 504	1 148	1 515	2 377	6 221	8 445	7 625	Milliers de tonnes
Metric tons per capita	0.2	0.1	0.1	0.1	0.1	0.2	0.3	0.3	Tonnes par habitant
Myanmar									**Myanmar**
Thousand metric tons	3 927	5 735	6 727	10 477	7 906	18 671	20 899	30 405	Milliers de tonnes
Metric tons per capita	0.1	0.2	0.2	0.2	0.2	0.4	0.4	0.6	Tonnes par habitant
Namibia									**Namibie**
Thousand metric tons	...	...	1 794	2 493	3 079	3 858	3 983	4 037	Milliers de tonnes
Metric tons per capita	...	...	1.1	1.2	1.4	1.6	1.6	1.6	Tonnes par habitant
Nepal									**Népal**
Thousand metric tons	319	551	1 763	3 074	4 122	5 694	8 504	10 114	Milliers de tonnes
Metric tons per capita	~0.0	~0.0	0.1	0.1	0.2	0.2	0.3	0.3	Tonnes par habitant
Netherlands									**Pays-Bas**
Thousand metric tons	131 962	138 397	163 583	167 490	170 762	157 858	158 034	155 574	Milliers de tonnes
Metric tons per capita	9.7	9.6	10.6	10.3	10.3	9.3	9.3	9.1	Tonnes par habitant
New Zealand									**Nouvelle-Zélande**
Thousand metric tons	16 430	18 905	23 934	33 690	30 348	31 259	30 435	32 242	Milliers de tonnes
Metric tons per capita	5.3	5.8	6.5	8.1	7.0	6.7	6.4	6.7	Tonnes par habitant
Nicaragua									**Nicaragua**
Thousand metric tons	1 850	1 806	2 514	4 032	4 277	5 055	5 113	5 106	Milliers de tonnes
Metric tons per capita	0.7	0.5	0.5	0.8	0.7	0.8	0.8	0.8	Tonnes par habitant
Niger									**Niger**
Thousand metric tons	...	...	...	736	1 359	1 954	1 952	2 049	Milliers de tonnes
Metric tons per capita	...	...	...	0.1	0.1	0.1	0.1	0.1	Tonnes par habitant
Nigeria									**Nigéria**
Thousand metric tons	10 816	31 785	32 775	56 558	55 418	82 589	84 738	85 989	Milliers de tonnes
Metric tons per capita	0.2	0.4	0.3	0.4	0.3	0.5	0.5	0.5	Tonnes par habitant
Norway									**Norvège**
Thousand metric tons	23 603	26 416	31 408	34 500	37 291	35 891	35 281	34 761	Milliers de tonnes
Metric tons per capita	5.9	6.4	7.2	7.5	7.6	6.9	6.7	6.6	Tonnes par habitant
Oman									**Oman**
Thousand metric tons	722	5 636	14 692	25 182	42 368	63 636	63 138	65 499	Milliers de tonnes
Metric tons per capita	0.8	3.8	6.7	10.0	13.9	15.2	14.3	14.1	Tonnes par habitant
Pakistan									**Pakistan**
Thousand metric tons	19 982	36 499	79 249	114 970	129 169	150 689	164 184	183 447	Milliers de tonnes
Metric tons per capita	0.3	0.4	0.6	0.7	0.8	0.8	0.9	0.9	Tonnes par habitant
Panama									**Panama**
Thousand metric tons	3 097	2 666	4 092	6 776	8 879	10 102	10 191	9 612	Milliers de tonnes
Metric tons per capita	1.8	1.2	1.5	2.0	2.4	2.5	2.5	2.3	Tonnes par habitant
Paraguay									**Paraguay**
Thousand metric tons	704	1 423	3 490	3 473	4 792	5 849	6 803	7 655	Milliers de tonnes
Metric tons per capita	0.3	0.4	0.7	0.6	0.8	0.9	1.0	1.1	Tonnes par habitant
Peru									**Pérou**
Thousand metric tons	18 240	18 052	23 311	28 633	41 544	49 725	52 187	49 694	Milliers de tonnes
Metric tons per capita	1.2	0.9	1.0	1.0	1.4	1.6	1.6	1.5	Tonnes par habitant
Philippines									**Philippines**
Thousand metric tons	29 244	29 268	57 258	71 502	77 128	103 891	114 752	126 488	Milliers de tonnes
Metric tons per capita	0.7	0.5	0.8	0.8	0.8	1.0	1.1	1.2	Tonnes par habitant
Poland									**Pologne**
Thousand metric tons	338 900	422 392	333 338	296 261	307 493	282 708	293 211	305 842	Milliers de tonnes
Metric tons per capita	10.0	11.4	8.7	7.8	8.0	7.4	7.6	8.0	Tonnes par habitant
Portugal [13]									**Portugal** [13]
Thousand metric tons	18 031	23 925	47 231	61 386	47 561	46 931	46 423	50 758	Milliers de tonnes
Metric tons per capita	2.0	2.4	4.7	5.8	4.5	4.5	4.5	4.9	Tonnes par habitant
Qatar									**Qatar**
Thousand metric tons	4 928	10 686	16 832	33 212	55 503	77 645	79 084	80 117	Milliers de tonnes
Metric tons per capita	30.0	28.8	32.8	38.4	31.2	31.3	30.8	30.4	Tonnes par habitant
Republic of Korea									**République de Corée**
Thousand metric tons	77 728	155 730	357 306	457 672	550 916	582 047	589 212	600 034	Milliers de tonnes
Metric tons per capita	2.2	3.8	7.9	9.5	11.1	11.4	11.5	11.7	Tonnes par habitant
Republic of Moldova									**République de Moldova**
Thousand metric tons	...	...	11 893	7 810	7 947	7 579	7 711	7 527	Milliers de tonnes
Metric tons per capita	...	...	3.2	2.2	2.2	2.1	2.2	2.1	Tonnes par habitant

CO2 emission estimates *(continued)*
From fossil fuel combustion (thousand metric tons of carbon dioxide) and per capita

Estimation des émissions de CO2 *(suite)*
Dues à la combustion de combustibles fossiles (milliers de tonnes de dioxyde de carbone) et par habitant

Country or area[&]	1975	1985	1995	2005	2010	2015	2016	2017	Pays ou zone[&]
Romania									**Roumanie**
Thousand metric tons	140 600	174 876	117 588	92 633	74 725	69 559	67 963	70 789	Milliers de tonnes
Metric tons per capita	6.6	7.7	5.2	4.3	3.7	3.5	3.5	3.6	Tonnes par habitant
Russian Federation									**Fédération de Russie**
Thousand metric tons	...	...	1 548 252	1 481 897	1 529 228	1 534 458	1 510 558	1 536 879	Milliers de tonnes
Metric tons per capita	...	...	10.4	10.3	10.7	10.6	10.5	10.6	Tonnes par habitant
Saudi Arabia									**Arabie saoudite**
Thousand metric tons	22 519	117 802	191 653	298 037	419 164	531 554	526 887	532 182	Milliers de tonnes
Metric tons per capita	3.0	8.9	10.2	12.5	15.3	16.8	16.3	16.2	Tonnes par habitant
Senegal									**Sénégal**
Thousand metric tons	1 609	2 125	2 479	4 626	5 461	7 517	8 160	8 312	Milliers de tonnes
Metric tons per capita	0.3	0.3	0.3	0.4	0.4	0.5	0.5	0.5	Tonnes par habitant
Serbia									**Serbie**
Thousand metric tons	...	...	44 549	50 320	45 610	44 460	45 474	46 130	Milliers de tonnes
Metric tons per capita	...	...	4.3	6.8	6.3	6.3	6.4	6.6	Tonnes par habitant
Singapore									**Singapour**
Thousand metric tons	8 440	16 605	37 582	36 901	42 414	45 496	46 065	47 407	Milliers de tonnes
Metric tons per capita	3.7	6.1	10.7	8.7	8.4	8.2	8.2	8.4	Tonnes par habitant
Slovakia									**Slovaquie**
Thousand metric tons	43 154	54 413	41 216	37 262	34 572	29 445	30 160	32 212	Milliers de tonnes
Metric tons per capita	9.1	10.5	7.7	6.9	6.4	5.4	5.6	5.9	Tonnes par habitant
Slovenia									**Slovénie**
Thousand metric tons	...	...	14 064	15 443	15 447	12 805	13 586	13 411	Milliers de tonnes
Metric tons per capita	...	...	7.1	7.7	7.5	6.2	6.6	6.5	Tonnes par habitant
South Africa									**Afrique du Sud**
Thousand metric tons	202 999	222 953	259 773	372 314	418 801	418 259	418 658	421 682	Milliers de tonnes
Metric tons per capita	7.7	6.6	6.2	7.6	8.1	7.6	7.5	7.4	Tonnes par habitant
South Sudan									**Soudan du sud**
Thousand metric tons	...	...	...	...	...	2 001	1 765	1 549	Milliers de tonnes
Metric tons per capita	...	...	...	...	...	0.2	0.1	0.1	Tonnes par habitant
Spain									**Espagne**
Thousand metric tons	155 843	173 024	228 207	333 710	262 055	247 067	237 400	253 423	Milliers de tonnes
Metric tons per capita	4.3	4.4	5.7	7.6	5.6	5.3	5.1	5.4	Tonnes par habitant
Sri Lanka									**Sri Lanka**
Thousand metric tons	2 637	3 485	5 454	13 393	12 409	19 490	20 899	23 103	Milliers de tonnes
Metric tons per capita	0.2	0.2	0.3	0.7	0.6	0.9	1.0	1.1	Tonnes par habitant
Sudan									**Soudan**
Thousand metric tons	3 213	3 980	4 309	9 928	15 123	16 354	18 923	18 778	Milliers de tonnes
Metric tons per capita	0.2	0.2	0.1	0.3	0.3	0.4	0.5	0.5	Tonnes par habitant
Suriname									**Suriname**
Thousand metric tons	...	...	...	1 653	1 696	2 063	1 910	1 928	Milliers de tonnes
Metric tons per capita	...	...	...	3.3	3.2	3.7	3.4	3.4	Tonnes par habitant
Sweden									**Suède**
Thousand metric tons	79 041	58 386	56 935	49 106	46 063	37 112	37 989	37 644	Milliers de tonnes
Metric tons per capita	9.6	7.0	6.5	5.4	4.9	3.8	3.8	3.7	Tonnes par habitant
Switzerland									**Suisse**
Thousand metric tons	36 753	41 773	41 451	44 007	43 258	37 323	37 852	37 136	Milliers de tonnes
Metric tons per capita	5.7	6.4	5.8	5.9	5.5	4.5	4.5	4.4	Tonnes par habitant
Syrian Arab Republic									**République arabe syrienne**
Thousand metric tons	8 261	19 536	31 133	53 466	57 271	23 872	23 086	23 031	Milliers de tonnes
Metric tons per capita	1.1	1.8	2.2	2.9	2.7	1.3	1.3	1.3	Tonnes par habitant
Tajikistan									**Tadjikistan**
Thousand metric tons	...	...	2 460	2 347	2 303	4 212	5 428	5 844	Milliers de tonnes
Metric tons per capita	...	...	0.4	0.3	0.3	0.5	0.6	0.7	Tonnes par habitant
Thailand									**Thaïlande**
Thousand metric tons	21 152	42 059	139 938	200 204	223 419	248 040	244 125	244 255	Milliers de tonnes
Metric tons per capita	0.5	0.8	2.4	3.1	3.3	3.6	3.5	3.5	Tonnes par habitant
North Macedonia									**Macédoine du Nord**
Thousand metric tons	...	...	8 306	8 917	8 320	7 134	6 948	7 441	Milliers de tonnes
Metric tons per capita	...	...	4.2	4.3	4.0	3.4	3.3	3.6	Tonnes par habitant
Togo									**Togo**
Thousand metric tons	317	297	579	963	2 076	1 906	1 998	2 082	Milliers de tonnes
Metric tons per capita	0.1	0.1	0.1	0.2	0.3	0.3	0.3	0.3	Tonnes par habitant

24

CO2 emission estimates *(continued)*
From fossil fuel combustion (thousand metric tons of carbon dioxide) and per capita

Estimation des émissions de CO2 *(suite)*
Dues à la combustion de combustibles fossils (milliers de tonnes de dioxyde de carbone) et par habitant

Country or area[&]	1975	1985	1995	2005	2010	2015	2016	2017	Pays ou zone[&]
Trinidad and Tobago									**Trinité-et-Tobago**
Thousand metric tons	4 575	6 654	8 163	17 176	21 849	21 280	17 457	18 008	Milliers de tonnes
Metric tons per capita	4.5	5.7	6.5	13.2	16.5	15.6	12.8	13.2	Tonnes par habitant
Tunisia									**Tunisie**
Thousand metric tons	4 846	9 662	14 036	19 473	23 294	25 615	25 212	26 157	Milliers de tonnes
Metric tons per capita	0.9	1.3	1.5	1.9	2.2	2.3	2.2	2.3	Tonnes par habitant
Turkey									**Turquie**
Thousand metric tons	59 631	95 358	154 030	215 893	267 846	318 974	338 874	378 631	Milliers de tonnes
Metric tons per capita	1.5	1.9	2.6	3.2	3.7	4.1	4.3	4.7	Tonnes par habitant
Turkmenistan									**Turkménistan**
Thousand metric tons	...	...	33 256	48 103	56 920	69 105	68 972	68 999	Milliers de tonnes
Metric tons per capita	...	...	7.9	10.1	11.2	12.4	12.2	12.0	Tonnes par habitant
Ukraine									**Ukraine**
Thousand metric tons	...	...	395 842	290 620	266 581	187 590[14]	197 626[14]	171 300[14]	Milliers de tonnes
Metric tons per capita	...	...	7.7	6.2	5.8	4.2[14]	4.4[14]	3.8[14]	Tonnes par habitant
United Arab Emirates									**Émirats arabes unis**
Thousand metric tons	4 919	35 636	69 659	111 145	154 590	186 576	192 071	196 510	Milliers de tonnes
Metric tons per capita	8.9	25.6	28.4	24.3	18.7	20.4	20.7	20.9	Tonnes par habitant
United Kingdom									**Royaume-Uni**
Thousand metric tons	576 042	543 545	513 796	531 649	476 626	394 115	372 558	358 731	Milliers de tonnes
Metric tons per capita	10.2	9.6	8.9	8.8	7.6	6.1	5.7	5.4	Tonnes par habitant
United Rep. of Tanzania									**Rép.-Unie de Tanzanie**
Thousand metric tons	1 405	1 463	2 492	5 119	6 217	10 473	9 677	10 132	Milliers de tonnes
Metric tons per capita	0.1	0.1	0.1	0.1	0.1	0.2	0.2	0.2	Tonnes par habitant
United States of America [15]									**États-Unis d'Amérique** [15]
Thousand metric tons	4 355 839	4 514 313	5 073 896	5 703 220	5 352 120	4 928 611	4 838 476	4 761 302	Milliers de tonnes
Metric tons per capita	20.2	18.9	19.0	19.3	17.3	15.3	14.9	14.6	Tonnes par habitant
Uruguay									**Uruguay**
Thousand metric tons	5 334	3 011	4 392	5 152	5 960	6 375	6 326	5 873	Milliers de tonnes
Metric tons per capita	1.9	1.0	1.4	1.5	1.8	1.9	1.8	1.7	Tonnes par habitant
Uzbekistan									**Ouzbékistan**
Thousand metric tons	...	...	94 584	105 600	100 563	92 162	81 343	81 156	Milliers de tonnes
Metric tons per capita	...	...	4.2	4.0	3.5	2.9	2.6	2.5	Tonnes par habitant
Venezuela (Boliv. Rep. of)									**Venezuela (Rép. boliv. du)**
Thousand metric tons	56 070	85 139	106 098	137 702	171 469	140 539	127 366	113 718	Milliers de tonnes
Metric tons per capita	4.2	4.9	4.8	5.1	5.9	4.5	4.0	3.6	Tonnes par habitant
Viet Nam									**Viet Nam**
Thousand metric tons	16 954	17 435	27 462	79 230	126 659	182 589	193 612	191 244	Milliers de tonnes
Metric tons per capita	0.3	0.3	0.4	0.9	1.4	2.0	2.0	2.0	Tonnes par habitant
Yemen									**Yémen**
Thousand metric tons	1 752	4 857	9 436	18 836	22 389	11 662	9 389	8 920	Milliers de tonnes
Metric tons per capita	0.3	0.5	0.6	0.9	0.9	0.4	0.3	0.3	Tonnes par habitant
Zambia									**Zambie**
Thousand metric tons	4 326	2 696	2 002	2 121	1 637	3 476	3 732	6 008	Milliers de tonnes
Metric tons per capita	0.9	0.4	0.2	0.2	0.1	0.2	0.2	0.4	Tonnes par habitant
Zimbabwe									**Zimbabwe**
Thousand metric tons	7 169	9 730	15 089	10 273	9 465	11 822	10 369	9 715	Milliers de tonnes
Metric tons per capita	1.2	1.1	1.3	0.8	0.7	0.7	0.6	0.6	Tonnes par habitant

Source:

International Energy Agency, IEA World Energy Balances 2019 and 2006 IPCC Guidelines for Greenhouse Gas Inventories, last accessed July 2020.

Source:

Agence internationale de l'énergie, AIE balances energétiques 2019 et lignes directrices 2006 du GIEC pour les inventaires de gaz à effet de serre, dernier accès juillet 2020.

1   Excluding overseas territories.
2   Data refer to fiscal years beginning 1 July.

3   For statistical purposes, the data for China do not include those for the Hong Kong Special Administrative Region (Hong Kong SAR), Macao Special Administrative Region (Macao SAR) and Taiwan Province of China.

1   Non compris les départements d'outre-mer.
2   Les données se réfèrent aux exercices budgétaires commençant le 1er juillet.

3   Pour la présentation des statistiques, les données pour la Chine ne comprennent pas la région administrative spéciale de Hong Kong (RAS de Hong Kong), la région administrative spéciale de Macao (RAS de Macao) et la province chinoise de Taïwan.

24

CO2 emission estimates *(continued)*
From fossil fuel combustion (thousand metric tons of carbon dioxide) and per capita

Estimation des émissions de CO2 *(suite)*
Dues à la combustion de combustibles fossiles (milliers de tonnes de dioxyde de carbone) et par habitant

4	Excluding northern Cyprus.	4	Chypre du nord non compris.
5	Refers to Czechia and Slovakia.	5	Désigne la Tchéquie et la Slovaquie.
6	Excluding the Faroe Islands and Greenland.	6	Non compris les Îles Féroé et le Groenland.
7	Including Eritrea.	7	Y compris Erythrée.
8	Including Monaco.	8	Y compris Monaco.
9	From 2011 onwards, data include Monaco and the overseas departments (Guadeloupe, French Guiana, Martinique, Mayotte and Réunion), excluding the overseas collectivities: New Caledonia, French Polynesia, Saint Barthélemy, Saint Martin, St. Pierre and Miquelon, and Wallis and Futuna.	9	À partir de 2011, les données incluent Monaco et les départements d'outre-mer (Guadeloupe, Guyane française, Martinique, Mayotte et Réunion), à l'exclusion des collectivités d'outre-mer: Nouvelle-Calédonie, Polynésie française, Saint-Barthélemy, Saint-Martin, Saint-Pierre et Miquelon, Wallis et Futuna.
10	Data refer to the Iranian Year which begins on 21 March and ends on 20 March of the following year.	10	Les données concernent l'année iranienne, qui commence le 21 mars et se termine le 20 mars de l'année suivante.
11	Including San Marino.	11	Y compris Saint-Marin.
12	Data include Okinawa.	12	Les données incluent Okinawa.
13	Data includes the Azores and Madeira.	13	Les données comprennent Azores et Madère.
14	The Government of Ukraine has informed the United Nations that it is not in a position to provide statistical data concerning the Autonomous Republic of Crimea and the city of Sevastopol.	14	Le Gouvernement ukrainien a informé l'Organisation des Nations Unies qu'il n'est pas en mesure de fournir des données statistiques concernant la République autonome de Crimée et Sébastopol.
15	Including overseas territories.	15	Y compris le territoire à l'étranger.

25

Water supply and sanitation services
Proportion of population using

Services d'alimentation en eau potable et d'assainissement
Proportion de la population utilisant des services

Country or area& Pays ou zone&	Year Année	Proportion of population using: - Proportion de la population utilisant des:					
		Safely managed drinking water services Services d'alimentation en eau potable gérés en toute sécurité			Safely managed sanitation facilities Services d'assainissement gérés en toute sécurité		
		Urban (%) Urbaine (%)	Rural (%) Rurale (%)	Total (%) Totale (%)	Urban (%) Urbaine (%)	Rural (%) Rurale (%)	Total (%) Totale (%)
Total, all countries or areas	**2005**	**86.2**	**43.0**	**64.2**	**37.0**	**26.1**	**31.5**
Total, tous pays ou zones	**2010**	**85.9**	**45.8**	**66.5**	**41.3**	**32.5**	**37.1**
	2017	**85.1**	**53.0**	**70.6**	**47.0**	**42.5**	**45.0**
Northern Africa	2005	...	...	...	32.8	...	20.1
Afrique septentrionale	2010	...	...	...	35.7	...	23.8
	2017	...	...	...	39.3	...	28.8
Sub-Saharan Africa	2005	43.7	7.4	19.6	18.4	14.9	16.1
Afrique subsaharienne	2010	46.0	8.9	22.4	19.1	16.1	17.2
	2017	50.0	11.6	26.9	19.8	17.5	18.4
Eastern Africa	2005	40.6	4.2	12.4	...	...	...
Afrique orientale	2010	45.6	5.8	15.5	...	...	...
	2017	53.2	8.9	21.1	...	...	...
Southern Africa	2005	89.3	...	...	...	...	...
Afrique australe	2010	87.2	...	...	...	...	...
	2017	81.9	...	...	...	...	...
Western Africa	2005	33.2	10.5	19.1	20.5	15.7	17.5
Afrique occidentale	2010	33.3	12.4	21.0	21.2	16.3	18.3
	2017	33.6	15.4	23.7	21.9	17.0	19.3
Northern America	2005	99.6	...	98.9	89.6	...	78.1
Amérique septentrionale	2010	99.6	...	99.0	90.1	...	79.0
	2017	99.6	...	99.0	90.2	...	79.8
Latin America & the Caribbean	2005	82.4	...	57.5	18.0	...	14.6
Amérique latine et Caraïbes	2010	82.3	39.0	73.0	25.0	...	20.7
	2017	82.3	41.7	74.3	37.0	...	31.3
Caribbean Caraïbes	2000	...	...	...	12.6	...	...
Central America	2005	...	37.3	43.8	19.5	...	15.0
Amérique centrale	2010	...	39.0	45.1	29.2	...	23.0
	2017	...	41.6	46.8	44.0	...	35.7
South America	2005	86.5	36.4	77.0	18.0	...	15.1
Amérique du Sud	2010	86.7	38.8	78.3	24.6	...	20.9
	2017	86.9	41.8	79.7	36.5	...	31.6
Asia	2005	86.1	46.8	62.9	27.3	23.7	29.8
Asie	2010	86.1	50.4	66.4	33.7	32.0	32.7
	2017	85.8	59.8	72.6	42.7	46.0	44.4
Central Asia	2005	85.2	34.4	58.2	46.6	...	...
Asie centrale	2010	87.6	41.6	63.7	49.0	...	...
	2017	90.4	52.9	71.0	49.0	...	...
Eastern Asia	2005	94.0	...	...	46.2	30.0	37.8
Asie orientale	2010	93.8	...	...	59.3	38.0	49.6
	2017	93.3	...	...	78.2	56.2	69.8
Southern Asia	2005	62.3	38.6	45.9	...	14.4	...
Asie méridionale	2010	60.7	47.1	51.5	...	24.3	...
	2017	58.5	59.9	59.4	...	38.7	...
Western Asia	2005	...	...	67.9	57.2	...	38.4
Asie occidentale	2010	...	...	71.8	60.9	...	42.4
	2017	...	...	75.8	64.0	...	45.9
Europe	2005	...	...	91.0	74.3	43.0	65.5
Europe	2010	...	...	92.4	77.9	50.1	75.6
	2017	...	...	93.4	81.1	53.3	78.9
Eastern Europe	2005	...	...	79.7	53.8	...	45.5
Europe orientale	2010	...	...	82.7	56.1	...	48.9
	2017	...	...	85.0	61.4	...	54.8
Northern Europe	2005	...	...	98.1	94.8	69.8	92.9
Europe septentrionale	2010	...	...	98.8	95.6	71.1	93.9
	2017	...	...	99.3	96.5	72.4	95.0
Southern Europe	2005	...	...	88.4	73.2	40.6	62.7
Europe méridionale	2010	...	...	91.1	82.6	63.2	76.6
	2017	...	...	94.0	85.2	65.4	79.5

Country or area& Pays ou zone&	Year Année	Proportion of population using: - Proportion de la population utilisant des:					
		Safely managed drinking water services Services d'alimentation en eau potable gérés en toute sécurité			Safely managed sanitation facilities Services d'assainissement gérés en toute sécurité		
		Urban (%) Urbaine (%)	Rural (%) Rurale (%)	Total (%) Totale (%)	Urban (%) Urbaine (%)	Rural (%) Rurale (%)	Total (%) Totale (%)
Western Europe Europe occidentale	2005	...	...	98.6	97.2	85.6	95.8
	2010			98.7	97.8	85.7	96.4
	2017	...	...	99.0	98.4	85.9	96.9
Oceania Océanie	2005	93.4	...	...	57.9	22.1	46.4
	2010	95.3	...	...	61.6	22.8	49.2
	2017	96.1	...	...	66.7	23.5	52.9
Australia and New Zealand Australie et Nouvelle-Zélande	2005	93.9	...	...	...	...	61.9
	2010	95.7	...	...	...	...	66.1
	2017	96.5	...	...	...	...	71.9
Micronesia Micronésie	2005	86.0	...	73.9	...	...	...
	2010	87.3	...	75.9	...	...	...
	2017	89.5	...	79.2	...	...	...
Polynesia Polynésie	2005	...	...	47.5	...	46.0	...
	2010	...	...	48.6	...	46.5	...
	2017	...	...	49.4	...	46.2	...
Albania Albanie	2005	...	...	52.6	39.7	36.2	37.8
	2010	...	...	62.0	40.0	37.2	38.6
	2017	...	...	70.0	40.2	39.4	39.9
Algeria Algérie	2005	...	...	...	17.5	19.8	18.3
	2010	...	...	...	17.0	20.3	18.1
	2017	...	...	...	16.5	20.8	17.7
American Samoa Samoa américaines	2005	...	...	12.5	...	...	...
	2010	...	...	12.5	...	...	...
	2017	...	...	12.6	...	...	...
Andorra Andorre	2005	...	...	90.6	50.5	50.5	50.5
	2010	...	...	90.6	86.5	86.5	86.5
	2017	...	...	90.6	100.0	100.0	100.0
Armenia Arménie	2005	...	...	43.9	45.5	...	47.9
	2010	...	...	61.7	45.5	...	48.1
	2017	...	...	86.5	45.3	...	48.2
Australia Australie	2005	98.3	...	...	...	...	65.1
	2010	98.7	...	...	...	...	69.5
	2017	98.8	...	...	...	...	75.6
Austria Autriche	2005	...	...	98.1	100.0	92.3	96.8
	2010	...	...	98.5	100.0	92.3	96.7
	2017	...	...	98.9	100.0	92.3	96.7
Azerbaijan Azerbaïdjan	2005	...	...	55.9	75.4	...	...
	2010	...	...	68.7	84.8	...	...
	2017	...	...	73.6	92.2	...	...
Bahrain Bahreïn	2005	...	...	98.9	...	...	95.9
	2010	...	...	99.0	...	...	96.0
	2017	...	...	99.0	...	...	96.0
Bangladesh Bangladesh	2005	44.6	60.0	55.9	...	18.6	...
	2010	44.6	60.6	55.7	...	24.1	...
	2017	44.6	61.5	55.4	...	32.3	...
Belarus Bélarus	2005	...	...	83.9	87.8	91.4	88.8
	2010	...	...	90.1	85.8	84.7	85.5
	2017	...	...	94.5	81.7	76.4	80.5
Belgium Belgique	2005	...	...	99.5	...	...	86.9
	2010	...	...	99.5	...	...	90.3
	2017	...	...	99.5	...	...	97.1
Bhutan Bhoutan	2005	48.7	23.6	31.4	...	...	...
	2010	48.8	25.5	33.6	...	...	...
	2017	48.9	27.6	36.2	...	...	...
Bolivia (Plurin. State of) Bolivie (État plurin. de)	2005	...	...	...	17.6	...	15.1
	2010	...	...	...	20.2	...	18.1
	2017	...	...	...	24.7	...	22.9
Bosnia and Herzegovina Bosnie-Herzégovine	2005	...	...	88.0	7.2	...	19.1
	2010	...	...	88.5	8.6	...	19.9
	2017	...	...	88.8	11.3	...	21.6

Country or area& Pays ou zone&	Year Année	Safely managed drinking water services Services d'alimentation en eau potable gérés en toute sécurité			Safely managed sanitation facilities Services d'assainissement gérés en toute sécurité		
		Urban (%) Urbaine (%)	Rural (%) Rurale (%)	Total (%) Totale (%)	Urban (%) Urbaine (%)	Rural (%) Rurale (%)	Total (%) Totale (%)
Botswana	2005	83.7	...	...	...	...	...
Botswana	2010	83.7	...	...	...	...	...
	2017	83.2	...	...	...	...	...
Brazil	2005	91.5	...	...	29.1	...	27.7
Brésil	2010	91.8	...	...	36.5	...	34.8
	2017	92.3	...	...	51.6	...	49.3
Bulgaria	2005	...	...	96.7	55.2	...	47.6
Bulgarie	2010	...	...	96.8	58.8	...	51.2
	2017	...	...	96.9	72.9	...	64.4
Cambodia	2005	47.3	12.5	19.2	...	...	...
Cambodge	2010	51.2	14.3	21.8	...	...	...
	2017	56.6	16.7	25.8	...	...	...
Canada	2005	...	...	98.3	78.9	78.7	78.8
Canada	2010	...	...	98.5	82.0	81.5	81.9
	2017	...	...	98.9	82.2	81.4	82.1
Channel Islands	2010	...	...	92.0	...	...	90.0
Îles Anglo-Normandes	2017	...	...	92.0	...	...	90.0
Chile	2005	98.5	...	94.3	52.6	...	53.1
Chili	2010	98.6	...	96.6	66.7	...	63.2
	2017	98.6	...	98.6	81.4	...	77.5
China [1]	2005	93.0	...	...	41.0	28.7	33.9
Chine [1]	2010	92.7	...	...	58.3	37.1	47.6
	2017	92.3	...	...	83.7	56.1	72.1
China, Hong Kong SAR	2005	88.2	...	88.2	92.1	...	92.1
Chine, RAS de Hong Kong	2010	97.2	...	97.2	91.9	...	91.9
	2017	100.0	...	100.0	91.8	...	91.8
China, Macao SAR	2005	100.0	...	60.8	...	...	...
Chine, RAS de Macao	2010	100.0	...	80.2	...	...	...
	2017	100.0	...	100.0	...	...	...
Colombia	2005	81.2	35.0	70.1	14.2	...	14.6
Colombie	2010	81.3	37.1	71.6	14.9	...	15.6
	2017	81.3	40.1	73.2	15.8	...	17.0
Congo	2005	45.8	8.4	31.2	...	...	...
Congo	2010	55.4	12.4	39.6	...	...	...
	2017	58.6	19.1	45.4	...	...	...
Costa Rica	2005	95.9	77.1	89.5	...	...	...
Costa Rica	2010	96.1	80.4	91.7	...	...	...
	2017	96.4	84.4	93.8	...	...	...
Côte d'Ivoire	2005	56.6	16.4	34.6	...	...	...
Côte d'Ivoire	2010	56.0	17.0	35.5	...	...	...
	2017	55.1	17.7	36.5	...	...	...
Croatia	2005	...	...	91.5	64.1	...	58.0
Croatie	2010	...	...	92.6	64.2	...	58.2
	2017	...	...	90.0	64.3	...	58.5
Cuba	2005	...	...	...	32.6	...	34.5
Cuba	2010	...	...	...	36.2	...	38.4
	2017	...	...	...	41.9	...	44.3
Cyprus	2005	...	...	96.3	86.4	...	76.2
Chypre	2010	...	...	98.5	86.3	...	75.9
	2017	...	...	99.6	86.3	...	75.5
Czechia	2005	...	...	96.8	88.0	77.3	85.2
Tchéquie	2010	...	...	97.4	92.4	80.8	89.3
	2017	...	...	97.9	97.8	85.1	94.5
Dem. People's Rep. Korea	2005	78.6	54.3	68.8	...	23.8	...
Rép. pop. dém. de Corée	2010	78.0	52.4	67.8	...	18.4	...
	2017	77.2	49.6	66.6	...	5.1	...
Denmark	2005	...	...	94.5	...	...	92.1
Danemark	2010	...	...	96.0	...	...	93.0
	2017	...	...	96.7	...	...	94.8
Djibouti	2005	...	...	...	31.2	12.2	26.8
Djibouti	2010	...	...	...	35.6	15.0	30.8
	2017	...	...	...	41.5	18.9	36.4

Services d'alimentation en eau potable et d'assainissement *(suite)*
Proportion de la population utilisant des services

Country or area& Pays ou zone&	Year Année	Proportion of population using: - Proportion de la population utilisant des:					
		Safely managed drinking water services Services d'alimentation en eau potable gérés en toute sécurité			Safely managed sanitation facilities Services d'assainissement gérés en toute sécurité		
		Urban (%) Urbaine (%)	Rural (%) Rurale (%)	Total (%) Totale (%)	Urban (%) Urbaine (%)	Rural (%) Rurale (%)	Total (%) Totale (%)
Ecuador Équateur	2005	79.6	52.0	69.0	38.0	47.4	41.6
	2010	82.0	54.4	71.7	36.3	51.5	42.0
	2017	84.9	57.9	75.1	33.4	57.2	42.0
Egypt Égypte	2005	...	...	...	64.9	...	54.7
	2010	...	...	...	67.0	...	57.1
	2017	...	...	...	70.7	...	60.7
El Salvador El Salvador	2005	81.8	...	...	...	...	...
	2010	76.1	...	...	...	...	...
	2017	77.3	...	...	...	...	...
Estonia Estonie	2005	...	...	94.4	97.3	93.6	96.1
	2010	...	...	95.4	97.4	93.9	96.3
	2017	...	...	93.3	98.7	94.4	97.4
Eswatini Eswatini	2005	75.0	...	...	...	...	...
	2010	83.0	...	...	...	...	...
	2017	88.7	...	...	...	...	...
Ethiopia Éthiopie	2005	36.0	0.5	6.1	...	2.0	...
	2010	37.0	1.7	7.9	...	2.8	...
	2017	38.4	4.6	11.4	...	3.8	...
Finland Finlande	2005	...	...	95.4	99.0	...	99.1
	2010	...	...	98.4	99.1	...	99.1
	2017	...	...	99.6	99.3	...	99.2
France France	2005	...	...	97.0	...	...	89.2
	2010	...	...	97.3	...	...	88.8
	2017	...	...	97.9	...	...	88.4
French Guiana Guyane française	2005	...	...	88.8	...	...	...
	2010	...	...	89.6	...	...	...
	2017	...	...	90.8	...	...	...
Gambia Gambie	2005	50.1	...	...	...	...	...
	2010	59.2	...	...	...	...	...
	2017	68.3	...	...	...	...	...
Georgia Géorgie	2005	...	...	76.4	7.0	...	22.9
	2010	...	...	78.5	10.7	...	24.6
	2017	...	...	80.0	15.9	...	27.2
Germany Allemagne	2005	...	...	99.8	97.5	90.5	95.8
	2010	...	...	99.8	98.2	91.1	96.5
	2017	...	...	99.8	98.8	91.8	97.2
Ghana Ghana	2005	36.0	2.6	18.4	...	...	...
	2010	44.3	5.9	25.4	...	...	...
	2017	56.5	11.5	36.4	...	...	...
Gibraltar Gibraltar	2005	100.0	...	100.0	...	...	...
	2010	100.0	...	100.0	...	...	...
	2017	100.0	...	100.0	...	...	...
Greece Grèce	2005	...	...	99.4	86.8	...	79.9
	2010	...	...	99.8	90.8	...	84.0
	2017	...	...	100.0	96.6	...	90.4
Greenland Groenland	2005	...	...	94.5	...	...	92.1
	2010	...	...	96.0	...	...	93.0
	2017	...	...	96.7	...	...	94.8
Grenada Grenade	2005	...	...	83.2	...	...	...
	2010	...	...	87.1	...	...	...
	2017	...	...	87.1	...	...	...
Guadeloupe Guadeloupe	2005	...	...	96.9	...	...	...
	2010	...	...	97.1	...	...	...
	2017	...	...	97.4	...	...	...
Guam Guam	2005	...	...	99.4	...	...	...
	2010	...	...	99.5	...	...	...
	2017	...	...	99.5	...	...	...
Guatemala Guatemala	2005	58.4	41.4	49.4	...	...	...
	2010	61.6	43.4	52.2	...	...	...
	2017	65.6	46.1	56.0	...	...	...

Country or area& Pays ou zone&	Year Année	Proportion of population using: - Proportion de la population utilisant des:					
		Safely managed drinking water services Services d'alimentation en eau potable gérés en toute sécurité			Safely managed sanitation facilities Services d'assainissement gérés en toute sécurité		
		Urban (%) Urbaine (%)	Rural (%) Rurale (%)	Total (%) Totale (%)	Urban (%) Urbaine (%)	Rural (%) Rurale (%)	Total (%) Totale (%)
Honduras Honduras	2005	...	16.5	...	...	33.6	...
	2010	...	17.4	...	...	34.0	...
	2017	...	18.5	...	...	34.5	...
Hungary Hongrie	2005	...	...	56.1	95.2	98.2	96.2
	2010	...	...	70.0	95.0	98.2	96.0
	2017	...	...	89.6	94.7	98.2	95.7
Iceland Islande	2005	...	...	92.7	...	...	55.0
	2010	...	...	95.8	...	...	65.9
	2017	...	...	100.0	...	...	81.8
India Inde	2005	...	29.5	...	...	11.4	...
	2010	...	40.0	...	...	22.6	...
	2017	...	56.0	...	...	39.0	...
Iran (Islamic Republic of) Iran (Rép. islamique d')	2005	95.4	83.2	91.4	...	...	...
	2010	95.1	82.9	91.5	...	...	...
	2017	94.9	82.7	91.8	...	...	...
Iraq Iraq	2005	61.6	32.8	52.6	32.5	35.4	33.4
	2010	62.6	38.5	55.2	35.1	39.2	36.3
	2017	64.1	46.5	58.8	39.4	45.0	41.1
Ireland Irlande	2005	...	...	94.5	59.6	65.8	62.0
	2010	...	...	95.9	74.2	68.8	72.1
	2017	...	...	97.3	88.5	72.1	82.4
Isle of Man Île de Man	2010	...	...	97.2	...	...	...
	2017	...	...	97.2	...	...	...
Israel Israël	2005	99.9	100.0	99.9	83.7	82.0	83.6
	2010	99.8	99.7	99.8	87.9	86.1	87.8
	2017	99.4	99.2	99.4	93.8	91.8	93.7
Italy Italie	2005	...	...	89.2	...	...	...
	2010	...	...	91.8	96.2	96.1	96.2
	2017	...	...	95.0	96.3	96.1	96.2
Japan Japon	2005	...	...	97.9	...	...	98.2
	2010	...	...	98.1	...	...	98.7
	2017	...	...	98.5	...	...	98.8
Jordan Jordanie	2005	...	...	93.8	83.4	...	76.6
	2010	...	...	93.9	83.3	...	79.0
	2017	...	...	93.8	83.2	...	80.6
Kazakhstan Kazakhstan	2005	...	...	65.5	92.4	...	...
	2010	...	...	75.4	91.6	...	...
	2017	...	...	89.5	90.5	...	...
Kenya Kenya	2005	60.3	...	...	...	...	...
	2010	55.9	...	...	...	...	...
	2017	50.0	...	...	...	...	...
Kuwait Koweït	2005	...	...	100.0	...	...	100.0
	2010	...	...	100.0	...	...	100.0
	2017	...	...	100.0	...	...	100.0
Kyrgyzstan Kirghizistan	2005	82.1	30.5	48.7	...	...	...
	2010	87.5	40.7	57.2	...	...	...
	2017	93.5	53.9	68.2	...	...	...
Lao People's Dem. Rep. Rép. dém. populaire lao	2005	22.9	7.0	11.3	50.7	27.5	33.8
	2010	24.3	8.6	13.3	55.5	39.5	44.3
	2017	26.3	10.8	16.1	62.4	55.8	58.1
Latvia Lettonie	2005	...	...	93.0	85.6	66.9	79.6
	2010	...	...	93.8	86.9	70.9	81.8
	2017	...	...	95.2	90.2	76.5	85.8
Lebanon Liban	2005	...	...	45.2	...	...	18.1
	2010	...	...	46.3	...	...	19.6
	2017	...	...	47.7	...	...	21.8
Libya Libye	2005	...	...	...	...	...	28.3
	2010	...	...	...	...	...	27.3
	2017	...	...	...	...	...	26.1
Liechtenstein Liechtenstein	2005	...	...	100.0	...	...	99.7
	2010	...	...	100.0	...	...	99.7
	2017	...	...	100.0	...	...	99.7

Country or area& Pays ou zone&	Year Année	Proportion of population using: - Proportion de la population utilisant des:					
		Safely managed drinking water services Services d'alimentation en eau potable gérés en toute sécurité			Safely managed sanitation facilities Services d'assainissement gérés en toute sécurité		
		Urban (%) Urbaine (%)	Rural (%) Rurale (%)	Total (%) Totale (%)	Urban (%) Urbaine (%)	Rural (%) Rurale (%)	Total (%) Totale (%)
Lithuania Lituanie	2005	...	...	73.1	92.3	70.5	85.0
	2010	...	...	81.9	93.5	75.8	87.6
	2017	...	...	92.0	95.2	83.3	91.3
Luxembourg Luxembourg	2005	100.0	100.0	100.0	92.2	84.8	91.2
	2010	100.0	100.0	100.0	93.4	85.8	92.5
	2017	100.0	97.0	99.7	97.4	89.3	96.6
Malaysia Malaisie	2005	...	...	93.2	...	...	78.8
	2010	...	...	93.3	...	...	81.5
	2017	...	...	93.3	...	...	88.6
Mali Mali	2005	...	...	...	7.7	11.7	10.4
	2010	...	...	...	8.3	16.9	13.8
	2017	...	...	...	9.1	25.5	18.7
Malta Malte	2005	...	...	100.0	93.0	93.0	93.0
	2010	...	...	100.0	93.0	93.0	93.0
	2017	...	...	100.0	93.0	93.0	93.0
Martinique Martinique	2005	...	...	99.1	...	...	...
	2010	...	...	99.1	...	...	...
	2017	...	...	98.9	...	...	...
Mayotte Mayotte	2010	...	...	83.7	...	...	...
	2017	...	...	83.7	...	...	...
Mexico Mexique	2005	...	...	40.1	24.3	...	23.8
	2010	...	...	41.3	35.3	...	34.1
	2017	...	...	42.9	52.3	...	50.4
Monaco Monaco	2005	100.0	...	100.0	100.0	...	100.0
	2010	100.0	...	100.0	100.0	...	100.0
	2017	100.0	...	100.0	100.0	...	100.0
Mongolia Mongolie	2005	...	...	23.5	...	...	...
	2010	...	...	24.3	...	...	...
	2017	...	...	23.7	...	...	...
Montenegro Monténégro	2010	94.6	...	89.1	30.6	...	...
	2017	93.8	...	93.6	29.8	...	...
Morocco Maroc	2005	87.0	25.5	59.4	38.0	...	34.6
	2010	87.9	32.1	64.4	39.4	...	36.9
	2017	88.9	39.9	70.3	40.2	...	38.8
Mozambique Mozambique	2005	...	...	...	...	5.6	...
	2010	...	...	...	...	9.8	...
	2017	...	...	...	...	16.3	...
Nepal Népal	2005	34.7	23.2	25.0	...	...	...
	2010	34.5	24.2	25.9	...	...	...
	2017	34.1	25.6	27.2	...	...	...
Netherlands Pays-Bas	2005	...	...	100.0	97.5	97.4	97.5
	2010	...	...	100.0	97.5	97.4	97.5
	2017	...	...	100.0	97.5	97.4	97.5
New Caledonia Nouvelle-Calédonie	2005	...	...	88.7	...	...	...
	2010	...	...	92.8	...	...	...
	2017	...	...	96.7	...	...	...
New Zealand Nouvelle-Zélande	2005	...	...	78.1	...	...	81.5
	2010	...	...	88.7	...	...	84.5
	2017	...	...	100.0	...	...	88.7
Nicaragua Nicaragua	2005	66.6	30.1	50.5	...	...	...
	2010	67.0	29.8	51.0	...	...	...
	2017	67.4	29.5	51.6	...	...	...
Niger Niger	2005	...	...	...	18.0	3.2	5.6
	2010	...	...	...	20.3	5.0	7.5
	2017	...	...	...	23.4	6.9	9.6
Nigeria Nigéria	2005	23.8	12.6	17.0	25.7	24.9	25.2
	2010	24.1	14.0	18.4	27.4	24.6	25.8
	2017	24.6	15.7	20.1	29.5	23.9	26.7
Niue Nioué	2005	...	...	98.1	...	...	...
	2010	...	...	97.6	...	...	...
	2017	...	...	97.2	...	...	...

Water supply and sanitation services *(continued)*
Proportion of population using

Services d'alimentation en eau potable et d'assainissement *(suite)*
Proportion de la population utilisant des services

Country or area& Pays ou zone&	Year Année	Proportion of population using: - Proportion de la population utilisant des:					
		Safely managed drinking water services Services d'alimentation en eau potable gérés en toute sécurité			Safely managed sanitation facilities Services d'assainissement gérés en toute sécurité		
		Urban (%) Urbaine (%)	Rural (%) Rurale (%)	Total (%) Totale (%)	Urban (%) Urbaine (%)	Rural (%) Rurale (%)	Total (%) Totale (%)
Northern Mariana Islands	2005	...	...	83.7	...	...	...
Îles Mariannes du Nord	2010	...	...	86.5	...	...	...
	2017	...	...	90.2	...	...	...
Norway	2005	...	...	100.0	...	...	73.9
Norvège	2010	...	...	99.4	...	...	74.9
	2017	...	...	98.3	...	...	76.3
Oman	2005	...	...	75.1	...	...	...
Oman	2010	...	...	82.5	...	...	...
	2017	...	...	90.3	...	...	...
Pakistan	2005	49.3	31.9	37.8	...	...	...
Pakistan	2010	45.4	32.2	36.8	...	...	...
	2017	40.0	32.6	35.3	...	...	...
Paraguay	2005	69.0	33.9	54.1	50.7	45.3	48.4
Paraguay	2010	70.3	41.0	58.4	51.9	54.1	52.8
	2017	72.2	50.7	63.9	53.6	66.2	58.5
Peru	2005	57.2	16.0	46.9	23.7	...	19.6
Pérou	2010	57.9	18.0	48.5	34.9	...	28.8
	2017	58.8	20.8	50.4	51.2	...	42.8
Philippines	2005	60.3	30.7	44.2	48.9	38.7	43.4
Philippines	2010	60.8	32.3	45.2	50.7	42.9	46.4
	2017	61.5	33.7	46.7	54.0	49.6	51.6
Poland	2005	...	...	94.0	...	...	83.1
Pologne	2010	...	...	95.3	...	...	87.7
	2017	...	...	99.2	...	...	93.3
Portugal	2005	...	...	94.1	58.5	...	54.3
Portugal	2010	...	...	94.8	74.1	...	67.8
	2017	...	...	95.3	92.7	...	84.7
Puerto Rico	2005	...	...	75.0	...	...	32.5
Porto Rico	2010	...	...	80.3	...	...	32.5
	2017	...	...	94.1	...	...	32.5
Qatar	2005	...	...	96.6	...	...	86.3
Qatar	2010	...	...	96.6	...	...	88.5
	2017	...	...	96.2	...	...	96.0
Republic of Korea	2005	...	...	96.8	...	...	90.8
République de Corée	2010	...	...	97.7	...	...	95.7
	2017	...	...	98.2	...	...	99.9
Republic of Moldova	2005	...	...	50.5	74.1	...	...
République de Moldova	2010	...	...	62.2	75.2	...	...
	2017	...	...	72.9	77.9	...	...
Réunion	2005	...	...	95.8	...	...	...
Réunion	2010	...	...	96.0	...	...	...
	2017	...	...	96.2	...	...	...
Romania	2005	...	...	81.7	...	...	55.7
Roumanie	2010	...	...	81.9	...	...	63.3
	2017	...	...	81.9	...	...	76.5
Russian Federation	2005	...	...	74.9	61.4	43.6	56.7
Fédération de Russie	2010	...	...	75.3	62.2	48.4	58.6
	2017	...	...	76.0	63.4	55.2	61.3
Rwanda	2005	29.7	...	...	...	...	...
Rwanda	2010	35.2	...	...	...	...	...
	2017	43.4	...	...	...	...	...
Saint Helena	2005	...	...	88.7	...	...	...
Sainte-Hélène	2010	...	...	88.9	...	...	...
	2017	...	...	89.2	...	...	...
Saint Pierre and Miquelon	2010	...	...	83.1	...	...	...
Saint-Pierre-et-Miquelon	2017	...	...	83.1	...	...	...
Samoa	2005	...	...	57.2	40.5	52.0	49.6
Samoa	2010	...	...	58.0	39.6	51.8	49.3
	2017	...	...	58.8	37.7	50.9	48.5
San Marino	2005	...	...	100.0	...	...	77.2
Saint-Marin	2010	...	...	100.0	...	...	77.2
	2017	...	...	100.0	...	...	77.2

Country or area& Pays ou zone&	Year Année	Proportion of population using: - Proportion de la population utilisant des:					
		Safely managed drinking water services Services d'alimentation en eau potable gérés en toute sécurité			Safely managed sanitation facilities Services d'assainissement gérés en toute sécurité		
		Urban (%) Urbaine (%)	Rural (%) Rurale (%)	Total (%) Totale (%)	Urban (%) Urbaine (%)	Rural (%) Rurale (%)	Total (%) Totale (%)
Saudi Arabia Arabie saoudite	2005	...	...	...	...	...	69.8
	2010	...	...	...	...	...	73.1
	2017	...	...	...	...	...	77.8
Senegal Sénégal	2005	...	...	...	16.1	15.6	15.8
	2010	...	...	...	16.9	17.8	17.4
	2017	...	...	...	21.9	21.1	21.5
Serbia Serbie	2005	81.5	66.5	74.6	18.8	...	26.6
	2010	81.4	66.4	74.7	20.2	...	25.1
	2017	81.3	66.4	74.7	23.2	...	24.7
Sierra Leone Sierra Leone	2005	11.0	2.9	5.9	17.5	5.6	10.0
	2010	11.5	4.8	7.4	18.6	6.7	11.3
	2017	12.1	8.3	9.9	20.3	8.4	13.3
Singapore Singapour	2005	100.0	...	100.0	100.0	...	100.0
	2010	100.0	...	100.0	100.0	...	100.0
	2017	100.0	...	100.0	100.0	...	100.0
Slovakia Slovaquie	2005	...	...	94.7	89.5	76.5	83.7
	2010	...	...	97.9	89.0	76.2	83.2
	2017	...	...	99.8	88.4	75.7	82.5
Slovenia Slovénie	2005	...	...	83.7	...	...	76.0
	2010	...	...	90.1	...	...	79.4
	2017	...	...	98.1	...	...	83.0
South Africa Afrique du Sud	2005	90.4	...	...	...	...	...
	2010	87.3	...	...	...	...	...
	2017	81.9	...	...	...	...	...
Spain Espagne	2005	...	...	98.7	94.9	93.9	94.7
	2010	...	...	98.6	95.8	95.3	95.7
	2017	...	...	98.4	96.6	96.7	96.6
Sri Lanka Sri Lanka	2005	86.2	...	...	...	...	...
	2010	88.1	...	...	...	...	...
	2017	90.8	...	...	...	...	...
State of Palestine État de Palestine	2005	...	...	...	59.0	...	54.3
	2010	...	...	...	61.4	...	57.4
	2017	...	...	...	64.7	...	61.2
Sweden Suède	2005	...	...	99.9	93.7	87.5	92.7
	2010	...	...	99.9	93.9	87.7	93.0
	2017	...	...	99.9	94.2	87.8	93.4
Switzerland Suisse	2005	...	...	93.3	98.5	98.3	98.5
	2010	...	...	94.5	99.3	98.5	99.1
	2017	...	...	95.5	99.9	98.5	99.5
Tajikistan Tadjikistan	2005	...	...	41.5	...	...	...
	2010	...	...	46.0	...	...	...
	2017	...	...	47.9	...	...	...
North Macedonia Macédoine du Nord	2005	97.8	95.1	96.7	11.3	...	13.5
	2010	92.9	89.1	91.3	8.6	...	14.5
	2017	89.9	68.8	81.0	8.2	...	16.6
Tunisia Tunisie	2005	...	...	63.2	77.7	...	63.9
	2010	...	...	86.3	82.2	...	70.2
	2017	...	...	92.7	88.3	...	78.1
Turkey Turquie	2005	...	...	...	63.5	...	56.2
	2010	...	...	...	66.6	...	60.6
	2017	...	...	...	69.6	...	65.2
Turkmenistan Turkménistan	2005	85.9	61.3	72.9	...	...	...
	2010	92.2	73.5	82.6	...	...	...
	2017	96.9	90.7	93.9	...	...	...
Tuvalu Tuvalu	2005	49.2	...	...	5.2	4.3	4.8
	2010	49.5	...	...	4.7	7.8	6.1
	2017	49.8	...	...	4.2	9.7	6.3
Uganda Ouganda	2005	22.8	1.9	5.5	...	...	...
	2010	19.9	2.9	6.2	...	...	...
	2017	15.7	4.5	7.1	...	...	...

Water supply and sanitation services *(continued)*
Proportion of population using

Services d'alimentation en eau potable et d'assainissement *(suite)*
Proportion de la population utilisant des services

Country or area& Pays ou zone&	Year Année	Proportion of population using: - Proportion de la population utilisant des:					
		Safely managed drinking water services Services d'alimentation en eau potable gérés en toute sécurité			Safely managed sanitation facilities Services d'assainissement gérés en toute sécurité		
		Urban (%) Urbaine (%)	Rural (%) Rurale (%)	Total (%) Totale (%)	Urban (%) Urbaine (%)	Rural (%) Rurale (%)	Total (%) Totale (%)
Ukraine Ukraine	2005	...	...	71.4	38.5	...	44.1
	2010			84.6	45.9	...	50.9
	2017	...	...	92.0	65.8	...	68.5
United Arab Emirates Émirats arabes unis	2005	...	...	...	...	...	91.3
	2010	...	...	...	...	...	93.4
	2017	...	...	...	...	...	96.3
United Kingdom Royaume-Uni	2005	...	...	100.0	99.0	91.8	97.5
	2010	...	...	100.0	99.0	91.8	97.6
	2017	...	...	100.0	99.0	91.8	97.8
United Rep. of Tanzania Rép.-Unie de Tanzanie	2005	10.3	...	...	16.9	8.8	10.8
	2010	28.0	...	...	24.0	15.0	17.6
	2017	35.0	...	...	31.4	22.4	25.4
United States of America États-Unis d'Amérique	2005	99.7	...	98.9	94.9	...	88.8
	2010	99.7	...	99.0	95.2	...	89.3
	2017	99.7	...	99.0	95.5	...	90.0
Uruguay Uruguay	2005	93.9	...	...	...	...	...
	2010	94.2	...	...	...	...	...
	2017	94.6	...	...	...	...	...
Uzbekistan Ouzbékistan	2005	84.8	30.9	57.1	...	...	...
	2010	85.4	30.2	58.3	...	...	...
	2017	86.1	31.1	58.9	...	...	...
Vanuatu Vanuatu	2005	...	...	40.0	...	...	...
	2010	...	...	41.8	...	...	...
	2017	...	...	44.1	...	...	...
Venezuela (Boliv. Rep. of) Venezuela (Rép. boliv. du)	2005	...	...	...	...	...	28.5
	2010	...	...	...	...	...	26.2
	2017	...	...	...	...	...	23.8
Yemen Yémen	2005	...	...	...	67.7	...	...
	2010	...	...	...	67.4	...	...
	2017	...	...	...	67.0	...	...
Zambia Zambie	2005	47.8	...	...	...	...	...
	2010	47.1	...	...	...	...	...
	2017	46.2	...	...	...	...	...
Zimbabwe Zimbabwe	2005	...	...	...	22.3	...	...
	2010	...	...	...	19.8	...	...
	2017	...	...	...	16.3	...	...

Source:

World Health Organization (WHO) and United Nations Children's Fund (UNICEF), Geneva and New York, the WHO/UNICEF Joint Monitoring Programme for the Water and Sanitation database, last accessed May 2019.

& The figures are estimated by the international agency, when corresponding country data on a specific year or set of years are not available, or when multiple sources exist, or there are issues of data quality. Estimates are based on national data, such as surveys or administrative records, or other sources but on the same variable being estimated.

1   For statistical purposes, the data for China do not include those for the Hong Kong Special Administrative Region (Hong Kong SAR), Macao Special Administrative Region (Macao SAR) and Taiwan Province of China.

Source:

Organisation mondiale de la santé (OMS) et Fonds des Nations Unies pour l'enfance (UNICEF), Genève et New York, base de données du Programme commun OMS/UNICEF de surveillance de l'eau et de l'assainissement, dernier accès mai 2019.

& Lorsque les données d'un pays sur une ou plusieurs années ne sont pas disponibles, ou lorsque plusieurs sources existent, ou s'il y a un problème de qualité des données, les chiffres sont estimés par l'organisme international. Ces estimations sont basées sur de données nationales comme les enquêtes, les registres administratifs, ou autres sources de la même variable estimée.

1   Pour la présentation des statistiques, les données pour la Chine ne comprennent pas la région administrative spéciale de Hong Kong (RAS de Hong Kong), la région administrative spéciale de Macao (RAS de Macao) et la province chinoise de Taïwan.

26

Population employed in research and development (R&D)
Full-time equivalent (FTE)

Population employé dans la recherche et le développement (R-D)
Equivalent temps plein (ETP)

Country or area / Pays ou zone	Year / Année	Total R & D personnel / Total du personnel de R - D	Researchers / Chercheurs Total M & F / Total H & F	Females / Femmes	Technicians and equivalent staff / Techniciens et personnel assimilé Total M & F / Total H & F	Females / Femmes	Other supporting staff / Autre personnel de soutien Total M & F / Total H & F	Females / Femmes
Albania [1] / Albanie [1]	2008	779	467	207	120	...	192	...
Algeria / Algérie	2005[1]	7 331	5 593	2 043	1 134	...	604	...
	2017	# 38 046	# 33 912	15 841	# 1 733	646[2]	# 2 401	973[2]
American Samoa [1] / Samoa américaines [1]	2005	6	6	...	...	...	...	...
Angola / Angola	2011	2 038	1 150	320	858	242	30	6[3]
	#2016	...	543	157	...	...	...	...
Argentina / Argentine	2005	45 361	31 868	15 416	7 788	...	5 705	...
	2008	56 987	41 523	20 690	8 236	...	7 228	...
	2010	...	45 960	22 901	...	...	...	...
	2017	...	52 383	27 911	...	...	...	...
Armenia [3] / Arménie [3]	2005	6 892[4]	5 056[1]	2 329[1]	345[1]	...	1 491[4]	...
	2010	6 558[4]	4 981[1]	2 261[1]	479[1]	...	672[1]	...
	2017	4 822[4]	3 588[5]	1 868[5]	235[5]	190[5,6]	531[5]	283[5]
Australia / Australie	2004	116 194	81 192	...	17 600	...	17 402	...
	2008	137 489	92 649	...	24 243	...	20 597	...
	2010	* 147 809	100 414	...	...	...	...	...
Austria [7] / Autriche [7]	2004	42 891	25 955	4 740	12 067	2 901	4 869	2 471
	2005	47 625	28 470	...	...	...	...	...
	2009	56 438	34 664	7 765	16 709	3 903	5 065	2 398
	2010	59 923	36 581	...	...	...	...	...
	2015	71 396	43 562	10 114	22 387	4 651	5 447	2 326
	2016	74 897	44 933	...	...	...	...	...
	2017	77 880	...	...	...	...	...	...
Azerbaijan [3] / Azerbaïdjan [3]	2005	18 164[4]	11 603	6 056	1 825	...	3 086	...
	2010	17 924[4]	11 037	6 101	1 819	2 174[5]	3 531	1 866
	2017	20 580[4]	14 732	8 698	1 902	2 014[5]	2 244	1 325
Bahrain / Bahreïn	2014	562	493	205	23	12	94[3]	16
Belarus [3] / Bélarus [3]	2005	30 222[4]	18 267	7 897	2 112	...	5 763	...
	2010	31 712[4]	19 879	8 392	2 248	...	9 585[4]	...
	2017	26 483[4]	17 089	6 785	1 691	...	7 703[4]	...
Belgium / Belgique	2005	53 517	33 146	9 769	15 047	4 585	5 324	2 702
	2010	60 075	40 832	12 962	14 401	5 079	4 841	2 517
	2011	62 895	42 686	13 545	15 176	5 232	5 033	2 575
	*2017	84 046	56 484	...	...	...	...	...
Benin [1,3] / Bénin [1,3]	*2007	...	1 000	...	...	...	...	...
Bermuda [3] / Bermudes [3]	2010	80	41	17	...	...	29	13
	2015	60	34	11	...	...	22	12
Bolivia (Plurin. State of) / Bolivie (État plurin. de)	2002	1 090	1 040	...	...	...	50	...
	2010	2 497	1 646	...	258	...	593	...
Bosnia and Herzegovina / Bosnie-Herzégovine	2005[1]	731	253	...	198	...	280	...
	2007[1]	1 554	745	...	270	...	536	...
	2017	2 426	1 627	748	224	119	205	131
Botswana / Botswana	2005[3]	...	...	533	...	...	...	...
	2013	1 214	382	225[3]	258	89	574	249
Brazil / Brésil	2005	...	94 742	...	...	...	...	...
	2010	243 560	134 284[8]	...	147 681[8]	...	...	...
	2014	316 495	179 989[8]	...	196 661[8]	...	...	...
Brunei Darussalam / Brunéi Darussalam	2003	140	98	78[3]	...	...	...	...
	2004	...	# 102	99[3]	...	...	...	...
Bulgaria / Bulgarie	2005	15 853	10 053	4 673	3 778	2 256	2 022	1 349
	2010	16 574	10 979	5 506	3 704	2 189	1 891	1 172
	2011	16 986	11 902	5 940	3 263	1 970	1 821	1 139
	2016	25 060	16 001	7 780	...	...	...	...
	2017	23 290	15 094	...	...	...	...	...

Country or area Pays ou zone	Year Année	Total R & D personnel Total du personnel de R - D	Researchers Chercheurs Total M & F Total H & F	Females Femmes	Technicians and equivalent staff Techniciens et personnel assimilé Total M & F Total H & F	Females Femmes	Other supporting staff Autre personnel de soutien Total M & F Total H & F	Females Femmes
Burkina Faso [3]	2005	942[1]	301[1]	37	225[1]	...	416[1]	...
Burkina Faso [3]	2010	# 2 548	# 1 144	# 264	# 608	298[5]	# 796	# 256
	2017	4 182[5]	2 050[5]	349[5]	407[5]	110[6]	1 725[5]	602[5]
Burundi [3]	2010	744[1]	374[1]	56	117[1]	...	253[1]	...
Burundi [3]	2011	746[1]	379[1]	55	125[1]	...	242[1]	...
Cabo Verde	2002[1]	151	60	...	15	...	76	...
Cabo Verde	2011	# 37	# 25	9	# 4	* 2	# 8	5
Cambodia	*2002[1]	494	223	50	170	...	102	...
Cambodge	2015	# 1 895	# 471	# 126	# 945	330	# 478	216
Cameroon [3]								
Cameroun [3]	2008	5 600	...	994	338	...	...	...
Canada	2005	218 590	136 700	...	52 825	...	29 072	...
Canada	2010	233 060	158 660	...	51 930	...	22 470	...
	2016	223 146	155 128	...	44 047	...	23 980	...
Central African Republic [3]	2005[1]	...	11	...	...	...	...	...
République centrafricaine [3]	2007	...	41[1]	17[9]	...	...	...	...
	2009[1]	...	134	...	...	...	...	...
Chad [5]								
Tchad [5]	2016	1 097	843	43	121	17	133	18
Chile [7]	2010	11 491	5 440	1 671	3 909	1 590	2 142	941
Chili [7]	2016	16 633	8 993	2 979	5 402	2 398	2 238	829
China	2005[7]	1 364 799	1 118 698	...	...	...	...	...
Chine	2010	2 553 829	1 210 841	...	...	...	...	...
	2017	4 033 597	1 740 442	...	...	...	...	...
China, Hong Kong SAR	2005	22 053	18 024	...	2 346	...	1 683	...
Chine, RAS de Hong Kong	2010	25 174	21 697	...	2 159	...	1 319	...
	2017	32 355	27 635	...	2 908	...	1 811	...
China, Macao SAR	#2005	413	298	77	110	...	5	...
Chine, RAS de Macao	2010[1]	676	350	116	313	158	13	9
	2017[1]	2 184	2 009	790	136	58	38	28
Colombia								
Colombie	2017	...	4 305	1 621	...	...	...	...
Congo								
Congo	2000	217[1]	102[1]	13	111[1]	22	4[1]	...
Costa Rica [3]	2005	...	1 144	569	...	...	...	...
Costa Rica [3]	2010	6 156[5]	3 569[5]	1 475[5]	1 326[5]	388[5]	1 261[5]	476
	2016[5]	5 525	3 885	1 663	815	310[6]	825	248
	2017[5]	...	3 834	1 700	...	...	...	...
Côte d'Ivoire [3]	2005[1]	...	...	395	...	...	...	...
Côte d'Ivoire [3]	2016	5 729[1]	...	# 728	1 214[1]	1 012[5,10]	229[1]	52[1]
Croatia	2005	9 270	5 727	2 710	2 633	1 196	910	584
Croatie	2010	10 859	7 104	3 485	2 601	1 280	1 154	768
	2016	11 536	7 788	3 762	2 686	1 338	1 062	741
	2017	11 778	7 815	...	...	...	...	...
Cuba [3]	2005	33 988	5 526	2 703	...	...	28 462[11]	...
Cuba [3]	2010	16 641	4 872	2 381	...	...	11 769	...
	2017	18 729	6 878	3 370	...	...	11 851	...
Cyprus	2005	1 157	682	239	273	98	201	105
Chypre	2010	1 302	905	337	216	89	181	101
	2016	1 356	898	332	232	98	225	121
	*2017	1 485	1 015	...	...	...	...	...
Czechia	#2005	43 370	24 169	6 349	13 773	5 153	5 429	2 633
Tchéquie	2010	52 290	29 228	7 429	15 971	5 141	7 092	3 369
	2016	65 783	37 338	8 610	19 421	5 813	9 024	4 237
	*2017	69 736	39 181	9 060	20 826	5 918	...	4 612
Dem. Rep. of the Congo [3]	2005[4]	33 478	10 411	...	1 510	...	21 557	...
Rép. dém. du Congo [3]	2009[4]	34 820	12 470	...	1 843	...	20 507	...
	2015	2 876[4]	# 1 310	114[1]	# 703	112[1]	# 863	...

Population employed in research and development (R&D) *(continued)*
Full-time equivalent (FTE)

Population employé dans la recherche et le développement (R-D) *(suite)*
Equivalent temps plein (ETP)

Country or area Pays ou zone	Year Année	Total R & D personnel Total du personnel de R - D	Researchers Chercheurs		Technicians and equivalent staff Techniciens et personnel assimilé		Other supporting staff Autre personnel de soutien	
			Total M & F Total H & F	Females Femmes	Total M & F Total H & F	Females Femmes	Total M & F Total H & F	Females Femmes
Denmark	2005	43 499	28 179	8 113	10 781	21 508	4 538	2 534
Danemark	2010	56 623	37 435	* 11 654	12 557	19 155[7]	6 631	* 3 433
	2011	57 585	39 181	12 376	11 856	18 600	6 548	3 112
	2015	60 243	42 826	13 649	...	...	...	...
	*2017	62 911	45 277	...	...	...	...	...
Ecuador	2003	...	645	...	...	...	...	...
Équateur	2010	4 769	2 110	854	1 029	300	1 630	783
	2014	8 948	6 373	2 630	1 435	714	1 140	649
Egypt	2010	86 455[1]	40 752[1]	16 972	20 758[1]	...	24 945[1]	...
Égypte	2017	122 142	65 301	28 475	35 799	14 365	21 042	8 965
El Salvador [3]	2005	...	260	81	...	...	...	...
El Salvador [3]	2010	...	516	190	...	...	...	...
	2016	1 036	941	369	89	* 41	6	* 4
	2017	...	981	379	...	...	...	...
Estonia	2005	4 362	3 331	1 317	567	274	464	305
Estonie	2010	5 277	4 077	1 688	907	404	293	211
	2016	5 772	4 338	1 793	935	478	498	328
	2017	6 048	4 674	...	...	...	...	...
Eswatini								
Eswatini	2015	408	157	71	40	20	211	93
Ethiopia	2005	5 112	1 608	111	779	...	2 725	...
Éthiopie	2007	6 051	1 615	125	978	...	3 458	...
	#2010	8 282	3 701	...	1 441	...	3 140	...
	2013	11 501	4 267	556	3 157	757	4 078	1 316
	2017	...	9 632	1 184	...	...	...	...
Faroe Islands								
Îles Féroé	2003	131	86	21	41	...	4	...
Finland	2005	57 471	39 582	...	...	...	...	...
Finlande	2010	55 897	41 425	...	...	...	...	...
	*2017	48 999	37 047	...	...	...	...	...
France	2005	349 681	202 507	...	105 171	...	42 003	...
France	2010	# 397 756	# 243 533	* 46 001	# 118 364	...	# 35 860	...
	2015	428 643	277 631	* 74 762	115 910	...	35 102	...
	*2017	434 670	288 579	...	...	...	...	...
Gabon [3]	2004[1]	188	80	25	68	...	...	...
Gabon [3]	2009	# 839	# 531	# 118	# 142	55[1]	...	66[1]
Gambia [3]	2005[1]	84	46	4	28	...	10	...
Gambie [3]	2008	# 855	# 155	31	# 200	...	# 500	...
	2009	926	179	...	198	...	549	...
	2011	# 1 055	# 60	12	# 737	...	# 233	...
Georgia [1]								
Géorgie [1]	2017	6 935	5 241	2 733	783	459	907	493
Germany	2005	475 278	272 148	47 666	94 578	29 657	108 553	44 729
Allemagne	2009	534 975	317 307	65 258	111 660	34 277	106 008	44 018
	2010	548 723	* 327 996	...	* 113 211	...	* 107 515	...
	2015	640 516	387 982	87 756	156 202	41 497	96 332	45 205
	2016	657 894	399 605	...	159 925	...	98 364	...
	*2017	681 552	413 542	...	...	...	...	...
Ghana								
Ghana	2010	# 3 005	# 941	163	# 731	186	# 1 333	288
Greece	2005[7]	33 603	19 593	6 213	8 450	3 070	5 559	3 007
Grèce	2007[7]	35 531	21 014	...	...	...	...	...
	#2011	36 913	24 674	9 602	6 336	2 973	5 903	2 897
	2015[7]	49 658	34 708	12 370	...	...	...	...
	2017[7]	48 226	35 185	...	...	...	...	...
Greenland								
Groenland	2004	48	40	11	8	...	...	...
Guam								
Guam	2005	51	48	...	...	...	...	...

Country or area Pays ou zone	Year Année	Total R & D personnel Total du personnel de R - D	Researchers Chercheurs Total M & F Total H & F	Researchers Chercheurs Females Femmes	Technicians and equivalent staff Techniciens et personnel assimilé Total M & F Total H & F	Technicians and equivalent staff Females Femmes	Other supporting staff Autre personnel de soutien Total M & F Total H & F	Other supporting staff Females Femmes
Guatemala [1] Guatemala [1]	2005	851	388	...	139	...	324	...
	2010	876	363	145	273	...	240	...
	2015	1 259	360	223	416	230	483	...
	2017	...	238	126	...	...	...	...
Guinea [3] Guinée [3]	2000	3 711[4]	2 117[1]	122[1]	768[1]	...	826[1]	...
	2013	# 752	# 214	# 21	# 33	3[1]	75[1]	22[1]
Honduras Honduras	2003[3]	2 280	539	143	...	...	1 741	731
	2015	# 304[3]	# 207[3]	# 85[3]	91[1]	47[1,3]	# 6[3]	# 3[3]
	2017[3]	...	538	196	...	...	...	...
Hungary Hongrie	2005	23 239	15 878	...	4 591	...	2 770	...
	2010	31 480	21 342	6 447	5 967	3 230	4 171	2 346
	2016	35 757	25 804	6 884	6 252	3 232	3 701	1 958
	*2017	40 432	28 426	...	...	...	...	...
Iceland Islande	2005	3 226	2 155	784	669	299	402	181
	2009	3 397	2 505	1 000	626	279	266	96
	#2011	3 244	2 258	812	604	192	381	246
	2016	3 247	2 206	...	697	...	345	...
India Inde	2000	318 443	115 936	11 304[12]	90 045[2]	10 363	112 462[2]	19 531
	2005	391 149	154 827	19 707[12]	105 808[2]	...	130 514[2]	...
	2010	441 126	192 819	27 532	124 188[2]	...	124 119[2]	...
	2015	528 219	282 994	39 389	125 184	15 644	120 041	22 673
Indonesia Indonésie	2001	51 544	42 722	...	...	...	...	...
	* #2009	...	21 349	...	...	...	...	...
	2017	64 635	56 950	24 897	4 628	1 113[2]	3 057[2]	1 141[2]
Iran (Islamic Republic of) Iran (Rép. islamique d')	2010	...	54 813	14 775	...	...	...	...
	2015	91 722	64 778	22 216	12 605	4 638	14 339	4 675
	2017	...	118 987	37 146	...	...	...	...
Iraq Iraq	2010	16 857[4]	12 849[4]	4 380[5]	1 927[4]	...	1 988[4]	...
	2017	5 041	3 978	1 664	724	335	339	100
Ireland Irlande	2005	16 690	11 587	3 241	3 043	797	2 060	881
	*2010	19 722	14 176	4 672	3 052	813	2 494	1 044
	2015	32 085	22 259	7 623	5 406	1 280	4 420	2 186
	2016	29 849	19 791	...	5 409	...	4 649	...
	*2017	29 405	19 559	...	...	...	...	...
Israel [7] Israël [7]	2011	70 401	55 184	11 700	9 818	2 320	5 399	2 006
	2012	77 143	63 521	...	7 676	...	5 946	...
Italy Italie	2005	175 248	82 489	26 797	...	...	...	...
	2010	225 632	103 424	35 792	...	...	...	...
	#2016	290 040	133 706	47 481	...	...	...	...
	*2017	291 516	136 204	...	...	...	...	...
Japan [7] Japon [7]	2005	896 855	680 631	102 948[3]	71 726	27 562[3]	144 498	65 753[3]
	2010	877 928	656 032	123 181[3]	74 857	30 404[3]	147 039	68 344[3]
	2017	890 749	676 292	150 545[3]	66 386	31 603	148 072	76 249[3]
Jordan Jordanie	2003[3]	...	...	...	...	...	6 940	2 101
	#2015	3 348	2 339	387	1 009	239	...	...
	2017	...	5 832[1]	1 230	...	...	...	...
Kazakhstan Kazakhstan	2010	8 325	6 022	...	454	...	1 179	1 506[3]
	2017	15 841	12 044	...	2 238	...	1 559	1 091[3]
Kenya Kenya	2010	# 42 566	# 9 305	1 861	# 26 384	12 024	# 6 877	2 735
Kuwait Koweït	2005[1]	800	384	...	96	...	320	...
	2010[1]	829	407	152	87	23	335	145
	2015	2 631[5]	1 518[5]	# 733	210[5]	59[5]	862[5]	363[5]
	2017[5]	...	2 034	1 028	207	61	722	335
Kyrgyzstan [3] Kirghizistan [3]	2005	3 419[4]	2 187	977	226	...	498	...
	2010	3 129[4]	1 974	876	261	...	428	...
	2017	4 300[4]	3 281[6]	1 525[6]	318[6]	192[5,13]	413[6]	250[6]
Lao People's Dem. Rep. Rép. dém. populaire lao	2002	268	87	* 48[3]	...	...	...	...

Country or area Pays ou zone	Year Année	Total R & D personnel Total du personnel de R - D	Researchers Chercheurs Total M & F Total H & F	Females Femmes	Technicians and equivalent staff Techniciens et personnel assimilé Total M & F Total H & F	Females Femmes	Other supporting staff Autre personnel de soutien Total M & F Total H & F	Females Femmes
Latvia	2005	5 483	3 282	1 636	1 062	554	1 139	594
Lettonie	2010	5 563	3 896	1 823	915	401	752	439
	2011	5 432	3 947	2 045	819	387	666	440
	2016	5 120	3 152	1 580	...	...	...	...
	2017	5 378	3 482	...	...	...	...	...
Lesotho	2004	51[1]	20[1]	10[12]	21[1]	...	10[1]	...
Lesotho	2009[1]	105	46	16	47	...	11	...
	2015[5]	72	50	20	14	7	8	2
Libya [3]	2004[1]	772	215	...	164	...	...	...
Libye [3]	2009	1 131[1]	460[1]	101	229[1]	...	268[1]	...
Lithuania	2005	11 002	7 637	3 706	1 436	939	1 929	1 280
Lituanie	2010	12 315	8 599	4 367	1 691	887	2 025	1 281
	2011	11 173	8 390	4 099	1 426	812	1 357	888
	2016	10 924	8 525	3 987	...	...	...	...
	2017	11 520	8 709	...	...	...	...	...
Luxembourg	2005	4 392	2 227	392	1 558	258	607	250
Luxembourg	2009	4 711	2 396	534	1 423	384	891	437
	2010	4 972	2 613	...	1 708	...	651	...
	2015	5 227	2 539	720	1 862	345	826	285
	2016	5 312	* 2 704	...	* 1 801	...	807	...
	*2017	5 322	2 732	...	...	...	...	...
Madagascar	2005	1 686[1]	879[1]	298	195[1]	...	612[1]	...
Madagascar	2010	# 1 785	# 1 099	371	# 326	...	# 360	...
	2017[5]	2 247	783	267	275	131	764	273
Malawi								
Malawi	2010	1 721	732	136	873	155	116	15
Malaysia	2004	17 887	12 670	4 701	1 598	...	3 619	...
Malaisie	2010	50 484	41 253	19 029	3 676	...	5 555	...
	2016	89 178	73 537	36 903	# 8 078	# 2 447	# 7 564	# 3 664
Mali	2010	856	443	62	342	* 44	71	34
Mali	2017[1]	1 451	608	87	440	87	403	115
Malta	2005	825	479	121	222	20	124	65
Malte	2010	1 102	587	150	335	36	179	87
	2016	1 505	896	238	324	36	284	132
	2017	1 481	894	...	...	...	...	...
Mauritania [3]								
Mauritanie [3]	2016	2 286[7]	2 263[7]	523[7]	14[1]	2[5,10]	9[1]	3[1]
Mauritius	2012[5]	627	228	94	68	34	331	57
Maurice	#2017	...	985	482	...	...	...	...
Mexico	2003	59 875	33 558	* 14 073[3]	15 304	13 342[5,10]	11 013	* 6 709[3]
Mexique	2005	83 685	43 922	...	25 796	...	13 967	...
	2010	70 997	38 497	...	20 760	...	11 740	...
	2013	59 073	29 921	13 943[3]	16 345	11 917[5]	12 807	5 918[3]
Monaco [1]								
Monaco [1]	2005	18	10	5	5	...	3	...
Mongolia [3]	2000	2 113[1]	1 631[1]	...	294[1]	150	188[1]	...
Mongolie [3]	2005	2 283[1]	1 731[1]	819	81[1]	...	471[1]	...
	2010	2 517[1]	1 739[1]	865[1]	129[1]	48	649[1]	399
	2017[1]	3 291	1 799	1 034	242	101	1 250	719
Montenegro	2015	673	523	239	81	39	68	47
Monténégro	2016	624	449	...	110	...	65	...
Morocco	2010	28 041[1]	23 280[1]	7 744	1 697[1]	...	1 747[1]	...
Maroc	2016	40 543[1]	37 709	12 851[5]	1 414[1]	217[10]	1 420[1]	341[14]
Mozambique	2008	1 555[1]	444[1]	148[1]	673[1]	* 374	438[1]	...
Mozambique	2010	# 2 164	# 912	294	# 1 093	...	# 159	...
	2015	2 320	1 162	336	723	217	435	144
Myanmar	2002[1]	7 418	837	...	6 499	...	82	...
Myanmar	2017	# 3 142	# 1 552	1 163[5]	# 998	746[5]	# 513	329[5]
Namibia [3]	2010	949	748	327	118	...	83	41
Namibie [3]	2014[1]	1 132	749	290	255	95	128	79

Country or area Pays ou zone	Year Année	Total R & D personnel Total du personnel de R - D	Researchers Chercheurs Total M & F Total H & F	Females Femmes	Technicians and equivalent staff Techniciens et personnel assimilé Total M & F Total H & F	Females Femmes	Other supporting staff Autre personnel de soutien Total M & F Total H & F	Females Femmes
Nauru [1,3] Nauru [1,3]	2003	77	19	3	18	...	36	...
Nepal [3] Népal [3]	*2002	13 500	3 000	450	6 000	...	4 500	...
	2010	# 41 911	# 5 123	399	# 12 053	...	# 21 167	...
Netherlands	2005	93 599	47 854	...	23 265	...	22 480	...
Pays-Bas	2010	100 544	53 703	...	22 128	...	24 714	...
	#2011	117 436	61 335	15 629	34 107	7 340	21 993	8 723
	2016	132 867	81 117	21 786	...	...	...	...
	*2017	138 292	85 300	...	...	...	...	...
New Zealand	2005	18 929	12 986	...	3 200	...	2 800	...
Nouvelle-Zélande	2009	23 200	16 100	...	4 100	...	2 900	...
	2015	26 400	18 700	...	4 700	...	2 600	...
Nicaragua [3] Nicaragua [3]	2002	456	...	96[12]	...	...	...	...
	2004	371	...	...	45	15	...	...
	2012	1 225	...	...	231	...	...	...
Niger [1] Niger [1]	2005	595	101	...	137	...	357	...
Nigeria [3] Nigéria [3]	2005[1]	66 574	28 533	4 839	10 854	...	27 187	...
	#2007	32 802	17 624	4 106	4 647	1 026	10 531	3 759
North Macedonia	2005	1 434	1 113	576	168	* 94	153	81
Macédoine du Nord	2010	1 434	1 102	620	170	104	162	106
	2017	1 870	1 519	856	191	101	160	69
Norway	2005	29 966	21 200	...	...	...	...	...
Norvège	2010	36 121	26 451	...	...	...	...	...
	*2017	46 989	34 367	...	...	...	...	...
Oman [1] Oman [1]	2017	1 643	1 131	343	200	98	312	335[8]
Pakistan	2005	53 159[5]	12 689[5]	2 053	6 471[5]	...	33 999[5]	...
Pakistan	2009	74 695[5]	27 602[5]	6 534	10 993[5]	...	36 100[5]	...
	2017[5]	101 437	69 769	26 213	6 611	274	25 057	1 371
Panama	2002	1 331[10]	297	...	...	...	1 034	...
Panama	2005	1 302[10]	344	...	...	...	...	...
	2008	1 449	463	...	377	...	609	...
	2009	530[10]	394	...	...	...	# 137	...
	#2012	792	142	67	350	144	300	113
	2013	...	150	74	595	298	433	166
Papua New Guinea Papouasie-Nvl-Guinée	2016	593[1]	294[1]	85[5]	89[1]	30[5]	210[1]	82[5]
Paraguay	2005	# 614	419	...	...	...	# 195	...
Paraguay	2008	667	466	...	...	...	201	...
	2016	# 1 526	821[5]	399[5]	# 525	242[5]	179[5]	110[5]
	2017[5]	...	928	450	...	...	...	...
Peru [3]	2004	8 434	4 965	...	1 757	...	1 712	...
Pérou [3]	#2010	...	434	...	...	...	...	...
	2015	5 408	3 374	1 076	1 195	440	837	336
	#2017	...	1 529	457	...	...	...	...
Philippines	2005	9 407[4]	6 896	3 500	897	...	1 440	...
Philippines	2009	10 366	7 505	3 882	1 116	381	1 743	708
	2013	26 577	18 481	8 872	2 765	1 041	5 140	2 086
	2015	...	10 791	5 267	...	...	...	...
Poland	2005	76 761	62 162	24 521	8 947	...	5 652	...
Pologne	2010	81 843	64 511	24 745	10 939	...	6 393	...
	2016	111 789	88 165	30 158	15 187	5 620	8 437	4 645
	*2017	121 428	96 497	...	...	...	...	...
Portugal	2005	25 728	21 126	9 530	2 918	1 177	1 683	954
Portugal	2010	47 616	41 523	18 175	4 004	1 481	2 088	894
	2016	50 406	41 349	17 751	7 239	3 085	1 818	943
	*2017	54 091	44 322	...	...	...	...	...
Puerto Rico [3]	2009	5 776	2 986	...	2 790	...	...	...
Porto Rico [3]	2015	5 500	2 070	...	3 040	...	390[2]	...

Country or area Pays ou zone	Year Année	Total R & D personnel Total du personnel de R - D	Researchers Chercheurs Total M & F Total H & F	Females Femmes	Technicians and equivalent staff Techniciens et personnel assimilé Total M & F Total H & F	Females Femmes	Other supporting staff Autre personnel de soutien Total M & F Total H & F	Females Femmes
Qatar Qatar	2015	3 016	1 498	451	1 002	424	516	335
Republic of Korea République de Corée	2005[7]	215 345	179 812	...	26 272	...	9 261	...
	2010	335 228	264 118	...	47 557	...	23 554	...
	2017	471 201	383 100	...	63 927	...	24 174	...
Republic of Moldova République de Moldova	2005	4 672[12]	2 583[12]	1 120	334[12]	...	1 755[12]	...
	2010	4 316	2 709	1 258	287	202	1 320	773
	2017	3 900	2 568	1 270	251	173	1 081	553
Romania Roumanie	2005	33 222	22 958	10 617	4 998	2 859	5 266	2 414
	2010	26 171	19 780	8 797	3 139	1 695	3 252	1 424
	2016	32 232	18 046	8 209	5 451	2 336	8 735	3 917
	*2017	32 586	17 518	...*	...	...	...	...
Russian Federation Fédération de Russie	2005	919 716	464 577	165 993[3]	74 253	...	380 886	...
	2010	839 992	442 071	153 863[3]*	68 042	...	329 879	...
	2017	778 155	410 617	142 290[3]	65 667	...	301 871	...
Rwanda [3] Rwanda [3]	2009	1 001[1]	564[1]	123[9]	8[1]	...	429[1]	...
	#2016	...	530	120	...	...	...	...
Saint Helena Sainte-Hélène	2000	33[1]	2[1]	...	8[1]	4	23[1]	...
Saint Vincent & Grenadines [3] Saint-Vincent-Grenadines [3]	2002	131	21	...	110	...	...	...
Saudi Arabia [3] Arabie saoudite [3]	2002[1]	4 182	1 513	263	1 674	...	995	...
	2009	2 655[1]	1 271[1]	18	658[1]	...	726[1]	...
	2013	# 751 927	# 35 324	# 8 198	# 100 053	39 420[4]	# 616 550	276 272[4]
Senegal Sénégal	2010	5 642	4 679	1 162	441	* 101	523	161
	2015[5]	9 329	8 227	2 486	538	166	563	150
Serbia Serbie	2010	17 274[13]	10 985[13]	5 370[13]	2 428[13]	1 475[2]	3 861[13]	1 954[13]
	2017	20 788[13]	14 557[13]	7 237	2 877[13]	1 453	3 354[13]	1 679
Seychelles [3] Seychelles [3]	2005[1]	199	14	5	64	...	121	...
	2016	# 442	# 149	# 52	141	57	# 152	86
Singapore Singapour	2005	28 586	23 789	...	2 375	...	2 422	...
	2010	37 013	32 031	...	2 342	...	2 641	...
	2014	42 543	36 666	...	2 490	...	3 387	...
Slovakia Slovaquie	2005	14 404	10 921	4 484	2 245	1 218	1 238	670
	2010	18 188	15 183	6 376	2 087	1 046	918	589
	2016	17 768	14 149	5 685	2 298	859	1 322	800
	2017	19 011	15 226	...	...	...	...	...
Slovenia Slovénie	2005	8 994	5 253	1 777	2 820	...	921	501
	2010	12 940	7 703	2 668	3 928	...	1 309	642
	2016	14 403	8 119	2 694	4 924	...	1 361	596
	*2017	14 713	9 293	...	...	...	...	...
South Africa Afrique du Sud	2005	28 798	17 303	6 272	5 248	1 749	6 247	2 928
	2010	29 486	18 720	7 649	5 410	2 016	5 357	2 546
	2016	42 533	27 656	12 344	7 563	* 2 992	7 314	3 558
Spain Espagne	2005	174 773	109 720	41 371	39 904	13 259	25 149	11 390
	2010[7]	222 022	134 653	51 831	60 697	24 052	26 672	12 988
	2016[7]	205 873	126 633	49 541	55 458	21 767	23 781	11 805
	2017[7]	215 713	133 195	...	...	...	...	...
Sri Lanka Sri Lanka	#2004	5 475	2 679	861	1 474	...	1 322	...
	2010	5 714	2 140	842	1 851	...	1 723	...
	2015	5 461	2 216	1 018	1 562	675	1 683	495
State of Palestine État de Palestine	2007	566[15]	280[13]	94	91[13]	...	195[13]	...
	2010	2 074[5]	1 312[5]	...	291[5]	* 145	471[16]	...
	2013	5 161[5]	2 492[5]	...	772[5]	370[5]	# 1 483	...
Sudan [3] Soudan [3]	2005	* 23 726[4]	* 11 208[4]	* 4 483	* 5 569[4]	...	6 949[4]	...
Sudan [former] [3] Soudan [anc.] [3]	*2005	23 726	11 208	4 483	5 569	...	6 949	...

Country or area Pays ou zone	Year Année	Total R & D personnel Total du personnel de R - D	Researchers Chercheurs		Technicians and equivalent staff Techniciens et personnel assimilé		Other supporting staff Autre personnel de soutien	
			Total M & F Total H & F	Females Femmes	Total M & F Total H & F	Females Femmes	Total M & F Total H & F	Females Femmes
Eswatini Eswatini	2015	408	157	71	40	20	211	93
Sweden Suède	#2005	77 557	55 001	15 960	...	...	...	...
	2009	* 77 363	* 47 308	* 14 080	39 372[10]	* 4 849	* 10 369	* 3 817
	*2010	77 418	49 312	...	...	...	...	...
	2011	* 78 445	* 48 702	* 14 721	38 388[10]	* 4 860	* 10 551	* 3 941
	*2015	83 551	66 734	18 195	...	...	...	...
	*2017	89 268	75 247	...	...	...	...	...
Switzerland Suisse	2004	52 250	25 400	11 555[3]	17 130	7 180[5]	9 720	10 960[3]
	2008	62 066	25 142	13 846[3]	21 763	9 140[5]	15 161	13 245[3]
	2015	81 451	43 740	23 762[3]	24 353	15 090[5]	13 359	10 916[3]
Syrian Arab Republic République arabe syrienne	2015	2 860[15]	1 637[5]	575[5]	1 223[5]	544[5]	...	...
Tajikistan [3] Tadjikistan [3]	2004	2 487[4]	1 548	407	247	...	692[4]	...
	2005	3 220[4]	1 993	...	324	...	903[4]	...
	2006	3 110[4]	1 895	735	202	...	1 013[4]	...
	2010	2 827[4]	1 802[5]	...	329[5]	...	427[5]	...
	2017	3 720[4]	2 562[5]	984[5]	332[5]	116[5]	533[5]	241[5]
Thailand Thaïlande	2005	36 967	20 506	10 241	...	...	5 941	...
	2009	# 60 344	22 000	11 064	...	...	# 23 308	...
	2016	112 386	83 349	39 953[12]	...	8 991[12]	6 982	3 990[12]
	2017	...	93 457	# 45 376	...	...	...	...
Togo Togo	#2005	312	186	...	126	...	...	...
	2010	# 444	# 220	21	# 54	* 10	# 169	14
	2017	362[1]	298[5]	27[5]	18[1]	1[1]	45[1]	16[1]
Trinidad and Tobago [3] Trinité-et-Tobago [3]	2005	954	548	183	406	180	...	...
	2010	1 351	951	462	400	152	...	...
	2016	2 636	1 375	684	476	190	785	333
	2017	...	1 506	842	...	...	...	...
Tunisia Tunisie	2010	15 589	14 727	7 654	499[14]	197[10]	363[14]	228[14]
	2016	23 590	22 407	13 384	717[14]	300[10]	466[14]	284[14]
Turkey Turquie	2005	* 49 251	39 139	13 381	* 4 753	* 988	* 5 360	* 978
	2010	* 81 792	64 341	21 056	* 10 352	* 1 741	* 7 099	* 1 551
	2017	153 552	111 893	36 677	28 694	8 078	12 965	4 480
Uganda [3] Ouganda [3]	2005	1 686	776	291	472	...	438	...
	2010	4 270	# 2 823	687	# 922	254	# 525	155
	2014	# 2 881	# 1 942	# 578	# 599	205	# 340	135
Ukraine Ukraine	2007	132 926[12]	67 493[12]	29 620	15 045[12]	...	25 160[12]	...
	2010[12]	116 321	60 812	...	13 053	...	21 593	...
	2017	67 806[13]	42 164[13]	18 252	6 768[13]	3 929	18 875[13]	8 768
United Arab Emirates Émirats arabes unis	*2011	11 400	...	...	...	...	...	...
	2016		22 308	...	...	...	...	...
United Kingdom Royaume-Uni	2005	# 324 917	# 248 599	...	* 41 494	...	* 34 824	...
	*2010	350 766	256 585	...	59 290	...	34 891	...
	*2016	417 390	288 922	...	86 547	...	41 921	...
	*2017	424 510	289 674	...	...	...	...	...
United Rep. of Tanzania Rép.-Unie de Tanzanie	2010	2 929	1 600	393	472	112	857	310
	2013[1]	1 967	929	228	301	62	737	277
United States of America États-Unis d'Amérique	*2005	...	1 104 019	...	...	...	...	...
	*2010	...	1 200 535	...	...	...	...	...
	*2016	...	1 371 290	...	...	...	...	...
United States Virgin Islands [1,3] Îles Vierges américaines [1,3]	2000	33	11	2	6		16	
	2005	37	6	...	12		11	
	2007	42	6	...	13		14	
Uruguay Uruguay	2002	1 412	1 242	...	...	...	170	...
	2010	...	2 105	1 024	...	...	...	...
	2017	...	2 374	1 161	...	...	...	...
Uzbekistan Ouzbékistan	2005	24 132[4]	16 723	6 663	2 206	1 099	3 113	1 547
	2010	21 555[4]	15 540	6 193	1 900	955	1 978	988
	2017	20 763[4]	15 838	6 157	1 460	712	2 086	839

Country or area Pays ou zone	Year Année	Total R & D personnel Total du personnel de R - D	Researchers Chercheurs Total M & F Total H & F	Females Femmes	Technicians and equivalent staff Techniciens et personnel assimilé Total M & F Total H & F	Females Femmes	Other supporting staff Autre personnel de soutien Total M & F Total H & F	Females Femmes
Venezuela (Boliv. Rep. of) [1] Venezuela (Rép. boliv. du) [1]	2005	...	3 248	...	...	...	...	...
	2009	...	5 209	2 782	...	...	...	...
	2010	...	5 803	...	...	...	...	...
	2015	...	7 488	4 615	...	...	...	...
	2016	...	8 963	...	...	...	...	...
Viet Nam Viet Nam	2002	11 356	9 328	...	...	...	...	...
	2015	81 222	62 887	28 167	6 077	2 617	8 263	4 623
	2017	84 733	66 953	...	6 763	...	# 11 017	...
Zambia Zambie	2005[3]	3 285[1]	792[1]	116[12]	1 240[1]	...	1 253[1]	...
	#2008	2 219[3]	612[3]	188[3]	835[3]	270[3]	772[3]	354
Zimbabwe Zimbabwe	2012	1 741[5]	1 305[5]	332	141[5]	41	295[5]	100

Source:

United Nations Educational, Scientific and Cultural Organization (UNESCO), Montreal, the UNESCO Institute for Statistics (UIS) statistics database, last accessed June 2020.

Source:

Organisation des Nations Unies pour l'éducation, la science et la culture (UNESCO), Montréal, base de données statistiques de l'Institut de statistique (ISU) de l'UNESCO, dernier accès juin 2020.

1	Partial data.
2	Excluding Higher Education.
3	Head count instead of Full-time equivalent.
4	Overestimated or based on overestimated data.
5	Excluding business enterprise.
6	Excluding private non-profit.
7	Do not correspond exactly to Frascati Manual recommendations.
8	The sum of the breakdown does not add to the total.
9	Higher Education only.
10	Excluding technicians and equivalent staff.
11	Including technicians and equivalent staff.
12	Underestimated or based on underestimated data.
13	Excluding data from some regions, provinces or states.
14	Government only.
15	Excluding data for other supporting staff.
16	Included in others/Not specified.

1	Données partielles.
2	Non compris l'enseignement supérieur.
3	Personnes physiques au lieu d'Equivalents temps plein.
4	Surestimé ou fondé sur des données surestimées.
5	Ne comprend pas les entreprises commerciales.
6	Non compris les organisations privées à but non lucratif.
7	Ne corresponds pas exactement aux recommandations du Manuel de Frascati.
8	La somme de toutes les valeurs diffère du total.
9	Enseignement supérieur seulement.
10	Non compris les techniciens y le personnel assimilé.
11	Y compris les techniciens y le personnel assimilé.
12	Sous-estimé ou basé sur des données sous-estimées.
13	Non compris les données de certaines régions, provinces ou états.
14	Etat seulement.
15	Non compris les données pour le personnel de soutien.
16	Inclus dans autres/Non spécifié.

27

Gross domestic expenditure on research and development (R&D)
As a percentage of GDP and by source of funds

Dépenses intérieures brutes de recherche et développement (R-D)
En pourcentage du PIB et répartition par source de financement

Country or area Pays ou zone	Year Année	Expenditure on R&D as a % of GDP Dépenses en R&D en % du PIB	Source of funds (%) / Source de financement (%)					
			Business enterprises Entreprises	Govern- ment Etat	Higher education Enseigne- ment supérieur	Private non-profit institut. Privées sans but lucratif	Funds from abroad Fonds de l'étranger	Not specified/ Non précisé
Total, all countries or areas	**2005**	**1.5**	...	...	...	...	...	...
Total, tous pays ou zones	**2010**	**1.6**	...	...	...	...	...	...
	2015	**1.7**	...	...	...	...	...	...
	2017	**1.7**	...	...	...	...	...	...
Northern Africa	2005	0.3	...	...	...	...	...	...
Afrique septentrionale	2010	0.5	...	...	...	...	...	...
	2015	0.6	...	...	...	...	...	...
	2017	0.6	...	...	...	...	...	...
Sub-Saharan Africa	2005	0.4	...	...	...	...	...	...
Afrique subsaharienne	2010	0.4	...	...	...	...	...	...
	2015	0.4	...	...	...	...	...	...
	2017	0.4	...	...	...	...	...	...
Northern America	2005	2.5	...	...	...	...	...	...
Amérique septentrionale	2010	2.7	...	...	...	...	...	...
	2015	2.6	...	...	...	...	...	...
	2017	2.7	...	...	...	...	...	...
Latin America & the Caribbean	2005	0.6	...	...	...	...	...	...
Amérique latine et Caraïbes	2010	0.7	...	...	...	...	...	...
	2015	0.7	...	...	...	...	...	...
	2017	0.7	...	...	...	...	...	...
Central Asia	2005	0.2	...	...	...	...	...	...
Asie centrale	2010	0.2	...	...	...	...	...	...
	2015	0.2	...	...	...	...	...	...
	2017	0.2	...	...	...	...	...	...
Eastern Asia	2005	2.0	...	...	...	...	...	...
Asie orientale	2010	2.2	...	...	...	...	...	...
	2015	2.4	...	...	...	...	...	...
	2017	2.5	...	...	...	...	...	...
South-eastern Asia	2005	0.6	...	...	...	...	...	...
Asie du Sud-Est	2010	0.7	...	...	...	...	...	...
	2015	0.9	...	...	...	...	...	...
	2017	1.0	...	...	...	...	...	...
Southern Asia	2005	0.7	...	...	...	...	...	...
Asie méridionale	2010	0.7	...	...	...	...	...	...
	2015	0.6	...	...	...	...	...	...
	2017	0.6	...	...	...	...	...	...
Western Asia	2005	0.5	...	...	...	...	...	...
Asie occidentale	2010	0.5	...	...	...	...	...	...
	2015	0.6	...	...	...	...	...	...
	2017	0.6	...	...	...	...	...	...
Europe	2005	1.6	...	...	...	...	...	...
Europe	2010	1.7	...	...	...	...	...	...
	2015	1.8	...	...	...	...	...	...
	2017	1.9	...	...	...	...	...	...
Australia and New Zealand	2005	1.9	...	...	...	...	...	...
Australie et Nouvelle-Zélande	2010	2.2	...	...	...	...	...	...
	2015	1.8	...	...	...	...	...	...
	2017	1.8	...	...	...	...	...	...
Albania [1] Albanie [1]	2008	0.2	3.3	80.8	8.6	...	7.4	...
Algeria	2005[1]	0.1	...	...	...	...	...	...
Algérie	2017	# 0.5	6.7	93.1	...	...	~0.0	~0.0
American Samoa [1]	2005	0.4	...	...	...	...	...	...
Samoa américaines [1]	2006	0.4	...	...	...	...	...	...
Angola [1,2,3] Angola [1,2,3]	2016	~0.0	...	100.0[4]	...	...	...	...

Gross domestic expenditure on research and development (R&D) *(continued)*
As a percentage of GDP and by source of funds

Dépenses intérieures brutes de recherche et développement (R-D) *(suite)*
En pourcentage du PIB et répartition par source de financement

Country or area Pays ou zone	Year Année	Expenditure on R&D as a % of GDP Dépenses en R&D en % du PIB	Source of funds (%) / Source de financement (%)					
			Business enterprises Entreprises	Govern- ment Etat	Higher education Enseigne- ment supérieur	Private non- profit Institut. Privées sans but lucratif	Funds from abroad Fonds de l'étranger	Not specified/ Non précisé
Argentina	2005	0.4	31.0	59.6	5.7	3.0	0.7	...
Argentine	2008	0.5	26.5	67.6	4.4	1.0	0.6	...
	2010	0.6	...	...	...	...	...	...
	2015	0.6	19.2	74.8	2.0	0.5	3.5	...
	2017	0.5	16.5	72.6	1.8	0.6	8.5	...
Armenia	2005[1]	0.3	...	77.5	...	...	4.7	17.8
Arménie	2010[1]	0.2	...	84.5	...	...	11.7	3.8
	2015[2,3]	0.3	...	73.8	...	...	2.3	23.9
	2018[2,3]	0.2	16.7	# 68.7	...	...	5.6	9.1
Australia	2004	1.9	54.6	40.3	0.4	1.9	2.9	...
Australie	2008	2.4	61.9	34.6	0.1	1.8	1.6	...
	*2010	2.4	...	...	...	...	...	...
	*2015	1.9	...	...	...	...	...	...
	*2017	1.9	...	...	...	...	...	...
Austria	2004	2.2	47.2	32.6	0.4	0.5	19.4	...
Autriche	*2005	2.4	45.6	35.9	...	0.4	18.0	...
	2009	2.6	47.1	34.9	0.7	0.6	16.8	...
	*2010	2.7	45.1	38.3[5]	...	0.5	16.1	...
	2015	3.0	49.7	32.6	0.6	0.5	16.6	...
	2017	3.1	54.7	27.6	0.8	0.3	16.6	...
	*2018	3.2	54.4	29.4	...	0.6	15.6	...
Azerbaijan	2005	0.2[6]	18.7	77.5	~0.0	1.3	2.4	...
Azerbaïdjan	2010	0.2	# 9.6	# 88.2	0.3	1.9	~0.0	...
	2014	0.2	30.5	67.6	0.8	0.9	0.2	...
	2015	0.2	32.2	65.8	0.4	1.7	...	...
	2016	0.2	29.9	68.5	1.4	0.2	...	...
	2017	0.2	32.0	67.2	...	0.7	0.1	...
	2018	0.2	30.8	68.7	...	0.5	...	...
Bahrain Bahreïn	2014	0.1	21.8	41.5	...	2.0	12.4	1.1
Belarus	2005	0.7[6]	21.2	71.9	0.7	...	6.3	...
Bélarus	2008	0.7[6]	36.5	57.6	0.3	0.1	5.5	...
	2010	0.7[6]	27.1	58.7	...	0.6	13.6	...
	2015	0.5[6]	41.3	46.0	...	...	12.7	...
	2018	0.6	45.0	41.8	...	...	13.2	...
Belgium	2005	1.8	59.7	24.7	2.6	0.6	12.4	...
Belgique	2010	2.1	57.6	25.4	3.1	0.6	13.3	...
	2015	2.5	58.6	22.5	2.0	0.4	16.5	...
	2017	2.7	63.5	20.0	3.0	0.5	13.0	...
	*2018	2.8	...	...	...	...	...	...
Bermuda [7]	2010	0.2	...	...	...	...	...	...
Bermudes [7]	2015	0.2	...	...	...	...	...	...
	2018	0.3	...	...	...	...	...	...
Bolivia (Plurin. State of)	2002	0.3	16.0	20.0	31.0	19.0	14.0	...
Bolivie (État plurin. de)	#2009	0.2	5.2	51.2	26.5	2.1	1.9	13.2
Bosnia and Herzegovina	2005[1]	~0.0	...	...	...	...	...	...
Bosnie-Herzégovine	2009[1]	~0.0	...	...	...	...	...	...
	2013	0.3	1.8	25.3	...	...	53.9	18.9
	2015	0.2	31.4	37.6	...	~0.0	16.9	...
	2017	0.2	29.1	41.2	...	0.1	16.4	0.1
	2018	0.2	28.9	40.9	...	~0.0	20.4	...
Botswana	2005	0.5	...	...	...	...	...	0.2
Botswana	#2012	0.3	5.8	73.9	...	0.7	6.8	...
	2013	0.5	17.7	59.7	...	...	21.7	...
Brazil	2005	1.0	50.4	47.7	1.9	...	...	...
Brésil	2010	1.2	47.0	51.1	1.8	...	...	...
	2015	1.3	45.5	52.2	2.2	...	...	...
	2017	1.3	47.5	49.7	2.8	...	...	...

Gross domestic expenditure on research and development (R&D) *(continued)*
As a percentage of GDP and by source of funds

Dépenses intérieures brutes de recherche et développement (R-D) *(suite)*
En pourcentage du PIB et répartition par source de financement

Country or area Pays ou zone	Year Année	Expenditure on R&D as a % of GDP Dépenses en R&D en % du PIB	Source of funds (%) / Source de financement (%)					
			Business enterprises Entreprises	Govern-ment Etat	Higher education Enseigne-ment supérieur	Private non-profit Institut. Privées sans but lucratif	Funds from abroad Fonds de l'étranger	Not specified/ Non précisé
Brunei Darussalam	2003	~0.0	6.7	86.8	...	...	6.6	...
Brunéi Darussalam	#2004	~0.0[1]	1.6	91.0	...	...	...	...
	2018[8]	# 0.3	...	# 97.0	...	...	# 0.1	0.6
Bulgaria	2005	0.4	27.8	63.9	0.4	0.3	7.6	...
Bulgarie	2010	0.6	16.7	43.2	0.5	0.1	39.6	...
	2015	1.0	35.6	20.3	0.1	0.1	43.8	...
	2017	0.8	43.2	24.3	0.1	0.2	32.2	...
	2018	0.8	...	...	...	...	...	...
Burkina Faso	2005	0.2[1]	...	100.0	...	...	...	...
Burkina Faso	2009	0.2	11.9	9.1	12.2	1.3	59.6	5.9
	#2014[3]	0.2	...	98.4	~0.0	0.1	1.5	...
	2017[3]	0.7	...	93.6	1.6	...	4.8	...
Burundi	2008[1]	0.2	...	59.9	...	...	39.9	...
Burundi	2010[1]	0.1	...	...	...	...	...	...
	2012[1]	0.1	...	...	...	...	...	...
	2018	# 0.2	8.8[1]	# 64.8[1,4]	...	# 26.4[1]	...	...
Cabo Verde [1,8]								
Cabo Verde [1,8]	2011	0.1	...	100.0	...	...	...	...
Cambodia	2002[1]	~0.0	...	17.9	...	43.0	28.4	10.6
Cambodge	#2015	0.1	19.4	23.5	...	22.1	34.9	...
Canada	2005	2.0	49.3	* 31.8	* 7.3	2.8	8.8	...
Canada	2010	1.8	47.2	* # 34.9	* 7.9	3.5	6.6	...
	2015	1.7	44.0	* 31.6	* 10.0[9]	4.0[9]	9.8	...
	*2018	1.6	41.1	33.1	11.1[9]	4.5[9]	9.3	...
Chad [2,3]								
Tchad [2,3]	2016	0.3	...	100.0[4]	...	...	...	...
Chile	2010	0.3	25.4	40.4	12.7	1.7	19.8	...
Chili	2015	0.4	32.8	42.6	11.1	0.6	12.9	...
	*2017	0.4	31.4	47.0	15.4	1.7	4.5	...
China [10]	2005	1.3	67.0	26.3	...	...	0.9	...
Chine [10]	2010	1.7	71.7	24.0	...	...	1.3	...
	2015	2.1	74.7	21.3	...	...	0.7	...
	2018	2.2	76.6	20.2	...	...	0.4	...
China, Hong Kong SAR	2005	0.8	53.0[11]	44.1	0.4	...	2.5	...
Chine, RAS de Hong Kong	2010	0.7	47.6[11]	47.3	0.1	...	4.9	...
	2015	0.8	47.4[11]	47.1	~0.0	...	5.5	...
	2018	0.9	49.1[11]	46.9	0.2	...	3.7	...
China, Macao SAR	2005	0.1[1]	* 0.2	88.0	...	0.4	...	1.4
Chine, RAS de Macao	2007	# 0.1[1]	0.1	89.3	...	2.8	0.6	1.6
	2008	0.1[1]	0.2	91.7	...	1.4	...	0.3
	2010[1]	0.1	...	...	...	...	...	...
	2015[1]	0.1	...	87.2	...	0.5	...	6.1
	2018[1]	0.2	...	66.7	...	0.3	...	29.0
Colombia	2005	0.2	...	...	...	...	...	...
Colombie	2010	0.2	23.1	8.9	39.9	27.2	1.0	...
	2015	0.3	44.7	9.6	28.6	16.7	0.4	...
	2017	0.2	49.1	8.2	22.8	19.1	0.5	0.4
	2018	0.2	...	...	...	...	...	...
Costa Rica	2004	0.4	...	...	...	...	...	...
Costa Rica	2009	0.5	28.7	53.0	...	2.8	1.7	13.7
	2010	0.5	...	...	...	...	...	...
	2015	0.4	4.7	57.4	...	2.9	3.7	31.2
	2017	0.4	3.7[3]	53.6[3]	...	~0.0[3]	6.7[3]	36.0[12]
Côte d'Ivoire [1,3]								
Côte d'Ivoire [1,3]	2016	0.1	...	...	...	...	...	...

Dépenses intérieures brutes de recherche et développement (R-D) *(suite)*
En pourcentage du PIB et répartition par source de financement

Country or area Pays ou zone	Year Année	Expenditure on R&D as a % of GDP Dépenses en R&D en % du PIB	Source of funds (%) / Source de financement (%)					
			Business enterprises Entreprises	Govern-ment Etat	Higher education Enseigne-ment supérieur	Private non-profit Institut. Privées sans but lucratif	Funds from abroad Fonds de l'étranger	Not specified/ Non précisé
Croatia	2005	0.9	34.3	58.1	4.9	~0.0	2.6	...
Croatie	2010	0.7	38.8	49.2	2.0	0.2	9.9	...
	2015	0.8	46.6	36.4	2.0	0.5	14.5	...
	2017	0.9	42.6	43.1	3.5	0.1	10.8	...
	*2018	1.0	...	...	...	...	...	...
Cuba	2005	0.5	35.0	60.0	...	...	5.0	...
Cuba	2010	0.6	15.0	75.0	...	...	10.0	...
	2015	0.4	40.0	55.0	...	...	5.0	...
	2016	0.3	34.5	62.0	...	...	2.0	1.5
	2017	0.4	33.0	66.0	...	...	1.0	...
	2018	...	42.0	56.4	...	...	1.6	...
Cyprus	2005	0.4	16.8	67.0	4.2	1.2	10.9	...
Chypre	2010	0.4	12.7	68.3	3.5	0.5	15.0	...
	2013	0.5	15.8	59.5	5.4	0.6	18.8	0.1
	2015	0.5	20.0	50.6	5.8	0.6	23.0	...
	2017	0.6	32.8	38.5	5.4	0.9	22.5	...
	*2018	0.6	...	...	...	...	...	...
Czechia	2005	1.2	48.2	45.2	1.2	~0.0	5.4	...
Tchéquie	2010	1.3	40.8	44.4	0.9	~0.0	13.9	...
	2015	1.9	34.5	32.2	0.7	0.1	32.5	...
	*2018	1.9	33.0	34.1	1.0	0.1	31.8	...
Dem. Rep. of the Congo	2005	# 0.1[13,14]	...	100.0	...	...	...	...
Rép. dém. du Congo	2009	0.1[13,14]	...	100.0	...	...	...	...
	2015	# 0.4[3,7]	~0.0[3]	# 34.5	...	0.2[3]	1.4[3]	...
Denmark	2005	2.4	59.5	27.6	...	2.8	10.1	...
Danemark	2010	2.9	* 61.1	* 28.2[5]	...	* 3.5	* 7.2	...
	2015	3.1	59.1	30.2[5]	...	4.4	6.3	...
	*2017	3.0	58.5	27.2[5]	...	5.4	8.9	...
	*2018	3.1	...	...	...	...	...	...
Ecuador	2003	0.1	...	...	...	...	...	...
Équateur	2010	0.4	1.0[3]	40.2[3]	9.6[3]	0.5[3]	5.3[3]	43.4[12]
	2014	0.4	0.1[3]	42.4[3]	12.6[3]	0.1[3]	2.5[3]	42.3[12]
Egypt	2005[1,13]	0.2	...	...	...	...	...	...
Égypte	2010[2,3]	0.4	...	...	...	...	...	...
	2014	0.6	8.1	91.7[4]	...	0.1	0.1	...
	2015	0.7	6.2	93.7[4]	...	0.1	...	...
	2018	0.7	3.9	95.4	...	~0.0	0.5	...
El Salvador	2010	0.1	0.6	70.1	20.8	~0.0	8.3	0.1
El Salvador	2013	0.1	0.7	42.7	37.0	2.8	16.4	0.3
	#2015	0.1	41.9	29.0	21.2	1.1	6.8	...
	2017	0.2	31.2	39.2	20.6	1.3	7.7	~0.0
Estonia	2005	0.9	38.5	43.5	0.8	0.2	17.1	...
Estonie	2010	1.6	43.6	44.1	0.6	0.2	11.4	...
	2015	1.5	41.0	46.4	0.2	0.2	12.2	...
	2017	1.3	43.6	40.2	1.0	0.3	15.0	...
	*2018	1.4	...	...	...	...	...	...
Eswatini Eswatini	2015	0.3	22.3	41.7	...	2.5	33.5	...
Ethiopia	2005	0.2[1]	...	69.2	...	0.1	30.8	...
Éthiopie	2010	# 0.2	10.8	56.0	1.1	~0.0	30.0	2.2
	2013	0.6	0.7	79.1	1.8	0.2	2.1	16.0
	2017	# 0.3	1.5	73.4	3.1	1.5	19.1	1.4
Faroe Islands Îles Féroé	2003	0.9	20.4	...	...	0.3	18.7	60.6[4,7,15]

27

Gross domestic expenditure on research and development (R&D) *(continued)*
As a percentage of GDP and by source of funds

Dépenses intérieures brutes de recherche et développement (R-D) *(suite)*
En pourcentage du PIB et répartition par source de financement

Country or area Pays ou zone	Year Année	Expenditure on R&D as a % of GDP Dépenses en R&D en % du PIB	Source of funds (%) / Source de financement (%)					
			Business enterprises Entreprises	Govern-ment Etat	Higher education Enseigne-ment supérieur	Private non-profit Institut. Privées sans but lucratif	Funds from abroad Fonds de l'étranger	Not specified/ Non précisé
Finland Finlande	2005	3.3	66.9	25.7	0.2	1.0	# 6.3	...
	2010	3.7	66.1	25.7	0.2	1.1	6.9	...
	2015	2.9	54.8	28.9	0.3	1.5	14.5	...
	2017	2.8	58.0	29.0	0.5	1.7	10.8	...
	2018	2.8	...	...	...	...	...	...
France France	2005	2.1	51.9	38.6	1.0	0.9	7.5	...
	#2010	2.2	53.5	37.1	1.0	0.8	7.5	...
	2015	2.3	54.0	34.8	2.6	0.9	7.6	...
	*2017	2.2	56.1	32.4	2.7	1.0	7.8	...
	*2018	2.2	...	...	...	...	...	...
Gabon Gabon	2009	0.6	29.3	58.1	9.5	...	3.1	~0.0
Gambia Gambie	2009[1]	~0.0	...	...	...	...	...	...
	2011[7]	0.1	...	38.5	...	45.6	15.9	...
	#2018[1,2]	0.1	...	...	...	...	...	...
Georgia Géorgie	2005	0.2	...	...	...	...	...	...
	2013[1,8]	# 0.1[16]	...	46.7[17]	...	3.1[17]	14.7[17]	0.4[17]
	2015[1,2,3]	0.3	...	...	...	...	...	...
	2018[1]	0.3[2,3]	1.7[8,17]	42.5[8,17]	...	1.0[2,3]	10.3[2,3]	1.7[2,3]
Germany Allemagne	2005	2.4	67.5[5]	28.5[5]	...	0.3[5]	3.7[5]	...
	2010	2.7	65.5[5]	30.4[5]	...	0.2[5]	3.9[5]	...
	2015	2.9	65.6[5]	27.9[5]	...	0.4[5]	6.2[5]	...
	2017	3.0	66.2[5]	27.7[5]	...	0.3[5]	5.8[5]	...
	*2018	3.1	...	...	...	...	...	...
Ghana Ghana	2010	# 0.4	# 0.1	# 68.3	...	0.1	31.2	...
Greece Grèce	2005	0.6	31.1	46.8	1.7	1.5	19.0	...
	*2010	0.6	36.5	48.3	2.3	1.0	11.9	...
	2015	1.0	31.4	53.1	2.5	0.4	12.7	...
	*2018	1.2	42.6	40.6	1.9	0.6	14.2	...
Greenland Groenland	2004	0.6	...	...	...	...	...	...
Guam Guam	2001	...	...	100.0	...	...	...	...
	2005	0.3	...	...	...	...	...	...
Guatemala [1] Guatemala [1]	2005	~0.0	...	42.1	57.9	...	...	...
	2010	~0.0	...	18.3	30.9	...	50.8	...
	2015	~0.0	...	27.8	28.2	...	44.0	~0.0
	2017	~0.0	10.3	10.2	79.5	...	...	...
Honduras Honduras	2004	~0.0	...	...	...	...	...	...
	2015[1]	# ~0.0	...	82.5	...	...	...	...
	2017	~0.0	10.4	44.9	...	13.8	3.5	...
Hungary Hongrie	2005	0.9	39.4[5]	49.4[5]	...	0.3[5]	10.7[5]	...
	2010	1.1	47.4	39.3	...	0.9	12.4	...
	2015	1.4	49.7	34.6	...	0.7	15.0	...
	2017	1.3	52.7	31.9	...	0.5	14.9	...
	2018	1.6	...	...	...	...	...	...
Iceland Islande	2005	2.7	48.0	40.5	...	0.3	11.2	...
	2009	2.6	47.8	40.2	...	0.6	11.4	...
	2015	2.2	35.8	30.8	4.0	4.1	25.4	...
	2018	2.0	40.2	36.0	3.3	1.9	18.6	...
India Inde	2005	0.8	...	...	...	...	...	...
	2010	0.8	...	...	...	...	...	...
	2015	0.7	...	...	...	...	...	...
	2017	0.7	36.8[18]	63.2[18]	...	...	...	...
	2018	0.7	...	...	...	...	...	...

27 Gross domestic expenditure on research and development (R&D) *(continued)*
As a percentage of GDP and by source of funds

Dépenses intérieures brutes de recherche et développement (R-D) *(suite)*
En pourcentage du PIB et répartition par source de financement

Country or area Pays ou zone	Year Année	Expenditure on R&D as a % of GDP Dépenses en R&D en % du PIB	Source of funds (%) / Source de financement (%)					
			Business enterprises Entreprises	Government Etat	Higher education Enseignement supérieur	Private non-profit Institut. Privées sans but lucratif	Funds from abroad Fonds de l'étranger	Not specified/ Non précisé
Indonesia	2001	~0.0	14.7[1,11]	84.5	...	...	...	0.7
Indonésie	#2009[1]	0.1	...	...	...	...	...	...
	2013	0.1	...	...	...	...	...	...
	2018	0.2	8.0	87.7	...	0.2	0.1	1.0
Iran (Islamic Republic of)	2005	0.6	12.2	76.2	11.6	...	...	...
Iran (Rép. islamique d')	2008	0.6	30.9	61.6	7.4	...	...	...
	2010[2,19]	0.3	...	...	...	...	...	...
	2015	0.4	...	...	...	...	...	...
	#2017	0.8	...	...	...	...	...	...
Iraq	2010	~0.0[2,3,16]	...	100.0[4]	...	...	...	...
Iraq	2015	~0.0	1.1	96.4	...	0.3	0.1	...
	2016	~0.0	1.2	96.0	...	0.7	0.1	...
	2018	~0.0	1.8	97.3	...	0.3	...	...
Ireland	2005	1.2	57.4	32.0	1.7	0.2	8.6	...
Irlande	*2010	1.6	52.2	29.4	0.9	0.5	17.0	...
	*2015	1.2	48.7	26.1	1.0	0.6	23.6	...
	*2016	1.2	49.0	25.8	0.8	0.8	23.6	...
	*2018	1.1	...	...	...	...	...	...
Israel [5]	2005	4.1	56.2	14.5	2.8	1.8	24.7	...
Israël [5]	2010	3.9	36.2	14.2	1.2	1.1	47.3	...
	2015	4.3	33.2	12.8	0.7	0.8	52.5	...
	2017	* 4.8	* 35.8	* 10.6	# 0.3	* 0.8	* 52.6	...
	*2018	5.0	...	...	...	...	...	...
Italy	2005	1.0	39.7	50.7	0.1	1.6	8.0	...
Italie	2010	1.2	44.7	41.6	0.9	3.1	9.8	...
	2015	1.3	50.0	38.0	1.0	2.7	8.3	...
	2017	1.4	53.7	32.3	0.8	1.5	11.7	...
	*2018	1.4	...	...	...	...	...	...
Jamaica			...	...	...	...	...	...
Jamaïque	2002	0.1	...	...	...	...	...	...
Japan	2005	3.2	76.1	* 16.8	* 6.1	0.7	0.3	...
Japon	2010	3.1	75.9	* 17.2	* 5.7	0.8	0.4	...
	2015	3.3	78.0	* 15.4	* 5.4	0.7	0.5	...
	2018	# 3.3	# 79.1	* 14.6	* 5.1	# 0.7	# 0.6	...
Jordan	2002	0.3	...	...	...	...	...	...
Jordanie	2008	0.4	...	...	...	...	...	...
	#2016[7]	0.7	...	...	...	...	...	...
Kazakhstan	2005	0.3	39.1	44.5	13.4	1.3	1.5	...
Kazakhstan	2010	0.2	36.6	36.7	17.2	8.9	0.6	...
	2011	0.2	51.6	24.9	16.3	6.9	0.3	...
	2015	0.2	36.6	58.8	...	...	1.8	2.8
	2018	0.1	47.4	44.5	...	...	2.7	5.4
Kenya								
Kenya	#2010	0.8	4.3	26.0	...	3.5	47.1	...
Kuwait	2004[13]	0.1[1]	6.0	93.2	...	...	0.8	...
Koweït	2005[13]	0.1[1]	7.3	92.3	...	0.4	...	...
	2009[13]	0.1[1]	2.3	96.5	...	...	1.2	...
	2010[13]	0.1[1]	5.2	94.8	...	~0.0	...	...
	2014[2,3]	0.4[7]	1.0	90.2	...	1.1	...	2.3
	#2015[1,2,3]	0.1	...	...	...	...	...	...
	2018[1,2,3]	0.1	...	...	...	...	...	...
Kyrgyzstan	2003	0.2	53.7	45.1	0.1	...	1.1	...
Kirghizistan	2005	0.2	36.4	63.6	...	...	~0.0	...
	2010	0.2	...	...	...	...	...	...
	2015[2]	0.1	8.7	89.2	0.2	...	1.0	0.8
	2017[2]	0.1	6.4	89.5	0.2	...	3.1	0.7
Lao People's Dem. Rep.								
Rép. dém. populaire lao	2002	~0.0	36.0	8.0[1]	...	...	54.0[1]	...

27

Gross domestic expenditure on research and development (R&D) *(continued)*
As a percentage of GDP and by source of funds

Dépenses intérieures brutes de recherche et développement (R-D) *(suite)*
En pourcentage du PIB et répartition par source de financement

Country or area / Pays ou zone	Year / Année	Expenditure on R&D as a % of GDP / Dépenses en R&D en % du PIB	Business enterprises / Entreprises	Government / Etat	Higher education / Enseignement supérieur	Private non-profit Institut. / Privées sans but lucratif	Funds from abroad / Fonds de l'étranger	Not specified/ Non précisé
Latvia	2005	0.5	34.3	46.0	1.2	...	18.5	...
Lettonie	2010	0.6	38.8	26.4	1.4	...	33.4	...
	2015	0.6	20.0	32.7	2.2	...	45.0	...
	2017	0.5	24.1	43.6	2.5	...	29.8	...
	2018	0.6	...	...	...	...	...	...
Lesotho	2004[1]	0.1	...	...	...	...	...	...
Lesotho	2009[1]	~0.0	3.4	15.0	...	...	...	78.9
	2011[1]	~0.0[8]	...	...	...	...	3.4	51.9
	2015[3]	~0.0[2]	0.8	91.1[2]	...	0.3[2]	7.8[2]	...
Lithuania	2005	0.7	20.8	62.7	5.7	0.2	10.5	...
Lituanie	2010	0.8	32.4	46.0	1.5	0.2	19.9	...
	2015	1.0	28.5	35.3	1.5	0.3	34.3	...
	2017	0.9	35.4	36.4	3.7	0.1	24.4	...
	*2018	0.9	...	...	...	...	...	...
Luxembourg	2005	1.6	79.7	16.6	~0.0	0.1	3.6	...
Luxembourg	2010	1.5	43.5	35.1	0.6	0.1	20.6	...
	2015	1.3	47.1	47.7	1.6	0.2	3.4	...
	2017	1.3	49.6	43.1	1.4	0.3	5.7	...
	*2018	1.2	...	...	...	...	...	...
Madagascar	2005	0.2[1]	...	89.8[4]	...	...	10.2	...
Madagascar	2009	0.1[1]	...	89.4[4]	...	...	10.6	...
	2010	0.1[1]	...	# 100.0[4]	...	...	...	...
	2011	0.1[1]	...	100.0[15]	...	...	...	...
	#2014[1,13]	~0.0	...	...	...	...	...	...
	2017[1,13]	~0.0	...	...	...	...	...	...
Malaysia	2004	0.6	71.2	21.5	6.9	...	0.4	...
Malaisie	2010	1.0	59.6	36.4	3.5	...	0.4	0.1
	2015	1.3	# 49.6	# 35.8	7.0	...	1.7	# 6.0[18]
	2016	1.4	# 56.9	# 28.8	# 12.8	...	# 0.9	# 0.7
Mali	2007[1]	0.2[19]	10.1	40.9	...	...	49.0	...
Mali	2010	0.6	...	# 91.2	...	...	8.8	...
	2015[3]	0.3	0.9	43.6	...	0.3	32.7	22.4
	2017[1]	0.3[3]	0.8[3]	46.0	...	3.0[3]	50.2[3]	...
Malta	2005	0.5	# 46.8	# 25.9	0.4	0.1	26.9	...
Malte	2010	0.6	52.5	34.4	1.3	0.1	11.7	...
	2015	0.7	45.6	32.8	1.1	0.1	20.4	...
	2017	0.6	56.4	31.3	1.3	0.3	10.8	...
	*2018	0.6	...	...	...	...	...	...
Mauritania [1,8]								
Mauritanie [1,8]	2018	~0.0	...	92.8	...	7.2	...	...
Mauritius	2005[7,16]	0.4	...	100.0	...	...	...	...
Maurice	2012	# 0.2[7]	0.3[3]	72.4[3]	...	0.1[3]	6.4[3]	...
	2018	0.3	4.1	79.4	...	...	1.0	11.0
Mexico	2005	0.4	41.5	49.2	7.3	0.9	1.1	...
Mexique	2010	0.5	33.0	64.0	2.0	0.5	0.5	...
	2015	0.4	17.4	79.7	1.7	0.5	0.6	...
	*2018	0.3	18.6	76.8	2.8	0.8	0.9	...
Monaco [1]								
Monaco [1]	2005	~0.0	...	98.8	...	...	...	1.2
Mongolia	2005	0.2[1]	10.4	77.8	0.8	...	4.4	6.5
Mongolie	2010[1]	0.2	7.2	61.1	1.5	...	4.2	25.9
	2014[1]	0.2	7.5	75.8	3.2	...	2.8	10.7
	2015[1]	0.2	7.3	80.1	9.7	...	...	2.9
	2016[1]	0.2	4.9	86.3	3.7	0.8	2.1	2.1
	2018[1]	0.1	8.1	80.9	7.1	...	3.5	0.4

27

Gross domestic expenditure on research and development (R&D) *(continued)*
As a percentage of GDP and by source of funds

Dépenses intérieures brutes de recherche et développement (R-D) *(suite)*
En pourcentage du PIB et répartition par source de financement

Country or area Pays ou zone	Year Année	Expenditure on R&D as a % of GDP Dépenses en R&D en % du PIB	Source of funds (%) / Source de financement (%)					
			Business enterprises Entreprises	Government Etat	Higher education Enseignement supérieur	Private non-profit Institut. Privées sans but lucratif	Funds from abroad Fonds de l'étranger	Not specified/ Non précisé
Montenegro	2005	0.9	...	...	...	...	...	...
Monténégro	2007	1.1	...	...	...	...	...	...
	2015	0.4	29.9	57.8	...	~0.0	5.9	...
	2017	0.3	18.7	64.1	...	...	10.3	...
	2018	0.4	...	...	...	...	...	...
Morocco	2003	0.6	12.3	40.3	47.4	...	...	...
Maroc	2010	0.7	29.9	23.1	45.3	...	1.7	...
Mozambique	2002[7,14]	0.4	...	34.7	...	...	65.3	...
Mozambique	2010	# 0.4[3]	...	18.8[4]	...	3.0	78.1	...
	2015	0.3	0.5[1]	43.5	...	...	39.9	2.8
Myanmar	2002[1]	0.2	...	...	...	...	...	...
Myanmar	2017[2,3]	# ~0.0[1]	...	77.4[4]	...	~0.0	22.5	...
Namibia	2010	0.1[1,19]	19.8	78.6	...	...	1.5	...
Namibie	2014[1]	0.3	11.1	63.2	...	3.9	15.8	...
Nepal [16]								
Népal [16]	#2010	0.3	...	...	...	...	...	...
Netherlands	2005	1.8	46.3	38.8	0.3	2.6	12.0	...
Pays-Bas	2009	1.7	45.1	40.9	0.3	2.8	10.8	...
	2010	1.7	...	...	...	...	...	...
	2015	2.0	48.6	33.1	0.2	2.6	15.5	...
	2017	2.0	51.6	31.4	0.2	2.5	14.3	...
	* #2018	2.2	...	...	...	...	...	...
New Zealand	2005	1.1	41.1	43.2	...	1.7	5.2	...
Nouvelle-Zélande	2009	1.3	39.0	44.7	...	2.8	5.2	...
	2015	1.2	43.8	37.1	...	3.1	7.7	...
	2017	1.4	46.4	35.8	...	2.5	7.7	...
Nicaragua	2002	~0.0	...	...	...	...	...	...
Nicaragua	2015[8]	0.1	...	...	...	...	...	...
Nigeria								
Nigéria	2007	0.1	0.2	96.4	0.1	1.7	1.0	0.6
North Macedonia	2002	0.2	* 7.8	76.3	7.3	~0.0	8.6	...
Macédoine du Nord	2005	0.2	...	...	...	...	...	...
	2010	0.2	...	...	...	...	...	...
	2015	0.4	16.8	52.9	25.0	0.1	5.2	...
	2018	0.4	30.1	45.2	20.2	0.2	4.3	...
Norway	2005	1.5	46.8	43.6	0.7	0.9	8.1	...
Norvège	2009	1.7	43.6	46.8	0.4	1.0	8.2	...
	2010	1.6	...	...	...	...	...	...
	2015	1.9	44.2	44.9	0.4	1.2	9.2	...
	2017	2.1	42.8	46.7	0.4	1.2	8.8	...
	*2018	2.1	...	...	...	...	...	...
Oman	2012	0.2	29.9	47.8	...	0.3	~0.0	...
Oman	2013	0.2	24.5	48.6	...	0.1	...	2.3
	2015	0.2	21.4	55.7	...	0.2	...	...
	2018[1]	0.2	31.8	43.3	...	4.3	1.5	...
Pakistan	2005	0.4[2,3]	...	87.0	11.9	...	0.3	0.8
Pakistan	2009	0.4[2,3]	...	84.0	12.1	1.7	0.9	1.3
	2015[2,3]	0.2	...	67.0	25.5	0.3	2.7	4.6
	2017	0.2[2,3]	...	61.8	35.1	0.3	1.3	1.4
Panama	2003	0.3	0.6	25.5	1.8	1.0	71.0	0.1
Panama	2005	0.2	0.4	38.5	1.4	0.7	58.9	...
	2010	0.1	3.4	53.9	6.0	14.0	22.7	~0.0
	2015	0.1	0.9	26.4	0.8	14.8	57.2	~0.0
	2016	0.1	0.5	48.0	6.0	6.7	38.8	...
	2017	0.1	1.5	55.7	...	8.0	34.7	0.1
Papua New Guinea [3]								
Papouasie-Nvl-Guinée [3]	2016	~0.0[1]	4.5	38.7	...	0.8	39.7	8.8

Gross domestic expenditure on research and development (R&D) *(continued)*
As a percentage of GDP and by source of funds

Dépenses intérieures brutes de recherche et développement (R-D) *(suite)*
En pourcentage du PIB et répartition par source de financement

Country or area Pays ou zone	Year Année	Expenditure on R&D as a % of GDP Dépenses en R&D en % du PIB	Source of funds (%) / Source de financement (%)					
			Business enterprises Entreprises	Govern-ment Etat	Higher education Enseigne-ment supérieur	Private non-profit Institut. Privées sans but lucratif	Funds from abroad Fonds de l'étranger	Not specified/ Non précisé
Paraguay Paraguay	2005	0.1	# 0.3	# 74.9	# 8.6	# 2.0	# 14.2	...
	2008	~0.0	0.3	76.2	9.2	2.1	12.3	...
	2015[3]	0.1	0.3	73.1	2.1	4.2	10.3	10.1
	2017[3]	0.1	0.2	77.4	3.9	2.8	11.5	4.3
Peru Pérou	2004	0.2	...	...	...	...	...	...
	2015	0.1	...	...	...	...	...	...
	2018	0.1	...	...	...	...	...	...
Philippines Philippines	2005	0.1	62.6	25.6	6.0	0.7	4.8	0.3
	2009	0.1	57.5	26.7	7.8	0.4	4.2	3.4
	2015	0.2	38.0	49.4	9.9	0.4	1.8	0.4
Poland Pologne	2005	0.6	33.4	57.7	2.9	0.3	5.7	...
	2010	0.7	24.4	60.9	2.5	0.3	11.8	...
	2015	1.0	39.0	41.8	2.2	0.2	16.7	...
	2017	1.0	52.5	38.3	3.0	0.3	6.0	...
	*2018	1.2	...	...	...	...	...	...
Portugal Portugal	2005	0.8	36.3	55.2	1.0	2.8	4.7	...
	2010	1.5	43.9	45.1	3.2	4.6	3.2	...
	2015	1.2	42.7	44.3	4.4	1.3	7.4	...
	2017	1.3	46.5	41.0	3.9	1.2	7.3	...
	*2018	1.4	...	...	...	...	...	...
Puerto Rico Porto Rico	2009	0.5	...	...	...	...	...	...
	2015	0.4	69.4	23.1	...	0.3	...	0.6
Qatar Qatar	2015	0.5	7.1	42.6	...	27.8	1.9	~0.0
	2018	0.5	9.3	32.4	...	12.7	0.5	~0.0
Republic of Korea République de Corée	2005[5]	2.6	75.0	23.0	0.9	0.4	0.7	...
	2010	3.5	71.8	26.7	0.9	0.4	0.2	...
	2015	4.2	74.5	23.7	0.6	0.4	0.8	...
	2018	4.8	76.6	20.5	0.6	0.3	1.9	...
Republic of Moldova République de Moldova	2005	0.4	...	...	...	...	3.8	96.2[18]
	2010	0.4	...	...	...	...	7.4	92.6[18]
	2015	0.3	...	...	...	...	11.6	88.4[18]
	2016	0.3	...	...	...	...	4.2	95.8[18]
	2018	0.3	15.5	76.7	2.8	...	5.0	...
Romania Roumanie	2005	0.4	37.2	53.5	4.0	~0.0	5.3	...
	2010	0.5	32.3	54.4	2.2	~0.0	11.1	...
	2015	0.5	37.3	41.7	1.7	0.1	19.2	...
	2017	0.5	54.4	35.9	1.7	~0.0	7.9	...
	2018	0.5	...	...	...	...	...	...
Russian Federation Fédération de Russie	2005	1.1	30.0	61.9	0.4	~0.0	7.6	...
	2010	1.1	25.5	70.3	0.5	0.1	3.5	...
	2015	1.1	26.5	69.5	1.2	0.2	2.6	...
	2018	1.0	29.5	67.0	0.9	0.3	2.3	...
Rwanda Rwanda	2016	0.7	0.6	64.5	...	0.7	33.7	...
Saint Vincent & Grenadines Saint-Vincent-Grenadines	2002	0.1	...	...	...	...	...	...
Saudi Arabia [16] Arabie saoudite [16]	2005[1]	~0.0	...	...	...	...	...	...
	#2010[7]	0.9	...	...	...	...	...	...
	2013[7]	0.8	...	...	...	...	...	...
Senegal Sénégal	2010	0.4	4.1	47.6	~0.0	3.2	40.5	4.5
	2015[3]	0.6	2.1	85.4	0.1	4.5	7.9	...
Serbia Serbie	2005[5,20]	0.4	...	...	...	...	...	...
	2010	0.7[20]	8.6	59.4	...	~0.0	3.6	...
	2015	0.8[20]	12.8	50.6	...	~0.0	12.6	...
	2018	0.9[20]	10.0	43.1	...	~0.0	21.6	...
Seychelles Seychelles	2005	0.3	...	...	...	...	...	...
	2016	# 0.2	2.0[3]	56.1[3]	...	3.2[3]	33.9[3]	0.3[3]

27

Gross domestic expenditure on research and development (R&D) *(continued)*
As a percentage of GDP and by source of funds

Dépenses intérieures brutes de recherche et développement (R-D) *(suite)*
En pourcentage du PIB et répartition par source de financement

Country or area Pays ou zone	Year Année	Expenditure on R&D as a % of GDP Dépenses en R&D en % du PIB	Source of funds (%) / Source de financement (%)					
			Business enterprises Entreprises	Govern-ment Etat	Higher education Enseigne-ment supérieur	Private non-profit Institut. Privées sans but lucratif	Funds from abroad Fonds de l'étranger	Not specified/ Non précisé
Singapore	2005	2.1	58.6	35.7	1.3	...	4.4	...
Singapour	2010	1.9	51.8	41.2	2.0	...	5.0	...
	2015	2.2	52.8	38.2	2.2	...	6.8	...
	2017	1.9	52.2	37.4	3.3	...	7.1	...
Slovakia	2005	0.5	36.6	* 57.0	0.3	~0.0	6.0	...
Slovaquie	2010	0.6	35.1	* 49.6	0.4	0.3	14.7	...
	2015	1.2	25.1	31.9	3.3	0.3	39.4	...
	2018	0.8	48.8	38.0	1.7	0.3	11.2	...
Slovenia	2005	1.4	54.8	37.2	0.7	~0.0	7.3	...
Slovénie	2010	2.1	58.4	35.3	0.3	0.1	6.0	...
	2015	2.2	69.2	19.9	0.3	~0.0	10.6	...
	2017	1.9	63.1	22.9	0.5	0.4	13.1	...
	*2018	1.9	...	...	...	...	...	...
South Africa	2005	0.9	43.9	38.2	3.0	1.4	13.6	...
Afrique du Sud	2010	0.7	40.1	44.5	0.1	3.2	12.1	...
	2015	0.8	38.9	44.6	0.1	3.3	13.0	...
	2017	0.8	41.5	46.7	0.2	1.5	10.2	...
Spain	2005	1.1	46.3	43.0	4.1	0.9	5.7	...
Espagne	2010	1.3	43.0	46.6	3.9	0.7	5.7	...
	2015	1.2	45.8	40.9	4.3	0.9	8.0	...
	2017	1.2	47.8	38.9	4.3	0.8	8.2	...
	2018	1.2	...	...	...	...	...	...
Sri Lanka	#2000	0.1[1]	* 7.7	51.7[1]	18.5[1]	...	4.5[1]	17.5[1]
Sri Lanka	#2004	0.2	0.6	67.5[4]	...	...	22.6	9.3
	2010	0.1	# 40.9	55.9	0.2	...	2.7	0.3
	2015	0.1	34.4	59.6	...	2.3	1.5	2.1
State of Palestine [3]	2010	0.4	0.9	21.3	...	4.9	52.4	18.2
État de Palestine [3]	2013	0.5	3.8	29.4	...	17.1	24.2	21.1
Sudan [7]								
Soudan [7]	2005	0.3	...	...	...	...	...	...
Sweden	#2005	3.4	63.9	24.4	0.7	2.9	8.1	...
Suède	2009	3.4	59.5	27.0	0.6	2.6	10.3	...
	*2010	3.2	...	...	...	...	...	...
	*2013	3.3	61.0	28.3	1.0	3.1	6.7	...
	2015	3.3[17]	57.3	...	0.9	3.3	...	...
	2017	3.4[17]	60.8	25.0	0.7	3.3	10.1	...
	*2018	3.3	...	...	...	...	...	...
Switzerland	2004	2.7	69.7	22.7	1.5	0.8	5.2	...
Suisse	2008	2.7	68.2	22.8	2.3	0.7	6.0	...
	2015	3.4	63.5	24.4	1.5	0.5	10.2	...
	2017	3.4	67.0	25.9	1.4	0.5	5.2	...
Tajikistan	2001	0.1	0.6	97.3	...	...	0.2	1.9
Tadjikistan	2005	0.1	2.2[17]	91.5[17]	...	...	...	5.5[17]
	2006	0.1	0.2[17]	76.3[17]	...	...	0.6[17]	19.9[17]
	2010	0.1[2,3]	1.9[17]	76.2[17]	...	...	...	19.7[17]
	2011	0.1[2,3]	1.6[17]	82.1[17]	...	...	...	15.1[17]
	2013	0.1[2,3]	...	92.5	...	...	0.2	7.1
	2015[2,3]	0.1	...	100.0	...	...	...	...
	2018[2,3]	0.1	...	100.0	...	...	...	...
Thailand	2005	0.2	48.7	31.5	14.9	0.7	1.8	2.4
Thaïlande	2009	0.2	41.4	37.9	17.8	0.3	1.0	1.6
	2015	0.6	66.2	20.5	5.5	0.1	1.5	6.0
	2017	1.0	80.8	12.2	5.7	0.5	0.7	0.1
Togo	2010	0.2	...	88.3	...	...	11.7	...
Togo	2012	0.2[3]	...	84.9	...	3.1	12.1	...
	2014[3]	0.3[2]	...	94.5	...	...	5.5	...

27 Gross domestic expenditure on research and development (R&D) *(continued)*
As a percentage of GDP and by source of funds

Dépenses intérieures brutes de recherche et développement (R-D) *(suite)*
En pourcentage du PIB et répartition par source de financement

Country or area Pays ou zone	Year Année	Expenditure on R&D as a % of GDP Dépenses en R&D en % du PIB	Source of funds (%) / Source de financement (%)					
			Business enterprises Entreprises	Govern-ment Etat	Higher education Enseigne-ment supérieur	Private non-profit Institut. Privées sans but lucratif	Funds from abroad Fonds de l'étranger	Not specified/ Non précisé
Trinidad and Tobago Trinité-et-Tobago	2005	0.1	...	...	...	...	...	...
	2010	~0.0	...	...	...	...	...	...
	2015	0.1	...	...	...	...	...	...
	2017	0.1	8.2	75.0	...	...	16.8	...
Tunisia Tunisie	2005	0.7	14.4	79.2	...	...	6.4	...
	2010	0.7	17.1	78.1	...	...	4.8	...
	2015	0.6	18.9	77.1	...	...	3.9	...
	2018	0.6	...	...	...	...	...	...
Turkey Turquie	2005	0.6	43.3[5]	50.1[5]	...	5.8[5]	0.8	...
	2010	0.8	38.2	43.1	16.8	0.1	1.7	...
	2015	0.9	44.6	38.5	15.0	~0.0	1.9	...
	2017	1.0	49.4	33.6	13.3	0.1	3.5	...
Uganda Ouganda	2005	0.2	1.7	41.5	...	...	56.9	...
	2010	0.5	13.7	21.9	...	6.0	57.3	...
	2014	# 0.2	# 3.4	37.9	...	3.3	52.4	0.7
Ukraine Ukraine	2005	1.0	# 32.3	# 40.1	# 0.1	# 0.4	# 24.4	# 2.8
	2010	0.8	26.2	46.7	0.2	0.1	25.7	1.1
	2014	0.7[20]	35.2	43.8	0.2	~0.0	19.8	1.1
	2015	0.6[20]	40.3	39.4	0.2		18.2	2.0
	2018	0.5[20]	30.5	46.3	0.3	0.1	21.7	1.1
United Arab Emirates Émirats arabes unis	2014	0.7	74.3[21]	25.7[13]	...	...	...	...
	2015	0.9	...	...	...	...	...	...
	#2018	1.3	...	...	...	...	...	...
United Kingdom Royaume-Uni	2005	1.6	42.1	32.7	1.2	4.7	19.3	...
	*2010	1.7	44.0	32.3	1.2	4.8	17.6	...
	2015	1.7	49.0	27.7	1.4	4.9	17.1	...
	2017	1.7	53.7	26.0	0.7	5.2	14.4	...
	*2018	1.7	...	...	...	...	...	...
United Rep. of Tanzania Rép.-Unie de Tanzanie	2010	0.4[1,3]	0.1	57.5	0.3	0.1	42.0	...
	2013[3]	0.5	...	...	...	...	...	...
United States of America États-Unis d'Amérique	2005[5]	2.5	63.3	30.8	2.8	3.1		...
	2010	2.7[5]	56.9[5]	32.6[5]	3.0[5]	3.8[5]	3.7	...
	2015	2.7[5]	62.5[5]	25.3[5]	3.5[5]	3.7[5]	5.0	...
	2018	* 2.8[5]	* 62.4[5]	* 23.0[5]	* 3.6[5]	* 3.7[5]	* 7.3	...
United States Virgin Islands [1] Îles Vierges américaines [1]	2002	0.1	...	70.8	...	1.2	...	...
	2005	~0.0	...	100.0	...	...	...	...
	2007	~0.0	...	100.0	...	...	...	...
Uruguay Uruguay	2000	0.2	39.3	20.3	35.7	...	4.8	~0.0
	2002	0.2	46.7	17.1	31.4	0.1	4.7	...
	2010	0.3	47.1	22.9	26.6	0.9	1.7	0.8
	2011	0.3	8.5	30.8	45.2	0.1	6.5	8.9
	2015	0.4	4.6	28.6	59.2	0.3	7.4	...
	2017	0.5	4.6	28.2	59.5	0.3	7.4	...
Uzbekistan Ouzbékistan	2005	0.2	52.7	43.1[4]	...	...	0.6	3.6
	2010	0.2	35.1	57.8[4]	...	...	2.4	4.7
	2015	0.2	38.9	57.0[4]	...	...	1.2	2.9
	2018	0.1	42.4	54.3[4]	...	...	0.3	3.0
Venezuela (Boliv. Rep. of) Venezuela (Rép. boliv. du)	2005	0.2	...	...	...	...	...	...
	2010	0.2	...	...	...	...	...	...
	2014	0.3	...	59.6	...	...	...	32.0
	2015	...	...	89.1	...	...	...	...
	#2016	...	...	91.1	...	...	...	...
Viet Nam Viet Nam	2002	0.2	18.1	74.1	...	...	6.3	0.8
	2015	0.4	58.1	33.0	...	...	2.9	5.0
	2017	0.5	64.1	26.9	...	...	4.5	3.1
Zambia Zambie	2005[1]	~0.0	...	...	...	...	...	...
	#2008	0.3	3.2	94.8	...	0.3	1.6	...

27

Gross domestic expenditure on research and development (R&D) *(continued)*
As a percentage of GDP and by source of funds

Dépenses intérieures brutes de recherche et développement (R-D) *(suite)*
En pourcentage du PIB et répartition par source de financement

Source:

United Nations Educational, Scientific and Cultural Organization (UNESCO), Montreal, the UNESCO Institute for Statistics (UIS) statistics database, last accessed June 2020.

Source:

Organisation des Nations Unies pour l'éducation, la science et la culture (UNESCO), Montréal, base de données statistiques de l'Institut de statistique (ISU) de l'UNESCO, dernier accès juin 2020.

1	Partial data.	1	Données partielles.
2	Excluding private non-profit.	2	Non compris les organisations privées à but non lucratif.
3	Excluding business enterprise.	3	Ne comprend pas les entreprises commerciales.
4	Including higher education.	4	Y compris l'enseignement supérieur.
5	Do not correspond exactly to Frascati Manual recommendations.	5	Ne corresponds pas exactement aux recommandations du Manuel de Frascati.
6	Data have been converted from the former national currency using the appropriate conversion rate.	6	Les données ont été converties à partir de l'ancienne monnaie nationale et du taux de conversion approprié.
7	Overestimated or based on overestimated data.	7	Surestimé ou fondé sur des données surestimées.
8	Higher Education only.	8	Enseignement supérieur seulement.
9	Underestimated or based on underestimated data.	9	Sous-estimé ou basé sur des données sous-estimées.
10	For statistical purposes, the data for China do not include those for the Hong Kong Special Administrative Region (Hong Kong SAR), Macao Special Administrative Region (Macao SAR) and Taiwan Province of China.	10	Pour la présentation des statistiques, les données pour la Chine ne comprennent pas la région administrative spéciale de Hong Kong (RAS de Hong Kong), la région administrative spéciale de Macao (RAS de Macao) et la province chinoise de Taïwan.
11	Including private non-profit.	11	Y compris les fonds privés à but non lucratif.
12	Including business enterprise.	12	Y compris les fonds d'entreprises.
13	Government only.	13	Etat seulement.
14	S&T budget instead of R&D expenditure.	14	Budget pour la science et technologie au lieu des dépenses de recherche et développement.
15	Including Government.	15	Y compris l'état.
16	Based on R&D budget instead of R&D expenditure.	16	Basé sur le budget de la recherche-développement au lieu des dépenses.
17	The sum of the breakdown does not add to the total.	17	La somme de toutes les valeurs diffère du total.
18	Including other classes.	18	Comprend d'autres catégories.
19	Excluding government.	19	Non compris l'état.
20	Excluding data from some regions, provinces or states.	20	Non compris les données de certaines régions, provinces ou états.
21	Business enterprise only.	21	Les entreprises commerciales seulement.

Region, country or area	1985	1995	2005	2010	2016	2017	2018	Région, pays ou zone
Total, all countries or areas								**Total, tous pays ou zones**
Grants of patents	397 580	430 700	633 100	914 800	1 345 800	1 397 900	1 422 800	Brevets délivrés
Africa								**Afrique**
Grants of patents	...	...	4 800	9 600	7 900	9 400	8 700	Brevets délivrés
Northern America								**Amérique septentrionale**
Grants of patents	...	...	159 300	238 700	329 500	342 900	331 300	Brevets délivrés
Latin America & the Caribbean								**Amérique latine et Caraïbes**
Grants of patents	...	...	14 200	17 100	18 900	20 300	24 700	Brevets délivrés
Asia								**Asie**
Grants of patents	...	...	288 700	469 700	765 900	796 400	812 000	Brevets délivrés
Europe								**Europe**
Grants of patents	...	...	150 900	160 800	195 900	203 700	226 900	Brevets délivrés
Oceania								**Océanie**
Grants of patents	...	...	15 200	18 900	27 700	25 200	19 200	Brevets délivrés
Albania								**Albanie**
Resident filings (per mil. pop.)	...	...	...	...	8	6	5	Dem. de rés. (par mil. d'hab.)
Grants of patents	...	...	395	349	5	10	12	Brevets délivrés
Patents in force	...	...	...	349	1 645	4 946	5 021	Brevets en vigueur
Algeria								**Algérie**
Resident filings (per mil. pop.)	...	1	2	2	3	4	4	Dem. de rés. (par mil. d'hab.)
Grants of patents	...	118	443	1 076	383	256	162	Brevets délivrés
Patents in force	...	...	498	...	5 618	2 171	2 084	Brevets en vigueur
Andorra								**Andorre**
Resident filings (per mil. pop.)	...	...	...	...	...	...	13	Dem. de rés. (par mil. d'hab.)
Grants of patents	...	...	...	...	...	4	6	Brevets délivrés
Patents in force	...	...	...	...	...	4	10	Brevets en vigueur
Antigua and Barbuda								**Antigua-et-Barbuda**
Resident filings (per mil. pop.)	...	...	...	...	...	...	52	Dem. de rés. (par mil. d'hab.)
Patents in force	...	...	...	...	...	...	78	Brevets en vigueur
Argentina								**Argentine**
Resident filings (per mil. pop.)	...	19	27	14	20	9	10	Dem. de rés. (par mil. d'hab.)
Grants of patents	...	1 003	1 798	1 366	1 879	2 302	1 525	Brevets délivrés
Patents in force	...	...	...	...	...	13 115	...	Brevets en vigueur
Armenia								**Arménie**
Resident filings (per mil. pop.)	...	58	69	49	44	37	35	Dem. de rés. (par mil. d'hab.)
Grants of patents	...	52	126	124	93	74	100	Brevets délivrés
Patents in force	...	...	110	278	226	209	209	Brevets en vigueur
Australia								**Australie**
Resident filings (per mil. pop.)	...	99	125	109	108	102	110	Dem. de rés. (par mil. d'hab.)
Grants of patents	6 764	9 406	10 979	14 557	23 744	22 742	17 065	Brevets délivrés
Patents in force	...	...	96 403	96 293	132 994	144 555	156 244	Brevets en vigueur
Austria								**Autriche**
Resident filings (per mil. pop.)	300	217	404	497	471	489	489	Dem. de rés. (par mil. d'hab.)
Grants of patents	2 571	1 777	938	1 130	1 135	1 102	1 189	Brevets délivrés
Patents in force	...	...	95 618	102 113	142 875	146 880	167 594	Brevets en vigueur
Azerbaijan								**Azerbaïdjan**
Resident filings (per mil. pop.)	...	29	33	30	19	24	19	Dem. de rés. (par mil. d'hab.)
Grants of patents	...	9	195	126	131	67	64	Brevets délivrés
Patents in force	...	...	...	...	345	236	253	Brevets en vigueur
Bahamas								**Bahamas**
Resident filings (per mil. pop.)	13	...	...	...	8	10	...	Dem. de rés. (par mil. d'hab.)
Grants of patents	66	...	...	...	47	20	...	Brevets délivrés
Patents in force	...	...	...	...	1 077	1 082	...	Brevets en vigueur
Bahrain								**Bahreïn**
Resident filings (per mil. pop.)	...	...	...	...	6	9	10	Dem. de rés. (par mil. d'hab.)
Grants of patents	31	...	...	...	...	...	15	Brevets délivrés
Patents in force	...	...	...	...	66	53	60	Brevets en vigueur
Bangladesh								**Bangladesh**
Resident filings (per mil. pop.)	...	1	...	...	...	...	...	Dem. de rés. (par mil. d'hab.)
Grants of patents	118	80	182	92	106	144	138	Brevets délivrés
Patents in force	...	...	...	...	890	995	990	Brevets en vigueur
Barbados								**Barbade**
Grants of patents	...	...	7	...	26	...	...	Brevets délivrés
Patents in force	...	...	49	57	...	...	...	Brevets en vigueur

Patents *(continued)*
Resident filings (per million population), grants and patents in force

Brevets *(suite)*
Demandes émanant de résidents (par million d'habitants), délivrances et brevets en vigueur

Region, country or area	1985	1995	2005	2010	2016	2017	2018	Région, pays ou zone
Belarus								**Bélarus**
Resident filings (per mil. pop.)	...	61	121	197	60	59	60	Dem. de rés. (par mil. d'hab.)
Grants of patents	...	633	955	1 222	949	861	627	Brevets délivrés
Patents in force	...	...	...	4 444	2 503	2 250	1 991	Brevets en vigueur
Belgium								**Belgique**
Resident filings (per mil. pop.)	78	72	208	244	286	278	285	Dem. de rés. (par mil. d'hab.)
Grants of patents	1 976	1 216	708	532	1 620	1 016	1 019	Brevets délivrés
Patents in force	...	...	...	89 999	97 639	130 967	...	Brevets en vigueur
Belize								**Belize**
Grants of patents	...	...	...	...	4	...	...	Brevets délivrés
Patents in force	...	...	...	...	132	...	1 409	Brevets en vigueur
Benin								**Bénin**
Resident filings (per mil. pop.)	...	...	1	...	...	...	...	Dem. de rés. (par mil. d'hab.)
Bhutan								**Bhoutan**
Resident filings (per mil. pop.)	...	...	...	...	5	...	...	Dem. de rés. (par mil. d'hab.)
Patents in force	...	...	...	...	1	1	...	Brevets en vigueur
Bolivia (Plurin. State of)								**Bolivie (État plurin. de)**
Resident filings (per mil. pop.)	1	2	...	...	1	5	...	Dem. de rés. (par mil. d'hab.)
Grants of patents	62	47	...	...	86	63	...	Brevets délivrés
Bosnia and Herzegovina								**Bosnie-Herzégovine**
Resident filings (per mil. pop.)	...	...	18	15	18	26	25	Dem. de rés. (par mil. d'hab.)
Grants of patents	...	...	46	173	12	4	5	Brevets délivrés
Patents in force	...	...	120	716	375	367	234	Brevets en vigueur
Botswana								**Botswana**
Resident filings (per mil. pop.)	...	...	...	...	...	1	...	Dem. de rés. (par mil. d'hab.)
Grants of patents	...	...	...	...	3	4	...	Brevets délivrés
Patents in force	...	...	...	...	1 999	2 035	2 038	Brevets en vigueur
Brazil								**Brésil**
Resident filings (per mil. pop.)	14	17	22	22	25	26	24	Dem. de rés. (par mil. d'hab.)
Grants of patents	3 934	2 659	2 439	3 251	4 195	5 450	9 966	Brevets délivrés
Patents in force	...	...	32 571	40 022	24 153	25 664	31 977	Brevets en vigueur
Brunei Darussalam								**Brunéi Darussalam**
Resident filings (per mil. pop.)	...	...	...	...	38	19	56	Dem. de rés. (par mil. d'hab.)
Grants of patents	...	42	26	40	...	41	...	Brevets délivrés
Patents in force	...	...	...	...	74	103	113	Brevets en vigueur
Bulgaria								**Bulgarie**
Resident filings (per mil. pop.)	...	44	36	34	35	33	30	Dem. de rés. (par mil. d'hab.)
Grants of patents	130	375	313	251	42	77	181	Brevets délivrés
Patents in force	...	...	2 203	6 812	11 511	12 039	13 393	Brevets en vigueur
Burundi								**Burundi**
Grants of patents	...	1	...	...	6	27	28	Brevets délivrés
Cabo Verde								**Cabo Verde**
Resident filings (per mil. pop.)	...	...	...	...	4	4	6	Dem. de rés. (par mil. d'hab.)
Grants of patents	...	...	...	...	...	...	1	Brevets délivrés
Patents in force	...	...	...	...	...	...	1	Brevets en vigueur
Cambodia								**Cambodge**
Grants of patents	...	...	...	...	19	23	56	Brevets délivrés
Cameroon								**Cameroun**
Resident filings (per mil. pop.)	...	...	1	...	2	1	2	Dem. de rés. (par mil. d'hab.)
Canada								**Canada**
Resident filings (per mil. pop.)	81	83	161	134	113	111	117	Dem. de rés. (par mil. d'hab.)
Grants of patents	18 697	9 139	15 516	19 120	26 424	24 099	23 499	Brevets délivrés
Patents in force	...	...	125 110	133 355	175 236	180 727	184 559	Brevets en vigueur
Central African Republic								**République centrafricaine**
Resident filings (per mil. pop.)	...	...	...	...	...	...	1	Dem. de rés. (par mil. d'hab.)
Chad								**Tchad**
Resident filings (per mil. pop.)	...	...	...	...	...	...	1	Dem. de rés. (par mil. d'hab.)
Chile								**Chili**
Resident filings (per mil. pop.)	10	12	22	19	21	23	22	Dem. de rés. (par mil. d'hab.)
Grants of patents	448	133	311	1 020	2 077	1 574	1 599	Brevets délivrés
Patents in force	...	...	...	8 121	12 512	12 389	13 795	Brevets en vigueur
China [1]								**Chine** [1]
Resident filings (per mil. pop.)	4	8	72	219	874	899	1 001	Dem. de rés. (par mil. d'hab.)
Grants of patents	44	3 393	53 305	135 110	404 208	420 144	432 147	Brevets délivrés
Patents in force	...	...	182 396	564 760	1 772 203	2 085 367	2 366 314	Brevets en vigueur

Region, country or area	1985	1995	2005	2010	2016	2017	2018	Région, pays ou zone
China, Hong Kong SAR								**Chine, RAS de Hong Kong**
Resident filings (per mil. pop.)	3	4	23	19	32	44	42	Dem. de rés. (par mil. d'hab.)
Grants of patents	1 030	1 960	6 518	5 353	5 698	6 671	9 651	Brevets délivrés
Patents in force	...	...	...	33 225	43 359	45 059	49 922	Brevets en vigueur
China, Macao SAR								**Chine, RAS de Macao**
Resident filings (per mil. pop.)	...	...	6	7	...	2	2	Dem. de rés. (par mil. d'hab.)
Grants of patents	...	2	5	156	57	21	27	Brevets délivrés
Patents in force	...	...	12	377	467	416	387	Brevets en vigueur
Colombia								**Colombie**
Resident filings (per mil. pop.)	2	4	2	3	11	12	8	Dem. de rés. (par mil. d'hab.)
Grants of patents	169	365	256	639	917	1 164	1 271	Brevets délivrés
Patents in force	...	...	...	...	6 623	7 024	7 403	Brevets en vigueur
Congo								**Congo**
Resident filings (per mil. pop.)	...	...	1	...	...	...	...	Dem. de rés. (par mil. d'hab.)
Grants of patents	...	15	...	...	...	...	...	Brevets délivrés
Costa Rica								**Costa Rica**
Resident filings (per mil. pop.)	...	...	...	2	2	4	1	Dem. de rés. (par mil. d'hab.)
Grants of patents	...	...	...	45	67	190	168	Brevets délivrés
Patents in force	...	...	...	239	678	834	925	Brevets en vigueur
Côte d'Ivoire								**Côte d'Ivoire**
Resident filings (per mil. pop.)	...	...	...	...	1	1	1	Dem. de rés. (par mil. d'hab.)
Croatia								**Croatie**
Resident filings (per mil. pop.)	...	57	84	64	45	38	33	Dem. de rés. (par mil. d'hab.)
Grants of patents	...	25	140	82	35	20	21	Brevets délivrés
Patents in force	...	...	1 094	2 134	6 606	7 845	8 945	Brevets en vigueur
Cuba								**Cuba**
Resident filings (per mil. pop.)	...	10	9	...	3	3	3	Dem. de rés. (par mil. d'hab.)
Grants of patents	18	77	64	...	93	74	93	Brevets délivrés
Patents in force	...	...	653	...	857	816	727	Brevets en vigueur
Cyprus								**Chypre**
Resident filings (per mil. pop.)	...	...	54	35	43	51	46	Dem. de rés. (par mil. d'hab.)
Grants of patents	43	...	68	19	...	...	...	Brevets délivrés
Patents in force	...	...	3 521	333	79	37	12	Brevets en vigueur
Czechia								**Tchéquie**
Resident filings (per mil. pop.)	...	61	65	99	93	94	87	Dem. de rés. (par mil. d'hab.)
Grants of patents	...	1 299	1 551	911	781	669	512	Brevets délivrés
Patents in force	...	...	10 165	23 415	37 889	41 606	45 016	Brevets en vigueur
Dem. People's Rep. Korea								**Rép. pop. dém. de Corée**
Resident filings (per mil. pop.)	...	...	245	327	...	...	...	Dem. de rés. (par mil. d'hab.)
Grants of patents	...	...	3 583	6 290	...	...	...	Brevets délivrés
Denmark								**Danemark**
Resident filings (per mil. pop.)	167	236	523	625	597	626	629	Dem. de rés. (par mil. d'hab.)
Grants of patents	1 054	1 120	389	155	409	419	322	Brevets délivrés
Patents in force	...	...	56 978	47 732	55 715	58 494	62 408	Brevets en vigueur
Dominican Republic								**République dominicaine**
Resident filings (per mil. pop.)	...	...	1	2	3	2	2	Dem. de rés. (par mil. d'hab.)
Grants of patents	...	...	...	91	100	127	95	Brevets délivrés
Patents in force	...	...	...	...	265	282	635	Brevets en vigueur
Ecuador								**Équateur**
Resident filings (per mil. pop.)	...	1	1	...	3	1	2	Dem. de rés. (par mil. d'hab.)
Grants of patents	...	90	38	28	10	17	10	Brevets délivrés
Patents in force	...	...	38	199	...	63	65	Brevets en vigueur
Egypt								**Égypte**
Resident filings (per mil. pop.)	3	7	6	7	10	11	10	Dem. de rés. (par mil. d'hab.)
Grants of patents	298	346	147	321	450	581	690	Brevets délivrés
Patents in force	...	...	...	3 316	5 757	5 779	5 706	Brevets en vigueur
El Salvador								**El Salvador**
Resident filings (per mil. pop.)	3	1	...	...	1	1	...	Dem. de rés. (par mil. d'hab.)
Grants of patents	70	61	...	...	40	24	36	Brevets délivrés
Estonia								**Estonie**
Resident filings (per mil. pop.)	...	11	19	83	55	69	54	Dem. de rés. (par mil. d'hab.)
Grants of patents	...	...	163	120	27	15	14	Brevets délivrés
Patents in force	...	...	1 395	5 317	8 924	9 710	10 452	Brevets en vigueur
Eswatini								**Eswatini**
Grants of patents	30	...	...	...	...	...	...	Brevets délivrés

Patents *(continued)*
Resident filings (per million population), grants and patents in force

Brevets *(suite)*
Demandes émanant de résidents (par million d'habitants), délivrances et brevets en vigueur

Region, country or area	1985	1995	2005	2010	2016	2017	2018	Région, pays ou zone
Ethiopia								**Éthiopie**
Grants of patents	...	...	9	...	11	6	10	Brevets délivrés
Fiji								**Fidji**
Grants of patents	15	...	...	...	...	...	...	Brevets délivrés
Finland								**Finlande**
Resident filings (per mil. pop.)	352	403	637	628	560	584	564	Dem. de rés. (par mil. d'hab.)
Grants of patents	2 160	2 347	1 757	923	815	704	533	Brevets délivrés
Patents in force	...	...	39 450	46 622	48 588	50 764	52 140	Brevets en vigueur
France								**France**
Resident filings (per mil. pop.)	213	209	354	373	370	374	369	Dem. de rés. (par mil. d'hab.)
Grants of patents	24 195	17 918	11 473	9 899	12 374	11 865	12 249	Brevets délivrés
Patents in force	...	...	343 568	435 915	535 554	563 695	602 084	Brevets en vigueur
Gabon								**Gabon**
Resident filings (per mil. pop.)	...	...	3	...	2	1	1	Dem. de rés. (par mil. d'hab.)
Gambia								**Gambie**
Grants of patents	...	...	2	...	2	4	...	Brevets délivrés
Patents in force	...	...	...	...	4	8	16	Brevets en vigueur
Georgia								**Géorgie**
Resident filings (per mil. pop.)	...	62	58	48	26	20	28	Dem. de rés. (par mil. d'hab.)
Grants of patents	...	133	320	258	177	206	133	Brevets délivrés
Patents in force	...	...	1 040	1 044	1 394	1 172	1 312	Brevets en vigueur
Germany								**Allemagne**
Resident filings (per mil. pop.)	415	467	875	910	893	887	884	Dem. de rés. (par mil. d'hab.)
Grants of patents	19 500	16 000	17 063	13 678	15 652	15 653	16 367	Brevets délivrés
Patents in force	...	...	434 663	514 046	617 307	657 749	703 606	Brevets en vigueur
Ghana								**Ghana**
Resident filings (per mil. pop.)	...	...	...	...	...	1	...	Dem. de rés. (par mil. d'hab.)
Grants of patents	...	...	...	...	25	5	9	Brevets délivrés
Patents in force	...	...	...	...	25	30	...	Brevets en vigueur
Greece								**Grèce**
Resident filings (per mil. pop.)	113	25	48	73	63	56	51	Dem. de rés. (par mil. d'hab.)
Grants of patents	3 294	350	320	479	271	261	240	Brevets délivrés
Patents in force	...	...	...	32 120	26 479	26 936	27 426	Brevets en vigueur
Grenada								**Grenade**
Grants of patents	...	...	...	...	14	...	...	Brevets délivrés
Guatemala								**Guatemala**
Resident filings (per mil. pop.)	9	3	1	...	...	...	...	Dem. de rés. (par mil. d'hab.)
Grants of patents	166	22	104	104	52	50	30	Brevets délivrés
Patents in force	...	...	...	590	883	908	914	Brevets en vigueur
Guyana								**Guyana**
Resident filings (per mil. pop.)	1	...	...	...	1	...	3	Dem. de rés. (par mil. d'hab.)
Grants of patents	22	...	...	...	10	21	6	Brevets délivrés
Patents in force	...	...	...	...	29	...	...	Brevets en vigueur
Haiti								**Haïti**
Resident filings (per mil. pop.)	1	...	...	...	...	...	...	Dem. de rés. (par mil. d'hab.)
Grants of patents	9	3	11	10	...	...	...	Brevets délivrés
Honduras								**Honduras**
Resident filings (per mil. pop.)	3	1	...	...	1	...	1	Dem. de rés. (par mil. d'hab.)
Grants of patents	19	...	85	81	53	54	88	Brevets délivrés
Patents in force	...	...	...	...	...	1 654	1 765	Brevets en vigueur
Hungary								**Hongrie**
Resident filings (per mil. pop.)	273	106	78	75	74	61	54	Dem. de rés. (par mil. d'hab.)
Grants of patents	2 095	1 910	1 126	65	271	155	156	Brevets délivrés
Patents in force	...	...	9 125	13 853	23 782	26 225	28 677	Brevets en vigueur
Iceland								**Islande**
Resident filings (per mil. pop.)	87	71	253	343	218	268	252	Dem. de rés. (par mil. d'hab.)
Grants of patents	21	11	101	139	22	36	16	Brevets délivrés
Patents in force	...	...	349	1 892	5 941	6 613	7 380	Brevets en vigueur
India								**Inde**
Resident filings (per mil. pop.)	1	2	4	7	10	11	12	Dem. de rés. (par mil. d'hab.)
Grants of patents	1 814	1 613	4 320	7 138	8 248	12 387	13 908	Brevets délivrés
Patents in force	...	...	16 419	47 224	49 575	60 777	60 865	Brevets en vigueur
Indonesia								**Indonésie**
Resident filings (per mil. pop.)	...	...	1	2	4	9	5	Dem. de rés. (par mil. d'hab.)
Grants of patents	...	...	...	...	3 005	2 309	6 374	Brevets délivrés
Patents in force	...	...	...	...	...	...	22 584	Brevets en vigueur

Region, country or area	1985	1995	2005	2010	2016	2017	2018	Région, pays ou zone
Iran (Islamic Republic of)								**Iran (Rép. islamique d')**
Resident filings (per mil. pop.)	4	5	58	151	188	189	146	Dem. de rés. (par mil. d'hab.)
Grants of patents	339	166	2 890	5 372	3 268	4 151	3 367	Brevets délivrés
Patents in force	...	...	...	...	46 552	42 447	48 859	Brevets en vigueur
Iraq								**Iraq**
Resident filings (per mil. pop.)	19	4	...	...	...	16	17	Dem. de rés. (par mil. d'hab.)
Grants of patents	103	32	...	...	...	388	426	Brevets délivrés
Patents in force	...	...	...	...	2 085	2 427	2 784	Brevets en vigueur
Ireland								**Irlande**
Resident filings (per mil. pop.)	205	...	...	...	159	139	181	Dem. de rés. (par mil. d'hab.)
Grants of patents	1 042	3 208	226	87	64	60	52	Brevets délivrés
Patents in force	...	...	...	79 040	147 125	169 453	196 707	Brevets en vigueur
Israel								**Israël**
Resident filings (per mil. pop.)	187	228	241	190	152	165	170	Dem. de rés. (par mil. d'hab.)
Grants of patents	1 636	2 029	2 269	2 293	4 938	...	4 107	Brevets délivrés
Patents in force	...	...	...	26 494	30 922	32 764	33 951	Brevets en vigueur
Italy								**Italie**
Resident filings (per mil. pop.)	35	...	...	219	215	215	220	Dem. de rés. (par mil. d'hab.)
Grants of patents	...	9 164	5 534	16 106	6 429	4 855	6 424	Brevets délivrés
Patents in force	...	...	...	229 648	287 499	297 672	306 768	Brevets en vigueur
Jamaica								**Jamaïque**
Resident filings (per mil. pop.)	...	3	4	5	7	4	9	Dem. de rés. (par mil. d'hab.)
Grants of patents	...	4	...	...	5	2	...	Brevets délivrés
Patents in force	...	...	527	...	328	265	...	Brevets en vigueur
Japan								**Japon**
Resident filings (per mil. pop.)	2 272	2 661	2 880	2 265	2 049	2 053	2 005	Dem. de rés. (par mil. d'hab.)
Grants of patents	50 100	109 100	122 944	222 693	203 087	199 577	194 525	Brevets délivrés
Patents in force	...	...	1 123 055	1 423 432	1 980 985	2 013 685	2 054 276	Brevets en vigueur
Jordan								**Jordanie**
Resident filings (per mil. pop.)	...	...	8	6	2	3	2	Dem. de rés. (par mil. d'hab.)
Grants of patents	...	...	55	64	121	119	167	Brevets délivrés
Patents in force	...	...	...	312	463	407	532	Brevets en vigueur
Kazakhstan								**Kazakhstan**
Resident filings (per mil. pop.)	...	65	101	105	59	63	49	Dem. de rés. (par mil. d'hab.)
Grants of patents	...	1 281	...	1 868	1 011	869	778	Brevets délivrés
Patents in force	...	...	...	581	3 218	2 625	...	Brevets en vigueur
Kenya								**Kenya**
Resident filings (per mil. pop.)	...	...	1	2	3	3	5	Dem. de rés. (par mil. d'hab.)
Grants of patents	98	...	48	54	26	43	26	Brevets délivrés
Kiribati								**Kiribati**
Grants of patents	1	...	...	...	...	...	...	Brevets délivrés
Kuwait								**Koweït**
Resident filings (per mil. pop.)	...	...	...	...	5	...	4	Dem. de rés. (par mil. d'hab.)
Kyrgyzstan								**Kirghizistan**
Resident filings (per mil. pop.)	...	26	...	26	15	23	...	Dem. de rés. (par mil. d'hab.)
Grants of patents	...	133	...	109	120	78	110	Brevets délivrés
Patents in force	...	...	...	112	274	256	253	Brevets en vigueur
Lao People's Dem. Rep.								**Rép. dém. populaire lao**
Resident filings (per mil. pop.)	...	...	1	...	...	...	...	Dem. de rés. (par mil. d'hab.)
Grants of patents	...	...	...	...	2	3	5	Brevets délivrés
Latvia								**Lettonie**
Resident filings (per mil. pop.)	...	85	53	101	55	54	51	Dem. de rés. (par mil. d'hab.)
Grants of patents	...	629	122	184	68	87	51	Brevets délivrés
Patents in force	...	...	4 012	5 680	7 419	8 808	9 475	Brevets en vigueur
Lesotho								**Lesotho**
Resident filings (per mil. pop.)	...	4	...	...	...	...	...	Dem. de rés. (par mil. d'hab.)
Grants of patents	...	7	...	...	...	...	...	Brevets délivrés
Libya								**Libye**
Resident filings (per mil. pop.)	...	1	...	...	...	...	...	Dem. de rés. (par mil. d'hab.)
Liechtenstein								**Liechtenstein**
Resident filings (per mil. pop.)	...	...	4 380	8 056	10 000	10 053	11 372	Dem. de rés. (par mil. d'hab.)
Lithuania								**Lituanie**
Resident filings (per mil. pop.)	...	29	21	38	43	37	42	Dem. de rés. (par mil. d'hab.)
Grants of patents	...	494	116	84	103	143	92	Brevets délivrés
Patents in force	...	...	768	642	522	...	474	Brevets en vigueur

Region, country or area	1985	1995	2005	2010	2016	2017	2018	Région, pays ou zone
Luxembourg								**Luxembourg**
Resident filings (per mil. pop.)	221	86	441	990	1 069	1 201	992	Dem. de rés. (par mil. d'hab.)
Grants of patents	418	...	29	87	184	487	423	Brevets délivrés
Patents in force	...	...	...	42 805	65 137	71 708	98 245	Brevets en vigueur
Madagascar								**Madagascar**
Resident filings (per mil. pop.)	...	2	...	...	...	...	...	Dem. de rés. (par mil. d'hab.)
Grants of patents	...	25	32	55	19	23	31	Brevets délivrés
Patents in force	...	...	249	387	386	206	229	Brevets en vigueur
Malawi								**Malawi**
Grants of patents	43	23	...	1	7	...	...	Brevets délivrés
Malaysia								**Malaisie**
Resident filings (per mil. pop.)	1	7	20	44	36	37	35	Dem. de rés. (par mil. d'hab.)
Grants of patents	1 150	1 753	2 508	2 160	3 324	5 063	4 287	Brevets délivrés
Patents in force	...	...	...	20 908	25 117	25 313	26 572	Brevets en vigueur
Mali								**Mali**
Resident filings (per mil. pop.)	...	...	...	...	1	...	...	Dem. de rés. (par mil. d'hab.)
Malta								**Malte**
Resident filings (per mil. pop.)	...	29	...	104	204	...	...	Dem. de rés. (par mil. d'hab.)
Grants of patents	20	19	...	4	6	...	...	Brevets délivrés
Patents in force	...	...	...	832	423	...	...	Brevets en vigueur
Mauritius								**Maurice**
Resident filings (per mil. pop.)	4	3	...	...	2	1	13	Dem. de rés. (par mil. d'hab.)
Grants of patents	4	3	...	8	2	4	7	Brevets délivrés
Patents in force	...	...	...	...	...	46	53	Brevets en vigueur
Mexico								**Mexique**
Resident filings (per mil. pop.)	8	5	6	8	11	11	12	Dem. de rés. (par mil. d'hab.)
Grants of patents	977	3 538	8 098	9 399	8 652	8 510	8 921	Brevets délivrés
Patents in force	...	...	48 374	82 017	109 238	112 617	113 286	Brevets en vigueur
Monaco								**Monaco**
Resident filings (per mil. pop.)	521	423	503	562	1 129	1 198	724	Dem. de rés. (par mil. d'hab.)
Grants of patents	66	36	9	5	9	10	28	Brevets délivrés
Patents in force	...	...	37 483	53 859	85 132	88 453	115 893	Brevets en vigueur
Mongolia								**Mongolie**
Resident filings (per mil. pop.)	...	57	40	40	37	40	26	Dem. de rés. (par mil. d'hab.)
Grants of patents	5	117	197	96	157	105	76	Brevets délivrés
Patents in force	...	...	13 663	2 645	4 324	...	1 030	Brevets en vigueur
Montenegro								**Monténégro**
Resident filings (per mil. pop.)	...	...	...	37	16	...	5	Dem. de rés. (par mil. d'hab.)
Grants of patents	...	...	...	264	8	...	11	Brevets délivrés
Patents in force	...	...	...	264	...	...	...	Brevets en vigueur
Morocco								**Maroc**
Resident filings (per mil. pop.)	2	3	5	5	7	6	5	Dem. de rés. (par mil. d'hab.)
Grants of patents	313	354	556	808	352	413	600	Brevets délivrés
Patents in force	...	...	9 872	...	...	4 145	8 364	Brevets en vigueur
Mozambique								**Mozambique**
Resident filings (per mil. pop.)	...	...	...	1	1	1	1	Dem. de rés. (par mil. d'hab.)
Grants of patents	...	...	14	...	35	...	...	Brevets délivrés
Patents in force	...	...	...	...	1 582	2 029	2 531	Brevets en vigueur
Namibia								**Namibie**
Resident filings (per mil. pop.)	...	...	...	...	8	4	9	Dem. de rés. (par mil. d'hab.)
Grants of patents	...	...	...	...	28	16	4	Brevets délivrés
Patents in force	...	...	...	...	479	451	623	Brevets en vigueur
Nepal								**Népal**
Resident filings (per mil. pop.)	...	...	...	...	...	1	...	Dem. de rés. (par mil. d'hab.)
Grants of patents	1	1	3	...	...	...	...	Brevets délivrés
Netherlands								**Pays-Bas**
Resident filings (per mil. pop.)	134	137	614	511	536	541	537	Dem. de rés. (par mil. d'hab.)
Grants of patents	2 145	673	2 373	1 947	1 914	2 307	1 972	Brevets délivrés
Patents in force	...	...	135 215	135 127	164 264	165 879	194 393	Brevets en vigueur
New Zealand								**Nouvelle-Zélande**
Resident filings (per mil. pop.)	310	350	458	364	229	212	208	Dem. de rés. (par mil. d'hab.)
Grants of patents	1 732	2 641	4 189	4 347	3 910	2 430	2 039	Brevets délivrés
Patents in force	...	...	34 182	34 800	38 906	36 157	33 331	Brevets en vigueur
Nicaragua								**Nicaragua**
Resident filings (per mil. pop.)	1	...	...	...	...	...	...	Dem. de rés. (par mil. d'hab.)
Grants of patents	25	1	...	...	...	...	...	Brevets délivrés

Region, country or area	1985	1995	2005	2010	2016	2017	2018	Région, pays ou zone
Nigeria								**Nigéria**
Resident filings (per mil. pop.)	...	...	...	...	...	1	1	Dem. de rés. (par mil. d'hab.)
Grants of patents	...	...	...	...	886	552	842	Brevets délivrés
North Macedonia								**Macédoine du Nord**
Resident filings (per mil. pop.)	...	50	26	13	...	...	...	Dem. de rés. (par mil. d'hab.)
Grants of patents	...	163	373	406	...	...	...	Brevets délivrés
Norway								**Norvège**
Resident filings (per mil. pop.)	222	259	247	334	335	319	318	Dem. de rés. (par mil. d'hab.)
Grants of patents	2 165	2 014	542	1 631	2 525	2 147	1 548	Brevets délivrés
Patents in force	...	...	...	16 534	27 930	33 150	37 434	Brevets en vigueur
Oman								**Oman**
Resident filings (per mil. pop.)	...	...	...	...	1	2	...	Dem. de rés. (par mil. d'hab.)
Grants of patents	...	...	...	...	17	17	136	Brevets délivrés
Pakistan								**Pakistan**
Resident filings (per mil. pop.)	...	...	1	1	1	1	1	Dem. de rés. (par mil. d'hab.)
Grants of patents	...	474	393	238	214	169	265	Brevets délivrés
Patents in force	...	...	...	...	1 848	1 745	1 835	Brevets en vigueur
Panama								**Panama**
Resident filings (per mil. pop.)	6	6	...	...	17	8	32	Dem. de rés. (par mil. d'hab.)
Grants of patents	72	80	228	378	13	4	147	Brevets délivrés
Patents in force	...	...	...	378	1 358	1 289	1 338	Brevets en vigueur
Paraguay								**Paraguay**
Resident filings (per mil. pop.)	2	...	4	3	...	...	...	Dem. de rés. (par mil. d'hab.)
Grants of patents	8	...	...	...	...	...	13	Brevets délivrés
Patents in force	...	...	...	...	...	...	347	Brevets en vigueur
Peru								**Pérou**
Resident filings (per mil. pop.)	2	...	1	1	2	3	3	Dem. de rés. (par mil. d'hab.)
Grants of patents	148	...	388	365	403	510	625	Brevets délivrés
Patents in force	...	...	2 252	2 435	2 779	2 791	3 098	Brevets en vigueur
Philippines								**Philippines**
Resident filings (per mil. pop.)	2	2	2	2	3	3	5	Dem. de rés. (par mil. d'hab.)
Grants of patents	1 281	589	1 642	1 153	4 006	1 645	3 435	Brevets délivrés
Patents in force	...	...	...	...	19 995	21 254	23 405	Brevets en vigueur
Poland								**Pologne**
Resident filings (per mil. pop.)	138	67	56	90	123	115	125	Dem. de rés. (par mil. d'hab.)
Grants of patents	4 467	2 608	2 522	3 004	3 548	2 904	2 980	Brevets délivrés
Patents in force	...	...	14 578	30 021	65 006	75 982	82 618	Brevets en vigueur
Portugal								**Portugal**
Resident filings (per mil. pop.)	8	8	19	55	85	77	86	Dem. de rés. (par mil. d'hab.)
Grants of patents	960	960	231	140	38	55	69	Brevets délivrés
Patents in force	...	...	35 871	39 076	35 649	36 821	38 193	Brevets en vigueur
Qatar								**Qatar**
Resident filings (per mil. pop.)	...	...	...	...	9	10	...	Dem. de rés. (par mil. d'hab.)
Grants of patents	...	...	...	...	...	37	...	Brevets délivrés
Republic of Korea								**République de Corée**
Resident filings (per mil. pop.)	66	1 313	2 536	2 660	3 189	3 091	3 148	Dem. de rés. (par mil. d'hab.)
Grants of patents	2 268	12 512	73 512	68 843	108 875	120 662	119 012	Brevets délivrés
Patents in force	...	...	420 906	640 412	950 526	970 889	1 001 163	Brevets en vigueur
Republic of Moldova								**République de Moldova**
Resident filings (per mil. pop.)	...	73	105	42	26	21	26	Dem. de rés. (par mil. d'hab.)
Grants of patents	...	227	269	132	70	62	79	Brevets délivrés
Patents in force	...	...	1 108	1 018	343	333	324	Brevets en vigueur
Romania								**Roumanie**
Resident filings (per mil. pop.)	185	80	43	69	53	59	59	Dem. de rés. (par mil. d'hab.)
Grants of patents	2 786	1 860	759	447	355	407	363	Brevets délivrés
Patents in force	...	...	8 627	2 915	18 906	20 711	22 732	Brevets en vigueur
Russian Federation								**Fédération de Russie**
Resident filings (per mil. pop.)	...	118	166	203	188	160	175	Dem. de rés. (par mil. d'hab.)
Grants of patents	...	25 633	23 390	30 322	33 536	34 254	35 774	Brevets délivrés
Patents in force	...	...	123 089	181 904	230 870	244 217	256 419	Brevets en vigueur
Rwanda								**Rwanda**
Grants of patents	1	...	3	...	...	176	...	Brevets délivrés
Patents in force	...	...	...	...	...	456	309	Brevets en vigueur
Saint Lucia								**Sainte-Lucie**
Resident filings (per mil. pop.)	...	...	...	...	28	17	11	Dem. de rés. (par mil. d'hab.)

Patents *(continued)*
Resident filings (per million population), grants and patents in force

Brevets *(suite)*
Demandes émanant de résidents (par million d'habitants), délivrances et brevets en vigueur

Region, country or area	1985	1995	2005	2010	2016	2017	2018	Région, pays ou zone
Saint Vincent & Grenadines								**Saint-Vincent-Grenadines**
Grants of patents	...	...	...	...	...	10	8	Brevets délivrés
Patents in force	...	...	...	...	...	10	8	Brevets en vigueur
Samoa								**Samoa**
Resident filings (per mil. pop.)	...	...	...	...	...	...	5	Dem. de rés. (par mil. d'hab.)
Grants of patents	4	2	...	...	...	...	...	Brevets délivrés
Patents in force	...	...	...	...	51	51	52	Brevets en vigueur
San Marino								**Saint-Marin**
Resident filings (per mil. pop.)	...	...	...	...	627	475	740	Dem. de rés. (par mil. d'hab.)
Grants of patents	...	...	...	...	467	624	686	Brevets délivrés
Sao Tome and Principe								**Sao Tomé-et-Principe**
Grants of patents	...	...	...	...	1	3	8	Brevets délivrés
Patents in force	...	...	...	...	11	11	19	Brevets en vigueur
Saudi Arabia								**Arabie saoudite**
Resident filings (per mil. pop.)	...	2	6	12	41	37	50	Dem. de rés. (par mil. d'hab.)
Grants of patents	...	3	225	194	595	501	569	Brevets délivrés
Patents in force	...	...	...	...	3 104	3 277	3 383	Brevets en vigueur
Senegal								**Sénégal**
Resident filings (per mil. pop.)	...	...	1	...	2	1	1	Dem. de rés. (par mil. d'hab.)
Serbia								**Serbie**
Resident filings (per mil. pop.)	...	...	50	40	27	26	25	Dem. de rés. (par mil. d'hab.)
Grants of patents	...	...	265	427	68	47	44	Brevets délivrés
Patents in force	...	...	...	1 477	3 790	4 644	5 685	Brevets en vigueur
Seychelles								**Seychelles**
Grants of patents	2	1	...	...	9	29	11	Brevets délivrés
Patents in force	...	...	...	...	169	198	209	Brevets en vigueur
Sierra Leone								**Sierra Leone**
Grants of patents	...	5	...	...	...	...	...	Brevets délivrés
Singapore								**Singapour**
Resident filings (per mil. pop.)	1	41	133	176	286	287	279	Dem. de rés. (par mil. d'hab.)
Grants of patents	416	1 750	7 530	4 442	7 341	6 217	5 172	Brevets délivrés
Patents in force	...	...	43 024	43 591	48 603	49 514	48 105	Brevets en vigueur
Slovakia								**Slovaquie**
Resident filings (per mil. pop.)	...	50	32	48	48	41	49	Dem. de rés. (par mil. d'hab.)
Grants of patents	...	381	560	376	122	82	109	Brevets délivrés
Patents in force	...	...	4 033	10 565	16 363	17 815	19 247	Brevets en vigueur
Slovenia								**Slovénie**
Resident filings (per mil. pop.)	...	158	215	282	...	...	172	Dem. de rés. (par mil. d'hab.)
Grants of patents	...	380	285	250	...	...	232	Brevets délivrés
Patents in force	...	...	5 201	1 485	...	...	1 343	Brevets en vigueur
Solomon Islands								**Îles Salomon**
Grants of patents	4	...	...	...	...	...	...	Brevets délivrés
Somalia								**Somalie**
Grants of patents	7	...	...	...	...	...	...	Brevets délivrés
South Africa								**Afrique du Sud**
Resident filings (per mil. pop.)	124	21	21	16	13	13	11	Dem. de rés. (par mil. d'hab.)
Grants of patents	6 768	5 113	1 831	5 331	4 255	5 535	4 746	Brevets délivrés
Patents in force	...	...	...	...	58 235	63 151	73 270	Brevets en vigueur
Spain								**Espagne**
Resident filings (per mil. pop.)	56	52	92	107	93	83	71	Dem. de rés. (par mil. d'hab.)
Grants of patents	9 115	686	2 769	2 773	2 308	2 011	1 760	Brevets délivrés
Patents in force	...	...	39 297	175 687	115 070	108 732	81 957	Brevets en vigueur
Sri Lanka								**Sri Lanka**
Resident filings (per mil. pop.)	2	4	8	11	13	13	16	Dem. de rés. (par mil. d'hab.)
Grants of patents	112	159	180	504	123	178	212	Brevets délivrés
Patents in force	...	...	...	...	710	826	850	Brevets en vigueur
Sudan								**Soudan**
Resident filings (per mil. pop.)	...	...	...	7	7	7	8	Dem. de rés. (par mil. d'hab.)
Grants of patents	...	...	174	125	164	177	204	Brevets délivrés
Patents in force	...	...	...	...	164	177	204	Brevets en vigueur
Sweden								**Suède**
Resident filings (per mil. pop.)	460	446	555	614	563	574	578	Dem. de rés. (par mil. d'hab.)
Grants of patents	5 681	1 541	1 911	1 380	866	1 031	1 063	Brevets délivrés
Patents in force	...	...	102 741	96 796	93 545	96 876	100 974	Brevets en vigueur

Region, country or area	1985	1995	2005	2010	2016	2017	2018	Région, pays ou zone
Switzerland								**Suisse**
Resident filings (per mil. pop.)	493	410	897	1 069	1 042	1 020	1 081	Dem. de rés. (par mil. d'hab.)
Grants of patents	6 421	1 303	...	741	617	771	614	Brevets délivrés
Patents in force	...	...	99 531	123 033	193 883	208 022	244 581	Brevets en vigueur
Syrian Arab Republic								**République arabe syrienne**
Resident filings (per mil. pop.)	...	9	6	...	...	7	6	Dem. de rés. (par mil. d'hab.)
Grants of patents	...	71	72	...	32	3	37	Brevets délivrés
Patents in force	...	...	...	...	...	13	...	Brevets en vigueur
Tajikistan								**Tadjikistan**
Resident filings (per mil. pop.)	...	6	4	1	...	...	...	Dem. de rés. (par mil. d'hab.)
Grants of patents	...	47	...	3	...	...	...	Brevets délivrés
Patents in force	...	...	...	248	...	...	...	Brevets en vigueur
Thailand								**Thaïlande**
Resident filings (per mil. pop.)	1	2	14	18	16	14	13	Dem. de rés. (par mil. d'hab.)
Grants of patents	45	470	553	772	1 838	3 080	3 818	Brevets délivrés
Patents in force	...	...	...	10 201	12 193	16 591	15 696	Brevets en vigueur
Togo								**Togo**
Resident filings (per mil. pop.)	...	...	...	...	1	...		Dem. de rés. (par mil. d'hab.)
Trinidad and Tobago								**Trinité-et-Tobago**
Resident filings (per mil. pop.)	...	19	1	...	2	...	3	Dem. de rés. (par mil. d'hab.)
Grants of patents	...	87	...	...	60	66	26	Brevets délivrés
Tunisia								**Tunisie**
Resident filings (per mil. pop.)	2	3	6	11	21	15	16	Dem. de rés. (par mil. d'hab.)
Grants of patents	...	141	338	620	583	555	451	Brevets délivrés
Patents in force	...	...	...	...	5 672	6 231	...	Brevets en vigueur
Turkey								**Turquie**
Resident filings (per mil. pop.)	3	3	15	48	84	112	94	Dem. de rés. (par mil. d'hab.)
Grants of patents	385	763	823	...	1 764	1 900	2 882	Brevets délivrés
Patents in force	...	...	...	24 969	63 575	68 886	75 363	Brevets en vigueur
Uganda								**Ouganda**
Grants of patents	26	...	...	...	...	2	2	Brevets délivrés
Patents in force	...	...	...	...	19	...	...	Brevets en vigueur
Ukraine								**Ukraine**
Resident filings (per mil. pop.)	...	93	75	56	50	51	47	Dem. de rés. (par mil. d'hab.)
Grants of patents	...	1 350	3 719	3 874	2 813	2 590	2 469	Brevets délivrés
Patents in force	...	...	37 336	24 622	24 760	23 705	22 977	Brevets en vigueur
United Arab Emirates								**Émirats arabes unis**
Resident filings (per mil. pop.)	...	...	...	...	...	9	9	Dem. de rés. (par mil. d'hab.)
Grants of patents	...	...	...	...	222	...	451	Brevets délivrés
Patents in force	...	...	...	...	673	874	1 302	Brevets en vigueur
United Kingdom								**Royaume-Uni**
Resident filings (per mil. pop.)	348	321	372	333	290	282	280	Dem. de rés. (par mil. d'hab.)
Grants of patents	20 880	9 473	10 159	5 594	5 602	6 311	5 982	Brevets délivrés
Patents in force	...	...	...	413 177	485 326	516 965	572 063	Brevets en vigueur
United Rep. of Tanzania								**Rép.-Unie de Tanzanie**
Grants of patents	30	...	3	1	...	...	6	Brevets délivrés
United States of America								**États-Unis d'Amérique**
Resident filings (per mil. pop.)	268	466	703	782	914	904	871	Dem. de rés. (par mil. d'hab.)
Grants of patents	71 661	101 419	143 806	219 614	303 049	318 829	307 759	Brevets délivrés
Patents in force	...	...	1 683 968	2 017 318	2 763 055	2 984 825	3 063 494	Brevets en vigueur
Uruguay								**Uruguay**
Resident filings (per mil. pop.)	21	11	7	7	...	7	...	Dem. de rés. (par mil. d'hab.)
Grants of patents	196	36	...	29	...	27	...	Brevets délivrés
Patents in force	...	...	...	877	...	410	...	Brevets en vigueur
Uzbekistan								**Ouzbékistan**
Resident filings (per mil. pop.)	...	46	10	13	11	11	14	Dem. de rés. (par mil. d'hab.)
Grants of patents	...	1 233	407	192	166	205	219	Brevets délivrés
Patents in force	...	...	1 263	1 253	977	952	966	Brevets en vigueur
Venezuela (Boliv. Rep. of)								**Venezuela (Rép. boliv. du)**
Resident filings (per mil. pop.)	13	...	5	2	1	3	...	Dem. de rés. (par mil. d'hab.)
Grants of patents	351	...	...	...	...	...	...	Brevets délivrés
Viet Nam								**Viet Nam**
Resident filings (per mil. pop.)	...	...	2	3	6	6	7	Dem. de rés. (par mil. d'hab.)
Grants of patents	...	56	668	822	1 423	1 745	2 219	Brevets délivrés
Patents in force	...	...	...	9 103	14 398	15 226	12 965	Brevets en vigueur

28

Patents *(continued)*
Resident filings (per million population), grants and patents in force

Brevets *(suite)*
Demandes émanant de résidents (par million d'habitants), délivrances et brevets en vigueur

Region, country or area	1985	1995	2005	2010	2016	2017	2018	Région, pays ou zone
Yemen								**Yémen**
Resident filings (per mil. pop.)	...	...	1	1	1	1	...	Dem. de rés. (par mil. d'hab.)
Grants of patents	...	...	...	...	...	28	8	Brevets délivrés
Patents in force	...	...	...	...	...	...	35	Brevets en vigueur
Zambia								**Zambie**
Resident filings (per mil. pop.)	...	...	...	...	1	1	...	Dem. de rés. (par mil. d'hab.)
Grants of patents	74	43	14	12	27	18	...	Brevets délivrés
Patents in force	...	...	2 695	3 858	7 259	7 705	...	Brevets en vigueur
Zimbabwe								**Zimbabwe**
Resident filings (per mil. pop.)	4	5	...	...	1	...	...	Dem. de rés. (par mil. d'hab.)
Grants of patents	212	105	...	...	...	...	...	Brevets délivrés

Source:

World Intellectual Property Organization (WIPO), Geneva, WIPO statistics database, last accessed May 2020.

Source:

Organisation mondiale de la propriété intellectuelle (OMPI), Genève, la base de données statistiques de l'OMPI, dernier accès mai 2020.

1 For statistical purposes, the data for China do not include those for the Hong Kong Special Administrative Region (Hong Kong SAR), Macao Special Administrative Region (Macao SAR) and Taiwan Province of China.

1 Pour la présentation des statistiques, les données pour la Chine ne comprennent pas la région administrative spéciale de Hong Kong (RAS de Hong Kong), la région administrative spéciale de Macao (RAS de Macao) et la province chinoise de Taïwan.

Internet usage
Percentage of individuals per country

Utilisation d'Internet
Pourcentage de personnes par pays

Country or area Total, all countries or areas	2000 6.5	2005 15.7	2010 28.7	2015 41.5	2016 44.6	2017 49.7	2018 51.4	Pays ou zone Total, tous pays ou zones
Northern Africa	0.6	9.2	24.6	38.8	39.2	45.8	44.1	Afrique septentrionale
Sub-Saharan Africa	0.5	2.1	6.5	20.5	19.5	25.2	26.0	Afrique subsaharienne
Eastern Africa	0.2	1.3	4.5	14.5	15.0	18.0	17.6	Afrique orientale
Middle Africa	0.1	0.7	2.1	8.7	10.6	12.4	13.9	Afrique centrale
Southern Africa	4.9	7.0	22.0	49.1	51.4	54.6	54.9	Afrique australe
Western Africa	0.1	2.5	7.7	27.2	...	33.7	35.8	Afrique occidentale
Northern America	43.9	68.3	72.5	76.1	86.1	87.6	89.2	Amérique septentrionale
Latin America & the Caribbean	3.9	16.6	34.7	54.6	57.4	63.2	66.3	Amérique latine et Caraïbes
Caribbean	2.9	12.5	23.7	39.6	44.4	50.2	58.7	Caraïbes
Latin America	4.0	16.9	35.5	55.7	58.3	64.1	66.8	Amérique latine
Asia	3.0	9.0	22.6	35.7	39.5	45.3	47.3	Asie
Central Asia	0.5	3.3	18.4	43.7	47.4	50.9	51.3	Asie centrale
Eastern Asia	6.0	16.1	39.5	54.4	57.2	58.6	59.1	Asie orientale
South-central Asia	0.5	2.8	8.0	18.4	22.6	32.3	34.1	Asie centrale et du Sud
South-eastern Asia	2.4	8.7	18.8	31.9	39.9	45.3	48.2	Asie du Sud-Est
Southern Asia	0.5	2.8	7.6	17.5	21.7	31.6	33.5	Asie méridionale
Western Asia	3.6	11.1	32.7	56.5	54.5	62.6	67.6	Asie occidentale
Europe	15.2	39.8	61.3	74.3	76.3	78.5	82.0	Europe
Oceania	34.7	46.9	57.3	65.7	67.4	68.2	...	Océanie
Australia and New Zealand	46.9	63.0	76.7	85.2	86.9	87.2	86.9	Australie et Nouvelle-Zélande
Afghanistan	...	1.2	* 4.0	* 8.3	11.2[1]	13.5[1]	...	Afghanistan
Albania	0.1	6.0	45.0	* 63.3	* 66.4	* 71.8	...	Albanie
Algeria	0.5	5.8	12.5	* 38.2	* 42.9	* 47.7	49.0	Algérie
Andorra	10.5	37.6	81.0	* 96.9	* 97.9	91.6	...	Andorre
Angola	0.1	1.1	* 2.8	* 12.4	* 13.0	* 14.3	...	Angola
Anguilla	22.4	* 29.0	* 49.6	* 76.0	* 81.6	...	...	Anguilla
Antigua and Barbuda	6.5	* 27.0	* 47.0	* 70.0	* 73.0	76.0	...	Antigua-et-Barbuda
Argentina	7.0	17.7	* 45.0	68.0	71.0	74.3	...	Argentine
Armenia	1.3	5.3	* 25.0	* 59.1	64.3	64.7	...	Arménie
Aruba	15.4	* 25.4	* 62.0	* 88.7	* 93.5	* 97.2	...	Aruba
Australia	46.8	63.0[2]	* 76.0	84.6[2]	* 86.5	86.5[2,3]	...	Australie
Austria	33.7[4]	58.0[5]	75.2[5]	83.9[5]	84.3[5,6]	87.9[5,6]	87.5	Autriche
Azerbaijan	0.1	8.0	46.0[7]	77.0[7]	78.2	79.0	79.8	Azerbaïdjan
Bahamas	* 8.0	* 25.0	* 43.0	* 78.0	* 80.0	* 85.0	...	Bahamas
Bahrain	6.2	21.3	55.0	93.5[2]	* 98.0	* 95.9	98.6	Bahreïn
Bangladesh	* 0.1	* 0.2	* 3.7	* 14.4	* 18.0	15.0[1]	...	Bangladesh
Barbados	4.0	* 52.5	* 65.1	* 76.1	* 79.5	* 81.8	...	Barbade
Belarus	1.9		31.8[8]	62.2[9]	71.1[9]	74.4[9]	79.1	Bélarus
Belgium	29.4	* 55.8	75.0	85.1[5,6]	86.5[5,6]	87.7	88.7	Belgique
Belize	6.0	* 17.0	28.2[10]	* 41.6	* 44.6	* 47.1	...	Belize
Benin	0.2	1.3	3.1	* 11.3	* 12.0	20.0[1]	...	Bénin
Bermuda	42.9	65.4	* 84.2	* 98.3	* 98.0	* 98.4	...	Bermudes
Bhutan	0.4	3.8	* 13.6	* 39.8	* 41.8	* 48.1	...	Bhoutan
Bolivia (Plurin. State of)	* 1.4	5.2	* 22.4	* 35.6	* 39.7	* 43.8	44.3	Bolivie (État plurin. de)
Bosnia and Herzegovina	1.1	21.3	* 42.8	* 52.6	* 60.3	64.9	70.1	Bosnie-Herzégovine
Botswana	2.9	* 3.3	6.0	* 37.3	* 39.4	47.0[1]	...	Botswana
Brazil	2.9	21.0[6,11]	40.7[6,11]	58.3	60.9	67.5	70.4	Brésil
British Virgin Islands	...	...	37.0	...	77.7	77.7	...	Îles Vierges britanniques
Brunei Darussalam	9.0	36.5	* 53.0	* 71.2	90.0	* 94.9	...	Brunéi Darussalam
Bulgaria	5.4	20.0[5]	46.2[5]	56.7[5]	59.8	63.4	64.8	Bulgarie
Burkina Faso	0.1	0.5	* 2.4	14.0[1,12]	* 14.0	16.0[1,12]	...	Burkina Faso
Burundi	0.1	0.5	* 1.0	* 4.9	* 5.2	2.7	...	Burundi
Cabo Verde	1.8	6.1	* 30.0	42.7	50.3[11]	57.2[11]	...	Cabo Verde
Cambodia	~0.0	0.3	1.3	6.4	32.4	32.4	40.0	Cambodge
Cameroon	0.3	1.4	* 4.3	* 20.7	* 23.2	23.2	...	Cameroun
Canada	51.3	71.7[8]	80.3[8]	90.0[1]	91.2	91.0[1]	...	Canada
Cayman Islands	...	38.0	* 66.0	* 77.0	* 79.0	* 81.1	...	Îles Caïmanes
Central African Republic	0.1	* 0.3	* 2.0	* 3.8	* 4.0	* 4.3	...	République centrafricaine
Chad	~0.0	0.4	* 1.7	* 3.5	* 5.0	* 6.5	...	Tchad

Country or area	2000	2005	2010	2015	2016	2017	2018	Pays ou zone
Chile	16.6[10]	* 31.2[10]	* 45.0[10]	76.6	83.6[2]	82.3[2]	...	Chili
China [13]	1.8	8.5	34.3	* 50.3[14,15,16]	53.2	54.3	...	Chine [13]
China, Hong Kong SAR	27.8[9,11]	56.9[11]	72.0[11]	84.9[11]	87.5	89.4[9,11]	90.5	Chine, RAS de Hong Kong
China, Macao SAR	* 13.6	* 34.9	55.2[17]	77.6[17]	81.6[6,17]	83.2[6,17]	83.8	Chine, RAS de Macao
Colombia	2.2	11.0	36.5[10]	55.9[10]	58.1	62.3[10]	64.1	Colombie
Comoros	0.3	* 2.0	* 5.1	* 7.5	* 7.9	* 8.5	...	Comores
Congo	~0.0	* 1.5	* 5.0	* 7.6	* 8.1	* 8.7	...	Congo
Costa Rica	5.8	22.1[10]	36.5[6,10]	59.8[6,10]	65.9	71.4	74.1	Costa Rica
Côte d'Ivoire	0.2	1.0	* 2.7	38.4	41.2	43.8	46.8	Côte d'Ivoire
Croatia	6.6	33.1[5]	56.6[5]	69.8[5]	72.7[6]	67.1[6]	75.3	Croatie
Cuba	0.5[18]	9.7[19]	15.9[19]	37.3[14]	43.0	57.1	...	Cuba
Curaçao	...	...	...	...	61.9	68.1	...	Curaçao
Cyprus	15.3	32.8[5]	53.0[5]	71.7[5]	75.9	80.7	84.4	Chypre
Czechia	9.8	35.3[5]	68.8[5]	75.7[8]	76.5[8]	78.7[6]	80.7	Tchéquie
Dem. People's Rep. Korea	0.0[20]	0.0[20]	* 0.0	...	...	...	...	Rép. pop. dém. de Corée
Dem. Rep. of the Congo	* ~0.0	* 0.2	* 0.7	* 3.8	* 6.2	* 8.6	...	Rép. dém. du Congo
Denmark	39.2[21]	82.7[5]	88.7[5]	96.3[5]	97.0[6]	97.1[6]	97.3	Danemark
Djibouti	0.2	1.0	* 6.5	* 11.9	* 13.1	55.7	...	Djibouti
Dominica	8.8	* 38.5	47.5	* 65.0	* 67.0	* 69.6	...	Dominique
Dominican Republic	3.7	11.5	* 31.4	54.2[22]	63.9[9]	67.6	74.8	République dominicaine
Ecuador	1.5	* 6.0	29.0[10]	48.9[10]	54.1[10]	57.3[10]	...	Équateur
Egypt	* 0.6	12.8	21.6[14]	37.8[14]	41.2	45.0	46.9	Égypte
El Salvador	1.2	* 4.2[11]	15.9[11]	26.8	* 29.0	33.8	...	El Salvador
Equatorial Guinea	0.1	1.1	6.0	* 21.3	* 23.8	* 26.2	...	Guinée équatoriale
Eritrea	0.1	...	* 0.6	* 1.1	* 1.2	* 1.3	...	Érythrée
Estonia	28.6	61.5[5]	74.1[5,6]	88.4	87.2	88.1	89.4	Estonie
Eswatini	0.9	* 3.7	11.0	* 25.6	* 28.6	47.0[1,12]	...	Eswatini
Ethiopia	~0.0	0.2	* 0.8	13.9	15.4	* 18.6	...	Éthiopie
Falkland Islands (Malvinas)	58.6	* 84.0	95.8	* 98.3	* 99.0	...	...	Îles Falkland (Malvinas)
Faroe Islands	32.9	* 67.9	75.2	* 94.2	* 95.1	* 97.6	...	Îles Féroé
Fiji	1.5	8.5	* 20.0	* 42.5	* 46.5	* 50.0	...	Fidji
Finland	37.2[2,6]	74.5[5]	86.9[5]	86.4[23]	87.7[23]	87.5	88.9	Finlande
France	14.3[2,9]	42.9[24,25]	77.3[5]	# 78.0[2]	79.3[2,6]	80.5[2,6]	82.0	France
French Polynesia	6.4	21.5	49.0	* 64.6	* 68.4	* 72.7	...	Polynésie française
Gabon	1.2	4.9	* 13.0	* 45.8	* 48.1	62.0[1,12]	...	Gabon
Gambia	0.9	* 3.8	9.2	* 16.5	* 18.5	* 19.8	...	Gambie
Georgia	0.5	* 6.1	26.9	# 47.6[6,14]	58.5[6,14]	59.7[6,14]	62.7	Géorgie
Germany	30.2	68.7[5]	82.0[5]	87.6[6]	84.2[6]	84.4	89.7	Allemagne
Ghana	0.2	1.8	# 7.8[22]	25.0[1]	* 34.7	39.0[1]	...	Ghana
Gibraltar	19.1	* 39.1	65.0	...	* 94.4	...	...	Gibraltar
Greece	9.1	24.0[5]	44.4[5]	66.8[5]	69.1	70.5	73.0	Grèce
Greenland	31.7	57.7	63.0	* 67.6	* 68.5	* 69.5	...	Groenland
Grenada	4.1	* 20.5	* 27.0	* 53.8	* 55.9	* 59.1	...	Grenade
Guam	16.1	38.6	* 54.0	* 73.1	* 77.0	* 80.5	...	Guam
Guatemala	0.7	5.7	* 10.5	* 28.8	* 34.5	65.0[26]	...	Guatemala
Guernsey	31.9	73.6	...	...	...	...	...	Guernesey
Guinea	0.1	0.5	* 1.0	* 8.2	* 9.8	18.0[1,12]	...	Guinée
Guinea-Bissau	0.2	1.9	* 2.5	* 3.5	* 3.8	* 3.9	...	Guinée-Bissau
Guyana	6.6	...	29.9	* 34.0	* 35.7	37.3	...	Guyana
Haiti	0.2	* 6.4	* 8.4	* 12.2	* 12.2	* 12.3	32.5	Haïti
Honduras	1.2	6.5[10]	11.1	27.1[6]	29.5[6]	31.7[6]	...	Honduras
Hungary	7.0	39.0[5]	65.0[5]	72.8[5]	79.3[6]	76.8[6]	76.1	Hongrie
Iceland	44.5	87.0[5]	93.4[5,6]	* 98.2	* 98.2	98.3	99.0	Islande
India	0.5	* 2.4	* 7.5	17.0[1]	22.0[1]	34.5	...	Inde
Indonesia	0.9	3.6	10.9	22.0[10]	25.4	32.3	39.9	Indonésie
Iran (Islamic Republic of)	0.9	* 8.1	15.9[14]	* 45.3	53.2[14]	* 64.0[14]	70.0	Iran (Rép. islamique d')
Iraq	...	* 0.9	2.5	58.0[2,27]	* 21.2	49.4	75.0	Iraq
Ireland	17.9[2]	41.6[5]	69.9[5]	83.5[5,6]	* 85.0	84.1	84.5	Irlande
Israel	20.9	25.2	67.5[28]	77.4[28]	79.7	81.6	83.7	Israël
Italy	23.1	35.0[5]	53.7[5]	58.1[14]	* 61.3	63.1	74.4	Italie
Jamaica	3.1	* 12.8	27.7[4]	* 42.2	44.4	* 55.1	...	Jamaïque
Japan	30.0[29]	66.9[14]	78.2[14]	91.1	93.2[9,30]	84.6	91.3	Japon
Jersey	9.2	31.3	...	...	...	...	...	Jersey

Country or area	2000	2005	2010	2015	2016	2017	2018	Pays ou zone
Jordan	2.6	12.9	27.2[10]	* 60.1	* 62.3	* 66.8	...	Jordanie
Kazakhstan	0.7	3.0	31.6[5]	70.8[31]	74.6	76.4	78.9	Kazakhstan
Kenya	0.3	3.1	7.2	16.6	16.6	* 17.8	...	Kenya
Kiribati	* 1.8	* 4.0	9.1	* 13.0	* 13.7	14.6	...	Kiribati
Kuwait	6.7	25.9	* 61.4	* 72.0	* 78.4	100.0	99.6	Koweït
Kyrgyzstan	1.0	10.5	* 16.3	* 30.2	37.0[1]	38.0[1]	...	Kirghizistan
Lao People's Dem. Rep.	0.1	0.9	7.0	* 18.2	* 21.9	* 25.5	...	Rép. dém. populaire lao
Latvia	6.3	46.0[5]	68.4[5]	79.2[5]	79.8[6]	80.1[6]	83.6	Lettonie
Lebanon	8.0	10.1[14]	* 43.7[2]	* 74.0	* 76.1	* 78.2	...	Liban
Lesotho	0.2	* 2.6	* 3.9	* 25.0	27.4	29.0[1,12]	...	Lesotho
Liberia	~0.0	...	2.3	33.0[1,25]	* 7.3	* 8.0	...	Libéria
Libya	0.2	* 3.9	* 14.0	* 19.0	* 20.3	* 21.8	...	Libye
Liechtenstein	36.5	63.4	* 80.0	* 96.6	* 98.1	* 98.1	...	Liechtenstein
Lithuania	6.4	36.2[5,9]	62.1[5,9]	71.4[5]	74.4[5]	77.6[5]	79.7	Lituanie
Luxembourg	22.9	70.0[5]	90.6[5]	96.4	* 98.1	97.4	97.1	Luxembourg
Madagascar	0.2	* 0.6	* 1.7	* 4.2	* 4.7	9.8	...	Madagascar
Malawi	0.1	0.4	2.3	* 5.3	11.5	* 13.8	...	Malawi
Malaysia	21.4	48.6	56.3	71.1[2]	78.8	80.1	81.2	Malaisie
Maldives	* 2.2[32]	* 6.9	26.5[2]	* 54.5	* 59.1	* 63.2	...	Maldives
Mali	0.1	0.5	* 2.0	* 10.3	11.1	13.0[1,12]	...	Mali
Malta	13.1	41.2[5]	63.0[5]	76.0[6]	78.1[6]	81.0[6]	81.7	Malte
Marshall Islands	1.5	3.9	* 7.0	* 19.3	* 29.8	* 38.7	...	Îles Marshall
Mauritania	0.2	0.7	* 4.0	* 15.2	* 18.0	* 20.8	...	Mauritanie
Mauritius	7.3	* 15.2	28.3[10]	50.1[10]	52.2	* 55.4	58.6	Maurice
Mayotte	1.2	...	...	...	...	...	...	Mayotte
Mexico	5.1	* 17.2	* 31.1	# 57.4[14]	59.5[14,33]	63.9[14,34]	65.8	Mexique
Micronesia (Fed. States of)	3.7	11.9	* 20.0	* 31.5	* 33.4	* 35.3	...	Micronésie (États féd. de)
Monaco	42.2	55.5	75.0	* 93.4	* 95.2	* 97.1	...	Monaco
Mongolia	1.3	...	10.2	22.5	22.3	* 23.7	47.2	Mongolie
Montenegro	...	* 27.1	* 37.5	68.1[5]	69.9	71.3	71.5	Monténégro
Montserrat	...	...	35.0	...	...	...	...	Montserrat
Morocco	0.7	15.1[25,35]	52.0[31,36]	57.1[6,10]	58.3	61.8	64.8	Maroc
Mozambique	0.1	* 0.9	4.2	* 16.9	* 17.5	10.0[26]	...	Mozambique
Myanmar	...	0.1	0.3	* 21.7	* 25.1	* 30.7	...	Myanmar
Namibia	1.6	* 4.0	11.6	* 25.7	* 31.0	51.0[1,12]	...	Namibie
Nauru	...	...	...	...	...	* 57.0	...	Nauru
Nepal	0.2	0.8	7.9[37]	* 17.6	* 19.7	34.0	...	Népal
Netherlands	44.0	81.0[5,9]	90.7[5,9]	91.7[22]	90.4	93.2	94.7	Pays-Bas
New Caledonia	13.9	32.4	* 42.0	* 74.0	...	* 82.0	...	Nouvelle-Calédonie
New Zealand	* 47.4	* 62.7	* 80.5	* 88.2	* 88.5	* 90.8	...	Nouvelle-Zélande
Nicaragua	1.0	2.6	* 10.0	* 19.7	* 24.6	* 27.9	...	Nicaragua
Niger	~0.0	* 0.2	* 0.8	* 2.5	* 4.3	10.2	5.3	Niger
Nigeria	0.1	* 3.5	* 11.5	36.0[1]	* 25.7	42.0[1]	...	Nigéria
Niue	26.5	51.7	* 77.0	...	...	...	...	Nioué
North Macedonia	2.5	* 26.5[5]	51.9[38]	70.4[5]	72.2[6]	74.5	79.2	Macédoine du Nord
Norway	* 52.0	82.0[5]	93.4[5]	96.8[5]	97.3[6]	96.4[6]	96.5	Norvège
Oman	* 3.5	6.7	35.8[10]	* 73.5	76.8	* 80.2	...	Oman
Other non-specified areas	28.1	58.0	71.5	78.0[22]	79.7	92.8	86.2	Autres zones non-spécifiées
Pakistan	...	6.3	* 8.0	* 14.0	12.4	15.5	...	Pakistan
Panama	6.6	11.5	40.1[39]	51.2[11]	* 54.0	* 57.9	...	Panama
Papua New Guinea	0.8	1.7	1.3[11]	* 7.9	* 9.6	* 11.2	...	Papouasie-Nvl-Guinée
Paraguay	0.7	7.9[6,11]	19.8[6,11]	49.7[11]	53.4	61.1	65.0	Paraguay
Peru	* 3.1	* 17.1	34.8[14]	40.9	45.5	48.7[25]	52.5	Pérou
Philippines	2.0	* 5.4	25.0	36.0[1]	* 55.5	* 60.1	...	Philippines
Poland	7.3	38.8[5]	62.3[5]	68.0[5,6]	73.3	76.0[5,6]	77.5	Pologne
Portugal	* 16.4	35.0[5]	53.3[5]	68.6[5]	70.4	73.8	74.7	Portugal
Puerto Rico	10.5	* 23.4	45.3[22]	63.5	68.6[6]	* 70.6	...	Porto Rico
Qatar	4.9	24.7	69.0	92.9[2]	95.1	97.4	99.7	Qatar
Republic of Korea	44.7[17,25]	73.5[17]	83.7[17]	89.9[5]	92.8[5]	95.1[5]	96.0	République de Corée
Republic of Moldova	1.3	14.6	* 32.3	69.0	71.0[9,40]	* 76.1	...	République de Moldova
Romania	3.6	* 21.5[5]	39.9[5]	55.8[5]	59.5[6]	63.7[6]	70.7	Roumanie
Russian Federation	2.0	15.2	43.0[5]	70.1[6,41]	73.1[9,41]	76.0[6,38]	80.9	Fédération de Russie
Rwanda	0.1	* 0.6	8.0	* 18.0	* 20.0	* 21.8	...	Rwanda

Country or area	2000	2005	2010	2015	2016	2017	2018	Pays ou zone
Saint Helena	5.9	15.9	24.9	...	...	...	...	Sainte-Hélène
Ascension	34.9	...	35.0	...	...	...	...	Ascension
Saint Kitts and Nevis	5.9	* 34.0	63.0	* 75.7	* 76.8	* 80.7	...	Saint-Kitts-et-Nevis
Saint Lucia	5.1	21.6	* 32.5	* 42.5	* 46.7	* 50.8	...	Sainte-Lucie
Saint Vincent & Grenadines	* 3.2	* 9.2	* 33.7	17.1	20.7	22.0	22.4	Saint-Vincent-Grenadines
Samoa	0.6	3.4	* 7.0	* 25.4	* 29.4	* 33.6	...	Samoa
San Marino	48.8	50.3	...	...	...	* 60.2	...	Saint-Marin
Sao Tome and Principe	4.6	* 13.8	18.8	* 25.8	* 28.0	* 29.9	...	Sao Tomé-et-Principe
Saudi Arabia	2.2	12.7	41.0	69.6[35]	74.9	82.1	93.3	Arabie saoudite
Senegal	0.4	4.8	* 8.0[22]	27.0[1]	25.7[1]	46.0[1]	...	Sénégal
Serbia	...	* 26.3[5]	40.9	65.3[5]	67.1	70.3	73.4	Serbie
Seychelles	* 7.4	25.4	* 41.0	* 54.3	* 56.5	* 58.8	...	Seychelles
Sierra Leone	0.1	0.2	* 0.6	* 6.3	* 11.8	9.0[6]	...	Sierra Leone
Singapore	36.0	61.0[2]	* 71.0[7]	79.0	84.5	84.4	88.2	Singapour
Slovakia	9.4	55.2[5]	75.7[5,6]	77.6[5,6]	80.5[5,6]	81.6[5,6]	80.7	Slovaquie
Slovenia	15.1	46.8[6]	70.0[5]	73.1[5]	75.5[5,6]	78.9[5,6]	79.8	Slovénie
Solomon Islands	0.5	0.8	* 5.0	* 10.0	* 11.0	* 11.9	...	Îles Salomon
Somalia	~0.0	* 1.1	...	* 1.8	* 1.9	* 2.0	...	Somalie
South Africa	5.3	7.5	* 24.0	* 51.9	* 54.0	* 56.2	...	Afrique du Sud
South Sudan	...	...	...	5.5	6.7	8.0	...	Soudan du sud
Spain	13.6[4,42]	47.9[5,9]	65.8[11]	78.7[5]	80.6	84.6[6]	86.1	Espagne
Sri Lanka	0.6	* 1.8	12.0	12.1	16.4	* 34.1	...	Sri Lanka
State of Palestine	1.1	* 16.0[11]	* 37.4	* 57.4	* 61.2	* 65.2	64.4	État de Palestine
Sudan	~0.0	1.3	* 16.7	* 26.6	14.1	* 30.9	...	Soudan
Suriname	2.5	6.4	31.6	* 42.8	* 45.4	* 48.9	...	Suriname
Sweden	45.7	84.8[5]	90.0[43]	90.6[5]	89.7	95.5	92.1	Suède
Switzerland	47.1[4,16]	70.1[4,16]	83.9[4,16]	87.5[4,16]	89.1	89.7	...	Suisse
Syrian Arab Republic	0.2	* 5.6	20.7	* 30.0	* 31.9	* 34.3	...	République arabe syrienne
Tajikistan	~0.0	0.3	* 11.6	* 19.0	* 20.5	* 22.0	...	Tadjikistan
Thailand	3.7	15.0	22.4	39.3[14]	47.5[14]	52.9[14]	56.8	Thaïlande
Timor-Leste	...	0.1	* 3.0	* 23.0	* 25.2	* 27.5	...	Timor-Leste
Togo	* 0.8	* 1.8	* 3.0	* 7.1	* 11.3	12.4	...	Togo
Tonga	2.4	* 4.9	* 16.0	* 38.7	* 40.0	* 41.2	...	Tonga
Trinidad and Tobago	7.7	* 29.0	* 48.5	* 69.2	* 73.3	* 77.3	...	Trinité-et-Tobago
Tunisia	2.8	9.7	36.8	46.5	49.6	64.2	64.2	Tunisie
Turkey	3.8[5]	15.5[5,9]	39.8[5,9]	53.7[5]	58.3[6]	64.7[6]	71.0	Turquie
Turkmenistan	0.1	* 1.0	* 3.0	* 15.0	* 18.0	* 21.3	...	Turkménistan
Tuvalu	5.2	...	* 25.0	* 42.7	* 46.0	* 49.3	...	Tuvalu
Uganda	0.2	1.7	12.5	* 17.8	* 21.9	* 23.7	...	Ouganda
Ukraine	0.7	* 3.7[25,44]	23.3	48.9	53.0	58.9	62.6	Ukraine
United Arab Emirates	23.6	* 40.0	68.0	* 90.5	90.6[6]	* 94.8[6,38]	98.5	Émirats arabes unis
United Kingdom	26.8[6,8]	70.0[5]	85.0[5]	92.0[5]	94.8[6]	* 94.6	94.9	Royaume-Uni
United Rep. of Tanzania	0.1	* 1.1	* 2.9	20.0[1]	* 13.0	25.0[1]	...	Rép.-Unie de Tanzanie
United States of America	* 43.1	* 68.0	71.7[17]	74.6[17]	85.5	87.3	...	États-Unis d'Amérique
United States Virgin Islands	13.8	* 27.3	* 31.2	* 54.8	* 59.6	* 64.4	...	Îles Vierges américaines
Uruguay	10.5	20.1	46.4[14]	64.6	66.4	* 68.3	74.8	Uruguay
Uzbekistan	0.5	3.3	* 15.9	* 42.8	* 46.8	* 52.3	55.2	Ouzbékistan
Vanuatu	2.1	5.1	8.0	* 22.4	* 24.0	* 25.7	...	Vanuatu
Venezuela (Boliv. Rep. of)	3.4	12.6	* 37.4	* 64.0	* 60.0	72.0	...	Venezuela (Rép. boliv. du)
Viet Nam	0.3	12.7	30.7	45.0[1]	53.0[1]	58.1	70.3	Viet Nam
Wallis and Futuna Islands	4.8	6.7	8.2	...	...	...	...	Îles Wallis-et-Futuna
Yemen	0.1	* 1.0	12.4	* 24.1	* 24.6	* 26.7	...	Yémen
Zambia	0.2	* 2.9	10.0	* 21.0	* 25.5	* 27.9	14.3	Zambie
Zimbabwe	* 0.4	* 2.4	* 6.4	* 22.7	* 23.1	* 27.1	...	Zimbabwe

Source:

International Telecommunication Union (ITU), Geneva, the ITU database, last accessed January 2020.

Source:

Union internationale des télécommunications (UIT), Genève, la base de données de l'UIT, dernier accès janvier 2020.

1	Population aged 18 years and over.
2	Population aged 15 years and over.
3	Accessed the internet for personal use in a typical week.
4	Population aged 14 years and over.
5	Population aged 16 to 74 years.
6	Users in the last 3 months.
7	Population aged 7 years and over.
8	Population aged 16 years and over.
9	Users in the last 12 months.
10	Population aged 5 years and over.
11	Population aged 10 years and over.
12	At least once a month.
13	For statistical purposes, the data for China do not include those for the Hong Kong Special Administrative Region (Hong Kong SAR), Macao Special Administrative Region (Macao SAR) and Taiwan Province of China.
14	Population aged 6 years and over.
15	Data refer to permanent residents.
16	Users in the last 6 months.
17	Population aged 3 years and over.
18	Refers only to users with access to the international network.
19	Including users of the international network and also those having access only to the Cuban network.
20	Commercially not available. Local Intranet available in country.
21	E-mail users.
22	Population aged 12 years and over.
23	Population aged 16 to 89 years.
24	Population aged 11 years and over.
25	Users in the last month.
26	Population aged 15 to 65 years.
27	Last week.
28	Population aged 20 years and over.
29	PC-based only.
30	Estimated by the following method: (The estimation population of more than 6 years old)×(Survey result(%)).
31	Population aged 6 to 74 years.
32	Mobile internet users are not included.
33	Data referring to the month of May 2016.
34	Data referring to the month of May 2017.
35	Population aged 12 to 65 years.
36	Living in electrified areas.
37	Data as at the end of December.
38	Population aged 15 to 74 years.
39	Multipliers were applied to residential and commercial subscriptions, taking into account the average size of households and employees per business.
40	At least once a day.
41	Population aged 15 to 72 years.
42	November.
43	Population aged 16 to 75 years.
44	Population aged 15 to 59 years.

1	Population âgée de 18 ans et plus.
2	Population âgée de 15 ans et plus.
3	Accès à Internet pour un usage personnel au cours d'une semaine typique.
4	Population âgée de 14 ans et plus.
5	Population âgée de 16 à 74 ans.
6	Utilisateurs au cours des 3 derniers mois.
7	Population âgée de 7 ans et plus.
8	Population âgée de 16 ans et plus.
9	Utilisateurs au cours des 12 derniers mois.
10	Population âgée de 5 ans et plus.
11	Population âgée de 10 ans et plus.
12	Au moins une fois par mois.
13	Pour la présentation des statistiques, les données pour la Chine ne comprennent pas la région administrative spéciale de Hong Kong (RAS de Hong Kong), la région administrative spéciale de Macao (RAS de Macao) et la province chinoise de Taïwan.
14	Population âgée de 6 ans et plus.
15	Les données concernent les résidents permanents.
16	Utilisateurs au cours des 6 derniers mois.
17	Population âgée de 3 ans et plus.
18	Uniquement utilisateurs ayant accès au réseau international.
19	Y compris les utilisateurs du réseau international et ceux qui n'ont accès qu'au réseau cubain.
20	Non disponible commercialement, seul l'intranet local est accessible dans le pays.
21	Utilisateurs du courrier électronique
22	Population âgée de 12 ans et plus.
23	Population âgée de 16 à 89 ans.
24	Population âgée de 11 ans et plus.
25	Utilisateurs au cours du mois passé.
26	Population âgée de 15 à 65 ans.
27	La semaine derniere.
28	Population âgée de 20 ans et plus.
29	Sur ordinateur PC seulement.
30	Estimation par la méthode suivante: (La population estimée de plus de 6 ans) × (Résultat de l'enquête (%)).
31	Population âgée de 6 à 74 ans.
32	Les utilisateurs de l'Internet mobile ne sont pas inclus.
33	Données se référant au mois de mai 2016.
34	Données se référant au mois de mai 2017.
35	Population âgée de 12 à 65 ans.
36	Vivant dans des zones électrifiées.
37	Données à la fin de décembre.
38	Population âgée de 15 à 74 ans.
39	Des multiplicateurs ont été appliqués aux abonnements résidentiels et commerciaux, en tenant compte de la taille moyenne des ménages et des employés par entreprise.
40	Au moins une fois par jour.
41	Population âgée de 15 à 72 ans.
42	Novembre.
43	Population âgée de 16 à 75 ans.
44	Population âgée de 15 à 59 ans.

Tourist/visitor arrivals and tourism expenditure
Thousands arrivals and millions of US dollars

Arrivées de touristes/visiteurs et dépenses touristiques
Milliers d'arrivées et millions de dollars É.-U.

Country or area of destination	Series& Série&	1995	2005	2010	2016	2017	2018	Pays ou zone de destination
Afghanistan								**Afghanistan**
Tourism expenditure		...	...	147	62	16	50	Dépenses touristiques
Albania								**Albanie**
Tourist/visitor arrivals [1]	TF	...	...	2 191	4 070	4 643	5 340	Arrivées de touristes/visiteurs [1]
Tourism expenditure		70	880	1 778	1 821	2 050	2 306	Dépenses touristiques
Algeria								**Algérie**
Tourist/visitor arrivals [2]	VF	520	1 443	2 070	2 039	2 451	2 657	Arrivées de touristes/visiteurs [2]
Tourism expenditure		...	477	324	246	172	...	Dépenses touristiques
American Samoa								**Samoa américaines**
Tourist/visitor arrivals	TF	34	25	23	20	20	20	Arrivées de touristes/visiteurs
Tourism expenditure [3]		...	...	...	22	22	...	Dépenses touristiques [3]
Andorra								**Andorre**
Tourist/visitor arrivals	TF	...	2 418	# 1 808	2 819	3 003	3 042	Arrivées de touristes/visiteurs
Angola								**Angola**
Tourist/visitor arrivals	TF	9	210	425	397	261	218	Arrivées de touristes/visiteurs
Tourism expenditure		27	103	726	628	884	557	Dépenses touristiques
Anguilla								**Anguilla**
Tourist/visitor arrivals [1]	TF	39	62	62	79	68	55	Arrivées de touristes/visiteurs [1]
Tourism expenditure [3]		50	86	99	136	141	102	Dépenses touristiques [3]
Antigua and Barbuda								**Antigua-et-Barbuda**
Tourist/visitor arrivals [1]	TF	220	245[4]	230[4]	265[4]	247[4]	269[4]	Arrivées de touristes/visiteurs [1]
Tourism expenditure [3]		247	309	298	753	737	881	Dépenses touristiques [3]
Argentina								**Argentine**
Tourist/visitor arrivals	TF	2 289	3 823	# 6 800	# 6 668	6 711	6 942	Arrivées de touristes/visiteurs
Tourism expenditure		2 550	3 209	5 605	5 466	5 835	5 999	Dépenses touristiques
Armenia								**Arménie**
Tourist/visitor arrivals	TF	12	319	684	1 260	1 495	1 652	Arrivées de touristes/visiteurs
Tourism expenditure		14	243	694	988	1 140	1 237	Dépenses touristiques
Aruba								**Aruba**
Tourist/visitor arrivals [4]	TF	619	733	824	1 102	1 071	1 082	Arrivées de touristes/visiteurs [4]
Tourism expenditure		554	1 097	1 254	1 764	1 857	2 024	Dépenses touristiques
Australia								**Australie**
Tourist/visitor arrivals [5]	VF	3 726	5 499	5 790	8 269	8 815	9 246	Arrivées de touristes/visiteurs [5]
Tourism expenditure		10 370	19 719	31 064	39 059	43 975	47 327	Dépenses touristiques
Austria								**Autriche**
Tourist/visitor arrivals [6]	TCE	17 173	19 952	22 004	28 121	29 460	30 816	Arrivées de touristes/visiteurs [6]
Tourism expenditure [3]		13 435	16 243	18 751	19 244	20 333	23 233	Dépenses touristiques [3]
Azerbaijan								**Azerbaïdjan**
Tourist/visitor arrivals	TF	...	693	1 280	2 044	2 454	2 633	Arrivées de touristes/visiteurs
Tourism expenditure		87	100	792	2 855	3 214	2 830	Dépenses touristiques
Bahamas								**Bahamas**
Tourist/visitor arrivals	TF	1 598	1 608	1 370	1 500	1 442	1 633	Arrivées de touristes/visiteurs
Tourism expenditure		1 356	2 081	2 159	3 091	3 017	3 383	Dépenses touristiques
Bahrain								**Bahreïn**
Tourist/visitor arrivals [1]	VF	2 311	6 313	11 952	# 10 158	11 374	12 045	Arrivées de touristes/visiteurs [1]
Tourism expenditure		593	1 603	2 163	4 021	4 380	3 834	Dépenses touristiques
Bangladesh								**Bangladesh**
Tourist/visitor arrivals	TF	156	208	303	830	1 026	...	Arrivées de touristes/visiteurs
Tourism expenditure		...	82	103	214	348	357	Dépenses touristiques
Barbados								**Barbade**
Tourist/visitor arrivals	TF	442	548	532	632	664	680	Arrivées de touristes/visiteurs
Tourism expenditure		630	1 081	1 074	...	...	...	Dépenses touristiques
Belarus								**Bélarus**
Tourist/visitor arrivals	TF	161[7]	91[7]	119[7]	10 935[8]	11 060[8]	11 502[8]	Arrivées de touristes/visiteurs
Tourism expenditure		28	346	665	1 019	1 124	1 221	Dépenses touristiques
Belgium								**Belgique**
Tourist/visitor arrivals	TCE	5 560	6 747	7 186	# 7 481	8 385	9 119	Arrivées de touristes/visiteurs
Tourism expenditure		...	10 881	12 680	8 784	9 636	10 381	Dépenses touristiques
Belize								**Belize**
Tourist/visitor arrivals	TF	131	237	242	386	427	489	Arrivées de touristes/visiteurs
Tourism expenditure [3]		78	214	264	391	427	487	Dépenses touristiques [3]
Benin								**Bénin**
Tourist/visitor arrivals	TF	138	176	199	267	281	295	Arrivées de touristes/visiteurs
Tourism expenditure		...	108	149	129	160	...	Dépenses touristiques

30 Tourist/visitor arrivals and tourism expenditure *(continued)*
Thousands arrivals and millions of US dollars

Arrivées de touristes/visiteurs et dépenses touristiques *(suite)*
Milliers d'arrivées et millions de dollars É.-U.

Country or area of destination	Series& Série&	1995	2005	2010	2016	2017	2018	Pays ou zone de destination
Bermuda								**Bermudes**
Tourist/visitor arrivals [1,4]	TF	387	270	232	244	270	282	Arrivées de touristes/visiteurs [1,4]
Tourism expenditure		488[3]	429[3]	442[3]	441	513	583	Dépenses touristiques
Bhutan								**Bhoutan**
Tourist/visitor arrivals	TF	5	14	# 41[9]	210	255	274	Arrivées de touristes/visiteurs
Tourism expenditure		5	19	64	139	153	121	Dépenses touristiques
Bolivia (Plurin. State of)								**Bolivie (État plurin. de)**
Tourist/visitor arrivals	TF	284	524	679	961	1 109	1 142	Arrivées de touristes/visiteurs
Tourism expenditure		92	345	339	827	912	970	Dépenses touristiques
Bonaire								**Bonaire**
Tourist/visitor arrivals	TF	59	63	71	...	...	...	Arrivées de touristes/visiteurs
Tourism expenditure [3]		37	87	...	...	...	...	Dépenses touristiques [3]
Bosnia and Herzegovina								**Bosnie-Herzégovine**
Tourist/visitor arrivals	TCE	...	217	365	778	923	1 053	Arrivées de touristes/visiteurs
Tourism expenditure		...	557	662	876	985	1 081	Dépenses touristiques
Botswana								**Botswana**
Tourist/visitor arrivals	TF	521	1 474	1 973	1 574	1 623	...	Arrivées de touristes/visiteurs
Tourism expenditure		176	563	440	505	542	575	Dépenses touristiques
Brazil								**Brésil**
Tourist/visitor arrivals [2]	TF	1 991	5 358	5 161	6 547	6 589	6 621	Arrivées de touristes/visiteurs [2]
Tourism expenditure		1 085	4 168	5 522	6 613	6 175	6 324	Dépenses touristiques
British Virgin Islands								**Îles Vierges britanniques**
Tourist/visitor arrivals	TF	219	337	330	408	335	192	Arrivées de touristes/visiteurs
Tourism expenditure		211	412	389	...	...	...	Dépenses touristiques
Brunei Darussalam								**Brunéi Darussalam**
Tourist/visitor arrivals [4]	TF	...	126	214	219	259	278	Arrivées de touristes/visiteurs [4]
Tourism expenditure [3]		...	191	...	144	177	190	Dépenses touristiques [3]
Bulgaria								**Bulgarie**
Tourist/visitor arrivals	TF	3 466	4 837	6 047	8 252	8 883	9 273	Arrivées de touristes/visiteurs
Tourism expenditure		662	3 063	3 807	4 164	4 678	5 072	Dépenses touristiques
Burkina Faso								**Burkina Faso**
Tourist/visitor arrivals	THS	124	245	274	152	143	144	Arrivées de touristes/visiteurs
Tourism expenditure		...	46	105	172	172	...	Dépenses touristiques
Burundi								**Burundi**
Tourist/visitor arrivals [2]	TF	34	148	# 142	187	299	...	Arrivées de touristes/visiteurs [2]
Tourism expenditure		2	2	2	...	...	...	Dépenses touristiques
Cabo Verde								**Cabo Verde**
Tourist/visitor arrivals	TF	28[4]	198[10]	336[10]	598[10]	668[10]	710[10]	Arrivées de touristes/visiteurs
Tourism expenditure		29	177	387	397	450	524	Dépenses touristiques
Cambodia								**Cambodge**
Tourist/visitor arrivals	TF	220[4]	1 422[11]	2 508[11]	5 012[11]	5 602[11]	6 201[11]	Arrivées de touristes/visiteurs
Tourism expenditure		71	929	1 671	3 523	4 024	4 832	Dépenses touristiques
Cameroon								**Cameroun**
Tourist/visitor arrivals	VF	...	...	573	994	1 081	...	Arrivées de touristes/visiteurs
Tourism expenditure		75	229	171	508	543	633	Dépenses touristiques
Canada								**Canada**
Tourist/visitor arrivals	TF	16 932	18 771	16 219	19 971	20 883	21 134	Arrivées de touristes/visiteurs
Tourism expenditure		9 176	15 887	18 439	...	...	...	Dépenses touristiques
Cayman Islands								**Îles Caïmanes**
Tourist/visitor arrivals [4]	TF	361	168	288	385	418	463	Arrivées de touristes/visiteurs [4]
Tourism expenditure		394	356	465	696	782	880	Dépenses touristiques
Central African Republic [12]								**République centrafricaine [12]**
Tourist/visitor arrivals	TF	26	12	54	82	107	...	Arrivées de touristes/visiteurs
Tourism expenditure		4	7	14	...	...	...	Dépenses touristiques
Chad								**Tchad**
Tourist/visitor arrivals [4]	TF	...	...	71	98	87	...	Arrivées de touristes/visiteurs [4]
Tourism expenditure		43	...	...	...	...	...	Dépenses touristiques
Chile								**Chili**
Tourist/visitor arrivals	TF	1 540	2 027	2 801[2]	5 641[2]	6 450[2]	5 723[2]	Arrivées de touristes/visiteurs
Tourism expenditure		1 186	1 608	2 362	3 744	4 372	3 972	Dépenses touristiques
China [13]								**Chine [13]**
Tourist/visitor arrivals	TF	20 034	46 809	55 664	59 270	60 740	62 900	Arrivées de touristes/visiteurs
Tourism expenditure [3]		8 730	29 296	45 814	44 432	38 559	40 386	Dépenses touristiques [3]

30

Tourist/visitor arrivals and tourism expenditure *(continued)*
Thousands arrivals and millions of US dollars

Arrivées de touristes/visiteurs et dépenses touristiques *(suite)*
Milliers d'arrivées et millions de dollars É.-U.

Country or area of destination	Series& Série&	1995	2005	2010	2016	2017	2018	Pays ou zone de destination
China, Hong Kong SAR								**Chine, RAS de Hong Kong**
Tourist/visitor arrivals	TF	...	14 773	20 085	26 553	27 884	29 263	Arrivées de touristes/visiteurs
Tourism expenditure		...	13 588	27 208	37 838	38 170	41 870	Dépenses touristiques
China, Macao SAR								**Chine, RAS de Macao**
Tourist/visitor arrivals	TF	4 202	9 014	11 926[14]	15 704[14]	17 255[14]	18 493[14]	Arrivées de touristes/visiteurs
Tourism expenditure		3 233	7 181	22 688	31 015	36 465	40 358	Dépenses touristiques
Colombia								**Colombie**
Tourist/visitor arrivals	TF	1 399	933	1 405	3 254	3 631	3 904	Arrivées de touristes/visiteurs
Tourism expenditure		887	1 891	3 441	5 584	5 882	6 617	Dépenses touristiques
Comoros								**Comores**
Tourist/visitor arrivals [4]	TF	23	26	15	27	28	36	Arrivées de touristes/visiteurs [4]
Tourism expenditure		22	24	35	51	61	77	Dépenses touristiques
Congo								**Congo**
Tourist/visitor arrivals [2]	TF	...	35	194	211	149	156	Arrivées de touristes/visiteurs [2]
Tourism expenditure		15	...	39	43	...	...	Dépenses touristiques
Cook Islands								**Îles Cook**
Tourist/visitor arrivals	TF	48	88	104	146	161	169	Arrivées de touristes/visiteurs
Tourism expenditure		28	91	111	137	153	...	Dépenses touristiques
Costa Rica								**Costa Rica**
Tourist/visitor arrivals	TF	785	1 679	2 100	2 925	2 960	3 017	Arrivées de touristes/visiteurs
Tourism expenditure		763	2 008	2 426	3 776	3 826	3 995	Dépenses touristiques
Côte d'Ivoire								**Côte d'Ivoire**
Tourist/visitor arrivals [15]	VF	...	...	252	1 583	1 800	1 965	Arrivées de touristes/visiteurs [15]
Tourism expenditure		103	93	213	477	508	...	Dépenses touristiques
Croatia								**Croatie**
Tourist/visitor arrivals	TCE	1 485	# 7 743	9 111[16]	13 809[16]	15 593[16]	16 645[16]	Arrivées de touristes/visiteurs
Tourism expenditure		...	7 625	8 299	9 820	11 128	12 075	Dépenses touristiques
Cuba								**Cuba**
Tourist/visitor arrivals [4]	TF	742	2 261	2 507	3 975	4 594	4 684	Arrivées de touristes/visiteurs [4]
Tourism expenditure		1 100	2 591	2 396	3 069	3 302	2 969	Dépenses touristiques
Curaçao								**Curaçao**
Tourist/visitor arrivals [4]	TF	224	222	342	441	399	432	Arrivées de touristes/visiteurs [4]
Tourism expenditure		175	244	438	644	572	605	Dépenses touristiques
Cyprus								**Chypre**
Tourist/visitor arrivals	TF	2 100	2 470	2 173	3 187	3 652	3 939	Arrivées de touristes/visiteurs
Tourism expenditure		2 018	2 644	2 137	2 870	3 274	3 449	Dépenses touristiques
Czechia								**Tchéquie**
Tourist/visitor arrivals	TF	...	9 404	8 629	12 808	13 665	...	Arrivées de touristes/visiteurs
Tourism expenditure		...	5 772	8 068	7 041	7 695	8 291	Dépenses touristiques
Dem. Rep. of the Congo								**Rép. dém. du Congo**
Tourist/visitor arrivals	TF	35	61	81[4]	351	...	...	Arrivées de touristes/visiteurs
Tourism expenditure [3]		...	3	11	4	6	61	Dépenses touristiques [3]
Denmark								**Danemark**
Tourist/visitor arrivals	TCE	...	# 9 587	9 425	10 781	# 12 426	12 749	Arrivées de touristes/visiteurs
Tourism expenditure [3]		3 691	5 293	5 704	7 494	8 508	9 097	Dépenses touristiques [3]
Djibouti								**Djibouti**
Tourist/visitor arrivals	THS	21	30	51	...	...	...	Arrivées de touristes/visiteurs
Tourism expenditure [3]		5	7	18	34	36	57	Dépenses touristiques [3]
Dominica								**Dominique**
Tourist/visitor arrivals	TF	60	79	77	78	72	63	Arrivées de touristes/visiteurs
Tourism expenditure [3]		42	57	94	198	161	111	Dépenses touristiques [3]
Dominican Republic								**République dominicaine**
Tourist/visitor arrivals [2,4]	TF	1 776[17]	3 691	4 125	5 959	6 188	6 569	Arrivées de touristes/visiteurs [2,4]
Tourism expenditure [3]		1 571	3 518	4 162	6 720	7 184	7 561	Dépenses touristiques [3]
Ecuador								**Équateur**
Tourist/visitor arrivals	VF	440[1]	860[1]	1 047[1]	1 569[2]	1 806[2]	2 535[2]	Arrivées de touristes/visiteurs
Tourism expenditure		315	488	786	1 450	1 554	1 878	Dépenses touristiques
Egypt								**Égypte**
Tourist/visitor arrivals	TF	2 871	8 244	14 051	5 258	8 157	11 196	Arrivées de touristes/visiteurs
Tourism expenditure		2 954	7 206	13 633	3 306	8 636	12 704	Dépenses touristiques
El Salvador								**El Salvador**
Tourist/visitor arrivals	TF	235	1 127	1 150	1 434	1 556	1 677	Arrivées de touristes/visiteurs
Tourism expenditure		152	656	646	1 161	1 227	1 370	Dépenses touristiques
Equatorial Guinea								**Guinée équatoriale**
Tourism expenditure		1	...	...	...	...	...	Dépenses touristiques

30 Tourist/visitor arrivals and tourism expenditure *(continued)*
Thousands arrivals and millions of US dollars

Arrivées de touristes/visiteurs et dépenses touristiques *(suite)*
Milliers d'arrivées et millions de dollars É.-U.

Country or area of destination	Series& Série&	1995	2005	2010	2016	2017	2018	Pays ou zone de destination
Eritrea								**Érythrée**
Tourist/visitor arrivals [2]	VF	315	83	84	142	...	...	Arrivées de touristes/visiteurs [2]
Tourism expenditure		58	66	...	48	...	...	Dépenses touristiques
Estonia								**Estonie**
Tourist/visitor arrivals	TF	530	1 917[18,19]	2 511[18,20]	3 131[18,20]	3 244[18,20]	3 234[18,20]	Arrivées de touristes/visiteurs
Tourism expenditure		452	1 229	...	1 916	2 126	2 332	Dépenses touristiques
Eswatini								**Eswatini**
Tourist/visitor arrivals	TF	300[21]	837	868	947	921	782	Arrivées de touristes/visiteurs
Tourism expenditure		54	77	51	13	13	16	Dépenses touristiques
Ethiopia								**Éthiopie**
Tourist/visitor arrivals	TF	103[22]	227[2,23]	468[2,23]	871[2,23]	933[2,23]	849[2,23]	Arrivées de touristes/visiteurs
Tourism expenditure		177	533	1 434	2 138	2 505	3 548	Dépenses touristiques
Fiji								**Fidji**
Tourist/visitor arrivals [1]	TF	318	545	632	792	843	870	Arrivées de touristes/visiteurs [1]
Tourism expenditure		369	722	825	1 149	1 243	1 370	Dépenses touristiques
Finland								**Finlande**
Tourist/visitor arrivals	TCE	1 779	# 2 080	2 319	2 789	3 180	3 224	Arrivées de touristes/visiteurs
Tourism expenditure		2 383	3 069	4 497	4 016	5 207	5 663	Dépenses touristiques
France								**France**
Tourist/visitor arrivals	TF	60 033[24]	74 988[25]	76 647[25]	82 682[25]	86 758[25]	* 89 322[25]	Arrivées de touristes/visiteurs
Tourism expenditure		31 295	52 126	56 178	63 557	67 936	73 125	Dépenses touristiques
French Guiana								**Guyane française**
Tourist/visitor arrivals [26]	TF	...	95	...	96	111	...	Arrivées de touristes/visiteurs [26]
Tourism expenditure		...	44	...	...	...	...	Dépenses touristiques
French Polynesia								**Polynésie française**
Tourist/visitor arrivals [1,4]	TF	172	208	154	192	199	216	Arrivées de touristes/visiteurs [1,4]
Tourism expenditure		326	759	630	782	...	...	Dépenses touristiques
Gabon								**Gabon**
Tourist/visitor arrivals [27]	TF	125	269	...	...	...	...	Arrivées de touristes/visiteurs [27]
Tourism expenditure		94	13	89	29	...	...	Dépenses touristiques
Gambia								**Gambie**
Tourist/visitor arrivals [2]	TF	45[28]	108[28]	91[28]	450	522	552	Arrivées de touristes/visiteurs [2]
Tourism expenditure		...	59	80	120	116	168	Dépenses touristiques
Georgia								**Géorgie**
Tourist/visitor arrivals	TF	...	...	1 067	3 297	4 069	4 757	Arrivées de touristes/visiteurs
Tourism expenditure		...	287	737	2 315	2 971	3 518	Dépenses touristiques
Germany								**Allemagne**
Tourist/visitor arrivals	TCE	14 847	21 500	26 875	35 555	37 452	38 881	Arrivées de touristes/visiteurs
Tourism expenditure		24 053	40 518	49 116	52 229	56 330	60 260	Dépenses touristiques
Ghana								**Ghana**
Tourist/visitor arrivals [2]	TF	286	429	931	...	...	...	Arrivées de touristes/visiteurs [2]
Tourism expenditure		30	867	706	952	919	996	Dépenses touristiques
Greece								**Grèce**
Tourist/visitor arrivals	TF	10 130	14 765	15 007	24 799	27 194	30 123	Arrivées de touristes/visiteurs
Tourism expenditure		4 182	13 455	13 857	16 811	19 139	21 594	Dépenses touristiques
Grenada								**Grenade**
Tourist/visitor arrivals	TF	108	99	110	156	168	185	Arrivées de touristes/visiteurs
Tourism expenditure [3]		76	71	112	437	482	548	Dépenses touristiques [3]
Guadeloupe								**Guadeloupe**
Tourist/visitor arrivals [4,29]	TF	640[30]	372	392	581	650	735	Arrivées de touristes/visiteurs [4,29]
Tourism expenditure		458	306	510	...	...	860	Dépenses touristiques
Guam								**Guam**
Tourist/visitor arrivals	TF	1 362	1 228	1 197	1 536	1 545	1 549	Arrivées de touristes/visiteurs
Guatemala								**Guatemala**
Tourist/visitor arrivals	TF	...	...	1 119	1 585	1 660	1 781	Arrivées de touristes/visiteurs
Tourism expenditure [3]		213	791	1 378	1 550	1 566	1 549	Dépenses touristiques [3]
Guinea								**Guinée**
Tourist/visitor arrivals [31]	TF	...	45	12	63	99	...	Arrivées de touristes/visiteurs [31]
Tourism expenditure		1	...	2	17	17	8	Dépenses touristiques
Guinea-Bissau								**Guinée-Bissau**
Tourist/visitor arrivals [4]	TF	...	5	22	45	...	...	Arrivées de touristes/visiteurs [4]
Tourism expenditure [3]		...	2	13	12	16	20	Dépenses touristiques [3]
Guyana								**Guyana**
Tourist/visitor arrivals	TF	106	117	152	235	247	287	Arrivées de touristes/visiteurs
Tourism expenditure [3]		33	35	80	104	95	28	Dépenses touristiques [3]

30
Tourist/visitor arrivals and tourism expenditure *(continued)*
Thousands arrivals and millions of US dollars

Arrivées de touristes/visiteurs et dépenses touristiques *(suite)*
Milliers d'arrivées et millions de dollars É.-U.

Country or area of destination	Series& Série&	1995	2005	2010	2016	2017	2018	Pays ou zone de destination
Haiti								**Haïti**
Tourist/visitor arrivals [4]	TF	145	112	255[2]	445[2]	467[2]	447[2]	Arrivées de touristes/visiteurs [4]
Tourism expenditure [3]		90	80	383	511	460	620	Dépenses touristiques [3]
Honduras								**Honduras**
Tourist/visitor arrivals	TF	271	673	863	838	851	...	Arrivées de touristes/visiteurs
Tourism expenditure		85	465	627	700	722	745	Dépenses touristiques
Hungary								**Hongrie**
Tourist/visitor arrivals	TF	...	9 979	9 510	15 255	15 785	17 552	Arrivées de touristes/visiteurs
Tourism expenditure		2 938	4 761	6 595	7 481	8 448	9 595	Dépenses touristiques
Iceland								**Islande**
Tourist/visitor arrivals	TF	190	374	489	1 792	2 225	2 344	Arrivées de touristes/visiteurs
Tourism expenditure [3]		186	413	562	2 411	3 024	3 128	Dépenses touristiques [3]
India								**Inde**
Tourist/visitor arrivals	TF	2 124[1]	3 919[1]	5 776[1]	14 570[2]	15 543[2]	17 423[2]	Arrivées de touristes/visiteurs
Tourism expenditure		...	7 659	...	23 111	27 878	29 143	Dépenses touristiques
Indonesia								**Indonésie**
Tourist/visitor arrivals	VF	4 324	5 002	7 003	11 519	14 040	15 810	Arrivées de touristes/visiteurs
Tourism expenditure		...	5 094	7 618	12 566	14 691	15 600	Dépenses touristiques
Iran (Islamic Republic of)								**Iran (Rép. islamique d')**
Tourist/visitor arrivals	VF	568	...	2 938	4 942	4 867	7 295	Arrivées de touristes/visiteurs
Tourism expenditure		205	1 025	2 631	3 914	4 632	...	Dépenses touristiques
Iraq								**Iraq**
Tourist/visitor arrivals	VF	61	...	1 518	...	...	...	Arrivées de touristes/visiteurs
Tourism expenditure		...	186	1 736	3 120	2 959	1 986	Dépenses touristiques
Ireland								**Irlande**
Tourist/visitor arrivals [32]	TF	4 818	7 333	# 7 134	10 100	10 338	10 926	Arrivées de touristes/visiteurs [32]
Tourism expenditure		2 698	6 779	8 185	11 429	14 294	14 658	Dépenses touristiques
Israel								**Israël**
Tourist/visitor arrivals [1]	TF	2 215	1 903	2 803	2 900	3 613	4 121	Arrivées de touristes/visiteurs [1]
Tourism expenditure [33]		3 491	2 750	5 621	6 587	7 578	8 073	Dépenses touristiques [33]
Italy								**Italie**
Tourist/visitor arrivals [34]	TF	31 052	36 513	43 626	52 372	58 253	61 567	Arrivées de touristes/visiteurs [34]
Tourism expenditure		30 411	38 364	...	42 423	46 719	51 602	Dépenses touristiques
Jamaica								**Jamaïque**
Tourist/visitor arrivals [35,36]	TF	1 147	1 479	1 922	2 182	2 353	2 473	Arrivées de tourist./visiteurs [35,36]
Tourism expenditure [3]		1 069	1 545	2 001	2 539	2 809	3 099	Dépenses touristiques [3]
Japan								**Japon**
Tourist/visitor arrivals [1]	VF	3 345	6 728	8 611	24 040	28 691	31 192	Arrivées de touristes/visiteurs [1]
Tourism expenditure		4 894	15 554	15 356	33 456	36 978	45 276	Dépenses touristiques
Jordan								**Jordanie**
Tourist/visitor arrivals [2]	TF	1 075	# 2 987	4 207	3 567	3 844	4 150	Arrivées de touristes/visiteurs [2]
Tourism expenditure		973	1 759	4 390	4 943	5 549	6 221	Dépenses touristiques
Kazakhstan								**Kazakhstan**
Tourist/visitor arrivals	TF	...	3 143	2 991	...	...	...	Arrivées de touristes/visiteurs
Tourism expenditure		155	801	1 236	2 038	2 356	2 651	Dépenses touristiques
Kenya								**Kenya**
Tourist/visitor arrivals [1]	TF	918	1 399	1 470	1 268	1 364	...	Arrivées de touristes/visiteurs [1]
Tourism expenditure		785	969	1 620	1 471	1 564	...	Dépenses touristiques
Kiribati								**Kiribati**
Tourist/visitor arrivals [37]	TF	4	4	5	6	6	7	Arrivées de touristes/visiteurs [37]
Tourism expenditure [3]		...	...	4	3	4	...	Dépenses touristiques [3]
Kuwait								**Koweït**
Tourist/visitor arrivals	VF	1 443	3 474	5 208	7 055	7 407	8 508	Arrivées de touristes/visiteurs
Tourism expenditure		307	413	574	831	643	919	Dépenses touristiques
Kyrgyzstan								**Kirghizistan**
Tourist/visitor arrivals	VF	...	319	1 224	3 853	4 568	6 947	Arrivées de touristes/visiteurs
Tourism expenditure		...	94	212	477	480	487	Dépenses touristiques
Lao People's Dem. Rep.								**Rép. dém. populaire lao**
Tourist/visitor arrivals	TF	60	672	1 670	3 315	3 257	3 770	Arrivées de touristes/visiteurs
Tourism expenditure		52	143	385	717	655	757	Dépenses touristiques
Latvia								**Lettonie**
Tourist/visitor arrivals [38]	TF	539	1 116	1 373	1 793	1 949	1 946	Arrivées de touristes/visiteurs [38]
Tourism expenditure		37	446	...	...	...	...	Dépenses touristiques

30 Tourist/visitor arrivals and tourism expenditure *(continued)*
Thousands arrivals and millions of US dollars

Arrivées de touristes/visiteurs et dépenses touristiques *(suite)*
Milliers d'arrivées et millions de dollars É.-U.

Country or area of destination	Series[&] Série[&]	1995	2005	2010	2016	2017	2018	Pays ou zone de destination
Lebanon								**Liban**
Tourist/visitor arrivals [39]	TF	450	1 140	2 168	1 688	1 857	1 964	Arrivées de touristes/visiteurs [39]
Tourism expenditure		710	5 969	8 026	7 373	8 086	8 694	Dépenses touristiques
Lesotho								**Lesotho**
Tourist/visitor arrivals	VF	209	304	426	# 1 196	# 1 137	# 1 173	Arrivées de touristes/visiteurs
Tourism expenditure [3]		27	27	23	48	23	24	Dépenses touristiques [3]
Liberia [3]								**Libéria** [3]
Tourism expenditure		...	67	...	...	...	...	Dépenses touristiques
Libya								**Libye**
Tourist/visitor arrivals	THS	...	81	...	...	...	...	Arrivées de touristes/visiteurs
Tourism expenditure		4	301	170	...	...	...	Dépenses touristiques
Liechtenstein								**Liechtenstein**
Tourist/visitor arrivals	TCE	...	...	64	69[40]	79[40]	85[40]	Arrivées de touristes/visiteurs
Lithuania								**Lituanie**
Tourist/visitor arrivals	TF	650	2 000	1 507	2 296	2 523	2 825	Arrivées de touristes/visiteurs
Tourism expenditure [3]		77	920	958	1 210	1 325	1 419	Dépenses touristiques [3]
Luxembourg								**Luxembourg**
Tourist/visitor arrivals	TCE	768	913	805	1 054	1 046	1 018	Arrivées de touristes/visiteurs
Tourism expenditure		...	3 770	4 519	4 766	4 993	5 537	Dépenses touristiques
Madagascar								**Madagascar**
Tourist/visitor arrivals [36]	TF	75	277	196	293	255	291	Arrivées de touristes/visiteurs [36]
Tourism expenditure		106	275	425	913	849	879	Dépenses touristiques
Malawi								**Malawi**
Tourist/visitor arrivals [41]	TF	192	438	746	849	837	871	Arrivées de touristes/visiteurs [41]
Tourism expenditure		22	48	45	30	35	43	Dépenses touristiques
Malaysia								**Malaisie**
Tourist/visitor arrivals [42]	TF	7 469	16 431	24 577	26 757	25 948	25 832	Arrivées de touristes/visiteurs [42]
Tourism expenditure		5 044	10 389	19 619	19 682	20 311	21 774	Dépenses touristiques
Maldives								**Maldives**
Tourist/visitor arrivals [4]	TF	315	395	792	1 286	1 390	1 484	Arrivées de touristes/visiteurs [4]
Tourism expenditure		...	...	...	2 640	2 771	3 054	Dépenses touristiques
Mali								**Mali**
Tourist/visitor arrivals	TF	...	...	169	173	193	...	Arrivées de touristes/visiteurs
Tourism expenditure		26	149	208	202	206	...	Dépenses touristiques
Malta								**Malte**
Tourist/visitor arrivals	TF	1 116	1 171[43]	1 339[43]	1 966[43]	2 274[43]	2 599[43]	Arrivées de touristes/visiteurs
Tourism expenditure [3]		656	755	1 066	1 451	1 746	1 845	Dépenses touristiques [3]
Marshall Islands								**Îles Marshall**
Tourist/visitor arrivals	TF	6[4]	9[44]	5[4]	5[4]	6[4]	7[4]	Arrivées de touristes/visiteurs
Tourism expenditure		3	4	4	30	18	20	Dépenses touristiques
Martinique								**Martinique**
Tourist/visitor arrivals	TF	457	484	478	519	536	537	Arrivées de touristes/visiteurs
Tourism expenditure		384	280	472	348	510	530	Dépenses touristiques
Mauritania								**Mauritanie**
Tourism expenditure		...	...	...	33	24	6	Dépenses touristiques
Mauritius								**Maurice**
Tourist/visitor arrivals	TF	422	761	935	1 275	1 342	1 399	Arrivées de touristes/visiteurs
Tourism expenditure		616	1 189	1 585	1 824	2 005	2 161	Dépenses touristiques
Mexico								**Mexique**
Tourist/visitor arrivals [2]	TF	20 241	21 915	23 290	35 079	39 291	41 313	Arrivées de touristes/visiteurs [2]
Tourism expenditure		6 847	12 801	12 628	20 619	22 467	23 802	Dépenses touristiques
Micronesia (Fed. States of)								**Micronésie (États féd. de)**
Tourist/visitor arrivals [45]	TF	...	19	45	30	...	19	Arrivées de touristes/visiteurs [45]
Tourism expenditure [3]		...	...	24	...	...	...	Dépenses touristiques [3]
Monaco								**Monaco**
Tourist/visitor arrivals	THS	233	286	279	336	355	347	Arrivées de touristes/visiteurs
Mongolia								**Mongolie**
Tourist/visitor arrivals	TF	...	339	456	404	469	529	Arrivées de touristes/visiteurs
Tourism expenditure		33	203	288	379	462	526	Dépenses touristiques
Montenegro								**Monténégro**
Tourist/visitor arrivals	TCE	...	272	1 088	1 662	1 877	2 077	Arrivées de touristes/visiteurs
Tourism expenditure		...	...	765	978	1 110	1 224	Dépenses touristiques
Montserrat								**Montserrat**
Tourist/visitor arrivals	TF	18	10	6	9	9	9	Arrivées de touristes/visiteurs
Tourism expenditure [3]		17	9	6	9	8	11	Dépenses touristiques [3]

30 Tourist/visitor arrivals and tourism expenditure *(continued)*
Thousands arrivals and millions of US dollars

Arrivées de touristes/visiteurs et dépenses touristiques *(suite)*
Milliers d'arrivées et millions de dollars É.-U.

Country or area of destination	Series& Série&	1995	2005	2010	2016	2017	2018	Pays ou zone de destination
Morocco								**Maroc**
Tourist/visitor arrivals [2]	TF	2 602	5 843	9 288	10 332	11 349	12 289	Arrivées de touristes/visiteurs [2]
Tourism expenditure		1 469	5 426	8 176	7 922	9 086	9 523	Dépenses touristiques
Mozambique								**Mozambique**
Tourist/visitor arrivals	TF	...	578[46]	# 1 718[47]	1 639[47]	1 447[47]	2 743[47]	Arrivées de touristes/visiteurs
Tourism expenditure		...	138	135	114	164	331	Dépenses touristiques
Myanmar								**Myanmar**
Tourist/visitor arrivals	TF	194	660	792	# 2 907	3 443	3 551	Arrivées de touristes/visiteurs
Tourism expenditure		169	83	91	2 289	1 988	1 670	Dépenses touristiques
Namibia								**Namibie**
Tourist/visitor arrivals	TF	272	778	984	1 469	1 499	...	Arrivées de touristes/visiteurs
Tourism expenditure		...	363	473	349	449	488	Dépenses touristiques
Nauru								**Nauru**
Tourism expenditure		...	...	1	3	4	2	Dépenses touristiques
Nepal								**Népal**
Tourist/visitor arrivals [48]	TF	363	375	603	753	940	1 173	Arrivées de touristes/visiteurs [48]
Tourism expenditure		232	160	378	498	712	744	Dépenses touristiques
Netherlands								**Pays-Bas**
Tourist/visitor arrivals	TCE	6 574	10 012	10 883	15 828	17 924	18 780	Arrivées de touristes/visiteurs
Tourism expenditure		10 611	...	...	21 151	23 414	25 850	Dépenses touristiques
New Caledonia								**Nouvelle-Calédonie**
Tourist/visitor arrivals [2]	TF	86	101	99	116	121	120	Arrivées de touristes/visiteurs [2]
Tourism expenditure [3]		108	149	129	159	...	...	Dépenses touristiques [3]
New Zealand								**Nouvelle-Zélande**
Tourist/visitor arrivals	TF	...	2 353	2 435	3 370	3 555	3 686	Arrivées de touristes/visiteurs
Tourism expenditure [3]		2 318	6 486	6 523	9 773	10 594	10 961	Dépenses touristiques [3]
Nicaragua								**Nicaragua**
Tourist/visitor arrivals	TF	281	712[2]	1 011[2]	1 504[2]	1 787[2]	1 256[2]	Arrivées de touristes/visiteurs
Tourism expenditure [3]		50	206	314	642	841	544	Dépenses touristiques [3]
Niger								**Niger**
Tourist/visitor arrivals	TF	35	58	74	152	164	157	Arrivées de touristes/visiteurs
Tourism expenditure		...	44	106	84	91	...	Dépenses touristiques
Nigeria								**Nigéria**
Tourist/visitor arrivals	TF	656	1 010	1 555	1 889	...	...	Arrivées de touristes/visiteurs
Tourism expenditure		47	139	736	1 088	2 615	1 977	Dépenses touristiques
Niue								**Nioué**
Tourist/visitor arrivals [49]	TF	2	3	6	9	10	...	Arrivées de touristes/visiteurs [49]
Tourism expenditure		2	1	2	...	...	...	Dépenses touristiques
North Macedonia								**Macédoine du Nord**
Tourist/visitor arrivals	TCE	147	197	262	510	631	707	Arrivées de touristes/visiteurs
Tourism expenditure		...	116	199	283	331	387	Dépenses touristiques
Northern Mariana Islands								**Îles Mariannes du Nord**
Tourist/visitor arrivals [4]	TF	669	498	375	526	656	517	Arrivées de touristes/visiteurs [4]
Tourism expenditure		655	...	...	...	...	...	Dépenses touristiques
Norway								**Norvège**
Tourist/visitor arrivals	TF	2 880[50]	3 824[51]	4 767[51]	5 960[30]	6 252[30]	5 688[30]	Arrivées de touristes/visiteurs
Tourism expenditure		2 730	4 243	5 299	6 285	6 840	7 096	Dépenses touristiques
Oman								**Oman**
Tourist/visitor arrivals	TF	...	891	1 441	2 335	2 316	2 301	Arrivées de touristes/visiteurs
Tourism expenditure		...	627	1 072	2 390	2 717	2 975	Dépenses touristiques
Other non-specified areas								**Autres zones non-spécifiées**
Tourist/visitor arrivals [2]	VF	2 332	3 378	5 567	10 690	10 740	11 067	Arrivées de touristes/visiteurs [2]
Tourism expenditure		3 985	5 740	10 387	15 825	14 847	16 366	Dépenses touristiques
Pakistan								**Pakistan**
Tourist/visitor arrivals	TF	378	798	907	...	...	...	Arrivées de touristes/visiteurs
Tourism expenditure		582	828	998	791	866	818	Dépenses touristiques
Palau								**Palaos**
Tourist/visitor arrivals [52]	TF	53	81	85	138	123	106	Arrivées de touristes/visiteurs [52]
Tourism expenditure		...	63	76	148	123	...	Dépenses touristiques
Panama								**Panama**
Tourist/visitor arrivals	TF	345	702	1 324	1 921	1 843	1 785	Arrivées de touristes/visiteurs
Tourism expenditure		372	1 108	2 621	6 280	6 824	5 615	Dépenses touristiques
Papua New Guinea								**Papouasie-Nvl-Guinée**
Tourist/visitor arrivals	TF	42	69	140	179	139	140	Arrivées de touristes/visiteurs
Tourism expenditure		...	9	2	2	15	...	Dépenses touristiques

30

Tourist/visitor arrivals and tourism expenditure *(continued)*
Thousands arrivals and millions of US dollars

Arrivées de touristes/visiteurs et dépenses touristiques *(suite)*
Milliers d'arrivées et millions de dollars É.-U.

Country or area of destination	Series& Série&	1995	2005	2010	2016	2017	2018	Pays ou zone de destination
Paraguay								**Paraguay**
Tourist/visitor arrivals [5]	TF	438	341	465	1 308	1 584	1 181	Arrivées de touristes/visiteurs [5]
Tourism expenditure		162	96	243	356	399	393	Dépenses touristiques
Peru								**Pérou**
Tourist/visitor arrivals [2]	TF	479	1 571[53]	2 299[53]	3 744[53]	4 032[53]	4 419[53]	Arrivées de touristes/visiteurs [2]
Tourism expenditure		521	1 438	2 475	4 288	4 573	4 894	Dépenses touristiques
Philippines								**Philippines**
Tourist/visitor arrivals [2]	TF	1 760	2 623	3 520	5 967	6 621	7 168	Arrivées de touristes/visiteurs [2]
Tourism expenditure		1 141	2 863	3 441	6 289	8 349	9 730	Dépenses touristiques
Poland								**Pologne**
Tourist/visitor arrivals	TF	19 215[18]	15 200[18]	12 470[18]	17 471	18 258	19 622	Arrivées de touristes/visiteurs
Tourism expenditure		6 927	7 161	10 036	12 052	14 083	15 748	Dépenses touristiques
Portugal								**Portugal**
Tourist/visitor arrivals	TCE	4 572	5 769	6 756	13 359[54]	15 432[54]	16 186[54]	Arrivées de touristes/visiteurs
Tourism expenditure		5 646	9 038	12 984	17 347	21 586	24 105	Dépenses touristiques
Puerto Rico								**Porto Rico**
Tourist/visitor arrivals [36]	TF	3 131	3 686	3 186	3 736	3 513	3 068	Arrivées de touristes/visiteurs [36]
Tourism expenditure [55]		1 828	3 239	3 211	3 974	3 848	3 282	Dépenses touristiques [55]
Qatar								**Qatar**
Tourist/visitor arrivals	TF	...	...	1 700	2 938	2 257	1 819	Arrivées de touristes/visiteurs
Tourism expenditure		...	...	...	12 593	15 757	15 239	Dépenses touristiques
Republic of Korea								**République de Corée**
Tourist/visitor arrivals [56]	VF	3 753	6 023	8 798	17 242	13 336	15 347	Arrivées de touristes/visiteurs [56]
Tourism expenditure		6 670	8 282	14 315	20 924	17 173	19 856	Dépenses touristiques
Republic of Moldova								**République de Moldova**
Tourist/visitor arrivals [57]	TCE	...	67	64	121	145	160	Arrivées de touristes/visiteurs [57]
Tourism expenditure		71	138	222	344	443	500	Dépenses touristiques
Réunion								**Réunion**
Tourist/visitor arrivals [4]	TF	304	409	420	458	508	535	Arrivées de touristes/visiteurs [4]
Tourism expenditure		216	364	392	343	427	495	Dépenses touristiques
Romania								**Roumanie**
Tourist/visitor arrivals	VF	5 445	5 839	7 498	10 223	10 926	11 720	Arrivées de touristes/visiteurs
Tourism expenditure		689	1 324	1 631	2 172	3 008	3 261	Dépenses touristiques
Russian Federation								**Fédération de Russie**
Tourist/visitor arrivals	VF	10 290	22 201	22 281	24 571	24 390	24 551	Arrivées de touristes/visiteurs
Tourism expenditure		...	7 805	13 239	12 822	14 983	18 670	Dépenses touristiques
Rwanda								**Rwanda**
Tourist/visitor arrivals	TF	...	...	504	932	...	...	Arrivées de touristes/visiteurs
Tourism expenditure		4	67	224	443	548	528	Dépenses touristiques
Saba								**Saba**
Tourist/visitor arrivals	TF	10	12	12	...	...	...	Arrivées de touristes/visiteurs
Saint Kitts and Nevis								**Saint-Kitts-et-Nevis**
Tourist/visitor arrivals [36]	TF	79	141	98	116	115	125	Arrivées de touristes/visiteurs [36]
Tourism expenditure [3]		63	121	90	332	355	367	Dépenses touristiques [3]
Saint Lucia								**Sainte-Lucie**
Tourist/visitor arrivals [1]	TF	231	318	306	348	386	395	Arrivées de touristes/visiteurs [1]
Tourism expenditure [3]		230	382	309	776	875	989	Dépenses touristiques [3]
Saint Vincent & Grenadines								**Saint-Vincent-Grenadines**
Tourist/visitor arrivals [36]	TF	60	96	72	79	76	80	Arrivées de touristes/visiteurs [36]
Tourism expenditure [3]		53	104	86	216	211	235	Dépenses touristiques [3]
Samoa								**Samoa**
Tourist/visitor arrivals	TF	68	102	122	134	146	164	Arrivées de touristes/visiteurs
Tourism expenditure		36	74	124	149	167	191	Dépenses touristiques
San Marino [58]								**Saint-Marin** [58]
Tourist/visitor arrivals	THS	28	50	120	60	78	84	Arrivées de touristes/visiteurs
Sao Tome and Principe								**Sao Tomé-et-Principe**
Tourist/visitor arrivals	TF	6	16	8	29	29	33	Arrivées de touristes/visiteurs
Tourism expenditure		...	...	...	69	66	72	Dépenses touristiques
Saudi Arabia								**Arabie saoudite**
Tourist/visitor arrivals	TF	3 325	8 037	10 850	18 044	16 109	15 334	Arrivées de touristes/visiteurs
Tourism expenditure		...	...	7 536	13 438	15 020	16 975	Dépenses touristiques
Senegal								**Sénégal**
Tourist/visitor arrivals	TF	...	769	* 900	* 1 210	* 1 365	...	Arrivées de touristes/visiteurs
Tourism expenditure		168	334	464	438	468	...	Dépenses touristiques

30

Tourist/visitor arrivals and tourism expenditure *(continued)*
Thousands arrivals and millions of US dollars

Arrivées de touristes/visiteurs et dépenses touristiques *(suite)*
Milliers d'arrivées et millions de dollars É.-U.

Country or area of destination	Series[&] Série[&]	1995	2005	2010	2016	2017	2018	Pays ou zone de destination
Serbia								**Serbie**
Tourist/visitor arrivals	TCE	...	453	683	1 281	1 497	1 711	Arrivées de touristes/visiteurs
Tourism expenditure		...	308	950	1 461	1 706	1 921	Dépenses touristiques
Seychelles								**Seychelles**
Tourist/visitor arrivals	TF	121	129	175	303	350	362	Arrivées de touristes/visiteurs
Tourism expenditure		224	269	352	505	585	611	Dépenses touristiques
Sierra Leone								**Sierra Leone**
Tourist/visitor arrivals	TF	14[4]	40[4]	39[4]	55[4]	51	57	Arrivées de touristes/visiteurs
Tourism expenditure [3]		57	64	26	41	39	39	Dépenses touristiques [3]
Singapore								**Singapour**
Tourist/visitor arrivals [59]	TF	6 070	7 079	9 161	12 913	13 903	14 673	Arrivées de touristes/visiteurs [59]
Tourism expenditure [3]		7 611	6 209	14 178	18 944	19 891	20 416	Dépenses touristiques [3]
Sint Eustatius [60]								**Saint-Eustache [60]**
Tourist/visitor arrivals	TF	9	10	11	...	...	...	Arrivées de touristes/visiteurs
Sint Maarten (Dutch part)								**St-Martin (partie néerland.)**
Tourist/visitor arrivals [61]	TF	460	468	443	528	402	178	Arrivées de touristes/visiteurs [61]
Tourism expenditure		...	...	681	871	646	468	Dépenses touristiques
Slovakia								**Slovaquie**
Tourist/visitor arrivals [62]	TCE	903	1 515	1 327	2 027	2 162	2 256	Arrivées de touristes/visiteurs [62]
Tourism expenditure		630	1 282	2 334	2 812	3 024	3 318	Dépenses touristiques
Slovenia								**Slovénie**
Tourist/visitor arrivals	TCE	732	1 555	2 049	3 397	3 991	4 425	Arrivées de touristes/visiteurs
Tourism expenditure		1 128	1 894	2 808	2 717	3 057	3 378	Dépenses touristiques
Solomon Islands								**Îles Salomon**
Tourist/visitor arrivals	TF	12	9[63]	21	23	26	28	Arrivées de touristes/visiteurs
Tourism expenditure		17	6	51	71	79	92	Dépenses touristiques
South Africa								**Afrique du Sud**
Tourist/visitor arrivals	TF	4 488[64]	7 369[64]	# 8 074	# 10 044[65]	10 285[65]	10 472[65]	Arrivées de touristes/visiteurs
Tourism expenditure		2 654	8 629	10 309	8 807	9 706	9 789	Dépenses touristiques
South Sudan								**Soudan du sud**
Tourism expenditure		...	...	...	24	26	12	Dépenses touristiques
Spain								**Espagne**
Tourist/visitor arrivals	TF	32 971	55 914	52 677	# 75 315	81 869	82 773	Arrivées de touristes/visiteurs
Tourism expenditure [3]		25 368	51 959	58 348	66 982	75 906	81 250	Dépenses touristiques [3]
Sri Lanka								**Sri Lanka**
Tourist/visitor arrivals [1]	TF	403	549	654	2 051	2 116	2 334	Arrivées de touristes/visiteurs [1]
Tourism expenditure		367	729	1 044	4 591	5 083	5 608	Dépenses touristiques
State of Palestine								**État de Palestine**
Tourist/visitor arrivals	THS	...	88	522	400[66]	503[66]	606[66]	Arrivées de touristes/visiteurs
Tourism expenditure [3,67]		255	52	409	235	225	245	Dépenses touristiques [3,67]
Sudan								**Soudan**
Tourist/visitor arrivals	TF	29	246[2]	495[2]	800[2]	813[2]	836[2]	Arrivées de touristes/visiteurs
Tourism expenditure [3]		8	114	82	1 009	1 029	1 043	Dépenses touristiques [3]
Suriname								**Suriname**
Tourist/visitor arrivals	TF	43[68]	161	205	256	278	...	Arrivées de touristes/visiteurs
Tourism expenditure		52	96	69	74	61	73	Dépenses touristiques
Sweden								**Suède**
Tourist/visitor arrivals	TCE	2 310	4 883	5 183	6 782	7 054	7 440	Arrivées de touristes/visiteurs
Tourism expenditure [3]		3 471	6 554	8 336	12 764	14 168	14 926	Dépenses touristiques [3]
Switzerland								**Suisse**
Tourist/visitor arrivals	THS	6 946	7 229	8 628	9 205	9 889	10 362	Arrivées de touristes/visiteurs
Tourism expenditure		11 354	11 952	17 614	19 042	19 654	20 276	Dépenses touristiques
Syrian Arab Republic								**République arabe syrienne**
Tourist/visitor arrivals	TCE	815	3 571[2]	8 546[2,69]	...	...	...	Arrivées de touristes/visiteurs
Tourism expenditure		...	2 035	6 308	...	...	...	Dépenses touristiques
Tajikistan								**Tadjikistan**
Tourist/visitor arrivals	VF	...	...	160	344	431	1 035	Arrivées de touristes/visiteurs
Tourism expenditure		...	9	142	150	172	171	Dépenses touristiques
Thailand								**Thaïlande**
Tourist/visitor arrivals	TF	6 952[2]	11 567[2]	15 936	32 530	35 592	38 178	Arrivées de touristes/visiteurs
Tourism expenditure		9 257	12 103	23 796	48 459	57 057	65 242	Dépenses touristiques
Timor-Leste								**Timor-Leste**
Tourist/visitor arrivals [70]	TF	...	...	40	66	74	75	Arrivées de touristes/visiteurs [70]
Tourism expenditure [3]		...	...	24	58	73	78	Dépenses touristiques [3]

30

Tourist/visitor arrivals and tourism expenditure *(continued)*
Thousands arrivals and millions of US dollars

Arrivées de touristes/visiteurs et dépenses touristiques *(suite)*
Milliers d'arrivées et millions de dollars É.-U.

Country or area of destination	Series& Série&	1995	2005	2010	2016	2017	2018	Pays ou zone de destination
Togo								**Togo**
Tourist/visitor arrivals	THS	53	81	202	338	514	573	Arrivées de touristes/visiteurs
Tourism expenditure		...	27	105	223	245	...	Dépenses touristiques
Tonga								**Tonga**
Tourist/visitor arrivals [4]	TF	29	42	47	59	63	54	Arrivées de touristes/visiteurs [4]
Tourism expenditure		...	15	17	53	49	48	Dépenses touristiques
Trinidad and Tobago								**Trinité-et-Tobago**
Tourist/visitor arrivals [4]	TF	260	463	388	409	395	375	Arrivées de touristes/visiteurs [4]
Tourism expenditure		232	593	630	708	717	541	Dépenses touristiques
Tunisia								**Tunisie**
Tourist/visitor arrivals	TF	4 120[1]	6 378[1]	7 828	5 724	7 052	8 299	Arrivées de touristes/visiteurs
Tourism expenditure		1 838	2 800	3 477	1 706	1 782	2 320	Dépenses touristiques
Turkey								**Turquie**
Tourist/visitor arrivals	TF	7 083	20 273	31 364[71]	30 289[71]	37 601[71]	45 768[71]	Arrivées de touristes/visiteurs
Tourism expenditure		...	20 760	26 318	26 788	31 870	37 140	Dépenses touristiques
Turkmenistan								**Turkménistan**
Tourist/visitor arrivals	TF	218	12	...	...	...	...	Arrivées de touristes/visiteurs
Turks and Caicos Islands								**Îles Turques-et-Caïques**
Tourist/visitor arrivals	TF	79	176	281	449	416	441	Arrivées de touristes/visiteurs
Tourism expenditure		53	...	...	...	...	...	Dépenses touristiques
Tuvalu								**Tuvalu**
Tourist/visitor arrivals [3]	TF	1	1	2	3	3	3	Arrivées de touristes/visiteurs
Tourism expenditure [3]		...	1	2	...	...	...	Dépenses touristiques [3]
Uganda								**Ouganda**
Tourist/visitor arrivals	TF	160	468	946	1 323	1 402	...	Arrivées de touristes/visiteurs
Tourism expenditure		...	382	802	1 118	957	1 044	Dépenses touristiques
Ukraine								**Ukraine**
Tourist/visitor arrivals	TF	3 716	17 631	21 203	13 333	14 230	14 104	Arrivées de touristes/visiteurs
Tourism expenditure		...	3 542	4 696	1 723	2 019	2 269	Dépenses touristiques
United Arab Emirates								**Émirats arabes unis**
Tourist/visitor arrivals [72]	THS	2 315	7 126	...	18 967	20 394	21 286	Arrivées de touristes/visiteurs [72]
Tourism expenditure		632	3 218	8 577	19 496	21 048	21 390	Dépenses touristiques
United Kingdom								**Royaume-Uni**
Tourist/visitor arrivals	TF	21 719	28 039	28 295	35 814	37 651	36 316	Arrivées de touristes/visiteurs
Tourism expenditure [3]		27 577	32 948	34 715	47 777	47 719	48 515	Dépenses touristiques [3]
United Rep. of Tanzania								**Rép.-Unie de Tanzanie**
Tourist/visitor arrivals	TF	285	590	754	1 233	1 275	1 378	Arrivées de touristes/visiteurs
Tourism expenditure		...	835	1 279	2 149	2 265	2 465	Dépenses touristiques
United States of America								**États-Unis d'Amérique**
Tourist/visitor arrivals	TF	43 318	49 206	60 010	# 76 407	77 187	79 746	Arrivées de touristes/visiteurs
Tourism expenditure		93 743	122 077	167 996	245 991	251 544	256 145	Dépenses touristiques
United States Virgin Islands								**Îles Vierges américaines**
Tourist/visitor arrivals	TF	454	594	572	667	535	381	Arrivées de touristes/visiteurs
Tourism expenditure		822	1 432	1 223	1 343	1 202	1 046	Dépenses touristiques
Uruguay								**Uruguay**
Tourist/visitor arrivals	TF	2 022	1 808	2 353	3 037	3 674	3 469	Arrivées de touristes/visiteurs
Tourism expenditure		725	699	1 669	2 182	2 660	2 439	Dépenses touristiques
Uzbekistan								**Ouzbékistan**
Tourist/visitor arrivals	TF	92	242	975	2 027	2 690	5 346	Arrivées de touristes/visiteurs
Tourism expenditure [3]		...	28	121	458	689	1 144	Dépenses touristiques [3]
Vanuatu								**Vanuatu**
Tourist/visitor arrivals	TF	44	62	97	95	109	116	Arrivées de touristes/visiteurs
Tourism expenditure		...	104	242	275	289	325	Dépenses touristiques
Venezuela (Boliv. Rep. of)								**Venezuela (Rép. boliv. du)**
Tourist/visitor arrivals	TF	700	706	526	601	427	...	Arrivées de touristes/visiteurs
Tourism expenditure		995	722	885	546	...	...	Dépenses touristiques
Viet Nam								**Viet Nam**
Tourist/visitor arrivals	VF	1 351	3 477	5 050	10 013	12 922	15 498	Arrivées de touristes/visiteurs
Tourism expenditure		...	2 300	4 450	8 500	8 890	10 080	Dépenses touristiques
Yemen								**Yémen**
Tourist/visitor arrivals	TF	61	336	1 025[2]	...	...	...	Arrivées de touristes/visiteurs
Tourism expenditure		...	...	1 291	116	...	...	Dépenses touristiques
Zambia								**Zambie**
Tourist/visitor arrivals	TF	163	669	815	956	1 083	1 072	Arrivées de touristes/visiteurs
Tourism expenditure [3]		...	447	492	683	653	742	Dépenses touristiques [3]

30

Tourist/visitor arrivals and tourism expenditure *(continued)*
Thousands arrivals and millions of US dollars

Arrivées de touristes/visiteurs et dépenses touristiques *(suite)*
Milliers d'arrivées et millions de dollars É.-U.

Country or area of destination	Series& Série&	1995	2005	2010	2016	2017	2018	Pays ou zone de destination
Zimbabwe								**Zimbabwe**
Tourist/visitor arrivals	VF	1 416	1 559	2 239	2 168	2 423	2 580	Arrivées de touristes/visiteurs
Tourism expenditure		145	99	135	194	158	...	Dépenses touristiques

Source:

World Tourism Organization (UNWTO), Madrid, the UNWTO Statistics Database, last accessed January 2020.

The majority of the expenditure data have been provided to the WTO by the International Monetary Fund (IMF). & Series (by order of priority, see Annex II): TF: Arrivals of non-resident tourists at national borders. VF: Arrivals of non-resident visitors at national borders. TCE: Arrivals of non-resident tourists in all types of accommodation establishments. THS: Arrivals of non-resident tourists in hotels and similar establishments.

1 Excluding nationals residing abroad.
2 Including nationals residing abroad.
3 Excluding passenger transport.
4 Arrivals by air.
5 Excluding nationals residing abroad and crew members.
6 Only paid accommodation; excluding stays at friends and relatives and second homes.
7 Excludes the Belarusian-Russian border segment.
8 Includes estimation of the Belarusian-Russian border segment.
9 Including regional high end tourists.
10 Non-resident tourists staying in hotels and similar establishments.
11 Arrivals by all means of transport.
12 Arrivals by air at Bangui only.
13 For statistical purposes, the data for China do not include those for the Hong Kong Special Administrative Region (Hong Kong SAR), Macao Special Administrative Region (Macao SAR) and Taiwan Province of China.
14 Does not include other non-residents namely workers, students, etc.
15 Arrivals to Félix Houphouët Boigny Airport only.
16 Excluding arrivals in ports of nautical tourism.
17 Excluding the passengers at Herrera airport.
18 Border statistics are not collected any more, surveys used instead.
19 Calculated on the basis of accommodation statistics and "Foreign Visitor Survey" carried out by the Statistical Office of Estonia.
20 Based on mobile positioning data.
21 Arrivals in hotels only.
22 Arrivals to Bole airport only.
23 Arrivals through all ports of entry.
24 Estimated based on surveys at national borders.
25 Arrivals of non-resident visitors.
26 Survey at Cayenne-Rochambeau airport on departure.
27 Arrivals of non-resident tourists at Libreville airport.
28 Arrivals by air only.
29 Excluding the north islands, Saint Barthélemy and Saint Martin (French part).
30 Non-resident tourists staying in all types of accommodation establishments.
31 Arrivals by air at Conakry airport.
32 Including tourists from Northern Ireland.

Source:

Organisation mondiale du tourisme (OMT), Madrid, base de données statistiques de l'OMT, dernier accés janvier 2020.

La majorité des données sur les dépenses touristiques sont celles que le Fonds monétaire international (FMI) a fournies à l'Organisation mondiale du tourisme (OMT). & Série (par ordre de priorite, voir annexe II): TF: Arrivées de touristes non résidents aux frontières nationales. VF: Arrivées de visiteurs non résidents aux frontières nationales. TCE: Arrivées de touristes non résidents dans tous les types d'établissements d'hébergement touristique. THS: Arrivées de touristes non résidents dans les hôtels et établissements assimilés.

1 À l'exclusion des nationaux résidant à l'étranger.
2 Y compris les nationaux du pays résidant à l'étranger.
3 Non compris le transport de passagers.
4 Arrivées par voie aérienne.
5 À l'exclusion des nationaux du pays résidant à l'étranger et des membres des équipages.
6 Seulement logement payé; sont exclus les séjours chez des amis et membres de la famille et des résidences secondaires.
7 Exclut le segment de la frontière biélorusse-russe.
8 Comprend l'estimation du segment frontalier biélorusse-russe.
9 Y compris les touristes régionaux haut de gamme.
10 Non résidents touristes dans les hôtels et établissements assimilés.
11 Arrivées par tous moyens de transport confondus.
12 Arrivées par voie aérienne à Bangui uniquement.
13 Pour la présentation des statistiques, les données pour la Chine ne comprennent pas la région administrative spéciale de Hong Kong (RAS de Hong Kong), la région administrative spéciale de Macao (RAS de Macao) et la province chinoise de Taïwan.
14 Ne comprend pas d'autres catégories de non-résidents tels que les travailleurs, les étudiants, etc.
15 Arrivées à l'aéroport Félix Houphouët Boigny seulement.
16 À l'exclusion des arrivées dans des ports à tourisme nautique.
17 A l'exclusion des passagers à l'aéroport de Herrera.
18 Statistiques frontaliers ne sont plus collectés, les enquêtes utilisées à la place.
19 Calculé sur la base des statistiques d'hébergement et de la « Foreign Visitor Survey » menée par la « Statistical Office of Estonia ». À partir de 2004, les statistiques de frontière ne sont plus collectées.
20 Basé sur les données de positionnement mobile.
21 Arrivées dans les hôtels uniquement.
22 Arrivées à l'aéroport de Bole uniquement.
23 Arrivées à travers tous les ports d'entrée.
24 Estimations à partir d'enquêtes aux frontières.
25 Arrivées de touristes non résidents.
26 Enquête au départ de l'aéroport de Cayenne-Rochambeau.
27 Arrivées de touristes non résidents à l'aéroport de Libreville.
28 Arrivées par avion uniquement.
29 Les îles du Nord, Saint-Barthélemy et Saint-Martin (partie française) sont exclues.
30 Arrivées de touristes non résidents dans tous les types d'établissements d'hébergement touristique.
31 Arrivées par voie aérienne à l'aéroport de Conakry.
32 Y compris touristes à Irlande du Nord.

30

Tourist/visitor arrivals and tourism expenditure *(continued)*
Thousands arrivals and millions of US dollars

Arrivées de touristes/visiteurs et dépenses touristiques *(suite)*
Milliers d'arrivées et millions de dollars É.-U.

33	Including the expenditures of foreign workers in Israel.	33	Y compris les dépenses des travailleurs étrangers en Israël.
34	Excluding seasonal and border workers.	34	À l'exclusion des travailleurs saisonniers et frontaliers.
35	Including nationals residing abroad; E/D cards.	35	Y compris les nationaux résidant à l'étranger; cartes d'embarquement.
36	Arrivals of non-resident tourists by air.	36	Arrivées de touristes non résidents par voie aérienne.
37	Air arrivals. Tarawa and Christmas Island.	37	Arrivées par voie aérienne. Tarawa et île Christmas.
38	Non-resident departures. Survey of persons crossing the state border.	38	Départs de non-résidents. Enquête menée auprès de personnes franchissant la frontière de l'État.
39	Excluding the Lebanon, Syria and Palestine nationalities.	39	À l'exclusion des nationalités libanaise, syrienne et palestinienne.
40	Excluding long term tourists on campgrounds and in holiday flats.	40	À l'exclusion des touristes à long terme en camping ou dans des appartements de vacances.
41	Departures.	41	Départs.
42	Including Singapore residents crossing the frontier by road through Johore Causeway.	42	Y compris les résidents de Singapour traversant la frontière par voie terrestre à travers le Johore Causeway.
43	Departures by air and by sea.	43	Départs par voies aérienne et maritime.
44	Air and sea arrivals.	44	Arrivées par voie aérienne et maritime.
45	Arrivals in the States of Kosrae, Chuuk, Pohnpei and Yap; excluding FSM citizens.	45	Arrivées dans les États de Kosrae, Chuuk, Pohnpei et Yap; non compris les citoyens FSM.
46	The data correspond only to 12 border posts.	46	les données ne couvrent que 12 postes frontière.
47	The data of all the border posts of the country are used.	47	Les données de l'ensemble des postes frontières du pays sont utilisées.
48	Including arrivals from India.	48	Y compris les arrivées à Inde.
49	Including Niueans residing usually in New Zealand.	49	Y compris les nationaux de Nioué résidant habituellement en Nouvelle-Zélande.
50	Non-resident tourists staying in registered hotels.	50	Non résidents touristes dans les hôtels enregistrés.
51	Arrivals of non-resident tourists at national borders.	51	Arrivées de touristes non résidents aux frontières nationales.
52	Air arrivals (Palau International Airport).	52	Arrivées par voie aérienne (Aéroport international de Palaos).
53	Including tourists with identity document other than a passport.	53	Nouvelle série estimée comprenant les touristes avec une pièce d'identité autre qu'un passeport.
54	Include hotels, apartment hotels, "pousadas", tourist apartments, tourist villages, camping sites, recreation centres, tourism in rural areas and local accommodation.	54	Inclure les hôtels, les appart-hôtels, les pousadas, les appartements touristiques, les villages touristiques, les terrains de camping, les centres de loisirs, le tourisme dans les zones rurales et les hébergements locaux.
55	Data refer to fiscal years beginning 1 July.	55	Les données se réfèrent aux exercices budgétaires commençant le 1er juillet.
56	Including nationals residing abroad and crew members.	56	Y compris les nationaux résidant à l'étranger et membres des équipages.
57	Excluding the left side of the river Nistru and the municipality of Bender.	57	La rive gauche de la rivière Nistru et la municipalité de Bender sont exclues.
58	Including Italian tourists.	58	Y compris les touristes italiens.
59	Excluding Malaysian citizens arriving by land.	59	Non compris les arrivées de malaysiens par voie terrestre.
60	Excluding Netherlands Antillean residents.	60	A l'exclusion des résidents des Antilles Néerlandaises.
61	Arrivals by air. Including arrivals to Saint Martin (French part).	61	Arrivées par voie aérienne. Y compris les arrivées à Saint-Martin (partie française).
62	Non-resident tourists staying in commercial accommodation only (representing approximately 25% of all tourists).	62	Les touristes non-résidents séjournant dans un logement commercial seulement (représentant environ 25% de tous les touristes).
63	Without first quarter.	63	Sans premier trimestre.
64	Excluding arrivals for work and contract workers.	64	À l'exclusion des arrivées par travail et les travailleurs contractuels.
65	Excluding transit.	65	À l'exclusion des personnes en transit.
66	West Bank only.	66	Cisjordanie seulement.
67	West Bank and Gaza.	67	Cisjordanie et Gaza.
68	Arrivals at Zanderij Airport.	68	Arrivées à l'aéroport de Zanderij.
69	Including Iraqi nationals.	69	Y compris les ressortissants iraquiens.
70	Arrivals by air at Dili Airport.	70	Arrivées par voie aérienne à l'aéroport de Dili.
71	Turkish citizens resident abroad are included.	71	Citoyens turcs résidant à l'étranger sont inclus.
72	Arrivals in hotels only. Including domestic tourism and nationals of the country residing abroad.	72	Arrivées dans les hôtels uniquement. Y compris le tourisme interne et les nationaux résidant à l'étranger.

31

Net disbursements of official development assistance to recipients
Total, bilateral and multilateral aid (millions of US dollars); and as a percentage of Gross National Income (GNI)

Décaissements nets d'aide publique au développement aux bénéficiaires
Total, bilatérale et multilatérale d'aide (millions de dollars É.-U.); et en pourcentage du Revenu National Brut (RNB)

Region, country or area[&]	1985	1995	2005	2010	2015	2016	2017	2018	Région, pays ou zone[&]
Total, all countries or areas [1]									**Total, tous pays ou zones [1]**
Bilateral	25 604	46 875	81 833	92 131	111 374	118 315	123 597	121 932	**Bilatérale**
Multilateral	5 920	11 004	25 620	37 133	35 368	40 493	41 429	44 346	**Multilatérale**
Total	31 524	57 879	107 452	129 264	146 741	158 808	165 026	166 278	**Total**
% of GNI	1.3	1.0	1.2	0.7	0.6	0.6	0.6	0.6	**% du RNB**
Africa [1]									**Afrique [1]**
Bilateral	10 076	16 828	24 081	30 087	33 959	31 563	34 345	34 597	Bilatérale
Multilateral	2 247	5 015	11 740	17 732	16 137	18 794	19 455	20 660	Multilatérale
Total	12 323	21 843	35 821	47 820	50 096	50 357	53 800	55 257	Total
% of GNI	3.6	4.4	3.4	2.6	2.2	2.3	2.4	2.4	% du RNB
Northern Africa [1,2]									**Afrique septentrionale [1,2]**
Bilateral	2 849	2 703	1 705	1 844	3 712	3 585	...	...	Bilatérale
Multilateral	142	277	980	823	1 294	1 783	...	...	Multilatérale
Total	2 991	2 981	2 685	2 667	5 006	5 368	...	...	Total
% of GNI	2.7	1.9	0.8	0.5	0.8	0.9	...	...	% du RNB
Sub-Saharan Africa [1,3]									**Afrique subsaharienne [1,3]**
Bilateral	7 017	13 771	21 889	27 172	28 572	25 949	30 130	29 418	Bilatérale
Multilateral	1 968	4 594	10 532	16 425	14 268	15 880	16 616	18 027	Multilatérale
Total	8 985	18 365	32 420	43 597	42 840	41 829	46 745	47 445	Total
% of GNI	3.9	5.4	4.5	3.4	2.7	2.8	2.9	2.9	% du RNB
Americas [1]									**Amériques [1]**
Bilateral	2 664	5 249	4 328	6 856	8 184	8 959	6 209	7 976	Bilatérale
Multilateral	398	935	2 106	2 854	2 027	2 342	2 481	2 518	Multilatérale
Total	3 062	6 184	6 434	9 710	10 211	11 301	8 690	10 494	Total
% of GNI	0.4	0.3	0.2	0.2	0.2	0.3	0.2	0.2	% du RNB
North America [1]									**Amérique du Nord [1]**
Bilateral	1 989	2 988	2 285	4 974	3 652	5 675	...	...	Bilatérale
Multilateral	203	513	1 011	1 886	916	1 210	...	...	Multilatérale
Total	2 193	3 501	3 296	6 860	4 567	6 885	...	...	Total
% of GNI	0.9	0.8	0.3	0.5	0.3	0.5	...	...	% du RNB
South America [1]									**Amérique du Sud [1]**
Bilateral	743	2 186	1 962	1 726	3 393	2 789	1 851	3 640	Bilatérale
Multilateral	150	344	792	858	928	1 003	1 151	1 033	Multilatérale
Total	892	2 531	2 754	2 584	4 321	3 793	3 002	4 673	Total
% of GNI	0.2	0.2	0.2	0.1	0.1	0.1	0.1	0.2	% du RNB
Asia									**Asie**
Bilateral	8 655	13 082	38 172	25 914	30 732	33 313	38 774	36 493	Bilatérale
Multilateral	2 747	4 415	7 579	9 896	9 737	10 735	10 644	12 746	Multilatérale
Total [1]	11 402	17 497	45 750	35 810	40 469	44 048	49 418	49 239	Total [1]
% of GNI [1]	0.8	0.6	0.9	0.3	0.2	0.3	0.3	0.2	% du RNB [1]
Eastern and South-Eastern Asia [1,4]									**Asie orientale et du Sud-Est [1,4]**
Bilateral	2 448	7 387	6 613	5 019	3 496	2 571	...	...	Bilatérale
Multilateral	498	1 411	1 779	2 515	1 901	1 915	...	...	Multilatérale
Total	2 946	8 798	8 391	7 534	5 397	4 486	...	...	Total
% of GNI	0.5	0.4	0.3	0.1	~0.0	~0.0	...	...	% du RNB
South-central Asia									**Asie centrale et du Sud**
Bilateral [1,5]	2 327	3 296	6 818	12 530	13 628	11 206	12 733	9 207	Bilatérale [1,5]
Multilateral [1,5]	1 998	2 409	4 395	5 499	6 155	6 915	6 439	7 296	Multilatérale [1,5]
Total [1,5]	4 326	5 705	11 213	18 029	19 783	18 121	19 172	16 503	Total [1,5]
% of GNI	1.5	1.1	1.0	0.8	0.6	0.6	0.5	0.4	% du RNB
Western Asia [1,6]									**Asie occidentale [1,6]**
Bilateral	3 856	2 449	24 324	7 766	12 535	18 817	21 756	24 835	Bilatérale
Multilateral	181	504	1 182	1 709	1 530	1 715	2 154	2 472	Multilatérale
Total	4 037	2 954	25 506	9 475	14 065	20 531	23 910	27 308	Total
% of GNI	0.9	0.7	3.5	1.2	2.0	2.8	3.1	7.5	% du RNB
Europe [1,7]									**Europe [1,7]**
Bilateral	383	1 753	2 446	3 123	2 782	3 353	3 814	2 548	Bilatérale
Multilateral	28	534	1 605	2 787	4 002	4 802	4 598	3 900	Multilatérale
Total	410	2 288	4 051	5 910	6 783	8 154	8 412	6 449	Total
% of GNI	0.6	1.0	0.6	0.5	0.6	0.8	0.8	0.6	% du RNB

Net disbursements of official development assistance to recipients *(continued)*
Total, bilateral and multilateral aid (millions of US dollars); and as a percentage of Gross National Income (GNI)

Décaissements nets d'aide publique au développement aux bénéficiaires *(suite)*
Total, bilatérale et multilatérale d'aide (millions de dollars É.-U.); et en pourcentage du Revenu National Brut (RNB)

Region, country or area[&]	1985	1995	2005	2010	2015	2016	2017	2018	Région, pays ou zone[&]
Oceania [1]									**Océanie** [1]
Bilateral	849	1 768	799	1 580	1 624	1 229	1 446	1 683	Bilatérale
Multilateral	38	62	341	269	295	454	551	603	Multilatérale
Total	887	1 829	1 141	1 849	1 919	1 683	1 997	2 286	Total
% of GNI	14.2	12.1	11.6	9.6	6.4	5.7	6.4	7.0	% du RNB
Micronesia [1]									**Micronésie** [1]
Bilateral	...	71	102	63	77	42	82	75	Bilatérale
Multilateral	...	3	3	1	4	9	16	24	Multilatérale
Total	...	74	105	64	81	51	98	99	Total
% of GNI	...	31.4	40.5	20.8	21.7	13.2	25.1	24.8	% du RNB
Areas not specified									**Zones non spécifiées**
Bilateral	2 977	8 196	12 007	24 571	34 092	39 899	39 010	38 635	Bilatérale
Multilateral	462	42	2 248	3 595	3 171	3 365	3 700	3 919	Multilatérale
Total	3 439	8 238	14 254	28 166	37 263	43 265	42 710	42 554	Total
Afghanistan									**Afghanistan**
Bilateral	7	129	2 273	5 522	3 908	3 506	3 202	3 027	Bilatérale
Multilateral	9	84	542	713	366	564	610	765	Multilatérale
Total	16	213	2 815	6 235	4 274	4 069	3 812	3 792	Total
% of GNI	...	...	...	39.3	21.3	20.9	18.8	19.5	% du RNB
Albania									**Albanie**
Bilateral	...	118	192	253	233	89	81	154	Bilatérale
Multilateral	...	63	123	112	102	82	87	190	Multilatérale
Total	...	181	315	365	335	171	168	344	Total
% of GNI	...	7.4	3.8	3.1	2.9	1.4	1.3	2.3	% du RNB
Algeria									**Algérie**
Bilateral	161	272	252	131	20	90	109	76	Bilatérale
Multilateral	11	24	96	71	51	54	66	69	Multilatérale
Total	172	296	347	201	71	145	175	144	Total
% of GNI	0.3	0.8	0.4	0.1	~0.0	0.1	0.1	0.1	% du RNB
Angola									**Angola**
Bilateral	72	304	217	146	276	62	76	47	Bilatérale
Multilateral	19	113	198	89	104	144	147	116	Multilatérale
Total	90	416	415	235	380	207	223	163	Total
% of GNI	1.4	8.7	1.3	0.3	0.4	0.2	0.2	0.2	% du RNB
Anguilla									**Anguilla**
Bilateral	2	3	4	-1	...	...	...	...	Bilatérale
Multilateral	1	1	~0	9	...	...	...	...	Multilatérale
Total	3	3	4	8	...	...	...	...	Total
Antigua and Barbuda									**Antigua-et-Barbuda**
Bilateral	2	2	7	6	1	-2	-21	6	Bilatérale
Multilateral	1	~0	1	14	1	2	31	11	Multilatérale
Total	3	2	8	20	1	~0	10	17	Total
% of GNI	1.2	0.4	0.8	1.8	0.1	~0.0	0.7	1.1	% du RNB
Argentina									**Argentine**
Bilateral	30	131	62	100	-45	-200	-34	-21	Bilatérale
Multilateral	9	17	32	30	26	203	33	93	Multilatérale
Total	39	148	94	130	-19	3	-1	73	Total
% of GNI	0.1	0.1	0.1	~0.0	0.0	0.0	0.0	~0.0	% du RNB
Armenia									**Arménie**
Bilateral	...	111	105	209	174	143	150	61	Bilatérale
Multilateral	...	107	67	111	173	183	107	80	Multilatérale
Total	...	218	173	320	347	326	257	141	Total
% of GNI	...	14.9	3.4	3.3	3.2	3.0	2.1	1.1	% du RNB
Aruba									**Aruba**
Bilateral	...	23	...	...	...	...	...	...	Bilatérale
Multilateral	...	3	...	...	...	...	...	...	Multilatérale
Total	12	26	...	...	...	...	...	...	Total
% of GNI	...	2.0	...	...	...	...	...	...	% du RNB
Azerbaijan									**Azerbaïdjan**
Bilateral	...	67	119	77	23	36	48	48	Bilatérale
Multilateral	...	53	91	80	47	44	75	39	Multilatérale
Total	...	120	210	156	70	79	124	87	Total
% of GNI	...	3.9	1.8	0.3	0.1	0.2	0.3	0.2	% du RNB

Net disbursements of official development assistance to recipients *(continued)*
Total, bilateral and multilateral aid (millions of US dollars); and as a percentage of Gross National Income (GNI)

Décaissements nets d'aide publique au développement aux bénéficiaires *(suite)*
Total, bilatérale et multilatérale d'aide (millions de dollars É.-U.); et en pourcentage du Revenu National Brut (RNB)

Region, country or area&	1985	1995	2005	2010	2015	2016	2017	2018	Région, pays ou zone&
Bahamas									**Bahamas**
Bilateral	~0	3	...	...	...	...	...	...	Bilatérale
Multilateral	1	2	...	...	...	...	...	...	Multilatérale
Total	1	4	...	...	...	...	...	...	Total
% of GNI	~0.0	0.1	...	...	...	...	...	...	% du RNB
Bahrain									**Bahreïn**
Bilateral	73	100	...	...	...	...	...	...	Bilatérale
Multilateral	1	~0	...	...	...	...	...	...	Multilatérale
Total	74	100	...	...	...	...	...	...	Total
% of GNI	2.2	1.7	...	...	...	...	...	...	% du RNB
Bangladesh									**Bangladesh**
Bilateral	475	658	521	505	1 629	1 400	2 599	1 337	Bilatérale
Multilateral	508	375	731	822	964	1 133	1 183	1 707	Multilatérale
Total	983	1 033	1 252	1 327	2 593	2 533	3 782	3 044	Total
% of GNI	4.3	2.6	1.7	1.1	1.3	1.1	1.5	1.1	% du RNB
Barbados									**Barbade**
Bilateral	5	-~0	-3	-2	...	...	...	...	Bilatérale
Multilateral	1	1	3	18	...	...	...	...	Multilatérale
Total	6	1	-1	16	...	...	...	...	Total
% of GNI	...	~0.0	-~0.0	0.4	...	...	...	...	% du RNB
Belarus									**Bélarus**
Bilateral	...	...	40	94	71	-66	-296	81	Bilatérale
Multilateral	...	...	18	42	34	43	46	38	Multilatérale
Total	...	...	58	136	105	-22	-250	119	Total
% of GNI	...	...	0.2	0.2	0.2	-0.1	-0.5	0.2	% du RNB
Belize									**Belize**
Bilateral	21	12	6	8	11	6	13	15	Bilatérale
Multilateral	1	7	6	16	17	29	21	19	Multilatérale
Total	22	19	12	24	28	35	34	34	Total
% of GNI	10.8	3.2	1.2	1.9	1.7	2.1	2.0	1.9	% du RNB
Benin									**Bénin**
Bilateral	62	229	175	388	256	252	381	323	Bilatérale
Multilateral	32	52	174	301	180	249	299	251	Multilatérale
Total	94	281	349	689	437	501	680	574	Total
% of GNI	9.2	13.2	7.3	10.0	5.3	5.9	7.4	5.6	% du RNB
Bermuda									**Bermudes**
Bilateral	1	-2	...	...	...	...	...	...	Bilatérale
Multilateral	~0	0	...	...	...	...	...	...	Multilatérale
Total	1	-2	...	...	...	...	...	...	Total
% of GNI	0.1	-0.1	...	...	...	...	...	...	% du RNB
Bhutan									**Bhoutan**
Bilateral	6	60	40	53	59	32	-42	36	Bilatérale
Multilateral	14	10	38	44	38	20	161	69	Multilatérale
Total	21	69	79	97	97	52	119	106	Total
% of GNI	15.0	26.1	9.8	6.5	5.1	2.5	5.1	4.5	% du RNB
Bolivia (Plurin. State of)									**Bolivie (État plurin. de)**
Bilateral	129	526	386	412	589	524	787	617	Bilatérale
Multilateral	30	153	157	148	203	173	162	113	Multilatérale
Total	159	679	543	560	791	696	949	730	Total
% of GNI	3.2	10.4	5.9	3.0	2.5	2.1	2.6	1.9	% du RNB
Bosnia and Herzegovina									**Bosnie-Herzégovine**
Bilateral	...	900	309	290	120	197	85	168	Bilatérale
Multilateral	...	66	231	222	236	249	355	186	Multilatérale
Total	...	966	540	511	356	446	441	354	Total
% of GNI	...	59.4	4.6	2.9	2.2	2.6	2.5	1.8	% du RNB
Botswana									**Botswana**
Bilateral	71	71	8	95	41	65	63	65	Bilatérale
Multilateral	24	19	40	60	24	25	39	21	Multilatérale
Total	96	90	48	155	66	91	102	86	Total
% of GNI	9.4	1.9	0.5	1.3	0.5	0.6	0.6	0.5	% du RNB
Brazil									**Brésil**
Bilateral	54	230	113	377	719	572	-2	343	Bilatérale
Multilateral	31	34	104	88	284	103	276	99	Multilatérale
Total	85	264	217	465	1 003	675	274	443	Total
% of GNI	~0.0	~0.0	~0.0	~0.0	0.1	~0.0	~0.0	~0.0	% du RNB

31

Net disbursements of official development assistance to recipients *(continued)*
Total, bilateral and multilateral aid (millions of US dollars); and as a percentage of Gross National Income (GNI)

Décaissements nets d'aide publique au développement aux bénéficiaires *(suite)*
Total, bilatérale et multilatérale d'aide (millions de dollars É.-U.); et en pourcentage du Revenu National Brut (RNB)

Region, country or area&	1985	1995	2005	2010	2015	2016	2017	2018	Région, pays ou zone&
British Virgin Islands									**Îles Vierges britanniques**
Bilateral	2	~0	...	...	...	...	...	...	Bilatérale
Multilateral	~0	1	...	...	...	...	...	...	Multilatérale
Total	2	1	...	...	...	...	...	...	Total
Brunei Darussalam									**Brunéi Darussalam**
Bilateral	1	4	...	...	...	...	...	...	Bilatérale
Multilateral	~0	~0	...	...	...	...	...	...	Multilatérale
Total	1	4	...	...	...	...	...	...	Total
% of GNI	...	0.1	...	...	...	...	...	...	% du RNB
Burkina Faso									**Burkina Faso**
Bilateral	134	350	382	554	527	492	498	474	Bilatérale
Multilateral	54	140	316	491	471	538	394	640	Multilatérale
Total	188	490	698	1 045	998	1 029	892	1 114	Total
% of GNI	12.2	20.7	12.8	12.0	9.9	9.8	7.5	7.9	% du RNB
Burundi									**Burundi**
Bilateral	91	147	163	279	185	560	241	236	Bilatérale
Multilateral	46	140	202	349	181	183	195	215	Multilatérale
Total	137	287	366	628	367	743	436	451	Total
% of GNI	12.1	29.0	33.3	31.1	11.8	25.1	13.8	14.7	% du RNB
Cabo Verde									**Cabo Verde**
Bilateral	42	91	112	248	111	77	87	56	Bilatérale
Multilateral	22	25	51	79	42	38	36	28	Multilatérale
Total	64	116	163	327	153	115	123	84	Total
% of GNI	48.0	23.9	17.4	20.6	10.0	7.2	7.2	4.3	% du RNB
Cambodia									**Cambodge**
Bilateral	9	389	288	471	522	552	702	548	Bilatérale
Multilateral	5	117	165	210	157	177	155	224	Multilatérale
Total	14	506	453	681	679	728	856	773	Total
% of GNI	...	15.0	7.5	6.4	4.0	3.9	4.1	3.4	% du RNB
Cameroon									**Cameroun**
Bilateral	134	380	279	303	434	489	685	792	Bilatérale
Multilateral	18	64	138	237	230	267	531	374	Multilatérale
Total	152	444	417	540	664	757	1 217	1 166	Total
% of GNI	1.9	4.9	2.4	2.1	2.2	2.4	3.6	3.1	% du RNB
Cayman Islands									**Îles Caïmanes**
Bilateral	-~0	-1	...	...	...	...	...	...	Bilatérale
Multilateral	~0	~0	...	...	...	...	...	...	Multilatérale
Total	~0	-1	...	...	...	...	...	...	Total
Central African Republic									**République centrafricaine**
Bilateral	73	126	37	78	295	268	260	338	Bilatérale
Multilateral	31	42	52	183	192	239	252	317	Multilatérale
Total	104	168	89	261	487	507	512	656	Total
% of GNI	12.1	15.3	6.7	12.1	28.4	27.4	23.6	27.5	% du RNB
Chad									**Tchad**
Bilateral	118	165	166	275	1	276	323	485	Bilatérale
Multilateral	61	70	221	215	606	348	326	390	Multilatérale
Total	179	235	386	490	606	624	649	875	Total
% of GNI	17.4	16.3	6.9	4.8	5.7	6.3	6.6	7.9	% du RNB
Chile									**Chili**
Bilateral	46	151	88	138	36	163	48	...	Bilatérale
Multilateral	3	9	83	44	18	16	22	...	Multilatérale
Total	49	161	171	182	54	178	70	...	Total
% of GNI	0.3	0.2	0.2	0.1	~0.0	0.1	~0.0	...	% du RNB
China									**Chine**
Bilateral	697	2 543	1 470	344	-558	-981	-1 143	-922	Bilatérale
Multilateral	242	921	329	327	252	190	153	216	Multilatérale
Total [8]	939	3 464	1 798	672	-306	-791	-990	-706	Total [8]
% of GNI [8]	0.3	0.5	0.1	~0.0	0.0	-~0.0	-~0.0	-~0.0	% du RNB [8]
China, Hong Kong SAR									**Chine, RAS de Hong Kong**
Bilateral	18	14	...	...	...	...	...	...	Bilatérale
Multilateral	2	4	...	...	...	...	...	...	Multilatérale
Total	20	18	...	...	...	...	...	...	Total
% of GNI	0.1	~0.0	...	...	...	...	...	...	% du RNB

31

Net disbursements of official development assistance to recipients *(continued)*
Total, bilateral and multilateral aid (millions of US dollars); and as a percentage of Gross National Income (GNI)

Décaissements nets d'aide publique au développement aux bénéficiaires *(suite)*
Total, bilatérale et multilatérale d'aide (millions de dollars É.-U.); et en pourcentage du Revenu National Brut (RNB)

Region, country or area&	1985	1995	2005	2010	2015	2016	2017	2018	Région, pays ou zone&
China, Macao SAR									**Chine, RAS de Macao**
Bilateral	~0	-4	...	...	...	...	...	...	Bilatérale
Multilateral	~0	0	...	...	...	...	...	...	Multilatérale
Total	~0	-4	...	...	...	...	...	...	Total
% of GNI	~0.0	-0.1	...	...	...	...	...	...	% du RNB
Colombia									**Colombie**
Bilateral	36	170	560	575	1 275	1 003	596	1 630	Bilatérale
Multilateral	17	12	83	98	81	103	254	142	Multilatérale
Total	53	182	643	673	1 356	1 107	850	1 772	Total
% of GNI	0.2	0.2	0.5	0.2	0.5	0.4	0.3	0.6	% du RNB
Comoros									**Comores**
Bilateral	32	27	5	23	30	21	30	51	Bilatérale
Multilateral	15	15	18	47	36	33	38	40	Multilatérale
Total	47	42	23	70	66	54	67	91	Total
% of GNI	24.1	10.4	3.6	7.7	6.6	5.2	6.3	7.8	% du RNB
Congo									**Congo**
Bilateral	55	117	1 350	1 048	38	34	47	74	Bilatérale
Multilateral	14	10	76	267	51	53	60	72	Multilatérale
Total	69	127	1 426	1 315	89	87	107	146	Total
% of GNI	3.4	10.3	35.4	14.6	1.1	1.0	1.4	1.5	% du RNB
Cook Islands									**Îles Cook**
Bilateral	8	10	6	13	22	-9	5	29	Bilatérale
Multilateral	1	1	1	1	4	27	14	5	Multilatérale
Total	9	11	7	14	26	17	19	34	Total
Costa Rica									**Costa Rica**
Bilateral	237	33	19	85	87	74	66	60	Bilatérale
Multilateral	14	13	13	16	25	27	33	39	Multilatérale
Total	252	46	33	101	111	101	99	99	Total
% of GNI	6.9	0.4	0.2	0.3	0.2	0.2	0.2	0.2	% du RNB
Côte d'Ivoire									**Côte d'Ivoire**
Bilateral	110	949	16	478	301	203	349	529	Bilatérale
Multilateral	7	264	75	368	351	413	480	424	Multilatérale
Total	117	1 212	91	845	652	616	829	954	Total
% of GNI	1.9	12.1	0.6	3.5	2.0	1.8	2.3	2.3	% du RNB
Croatia									**Croatie**
Bilateral	...	48	58	11	...	...	...	...	Bilatérale
Multilateral	...	5	65	121	...	...	...	...	Multilatérale
Total	...	53	123	132	...	...	...	...	Total
% of GNI	...	0.2	0.3	0.2	...	...	...	...	% du RNB
Cuba									**Cuba**
Bilateral	31	46	67	82	533	2 670	701	724	Bilatérale
Multilateral	11	17	23	51	25	28	34	25	Multilatérale
Total	42	64	90	132	558	2 698	735	750	Total
% of GNI	0.2	0.2	0.2	0.2	0.7	...	...	...	% du RNB
Cyprus									**Chypre**
Bilateral	31	15	...	...	...	...	...	...	Bilatérale
Multilateral	6	7	...	...	...	...	...	...	Multilatérale
Total	37	21	...	...	...	...	...	...	Total
% of GNI	1.5	0.2	...	...	...	...	...	...	% du RNB
Dem. People's Rep. Korea									**Rép. pop. dém. de Corée**
Bilateral	...	3	33	28	104	86	83	82	Bilatérale
Multilateral	...	11	54	50	27	34	50	38	Multilatérale
Total	6	13	87	79	131	120	133	121	Total
Dem. Rep. of the Congo									**Rép. dém. du Congo**
Bilateral	223	136	1 094	1 042	1 663	1 058	1 394	1 410	Bilatérale
Multilateral	83	59	788	2 442	936	1 044	899	1 103	Multilatérale
Total	305	195	1 882	3 484	2 599	2 102	2 293	2 513	Total
% of GNI	...	4.0	16.4	16.9	7.4	5.8	6.2	5.5	% du RNB
Djibouti									**Djibouti**
Bilateral	71	94	46	105	140	141	101	120	Bilatérale
Multilateral	11	12	29	27	33	44	41	59	Multilatérale
Total	81	106	74	132	173	185	142	179	Total
% of GNI	...	...	...	...	9.8	9.8	7.3	8.7	% du RNB

31

Net disbursements of official development assistance to recipients *(continued)*
Total, bilateral and multilateral aid (millions of US dollars); and as a percentage of Gross National Income (GNI)

Décaissements nets d'aide publique au développement aux bénéficiaires *(suite)*
Total, bilatérale et multilatérale d'aide (millions de dollars É.-U.); et en pourcentage du Revenu National Brut (RNB)

Region, country or area[&]	1985	1995	2005	2010	2015	2016	2017	2018	Région, pays ou zone[&]
Dominica									**Dominique**
Bilateral	13	18	13	3	4	-2	-3	3	Bilatérale
Multilateral	4	7	8	30	8	11	22	24	Multilatérale
Total	17	25	21	32	12	9	19	27	Total
% of GNI	14.2	9.6	6.3	6.7	2.3	1.5	3.9	5.3	% du RNB
Dominican Republic									**République dominicaine**
Bilateral	155	94	28	78	241	125	75	13	Bilatérale
Multilateral	12	13	67	116	39	51	43	75	Multilatérale
Total	167	108	95	194	280	177	118	88	Total
% of GNI	3.5	0.7	0.3	0.4	0.4	0.3	0.2	0.1	% du RNB
Ecuador									**Équateur**
Bilateral	61	161	184	119	172	126	122	229	Bilatérale
Multilateral	19	27	74	49	146	118	81	173	Multilatérale
Total	79	188	258	169	318	244	203	402	Total
% of GNI	0.5	0.8	0.7	0.3	0.3	0.3	0.2	0.4	% du RNB
Egypt									**Égypte**
Bilateral	1 692	1 873	730	412	2 341	2 035	-353	1 719	Bilatérale
Multilateral	82	155	316	187	184	403	386	351	Multilatérale
Total	1 774	2 028	1 046	599	2 525	2 437	33	2 070	Total
% of GNI	5.0	3.4	1.2	0.3	0.8	0.7	~0.0	0.9	% du RNB
El Salvador									**El Salvador**
Bilateral	308	260	146	224	66	72	120	146	Bilatérale
Multilateral	18	19	72	78	24	57	32	107	Multilatérale
Total	325	279	218	302	90	129	152	253	Total
% of GNI	8.8	3.2	1.5	1.7	0.4	0.6	0.6	1.0	% du RNB
Equatorial Guinea									**Guinée équatoriale**
Bilateral	9	23	18	75	3	3	-1	-7	Bilatérale
Multilateral	8	10	20	10	5	4	7	13	Multilatérale
Total	17	33	38	85	7	7	7	6	Total
% of GNI	29.5	28.3	0.9	0.9	0.1	0.1	0.1	0.1	% du RNB
Eritrea									**Érythrée**
Bilateral	...	119	229	49	54	16	36	25	Bilatérale
Multilateral	...	29	121	114	40	51	43	59	Multilatérale
Total	...	148	350	162	94	67	79	84	Total
% of GNI	...	25.3	32.1	7.7	...	...	...	...	% du RNB
Eswatini									**Eswatini**
Bilateral	18	49	-1	21	42	77	88	78	Bilatérale
Multilateral	6	9	47	70	51	70	60	43	Multilatérale
Total	24	58	47	91	93	147	148	120	Total
% of GNI	...	3.2	1.4	2.2	2.3	3.9	3.4	2.6	% du RNB
Ethiopia									**Éthiopie**
Bilateral	541	653	1 205	2 223	2 243	2 502	2 572	2 638	Bilatérale
Multilateral	177	224	724	1 232	996	1 582	1 553	2 302	Multilatérale
Total	718	877	1 929	3 455	3 239	4 084	4 125	4 941	Total
% of GNI	7.6	11.5	15.6	11.6	5.0	5.5	5.1	5.9	% du RNB
Fiji									**Fidji**
Bilateral	28	39	32	56	73	95	85	92	Bilatérale
Multilateral	3	4	34	19	30	23	61	25	Multilatérale
Total	31	43	66	76	102	117	146	116	Total
% of GNI	2.8	2.2	2.2	2.5	2.3	2.5	3.0	2.3	% du RNB
French Polynesia									**Polynésie française**
Bilateral	171	448	...	...	...	...	...	...	Bilatérale
Multilateral	1	3	...	...	...	...	...	...	Multilatérale
Total	172	451	...	...	...	...	...	...	Total
% of GNI	11.4	11.3	...	...	...	...	...	...	% du RNB
Gabon									**Gabon**
Bilateral	55	140	1	82	81	22	86	101	Bilatérale
Multilateral	6	4	50	24	17	19	21	15	Multilatérale
Total	61	144	50	106	99	42	106	116	Total
% of GNI	2.0	3.4	0.6	0.9	0.8	0.3	0.8	0.7	% du RNB
Gambia									**Gambie**
Bilateral	33	25	7	52	75	7	127	107	Bilatérale
Multilateral	15	20	53	70	39	85	151	127	Multilatérale
Total	48	45	61	121	114	92	278	234	Total
% of GNI	19.1	5.9	10.1	13.1	8.4	6.5	19.1	14.7	% du RNB

31

Net disbursements of official development assistance to recipients *(continued)*
Total, bilateral and multilateral aid (millions of US dollars); and as a percentage of Gross National Income (GNI)

Décaissements nets d'aide publique au développement aux bénéficiaires *(suite)*
Total, bilatérale et multilatérale d'aide (millions de dollars É.-U.); et en pourcentage du Revenu National Brut (RNB)

Region, country or area[&]	1985	1995	2005	2010	2015	2016	2017	2018	Région, pays ou zone[&]
Georgia									**Géorgie**
Bilateral	...	104	183	319	255	210	207	287	Bilatérale
Multilateral	...	106	110	270	194	252	241	302	Multilatérale
Total	...	209	293	589	449	463	447	590	Total
% of GNI	...	8.1	4.5	5.2	3.3	3.4	3.1	3.8	% du RNB
Ghana									**Ghana**
Bilateral	105	362	660	1 132	1 024	716	722	704	Bilatérale
Multilateral	89	288	493	565	746	603	541	363	Multilatérale
Total	194	650	1 153	1 697	1 770	1 319	1 263	1 068	Total
% of GNI	4.4	10.3	10.9	5.4	3.7	2.4	2.2	1.7	% du RNB
Gibraltar									**Gibraltar**
Bilateral	...	~0	...	...	...	...	...	...	Bilatérale
Multilateral	...	0	...	...	...	...	...	...	Multilatérale
Total	29	~0	...	...	...	...	...	...	Total
Grenada									**Grenade**
Bilateral	32	8	33	10	7	-4	-8	-53	Bilatérale
Multilateral	2	3	20	24	17	13	14	84	Multilatérale
Total	34	11	53	34	24	9	6	32	Total
% of GNI	21.2	3.3	7.9	4.6	2.7	0.9	0.6	2.9	% du RNB
Guatemala									**Guatemala**
Bilateral	64	178	204	335	331	199	282	314	Bilatérale
Multilateral	12	27	65	67	80	67	85	85	Multilatérale
Total	76	205	269	402	411	265	367	399	Total
% of GNI	0.8	1.4	1.0	1.0	0.7	0.4	0.5	0.5	% du RNB
Guinea									**Guinée**
Bilateral	74	305	89	47	247	248	259	338	Bilatérale
Multilateral	39	111	104	174	292	319	213	256	Multilatérale
Total	113	416	193	221	539	567	472	594	Total
% of GNI	...	11.5	7.3	3.5	6.3	6.7	4.8	5.7	% du RNB
Guinea-Bissau									**Guinée-Bissau**
Bilateral	34	95	8	-32	29	130	21	21	Bilatérale
Multilateral	22	23	59	161	66	67	93	133	Multilatérale
Total	56	118	67	129	95	197	113	154	Total
% of GNI	35.3	49.8	11.6	15.3	8.9	16.3	8.4	10.6	% du RNB
Guyana									**Guyana**
Bilateral	5	41	32	45	12	15	17	38	Bilatérale
Multilateral	6	27	70	62	20	55	34	66	Multilatérale
Total	11	68	101	106	32	70	51	104	Total
% of GNI	2.8	12.7	12.6	4.7	1.0	2.0	1.4	2.9	% du RNB
Haiti									**Haïti**
Bilateral	109	535	201	2 189	837	828	791	740	Bilatérale
Multilateral	29	120	165	700	209	244	190	256	Multilatérale
Total	138	655	367	2 890	1 046	1 072	981	996	Total
% of GNI	6.9	23.2	8.6	43.5	11.9	13.4	11.6	10.3	% du RNB
Honduras									**Honduras**
Bilateral	213	274	467	273	412	308	322	538	Bilatérale
Multilateral	25	101	183	198	128	105	120	126	Multilatérale
Total	238	375	649	471	541	412	442	664	Total
% of GNI	4.7	7.4	7.0	3.1	2.8	2.1	2.1	3.0	% du RNB
India									**Inde**
Bilateral	844	871	669	1 639	1 801	935	1 767	1 049	Bilatérale
Multilateral	743	862	1 207	1 192	1 373	1 743	1 431	1 413	Multilatérale
Total	1 587	1 733	1 876	2 831	3 174	2 679	3 198	2 462	Total
% of GNI	0.7	0.5	0.2	0.2	0.2	0.1	0.1	0.1	% du RNB
Indonesia									**Indonésie**
Bilateral	508	1 201	2 208	901	-162	-286	-12	837	Bilatérale
Multilateral	83	50	281	423	133	178	293	124	Multilatérale
Total	591	1 252	2 489	1 324	-28	-108	280	962	Total
% of GNI	0.7	0.6	0.9	0.2	0.0	-~0.0	~0.0	0.1	% du RNB
Iran (Islamic Republic of)									**Iran (Rép. islamique d')**
Bilateral	2	162	61	72	91	79	111	134	Bilatérale
Multilateral	9	25	40	40	19	37	29	33	Multilatérale
Total	11	187	101	112	111	116	140	166	Total
% of GNI	~0.0	0.2	0.1	~0.0	~0.0	~0.0	~0.0	...	% du RNB

31

Net disbursements of official development assistance to recipients *(continued)*
Total, bilateral and multilateral aid (millions of US dollars); and as a percentage of Gross National Income (GNI)

Décaissements nets d'aide publique au développement aux bénéficiaires *(suite)*
Total, bilatérale et multilatérale d'aide (millions de dollars É.-U.); et en pourcentage du Revenu National Brut (RNB)

Region, country or area&	1985	1995	2005	2010	2015	2016	2017	2018	Région, pays ou zone&
Iraq									**Iraq**
Bilateral	19	273	21 999	2 040	1 347	2 106	2 717	2 040	Bilatérale
Multilateral	1	60	58	138	136	182	191	260	Multilatérale
Total	20	333	22 057	2 178	1 483	2 288	2 908	2 300	Total
% of GNI	~0.0	...	43.5	1.6	0.8	1.4	1.5	1.0	% du RNB
Israel									**Israël**
Bilateral	1 978	334	...	...	...	...	...	...	Bilatérale
Multilateral	~0	2	...	...	...	...	...	...	Multilatérale
Total	1 978	336	...	...	...	...	...	...	Total
% of GNI	7.8	0.3	...	...	...	...	...	...	% du RNB
Jamaica									**Jamaïque**
Bilateral	159	88	-5	-8	15	-17	26	55	Bilatérale
Multilateral	7	27	48	150	44	44	35	45	Multilatérale
Total	166	115	44	141	59	27	61	100	Total
% of GNI	9.1	1.9	0.4	1.1	0.4	0.2	0.4	0.7	% du RNB
Jordan									**Jordanie**
Bilateral	598	462	593	692	1 900	2 415	2 699	2 253	Bilatérale
Multilateral	9	78	117	263	241	313	281	273	Multilatérale
Total	607	540	710	955	2 141	2 728	2 980	2 526	Total
% of GNI	12.4	8.4	5.5	3.6	5.7	7.0	7.4	6.0	% du RNB
Kazakhstan									**Kazakhstan**
Bilateral	...	48	194	140	5	29	-9	63	Bilatérale
Multilateral	...	11	31	72	77	33	68	17	Multilatérale
Total	...	59	225	212	82	63	59	80	Total
% of GNI	...	0.3	0.4	0.2	0.1	0.1	~0.0	0.1	% du RNB
Kenya									**Kenya**
Bilateral	366	506	475	1 163	1 655	1 379	1 629	1 455	Bilatérale
Multilateral	61	227	281	468	809	809	852	1 035	Multilatérale
Total	427	733	757	1 631	2 464	2 188	2 480	2 490	Total
% of GNI	7.2	8.4	4.0	4.1	3.9	3.2	3.2	2.9	% du RNB
Kiribati									**Kiribati**
Bilateral	11	13	18	22	50	49	58	17	Bilatérale
Multilateral	1	2	8	2	15	12	19	58	Multilatérale
Total	12	15	27	24	65	61	77	75	Total
% of GNI	38.1	16.0	16.6	10.4	18.5	17.5	21.2	20.7	% du RNB
Kosovo									**Kosovo**
Bilateral	...	...	...	215	251	236	141	201	Bilatérale
Multilateral	...	...	0	312	186	134	251	145	Multilatérale
Total	...	...	...	528	438	370	392	345	Total
% of GNI	...	...	...	8.9	6.7	5.4	5.3	4.3	% du RNB
Kuwait									**Koweït**
Bilateral	3	4	...	...	...	...	...	...	Bilatérale
Multilateral	1	~0	...	...	...	...	...	...	Multilatérale
Total	4	4	...	...	...	...	...	...	Total
% of GNI	~0.0	~0.0	...	...	...	...	...	...	% du RNB
Kyrgyzstan									**Kirghizistan**
Bilateral	...	151	147	245	602	315	304	280	Bilatérale
Multilateral	...	94	91	127	172	205	161	135	Multilatérale
Total	...	245	238	372	775	519	465	416	Total
% of GNI	...	15.1	10.0	8.3	12.1	8.0	6.3	5.3	% du RNB
Lao People's Dem. Rep.									**Rép. dém. populaire lao**
Bilateral	15	191	105	261	394	283	348	-376	Bilatérale
Multilateral	21	55	137	128	77	117	132	944	Multilatérale
Total	36	246	241	389	471	399	480	568	Total
% of GNI	1.5	14.0	9.0	5.8	3.4	2.6	3.0	3.3	% du RNB
Lebanon									**Liban**
Bilateral	65	147	142	319	779	960	1 083	1 183	Bilatérale
Multilateral	17	44	89	126	187	169	220	240	Multilatérale
Total	82	191	231	445	966	1 129	1 303	1 422	Total
% of GNI	...	1.6	1.1	1.2	2.0	2.2	2.4	2.6	% du RNB
Lesotho									**Lesotho**
Bilateral	65	81	26	92	43	50	77	73	Bilatérale
Multilateral	28	31	42	164	43	62	68	81	Multilatérale
Total	92	113	68	256	86	112	146	154	Total
% of GNI	18.4	8.4	3.1	8.5	3.1	4.3	5.0	4.9	% du RNB

31

Net disbursements of official development assistance to recipients *(continued)*
Total, bilateral and multilateral aid (millions of US dollars); and as a percentage of Gross National Income (GNI)

Décaissements nets d'aide publique au développement aux bénéficiaires *(suite)*
Total, bilatérale et multilatérale d'aide (millions de dollars É.-U.); et en pourcentage du Revenu National Brut (RNB)

Region, country or area[&]	1985	1995	2005	2010	2015	2016	2017	2018	Région, pays ou zone[&]
Liberia									**Libéria**
Bilateral	72	51	118	959	764	570	451	366	Bilatérale
Multilateral	19	72	104	457	330	249	180	207	Multilatérale
Total	90	123	222	1 416	1 094	819	631	573	Total
% of GNI	...	...	28.0	77.9	37.8	27.3	21.1	20.4	% du RNB
Libya									**Libye**
Bilateral	3	4	17	1	132	149	365	232	Bilatérale
Multilateral	2	2	6	7	26	30	66	71	Multilatérale
Total	5	6	24	8	157	179	432	303	Total
% of GNI	...	...	0.1	~0.0	0.5	0.7	1.1	0.6	% du RNB
Madagascar									**Madagascar**
Bilateral	118	192	517	264	400	246	359	343	Bilatérale
Multilateral	67	107	399	214	277	376	420	350	Multilatérale
Total	185	299	916	477	678	622	779	693	Total
% of GNI	6.7	10.0	18.5	5.5	7.2	6.5	7.0	5.9	% du RNB
Malawi									**Malawi**
Bilateral	72	286	301	560	694	773	986	852	Bilatérale
Multilateral	41	149	272	456	355	469	532	423	Multilatérale
Total	112	435	574	1 017	1 049	1 242	1 518	1 275	Total
% of GNI	10.4	32.2	15.9	14.8	16.9	23.0	24.2	18.1	% du RNB
Malaysia									**Malaisie**
Bilateral	217	102	17	-33	-14	-64	-55	-48	Bilatérale
Multilateral	10	5	12	27	13	13	26	13	Multilatérale
Total	227	107	29	-6	-1	-52	-29	-35	Total
% of GNI	0.8	0.1	~0.0	0.0	0.0	-~0.0	-~0.0	-~0.0	% du RNB
Maldives									**Maldives**
Bilateral	6	45	46	49	14	10	25	108	Bilatérale
Multilateral	3	7	27	40	10	13	19	12	Multilatérale
Total	9	52	72	88	24	23	43	119	Total
% of GNI	7.5	13.9	6.4	3.9	0.6	0.6	1.0	2.5	% du RNB
Mali									**Mali**
Bilateral	308	401	395	770	788	725	867	944	Bilatérale
Multilateral	70	139	330	322	414	480	493	555	Multilatérale
Total	379	540	725	1 091	1 202	1 205	1 360	1 500	Total
% of GNI	27.7	20.3	12.0	10.6	9.4	8.8	9.1	9.0	% du RNB
Malta									**Malte**
Bilateral	18	7	...	...	...	...	...	...	Bilatérale
Multilateral	~0	2	...	...	...	...	...	...	Multilatérale
Total	18	9	...	...	...	...	...	...	Total
% of GNI	1.5	0.3	...	...	...	...	...	...	% du RNB
Marshall Islands									**Îles Marshall**
Bilateral	...	31	55	18	56	12	68	11	Bilatérale
Multilateral	...	2	2	7	1	1	4	43	Multilatérale
Total	...	33	56	25	57	13	73	54	Total
% of GNI	...	21.8	31.5	12.5	23.0	4.8	27.0	19.5	% du RNB
Mauritania									**Mauritanie**
Bilateral	179	163	91	277	252	191	170	291	Bilatérale
Multilateral	28	67	97	97	78	117	122	156	Multilatérale
Total	208	230	189	374	329	307	292	447	Total
% of GNI	32.9	17.2	8.4	8.8	7.1	6.7	6.0	8.4	% du RNB
Mauritius									**Maurice**
Bilateral	24	16	13	41	30	-31	-10	35	Bilatérale
Multilateral	3	8	22	84	48	73	22	34	Multilatérale
Total	27	24	34	125	78	42	12	69	Total
% of GNI	2.6	0.6	0.5	1.3	0.6	0.3	0.1	0.4	% du RNB
Mayotte									**Mayotte**
Bilateral	20	107	201	603	...	...	...	...	Bilatérale
Multilateral	~0	1	~0	1	...	...	0	...	Multilatérale
Total	21	108	201	604	...	...	...	...	Total
Mexico									**Mexique**
Bilateral	128	386	171	398	270	643	648	515	Bilatérale
Multilateral	23	24	29	56	51	166	107	33	Multilatérale
Total	151	411	200	455	321	809	755	548	Total
% of GNI	0.1	0.1	~0.0	~0.0	~0.0	0.1	0.1	0.1	% du RNB

31

Net disbursements of official development assistance to recipients *(continued)*
Total, bilateral and multilateral aid (millions of US dollars); and as a percentage of Gross National Income (GNI)

Décaissements nets d'aide publique au développement aux bénéficiaires *(suite)*
Total, bilatérale et multilatérale d'aide (millions de dollars É.-U.); et en pourcentage du Revenu National Brut (RNB)

Region, country or area[&]	1985	1995	2005	2010	2015	2016	2017	2018	Région, pays ou zone[&]
Mongolia									**Mongolie**
Bilateral	...	128	135	206	191	241	638	184	Bilatérale
Multilateral	...	25	61	81	45	84	127	149	Multilatérale
Total	5	153	195	287	236	326	765	333	Total
% of GNI	0.2	10.8	7.9	4.3	2.2	3.2	7.8	2.9	% du RNB
Montenegro									**Monténégro**
Bilateral	...	...	4	54	27	25	3	20	Bilatérale
Multilateral	...	...	0	26	73	60	115	136	Multilatérale
Total	...	...	4	80	100	86	118	156	Total
% of GNI	...	...	0.2	2.0	2.4	1.9	2.4	2.8	% du RNB
Montserrat									**Montserrat**
Bilateral	2	9	27	16	...	39	35	36	Bilatérale
Multilateral	~0	1	1	10	...	~0	1	6	Multilatérale
Total	2	9	28	26	52	39	36	42	Total
Morocco									**Maroc**
Bilateral	836	447	395	708	873	1 259	1 616	493	Bilatérale
Multilateral	30	54	338	278	645	803	801	324	Multilatérale
Total	866	501	733	986	1 518	2 062	2 417	818	Total
% of GNI	6.0	1.3	1.2	1.1	1.5	2.0	2.3	0.7	% du RNB
Mozambique									**Mozambique**
Bilateral	242	799	806	1 432	1 310	942	1 357	1 331	Bilatérale
Multilateral	54	264	483	512	509	592	449	493	Multilatérale
Total	296	1 063	1 290	1 943	1 819	1 534	1 806	1 823	Total
% of GNI	6.8	44.1	17.5	19.8	12.5	14.4	14.7	12.9	% du RNB
Myanmar									**Myanmar**
Bilateral	205	119	34	212	927	1 126	1 194	1 301	Bilatérale
Multilateral	107	42	111	143	242	410	348	389	Multilatérale
Total	311	160	145	355	1 169	1 537	1 542	1 690	Total
% of GNI	...	...	1.2	0.7	2.0	2.5	2.4	2.4	% du RNB
Namibia									**Namibie**
Bilateral	...	170	56	207	106	74	98	87	Bilatérale
Multilateral	...	20	58	55	37	97	88	64	Multilatérale
Total	5	190	113	261	142	170	187	152	Total
% of GNI	0.4	4.6	1.6	2.4	1.2	1.5	1.4	1.1	% du RNB
Nauru									**Nauru**
Bilateral	...	3	9	27	30	21	-84	22	Bilatérale
Multilateral	...	~0	~0	1	1	2	109	10	Multilatérale
Total	~0	3	9	28	31	23	26	32	Total
% of GNI	...	...	...	48.7	25.2	17.7	17.8	21.5	% du RNB
Nepal									**Népal**
Bilateral	62	254	268	397	819	646	861	810	Bilatérale
Multilateral	126	126	139	370	406	419	408	641	Multilatérale
Total	188	381	407	767	1 224	1 065	1 269	1 452	Total
% of GNI	7.2	8.6	5.0	4.8	5.6	5.0	5.0	5.0	% du RNB
Netherlands Antilles [former]									**Antilles néerlandaises [anc.]**
Bilateral	64	97	...	...	...	...	...	...	Bilatérale
Multilateral	1	2	...	...	0	0	...	...	Multilatérale
Total	65	98	...	...	...	...	...	...	Total
New Caledonia									**Nouvelle-Calédonie**
Bilateral	145	448	...	...	...	...	...	...	Bilatérale
Multilateral	~0	3	...	...	...	...	...	...	Multilatérale
Total	145	451	...	...	...	...	...	...	Total
% of GNI	17.0	12.4	...	...	...	...	...	...	% du RNB
Nicaragua									**Nicaragua**
Bilateral	84	505	486	390	341	305	442	240	Bilatérale
Multilateral	17	65	171	121	117	126	121	114	Multilatérale
Total	101	569	656	511	458	431	563	354	Total
% of GNI	4.0	15.1	10.6	6.0	3.7	3.3	4.2	2.8	% du RNB
Niger									**Niger**
Bilateral	226	211	270	402	491	491	667	670	Bilatérale
Multilateral	72	61	254	339	379	462	557	527	Multilatérale
Total	298	272	523	741	869	952	1 225	1 197	Total
% of GNI	21.3	14.9	15.4	13.1	12.3	12.9	15.4	13.2	% du RNB

Net disbursements of official development assistance to recipients *(continued)*
Total, bilateral and multilateral aid (millions of US dollars); and as a percentage of Gross National Income (GNI)

Décaissements nets d'aide publique au développement aux bénéficiaires *(suite)*
Total, bilatérale et multilatérale d'aide (millions de dollars É.-U.); et en pourcentage du Revenu National Brut (RNB)

Region, country or area[&]	1985	1995	2005	2010	2015	2016	2017	2018	Région, pays ou zone[&]
Nigeria									**Nigéria**
Bilateral	19	88	5 954	1 072	1 492	1 362	2 195	1 950	Bilatérale
Multilateral	13	122	448	980	939	1 137	1 164	1 355	Multilatérale
Total	32	211	6 402	2 052	2 432	2 498	3 359	3 305	Total
% of GNI	~0.0	0.5	3.9	0.6	0.5	0.6	0.9	0.9	% du RNB
Niue									**Nioué**
Bilateral	...	8	19	14	19	13	11	16	Bilatérale
Multilateral	...	~0	2	1	~0	1	4	3	Multilatérale
Total	4	8	21	15	20	14	15	19	Total
North Macedonia									**Macédoine du Nord**
Bilateral	...	34	154	127	55	54	-3	39	Bilatérale
Multilateral	...	45	74	67	159	115	153	131	Multilatérale
Total	...	79	227	194	214	168	150	170	Total
% of GNI	...	1.7	3.7	2.1	2.2	1.6	1.4	1.4	% du RNB
Northern Mariana Islands									**Îles Mariannes du Nord**
Bilateral	158	~0	...	...	...	...	...	...	Bilatérale
Multilateral	1	-1	0	...	...	...	...	...	Multilatérale
Total	159	-1	...	...	...	...	...	...	Total
Oman									**Oman**
Bilateral	75	74	15	-24	...	...	...	...	Bilatérale
Multilateral	2	1	4	2	...	...	...	...	Multilatérale
Total	78	75	19	-22	...	...	...	...	Total
% of GNI	0.8	0.6	0.1	-~0.0	...	...	...	...	% du RNB
Pakistan									**Pakistan**
Bilateral	305	152	746	2 093	2 318	1 799	1 488	618	Bilatérale
Multilateral	363	349	731	840	1 446	1 162	876	749	Multilatérale
Total	668	501	1 477	2 933	3 764	2 961	2 364	1 367	Total
% of GNI	2.0	0.8	1.3	1.6	1.3	1.0	0.7	0.4	% du RNB
Palau									**Palaos**
Bilateral	...	142	23	28	13	15	20	82	Bilatérale
Multilateral	...	0	~0	1	1	3	2	2	Multilatérale
Total	...	142	24	29	14	18	22	85	Total
% of GNI	...	...	13.1	15.8	5.1	6.1	7.9	28.0	% du RNB
Panama									**Panama**
Bilateral	41	39	5	116	-2	2	-36	11	Bilatérale
Multilateral	8	8	23	14	12	20	78	28	Multilatérale
Total	49	47	28	130	10	23	42	39	Total
% of GNI	0.8	0.5	0.2	0.5	~0.0	~0.0	0.1	0.1	% du RNB
Papua New Guinea									**Papouasie-Nvl-Guinée**
Bilateral	237	330	214	420	484	424	440	561	Bilatérale
Multilateral	16	28	54	94	107	107	92	229	Multilatérale
Total	253	358	268	514	591	532	533	790	Total
% of GNI	10.8	8.2	5.9	3.9	2.8	2.6	2.5	3.5	% du RNB
Paraguay									**Paraguay**
Bilateral	25	112	51	61	30	43	74	73	Bilatérale
Multilateral	8	10	13	51	30	46	69	91	Multilatérale
Total	34	121	64	112	60	89	143	164	Total
% of GNI	...	1.5	0.7	0.4	0.2	0.3	0.4	0.4	% du RNB
Peru									**Pérou**
Bilateral	286	356	376	-368	295	251	-135	369	Bilatérale
Multilateral	21	31	89	69	39	69	133	80	Multilatérale
Total	307	387	465	-299	335	320	-2	449	Total
% of GNI	2.0	0.8	0.7	-0.2	0.2	0.2	0.0	0.2	% du RNB
Philippines									**Philippines**
Bilateral	418	798	510	431	409	177	57	443	Bilatérale
Multilateral	37	60	77	151	106	106	104	104	Multilatérale
Total	455	858	588	582	515	284	160	547	Total
% of GNI	1.6	1.1	0.5	0.2	0.1	0.1	~0.0	0.1	% du RNB
Qatar									**Qatar**
Bilateral	1	4	...	...	...	...	...	...	Bilatérale
Multilateral	1	-~0	...	...	...	...	...	...	Multilatérale
Total	2	4	...	...	...	...	...	...	Total
% of GNI	~0.0	0.1	...	...	...	...	...	...	% du RNB

31

Net disbursements of official development assistance to recipients *(continued)*
Total, bilateral and multilateral aid (millions of US dollars); and as a percentage of Gross National Income (GNI)

Décaissements nets d'aide publique au développement aux bénéficiaires *(suite)*
Total, bilatérale et multilatérale d'aide (millions de dollars É.-U.); et en pourcentage du Revenu National Brut (RNB)

Region, country or area[&]	1985	1995	2005	2010	2015	2016	2017	2018	Région, pays ou zone[&]
Republic of Korea									**République de Corée**
Bilateral	-13	54	...	...	...	...	...	...	Bilatérale
Multilateral	4	3	...	...	...	...	...	...	Multilatérale
Total	-9	57	...	...	...	...	...	...	Total
% of GNI	-~0.0	~0.0	...	...	...	...	...	...	% du RNB
Republic of Moldova									**République de Moldova**
Bilateral	...	...	94	213	204	80	87	110	Bilatérale
Multilateral	...	...	75	260	108	182	156	120	Multilatérale
Total	...	...	170	473	313	262	243	230	Total
% of GNI	...	...	5.1	6.3	3.8	3.1	2.4	1.9	% du RNB
Rwanda									**Rwanda**
Bilateral	123	403	271	602	716	636	720	560	Bilatérale
Multilateral	54	291	302	431	373	515	512	560	Multilatérale
Total	177	695	573	1 033	1 088	1 150	1 231	1 119	Total
% of GNI	10.4	53.5	21.6	18.0	13.5	13.9	13.8	12.0	% du RNB
Saint Helena									**Sainte-Hélène**
Bilateral	...	12	22	...	82	102	65	58	Bilatérale
Multilateral	...	~0	~0	...	~0	4	1	9	Multilatérale
Total	12	13	23	54	82	106	66	67	Total
Saint Kitts and Nevis									**Saint-Kitts-et-Nevis**
Bilateral	3	2	1	-2	...	...	...	...	Bilatérale
Multilateral	1	2	2	13	...	...	...	...	Multilatérale
Total	4	4	3	11	...	...	...	...	Total
% of GNI	4.0	1.3	0.5	1.6	...	...	...	...	% du RNB
Saint Lucia									**Sainte-Lucie**
Bilateral	4	31	4	~0	1	-7	6	-~0	Bilatérale
Multilateral	3	17	6	41	13	22	10	9	Multilatérale
Total	7	48	11	41	14	15	15	9	Total
% of GNI	2.9	8.0	1.2	3.0	0.9	1.0	0.9	0.5	% du RNB
Saint Vincent & Grenadines									**Saint-Vincent-Grenadines**
Bilateral	3	32	4	-~0	3	-5	6	8	Bilatérale
Multilateral	3	15	4	17	11	14	5	10	Multilatérale
Total	5	48	8	17	14	9	12	18	Total
% of GNI	3.8	15.6	1.5	2.5	1.6	1.1	1.4	2.1	% du RNB
Samoa									**Samoa**
Bilateral	12	34	23	75	63	-14	87	87	Bilatérale
Multilateral	6	5	20	50	31	102	45	34	Multilatérale
Total	18	38	43	124	94	89	131	121	Total
% of GNI	25.9	...	10.1	20.0	11.9	11.5	16.1	14.5	% du RNB
Sao Tome and Principe									**Sao Tomé-et-Principe**
Bilateral	6	72	10	36	33	24	16	14	Bilatérale
Multilateral	6	12	23	14	16	24	25	32	Multilatérale
Total	12	84	33	50	49	47	40	46	Total
% of GNI	...	...	24.4	25.4	15.4	13.5	10.8	10.9	% du RNB
Saudi Arabia									**Arabie saoudite**
Bilateral	16	17	23	...	...	...	...	...	Bilatérale
Multilateral	12	~0	2	...	...	...	...	...	Multilatérale
Total	27	17	25	...	...	...	...	...	Total
% of GNI	~0.0	~0.0	~0.0	...	...	...	...	...	% du RNB
Senegal									**Sénégal**
Bilateral	249	489	429	654	618	428	602	678	Bilatérale
Multilateral	42	163	272	283	251	303	305	319	Multilatérale
Total	290	652	701	936	869	731	908	997	Total
% of GNI	8.0	10.8	6.4	5.8	5.0	4.0	4.4	4.3	% du RNB
Serbia									**Serbie**
Bilateral	...	92	838	300	-75	219	1 255	510	Bilatérale
Multilateral	...	3	231	361	387	414	433	560	Multilatérale
Total	...	95	1 068	661	312	633	1 688	1 070	Total
% of GNI	...	...	3.9	1.6	0.8	1.7	4.1	2.2	% du RNB
Seychelles									**Seychelles**
Bilateral	19	12	12	43	1	-7	5	...	Bilatérale
Multilateral	3	2	6	11	6	13	11	...	Multilatérale
Total	22	13	17	54	7	6	16	...	Total
% of GNI	13.5	2.7	1.9	5.9	0.5	0.4	1.2	...	% du RNB

31

Net disbursements of official development assistance to recipients *(continued)*
Total, bilateral and multilateral aid (millions of US dollars); and as a percentage of Gross National Income (GNI)

Décaissements nets d'aide publique au développement aux bénéficiaires *(suite)*
Total, bilatérale et multilatérale d'aide (millions de dollars É.-U.); et en pourcentage du Revenu National Brut (RNB)

Region, country or area&	1985	1995	2005	2010	2015	2016	2017	2018	Région, pays ou zone&
Sierra Leone									**Sierra Leone**
Bilateral	43	136	131	221	708	471	339	331	Bilatérale
Multilateral	20	76	209	237	239	223	203	177	Multilatérale
Total	64	212	340	458	947	693	541	508	Total
% of GNI	7.7	26.0	21.1	17.6	22.8	21.2	14.9	13.4	% du RNB
Singapore									**Singapour**
Bilateral	21	16	...	...	...	...	...	...	Bilatérale
Multilateral	2	1	...	...	...	...	...	...	Multilatérale
Total	23	17	...	...	...	...	...	...	Total
% of GNI	0.1	~0.0	...	...	...	...	...	...	% du RNB
Slovenia									**Slovénie**
Bilateral	...	40	...	...	...	...	...	...	Bilatérale
Multilateral	...	12	...	...	...	...	...	...	Multilatérale
Total	...	53	...	...	...	...	...	...	Total
% of GNI	...	0.3	...	...	...	...	...	...	% du RNB
Solomon Islands									**Îles Salomon**
Bilateral	14	42	165	293	170	152	84	168	Bilatérale
Multilateral	5	6	32	40	21	23	103	28	Multilatérale
Total	19	48	197	333	190	176	187	196	Total
% of GNI	12.4	14.9	47.3	67.0	17.0	15.1	15.3	14.6	% du RNB
Somalia									**Somalie**
Bilateral	249	134	117	309	1 035	969	1 402	1 245	Bilatérale
Multilateral	102	54	123	197	225	215	359	330	Multilatérale
Total	351	188	240	506	1 261	1 184	1 760	1 575	Total
% of GNI	42.4	...	...	...	31.4	28.4	39.3	33.6	% du RNB
South Africa									**Afrique du Sud**
Bilateral	...	358	423	800	901	929	806	683	Bilatérale
Multilateral	...	28	259	236	519	251	209	238	Multilatérale
Total	...	386	681	1 036	1 420	1 180	1 015	921	Total
% of GNI	...	0.3	0.3	0.3	0.5	0.4	0.3	0.3	% du RNB
South Sudan									**Soudan du sud**
Bilateral	...	...	...	...	1 407	1 297	1 791	1 389	Bilatérale
Multilateral	...	...	...	...	267	290	392	188	Multilatérale
Total	...	...	...	...	1 675	1 587	2 183	1 577	Total
% of GNI	...	...	...	...	14.8	60.5	...	...	% du RNB
Sri Lanka									**Sri Lanka**
Bilateral	314	329	777	263	191	36	90	-769	Bilatérale
Multilateral	125	142	263	296	254	337	223	513	Multilatérale
Total	439	471	1 040	559	445	373	313	-256	Total
% of GNI	7.4	3.7	4.3	1.0	0.6	0.5	0.4	-0.3	% du RNB
State of Palestine									**État de Palestine**
Bilateral	...	374	640	1 818	1 396	1 970	1 691	1 709	Bilatérale
Multilateral	...	140	376	695	477	432	456	532	Multilatérale
Total	...	514	1 016	2 513	1 872	2 402	2 147	2 241	Total
% of GNI	...	13.8	19.6	26.4	13.0	15.7	13.0	13.2	% du RNB
Sudan									**Soudan**
Bilateral	972	183	1 450	1 557	821	590	662	688	Bilatérale
Multilateral	153	54	376	469	148	219	200	279	Multilatérale
Total	1 125	237	1 826	2 026	970	809	862	966	Total
% of GNI	9.4	1.8	7.4	3.4	1.1	0.9	0.8	2.6	% du RNB
Suriname									**Suriname**
Bilateral	8	74	30	76	11	10	7	7	Bilatérale
Multilateral	2	3	13	25	5	6	13	7	Multilatérale
Total	10	77	43	101	16	17	20	14	Total
% of GNI	1.1	11.1	2.5	2.4	0.3	0.6	0.8	0.5	% du RNB
Syrian Arab Republic									**République arabe syrienne**
Bilateral	591	306	-3	-31	4 698	8 610	10 115	9 457	Bilatérale
Multilateral	19	50	74	162	222	289	313	535	Multilatérale
Total	610	356	71	131	4 920	8 900	10 428	9 992	Total
% of GNI	3.6	3.1	0.3	...	...	...	...	...	% du RNB
Tajikistan									**Tadjikistan**
Bilateral	...	49	116	210	286	214	84	226	Bilatérale
Multilateral	...	16	110	178	147	146	245	173	Multilatérale
Total	...	65	226	388	432	360	328	399	Total
% of GNI	...	5.5	10.1	5.6	4.6	4.4	4.0	4.5	% du RNB

31

Net disbursements of official development assistance to recipients *(continued)*
Total, bilateral and multilateral aid (millions of US dollars); and as a percentage of Gross National Income (GNI)

Décaissements nets d'aide publique au développement aux bénéficiaires *(suite)*
Total, bilatérale et multilatérale d'aide (millions de dollars É.-U.); et en pourcentage du Revenu National Brut (RNB)

Region, country or area[&]	1985	1995	2005	2010	2015	2016	2017	2018	Région, pays ou zone[&]
Thailand									**Thaïlande**
Bilateral	392	812	-237	-132	-2	170	195	-462	Bilatérale
Multilateral	55	25	72	111	61	58	56	43	Multilatérale
Total	447	836	-165	-20	59	228	250	-420	Total
% of GNI	1.2	0.5	-0.1	-~0.0	~0.0	0.1	0.1	-0.1	% du RNB
Timor-Leste									**Timor-Leste**
Bilateral	...	~0	149	250	174	178	179	174	Bilatérale
Multilateral	...	0	35	40	39	46	53	33	Multilatérale
Total	...	~0	185	290	212	224	232	207	Total
% of GNI	...	...	21.8	8.7	7.6	9.9	10.2	8.8	% du RNB
Togo									**Togo**
Bilateral	74	156	42	205	110	67	130	163	Bilatérale
Multilateral	37	35	41	198	90	101	215	134	Multilatérale
Total	111	191	83	403	199	168	345	297	Total
% of GNI	15.3	15.1	3.7	11.9	4.6	3.8	7.2	5.6	% du RNB
Tokelau									**Tokélaou**
Bilateral	2	3	16	14	...	14	7	27	Bilatérale
Multilateral	~0	~0	~0	~0	...	~0	~0	~0	Multilatérale
Total	2	4	16	15	9	14	7	27	Total
Tonga									**Tonga**
Bilateral	10	30	23	55	52	63	71	34	Bilatérale
Multilateral	2	2	9	11	16	20	15	54	Multilatérale
Total	13	32	33	66	68	83	87	88	Total
% of GNI	20.2	15.6	12.6	17.4	15.5	20.5	19.9	19.2	% du RNB
Trinidad and Tobago									**Trinité-et-Tobago**
Bilateral	4	13	-11	2	...	...	...	...	Bilatérale
Multilateral	4	11	9	2	...	...	...	...	Multilatérale
Total	7	24	-2	4	...	...	...	...	Total
% of GNI	0.1	0.5	-~0.0	~0.0	...	...	...	...	% du RNB
Tunisia									**Tunisie**
Bilateral	144	49	240	426	165	235	417	457	Bilatérale
Multilateral	17	27	128	124	331	412	394	349	Multilatérale
Total	160	75	368	550	496	647	812	807	Total
% of GNI	2.0	0.4	1.2	1.3	1.2	1.6	2.1	2.1	% du RNB
Turkey									**Turquie**
Bilateral	168	297	-57	715	135	1 024	1 072	-385	Bilatérale
Multilateral	12	16	457	334	2 006	2 585	2 076	1 575	Multilatérale
Total	180	314	399	1 050	2 141	3 609	3 147	1 190	Total
% of GNI	0.3	0.2	0.1	0.1	0.3	0.4	0.4	0.2	% du RNB
Turkmenistan									**Turkménistan**
Bilateral	...	27	20	29	12	18	5	9	Bilatérale
Multilateral	...	4	10	15	11	14	24	11	Multilatérale
Total	...	31	29	44	23	32	28	20	Total
% of GNI	...	1.2	0.4	0.2	0.1	0.1	0.1	0.1	% du RNB
Turks and Caicos Islands									**Îles Turques-et-Caïques**
Bilateral	5	5	3	...	...	...	...	...	Bilatérale
Multilateral	1	1	2	...	...	...	...	...	Multilatérale
Total	6	6	5	...	...	...	...	...	Total
Tuvalu									**Tuvalu**
Bilateral	3	7	5	13	42	-30	20	14	Bilatérale
Multilateral	~0	1	4	~0	8	54	7	6	Multilatérale
Total	3	7	9	14	50	24	27	20	Total
% of GNI	...	...	24.4	27.3	88.7	44.4	45.7	31.6	% du RNB
Uganda									**Ouganda**
Bilateral	84	571	699	1 112	1 137	1 142	1 472	1 307	Bilatérale
Multilateral	96	263	497	578	502	620	537	636	Multilatérale
Total	179	834	1 195	1 690	1 638	1 763	2 009	1 943	Total
% of GNI	5.2	14.6	13.7	8.5	6.2	7.5	7.9	7.3	% du RNB
Ukraine [9]									**Ukraine** [9]
Bilateral	...	...	248	442	1 198	1 062	837	861	Bilatérale
Multilateral	...	...	156	214	251	461	343	363	Multilatérale
Total	...	...	404	657	1 449	1 523	1 181	1 223	Total
% of GNI	...	...	0.5	0.5	1.6	1.7	1.1	1.0	% du RNB

Net disbursements of official development assistance to recipients *(continued)*
Total, bilateral and multilateral aid (millions of US dollars); and as a percentage of Gross National Income (GNI)

Décaissements nets d'aide publique au développement aux bénéficiaires *(suite)*
Total, bilatérale et multilatérale d'aide (millions de dollars É.-U.); et en pourcentage du Revenu National Brut (RNB)

Region, country or area[&]	1985	1995	2005	2010	2015	2016	2017	2018	Région, pays ou zone[&]
United Arab Emirates									**Émirats arabes unis**
Bilateral	3	6	...	...	...	...	...	...	Bilatérale
Multilateral	1	-~0	...	...	...	...	...	...	Multilatérale
Total	4	5	...	...	...	...	...	...	Total
United Rep. of Tanzania									**Rép.-Unie de Tanzanie**
Bilateral	400	613	823	1 923	1 718	1 508	1 207	1 532	Bilatérale
Multilateral	77	258	670	1 037	866	810	1 379	923	Multilatérale
Total	477	871	1 492	2 960	2 585	2 318	2 586	2 455	Total
% of GNI	...	17.0	8.3	9.4	5.6	4.8	5.0	4.4	% du RNB
Uruguay									**Uruguay**
Bilateral	6	62	2	29	12	4	31	...	Bilatérale
Multilateral	2	6	17	17	12	14	10	...	Multilatérale
Total	8	69	18	46	23	18	41	...	Total
% of GNI	0.2	0.4	0.1	0.1	0.1	~0.0	0.1	...	% du RNB
Uzbekistan									**Ouzbékistan**
Bilateral	...	76	128	117	290	342	474	363	Bilatérale
Multilateral	...	8	41	81	161	169	165	195	Multilatérale
Total	...	84	169	198	451	511	639	558	Total
% of GNI	...	0.6	1.2	0.5	0.5	0.6	1.1	1.1	% du RNB
Vanuatu									**Vanuatu**
Bilateral	19	42	30	106	169	81	112	100	Bilatérale
Multilateral	2	2	11	3	18	48	20	30	Multilatérale
Total	21	45	40	109	187	129	132	130	Total
% of GNI	17.2	20.6	10.9	16.2	25.8	16.5	15.7	14.9	% du RNB
Venezuela (Boliv. Rep. of)									**Venezuela (Rép. boliv. du)**
Bilateral	14	36	12	33	22	30	73	117	Bilatérale
Multilateral	2	8	36	20	15	14	14	32	Multilatérale
Total	17	45	49	53	37	43	87	149	Total
% of GNI	~0.0	0.1	~0.0	~0.0	...	...	...	...	% du RNB
Viet Nam									**Viet Nam**
Bilateral	113	667	1 169	1 831	2 250	2 039	1 750	841	Bilatérale
Multilateral	38	111	525	938	918	867	654	798	Multilatérale
Total	151	778	1 693	2 770	3 167	2 906	2 404	1 638	Total
% of GNI	...	3.8	3.0	2.5	1.7	1.5	1.1	0.7	% du RNB
Wallis and Futuna Islands									**Îles Wallis-et-Futuna**
Bilateral	~0	1	72	123	106	85	89	36	Bilatérale
Multilateral	~0	~0	~0	5	~0	~0	1	12	Multilatérale
Total	~0	1	72	127	106	85	90	48	Total
Yemen									**Yémen**
Bilateral	342	109	127	418	1 632	2 090	2 698	7 492	Bilatérale
Multilateral	89	63	169	249	146	211	536	493	Multilatérale
Total	431	172	296	667	1 778	2 301	3 234	7 985	Total
% of GNI	...	4.2	2.0	2.3	4.3	7.5	12.1	29.7	% du RNB
Zambia									**Zambie**
Bilateral	244	1 765	692	654	564	633	771	634	Bilatérale
Multilateral	75	266	478	266	234	334	270	362	Multilatérale
Total	319	2 031	1 169	919	797	966	1 040	996	Total
% of GNI	15.9	57.0	15.2	4.9	3.8	4.7	4.2	3.8	% du RNB
Zimbabwe									**Zimbabwe**
Bilateral	218	438	162	478	507	398	519	481	Bilatérale
Multilateral	18	53	211	234	281	257	207	314	Multilatérale
Total	235	492	373	713	788	654	726	794	Total
% of GNI	4.3	7.2	6.8	6.7	4.4	3.5	3.5	2.6	% du RNB

Source:

Organisation for Economic Co-operation and Development (OECD), Paris, the OECD Development Assistance Committee (DAC) database, last accessed June 2020.

Official Development Assistance (ODA) is defined as those flows to developing countries and multilateral institutions provided by official

Source:

Organisation de coopération et de développement économiques (OCDE), Paris, base de données du Comité d'aide au développement (CAD) de l'OCDE, dernier accès juin 2020.

On entend par Aide publique au développement (APD), l'ensemble des flux financiers à destination des pays en développement et des institutions

31

Net disbursements of official development assistance to recipients *(continued)*
Total, bilateral and multilateral aid (millions of US dollars); and as a percentage of Gross National Income (GNI)

Décaissements nets d'aide publique au développement aux bénéficiaires *(suite)*
Total, bilatérale et multilatérale d'aide (millions de dollars É.-U.); et en pourcentage du Revenu National Brut (RNB)

agencies, including state and local governments, or by their executive agencies, each transaction of which meets the following tests: i) it is administered with the promotion of the economic development and welfare of developing countries as its main objective; and ii) it is concessional in character and conveys a grant element of at least 25 per cent.

multilatérales par des organismes publics (y compris les autorités étatiques et locales) ou par leurs organes exécutifs satisfaisant les critères suivants: i) elle est administrée dans le but premier de promouvoir le développement économique et social des pays en développement ; ii) elle est accordée à des conditions de faveur et comporte une élément de subvention d'au moins 25 pour cent.

1	Including regional aid disbursements in addition to the disbursements made to individual countries and areas.	1	Y compris les versements d'aides régionales en plus des versements effectués aux aux différents pays et régions.
2	Excluding Sudan.	2	Exclut le Soudan.
3	Including Sudan.	3	Y compris le Soudan.
4	Excludes Myanmar.	4	Non compris Myanmar.
5	Includes Armenia, Azerbaijan, Georgia and Myanmar. Excludes Iran (Islamic Rep. of).	5	Y compris l'Arménie, l'Azerbaïdjan, la Géorgie et le Myanmar. Non compris la Rép. Islamique d 'Iran.
6	Excluding Armenia, Azerbaijan, Cyprus, Georgia and Turkey. Includes Iran (Islamic Rep. of).	6	Non compris l'Arménie, l'Azerbaïdjan, Chypre, la Géorgie et la Turquie. Y compris la Rép. Islamique d 'Iran.
7	Including Turkey and Cyprus.	7	Y compris la Turquie et Chypre.
8	For statistical purposes, the data for China do not include those for the Hong Kong Special Administrative Region (Hong Kong SAR), Macao Special Administrative Region (Macao SAR) and Taiwan Province of China.	8	Pour la présentation des statistiques, les données pour la Chine ne comprennent pas la région administrative spéciale de Hong Kong (RAS de Hong Kong), la région administrative spéciale de Macao (RAS de Macao) et la province chinoise de Taïwan.
9	The Government of Ukraine has informed the United Nations that it is not in a position to provide statistical data concerning the Autonomous Republic of Crimea and the city of Sevastopol.	9	Le Gouvernement ukrainien a informé l'Organisation des Nations Unies qu'il n'est pas en mesure de fournir des données statistiques concernant la République autonome de Crimée et Sébastopol.

Net disbursements of official development assistance from donors
Millions of US dollars and as a percentage of gross national income (GNI)

Décaissements nets d'aide publique au développement par des donateurs
Millions de dollares É.-U. et en pourcentage du revenu national brut (RNB)

Country or area	1975	1985	1995	2005	2010	2015	2017	2018	2019	Pays ou zone
Total										**Total**
$ millions	20 183	33 855	65 424	120 771	147 644	156 882	180 811	187 308	181 345	$millions
DAC total										**CAD total**
$ millions	13 315	28 858	58 896	108 397	128 484	131 563	147 169	150 059	147 373	$millions
% of GNI	0.34	0.33	0.26	0.32	0.31	0.30	0.31	...	...	% du RNB
Australia [1]										**Australie** [1]
$ millions	552	749	1 194	1 680	3 826	3 494	3 036	3 149	2 949	$millions
% of GNI	0.65	0.48	0.34	0.25	0.32	0.29	0.23	...	...	% du RNB
Austria [1]										**Autriche** [1]
$ millions	79	248	620	1 573	1 208	1 324	1 251	1 167	1 208	$millions
% of GNI	0.21	0.38	0.27	0.52	0.32	0.35	0.30	...	...	% du RNB
Azerbaijan										**Azerbaïdjan**
$ millions	...	...	...	...	...	13	19	28	...	$millions
% of GNI	...	...	...	...	...	0.02	0.05	...	...	% du RNB
Belgium [1]										**Belgique** [1]
$ millions	378	440	1 034	1 963	3 004	1 904	2 196	2 348	2 211	$millions
% of GNI	0.60	0.55	0.38	0.53	0.64	0.42	0.45	...	...	% du RNB
Bulgaria										**Bulgarie**
$ millions	...	...	...	...	40	41	62	69	65	$millions
% of GNI	...	...	...	...	0.09	0.09	0.11	...	...	% du RNB
Canada [1]										**Canada** [1]
$ millions	880	1 631	2 067	3 756	5 214	4 277	4 305	4 641	4 514	$millions
% of GNI	0.54	0.49	0.38	0.34	0.34	0.28	0.26	...	...	% du RNB
Croatia										**Croatie**
$ millions	...	...	...	...	...	51	54	79	78	$millions
% of GNI	...	...	...	...	...	0.09	0.10	...	...	% du RNB
Cyprus [2]										**Chypre** [2]
$ millions	...	...	...	15	51	18	...	25	45	$millions
% of GNI	...	...	...	0.09	0.23	0.09	...	...	...	% du RNB
Czechia [1]										**Tchéquie** [1]
$ millions	...	...	...	135	228	199	304	305	306	$millions
% of GNI	...	...	...	0.11	0.13	0.12	0.15	...	...	% du RNB
Denmark [1]										**Danemark** [1]
$ millions	205	440	1 623	2 109	2 871	2 566	2 448	2 577	2 534	$millions
% of GNI	0.55	0.80	0.96	0.81	0.91	0.85	0.74	...	...	% du RNB
Estonia										**Estonie**
$ millions	...	...	...	10	19	34	43	49	42	$millions
% of GNI	...	...	...	0.08	0.10	0.15	0.16	...	...	% du RNB
Finland [1]										**Finlande** [1]
$ millions	48	211	388	902	1 333	1 288	1 084	984	1 144	$millions
% of GNI	0.17	0.40	0.31	0.46	0.55	0.55	0.42	...	...	% du RNB
France [1]										**France** [1]
$ millions	1 493	3 134	8 443	10 026	12 915	9 039	11 331	12 840	11 980	$millions
% of GNI	0.44	0.61	0.55	0.47	0.50	0.37	0.43	...	...	% du RNB
Germany [1]										**Allemagne** [1]
$ millions	1 689	2 942	7 524	10 082	12 985	17 940	25 005	25 670	23 729	$millions
% of GNI	0.40	0.47	0.31	0.36	0.39	0.52	0.67	...	...	% du RNB
Greece [1]										**Grèce** [1]
$ millions	...	...	...	384	508	239	314	290	308	$millions
% of GNI	...	...	...	0.17	0.17	0.12	0.16	...	...	% du RNB
Hungary [1]										**Hongrie** [1]
$ millions	29	84	...	100	114	156	149	285	317	$millions
% of GNI	...	...	...	0.11	0.09	0.13	0.11	...	...	% du RNB
Iceland [1]										**Islande** [1]
$ millions	...	...	...	27	29	40	68	74	67	$millions
% of GNI	...	...	...	0.18	0.26	0.24	0.28	...	...	% du RNB
Ireland [1]										**Irlande** [1]
$ millions	8	39	153	719	895	718	838	934	935	$millions
% of GNI	0.09	0.24	0.29	0.42	0.52	0.32	0.32	...	...	% du RNB
Israel										**Israël**
$ millions	...	...	...	95	145	233	408	365	278	$millions
% of GNI	...	...	...	0.07	0.07	0.08	0.12	...	...	% du RNB

32 Net disbursements of official development assistance from donors *(continued)*
Millions of US dollars and as a percentage of gross national income (GNI)

Décaissements nets d'aide publique au développement par des donateurs *(suite)*
Millions de dollars É.-U. et en pourcentage du revenu national brut (RNB)

Country or area	1975	1985	1995	2005	2010	2015	2017	2018	2019	Pays ou zone
Italy [1]										**Italie [1]**
$ millions	182	1 098	1 623	5 091	2 996	4 003	5 858	5 098	4 733	$millions
% of GNI	0.10	0.26	0.15	0.29	0.15	0.22	0.30	...	...	% du RNB
Japan [1]										**Japon [1]**
$ millions	1 148	3 797	14 489	13 126	11 058	9 203	11 463	10 064	11 639	$millions
% of GNI	0.23	0.29	0.27	0.28	0.20	0.20	0.23	...	...	% du RNB
Kazakhstan										**Kazakhstan**
$ millions	...	...	...	...	...	43	35	40	...	$millions
% of GNI	...	...	...	...	...	0.02	0.02	...	...	% du RNB
Kuwait										**Koweït**
$ millions	859[3]	647[3]	384[3]	218[3]	232[3]	304[3]	570[4]	273[4]	...	$millions
% of GNI	...	...	...	...	...	...	0.41	...	...	% du RNB
Latvia										**Lettonie**
$ millions	...	...	...	11	16	23	32	34	34	$millions
% of GNI	...	...	...	0.07	0.06	0.09	0.11	...	...	% du RNB
Liechtenstein										**Liechtenstein**
$ millions	...	...	...	...	27	24	24	26	...	$millions
% of GNI	...	...	...	...	0.62	...	...	...	...	% du RNB
Lithuania										**Lituanie**
$ millions	...	...	...	16	37	48	59	65	58	$millions
% of GNI	...	...	...	0.06	0.10	0.12	0.13	...	...	% du RNB
Luxembourg [1]										**Luxembourg [1]**
$ millions	...	8	65	256	403	363	424	473	474	$millions
% of GNI	...	0.17	0.36	0.79	1.05	0.95	1.00	...	...	% du RNB
Malta										**Malte**
$ millions	...	...	...	...	14	17	25	33	40	$millions
% of GNI	...	...	...	...	0.18	0.17	0.21	...	...	% du RNB
Netherlands [1]										**Pays-Bas [1]**
$ millions	608	1 136	3 226	5 115	6 357	5 726	4 958	5 617	5 292	$millions
% of GNI	0.74	0.91	0.81	0.82	0.81	0.75	0.60	...	...	% du RNB
New Zealand [1]										**Nouvelle-Zélande [1]**
$ millions	66	54	123	274	342	442	450	556	559	$millions
% of GNI	0.52	0.25	0.23	0.27	0.26	0.27	0.23	...	...	% du RNB
Norway [1]										**Norvège [1]**
$ millions	184	574	1 244	2 794	4 372	4 278	4 125	4 258	4 292	$millions
% of GNI	0.65	1.01	0.86	0.94	1.05	1.05	0.99	...	...	% du RNB
Other non-specified areas										**Autres zones non-spécifiées**
$ millions	...	...	92	483	381	255	319	292	293	$millions
% of GNI	...	...	...	0.14	0.10	0.05	0.06	...	...	% du RNB
Poland [1]										**Pologne [1]**
$ millions	32	19	...	205	378	441	679	759	669	$millions
% of GNI	...	...	...	0.07	0.08	0.10	0.13	...	...	% du RNB
Portugal [1]										**Portugal [1]**
$ millions	...	10	258	377	649	308	381	388	344	$millions
% of GNI	...	0.05	0.25	0.21	0.29	0.16	0.18	...	...	% du RNB
Republic of Korea [1]										**République de Corée [1]**
$ millions	...	...	116	752	1 174	1 915	2 201	2 423	2 575	$millions
% of GNI	...	...	0.02	0.10	0.12	0.14	0.14	...	...	% du RNB
Romania										**Roumanie**
$ millions	...	...	...	...	114	158	220	249	251	$millions
% of GNI	...	...	...	...	0.07	0.09	0.11	...	...	% du RNB
Russian Federation										**Fédération de Russie**
$ millions	...	...	...	...	472	1 161[5]	1 190[5]	999[5]	...	$millions
% of GNI	...	...	...	...	0.03	0.09[5]	0.08[5]	...	...	% du RNB
Saudi Arabia										**Arabie saoudite**
$ millions	2 569	2 443	305	1 026	3 480	859[6]	1 932[6]	4 779[6]	4 847[6]	$millions
Slovakia [1]										**Slovaquie [1]**
$ millions	...	...	...	57	74	85	119	138	129	$millions
% of GNI	...	...	...	...	0.09	0.10	0.13	...	...	% du RNB
Slovenia [1]										**Slovénie [1]**
$ millions	...	...	...	35	59	63	76	84	86	$millions
% of GNI	...	...	...	0.11	0.13	0.15	0.16	...	...	% du RNB
Spain [1]										**Espagne [1]**
$ millions	...	169	1 348	3 018	5 949	1 397	2 560	2 590	2 662	$millions
% of GNI	...	0.10	0.24	0.27	0.43	0.12	0.19	...	...	% du RNB

Net disbursements of official development assistance from donors *(continued)*
Millions of US dollars and as a percentage of gross national income (GNI)

Décaissements nets d'aide publique au développement par des donateurs *(suite)*
Millions de dollares É.-U. et en pourcentage du revenu national brut (RNB)

Country or area	1975	1985	1995	2005	2010	2015	2017	2018	2019	Pays ou zone
Sweden [1]										**Suède** [1]
$ millions	566	840	1 704	3 362	4 533	7 089	5 563	6 000	5 396	$millions
% of GNI	0.78	0.86	0.77	0.94	0.97	1.40	1.02	...	...	% du RNB
Switzerland [1]										**Suisse** [1]
$ millions	104	303	1 084	1 772	2 300	3 529	3 147	3 097	3 089	$millions
% of GNI	0.18	0.31	0.33	0.42	0.39	0.51	0.47	...	...	% du RNB
Thailand										**Thaïlande**
$ millions	...	...	...	...	4	62	133	...	...	$millions
% of GNI	...	...	...	...	~0.00	0.02	0.03	...	...	% du RNB
Timor-Leste										**Timor-Leste**
$ millions	...	...	...	...	...	4	...	...	...	$millions
Turkey										**Turquie**
$ millions	...	...	107	601	967	3 919	8 121	8 612	8 652	$millions
% of GNI	...	...	0.06	0.17	0.13	0.50	0.95	...	...	% du RNB
United Arab Emirates [7]										**Émirats arabes unis** [7]
$ millions	1 998	366	243	510	414	4 381	3 957	4 116	2 478	$millions
% of GNI	...	...	...	...	0.14	1.18	1.03	...	...	% du RNB
United Kingdom [1]										**Royaume-Uni** [1]
$ millions	904	1 530	3 202	10 772	13 053	18 553	18 103	19 462	19 343	$millions
% of GNI	0.38	0.33	0.29	0.47	0.57	0.70	0.70	...	...	% du RNB
United States of America [1]										**États-Unis d'Amérique** [1]
$ millions	4 161	9 403	7 367	27 935	29 656	30 986	34 732	33 787	33 889	$millions
% of GNI	0.27	0.24	0.10	0.23	0.20	0.17	0.18	...	...	% du RNB
European Union (EU) [1,8]										**Union européenne (UE)** [1,8]
$ millions	722	1 510	5 398	9 390	12 747	13 670	16 440	17 116	15 154	$millions

Source:

Organisation for Economic Co-operation and Development (OECD), Paris, the OECD Development Assistance Committee (DAC) database, last accessed June 2020.

Source:

Organisation de coopération et de développement économiques (OCDE), Paris, base de données du Comité d'aide au développement (CAD) de l'OCDE, dernier accès juin 2020.

1 Development Assistance Committee member (OECD).
2 Data refer to government controlled areas.

3 Includes Kuwait Fund grants only.
4 Includes Kuwait Fund grants, State of Kuwait grants administered by Kuwait Fund as well as State of Kuwait grants.

5 Some of the debt relief reported may correspond to the credits. Statistics currently published on ODA by Russia and the estimates from the previous Chairman's reports should not be used at the same time.
6 Saudi Arabia's reporting to the OECD on its development co-operation programme consists of aggregate figures on humanitarian and development assistance by region, multilateral aid and loan disbursements and repayments by the Saudi Fund for Development.

7 Data reported at activity level, represent flows from all government agencies.
8 Refers to European Union institutions.

1 Le Comité d'aide au développement (l'OCDE).
2 Les données se rapportent aux zones contrôlées par le Gouvernement.
3 Inclut les subventions du Fonds koweïtien seulement.
4 Inclut les subventions du Fonds koweïtien, les subventions de l'État du Koweït administrées par le Kuwait Fund ainsi que les subventions de l'État du Koweït.

5 Une partie de l'allégement de la dette rapporté peut correspondre aux crédits. Les statistiques actuellement publiées sur l'APD par la Russie et les estimations des précédents rapports du Président ne devraient pas être utilisées en même temps.
6 La déclaration de l'Arabie saoudite auprès de l'OCDE relatif au programme de coopération au développement est constituée de données globales sur l'aide humanitaire, l'aide au développement par région, l'aide multilatérale, et les débousements et les remboursements de prêts par les Fonds saoudien pour le développement.

7 Les données rapportées au niveau d'activité, ces données représentent les flux de tous les organismes gouvernementaux.
8 Se référent aux institutions de l'Union Européenne.

Annex I - Country and area nomenclature, regional and other groupings

The *Statistical Yearbook* lists countries or areas based on the United Nations Standard Country Codes (Series M, No. 49), prepared by the Statistics Division of the United Nations Secretariat and first issued in 1970[1]. The list of countries or areas; the composition of geographical regions and economic, trade and other groupings used within this yearbook (as at 31 July 2018) are presented in this Annex. The names of countries or areas refer to their short form used in day-to-day operations of the United Nations and not necessarily to their official name as used in formal documents[2]. As an aid to statistical data processing, a unique standard three-digit numerical code is assigned to each country or area and to each geographical region and grouping of countries or areas. For reference, these codes, where applicable, are presented to the left of each country or area listed in this Annex. These codes range from 000 to 899, inclusive.

A.   Changes in country or area names (since 31 July 2008)

The geographical extent of a country or area, or the composition of a geographical region, may change over time and users should take such changes into account in interpreting the tables in this Yearbook. A change in the name of a country or area while its geographical coverage remains the same is not usually accompanied by a change in its numerical code. Changes in numerical codes and names in the general period covered by the statistics (since 31 July 2008) in the *Yearbook*, are shown below;

Numerical code	Country or area (added or changed)	Date of change	Numerical code	Country or area (Name changes with no change in code)	Date of change
728	South Sudan	2011	748	Eswatini, *previously Swaziland*	2018
729	Sudan	2011	203	Czechia, *previously Czech Republic*	2016
531	Curaçao	2010	132	Cabo Verde, *previously Cape Verde*	2013
534	Sint Maarten (Dutch part)	2010	275	State of Palestine, *previously Occupied Palestinian Territory*	2013
535	Bonaire, Sint Eustatius and Saba	2010	434	Libya, *previously Libyan Arab Jamahiriya*	2011
			068	Bolivia (Plurinational State of), *previously Bolivia*	2009
			807	North Macedonia, *previously the former Yugoslav Republic of Macedonia*	2019
			498	Republic of Moldova, *previously Moldova*	2008

B.   Regional groupings

The scheme of regional groupings given on the next page is based mainly on 6 continents; these continental regions, except Antarctica, are further subdivided into 22 sub-regions and 2 intermediary regions (Sub-Saharan Africa and Latin America and the Caribbean) that are drawn as to obtain greater homogeneity in sizes of population, demographic circumstances and accuracy of demographic statistics. This nomenclature is widely used in international statistics and is followed to the greatest extent possible in the present *Yearbook* in order to promote consistency and facilitate comparability and analysis. However, it is by no means universal in international statistical compilation, even at the level of continental regions, and variations in international statistical sources and methods dictate many unavoidable differences in particular fields in the present *Yearbook*. General differences are indicated in the footnotes to the classification presented below. More detailed differences are given in the footnotes and technical notes to individual tables.

Neither is there international standardization in the use of the terms "developed" and "developing" countries, areas or regions. These terms are used in the present publication to refer to regional groupings generally considered as "developed": these are Northern America (numerical code 021), Europe (150), Cyprus (196), Israel (376), Japan (392) and Australia and New Zealand (053). These designations are intended for statistical convenience and do not necessarily express a judgement about the stage reached by a particular country or area in the development process. Differences from this usage are indicated in the notes to individual tables.

---

[1] Four revisions of this document were published in 1975, 1982, 1996 and 1999. Further revisions are now published on the United Nations Statistics Division website under the M49 section.

[2] A listing in the 6 official languages of the United Nations is contained in Terminology Bulletin No. 347/Rev.1 or the UNTERM website, prepared by the Department of General Assembly Affairs and Conference Services of the United Nations Secretariat.

001			World			
002			Africa			
202			Sub-Saharan Africa		015	Northern Africa

014 Eastern Africa
086	British Indian Ocean Territory
108	Burundi
174	Comoros
262	Djibouti
232	Eritrea
231	Ethiopia
260	French Southern Territories
404	Kenya
450	Madagascar
454	Malawi
480	Mauritius
175	Mayotte
508	Mozambique
638	Réunion
646	Rwanda
690	Seychelles
706	Somalia
728	South Sudan note 736
800	Uganda

834	United Republic of Tanzania note /a
894	Zambia
716	Zimbabwe

017 Middle Africa
024	Angola
120	Cameroon
140	Central African Republic
148	Chad
178	Congo
180	Democratic Republic of the Congo
226	Equatorial Guinea
266	Gabon
678	Sao Tome and Principe

018 Southern Africa
072	Botswana
748	Eswatini
426	Lesotho
516	Namibia
710	South Africa

011 Western Africa
204	Benin
854	Burkina Faso
132	Cabo Verde
384	Côte d'Ivoire
270	Gambia
288	Ghana
324	Guinea
624	Guinea-Bissau
430	Liberia
466	Mali
478	Mauritania
562	Niger
566	Nigeria
654	Saint Helena note /b
686	Senegal
694	Sierra Leone
768	Togo

015 Northern Africa
012	Algeria
818	Egypt
434	Libya
504	Morocco
729	Sudan note 736
788	Tunisia
732	Western Sahara

Note	Tables may list
736	Sudan [former]
/a	Includes
---	Zanzibar
/b	Includes
---	Ascension
---	Tristan da Cunha

019			Americas			
419			Latin America and the Caribbean		021	Northern America note 003

029 Caribbean
660	Anguilla
028	Antigua and Barbuda
533	Aruba
044	Bahamas
052	Barbados
535	Bonaire, note 530 Sint Eustatius and Saba
092	British Virgin Islands
136	Cayman Islands
192	Cuba
531	Curaçao note 530
212	Dominica
214	Dominican Republic
308	Grenada
312	Guadeloupe
332	Haiti
388	Jamaica
474	Martinique
500	Montserrat
630	Puerto Rico
652	Saint Barthélemy

659	Saint Kitts and Nevis
662	Saint Lucia
663	Saint Martin (French part)
670	Saint Vincent and the Grenadines
534	Sint Maarten note 530 (Dutch part)
780	Trinidad and Tobago
796	Turks and Caicos Islands
850	United States Virgin Islands

013 Central America
084	Belize
188	Costa Rica
222	El Salvador
320	Guatemala
340	Honduras
484	Mexico
558	Nicaragua
591	Panama

005 South America
032	Argentina
068	Bolivia (Plurinational State of)
074	Bouvet Island
076	Brazil
152	Chile
170	Colombia
218	Ecuador
238	Falkland Islands (Malvinas)
254	French Guiana
328	Guyana
600	Paraguay
604	Peru
740	Suriname
239	South Georgia and the South Sandwich Islands
858	Uruguay
862	Venezuela (Bolivarian Republic of)

021 Northern America note 003
060	Bermuda
124	Canada
304	Greenland
666	Saint Pierre and Miquelon
840	United States of America

Note	
003	The continent of **North America** comprises Northern America, Caribbean and Central America.

Tables may list	
530	Netherlands Antilles [former]

010	Antarctica

001				World				

001 World

142 Asia

143	**Central Asia**	496	Mongolia	034	**Southern Asia**	196	Cyprus
398	Kazakhstan	410	Republic of Korea	004	Afghanistan	268	Georgia
417	Kyrgyzstan			050	Bangladesh	368	Iraq
762	Tajikistan	**035**	**South-eastern Asia**	064	Bhutan	376	Israel
795	Turkmenistan	096	Brunei Darussalam	356	India	400	Jordan
860	Uzbekistan	116	Cambodia	364	Iran (Islamic	414	Kuwait
		360	Indonesia		Republic of)	422	Lebanon
030	**Eastern Asia**	418	Lao People's	462	Maldives	512	Oman
156	China		Democratic Republic	524	Nepal	634	Qatar
344	China, Hong Kong Special	458	Malaysia	586	Pakistan	682	Saudi Arabia
	Administrative Region	104	Myanmar	144	Sri Lanka	275	State of Palestine
446	China, Macao Special	608	Philippines			760	Syrian Arab Republic
	Administrative Region	702	Singapore	**145**	**Western Asia**	792	Turkey
408	Democratic People's	764	Thailand	051	Armenia	784	United Arab Emirates
	Republic of Korea	626	Timor-Leste	031	Azerbaijan	887	Yemen
392	Japan	704	Viet Nam	048	Bahrain		

150 Europe

151	**Eastern Europe**	831	Guernsey note 830	039	**Southern Europe**	155	**Western Europe**
112	Belarus	352	Iceland	008	Albania	040	Austria
100	Bulgaria	372	Ireland	020	Andorra	056	Belgium
203	Czechia	833	Isle of Man	070	Bosnia and Herzegovina	250	France
348	Hungary	832	Jersey note 830	191	Croatia	276	Germany
616	Poland	428	Latvia	292	Gibraltar	438	Liechtenstein
498	Republic of Moldova	440	Lithuania	300	Greece	442	Luxembourg
642	Romania	578	Norway	336	Holy See	492	Monaco
643	Russian Federation	744	Svalbard and Jan	380	Italy	528	Netherlands
703	Slovakia		Mayen Islands	470	Malta	756	Switzerland
804	Ukraine	752	Sweden	499	Montenegro note 891		
		826	United Kingdom of	807	North Macedonia	**Note**	**Tables may list**
154	**Northern Europe**		Great Britain and	620	Portugal	830	Channel Islands
248	Åland Islands		Northern Ireland	674	San Marino	891	Serbia and
208	Denmark			688	Serbia note 891 & /c		Montenegro [former]
233	Estonia			705	Slovenia	/c	Kosovo
234	Faroe Islands			724	Spain		
246	Finland						

009 Oceania

053	**Australia and New Zealand**	057	**Micronesia**	061	**Polynesia**
036	Australia	316	Guam	016	American Samoa
162	Christmas Island	296	Kiribati	184	Cook Islands
166	Cocos (Keeling) Islands	584	Marshall Islands	258	French Polynesia
334	Heard Island and McDonald Islands	583	Micronesia (Federated States of)	570	Niue
554	New Zealand	520	Nauru	612	Pitcairn
574	Norfolk Island	580	Northern Mariana Islands	882	Samoa
		585	Palau	772	Tokelau
054	**Melanesia**	581	United States minor outlying islands	776	Tonga
242	Fiji			798	Tuvalu
540	New Caledonia			876	Wallis and Futuna Islands
598	Papua New Guinea				
090	Solomon Islands				
548	Vanuatu				

Other groupings

Following is a list of other groupings and their compositions presented in the *Yearbook*. These groupings are organized mainly around economic and trade interests in regional associations.

063	Andean Common Market (ANCOM)						
068	Bolivia (Plurinational State of)	170	Colombia	218	Ecuador	604	Peru

066 — Asia-Pacific Economic Cooperation (APEC)

036	Australia	344	China, Hong Kong Special Administrative Region	554	New Zealand	702	Singapore
096	Brunei Darussalam			598	Papua New Guinea	158	Taiwan Province of China
		360	Indonesia	604	Peru	764	Thailand
124	Canada	392	Japan	608	Philippines	840	United States of America
152	Chile	458	Malaysia	410	Republic of Korea	704	Viet Nam
156	China	484	Mexico	643	Russian Federation		

073 — Association of Southeast Asian Nations (ASEAN)

096	Brunei Darussalam	360	Indonesia	458	Malaysia	608	Philippines	764	Thailand
116	Cambodia	418	Lao PDR	104	Myanmar	702	Singapore	704	Viet Nam

130 — Caribbean Community and Common Market (CARICOM)

028	Antigua and Barbuda	084	Belize	332	Haiti	662	Saint Lucia
044	Bahamas (member of the Community only)	212	Dominica	388	Jamaica	670	Saint Vincent and the Grenadines
		308	Grenada	500	Montserrat	740	Suriname
052	Barbados	328	Guyana	659	Saint Kitts and Nevis	780	Trinidad and Tobago

395 — Central American Common Market (CACM)

188	Costa Rica	222	El Salvador	320	Guatemala	340	Honduras	558	Nicaragua

171 — Common Market for Eastern and Southern Africa (COMESA)

108	Burundi	818	Egypt	434	Libya	690	Seychelles	894	Zambia
174	Comoros	232	Eritrea	450	Madagascar	706	Somalia	716	Zimbabwe
180	Democratic Republic of the Congo	748	Eswatini	454	Malawi	729	Sudan		
		231	Ethiopia	480	Mauritius	788	Tunisia		
262	Djibouti	404	Kenya	646	Rwanda	800	Uganda		

172 — Commonwealth of Independent States (CIS)[3]

051	Armenia	398	Kazakhstan	643	Russian Federation	804	Ukraine
031	Azerbaijan	417	Kyrgyzstan	762	Tajikistan	860	Uzbekistan
112	Belarus	498	Republic of Moldova	795	Turkmenistan		

692 — Economic and Monetary Community of Central Africa (EMCCA)

120	Cameroon	140	Central African Republic	148	Chad	178	Congo	226	Equatorial Guinea	266	Gabon

892 — Economic Community of West African States (ECOWAS)

204	Benin	384	Côte d'Ivoire	324	Guinea	466	Mali	686	Senegal
854	Burkina Faso	270	Gambia	624	Guinea-Bissau	562	Niger	694	Sierra Leone
132	Cabo Verde	288	Ghana	430	Liberia	566	Nigeria	768	Togo

098 — Euro Area

040	Austria	246	Finland	372	Ireland	442	Luxembourg	703	Slovakia
056	Belgium	250	France	380	Italy	470	Malta	705	Slovenia
196	Cyprus	276	Germany	428	Latvia	528	Netherlands	724	Spain
233	Estonia	300	Greece	440	Lithuania	620	Portugal		

197 — European Free Trade Association (EFTA)

352	Iceland	438	Liechtenstein	578	Norway	756	Switzerland

097 — European Union (EU)

040	Austria	208	Denmark	348	Hungary	470	Malta	705	Slovenia
056	Belgium	233	Estonia	372	Ireland	528	Netherlands	724	Spain

[3] Georgia (numerical code 268) can be listed as part of this group; for example, in International Merchandise Trade statistics.

097   European Union (EU) *(Continued)*

100	Bulgaria	246	Finland	380	Italy	616	Poland	752	Sweden
191	Croatia	250	France	428	Latvia	620	Portugal	826	United Kingdom
196	Cyprus	276	Germany	440	Lithuania	642	Romania		
203	Czechia	300	Greece	442	Luxembourg	703	Slovakia		

095   Latin American Integration Association (LAIA)

032	Argentina	170	Colombia	591	Panama	862	Venezuela (Bolivarian Republic of)
068	Bolivia (Plurinational State of)	192	Cuba	600	Paraguay		
076	Brazil	218	Ecuador	604	Peru		
152	Chile	484	Mexico	858	Uruguay		

199   Least developed countries (LDCs)

004	Afghanistan	262	Djibouti	454	Malawi	728	South Sudan
024	Angola	232	Eritrea	466	Mali	729	Sudan
050	Bangladesh	231	Ethiopia	478	Mauritania	626	Timor-Leste
204	Benin	270	Gambia	508	Mozambique	768	Togo
064	Bhutan	324	Guinea	104	Myanmar	798	Tuvalu
854	Burkina Faso	624	Guinea-Bissau	524	Nepal	800	Uganda
108	Burundi	332	Haiti	562	Niger	834	United Republic of Tanzania
116	Cambodia	296	Kiribati	646	Rwanda		
140	Central African Republic	418	Lao People's Democratic Republic	678	Sao Tome and Principe	548	Vanuatu
148	Chad			686	Senegal	887	Yemen
174	Comoros	426	Lesotho	694	Sierra Leone	894	Zambia
180	Democratic Republic of the Congo	430	Liberia	090	Solomon Islands		
		450	Madagascar	706	Somalia		

071   North American Free Trade Agreement (NAFTA)

124	Canada	484	Mexico	840	United States of America

198   Organisation for Economic Co-operation and Development (OECD)

036	Australia	250	France	428	Latvia	410	Republic of Korea
040	Austria	276	Germany	440	Lithuania	703	Slovakia
056	Belgium	300	Greece	442	Luxembourg	705	Slovenia
124	Canada	348	Hungary	484	Mexico	724	Spain
152	Chile	352	Iceland	528	Netherlands	752	Sweden
203	Czech Republic	372	Ireland	554	New Zealand	756	Switzerland
208	Denmark	376	Israel	578	Norway	792	Turkey
233	Estonia	380	Italy	616	Poland	826	United Kingdom of Great Britain and Northern Ireland
246	Finland	392	Japan	620	Portugal	840	United States of America

399   Organization of the Petroleum Exporting Countries (OPEC)

012	Algeria	226	Equatorial Guinea	414	Kuwait	784	United Arab Emirates
024	Angola	266	Gabon	434	Libya	862	Venezuela (Bolivarian Republic of)
178	Congo	364	Iran (Islamic Republic of)	566	Nigeria		
218	Ecuador	368	Iraq	682	Saudi Arabia		

711   Southern African Customs Union (SACU)

072	Botswana	748	Eswatini	426	Lesotho	516	Namibia	710	South Africa

069   Southern Common Market (MERCOSUR)

032	Argentina	076	Brazil	858	Uruguay
068	Bolivia (Plurinational State of)	600	Paraguay	862	Venezuela (Bolivarian Republic of)

Annexe I - Nomenclature des pays ou zones, groupements régionaux et autres groupements

L'Annuaire statistique répertorie de pays ou de zones sur la base de l'opuscule United Nations Standard Country Codes (Série M, nº 49) rédigée par la Division de statistique du Secrétariat de l'Organisation des Nations Unies et publiée en 1970[1]. La liste des pays ou zones; la composition des régions géographiques et économiques, commerciales et d'autres groupements utilisés dans cet annuaire (au 31 juillet 2018) sont présentées dans la présente annexe. On a eu recours à la forme brève des noms des pays et des zones usitées au cours des activités courantes des Nations Unies, et pas nécessairement aux désignations officielles utilisées dans les documents officiels[2]. Afin de faciliter le traitement des données statistiques, un code numérique unique et standard à trois chiffres est attribué à chaque pays ou zone et à chaque région géographique et groupement de pays ou de zones. Pour référence, ces codes, le cas échéant, sont présentés à la gauche de chaque pays ou zone visées dans cette annexe. Ces codes s'échelonnent entre 000 et 899.

A. Changements dans le nom des pays ou zones (depuis 31 juillet 2008)

L'étendue géographique d'un pays ou d'une zone ou la composition d'une région géographique peuvent varier au fil du temps et les utilisateurs devront tenir compte de telles modifications lorsqu'ils ont recours aux codes indiques dans la présente publication et qu'ils établissent des rapports entre les données portant sur différentes périodes. La modification du nom d'un pays ou d'une zone alors que son espace géographique demeure le même n'est pas habituellement accompagnée d'un changement de son code numérique. Changements dans les codes numériques et noms dans la période générale couverts par les statistiques (depuis le 31 juillet 2008) dans l'Annuaire, sont présentés ci-dessous;

Code numérique	Pays ou region (nouveaux codes et codes modifies)	Date de la modification	Code numérique	Pays ou region (Changements de nom sans modification du code)	Date de la modification
728	Soudan du Sud	2011	748	Eswatini, *ex-Swaziland*	2018
729	Soudan	2011	203	Tchéquie, *ex-République tchèque*	2016
531	Curaçao	2010	132	Cabo Verde, *ex-Cap-Vert*	2013
534	Saint-Martin (partie néerlandaise)	2010	434	État de Palestine, *ex-Territoire palestinien occupé*	2013
535	Bonaire, Saint-Eustache et Saba	2010	275	Libye, *ex-Jamahiriya arabe libyenne*	2011
			068	Bolivie (État plurinational de), *ex-Bolivie*	2009
				Macédoine du Nord, *Ancienne république yougoslave de Macédoine*	2019
			498	République de Moldova, *ex-Moldova*	2008

B. Groupements régionaux

Le système des groupements régionaux à la page suivante est principalement basé sur les 6 continents; ces régions continentales, à l'exception de l'Antarctique, sont subdivisées en 22 sous-régions et 2 régions intermédiaires (Afrique subsaharienne et l'Amérique latine et Caraïbes) afin d'obtenir une homogénéité accrue les effectifs de population, les situations démographiques et la précision des statistiques démographiques. Cette nomenclature est couramment utilisée aux fins des statistiques internationales et a été appliquée autant qu'il a été possible dans le présent *Annuaire* en vue de renforcer la cohérence et de faciliter la comparaison et l'analyse. Son utilisation pour l'établissement des statistiques internationales n'est cependant rien moins qu'universelle, même au niveau des régions continentales, et les variations que présentent les sources et méthodes statistiques internationales entraînent inévitablement de nombreuses différences dans certains domaines de cet *Annuaire*. Les différences d'ordre général sont indiquées dans les notes figurant au bas de la classification présentée ci-dessous. Les différences plus spécifiques sont mentionnées dans les notes techniques et notes de bas de page accompagnant les divers tableaux.

L'application des expressions "développés" et "en développement" aux pays, zones ou régions n'est pas non plus normalisée à l'échelle internationale. Ces expressions sont utilisées dans la présente publication en référence aux groupements régionaux généralement considérés comme "développés", à savoir l'Amérique septentrionale (code numérique 021), l'Europe (150), Chypre (196), Israël (376), le Japon (392) et l'Australie et la Nouvelle-Zélande (053). Ces appellations sont employées pour des raisons de commodité statistique et n'expriment pas nécessairement un jugement sur le stade de développement atteint par tel ou tel pays ou zone. Les cas différant de cet usage sont signalés dans les notes accompagnant les tableaux concernés.

---

[1] Quatre révisions de ce document ont été publiés en 1975, 1982, 1996 et 1999. D'autres révisions sont maintenant publiés sur le site internet de la Division de statistique des Nations Unies.

[2] Le Bulletin terminologique No 347/Rev.1 ou UNTERM website, intitulé "Noms de pays" établi par le Département des affaires de l'Assemblée générale et des services de conférence du Secrétariat de l'Organisation des Nations Unies, répertorie les noms des États Membres dans les six langues de l'Organisation.

001	Monde					

002	Afrique					

202	Afrique subsaharienne				015	Afrique septentrionale

014 Afrique orientale

108	Burundi	086	Territoire britannique de l'océan Indien	426	Lesotho
174	Comores			516	Namibie
262	Djibouti	894	Zambie		
232	Érythrée	716	Zimbabwe	**011**	**Afrique occidentale**
231	Éthiopie			204	Bénin
404	Kenya	**017**	**Afrique centrale**	854	Burkina Faso
450	Madagascar	024	Angola	132	Cabo Verde
454	Malawi	120	Cameroun	384	Côte d'Ivoire
480	Maurice	178	Congo	270	Gambie
175	Mayotte	266	Gabon	288	Ghana
508	Mozambique	226	Guinée équatoriale	324	Guinée
800	Ouganda	140	République centrafricaine	624	Guinée-Bissau
834	République-Unie de Tanzanie note /a			430	Libéria
		180	République démocratique du Congo	466	Mali
638	Réunion			478	Mauritanie
646	Rwanda	678	Sao Tomé-et-Principe	562	Niger
690	Seychelles	148	Tchad	566	Nigéria
706	Somalie			654	Sainte-Hélène note /b
728	Soudan du Sud note 736	**018**	**Afrique australe**	686	Sénégal
260	Terres australes françaises	710	Afrique du Sud	694	Sierra Leone
		072	Botswana	768	Togo
		748	Eswatini		

015 Afrique septentrionale

012	Algérie
818	Égypte
434	Libye
504	Maroc
732	Sahara occidental
729	Soudan note 736
788	Tunisie

Note	**Certains tableaux peuvent**
736	*Soudan [anc.]*
/a	Incluent
---	*Zanzibar*
/b	Incluent
---	*Ascension*
---	*Tristan da Cunha*

019	Amériques					

419	Amérique latine et Caraïbes				021	Amérique septentrionale

029 Caraïbes

660	Anguilla	652	Saint-Barthélemy	**005**	**Amérique du Sud**
028	Antigua-et-Barbuda	659	Saint-Kitts-et-Nevis	032	Argentine
533	Aruba	662	Sainte-Lucie	068	Bolivie (État plurinational de)
044	Bahamas	663	Saint-Martin (partie française)		
052	Barbade			076	Brésil
535	Bonaire, note 530 Saint-Eustache et Saba	534	Saint-Martin note 530 (partie néerlandaise)	152	Chili
		670	Saint-Vincent-et-les Grenadines	170	Colombie
192	Cuba			218	Équateur
531	Curaçao note 530	780	Trinité-et-Tobago	239	Géorgie du Sud-et-les Îles Sandwich du Sud
212	Dominique				
308	Grenade	**013**	**Amérique centrale**	328	Guyana
312	Guadeloupe	084	Belize	254	Guyane française
332	Haïti	188	Costa Rica	074	Île Bouvet
136	Îles Caïmanes	222	El Salvador	238	Îles Falkland (Malvinas)
796	Îles Turques-et-Caïques	320	Guatemala		
850	Îles Vierges américaines	340	Honduras	600	Paraguay
092	Îles Vierges britanniques	484	Mexique	604	Pérou
388	Jamaïque	558	Nicaragua	740	Suriname
474	Martinique	591	Panama	858	Uruguay
500	Montserrat			862	Venezuela (République bolivarienne du)
630	Porto Rico				
214	République dominicaine				

021 Amérique septentrionale note 003

060	Bermudes
124	Canada
840	États-Unis d'Amérique
304	Groenland
666	Saint-Pierre-et-Miquelon

Note	
003	*Le continent de l'Amérique du Nord comprend l'Amérique septentrionale, les Caraïbes et l'Amérique centrale*
	Certains tableaux peuvent
530	*Antilles néerlandaises [anc.]*

010	Antarctique					

Monde

142 Asie

143 Asie centrale		**035 Asie du Sud-Est**		**034 Asie méridionale**		784	Émirats arabes unis

143 Asie centrale
398 Kazakhstan
417 Kirghizistan
860 Ouzbékistan
762 Tadjikistan
795 Turkménistan

030 Asie orientale
156 Chine
344 Chine, région administrative spéciale de Hong Kong
446 Chine, région administrative spéciale de Macao
392 Japon
496 Mongolie
410 République de Corée
408 République populaire démocratique de Corée

035 Asie du Sud-Est
096 Brunéi Darussalam
116 Cambodge
360 Indonésie
458 Malaisie
104 Myanmar
608 Philippines
418 République démocratique populaire lao
702 Singapour
764 Thaïlande
626 Timor-Leste
704 Viet Nam

034 Asie méridionale
004 Afghanistan
050 Bangladesh
064 Bhoutan
356 Inde
364 Iran (République islamique d')
462 Maldives
524 Népal
586 Pakistan
144 Sri Lanka

145 Asie occidentale
682 Arabie saoudite
051 Arménie
031 Azerbaïdjan
048 Bahreïn
196 Chypre
784 Émirats arabes unis
275 État de Palestine
268 Géorgie
368 Iraq
376 Israël
400 Jordanie
414 Koweït
422 Liban
512 Oman
634 Qatar
760 République arabe syrienne
792 Turquie
887 Yémen

150 Europe

151 Europe orientale
112 Bélarus
100 Bulgarie
643 Fédération de Russie
348 Hongrie
616 Pologne
498 République de Moldova
642 Roumanie
703 Slovaquie
203 Tchéquie
804 Ukraine

154 Europe septentrionale
208 Danemark
233 Estonie
246 Finlande
831 Guernesey   note 830
833 Île de Man
248 Îles d'Åland
234 Îles Féroé
744 Îles Svalbard-et-Jan Mayen
372 Irlande
352 Islande
832 Jersey   380
428 Lettonie
440 Lituanie
578 Norvège
826 Royaume-Uni de Grande-Bretagne et d'Irlande du Nord
752 Suède

039 Europe méridionale
008 Albanie
020 Andorre
070 Bosnie-Herzégovine
191 Croatie
724 Espagne
292 Gibraltar
300 Grèce
380 Italie
807 Macédoine du Nord
470 Malte
499 Monténégro   note 891
620 Portugal
674 Saint-Marin
336 Saint-Siège
688 Serbie   note 891 & /c
705 Slovénie

155 Europe occidentale
276 Allemagne
040 Autriche
056 Belgique
250 France
438 Liechtenstein
442 Luxembourg
492 Monaco
528 Pays-Bas
756 Suisse

Note   Certains tableaux peuvent énumérer
830   Îles Anglo-Normandes
891   Serbie-et-Monténégro [anc.]
/c   Kosovo

009 Océanie

053 Australie et Nouvelle-Zélande
036 Australie
162 Île Christmas
334 Île Heard-et-Îles MacDonald
574 Île Norfolk
166 Îles des Cocos (Keeling)
554 Nouvelle-Zélande

054 Mélanésie
242 Fidji
090 Îles Salomon
540 Nouvelle-Calédonie
598 Papouasie-Nouvelle-Guinée
548 Vanuatu

057 Micronésie
316 Guam
580 Îles Mariannes du Nord
584 Îles Marshall
581 Îles mineures éloignées des États-Unis
296 Kiribati
583 Micronésie (États fédérés de)
520 Nauru
585 Palaos

061 Polynésie
184 Îles Cook
876 Îles Wallis-et-Futuna
570 Nioué
612 Pitcairn
258 Polynésie française
882 Samoa
016 Samoa américaines
772 Tokélaou[corrigée]
776 Tonga
798 Tuvalu

C. Autres groupements

On trouvera ci-après une liste des autres groupements et de leur composition, présentée dans l'*Annuaire*. Ces groupements correspondent essentiellement à des intérêts économiques et commerciaux d'après les associations régionales.

071	**Accord de libre-échange nord-américain (ALENA)**				
124	Canada	840	États-Unis d'Amérique	484	Mexique

073	**Association des nations de l'Asie du Sud-Est (ANASE)**							
096	Brunéi Darussalam	360	Indonésie	104	Myanmar	418	République démocratique populaire lao	764	Thaïlande
116	Cambodge	458	Malaisie	608	Philippines	702	Singapour	704	Viet Nam

197	**Association européenne de libre-échange (AELE)**				
352	Islande	438	Liechtenstein	578	Norvège	756	Suisse

095	**Association latino-américaine d'intégration (ALAI)**				
032	Argentine	170	Colombie	591	Panama	862	Venezuela (République bolivarienne du)
068	Bolivie (État plurinational de)	192	Cuba	600	Paraguay		
076	Brésil	218	Équateur	604	Pérou		
152	Chili	484	Mexique	858	Uruguay		

130	**Communauté des Caraïbes et Marché commun des Caraïbes (CARICOM)**				
028	Antigua-et-Barbuda	084	Belize	332	Haïti	662	Sainte-Lucie
044	Bahamas (membre de la communauté seulement)	212	Dominique	388	Jamaïque	670	Saint-Vincent-et-les Grenadines
		308	Grenade	500	Montserrat	740	Suriname
052	Barbade	328	Guyana	659	Saint-Kitts-et-Nevis	780	Trinité-et-Tobago

172	**Communauté d'Etats indépendants (CEI)[3]**				
051	Arménie	643	Fédération de Russie	417	Kirghizistan	762	Tadjikistan
031	Azerbaïdjan	268	Géorgie	860	Ouzbékistan	795	Turkménistan
112	Bélarus	398	Kazakhstan	498	République de Moldova	804	Ukraine

892	**Communauté économique des Etats de l'Afrique de l'Ouest (CEDEAO)**				
204	Bénin	384	Côte d'Ivoire	324	Guinée	466	Mali	686	Sénégal
854	Burkina Faso	270	Gambie	624	Guinée-Bissau	562	Niger	694	Sierra Leone
132	Cabo Verde	288	Ghana	430	Libéria	566	Nigéria	768	Togo

692	**Communauté économique et monétaire des Etats de l'Afrique Centrale (CEMAC)**				
120	Camerou n	178	Congo	266	Gabon	226	Guinée équatoriale	140	République centrafricaine	148	Tchad

066	**Coopération économique Asie-Pacifique (CEAP)**				
036	Australie	840	États-Unis d'Amérique	598	Papouasie-Nouvelle-Guinée	704	Viet Nam
096	Brunéi Darussalam	643	Fédération de Russie	604	Pérou		
124	Canada	360	Indonésie	608	Philippines		
152	Chili	392	Japon	158	Province chinoise de Taïwan		
156	Chine	458	Malaisie	410	République de Corée		
344	Chine, région administrative spéciale de Hong Kong	484	Mexique	702	Singapour		
		554	Nouvelle-Zélande	764	Thaïlande		

063	**Marché commun andin (ANCOM)**				
068	Bolivie (État plurinational de)	170	Colombie	218	Équateur	604	Pérou

395	**Marché commun centraméricain (MCCA)**				
188	Costa Rica	222	El Salvador	320	Guatemala	340	Honduras	558	Nicaragua

171	**Marché commun de l'Afrique de l'Est et de l'Afrique australe (COMESA)**				
108	Burundi	748	Eswatini	454	Malawi	646	Rwanda	788	Tunisie
174	Comores	231	Éthiopie	480	Maurice	690	Seychelles	894	Zambie

---

[3] La Géorgie (code numérique 268) peut figurer dans ce groupe; par exemple, dans le cadre des statistiques du commerce international de marchandises.

262	Djibouti	404	Kenya	800	Ouganda	706	Somalie	716	Zimbabwe
818	Égypte	434	Libye	180	République	729	Soudan		
232	Érythrée	450	Madagascar		dém. du Congo				

069 — Marché commun du Sud (MERCOSUR)

| 032 | Argentine | 076 | Brésil | 858 | Uruguay |
| 068 | Bolivie (État plurinational de) | 600 | Paraguay | 862 | Venezuela (République bolivarienne du) |

198 — Organisation de coopération et de développement économiques (OCDE)

276	Allemagne	840	États-Unis d'Amérique	392	Japon	203	République tchèque
036	Australie	246	Finlande	442	Luxembourg	826	Royaume-Uni de Grande-Bretagne et d'Irlande du Nord
040	Autriche	250	France	484	Mexique		
056	Belgique	300	Grèce	578	Norvège		
124	Canada	348	Hongrie	554	Nouvelle-Zélande	703	Slovaquie
152	Chili	372	Irlande	528	Pays-Bas	705	Slovénie
208	Danemark	376	Israël	616	Pologne	752	Suède
724	Espagne	352	Islande	620	Portugal	756	Suisse
233	Estonie	380	Italie	410	République de Corée	792	Turquie

399 — Organisation des pays exportateurs de pétrole (OPEP)

012	Algérie	218	Équateur	364	Iran (République Islamique d')	566	Nigéria
024	Angola	266	Gabon			634	Qatar
682	Arabie saoudite	226	Guinée équatoriale	368	Iraq	862	Venezuela (République bolivarienne du)
178	Congo	360	Indonésie	434	Libye		
784	Émirats arabes unis			414	Koweït		

199 — Pays les moins avancés (PMA)

004	Afghanistan	270	Gambie	508	Mozambique	694	Sierra Leone
024	Angola	324	Guinée	104	Myanmar	706	Somalie
050	Bangladesh	624	Guinée-Bissau	524	Népal	728	Soudan du Sud
204	Bénin	332	Haïti	562	Niger	729	Soudan
064	Bhoutan	090	Îles Salomon	800	Ouganda	148	Tchad
854	Burkina Faso	296	Kiribati	140	République centrafricaine	626	Timor-Leste
108	Burundi	426	Lesotho	180	République démocratique du Congo	768	Togo
116	Cambodge	430	Libéria	418	République démocratique populaire lao	798	Tuvalu
174	Comores	450	Madagascar	834	République-Unie de Tanzanie	548	Vanuatu
262	Djibouti	454	Malawi	646	Rwanda	887	Yémen
232	Érythrée	466	Mali	678	Sao Tomé-et-Principe	894	Zambie
231	Éthiopie	478	Mauritanie	686	Sénégal		

711 — Union douanière d'Afrique australe

| 710 | Afrique du Sud | 072 | Botswana | 748 | Eswatini | 426 | Lesotho | 516 | Namibie |

097 — Union européenne (UE)

276	Allemagne	208	Danemark	348	Hongrie	470	Malte	826	Royaume-Uni de Grande-Bretagne et d'Irlande du Nord
040	Autriche	724	Espagne	372	Irlande	528	Pays-Bas		
056	Belgique	233	Estonie	380	Italie	616	Pologne		
100	Bulgarie	246	Finlande	428	Lettonie	620	Portugal	703	Slovaquie
191	Croatie	250	France	440	Lituanie	203	République tchèque	705	Slovénie
196	Chypre	300	Grèce	442	Luxembourg	642	Roumanie	752	Suède

098 — Zone euro

276	Allemagne	724	Espagne	300	Grèce	440	Lituania	620	Portugal
040	Autriche	233	Estonie	372	Irlande	442	Luxembourg	703	Slovaquie
056	Belgique	246	Finlande	380	Italie	470	Malte	705	Slovénie
196	Chypre	250	France	428	Lettonie	528	Pays-Bas		

Annex II: Technical notes

Chapter I: World summary

Table 1: World statistics – selected series

These world aggregates are obtained from other tables in this *Yearbook*, where available, and are compiled from statistical publications and databases of the United Nations and the specialized agencies and other institutions. The technical notes of the relevant table in this *Yearbook* should be consulted for detailed information on definition, source, compilation and coverage.

Chapter II: Population and migration

Table 2: Population, surface area and density

The total, male and female population, sex ratio, population age distribution and population density are taken from the estimates and projections prepared by the United Nations Population Division, published in *World Population Prospects: The 2019 Revision*. Surface area are obtained from the *Demographic Yearbook*, through this source only official national data are reported.

Total, male and female population refers to the de facto population in a country, area or region as of 1 July of the year indicated, unless otherwise stated in a footnote. Figures are presented in millions. The total population of a country may comprise either all usual residents of the country (de jure population) or all persons present in the country (de facto population) at the time of the census; for purposes of international comparisons, the de facto definition is used, unless otherwise stated in a footnote.

Population aged 0-14 years / 60 years and over refers to the percentage of the population aged 0-14 years and aged 60 years and older, respectively as of 1 July of the year indicated, unless otherwise stated in a footnote.

Population density refers to the population, as of 1 July of the year indicated, per square kilometre of surface area, unless otherwise stated in a footnote.

Sex ratio is calculated as the ratio of the population of men to that of 100 women as of 1 July of the year indicated, unless otherwise stated in a footnote.

Surface area refers to land area plus inland water, unless otherwise stated in a footnote.

Table 3: International migrants and refugees

International migrant stock are taken from the estimates and projections prepared by the United Nations Population Division, published in *International migrant stock: The 2019 Revision*. "Refugees and others of concern to UNHCR" are obtained from the United Nations High Commissioner for Refugees, published in the Population Statistics database.

International migrant stock represents the number of persons born in a country other than that in which they live. When information on country of birth was not recorded, data on the number of persons having foreign citizenship was used instead. In the absence of any empirical data, estimates were imputed. Figures for international migrant stock as a percentage of the population are the outcome of dividing the estimated international migrant stock by the estimated total population and multiplying the result by 100.

Refugees include individuals recognised under the 1951 Convention relating to the Status of Refugees; its 1967 Protocol; the 1969 OAU Convention Governing the Specific Aspects of Refugee Problems in Africa; those recognised in accordance with the UNHCR Statute; individuals granted complementary forms of protection; or those enjoying temporary protection. Since 2007, the refugee population also includes people in a refugee-like situation.

Asylum-seekers are individuals who have sought international protection and whose claims for refugee status have not yet been determined, irrespective of when they may have been lodged.

"Other" represents the following 5 categories:

- Internally displaced persons (IDPs) are people or groups of individuals who have been forced to leave their homes or places of habitual residence, in particular as a result of, or in order to avoid the effects of armed conflict, situations of generalised violence, violations of human rights, or natural or man-made disasters, and who have not crossed an international border. For the purposes of UNHCR's statistics, this population only includes conflict-generated IDPs to whom the Office extends protection and/or assistance. Since 2007, the IDP population also includes people in an IDP-like situation. For global IDP estimates, see www.internal-displacement.org.

- Returned refugees are former refugees who have returned to their country of origin spontaneously or in an organised fashion but are yet to be fully integrated. Such return would normally only take place in conditions of safety and dignity.

- Returned IDPs refer to those IDPs who were beneficiaries of UNHCR's protection and assistance activities and who returned to their areas of origin or habitual residence during the year.

- Stateless persons are defined under international law as persons who are not considered as nationals by any State under the operation of its law. In other words, they do not possess the nationality of any State. UNHCR statistics refer to persons who fall under the agency's statelessness mandate because they are stateless according to this international definition, but data from some countries may also include persons with undetermined nationality.

- Others of concern refers to individuals who do not necessarily fall directly into any of the groups above, but to whom UNHCR extends its protection and/or assistance services, based on humanitarian or other special grounds.

Chapter III: Gender

Table 4: Proportion of seats held by women in national parliament

The table shows the percentage of seats held by women members in single or lower chambers of national parliaments as at January/ February each year (see table footnotes for specific details). National parliaments can be bicameral or unicameral. This table covers the single chamber in unicameral parliaments and the lower chamber in bicameral parliaments. It does not cover the upper chamber of bi-cameral parliaments. Seats are usually won by members in general parliamentary elections. Seats may also be filled by nomination, appointment, indirect election, rotation of members and by-election. The proportion of seats held by women in national parliament is derived by dividing the total number of seats occupied by women by the total number of seats in parliament. There is no weighting or normalising of statistics. The source for this table is the Inter-Parliamentary Union (IPU), see www.ipu.org for further information.

Table 5: Ratio of girls to boys in primary, secondary and tertiary education

The ratio of girls to boys (gender parity index) in primary, secondary and tertiary education is the ratio of the number of female students enrolled at primary, secondary and tertiary levels of education to the number of male students in each level. To standardise the effects of the population structure of the appropriate age groups, the Gender Parity Index (GPI) of the Gross Enrolment Ratio (GER) for each level of education is used. The source for this table is the UNESCO Institute for Statistics (UIS), see www.uis.unesco.org for further information.

Chapter IV: Education

Data in Tables 6 and 7 are presented using the 2011 revision of UNESCO's International Standard Classification of Education (ISCED). Data are presented in the tables based on the three main levels of educations defined as follows;

"Primary education" (ISCED level 1) programmes are typically designed to provide students with fundamental skills in reading, writing and mathematics (i.e. literacy and numeracy) and establish a solid foundation for learning and understanding core areas of knowledge, personal and social development, in preparation for lower secondary education. It focuses on learning at a basic level of complexity with little, if any, specialisation.

"Secondary education" (ISCED level 2 and 3) is divided into two different stages, i.e. lower secondary and upper secondary. Lower secondary education programmes are typically designed to build on the learning outcomes from primary. Usually, they aim to lay the foundation for lifelong learning and human development upon which education systems may then expand further educational opportunities. Upper secondary education programmes are typically designed to complete secondary education in preparation for tertiary education or provide skills relevant to employment, or both. Programmes at this level offer students more varied, specialised and in-depth instruction than programmes at lower secondary. They are more differentiated, with an increased range of options and streams available. Teachers are often highly qualified in the subjects or fields of specialisation they teach, particularly in the higher grades.

Tertiary education (ISCED levels 5-8) builds on secondary education, providing learning activities in specialised fields of education. It aims at learning at a high level of complexity and specialisation. Tertiary education includes what is commonly understood as academic education but also includes advanced vocational or professional education. It comprises ISCED levels 5, 6, 7 and 8, which are labelled as short-cycle tertiary education, Bachelor's or equivalent level,

Master's or equivalent level, and doctoral or equivalent level, respectively. The content of programmes at the tertiary level is more complex and advanced than in lower ISCED levels.

For more information about the International Standard Classification of Education (ISCED) 2011 please refer to: http://www.uis.unesco.org/Education/Documents/isced-2011-en.pdf

Table 6: Education at the primary, secondary and tertiary levels

The table shows the number of students enrolled as well as the gross enrolment ratio which is the number of students enrolled, regardless of age, expressed as a percentage of the eligible official school-age population corresponding to the same level of education in a given school year. Enrolment is measured at the beginning of the school or academic year. The gross enrolment ratio at each level will include all pupils whatever their ages, whereas the population is limited to the range of official school ages. Therefore, for countries with almost universal education among the school-age population, the gross enrolment ratio can exceed 100 if the actual age distribution of pupils extends beyond the official school ages.

Table 7: Teaching staff at the primary, secondary and tertiary levels

The table shows the total number of teachers at a given level of education, as well as the proportion of female teachers expressed as a percentage of the total (male and female) at the same level in a given school year. The data sources include school census or surveys and teachers' records. Teachers (or teaching staff) are defined as persons employed full-time or part-time in an official capacity to guide and direct the learning experience of pupils and students, irrespective of their qualifications or the delivery mechanism, i.e. face-to-face and/or at a distance. This definition excludes educational personnel who have no active teaching duties (e.g. headmasters, headmistresses or principals who do not teach) or who work occasionally or in a voluntary capacity in educational institutions.

Table 8: Public expenditure on education

Public expenditure on education consists of current and capital expenditures on education by local, regional and national governments, including municipalities. Household contributions are excluded. Current expenditure on education includes expenditure for goods and services consumed within the current year and which would need to be renewed if needed the following year. It includes expenditure on: staff salaries and benefits; contracted or purchased services; other resources including books and teaching materials; welfare services; and other current expenditure such as subsidies to students and households, furniture and equipment, minor repairs, fuel, telecommunications, travel, insurance and rents. Capital expenditure on education includes expenditure for assets that last longer than one year. It includes expenditure for construction, renovation and major repairs of buildings and the purchase of heavy equipment or vehicles.

Chapter V: Health

Table 9: Health personnel

The table shows four main categories of health personnel (out of 9 categories available in the source); Physicians which includes generalist medical practitioners and specialist medical practitioners; Nursing and midwifery personnel which includes nursing professionals, midwifery professionals, nursing associate professionals and midwifery associate professionals. Traditional midwives are not included here; Dentistry personnel includes dentists, dental assistants, dental technicians and related occupations; and Pharmaceutical personnel which includes pharmacists, pharmaceutical assistants, pharmaceutical technicians and related occupations.

The data are obtained from the World Health Organisation's (WHO) Global Health Workforce Statistics database which are compiled from several sources such as national population censuses, labour force and employment surveys, national statistical products and routine administrative information systems. As a result, considerable variability remains across countries in the coverage, quality and reference year of the original data. In general, the denominator data for health workforce density (i.e. national population estimates) were obtained from the United Nations Population Division's *World Population Prospects* publication. In some cases, the official report provided only workforce density indicators, from which estimates of the stock were then calculated.

The classification of health workers used is based on criteria for vocational education and training, regulation of health professions, and activities and tasks of jobs, i.e. a framework for categorizing key workforce variables according to shared characteristics. The WHO framework largely draws on the latest revisions to the internationally standardized classification systems of the International Labour Organization (International Standard Classification of Occupations), United Nations Educational, Scientific and Cultural Organization (International Standard Classification of Education), and the United Nations Statistics Division (International Standard Industrial Classification of All Economic Activities). Depending on the nature of each country's situation and the means of measurement, data are available for up to 9 categories of health workers in the aggregated set, and up to 18 categories in the disaggregated set. The latter essentially reflects attempts to better distinguish some subgroups of the workforce according to assumed differences in skill level and skill specialization.

Table 10: Expenditure on health

The series "Current expenditure" refers to all health care goods and services used or consumed during a year excluding capital spending, or rather "gross capital formation", which is the purchase of new assets used repeatedly over several years. These estimates are in line with the 2011 System of Health Accounts (SHA). Current expenditure is expressed as a proportion of Gross Domestic Product (GDP). The series Domestic General government expenditures are composed of public and private domestic sources. The Domestic public sources include domestic revenue as internal transfers and grants, transfers, subsidies to voluntary health insurance beneficiaries, Non-profit institutions serving households (NPISH) or enterprise financing schemes as well as compulsory prepayment and social health insurance contributions. All these transfers and subsidies represent public sources for health and indicate the overall governments' contribution to funding healthcare relative to other sources of funding from domestic private and external sources. Domestic General government expenditure is expressed as a proportion of general government expenditures.

Chapter VI: Crime

Table 11: Intentional homicides and other crimes

"Intentional homicides" and "other crimes" are taken from the United Nations Office on Drugs and Crime, published in their statistics database.

"Intentional Homicide" means unlawful death purposefully inflicted on a person by another person. Data on intentional homicide should also include serious assault leading to death and death as a result of a terrorist attack. It should exclude attempted homicide, manslaughter, death due to legal intervention, justifiable homicide in self-defence and death due to armed conflict.

"Assault" means physical attack against the body of another person resulting in serious bodily injury, excluding indecent/sexual assault, threats and slapping/punching. 'Assault' leading to death should also be excluded.

"Kidnapping" means unlawfully detaining a person or persons against their will (including through the use of force, threat, fraud or enticement) for the purpose of demanding for their liberation an illicit gain or any other economic gain or other material benefit, or in order to oblige someone to do or not to do something. "Kidnapping" excludes disputes over child custody.

"Theft" means depriving a person or organisation of property without force with the intent to keep it . "Theft" excludes Burglary, housebreaking, Robbery, and Theft of a Motor Vehicle, which are recorded separately.

Total "Sexual violence" means rape and sexual assault, including Sexual Offences against Children.

Chapter VII: National accounts

The National Accounts Main Aggregates Database (available at http://unstats.un.org/unsd/snaama) presents national accounts data for more than 200 countries and areas of the world. It is the basis for the publication of National Account Statistics: Analysis of Main Aggregates (AMA), a publication prepared by the Statistics Division of the Department for Economic and Social Affairs of the United Nations Secretariat with the generous co-operation of national statistical offices. The database is updated in December of each year with newly available national accounts data for all countries and areas.

The National Accounts Main Aggregates Database is based on the data obtained from the United Nations National Accounts Questionnaire (NAQ) introduced in October 1999, which in turn is based on the System of National Accounts 1993 (1993 SNA). The data are supplemented with estimates prepared by the Statistics Division. The updated SNA, called the System of National Accounts 2008 (2008 SNA) was finalised in September 2009. As of 2018, 105 countries and territories have implemented 2008 SNA. These countries are the European Member States, Andorra, Argentina, Armenia, Australia, Bahamas, Belarus, Bosnia and Herzegovina, Brazil, British Virgin Islands, Brunei Darussalam, Cameroon, Canada, Cayman Islands, Chile, China (mainland), China, Hong Kong SAR, China, Macao SAR, Colombia, Costa Rica, Djibouti, Dominican Republic, Ecuador, El Salvador, Eswatini, Fiji, Gambia, Ghana, Greenland, Iceland, India, Indonesia, Israel, Japan, Kenya, Kosovo, Lao People's Democratic Republic, Lebanon, Liechtenstein, Malaysia,

Maldives, Mauritius, Mexico, Mongolia, Montenegro, Morocco, New Zealand, Niger, Nigeria, Norway, Pakistan, Paraguay, Peru, Philippines, Republic of Korea, Republic of Moldova, Russian Federation, Samoa, Saudi Arabia, Senegal, Serbia, Singapore, Sint Maarten, South Africa, Sri Lanka, Switzerland, North Macedonia, Thailand, Timor-Leste, Turkey, Uganda, Ukraine, United Arab Emirates, the United Kingdom, United Republic of Tanzania, the United States of America and Zambia.

Every effort has been made to present the estimates of the various countries or areas in a form designed to facilitate international comparability. To this end, important differences in concept, scope, coverage and classification have been described in the footnotes for individual countries. Such differences should be taken into account to avoid misleading comparisons. Data contained in the tables relate to the calendar year for which they are shown, except in several cases. These special cases are posted on the National Accounts Main Aggregates Database website (http://unstats.un.org/unsd/snaama/notes.asp). The figures shown are the most recent estimates and revisions available at the time of compilation. In general, figures for the most recent year are to be regarded as provisional. The sums of the components in the tables may not necessarily add up to totals shown because of rounding.

Table 12: Gross domestic product and gross domestic product per capita

This table shows gross domestic product (GDP) and GDP per capita in US dollars at current prices, GDP at constant 2015 prices and the corresponding real rates of growth. The tables are intended to facilitate international comparisons of levels of income generated in production. Official data and estimates of total and per capita GDP at current prices have been converted to US dollars, while total GDP at constant prices are converted to 2015 prices before conversion to US dollars using the 2015 exchange rates. The conversion methodology to US dollars is described in the document on the methodology for the National Accounts Main Aggregates Database (http://unstats.un.org/unsd/snaama/methodology.pdf). For inter-country comparisons over time, it would be more appropriate to use the growth rate in the table based on constant price data, which are more indicative of inter-country and intra-grouping comparisons of trends in total GDP. The growth rate shown in the table is computed as geometric mean of annual growth rates expressed as percentages for the years.

Table 13: Gross value added by kind of economic activity

This table presents the shares of the components of gross value added at current prices by kind of economic activity.

Sector	Comprises of (in terms of ISIC 3):
Agriculture	Agriculture, hunting, forestry and fishing (ISIC A-B)
Industry	Mining and quarrying, Manufacturing, Electricity, gas and water supply (ISIC C-E) Construction (ISIC F)
Services	Wholesale and retail trade; repair of motor vehicles, motorcycles and personal and household goods, Hotels and restaurants (ISIC G-H) Transport, storage and communications (ISIC I) Other activities which includes financial intermediation, real estate, renting and business activities, public administration and defense; compulsory social security, education, health and social work, other community, social and personal service activities, private households with employed persons (ISIC J-P).

Chapter VIII: Finance

Detailed information and current figures relating to table 14 are contained in International Financial Statistics, published by the International Monetary Fund (see also http://elibrary-data.imf.org) and in the United Nations Monthly Bulletin of Statistics.

Table 14: Balance of payments summary

A balance of payments can be broadly described as the record of an economy's international economic transactions. It shows (a) transactions in goods, services and income between an economy and the rest of the world, (b) changes of ownership and other changes in that economy's monetary gold, special drawing rights (SDRs) and claims on and liabilities to the rest of the world, and (c) unrequited transfers and counterpart entries needed to balance in the accounting sense any entries for the foregoing transactions and changes which are not mutually offsetting. The balance of payments data are presented on the basis of the methodology and presentation of the sixth edition of the Balance of Payments

Manual (BPM6), published by the International Monetary Fund in November 2013. The BPM6 incorporates several major changes to take account of developments in international trade and finance over the years, and to better harmonize the Fund's balance of payments methodology with the methodology of the 2008 System of National Accounts (SNA). The detailed definitions concerning the content of the basic categories of the balance of payments are given in the Balance of Payments Manual (sixth edition)

Brief explanatory notes are given below to clarify the scope of the major items.

Current account is a record of all transactions in the balance of payments covering the exports and imports of goods and services, payments of income, and current transfers between residents of a country and non-residents.

Capital account, n.i.e. refers mainly to capital transfers linked to the acquisition of a fixed asset other than transactions relating to debt forgiveness plus the disposal of nonproduced, nonfinancial assets, and to capital transfers linked to the disposal of fixed assets by the donor or to the financing of capital formation by the recipient, plus the acquisition of nonproduced, nonfinancial assets.

Financial account, n.i.e. is the net sum of the balance of direct investment, portfolio investment, and other investment transactions.

Reserves and related items is the sum of transactions in reserve assets, LCFARs, exceptional financing, and use of Fund credit and loans.

Table 15: Exchange rates

Foreign exchange rates are shown in units of national currency per US dollar. The exchange rates are classified into three broad categories, reflecting both the role of the authorities in the determination of the exchange and/or the multiplicity of exchange rates in a country. The market rate is used to describe exchange rates determined largely by market forces; the official rate is an exchange rate deter-mined by the authorities, sometimes in a flexible manner. For countries maintaining multiple exchange arrangements, the rates are labelled principal rate, secondary rate, and tertiary rate. Unless otherwise stated, the table refers to end of period and period averages of market exchange rates or official exchange rates.

Chapter IX: Labour market

A comparable and comprehensive collection of data on labour force and related topics are available from the International Labour Organisation's (ILO) *Key Indicators of the Labour Market (KILM)* publication, which is updated every 2 years. More timely information is contained in the ILO's ILOSTAT data repository (see www.ilo.org/ilostat) which publishes data as it is received from the countries either on an annual, quarterly or monthly basis but does not include all the consistency checks nor include all the sources used by KILM. For various reasons, national definitions of employment and unemployment often differ from the recommended international standard definitions and thereby limit international comparability. Inter-country comparisons are also complicated by a variety of types of data collection systems used to obtain information on employed and unemployed persons. The ILOSTAT website provides a comprehensive description of the methodology underlying the labour series.

Table 16: Labour force and unemployment

Labour force participation rate is calculated by expressing the number of persons in the labour force as a percentage of the working-age population. The labour force is the sum of the number of persons employed and the number of unemployed (see ILO's current International Recommendations on Labour Statistics). The working-age population is the population above a certain age, prescribed for the measurement of economic characteristics. The data refer to the age group of 15 years and over and are based on ILO's modelled estimates, unless otherwise stated in a footnote.

Unemployment" is defined to include persons above a certain age who, during a specified period of time were:

(a) "Without work", i.e. were not in paid employment or self-employment;

(b) "Currently available for work", i.e. were available for paid employment or self-employment during the reference period; and

(c) "Seeking work", i.e. had taken specific steps in a specified period to find paid employment or self-employment

Persons not considered to be unemployed include:

(a) Persons intending to establish their own business or farm, but who had not yet arranged to do so and who were not seeking work for pay or profit;

(b) Former unpaid family workers not at work and not seeking work for pay or profit.

The series generally represent the total number of persons wholly unemployed or temporarily laid-off. Percentage figures, where given, are calculated by comparing the number of unemployed to the total members of that group of the labour force on which the unemployment data are based.

Table 17: Employment by economic activity

The employment table presents the percentage distribution of employed persons by economic activity, according to International Standard Industry Classification (ISIC) version 4.

Chapter X: Price and production indices

Table 18: Consumer price indices

A consumer price index is usually estimated as a series of summary measures of the period-to-period proportional change in the prices of a fixed set of consumer goods and services of constant quantity and characteristics, acquired, used or paid for by the reference population. Each summary measure is constructed as a weighted average of a large number of elementary aggregate indices. Each of the elementary aggregate indices is estimated using a sample of prices for a defined set of goods and services obtained in, or by residents of, a specific region from a given set of outlets or other sources of consumption goods and services. The table presents the general consumer price index for all groups of consumption items combined, and the food index including non-alcoholic beverages only. Where alcoholic beverages and/or tobacco are included, this is indicated in footnotes.

Chapter XI: International merchandise trade

The *International Trade Statistics Yearbook* (ITSY) provides an overview of the latest trends of trade in goods and services of most countries and areas in the world, a publication prepared by the Statistics Division of the Department for Economic and Social Affairs of the United Nations Secretariat. The yearbook, see http://comtrade.un.org/pb/, is released in two volumes; Volume I is compiled earlier in the year to present an advanced overview of international merchandise trade from the previous year, Volume II, generally released six months later, contains detailed tables showing international trade for individual commodities and 11 world trade tables covering trade values and indices. Volume II also contains updated versions of world trade tables. The table in this yearbook are also updated monthly in the United Nations Monthly Bulletin of Statistics and on the trade statistics website, see http://unstats.un.org/unsd/trade/data/tables.asp#annual.

The statistics in this Yearbook have been compiled by national statistical authorities largely consistent with the United Nations recommended International Merchandise Trade Statistics, Concepts and Definitions 2010 (IMTS 2010). Depending on what parts of the economic territory are included in the statistical territory, the trade data-compilation system adopted by a country (its trade system) may be referred to as general or special.

General trade system	The statistical territory coincides with the economic territory. Consequently, it is recommended that the statistical territory of a country applying the general trade system comprises all applicable territorial elements. In this case, imports include goods entering the free circulation area, premises for inward processing, industrial free zones, premises for customs warehousing or commercial free zones and exports include goods leaving those territorial elements
Special trade system	(strict definition) The statistical territory comprises only a particular part of the economic territory, so that certain flows of goods which are in the scope of IMTS 2010 are not included in either import or export statistics of the compiling country. The strict definition of the special trade system is in use when the statistical territory comprises only the free circulation area, that is, the part within which goods "may be disposed of without customs restriction". Consequently, in such a case, imports include only goods entering the free circulation area of a compiling country and exports include only goods leaving the free circulation area of a compiling country
	(relaxed definition) (a) goods that enter a country for, or leave it after, inward processing, as well as (b) goods that enter or leave an industrial free zone, are also recorded and included in international merchandise trade statistics

Generally, all countries report their detailed merchandise trade data according to the Harmonized Commodity Description and Coding System (HS) and the data correspond and are then presented by Standard International Trade Classifications (SITC, Rev.3). Data refer to calendar years; however, for those countries which report according to some other reference year, the data are presented in the year which covers the majority of the reference year used by the country.

FOB-type values include the transaction value of the goods and the value of services performed to deliver goods to the border of the exporting country. CIF-type values include the transaction value of the goods, the value of services performed to deliver goods to the border of the exporting country and the value of the services performed to deliver the goods from the border of the exporting country to the border of the importing country. Therefore, data for the statistical value of imported goods are presented as a CIF-type value and the statistical value of exported goods as an FOB-type value.

Conversion of values from national currencies into United States dollars is done by means of currency conversion factors based on official exchange rates. Values in currencies subject to fluctuation are converted into United States dollars using weighted average exchange rates specially calculated for this purpose. The weighted average exchange rate for a given currency for a given year is the component monthly factors, furnished by the International Monetary Fund in its International Financial Statistics publication, weighted by the value of the relevant trade in each month; a monthly factor is the exchange rate (or the simple average rate) in effect during that month. These factors are applied to total imports and exports and to the trade in individual commodities with individual countries.

Table 19: Total imports, exports and balance of trade

Figures on the total imports and exports of countries (or areas) presented in this table are mainly taken from International Financial Statistics published monthly by the International Monetary Fund (IMF) but also from other sources such as national publications and websites and the United Nations *Monthly Bulletin of Statistics* Questionnaire, see the *International Trade Statistics Yearbook* for further details. Estimates for missing data are made in order to arrive to regional totals but are otherwise not shown. The estimation process is automated using quarterly year-on-year growth rates for the extrapolation of missing quarterly data (unless quarterly data can be estimated using available monthly data within the quarter). The conversion factors applied to data in this table are published quarterly in the United Nations *Monthly Bulletin of Statistics* and are also available on the United Nations trade statistics website: http://unstats.un.org/unsd/trade/data/tables.asp#annual.

Table 20: Major trading partners

Figures on major trading partners show the three largest trade partners (countries of last known destination and origin or consignment) in international merchandise trade transactions. In some cases a special partner is shown (i.e. Areas nes, bunkers, etc.) instead of a country and refers to one of the following special categories. Areas not elsewhere specified (i.e. Areas nes) is used (a) for low value trade, (b) if the partner designation was unknown to the country or if an error was made in the partner assignment and (c) for reasons of confidentiality. If a specific geographical location can be identified within Areas nes, then they are recorded accordingly (i.e. Asia nes). Bunkers are ship stores and aircraft supplies, which consists mostly of fuels and food. Free zones belong to the geographical and economic territory of a country but not to its customs territory. For the purpose of trade statistics the transactions between the customs territory and the free zones are recorded, if the reporting country uses the Special Trade System. Free zones can be commercial free zones (duty free shops) or industrial free zones. Data are expressed as percentages of total exports and of total imports of the country, area or special partner.

Data in this table consists of data as reported by UN Comtrade (at three-digit level of SITC Rev. 3 and detailed trading partners breakdown) and estimated data for missing reporters. The data are estimated either through the extrapolation of the data of the two adjacent years, or, if this is not possible, through the use of the data reported by the trading partners (so called mirror data). Mirror statistics is also used in case the partner distribution or confidential data make it necessary to adjust the reported data. In addition, modifications to the received data are made in cases where the provided data are obviously incomplete, in particular in the case of unreported petroleum oils exports in merchandise data.

Chapter XII: Energy

The Energy Statistics Yearbook (available at http://unstats.un.org/unsd/energy/yearbook) is a comprehensive collection of international energy statistics for over 220 countries and areas. The yearbook is prepared by the Statistics Division of the Department for Economic and Social Affairs of the United Nations Secretariat. The yearbook is produced every year with newly available data on energy production, trade, stock changes, bunkers and consumption for all countries and areas, and a historical series back to 1950 are available. The data are compiled primarily from the annual energy questionnaire distributed by the United Nations Statistics Division and supplemented by official national statistical publications, as well as publications from international and regional organizations. Where official data are not available or are inconsistent, estimates are made by the Statistics Division based on governmental, professional or commercial materials.

The period to which the data refer is the calendar year, with the exception of the data of the following countries which refer to the fiscal year: Afghanistan and Iran (Islamic Rep. of) – beginning 21 March of the year stated; Australia, Bangladesh, Bhutan, Egypt (for the latter two, electricity only), Nepal - ending June of the year stated; Pakistan - starting July of the year stated; India, Myanmar and New Zealand – beginning April of the year stated. Data on a per capita basis use population data from the United Nations Population Division as a denominator.

Table 21: Production, trade and consumption of energy

Data are presented in petajoules (gigajoules per capita), to which the individual energy commodities are converted in the interests of international uniformity and comparability. To convert from original units to joules, the data in original units (metric tons, metric tons of oil equivalent, kilowatt hours, cubic metres) are multiplied by conversion factors. For a list of the relevant conversion factors and a detailed description of methods, see the Energy Statistics Yearbook.

Included in the production of primary energy for solids are hard coal, lignite, peat and oil shale, primary solid biofuels and wastes; liquids are comprised of crude oil, natural gas liquids, other hydrocarbons, additives and oxygenates, and liquid biofuels; gas comprises natural gas and biogas; and electricity is comprised of primary electricity generation from hydro, wind, tide, wave and solar sources. Heat comprises primary heat from nuclear, geothermal, chemical and solar sources.

Net imports (imports less exports and bunkers) and changes in stocks, refer to all primary and secondary forms of energy (including feedstocks). Within net imports; bunkers refer to bunkers of aviation gasoline, jet fuel and of hard coal, gas diesel oil and residual fuel oil. International trade of energy commodities is based on the "general trade" system, that is, all goods entering and leaving the national boundary of a country are recorded as imports and exports.

Supply is calculated as primary energy production plus import minus exports minus international bunkers (aviation and marine) minus stock changes.

Chapter XIII: Environment

Table 22: Land

The data on land are compiled by the Food and Agriculture Organization of the United Nations (FAO). FAO's definitions of the land categories are as follows:

Land area	Total area excluding area under inland water bodies. The definition of inland water bodies generally includes major rivers and lakes
Arable land	Land under temporary crops (multiple cropped areas are counted only once); temporary meadows for mowing or pasture; land under market and kitchen gardens; and land temporarily fallow (less than five years). Abandoned land resulting from shifting cultivation is not included in this category. Data for "arable land" are not meant to indicate the amount of land that is potentially cultivable.
Permanent crops	Land cultivated with crops that occupy the land for long periods and need not be replanted after each harvest, such as cocoa, coffee and rubber. This category includes land under flowering shrubs, fruit trees, nut trees and vines, but excludes land under trees grown for wood or timber
Forest	In the Global Forest Resources Assessment 2010 the following definition is used for forest: Land spanning more than 0.5 hectares with trees higher than 5 metres and a canopy cover of more than 10 percent, or trees able to reach these thresholds in situ. It does not include land that is predominantly under agricultural or urban land use.
Sites protected	Land which contributes significantly to the global persistence of biodiversity measured as a proportion of which is wholly covered by a designated protected area. Data are based on spatial

for terrestrial biodiversity	overlap between polygons for Key Biodiversity Areas from the World Database of key Biodiversity Areas and polygons for protected areas from the World Database on Protected Areas. Figures for each region are calculated as the proportion of each Key Biodiversity Area covered by protected areas, averaged (i.e. calculated as the mean) across all Key Biodiversity Areas within the region.

Table 23: Threatened species

Data on the number of threatened species in each group of animals and plants are compiled by the World Conservation Union (IUCN)/ Species Survival Commission (SSC) and published in the IUCN Red List of Threatened Species. The list provides a catalogue of those species that are considered globally threatened. The number of threatened species for any particular country will change between years for a number of reasons, including:

- New information being available to refine the assessment (e.g., confirmation that the species occurs or does not occur in a particular country, confirmation that the species is or is not threatened, etc.)

- Taxonomic changes (e.g., what was previously recognised as one species is now split into several separate species, or has now been merged with another species).

- Corrections (e.g., the previous assessment may have missed a particular country out of its country occurrence list or included a specific country by mistake).

- Genuine status changes (e.g., a species may have genuinely deteriorated or improved in status and therefore has moved into or out of the threatened categories).

The categories used in the Red List are as follows; extinct, extinct in the wild, critically endangered; endangered, vulnerable, near threatened and data deficient.

Table 24: Carbon dioxide emission estimates

Carbon dioxide (CO2) represent total CO2 emissions from fuel combustion. This includes CO2 emissions from fuel combustion in IPCC Source/Sink Category 1 A Fuel Combustion Activities and those which may be reallocated to IPCC Source/Sink Category 2 Industrial Processes and Product Use under the 2006 GLs.

Table 25: Water supply and sanitation services

Population using safely managed drinking water sources is currently being measured by the proportion of population in urban and rural areas, according to national definitions, meeting the criteria for using safely managed drinking water sources (SDG 6.1.1) by using an improved basic drinking water source which is located on premises, available when needed and free of faecal and priority chemical contamination. Improved drinking watersources are those that have the potential to deliver safe water by nature of their design and construction, and include: piped water, boreholes or tubewells, protected dug wells, protected springs, rainwater, and packaged or delivered water.

Population using safely managed sanitation facilities is currently being measured by the proportion of the population in urban and rural areas, according to national definitions, meeting the criteria for having a safely managed sanitation service (SDG 6.2.1a) by using a basic sanitation facility which is not shared with other households and where excreta is safely disposed in situ or transported and treated off-site. Improved sanitation facilities are those designed to hygienically separate excreta from human contact, and include: flush/pour flush to piped sewer system, septic tanks or pit latrines; ventilated improved pit latrines, composting toilets or pit latrines with slabs.

Chapter XIV: Science and technology

Table 26: Human resources in research and development (R&D)

The data presented on human resources in research and development (R&D) are compiled by the UNESCO Institute for Statistics. Data for certain countries are provided to UNESCO by OECD, Eurostat and the Latin-American Network on Science and Technology Indicators (RICYT). The definitions and classifications applied by UNESCO in the table are based on those set out in the Frascati Manual (OECD, 2002). The three categories of personnel shown are defined as follows:

Researchers	Professionals engaged in the conception or creation of new knowledge, products, processes, methods and systems and also in the management of the projects concerned. Postgraduate students at the PhD level (ISCED level 8) engaged in R&D are considered as researchers.
Technicians and equivalent staff	Persons whose main tasks require technical knowledge and experience in one or more fields of engineering, physical and life sciences (technicians) or social sciences and humanities (equivalent staff). They participate in R&D by performing scientific and technical tasks involving the application of concepts and operational methods, normally under the supervision of researchers.
Other supporting staff	Skilled and unskilled craftsmen, secretarial and clerical staff participating in R&D projects or directly associated with (or providing services to researchers involved in) such projects.

Headcount data reflect the total number of persons employed in R&D, independently from their dedication. Full-time equivalent (FTE) may be thought of as one person-year. Thus, a person who normally spends 30% of his/her time on R&D and the rest on other activities (such as teaching, university administration and student counselling) should be considered as 0.3 FTE. Similarly, if a full-time R&D worker is employed at an R&D unit for only six months, this results in an FTE of 0.5.

Table 27: Gross domestic expenditure on research and development (R&D)

The data presented on gross domestic expenditure on research and development are compiled by the UNESCO Institute for Statistics. Data for certain countries are provided to UNESCO by OECD, EUROSTAT and the Network on Science and Technology Indicators (RICYT). Gross domestic expenditure on R&D (GERD) is total intramural expenditure on R&D performed on the national territory during a given period. It includes R&D performed within a country and funded from abroad but excludes payments made abroad for R&D. The sources of funds for GERD are classified according to the following five categories:

Business enterprise funds	Funds allocated to R&D by all firms, organizations and institutions whose primary activity is the market production of goods and services (other than the higher education sector) for sale to the general public at an economically significant price, and those private non-profit institutes mainly serving these firms, organizations and institutions.
Government funds	Funds allocated to R&D by all departments, offices and other bodies which furnish, but normally do not sell to the community, those common services, other than higher education, which cannot otherwise be conveniently and economically provided, as well as those that administer the state and the economic and social policy of the community. Public enterprises, mainly engaged in market production and sale of goods and services, funds are included in the business enterprise funds sector. Government funds also include private non-profit institutes controlled and mainly financed by government, not administered by the higher education sector.
Higher education funds	Funds allocated to R&D by institutions of higher education comprising all universities, colleges of technology, other institutions providing tertiary education (i.e. ISCED 5, 6, 7 or 8), whatever their source or finance or legal status. They also include all research institutes, experimental stations and clinics operating under the direct control of or administered by or associated with higher education institutions.
Private non-profit funds	Funds allocated to R&D by non-market, private non-profit institutions serving households (i.e. the general public), as well as by private individuals and households.
Funds from abroad	Funds allocated to R&D by all institutions and individuals located outside the political borders of a country; and all international organizations (except business enterprises), including facilities and operations within the country's borders.

The absolute figures for R&D expenditure should not be compared country by country. Such comparisons would require the conversion of national currencies into a common currency by means of special R&D exchange rates. Official exchange rates do not always reflect the real costs of R&D activities and comparisons that are based on such rates can result in misleading conclusions, although they can be used to indicate a gross order of magnitude.

Table 28: Patents

A patent is granted by a national patent office or by a regional office that does the work for a number of countries, such as the European Patent Office and the African Regional Intellectual Property Organisation. Under such regional systems, an applicant requests protection for the invention in one or more countries, and each country decides as to whether to offer patent protection within its borders. The World Intellectual Property Organisation (WIPO) administered Patent Cooperation Treaty (PCT) provides for the filling of a single international patent application which has the same effect as national applications filed in the designated countries. Data include resident intensity, patents granted and patents in force. Patent intensity is presented as the resident patent fillings per million population, where as resident Intellectual Property (IP) filling refers to an application filed by an applicant at its national IP office. IP grant (registration) data are based on the same concept. In force refers to a patent or other form of IP protection that is currently valid. Country of origin is used to categorise IP data by resident (domestic) and non-resident (foreign). The residence of the first-named applicant (or inventor) recorded in the IP document (e.g. patent or trademark application) is used to classify IP data by country of origin. The data are compiled and published by the WIPO.

Chapter XV: Communication

Table 29: Internet usage

The table shows percentage of individuals using the internet and replaces the statistics shown in previous yearbooks such as the "Number (thousands) of fixed (wired) internet subscriptions" and "fixed (wired) internet subscriptions per 100 inhabitants". Besides capturing the use of the Internet, this indicator is able to measure changes in Internet access and use. In countries where many people access the Internet at work, at school, at cybercafés or other public locations, increases in public access serve to increase the number of users despite limited numbers of Internet subscriptions and of households with Internet access. Developing countries especially tend to have many Internet users per Internet subscriptions, reflecting that home access is not the primary location of access.

Chapter XVI: International tourism and transport

The data on international tourism have been supplied by the World Tourism Organization (UNWTO) from detailed tourism information published in either the *Yearbook of Tourism Statistics* or *Compendium of Tourism Statistics,* see www.unwto.org/statistics for further information. For statistical purposes, the term "international visitor" describes "any person who travels to a country other than that in which he/she has his/her usual residence but outside his/her usual environment for a period not exceeding 12 months and whose main purpose of visit is other than the exercise of an activity remunerated from within the country visited". There are four series presented in the UNWTO *yearbook* and *compendium*, but only one series is selected to be presented in this yearbook, generally based on the following priority order to best describe an "international visitor";

Order	Series code	Series name
1	TF	*Arrivals of non-resident tourists at national borders* are visitors who stay at least one night in a collective or private accommodation in the country visited (excludes same-day visitors)
2	VF	*Arrivals of non-resident visitors at national borders* are visitors as defined in series "TF" as well as same-day visitors who do not spend the night in a collective or private accommodation in the country visited
3	TCE	*Arrivals of non-resident tourists in all types of accommodation establishments*
4	THS	*Arrivals of non-resident tourists in hotels and similar establishments*

The figures do not include immigrants, residents in a frontier zone, persons domiciled in one country or area and working in an adjoining country or area, members of the armed forces and diplomats and consular representatives when they travel from their country of origin to the country in which they are stationed and vice-versa. The figures also exclude persons in transit who do not formally enter the country through passport control, such as air transit passengers who remain for a short period in a designated area of the air terminal or ship passengers who are not permitted to disembark. This category includes passengers transferred directly between airports or other terminals. Other passengers in transit through a country are classified as visitors.

Table 30: Tourist/visitor arrivals and tourism expenditure

Data on arrivals of non-resident (or international) visitors may be obtained from different sources. In some cases data are obtained from border statistics derived from administrative records (police, immigration, traffic counts and other types of controls), border surveys and registrations at accommodation establishments. Totals correspond to the total number of arrivals from the regions indicated in the table. When a person visits the same country several times a year, an equal number of arrivals is recorded. Likewise, if a person visits several countries during the course of a single trip, his/her arrival in each country is recorded separately. Consequently, arrivals cannot be assumed to be equal to the number of persons travelling.

Expenditure associated with tourism activity of visitors has been traditionally identified with the travel item of the Balance of Payments (BOP): in the case of inbound tourism, those expenditures in the country of reference associated with non-resident visitors are registered as "credits" in the BOP and refer to "travel receipts". The new conceptual framework approved by the United Nations Statistical Commission in relation to the measurement of tourism macroeconomic activity (the so-called Tourism Satellite Account) considers that "tourism industries and products" includes transport of passengers. Consequently, a better estimate of tourism-related expenditures by resident and non-resident visitors in an international scenario would be, in terms of the BOP, the value of the travel item plus that of the passenger transport item. Nevertheless, users should be aware that BOP estimates include, in addition to expenditures associated with visitors, those related to other types of individuals. The data published should allow international comparability and therefore correspond to those published by the International Monetary Fund and provided by the Central Banks, any exceptions are listed within the *Compendium of Tourism Statistics* and the *Yearbook of Tourism Statistics,* see www.unwto.org/statistics for further information.

Chapter XVII: Development assistance

Table 31: Net disbursements of official development assistance to recipients

The table presents estimates of flows of financial resources to individual recipients either directly (bilaterally) or through multilateral institutions (multilaterally). The multilateral institutions include the World Bank Group, regional banks, financial institutions of the European Union and a number of United Nations institutions, programmes and trust funds. The source of data is the Development Assistance Committee (DAC) of OECD to which member countries reported data on their flow of resources to developing countries and territories, countries and territories in transition, and multilateral institutions. Additional information on definitions, methods and sources can be found in OECD's *Geographical Distribution of Financial Flows to Developing Countries* publication, also see http://stats.oecd.org/ for further information.

Table 32: Net disbursements of official development assistance from donors

The table presents the development assistance expenditures of donor countries. This table includes donors' contributions to multilateral agencies; therefore, the overall totals differ from those in table 32, which include disbursements by multilateral agencies.

Annexe II : Notes techniques

Chapitre I: Aperçu mondial

Tableau 1: Statistiques mondiales – séries principales

Ces séries d'agrégats mondiaux sont obtenues à partir d'autres tableaux figurant dans le présent *Annuaire*, lorsque c'est possible, et sont établies à partir de publications et de bases de données statistiques des Nations Unies et des organismes spécialisés ainsi que d'autres institutions. Pour davantage d'information sur les définitions, les sources, les méthodes de compilation et la couverture des données, il convient de se référer aux notes techniques du tableau correspondant dans le présent *Annuaire*.

Chapitre II: Population et migration

Tableau 2: Population, superficie et densité

Les données concernant la population totale, masculine et féminine, le rapport des sexes, la répartition de la population par âge et la densité de la population proviennent des estimations et des projections préparées par la Division de la population de l'Organisation des Nations Unies, qui sont publiées dans *Perspectives de la population mondiale : Révision de 2019*. Les données concernant la superficie sont extraites de l'*Annuaire démographique*, qui ne contient que les données nationales officielles.

La population totale, masculine et féminine correspond à la population de fait dans un pays, un territoire ou une région à compter du 1er juillet de l'année indiquée, sauf indication contraire dans une note en bas de page. Les chiffres sont présentés en millions. La population totale d'un pays peut consister de tous les résidents habituels (population de droit) ou toutes les personnes présentes dans le pays (population de fait) au moment du recensement ; pour permettre les comparaisons internationales, la population de fait est utilisée, sauf indication contraire dans une note en bas de page.

La population âgée de 0 à 14 ans/ 60 ans et plus correspond au pourcentage de la population âgée de 0 à 14 ans et 60 ans et plus, respectivement à compter du 1er juillet de l'année indiquée, sauf indication contraire dans une note en bas de page.

La densité de la population correspond à la population, à compter du 1er juillet de l'année indiquée, par kilomètre carré de superficie, sauf indication contraire dans une note en bas de page.

Le rapport des sexes est calculé en tant que le rapport de la population des hommes à celui de 100 femmes à compter du 1er juillet de l'année indiquée, sauf indication contraire dans une note en bas de page.

La superficie correspond aux territoires plus eaux intérieures, sauf indication contraire dans une note en bas de page.

Tableau 3: Migrants internationaux et réfugiés

Le stock international de migrants provient d'estimations et de projections préparées par la Division de la population de l'Organisation des Nations Unies, publiées dans le *Stock de migrants internationaux: Révision 2019*. Les données sur les « réfugiés et autres personnes relevant de la compétence du HCR » ont été obtenues auprès du Haut-Commissaire des Nations Unies pour les réfugiés, et sont publiées dans la base de données de statistiques démographiques.

Le stock international de migrants représente le nombre de personnes nées dans un autre pays que celui dans lequel elles vivent. Lorsque les informations concernant le pays d'origine font défaut, on a utilisé les données sur le nombre de personnes de nationalité étrangère. Et à défaut de données empiriques, on a eu recours à des estimations. Les données font référence au milieu de l'année 2015. Le stock international de migrants en pourcentage de la population est obtenu en divisant le stock international de migrants estimé par la population totale estimée et en multipliant le résultat par 100.

Les réfugiés sont les personnes reconnues comme telles au sens de la Convention de 1951 relative au statut des réfugiés, de son protocole de 1967 ou de la Convention de l'OUA de 1969 régissant les aspects propres aux problèmes des réfugiés en Afrique; celles reconnues comme réfugiés conformément au Statut du HCR; les personnes qui bénéficient d'une forme de protection complémentaire ou jouissent d'une protection temporaire. Depuis 2007, la population des réfugiés inclut également les personnes dont la situation est assimilable à celle des réfugiés

Les demandeurs d'asile sont des personnes qui ont déposé une demande de protection internationale et qui n'ont pas encore obtenu le statut de réfugié, quelle que soit la date à laquelle la demande a été présentée.

Les « autres personnes relevant de la compétence du HCR » se composent des cinq catégories suivantes :

Les personnes déplacées sont des personnes ou groupes de personnes qui ont été forcés ou contraints de fuir ou de quitter leurs foyers ou leur lieu de résidence habituel, notamment en raison d'un conflit armé, de situations de violence généralisée, de violations des droits de l'homme ou de catastrophes naturelles ou provoquées par l'homme, ou pour en éviter les effets, et qui n'ont pas franchi les frontières internationalement reconnues d'un État. Aux fins des statistiques du HCR, cette population ne comprend que les personnes déplacées en raison d'un conflit qui bénéficient de la protection et/ou de l'assistance du HCR. Depuis 2007, la population de personnes déplacées inclut également les personnes dont la situation est assimilable à celle des personnes déplacées. On trouvera des estimations de la population mondiale des personnes déplacées sur le site www.internal-displacement.org.

Les réfugiés de retour sont d'anciens réfugiés rentrés dans leur pays d'origine, soit spontanément, soit de façon organisée, mais qui ne sont pas encore pleinement intégrés. Ces retours ne se font normalement que lorsque leur sécurité et leur dignité peuvent être garanties.

Les déplacés de retour sont des personnes déplacées qui bénéficiaient des activités de protection et d'assistance du HCR et qui sont revenues à leur lieu d'origine ou de résidence habituel au cours de l'année.

Les apatrides sont définis par le droit international comme des personnes qu'aucun État ne considère comme ses ressortissants par application de sa législation. En d'autres termes, les apatrides ne possèdent la nationalité d'aucun État. Les statistiques du HCR incluent les personnes qui relèvent de sa compétence en vertu de cette définition, mais les données de certains pays peuvent aussi inclure des personnes de nationalité indéterminée.

Les autres personnes relevant de la compétence du HCR sont des personnes qui ne relèvent pas directement d'une des catégories ci-dessus, mais auxquelles le HCR assure protection et/ou assistance pour des raisons humanitaires ou d'autre motifs particuliers.

Chapitre III: La situation des femmes

Tableau 4: Proportion de sièges occupés par des femmes au parlement national

Ce tableau indique le pourcentage des sièges des chambres uniques ou basses des parlements nationaux occupés par des femmes, en janvier ou février de chaque année (voir les notes du tableau pour plus de détails). Les parlements nationaux peuvent être bicaméraux ou unicaméraux. Ce tableau porte sur la chambre unique des parlements unicaméraux et sur la chambre basse des parlements bicaméraux. Il ne porte pas sur la chambre haute des parlements bicaméraux. Les sièges sont habituellement attribués aux membres à l'issue d'élections parlementaires générales. Certains sièges peuvent aussi être pourvus à l'issue de nominations, de désignations, d'élections indirectes, de roulement des membres et d'élections partielles. La proportion d'élues est obtenue en divisant le nombre total de sièges occupés par des femmes par le nombre total de sièges que compte le parlement. Les statistiques ne sont ni pondérées ni normalisées. La source de ce tableau est l'Union interparlementaire, voir www.ipu.org pour plus d'informations

Tableau 5: Rapport filles/garçons dans l'enseignement primaire, secondaire et supérieur

Ce tableau indique la proportion de filles par rapport aux garçons (indice de parité des sexes) dans l'enseignement primaire, secondaire et supérieur, à savoir le rapport entre le nombre de filles inscrites dans l'enseignement primaire, secondaire et supérieur et le nombre de garçons à chaque niveau. Pour normaliser les effets de la pyramide des âges, l'indice de parité des sexes du taux brut de scolarisation pour chaque niveau d'enseignement est utilisé. La source de ce tableau est l'Institut de statistique de l'UNESCO, voir www.uis.unesco.org pour plus d'informations.

Chapitre IV: Éducation

Les données des tableaux 6 et 7 sont présentées conformément à la Classification internationale type de l'éducation de l'UNESCO (CITE, révision de 2011). Les données sont présentées dans les tableaux sur la base des trois principaux niveaux d'éducation, présentés comme suit :

L'enseignement primaire (CITE niveau 1) désigne les programmes éducatifs habituellement conçus pour apporter aux élèves les compétences fondamentales en lecture, écriture et en mathématiques (c'est-à-dire en calcul) afin d'établir une base solide pour la compréhension et l'apprentissage des principaux domaines de la connaissance et favoriser le développement personnel et social dans le but de les préparer à l'entrée dans le premier cycle de l'enseignement secondaire. Il privilégie l'enseignement à un niveau de complexité élémentaire avec peu ou pas de spécialisation.

L'enseignement secondaire (niveaux 2 et 3 de la CITE) est divisé en deux parties : le premier et le second cycles du secondaire. Les programmes du premier cycle de l'enseignement secondaire sont généralement conçus de manière à renforcer les acquis scolaires du primaire. L'objectif consiste habituellement à établir la base d'un apprentissage et d'un développement humain valables pour toute la vie et que les systèmes éducatifs pourront ensuite enrichir par de nouvelles possibilités d'éducation. Les programmes du deuxième cycle de l'enseignement secondaire visent en général à achever l'enseignement secondaire et à préparer à l'entrée dans l'enseignement supérieur et/ou à enseigner des compétences utiles à l'exercice d'un emploi. Les programmes de ce niveau offrent aux élèves un enseignement plus varié, spécialisé et approfondi que les programmes du premier cycle. Ils sont davantage différenciés et proposent un éventail plus large d'options et de filières. Les enseignants sont souvent hautement qualifiés dans les matières ou domaines spécialisés qu'ils enseignent, en particulier dans les classes supérieures.

L'enseignement supérieur (niveaux 5 à 8 de la CITE) se fonde sur les acquis de l'enseignement secondaire et offre des activités d'apprentissage dans des domaines d'éducation spécialisés. Il vise à transmettre des connaissances très spécialisées et d'un niveau de complexité élevé. L'enseignement supérieur inclut ce que l'on qualifie habituellement d'enseignement académique mais il comprend aussi l'enseignement technique ou professionnel avancé. Il comprend les niveaux 5, 6, 7 et 8 de la CITE, appelés respectivement enseignement supérieur de cycle court, enseignement du niveau de la licence ou équivalent, niveau master ou équivalent, et niveau doctorat ou équivalent. Le contenu des programmes de l'enseignement supérieur est plus complexe et plus avancé que celui des niveaux inférieurs de la CITE.

On trouvera davantage d'informations sur la Classification internationale type de l'éducation (CITE) 2011 sur le site : http://www.uis.unesco.org/Education/Documents/isced-2011-fr.pdf.

Tableau 6: Inscriptions aux niveaux primaire, secondaire et supérieur

Le tableau montre le nombre d'élèves scolarisés ainsi que le taux de scolarisation brut qui est le nombre d'étudiants inscrits, quel que soit leur âge, exprimé en pourcentage de la population d'âge scolaire officiellement admissible correspondant au même niveau d'enseignement pour une année scolaire donnée. Les inscriptions sont mesurées au début de l'année scolaire ou universitaire. Le taux de scolarisation brut pour chaque niveau comprend tous les élèves, quel que soit leur âge, tandis que la population générale considérée ne comprend que ceux dont l'âge correspond à l'âge scolaire officiel. De ce fait, pour les pays dont la population d'âge scolaire est quasi totalement scolarisée, le taux de scolarisation brut peut dépasser 100 si la répartition des âges effectifs des élèves s'étend au-delà des âges scolaires officiels.

Tableau 7: Personnel enseignant au niveau primaire, secondaire et supérieur

Le tableau montre le nombre total d'enseignants à chaque niveau ainsi que la proportion des enseignantes exprimée en pourcentage du nombre total d'enseignants (hommes et femmes) au même niveau au cours d'une année scolaire donnée. Les données proviennent de recensements ou d'enquêtes dans les écoles et des dossiers des enseignants.

Les enseignants (ou personnel enseignant) sont définis comme des personnes qui, dans l'exercice de leur métier, guident et dirigent le parcours didactique des élèves et étudiants, indépendamment de leurs qualifications et du mécanisme de transmission des connaissances (autrement dit soit face-à-face et/ou à distance). L'enseignement consiste à planifier, organiser, et mener des activités de groupe ou les connaissances, aptitudes et compétences des élèves sont développés comme précisé dans le programme d'éducation. Cette définition exclut le personnel enseignant qui n'a pas de fonctions pédagogiques à la période de référence (par exemple les directeurs ou chefs d'établissements scolaires qui n'enseignent pas) et les personnes qui travaillent ponctuellement ou bénévolement dans des établissements d'enseignement.

Le personnel enseignant universitaire est le personnel employé dont la mission principale est l'enseignement et /ou la recherche. Cela comprend le personnel qui détient un grade universitaire avec des titres tels que professeur,

professeur agrégé, professeur adjoint, maitre de conférences ou l'équivalent. Le personnel, comme par exemple doyen, directeur, vice-doyen, doyen adjoint, président ou chef de département, est également inclus si leur activité principale est l'enseignement ou la recherche.

Tableau 8: Dépenses publiques afférentes à l'éducation

Les dépenses publiques afférentes à l'éducation consistent en dépenses courantes et dépenses en capital engagées par l'administration aux niveaux local, régional et national, y compris les municipalités. Les contributions des ménages sont exclues. Les dépenses d'éducation courantes comprennent les dépenses en biens et en services consommés dans l'année en cours et qui devront être renouvelées au besoin l'année suivante. Elles comprennent les dépenses au titre des salaires et avantages du personnel; des services achetés ou obtenus par contrat; d'autres ressources, notamment de manuels et autres matériels d'enseignement; des services sociaux; et d'autres dépenses courantes telles que les subventions aux étudiants et aux ménages, l'ameublement et le matériel, les petites réparations, le combustible, les télécommunications, les voyages, l'assurance et les loyers. Les dépenses en capital pour l'éducation consistent en achats de biens dont la durée dépasse une année. Elles comprennent les dépenses de construction, de rénovation et de grosses réparations de bâtiments ainsi que l'achat de matériel lourd et de véhicules.

Chapitre V: Santé

Tableau 9: Le personnel de santé

Le tableau présente quatre grandes catégories de personnel de santé (sur les 9 catégories disponibles à la source) : la catégorie des médecins, qui comprend les médecins généralistes et les spécialistes; celle des infirmiers et sages-femmes comprend les infirmiers et sages-femmes qualifiés, les infirmiers auxiliaires professionnels et les sages-femmes auxiliaires professionnelles. Les accoucheuses traditionnelles ne sont pas incluses; le personnel de dentisterie comprend les dentistes, les assistants dentaires, les techniciens dentaires et les professions associées; et le personnel du secteur pharmaceutique comprend les pharmaciens, les pharmaciens assistants, les préparateurs en pharmacie et les professions associées.

Les données sont extraites des statistiques mondiales des personnels de santé de la base de données de l'Organisation mondiale de la Santé (OMS), qui sont établies à partir de plusieurs sources comme les recensements de population nationaux, les enquêtes sur la population active et l'emploi, les productions statistiques nationales et les données régulières des administrations. Il existe de ce fait d'un pays à l'autre une variabilité considérable dans la couverture, la qualité et l'année de référence des données. Généralement, les données du dénominateur pour le calcul de la densité du personnel de santé (c'est-à-dire les estimations de la population nationale) sont extraites des *Perspectives de la population mondiale* publiées par la Division de la population de l'Organisation des Nations Unies. Parfois le rapport officiel ne fournit que les indicateurs de la densité du personnel de santé, à partir desquels le stock est ensuite estimé.

La classification des personnels du secteur de la santé utilisée repose sur les critères de l'enseignement et formation techniques et professionnels, la réglementation des professions de santé et les activités et tâches des postes, c'est-à-dire sur un cadre de catégorisation des principales variables des personnels selon des caractéristiques communes. Le cadre de l'OMS repose en grande partie sur les révisions les plus récentes des systèmes de classification internationaux normalisés de l'Organisation internationale du Travail (Classification internationale type des professions), de l'Organisation des Nations Unies pour l'éducation, la science et la culture (Classification internationale type de l'éducation) et de la Division de statistique de l'ONU (Classification internationale type, par industrie, de toutes les branches d'activité économique). En fonction de la situation propre à chaque pays et des moyens de mesure, les données disponibles dans l'ensemble agrégé décrivent jusqu'à 9 catégories de personnels de santé, et jusqu'à 18 catégories dans l'ensemble désagrégé. Ce dernier reflète essentiellement une tentative de mieux distinguer certains sous-groupes des personnels du secteur de la santé en fonction de différences supposées dans les niveaux de compétence et de spécialisation.

Tableau 10: Dépenses de santé

La série « Dépenses courantes » fait référence aux biens et aux services de santé utilisés ou consommés au cours d'une année, à l'exclusion des dépenses en capital, ou plutôt de la « formation brute de capital », qui correspond à l'achat de nouveaux actifs sur plusieurs années. Ces estimations sont conformes au Système de comptes de la santé (SCS) de 2011. La dépense courante est exprimée en proportion du produit intérieur brut (PIB). Les séries des dépenses des administrations publiques générales sont composées de sources nationales publiques et privées. Les séries des dépenses des administrations publiques générales sont composées de sources nationales publiques et privées. Les sources publiques nationales comprennent les recettes intérieures sous forme de transferts et de subventions internes, les transferts, les subventions aux bénéficiaires de l'assurance maladie volontaire, les institutions sans but lucratif au service des ménages ou les régimes de financement des entreprises ainsi que les cotisations obligatoires. Tous ces transferts et subventions représentent des sources publiques de santé et indiquent la contribution globale des gouvernements au financement des soins de santé par rapport à d'autres sources de financement provenant de sources privées et extérieures nationales. Les dépenses des administrations publiques nationales sont exprimées en proportion des dépenses des administrations publiques. (Voir http://apps.who.int/nha/database/DocumentationCentre/Index/fr).

Chapitre VI: Criminalité

Tableau 11: Homicides intentionnels et autres crimes

Les données des « homicides intentionnels » et des « autres crimes » proviennent des données recueillies dans la base de données statistiques de l'Office des Nations Unies contre la drogue et le crime.

L'homicide intentionnel est défini comme la mort illégale d'une personne causée par une autre ayant l'intention de tuer ou de blesser gravement. Les données de l'homicide intentionnel doivent aussi inclure les violences suivies de mort et la mort résultant d'une attaque terroriste. Elles excluent la tentative d'homicide intentionnel, l'homicide involontaire, la mort causée par une intervention légale, l'homicide justifiable en état de légitime défense et la mort causée par un conflit armé.

L'agression est une atteinte à l'intégrité physique d'une autre personne entraînant des dommages corporels graves, à l'exclusion des actes préjudiciables à caractère sexuel, des menaces et des gifles/coups de poing. Les agressions graves ayant entraîné la mort sont également exclues.

L'enlèvement désigne la détention et soustraction illégales d'une ou de plusieurs personnes contre leur volonté (y compris par le recours à la force, aux menaces, à la fraude ou à l'incitation) aux fins d'exiger pour leur libération un gain illicite ou un autre avantage économique ou matériel, ou pour contraindre une personne à suivre ou à ne pas suivre une ligne de conduite. L'enlèvement exclut les différends relatifs à la garde d'un enfant.

Le vol est l'appropriation ou l'obtention illégale d'un bien dans l'intention d'en priver une personne ou une organisation de manière permanente sans son consentement et sans recours à la force. Le vol exclut le cambriolage, l'entrée avec effraction, le vol qualifié et le vol de véhicule motorisé, qui sont comptabilisés séparément.

La violence sexuelle désigne le viol et l'agression sexuelle, y compris les agressions sexuelles contre les enfants.

Chapitre VII: Comptes nationaux

La base de données des principaux agrégats des comptes nationaux (consultable sur le site http://unstats.un.org/unsd/snaama) présente les données des comptes nationaux de plus de 200 pays et régions du monde. Elle constitue la base de l'analyse des principaux agrégats des statistiques de la comptabilité nationale (*Statistiques de la comptabilité nationale : analyse des principaux agrégats*), une publication préparée par la Division de statistique du Département des affaires économiques et sociales du Secrétariat des Nations Unies avec le généreux concours des offices nationaux de la statistique. La base de données est mise à jour chaque année au mois de décembre avec les données nouvellement disponibles des comptes nationaux de tous les pays et régions.

La base de données des principaux agrégats des comptes nationaux repose sur les données extraites du Questionnaire sur la comptabilité nationale des Nations Unies (NAQ) introduit en octobre 1999, qui lui-même repose sur le Système de comptes nationaux 1993 (SCN 1993). Les données sont complétées par des estimations préparées par la Division de statistique. Le SCN actualisé, appelé Système de comptes nationaux 2008 (SCN 2008) a été finalisé en septembre 2009. A partir de 2018, 105 pays et territoires (États membres de l'Union européenne, Afrique du Sud, Albanie, Andorre, Arabie saoudite, Argentine, Arménie, Australie, Bahamas, Bélarus, Bosnie-Herzégovine, Brésil, Brunéi Darussalam, Cameroun, Canada, Chili, Chine, Chine, RAS de Hong Kong, Chine, RAS de Macao, Colombie, Costa Rica, Djibouti, El Salvador, Émirats arabes unis, Équateur, Eswatini, États-Unis d'Amérique, Fédération de Russie, Fidji, Gambie, Ghana, Groenland, Îles Caïmanes, Îles Vierges britanniques, Inde, Indonésie, Islande, Israël, Japon, Kenya, Kosovo, Liban, Liechtenstein, Macédoine du Nord, Malaisie, Maldives, Maroc, Maurice, Mexique, Mongolie, Monténégro, Nouvelle-Zélande, Niger, Nigéria, Norvège, Pakistan, Paraguay, Pérou, Philippines, République de Corée, République démocratique populaire lao,

République de Moldova, République dominicaine, République-Unie de Tanzanie, Samoa, Royaume-Uni de Grande-Bretagne, Sénégal, Serbie, Singapour, St-Martin, Sri Lanka, Suisse, Thaïlande, Timor-Leste, Turquie, Ouganda, Ukraine, et Zambie) ont implémenté des données conformément au SCN 2008.

Tout est mis en œuvre pour présenter les estimations des divers pays ou régions sous une forme conçue pour faciliter la comparabilité internationale. À cette fin, les différences importantes entre les concepts, la portée, la couverture et la classification sont décrites dans les notes de chaque pays. Ces différences doivent être prises en compte afin d'éviter les comparaisons fallacieuses. Les données contenues dans les tableaux se rapportent à l'année civile pour laquelle elles sont présentées, sauf exceptions. Ces exceptions sont affichées sur le site Web de la base de données des principaux agrégats des comptes nationaux (http://unstats.un.org/unsd/snaama/notes.asp). Les chiffres présentés sont les estimations et révisions les plus récentes disponibles au moment de leur établissement. En général, les chiffres de l'année la plus récente doivent être considérés comme provisoires. Les sommes des composantes des tableaux ne correspondent pas nécessairement aux totaux indiqués en raison des arrondis.

Tableau 12: Produit intérieur brut et produit intérieur brut par habitant

Ce tableau présente le produit intérieur brut (PIB) et le PIB par habitant en dollars des États-Unis aux prix courants, le PIB à prix constants de 2015 et les taux de croissance réels correspondants. Les tableaux sont destinés à faciliter les comparaisons internationales des niveaux de revenu générés par la production. Les données et les estimations officielles du PIB total et du PIB par habitant aux prix courants sont converties en dollars des États-Unis, tandis que celles du PIB total à prix constants sont converties aux prix de 2015 avant conversion en dollars aux taux de change en vigueur en 2015. La méthode de conversion en dollars des États-Unis est décrite dans le document sur la méthodologie de la base de données des principaux agrégats des comptes nationaux (http://unstats.un.org/unsd/snaama/methodology.pdf). Pour les comparaisons entre pays sur la durée, il est plus approprié d'utiliser les taux de croissance à prix constants du tableau, qui représentent mieux les tendances du PIB total dans les comparaisons entre pays et entre groupes de pays. Le taux de croissance indiqué dans le tableau est calculé comme la moyenne géométrique des taux de croissance annuelle exprimés en pourcentages pour les années.

Tableau 13: Valeur ajoutée brute par type d'activité économique

Ce tableau présente les parts des composantes de la valeur ajoutée brute aux prix courants par type d'activité économique.

Secteur	Composé de (selon la nomenclature CITI 3)
Agriculture	Agriculture, chasse, sylviculture et pêches (CITI A-B)
Industrie	Activités extractives, activités de fabrication, production et distribution d'électricité, de gaz et d'eau (CITI C-E) Construction (CITI F)
Services	Commerce de gros et de détail ; réparation de véhicules automobiles, de motocycles et de biens personnels et domestiques, hôtels et restaurants (CITI G-H) Transports, entreposage et communications (CITI I) Autres activités, y compris intermédiation financière, immobilier, location et activités de services aux entreprises, administration publique et défense, sécurité sociale obligatoire, éducation, santé et action sociale, autres activités de services collectifs, sociaux et personnels, ménages privés employant du personnel domestique (CITI J-P).

Chapitre VIII: Finances

Des informations détaillées et les chiffres courants concernant le tableau 14 figurent dans *Statistiques financières internationales*, une publication du Fonds monétaire international (voir aussi http://elibrary-data.imf.org) et dans le *Bulletin mensuel de statistique des Nations Unies*.

Tableau 14: Résumé de la balance des paiements

La balance des paiements peut être décrite d'une façon générale comme l'enregistrement des transactions économiques internationales d'une économie. Elle présente : a) les transactions en biens, services et revenus entre une économie et le reste du monde, b) les changements de propriété et les autres changements des avoirs de cette économie en or monétaire, droits de tirage spéciaux (DTS) et en créances et engagements envers le reste du monde, et c) les transferts sans contrepartie et les écritures de contrepartie nécessaires pour équilibrer au sens comptable les écritures au titre des transactions et changements susmentionnés qui ne s'annulent pas mutuellement. Les données de la balance des paiements sont présentées sur la base de la méthodologie et de la présentation de la sixième édition du *Manuel de la balance des paiements* (MBP6), publiée par le Fonds monétaire international en novembre 2013. Le MBP6 incorpore plusieurs modifications majeures pour tenir compte des évolutions du commerce international et de la finance internationale au fil des années, et de mieux harmoniser la méthodologie de la balance des paiements du Fonds avec celle du Système de comptes nationaux 2008 (SCN 2008). Les définitions détaillées concernant le contenu des catégories fondamentales de la balance des paiements sont données dans le *Manuel de la balance des paiements* (sixième édition).

De brèves notes explicatives sont données ci-dessous pour clarifier la portée des principaux éléments.

Le compte des transactions courantes enregistre toutes les transactions de la balance des paiements couvrant les exportations et les importations de biens et de services, les revenus et les transferts courants entre les résidents d'un pays et des non-résidents.

Le compte de capital, n.i.a. porte principalement sur les transferts de capital liés à l'acquisition d'un actif fixe autres que les transactions relatives à l'annulation de la dette, plus la cession d'actifs non financiers non produits, et les transferts de capital liés à la cession d'actifs fixes par le donateur ou au financement de la formation de capital par le récipiendaire, plus l'acquisition d'actifs non financiers non produits.

Le compte d'opérations financières, n.i.a. représente le solde net de l'investissement direct, de l'investissement de portefeuille et des autres transactions d'investissement.

Les réserves sont la somme des transactions sur actifs de réserve, les engagements constituant des avoirs de réserve pour les autorités étrangères, le financement exceptionnel et l'utilisation des crédits du FMI.

Tableau 15: Cours des changes

Les taux des changes sont exprimés par le nombre d'unités de monnaie nationale pour un dollar des Etats-Unis. Les taux de change sont classés en trois catégories, qui dénotent le rôle des autorités dans l'établissement des taux de change et/ou la multiplicité des taux de change dans un pays. Par taux du marché, on entend les taux de change déterminés essentiellement par les forces du marché; le taux officiel est un taux de change établi par les autorités, parfois selon des dispositions souples. Pour les pays qui continuent à mettre en œuvre des régimes de taux de change multiples, les taux sont désignés par les appellations suivantes: "taux principal", "taux secondaire" et "taux tertiaire". Sauf indication contraire, le tableau indique des taux de fin de période et les moyennes sur la période, des taux de change du marché ou des taux de change officiels.

Chapitre IX: Marché du travail

Une collection complète de données comparables sur la population active et les sujets connexes est disponible sous la forme des *Indicateurs clé du marché du travail* (KILM) publiés par l'Organisation internationale du Travail (OIT), et mis à jour tous les deux ans. Des données plus contemporaines sont accessibles sur ILOSTAT (www.ilo.org/ilostat), le dépôt de données de l'OIT, qui publie des données annuellement, trimestriellement ou mensuellement à mesure de leur communication par les pays mais sans procéder à toutes les vérifications de leur cohérence ni inclure toutes les sources utilisées par les KILM. Pour diverses raisons, les définitions nationales de l'emploi et du chômage diffèrent souvent des définitions internationales normalisées recommandées, ce qui limite la comparabilité internationale. Les comparaisons entre pays se trouvent en outre compliquées par la diversité des systèmes de collecte de données utilisés pour recueillir des informations sur les personnes employées et les chômeurs. Le site Web d'ILOSTAT offre une description complète de la méthodologie employée pour établir les séries sur la main-d'œuvre.

Tableau 16: Taux d'activité et taux de chômage

Le taux de participation à la population active est calculé en exprimant le nombre de personnes de la population active sous forme de pourcentage de la population en âge de travailler. La population active est la somme du nombre de personnes employées et du nombre de personnes sans emploi (voir les Recommandations internationales en vigueur sur les statistiques du travail de l'OIT). La population en âge de travailler est la population d'âge supérieur à un certain seuil, prescrit pour la mesure des caractéristiques économiques. Les données concernent le groupe des personnes de 15 ans et plus et reposent sur les estimations modélisées de l'OIT, sauf indication contraire en note de bas de page.

La définition du chômage inclut les personnes en âge de travailler qui, au cours d'une certaine période, étaient :

a)   « Sans emploi », c'est-à-dire sans emploi rémunéré ou indépendant;

b)   « Disponibles », c'est-à-dire libres de contracter un emploi rémunéré ou de pratiquer un emploi indépendant au cours de la période de référence; et

c)   « À la recherche d'un emploi », c'est-à-dire qui ont pris des mesures déterminées pour trouver un emploi rémunéré ou indépendant au cours de la période spécifiée

Ne sont pas considérées comme sans emploi :

a)   Les personnes qui ont l'intention d'établir leur propre activité ou exploitation agricole, mais n'ont pas encore pris les dispositions nécessaires à cet effet et ne recherchent pas un emploi en vue d'une rémunération ou d'un profit;

b)   Les anciens travailleurs familiaux non rémunérés qui n'ont pas d'emploi et ne sont pas à la recherche d'un emploi pour rémunération ou profit.

Les séries représentent généralement le nombre total des personnes au chômage complet ou temporairement mises à pied. Les données exprimées en pourcentages, lorsqu'elles figurent dans le tableau, sont calculées en comparant le nombre des chômeurs au total des membres du groupe de la population active sur lequel les données du chômage sont basées.

Tableau 17: Emploi par activité économique

Le tableau de l'emploi présente, exprimée en pourcentages, la répartition des personnes employées par activité économique, conformément à la Classification internationale type, par industrie, de toutes les branches d'activité économique (CITI) version 4.

Chapitre X: Indices des prix et de la production

Tableau 18 : Indices des prix à la consommation

Un indice des prix à la consommation est généralement estimé sous forme d'une série de mesures synthétiques des variations relatives, d'une période à l'autre, des prix d'un ensemble fixe de biens et de services de consommation d'une quantité et de caractéristiques constantes, acquis, utilisés ou payés par la population de référence. Chaque mesure synthétique est construite comme la moyenne pondérée d'un grand nombre d'indices d'agrégats élémentaires. L'indice de chaque agrégat élémentaire est estimé au moyen d'un échantillon de prix pour un ensemble défini de biens et de services obtenus dans une région donnée ou par ses résidents auprès d'un ensemble donné de points de vente ou d'autres sources de biens et de services de consommation. Le tableau présente les indices généraux des prix à la consommation pour tous les groupes d'articles de consommation combinés, et un indice des prix des produits alimentaires ne comprenant que les boissons non alcoolisées. Lorsque les prix des boissons alcoolisées et/ou du tabac sont inclus, cela est indiqué en note.

Chapitre XI: Commerce international des marchandises

Préparé par la Division de statistique du Département des affaires économiques et sociales du Secrétariat des Nations Unies, l'*Annuaire statistique du commerce international* (ITSY) offre un aperçu des tendances récentes du commerce de biens et de services de la plupart des pays et régions du monde. L'*Annuaire*, voir http://comtrade.un.org/pb/, est publié en deux volumes; le Volume I est établi plus tôt dans l'année pour présenter un aperçu préliminaire du commerce international de marchandises de l'année précédente; le Volume II, publié généralement six mois plus tard, contient des tableaux détaillés qui présentent le commerce international par produit et 11 tableaux du commerce mondial couvrant les valeurs commerciales et les indices. Le Volume II contient également des versions actualisées des tableaux du commerce mondial. Les tableaux de cet *Annuaire* sont également mis à jour mensuellement dans le Bulletin mensuel de statistique des Nations Unies et sur le site des statistiques du commerce, voir http://unstats.un.org/unsd/trade/data/tables.asp#annual.

Les statistiques présentées dans cet *Annuaire* sont établies par les autorités statistiques nationales de façon largement conforme aux concepts et définitions des statistiques du commerce international de marchandises recommandés par les Nations Unies en 2010 (IMTS 2010). En fonction des parties du territoire économique incluses dans le territoire statistique, le système d'établissement des données du commerce adopté par un pays (son système de commerce) sera appelé général ou spécial.

Système de commerce général	Le territoire statistique coïncide avec le territoire économique. Il est donc recommandé que le territoire statistique d'un pays qui applique le système de commerce général englobe tous les éléments territoriaux applicables. Dans ce cas, les importations comprennent les biens qui entrent dans la zone de libre circulation, les installations de perfectionnement actif, les zones franches industrielles, les entrepôts sous douane ou les zones franches commerciales, et les exportations comprennent les biens qui quittent ces éléments territoriaux.
Système de commerce spécial	(Définition stricte) Le territoire statistique ne comprend qu'une partie spécifique du territoire économique, de sorte que certains flux de marchandises auxquels les recommandations IMTS 2010 sont applicables ne sont inclus ni dans les statistiques d'importation ni dans les statistiques d'exportation du pays déclarant. La définition stricte du système de commerce spécial est utilisée lorsque le territoire statistique ne comprend que la zone de libre circulation, c'est-à-dire la partie dans laquelle les marchandises « peuvent être écoulées sans restriction douanière ». Par conséquent, dans ce cas, les importations ne comprennent que les marchandises qui entrent dans la zone de libre circulation du pays déclarant et les exportations ne comprennent que les marchandises qui quittent la zone de libre circulation du pays déclarant.
	(Définition assouplie) a) les marchandises qui entrent dans un pays aux fins du perfectionnement actif ou en ressortent après, ainsi que b) les marchandises qui entrent dans une zone franche industrielle ou en sortent, sont aussi enregistrées et incluses dans les statistiques du commerce international de marchandises.

Tous les pays communiquent en général leurs données détaillées du commerce de marchandises conformément au Système harmonisé de désignation et de codification des marchandises (SH) et les données correspondent à la Classification type pour le commerce international (CTCI, rév. 3), dans laquelle elles sont ensuite présentées. Les données se réfèrent à des années civiles; cependant, pour les pays qui communiquent leurs données selon une autre année de référence, les données sont présentées dans l'année qui couvre la plus grande partie de l'année de référence utilisée par le pays.

Les valeurs FOB comprennent la valeur transactionnelle des marchandises et la valeur des services fournis pour livrer les marchandises à la frontière du pays exportateur. Les valeurs CIF comprennent la valeur transactionnelle des marchandises, la valeur des services fournis pour livrer les marchandises à la frontière du pays exportateur et la valeur des services fournis pour livrer les marchandises depuis la frontière du pays exportateur jusqu'à la frontière du pays importateur. De ce fait, les données de la valeur statistique des marchandises importées sont présentées dans le format CIF et celles de la valeur statistique des marchandises exportées dans le format FOB.

La conversion des valeurs libellées en monnaies nationales en dollars des États-Unis s'effectue au moyen de facteurs de conversion de devises fondés sur les taux de change officiels. Les valeurs libellées en monnaies sujettes à des fluctuations sont converties en dollars des États-Unis au moyen de taux de change moyens pondérés calculés spécialement à cette fin. Le taux de change moyen pondéré d'une monnaie donnée pour une année donnée est donné par les facteurs composants mensuels, fournis par le Fonds monétaire international dans sa publication *Statistiques financières internationales*, pondérés par la valeur du commerce concerné pour chaque mois; les facteurs mensuels sont les taux de change (ou les taux moyens simples) en vigueur au cours de ce mois.

Ces facteurs sont appliqués aux importations et aux exportations totales et au commerce de chaque produit avec chaque pays.

Tableau 19: Total des importations, des exportations et balance commerciale

Les données des importations totales et des exportations totales des pays (ou régions) présentées dans ce tableau proviennent principalement des *Statistiques financières internationales* publiées mensuellement par le Fonds monétaire international (FMI) mais aussi d'autres sources comme les publications et les sites web nationaux et le Questionnaire du *Bulletin mensuel de statistique* des Nations Unies, voir l'*Annuaire statistique du commerce international* pour plus de détails. Les données manquantes sont estimées afin de parvenir à des totaux régionaux mais ne sont pas présentées. La procédure d'estimation est automatisée au moyen des taux de croissance en glissement annuel trimestriels pour l'extrapolation des données trimestrielles manquantes (sauf si les données trimestrielles peuvent être estimées au moyen des données mensuelles disponibles au cours du trimestre). Les facteurs de conversion appliqués aux données de ce tableau sont publiés trimestriellement dans le *Bulletin mensuel de statistique* des Nations Unies et sont aussi disponibles sur le site Web des statistiques du commerce de l'ONU : http://unstats.un.org/unsd/trade/data/tables.asp#annual.

Tableau 20 : Principaux partenaires commerciaux

Les chiffres sur les principaux partenaires commerciaux montrent les trois plus grands partenaires commerciaux (les pays de dernière destination et d'origine ou de provenance) dans les transactions du commerce international de marchandises. Dans certains cas un partenaire privilégié est présenté (zones nca, abris fortifiés, etc.). Les zones ni compris ailleurs (zones nca) sont utilisées (a) pour le commerce de faible valeur, (b)si le partenaire choisi est inconnu ou si une erreur a été commise en choisissant le partenaire et (c) pour des raisons de confidentialité. Si un emplacement géographique précis peut être identifie dans zones nca, elles sont alors enregistrées en conséquence (par exemple, Asie nca). Les abris fortifiés sont des magasins de navires et d'aéronefs, qui consistent pour la plupart de combustibles et de denrées alimentaires. Les zones franches appartiennent au territoire économique et géographique d'un pays et non à leurs territoires douaniers. Aux fins des statistiques sur le commerce les opérations entre les territoires douaniers et les zones franches sont enregistrées, si le pays déclarant utilise le Système de Commerce Spécial. Les zones franches peuvent être des zones franches commerciales (boutiques hors taxes) ou des zones franches industrielles. Les données sont exprimées en pourcentage des exportations totales et des importations totales d'un pays, zone ou partenaire privilégié.

Les données dans ce tableau sont des données telles que rapportées par l'UN Comtrade (au niveau à trois chiffres de la CTCI Rév. 3 et une ventilation détaillée des partenaires commerciaux) et des données estimées pour les rapporteurs manquants. Les données sont estimées soit par extrapolation des données des deux années adjacentes, soit, si cela n'est pas possible, par l'utilisation des données déclarées par les partenaires commerciaux (données dites miroir). Les statistiques de miroir sont également utilisées dans le cas où la distribution du partenaire ou des données confidentielles rendent nécessaire l'ajustement des données rapportées. En outre, des modifications sont apportées aux données reçues dans les cas où les données fournies sont manifestement incomplètes, en particulier dans le cas d'exportations d'huiles de pétrole non déclarées dans les données sur les marchandises.

Chapitre XII: Énergie

L'*Annuaire statistique de l'énergie* (consultable sur le site http://unstats.un.org/unsd/energy/yearbook) est une collection complète de statistiques internationales de l'énergie qui couvre plus de 220 pays et régions. L'*Annuaire* est préparé par la Division de statistique du Département des affaires économiques et sociales du Secrétariat des Nations Unies. L'*Annuaire* est produit chaque année avec les nouvelles données disponibles sur la production d'énergie, le commerce, les variations de stocks, les réserves et la consommation de tous les pays et régions, et une série historique remontant à 1950 est disponible. Les données sont établies essentiellement à partir du questionnaire annuel sur l'énergie diffusé par la Division de statistique des Nations Unies et complétées par des publications statistiques officielles nationales, ainsi que des publications des organisations internationales et régionales. Lorsque les données officielles ne sont pas disponibles ou ne sont pas cohérentes, la Division de statistique établit des estimations en s'appuyant sur des éléments d'origine gouvernementale, professionnelle ou commerciale.

Les données se réfèrent à l'année civile, sauf celles des pays suivants qui se rapportent à l'exercice budgétaire : Afghanistan et Iran (République islamique d') – commençant le 21 mars de l'année indiquée; Australie, Bangladesh, Bhoutan, Égypte (électricité seulement pour ces deux derniers pays), Népal – finissant en juin de l'année indiquée; Pakistan – commençant en juillet de l'année indiquée; Inde, Myanmar et Nouvelle-Zélande –

commençant en avril de l'année indiquée. Les données exprimées par habitant utilisent comme dénominateur les données démographiques de la Division de la population de l'Organisation des Nations Unies.

Tableau 21: Production, commerce et consommation d'énergie

Les données sont présentées en pétajoules (ou en gigajoules par habitant), unités auxquelles chaque produit énergétique est converti afin d'assurer l'uniformité et la comparabilité internationales des données. Pour convertir en joules les unités originelles, celles-ci (tonnes métriques, tonnes métriques d'équivalent pétrole, kilowattheures, mètres cubes) sont multipliées par des facteurs de conversion. Voir l'*Annuaire statistique de l'énergie* pour une liste des facteurs de conversion et une description détaillée des méthodes utilisées.

Les combustibles solides inclus dans la production commerciale d'énergie primaire sont l'anthracite, la lignite, la tourbe et le schiste bitumineux; les liquides comprennent le pétrole brut, les condensats de gaz naturel, les autres hydrocarbures, additifs et oxygénats, et les biocarburants liquides; les gaz comprennent le gaz naturel et la vapeur/chaleur primaire; et l'électricité comprend la production primaire d'électricité d'origine hydraulique, nucléaire, géothermique, éolienne, marémotrice, houlomotrice et solaire.

Les importations nettes (importations moins exportations et bunkers) et les variations des stocks font référence à toutes les formes d'énergie primaire et secondaire (y compris les produits intermédiaires). Dans les importations nettes, les bunkers font référence aux bunkers d'essence aviation, de carburéacteur et d'anthracite, de gazole/carburant diesel et de fiouls résiduels. Le commerce international de produits énergétiques repose sur le système du « commerce général », c'est-à-dire que toutes les marchandises entrant sur le territoire national d'un pays ou en sortant sont enregistrées comme importations ou exportations.

La consommation d'énergie comprend les formes primaires des combustibles solides, les importations nettes et les variations des stocks des combustibles secondaires; les liquides comprennent les produits pétroliers utilisés à des fins de production d'énergie y compris les produits intermédiaires, le gaz de raffinerie et le pétrole brut utilisé directement; les gaz comprennent la consommation de gaz naturel et de chaleur primaire, les importations nettes et les variations des stocks de gaz manufacturés; et l'électricité comprend la production primaire d'électricité et les importations nettes d'électricité. La consommation de certains produits pétroliers est négative en raison de l'exclusion des calculs des transferts entre produits. La consommation négative d'électricité est due à une production d'électricité primaire négligeable par rapport aux exportations nettes. Plus généralement, une consommation négative peut représenter une différence résiduelle ou statistique entre la production et les exportations lorsqu'un produit donné est principalement exporté.

Chapitre XIII: Environnement

Tableau 22: Terres

Les données relatives aux terres sont compilées par l'Organisation des Nations Unies pour l'alimentation et l'agriculture (FAO). Les définitions de la FAO en ce qui concerne les terres sont les suivantes:

Superficie totale des terres	Superficie totale, à l'exception des eaux intérieures. Les eaux intérieures désignent généralement les principaux fleuves et lacs.
Terres arables	Terres affectées aux cultures temporaires (les terres sur lesquelles est pratiquée la double culture ne sont comptabilisées qu'une fois); prairies temporaires à faucher ou à pâturer, jardins maraîchers ou potagers et terres en jachère temporaire (moins de cinq ans). Cette définition ne comprend pas les terres abandonnées du fait de la culture itinérante. Les données relatives aux terres arables ne peuvent être utilisées pour calculer la superficie des terres aptes à l'agriculture.
Cultures permanentes	Superficie des terres avec des cultures qui occupent la terre pour de longues périodes et qui ne nécessitent pas d'être replantées après chaque récolte, comme le cacao, le café et le caoutchouc. Cette catégorie comprend les terres plantées d'arbustes à fleurs, d'arbres fruitiers, d'arbres à noix et de vignes, mais ne comprend pas les terres plantées d'arbres destinés à la coupe.
Superficie	Dans l'Évaluation des ressources forestières mondiales 2010, la FAO a défini les forêts comme suit : Terres occupant une superficie de plus de 0,5 hectares avec des arbres

forestière	atteignant une hauteur supérieure à cinq mètres et un couvert arboré de plus de dix pour cent, ou avec des arbres capables d'atteindre ces seuils en situ. Sont exclues les terres à vocation agricole ou urbaine prédominante.
Sites importants pour la biodiversité terrestre dans les aires protégées	Les terres contribuant énormément à la persistance globale de la biodiversité mesurées en proportion entièrement couverte par des zones protégées désignées. Les données sont fondées sur un chevauchement entre les polygones pour les zones clés de la biodiversité provenant de la base des données mondiales sur les zones clés pour la biodiversité et les polygones pour les zones protégées provenant de la base des données mondiales sur les zones protégées. Les chiffres pour chaque région sont calculés comme la proportion de chaque zone clé pour la biodiversité couverte par des zones protégées, moyennés (c'est-à-dire, calculés comme la moyenne) à travers toutes les zones clés de la biodiversité dans la région.

Tableau 23: Espèces menacées

Les données relatives au nombre d'espèces menacées dans chaque groupe d'animaux et de plantes sont établies par l'Union internationale pour la conservation de la nature et de ses ressources (UICN)/ Commission de sauvegarde des espèces (CSE) et publiées dans la liste rouge des espèces menacées de l'UICN. Cette liste fournit le catalogue des espèces considérées comme menacées au niveau mondial. Le nombre d'espèces menacées dans un pays donné change au cours des années pour diverses raisons, entre autres :

- La disponibilité d'informations nouvelles permet de raffiner l'évaluation (de confirmer par exemple que l'espèce est ou n'est pas présente dans un pays donné, que l'espèce est ou n'est pas menacée, etc.);

- L'évolution de la taxonomie (par exemple ce qu'on reconnaissait auparavant comme une certaine espèce est à présent réparti entre plusieurs espèces distinctes, ou fusionné avec une autre espèce);

- Les corrections (par exemple l'évaluation précédente peut avoir omis d'inscrire un pays donné dans la liste appropriée ou avoir inclus un pays donné par erreur);

- Changement de statut réel (par exemple la situation d'une espèce peut s'être réellement détériorée ou améliorée et l'espèce avoir par conséquent été incorporée aux catégories menacées ou en avoir été retirée).

Les catégories utilisées dans la Liste rouge sont les suivantes : espèce éteinte, éteinte à l'état sauvage, gravement menacée d'extinction; menacée d'extinction, vulnérable, quasi menacée et données insuffisantes.

Tableau 24: Estimations des émissions de CO2

Les estimations des émissions de CO_2 représentent les émissions totales de CO_2 provenant de la combustion de carburant. Cela comprend les émissions de CO_2 provenant de la combustion de combustibles dans les activités de combustion de sources / puits de catégorie 1 A du GIEC et celles qui peuvent être réaffectées aux processus industriels et à l'utilisation des produits de la catégorie 2 des sources / puits du GIEC dans le cadre des GL 2006.

Tableau 25: Services d'alimentation en eau potable et d'assainissement

La population utilisant des services d'alimentation en eau potable est actuellement mesurée par la proportion de la population dans les zones urbaines et rurales, selon les définitions nationales, répondant aux critères pour l'utilisation des services d'alimentation en eau potable (SDG 6.1.1) en utilisant une source d'eau potable de base améliorée située sur place, disponible en cas de besoin et exempte de contamination fécale et chimique prioritaire. Les sources d'eau potable améliorées sont celles qui ont le potentiel de fournir de l'eau salubre de par la nature de leur conception et de leur construction, et comprennent : l'eau courante, les forages ou puits tubulaires, les puits creusés protégés, les sources protégées, l'eau de pluie et l'eau conditionnée ou livrée. La Population utilisant des services d'assainissement gérés en toute sécurité est actuellement mesurée par la proportion de la population dans les zones urbaines et rurales, selon les définitions nationales, remplissant les critères pour avoir un service d'assainissement géré en toute sécurité (SDG 6.2.1a) en utilisant une installation d'assainissement de base qui n'est pas partagée avec d'autres ménages et où les excréments sont éliminés en toute sécurité sur place ou transportés et traités hors site. Les installations sanitaires améliorées sont celles conçues pour séparer de manière hygiénique les excréments du contact humain et comprennent : la chasse d'eau / déversement dans le système d'égout, les fosses septiques ou les latrines à fosse ; latrines à fosse ventilées améliorées, toilettes à compost ou latrines à fosse avec dalles.

Chapitre XIV: Science et technologie

La recherche et le développement expérimental (R-D) englobe tous les travaux de création entrepris de façon systématique en vue d'accroître la somme des connaissances, y compris la connaissance de l'homme, de la culture et de la société, ainsi que l'utilisation de cette somme de connaissances pour de nouvelles applications. Pour tout renseignement complémentaire, voir le site Web de l'Institut de statistique de l'UNESCO www.uis.unesco.org.

Tableau 26: Personnel employé dans la recherche et le développement (R–D)

Les données présentées sur le personnel employé dans la recherche et le développement (R-D) sont compilées par l'Institut de statistique de l'UNESCO. Les données de certains pays ont été fournies à l'UNESCO par l'OCDE, EUROSTAT et "la Red de Indicadores de Ciencia y Technología (RICYT)". Les définitions et classifications appliquées par l'UNESCO sont basées sur le Manuel de Frascati (OCDE, 2002).

Les trois catégories du personnel présentées sont définies comme suivant:

Les chercheurs	Les chercheurs sont des spécialistes travaillant à la conception ou à la création de connaissances, de produits, de procédés, de méthodes et de systèmes nouveaux et à la gestion des projets concernés. Les étudiants diplômés au niveau du doctorat (CITE niveau 8) ayant des activités de R-D sont considérés comme des chercheurs.
Techniciens et personnel assimilé	Personnes dont les tâches principales requièrent des connaissances et une expérience technique dans un ou plusieurs domaines de l'ingénierie, des sciences physiques et de la vie ou des sciences sociales et humaines. Ils participent à la R-D en exécutant des tâches scientifiques et techniques faisant intervenir l'application de principes et de méthodes opérationnelles, généralement sous le contrôle de chercheurs.
Autre personnel de soutien	Les travailleurs, qualifiés ou non, et le personnel de secrétariat et de bureau participant à l'exécution des projets de R-D ou qui sont directement associés à l'exécution de tels projets.

Personnes physiques est le nombre total de personnes qui sont principalement ou partiellement affectées à la R-D. Ce dénombrement inclut les employés à 'temps plein' et les employés à 'temps partiel'. Équivalent temps plein (ETP) peut être considéré comme une année-personne. Ainsi, une personne qui consacre 30% de son temps en R&D et le reste à d'autres activités (enseignement, administration universitaire ou direction d'étudiants) compte pour 0.3 ETP en R&D. De façon analogue, si un employé travaille à temps plein dans un centre de R&D pendant six mois seulement, il compte pour 0.5 ETP.

Tableau 27: Dépenses intérieures brutes de recherche et développement (R–D)

Les données présentées sur les dépenses intérieures brutes de recherche et développement sont compilées par l'Institut de statistique de l'UNESCO. Les données de certains pays ont été fournies à l'UNESCO par l'OCDE, EUROSTAT et "la Red de Indicadores de Ciencia y Technología (RICYT)". La dépense intérieure brute de R-D (DIRD) est la dépense totale intra-muros afférente aux travaux de R-D exécutés sur le territoire national pendant une période donnée. Elle comprend la R-D exécutée sur le territoire national et financée par l'étranger mais ne tient pas compte des paiements effectués à l'étranger pour des travaux de R-D. Les sources de financement pour la DIRD sont classées selon les cinq catégories suivantes:

Les fonds des entreprises	Les fonds alloués à la R-D par toutes les firmes, organismes et institutions dont l'activité première est la production marchande de biens ou de services (autres que dans le secteur d'enseignement supérieur) en vue de leur vente au public, à un prix qui correspond à la réalité économique, et les institutions privées sans but lucratif principalement au service de ces entreprises, organismes et institutions.
Les fonds de l'État	Les fonds fournis à la R-D par le gouvernement central (fédéral), d'état ou par les autorités locales. Ceci inclut tous les ministères, bureaux et autres organismes qui fournissent, sans normalement les vendre, des services collectifs autres que d'enseignement supérieur, qu'il n'est pas possible d'assurer de façon pratique et économique par d'autres moyens et qui, de surcroît, administrent les affaires publiques et appliquent la politique économique et sociale de la collectivité. Les fonds des entreprises publiques sont compris dans ceux du secteur des

	entreprises. Les fonds de l'État incluent également les institutions privées sans but lucratif contrôlées et principalement financées par l'État.
Les fonds de l'enseignement supérieur	Les fonds fournis à la R-D par les établissements d'enseignement supérieur tels que toutes les universités, grandes écoles, instituts de technologie et autres établissements postsecondaires, ainsi que tous les instituts de recherche, les stations d'essais et les cliniques qui travaillent sous le contrôle direct des établissements d'enseignement supérieur ou qui sont administrés par ces derniers ou leur sont associés
Les fonds d'institutions privées sans but lucratif	Les fonds destinés à la R-D par les institutions privées sans but lucratif non marchandes au service du public, ainsi que par les simples particuliers ou les ménages.
Les fonds étrangers	Les fonds destinés à la R-D par les institutions et les individus se trouvant en dehors des frontières politiques d'un pays, à l'exception des véhicules, navires, avions et satellites utilisés par des institutions nationales, ainsi que des terrains d'essai acquis par ces institutions, et par toutes les organisations internationales (à l'exception des entreprises), y compris leurs installations et leurs activités à l'intérieur des frontières d'un pays

Il faut éviter de comparer les chiffres absolus concernant les dépenses de R-D d'un pays à l'autre. On ne pourrait procéder à des comparaisons détaillées qu'en convertissant en une même monnaie les sommes libellées en monnaie nationale au moyen de taux de change spécialement applicables aux activités de R-D. Les taux de change officiels ne reflètent pas toujours le coût réel des activités de R-D, et les comparaisons établies sur la base de ces taux peuvent conduire à des conclusions trompeuses; toutefois, elles peuvent être utilisées pour donner une idée de l'ordre de grandeur.

Tableau 28: Brevets

Les brevets sont accordés par un office national des brevets ou un office régional qui accomplit cette tâche pour de nombreux pays, comme l'Office européen des brevets et l'African Regional Intellectual Property Organisation. Dans le cadre de ces systèmes régionaux, le requérant demande que son invention soit protégée dans un ou plusieurs pays, et il appartient à chaque pays d'accorder ou non la protection d'un brevet sur son territoire. Le Traité de coopération en matière de brevets (PCT), administré par l'Organisation mondiale de la propriété intellectuelle (OMPI) prévoit le dépôt d'une demande de brevet international unique dotée de la même validité que des demandes nationales déposées dans les pays désignés. Les données comprennent l'intensité de l'activité des résidents, les brevets délivrés et les brevets en vigueur. L'intensité du dépôt de brevets est présentée comme le nombre de demandes de brevet déposées par des résidents par million d'habitants, tandis que le dépôt d'une demande de propriété intellectuelle (PI) par des résidents fait référence à une demande déposée par un requérant auprès de son office national de la propriété intellectuelle. Les statistiques des droits de propriété intellectuelle (enregistrement) reposent sur le même concept. L'expression « en vigueur » désigne un brevet ou une autre forme de protection de la PI en cours de validité. Le pays d'origine sert à catégoriser les données de PI en PI résidente (intérieure) et non résidente (étrangère). La résidence du premier demandeur cité (ou inventeur) enregistré dans le document de PI (par exemple une demande de brevet ou de dépôt de marque) sert à classer les données de PI par pays d'origine. Les données sont établies et publiées par l'OMPI.

Chapitre XV: Communication

Tableau 29: Utilisation d'Internet

Le tableau indique le pourcentage de personnes qui utilisent Internet et remplace les statistiques présentées dans les annuaires précédents comme le « Nombre (en milliers) d'abonnements à l'Internet fixe (filaire) » et le « Nombre d'abonnements à l'Internet fixe (filaire) pour 100 habitants ». Cet indicateur, outre qu'il saisit l'usage d'Internet, permet de mesurer les évolutions de l'accès à Internet et de son utilisation. Dans les pays où de nombreuses personnes accèdent à Internet au travail, à l'école, dans les cybercafés ou d'autres lieux publics, la multiplication des accès publics accroît le nombre d'utilisateurs malgré le nombre limité des abonnements et des foyers qui ont accès à Internet. Les pays en développement en particulier comptent souvent de nombreux utilisateurs par abonnement à Internet, ce qui traduit le fait que le foyer n'est pas le lieu principal d'accès.

Chapitre XVI: Tourisme et transport internationaux

Les données sur le tourisme international sont fournies par l'Organisation mondiale du tourisme (OMT) qui publie des renseignements détaillés sur le tourisme dans l'*Annuaire des statistiques du tourisme* ou le *Compendium des statistiques du tourisme*, voir www.unwto.org/statistics pour des informations plus complètes. Aux fins de l'établissement des statistiques, l'expression « visiteur international » décrit « toute personne qui se rend dans un pays autre que celui dans lequel il ou elle a son lieu de résidence habituelle, mais différent de son environnement habituel, pour une période de 12 mois au maximum, dans un but principal autre que celui d'y exercer une activité rémunérée ». L'*Annuaire* et le *Compendium* de l'OMT comportent quatre séries distinctes, mais une seule est retenue pour inclusion dans le présent *Annuaire*, en fonction en général de l'ordre de priorité suivant afin de décrire au mieux le « visiteur international »;

Ordre	Code de la série	Nom de la série
1	TF	*Arrivées de touristes non-résidents aux frontières nationales* désigne les visiteurs qui passent au moins une nuit dans un logement collectif ou privé dans le pays visité (exclut les visiteurs d'un jour)
2	VF	*Arrivées de visiteurs non résidents aux frontières nationales* désigne les visiteurs définis dans la série « TF » ainsi que les visiteurs d'un jour qui ne passent pas la nuit dans un logement collectif ou privé dans le pays visité
3	TCE	*Arrivées de touristes non résidents dans tous les types d'établissements d'hébergement*
4	THS	*Arrivées de touristes non résidents dans les hôtels et établissements similaires*

Ces chiffres ne comprennent pas les immigrants, les résidents frontaliers, les personnes domiciliées dans un pays ou une région et qui travaillent dans un pays ou une région limitrophe, les membres des forces armées et les diplomates et les représentants consulaires lorsqu'ils se rendent de leur pays d'origine au pays où ils sont en poste et vice-versa. Ne sont pas inclus non plus les voyageurs en transit qui n'entrent pas formellement dans le pays en faisant viser leur passeport, comme les passagers d'un vol en escale qui demeurent pendant un court laps de temps dans une zone distincte d'une aérogare ou les passagers d'un navire qui ne sont pas autorisés à débarquer. Cette catégorie inclut les passagers transférés directement d'une aérogare à une autre ou à un autre terminal. Les autres passagers en transit dans un pays sont classés comme visiteurs.

Tableau 30: Arrivées de touristes/visiteurs et dépenses touristiques

Les données relatives aux arrivées de visiteurs non résidents (ou internationaux) peuvent être obtenues de différentes sources. Dans certains cas, elles proviennent des statistiques frontalières tirées des registres administratifs (contrôles de police, de l'immigration, comptages du trafic routier et autres types de contrôle), des enquêtes statistiques aux frontières et des enregistrements d'établissements d'hébergement. Les totaux correspondent au nombre total d'arrivées depuis les régions indiquées dans le tableau. Lorsqu'une personne visite le même pays plusieurs fois dans l'année, un même nombre d'arrivées est enregistré. De même, si une personne visite plusieurs pays au cours d'un même voyage, son arrivée dans chaque pays est enregistrée séparément. On ne peut donc pas supposer que le nombre des arrivées soit égal au nombre de personnes qui voyagent.

Les dépenses associées à l'activité touristique des visiteurs sont traditionnellement identifiées au poste « Voyages » de la balance des paiements (BDP): dans le cas du tourisme dans le pays récepteur, les dépenses dans le pays de référence associées aux visiteurs non résidents sont enregistrées comme « crédits » dans la BDP et il s'agit de « recettes au titre des voyages ». Le nouveau cadre conceptuel approuvé par la Commission de statistique des Nations Unies concernant la mesure de l'activité touristique à l'échelle macroéconomique (le compte satellite du tourisme) considère que la notion « industries et produits touristiques » inclut le transport de passagers. Par conséquent, une meilleure estimation des dépenses liées au tourisme par des visiteurs résidents et non résidents dans un scénario international serait, du point de vue de la BDP, la somme des valeurs du poste « Voyages » et du poste « Transport de passagers ». Néanmoins, les utilisateurs doivent être conscients de ce que les estimations de la BDP comprennent, outre les dépenses associées aux visiteurs, celles liées à d'autres types d'individus. Les données publiées doivent permettre la comparabilité internationale et donc correspondre à celles publiées par le Fonds monétaire international et fournies par les banques centrales, les exceptions sont listées dans le

Compendium des statistiques du tourisme et l'*Annuaire des statistiques du tourisme*, voir www.unwto.org/statistics pour des informations plus complètes.

Chapitre XVII: Aide au développement

Tableau 31: Décaissements nets d'aide publique au développement aux bénéficiaires

Le tableau présente des estimations des flux de ressources financières à destination des pays bénéficiaires soit directement (aide bilatérale) soit par l'intermédiaire d'institutions multilatérales (aide multilatérale). Les institutions multilatérales comprennent le Groupe de la Banque mondiale, des banques régionales, les institutions financières de l'Union européenne et un certain nombre d'institutions, de programmes et de fonds d'affectation spéciale des Nations Unies. Les données ont été obtenues auprès du Comité d'aide au développement (CAD) de l'OCDE, auquel les pays membres communiquent des données sur les flux de ressources qu'ils mettent à la disposition de pays et territoires en développement, de pays et territoires en transition, et des institutions multilatérales. On trouvera davantage d'informations sur les définitions, les méthodes et les sources dans la publication de l'OCDE intitulée *Répartition géographique des ressources financières allouées aux pays en développement*, ainsi que sur le site http://stats.oecd.org/.

Tableau 32: Décaissements nets d'aide publique au développement par des donateurs

Le tableau présente les dépenses d'aide au développement des pays donateurs. Ce tableau inclut les contributions des donateurs aux institutions multilatérales; les totaux diffèrent donc de ceux du tableau 32, qui incluent les décaissements des institutions multilatérales.

***

Annex III

Conversion coefficients and factors

The metric system of weights and measures is employed in the *Statistical Yearbook*. In this system, the relationship between units of volume and capacity is: 1 litre = 1 cubic decimetre (dm^3) exactly (as decided by the 12th International Conference of Weights and Measures, New Delhi, November 1964).

Section A shows the equivalents of the basic metric, British imperial and United States units of measurements. According to an agreement between the national standards institutions of English-speaking nations, the British and United States units of length, area and volume are now identical, and based on the yard = 0.9144 metre exactly. The weight measures in both systems are based on the pound = 0.45359237 kilogram exactly (Weights and Measures Act 1963 (London), and *Federal Register announcement of 1 July 1959: Refinement of Values for the Yard and Pound* (Washington D.C.)).

Section B shows various derived or conventional conversion coefficients and equivalents.

Section C shows other conversion coefficients or factors which have been utilized in the compilation of certain tables in the *Statistical Yearbook*. Some of these are only of an approximate character and have been employed solely to obtain a reasonable measure of international comparability in the tables.

For a comprehensive survey of international and national systems of weights and measures and of units' weights for a large number of commodities in different countries, see *World Weights and Measures*.

Annexe III

Coefficients et facteurs de conversion

L'*Annuaire statistique* utilise le système métrique pour les poids et mesures. La relation entre unités métriques de volume et de capacité est: 1 litre = 1 décimètre cube (dm^3) exactement (comme fut décidé à la Conférence internationale des poids et mesures, New Delhi, novembre 1964).

La section A fournit les principaux équivalents des systèmes de mesure métrique, britannique et américain. Suivant un accord entre les institutions de normalisation nationales des pays de langue anglaise, les mesures britanniques et américaines de longueur, superficie et volume sont désormais identiques, et sont basées sur le yard = 0.9144 mètre exactement. Les mesures de poids se rapportent, dans les deux systèmes, à la livre (pound) = 0.45359237 kilogramme exactement (*Weights and Measures Act 1963* (Londres), et *Federal Register Announcement of 1 July 1959: Refinement of Values for the Yard and Pound* (Washington, D.C.)).

La section B fournit divers coefficients et facteurs de conversion conventionnels ou dérivés.

La section C fournit d'autres coefficients ou facteurs de conversion utilisés dans l'élaboration de certains tableaux de l'*Annuaire statistique*. Certains coefficients ou facteurs de conversion ne sont que des approximations et ont été utilisés uniquement pour obtenir un degré raisonnable de comparabilité sur le plan international.

Pour une étude d'ensemble des systèmes internationaux et nationaux de poids et mesures, et d'unités de poids pour un grand nombre de produits dans différents pays, voir *World Weights and Measures*.

A. Equivalents of metric, British imperial and United States units of measure

A. Equivalents des unités métriques, britanniques et des Etats-Unis

Metric units / Unités métriques	British imperial and US equivalents / Equivalents en mesures britanniques et des Etats-Unis		British imperial and US units / Unités britanniques et des Etats-Unis	Metric equivalents / Equivalents en mesures métriques
Length — Longueur				
1 centimetre – centimètre (cm)	0.3937008	inch	1 inch	2.540 cm
1 metre – mètre (m)	3.280840	feet	1 foot	30.480 cm
	1.093613	yard	1 yard	0.9144 m
1 kilometre – kilomètre (km)	0.6213712	mile	1 mile	1609.344 m
	0.5399568	international nautical mile	1 international nautical mile	1852.000 m
Area — Superficie				
1 square centimetre – (cm^2)	0.1550003	square inch	1 square inch	6.45160 cm^2
1 square metre – (m^2)	10.763910	square feet	1 square foot	9.290304 dm^2
	1.195990	square yards	1 square yard	0.83612736 m^2
1 hectare – (ha)	2.471054	acres	1 acre	0.4046856 ha
1 square kilometre – (km^2)	0.3861022	square mile	1 square mile	2.589988 km^2
Volume				
1 cubic centimetre – (cm^3)	0.06102374	cubic inch	1 cubic inch	16.38706 cm^3
1 cubic metre – (m^3)	35.31467	cubic feet	1 cubic foot	28.316847 dm^3
	1.307951	cubic yards	1 cubic yard	0.76455486 m^3
Capacity — Capacité				
1 litre (l)	0.8798766	British imperial quart	1 British imperial quart	1.136523 l
	1.056688	U.S. liquid quart	1 U.S. liquid quart	0.9463529 l
	0.908083	U.S. dry quart	1 U.S. dry quart	1.1012208 l
1 hectolitre (hl)	21.99692	British imperial gallons	1 British imperial gallon	4.546092 l
	26.417200	U.S. gallons	1 U.S. gallon	3.785412 l
	2.749614	British imperial bushels	1 imperial bushel	36.368735 l
	2.837760	U.S. bushels	1 U.S. bushel	35.239067 l

Metric units Unités métriques	British imperial and US equivalents Equivalents en mesures britanniques et des Etats-Unis		British imperial and US units Unités britanniques et des Etats-Unis	Metric equivalents Equivalents en mesures métriques
Weight or mass — Poids				
1 kilogram (kg)	35.27396	av. ounces	1 av. ounce	28.349523 g
	32.15075	troy ounces	1 troy ounce	31.10348 g
	2.204623	av. pounds	1 av. pound	453.59237 g
			1 cental (100 lb.)	45.359237 kg
			1 hundredweight (112 lb.)	50.802345 kg
1 ton – tonne (t)	1.1023113	short tons	1 short ton (2 000 lb.)	0.9071847 t
	0.9842065	long tons	1 long ton (2 240 lb.)	1.0160469 t

B. Various conventional or derived coefficients

Air transport
1 passenger-mile = 1.609344 passenger kilometre
1 short ton-mile = 1.459972 tonne-kilometre
1 long ton-mile = 1.635169 tonne kilometre

Electric energy
1 Kilowatt (kW) = 1.34102 British horsepower (hp)
1.35962 cheval vapeur (cv)

C. Other coefficients or conversion factors employed in *Statistical Yearbook* tables

Roundwood
Equivalent in solid volume without bark.

Sugar
1 metric ton raw sugar = 0.9 metric ton refined sugar

For the United States and its possessions:
1 metric ton refined sugar = 1.07 metric tons raw sugar

Energy

1 metric ton peat = .325 metric ton of coal oil equivalent
1 ton oil equivalent = .4186 GJ or 11.63 MWh

B. Divers coefficients conventionnels ou dérivés

Transport aérien
1 voyageur (passager) – kilomètre = 0.621371 passenger-mile
1 tonne-kilomètre = 0.684945 short ton-mile
0.611558 long ton-mile

Energie électrique
1 British horsepower (hp) = 0.7457 kW
1 cheval vapeur (cv) = 0.735499 kW

C. Autres coefficients ou facteurs de conversion utilisés dans les tableaux de l'*Annuaire statistique*

Bois rond
Equivalences en volume solide sans écorce.

Sucre
1 tonne métrique de sucre brut = 0.9 tonne métrique de sucre raffiné

Pour les États-Unis et leurs possessions:
1 tonne métrique de sucre raffiné = 1.07 tonne métrique de sucre brut

Energie

1 tonne métrique d'équivalent charbon = 3.08 tonnes métrique de tourbe
1 GJ = 2.39 tonne d'équivalent pétrol or 1 MWh = .086 tonne métrique d'équivalent pétrol

Annex IV - Tables added, omitted and discontinued

A. Tables added

The present issue of the *Statistical Yearbook* includes the following tables which were not presented in the previous issue:

> Table 24   Carbon dioxide (CO2) emission estimates

B. Tables omitted

The following tables which were presented in previous issues are not presented in the present issue. They will be updated in future issues of the *Yearbook* when new data become available:

- Population growth and indicators of fertility and morality
- Population in the capital city, urban and rural areas
- Agricultural production indices

C. Tables discontinued

- Mobile telephone subscriptions
- Index of industrial production

Annexe IV - Tableaux ajoutés, supprimés et discontinués

A. Tableaux ajoutés

Dans ce numéro de l'Annuaire statistique, les tableaux suivants n'ont pas été présentés dans le numéro antérieur, et ont été ajoutés:

Tableau 24   Estimation des émissions de dioxyde de carbone (CO2)

B. Tableaux supprimés

Les tableaux suivants qui ont été repris dans les éditions antérieures n'ont pas été repris dans la présente édition. Ils seront actualisés dans les futures livraisons de l'Annuaire à mesure que des données nouvelles deviendront disponibles:

- Croissance démographique et indicateurs de fécondité et mortalité
- Population et taux de croissance dans les zones urbaines et capitales
- Indices de la production agricole

C. Tableaux discontinués

Les tableaux suivants ont été discontinués

- Abonnements aux services de téléphone cellulaire mobile
- Indices de la production industrielle